# Greens Sheriff Court Rules 2013/2014

D1795160

# Greens Sheriff Court Rules 2013/2014

REPRINTED FROM DIVISION D (COURTS, LOWER)
AND DIVISION K (FAMILY LAW) OF THE PARLIA-
MENT HOUSE BOOK

**W. GREEN**

 THOMSON REUTERS

Published in 2013 by
W. Green, 21 Alva Street, Edinburgh EH2 4PS
Part of Thomson Reuters (Professional) UK Limited
(Registered in England & Wales, Company No 1679046.
Registered Office and address for service:
Aldgate House, 33 Aldgate High Street, London EC3N 1DL)
*Printed and bound by CPI Group (UK) Ltd, Croydon, CR0 4YY*
No natural forests were destroyed to make this product;
only farmed timber was used and replanted
A CIP catalogue record for this book is available from the British Library

ISBN 9780414019065

Thomson Reuters and the Thomson Reuters Logo are trademarks of Thomson
Reuters.
All rights reserved. UK statutory material in this publication is acknowledged as
Crown copyright. No part of this publication may be reproduced or transmitted in
any form or by any means, or stored in any retrieval system of any nature, without
prior written permission of the copyright holder and publisher, except for permitted
fair dealing under the Copyright, Designs and Patents Act 1988, or in accordance
with the terms of a licence issued by the Copyright Licensing Agency in respect of
photocopying and/or reprographic reproduction. Full acknowledgment of publisher
and source must be given. Material is contained in this publication for which
publishing permission has been sought, and for which copyright is acknowledged.
Permission to reproduce such material cannot be granted by the publishers and application must be made to the copyright holders.

© 2013 Thomson Reuters (Professional) UK Limited

Reprinted from the *Parliament House Book*, published in looseleaf form and updated five times a year by W. Green, the Scottish Law Publisher

| | |
|---|---|
| *The following paperback titles are also available in the series:* | |
| Annotated Rules of the Court of Session 2013/2014 | |
| Solicitors Professional Handbook 2013/2014 | |
| *Parliament House Book consists of the following Divisions:* | |
| A Fees and Stamps | |
| B Courts, Upper | |
| C Court of Session Practice | |
| D Courts, Lower | |
| E Licensing | |
| F Solicitors | |
| G Legal Aid | |
| H Bankruptcy and other Mercantile Statutes | |
| I Companies | |
| J Conveyancing, Land Tenure and Registration | |
| K Family Law | |
| L Landlord and Tenant | |
| M Succession, Trusts, Liferents and Judicial Factors | |

# MAIN TABLE OF CONTENTS

*Volume 1*

## COURTS, LOWER: ACTS OF COURT AND PRACTICE NOTES

## COURTS, LOWER: NOTES FOR GUIDANCE

# STATUTES

# NOTICE OF ACCIDENTS ACT 1894

(57 & 58 VICT. C.28)

An Act to provide for notice of and inquiry into accidents occurring in certain employments and industries.

[20th July 1894]

*[Repealed subject to savings by the Transport and Works Act 1992 (c.42), Sch.4(1), para.1 (effective February 26, 1998).]*

## SHERIFF COURTS (SCOTLAND) ACT 1907

(7 Edw. 7 c. 51)

**D1.2**

An Act to regulate and amend the laws and practice relating to the civil procedure in sheriff courts in Scotland, and for other purposes.[1, 2]

[28th August 1907]

*Preliminary*

### Short title

**1.** This Act may be cited for all purposes as the Sheriff Courts (Scotland) Act 1907.

**D1.3**

**2.** *[Repealed by the Statute Law Revision Act 1927, (c.42).]*

### Interpretation

**3.** In construing this Act (unless where the context is repugnant to such construction)—

**D1.4**

    (a)[3]  "Sheriff principal" includes sheriff;

    (b)  "Tenant" includes sub-tenant;

    (c)  "Lease" includes sub-lease;

    (d)[4]  "Action" or "cause" includes every civil proceeding competent in the ordinary sheriff court;

    (e)  "Person" includes company, corporation, or association and firm of any description nominate or descriptive, or any Board corporate or unincorporate;

    (f)  "Sheriff-clerk" includes sheriff-clerk depute;

    (g)  "Agent" means a law-agent enrolled in terms of the Law Agents (Scotland) Act 1873;

    (h)  "Final judgment" means an interlocutor which, by itself, or taken along with previous interlocutors, disposes of the subject-matter of the cause, notwithstanding that judgment may not have been pronounced on every question raised, and that the expenses found due may not have been modified, taxed or decerned for;

    (i)  *[Repealed by the Sheriff Courts (Scotland) Act 1971 (c.58), Sch.2.]*

    (j)  "Small Debt Acts" means and includes the Small Debt (Scotland) Acts 1887 to 1889, and Acts explaining or amending the same;

    (k)  "Initial writ" means the statement of claim, petition, note of appeal, or other document by which the action is initiated;

    (l)  "Procurator-Fiscal" means procurator-fiscal in the sheriff court;

    (m)  *[Repealed by the Statute Law (Repeals) Act 1989 (c.43), Sch.1, Pt I.]*

    (n)  "Pursuer" means and includes any person making a claim or demand, or seeking any warrant or order competent in the sheriff court;

---

[1] As amended by the Sheriff Courts (Scotland) Act 1913 (2 & 3 Geo. V, c. 28). Applied by the Agricultural Holdings (Scotland) Act 1991 (c.55), s.21(4), (5).

[2] For the interpretation of the terms "sheriff" and "sheriff-substitute" throughout this Act, see now the Sheriff Courts (Scotland) Act 1971 (c.58), s.4, and the Interpretation Act 1978 (c.30), Sched. 1.

[3] As substituted by the Sheriff Courts (Scotland) Act 1971 (c.58), s.4.

[4] As amended by the Sheriff Courts (Scotland) Act 1913 (c.28), Sch.1.

(o) "Defender" means and includes any person who is required to be called in any action;

(p)[1] "Summary application" means and includes all applications of a summary nature brought under the common law jurisdiction of the sheriff principal, and all applications, whether by appeal or otherwise, brought under any Act of Parliament which provides, or, according to any practice in the sheriff court, which allows that the same shall be disposed of in a summary manner, but which does not more particularly define in what form the same shall be heard, tried, and determined;

(q) *[Repealed by the Law Reform (Miscellaneous Provisions) (Scotland) Act 1980 (c.55), Sch.3.]*

*Jurisdiction*

**Jurisdiction**

**D1.5**

**4.**[2, 3]  The jurisdiction of the sheriffs principal, within their respective sheriffdoms, shall extend to and include all navigable rivers, ports, harbours, creeks, shores, and anchoring grounds in or adjoining such sheriffdoms. And the powers and jurisdictions formerly competent to the High Court of Admiralty in Scotland in all maritime causes and proceedings, civil and criminal, including such as may apply to persons furth of Scotland, shall be competent to the sheriffs principal, provided the defender shall upon any legal ground of jurisdiction be amenable to the jurisdiction of the sheriff principal before whom such cause or proceeding may be raised, and provided also that it shall not be competent to the sheriffs principal to try any crime committed on the seas which it would not be competent for him to try if the crime had been committed on land: Provided always that where sheriffdoms are separated by a river, firth, or estuary, the sheriffs on either side shall have concurrent jurisdictions over the intervening space occupied by water.

**Extension of jurisdiction**

**D1.6**

**5.**[4]  Nothing herein contained shall derogate from any jurisdiction, powers, or authority presently possessed or in use to be exercised by the sheriffs principal of Scotland, and such jurisdiction shall extend to and include—

(1)[5, 6]  Actions of declarator;

(1A)  *[Repealed by the Law Reform (Parent and Child) (Scotland) Act 1986 (c.9) Sch.2.]*

(2)[7]  Actions for aliment or separation (other than any action mentioned in subsection (2A) below):

---

[1] As substituted by the Sheriff Courts (Scotland) Act 1971 (c.58), s.4.

[2] Repealed, so far as relating to criminal proceedings, by the Criminal Procedure (Scotland) Act 1975 (c.21) Sch.10.

[3] As substituted by the Sheriff Courts (Scotland) Act 1971 (c.58) s.4.

[4] Explained (legal aid): see SI 1958/1872, r.2(2). Excluded by the Land Registration (Scotland) Act 1979 (c.33), ss.21(6) and 22(7). As amended by the Law Reform (Miscellaneous Provisions) (Scotland) Act 1980 (c.55), s.15(a) and Sch.3, and the Civil Jurisdiction and Judgments Act 1982 (c.27), Sch.14.

[5] As amended by the Law Reform (Parent and Child) (Scotland) Act 1986 (c.9), Sch.2.

[6] As amended by the Family Law (Scotland) Act 2006 (asp 2), s.4 (effective May 4, 2006 (SSI 2006/212)).

[7] As substituted by the Family Law (Scotland) Act 1985 (c.37), Sch.1, para.1. As amended by the Law Reform (Parent and Child) (Scotland) Act 1986 (c.9), Sch.2. See the Domicile and Matrimonial Proceedings Act 1973 (c.45), Sch.2.

(2A)[1]  Actions, arising out of an application under section 31(1) of the Maintenance Orders (Reciprocal Enforcement) Act 1972, for the recovery of maintenance:

(2B)[2]  Actions for divorce:

(2C)  *[Repealed by the Children (Scotland) Act 1995 (c.36), Sch.5.]*

(3)  Actions of division of commonty and of division or division and sale of common property, in which cases the Act of 1695 concerning the division of commonties shall be read and construed as if it conferred jurisdiction upon the sheriff court in the same manner as upon the Court of Session:

(4)  Actions relating to questions of heritable right or title (except actions of adjudication save in so far as now competent and actions of reduction) including all actions of declarator of irritancy and removing, whether at the instance of a superior against a vassal or of a landlord against a tenant:

(5)  Suspension of charges or threatened charges upon the decrees of court granted by the sheriff or upon decrees of registration proceeding upon bonds, bills, contracts or other obligations registered in the books of the sheriff court, the books of council and session, or any others competent.

### Power of sheriff to order sheriff clerk to execute deeds relating to heritage

**5A.**—[3](1)  This section applies where—                                              **D1.7**

    (a)  an action relating to heritable property is before the sheriff; or

    (b)  it appears to the sheriff that an order under this section is necessary to implement a decree of a sheriff relating to heritable property.

(2)  Where the grantor of any deed relating to the heritable property cannot be found or refuses or is unable or otherwise fails to execute the deed, the sheriff may—

    (a)  where subsection (1)(a) above applies, on application;

    (b)  where subsection (1)(b) above applies, on summary application, by the grantee, make an order dispensing with the execution of the deed by the grantor and directing the sheriff clerk to execute the deed.

(3)  Where in pursuance of an order under this section a deed is executed by the sheriff clerk, it shall have the like force and effect as if it had been executed by the grantor.

(4)  In this section—

"grantor" means a person who is under an obligation to execute the deed; and
"grantee" means the person to whom that obligation is owed.

### Action competent in sheriff court

**6.**[4, 5]  Subject to section 8 of the Domicile and Matrimonial Proceedings Act     **D1.8**
1973 and Chapter III of Part I of the Family Law Act 1986 any action competent in the sheriff court may be brought within the jurisdiction of the sheriff principal—

---

[1] As inserted by the Domestic Proceedings and Magistrates' Courts Act 1978 (c.22), Sch.2.

[2] As inserted by the Divorce Jurisdiction, Court Fees and Legal Aid (Scotland) Act 1983 (c.12) s.1.

[3] As inserted by the Law Reform (Miscellaneous Provisions) (Scotland) Act 1985 (c.73), s.17.

[4] Excluded by the Civil Jurisdiction and Judgments Act 1982 s.20(3). This section ceases to have effect in relation to actions to which s.45 of the Administration of Justice Act 1956 applies; ibid. s.45(6). As amended by the Domicile and Matrimonial Proceedings Act 1973 Sch.4 and by the Family Law Act 1986 Sch.1 para.3.

[5] As substituted by the Sheriff Courts (Scotland) Act 1971 (c.58) s.4.

(a)[1]   Where the defender (or when there are several defenders over each of whom a sheriff court has jurisdiction in terms of this Act, where one of them) resides within the jurisdiction, or having resided there for at least forty days has ceased to reside there for less than forty days and has no known residence in Scotland:

(b)[2]   Where a defender carries on business, and has a place of business within the jurisdiction, and is cited either personally or at such place of business:

(c)[3]   Where the defender is a person not otherwise subject to the jurisdiction of the courts of Scotland, and a ship or vessel of which he is the owner or part owner or demise charterer or master, or goods, debts, money, or other moveable property belonging to him, have been arrested within the jurisdiction:

(d)   Where the defender is the owner or part owner or tenant or joint tenant, whether individually or as a trustee of heritable property within the jurisdiction, and the action relates to such property or to his interest therein:

(e)   Where the action is for interdict against an alleged wrong being committed or threatened to be committed within the jurisdiction:

(f)   Where the action relates to a contract the place of execution or performance of which is within the jurisdiction, and the defender is personally cited there:

(g)   Where in an action of furthcoming or multiplepoinding the fund or subject *in medio* is situated within the jurisdiction; or the arrestee or holder of the fund is subject to the jurisdiction of the court:

(h)   Where the party sued is the pursuer in any action pending within the jurisdiction against the party suing:

(i)[4]   Where the action is founded on delict, and the delict forming the cause of action was committed within the jurisdiction:

(j)   Where the defender prorogates the jurisdiction of the court.

**Privative jurisdiction in causes under one thousand five hundred pounds value**

**D1.9**

**7.**[5]   All causes not exceeding £5000 in value exclusive of interest and expenses competent in the sheriff court shall be brought and followed forth in the sheriff court only, and shall not be subject to review by the Court of Session: Provided that nothing herein contained shall affect any right of appeal competent under any Act of Parliament in force for the time being.

**8.**   *[Repealed by the Sheriff Courts (Scotland) Act 1971 (c.58) Sch.2.]*

**9.**   *[Repealed by the Sheriff Courts (Scotland) Act 1971 (c.58) Sch.2.]*

---

[1] As amended by the Sheriff Courts (Scotland) Act 1913 (c.28) Sch.1.
[2] As substituted by the Sheriff Courts (Scotland) Act 1913 (c.28) Sch.1.
[3] As amended by the Bankruptcy and Diligence etc. (Scotland) Act 2007 (asp 3) Sch.4 para. 13 (effective July 10, 2010: subject to savings specified in SSI 2010/249 art.3).
[4] As substituted by the Law Reform (Jurisdiction in Delict) (Scotland) Act 1971 s.1(2).
[5] As amended by the Sheriff Courts (Scotland) Act 1971 (c.58) Pt III s.31. The figure is substituted subject to savings specified in SSI 2007/507 by the Sheriff Courts (Scotland) Act 1971 (Privative Jurisdiction and Summary Cause) Order (SSI 2007/507) art.2 (effective January 14, 2008).

## Privilege not to exempt from jurisdiction

**10.** No person shall be exempt from the jurisdiction of the sheriff court on account of privilege by reason of being a member of the College of Justice.

**D1.10**

*Sheriffs*

## Appointment of sheriffs and salaried sheriffs-substitute

**11.**[1] The right of appointing to the salaried offices of sheriff principal and salaried sheriff shall be vested in His Majesty, and shall be exercised on the recommendation of the Secretary of State.

**D1.11**

**12, 13.** *[Repealed by the Sheriff Courts (Scotland) Act 1971 (c.58), Sch.2.]*

## Salaries of sheriffs and sheriffs-substitute

**14.**[2] It shall be lawful to grant to any sheriff principal or sheriff such salary as to the Treasury may seem meet, and every such salary shall be paid quarterly or otherwise in every year as the Treasury may determine, and shall be charged upon and be payable out of the Consolidated Fund.

**D1.12**

**15, 16.** *[Repealed by the Sheriff Courts (Scotland) Act 1971 (c.58), Sch.2.]*

## Honorary sheriff-substitute

**17.**[3] The sheriff principal may by writing under his hand appoint such persons as he thinks proper to hold the office of honorary sheriff within his sheriffdom during his pleasure, and for whom he shall be answerable. An honorary sheriff, during the subsistence of his commission, shall be entitled to exercise the powers and duties appertaining to the office of sheriff. An honorary sheriff shall hold office, notwithstanding the death, resignation, or removal of the sheriff principal, until his commission shall be recalled by a succeeding sheriff principal. In this section "sheriff principal" does not include sheriff.

**D1.13**

**18, 19.** *[Repealed by the Sheriff Courts (Scotland) Act 1971 (c.58), Sch.2.]*

**20.** *[Repealed by the Sheriffs' Pensions (Scotland) Act 1961 (c.42), Sch.2.]*

**21.** *[Repealed by the Sheriff Courts (Scotland) Act 1971 (c.58), Sch.2.]*

**22–24.** *[Repealed by the Sheriff Courts and Legal Officers (Scotland) Act 1927 (c.35), Sch.]*

**25, 26.** *[Repealed by the Sheriff Courts (Scotland) Act 1971 (c.58), Sch.2.]*

---

[1] As substituted by the Sheriff Courts (Scotland) Act 1971 (c.58), s.4 and the Secretaries of State Act 1926 (c.18), s.1(3).

[2] As substituted by the Sheriff Courts (Scotland) Act 1971 (c.58), s.4 and amended by the Sheriffs' Pensions (Scotland) Act 1961 (c.42), Sch.1.

[3] As substituted by the Sheriff Courts (Scotland) Act 1971 (c.58), s.4.

*Appeals*

**Appeal to sheriff**

D1.14

27.[1]   Subject to the provisions of this Act an appeal to the sheriff principal shall be competent against all final judgments of the sheriff and also against interlocutors—

    (a)   Granting or refusing interdict, interim or final;

    (b)   Granting interim decree for payment of money other than a decree for expenses, or making an order *ad factum praestandum*;

    (c)   Sisting an action;

    (d)   Allowing or refusing or limiting the mode of proof;

    (e)   Refusing a reponing note; or

    (f)   Against which the sheriff either *ex proprio motu* or on the motion of any party grants leave to appeal;

Provided always that notwithstanding the death, resignation, or removal of a sheriff principal, appeals may be taken from the judgment of the sheriff, which appeals shall be heard by the succeeding sheriff principal when he shall enter upon office. It shall be competent for the sheriff principal, when the action is before him on appeal on any point, to open the record *ex proprio motu* if the record shall appear to him not to have been properly made up, or to allow further proof.

**Appeal to the Court of Session**

D1.15

28.—[2](1)   Subject to the provisions of this Act, it shall be competent to appeal to the Court of Session against a judgment either of a sheriff principal or of a sheriff if the interlocutor appealed against is a final judgment; or is an interlocutor—

    (a)   Granting interim decree for payment of money other than a decree for expenses; or

    (b)   Sisting an action; or

    (c)   Refusing a reponing note; or

    (d)   Against which the sheriff principal or sheriff, either *ex proprio motu* or on the motion of any party, grants leave to appeal.

(2)   Nothing in this section nor in section 27 of this Act contained shall affect any right of appeal or exclusion of such right provided by any Act of Parliament in force for the time being.

**Effect of appeal**

D1.16

29.[3]   An appeal shall be effectual to submit to review the whole of the interlocutors pronounced in the cause, and shall be available to and may be insisted in by all other parties in the cause notwithstanding they may not have noted separate appeals. An appeal shall not prevent immediate execution of warrants to take inventories, or place effects in custody *ad interim*, or warrants for interim preservation, and an interim interdict, although appealed against, shall be binding till recalled.

---

[1] As substituted by the Sheriff Courts (Scotland) Act 1971 (c.58), s.4 and amended by the Law Reform (Miscellaneous Provisions) (Scotland) Act 1980 (c.55), Sch.3.

[2] See SI 1949/2062. As substituted by the Sheriff Courts (Scotland) Act 1913 (c.28), s.2 and the Sheriff Courts (Scotland) Act 1971 (c.58), s.4 and amended by the Sheriff Courts (Scotland) Act 1971 (c.58), Sch.2.

[3] As amended by the Bankruptcy and Diligence etc. (Scotland) Act 2007 (asp 3) Sch.6(1) para.1 (effective April 22, 2009).

**30.** *[Repealed by the Law Reform (Miscellaneous Provisions) (Scotland) Act 1980 (c.55), Sch.3.]*

**31.** *[Repealed by the Law Reform (Miscellaneous Provisions) (Scotland) Act 1980 (c.55), s.11 and Sch.3.]*

**32.** *[Repealed by the Sheriff Courts (Scotland) Act 1913 (2 & 3 Geo. V, c.28),s.1.]*

**33.** *[Repealed by the Juries Act 1949 (c.27), Sch.3.]*

*Removings[1]*

**Removings**

**34.**[2]  Where lands exceeding two acres in extent are held under a probative lease specifying a term of endurance, and whether such lease contains an obligation upon the tenant to remove without warning or not, such lease, or an extract thereof from the books of any court of record shall have the same force and effect as an extract decree of removing obtained in an ordinary action at the instance of the lessor, or any one in his right, against the lessee or any party in possession, and such lease or extract shall along with authority in writing signed by the lessor or any one in his right or by his factor or law agent be sufficient warrant to any sheriff-officer or messenger-at-arms of the sheriffdom within which such lands or heritages are situated to eject such party in possession, his family, sub-tenants, cottars, and dependants, with their goods, gear, and effects, at the expiry of the term or terms of endurance of the lease: Provided that previous notice in writing to remove shall have been given—

**D1.17**

    (a)   When the lease is for three years and upwards not less than one year and not more than two years before the termination of the lease; and

    (b)   In the case of leases from year to year (including lands occupied by tacit relocation) or for any other period less than three years, not less than six months before the termination of the lease (or where there is a separate ish as regards land and houses or otherwise before that ish which is first in date):

Provided that if such written notice as aforesaid shall not be given the lease shall be held to be renewed by tacit relocation for another year, and thereafter from year to year: Provided further that nothing contained in this section shall affect the right of the landlord to remove a tenant who has been sequestrated under the Bankruptcy (Scotland) Act 1913, or against whom a decree of cessio has been pronounced under the Debtors (Scotland) Act 1880, or who by failure to pay rent has incurred any irritancy of his lease or other liability to removal: Provided further that removal or ejectment in virtue of this section shall not be competent after six weeks from the date of the ish last in date: Provided further that nothing herein contained shall be construed to prevent proceedings under any lease in common form; and that the foregoing provisions as to notice shall not apply to any stipulations in a lease entitling the landlord to resume land for building, planting, feuing, or other purposes or to subjects let for any period less than a year.

---

[1] The provisions of this Act relating to removings are, in the case of an agricultural holding, subject to the Agricultural Holdings (Scotland) Act 1991 (c.55), s.21: see subs. (4).

[2] Reference to the Bankruptcy (Scotland) Act 1913 inserted by virtue of the Interpretation Act 1889 (c.63), s.38 (1). The 1913 Act was repealed by the Bankruptcy (Scotland) Act 1985 (c.66): see s.5(1) and Sch.8.

**Letter of removal**

D1.18

**35.**[1] Where any tenant in possession of any lands exceeding two acres in extent (whether with or without a written lease) shall, either at the date of entering upon the lease or at any other time, have granted a letter of removal, such letter of removal shall have the same force and effect as an extract decree of removing, and shall be a sufficient warrant for ejection to the like effect as is provided in regard to a lease or extract thereof, and shall be operative against the granter of such letter of removal or any party in his right within the same time and in the same manner after the like previous notice to remove: Provided always that where such letter is dated and signed within twelve months before the date of removal or before the first ish, if there be more than one ish, it shall not be necessary that any notice of any kind shall be given by either party to the other.

**Notice to remove**

D1.19

**36.** Where lands exceeding two acres in extent are occupied by a tenant without any written lease, and the tenant has given to the proprietor or his agent no letter of removal, the lease shall terminate on written notice being given to the tenant by or on behalf of the proprietor, or to the proprietor by or on behalf of the tenant not less than six months before the determination of the tenancy, and such notice shall entitle the proprietor, in the event of the tenant failing to remove, to apply for and obtain a summary warrant of ejection against the tenant and every one deriving right from him.

**Notice of termination of tenancy**

D1.20

**37.**[2] In all cases where houses, with or without land attached, not exceeding two acres in extent, lands not exceeding two acres in extent let without houses, mills, fishings, shootings, and all other heritable subjects (excepting land exceeding two acres in extent) are let for a year or more, notice of termination of tenancy shall be given in writing to the tenant by or on behalf of the proprietor or to the proprietor by or on behalf of the tenant: Provided always that notice under this section shall not warrant summary ejection from the subjects let to a tenant, but such notice, whether given to or by or on behalf of the tenant, shall entitle the proprietor to apply to the sheriff principal for a warrant for summary ejection in common form against the tenant and every one deriving right from him: Provided further that the notice provided for by this section shall be given at least forty days before the fifteenth day of May when the termination of the tenancy is the term of Whit-sunday, and at least forty days before the eleventh day of November when the termination of the tenancy is the term of Martinmas.

**Exception for certain tenancies**

D1.21

**37A.**[3] The provisions of this Act relating to removings (including summary removings) shall not apply to or in relation to short limited duration tenancies or limited duration tenancies within the meaning of the Agricultural Holdings (Scotland) Act 2003 (asp 11).

---

[1] As amended by the Requirements of Writing (Scotland) Act 1995 (c.7) Sch.5 (effective August 1, 1995: s.15(2)).

[2] As substituted by the Sheriff Courts (Scotland) Act 1971 (c.58), s.4.

[3] As inserted by the Agricultural Holdings (Scotland) Act 2003 (asp 11), Sch., para.1 and brought into force by the Agricultural Holdings (Scotland) Act 2003 (Commencement No.3, Transitional and Savings Provisions) Order 2003 (SSI 2003/548), reg.2(i) (effective November 23, 2003).

*Summary Removings*

## Summary removing

**38.**[1, 2]   Where houses or other heritable subjects are let for a shorter period than a year, any person by law authorised may present to the sheriff principal a summary application for removing, and a decree pronounced in such summary cause shall have the full force and effect of a decree of removing and warrant of ejection. Where such a let is for a period not exceeding four months, notice of removal therefrom shall, in the absence of express stipulation, be given as many days before the ish as shall be equivalent to at least one-third of the full period of the duration of the let; and where the let exceeds four months, notice of removal shall, in the absence of express stipulation, be given at least forty days before the expiry of the said period. Provided that in no case shall notice of removal be given less than twenty-eight days before the date on which it is to take effect.

**D1.22**

## Notice of termination in respect of dwelling-houses

**38A.**[3]   Any notice of termination of tenancy or notice of removal given under sections 37 and 38 above in respect of a dwelling-house, on or after the date of the coming into operation of section 123 of the Housing Act 1974, shall be in writing and shall contain such information as may be prescribed by virtue of section 131 of the Rent (Scotland) Act 1971, and Rule 112 of Schedule 1 to this Act shall no longer apply to any such notice under section 37 above.

**D1.23**

## Lord Advocate as party to action for divorce

**38B.**   *[Repealed by the Family Law (Scotland) Act 2006 (asp.2), Sch.3 (effective May 4, 2006).]*

**D1.24**

**38C.**   *[Repealed by the Children (Scotland) Act 1995 (c.36), Sch.5 (effective November 1, 1996).]*

*Procedure Rules*

## Procedure rules

**39.**   Subject to the provisions of any Act of Parliament in force after the passing of this Act, the procedure in all civil causes shall be conform to the rules of procedure set forth in Schedule 1 hereto annexed. Such rules shall be construed and have effect as part of this Act.

**D1.25**

---

[1] Proviso added by the Rent (Scotland) Act 1971 (c.28), Sch.18.

[2] As substituted by the Sheriff Courts (Scotland) Act 1971 (c.58) s.4. In terms of s.3(a) of the 1907 Act, the meaning of the term "sheriff principal" includes "sheriff".

[3] As inserted by the Housing Act 1974 (c.44), Sch.13, para.1. For rule 112 read rule 105 of the rules substituted by SI 1983/747, and rule 34.7 of the rules substituted by SI 1993/1956.

**Court of Session to regulate fees, etc.**

D1.26

**40.**[1, 2](1)   The Court of Session may from time to time, by act of sederunt, make such regulations for regulating the fees of agents (other than such of the fees of agents as the Secretary of State may regulate under or by virtue of section 14A of the Legal Aid (Scotland) Act 1967), officers, shorthand writers, and others;

(2)   An Act of Sederunt under this section is subject to the negative procedure.

*Postal Charge*

**41.**   *[Repealed by the Administration of Justice (Scotland) Act 1933 (c.41), Sch.]*

*Small Debts Acts*

**42–48.**   *[Repealed by the Sheriff Courts (Scotland) Act 1971 (c.58), Sch.2]*

**49.**   *[Repealed by the Execution of Diligence (Scotland) Act 1926 (c.16), s.7.]*

*Summary Applications*

**Summary applications**

D1.27

**50.**[3]   In summary applications (where a hearing is necessary) the sheriff principal shall appoint the application to be heard at a diet to be fixed by him, and at that or any subsequent diet (without record of evidence unless the sheriff principal shall order a record) shall summarily dispose of the matter and give his judgment in writing: Provided that wherever in any Act of Parliament an application is directed to be heard, tried, and determined summarily or in the manner provided by section 52 of the Sheriff Courts (Scotland) Act 1876, such direction shall be read and construed as if it referred to this section of this Act: Provided also that nothing contained in this Act shall affect any right of appeal provided by any Act of Parliament under which a summary application is brought.

*The Poor's Roll*

**51.**   *[Repealed by the Statute Law (Repeals) Act 1973 (c.39).]*

*Repeal*

**52.**   *[Repealed by the Statute Law Revision Act 1927 (c.42).]*

D1.28

SCHEDULES

FIRST SCHEDULE[4]

---

[1] As amended by the Sheriff Courts (Scotland) Act 1913 (c.28), Sch.1, the Administration of Justice (Scotland) Act 1933 (c.41), Sch, the Divorce Jurisdiction, Court Fees and Legal Aid (Scotland) Act 1983 (c.12), Sch.1, para.7 and Sch.2, and substituted by the Secretaries of State Act 1926 (c.18), s.1(3).

[2] As amended by the Interpretation and Legislative Reform (Scotland) Act 2010 (Consequential, Savings and Transitional Provisions) Order 2011 (SSI 2011/396) para.3 (effective November 11, 2011).

[3] As substituted by the Sheriff Courts (Scotland) Act 1971 (c.58) s.4. In terms of s.3(a) of the 1907 Act, the meaning of the term "sheriff principal" includes "sheriff".

[4] As substituted by SI 1983/747, affecting any action or proceedings commenced on or after September 1, 1983. New First Schedule substituted in respect of causes commenced on or after January 1, 1994 by SI 1993/1956: see pp.D 44/29 et seq. Please note that we have now removed the pre-1993 Ordinary Cause Rules from this volume.

14

ORDINARY CAUSE RULES 1993[1]

Ordinary Cause Rules 1993

Arrangement of Ordinary Cause Rules

Initiation and Progress of Causes

*Chapter 1*

*Citation, Interpretation, Representation and Forms*

---

[1] The Ordinary Cause Rules were amended inter alia by SI 1996/2445, effective November 1, 1996. The amendments made thereby apply equally to causes commenced before that date: see SI 1996/2586

49.13        Arrestment before service

INITIATION AND PROGRESS OF CAUSES

Chapter 1

Citation, Interpretation, Representation and Forms

**D1.29**

**Citation1.1.**    These Rules may be cited as the Ordinary Cause Rules 1993.

**Interpretation**

**D1.30**

**1.2.**—(1)   In these Rules, unless the context otherwise requires—

"document" has the meaning assigned to it in section 9 of the Civil Evidence (Scotland) Act 1988;
"enactment" includes an enactment comprised in, or in an instrument made under, an Act of the Scottish Parliament;[1]
"period of notice" means the period determined under rule 3.6 (period of notice after citation).
"the Act of 2004" means the Vulnerable Witnesses (Scotland) Act 2004.[2]

(2)   For the purposes of these Rules—

    (a)   "affidavit" includes an affirmation and a statutory or other declaration; and

    (b)   an affidavit shall be sworn or affirmed before a notary public or any other competent authority.

(3)   Where a provision in these Rules requires a party to intimate or send a document to another party, it shall be sufficient compliance with that provision if the document is intimated or sent to the solicitor acting in the cause for that party.

(4)   Unless the context otherwise requires, anything done or required to be done under a provision in these Rules by a party may be done by the agent for that party acting on his behalf.

(5)   Unless the context otherwise requires, a reference to a specified Chapter, Part, rule or form, is a reference to the Chapter, Part, rule, or form in Appendix 1, so specified in these Rules; and a reference to a specified paragraph, sub-paragraph or head is a reference to that paragraph of the rule or form, that sub-paragraph of the paragraph or that head of the sub-paragraph, in which the reference occurs.

(6)[3]   In these Rules, references to a solicitor include a reference to a member of a body which has made a successful application under section 25 of the Law Reform (Miscellaneous Provisions) (Scotland) Act 1990 but only to the extent that the member is exercising rights acquired by virtue of section 27 of that Act.

**Representation**

**D1.31**

**1.3.**—(1)   Subject to paragraph (2), a party to any proceedings arising solely under the provisions of the Debtors (Scotland) Act 1987 shall be entitled to be represented by a person other than a solicitor or an advocate provided that the sheriff is satisfied that such person is a suitable representative and is duly authorised to represent that party.

(2)   Paragraph (1) shall not apply to an appeal to the Sheriff Principal.

(3)[4]   A party may be represented by any person authorised under any enactment to conduct proceedings in the sheriff court in accordance with the terms of that enactment.

(4)[5]   The person referred to in paragraph (3) may do everything for the preparation and conduct of an action as may have been done by an individual conducting his own action.

---

[1] As inserted by the Act of Sederunt (Ordinary Cause, Summary Application, Summary Cause and Small Claim Rules) Amendment (Miscellaneous) 2007 (SSI 2007/6), para.2(2) (effective January 29, 2007).

[2] As inserted by the Act of Sederunt (Ordinary Cause, Summary Application, Summary Cause and Small Claim Rules) Amendment (Vulnerable Witnesses (Scotland) Act 2004) 2007 (SSI 2007/463), r.2(2) (effective November 1, 2007).

[3] As inserted by the Act of Sederunt (Sheriff Court Rules Amendment) (Sections 25 to 29 of the Law Reform (Miscellaneous Provisions) (Scotland) Act 1990) 2009 (SSI 2009/164) r.2 (effective May 20, 2009).

[4] As inserted by the Act of Sederunt (Ordinary Cause, Summary Application, Summary Cause and Small Claim Rules) Amendment (Miscellaneous) 2007 (SSI 2007/6), para.2(3) (effective January 29, 2007).

[5] As inserted by the Act of Sederunt (Ordinary Cause, Summary Application, Summary Cause and Small Claim Rules) Amendment (Miscellaneous) 2007 (SSI 2007/6), para.2(3) (effective January 29, 2007).

**Lay support**

**1.3A.**—[1](1)    At any time during proceedings the sheriff may, on the request of a party litigant, permit    **D1.32**
a named individual to assist the litigant in the conduct of the proceedings by sitting beside or behind (as
the litigant chooses) the litigant at hearings in court or in chambers and doing such of the following for
the litigant as he or she requires—

 (a)    providing moral support;
 (b)    helping to manage the court documents and other papers;
 (c)    taking notes of the proceedings;
 (d)    quietly advising on—
  (i)    points of law and procedure;
  (ii)    issues which the litigant might wish to raise with the sheriff;
  (iii)    questions which the litigant might wish to ask witnesses.

(2)    It is a condition of such permission that the named individual does not receive from the litigant,
whether directly or indirectly, any remuneration for his or her assistance.

(3)    The sheriff may refuse a request under paragraph (1) only if—

 (a)    the sheriff is of the opinion that the named individual is an unsuitable person to act in that
  capacity (whether generally or in the proceedings concerned); or
 (b)    the sheriff is of the opinion that it would be contrary to the efficient administration of
  justice to grant it.

(4)    Permission granted under paragraph (1) endures until the proceedings finish or it is withdrawn
under paragraph (5); but it is not effective during any period when the litigant is represented.

(5)    The sheriff may, of his or her own accord or on the motion of a party to the proceedings, withdraw
permission granted under paragraph (1); but the sheriff must first be of the opinion that it would be
contrary to the efficient administration of justice for the permission to continue.

(6)    Where permission has been granted under paragraph (1), the litigant may—

 (a)    show the named individual any document (including a court document); or
 (b)    impart to the named individual any information,

which is in his or her possession in connection with the proceedings without being taken to contravene
any prohibition or restriction on the disclosure of the document or the information; but the named
individual is then to be taken to be subject to any such prohibition or restriction as if he or she were the
litigant.

(7)    Any expenses incurred by the litigant as a result of the support of an individual under paragraph
(1) are not recoverable expenses in the proceedings.

**Forms1.4.**    Where there is a reference to the use of a form in these Rules, that form in Appendix 1 or    **D1.33**
 Appendix 2, as the case may be, to these Rules, or a form substantially to the same effect, shall be
 used with such variation as circumstances may require.

Chapter 1A[2]

Lay Representation

**Application and interpretation**

**1A.1.**—(1)    This Chapter is without prejudice to any enactment (including any other provision in    **D1.34**
these Rules) under which provision is, or may be, made for a party to a particular type of case before the
sheriff to be represented by a lay representative.

(2)    In this Chapter, a "lay representative" means a person who is not—

 (a)    a solicitor;
 (b)    an advocate, or
 (c)    someone having a right to conduct litigation, or a right of audience, by virtue of section
  27 of the Law Reform (Miscellaneous Provisions) (Scotland) Act 1990.

**Lay representation for party litigants**

**1A.2.**—(1)    In any proceedings in respect of which no provision as mentioned in rule 1A.1(1) is in    **D1.35**
force, the sheriff may, on the request of a party litigant, permit a named individual (a "lay representative") to appear, along with the litigant, at a specified hearing for the purpose of making oral submissions
on behalf of the litigant at that hearing.

---

[1] As inserted by the Act of Sederunt (Sheriff Court Rules) (Miscellaneous Amendments) (No.2) 2010
 (SSI 2010/416) r.2 (effective January 1, 2011).
[2] As inserted by the Act of Sederunt (Sheriff Court Rules) (Lay Representation) 2013 (SSI 2013/91) r.2
 (effective April 4, 2013).

(2)    An application under paragraph (1)—

(a)    is to be made orally on the date of the first hearing at which the litigant wishes a named individual to make oral submissions; and

(b)    is to be accompanied by a document, signed by the named individual, in Form 1A.2.

(3)    The sheriff may grant an application under paragraph (1) only if the sheriff is of the opinion that it would assist his or her consideration of the case to grant it.

(4)    It is a condition of permission granted by the sheriff that the lay representative does not receive directly or indirectly from the litigant any remuneration or other reward for his or her assistance.

(5)    The sheriff may grant permission under paragraph (1) in respect of one or more specified hearings in the case; but such permission is not effective during any period when the litigant is legally represented.

(6)    The sheriff may, of his or her own accord or on the motion of a party to the proceedings, withdraw permission granted under paragraph (1).

(7)    Where permission has been granted under paragraph (1), the litigant may—

(a)    show the lay representative any document (including a court document); or

(b)    impart to the lay representative any information,

which is in his or her possession in connection with the proceedings without being taken to contravene any prohibition or restriction on the disclosure of the document or the information; but the lay representative is then to be taken to be subject to any such prohibition or restriction as if he or she were the litigant.

(8)    Any expenses incurred by the litigant in connection with lay representation under this rule are not recoverable expenses in the proceedings.

Chapter 2

Relief from Compliance with Rules

**Relief from failure to comply with rules**

**D1.36**

**2.1.**—(1)    The sheriff may relieve a party from the consequences of failure to comply with a provision in these Rules which is shown to be due to mistake, oversight or other excusable cause, on such conditions as he thinks fit.

(2)    Where the sheriff relieves a party from the consequences of a failure to comply with a provision in these Rules under paragraph (1), he may make such order as he thinks fit to enable the cause to proceed as if the failure to comply with the provision had not occurred.

Chapter 3

Commencement of Causes

**Form of initial writ**

**D1.37**

**3.1.**—(1)[1]    A cause shall be commenced—

(a)    in the case of an ordinary cause, by initial writ in Form G1; or

(b)    in the case of a commercial action within the meaning of Chapter 40, by initial writ in Form G1A.

or

(c)[2]    in the case of a personal injuries action within the meaning of Part AI of Chapter 36, by initial writ in Form PI1.

(2)    The initial writ shall be written, typed or printed on A4 size paper of durable quality and shall not be backed.

(3)    Where the pursuer has reason to believe that an agreement exists prorogating jurisdiction over the subject matter of the cause to another court, the initial writ shall contain details of that agreement.

(4)    Where the pursuer has reason to believe that proceedings are pending before another court involving the same cause of action and between the same parties as those named in the instance of the initial writ, the initial writ shall contain details of those proceedings.

(5)    An article of condescendence shall be included in the initial writ averring—

(a)    the ground of jurisdiction; and

(b)    the facts upon which the ground of jurisdiction is based.

---

[1] As inserted by the Act of Sederunt (Ordinary Cause Rules) Amendment (Commercial Actions) 2001 (SSI 2001/8) (effective March 1, 2001).

[2] As inserted by the Act of Sederunt (Ordinary Cause Rules Amendment) (Personal Injuries Actions) 2009 (SSI 2009/285) r.2 (effective November 2, 2009).

(6) Where the residence, registered office or place of business, as the case may be, of the defender is not known and cannot reasonably be ascertained, the pursuer shall set out in the instance that the whereabouts of the defender are not known and aver in the condescendence what steps have been taken to ascertain his present whereabouts.

(7) The initial writ shall be signed by the pursuer or his solicitor (if any) and the name and address of that solicitor shall be stated on the back of every service copy of that writ.

**Actions relating to heritable property**

**3.2.**—(1) In an action relating to heritable property, it shall not be necessary to call as a defender any person by reason only of any interest he may have as the holder of a heritable security over the heritable property.

(2) Intimation of such an action shall be made to the holder of the heritable security referred to in paragraph (1)—

    (a) where the action relates to any heritable right or title; and

    (b) in any other case, where the sheriff so orders.

(3) *[Repealed by the Act of Sederunt (Sheriff Court Rules) (Enforcement of Securities over Heritable Property) 2010 (SSI 2010/324) para.2 (effective September 30, 2010).]*

**D1.38**

**Actions relating to regulated agreements3.2A.**[1] In an action which relates to a regulated agreement within the meaning given by section 189(1) of the Consumer Credit Act 1974 the initial writ shall include an averment that such an agreement exists and details of that agreement.

**D1.39**

**Warrants of citation**

**3.3.**—[2, 3](1) The warrant of citation in any cause other than—

    (a) a family action within the meaning of rule 33.1(1),

    (b) an action of multiplepoinding,

    (c) an action in which a time to pay direction under the Debtors (Scotland) Act 1987 or a time order under the Consumer Credit Act 1974 may be applied for by the defender,

    (d) *[Repealed by the Act of Sederunt (Sheriff Court Rules) (Enforcement of Securities over Heritable Property) 2010 (SSI 2010/324) para.2 (effective September 30, 2010).]*

    (e)[4] a civil partnership action within the meaning of rule 33A.1(1) shall be in Form O1.

(2) In a cause in which a time to pay direction under the Debtors (Scotland) Act 1987 or a time order under the Consumer Credit Act 1974 may be applied for by the defender, the warrant of citation shall be in Form O2.

(3) In a cause in which a warrant for citation in accordance with Form O2 is appropriate, there shall be served on the defender (with the initial writ and warrant) a notice in Form O3.

(4) *[Repealed by the Act of Sederunt (Sheriff Court Rules) (Enforcement of Securities over Heritable Property) 2010 (SSI 2010/324) para.2 (effective September 30, 2010).]*

**D1.40**

**Warrants for arrestment to found jurisdiction**

**3.4.**—(1) Where an application for a warrant for arrestment to found jurisdiction may be made, it shall be made in the crave of the initial writ.

(2) Averments to justify the granting of such a warrant shall be included in the condescendence.

**D1.41**

---

[1] As inserted by the Act of Sederunt (Sheriff Court Rules) (Miscellaneous Amendments) 2009 (SSI 2009/294) r.2 (effective December 1, 2009) as substituted by the Act of Sederunt (Amendment of the Act of Sederunt (Sheriff Court Rules) (Miscellaneous Amendments) 2009) 2009 (SSI 2009/402) (effective November 30, 2009).

[2] Inserted by the Act of Sederunt (Amendment of Ordinary Cause Rules and Summary Applications, Statutory Applications and Appeals etc. Rules) (Applications under the Mortgage Rights (Scotland) Act 2001) 2002 (SSI 2002/7), para.2(3).

[3] As amended by the Act of Sederunt (Ordinary Cause, Summary Application, Summary Cause and Small Claim Rules) Amendment (Miscellaneous) 2007 (SSI 2007/6), para.2(4) (effective January 29, 2007).

[4] As amended by Act of Sederunt (Ordinary Cause Rules) Amendment (Family Law (Scotland) Act 2006 etc.) 2006 (SSI 2006/207), para.2 (effective May 4, 2006).

**Warrants and precepts for arrestment on dependence 3.5.** *[Repealed by the Act of Sederunt (Sheriff Court Rules Amendment) (Diligence) 2008 (SSI 2008/121) r.5(2) (effective April 1, 2008).]*

**Period of notice after citation**

**D1.42**

**3.6.**—(1) Subject to rule 5.6(1) (service where address of person is not known) and to paragraph (2) of this rule, a cause shall proceed after one of the following periods of notice has been given to the defender:—

 (a) where the defender is resident or has a place of business within Europe, 21 days after the date of execution of service; or

 (b) where the defender is resident or has a place of business outside Europe, 42 days after the date of execution of service.

(2) Subject to paragraph (3), the sheriff may, on cause shown, shorten or extend the period of notice on such conditions as to the method or manner of service as he thinks fit.

(3) A period of notice may not be reduced to a period of less than 2 days.

(4) Where a period of notice expires on a Saturday, Sunday, or public or court holiday, the period of notice shall be deemed to expire on the next day on which the sheriff clerk's office is open for civil court business.

Chapter 4

Caveats

*[Omitted by Act of Sederunt (Sheriff Court Caveat Rules) 2006 (SI 2006/198), effective April 28, 2006]*

Chapter 5

Citation, Service and Intimation

**Signature of warrants**

**D1.43**

**5.1.**—(1)[1] Subject to paragraph (2), a warrant for citation or intimation may be signed by the sheriff or sheriff clerk.

(2) The following warrants shall be signed by the sheriff:—

 (a) a warrant containing an order shortening or extending the period of notice or any other order other than a warrant which the sheriff clerk may sign;

 (b)[2,3] a warrant for arrestment to found jurisdiction (including the arrestment of a ship);

 (ba)[4,5] a warrant for arrestment on the dependence;

 (c) a warrant for intimation ordered under rule 33.8 (intimation where alleged association).

 (d)[6] a warrant for intimation ordered under rule 33A.8 (intimation where alleged association).

 (e)[7] a warrant for arrestment of a ship to found jurisdiction;

 (f)[8] a warrant for arrestment of a ship or cargo in rem;

 (g)[9] a warrant for arrestment of cargo.

(3) Where the sheriff clerk refuses to sign a warrant which he may sign, the party presenting the initial writ may apply to the sheriff for the warrant.

---

[1] As inserted by the Act of Sederunt (Ordinary Cause, Summary Application and Small Claim Rules) Amendment (Miscellaneous) 2004 (SSI 2004/197) para.2(3) (effective May 21, 2004).

[2] As inserted by the Act of Sederunt (Ordinary Cause, Summary Application and Small Claim Rules) Amendment (Miscellaneous) 2004 (SSI 2004/197) para.2(3) (effective May 21, 2004).

[3] As amended by the Act of Sederunt (Sheriff Court Rules) (Miscellaneous Amendments) 2012 (SSI 2012/188) para.10 (effective August 1, 2012).

[4] As inserted by the Act of Sederunt (Ordinary Cause, Summary Application and Small Claim Rules) Amendment (Miscellaneous) 2004 (SSI 2004/197) para.2(3) (effective May 21, 2004).

[5] As amended by Act of Sederunt (Ordinary Cause Rules) Amendment (Family Law (Scotland) Act 2006 etc.) 2006 (SSI 2006/207) para.2 (effective May 4, 2006).

[6] As inserted by Act of Sederunt (Ordinary Cause Rules) Amendment (Family Law (Scotland) Act 2006 etc.) 2006 (SSI 2006/207) para.2 (effective May 4, 2006).

[7] As inserted by the Act of Sederunt (Sheriff Court Rules) (Miscellaneous Amendments) 2012 (SSI 2012/188) para.10 (effective August 1, 2012).

[8] As inserted by the Act of Sederunt (Sheriff Court Rules) (Miscellaneous Amendments) 2012 (SSI 2012/188) para.10 (effective August 1, 2012).

[9] As inserted by the Act of Sederunt (Sheriff Court Rules) (Miscellaneous Amendments) 2012 (SSI 2012/188) para.10 (effective August 1, 2012).

### Form of citation and certificate

**5.2.**—[1, 2](1)  Subject to rule 5.6 (service where address of person is not known), in any cause other than—

    (a)    a family action within the meaning of rule 33.1(1),

    (aa)[3]  a civil partnership action within the meaning of rule 33A.1(1);

    (b)    an action of multiplepoinding,

    (c)    an action in which a time to pay direction under the Debtors (Scotland) Act 1987 or a time order under the Consumer Credit Act 1974 may be applied for by the defender, or

    (d)    *[Repealed by the Act of Sederunt (Sheriff Court Rules) (Enforcement of Securities over Heritable Property) 2010 (SSI 2010/324) para.2 (effective September 30, 2010).]*

citation by any person shall be in Form O4 which shall be attached to a copy of the initial writ and warrant of citation and shall have appended to it a notice of intention to defend in Form O7.

(2)  In a cause in which a time to pay direction under the Debtors (Scotland) Act 1987 or a time order under the Consumer Credit Act 1974 may be applied for by the defender, citation shall be in Form O5 which shall be attached to a copy of the initial writ and warrant of citation and shall have appended to it a notice of intention to defend in Form O7.

(2A)  *[Repealed by the Act of Sederunt (Sheriff Court Rules) (Enforcement of Securities over Heritable Property) 2010 (SSI 2010/324) para.2 (effective September 30, 2010).]*

(3)  The certificate of citation in any cause other than a family action within the meaning of rule 33.1(1) or an action of multiplepoinding shall be in Form O6 which shall be attached to the initial writ.

(4)  Where citation is by a sheriff officer, one witness shall be sufficient for the execution of citation.

(5)  Where citation is by a sheriff officer, the certificate of citation shall be signed by the sheriff officer and the witness and shall state—

    (a)    the method of citation; and

    (b)    where the method of citation was other than personal or postal citation, the full name and designation of any person to whom the citation was delivered.

(6)  Where citation is executed under paragraph (3) of rule 5.4 (depositing or affixing by sheriff officer), the certificate shall include a statement—

    (a)    of the method of service previously attempted;

    (b)    of the circumstances which prevented such service being executed; and

    (c)    that a copy was sent in accordance with the provisions of paragraph (4) of that rule.

**D1.44**

### Postal service or intimation

**5.3.**—(1)  In any cause in which service or intimation of any document or citation of any person may be by recorded delivery, such service, intimation or citation shall be by the first class recorded delivery service.

(2)  Notwithstanding the terms of section 4(2) of the Citation Amendment (Scotland) Act 1882 (time from which period of notice reckoned), where service or intimation is by post, the period of notice shall run from the beginning of the day after the date of posting.

(3)  On the face of the envelope used for postal service or intimation under this rule there shall be written or printed the following notice:—

"This envelope contains a citation to or intimation from (*specify the court*). If delivery cannot be made at the address shown it is to be returned immediately to:— The Sheriff Clerk (*insert address of sheriff clerk's office*)".

(4)  The certificate of citation or intimation in the case of postal service shall have attached to it any relevant postal receipts.

**D1.45**

### Service within Scotland by sheriff officer

**5.4.**—(1)  An initial writ, decree, charge, warrant or any other order or writ following upon such initial writ or decree served by a sheriff officer on any person shall be served—

**D1.46**

---

[1]  As amended by SI 1996/2445 (effective November 1, 1996) (clerical error) and further amended by the Act of Sederunt (Amendment of Ordinary Cause Rules and Summary Applications, Statutory Applications and Appeals etc. Rules) (Applications under the Mortgage Rights (Scotland) Act 2001) 2002 (SSI 2002/7), para.2(4).

[2]  As amended by the Act of Sederunt (Ordinary Cause, Summary Application, Summary Cause and Small Claim Rules) Amendment (Miscellaneous) 2007 (SSI 2007/6), para.2(5) (effective January 29, 2007).

[3]  As inserted by Act of Sederunt (Ordinary Cause Rules) Amendment (Family Law (Scotland) Act 2006 etc.) 2006, para.2 (SSI 2006/207) (effective May 4, 2006).

(a)    personally; or

(b)    by being left in the hands of a resident at the person's dwelling place or an employee at his place of business.

(2)    Where service is executed under paragraph (1)(b), the certificate of citation or service shall contain the full name and designation of any person in whose hands the initial writ, decree, charge, warrant or other order or writ, as the case may be, was left.

(3)    Where a sheriff officer has been unsuccessful in executing service in accordance with paragraph (1), he may, after making diligent enquiries, serve the document in question—

(a)    by depositing it in that person's dwelling place or place of business; or

(b)[1]    by leaving it at that person's dwelling place or place of business in such a way that it is likely to come to the attention of that person.

(4)    Subject to rule 6.1 (service of schedule of arrestment), where service is executed under paragraph (3), the sheriff officer shall, as soon as possible after such service, send a letter containing a copy of the document by ordinary first class post to the address at which he thinks it most likely that the person on whom service has been executed may be found.

(5)[2]    Where the firm which employs the sheriff officer has in its possession—

(a)    the document or a copy of it certified as correct by the pursuer's solicitor, the sheriff officer may serve the document upon the defender without having the document or certified copy in his possession, in which case he shall if required to do so by the person on whom service is executed and within a reasonable time of being so required, show the document or certified copy to the person; or

(b)    a certified copy of the interlocutor pronounced allowing service of the document, the sheriff officer may serve the document without having in his possession the certified copy interlocutor if he has in his possession a facsimile copy of the certified copy interlocutor (which he shall show, if required, to the person on whom service is executed).

(6)[3]    Where service is executed under paragraphs (1)(b) or (3), the document and the citation or notice of intimation, as the case may be, must be placed in an envelope bearing the notice "This envelope contains a citation to or intimation from (*insert name of sheriff court*)"and sealed by the sheriff officer.

### Service on persons furth of Scotland

**D1.47**

5.5.—[4](1)    Subject to the following provisions of this rule, an initial writ, decree, charge, warrant or any other order or writ following upon such initial writ or decree on a person furth of Scotland shall be served—

(a)    at a known residence or place of business in England, Wales, Northern Ireland, the Isle of Man, the Channel Islands or any country with which the United Kingdom does not have a convention providing for service of writs in that country—

(i)    in accordance with the rules for personal service under the domestic law of the place in which service is to be executed; or

(ii)    by posting in Scotland a copy of the document in question in a registered letter addressed to the person at his residence or place of business;

(b)[5]    in a country which is a party to the Hague Convention on the Service Abroad of Judicial and Extra-Judicial Documents in Civil and Commercial Matters dated 15th November 1965 or the Convention in Schedule 1 or 3C to the Civil Jurisdiction and Judgments Act 1982—

(i)    by a method prescribed by the internal law of the country where service is to be executed for the service of documents in domestic actions upon persons who are within its territory;

---

[1] As substituted by the Act of Sederunt (Sheriff Court Rules) (Miscellaneous Amendments) 2011 (SSI 2011/193) r.2 (effective April 4, 2011).

[2] As inserted by the Act of Sederunt (Ordinary Cause, Summary Application, Summary Cause and Small Claim Rules) Amendment (Miscellaneous) 2003 (SSI 2003/26), para.2(3) (effective January 24, 2003).

[3] As inserted by the Act of Sederunt (Sheriff Court Rules) (Miscellaneous Amendments) 2011 (SSI 2011/193) r.2 (effective April 4, 2011).

[4] As amended by SI 1996/2445 (effective November 1, 1996) and the Act of Sederunt (Ordinary Cause, Summary Application, Summary Cause and Small Claim Rules) Amendment (Miscellaneous) 2003 (SSI 2003/26), para.2(4) (effective January 24, 2003).

[5] As amended by the Act of Sederunt (Ordinary Cause, Summary Application and Small Claim Rules) Amendment (Miscellaneous) 2004 (SSI 2004/197) (effective May 21, 2004), para.2(4).

      (ii)[1]  by or through the central, or other appropriate, authority in the country where service is to be executed at the request of the Scottish Ministers;

      (iii)  by or through a British Consular Office in the country where service is to be executed at the request of the Secretary of State for Foreign and Commonwealth Affairs;

      (iv)  where the law of the country in which the person resides permits, by posting in Scotland a copy of the document in a registered letter addressed to the person at his residence; or

      (v)  where the law of the country in which service is to be executed permits, service by an huissier, other judicial officer or competent official of the country where service is to be executed; or

  (c)  in a country with which the United Kingdom has a convention on the service of writs in that country other than the conventions mentioned in sub-paragraph (b), by one of the methods approved in the relevant convention.

  (d)  *[Repealed by the Act of Sederunt (Ordinary Cause, Summary Application, Summary Cause and Small Claim Rules) Amendment (Miscellaneous) 2004 (SSI 2004/197) r.24(a) (effective May 21, 2004).]*

(1A)[2, 3]  In a country to which the EC Service Regulation applies, service—

  (a)  may be effected by the methods prescribed in paragraph (1)(b)(ii) and (iii) only in exceptional circumstances; and

  (b)  is effected only if the receiving agency has informed the person that acceptance of service may be refused on the ground that the document has not been translated in accordance with paragraph (6).

(2)  Any document which requires to be posted in Scotland for the purposes of this rule shall be posted by a solicitor or a sheriff officer; and on the face of the envelope there shall be written or printed the notice set out in rule 5.3(3).

(3)  In the case of service by a method referred to in paragraph (1)(b)(ii) and (iii), the pursuer shall—

  (a)[4]  send a copy of the writ and warrant for service with citation attached, or other document, as the case may be, with a request for service by the method indicated in the request to the Scottish Ministers or, as the case may be, the Secretary of State for Foreign and Commonwealth Affairs; and

  (b)  lodge in process a certificate signed by the authority which executed service stating that it has been, and the manner in which it was, served.

(4)  In the case of service by a method referred to in paragraph (1)(b)(v), the pursuer or the sheriff officer, shall—

  (a)  send a copy of the writ and warrant for service with citation attached, or other document, as the case may be, with a request for service by the method indicated in the request to the official in the country in which service is to be executed; and

  (b)  lodge in process a certificate of the official who executed service stating that it has been, and the method in which it was, served.

(5)  Where service is executed in accordance with paragraph (1)(a)(i) or (1)(b)(i) other than on another party in the United Kingdom, the Isle of Man or the Channel Islands, the party executing service shall lodge a certificate by a person who is conversant with the law of the country concerned and who practises or has practised law in that country or is a duly accredited representative of the Government of that country, stating that the method of service employed is in accordance with the law of the place where service was executed.

(6)  Every writ, document, citation or notice on the face of the envelope mentioned in rule 5.3(3) shall be accompanied by a translation in—

---

[1] As substituted by the Act of Sederunt (Sheriff Court Rules) (Miscellaneous Amendments) 2011 (SSI 2011/193) r.6 (effective April 4, 2011).

[2] As inserted by the Act of Sederunt (Ordinary Cause, Summary Application and Small Claim Rules) Amendment (Miscellaneous) 2004 (SSI 2004/197) (effective May 21, 2004), para.2(4) and substituted by the Act of Sederunt (Sheriff Court Ordinary Cause, Summary Application, Summary Cause and Small Claims Rules) Amendment (Council Regulation (EC) No. 1348 of 2000 Extension to Denmark) 2007 (SSI 2007/440) r.2(2) (effective October 9, 2007).

[3] As substituted by the Act of Sederunt (Sheriff Court Rules) (Miscellaneous Amendments) (No.2) 2008 (SSI 2008/365) r.7 (effective November 13, 2008).

[4] As amended by the Act of Sederunt (Sheriff Court Rules) (Miscellaneous Amendments) 2011 (SSI 2011/193) r.7 (effective April 4, 2011).

(a)[1]    an official language of the country in which service is to be executed; or

(b)[2]    in a country to which the EC Service Regulation applies, a language of the member state of transmission that is understood by the person on whom service is being executed.

(7)    A translation referred to in paragraph (6) shall be certified as correct by the person making it; and the certificate shall—

(a)    include his full name, address and qualifications; and

(b)    be lodged with the execution of citation or service.

(8)[3]    In this rule "the EC Service Regulation" means Regulation (EC) No. 1393/2007 of the European Parliament and of the Council of 13th November 2007 on the service in the Member States of judicial and extrajudicial documents in civil or commercial matters (service of documents), and repealing Council Regulation (EC) No. 1348/2000, as amended from time to time.

### Service where address of person is not known

**D1.48**

**5.6.**—(A1)[4]    Subject to rule 6.A7 this rule applies to service where the address of a person is not known.

(1)    Where the address of a person to be cited or served with a document is not known and cannot reasonably be ascertained, the sheriff shall grant warrant for citation or service upon that person—

(a)    by the publication of an advertisement in Form G3 in a specified newspaper circulating in the area of the last known address of that person, or

(b)    by displaying on the walls of court a copy of the instance and crave of the initial writ, warrant of citation and a notice in Form G4;

and the period of notice fixed by the sheriff shall run from the date of publication of the advertisement or display on the walls of court, as the case may be.

(2)    Where service requires to be executed under paragraph (1), the pursuer shall lodge a service copy of the initial writ and a copy of any warrant of citation with the sheriff clerk from whom they may be uplifted by the person for whom they are intended.

(3)    Where a person has been cited or served in accordance with paragraph (1) and, after the cause has commenced, his address becomes known, the sheriff may allow the initial writ to be amended subject to such conditions as to re-service, intimation, expenses, or transfer of the cause as he thinks fit.

(4)    Where advertisement in a newspaper is required for the purpose of citation or service under this rule, a copy of the newspaper containing the advertisement shall be lodged with the sheriff clerk by the pursuer.

(5)    Where display on the walls of court is required under paragraph (1)(b), the pursuer shall supply to the sheriff clerk for that purpose a certified copy of the instance and crave of the initial writ and any warrant of citation.

### Persons carrying on business under trading or descriptive name

**D1.49**

**5.7.**—[5](1)    A person carrying on a business under a trading or descriptive name may sue or be sued in such trading or descriptive name alone; and an extract—

(a)    of a decree pronounced in the sheriff court, or

(b)    of a decree proceeding upon any deed, decree arbitral, bond, protest of a bill, promissory note or banker's note or upon any other obligation or document on which execution may proceed, recorded in the sheriff court books,

against such person under such trading or descriptive name shall be a valid warrant for diligence against such person.

(2)    An initial writ, decree, charge, warrant or any other order or writ following upon such initial writ or decree in a cause in which a person carrying on business under a trading or descriptive name sues or is sued in that name may be served—

---

[1] As inserted by the Act of Sederunt (Ordinary Cause, Summary Application and Small Claim Rules) Amendment (Miscellaneous) 2004 (SSI 2004/197) (effective May 21, 2004), para.2(4) and substituted by the Act of Sederunt (Sheriff Court Ordinary Cause, Summary Application, Summary Cause and Small Claims Rules) Amendment (Council Regulation (EC) No. 1348 of 2000 Extension to Denmark) 2007 (SSI 2007/440) r.2(2) (effective October 9, 2007).

[2] As substituted by the Act of Sederunt (Sheriff Court Rules) (Miscellaneous Amendments) (No.2) 2008 (SSI 2008/365) r.7 (effective November 13, 2008).

[3] As substituted by the Act of Sederunt (Sheriff Court Rules) (Miscellaneous Amendments) (No.2) 2008 (SSI 2008/365) r.7 (effective November 13, 2008).

[4] As inserted by the Act of Sederunt (Sheriff Court Rules Amendment) (Diligence) 2008 (SSI 2008/121) r.5(3) (effective April 1, 2008).

[5] As amended by SI 1996/2445 (effective November 1, 1996).

(a)   at any place of business or office at which such business is carried on within the sheriffdom of the sheriff court in which the cause is brought; or

(b)   where there is no place of business within that sheriffdom, at any place where such business is carried on (including the place of business or office of the clerk or secretary of any company, corporation or association or firm).

**Endorsation unnecessary5.8.**   An initial writ, decree, charge, warrant or any other order or writ following upon such initial writ or decree may be served, enforced or otherwise lawfully executed anywhere in Scotland without endorsation by a sheriff clerk; and, if executed by a sheriff officer, may be so executed by a sheriff officer of the court which granted it or by a sheriff officer of the sheriff court district in which it is to be executed. **D1.50**

**Re-service5.9.**   Where it appears to the sheriff that there has been any failure or irregularity in citation or service on a person, he may order the pursuer to re-serve the initial writ on such conditions as he thinks fit. **D1.51**

## No objection to regularity of citation, service or intimation

**5.10.**—(1)   A person who appears in a cause shall not be entitled to state any objection to the regularity of the execution of citation, service or intimation on him; and his appearance shall remedy any defect in such citation, service or intimation. **D1.52**

(2)   Nothing in paragraph (1) shall preclude a party from pleading that the court has no jurisdiction.

Chapter 6

Interim Diligence[1]

*Annotations to Chapter 6 are by Tim Edward.*

GENERAL NOTE

The procedure for obtaining warrant to arrest to found jurisdiction is dealt with at rule 3.4. **D1.53**

The procedure for obtaining warrant for diligence on the dependence of an action is dealt with by Rule 6.A2, and by Part 1A of the Debtors (Scotland) Act 1987 (as inserted by the Bankruptcy and Diligence etc. (Scotland) Act 2007).

The 1987 Act, as amended, provides that the court may make an order granting warrant for diligence on the dependence of an action if it is satisfied, having had a hearing on the matter, that: the creditor has a prima facie case on the merits of the action; there is a real and substantial risk that enforcement by the creditor of any decree in the action would be defeated or prejudiced by reason of the debtor being insolvent or verging on insolvency or the likelihood of the debtor removing, disposing of, burdening, concealing or otherwise dealing with all or some of his assets; and that it is reasonable in all the circumstances to do so. An application for an order granting warrant for diligence must be intimated to the debtor and any other person having an interest (unless the application is for warrant to be granted before a hearing, as described below). Before making such an order, the court must give an opportunity to be heard to (a) any person to whom intimation of the date of the hearing was made; and (b) any other person the court is satisfied has an interest.

The court may make an order granting warrant for diligence without a hearing if it is satisfied that the creditor has a prima facie case, that it is reasonable to grant such an order, and that that there is a real and substantial risk that enforcement of any decree in the action in favour of the creditor would be defeated or prejudiced (again, due to insolvency or the risk of the debtor removing or otherwise dealing with his assets) if warrant were not granted in advance of a hearing.

In both cases, the onus is on the creditor to satisfy the court that the order should be made.

The 1987 Act now specifically provides that it is competent for the court to grant warrant for arrestment or inhibition on the dependence where the sum concluded for is a future or contingent debt. At common law, there had to be special circumstances justifying diligence in respect of a future or contingent debt, such as that the debtor was at significant risk of insolvency or was contemplating flight from the jurisdiction. However such special circumstances, as set out above, now have to be demonstrated in respect of all debts. Common law cases on future and contingent debts may now be of assistance in interpreting the rules applying to all cases under the new provisions.

---

[1] Chapter renamed by the Act of Sederunt (Sheriff Court Rules Amendment) (Diligence) 2008 (SSI 2008/121) r.5(4) (effective April 1, 2008).

Rule 6 sets out the procedure for execution of such arrestments and Rule 6.A4 deals with the recall of an arrestment.

### Interpretation

**D1.54**

6.A1.[1]  In this Chapter—

"the 1987 Act" means the Debtors (Scotland) Act 1987; and
"the 2002 Act" means the Debt Arrangement and Attachment (Scotland) Act 2002.

### Application for interim diligence

**D1.55**

6.A2.—[2](1)  The following shall be made by motion—

    (a)  an application under section 15D(1) of the 1987 Act for warrant for diligence by arrestment or inhibition on the dependence of an action or warrant for arrestment on the dependence of an admiralty action;

    (b)  an application under section 9C of the 2002 Act for warrant for interim attachment.

(2)  Such an application must be accompanied by a statement in Form G4A.

(3)  A certified copy of an interlocutor granting a motion under paragraph (1) shall be sufficient authority for the execution of the diligence concerned.

### Effect of authority for inhibition on the dependence

**D1.56**

6.A3.—[3](1)  Where a person has been granted authority for inhibition on the dependence of an action, a certified copy of the interlocutor granting the motion may be registered with a certificate of execution in the Register of Inhibitions and Adjudications.

(2)[4]  A notice of a certified copy of an interlocutor granting authority for inhibition under rule 6.A2 may be registered in the Register of Inhibitions and Adjudications; and such registration is to have the same effect as registration of a notice of inhibition under section 155(2) of the Titles to Land Consolidation (Scotland) Act 1868.

### Recall etc. of arrestment or inhibition

**D1.57**

6.A4.[5]  An application by any person having an interest—

    (a)  to loose, restrict, vary or recall an arrestment or an interim attachment; or

    (b)  to recall, in whole or in part, or vary, an inhibition,

shall be made by motion.

### Incidental applications in relation to interim diligence, etc

**D1.58**

6.A5.[6]  An application under Part 1A of the 1987 Act or Part 1A of the 2002 Act other than mentioned above shall be made by motion.

### Form of schedule of inhibition on the dependence

**6.A6.**  [*Revoked by the Act of Sederunt (Sheriff Court Rules Amendment) (Diligence) 2009 (SSI 2009/107) r.3 (effective April 22, 2009).*]

### Service of inhibition on the dependence where address of defender not known

**1.59**

6.A7.—[7](1)  Where the address of a defender is not known to the pursuer, an inhibition on the dependence shall be deemed to have been served on the defender if the schedule of inhibition is left with or deposited at the office of the sheriff clerk of the sheriff court district where the defender's last known address is located.

---

[1] As inserted by the Act of Sederunt (Sheriff Court Rules Amendment) (Diligence) 2008 (SSI 2008/121) r.5(5) (effective April 1, 2008).

[2] As inserted by the Act of Sederunt (Sheriff Court Rules Amendment) (Diligence) 2008 (SSI 2008/121) r.5(5) (effective April 1, 2008).

[3] As inserted by the Act of Sederunt (Sheriff Court Rules Amendment) (Diligence) 2008 (SSI 2008/121) r.5(5) (effective April 1, 2008).

[4] As substituted by the Act of Sederunt (Sheriff Court Rules Amendment) (Diligence) 2009 (SSI 2009/107) r.3 (effective April 22, 2009).

[5] As inserted by the Act of Sederunt (Sheriff Court Rules Amendment) (Diligence) 2008 (SSI 2008/121) r.5(5) (effective April 1, 2008).

[6] As inserted by the Act of Sederunt (Sheriff Court Rules Amendment) (Diligence) 2008 (SSI 2008/121) r.5(5) (effective April 1, 2008).

[7] As inserted by the Act of Sederunt (Sheriff Court Rules Amendment) (Diligence) 2008 (SSI 2008/121) r.5(5) (effective April 1, 2008).

(2)   Where service of an inhibition on the dependence is executed under paragraph (1), a copy of the schedule of inhibition shall be sent by the sheriff officer by first class post to the defender's last known address.

### Form of schedule of arrestment on the dependence[1]

**6.A8.**—(1)   An arrestment on the dependence shall be served by serving the schedule of arrestment on the arrestee in Form G4B.

**D1.60**

(2)   A certificate of execution shall be lodged with the sheriff clerk in Form G4C.

### Service of schedule of arrestment

**6.1**   If a schedule of arrestment has not been personally served on an arrestee, the arrestment shall have effect only if a copy of the schedule is also sent by registered post or the first class recorded delivery service to—

**D1.61**

(a)   the last known place of residence of the arrestee, or

(b)   if such place of residence is not known, or if the arrestee is a firm or corporation, to the arrestee's principal place of business if known, or, if not known, to any known place of business of the arrestee;

and the sheriff officer shall, on the certificate of execution, certify that this has been done and specify the address to which the copy of the schedule was sent.

#### "SCHEDULE OF ARRESTMENT"

What is delivered to the arrestee is the "schedule" of arrestment. This is a short copy of the warrant. The sheriff officer will then return an "execution" or report of arrestment which states that the arrestment was duly executed.

Both the schedule and the execution narrate the warrant for the arrestment, (giving its date and the designation of the parties), the arrestee, the sum or subjects arrested and the date of execution. These must conform to the warrant and craves of the initial writ (*Mactaggart v MacKillop* , 1938 S.L.T. 100).

A high degree of precision is required in the schedule. By statute, the schedule must be signed by the officer, and must contain such information as the date and time of the execution and the name, occupation and address of the witness: Citation Acts 1592 and 1693.

Erroneous or defective execution, if in the essentials, can be fatal. Misnaming the pursuer, for example, may be fatal: *Richards & Wallington (Earthmoving) Limited v Whatlings Limited* , 1982 S.L.T. 66. Here the Lord Ordinary (Maxwell) held that "(a) trivial spelling mistake, for example, might not invalidate, but ... I think that a high degree of accuracy in this field is required."

The same rule applies to naming the arrestee (*Henderson's Trs* (1831) 9 S. 618) and to the description of the capacity in which the funds or subjects are due to the common debtor: *Wilson v Mackie* (1875) 3 R. 18. So too does it apply to ambiguity in the description of the funds intended to be attached: *Lattimore v Singleton, Dunn & Co.* , 1911 2 S.L.T. 360.

It has been held that misnomer of the common debtor is not fatal if there is no risk of misunderstanding: *Pollock, Whyte & Waddell v Old Park Forge Limited* (1907) 15 S.L.T. 3. Similarly, misdescription of the capacity in which the arrestee holds any sum arrested need not be fatal if there is no difficulty in identifying the sums in the hands of the arrestee: *Huber v Banks* , 1986 S.L.T. 58.

Furthermore, a defective execution to a summons can be replaced by a correct one before being produced in judgement: *Henderson v Richardson* (1848) 10 D. 1035; *Hamilton v Monkland Iron & Steel Co.* (1863) 1 M. 672.

Where an arrestment has been made on the dependence of an action and subsequently decree is granted in favour of the arresting creditor, the arrestment is automatically transformed into an arrestment in execution and no further service of a schedule of arrestment is required: *Abercrombie v Edgar and Crerar Ltd.* , 1923 S.L.T. 271. In contrast to the diligence of poinding and sale, and arrestment against earnings, an arrestment on the dependence of an action or in execution proceeds without a charge having been served on the debtor.

#### "...PERSONALLY SERVED..."

(i)   Where the arrestee is an individual, the schedule of arrestment need not be served personally; it may also be served at his dwelling-place: *Campbell v Watson Trustees* (1898) 25 R. 690. Rule 6.1 provides that if the latter course is taken then the arrestment shall have effect only if a copy of the schedule of arrestment is also sent by registered post or the first class recorded delivery service to

---

[1] As inserted by the Act of Sederunt (Sheriff Court Rules Amendment) (Diligence) 2009 (SSI 2009/ 107) r.3 (effective April 22, 2009).

the last known place of residence of the arrestee, or, if such place of residence is not known, or if the arrestee is a firm or corporation, to the arrestee's principal place of business if known, or, if not known, to any known place of business of the arrestee. Postal service alone is incompetent, except in summary cause actions: Execution of Diligence (S) Act 1926, s.2 and *Dick Bros v Thomas C Gray Ltd* , 1958 S.L.T. (Sh. Ct.) 66.

(ii)   If the arrestee is a bank, the service of the arrestment should be made at its registered office, or the schedule should be delivered to an official at head office (see Macphail, *Sheriff Court Practice*, at 11.21. He also states that in all cases, notice by way of another schedule should be served at the branch where the account of the common debtor is kept).

(iii)   Where the arrestee is a corporation, the arrestment should name the corporation, and can be delivered to the hands of an employee: *Campbell v Watson's Trustee* (1898) 25 R. 690; *Gall v Stirling Water Commissioners* (1901) 9 S.L.T. (Sh. Ct.) 13. Service on a superior officer of a company does not appear to be essential, although it is a proper precaution according to Lord Young in *Campbell v Watson's Trustees* (1898) 25 R. 690. Delivery to the registered office is certainly competent, by virtue of the Companies Act 2006 s.1139(1).

In *McIntyre v Caledonian Railway Co.* (1909), 25 Sh. Ct Rep. 529, it was held that an arrestment by handing a schedule to a servant of a corporation within one of its branch offices was effectual, and rendered unnecessary the posting of a schedule to the corporation. However, this is authority only for the proposition that service at a branch office is only good in respect of subjects held at that branch.

It should be noted that in *Corson v Macmillan* , 1927 S.L.T. (Sh. Ct.) 13 it was found that service on a director at a place that was not a place of business was bad. This tends to suggest service at the registered office is the safest option. This should also attach subjects at branch offices.

(iv)   For a firm with a social name the arrestment should name the firm and be served at the place of business in the hands of an employee. Should the firm have a descriptive name then the arrestment should be served at its place of business and personally on or at the dwelling- places of three partners, should there be as many.

(v)   Where the arrestees are trustees, the schedule should be served on such trustees as are entitled to act (*Gracie v Gracie* , 1910 S.C. 899). The schedule should also state that the arrestment is served on each as a trustee and not as an individual: *Burns v Gillies* (1906) 8 F. 460.

Where the arrestment is not executed personally, and the arrestee in justifiable ignorance of it has paid away the arrested fund, he cannot be called upon to refund the money (*Laidlaw v Smith* 1838, 16 S. 367, aff'g. 2 Rob. App. 490; *Leslie v Lady Ashburton* , 1827, 6 S. 165)

**D1.62**

**Arrestment on dependence before service**

**6.2.**   *[Repealed by the Act of Sederunt (Sheriff Court Rules Amendment) (Diligence) 2008 (SSI 2008/ 121) r.5(6) (effective April 1, 2008).]*

RULE 6.2

**D1.63**

Rule 6.2 dealt with arrestment on the dependence of an action before service of the initial writ. This was repealed by the Act of Sederunt (Sheriff Court Rules Amendment) (Diligence) 2008 (SSI 2008/121) r.5(6) (effective 1 April 2008) and this area is now dealt with by Section 15G of the Debtors (Scotland) Act 1987.

**D1.64**

**Movement of arrested property**

**6.3.—**   [Omitted by the Act of Sederunt (Sheriff Court Rules) (Miscellaneous Amendments) 2012 (SSI 2012/188) para.10 (effective August 1, 2012).]

RULE 6.3

Rule 6.3, which allowed for an application to be made for a warrant authorising the movement of a vessel or cargo which is the subject of an arrestment, was omitted by the Act of Sederunt (Sheriff Court

Rules) (Miscellaneous Amendments) 2012 (SSI 2012/188) para.10 (effective 1 August 2012). Admiralty Actions are now dealt with by Rule 49 and section 47 of the Administration of Justice Act 1956.

Chapter 7

**D1.65**

Undefended Causes

### Application of this Chapter

**7.1.** This Chapter applies to any cause other than an action in which the sheriff may not grant decree without evidence.

**D1.66**

### Minute for granting of decree without attendance

**7.2.**—(1)[1] Subject to the following paragraphs, where the defender—

**D1.67**

   (a)   does not lodge a notice of intention to defend,

   (b)   does not lodge an application for a time to pay direction under the Debtors (Scotland) Act 1987 or a time order under the Consumer Credit Act 1974,

   (c)   has lodged such an application for a time to pay direction or time order and the pursuer does not object to the application or to any recall or restriction of an arrestment sought in the application,

the sheriff may, on the pursuer endorsing a minute for decree on the initial writ, at any time after the expiry of the period for lodging that notice or application, grant decree in absence or other order in terms of the minute so endorsed without requiring the attendance of the pursuer in court.

   (2)   The sheriff shall not grant decree under paragraph (1)—

   (a)   unless it appears ex facie of the initial writ that a ground of jurisdiction exists under the Civil Jurisdiction and Judgments Act 1982; and

   (b)   the cause is not a cause—

      (i)   in which decree may not be granted without evidence;

      (ii)   to which paragraph (4) applies; or

      (iii)[2] to which rule 33.31 (procedure in undefended family action for a section 11 order) applies.

   (3)   Where a defender is domiciled in another part of the United Kingdom or in another Contracting State, the sheriff shall not grant decree in absence until it has been shown that the defender has been able to receive the initial writ in sufficient time to arrange for his defence or that all necessary steps have been taken to that end; and for the purposes of this paragraph—

   (a)   the question whether a person is domiciled in another part of the United Kingdom shall be determined in accordance with sections 41 and 42 of the Civil Jurisdiction and Judgments Act 1982;

   (b)   the question whether a person is domiciled in another Contracting State shall be determined in accordance with Article 52 of the Convention in Schedule 1 or 3C to that Act; and

   (c)   the term "Contracting State" has the meaning assigned in section 1 of that Act.

   (4)   Where an initial writ has been served in a country to which the Hague Convention on the Service Abroad of Judicial and Extra-Judicial Documents in Civil or Commercial Matters dated 15th November 1965 applies, decree shall not be granted until it is established to the satisfaction of the sheriff that the requirements of Article 15 of that Convention have been complied with.

### Applications for time to pay directions or time orders in undefended causes

**7.3.**—(1) This rule applies to a cause in which—

**D1.68**

   (a)[3]   a time to pay direction may be applied for under the Debtors (Scotland) Act 1987; or

   (b)   a time order may be applied for under the Consumer Credit Act 1974.

   (2)   A defender in a cause which is otherwise undefended, who wishes to apply for a time to pay direction or time order, and where appropriate, to have an arrestment recalled or restricted, shall complete and lodge with the sheriff clerk the appropriate part of Form O3 before the expiry of the period of notice.

---

[1] As amended by the Act of Sederunt (Ordinary Cause, Summary Application, Summary Cause and Small Claim Rules) Amendment (Miscellaneous) 2007 (SSI 2007/6) r.2(6) (effective January 29, 2007).

[2] As amended by SI 1996/2167 (effective November 1, 1996) and SI 1996/2445 (effective November 1, 1996).

[3] As amended by the Act of Sederunt (Ordinary Cause, Summary Application, Summary Cause and Small Claim Rules) Amendment (Miscellaneous) 2007 (SSI 2007/6) r.2(7) (effective January 29, 2007).

(2A)[1]　As soon as possible after the application of the defender is lodged, the sheriff clerk shall send a copy of it to the pursuer by first class ordinary post.

(3)　Where the pursuer does not object to the application of the defender made in accordance with paragraph (2), he shall minute for decree in accordance with rule 7.2; and the sheriff may grant decree or other order in terms of the application and minute.

(4)[2]　Where the pursuer objects to the application of the defender made in accordance with paragraph (2) he shall on the same date—

 (a) complete and lodge with the sheriff clerk Form O3A;

 (b) minute for decree in accordance with rule 7.2; and

 (c) send a copy of Form O3A to the defender.

(4A)[3]　The sheriff clerk shall then fix a hearing on the application of the defender and intimate the hearing to the pursuer and the defender.

(4B)[4]　The hearing must be fixed for a date within 28 days of the date on which the Form O3A and the minute for decree are lodged.

(5)　The sheriff may determine an application in which a hearing has been fixed under paragraph (4) whether or not any of the parties appear.

**Decree for expenses**

**D1.69**

**7.4.**　On granting decree in absence or thereafter, the sheriff may grant decree for expenses.

**Finality of decree in absence**

**D1.70**

**7.5.**[5]　Subject to section 9(7) of the Land Tenure Reform (Scotland) Act 1974 (decree in action of removing for breach of condition of long lease to be final when extract recorded in Register of Sasines), a decree in absence which has not been recalled or brought under review by suspension or by reduction shall become final and shall have effect as a decree *in foro contentioso*—

 (a) on the expiry of six months from the date of the decree or from the date of a charge made under it, as the case may be, where the service of the initial writ or of the charge has been personal; and

 (b) in any event, on the expiry of 20 years from the date of the decree.

**Amendment of initial writ**

**D1.71**

**7.6.**—(1)　In an undefended cause, the sheriff may—

 (a) allow the pursuer to amend the initial writ in any way permitted by rule 18.2 (powers of sheriff to allow amendment); and

 (b) order the amended initial writ to be re-served on the defender on such period of notice as he thinks fit.

(2)　The defender shall not be liable for the expense occasioned by any such amendment unless the sheriff so orders.

(3)　Where an amendment has been allowed under paragraph (1), the amendment—

 (a) shall not validate diligence used on the dependence of a cause so as to prejudice the rights of creditors of the party against whom the diligence has been executed who are interested in defeating such diligence; and

 (b) shall preclude any objection to such diligence stated by a party or any person by virtue of a title acquired or in right of a debt contracted by him subsequent to the execution of such diligence.

**Disapplication of certain rules**

**D1.72**

**7.7**[6]　The following rules in Chapter 15 (motions) shall not apply to an action in which no notice of intention to defend has been lodged or to any action in so far as it proceeds as undefended—

rule 15.2 (intimation of motions),

rule 15.3 (opposition to motions),

---

[1] As inserted by the Act of Sederunt (Sheriff Court Rules) (Miscellaneous Amendments) 2009 (SSI 2009/294) r.2 (effective December 1, 2009).

[2] Para.(4) substituted for paras (4)–(4B) by the Act of Sederunt (Sheriff Court Rules) (Miscellaneous Amendments) 2009 (SSI 2009/294) r.2 (effective December 1, 2009).

[3] Para.(4) substituted for paras (4)–(4B) by the Act of Sederunt (Sheriff Court Rules) (Miscellaneous Amendments) 2009 (SSI 2009/294) r.2 (effective December 1, 2009).

[4] Para.(4) substituted for paras (4)–(4B) by the Act of Sederunt (Sheriff Court Rules) (Miscellaneous Amendments) 2009 (SSI 2009/294) r.2 (effective December 1, 2009).

[5] As amended by SI 1996/2445 (effective November 1, 1996).

[6] Inserted by SI 1996/2445 (effective November 1, 1996).

rule 15.5 (hearing of motions).

## Chapter 8

### Reponing

**Reponing**

**8.1.**—(1)  In any cause other than—

    (a)[1]  a cause mentioned in rule 33.1(a) to (h) or (n) to (p), (certain family actions), or

    (aa)[2]  a cause mentioned in rule 33A.1(a), (b) or (f) (certain civil partnership actions);

    (b)  a cause to which Chapter 37 (causes under the Presumption of Death (Scotland) Act 1977) applies,

the defender or any party with a statutory title or interest may apply to be reponed by lodging with the sheriff clerk, before implement in full of a decree in absence, a reponing note setting out his proposed defence or the proposed order or direction and explaining his failure to appear.

(2)  A copy of the note lodged under paragraph (1) shall be served on the pursuer and any other party—

(3)  The sheriff may, on considering the reponing note, recall the decree so far as not implemented subject to such order as to expenses as he thinks fit; and the cause shall thereafter proceed as if—

    (a)  the defender had lodged a notice of intention to defend and the period of notice had expired on the date on which the decree in absence was recalled; or

    (b)[3]  the party seeking the order or direction had lodged the appropriate application on the date when the decree was recalled.

(4)  A reponing note, when duly lodged with the sheriff clerk and served upon the pursuer, shall have effect to sist diligence.

(4A)[4]  Where an initial writ has been served on a defender furth of the United Kingdom under rule 5.5(1)(b) (service on persons furth of Scotland) and decree in absence has been pronounced against him as a result of his failure to enter appearance, the court may, on the defender applying to be reponed in accordance with paragraph (1) above, recall the decree and allow defences to be received if—

    (a)  without fault on his part, he did not have knowledge of the initial writ in sufficient time to defend;

    (b)  he has disclosed a prima facie defence to the action on the merits; and

    (c)  the reponing note is lodged within a reasonable time after he had knowledge of the decree or in any event before the expiry of one year from the date of decree.

(5)  Any interlocutor or order recalling, or incidental to the recall of, a decree in absence shall be final and not subject to appeal.

**D1.73**

## Chapter 9

### Standard Procedure in Defended Causes

**Notice of intention to defend**

**9.1.**—(1)[5, 6]  Subject to rules 33.34 (notice of intention to defend and defences in family action) 33A.34 (notice of intention to defend and defences in civil partnership action) and 35.8 (lodging of notice of appearance in action of multiplepoinding), where the defender intends to—

    (a)  challenge the jurisdiction of the court,

    (b)  state a defence, or

    (c)  make a counterclaim,

he shall, before the expiry of the period of notice, lodge with the sheriff clerk a notice of intention to defend in Form O7 and, at the same time, send a copy to the pursuer.

**D1.74**

---

[1] As amended by Act of Sederunt (Ordinary Cause Rules) Amendment (Family Law (Scotland) Act 2006 etc.) 2006 (SSI 2006/207) r.2 (effective May 4, 2006) and by the Act of Sederunt (Sheriff Court Rules) (Miscellaneous Amendments) (No.2) 2010 (SSI 2010/416) r.8 (effective January 1, 2011).

[2] Inserted by Act of Sederunt (Ordinary Cause Rules) Amendment (Family Law (Scotland) Act 2006 etc.) 2006 (SSI 2006/207) r.2 (effective May 4, 2006).

[3] Inserted by the Act of Sederunt (Ordinary Cause, Summary Application and Small Claim Rules) Amendment (Miscellaneous) 2004 (SSI 2004/197) r.2(5) (effective May 21, 2004).

[4] Inserted by SSI 2000/239 (effective October 2, 2000).

[5] As amended by the Act of Sederunt (Family Proceedings in the Sheriff Court) 1996 (SI 1996/2167) (effective November 1, 2000).

[6] As amended by Act of Sederunt (Ordinary Cause Rules) Amendment (Family Law (Scotland) Act 2006 etc.) 2006 (SSI 2006/207) r.2 (effective May 4, 2006).

(2) The lodging of a notice of intention to defend shall not imply acceptance of the jurisdiction of the court.

(3)[1] This Chapter shall not apply to a commercial action within the meaning of Chapter 40.

### Fixing date for Options Hearing

**D1.75**

**9.2.**—(1)[2] Subject to paragraph (1A), on the lodging of a notice of intention to defend, the sheriff clerk shall fix a date and time for an Options Hearing which date shall be on the first suitable court day occurring not sooner than 10 weeks after the expiry of the period of notice.

(1A)[3, 4] Where in a family action or a civil partnership action—

  (i)   the only matters in dispute are an order in terms of section 11 of the Children (Scotland) Act 1995 (court orders relating to parental responsibilities etc.); or

  (ii)  the matters in dispute include an order in terms of section 11 of that Act,

there shall be no requirement to fix an Options Hearing in terms of paragraph (1) above insofar as the matters in dispute relate to an order in terms of section 11(2) of the Children (Scotland) Act 1995.

(1B)[5]  In paragraph (1A) above—

  (a)   "family action" has the meaning given in rule 33.1(1); and

  (b)   "civil partnership action" has the meaning given in rule 33A.1(1).

(2)  On fixing the date for the Options Hearing, the sheriff clerk shall—

  (a)   forthwith intimate to the parties in Form G5—

    (i)    the last date for lodging defences;

    (ii)   the last date for adjustment; and

    (iii)  the date of the Options hearing; and

  (b)   prepare and sign an interlocutor recording those dates.

(3)[6]  The fixing of the date for the Options Hearing shall not affect the right of a party to make any incidental application to the court.

### Alteration of date for Options Hearing

**D1.76**

**9.2A.**—[7](1)  Subject to paragraph (2), at any time before the date and time fixed under rule 9.2 (fixing date for Options Hearing) or under this rule, the sheriff—

  (a)   may, of his own motion or on the motion of any party—

    (i)    discharge the Options Hearing; and

    (ii)   fix a new date and time for the Options Hearing; or

  (b)   shall, on the joint motion of the parties—

    (i)    discharge the Options Hearing; and

    (ii)   fix a new date and time for the Options Hearing.

(2)  The date and time to be fixed—

  (a)   under paragraph (1)(a)(ii) may be earlier or later than the date and time fixed for the discharged Options Hearing;

  (b)   under paragraph (1)(b)(ii) shall be earlier than the date and time fixed for the discharged Options Hearing.

---

[1] Inserted by the Act of Sederunt (Ordinary Cause Rules) Amendment (Commercial Actions) 2001 (SSI 2001/8) (effective March 1, 2001).

[2] As amended by the Act of Sederunt (Sheriff Court Ordinary Cause Rules Amendment) (Miscellaneous) 2000 (SSI 2000/239) (effective October 2, 2000).

[3] Added by the Act of Sederunt (Sheriff Court Ordinary Cause Rules Amendment) (Miscellaneous) 2000 (SSI 2000/239) (effective October 2, 2000).

[4] As amended by Act of Sederunt (Ordinary Cause Rules) Amendment (Family Law (Scotland) Act 2006 etc.) 2006 (SSI 2006/207) (effective May 4, 2006).

[5] Inserted by Act of Sederunt (Ordinary Cause Rules) Amendment (Family Law (Scotland) Act 2006 etc.) 2006 (SSI 2006/207) (effective May 4, 2006).

[6] As amended by the Act of Sederunt (Sheriff Court Ordinary Cause Rules Amendment) (Miscellaneous) 1996 (SI 1996/2445) (effective November 1, 1996).

[7] Inserted by the Act of Sederunt (Sheriff Court Ordinary Cause Rules Amendment) (Miscellaneous) 1996 (SI 1996/2445) (effective November 1, 1996) and substituted by the Act of Sederunt (Ordinary Cause and Summary Application Rules) Amendment (Miscellaneous) 2006 (SI 2006/410) (effective August 18, 2006).

(3)    Where the sheriff is considering making an order under paragraph (1)(a) of his own motion and in the absence of the parties, the sheriff clerk shall—

    (a)    fix a date, time and place for the parties to be heard; and

    (b)    inform the parties of that date, time and place.

(4)    The sheriff may discharge a hearing fixed under paragraph (3) on the joint motion of the parties.

(5)    On the discharge of the Options Hearing under paragraph (1), the sheriff clerk shall forthwith intimate to all parties—

    (a)    that the Options Hearing has been discharged under paragraph (1)(a) or (b), as the case may be;

    (b)    the last date for lodging defences, if appropriate;

    (c)    the last date for adjustment, if appropriate; and

    (d)    the new date and time fixed for the Options Hearing under paragraph (1)(a) or (b), as the case may be.

(6)    Any reference in these Rules to the Options Hearing or a continuation of it shall include a reference to an Options Hearing for which a date and time has been fixed under this rule.

**Return of initial writ**

**9.3.**    Subject to rule 9.4 (lodging of pleadings before Options Hearing), the pursuer shall return the initial writ, unbacked and unfolded, to the sheriff clerk within 7 days after the expiry of the period of notice.    **D1.77**

**Lodging of pleadings before Options Hearing**

**9.4.**    Where any hearing, whether by motion or otherwise, is fixed before the Options Hearing, each party shall lodge in process a copy of his pleadings, or, where the pleadings have been adjusted, the pleadings as adjusted, not later than 2 days before the hearing.    **D1.78**

**Process folder**

**9.5.**—(1)    On receipt of the notice of intention to defend, the sheriff clerk shall prepare a process folder which shall include—    **D1.79**

    (a)    interlocutor sheets;

    (b)    duplicate interlocutor sheets;

    (c)    a production file;

    (d)    a motion file; and

    (e)    an inventory of process.

(2)    Any production or part of process lodged in a cause shall be placed in the process folder.

**Defences**

**9.6.**—(1)    Where a notice of intention to defend has been lodged, the defender shall (subject to paragraph (3)) lodge defences within 14 days after the expiry of the period of notice.    **D1.80**

(2)    Subject to rule 19.1(3) (form of defences where counterclaim included), defences shall be in the form of answers in numbered paragraphs corresponding to the articles of the condescendence, and shall have appended a note of the pleas-in-law of the defender.

(3)[12]    In a family action (within the meaning of rule 33.1(1)) or a civil partnership action (within the meaning of rule 33A.1(1)), neither a crave nor averments need be made in the defences which relate to any order under section 11 of the Children (Scotland) Act 1995.

**Implied admissions**

**9.7.**    Every statement of fact made by a party shall be answered by every other party, and if such a statement by one party within the knowledge of another party is not denied by that other party, that other party shall be deemed to have admitted that statement of fact.    **D1.81**

**Adjustment of pleadings**

**9.8.**—(1)    Parties may adjust their pleadings until 14 days before the date of the Options Hearing or any continuation of it.    **D1.82**

(2)    Any adjustments shall be exchanged between parties and not lodged in process.

(3)    Parties shall be responsible for maintaining a record of adjustments made during the period for adjustment.

---

[1] Inserted by the Act of Sederunt (Family Proceedings in the Sheriff Court) 1996 (SI 1996/ 2167) (effective November 1, 2000).

[2] As amended by Act of Sederunt (Ordinary Cause Rules) Amendment (Family Law (Scotland) Act 2006 etc.) 2006 (SSI 2006/207) (effective May 4, 2006).

(4)   No adjustments shall be permitted after the period mentioned in paragraph (1) except with leave of the sheriff.

**Effect of sist on adjustment**

**D1.83**

**9.9.**—(1)   Where a cause has been sisted, any period for adjustment before the sist shall be reckoned as a part of the period for adjustment.

(2)   On recall of the sist of a cause, the sheriff clerk shall—

(a)   fix a new date for the Options Hearing;

(b)   prepare and sign an interlocutor recording that date; and

(c)   intimate that date to each party.

**Open record**

**D1.84**

**9.10.**   The sheriff may, at any time before the closing of the record in a cause to which this Chapter applies, of his own motion or on the motion of a party, order any party to lodge a copy of the pleadings in the form of an open record containing any adjustments and amendments made as at the date of the order.

**Record for Options Hearing**

**D1.85**

**9.11.**—(1)   The pursuer shall, at the end of the period for adjustment referred to in rule 9.8(1), and before the Options Hearing, make a copy of the pleadings and any adjustments and amendments in the form of a record.

(2)   Not later than 2 days before the Options Hearing, the pursuer shall lodge a certified copy of the record in process.

(3)[1]   Where the Options Hearing is continued under rule 9.12(5), and further adjustment or amendment is made to the pleadings, a copy of the pleadings as adjusted or amended, certified by the pursuer, shall be lodged in process not later than 2 days before the Options Hearing so continued.

**Options Hearing**

**D1.86**

**9.12.**—(1)   At the Options Hearing the sheriff shall seek to secure the expeditious progress of the cause by ascertaining from parties the matters in dispute and information about any other matter referred to in paragraph (3).

(2)   It shall be the duty of parties to provide the sheriff with sufficient information to enable him to conduct the hearing as provided for in this rule.

(3)   At the Options Hearing the sheriff shall, except where the cause is ordered to proceed under the procedure in Chapter 10 (additional procedure), close the record and—

(a)   appoint the cause to a proof and make such orders as to the extent of proof, the lodging of a joint minute of admissions or agreement, or such other matter as he thinks fit;

(b)   after having heard parties and considered any note lodged under rule 22.1 (note of basis of preliminary plea), appoint the cause to a proof before answer and make such orders as to the extent of proof, the lodging of a joint minute of admissions or agreement, or such other matter as he thinks fit; or

(c)[2]   after having heard parties and considered any note lodged under rule 22.1, appoint the cause to debate if satisfied that there is a preliminary matter of law which if established following debate would lead to decree in favour of any party, or to limitation of proof to any substantial degree.

(d)[3]   consider any child witness notice or vulnerable witness application that has been lodged where no order has been made, or

(e)[4]   ascertain whether there is or is likely to be a vulnerable witness within the meaning of section 11(1) of the Act of 2004 who is to give evidence at any proof or hearing and whether any order under section 12(1) of the Act of 2004 requires to be made.

---

[1] Inserted by SI 1996/2445 (effective November 1, 1996).

[2] As amended by the Act of Sederunt (Ordinary Cause, Summary Application and Small Claim Rules) Amendment (Miscellaneous) 2004 (SSI 2004/197) (effective May 21, 2004).

[3] As inserted by the Act of Sederunt (Ordinary Cause, Summary Application, Summary Cause and Small Claim Rules) Amendment (Vulnerable Witnesses (Scotland) Act 2004) 2007 (SSI 2007/463) r.2(3) (effective November 1, 2007).

[4] As inserted by the Act of Sederunt (Ordinary Cause, Summary Application, Summary Cause and Small Claim Rules) Amendment (Vulnerable Witnesses (Scotland) Act 2004) 2007 (SSI 2007/463) r.2(3) (effective November 1, 2007).

(f)[1]   where the cause has been appointed to proof or proof before answer and Chapter 33AA applies, assign a case management hearing.

(4)   At the Options Hearing the sheriff may, having heard parties—

   (a)   of his own motion or on the motion of any party, and

   (b)   on being satisfied that the difficulty or complexity of the cause makes it unsuitable for the procedure under this Chapter,

order that the cause proceed under the procedure in Chapter 10 (additional procedure).

(5)   The sheriff may, on cause shown, of his own motion or on the motion of any party, allow a continuation of the Options Hearing on one occasion only for a period not exceeding 28 days or to the first suitable court day thereafter.

(6)   On closing the record—

   (a)   where there are no adjustments made since the lodging of the record under rule 9.11(2), that record shall become the closed record; and

   (b)   where there are such adjustments, the sheriff may order that a closed record including such adjustments be lodged within 7 days after the date of the interlocutor closing the record.

(7)[2]   For the purposes of rules 16.2 (decrees where party in default), 33.37 (decree by default in family action) and 33A.37 (decree by default in civil partnership action), an Options Hearing shall be a diet in accordance with those rules.

(8)[3]   Where the cause is appointed, under paragraph (3), to a proof or proof before answer, the sheriff shall consider whether a pre-proof hearing should be fixed under rule 28A.1.

(9)[4]   Paragraph (8) does not apply where Chapter 33AA applies.

**9.13.–9.15.**   *[Omitted by the Act of Sederunt (Ordinary Cause, Summary Application and Small Claim Rules) Amendment (Miscellaneous) 2004 (SSI 2004/197) (effective May 21, 2004), r.2(7).]*

Chapter 9A[5]

Documents and Witnesses

**Application of this Chapter**

**9A.1.**   This Chapter applies to any cause proceeding under Chapters 9 and 10.      **D1.87**

**Inspection and recovery of documents**

**9A.2.**—(1)   Each party shall, within 14 days after the date of the interlocutor allowing proof or proof   **D1.88** before answer, intimate to every other party a list of the documents, which are or have been in his possession or control and which he intends to use or put in evidence at the proof, including the whereabouts of those documents.

(2)   A party who has received a list of documents from another party under paragraph (1) may inspect those documents which are in the possession or control of the party intimating the list at a time and place fixed by that party which is reasonable to both parties.

(3)   A party who seeks to use or put in evidence at a proof a document not on his list intimated under paragraph (1) shall, if any other party objects to such document being used or put in evidence, seek leave of the sheriff to do so; and such leave may be granted on such conditions, if any, as the sheriff thinks fit.

(4)   Nothing in this rule shall affect—

   (a)   the law relating to, or the right of a party to object, to the inspection of a document on the ground of privilege or confidentiality; or

   (b)   the right of a party to apply under rule 28.2 for a commission and diligence for recovery of documents or an order under section 1 of the Administration of Justice (Scotland) Act 1972.

---

[1] As inserted by the Act of Sederunt (Sheriff Court Rules)(Miscellaneous Amendments) (No.2) 2013 (SI 2013/139) para.2 (effective June 3, 2013).

[2] As amended by Act of Sederunt (Ordinary Cause Rules) Amendment (Family Law (Scotland) Act 2006 etc.) 2006 (SSI 2006/207) (effective May 4, 2006).

[3] Inserted by the Act of Sederunt (Ordinary Cause and Summary Application Rules) Amendment (Miscellaneous) 2006 (SSI 2006/410) (effective August 18, 2006).

[4] As inserted by the Act of Sederunt (Sheriff Court Rules)(Miscellaneous Amendments) (No.2) 2013 (SI 2013/139) para.2 (effective June 3, 2013).

[5] Inserted by the Act of Sederunt (Ordinary Cause, Summary Application and Small Claim Rules) Amendment (Miscellaneous) 2004 (SSI 2004/197) (effective May 21, 2004) and substituted by the Act of Sederunt (Ordinary Cause, Summary Application, Summary Cause and Small Claim Rules) Amendment (Miscellaneous) 2007 (SSI 2007/6) (effective January 29, 2007).

**Exchange of lists of witnesses**

**D1.89**

**9A.3.**—(1)   Within 28 days after the date of the interlocutor allowing a proof or proof before answer, each party shall—

(a)   intimate to every other party a list of witnesses, including any skilled witnesses, on whose evidence he intends to rely at proof; and

(b)   lodge a copy of that list in process.

(2)   A party who seeks to rely on the evidence of a person not on his list intimated under paragraph (1) shall, if any other party objects to such evidence being admitted, seek leave of the sheriff to admit that evidence whether it is to be given orally or not; and such leave may be granted on such conditions, if any, as the sheriff thinks fit.

(3)[1]   The list of witnesses intimated under paragraph (1) shall include the name, occupation (where known) and address of each intended witness and indicate whether the witness is considered to be a vulnerable witness within the meaning of section 11(1) of the Act of 2004 and whether any child witness notice or vulnerable witness application has been lodged in respect of that witness.

**Applications in respect of time to pay directions, arrestments and time orders**

**D1.90**

**9A.4.**   An application for—

(a)   a time to pay direction under section 1(1) of the Debtors (Scotland) Act 1987;

(b)   the recall or restriction of an arrestment under section 2(3) or 3(1) of that Act; or

(c)   a time order under section 129 of the Consumer Credit Act 1974,

in a cause which is defended, shall be made by motion lodged before the sheriff grants decree.

Chapter 10

Additional Procedure

**Additional period for adjustment**

**D1.91**

**10.1.**—(1)   Where, under rule 9.12(4) (order at Options Hearing to proceed under Chapter 10), the sheriff orders that a cause shall proceed in accordance with the procedure in this Chapter, he shall continue the cause for adjustment for a period of 8 weeks.

(2)   Paragraphs (2) and (3) of rule 9.8 (exchange and record of adjustments) shall apply to a cause in which a period for adjustment under paragraph (1) of this rule has been allowed as they apply to the period for adjustment under that rule.

**Effect of sist on adjustment period**

**D1.92**

**10.2.**   Where a cause has been sisted, any period for adjustment before the sist shall be reckoned as part of the period for adjustment.

**Variation of adjustment period**

**D1.93**

**10.3.**—(1)   At any time before the expiry of the period for adjustment the sheriff may close the record if parties, of consent or jointly, lodge a motion seeking such an order.

(2)   The sheriff may, if satisfied that there is sufficient reason for doing so, extend the period for adjustment for such period as he thinks fit, if any party—

(a)   lodges a motion seeking such an order; and

(b)   lodges a copy of the record adjusted to the date of lodging of the motion.

(3)   A motion lodged under paragraph (2) shall set out—

(a)   the reasons for seeking an extension of the period for adjustment; and

(b)   the period for adjustment sought.

**Order for open record**

**D1.94**

**10.4.**   The sheriff may, at any time before the closing of the record in a cause to which this of his own motion or on the motion of a party, order any party to lodge a copy of the pleadings in the form of an open record containing any adjustments and amendments made as at the date of the order.

**Closing record**

**D1.95**

**10.5.**—(1)   On the expiry of the period for adjustment, the record shall be closed and, without the attendance of parties, the sheriff clerk shall forthwith—

(a)   prepare and sign an interlocutor recording the closing of the record and fixing the date of

---

[1] As amended by the Act of Sederunt (Ordinary Cause, Summary Application, Summary Cause and Small Claim Rules) Amendment (Vulnerable Witnesses (Scotland) Act 2004) 2007 (SSI 2007/463) r.2(4) (effective November 1, 2007).

the Procedural Hearing under rule 10.6, which date shall be on the first suitable court day occurring not sooner than 21 days after the closing of the record; and

    (b)    intimate the date of the hearing to each party.

(2)    The pursuer shall, within 14 days after the date of the interlocutor closing the record, lodge a certified copy of the closed record in process.

(3)    The closed record shall contain only the pleadings of the parties.

### Procedural Hearing

**10.6.**—(1)    At the Procedural Hearing, the sheriff shall seek to secure the expeditious progress of the cause by ascertaining from parties the matters in dispute and information about any other matter referred to in paragraph (3).

**D1.96**

(2)    It shall be the duty of parties to provide the sheriff with sufficient information to enable him to conduct the hearing as provided for in this rule.

(3)    At the Procedural Hearing the sheriff shall—

    (a)    appoint the cause to a proof and make such orders as to the extent of proof, the lodging of a joint minute of admissions or agreement, or such other matter as he thinks fit;

    (b)    after having heard the parties and considered any note lodged under rule 22.1 (note of basis of preliminary plea), appoint the cause to a proof before answer and make such orders as to the extent of proof, the lodging of a joint minute of admissions or agreement, or such other matter as he thinks fit; or

    (c)[1]    after having heard parties and considered any note lodged under rule 22.1, appoint the cause to a debate if satisfied that there is a preliminary matter of law which if established following debate would lead to decree in favour of any party, or to limitation of proof to any substantial degree.

    (d)[2]    consider any child witness notice or vulnerable witness application that has been lodged where no order has been made, or

    (e)[3]    ascertain whether there is or is likely to be a vulnerable witness within the meaning of section 11(1) of the Act of 2004 who is to give evidence at any proof or hearing and whether any order under section 12(1) of the Act of 2004 requires to be made.

    (f)[1]    where the cause has been appointed to proof or proof before answer and Chapter 33AA applies, assign a case management hearing.

(4)[4]    For the purposes of rules 16.2 (decrees where party in default), 33.37 (decree by default in family action) and 33A.37 (decree by default in civil partnership action), a Procedural Hearing shall be a diet in accordance with those rules.

(5)[5]    Where the cause is appointed, under paragraph (3), to a proof or proof before answer, the sheriff shall consider whether a pre-proof hearing should be fixed under rule 28A.1.

(6)[4]    Paragraph (5) does not apply where Chapter 33AA applies.

Chapter 11

The Process

### Form and lodging of parts of process

**11.1.**    All parts of process shall be written, typed or printed on A4 size paper of durable quality and shall be lodged, unbacked and unfolded, with the sheriff clerk.

**D1.97**

### Custody of process

**11.2.**—(1)    The initial writ, and all other parts of process lodged in a cause, shall be placed by the sheriff clerk in the process folder.

**D1.98**

---

[1] As amended by the Act of Sederunt (Ordinary Cause, Summary Application and Small Claim Rules) Amendment (Miscellaneous) 2004 (SSI 2004/197) r.2(9) (effective May 21, 2004).

[2] As inserted by the Act of Sederunt (Ordinary Cause, Summary Application, Summary Cause and Small Claim Rules) Amendment (Vulnerable Witnesses (Scotland) Act 2004) 2007 (SSI 2007/463) r.2(5) (effective November 1, 2007).

[3] As inserted by the Act of Sederunt (Ordinary Cause, Summary Application, Summary Cause and Small Claim Rules) Amendment (Vulnerable Witnesses (Scotland) Act 2004) 2007 (SSI 2007/463) r.2(5) (effective November 1, 2007).

[4] As amended by the Act of Sederunt (Ordinary Cause and Summary Application Rules) Amendment (Miscellaneous) 2006 (SSI 2006/410) (effective August 18, 2006).

[5] Inserted by the Act of Sederunt (Ordinary Cause and Summary Application Rules) Amendment (Miscellaneous) 2006 (SSI 2006/410) (effective August 18, 2006).

(2) The initial writ, interlocutor sheets, borrowing receipts and the process folder shall remain in the custody of the sheriff clerk.

(3) The sheriff clerk may, on cause shown, authorise the initial writ to be borrowed by the pursuer, his solicitor or the solicitor's authorised clerk.

### Borrowing and returning of process

**D1.99**

11.3.—(1) Subject to paragraph (3), a process, or any part of a process which may be borrowed, may be borrowed only by a solicitor or by his authorised clerk.

(2) All remedies competent to enforce the return of a borrowed process may proceed on the warrant of the court from the custody of which the process was obtained.

(3) A party litigant—

  (a) may borrow a process only—
    (i) with leave of the sheriff; and
    (ii) subject to such conditions as the sheriff may impose; or
  (b) may inspect a process and obtain copies, where practicable, from the sheriff clerk.

(4) The sheriff may, on the motion of any party, ordain any other party who has borrowed a part of process to return it within such time as the sheriff thinks fit.

### Failure to return parts of process

**D1.100**

11.4.—(1) Where a solicitor or party litigant has borrowed any part of process and fails to return it for any diet or hearing at which it is required, the sheriff may impose on such solicitor or party litigant a fine not exceeding £50, which shall be payable to the sheriff clerk; but an order imposing a fine may, on cause shown, be recalled by the sheriff.

(2) An order made under this rule shall not be subject to appeal.

### Replacement of lost documents

**D1.101**

11.5. Where any part of process is lost or destroyed, a copy of it, authenticated in such manner as the sheriff thinks fit, may be substituted for and shall, for the purposes of the cause to which the process relates, be treated as having the same force and effect as the original.

### Intimation of parts of process and adjustments

**D1.102**

11.6.—[1](1) After a notice of intention to defend has been lodged, any party lodging a part of process or making an adjustment to his pleadings shall, at the same time, intimate such lodging or adjustment to every other party who has entered the process by delivering to every other party a copy of each part of process or adjustment, including, where practicable, copies of any documentary production.

(2) Unless otherwise provided in these Rules, the party required to give intimation under paragraph (1) shall deliver to every other party who has entered the process a copy of the part of process or adjustment or other document, as the case may be, by—

  (a) any of the methods of service provided for in Chapter 5 (citation, service and intimation); or
  (b) where intimation is to a party represented by a solicitor—
    (i) personal delivery,
    (ii) facsimile transmission,
    (iii) first class ordinary post,
    (iv) delivery to a document exchange,
    to that solicitor.

(3) Subject to paragraph (4), where intimation is given under—

  (a) paragraph (2)(b)(i) or (ii), it shall be deemed to have been given—
    (i) on the day of transmission or delivery where it is given before 5.00 p.m. on any day; or
    (ii) on the day after transmission or delivery where it is given after 5.00 p.m. on any day; or
  (b) paragraph (2)(b)(iii) or (iv), it shall be deemed to have been given on the day after posting or delivery.

(4) Where intimation is given or, but for this paragraph, would be deemed to be given on a Saturday, Sunday or public or court holiday, it shall be deemed to have been given on the next day on which the sheriff clerk's office is open for civil court business.

---

[1] As amended by SI 1996/2445 (effective November 1, 1996).

**Retention and disposal of parts of process by sheriff clerk**

**D1.103**

**11.7.**—(1)   Where any cause has been finally determined and the period for marking an appeal has expired without an appeal having been marked, the sheriff clerk shall—

    (a)   retain—

        (i)   the initial writ;

        (ii)   any closed record;

        (iii)   the interlocutor sheets;

        (iv)   any joint minute;

        (v)   any offer and acceptance of tender;

        (vi)   any report from a person of skill;

        (vii)   any affidavit; and

        (viii)   any extended shorthand notes of the proof; and

    (b)   dispose of all other parts of process (except productions) in such a manner as seems appropriate.

(2)   Where an appeal has been marked on the final determination of the cause, the sheriff clerk shall exercise his duties mentioned in paragraph (1) after the final disposal of the appeal and any subsequent procedure.

**Uplifting of productions from process**

**D1.104**

**11.8.**—(1)   Each party who has lodged productions in a cause shall—

    (a)   within 14 days after the final determination of the cause, where no subsequent appeal has been marked, or

    (b)   within 14 days after the disposal of any appeal marked on the final determination of the cause,

uplift the productions from process.

(2)   Where any production has not been uplifted as required by paragraph (1), the sheriff clerk shall intimate to—

    (a)   the solicitor who lodged the production, or

    (b)   where no solicitor is acting, the party himself or such other party as seems appropriate,

that if he fails to uplift the production within 28 days after the date of such intimation, it will be disposed of in such a manner as the sheriff directs.

Chapter 12

Interlocutors

**Signature of interlocutors by sheriff clerk**

**D1.105**

**12.1.**   In accordance with any directions given by the Sheriff Principal, any interlocutor other than a final interlocutor may be written and signed by the sheriff clerk and—

    (a)   any interlocutor written and signed by a sheriff clerk shall be treated for all purposes as if it had been written and signed by the sheriff; and

    (b)   any extract of such an interlocutor shall not be invalid by reason only of its being written and signed by a sheriff clerk.

**Further provisions in relation to interlocutors**

**D1.106**

**12.2.**—[1](1)   The sheriff may sign an interlocutor when outwith his or her sheriffdom.

(2)   At any time before extract, the sheriff may correct any clerical or incidental error in an interlocutor or note attached to it.

(3)   Paragraphs (4) and (5) apply in any cause other than—

    (a)   an undefended family action within the meaning of rule 33.1(1); or

    (b)   an undefended civil partnership action within the meaning of rule 33A.1(1).

(4)   At the conclusion of any hearing in which evidence has been led, the sheriff shall either—

    (a)   pronounce an extempore judgment in accordance with rule 12.3; or

    (b)   reserve judgment in accordance with rule 12.4.

(5)   In circumstances other than those mentioned in paragraph (4), the sheriff may, and must when requested by a party, append to the interlocutor a note setting out the reasons for the decision.

(6)   A party must make a request under paragraph (5) in writing within 7 days of the date of the interlocutor.

---

[1] As substituted by the Act of Sederunt (Sheriff Court Rules) (Miscellaneous Amendments) 2012 (SSI 2012/188) para.2 (effective August 1, 2012).

(7) Where a party requests a note of reasons other than in accordance with paragraph (6), the sheriff may provide such a note.

### Extempore judgments

**D1.107**

**12.3.**—[1](1) This rule applies where a sheriff pronounces an extempore judgment in accordance with rule 12.2(4)(a).

(2) The sheriff must state briefly the grounds of his or her decision, including the reasons for his or her decision on any questions of fact or law or of admissibility of evidence.

(3) The sheriff may, and must if requested to do so by a party, append to the interlocutor a note setting out the matters referred to in paragraph (2) and his or her findings in fact and law.

(4) A party must make a request under paragraph (3) in writing within 7 days of the date of the extempore judgment.

(5) Where a party requests a note of reasons other than in accordance with paragraph (4), the sheriff may provide such a note.

### Reserved judgments

**D1.108**

**12.4.**—[2](1) This rule applies where a sheriff reserves judgment in accordance with rule 12.2(4)(b).

(2) The sheriff must give to the sheriff clerk—

    (a) an interlocutor giving effect to the sheriff's decision and incorporating findings in fact and law; and

    (b) a note stating briefly the grounds of his or her decision, including the reasons for his or her decision on any questions of fact or law or of admissibility of evidence.

(3) The date of the interlocutor is the date on which it is received by the sheriff clerk.

(4) The sheriff clerk must forthwith send a copy of the documents mentioned in paragraph (2) to each party.

Chapter 13

Party Minuter Procedure

*Annotations to Chapters 13 to 18 by Sheriff Iain Peebles.*

### Person claiming title and interest to enter process as defender

**D1.109**

**13.1.**—(1) A person who has not been called as a defender or third party may apply by minute for leave to enter a process as a party minuter and to lodge defences.

(2) A minute under paragraph (1) shall specify—

    (a) the applicant's title and interest to enter the process; and

    (b) the grounds of the defence he proposes to state.

(3) Subject to paragraph (4), after hearing the applicant and any party, the sheriff may—

    (a) if he is satisfied that the applicant has shown title and interest to enter the process, grant the applicant leave to enter the process as a party minuter and to lodge defences; and

    (b) make such order as to expenses or otherwise as he thinks fit.

(4)[3] Where an application under paragraph (1) is made after the closing of the record or in a personal injuries action subject to personal injuries procedure after the date upon which the record is required to be lodged, the sheriff shall only grant leave under paragraph (3) if he is satisfied as to the reason why earlier application was not made.

### Procedure following leave to enter process

**D1.110**

**13.2.**—(1)[4] Where a party minuter lodges answers, the sheriff clerk shall fix a date and time under rule 9.2 for a hearing under rule 9.12 (Options Hearing) as if the party minuter had lodged a notice of intention to defend and the period of notice had expired on the date for lodging defences.

(2) At the Options Hearing, or at any time thereafter, the sheriff may grant such decree or other order as he thinks fit.

---

[1] As inserted by the Act of Sederunt (Sheriff Court Rules) (Miscellaneous Amendments) 2012 (SSI 2012/188) para.2 (effective August 1, 2012).

[2] As inserted by the Act of Sederunt (Sheriff Court Rules) (Miscellaneous Amendments) 2012 (SSI 2012/188) para.2 (effective August 1, 2012).

[3] As amended by the Act of Sederunt (Ordinary Cause Rules Amendment) (Personal Injuries Actions) 2009 (SSI 2009/285) r.2 (effective November 2, 2009).

[4] As amended by SI 1996/2445 (effective November 1, 1996).

(3) A decree or other order against the party minuter shall have effect and be extractable in the same way as a decree or other order against a defender.

(4)[1] Paragraphs (1), (2) and (3) shall not apply to a personal injuries action which is subject to personal injuries procedure.

(5)[2] Where the sheriff grants an application under rule 13.1 in a personal injuries action which is subject to personal injuries procedure, the sheriff may make such further order as he thinks fit.

GENERAL NOTE

The procedure set out in this rule is appropriate where a person believes he has title and interest to defend an action but he has not been called as a defender or introduced as a third party by a defender using third party procedure. This rule allows a minute to be lodged setting forth their title, interest and proposed ground of defence.

It is a matter of discretion for the court whether a person who establishes title and interest should be granted leave to enter the process in terms of this Rule of Court. If allowed to enter the process, defences are lodged in the usual form.

It may not be appropriate to allow the party to be sisted where no defence which has a reasonable chance of success has been stated (see: *Glasgow Corporation v Regent Oil Company Ltd* , 1971 S.L.T. (Sh.Ct) 61 per Sheriff Principal Sir Allan Walker at 62). It is important that a reasonably full statement of the proposed defence is set forth in the minute. For examples of situations where it was held not to be appropriate to grant see: *Laing's Sewing Machine Company v Norrie & Sons* , 1877 5 R. 29 and *Aberdeen Grit Company Ltd v The Corporation of the City of Aberdeen* , 1948 S.L.T. (N.) 44 (although the latter case may have been decided on a question of title and interest).

*"after closing of the record'.*

before leave is granted to enter the process the court must in addition be satisfied that there is a proper reason why an earlier application was not made.

*"procedure following leave to enter'.*

broadly follows that set out in Chapter 9.

### Chapter 13A[3]

**D1.111**

Interventions by the Commission for Equality and Human Rights

**Interpretation**

**13A.1.** In this Chapter "the CEHR" means the Commission for Equality and Human Rights.

**D1.112**

**Interventions by the CEHR**

**13A.2.**—(1) The CEHR may apply to the sheriff for leave to intervene in any cause in accordance with this Chapter.

**D1.113**

(2) This Chapter is without prejudice to any other entitlement of the CEHR by virtue of having title and interest in relation to the subject matter of any proceedings by virtue of section 30(2) of the Equality Act 2006 or any other enactment to seek to be sisted as a party in those proceedings.

(3) Nothing in this Chapter shall affect the power of the sheriff to make such other direction as he considers appropriate in the interests of justice.

(4) Any decision of the sheriff in proceedings under this Chapter shall be final and not subject to appeal.

**Applications to intervene**

**13A.3.**—(1) An application for leave to intervene shall be by way of minute of intervention in Form O7A and the CEHR shall—

**D1.114**

    (a) send a copy of it to all the parties; and

    (b) lodge it in process, certifying that subparagraph (a) has been complied with.

(2) A minute of intervention shall set out briefly—

---

[1] As inserted by the Act of Sederunt (Ordinary Cause Rules Amendment) (Personal Injuries Actions) 2009 (SSI 2009/285) r.2 (effective November 2, 2009).

[2] As inserted by the Act of Sederunt (Ordinary Cause Rules Amendment) (Personal Injuries Actions) 2009 (SSI 2009/285) r.2 (effective November 2, 2009).

[3] As inserted by the Act of Sederunt (Sheriff Court Rules) (Miscellaneous Amendments) 2008 (SSI 2008/223) r.4(2) (effective July 1, 2008).

(a)  the CEHR's reasons for believing that the proceedings are relevant to a matter in connection with which the CEHR has a function;

(b)  the issue in the proceedings which the CEHR wishes to address; and

(c)  the propositions to be advanced by the CEHR and the CEHR's reasons for believing that they are relevant to the proceedings and that they will assist the sheriff.

(3)  The sheriff may—

(a)  refuse leave without a hearing;

(b)  grant leave without a hearing unless a hearing is requested under paragraph (4);

(c)  refuse or grant leave after such a hearing.

(4)  A hearing, at which the applicant and the parties may address the court on the matters referred to in paragraph (6)(c), may be held if, within 14 days of the minute of intervention being lodged, any of the parties lodges a request for a hearing.

(5)  Any diet in pursuance of paragraph (4) shall be fixed by the sheriff clerk who shall give written intimation of the diet to the CEHR and all the parties.

(6)  The sheriff may grant leave only if satisfied that—

(a)  the proceedings are relevant to a matter in connection with which the CEHR has a function;

(b)  the propositions to be advanced by the CEHR are relevant to the proceedings and are likely to assist him; and

(c)  the intervention will not unduly delay or otherwise prejudice the rights of the parties, including their potential liability for expenses.

(7)  In granting leave the sheriff may impose such terms and conditions as he considers desirable in the interests of justice, including making provision in respect of any additional expenses incurred by the parties as a result of the intervention.

(8)  The sheriff clerk shall give written intimation of a grant or refusal of leave to the CEHR and all the parties.

**Form of intervention**

**D1.115**

**13A.4.**—(1)  An intervention shall be by way of a written submission which (including any appendices) shall not exceed 5000 words.

(2)  The CEHR shall lodge the submission and send a copy of it to all the parties by such time as the sheriff may direct.

(3)  The sheriff may in exceptional circumstances—

(a)  allow a longer written submission to be made;

(b)  direct that an oral submission is to be made.

(4)  Any diet in pursuance of paragraph (3)(b) shall be fixed by the sheriff clerk who shall give written intimation of the diet to the CEHR and all the parties.

Chapter 13B[1]

Interventions by the Scottish Commission for Human Rights

**Interpretation**

**D1.116**

**13B.1.**  In this Chapter—

"the Act of 2006" means the Scottish Commission for Human Rights Act 2006; and

"the SCHR" means the Scottish Commission for Human Rights.

**Application to intervene**

**D1.117**

**13B.2.**—(1)  An application for leave to intervene under section 14(2)(a) of the Act of 2006 shall be by way of minute of intervention in Form O7B and the SCHR shall—

(a)  send a copy of it to all the parties; and

(b)  lodge it in process, certifying that subparagraph (a) has been complied with.

(2)  In granting leave the sheriff may impose such terms and conditions as he considers desirable in the interests of justice, including making provision in respect of any additional expenses incurred by the parties as a result of the intervention.

(3)  The sheriff clerk shall give written intimation of a grant or refusal of leave to the SCHR and all the parties.

---

[1] As inserted by the Act of Sederunt (Sheriff Court Rules) (Miscellaneous Amendments) 2008 (SSI 2008/223) r.4(2) (effective July 1, 2008).

(4)   Any decision of the sheriff in proceedings under this Chapter shall be final and not subject to appeal.

### Invitation to intervene

**13B.3.**—(1)   An invitation to intervene under section 14(2)(b) of the Act of 2006 shall be in Form O7C and the sheriff clerk shall send a copy of it to the SCHR and all the parties.

**D1.118**

(2)   An invitation under paragraph (1) shall be accompanied by—
  (a)   a copy of the pleadings in the proceedings; and
  (b)   such other documents relating to those proceedings as the sheriff thinks relevant.

(3)   In issuing an invitation under section 14(2)(b) of the Act of 2006, the sheriff may impose such terms and conditions as he considers desirable in the interests of justice, including making provision in respect of any additional expenses incurred by the parties as a result of the intervention.

### Form of intervention

**13B.4.**—(1)   An intervention shall be by way of a written submission which (including any appendices) shall not exceed 5000 words.

**D1.119**

(2)   The SCHR shall lodge the submission and send a copy of it to all the parties by such time as the sheriff may direct.

(3)   The sheriff may in exceptional circumstances—
  (a)   allow a longer written submission to be made;
  (b)   direct that an oral submission is to be made.

(4)   Any diet in pursuance of paragraph (3)(b) shall be fixed by the sheriff clerk who shall give written intimation of the diet to the SCHR and all the parties.

Chapter 14

Applications by Minute

### Application of this Chapter

**14.1.**—(1)   Where an application may be made by minute, the form of the minute and the procedure to be adopted shall, unless otherwise provided in these Rules, be in accordance with this Chapter.

**D1.120**

(2)[1]   This Chapter shall not apply to—
  (a)   a minute of amendment;
  (b)   a minute of abandonment; or
  (c)   a joint minute.

GENERAL NOTE

The procedure set out in this rule is appropriate where a party is applying to the court for a decision on matters which cannot be dealt with by motion, and require a crave, supporting averments and plea-in-law.

### Form of minute

**D1.121**

**14.2.**   A minute to which this Chapter applies shall contain—
  (a)   a crave;
  (b)   where appropriate, a condescendence in the form of a statement of facts supporting the crave; and
  (c)   where appropriate, pleas-in-law.

"FORM OF MINUTES"

In all essential matters a minute will be in the same form as an Initial Writ.

### Lodging of minutes

**D1.122**

**14.3.**—[2](1)   Before intimating any minute, the minuter shall lodge the minute in process.

(2)   On the lodging of a minute, and any document under rule 21.1(1)(b) (lodging documents founded on or adopted), the sheriff—
  (a)   may make an order for answers to be lodged;
  (b)   may order intimation of the minute without making an order for answers; or
  (c)   where he considers it appropriate for the expeditious disposal of the minute or for any other specified reason, may fix a hearing.

---

[1] As amended by SI 1996/2445 (effective November 1, 1996).
[2] Substituted by SI 1996/2445 (effective November 1, 1996).

(3)   Any answers ordered to be lodged under paragraph (2)(a) shall, unless otherwise ordered by the sheriff, be lodged within 14 days after the date of intimation of the minute.

(4)   Where the sheriff fixes a hearing under paragraph (2)(c), the interlocutor fixing that hearing shall specify whether—

    (a)   answers are to be lodged;

    (b)   the sheriff will hear evidence at that hearing; and

    (c)   the sheriff will allow evidence by affidavit.

(5)   Any answers or affidavit evidence ordered to be lodged under paragraph (4) shall be lodged within such time as shall be specified in the interlocutor of the sheriff.

(6)   The following rules shall not apply to any hearing fixed under paragraph (2)(c):—

        rule 14.7 (opposition where no order for answers made),

        rule 14.8 (hearing of minutes where no opposition or no answers lodged),

        rule 14.10 (notice of opposition or answers lodged).

(7)   The sheriff clerk shall forthwith return the minute to the minuter with any interlocutor pronounced by the sheriff.

*"Lodging of Minutes"* After the lodging of the minute in process, depending on the nature of the decision sought and the whole circumstances as set out in the minute, the sheriff will make one of three orders regarding further procedure. If a hearing is fixed by the sheriff at this stage the interlocutor fixing this will further state (a) if evidence is to be heard at the hearing and (b) if evidence will be allowed in the form of affidavits. The normal reason for fixing a hearing at this stage is urgency in having the matter dealt with.

**D1.123**

### Intimation of minutes

**14.4.**—[1](1)   The party lodging a minute shall, on receipt from the sheriff clerk of the minute, intimate to every other party including any person referred to in rule 14.13(1)—

    (a)   a notice in Form G7A, G7B or G7C, as the case may be, by any of the methods provided for in rule 14.5 (methods of intimation); and

    (b)   a copy of—

        (i)   the minute;

        (ii)   any interlocutor; and

        (iii)   any document referred to in the minute.

(2)   The sheriff may, on cause shown, dispense with intimation.

*"Intimation of Minutes"* Intimation only occurs following the sheriff pronouncing an interlocutor in terms of 14.3(2).

**D1.124**

### Methods of intimation

**14.5.**—[2](1)   Intimation of a minute may be given by—

    (a)   any of the methods of service provided for in Chapter 5 (citation, service and intimation); or

    (b)   where intimation is to a party represented by a solicitor, by—

        (i)   personal delivery,

        (ii)   facsimile transmission,

        (iii)   first class ordinary post, or

        (iv)   delivery to a document exchange, to that solicitor.

(2)   Where intimation is given—

    (a)   under paragraph (1)(b)(i) or (ii), it shall be deemed to have been given—

        (i)   on the day of transmission or delivery where it is given before 5.00 p.m. on any day; or

        (ii)   on the day after transmission or delivery where it is given after 5.00 p.m. on any day; or

    (b)   under paragraph 1(b)(iii) or (iv), it shall be deemed to have been given on the day after the date of posting or delivery.

*"Method of Intimation"* The methods of intimation are the same as in respect to motions.

---

[1] Inserted by SI 1996/2445 (effective November 1, 1996).
[2] Inserted by SI 1996/2445 (effective November 1, 1996).

**Return of minute with evidence of intimation**

**14.6.**[1]   Where intimation of any minute has been given, the minute and a certificate of intimation in Form G8 shall be returned to the sheriff clerk within 5 days after the date of intimation.

**Opposition where no order for answers made**

**14.7.**—[2](1)   Where a party seeks to oppose a minute lodged under rule 14.3 (lodging of minutes) in which no order for answers has been made under paragraph (2)(a) of that rule, that party shall, within 14 days after the date of intimation of the minute to him—
    (a)   complete a notice of opposition in Form G9;
    (b)   lodge the notice with the sheriff clerk; and
    (c)   intimate a copy of that notice to every other party.
    (2)   Rule 14.5 (methods of intimation) and rule 14.6 (return of minute with evidence of intimation) shall apply to intimation of opposition to a minute under paragraph (1)(c) of this rule as they apply to intimation of a minute.
    (3)   The sheriff may, on cause shown, reduce or dispense with the period for lodging the notice mentioned in paragraph (1)(b).

The procedure to be followed where a minute is opposed and the sheriff has pronounced an interlocutor in terms of paragraph 2(a) of the Rule is as set out in 14.7.

**Hearing of minutes where no opposition or no answers lodged**

**14.8.**—[3](1)   Where no notice of opposition is lodged or where no answers have been lodged to the minute within the time allowed, the minute shall be determined by the sheriff in chambers without the attendance of parties, unless the sheriff otherwise directs.
    (2)   Where the sheriff requires to hear a party on a minute, the sheriff clerk shall—
    (a)   fix a date, time and place for the party to be heard; and
    (b)   inform that party—
        (i)   of that date, time and place; and
        (ii)   of the reasons for the sheriff wishing to hear him.
In the same way as with an unopposed motion an unopposed minute may be determined by the sheriff without the necessity of parties attending. As with an unopposed motion, if the sheriff believes it necessary he may order the attendance of parties to hear from them in relation to the minute.

**Intimation of interlocutor**

**14.9.**[4]   Where a minute has been determined in accordance with rule 14.8 (hearing of minutes where no opposition or no answers lodged), the sheriff clerk shall intimate the interlocutor determining that minute to the parties forthwith.

**Notice of opposition or answers lodged**

**14.10.**—[5](1)   Where a notice of opposition has, or answers have, been lodged to the minute, the sheriff clerk shall—
    (a)   assign a date, time and place for a hearing on the first suitable court day after the date of the lodging of the notice of opposition or answers, as the case may be; and
    (b)   intimate that date, time and place to the parties.
    (2)   The interlocutor fixing a hearing under paragraph (1) shall specify whether the sheriff will hear evidence at the hearing or receive evidence by affidavit.

*"Notice of Opposition or Answers Lodged"*. If a hearing is fixed and a notice of opposition or answers are lodged then, as with a hearing ordered in terms of paragraph 2(c), the sheriff will specify whether evidence will be heard and if so whether affidavit evidence will be allowed. If answers have been lodged, this interlocutor will normally also allow an adjustment period. Usually adjustment will be allowed until 2 weeks before the date of the hearing. The interlocutor may also direct the lodging of a record, however, the lodging thereof is not mandatory in terms of this rule. If a case proceeds to a hearing in which evidence is to be led the procedure will be the same as at a proof.

---

[1] Inserted by SI 1996/2445 (effective November 1, 1996).
[2] Inserted by SI 1996/2445 (effective November 1, 1996).
[3] Inserted by SI 1996/2445 (effective November 1, 1996).
[4] Inserted by SI 1996/2445 (effective November 1, 1996).
[5] Inserted by SI 1996/2445 (effective November 1, 1996).

**D1.130**

### Orders under section 11 of the Children (Scotland) Act 1995

**14.10A.**—[1](1)   This rule applies where a notice of opposition or answers are lodged in respect of a minute including a crave for an order under section 11 of the Children (Scotland) Act 1995 (court orders relating to parental responsibilities etc.).

(2)   The sheriff, having regard to the measures referred to in Chapter 33AA (expeditious resolution of certain causes), may make such orders as the sheriff considers appropriate to ensure the expeditious resolution of the issues in dispute.

### Procedure for hearing

**D1.131**

**14.11.**—[2](1)   A certified copy of the interlocutor assigning a hearing under this Chapter and requiring evidence to be led shall be sufficient warrant to a sheriff officer to cite a witness on behalf of a party.

(2)   At the hearing, the sheriff shall hear parties on the minute and any answers lodged, and may determine the minute or may appoint such further procedure as he considers necessary.

### Consent to minute

**D1.132**

**14.12.**[3]   Subject to paragraph (2) of rule 14.8 (hearing of minutes where no opposition or no answers lodged), where all parties to the action indicate to the sheriff, by endorsement of the minute or otherwise in writing, their intention to consent to the minute, the sheriff may forthwith determine the minute in chambers without the appearance of parties.

### Procedure following grant of minute

**D1.133**

**14.13.**—[4](1)   Where the minute includes a crave seeking leave—

    (a)   for a person—

        (i)    to be sisted as a party to the action, or

        (ii)   to appear in the proceedings, or

    (b)   for the cause to be transferred against the representatives of a party who has died or is under a legal incapacity,

the sheriff, on granting the minute, may order a hearing under rule 9.12 (Options Hearing) to be fixed or may appoint such further procedure as he thinks fit.

(2)   Where an Options Hearing is ordered under paragraph (1), the sheriff clerk shall—

    (a)   fix a date and time for such hearing, which date, unless the sheriff otherwise directs, shall be on the first suitable court day occurring not sooner than 10 weeks after the date of the interlocutor of the sheriff ordering such hearing be fixed;

    (b)   forthwith intimate to the parties in Form G5—

        (i)     where appropriate, the last date for lodging defences;

        (ii)    where appropriate, the last date for adjustment; and

        (iii)   the date of the Options Hearing; and

    (c)   prepare and sign an interlocutor recording those dates.

(3)   For the purpose of fixing the date for the Options Hearing referred to in paragraph (1), the date of granting the minute shall be deemed to be the date of expiry of the period of notice.

"*Expenses*". If expenses are sought the sheriff will deal with the issue in accordance with the general rules in respect of the awarding of expenses.

**D1.134**

### Chapter 15[5]

Motions

### Lodging of motions

**15.1.**—(1)   A motion may be made—

    (a)   orally with leave of the court during any hearing of a cause; or

    (b)   by lodging a written motion in Form G6.

(2)   Subject to paragraph (3), a written motion shall be lodged with the sheriff clerk within 5 days after the date of intimation of the motion required by rule 15.2 (intimation of motions) with—

    (a)   a certificate of intimation in Form G8; and

---

[1] As inserted by the Act of Sederunt (Sheriff Court Rules)(Miscellaneous Amendments) (No.2) 2013 (SI 2013/139) para.2 (effective June 3, 2013).

[2] Inserted by SI 1996/2445 (effective November 1, 1996).

[3] Inserted by SI 1996/2445 (effective November 1, 1996).

[4] Inserted by SI 1996/2445 (effective November 1, 1996).

[5] Substituted by SI 1996/2445 (effective November 1, 1996).

(b) so far as practicable any document referred to in the written motion and not already lodged in process.

(3) Where the period for lodging opposition to the motion is varied under rule 15.2(4) (variation of and dispensing with period of intimation) to a period of 5 days or less, the written motion and certificate to be lodged in terms of paragraph (2) shall be lodged no later than the day on which the period for lodging opposition expires.

GENERAL NOTE

A motion is the means by which the court is requested to make an order either procedural or substantive in the course of a depending action.

*"Orally with Leave of the Court"*. The vast majority of motions are made by lodging a written motion. However, it is competent to make an oral motion at the bar. Such motions most frequently occur in the course of a debate or proof when a party seeks leave to amend. Motions made during the course of a hearing may only be made with the leave of the court. The court will normally only allow such a motion to be made where there is firstly a good reason why a written motion was not lodged and secondly where there is no prejudice to the other party. Given the issue of prejudice to the other party it is often only with the consent of the other party that such a motion is allowed to be made. Where allowed to be made at the bar, such motions are often continued by the court in order to allow the other party time to prepare a reply and by this means the issue of possible prejudice to the other party is obviated.

**Intimation of motions**

D1.135

**15.2.**—(1) Subject to paragraphs (4) and (7), a party intending to lodge a motion in accordance with rule 15.1(1)(b) (lodging written motion) shall intimate the motion in Form G7, and a copy of any document referred to in the motion, to every other party.

(2) Intimation of a motion may be given by—

    (a) any of the methods of service provided for in Chapter 5 (citation, service and intimation); or

    (b) where intimation is to a party represented by a solicitor, by—

        (i) personal delivery,

        (ii) facsimile transmission,

        (iii) first class ordinary post, or

        (iv) delivery to a document exchange, to that solicitor.

(3) Where intimation is given—

    (a) under paragraph (2)(b)(i) or (ii), it shall be deemed to have been given—

        (i) on the day of transmission or delivery where it is given before 5.00 p.m. on any day; or

        (ii) on the day after transmission or delivery where it is given after 5.00 p.m. on any day; or

    (b) under paragraph (2)(b)(iii) or (iv), it shall be deemed to have been given on the day after posting or delivery.

(4) The sheriff may, on the application of a party intending to lodge a written motion, vary the period of 7 days specified in rule 15.3(1)(c) for lodging opposition to the motion or dispense with intimation.

(5) An application under paragraph (4) shall be made in the written motion, giving reasons for such variation or dispensation.

(6) Where the sheriff varies the period within which notice of opposition is to be lodged under rule 15.3(1)(c), the form of intimation required under rule 15.2(1) (intimation of motion in Form G7) shall state the date by which such notice requires to be lodged.

(7) A joint motion by all parties lodged in Form G6 need not be intimated.

*"Copy of any Document Referred to in the Motion"*. Such a copy shall be intimated to every party and where practicable lodged in court.

*"Intimation of Motion and Intimation of Opposition to a Motion"*. The method and timing of the intimation is the same in relation to both (see: 15.2(2) and (3)).

*"Intimation of Motion"*. Intimation is in accordance with Chapter 5 except where the other party is represented by a solicitor where the forms of intimation are considerably widened.

*"Vary the Period for Lodging Opposition...or Dispense with Intimation"*. Where such variation or dispensation is sought it should be sought in the written motion and must be supported by reasons. It should be noted that although lengthening of the period for lodging opposition is competent this is very rarely sought. Where shortening of the period is sought the usual reason given is urgency in having the matter dealt with by the court. The test as to whether the court will grant such shortening will be whether it is in the interests of justice to grant it, i.e. whether on balance the need for the matter being dealt with urgently outweighs any prejudice to the other party in shortening the period for lodging opposition.

As regards dispensing with intimation, this will only be granted on the basis of the most cogent of reasons. In terms of 15.5(7) where intimation has been dispensed with, the sheriff shall make such order as he thinks fit for intimation of his determination on those parties to whom intimation was dispensed with.

**Opposition to motions**

**D1.136**

**15.3.**—(1)   Where a party seeks to oppose a motion made in accordance with rule 15.1(1)(b) (written motion), he shall—

    (a)   complete a notice of opposition in Form G9;

    (b)   intimate a copy of that notice to every other party; and

    (c)   lodge the notice with the sheriff clerk within 7 days after the date of intimation of the motion or such other period as the sheriff may have determined under rule 15.2(6).

(2)   Paragraphs (2) and (3) of rule 15.2 (methods and time of intimation of motions) shall apply to the intimation of opposition to a motion under paragraph (1)(b) of this rule as they apply to intimation under that rule.

**Consent to motions**

**D1.137**

**15.4.**   Where a party consents to a written motion, he shall endorse the motion, or give notice to the sheriff clerk in writing, of his consent.

**Hearing of motions**

**D1.138**

**15.5.**—(1)   Subject to paragraph (2), where no notice of opposition is lodged with the sheriff clerk within the period specified in rule 15.3(1)(c), or ordered by virtue of rule 15.2(4), the motion shall be determined by the sheriff in chambers without the appearance of parties, unless the sheriff otherwise directs.

(2)   In accordance with any directions given by the sheriff principal, the sheriff clerk may determine any motion other than a motion which seeks a final interlocutor.

(3)   Where the sheriff clerk considers that a motion dealt with by him under paragraph (2) should not be granted, he shall refer that motion to the sheriff who shall deal with it in accordance with paragraph (1).

(4)   Where the sheriff requires to hear a party on a motion which is not opposed, the sheriff clerk shall—

    (a)   fix a date, time and place for the party to be heard, and

    (b)   inform that party—

       (i)   of that date, time and place; and

       (ii)   of the reasons for the sheriff wishing to hear him.

(5)   Where a notice of opposition is lodged in accordance with rule 15.3(1), the sheriff clerk shall—

    (a)   assign a date, time and place, on the first suitable court day after the lodging of the notice of opposition, for the motion to be heard; and

    (b)   intimate that date, time and place to the parties.

(6)   Where a motion has been determined under paragraph (1) or (2), the sheriff clerk shall intimate the interlocutor determining that motion to all parties forthwith.

(7)   Where the sheriff, under paragraph (4) of rule 15.2, dispenses with intimation required by paragraph (1) of that rule, he shall make such order as he thinks fit for intimation of his determination of the motion to every party to the action in respect of whom intimation has been so dispensed with.

(8)   Subject to paragraph (4), where all parties consent to a written motion, the sheriff may determine the motion in chambers without the appearance of parties.

(9)   Subject to paragraph (4) where a joint motion of all parties in Form G6 is lodged with the sheriff clerk, the sheriff may determine the motion in chambers without the appearance of parties.

"*Hearing of Motions*". Unlike in the Court of Session all unopposed motions may be granted without a hearing at which the appearance of counsel, solicitor or party litigant is necessary.

A sheriff principal may by direction delegate to the sheriff clerk the determination of any motions other than those which seek a final interlocutor. In practice the sheriffs principal have exercised this power in the same way and the list of motions which may be determined by the sheriff clerk is the same in each Sheriffdom. The motions which may be dealt with by the sheriff clerk are all minor and procedural.

An unopposed motion may be put out by a sheriff for a hearing. The sheriff will also give reasons for so ordering. Such a hearing may be procedural in nature or relate to the substance of the motion.

*Lengthy Hearings*. Where parties believe that an opposed motion is likely to require a lengthy hearing it is good practice to advise the sheriff clerk of the likelihood in order that necessary practical arrangements can be made for the hearing thereof.

**Motions to sist**

**15.6.**—[1](1)   Where a motion to sist is made, either orally or in writing in accordance with rule 15.1(1)(a) or (by—

(a)   the reason for the sist shall be stated by the party seeking the sist; and

(b)   that reason shall be recorded in the interlocutor.

(2)   Where a cause has been sisted, the sheriff may, after giving parties an opportunity to be heard, recall the sist.

"*Expenses*". Often the issue of expenses is not raised at the stage which the motion is dealt with by the court. If the issue is raised then the sheriff will deal with it in accordance with the general rules in respect of the awarding of expenses.

**D1.139**

**Dismissal of action due to delay**

**15.7.**—[2](1)   Any party to an action may, while that action is depending before the court, apply by written motion for the court to dismiss the action due to inordinate and inexcusable delay by another party or another party's agent in progressing the action, resulting in unfairness.

(2)   A motion under paragraph (1) shall—

(a)[3]   include a statement of the grounds on which it is proposed that the motion should be allowed; and

(b)   be lodged in accordance with rule 15.1.

(3)   A notice of opposition to the motion in Form G9 shall include a statement of the grounds of opposition to the motion.

(4)   In determining an application made under this rule, the court may dismiss the action if it appears to the court that—

(a)   there has been an inordinate and inexcusable delay on the part of any party or any party's agent in progressing the action; and

(b)   such delay results in unfairness specific to the factual circumstances, including the procedural circumstances, of that action.

(5)   In determining whether or not to dismiss an action under paragraph (4), the court shall take account of the procedural consequences, both for the parties and for the work of the court, of allowing the action to proceed.

**D1.140**

Chapter 16

Decrees by Default

**Application of this Chapter**

**16.1.**[4]   This Chapter applies to any cause other than—

(a)   an action to which rule 33.37 (decree by default in family action) applies;

(aa)[5]   an action to which rule 33A.37 (decree by default in a civil partnership action) applies;

(b)   an action of multiplepoinding;

(c)   a cause under the Presumption of Death (Scotland) Act 1977; or

(d)   a commercial action within the meaning of Chapter 40.

**D1.141**

**Decrees where party in default**

**16.2.**—(1)   In a cause to which this Chapter applies, where a party fails—

(a)   to lodge, or intimate the lodging of, any production or part of process within the period required under a provision in these Rules or an order of the sheriff,

(b)   to implement an order of the sheriff within a specified period,

(c)   to appear or be represented at any diet, or

(d)[6]   otherwise to comply with any requirement imposed upon that party by these Rules;

that party shall be in default.

**D1.142**

---

[1] Inserted by SSI 2000/239 (effective October 2, 2000).

[2] As inserted by the Act of Sederunt (Sheriff Court Rules) (Miscellaneous Amendments) 2009 (SSI 2009/294) r.14 (effective October 1, 2009).

[3] As amended by the Act of Sederunt (Sheriff Court Rules) (Miscellaneous Amendments) 2010 (SSI 2010/279) r.7(1) (effective July 29, 2010).

[4] As amended by SSI 2001/8 (effective March 1, 2001).

[5] Inserted by Act of Sederunt (Ordinary Cause Rules) Amendment (Family Law (Scotland) Act 2006 etc.) 2006 (SSI 2006/207) (effective May 4, 2006).

[6] Inserted by the Act of Sederunt (Ordinary Cause and Summary Application Rules) Amendment (Miscellaneous) 2006 (SSI 2006/410) (effective August 18, 2006).

(2)[1, 1]   Where a party is in default the sheriff may, as the case may be—

    (a)   grant decree as craved with expenses;

    (b)   grant decree of absolvitor with expenses;

    (c)   dismiss the cause with expenses; or

    (d)   make such other order as he thinks fit to secure the expeditious progress of the cause.

(3)   Where no party appears at a diet, the sheriff may dismiss the cause.

(4)   In this rule, "diet" includes—

    (a)   a hearing under rule 9.12 (Options Hearing);

    (b)   a hearing under rule 10.6 (Procedural Hearing);

    (c)   a proof or proof before answer; and

    (d)   a debate.

**D1.143**

**Prorogation of time where party in default**

**16.3.**   In an action to which this Chapter applies, the sheriff may, on cause shown, prorogate the time for lodging any production or part of process or for giving intimation or for implementing any order.

## General Note.

The purpose of the rule is to provide a discretionary remedy to the court in the event that a party to a defended action (being one in which a notice to defend has been lodged) prevents its proper progress by a failure to act in any of the ways specified in the rule.

NATURE OF DECREE.

A decree by default is (a) a final judgment and (b) if granted after the lodging of defences, and if other than a decree of dismissal, is a decree *in foro* founding a plea of res judicata. If granted prior to the lodging of defences it will not found a plea of res judicata (see: *Esso Petroleum Company Ltd v Law* , 1956, S.C. 33). A decree by default may be obtained prior to the lodging of defences in the event that defences are not lodged timeously (see: OCR 9.6(1)); namely, on the failure to comply with the foregoing rule.

It is a matter for the discretion of the court whether it is appropriate to grant absolvitor or dismissal. In considering whether to grant *absolvitor* or dismissal it is suggested that the court has to consider the issue of whether a decree of *absolvitor* is proportionate to the default and thus in all the circumstances in the interests of justice (see further below).

*Where the pursuer is in default* decree of *absolvitor* would normally be pronounced. However, in the case of *Group 4 Total Security v Jaymarke Developments Ltd* , 1995 S.C.L.R. 303 where a closed record was lodged late the court held it appropriate to grant only decree of dismissal, thus leaving it open for the action to be re-raised.

*Where the defender is in default*, the decree normally granted is that craved for.

*"Where no party appears at a diet"* the appropriate decree is a decree of dismissal with a finding of no expenses due to or by either party (pronounced on the basis of want of insistence).

DISCRETION.

In the exercise of discretion whether to grant decree by default, it is for the court in exercising said discretion to see that the interests of justice are met. The court should have regard to the following broad guidelines laid down by the Inner House in considering the interests of justice.

(a)   The court should have regard to whether there is a proper claim or defence. See *McKelvie v Scottish Steel Scaffolding* , 1938 S.C. 278 per Lord Moncrieffe at 281:

> "I would be most reluctant, in any case in which prima facie there appeared to be a proper defence put forward to allow decree to pass against the defender without investigation of that defence. Even if carelessness on the part of the defender or others for whom he had been responsible had delayed the course of the procedure of the action, I should, in such a case, always be willing to entertain an application of relief."

(b)   The court should have regard to whether the default has arisen as a result of the behaviour of the party to the action or his agent. If the default is due to his agent this should not normally result in decree by default. The appropriate finding would be an adverse award of expenses, and perhaps an adverse award of expenses against the agent personally.

---

[1] As amended by the Act of Sederunt (Ordinary Cause and Summary Application Rules) Amendment (Miscellaneous) 2006 (SSI 2006/410) (effective August 18, 2006).

(c)    The court should have regard to the seriousness of the default.

"PROROGATION OF TIME WHERE PARTY IN DEFAULT".

The court is given the specific power to prorogate. Cause must be shown and again the court will apply the test of what is in the interests of justice.

Apart from the specific power of prorogation in the rule the court may also be moved to exercise the dispensing power in OCR 2.1.(1).

Generally, if a party fails to appear at a calling of a case, the court will be slow to grant decree unless it can be satisfied that there is likely to be no acceptable reason for the failure (see: *Canmore Housing Association v Scott* , 2003 G.W.D. 9-243). No matter how nominally or informally a party is represented at a diet it is not appropriate for the court to grant decree by default (see: *Samson v Fielding* , 2003 S.L.T. (Sh. Ct) 48).

*Solicitor withdraws from acting.* in these circumstances the court must fix a peremptory diet (OCR 24.2(1)).

*Appeal* against decree by default can be made without leave. (See: *GAS Construction Co Ltd v Schrader* , 1992 S.L.T. 528). Appeal against refusal of a decree by default is only competent with the leave of the court.

Chapter 17

**D1.144**

Summary Decrees

**Application of this Chapter**

**17.1.**    This Chapter applies to any action other than—
(a)    a family action within the meaning of rule 33.1(1);
(aa)[1]    a civil partnership action within the meaning of rule 33A.1(1);
(b)    an action of multiplepoinding; or
(c)    an action under the Presumption of Death (Scotland) Act 1977.

**Applications for summary decree**

**17.2.**—[2](1)    Subject to paragraphs (2) to (4), a party to an action may, at any time after defences have been lodged, apply by motion for summary decree in accordance with rule 15.1(1)(b) (lodging of motions).

**D1.145**

(2)    An application may only be made on the grounds that—
(a)    an opposing party's case (or any part of it) has no real prospect of success; and
(b)    there exists no other compelling reason why summary decree should not be granted at that stage.

(3)    The party enrolling the motion may request the sheriff—
(a)    to grant decree in terms of all or any of the craves of the initial writ or counterclaim;
(b)    to dismiss a cause or to absolve any party from any crave directed against him or her;
(c)    to pronounce an interlocutor sustaining or repelling any plea-in-law; or
(d)    to dispose of the whole or part of the subject-matter of the cause.

(4)    The sheriff may—
(a)    grant the motion in whole or in part, if satisfied that the conditions in subparagraph (2) are met,
(b)    ordain any party, or a partner, director, officer or office-bearer of any party—
(i)    to produce any relevant document or article; or
(ii)    to lodge an affidavit in support of any assertion of fact made in the pleadings or at the hearing of the motion.

(5)    Notwithstanding the refusal of all or part of a motion for summary decree, a subsequent motion may be made where there has been a change in circumstances.

GENERAL NOTE

The rule may flow from comments made by Lord Stewart in *Ellon Castle Estates Company Ltd v MacDonald* , 1975 S.L.T. (News) 66. Although this case considerably predates the rule it is frequently founded upon as setting forth a definition of the type of defences the rule is intended to strike at.

---

[1] Inserted by Act of Sederunt (Ordinary Cause Rules) Amendment (Family Law (Scotland) Act 2006 etc.) 2006 (SSI 2006/207) r.2 (effective May 4, 2006).
[2] As substituted by the Act of Sederunt (Sheriff Court Rules) (Miscellaneous Amendments) 2012 (SSI 2012/188) para.3 (effective August 1, 2012).

The purpose of the introduction of this rule of court was summarised by Lord McDonald in an unreported decision of March 26, 1985: *McAlinden v Bearsden & Milngavie District Council* as follows:

"I have no doubt it is intended to deal with the regrettable situation where there is no valid stateable defence but procedural technicalities are founded upon to delay prompt settlement of an unanswerable claim."

In his judgment, in *McAlinden v Bearsden & Milngavie District Council* supra, Lord McDonald further stated—

"It (the summary decree motion) is not in my view intended to provide an opportunity on the motion roll for legal debate appropriate to the procedure roll."

This opinion has been followed in a number of cases (see example: *Mitchell v H A T Contracting Services Ltd (No. 2)* 1993 S.L.T. 734; and *Rankin v Reid*, 1987 S.L.T. 352). Thus a summary decree motion is not the appropriate forum for a decision on relevancy and if such an issue arises in the course of such a motion it should be sent to debate. However, Sheriff Principal Nicholson, Q.C., held in *Matthews v SLAB & Henderson*, 1995 S.C.L.R. 184 that where the sole issue in the course of the summary decree motion was whether there was a legal basis for the defence then it is not inappropriate for a sheriff to approach that issue in a manner which is not entirely different from that which would be appropriate at a debate. See also *Royal Bank of Scotland Ltd v Dinwoodie*, 1987 S.L.T. 82 and *McKays Stores Ltd v City Wall (Holdings) Ltd*, 1989 S.L.T. 835 at 836E per Lord McCluskey "The test which I have to apply at this stage: I have to ask myself if the question of law which is raised admits of a clear and obvious answer". If the answer to that question is yes then the matter can be appropriately dealt with by way of a summary decree motion.

It should not, however, be thought that a summary decree motion is a narrower procedure than a debate. Rather as Lord Caplan stated in *Frimobar v Mobile Technical Plant (International) Ltd*, 1990 S.L.T. 180 at 181L "A hearing in a summary decree motion is more far reaching (than a debate) because the rules of court specifically admit material extraneous to the pleadings such as affidavits or productions. Thus the court is concerned not only to test the relevancy of the defence but the authenticity of the defence."

*"at any time after a defender has lodged defences".*

A motion for summary decree may be moved at any time up to final decree. Such motions are due to their nature most commonly enrolled shortly after the lodging of defences.

*"no defence to the action".*

In considering whether no defence is disclosed the court should have regard to the pleadings before it at the time of the motion. Although, in exceptional cases, the court may have regard to a minute of amendment presented but not yet part of the pleadings (see: *Robinson v Thomson*, 1987 S.L.T. 120). The court is further entitled to have regard to documents extraneous to the pleadings which have been lodged together with the history of the case and any relevant background information (see: *Spink & Son Ltd v McColl*, 1992 S.L.T. 470).

What the court should have regard to is the substance of the defence and not the manner in which it is pled. The issue for the court is to decide whether there is a genuine issue to try raised by the defences. The court is not confined to merely considering the narrow issue of relevancy (see: *Frimobar UK Ltd v Mobile Tech Plant (International) Ltd* supra). In considering the defence the court should consider whether by adjustment or minute of amendment a case can be improved to enable a genuine defence to be stated. In that event summary decree should not be pronounced.

Before the court can properly grant a summary decree it must be satisfied that no defence is disclosed. The test should be applied at the time that the motion is made (see: *Frimobar* supra). The standard of satisfaction has been defined by the court as being one of more than probability but less than complete certainty (see: *Watson-Towers Ltd v McPhail*, 1986 S.L.T. 617) or as put by Lord Prosser in *P and M Sinclair v The Bamber Gray Partnership*, 1987 S.C. 203 at 206 near certainty was required in order to fulfil the test.

*Personal Injury Actions.*

Generally courts have been slow to grant summary decrees in personal injury actions. It has been made clear that the putting forward of such a motion merely on the basis that the defender has lodged skeletal defences would not of itself be sufficient to obtain a summary decree (see: *McManus v Speirs Dick & Smith Ltd*, 1989 S.L.T. 806 per Lord Caplan at 807L). However, summary decree has been granted (see *Campbell v Golding*, 1992 S.L.T. 889) where the pursuer was able to found on an extract conviction relative to the defender. In *Struthers v British Alcan Rolled Products Ltd* , 1995 S.L.T. 142 summary decree was granted where the pursuer was able to found on a report lodged by the defenders indicating fault on their part.

*Order to produce a document or lodge an affidavit.*

The court may order the production of a document or the lodging of an affidavit which it considers may be of assistance in deciding the issue of whether there is a genuine defence.

It has been held that the court is entitled on the basis of evidence contained in an affidavit to hold itself satisfied that a certain state of fact exists although a denial of that state of facts is contained within the defences. (See: *Ingram Coal Co. v Nugent* , 1991 S.L.T. 603).

*"Change of circumstances" giving rise to a subsequent motion.*

Such a change of circumstances may arise from, for example, on an alteration in the pleadings; the lodging of certain documents in process; and the production of an affidavit.

*Appeal.*

If as a result of a summary decree motion a final judgment is pronounced (see: s.27 of the 1907 Act) then such decree is appealable without leave. Otherwise any other decision made in the course of a motion for summary decree with the exception of an interlocutor making an order *ad factum praestandum*, for example the lodging of a document requires leave to appeal.

*Counterclaim.*

The above points are equally applicable where an application for summary decree is made by a defender in terms of a counterclaim.

## Chapter 18

**D1.146**

### Amendment of Pleadings

**Alteration of sum sued for**

18.1.—(1)[1]   In a cause in which all other parties have lodged defences or answers, the pursuer may, before the closing of the record, alter any sum sued for by amending the crave of the initial writ, and any record.

(2)   The pursuer shall forthwith intimate any such amendment in writing to every other party.

**Powers of sheriff to allow amendment**

18.2.—(1)   The sheriff may, at any time before final judgment, allow an amendment mentioned in paragraph (2).

**D1.147**

(2)   Paragraph (1) applies to the following amendments:—

    (a)    an amendment of the initial writ which may be necessary for the purpose of determining the real question in controversy between the parties, notwithstanding that in consequence of such amendment—

        (i)    the sum sued for is increased or restricted after the closing of the record; or

        (ii)    a different remedy from that originally craved is sought;

    (b)    an amendment which may be necessary—

        (i)    to correct or supplement the designation of a party to the cause;

        (ii)    to enable a party who has sued or has been sued in his own right to sue or be sued in a representative capacity;

        (iii)    to enable a party who has sued or has been sued in a representative capacity to sue or be sued in his own right or in a different representative capacity;

        (iv)    to add the name of an additional pursuer or person whose concurrence is necessary;

        (v)    where the cause has been commenced or presented in the name of the wrong person, or it is doubtful whether it has been commenced or presented in the name of the right person, to allow any other person to be sisted in substitution for, or in addition to, the original person; or

        (vi)    to direct a crave against a third party brought into an action under Chapter 20 (third party procedure);

---

[1] As amended by SI 1996/2445 (effective November 1, 1996).

   (c)    an amendment of a condescendence, defences, answers, pleas-in-law or other pleadings which may be necessary for determining the real question in controversy between the parties; and

   (d)    where it appears that all parties having an interest have not been called or that the cause has been directed against the wrong person, an amendment inserting in the initial writ an additional or substitute party and directing existing or additional craves, averments and pleas-in-law against that party.

GENERAL NOTE.

Before this rule amendment procedure in the Sheriff Court was governed by Rules 79 and 80 of Schedule 1 to the 1970 Act which were in wholly different terms from Rule 18.2. Cases decided in terms of the old Sheriff Court Rules are no longer of relevance.

Rule 18 is now in broadly similar terms to Rule 24 in the Court of Session and cases decided in terms of said latter rule are accordingly of relevance.

The power to allow amendment given by this rule is a wide one. However, amendment cannot cure fundamental nullity (see: *Rutherford v Vertue* , 1993 S.C.L.R. 886).

*Test as to allowing of Minute of amendment.*

In terms of para.8.2(2)(a) and (c) the test as to whether a minute of amendment should be allowed is a two-part one.

*"necessary for…determining the real question in controversy":*

Firstly, is the minute of amendment necessary to determine the real question in controversy between the parties.

Secondly, should the court in the exercise of its discretion allow the minute of amendment. In other words, is it in the interests of justice to allow the minute of amendment? (See: *Thomson v Glasgow Corporation* , 1962 S.C. (HL) 36 per Thomson LJC at 51).

The decision as to whether to allow a minute of amendment is a matter for the discretion of the court, even when the amendment required to determine the real question in controversy is radical in nature and even if presented outwith the triennium (see: *Sellars v IMI Yorkshire Imperial Ltd* , 1986 S.L.T. 629).

In terms of the first test the court must consider inter alia:

1.    Is the minute of amendment relevant?

2.    Does the minute of amendment cure or at least to a material extent cure the identified defect or defects in the party's case?

Turning to the second part of the test, in seeking to apply the test of whether it is fair and in the interests of justice to allow the minute of amendment the court will have regard to inter alia the following broad factors—

1.    The whole procedural history of the case.

2.    The extent to which the amendment seeks to alter the case already pled.

3.    The procedural stage at which the amendment is sought.

4.    The extent and nature of the prejudice to the other party by the allowance of the amendment.

5.    The extent to which such prejudice can be ameliorated/obviated by the awarding of expenses against the party seeking to amend or by the attachment of any other conditions to the granting of the minute of amendment. The most common condition attached is the discharge of a diet of proof in order to allow the party who is required to answer the minute of amendment to prepare to meet the amendment.

*Stage in Procedure when minute of Amendment is Presented*

*General Rule. "before final Judgment".*

A minute of amendment may be competently moved at any time before final judgment.

It can be broadly stated that the later in an action leave is sought the more likely it is that prejudice to the other side will not be capable of amelioration by an award of expenses or otherwise.

*Specific Stages at Which Leave to Amend May be Sought*

   (a)    Where leave to amend is sought at or before a diet of debate it will often be allowed as it is unlikely that at that stage any prejudice to the other party will be of such a nature or extent that it cannot properly be compensated by an appropriate award of expenses. Where leave to amend is sought at the commencement of or during the course of a debate then it will be necessary for the party seeking leave to be in a position to satisfy the court that he can or will be able to answer the points set forth in the Rule 22 Note which it is accepted require to be answered.

(b)    Where leave to amend is sought sufficiently prior to the proof not to require any adjournment it is likely to be allowed. On the other hand, if amendment is sought so close to the diet of proof as to require a discharge in order to allow investigation by the other side then leave to amend is more likely to be refused on the basis that it is not in the interests of justice that the other side should lose their diet of proof (see: *Dryburgh v NCB* 1962 S.C. 485 at 492 per Lord Guthrie). It will be of particular importance in persuading the court that leave should be allowed at this stage that there is some very good reason why the minute of amendment comes at such a late stage in the case.

(c)    Where minute of amendment is tendered in the course of proof. In considering whether leave should be granted at this stage of a case, the court will consider a number of factors:

   (i)    whether it has been presented at the first opportunity (see: *Cameron v Lanarkshire Health Board* , 1997 S.L.T. 1040 at 1043D to Eper Lord Gill and *Rafferty v Weir* , 1966 S.L.T. (News) 23).

   (ii)    whether there is a good explanation as to why the minute of amendment is presented at such a late stage.

   (iii)    prejudice to the other party.

At this stage it is often difficult to see how an award of expenses or any other condition could compensate for the prejudice which has arisen to the other side by the late stage at which leave to amend is being sought. However, it should be borne in mind in relation to the issue of countering any prejudice to the other party that witnesses can be recalled.

*Circumstances requiring an amendment during the course of a proof.* If it is sought to advance a ground not covered by the record (see: *Gunn v John McAdam & Son* , 1949 S.C. 31) then a minute of amendment is required.

A ground is not covered by record where it can be described as being other than a "variation, modification or development" of the case on record. (See Thompson LJC in *Burns v Dixon's Ironworks Ltd* , 1961 S.C. 102 at 107).

Such a motion to seek leave to amend will almost always arise on an objection of no record being made by the other side. Should the other side fail to object timeously to a line of evidence for which there is in fact no record and there should have been then amendment is not required (see: *McGlone v BRB* , 1966 S.C. (HL) 1).

(d)    Where a minute of amendment is presented after proof. Such a minute of amendment although competent would only be granted in the rarest of situations given the almost inevitable material prejudice to the other side by allowing it. An example of where such a minute of amendment has been allowed is *Moyes v Burntisland Shipping Company* , 1952 S.L.T. 417. Here a minute of amendment was allowed following a jury trial. In that case the circumstances were described as exceptional and in order to deal to some extent with the prejudice caused by the lateness of the minute of amendment a proof before answer was ordered rather than a further jury trial.

(e)    Where amendment is sought after the marking of an appeal. Frequently such amendment is allowed by the party which has lost at debate and then appeals. The considerations as to whether such an amendment should be allowed are broadly similar to those which are relevant where leave to amend is sought shortly before or at a diet of debate. However, following upon a hearing at which evidence has been led the granting of leave to appeal at this stage will be extremely rare. The factors referred to at (c) will again apply, however, with even more force.

(f)    Where amendment is sought after expiry of the time limit. The court will not, in general, allow a pursuer by amendment to substitute the right defender for the wrong defender, or to cure a radical incompetence in his action, or to change the basis of his case if he only seeks to make such amendments after the expiry of a time limit which would have prevented him at that stage from raising fresh proceedings: see *Pompa's Trustees v The Magistrates of Edinburgh* , 1942 S.C. 119 at 125 per Cooper L.JC.

The question which most frequently arises is what amounts to changing the basis of the case. Lord President Cooper in *McPhail v Lanarkshire County Council* , 1951 S.C. 301 at 309 elaborated on what he had said in *Pompa's Trustees v The Magistrates of Edinburgh supra* and gives the clearest statement of what amounts to the changing of the basis of the case:

I think the pursuer may well claim, not to have offered a new but only to have presented the old case but from a new angle, not to have changed the foundation of his action but only to have made certain alterations to the superstructure.

The appropriate time to consider the issue of time bar/prescription where it is raised in answer to the presentation of a minute of amendment is when the motion to allow the record to be amended is being heard (see: *Greenhorn v Smart* , 1979 S.C. 427 per Lord Cameron at 432 and *Stewart v Highlands & Islands Development Board* , 1991 S.L.T. 787).

The courts will not allow a new pursuer to be added by amendment post expiry of the relevant period of time bar or prescriptive period (see *MacLean v BRB* , 1966 S.L.T. 39).

"the sum sued for is increased:" Such amendment can be competently made following the expiry of a time limit in terms of the law of prescription or time bar (see *Mackie v Glasgow Corporation* , 1924 S.L.T. 510).

"a different remedy from that originally craved is sought:" A fundamental change in the form of the action is not competent see e.g. *Sleigh v City of Edinburgh District Council* , 1988 S.L.T. 253, in which a motion for leave to amend a petition for interdict to a petition for judicial review was refused under reference to Lord Cooper's opinion in *Pompa's Trustees supra.*

**D1.148**

### Applications to amend

**18.3.**—(1)   A party seeking to amend shall lodge a minute of amendment in process setting out his proposed amendment and, at the same time, lodge a motion—

  (a)   to allow the minute of amendment to be received; and

  (b)   to allow—

   (i)   amendment in terms of the minute of amendment and, where appropriate, to grant an order under rule 18.5(1)(a) (service of amendment for additional or substitute party); or

   (ii)   where the minute of amendment may require to be answered, any other person to lodge answers within a specified period.

  (2)   Where the sheriff has pronounced an interlocutor allowing a minute of amendment to be received and answered, he may allow a period of adjustment of the minute of amendment and answers and, on so doing, shall fix a date for parties to be heard on the minute of amendment and answers as adjusted.

  (3)[1]   Any adjustment to any minute of amendment or answers shall be exchanged between parties and not lodged in process.

  (4)[2]   Parties shall be responsible for maintaining a record of adjustment made and the date of their intimation.

  (5)[3]   No adjustments shall be permitted after the period of adjustment allowed, except with leave of the sheriff.

  (6)[4]   Each party shall, no later than 2 days before the hearing fixed in terms of paragraph (2), lodge in process a copy of their minute of amendment or answers with all adjustments made thereto in italic or bold type, or underlined.

"to add the name of an additional pursuer." The courts will allow this even when the pursuers title has been defective during the course of the action (see: *Donaghy v Rollo* , 1964 S.C. 278). A minute of sist is not required (see: Macphail, Sheriff Court Practice para. 10.09).

"Lodge a motion." The procedure as set out in OCR 15 should be followed.

"shall fix a date for parties to be heard on the minute of amendment." If there is opposition to the minute of amendment this is the appropriate stage for opposition to be made to the minute of amendment. Broadly, the only exception to this would be if the lodging of the minute of amendment due to the stage at which it is lodged gives rise to the issue of possible discharge of a proof or a debate. In such circumstances it would be appropriate to lodge opposition to the motion to have the minute of amendment received. The motion made at the hearing in terms of 18.3(2) for the record to be amended in terms of the minute of amendment and answers (if necessary as adjusted) is made orally as to do it by written motion would require the whole of OCR 15 to be followed.

"Each party shall no later than 2 days before the hearing—lodge in process a copy of their minute of amendment or answers with all adjustments made thereto in italics." It is important that this rule is complied with in that non compliance results in the court being unable to prepare for and conduct the hearing properly as in terms of 18.3(3) no copy of adjustments is lodged in court when adjustments are exchanged.

---

[1] Inserted by SSI 2000/239 (effective October 2, 2000).
[2] Inserted by SSI 2000/239 (effective October 2, 2000).
[3] Inserted by SSI 2000/239 (effective October 2, 2000).
[4] Inserted by SSI 2000/239 (effective October 2, 2000).

"Form of Minute of Amendment." It should begin with the instance and be followed by a preamble.

... for the pursuer/defender craved and hereby craves leave of the court to amend the initial writ/ defence or to open the closed record and to amend the same as follows—

Thereafter in numbered paragraphs the amendments should be set out.

At the end IN RESPECT WHEREOF should appear.

"Form of Answers:" It should begin with the instance and be followed by a preamble—

... for the pursuer/defender craved and hereby craves leave of the court to answer the minute of amendment number...of process as follows—

Thereafter in numbered paragraphs the answers should be set out.

At the end IN RESPECT WHEREOF should appear.

**Applications for diligence on amendment**

**18.4.**—(1)   Where a minute of amendment is lodged by a pursuer under rule 18.2(2)(d) (all parties not, or wrong person, called), he may apply by motion for warrant to use any form of diligence which could be used on the dependence of a separate action.

(2)   A copy certified by the sheriff clerk of the interlocutor granting warrant for diligence on the dependence applied for under paragraph (1) shall be sufficient authority for the execution of that diligence.

**D1.149**

**Service of amended pleadings**

**18.5.**—(1)[1]   Where an amendment under rule 18.2(2)(b)(iv), (v) or (vi) (additional or substitute defenders added by amendment) or rule 18.2(2)(d) (all parties not, or wrong person, called) has been made—

    (a)    the sheriff shall order that a copy of the initial writ or record, as the case may be, as so amended be served by the party who made the amendment on that additional or substitute party with—

        (i)[2]   in a cause in which a time to pay direction under the Debtors (Scotland) Act 1987 or a time order under the Consumer Credit Act 1974 may be applied for, a notice in Form 08 specifying the date by which a notice of intention must be lodged in process, a notice in Form 03 and a notice of intention to defend in Form 07; or

        (ii)  in any other cause, a notice in Form 09 specifying the date by which a notice of intention to defend must be lodged in process and a notice of intention to defend in Form 07; and

    (b)    the party who made the amendment shall lodge in process—

        (i)   a copy of the initial writ or record as amended;

        (ii)  a copy of the notice sent in Form 08 or Form 09; and

        (iii) a certificate of service.

(2)   When paragraph (1) has been complied with, the cause as so amended shall proceed in every respect as if that party had originally been made a party to the cause.

(3)   Where a notice of intention to defend is lodged by virtue of paragraph (1)(a), the sheriff clerk shall fix a date for a hearing under rule 9.12 (Options Hearing).

**D1.150**

GENERAL NOTE

Where in terms of the minute of amendment the parties to the action are intended to be altered then service of the writ or record as amended will be ordered. Service will require to conform to OCR 5.

**Expenses and conditions of amendment**

**18.6.**   The sheriff shall find the party making an amendment liable in the expenses occasioned by the amendment unless it is shown that it is just and equitable that the expenses occasioned by the amendment should be otherwise dealt with, and may attach such other conditions as he thinks fit.

**D1.151**

GENERAL NOTE

This rule specifically directs that the party amending will be found liable in the expenses occasioned by the amendment, unless it is just and equitable, to make any other type of award. The most common instance of where a party amending will not be found liable in expenses is where the other party adjusted

---

[1] As amended by SI 1996/2445 (effective November 1, 1996).

[2] As amended by the Act of Sederunt (Ordinary Cause, Summary Application, Summary Cause and Small Claim Rules) Amendment (Miscellaneous) 2007 (SSI 2007/6), para.2(9) (effective January 29, 2007).

shortly before the closing of the record not allowing adjustments in answer to be made timeously and thus requiring a minute of amendment to deal with these adjustments.

*expenses occasioned by the amendment*

will include the expenses of preparing answers (see: *Campbell v Henderson* , 1949 S.C. 172). Such awards of expenses may also cover more than merely the cost of preparing answers. If the lodging of the minute of amendment has resulted in either the procedure which has gone before in its entirety or to some specific prior stage for eg. the closing of the record being rendered worthless then the party amending may be found liable for either the whole of the procedure or to that specific stage (see: *Campbell v Henderson supra*). Further, where the lodging of a minute of amendment has resulted in the discharge of a debate or proof the party amending is likely to be found liable for the costs of the discharge (see e.g. *Mackenzie v Mackenzie* , 1951 S.C. 163 at 165–166).

**D1.152**

**Effect of amendment on diligence**

18.7.   Where an amendment has been allowed, the amendment—

(a)   shall not validate diligence used on the dependence of a cause so as to prejudice the rights of creditors of the party against whom the diligence has been executed who are interested in defeating such diligence; and

(b)   shall preclude any objection to such diligence stated by a party or any person by virtue of a title acquired or in right of a debt contracted by him subsequent to the execution of such diligence.

**Preliminary pleas inserted on amendment**

**D1.153**

18.8.—(1)   Where a party seeks to add a preliminary plea by amendment or answers to an amendment, or by adjustment thereto, a note of the basis for the plea shall be lodged at the same time as the minute, answers or adjustment, as the case may be.

(2)   If a party fails to comply with paragraph (1), that party shall be deemed to be no longer insisting on the preliminary plea and the plea shall be repelled by the sheriff.

If the minute of amendment or answers thereto seeks to add a preliminary plea, a note of the basis of that plea must be lodged at the same time as the minute, answers or adjustments thereto which introduces the plea (OCR 18.8(1))

"Appeal." Leave to appeal is required both in relation to a grant and refusal of a motion for leave to amend.

**D1.154**

Chapter 19

Counterclaims

*Annotations to Chapters 19 to 29 by Simon Di Rollo, Q.C.*

**Counterclaims**

19.1.—(1)As amended by theAct of Sederunt (Ordinary Cause Rules) Amendment (Family Law (Scotland) ct 2006 etc.) 2006 (SSI 2006/207) r.2 (effective May 4, 2006).   In any action other than a family action within the meaning of rule 33.1(1), a civil partnership action within the meaning of rule 33A.1(1) or an action of multiplepoinding, a defender may counterclaim against a pursuer—

(a)   where the counterclaim might have been made in a separate action in which it would not have been necessary to call as defender any person other than the pursuer; and

(b)   in respect of any matter—

(i)   forming part, or arising out of the grounds, of the action by the pursuer;

(ii)   the decision of which is necessary for the determination of the question in controversy between the parties; or

(iii)   which, if the pursuer had been a person not otherwise subject to the jurisdiction of the court, might have been the subject-matter of an action against that pursuer in which jurisdiction would have arisen by reconvention.

(2)   A counterclaim shall be made in the defences—

(a)   when the defences are lodged or during the period for adjustment;

(b)   by amendment at any other stage, with the leave of the sheriff and subject to such conditions, if any, as to expenses or otherwise as the sheriff thinks fit.

(3)   Defences which include a counterclaim shall commence with a crave setting out the counterclaim in such form as, if the counterclaim had been made in a separate action, would have been appropriate in the initial writ in that separate action and shall include—

(a)   answers to the condescendence of the initial writ as required by rule 9.6(2) (form of defences);

(b) a statement of facts in numbered paragraphs setting out the facts on which the counterclaim is founded, incorporating by reference, if necessary, any matter contained in the defences; and

(c) appropriate pleas-in-law.

NOTE

[1] As amended by Act of Sederunt (Ordinary Cause Rules) Amendment (Family Law (Scotland) Act 2006 etc.) 2006 (SSI 2006/207) r.2 (effective May 4, 2006).

GENERAL NOTE

The Ordinary Cause Rules 1993 made several important changes to sheriff court counterclaim procedure. Care is required in relation to earlier sheriff court decisions made under the old rules. The terms of the sheriff court rule are now practically identical to the current Court of Session rule (see RCS 1994, Chapter 25). The language of the latter is in similar terms to the earlier Court of Session rule. The older Court of Session cases remain of value.

The purpose of the counterclaim procedure is to allow the defender to obtain a decree (apart from absolvitor or dismissal) against the pursuer where he has a claim against him which is connected with the grounds of the pursuer's action. It is expedient to permit the parties to resolve the whole of their dispute in one process. Family actions have their own discrete rules (see Chapter 33) and are excluded from Chapter 19 as are, for obvious reasons, actions of multiplepoinding. In all other actions under the Ordinary Cause Rules a counterclaim is competent under this chapter. Provided the requirements of the rules are otherwise satisfied, it is competent to counterclaim for interdict (*Mclean v Marwhirn Developments Ltd* , 1976 S.L.T. (Notes) 47) or delivery (*Borthwick v Dean Warwick Ltd* , 1985 S.L.T. 269) and presumably in an appropriate case for other types of non-pecuniary decree.

A counterclaim is often (but not exclusively) used in response to an action for payment of the contract price where the defender seeks damages for breach of contract, or in the converse situation. It is important not to confuse two questions. The first question is whether in an action for debt it is relevant to plead in defence that a debt is due by the pursuer to the defender. The answer to that question is a matter of the substantive law (see Wilson, *Debt* (2nd ed., 1991), Chap.13 and McBryde, *Contract* (2nd ed., 2001), pp.499–501). For a detailed and comprehensive review of the authorities on the substantive law see *Inveresk Plc v Tullis Russell Papermakers Ltd* , 2010 S.L.T. 941; 2010 SC (UKSC) 106. The second question is in an action what types of claim can form the basis of a counterclaim under the rule in this chapter? That is a question to be answered by the terms of this rule. In this context if the defender seeks to withhold the price on the ground of the pursuer's breach of contract then it may not be necessary to lodge a counterclaim (see Macphail, *Sheriff Court Practice* (2nd ed., 1998), p.390 footnote 37), but he still requires to give fair notice in his defences of the precise basis upon which payment is withheld and to make adequate relevant averments (including specification of the amount of the damage) to permit the equitable doctrine of retention (see *Inveresk Plc* (above) at paras [60] to [107]) to be operated.

OCR, r.19.1(1)(a), (b)(i), (ii) and (iii) define the scope of the connection required between the pursuer's action and the defender's response which permit the latter to lodge a counterclaim.

RULE 19.1(1)(A)

First, it is essential that the counterclaim could have been brought by the same defender as a separate action against the same pursuer without having to call any other party as defender (*Tods Murray W.S. v Arakin Ltd* , 2001 S.C. 840, IH).

RULE 19.1(1)(B)(I) OR (II) OR (III)

Secondly, the subject matter of the counterclaim must either (i) form part of the pursuer's action, or (ii) arise out of its grounds, or (iii) be a matter the decision of which is necessary for the determination of the question in controversy between the parties, or (iv) arise from the common law principle of reconvention (in so far as that has not been swept away by the Civil Jurisdiction and Judgements Act 1982).

RULE 19.1(1)(B)(I)—"FORM PART OF THE PURSUER'S ACTION", OR "ARISE OUT OF ITS GROUNDS"

In the contractual context when a contract is one and indivisible, a counterclaim arising out of one item can be competently pursued in answer to a claim for payment on the whole contract. Often there is a series of transactions between the parties with each transaction or group representing a separate contract. In that event if the pursuer sues upon one contract the defender's counterclaim has to relate to that contract in order to be said to form part of the pursuer's action or arise out of its grounds (see *JW Chafer (Scotland) Ltd v Hope* , 1963 S.L.T. (Notes) 11). Nevertheless, the defender may be able to bring himself within rule 19.1(1)(b)(ii).

RULE 19.1(1)(B)(II) — "NECESSARY FOR THE DETERMINATION OF THE QUESTION IN CONTROVERSY BETWEEN THE PARTIES"

This permits a counterclaim to be maintained even though the defender is not allowed under the substantive law of contract to retain a sum in defence to the pursuer's claim for payment. In *Fulton Clyde Ltd v JF McCallum & Co. Ltd* , 1960 S.C. 78; 1960 S.L.T. 253 the pursuer sought payment of the price of goods delivered. The defenders did not dispute that the goods had been delivered or the contract price. They sought to retain the price in respect of a failure to deliver goods on an earlier occasion. It was held that the earlier failure in delivery was a separate contract and so the defender was not entitled to retain the contract price in respect of the later delivery. Decree was granted for the sum sought by the pursuer. However, the court allowed the counterclaim to proceed on the basis that the questions in controversy between the parties on the whole pleadings included whether the defender was entitled to damages for breach of contract due to the failure to make an earlier delivery (see also *Borthwick v Dean Warwick Ltd* , 1985 S.L.T. 269 where the court considered that on the pleadings it could not be said that the counterclaim did not arise out of the same contract).

RULE 19.1(1)(B)(III)

This only applies where the common law doctrine of reconvention can be invoked. Reconvention is a common law equitable doctrine that permits a pursuer who raises an action against the defender to be counterclaimed against where he would not otherwise be subject to the jurisdiction of the court. The basic principles involved are illustrated in *Thompson v Whitehead* (1862) 24 D. 331, and for a modern example where it was held to apply, see e.g. *MacKenzie v Macleod's Executor* , 1988 S.L.T. 207, OH. In the sheriff court the doctrine had statutory sanction by virtue of section 6(h) of the Sheriff Courts (Scotland) Act 1907 which provided that the sheriff had jurisdiction "where the party sued is the pursuer in any action pending within [his] jurisdiction against the party suing". Section 20 of the Civil Jurisdiction and Judgements Act 1982 provides that section 6 of the 1907 Act ceases to have effect to the extent that it determines jurisdiction in relation to any matter to which Schedule 8 applies. Paragraph 2(15)(c) of Schedule 8 to the 1982 Act provides that there is jurisdiction on a counterclaim arising from the same contract or facts on which the original claim was based, in the court in which the original claim is pending. The common law doctrine of reconvention can only be invoked in relation to those matters in Schedule 9 of the 1982 Act (see Anton, *Private International Law* (3rd ed., 2011), paras 8.331 and 8.332).

RULE 19.1(2)(A) AND (B)

Leave is required to lodge a counterclaim after the record has closed. Before that stage is reached, provided the counterclaim meets the requirement of the rules, there is no discretion to it being included in the defences.

RULE 19.1(3)

This prescribes how to set out the defences and counterclaim and should be followed in every case. The order is crave, answers to each article of condescendence, pleas-in-law relating to the answers, statement of facts and pleas in law relating to the statement of facts.

**D1.155**   **Warrants for diligence on counterclaims**

19.2.[1](1)   A defender who makes a counterclaim may apply for a warrant for interim diligence which would have been permitted had the warrant been sought in an initial writ in a separate action.

(2)–(4)   *[Repealed by the Act of Sederunt (Sheriff Court Rules) (Miscellaneous Amendments) 2009 (SSI 2009/294) r.10 (effective October 1, 2009).]*

GENERAL NOTE

See OCR 1993 Chapter 6 Interim Diligence. The law is codified in the Debtors (Scotland) Act 1987 ss.15A to 15N.

**D1.156**   **Form of record where counterclaim lodged**

19.2A.[2]   Where, under rule 9.10 (open record), 9.11 (record for Options Hearing), 10.4 (open record), or 10.5 (closed record), a record requires to be lodged in an action in which a counterclaim is included in the defences, the pleadings of the parties shall be set out in the record in the following order:—

    (a)   the crave of the initial writ;

    (b)   the condescendence and answers relating to the initial writ;

---

[1] As amended by the Act of Sederunt (Sheriff Court Rules) (Miscellaneous Amendments) 2009 (SSI 2009/294) r.10 (effective October 1, 2009).

[2] Inserted by SI 1996/2445 (effective November 1, 1996).

(c)   the pleas-in-law of the parties relating to the crave of the initial writ;

(d)   the crave of the counterclaim;

(e)   the statement of facts and answers relating to the counterclaim; and

(f)   the pleas-in-law of the parties relating to the counterclaim.

### General Note

This rule helpfully provides the correct format of the record where there is a counterclaim, and should be followed in every case.

**Effect of abandonment of cause**                                                                                   **D1.157**

19.3.—(1)   The right of a pursuer to abandon a cause under rule 23.1 shall not be affected by a counterclaim; and any expenses for which the pursuer is found liable as a condition of, or in consequence of, such abandonment shall not include the expenses of the counterclaim.

(2)   Notwithstanding abandonment by the pursuer, a defender may insist in his counterclaim; and the proceedings in the counterclaim shall continue in dependence as if the counterclaim were a separate action.

### General Note

The counterclaim, once it is born, has an existence independent of the principal action. It can proceed in conjunction with the principal action or on its own should that be abandoned.

**Disposal of counterclaims**                                                                                       **D1.158**

19.4.   The sheriff may—

(a)   deal with a counterclaim as if it had been stated in a separate action;

(b)   regulate the procedure in relation to the counterclaim as he thinks fit; and

(c)   grant decree for the counterclaim in whole or in part or for the difference between it and the sum sued for by the pursuer.

### General Note

Usually the counterclaim will be subject to the same procedure as the main action but there is scope for having separate enquires or debates. The parties should make it clear what procedure they desire in relation to both the principal action and the counterclaim and any interlocutor should be specific to each in relation to any procedure to take place. The court has the same powers in relation to the disposal of the counterclaim as it does with regard to the principal action.

Chapter 20                                                                           **D1.159**

Third Party Procedure

**Applications for third party notice**

20.1.—(1)   Where, in an action, a defender claims that—

(a)   he has in respect of the subject-matter of the action a right of contribution, relief or indemnity against any person who is not a party to the action, or

(b)   a person whom the pursuer is not bound to call as a defender should be made a party to the action along with the defender in respect that such person is—

(i)   solely liable, or jointly or jointly and severally liable with the defender, to the pursuer in respect of the subject-matter of the action, or

(ii)   liable to the defender in respect of a claim arising from or in connection with the liability, if any, of the defender to the pursuer,

he may apply by motion for an order for service of a third party notice upon that other person in Form O10 for the purpose of convening that other person as a third party to the action.

(2)[1]   Where—

(a)   a pursuer against whom a counterclaim has been made, or

(b)   a third party convened in the action,

seeks, in relation to the claim against him, to make against a person who is not a party, a claim mentioned in paragraph (1) as a claim which could be made by a defender against a third party, he shall apply by motion for an order for service of a third party notice in Form O10 in the same manner as a defender under that paragraph; and rules 20.2 to 20.6 shall, with the necessary modifications, apply to such a claim as they apply in relation to such a claim by a defender.

---

[1] As amended by SI 1996/2445 (effective November 1, 1996).

Like the counterclaim procedure (see Chapter 19) the purpose of the third party procedure is to permit matters arising out of a dispute to be resolved in one process. Where a defender considers that responsibility for the pursuer's claim lies ultimately in whole or in part with another person, he may introduce that person into the action as a third party. The procedure is available when a defender claims: (1) a right of contribution, relief or indemnity against a third party; or (2) that the third party is either solely liable or jointly or jointly and severally liable with him to the pursuer. Again like counterclaim procedure the rule is purely procedural (see *National Coal Board v Knight Bros* , 1972 S.L.T. (Notes) 24, OH; *R and Watson Ltd v David Traill & Sons Ltd* , 1972 S.L.T. (Notes) 38). The terms "contribution, relief or indemnity" in the rule are to be interpreted in a broad way and it is not essential that any separate action against the third party would be put into any particular pigeon-hole (see, e.g. *Nicol Homeworld Contractors Ltd v Charles Gray Builders Ltd* , 1986 S.L.T. 317, OH). Thereafter the rights of the parties must be worked out under reference to the substantive law. A pursuer in a counterclaim may also lodge a third party notice. A third party may counterclaim against a defender or lodge a further third party notice himself. In that event the further third party is referred to as "second third party".

Application to lodge a third party notice is made by motion for an order for service of a notice in Form O10. The notice requires specification of the basis upon which the third party is to be convened to the action, but the terms of any such notice do not prevent the defender from altering the pleadings against the third party from one of joint liability to sole fault or vice versa (*Beedie v Norrie* , 1966 S.C. 207; 1966 S.L.T. 295).

**D1.160**

### Averments where order for service of third party notice sought

**20.2.**—(1)   Where a defender intends to apply by motion for an order for service of a third party notice before the closing of the record, he shall, before lodging the motion, set out in his defences, by adjustment to those defences, or in a separate statement of facts annexed to those defences—

    (a)   averments setting out the grounds on which he maintains that the proposed third party is liable to him by contribution, relief or indemnity or should be made a party to the action; and

    (b)   appropriate pleas-in-law.

(2)   Where a defender applies by motion for an order for service of a third party notice after the closing of the record, he shall, on lodging the motion, lodge a minute of amendment containing—

    (a)   averments setting out the grounds on which he maintains that the proposed third party is liable to him by contribution, relief or indemnity or should be made a party to the action, and

    (b)   appropriate pleas-in-law,

unless those grounds and pleas-in-law have been set out in the defences in the closed record.

(3)   A motion for an order for service of a third party notice shall be lodged before the commencement of the hearing of the merits of the cause.

GENERAL NOTE

*Rule 20.2(3)*

Until the commencement of the hearing on the merits it is entirely a matter for the discretion of the court whether a motion to introduce a third party is granted or not. The length of time that a case has been in dependence, the inevitable delay caused by allowing a motion and the requirement to discharge a proof may each be important factors weighing against allowing a motion to allow an order for service of a third party notice being granted. It is not competent to lodge a third party notice after the commencement of the hearing on the merits.

**D1.161**

### Warrants for diligence on third party notice

**20.3.**[1](1)   A defender who applies for an order for service of a third party notice may apply for—

    (a)   a warrant for arrestment to found jurisdiction;

    (b)   a warrant for interim diligence,

which would have been permitted had the warrant been sought in an initial writ in a separate action.

(2)   Averments in support of the application for a warrant under paragraph (1)(a) shall be included in the defences or the separate statement of facts referred to in rule 20.2(1).

(3)   An application for a warrant under paragraph (1)(a) shall be made by motion—

    (a)   at the time of applying for the third party notice; or

(b)    if not applied for at that time, at any stage of the cause thereafter.

(4)    A certified copy of the interlocutor granting warrant for diligence applied for under paragraph (2) shall be sufficient authority for execution of the diligence.

GENERAL NOTE

A warrant for diligence may be sought (see generally OCR 1993 Chapter 6 Interim Diligence). The law is codified in the Debtors (Scotland) Act 1987 ss.15A to 15N) but an explanation for seeking it has to be made expressly in the pleadings.

**Service on third party**                                                                         D1.162

**20.4.**—(1)    A third party notice shall be served on the third party within 14 days after the date of the interlocutor allowing service of that notice.

(2)    Where service of a third party notice has not been made within the period specified in paragraph (1), the order for service of it shall cease to have effect; and no service of the notice may be made unless a further order for service of it has been applied for and granted.

(3)[1]    There shall be served with a third party notice—
    (a)    a copy of the pleadings (including any adjustments and amendments); and
    (b)    where the pleadings have not been amended in accordance with the minute of amendment referred to in rule 20.2, a copy of that minute.

(4)    A copy of the third party notice, with a certificate of service attached to it, shall be lodged in process by the defender.

GENERAL NOTE

*Rule 20.4(1), (2)*

It is essential to serve the third party notice within 14 days of the order for service. This prevents a defender from delaying bringing in the third party once an order for service has been made. If service is not effective during that period the defender must return to court and obtain a fresh order.

*Rule 20.4(3)*

The pleadings served with the third party notice must contain the averments anent the basis of the claim made by the defender against the third party.

**Answers to third party notice**                                                                 D1.163

**20.5.**—(1)    An order for service of a third party notice shall specify 28 days, or such other period as the sheriff on cause shown may specify, as the period within which the third party may lodge answers.

(2)    Answers for a third party shall be headed "Answers for [E.F.], Third Party in the action at the instance of [A.B.], Pursuer against [C.D.], Defender" and shall include—
    (a)    answers to the averments of the defender against him in the form of numbered paragraphs corresponding to the numbered articles of the condescendence annexed to the summons and incorporating, if the third party so wishes, answers to the averments of the pursuer; or
    (b)    where a separate statement of facts has been lodged by the defender under rule 20.2(1), answers to the statement of facts in the form of numbered paragraphs corresponding to the numbered paragraphs of the statement of facts; and
    (c)    appropriate pleas-in-law.

GENERAL NOTE

It is important that the answers for the third party are organised in such a way so as to make clear the response in relation to the pursuer's averments and thereafter the defenders averments. The answers should be headed "Answers to condescendence and answers to averments for the defender". The third party is entitled to be heard in relation to the pursuer's claim against the defender, including any plea to the relevancy or other preliminary plea.

---

[1] As amended by the Act of Sederunt (Sheriff Court Rules) (Miscellaneous Amendments) 2009 (SSI 2009/294) r.10 (effective October 1, 2009).

**D1.164**

**Consequences of failure to amend pleadings**

**20.5A.**[1]   Where the pleadings have not been amended in accordance with the minute of amendment referred to in rule 20.2, no motion for a finding, order or decree against a third party may be enrolled by the defender unless, at or before the date on which he enrols the motion, he enrols a motion to amend the pleadings in accordance with that minute.

**Procedure following answers**

**D1.165**

**20.6.**—(1)   Where a third party lodges answers, the sheriff clerk shall fix a date and time under rule 9.2 for a hearing under rule 9.12 (Options Hearing) as if the third party had lodged a notice of intention to defend and the period of notice had expired on the date for lodging answers.

(2)   At the Options Hearing, or at any time thereafter, the sheriff may grant such decree or other order as he thinks fit.

(3)   A decree or other order against the third party shall have effect and be extractable in the same way as a decree or other order against a defender.

GENERAL NOTE

A final date for adjustment should be specified. The pursuer and the defender may require to adjust their pleadings in the light of the answers for the third party. The pursuer requires to consider whether or not to adopt the defender's case against the third party and/or whether or not to adopt the third party's case against the defender. If the pursuer wishes to adopt a case against the third party he requires to insert a crave for decree against the third party (which he must do by amendment) and to insert an appropriate plea in law. In any such amendment for the pursuer it is competent (but not essential) to redesign the third party as a second defender. The original defender may develop his case against the third party beyond what is stated as the ground of action in the third party notice.

RULE 20.6(2)

This rule is expressed in exceedingly wide terms and at first sight appears to permit the sheriff to deal with the merits of the whole case at the options hearing. It is thought, however, that the intention is to permit as much flexibility as possible in regulating further procedure as between all of the parties. It is possible to have separate debates or proofs depending on whether there are separate issues between the parties that may be advantageously resolved at different stages.

**D1.166**

Chapter 21

Documents Founded on or Adopted in Pleadings

**Lodging documents founded on or adopted**

**21.1.**—(1)   Subject to any other provision in these Rules, any document founded on by a party, or adopted as incorporated, in his pleadings shall, so far as in his possession or within his control, be lodged in process as a production by him—

(a)[2]   when founded on or adopted in an initial writ, at the time of returning the initial writ under rule 9.3 or, in the case of a personal injuries action raised under Part AI of Chapter 36, when the initial writ is presented for warranting in accordance with rule 5.1;

(b)   when founded on or adopted in a minute, defences, counterclaim or answers, at the time of lodging that part of process; and

(c)   when founded on or adopted in an adjustment to any pleadings, at the time when such adjustment is intimated to any other party.

(2)   Paragraph (1) shall be without prejudice to any power of the sheriff to order the production of any document or grant a commission and diligence for recovery of it.

GENERAL NOTE

A document founded upon (by reference to it) or incorporated in the pleadings (by the use of a form of words expressly incorporating it) must be lodged. It is the original that must be lodged. A document is founded on if it is a document that forms the basis at least to some extent of the action. Typically, a contract, lease, title deed, will or invoice is apt to form the basis of an action. A document is incorporated in the pleadings if that is expressly stated, the traditional form of words being "The [the title of the document] is held as repeated herein *brevitatis causa*". A more modern form is "The [document] is held as incorporated here in full". Documents that contain assertions of fact or expressions of opinion from witnesses in relation to the issues in the case (such as expert reports or medical reports) should not under any

---

[1] As inserted by SSI 2003/26 r.2 (effective January 24, 2003).
[2] As amended by the Act of Sederunt (Ordinary Cause Rules Amendment) (Personal Injuries Actions) 2009 (SSI 2009/285) r.2 (effective November 2, 2009).

circumstances be founded on in pleadings, nor should such items be incorporated in the pleadings. The pleader should extract from such documents the material required to make specific averments based on that material. Otherwise difficulties can arise (see e.g. *Reid v Shetland Sea Ferries* , 1999 S.C.C.R. 735). At a debate on relevancy or specification the court can only look at the pleadings. If the document has been incorporated then the document forms part of the pleadings and the court may have regard to it. If it has not been incorporated then even if the document is referred to and founded upon the court may not consider the document (although it must have regard to such parts of it as actually form part of the pleadings).

By virtue of OCR, rule 1.2(1), "document" has the meaning assigned to it in section 9 of the Civil Evidence (Scotland) Act 1988 (i.e. it includes maps, plans, graphs or drawings, photographs, discs, film, negatives, tapes, sound tracks or other devices from which sounds or other data or visual images are recorded so as to be capable (with or without the aid of some other equipment) of being reproduced).

A party may be penalised in expenses if there has been any wasted procedure through failure to lodge a document founded upon or incorporated.

*Rule 21.1(2)*

The sheriff has residuary power (presumably on the motion of a party or ex propio motu) to order production of a document at any stage of the cause (see Macphail, *Sheriff Court Practice* (3rd ed.), para.15.48).

**Consequences of failure to lodge documents founded on or adopted**

**D1.167**

**21.2.** Where a party fails to lodge a document in accordance with rule 21.1(1), he may be found liable in the expenses of any order for production or recovery of it obtained by any other party.

GENERAL NOTE

This is without prejudice to other sanctions available to secure compliance with OCR.

**Objection to documents founded on**

**D1.168**

**21.3.**—(1) Where a deed or writing is founded on by a party, any objection to it by any other party may be stated and maintained by exception without its being reduced.

(2) Where an objection is stated under paragraph (1) and an action of reduction would otherwise have been competent, the sheriff may order the party stating the objection to find caution or give such other security as he thinks fit.

GENERAL NOTE

A document that has a patent defect that renders it void or *ipso jure* null (such as a document that is executed without the necessary statutory solemnities or is unstamped) will simply not be given effect in any proceedings. If a defect is not of that type or there is room for doubt then the document has to be set aside by reduction. An action of reduction is not competent in the sheriff court but it is competent in certain circumstances to state an objection *ope exceptionis*. If a deed or writing (not decree) founded upon by a party in a sheriff court action is objected to then that objection may be stated and maintained, i.e. insisted upon (see Macphail, *Sheriff Court Practice* (3rd ed.), paras 12.66 to 12.72). Fair notice of the objection is required by averments and a plea in law.

Chapter 22

**D1.169**

Preliminary Pleas

**Note of basis of preliminary plea**

**22.1.**—(1) A party intending to insist on a preliminary plea shall, not later than 3 days before the Options Hearing under rule 9.12 or the Procedural Hearing under rule 10.6—

(a) lodge in process a note of the basis for the plea; and

(b) intimate a copy of it to every other party.

(2)[1] Where the Options Hearing is continued under rule 9.12(5) and a preliminary plea is added by adjustment, a party intending to insist on that plea shall, not later than 3 days before the date of the Options Hearing so continued—

(a) lodge in process a note of the basis for the plea; and

(b) intimate a copy of it to every other party.

---

[1] As inserted by the Act of Sederunt (Sheriff Court Ordinary Cause Rules Amendment) (Miscellaneous) 1996 (SI 1996/2445) (effective November 1, 1996).

(3)   If a party fails to comply with paragraph (1) or (2), he shall be deemed to be no longer insisting on the preliminary plea; and the plea shall be repelled by the sheriff at the Options Hearing or Procedural Hearing.

(4)[1]   At any proof before answer or debate, parties may on cause shown raise matters in addition to those set out in the note mentioned in paragraph (1) or (2).

(5)[2]   Where a note of the basis of a preliminary plea has been lodged under paragraph (1), and the Options Hearing is continued under rule 9.12(5), unless the basis of the plea has changed following further adjustment, it shall not be necessary for a party who is insisting on the plea to lodge a further note before the Options Hearing so continued.

GENERAL NOTE

*Rule 22.1(1)*

One of the most useful innovations of OCR 1993 was the removal of the automatic right to debate together with the requirement to provide notice of the basis of a preliminary plea. At the options hearing the court requires to make an informed decision as to further procedure. To do that in addition to studying the pleadings the sheriff must have a clear indication of the basis upon which any preliminary plea is stated. Accordingly any party that has a preliminary plea must lodge a note under this rule three days before the hearing. Failure to comply means that the preliminary plea must be repelled at the options hearing (or continued options hearing)—although it may just be possible in certain circumstances to invoke the dispensing power under OCR, rule 2.1 (see *Colvin v Montgomery Preservations Ltd* , 1995 S.L.T. (Sh. Ct) 14—that case involved sending the case for additional procedure in terms of Chapter 10 and was an early decision (less latitude might be shown now)). See also *Humphrey v Royal Sun Alliance Plc* , 2005 S.L.T. (Sh. Ct) 31.

*Rule 22.1(2)*

Where a preliminary plea is added by adjustment between an options hearing and a continued options hearing a note of the basis of the plea must be lodged failing which it will be repelled. Likewise, where a preliminary plea is added by amendment (or answers thereto) it is necessary to lodge a note of argument failing which the plea must be repelled (see OCR, rule 18.8) (cf. *Sutherland v Duncan* , 1996 S.L.T. 428—another early case and where the sheriff's exercise of the dispensing power was not interfered with on appeal).

*Rule 22.1(4)*

On cause shown it is competent to make an argument in support of a preliminary plea not foreshadowed in the rule 22 note but if the argument is new, separate or distinct from the note of the basis of the plea as intimated it might, if successful, result in a penalty in expenses at least to some extent. On the other hand it is not competent to attempt at debate or by amendment to introduce a new or different plea (in relation to the same pleadings that have already been considered at the options hearing) or to reintroduce a plea that has been repelled already (see *George Martin (Builders) Ltd v Jamal* , 2001 S.L.T. (Sh. Ct) 119; see also *Bell v John Davidson (Pipes)* , 1995 S.L.T. (Sh. Ct) 15).

**D1.170**

## Chapter 23

### Abandonment

**Abandonment of causes**

**23.1.**—(1)   A pursuer may abandon a cause at any time before decree of absolvitor or dismissal by lodging a minute of abandonment and—

   (a)   consenting to decree of absolvitor; or
   (b)   seeking decree of dismissal.

(2)[3]   The sheriff shall not grant decree of dismissal under paragraph (1)(b) unless full judicial expenses have been paid to the defender, and any third party against whom the pursuer has directed any crave, within 28 days after the date of taxation.

---

[1] As amended by the Act of Sederunt (Sheriff Court Ordinary Cause Rules Amendment) (Miscellaneous) 2000 (SSI 2000/239) (effective October 2, 2000).
[2] As inserted by the Act of Sederunt (Sheriff Court Ordinary Cause Rules Amendment) (Miscellaneous) 1996 (SI 1996/2445) (effective November 1, 1996).
[3] As amended by SSI 2003/26, reg. 2 (effective from January 24, 2003).

(3)   If the pursuer fails to pay the expenses referred to in paragraph (2) to the party to whom they are due within the period specified in that paragraph, that party shall be entitled to decree of absolvitor with expenses.

General Note

A pursuer has a right to abandon an action against one or more defenders without reserving the ability to raise a fresh action against the same defender in respect of the same subject matter. Such abandonment without reservation will result in decree of absolvitor being pronounced in favour of the defender who will have the benefit of the plea of res judicata should the same pursuer raise the same action against him. The minute is in the following terms "[Name of Solicitor] for the pursuer stated and hereby stated to the court that the pursuer abandons the cause and consents to decree of absolvitor in terms of rule 23.2(1)(a) of the Ordinary Cause Rules". It is usual for the minute also to concede expenses, although this is not a prerequisite. The pursuer should enrol a motion to abandon in terms of the minute (*Walker v Walker* , 1995 S.C.L.R. 187). If the minute is silent as to expenses the defender should oppose the motion to abandon *quaod* the matter of expenses. Expenses as taxed will ordinarily be pronounced in favour of the defender unless, for example, the defender has wrongly misled the pursuer into raising an action against him in which case the pursuer may be able to persuade the court to award him expenses despite the abandonment.

The pursuer may want to reserve the right to raise a fresh action. To achieve that he must ensure that the court pronounces dismissal as opposed to absolvitor, and to do that he must comply with the peremptory terms of the rule. The court will not grant dismissal unless full judicial expenses are paid to the defender within 28 days of the date of taxation. The procedure is for a motion to be lodged for dismissal together with a minute stating "[Name of Solicitor] for the pursuer stated and hereby states to the court that the pursuer abandons the cause and seeks decree of dismissal in terms of rule 23.1(1)(b) of the Ordinary Cause Rules". The court allows the minute to be received, appoints the defender to lodge an account of expenses (within such period as the court may specify) and remits the same when lodged to the auditor of court to tax and to report. The pursuer has 28 days from the date of taxation in order to pay the account if he seeks dismissal as opposed to absolvitor. If he pays he should lodge the receipt in process together with a motion for dismissal in respect that the expenses as taxed due to the defender have been paid (or consigned) and the court then pronounces an interlocutor allowing the pursuer to abandon the cause and dismisses the action. If the expenses are not paid within the 28-day period the defender can enrol for absolvitor with expenses (see *VP Packaging Ltd v The ADF Partnership* , 2002 S.L.T. 1224; see also *Anderson v Hardie* , 1997 S.L.T. (Sh. Ct) 70), but the court still has a discretion to allow a pursuer to withdraw a minute of abandonment at any time before the final decree disposing of the action (subject to such conditions as to expenses as seem appropriate (see *Lee v Pollock's Trustees* (1906) F. 857)). Rule 23.1 makes no provision for the situation where parties agree on the amount of expenses without the account being taxed, and if that is done it has been held that the pursuer may be presumed to have abandoned any right to ask for dismissal in terms of the rule (see *VP Packaging* (above) but for a contrary view see *Beattie v The Royal Bank of Scotland Plc* , 2003 S.L.T. 564 which suggests that the dispensing power may be used in these circumstances).

**Application of abandonment to counterclaims**                                                    **D1.171**

**23.2.**   Rule 23.1 shall, with the necessary modifications, apply to the abandonment by a defender of his counterclaim as it applies to the abandonment of a cause.

Chapter 24

Withdrawal of Solicitors

**Intimation of withdrawal to court**

**24.1.**—(1)[1]   Subject to paragraph (3), where a solicitor withdraws from acting on behalf of a party,   **D1.172** he shall intimate his withdrawal by letter to the sheriff clerk and to every other party.

(2)[2]   The sheriff clerk shall forthwith lodge such letter in process.

(3)[3]   Where a solicitor withdraws from acting on behalf of a party in open court and in the presence of the other parties to the action or their representatives, paragraph (1) shall not apply.

---

[1] As amended by the Act of Sederunt (Sheriff Court Ordinary Cause Rules Amendment) (Miscellaneous) 2000 (SSI 2000/239) (effective October 2, 2000).
[2] As amended by the Act of Sederunt (Sheriff Court Ordinary Cause Rules Amendment) (Miscellaneous) 2000 (SSI 2000/239) (effective October 2, 2000).
[3] Inserted by the Act of Sederunt (Sheriff Court Ordinary Cause Rules Amendment) (Miscellaneous) 2000 (SSI 2000/239) (effective October 2, 2000).

GENERAL NOTE

An agent is entitled to withdraw from acting without asking for leave from the court but must intimate the withdrawal by letter to the sheriff clerk and every other party. The agent also has a duty to furnish the agents for the other parties with the address of his former client, if it is known to him (see *Sime, Sullivan & Dickson's Trustee v Adam* , 1908 S.C. 32). Of course, notwithstanding the requirements of this rule the court still has discretion to pronounce decree by default if a party is unrepresented at a diet (see Chapter 16 and for an example see *Munro & Miller (Pakistan) Ltd v Wyvern Structures Ltd* , 1997 S.C. 1).

**D1.173**

**Intimation to party whose solicitor has withdrawn**

**24.2.**—(1)[1]   Subject to paragraph (1A), the sheriff shall, of his own motion, or on the motion of any other party, pronounce an interlocutor ordaining the party whose solicitor has withdrawn from acting to appear or be represented at a specified diet fixed by the sheriff to state whether or not he intends to proceed, under certification that if he fails to do so the sheriff may grant decree or make such other order or finding as he thinks fit.

(1A)[2]   Where any previously fixed diet is to occur within 14 days from the date when the sheriff first considers the solicitor's withdrawal, the sheriff may either—

    (a)   pronounce an interlocutor in accordance with paragraph (1);

       or

    (b)   consider the matter at the previously fixed diet.

(2)   The diet fixed in the interlocutor under paragraph (1) shall not be less than 14 days after the date of the interlocutor unless the sheriff otherwise orders.

(3)   The party who has lodged the motion under paragraph (1), or any other party appointed by the sheriff, shall forthwith serve on the party whose solicitor has withdrawn a copy of the interlocutor and a notice in Form G10; and a certificate of service shall be lodged in process.

GENERAL NOTE

It is very important that the requirements of intimation, notice and certification are complied with to ensure the peremptory nature of the diet at which the now unrepresented party is required to appear.

**D1.174**

**Consequences of failure to intimate intention to proceed**

**24.3.**   Where a party on whom a notice and interlocutor has been served under rule 24.2(2) fails to appear or be represented at a diet fixed under rule 24.2(1) and to state his intention as required by that paragraph, the sheriff may grant decree or make such other order or finding as he thinks fit.

GENERAL NOTE

If the requirements of intimation, notice and certification are followed then, ordinarily, decree will be pronounced (see, e.g. *Connelly v Lanarkshire Health Board* , 1999 S.C. 364). The decree could be *de plano* in favour of a pursuer or dismissal in favour of a defender. It is competent to pronounce absolvitor in favour of a defender but generally the court will pronounce decree of dismissal. The decree is a decree *in foro*. If the requirements are followed then appeal though competent is unlikely to succeed (see *Connelly*).

**D1.175**

Chapter 25

Minutes of Sist and Transference

**Minutes of sist**

**25.1.**   Where a party dies or comes under legal incapacity while a cause is depending, any person claiming to represent that party or his estate may apply by minute to be sisted as a party to the cause.

GENERAL NOTE

Death of a party suspends all procedure in the cause at whatever stage it is at (including appeal) and any further procedure is inept unless the representatives of the deceased sist themselves to the cause, or the action is transferred (by amendment) against such representatives. Where a party becomes bankrupt during the dependence of the action the trustee has power (section 39(2)(b) of the Bankruptcy (Scotland) Act 1985) to carry it on (or continue to defend it) and if he so wishes he should sist himself as a party. By so doing he renders himself liable to the opposite party in the whole expenses of the action. If the trustee declines to sist himself as a party then the bankrupt, if he continues to have title to sue, may continue the

---

[1] As amended by the Act of Sederunt (Sheriff Court Ordinary Cause Rules Amendment) (Miscellaneous) 2000 (SSI 2000/239) (effective October 2, 2000).

[2] Inserted by the Act of Sederunt (Sheriff Court Ordinary Cause Rules Amendment) (Miscellaneous) 2000 (SSI 2000/239) (effective October 2, 2000).

action. If the bankrupt is a pursuer the court (if asked) will ordain him to find caution but not if he is a defender (see *William Dow (Potatoes) Ltd v Dow*, 2001 S.L.T. (Sh. Ct) 37). Where a party becomes insane the cause should be sisted so that a guardian may be appointed. Once appointed the guardian is entitled to sist himself as a party. If the guardian fails to sist himself as a party then the other party may apply for and obtain decree and expenses against the incapax (provided of course that proper intimation is made to the guardian).

In the case of corporate bodies, if a company is struck from the register under s.1000 of the Companies Act 2006 during the dependence of the action, the action should be sisted to allow an application to restore it to the register (see *Steans Fashions Ltd v General Assurance Society* [1995] B.C.C. 510—a decision of the English Court of Appeal). If a defender company goes into liquidation during the dependence of the action the permission of the court (in the liquidation process) is required to continue the proceedings against it (see section 130(2) of the Insolvency Act 1986). If the company is a pursuer then the liquidator has power to carry it on (see section 169(2) of the Insolvency Act 1986) and if he wishes to do so he should sist himself as a party to the action. In the case of a company in administration it is essential to obtain the permission of the administrator or the court (in the administration process) to continue proceedings against the company (see s.8 of the Insolvency Act 1988; Schedule B1 para.43(b)). It is unnecessary for an administrator or receiver to sist himself as a party to the action but the instance should be amended to narrate the position.

### Minutes of transference

**D1.176**

**25.2.**[1]   Where a party dies or comes under legal incapacity while a cause is depending and the provisions of rule 25.1 are not invoked, any other party may apply by minute to have the cause transferred in favour of or against, as the case may be, any person who represents that party or his estate.

GENERAL NOTE

If the representatives of a deceased or incapax do not sist themselves to the cause, then any other party may apply by minute of transference to have it transferred in favour of or against the person who represents the estate. Decree *cognitionis causa tantum* should be sought so as to constitute the debt against a deceased's estate. If no one comes to represent a pursuer then decree of absolvitor may be obtained.

CHAPTER 26

**D1.177**

TRANSFER AND REMIT OF CAUSES

### Transfer to another sheriff court

**26.1.**—(1)   The sheriff may, on cause shown, remit any cause to another sheriff court.

(2)   Subject to paragraph (4), where a cause in which there are two or more defenders has been brought in the sheriff court of the residence or place of business of one of them, the sheriff may transfer the cause to any other sheriff court which has jurisdiction over any of the defenders.

(3)   Subject to paragraph (4), where a plea of no jurisdiction is sustained, the sheriff may transfer the cause to the sheriff court before which it appears to him the cause ought to have been brought.

(4)   The sheriff shall not transfer a cause to another sheriff court under paragraph (2) or (3) except—

    (a)   on the motion of a party; and

    (b)   where he considers it expedient to do so having regard to the convenience of the parties and their witnesses.

(5)   On making an order under paragraph (1), (2) or (3), the sheriff—

    (a)   shall state his reasons for doing so in the interlocutor; and

    (b)   may make the order on such conditions as to expenses or otherwise as he thinks fit.

(6)   The court to which a cause is transferred under paragraph (1), (2) or (3) shall accept the cause.

(7)   A transferred cause shall proceed in all respects as if it had been originally brought in the court to which it is transferred.

(8)   An interlocutor transferring a cause may, with leave of the sheriff, be appealed to the sheriff principal but shall not be subject to appeal to the Court of Session.

GENERAL NOTE

The convenience of the parties and witnesses is the paramount consideration determining whether to transfer a cause from one sheriff court to another. The ability of the court to transfer rather than dismiss an action where it has no jurisdiction is based on expediency (see *Wilson v Ferguson*, 1957 S.L.T. (Sh. Ct) 52). It is necessary that either the transferring court or the court to which the cause is transferred

---

[1] As amended by the Act of Sederunt (Sheriff Court Ordinary Cause Rules Amendment) (Miscellaneous) 1996 (SI 1996/2445) (effective November 1, 1996).

otherwise has jurisdiction over the defender. It is essential that the sheriff sets out the reasons for the transfer in the interlocutor.

**D1.178**

### Remit to Court of Session

**26.2.**—(1) The sheriff clerk shall, within four days after the sheriff has pronounced an interlocutor remitting a cause to the Court of Session, transmit the process to the Deputy Principal Clerk of Session.

(2) The sheriff clerk shall, within the period specified in paragraph (1), send written notice of the remit to each party and certify on the interlocutor sheet that he has done so.

(3) Failure by a Sheriff Clerk to comply with paragraph (2) shall not affect the validity of a remit made under paragraph (1).

GENERAL NOTE

The general power to remit to the Court of Session is contained in section 37(1)(b) of the Sheriff Courts (Scotland) Act 1971, which provides:

"In the case of any ordinary cause brought in the sheriff court the sheriff—

(b)  may, subject to section 7 of the Sheriff Courts (Scotland) Act 1907, on the motion of any of the parties to the cause, if he is of the opinion that the *importance or difficulty* of the cause make it appropriate to do so, remit the cause to the Court of Session."

*"Importance or difficulty"*

The leading case is the five judge decision in *Mullan v Anderson* , 1993 S.L.T. 835. Despite the divergence of opinions it is submitted that there should not be much difficulty in practice in recognising a case that is suitable to be remitted to the Court of Session. In assessing the matter, the sheriff has a wide discretion and should consider the importance of the cause to the parties and weigh up the procedural implications as well as the expense and delay involved. He should also consider the public interest. In *Mullan* it was clearly appropriate that an allegation of murder be tried in the Supreme Court. In the personal injury field it is insufficient merely to assert that the claim is a substantial one to justify a remit (see *Butler v Thom* , 1982 S.L.T. (Sh. Ct) 57) but other considerations may justify a remit—see *Gallagher v Birse* , 2003 S.C.L.R. 623.

A decision to remit or not to remit may be appealed to the Court of Session without leave (see section 37(3)(b) of the Sheriff Courts (Scotland) Act 1971).

Section 37 of the Sheriff Courts (Scotland) Act 1971 also contains specific powers to remit in family actions and there are specific provisions under section 1 of the Presumption of Death (Scotland) Act 1977 and section 44 of the Crown Proceedings Act 1947.

If a remit is granted, the Sheriff Clerk must send the process to the Court of Session within four days. Once the process is received by him the Deputy Principal Clerk of Session writes the date of receipt on the interlocutor sheet and intimates that date to each party. Within 14 days after such intimation the party on whose motion the remit was made, or if the cause was remitted by the sheriff at his own instance, the pursuer makes up and lodges a process incorporating the sheriff court process in the General Department and makes a motion for such further procedure as he desires and thereafter the cause proceeds as though it had been initiated in the Court of Session (see RCS 1994, rr.32.3 and 32.4).

The other party is entitled to insist on the remit (RCS 1994, r.32.6), but if neither party enrols for further procedure the remit will be deemed to have been abandoned and the cause transmitted back to the sheriff clerk (RCS 1994, r.32.7).

The Court of Session also has power in terms of section 33 of the Court of Session Act to order transmission of a sheriff court process to it on the ground of contingency (see RCS 1994, r.32.2).

Once a cause is before the Court of Session it is incompetent (see *Baird v Scottish Motor Traction Co* , 1948 S.C. 526) to remit it back to the sheriff to consider questions relating to expenses (such as certification of the cause as suitable for the employment of counsel). There is no reason why such matters cannot be dealt with before a remit is granted. But if they have not been, then it is a matter for the Auditor of the Court of Session upon taxation to consider such issues relating to expenses relative to the whole action.

**D1.179**

### Remit from Court of Session

**26.3.**  On receipt of the process in an action which has been remitted from the Court of Session under section 14 of the Law Reform (Miscellaneous Provisions) (Scotland) Act 1985, the sheriff clerk shall—

(a)  record the date of receipt on the interlocutor sheet;

(b)  fix a hearing to determine further procedure on the first court day occurring not earlier than 14 days after the date of receipt of the process; and (c)　forthwith send written notice of the date of the hearing fixed under sub-paragraph (b) to each party.

GENERAL NOTE

The provision under section 14 of the Law Reform (Miscellaneous Provisions) (Scotland) Act 1985 (to allow the Court of Session to remit a cause to the sheriff, "where, in the opinion of the court the nature of the action makes it appropriate to do") was not introduced to effect a general redistribution of work between the courts but to meet the needs of particular cases (see *McIntosh v British Railways Board (No.1)* , 1990 S.L.T. 637 (see also *Gribb v Gribb* , 1993 S.L.T. 178). The power to remit should be exercised on grounds particular to the case concerned (see *Bell v Chief Constable of Strathclyde* , 2011 S.L.T. 244). For an example where a remit was granted see *Colin McKay v Lloyd's TSB Mortgages Ltd* , 2005 S.C.L.R. 547.

### Chapter 27

**D1.180**

### Caution and Security

**Application of this Chapter**

**27.1.**　This Chapter applies to—
(a)　any cause in which the sheriff has power to order a person to find caution or give other security; and
(b)　security for expenses ordered to be given by the election court or the sheriff under section 136(2)(i) of the Representation of the People Act 1983 in an election petition.

GENERAL NOTE

Caution or other security (usually but not necessarily consignation) may be ordered as a condition of recall of arrestment on the dependence. It may also be sought as an alternative to sisting a mandatary where the other party is not resident in an EU country (see *Deiter Rossmeier v Mounthooly Transport* , 2000 S.L.T. 208). Moreover, the court has power to order that a party find caution or consign a sum as security for expenses and/or the sum sought. There are certain particular provisions where caution consignation may be ordered, such as under OCR r.21.3(2) or section 100 of the Bills of Exchange Act 1882. Apart from these, the court has a general power within its discretion to make an order. In relation to natural persons, however, the court will generally not order that caution or security be found unless the party is an undischarged bankrupt, is a nominal pursuer or there are exceptional circumstances justifying an order. Being poor is not of itself a sufficient reason to require caution or security to be found since that would deprive a large section of the community of access to the court (see *Stevenson v Midlothian D.C.* , 1983 S.C. (H.L.) 50 and *McTear's Exr v Imperial Tobacco Ltd* , 1997 S.L.T. 530). If the case is patently without merit then an order may be granted, but such a situation is rare since agents have a professional duty not to prosecute or defend unstateable cases. Defenders are not generally required to find caution, nevertheless the terms of the defence will be scrutinised with care (and a defender with a counter claim falls to be treated in the same way as a pursuer: see *William Dow (Potatoes) Ltd v Dow* , 2001 S.L.T. (Sh Ct) 37). Limited companies as pursuers are required to find security under s.726(2) of the Companies Act 1985 (this is still in force; see Companies Act 2006 (Consequential Amendments Transitional Provisions and Savings) Order 2009 (SI 2009/1941)) if it appears by credible testimony that there is reason to believe that the company will be unable to pay the defender's expenses if successful in his defence. Absence of trading and the failure to comply with the requirements to lodge accounts or annual returns are relevant.

**Form of applications**

**D1.181**

**27.2.**—(1)　An application for an order for caution or other security or for variation or recall of such an order, shall be made by motion.

(2)　The grounds on which such an application is made shall be set out in the motion.

GENERAL NOTE

It is important to provide detail in the motion as to the reason for seeking security and any supporting documents should be lodged.

**Orders**

**D1.182**

**27.3.**　Subject to section 726(2) of the Companies Act 1985 (expenses by certain limited companies), an order to find caution or give other security shall specify the period within which such caution is to be found or such security given.

GENERAL NOTE

Section 726(2) of the Companies Act 1985 permits the action to be sisted pending the finding of security, but the court is also entitled to impose a time limit within which caution should be found in relation to which failure to comply would amount to default. At common law it is competent to ordain a defender company to find caution. A defender company with a counterclaim falls to be treated in the same way as a pursuer under section 726(2): see *William Dow (Potatoes) Ltd v Dow* , 2001 S.L.T. (Sh Ct) 37.

**D1.183**

### Methods of finding caution or giving security

    **27.4.**—(1)  A person ordered—
        (a)  to find caution, shall do so by obtaining a bond of caution; or
        (b)  to consign a sum of money into court, shall do so by consignation under the Sheriff Court Consignations (Scotland) Act 1893 in the name of the sheriff clerk.

    (2)  The sheriff may approve a method of security other than one mentioned in paragraph (1), including a combination of two or more methods of security.

    (3)  Subject to paragraph (4), any document by which an order to find caution or give other security is satisfied shall be lodged in process.

    (4)  Where the sheriff approves a security in the form of a deposit of a sum of money in the joint names of the agents of parties, a copy of the deposit receipt, and not the principal, shall be lodged in process.

    (5)  Any document lodged in process, by which an order to find caution or give other security is satisfied, shall not be borrowed from process.

GENERAL NOTE

    Joint deposit receipt is another form of security.

**D1.184**

### Cautioners and guarantors[1]

    **27.5.**[2]  A bond of caution or other security shall be given only by a person who is an "authorised person" within the meaning of section 31 of the Financial Services and Markets Act 2000.

GENERAL NOTE

    See *Greens Annotated Rules of the Court of Session* (W.Green, 2002) and the annotation to RCS 1994, r.33.5.

**D1.185**

### Form of bonds of caution and other securities

    **27.6.**—(1)  A bond of caution shall oblige the cautioner, his heirs and executors to make payment of the sums for which he has become cautioner to the party to whom he is bound, as validly and in the same manner as the party, his heirs and successors, for whom he is cautioner, are obliged.

    (2)[3]  A bond of caution or other security document given by a person shall state whether that person is an "authorised person" within the meaning of section 31 of the Financial Services and Markets Act 2000.

### Sufficiency of caution or security and objections

**D1.186**

    **27.7.**—(1)  The sheriff clerk shall satisfy himself that any bond of caution, or other document lodged in process under rule 27.4(3), is in proper form.

    (2)  A party who is dissatisfied with the sufficiency or form of the caution or other security offered in obedience to an order of the court may apply by motion for an order under rule 27.9 (failure to find caution or give security).

GENERAL NOTE

    Clearly it is in the interest of the party in whose favour the order has been granted to satisfy himself that the security is in proper form.

**D1.187**

### Insolvency or death of cautioner or guarantor

    **27.8.**  Where caution has been found by bond of caution or security has been given by guarantee and the cautioner or guarantor, as the case may be—
        (a)  becomes apparently insolvent within the meaning assigned by section 7 of the Bankruptcy (Scotland) Act 1985 (constitution of apparent insolvency),

---

[1] As substituted by the Act of Sederunt (Sheriff Court Ordinary Cause Rules Amendment) (Miscellaneous) 1996 (SI 1996/2445) r.3(31) (effective November 1, 1996).
[2] As amended by the Act of Sederunt (Ordinary Cause Rules) Amendment (Caution and Security) 2005 (SSI 2005/20) r.2(2) (effective February 1, 2005).
[3] As amended by the Act of Sederunt (Ordinary Cause Rules) Amendment (Caution and Security) 2005 (SSI 2005/20) r.2(3) (effective February 1, 2005).

(b)   calls a meeting of his creditors to consider the state of his affairs,

(c)   dies unrepresented, or

(d)   is a company and—

    (i)[1]   an administration, bank administration or building society special administration order or a winding up, bank insolvency or building society insolvency order has been made, or a resolution for a voluntary winding up has been passed, with respect to it,

    (ii)   a receiver of all or any part of its undertaking has been appointed, or

    (iii)   a voluntary arrangement (within the meaning assigned by section 1(1) of the Insolvency Act 1986) has been approved under Part I of that Act,

the party entitled to benefit from the caution or guarantee may apply by motion for a new security or further security to be given.

**Failure to find caution or give security**

**27.9.**   Where a party fails to find caution or give other security (in this rule referred to as "the party in default") any other party may apply by motion—

(a)   where he party in default is a pursuer, for decree of absolvitor; or

(b)   where the party in default is a defender or a third party, for decree by default or for such other finding or order as the sheriff thinks fit.

**D1.188**

GENERAL NOTE

See Chapter 16. A decree whether absolvitor or by default is in foro and is res judicata between the parties. A successful motion to award caution cannot be appealed without leave (see sections 27 and 28 of the Sheriff Courts (Scotland) Act 1907), but a decree of absolvitor or default can be and the earlier interlocutor ganting security will be opened up as a result: see *McCue v Scottish Daily Record and Sunday Mail* , 1998 S.C. 811.

Chapter 28

**D1.189**

Recovery of Evidence

*Application and interpretation of this Chapter*

**28.1.**—(1)   This Chapter applies to the recovery of any evidence in a cause depending before the sheriff.

(2)   In this Chapter, "the Act of 1972" means the Administration of Justice (Scotland) Act 1972.

GENERAL NOTE

An application for recovery under Chapter 28 refers to a cause depending before the sheriff. Before the commencement of an action, the court may grant applications to recover documents, inspect and preserve property, etc. (under the Administration of Justice (Scotland) Act 1972 (as amended)). Such applications require to be brought by summary application (see Act of Sederunt (Summary Applications, Statutory Applications and Appeals etc. Rules) 1999 (SI 1999/929) (reproduced at page D 488) and Part I, rules 3.1.1 and 3.1.2 (page D 513)).

**Applications for commission and diligence for recovery of documents or for orders under section 1 of the Act of 1972**

**D1.190**

**28.2.**—(1)   An application by a party for—

(a)   a commission and diligence for the recovery of a document, or

(b)   an order under section 1 of the Act of 1972,

shall be made by motion.

(2)   At the time of lodging a motion under paragraph (1), a specification of—

(a)   the document or other property sought to be inspected, photographed, preserved, taken into custody, detained, produced, recovered, sampled or experimented with or upon, as the case may be, or

(b)   the matter in respect of which information is sought as to the identity of a person who might be a witness or a defender,

shall be lodged in process.

(3)[2]   A copy of the specification lodged under paragraph (2) and the motion made under paragraph (1) shall be intimated by the applicant to—

---

[1] As substituted by the Act of Sederunt (Sheriff Court Rules) (Miscellaneous Amendments) 2009 (SSI 2009/294) r.16 (effective October 1, 2009).

[2] As substituted by SI 1996/2445 (effective November 1, 1996).

(a)   every other party;

(b)   in respect of an application under section 1(1) of the Act of 1972, any third party haver; and

(c)[1]  where necessary—

    (i)   the Advocate General for Scotland (in a case where the document or other property sought is in the possession of either a public authority exercising functions in relation to reserved matters within the meaning of Schedule 5 to the Scotland Act 1998, or a cross-border public authority within the meaning of section 88(5) of that Act); or

    (ii)  the Lord Advocate (in any other case),

    and, if there is any doubt, both.

(4)   Where the sheriff grants a motion under paragraph (1) in whole or in part, he may order the applicant to find such caution or give such other security as he thinks fit.

(5)   The Advocate General for Scotland or the Lord Advocate or both, as appropriate, may appear at the hearing of any motion under paragraph (1).

GENERAL NOTE

*Rule 28.2(1)(a)*

The common law process whereby evidence can be recovered and preserved for use in an action is termed commission and diligence. The commission is the written authority of the court to a person (normally a solicitor in practice at the sheriff court where the order is granted) to take the evidence of the witness (or haver) as to the existence or whereabouts of the document; and the diligence is the warrant to cite such witnesses or haver to appear before the commissioner.

*Rule 28.2(1)(b)*

Apart from the power to order recovery and inspection before the action is raised, the Administration of Justice (Scotland) Act 1972 also augments the common law powers of the court to order inspection, photographing, preservation, custody and detention of documents and other property which appear to be property as to which any question may relevantly arise in any existing civil proceedings before that court. Section 1A of the 1972 Act also gives power to the court to require any person to disclose such information as he has as to the identity of witnesses to the proceedings. The general rule that a litigant will not normally be permitted to recover or inspect property until after the closing of the record is thus modified, and cases, such as *Boyle v Glasgow Royal Infirmary and Associated Hospitals Board of Management* , 1969 S.C. 72, decided before this provision came into force, require to be read in the light of it. The judicial climate and the background culture has altered significantly not least because of the passing into law of the Freedom of Information (Scotland) Act 2002 and there is now no reason why there should be any difference between the test for recovery before and after the closing of the record (cf. *Moore v Greater Glasgow Health Board* , 1978 S.C. 123—it is unthinkable now that an application of the type made in *Moore* could be opposed successfully).

Whether the application for recovery is at common law or under the statute it must satisfy the test of relevancy. A call is relevant if it is designed to recover documents or items which would permit a party to make more detailed or specific averments that are already in the pleadings (including responding to the other side's pleadings). Further a call is relevant if it is designed to recover a document the purpose of which is to prove an averment. Fishing (that is, looking for documents in the hope that material will be obtained to make a case not yet pled) is not permitted.

*Rule 28.2(2)*

The application is made by motion (see Chapter 15) and at the same time a specification of document(s) or, as the case may be, specification of property or matter requires to be lodged in process. If the application is made before the options hearing the pleadings as adjusted to date should be lodged in process (see OCR, rule 9.4).

*"Specification"*

A specification is in the form of written calls specifying precisely the document or items sought. There are two types of call. The first is a named description of the document or item. This is appropriate where the document or item is known to exist or at least to have been in existence and can be readily identified

---

[1] As substituted by the Act of Sederunt (Ordinary Cause, Summary Application, Summary Cause and Small Claim Rules) Amendment (Miscellaneous) 2007 (SSI 2007/6) r.2(10) (effective January 29, 2007).

by a verbal description. The second type seeks a range of documents which may contain an entry relevant to the case. There is a tendency for practitioners to favour the second type of call. Nevertheless it is advantageous, wherever possible, to use the first type since that minimises the work of the haver in locating the particular document sought and thereafter of the commissioner in excerpting from the documents produced to him the relevant entries falling within the terms of the call. It is not necessary in any specification to identify the name of the haver, but it is helpful to all concerned if it is frequently done. Of course, frequently the haver is unknown and a series of diets of commission require to take place before the document or item is traced to any person.

*"Intimated"*

It is necessary to intimate the motion to every other party and to the Lord Advocate and/or the Advocate General where what is sought is in the possession of the Crown. Intimation to the Lord Advocate of an application to recover medical records is not necessary; see e.g. Practice Note No.2 of 2006 for Grampian, Highland and Islands (all the other Sherrifdoms have issued practice notes). It is also now necessary to intimate to the haver where what is sought is an order under section 1 of the Administration of Justice (Scotland) Act 1972. It is important therefore that the applicant is clear which of the court's powers is being invoked.

In the case of documents held by the Scottish Government, United Kingdom government departments or other public authorities an objection may be raised that recovery would be contrary to public policy. In that event the court, while accepting a statement to the effect that production would be contrary to the public interest, has to decide whether nevertheless justice requires that the order be granted in the interests of the individual party (*Glasgow Corporation v Central Land Board* , 1956 S.C. (H.L.) 1; *Rogers v Orr* , 1939 S.C. 492; *AB v Glasgow West of Scotland Blood Transfusion Service* , 1993 S.L.T. 36). The objection is frequently taken to protect information gathered by the Police, the Crown Office and Procurator Fiscal service. Whether the objection (which may be at the instance of a party or the haver or both) is successful depends upon the circumstances of the case, the nature of the application and the document sought to be recovered. (See generally, Walker, *Evidence* (3rd ed.), pp.193–198).

It is also the case that by virtue of art.8 of ECHR the Court may require the motion to other persons who may be affected; see *M v A Scottish Local Authority* , 2012 S.L.T. 6.

**Optional procedure before executing commission and diligence**

**28.3.**—(1)   The party who has obtained a commission and diligence for the recovery of a document under rule 28.2(1)(a) may, at any time before executing it against a haver, serve on the haver an order in Form G11 (in this rule referred to as "the order"); and if so, the provisions of this rule shall apply.

(2)[1]   The order and a copy of the specification referred to in rule 28.2(2) as approved by the court shall be served on the haver or his known solicitor and shall be complied with by the haver in the manner and within the period specified in the order.

(3)[2]   Not later than the day after the date on which the order, the certificate appended to Form G11 and any document is received by the sheriff clerk from a haver, he shall intimate that to each party.

(4)   No party, other than the party who served the order, may uplift such a document until after the expiry of 7 days after the date of intimation under paragraph (3).

(5)   Where the party who served the order fails to uplift such a document within 7 days after the date of intimation under paragraph (3), the sheriff clerk shall intimate that failure to every other party.

(6)   Where no party has uplifted such a document within 14 days after the date of intimation under paragraph (5), the sheriff clerk shall return it to the haver who delivered it to him.

(7)   Where a party who has uplifted such a document does not wish to lodge it, he shall return it to the sheriff clerk who shall—

    (a)   intimate the return of the document to every other party; and

    (b)   if no other party uplifts the document within 14 days of the date of intimation, return it to the haver.

(8)   If the party who served the order is not satisfied—

    (a)   that full compliance has been made with the order, or

    (b)   that adequate reasons for non-compliance have been given,

he may execute the commission and diligence under rule 28.4.

(9)   Where an extract from a book of any description (whether the extract is certified or not) is produced under the order, the sheriff may, on the motion of the party who served the order, order that that party shall be allowed to inspect the book and take copies of any entries falling within the specification.

**D1.191**

---

[1] As amended by SI 1996/2445 (effective November 1, 1996).
[2] As amended by SI 1996/2445 (effective November 1, 1996).

(10)   Where any question of confidentiality arises in relation to a book ordered to be inspected under paragraph (9), the inspection shall be made, and any copies shall be taken, at the sight of the commissioner appointed in the interlocutor granting the commission and diligence.

(11)[1]   The sheriff may, on cause shown, order the production of any book (not being a banker's book or book of public record) containing entries falling under a specification, notwithstanding the production of a certified extract from that book.

GENERAL NOTE

The vast majority of commissions proceed under the optional procedure and a diet of commission is not required. The procedure is designed to ensure that all documents falling within the terms of the calls of the specification are produced to the sheriff clerk so that all parties are aware of all of the documents recovered, giving all parties an opportunity of lodging them in process and in the event that they are not lodged ensuring their safe return to the haver. A demand for production (within seven days) in Form G11 (or "order") is served on the haver or his known solicitor together with the specification as approved by the court. The haver produces to the sheriff clerk the certificate appended to the Form G11 together with all documents in his possession falling within the specification. The haver certifies (1) that he has produced all documents in his possession sought under the specification; (2) a list of any other documents that are believed to be in the hands of other named persons; and (3) that there are no other documents falling within the terms of the calls of the specification. No later than the day after the order and documents are produced, the sheriff clerk intimates the returned Form G11 and any document to each party. The party seeking the documents may or may not choose to uplift them from the sheriff clerk within seven days. If he does not then the sheriff clerk must inform every other party of this to enable it to uplift the documents. If a party uplifts the document but decides not to lodge it, the document must be returned to the sheriff clerk within 14 days. The sheriff clerk must intimate the return to all parties and after 14 days of that intimation return the document to the haver.

**D1.192**

**Execution of commission and diligence for recovery of documents**

28.4.—(1)   The party who seeks to execute a commission and diligence for recovery of a document obtained under rule 28.2(1)(a) shall—

  (a)   provide the commissioner with a copy of the specification, a copy of the pleadings (including any adjustments and amendments) and a certified copy of the interlocutor of his appointment; and

  (b)   instruct the clerk and any shorthand writer considered necessary by the commissioner or any party; and

  (c)   be responsible for the fees of the commissioner and his clerk, and of any shorthand writer.

(2)   The Commissioner shall, in consultation with the parties, fix a diet for the execution of the commission.

(3)   The interlocutor granting such a commission and diligence shall be sufficient authority for citing a haver to appear before the commissioner.

(4)[2]   A citation in Form G13 shall be served on the haver with a copy of the specification and, where necessary for a proper understanding of the specification, a copy of the pleadings (including any adjustments and amendments) and the party citing the haver shall lodge a certificate of citation in Form G12.

(5)   The parties and the haver shall be entitled to be represented by a solicitor or person having a right of audience before the sheriff at the execution of the commission.

(6)[3]   At the commission, the commissioner shall—

  (a)   administer the oath de fideli administratione to any clerk and any shorthand writer appointed for the commission; and

  (b)   administer to the haver the oath in Form G14, or, where the haver elects to affirm, the affirmation in Form G15.

(7)   The report of the execution of the commission and diligence, any document recovered and an inventory of that document, shall be sent by the commissioner to the sheriff clerk.

(8)   Not later than the day after the date on which such a report, document and inventory, if any, are received by the sheriff clerk, he shall intimate to the parties that he has received them.

(9)   No party, other than the party who served the order, may uplift such a document until after the expiry of 7 days after the date of intimation under paragraph (8).

(10)   Where the party who served the order fails to uplift such a document within 7 days after the date of intimation under paragraph (8), the sheriff clerk shall intimate that failure to every other party.

---

[1] As amended by SI 1996/2445 (effective November 1, 1996).
[2] As amended by SI 1996/2445 (effective November 1, 1996).
[3] As amended by SI 1996/2445 (effective November 1, 1996).

(11)  Where no party has uplifted such a document within 14 days after the date of intimation under paragraph (10), the sheriff clerk shall return it to the haver.

(12)  Where a party who has uplifted such a document does not wish to lodge it, he shall return it to the sheriff clerk who shall—

(a)  intimate the return of the document to every other party; and

(b)  if no other party uplifts the document within 14 days of the date of intimation, return it to the haver.

GENERAL NOTE

This rule provides the standard procedure to be followed where a party decides not to use the optional procedure or is not satisfied that there has been full compliance with the G11 order or that adequate reasons for non-compliance have been given. The commissioner may or may not have been appointed in the original interlocutor allowing the commission and diligence. If he has not been appointed then it is necessary to ask the sheriff to make an appointment before the commission can proceed. As well as the commissioner it is necessary to instruct the clerk and any shorthand writer. It is not essential to instruct a shorthand writer, but it is very unwise to proceed without one. Normally the clerk to the commission is the shorthand writer who takes the oath *de fideli administratione* "to faithfully discharge the duties of clerk and shorthand writer at this commission". The haver is cited to the diet of commission by the party seeking to recover the documents. Failure to obtemper a citation is dealt with in the same way as with any witness citation (see OCR, rules 28.15 and 29.10). If the haver is not a natural person a responsible official or representative should be cited. Usually the organisation will identify a suitable person, if not then the managing director or chief executive of the organisation may require to be cited. At a commission the haver is placed on oath but the questions that may be asked is very limited (see JA Maclaren, *Court of Session Practice* (1916), 1079). Legitimate questions are (1) whether the witness has the document or item; (2) whether he has had the document or item at any time; (3) whether he has disposed of it; (4) whether he knows or suspects where it is or has been; (5) whether he is aware of whether anyone else has had, has or has disposed of the document or item; (6) whether the document or item has been destroyed and, if so, when by whom, why and how; and (7) any question designed to ascertain the whereabouts of the document or item or facilitate its recovery. It is illegitimate to use the commission to inquire into the merits of the cause and any such question clearly having that purpose as opposed to a legitimate purpose should simply be disallowed by the commissioner. The haver's representative and any other party (if they have decided to attend) may ask questions to clarify any ambiguities in relation to the answers given to the restricted permissible questions but again must not stray into the merits of the cause.

The clerk will prepare the report which will include a transcript of the proceedings together with an inventory of the documents recovered. These items are transmitted to the sheriff clerk and may be uplifted and lodged, failing which, returned to the haver.

**Execution of orders for production or recovery of documents or other property under section 1(1) of the Act of 1972**                                                                              **D1.193**

**28.5.**—(1)  An order under section 1(1) of the Act of 1972 for the production or recovery of a document or other property shall grant a commission and diligence for the production or recovery of that document or other property.

(2)  Rules 28.3 (optional procedure before executing commission and diligence) and 28.4 (execution of commission and diligence for recovery of documents) shall apply to an order to which paragraph (1) applies as they apply to a commission and diligence for the recovery of a document.

GENERAL NOTE

This rules makes it clear that an order for production or recovery of documents or other items under the 1972 Act is for a commission and diligence and that the optional procedure and standard procedure apply mutatis mutandis.

**Execution of orders for inspection etc. of documents or other property under section 1(1) of the Act of 1972**                                                                                     **D1.194**

**28.6.**—(1)  An order under section 1(1) of the Act of 1972 for the inspection or photographing of a document or other property, the taking of samples or the carrying out of any experiment thereon or therewith, shall authorise and appoint a specified person to photograph, inspect, take samples of, or carry out any experiment on or with, any such document or other property, as the case may be, subject to such conditions, if any, as the sheriff thinks fit.

(2)  A certified copy of the interlocutor granting such an order shall be sufficient authority for the person specified to execute the order.

(3)  When such an order is executed, the party who obtained the order shall serve on the haver a copy of the interlocutor granting it, a copy of the specification and, where necessary for a proper understanding of the specification, a copy of the pleadings (including any adjustments and amendments).

GENERAL NOTE

Rules 28.6 and 28.7 make specific provision where what is sought is inspection or preservation or documents or other property in terms of the 1972 Act as opposed to production and recovery.

**D1.195**

### Execution of orders for preservation etc. of documents or other property under section 1(1) of the Act of 1972

**28.7.**—[1](1)   An order under section 1(1) of the Act of 1972 for the preservation, custody and detention of a document or other property shall grant a commission and diligence for the detention and custody of that document or other property.

(2)   The party who has obtained an order under paragraph (1) shall—

    (a)  provide the commissioner with a copy of the specification, a copy of the pleadings (including any adjustments and amendments) and a certified copy of the interlocutor of his appointment;

    (b)  be responsible for the fees of the commissioner and his clerk; and

    (c)  serve a copy of the order on the haver.

(3)   The report of the execution of the commission and diligence, any document or other property taken by the commissioner and an inventory of such property, shall be sent by the commissioner to the sheriff clerk for the further order of the sheriff.

### Confidentiality

**D1.196**

**28.8.**—[2](1)   Where confidentiality is claimed for any evidence sought to be recovered under any of the following rules, such evidence shall, where practicable, be enclosed in a sealed packet:—

28.3 (optional procedure before executing commission and diligence),

28.4 (execution of commission and diligence for recovery of documents),

28.5 (execution of orders for production or recovery of documents or other property under section 1(1) of the Act of 1972),

28.7 (execution of orders for preservation etc. of documents or other property under section 1(1) of the Act of 1972).

(2)   A motion to have such a sealed packet opened up or such recovery allowed may be lodged by—

    (a)  the party who obtained the commission and diligence; or

    (b)  any other party after the date of intimation by the sheriff clerk under rule 28.3(5) or 28.4(10) (intimation of failure to uplift documents).

(3)   In addition to complying with rule 15.2 (intimation of motions), the party lodging such a motion shall intimate the terms of the motion to the haver by post by the first class recorded delivery service.

(4)   The person claiming confidentiality may oppose a motion made under paragraph (2).

GENERAL NOTE

Confidentiality can be claimed at the stage when a commission and diligence is sought and if successful will prevent the application being granted. Confidentiality can be claimed where the document (1) is a communication between a party and his solicitor (but the client that can plead or waive confidentiality and where the subject matter of the dispute involves an examination of the comunings between the client and agent there is no confidentiality (see *Micosta SA v Shetland Islands Council* , 1983 S.L.T. 483); (2) came into existence *post litam motam* (that is to say, material that a party has made in preparing his case but not otherwise; see *Komori v Tayside Health Board* , 2010 S.L.T. 387)—the full rigour of the *post litam motam* rule has been undermined by OCR, rule 9A.2 (entitlement to inspection and recovery of documents to be put in evidence at proof) and OCR, rule 36.17C (requirement to lodge medical reports to be relied on the action); (3) is a communication between a party or agents in an attempt to negotiate settlement; and (4) where art.8 of ECHR may be engaged see *M v A Scottish Local Authority* , 2012 S.L.T. 6. Where a party or the court has reason to anticipate that an issue of confidentiality may arise it is sensible to intimate the motion for a commission and diligence to the haver so that the issue may be dealt with at that stage. If confidentiality is claimed before the commission and diligence is granted the court may require all documents falling within the terms of the call to be produced to it so that it can determine the issue and it may (if there is a lot of material to be examined) appoint a commissioner for that purpose. Where a commissioner is appointed it remains for the court to determine whether or not any material identified by him as potentially confidential should be produced to the party seeking the recovery.

---

[1] As amended by SI 1996/2445 (effective November 1, 1996).
[2] As amended by SI 1996/2445 (effective November 1, 1996).

Frequently the first time that a haver will be in a position to claim confidentiality will be at a stage after he has been ordered to produce the documents or item. In that event the documents or item should, where practicable, be produced in a sealed packet. A motion is then made to open up the sealed packet which motion may be opposed by the haver.

**Warrants for production of original documents from public records**

D1.197

**28.9.**—(1)   Where a party seeks to obtain from the keeper of any public record production of the original of any register or deed in his custody for the purposes of a cause, he shall apply to the sheriff by motion.

(2)   Intimation of a motion under paragraph (1) shall be given to the keeper of the public record concerned at least 7 days before the motion is lodged.

(3)   In relation to a public record kept by the Keeper of the Registers of Scotland or the Keeper of the Records of Scotland, where it appears to the sheriff that it is necessary for the ends of justice that a motion under this rule should be granted, he shall pronounce an interlocutor containing a certificate to that effect; and the party applying for production may apply by letter (enclosing a copy of the interlocutor duly certified by the sheriff clerk), addressed to the Deputy Principal Clerk of Session, for an order from the Court of Session authorising the Keeper of the Registers or the Keeper of the Records, as the case may be, to exhibit the original of any register or deed to the sheriff.

(4)   The Deputy Principal Clerk of Session shall submit the application sent to him under paragraph (3) to the Lord Ordinary in chambers who, if satisfied, shall grant a warrant for production or exhibition of the original register or deed sought.

(5)   A certified copy of the warrant granted under paragraph (4) shall be served on the keeper of the public record concerned.

(6)   The expense of the production or exhibition of such an original register or deed shall be met, in the first instance, by the party who applied by motion under paragraph (1).

GENERAL NOTE

It may sometimes be necessary to obtain the original public record (for instance a coloured plan annexed to a deed, although any extract should also be in colour). If it is, then this rule provides the procedure. Normally an official extract of public record will suffice, and such a document is admissible (see Walkers, *Evidence* (1st ed.), para.227). Another approach is provided by s.6 of the Civil Evidence (Scotland) Act 1988.

**Commissions for examination of witnesses**

D1.198

**28.10.**—(1)[1]   This rule applies to a commission—

    (a)    to take the evidence of a witness who—

        (i)    is resident beyond the jurisdiction of the court;

        (ii)    although resident within the jurisdiction of the court, resides at some place remote from that court; or

        (iii)    by reason of age, infirmity or sickness, is unable to attend the diet of proof;

    (b)    in respect of the evidence of a witness which is in danger of being lost, to take the evidence to *lie in retentis*; or

    (c)    on special cause shown, to take evidence of a witness on a ground other than one mentioned in sub-paragraph (a) or (b).

(2)   An application by a party for a commission to examine a witness shall be made by motion; and that party shall specify in the motion the name and address of at least one proposed commissioner for approval and appointment by the sheriff.

(2A)[2]   A motion under paragraph (2) may include an application for authority to record the proceedings before the commissioner by video recorder.

(3)   The interlocutor granting such a commission shall be sufficient authority for citing the witness to appear before the commissioner.

(4)[3]   At the commission, the commissioner shall—

    (a)    administer the oath *de fideli administratione* to any clerk and any shorthand writer appointed for the commission; and

    (b)    administer to the witness the oath in Form G14, or where the witness elects to affirm, the affirmation in Form G15.

---

[1] As amended by SI 1996/2445 (effective November 1, 1996).
[2] As inserted by the Act of Sederunt (Sheriff Court Rules) (Miscellaneous Amendments) 2008 (SSI 2008/223) para.11 (effective July 1, 2008).
[3] As amended by SI 1996/2445 (effective November 1, 1996).

(5)   Where a commission is granted for the examination of a witness, the commission shall proceed without interrogatories unless, on cause shown, the sheriff otherwise directs.

GENERAL NOTE

The recovery of evidence for use in an action is termed commission and diligence. The commission is the written authority of the court to the person appointed commissioner (either a solicitor or advocate but there is no reason why the Sheriff hearing the proof should not appoint himself commissioner) to take the evidence of the witness and the diligence is the warrant to cite the witness to appear before the commissioner.

A commission to take the evidence of a witness may be granted where a party wishes evidence that is in danger of being lost (through death or serious illness or prolonged absence abroad) to be taken to *lie in retentis* pending a proof or where the witness is unable to attend through age or infirmity or sickness or is resident beyond the jurisdiction or because of a special cause (such as holiday or important professional commitments). There has been an increased willingness to use the procedure so as not to cause disproportionate inconvenience to witnesses.

**D1.199**

**Commissions on interrogatories**

**28.11.**—(1)   Where interrogatories have not been dispensed with, the party who obtained the commission to examine a witness under rule 28.10 shall lodge draft interrogatories in process.

(2)   Any other party may lodge cross-interrogatories.

(3)   The interrogatories and any cross-interrogatories, when adjusted, shall be extended and returned to the sheriff clerk for approval and the settlement of any dispute as to their contents by the sheriff.

(4)   The party who has obtained the commission shall—

(a)   provide the commissioner with a copy of the pleadings (including any adjustments and amendments), the approved interrogatories and any cross-interrogatories and a certified copy of the interlocutor of his appointment;

(b)   instruct the clerk; and

(c)   be responsible, in the first instance, for the fee of the commissioner and his clerk.

(5)   The commissioner shall, in consultation with the parties, fix a diet for the execution of the commission to examine the witness.

(6)   The executed interrogatories, any document produced by the witness and an inventory of that document, shall be sent by the commissioner to the sheriff clerk.

(7)   Not later than the day after the date on which the executed interrogatories, any document and an inventory of that document, are received by the sheriff clerk, he shall intimate to each party that he has received them.

(8)   The party who obtained the commission to examine the witness shall lodge in process—

(a)   the report of the commission; and

(b)   the executed interrogatories and any cross-interrogatories.

GENERAL NOTE

Unless dispensed with a commission proceeds upon interrogatories, that is a series of approved questions in writing for the witness to answer. This procedure is derived from the Court of Session where it was often used in divorce cases where the subject matter was exceedingly straightforward. Interrogatories are not ideal for anything but the simplest of cases. The exception is now the rule so that interrogatories are almost always dispensed with. See OCR r.28.10(5).

**D1.200**

**Commissions without interrogatories**

**28.12.**—(1)   Where interrogatories have been dispensed with, the party who has obtained a commission to examine a witness under rule 28.10 shall—

(a)   provide the commissioner with a copy of the pleadings (including any adjustments and amendments) and a certified copy of the interlocutor of his appointment;

(b)   fix a diet for the execution of the commission in consultation with the commissioner and every other party;

(c)   instruct the clerk and any shorthand writer; and

(d)[1]   be responsible in the first instance for the fees of the commissioner, his clerk and any shorthand writer.

(2)   All parties shall be entitled to be present and represented at the execution of the commission.

---

[1] As amended by the Act of Sederunt (Ordinary Cause, Summary Application, Summary Cause and Small Claim Rules) Amendment (Vulnerable Witnesses (Scotland) Act 2004) 2007, r.2(7) (effective November 1, 2007).

(3)   The report of the execution of the commission, any document produced by the witness and an inventory of that document, shall be sent by the commissioner to the sheriff clerk.

(4)   Not later than the day after the date on which such a report, any document and an inventory of that document are received by the sheriff clerk, he shall intimate to each party that he has received them.

(5)   The party who obtained the commission to examine the witness shall lodge the report in process.

GENERAL NOTE

The standard commission takes place without interrogatories. The party whose commission it is fixes the diet and should also instruct a shorthand writer who will act as clerk. A shorthand writer is not compulsory but it is unwise to proceed without one. The commissioner should place the shorthand writer ("I do swear that I will faithfully discharge the duties of clerk and shorthand writer to this commission. So help me God") and witness ("I swear by almighty God that I will tell the truth, the whole truth and nothing but the truth") on oath. If the witness affirms then it is "I solemnly, sincerely and truly declare and affirm that I will tell the truth, the whole truth and nothing but the truth". Productions to be put to the witness should be borrowed from process in advance for that purpose. A commission can take place at any location. The party whose commission it is examines the witness and cross-examination and reexamination follows in the usual way. Objections to questions or to the line of evidence are normally dealt with by allowing the evidence to be heard subject to competency and relevancy. The evidence thus heard should be noted on a paper apart so that it is easily identifiable for determination as to its admissibility by the sheriff due course. Once the commission has been completed, a written transcript and report will be made up by the clerk (and shorthand writer) and signed by him and the commissioner. The report of the commission must be lodged in process.

**Evidence taken on commission**

**D1.201**

**28.13.**—(1)   Subject to the following paragraphs of this rule and to all questions of relevancy and admissibility, evidence taken on commission under rule 28.11 or 28.12 may be used as evidence at any proof of the cause.

(2)   Any party may object to the use of such evidence at a proof; and the objection shall be determined by the sheriff.

(3)   Such evidence shall not be used at a proof if the witness becomes available to attend the diet of proof.

(4)   A party may use such evidence in accordance with the preceding paragraphs of this rule notwithstanding that it was obtained at the instance of another party.

GENERAL NOTE

If the evidence is to be relied upon it must be tendered before the party relying upon it closes its case. Any of the parties may do so. Although there is no modern reported decision there seems no reason in principle why a witness who gives evidence at a proof having made a statement at a commission may not be examined as to consistencies or cross examined as to inconsistencies (see section 3 of the Civil Evidence (Scotland) Act 1988; cf. *Forrests v Low's Trs* , 1907 S.C. 1240).

**Letters of request**

**D1.202**

**28.14.**—[1](1)   Subject to paragraph (7), this rule applies to an application for a letter of request to a court or tribunal outside Scotland to obtain evidence of the kind specified in paragraph (2), being evidence obtainable within the jurisdiction of that court or tribunal, for the purposes of a cause depending before the sheriff.

(2)[2]   An application to which paragraph (1) applies may be made in relation to a request—

    (a)   for the examination of a witness,

    (b)   for the inspection, photographing, preservation, custody, detention, production or recovery of, or the taking of samples of, or the carrying out of any experiment on or with, a document or other property, as the case may be,

    (c)   for the medical examination of any person,

    (d)   for the taking and testing of samples of blood from any person, or

    (e)   for any other order for obtaining evidence,

for which an order could be obtained from the sheriff.

(3)   Such an application shall be made by minute in Form G16 together with a proposed letter of request in Form G17.

---

[1] As amended by the Act of Sederunt (Taking of Evidence in the European Community) 2003 (SSI 2003/601).

[2] As amended by SI 1996/2445 (effective November 1, 1996).

(4)[1]   It shall be a condition of granting a letter of request that any solicitor for the applicant, or a party litigant, as the case may be, shall be personally liable, in the first instance, for the whole expenses which may become due and payable in respect of the letter of request to the court or tribunal obtaining the evidence and to any witness who may be examined for the purpose; and he shall consign into court such sum in respect of such expenses as the sheriff thinks fit.

(5)   Unless the court or tribunal to which a letter of request is addressed is a court or tribunal in a country or territory—

(a)   where English is an official language, or

(b)   in relation to which the sheriff clerk certifies that no translation is required,

then the applicant shall, before the issue of the letter of request, lodge in process a translation of that letter and any interrogatories and cross-interrogatories into the official language of that court or tribunal.

(6)[2]   The letter of request when issued; any interrogatories and cross-interrogatories adjusted as required by rule 28.11 and the translations (if any), shall be forwarded by the sheriff clerk to the Scottish Ministers or to such person and in such manner as the sheriff may direct.

(7)   This rule does not apply to any request for the taking of evidence under Council Regulation (EC) No. 1206/2001 of 28th May 2001 on cooperation between the courts of the Member States in the taking of evidence in civil or commercial matters.

GENERAL NOTE

There is no power to enforce the attendance of witnesses who are furth of Scotland but an application may be made to apply for evidence to be taken on commission or by letter of request. A commission still relies on co-operation of the witness outwith the jurisdiction. A letter of request enables the foreign court or tribunal to compel the witness to give evidence. In relation to witnesses in other parts of the United Kingdom, the sheriff appoints a commissioner to take the evidence and the attendance of that witness at a commission is compelled by the High Court in England and Wales and Northern Ireland (see Evidence (Proceedings in Other Jurisdictions) Act 1975, ss.1–4). Witnesses beyond the United Kingdom require to be considered under reference to the Hague Convention on the Taking of Evidence Abroad in Civil or Commercial Matters, March 18, 1970. OCR r.28.14 is for all practical purposes identical to the rule in the equivalent rule in the Court of Session (see *Greens Annotated Rules of the Court of Session* (W.Green, 2002), pp.C250–C253).

**D1.203**

### Taking of evidence in the European Community

**28.14A.**—[3](1)   This rule applies to any request—

(a)   for the competent court of another Member State to take evidence under Article 1.1(a) of the Council Regulation; or

(b)   that the court shall take evidence directly in another Member State under Article 1.1(b) of the Council Regulation.

(2)   An application for a request under paragraph (1) shall be made by minute in Form G16, together with the proposed request in form A or I (as the case may be) in the Annex to the Council Regulation.

(3)   In this rule, "the Council Regulation" means Council Regulation (EC) No. 1206/2001 of 28th May 2001 on cooperation between the courts of the Member States in the taking of evidence in civil or commercial matters.

### Citation of witnesses and havers

**D1.204**

**28.15.**   The following rules shall apply to the citation of a witness or haver to a commission under this Chapter as they apply to the citation of a witness for a proof:—

rule 29.7 (citation of witnesses) except paragraph 4,

rule 29.9 (second diligence against a witness),

rule 29.10 (failure of witness to attend).

GENERAL NOTE

A witness is cited for a commission as he would be for a proof and his attendance may likewise be enforced.

---

[1] As amended by SI 1996/2445 (effective November 1, 1996).

[2] As substituted by the Act of Sederunt (Sheriff Court Rules) (Miscellaneous Amendments) 2011 (SSI 2011/193) r.8 (effective April 4, 2011).

[3] As amended by the Act of Sederunt (Taking of Evidence in the European Community) 2003 (SSI 2003/601).

Chapter 28A[1]

Pre-Proof Hearing

**Pre-proof hearing**

**28A.1.**—(1)[2]  Subject to paragraph (1A) the appointment of a cause to a proof or proof before answer or thereafter on the motion of any party or of his own motion, the sheriff may appoint the cause to a pre-proof hearing.

(1A)[3]  Where Chapter 33AA applies, the sheriff will fix a pre-proof hearing at the case management hearing.

(2)  It shall be the duty of the parties to provide the sheriff with sufficient information to enable him to conduct the hearing as provided for in this rule.

(3)  At a pre-proof hearing the sheriff shall ascertain, so far as is reasonably practicable, whether the cause is likely to proceed to proof on the date fixed for that purpose and, in particular—

    (a)    the state of preparation of the parties; and

    (b)[4] [5]    the extent to which the parties have complied with their duties under rules 9A.2, 9A.3, 29.11 and 29.15 and any orders made by the sheriff under rules 9.12(3)(a), (b), (d), or (e) or 10.6(3)(a) or (b) or Chapter 33AA; and

    (c)[6]    consider any child witness notice or vulnerable witness application that has been lodged where no order has been made, or ascertain whether there is or is likely to be a vulnerable witness within the meaning of section 11(1) of the 2004 Act who is to give evidence at any proof or hearing and whether any order under section 12(1) of the Act of 2004 requires to be made.

(4)  At a pre-proof hearing the sheriff may—

    (a)    discharge the proof or proof before answer and fix a new date for such proof or proof before answer;

    (b)    adjourn the pre-proof hearing; or

    (c)    make such other order as he thinks fit to secure the expeditious progress of the cause.

(5)  For the purposes of rules 16.2 (decrees where party in default), 33.37 (decree by default in family action) and 33A.37 (decree by default in civil partnership action), a pre-proof hearing shall be a diet in accordance with those rules.

GENERAL NOTE

This is a particularly useful rule designed to allow effective management of court resources. The Sheriff is directed to find out whether parties are in a position to proceed and to check that they have complied with their obligations under the rules. There is sufficient flexibility to allow, if so advised, for the scope of the proof to be confined or restricted if appropriate.

Chapter 29

Proof

**Reference to oath**

**29.1.**—(1)  Where a party intends to refer any matter to the oath of his opponent he shall lodge a motion to that effect.

(2)  If a party fails to appear at the diet for taking his deposition on the reference to his oath, the sheriff may hold him as confessed and grant decree accordingly.

---

[1] Inserted by the Act of Sederunt (Ordinary Cause and Summary Application Rules) Amendment (Miscellaneous) 2006 (SSI 2006/410) (effective August 18, 2006).

[2] As inserted by the Act of Sederunt (Sheriff Court Rules)(Miscellaneous Amendments) (No.2) 2013 (SI 2013/139) para.2 (effective June 3, 2013).

[3] As inserted by the Act of Sederunt (Sheriff Court Rules)(Miscellaneous Amendments) (No.2) 2013 (SI 2013/139) para.2 (effective June 3, 2013).

[4] As amended by the Act of Sederunt (Ordinary Cause, Summary Application, Summary Cause and Small Claim Rules) Amendment (Vulnerable Witnesses (Scotland) Act 2004) 2007, r.2(6)(a) (effective November 1, 2007).

[5] As amended by the Act of Sederunt (Sheriff Court Rules)(Miscellaneous Amendments) (No.2) 2013 (SI 2013/139) para.2 (effective June 3, 2013).

[6] As inserted by the Act of Sederunt (Ordinary Cause, Summary Application, Summary Cause and Small Claim Rules) Amendment (Vulnerable Witnesses (Scotland) Act 2004) 2007, r.2(6)(b) (effective November 1, 2007).

GENERAL NOTE

The procedure is described in Walker's *Evidence*, Chapter 25. The Requirements of Writing (Scotland) Act 1995 has rendered the procedure of reference to oath of no practical importance although it remains theoretically possible that it could still be used in relation to events prior to the coming into force of that Act (see e.g. *McEleveen v McQuiilan's Executors* , 1997 S.L.T. (Sh Ct) 46.

**D1.207**

### Remit to person of skill

**29.2.**—(1)   The sheriff may, on a motion by any party or on a joint motion, remit to any person of skill, or other person, to report on any matter of fact.

(2)   Where a remit under paragraph (1) is made by joint motion or of consent of all parties, the report of such person shall be final and conclusive with respect to the subject-matter of the remit.

(3)   Where a remit under paragraph (1) is made—

    (a)   on the motion of one of the parties, the expenses of its execution shall, in the first instance, be met by that party; and

    (b)   on a joint motion or of consent of all parties, the expenses shall, in the first instance, be met by the parties equally, unless the sheriff otherwise orders.

GENERAL NOTE

There are no modern reported examples of the use of this procedure but there may well be cases where it could be usefully employed, particularly now that many issues of disputed fact are spoken to by experts. Perhaps if the sheriff were able to remit to a man of skill *ex proprio motu* the procedure would be used more often. The rule does not prevent a remit being made before the record has closed but it is normally better to know what the parties' final position is in relation to the dispute before a remit is made as it offends against OCR r.29.17.

**D1.208**

### Written statements

**29.3.**[1]   Where a statement in a document is admissible under section 2(1)(b) of the Civil Evidence (Scotland) Act 1988, any party who wishes to have that statement received in evidence shall—

    (a)   docquet that document as follows:—

        "(*Place and date*)

        This document contains a statement admissible under section 2(1)(b) of the Civil Evidence (Scotland) Act 1988.

        (*Signed*)

        (*Designation and address*)";

    (b)   lodge that document in process; and

    (c)   provide all other parties with a copy of that document.

GENERAL NOTE

Rule 29.3 addresses a *lacuna* in the Ordinary Cause Rules by providing for receiving into evidence written statements.

**D1.209**

### Renouncing probation

**29.4.**[2](1)   Where, at any time, the parties seek to renounce probation, they shall lodge in process a joint minute to that effect with or without a statement of admitted facts and any productions.

(2)   On the lodging of a joint minute under paragraph (1), the sheriff may make such order as he thinks fit to secure the expeditious progress of the cause.

GENERAL NOTE

Once a joint minute is lodged renouncing probation, both parties are contractually barred from leading evidence. Any attempt to amend is likely to be refused. The renunciation of probation is rare but does happen from time to time where parties are in agreement as to the material facts. If necessary a separate statement of agreed facts can be lodged. The diet of proof may be converted into a diet of debate.

---

[1] As inserted by the Act of Sederunt (Ordinary Cause, Summary Application and Small Claim Rules) Amendment (Miscellaneous) 2004 (SSI 2004/197) (effective May 21, 2004), para.2(11).

[2] As amended by the Act of Sederunt (Ordinary Cause and Summary Application Rules) Amendment (Miscellaneous) 2006 (SI 2006/410) (effective August 18, 2006).

**Orders for proof**

**D1.210**

**29.5.** Where proof is necessary in any cause, the sheriff shall fix a date for taking the proof and may limit the mode of proof.

GENERAL NOTE

In terms of OCR r.9.12(3), a proof will be ordered at the options hearing; but if after additional procedure, debate or amendment a proof is required, then this rule authorises that to be done at any procedural hearing or debate. This rule is also without prejudice to OCR r.28A(4).

The interlocutor allowing proof should make it clear whose averments are admitted to probation, and if any averments are not the subject of proof that should also be made clear. If the proof is a preliminary proof then the subject matter of the proof should be specified precisely in the interlocutor. Where there is a counter-claim the interlocutor should indicate whether the averments in the counterclaim are admitted to probation.

Proof by writ or oath has been abolished (see section 11 of the Requirements of Writing (Scotland) Act 1995) so the mode of proof will not be limited; but this is subject to section 14(3) which provides that the 1995 Act does not apply to anything done before the commencement of that Act.

**Hearing parts of proof separately**

**D1.211**

**29.6.**—(1)[1]   In any cause, the sheriff may—
    (a)   of his own motion, or
    (b)   on the motion of any party,
order that proof on liability or any specified issue be heard separately from proof on the question of the amount for which decree may be pronounced and determine the order in which the proofs shall be heard.

    (2)   The sheriff shall pronounce such interlocutor as he thinks fit at the conclusion of the first proof of any cause ordered to be heard in separate parts under paragraph (1).

GENERAL NOTE

This rule is designed to allow a certain amount of flexibility and to avoid wasted procedure.

The obvious examples are preliminary proof on the question of limitation or prescription and separation of proof on liability and quantum. Whether to split a proof is a matter for the discretion of the sheriff in the circumstances of any particular case. See also OCR r.28A(4).

**Citation of witnesses**

**D1.212**

**29.7.**—(1)   A witness shall be cited for a proof—
    (a)   by registered post or the first class recorded delivery service by the solicitor for the party on whose behalf he is cited; or
    (b)   by a sheriff officer—
        (i)   personally;
        (ii)   by a citation being left with a resident at the person's dwelling place or an employee at his place of business;
        (iii)   by depositing it in that person's dwelling place or place of business;
        (iv)   by affixing it to the door of that person's dwelling place or place of business; or
        (v)   by registered post or the first class recorded delivery service.

    (2)   Where service is executed under paragraph (1)(b)(iii) or (iv), the sheriff officer shall, as soon as possible after such service, send, by ordinary post to the address at which he thinks it most likely that the person may be found, a letter containing a copy of the citation.

    (3)   A certified copy of the interlocutor allowing a proof shall be sufficient warrant to a sheriff officer to cite a witness on behalf of a party.

    (4)   A witness shall be cited on a period of notice of 7 days in Form G13 and the party citing the witness shall lodge a certificate of citation in Form G12.

    (5)   A solicitor who cites a witness shall be personally liable for his fees and expenses.

    (6)   In the event of a solicitor intimating to a witness that his citation is cancelled, the solicitor shall advise him that the cancellation is not to affect any other citation which he may have received from another party.

GENERAL NOTE

This rule is without prejudice to OCR r.9A.3 (exchange of list of witnesses). It is not necessary to cite a witness to lead him in evidence as the purpose of citation is to compel attendance, but it is wise to cite

---

[1] As amended by SI 1996/2445 (effective November 1, 1996).

any witness that it is intended to call. The methods of citation are similar to the citation of parties. As soon as a proof is allowed the witnesses should be informed of its date and they should be cited with as much notice as possible. The seven-day period in the rule is a minimum period of notice. Parties should communicate with each other in order to minimise the inconvenience to witnesses. Fees of witnesses are set out in Act of Sederunt (Fees of Witnesses and Shorthand Writers in the Sheriff Court) 1992.

**D1.213**

### Citation of witnesses by party litigants

**29.8.**—(1)  Where a party to a cause is a party litigant, he shall—

    (a)  not later than 4 weeks before the diet of proof, apply to the sheriff by motion to fix caution in such sum as the sheriff considers reasonable having regard to the number of witnesses he proposes to cite and the period for which they may be required to attend court; and

    (b)  before instructing a sheriff officer to cite a witness, find caution for such expenses as can reasonably be anticipated to be incurred by the witness in answering the citation.

(2)  A party litigant who does not intend to cite all the witnesses referred to in his application under paragraph (1)(a), may apply by motion for variation of the amount of caution.

GENERAL NOTE

The sheriff clerk has a duty to assist party litigants to comply with the requirements of this rule.

**D1.214**

### Second diligence against a witness

**29.9.**—(1)  The sheriff may, on the motion of a party, grant a second diligence to compel the attendance of a witness under pain of arrest and imprisonment until caution can be found for his due attendance.

(2)  The warrant for a second diligence shall be effective without endorsation and the expenses of such a motion and diligence may be decerned for against the witness.

GENERAL NOTE

Where there is reason to think in advance of the proof that a witness will not attend, then a motion for second diligence to compel attendance may be made. The procedure is described in Maclaren *Court of Session Practice*, pp.343–344. The letters are issued by the sheriff clerk in the name of the sheriff principal and addressed to the sheriff officer, requiring him to apprehend the witness and imprison him within a named prison. Once caution is found the witness must be released. The appropriate sum as a penalty should now be £250 and the sheriff should fix the amount of caution. Letters of second diligence will not be granted unless the witness is essential, there has been effective citation failing which a clear attempt to evade it and that there is a real risk that the witness will not attend.

**D1.215**

### Failure of witness to attend

**29.10.**—(1)  Where a witness fails to answer a citation after having been duly cited, the sheriff may, on the motion of a party and on production of a certificate of citation, grant warrant for the apprehension of the witness and for bringing him to court; and the expenses of such a motion and apprehension may be decerned for against the witness.

(2)  Where a witness duly cited and after having demanded and been paid his travelling expenses, fails to attend a diet, either before the sheriff or before a commissioner, the sheriff may—

    (a)  ordain the witness to forfeit and pay a penalty not exceeding £250 unless a reasonable excuse be offered and sustained; and

    (b)  grant decree for that penalty in favour of the party on whose behalf the witness was cited.

GENERAL NOTE

Decree for the penalty is enforceable by civil diligence.

**D1.216**

### Lodging productions

**29.11.**—(1)[1, 2]  Where a proof has been allowed, all productions and affidavits which are intended to be used at the proof shall be lodged in process not later than 28 days before the diet of proof.

(2)  A production which is not lodged in accordance with paragraph (1) shall not be used or put in evidence at a proof unless—

    (a)  by consent of parties; or

    (b)  with leave of the sheriff on cause shown and on such conditions, if any, as to expenses or otherwise as the sheriff thinks fit.

---

[1]  As amended by SSI 2000/239 (effective October 2, 2000).

[2]  As amended by the Act of Sederunt (Ordinary Cause and Summary Application Rules) Amendment (Miscellaneous) 2006 (SSI 2006/410) (effective August 18, 2006).

GENERAL NOTE

This rule is without prejudice to OCR r.9A.2 (inspection and recovery of documents); OCR r.21.1 (lodging of documents founded on or adopted); or OCR r.36.17C (lodging of medical reports in actions of damages). It is not necessary to lodge under this rule a document used (usually in cross-examination) only to test the credibility of a witness (see *Paterson & Sons v Kit Coffee Co. Ltd* (1908) 16 S.L.T. 180) whether or not the witness is a party (Macphail, *Sheriff Court Practice* (2nd ed.), para.16.25, and see *Robertson v Anderson* , May 15, 2001 Unreported, OH Lord Carloway paras [64] to [68].

### Copy productions

**D1.217**

**29.12.**—(1)[1] A copy of every documentary production, marked with the appropriate number of process of the principal production, shall be lodged for the use of the sheriff at a proof not later than 48 hours before the diet of proof.

(2) Each copy production consisting of more than one sheet shall be securely fastened together by the party lodging it.

GENERAL NOTE

Copy productions should be legible and have the same page numbers as the principal.

### Returning borrowed parts of process and productions before proof

**D1.218**

**29.13.** All parts of process and productions which have been borrowed shall be returned to process before 12.30 pm on the day preceding the diet of proof.

GENERAL NOTE

This rule is without prejudice to OCR rr.11.3, 11.4 and 11.5. Failure to return a borrowed production may result in liability for expenses if any procedure is wasted.

### Notices to admit and notices of non-admission

**D1.219**

**29.14.**—(1)[2] At any time after the record has closed, a party may intimate to any other party a notice or notices calling on him to admit for the purposes of that cause only—

    (a) such facts relating to an issue averred in the pleadings as may be specified in the notice;

    (b) that a particular document lodged in process and specified in the notice is—

        (i) an original and properly authenticated document; or

        (ii) a true copy of an original and properly authenticated document.

(2) Where a party on whom a notice is intimated under paragraph (1)—

    (a) does not admit a fact specified in the notice, or

    (b) does not admit, or seeks to challenge, the authenticity of a document specified in the notice,

he shall, within 21 days after the date of intimation of the notice under paragraph (1), intimate a notice of non-admission to the party intimating the notice to him under paragraph (1) stating that he does not admit the fact or document specified.

(3) A party who fails to intimate a notice of non-admission under paragraph (2) shall be deemed to have admitted the fact or document specified in the notice intimated to him under paragraph (1); and such fact or document may be used in evidence at a proof if otherwise admissible in evidence, unless the sheriff, on special cause shown, otherwise directs.

(4) [Repealed by the Act of Sederunt (Sheriff Court Rules) (Miscellaneous Amendments) (No.2) 2008 (SSI 2008/365) para.4 (effective December 1, 2008).]

(5) The party serving a notice under paragraph (1) or (2) shall lodge a copy of it in process.

(6) A deemed admission under paragraph (3) shall not be used against the party by whom it was deemed to be made other than in the cause for the purpose for which it was deemed to be made or in favour of any person other than the party by whom the notice was given under paragraph (1).

(7)[3] The sheriff may, at any time, allow a party to amend or withdraw an admission made by him on such conditions, if any, as he thinks fit.

(8)[4] A party may, at any time, withdraw in whole or in part a notice of non admission by intimating a notice of withdrawal.

---

[1] As amended by SSI 2000/239 (effective October 2, 2000).
[2] As amended by SSI 2000/239 (effective October 2, 2000).
[3] Inserted by SSI 2000/239 (effective October 2, 2000).
[4] Inserted by SSI 2000/239 (effective October 2, 2000).

GENERAL NOTE

The record is supposed to be the place where parties identify with precision what is truly in dispute between them. Each fact averred requires to be carefully considered by the other party and if appropriate admitted. Frequently the parties respond with a general denial which covers at least some averments that are not in dispute. The whole system of written pleading proceeds on trust that parties will honestly answer averments by an opponent on matters within their knowledge and a party must admit averments that he knows to be true. Unfortunately for one reason or another parties do not always live up to these expectations. Furthermore, it is often the case that facts even not strictly speaking within the knowledge of the other party should be identified as not being in dispute. Sometimes there are facts (and there may well be documents) that are not necessarily the subject of averment but which may be relevant to the proof of a parties case that can be usefully identified as being capable of agreement.

This rule provides a mechanism apart from the written pleadings whereby a party can call upon the other to admit certain facts including the originality or authenticity of a document. A failure to respond results in a deemed admission and a response that turns out to be unjustified ought to result at the very least in liability in expenses for any unnecessary procedure. Admissions can be withdrawn and departed from on special cause being shown.

**D1.220**

**Instruction of shorthand writer**

**29.15.** Where a shorthand writer is to record evidence at a proof, the responsibility for instructing a shorthand writer shall lie with the pursuer.

GENERAL NOTE

Failure to instruct the shorthand writer means that the proof cannot proceed unless recording of the evidence by mechanical means is available or recording is dispensed with under r.29.18. Another option may be to seek to have the cause treated as a summary cause (under section 37(1)(a) of the Sheriff Courts (Scotland) Act 1971) but that will restrict any decree accordingly.

**D1.221**

**Administration of oath or affirmation to witnesses**

**29.16.** The sheriff shall administer the oath to a witness in Form G14 or, where the witness elects to affirm, the affirmation in Form G15.

GENERAL NOTE

"I swear by Almighty God that I will tell the truth, the whole truth and nothing but the truth"

"I solemnly sincerely and truly declare and affirm that I will tell the truth, the whole truth and nothing but the truth"

Children under 12 do not have the oath administered but are admonished to tell the truth. Between these ages whether to administer the oath is at the discretion of the Sheriff. The oath (or affirmation) should be administered where the child is 14 or over. It is unlawful to ask questions of a witness before he gives evidence intended to establish that he does not understand the duty to give truthful evidence or the difference between truth and lies (see Vulnerable Witnesses (Scotland) Act 2004 s.24).

**D1.222**

**Proof to be taken continuously**

**29.17.** A proof shall be taken continuously so far as possible; but the sheriff may adjourn the diet from time to time.

GENERAL NOTE

It is important that proof should proceed continuously so as to save time and expense and any adjournment for any period should be arranged with this rule in mind.

**D1.223**

**Recording of evidence**

**29.18.**—[1](1)[2] Evidence in a cause shall be recorded by—

    (a)   a shorthand writer, to whom the oath *de fideli administratione* in connection with the sheriff court service generally shall have been administered, or

    (b)   tape recording or other mechanical means approved by the court, unless the parties, by agreement and with the approval of the sheriff, dispense with the recording of evidence.

    (2)   Where a shorthand writer is employed to record evidence, he shall, in the first instance, be paid by the parties equally.

---

[1] As amended by SI 1996/2445 (effective November 1, 1996).
[2] As amended by SI 1996/2445 (effective November 1, 1996).

(3)   Where evidence is recorded by tape recording or other mechanical means, any fee payable shall, in the first instance, be paid by the parties equally.

(4)   The solicitors for the parties shall be personally liable for the fees payable under paragraph (2) or (3), and the sheriff may make an order directing payment to be made.

(5)   The record of the evidence at a proof shall include—
   (a)   any objection taken to a question or to the line of evidence;
   (b)   any submission made in relation to such an objection; and
   (c)   the ruling of the court in relation to the objection and submission.

(6)   A transcript of the record of the evidence shall be made only on the direction of the sheriff; and the cost shall, in the first instance, be borne—
   (a)   in an undefended cause, by the solicitor for the pursuer; and
   (b)   in a defended cause, by the solicitors for the parties in equal proportions.

(7)   The transcript of the record of the evidence provided for the use of the court shall be certified as a faithful record of the evidence by—
   (a)   the shorthand writer who recorded the evidence; or
   (b)   where the evidence was recorded by tape recording or other mechanical means, by the person who transcribed the record.

(8)   The sheriff may make such alterations to the transcript of the record of the evidence as appear to him to be necessary after hearing the parties; and, where such alterations are made, the sheriff shall authenticate the alterations.

(9)   Where a transcript of the record of the evidence has been made for the use of the sheriff, copies of it may be obtained by any party from the person who transcribed the record on payment of his fee.

(10)   Except with leave of the sheriff, the transcript of the record of the evidence may be borrowed from process only for the purpose of enabling a party to consider whether to appeal against the interlocutor of the sheriff on the proof.

(11)   Where a transcript of the record of the evidence is required for the purpose of an appeal but has not been directed to be transcribed under paragraph (6), the appellant—
   (a)   may request such a transcript from the shorthand writer or as the case may be, the cost of the transcript being borne by the solicitor for the appellant in the first instance; and
   (b)   shall lodge the transcript in process; and copies of it may be obtained by any party from the shorthand writer or as the case may be, on payment of his fee.

(12)   Where the recording of evidence has been dispensed with under paragraph (1), the sheriff, if called upon to do so, shall—
   (a)   in the case of an objection to—
      (i)   the admissibility of evidence on the ground of confidentiality, or
      (ii)   the production of a document on any ground,
      note the terms in writing of such objections and his decision on the objection; and
   (b)   in the case of any other objection, record, in the note to his interlocutor disposing of the merits of the cause, the terms of the objection and his decision on the objection.

(13)   This rule shall, with the necessary modifications, apply to the recording of evidence at a commission as it applies to the recording of evidence at a proof.

GENERAL NOTE

In the sheriff court the principal method of recording evidence remains the shorthand writer. It may seem curious that this superior form of recording the evidence should be retained in the ordinary sheriff court when it has disappeared from the Court of Session, High Court of Justiciary and solemn sheriff court procedure. Only in the ordinary sheriff court did (do) the parties pay for the shorthand writer. Further, if there was no shorthand writer then the clerk would have to remain in the court room to operate the tape recording equipment. This would have manning implications, particularly in the smaller courts.

*Rule 29.18(5)*

Parties themselves should keep a note of these matters as it is necessary to ask the sheriff to deal with reserved matters at the hearing on evidence. One of the advantages of a shorthand writer is that one can always ask for a note of these matters before they disappear at the end of the evidence.

*Rule 29.19(8)*

If the sheriff considers that the transcript is inaccurate he may correct it after hearing the parties and he may hear the witness again (see e.g. *Wilson v MacQueen* , 1925 S.L.T. (Sh Ct) 130.

**D1.224**

### Incidental appeal against rulings on confidentiality of evidence and production of documents

**29.19.**—(1)   Where a party or any other person objects to the admissibility of oral or documentary evidence on the ground of confidentiality or to the production of a document on any ground, he may, if dissatisfied with the ruling of the sheriff on the objection, express immediately his formal dissatisfaction with the ruling and, with leave of the sheriff, appeal to the sheriff principal.

(2)   The sheriff principal shall dispose of an appeal under paragraph (1) with the least possible delay.

(3)   Except as provided in paragraph (1), no appeal may be made during a proof against any decision of the sheriff as to the admissibility of evidence or the production of documents.

(4)   The appeal referred to in paragraph (1) shall not remove the cause from the sheriff who may proceed with the cause in relation to any issue which is not dependent on the ruling appealed against.

GENERAL NOTE

This is the only competent method of review as to the admissibility of evidence or production of a document during a proof. It would only be in exceptional circumstances that a sheriff would grant leave under this rule as any decision on admissibility can also be challenged following the final interlocutor (see section 27 of the Sheriff Courts (Scotland) Act 1907). Appeal from the sheriff principal also requires leave in terms of section 28 of the Sheriff Courts (Scotland) Act 1907.

**D1.225**

### Parties to be heard at close of proof

**29.20.**   At the close of the proof, or at an adjourned diet if for any reason the sheriff has postponed the hearing, the sheriff shall hear parties on the evidence and thereafter shall pronounce judgment with the least possible delay.

GENERAL NOTE

Parties should tell the court in precise terms what order they require. They should bear in mind that in terms of OCR r.12.2(3)(a) the sheriff is required to make findings in fact and law. Accordingly, parties should indicate what pleas-in-law are to be sustained and repelled and under reference to the pleadings, what averments of fact have been proved. Care should be taken to concentrate on findings necessary to resolve the issues (see *B v G* , 2012 S.L.T. 840 at para.48). If objection has been taken to evidence and the evidence allowed to be heard subject to competency and relevancy, then the party who has taken the objection should indicate whether he insists on the objection and if so justify such a position. Interest, the remuneration of witnesses attending but not called, the expenses of skilled witnesses and certification of the cause as suitable for the employment of counsel should be addressed at this stage. The question of expenses and any motion relating to modification or enhancement is normally better left until the outcome of the case is known.

**D1.226**

Chapter 30

Decrees, Extracts and Execution

### Interpretation of this Chapter

**30.1.**   In this Chapter, "decree" includes any judgment, deliverance, interlocutor, act, order, finding or authority which may be extracted.

### Taxes on funds under control of the court

**D1.227**

**30.2.**—(1)   Subject to paragraph (2), in a cause in which money has been consigned into court under the Sheriff Court Consignations (Scotland) Act 1893, no decree, warrant or order for payment to any person shall be granted until there has been lodged with the sheriff clerk a certificate by an authorised officer of the Inland Revenue stating that all taxes or duties payable to the Commissioners of Inland Revenue have been paid or satisfied.

(2)   In an action of multiplepoinding, it shall not be necessary for the grant of a decree, warrant or order for payment under paragraph (1) that all of the taxes or duties payable on the estate of a deceased claimant have been paid or satisfied.

### Decrees for payment in foreign currency

**D1.228**

**30.3.**—(1)   Where decree has been granted for payment of a sum of money in a foreign currency or the sterling equivalent, a party requesting extract of the decree shall do so by minute endorsed on or annexed to the initial writ stating the rate of exchange prevailing on the date of the decree sought to be extracted or the date, or within 3 days before the date, on which the extract is ordered, and the sterling equivalent at that rate for the principal sum and interest decerned for.

(2)   A certificate in Form G18, from the Bank of England or a bank which is an institution authorised under the Banking Act 1987 certifying the rate of exchange and the sterling equivalent shall be lodged with the minute requesting extract of the decree.

(3)   The extract decree issued by the sheriff clerk shall mention any certificate referred to in paragraph (2).

**When decrees extractable**

30.4.—(1)[1]   Subject to the following paragraphs:—

(a)   subject to sub-paragraph (c), a decree in absence may be extracted after the expiry of 14 days from the date of decree;

(b)   subject to sub-paragraph (c), any decree pronounced in a defended cause may be extracted at any time after whichever is the later of the following:—

(i)   the expiry of the period within which an application for leave to appeal may be made and no such application has been made;

(ii)   the date on which leave to appeal has been refused and there is no right of appeal from such refusal;

(iii)   the expiry of the period within which an appeal may be marked and no appeal has been marked; or

(iv)   the date on which an appeal has been finally disposed of; and

(c)   where, the sheriff has, in pronouncing decree, reserved any question of expenses, extract of that decree may be issued only after the expiry of 14 days from the date of the interlocutor disposing of the question of expenses unless the sheriff otherwise directs.

(2)   The sheriff may, on cause shown, grant a motion to allow extract to be applied for and issued earlier than a date referred to in paragraph (1).

(3)   In relation to a decree referred to in paragraph (1)(b) or (c), paragraph (2) shall not apply unless—

(a)   the motion under that paragraph is made in the presence of parties; or

(b)   the sheriff is satisfied that proper intimation of the motion has been made in writing to every party not present at the hearing of the motion.

(4)   Nothing in this rule shall affect the power of the sheriff to supersede extract.

**D1.229**

**Extract of certain awards notwithstanding appeal**

30.5.[2]   The sheriff clerk may issue an extract of an order under section 11 of the Children (Scotland) Act 1995 or in respect of aliment notwithstanding that an appeal has been made against an interlocutor containing such an award unless an order under rule 31.5 (appeals in connection with orders under section 11 of the Children (Scotland) Act 1995 or aliment) has been made excusing obedience to or implement of that interlocutor.

**D1.230**

**Form of extract decree**

30.6.—(1)   The extract of a decree mentioned in Appendix 2 shall be in the appropriate form for that decree in Appendix 2.

(2)   In the case of a decree not mentioned in Appendix 2, the extract of the decree shall be modelled on a form in that Appendix with such variation as circumstances may require.

**D1.231**

**Form of warrant for execution**

30.7.   An extract of a decree on which execution may proceed shall include a warrant for execution in the following terms:— "This extract is warrant for all lawful execution hereon.".

**D1.232**

**Date of decree in extract**

30.8.—(1)   Where the sheriff principal has adhered to the decision of the sheriff following an appeal, the date to be inserted in the extract decree as the date of decree shall be the date of the decision of the sheriff principal.

(2)   Where a decree has more than one date it shall not be necessary to specify in an extract what was done on each date.

**D1.233**

**Service of charge where address of defender not known**

30.9.—(1)   Where the address of a defender is not known to the pursuer, a charge shall be deemed to have been served on the defender if it is—

(a)   served on the sheriff clerk of the sheriff court district where the defender's last known address is located; and

(b)   displayed by the sheriff clerk on the walls of court for the period of the charge.

**D1.234**

---

[1] As amended by SI 1996/2445 (effective November 1, 1996).

[2] As substituted by the Act of Sederunt (Sheriff Court Rules) (Miscellaneous Amendments) (No.2) 2010 (SSI 2010/416) r.6 (effective January 1, 2011).

(2)   On receipt of such a charge, the sheriff clerk shall display it on the walls of court and it shall remain displayed for the period of the charge.

(3)   The period specified in the charge shall run from the first date on which it was displayed on the walls of court.

(4)   On the expiry of the period of charge, the sheriff clerk shall endorse a certificate on the charge certifying that it has been displayed in accordance with this rule and shall thereafter return it to the sheriff officer by whom service was executed.

**Expenses**

**D1.235**

**30.10.**[1]   A party who—

(a)   is or has been represented by a person authorised under any enactment to conduct proceedings in the sheriff court; and

(b)   would have been found entitled to expenses if he had been represented by a solicitor or an advocate,

may be awarded any expenses or outlays to which a party litigant may be found entitled under the Litigants in Person (Costs and Expenses) Act 1975 or any enactment under that Act.

Chapter 31

Appeals

**Time limit for appeal**

**D1.236**

**31.1.**   Subject to the provisions of any other enactment, an interlocutor which may be appealed against may be appealed within 14 days after the date of the interlocutor unless it has been extracted following a motion under rule 30.4(2) (early extract).

**Applications for leave to appeal**

**D1.237**

**31.2.**—(1)   Where leave to appeal is required, applications for leave to appeal against an interlocutor of a sheriff shall be made within 7 days after the date of the interlocutor against which it is sought to appeal unless the interlocutor has been extracted following a motion under rule 30.4(2) (early extract).

(2)   Subject to the provisions of any other enactment, where leave to appeal has been granted, an appeal shall be made within 7 days after the date when leave was granted.

(3)[2]   An application for leave to appeal from a decision in relation to—

(a)   a time to pay direction under section 1 of the Debtors (Scotland) Act 1987;

(b)   the recall or restriction of an arrestment made under section 3(4) of that Act; or

(c)   a time order under section 129 of the Consumer Credit Act 1974,

shall specify the question of law on which the appeal is made.

**Appeals in connection with interim diligence**

**D1.238**

**31.2A.**[3]   An interlocutor—

(a)   loosing, restricting, varying or recalling an arrestment or an interim attachment;

(b)   recalling in whole or in part, or varying an inhibition used on the dependence of an action; or

(c)   refusing to loose, restrict or recall such arrestment, attachment or inhibition,

may be appealed to the sheriff principal, without leave of the sheriff, within 14 days after the date of the interlocutor.

**Form of appeal to Court of Session**

**D1.239**

**31.3.**—[4](1)   An appeal to the Court of Session shall be marked by writing a note of appeal—

(a)   on the interlocutor sheet or other written record containing the interlocutor appealed against, or

(b)   where the decision appealed against is not available or the proceedings appealed against are recorded in an official book, on a separate sheet lodged with the sheriff clerk,

in the following terms:—"The pursuer [or defender or as the case may be] appeals to the Court of Session.".

---

[1] As inserted by the Act of Sederunt (Ordinary Cause, Summary Application, Summary Cause and Small Claim Rules) Amendment (Miscellaneous) 2007 (SSI 2007/6), para.2(11) (effective January 29, 2007).

[2] As substituted by the Act of Sederunt (Ordinary Cause, Summary Application, Summary Cause and Small Claim Rules) Amendment (Miscellaneous) 2007 (SSI 2007/6), para.2(12) (effective January 29, 2007).

[3] As inserted by the Act of Sederunt (Sheriff Court Rules) (Miscellaneous Amendments) (No.2) 2008 (SSI 2008/365) para.3 (effective December 1, 2008).

[4] Substituted by SI 1996/2445 (effective November 1, 1996).

(2)    A note of appeal under paragraph (1) shall—
    (a)    be signed by the appellant or his solicitor;
    (b)    bear the date on which it is signed; and
    (c)    where the appellant is represented, specify the name and address of the solicitor or other agent who will be acting for him in the appeal.

**Form of appeal to the sheriff principal**

**31.4.**—[1](1)    An appeal to the sheriff principal shall be marked by lodging a note of appeal in Form A1.

    **D1.240**

(2)    A note of appeal under paragraph (1) shall—
    (a)    be signed by the appellant or his solicitor;
    (b)    bear the date on which it is signed;
    (c)    where the appellant is represented, specify the name and address of the solicitor or other agent who will be acting for him in the appeal; and
    (d)    where a note has not been provided by the sheriff, request that the sheriff write a note setting out the reasons for his decision.

(3)    The grounds of appeal in a note of appeal shall consist of brief specific numbered propositions stating the grounds on which it is proposed to submit that the appeal should be allowed or as the case may be.

(4)    On making or lodging a note of appeal, the appellant shall send a copy of the note of appeal to every other party.

(5)    An appellant—
    (a)    may amend the grounds of appeal at any time up to 14 days before the date assigned for the hearing of the appeal; and
    (b)    shall at the same time send or deliver a copy of such amendment to every other party.

(6)    Where any party wishes to cross-appeal, he shall—
    (a)    lodge a note of the grounds of appeal in accordance with paragraph (1) not less than 7 days before the date assigned for the hearing of the appeal; and
    (b)    at the same time send a copy of the note to every other party.

(7)    The sheriff principal may, on cause shown, shorten or dispense with the time limits mentioned in paragraphs (5) and (6).

(8)    On a note of appeal being lodged, the sheriff clerk shall note on the interlocutor sheet that an appeal has been marked and the date of the appeal.

GENERAL NOTE

In *City of Edinburgh v Z* , 2005 S.L.T. (Sh Ct) 7, it was said that an appeal under s.2(3) of the Adults with Incapacity (Scotland) Act 2000 should follow the rules prescribed by rule 31.4.

**Transmission of process and notice to parties**

    **D1.241**

**31.5.**—[2](1)    Where an appeal is marked in terms of rule 31.3 (appeal to Court of Session) or 31.4 (appeal to sheriff principal), the sheriff clerk shall transmit the process of the cause—
    (a)    in an appeal to the sheriff principal, to him; or
    (b)    in an appeal to the Court of Session, to the Deputy Principal Clerk of Session, within the period specified in rule 40.6 of the Rules of the Court of Session 1994.

(2)    On transmitting the process in terms of paragraph (1), the sheriff clerk shall—
    (a)    send written notice of the appeal to every party; and
    (b)    certify on the interlocutor sheet that he has done so.

(3)    Failure of the sheriff clerk to comply with paragraph (2) shall not invalidate the appeal.

**Record of pleadings etc.**

    **D1.242**

**31.6**[3]    In an appeal to him, the sheriff principal may order the appellant to lodge a record of the pleadings containing all adjustments made in the cause with—
    (a)    a copy of all relevant interlocutors;
    (b)    any other document lodged in process by any party or produced by order of the sheriff, whether or not pursuant to the commission and diligence for its recovery; and
    (c)    any other document to which reference is intended to be made in the appeal, by any party.

---

[1] Substituted by SI 1996/2445 (effective November 1, 1996).
[2] Substituted by SI 1996/2445 (effective November 1, 1996).
[3] Substituted by SI 1996/2445 (effective November 1, 1996).

**Determination of appeal**

**D1.243**

31.7.[1]   In an appeal to him, the sheriff principal shall—

    (a)   hear parties at an oral hearing; or

    (b)   on the motion of the parties, and if he thinks fit, dispose of the appeal without ordering an oral hearing.

**Fixing of Options Hearing or making other order following appeal**

**D1.244**

31.8.[2]   On determination of an appeal from a decision of the sheriff made before or at an Options Hearing or any contribution of it, the sheriff principal may order the sheriff clerk to fix a new date for a hearing under rule 9.12 (options hearing) or may make such other order as he thinks fit.

**Appeals in connection with orders under section 11 of the Children (Scotland) Act 1995 or aliment**

**D1.245**

31.9.[3]   Where an appeal is marked against an interlocutor making an order under section 11 of the Children (Scotland) Act 1995 (court orders relating to parental responsibilities etc.) or in respect of aliment, the marking of that appeal shall not excuse obedience to or implement of that order unless by order of the sheriff, the sheriff principal or the Court of Session, as the case may be.

**Interim possession etc. pending appeal**

**D1.246**

31.10.—[4](1)   Notwithstanding an appeal, the sheriff or sheriff principal from whose decision an appeal has been taken shall have power—

    (a)   to regulate all matters relating to interim possession;

    (b)   to make any order for the preservation of any property to which the action relates or for its sale if perishable;

    (c)   to make provision for the preservation of evidence; or

    (d)   to make any interim order which a due regard to the interests of the parties may require.

(2)   An order made under paragraph (1) may be reviewed—

    (a)   by the sheriff principal, on an appeal to him; or

    (b)   the Court of Session, on an appeal to it.

**Abandonment of appeal**

**D1.247**

31.11.[5]   After an appeal to the sheriff principal has been marked, the appellant shall not be entitled to abandon his appeal unless—

    (a)   of consent of all other parties; or

    (b)   with leave of the sheriff principal.

## Chapter 32

### Taxation of Expenses

**Taxation before decree for expenses**

**D1.248**

32.1.   Expenses allowed in any cause, whether in absence or *in foro contentioso*, unless modified at a fixed amount, shall be taxed before decree is granted for them.

**Order to lodge account of expenses**

**D1.249**

32.1A.[6]   A party found liable in expenses may from 4 months after the date of the interlocutor finding him so liable apply by motion for an order ordaining the party entitled to expenses to lodge an account of those expenses in process.

**Decree for expenses in name of solicitor**

**D1.250**

32.2.   The sheriff may allow a decree for expenses to be extracted in the name of the solicitor who conducted the cause.

**Procedure for taxation**

**D1.251**

32.3.—(1)   Where an account of expenses awarded in a cause is lodged for taxation, the account and process shall be transmitted by the sheriff clerk to the auditor of court.

(2)   The auditor of court shall—

---

[1] Substituted by SI 1996/2445 (effective November 1, 1996).

[2] Inserted by SI 1996/2445 (effective November 1, 1996).

[3] Inserted by SI 1996/2445 (effective November 1, 1996).

[4] Former rule 31.6 renumbered by SI 1996/2445 (effective November 1, 1996).

[5] Former rule 31.7 renumbered by SI 1996/2445 (effective November 1, 1996).

[6] Inserted by the Act of Sederunt (Ordinary Cause, Summary Application and Small Claim Rules) Amendment (Miscellaneous) 2004 (SSI 2004/197) (effective May 21, 2004), para.2(12).

    (a)    assign a diet of taxation not earlier than 7 days from the date he receives the account from the sheriff clerk; and

    (b)    intimate that diet forthwith to the party who lodged the account.

(3)    The party who lodged the account of expenses shall, on receiving intimation from the auditor of court under paragraph (2)—

    (a)    send a copy of the account, and

    (b)    intimate the date, time and place of the diet of taxation,

to every other party.

(4)    After the account has been taxed, the auditor of court shall transmit the process with the account and his report to the sheriff clerk.

(5)    Where the auditor of court has reserved consideration of the account at the date of the taxation, he shall intimate his decision to the parties who attended the taxation.

(6)    Where no objections are lodged under rule 32.4 (objections to auditor's report), the sheriff may grant decree for the expenses as taxed.

**Objections to auditor's report**

**32.4.**—(1)    A party may lodge a note of objections to an account as taxed only where he attended the diet of taxation.         **D1.252**

(2)    Such a note shall be lodged within 7 days after—

    (a)    the diet of taxation; or

    (b)    where the auditor of court reserved consideration of the account under paragraph (5) of rule 32.3, the date on which the auditor of court intimates his decision under that paragraph.

(3)    The sheriff shall dispose of the objection in a summary manner, with or without answers.

Chapter 32A[1]

Live Links

**32A.1.**—(1)    On cause shown, a party may apply by motion for authority for the whole or part of—    **D1.253**

    (a)    the evidence of a witness or the party to be given; or

    (b)    a submission to be made,

through a live link.

(2)    In paragraph (1)—

"witness" means a person who has been or may be cited to appear before the court as a witness, except a vulnerable witness within the meaning of section 11(1) of the Act of 2004;

"submission" means any oral submission which would otherwise be made to the court by the party or his representative in person including an oral submission in support of a motion; and

"live link" means a live television link or such other arrangement as may be specified in the motion by which the witness, party or representative, as the case may be, is able to be seen and heard in the proceedings or heard in the proceedings and is able to see and hear or hear the proceedings while at a place which is outside the courtroom.

Special Provisions in Relation to Particular Causes

Chapter 33

Family Actions

Part I

General Provisions

**Interpretation of this Chapter**

**33.1.**—[2](1)    In this Chapter, "family action" means—    **D1.254**

    (a)    an action of divorce;

    (b)    an action of separation;

    (c)    an action of declarator of legitimacy;

    (d)    an action of declarator of illegitimacy;

    (e)    an action of declarator of parentage;

---

[1] As inserted by the Act of Sederunt (Ordinary Cause, Summary Application, Summary Cause and Small Claim Rules) Amendment (Miscellaneous) 2007 (SSI 2007/6) r.2(12) (effective January 29, 2007).

[2] As amended by SI 1996/2167 (effective November 1, 1996).

    (f)   an action of declarator of non-parentage;

    (g)   an action of declarator of legitimation;

    (h)   an action or application for, or in respect of, an order under section 11 of the Children (Scotland) Act 1995 (court orders relating to parental responsibilities etc.), except—

        (i)   an application for the appointment of a judicial factor mentioned in section 11(2)(g) of the Act of 1995 to which Part I of the Act of Sederunt (Judicial Factors Rules) 1992 applies;

        (ii)  *[Repealed by the Act of Sederunt (Sheriff Court Rules) (Miscellaneous Amendments) 2011 (SSI 2011/193) r.13 (effective April 4, 2011).]*

    (i)   an action of affiliation and aliment;

    (j)   an action of, or application for or in respect of, aliment;

    (k)   an action or application for financial provision after a divorce or annulment in an overseas country within the meaning of Part IV of the Matrimonial and Family Proceedings Act 1984;

    (l)   an action or application for an order under the Act of 1981;

    (m)  an application for the variation or recall of an order mentioned in section 8(1) of the Law Reform (Miscellaneous Provisions) (Scotland) Act 1966.

    (n)[1]  an action of declarator of marriage;

    (o)[2]  an action of declarator of nullity of marriage.

    (p)[3]  an action for declarator of recognition, or non-recognition, of a relevant foreign decree within the meaning of section 7(9) of the Domicile and Matrimonial Proceedings Act 1973.

    (q)[4]  an application under section 28 or 29 of the Act of 2006 (financial provision for former co-habitants).

  (2)  In this Chapter, unless the context otherwise requires—

"the Act of 1975" means the Children Act 1975;

"the Act of 1976" means the Divorce (Scotland) Act 1976;

"the Act of 1981" means the Matrimonial Homes (Family Protection) (Scotland) Act 1981;

"the Act of 1985" means the Family Law (Scotland) Act 1985;

"the Act of 1995" means the Children (Scotland) Act 1995;

"the Act of 2006" means the Family Law (Scotland) Act 2006;

"contact order" has the meaning assigned in section 11(2)(d) of the Act of 1995;

"full gender recognition certificate" and "interim gender recognition certificate" mean the certificates issued as such under section 4 or 5 of the Gender Recognition Act 2004;[5]

"Gender Recognition Panel" is to be construed in accordance with Schedule 1 to the Gender Recognition Act 2004;

"local authority" means a council constituted under section 2 of the Local Government etc. (Scotland) Act 1994;

"mental disorder" has the meaning assigned in section 328 of the Mental Health (Care and Treatment) (Scotland) Act 2003;[6]

"order for financial provision" means, except in Part VII of this Chapter (financial provision after overseas divorce or annulment), an order mentioned in section 8(1) of the Act of 1985;

"parental responsibilities" has the meaning assigned in section 1(3) of the Act 1995;

"parental rights" has the meaning assigned in section 2(4) of the Act of 1995;

"residence order" has the meaning assigned in section 11(2)(c) of the Act of 1995;

"section 11 order" means an order under section 11 of the Act of 1995.

  (3)  For the purposes of rules 33.2 (averments in actions of divorce or separation about other proceedings) and 33.3 (averments where section 11 order sought) and, in relation to proceedings in another

---

[1] Inserted or substituted by Act of Sederunt (Ordinary Cause Rules) Amendment (Family Law (Scotland) Act 2006 etc.) 2006 (SSI 2006/207) (effective May 4, 2006).

[2] Inserted or substituted by Act of Sederunt (Ordinary Cause Rules) Amendment (Family Law (Scotland) Act 2006 etc.) 2006 (SSI 2006/207) (effective May 4, 2006).

[3] As inserted by the Act of Sederunt (Sheriff Court Rules) (Miscellaneous Amendments) (No.2) 2010 (SSI 2010/416) r.8 (effective January 1, 2011).

[4] As inserted by the Act of Sederunt (Sheriff Court Rules) (Miscellaneous Amendments) 2012 (SSI 2012/188) para.5 (effective August 1, 2012).

[5] Inserted by the Act of Sederunt (Ordinary Cause Rules) Amendment (Gender Recognition Act 2004) 2005 (SSI 2005/189) (effective April 4, 2005).

[6] Inserted or substituted by Act of Sederunt (Ordinary Cause Rules) Amendment (Family Law (Scotland) Act 2006 etc.) 2006 (SSI 2006/207) (effective May 4, 2006).

jurisdiction, Schedule 3 to the Domicile and Matrimonial Proceedings Act 1973 (sisting of consistorial actions in Scotland), proceedings are continuing at any time after they have commenced and before they are finally disposed of.

**Averments in certain family actions about other proceedings**[1]

**33.2.**—[2](1)[3] This rule applies to an action of divorce, separation, declarator of marriage or declarator of nullity of marriage.

    (2)   In an action to which this rule applies, the pursuer shall state in the condescendence of the initial writ—

      (a)   whether to his knowledge any proceedings are continuing in Scotland or in any other country in respect of the marriage to which the initial writ relates or are capable of affecting its validity or subsistence; and

      (b)   where such proceedings are continuing—

          (i)   the court, tribunal or authority before which the proceedings have been commenced;

          (ii)   the date of commencement;

          (iii)   the names of the parties;

          (iv)   the date, or expected date of any proof (or its equivalent) in the proceedings; and

          (v)[4, 5]   such other facts as may be relevant to the question of whether or not the action before the sheriff should be sisted under Schedule 3 to the Domicile and Matrimonial Proceedings Act 1973 or Council Regulation (E.C.) No. 2201/2003 of 27th November 2003 concerning jurisdiction and the recognition and enforcement of judgments in matrimonial matters and matters of parental responsibility for the 1996 Convention on Jurisdiction, Applicable Law, Recognition, Enforcement and Co-operation in Respect of Parental Responsibility and Measures for the Protection of Children, signed at the Hague on 19th October 1996.

    (3)   Where—

      (a)   such proceedings are continuing;

      (b)   the action before the sheriff is defended; and

      (c)   either—

          (i)   the initial writ does not contain the statement referred to in paragraph (2)(a), or

          (ii)   the particulars mentioned in paragraph (2)(b) as set out in the initial writ are incomplete or incorrect,

any defences or minute, as the case may be, lodged by any person to the action shall include that statement and, where appropriate, the further or correct particulars mentioned in paragraph (2)(b).

**Averments where section 11 order sought**

**33.3.**—[6](1)   A party to a family action, who makes an application in that action for a section 11 order in respect of a child shall include in his pleadings—

      (a)[7]   where that action is an action of divorce, separation or declarator of nullity of marriage, averments giving particulars of any other proceedings known to him, whether in Scotland or elsewhere and whether concluded or not, which relate to the child in respect of whom the section 11 order is sought;

      (b)   in any other family action—

          (i)   the averments mentioned in paragraph (a); and

**D1.255**

**D1.256**

---

[1] As amended by Act of Sederunt (Ordinary Cause Rules) Amendment (Family Law (Scotland) Act 2006 etc.) 2006 (SSI 2006/207) (effective May 4, 2006).

[2] As amended by Act of Sederunt (Ordinary Cause Rules) Amendment (European Matrimonial and Parental Responsibility Jurisdiction and Judgments) 2001 (SSI 2001/144) (effective April 2, 2001).

[3] As amended by Act of Sederunt (Ordinary Cause Rules) Amendment (Family Law (Scotland) Act 2006 etc.) 2006 (SSI 2006/207) (effective May 4, 2006).

[4] As amended by Act of Sederunt (Ordinary Cause Rules) Amendment (Family Law (Scotland) Act 2006 etc.) 2006 (SSI 2006/207) (effective May 4, 2006).

[5] As amended by the Act of Sederunt (Sheriff Court Rules) (Miscellaneous Amendments) (No.2) 2012 (SSI 2012/221) para.3 (effective August 1, 2012).

[6] As amended by SI 1996/2167 (effective November 1, 1996) and SI 1996/2445 (effective November 1, 1996) (clerical error).

[7] As amended by Act of Sederunt (Ordinary Cause Rules) Amendment (Family Law (Scotland) Act 2006 etc.) 2006 (SSI 2006/207) (effective May 4, 2006).

> (ii) averments giving particulars of any proceedings known to him which are continuing, whether in Scotland or elsewhere, and which relate to the marriage of the parents of that child.
>
> (c)[1] where the party seeks an order such as is mentioned in any of paragraphs (a) to (e) of subsection (2) of that section, an averment that no permanence order (as defined in section 80(2) of the Adoption and Children (Scotland) Act 2007) is in force in respect of the child.

(2) Where such other proceedings are continuing or have taken place and the averments of the applicant for such a section 11 order—

> (a) do not contain particulars of the other proceedings, or
> (b) contain particulars which are incomplete or incorrect,

any defences or minute, as the case may be, lodged by any party to the family action shall include such particulars or such further or correct particulars as are known to him.

(3) In paragraph (1)(b)(ii), "child" includes a child of the family within the meaning assigned in section 42(4) of the Family Law Act 1986.

### Averments where identity or address of person not known

**D1.257**

**33.4.** In a family action, where the identity or address of any person referred to in rule 33.7 as a person in respect of whom a warrant for intimation requires to be applied for is not known and cannot reasonably be ascertained, the party required to apply for the warrant shall include in his pleadings an averment of that fact and averments setting out what steps have been taken to ascertain the identity or address, as the case may be, of that person.

### Averments about maintenance orders

**D1.258**

**33.5.** In a family action in which an order for aliment or periodical allowance is sought, or is sought to be varied or recalled, by any party, the pleadings of that party shall contain an averment stating whether and, if so, when and by whom, a maintenance order (within the meaning of section 106 of the Debtors (Scotland) Act 1987) has been granted in favour of or against that party or of any other person in respect of whom the order is sought.

### Averments where aliment or financial provision sought

**D1.259**

**33.6.**—[2](1) In this rule—

"the Act of 1991" means the Child Support Act 1991;
"child" has the meaning assigned in section 55 of the Act of 1991;
"crave relating to aliment" means—

> (a) for the purposes of paragraph (2), a crave for decree of aliment in relation to a child or for recall or variation of such a decree; and
> (b) for the purposes of paragraph (3), a crave for decree of aliment in relation to a child or for recall or variation of such a decree or for the variation or termination of an agreement on aliment in relation to a child;

"maintenance calculation" has the meaning assigned in section 54 of the Act of 1991.

(2) A family action containing a crave relating to aliment and to which section 8(6), (7), (8) or (10) of the Act of 1991 (top up maintenance orders) applies shall—

> (a) include averments stating, where appropriate—
>> (i) that a maintenance calculation under section 11 of that Act (maintenance calculations) is in force;
>> (ii) the date of the maintenance calculation;
>> (iii) the amount and frequency of periodical payments of child support maintenance fixed by the maintenance calculation; and
>> (iv) the grounds on which the sheriff retains jurisdiction under section 8(6), (7), (8) or (10) of that Act; and
> (b) unless the sheriff on cause shown otherwise directs, be accompanied by any document issued by the Secretary of State to the party intimating the making of the maintenance calculation referred to in sub-paragraph (a).

---

[1] As inserted by the Act of Sederunt (Sheriff Court Rules Amendment) (Adoption and Children (Scotland) Act 2007) 2009 (SSI 2009/284) (effective September 28, 2009).
[2] As amended by the Act of Sederunt (Ordinary Cause, Summary Application, Summary Cause and Small Claim Rules) Amendment (Miscellaneous) 2003 (SSI 2003/26) r.2(8) (effective January 24, 2003).

(3)   A family action containing a crave relating to aliment, and to which section 8(6), (7), (8) or (10) of the Act of 1991 does not apply, shall include averments stating—

    (a)   that the habitual residence of the absent parent, person with care or qualifying child, within the meaning of section 3 of that Act, is furth of the United Kingdom;

    (b)   that the child is not a child within the meaning of section 55 of that Act; or

    (c)   where the action is lodged for warranting before 7th April 1997, the grounds on which the sheriff retains jurisdiction.

(4)   In an action for declarator of non-parentage or illegitimacy—

    (a)   the initial writ shall include an article of condescendence stating whether the pursuer previously has been alleged to be the parent in an application for a maintenance calculation under section 4, 6 or 7 of the Act of 1991 (applications for maintenance calculation); and

    (b)   where an allegation of paternity has been made against the pursuer, the Secretary of State shall be named as a defender in the action.

(5)   A family action involving parties in respect of whom a decision has been made in any application, review or appeal under the Act of 1991 relating to any child of those parties, shall—

    (a)   include averments stating that such a decision has been made and giving details of that decision; and

    (b)   unless the sheriff on cause shown otherwise directs, be accompanied by any document issued by the Secretary of State to the parties intimating that decision.

### Application by survivor for provision on intestacy

**33.6A.**—[1](1)   In an action for an order under section 29(2) of the Act of 2006 (application by survivor for provision on intestacy), the pursuer shall call the deceased's executor as a defender.

    (2)   An application under section 29(9) of the Act of 2006 for variation of the date or method of payment of the capital sum shall be made by minute in the process of the action to which the application relates.

    (3)   Words and expressions used in this rule shall have the same meaning as in section 29 of the Act of 2006.

**D1.260**

### Warrants and forms for intimation

**33.7.**—[2](1)   Subject to paragraphs (5) and (7), in the initial writ in a family action, the pursuer shall include a crave for a warrant for intimation—

    (a)   in an action where the address of the defender is not known to the pursuer and cannot reasonably be ascertained, to—

        (i)[3,5]   every person who is a child of the family (as defined in section 12(4)(a) of the Act of 1995) who has reached the age of 16 years; and

        (ii)   one of the next-of-kin of the defender who has reached that age,

    unless the address of such a person is not known to the pursuer and cannot reasonably be ascertained, and a notice of intimation in Form F1 shall be attached to the copy of the initial writ intimated to any such person;

    (b)[4]   in an action of divorce where the pursuer alleges that the defender has committed adultery with another person, to that person, unless—

        (i)   that person is not named in the initial writ and, if the adultery is relied on for the purposes of section 1(2)(a) of the Act of 1976 (irretrievable breakdown of marriage by reason of adultery), the initial writ contains an averment that his or her identity is not known to the pursuer and cannot reasonably be ascertained; or

        (ii)   the pursuer alleges that the defender has been guilty of rape upon or incest with, that named person,

    and a notice of intimation in Form F2 shall be attached to the copy of the initial writ intimated to any such person;

    (c)   in an action where the defender is a person who is suffering from a mental disorder, to—

**D1.261**

---

[1] As inserted by the Act of Sederunt (Sheriff Court Rules) (Miscellaneous Amendments) 2012 (SSI 2012/188) para.5 (effective August 1, 2012).

[2] As amended by SI 1996/2167 (effective November 1, 1996) and SI 1996/2445 (effective November 1, 1996).

[3] As amended by the Act of Sederunt (Sheriff Court Rules) (Miscellaneous Amendments) 2012 (SSI 2012/188) para.5 (effective August 1, 2012).

[4] As amended by the Act of Sederunt (Sheriff Court Rules) (Miscellaneous Amendments) 2012 (SSI 2012/188) para.5 (effective August 1, 2012).

        (i)[1]   those persons mentioned in sub-paragraph (a)(i) and (ii), unless the address of such person is not known to the pursuer and cannot reasonably be ascertained;

        (ii)   the curator bonis to the defender, if one has been appointed,

and a notice of intimation in Form F3 shall be attached to the copy of the initial writ intimated to any such person;

        (iii)[2]  any person holding the office of guardian or continuing or welfare attorney to the defender under or by virtue of the Adults with Incapacity (Scotland) Act 2000,

(d)   in an action relating to a marriage which was entered into under a law which permits polygamy where—

        (i)   one of the decrees specified in section 2(2) of the Matrimonial Proceedings (Polygamous Marriages) Act 1972 is sought; and

        (ii)  either party to the marriage in question has any spouse additional to the other party,

to any such additional spouse, and a notice of intimation in Form F4 shall be attached to the initial writ intimated to any such person;

(e)[3]  in an action of divorce, separation or declarator of nullity of marriage where the sheriff may make a section 11 order in respect of a child—

        (i)   who is in the care of a local authority, to that authority and a notice of intimation in Form F5 shall be attached to the initial writ intimated to that authority;

        (ii)  who, being a child of one party to the marriage, has been accepted as a child of the family by the other party to the marriage and who is liable to be maintained by a third party, to that third party, and a notice of intimation in Form F5 shall be attached to the initial writ intimated to that third party; or

        (iii) in respect of whom a third party in fact exercises care and control, to that third party, and a notice of intimation in Form F6 shall be attached to the initial writ intimated to that third party;

(f)   in an action where the pursuer craves a section 11 order, to any parent or guardian of the child who is not a party to the action, and a notice of intimation in Form F7 shall be attached to the initial writ intimated to any such parent or guardian;

(g)   *[Repealed by the Act of Sederunt (Sheriff Court Rules) (Miscellaneous Amendments) (No.2) 2010 (SSI 2010/416) r.7 (effective January 1, 2011).]*

(h)   in an action which includes a crave for a section 11 order, to the child to whom such an order would relate if not a party to the action, and a notice of intimation in Form F9 shall be intimated to that child;

(i)   in an action where the pursuer makes an application for an order under section 8(1)(aa) of the Act of 1985 (transfer of property) and—

        (i)   the consent of a third party to such a transfer is necessary by virtue of an obligation, enactment or rule of law, or

        (ii)  the property is subject to a security,

to the third party or creditor, as the case may be, and a notice of intimation in Form F10 shall be attached to the initial writ intimated to any such person;

(j)   in an action where the pursuer makes an application for an order under section 18 of the Act of 1985 (which relates to avoidance transactions), to—

        (i)   any third party in whose favour the transfer of, or transaction involving, the property is to be or was made, and

        (ii)  any other person having an interest in the transfer of, or transaction involving, the property,

and a notice of intimation in Form F11 shall be attached to the initial writ intimated to any such person;

(k)   in an action where the pursuer makes an application for an order under the Act of 1981—

        (i)   where he is a non-entitled partner and the entitled partner has a spouse, to that spouse; or

        (ii)  where the application is under section 2(1)(e), 2(4)(a), 3(1), 3(2), 4, 7, 13 or 18

---

[1] As amended by Act of Sederunt (Ordinary Cause Rules) Amendment (Family Law (Scotland) Act 2006 etc.) 2006 (SSI 2006/207) r.2 (effective May 4, 2006).

[2] Inserted or substituted by Act of Sederunt (Ordinary Cause Rules) Amendment (Family Law (Scotland) Act 2006 etc.) 2006 (SSI 2006/207) r.2 (effective May 4, 2006).

[3] As amended by Act of Sederunt (Ordinary Cause Rules) Amendment (Family Law (Scotland) Act 2006 etc.) 2006 (SSI 2006/207) r.2 (effective May 4, 2006).

of that Act, and the entitled spouse or entitled partner is a tenant or occupies the matrimonial home by permission of a third party, to the landlord or the third party, as the case may be,

and a notice of intimation in Form F12 shall be attached to the initial writ intimated to any such person;

(l) in an action where the pursuer makes an application for an order under section 8(1)(ba) of the Act of 1985 (orders under section 12A of the Act of 1985 for pension lump sum), to the person responsible for the pension arrangement, and a notice of intimation in Form F12A shall be attached to the initial writ intimated to any such person;

(m)[1] in an action where a pursuer makes an application for an order under section 8(1)(baa) of the Act of 1985 (pension sharing orders), to the person responsible for the pension arrangement and a notice of intimation in Form F12B shall be attached to the initial writ intimated to any such person;

(n)[2] in an action where a pursuer makes an application for an order under section 8(1)(bab) of the Act of 1985 (pension compensation sharing order), to the Board of the Pension Protection Fund, and a notice of intimation in Form F12C shall be attached to the initial writ intimated to that Board; and

(o)[3] in an action where a pursuer makes an application for an order under section 8(1)(bb) of the Act of 1985 (an order under section 12B(2) of the Act of 1985 for pension compensation), to the Board of the Pension Protection Fund and a notice of intimation in Form F12D shall be attached to the initial writ intimated to that Board.

(p)[4] in an action where a pursuer makes an application for an order under section 29(2) of the Act of 2006 (application by survivor for provision on intestacy) to any person having an interest in the deceased's net estate, and a notice of intimation in Form F12E shall be attached to the initial writ intimated to any such person.

(2)[5] Expressions used in—

(a) paragraph (1)(k) which are also used in the Act of 1981; and

(b) paragraph (1)(p) which are also used in section 29 of the Act of 2006,

shall have the same meanings as in that Act or section, as the case may be.

(3) A notice of intimation under paragraph (1) shall be on a period of notice of 21 days unless the sheriff otherwise orders; but the sheriff shall not order a period of notice of less than 2 days.

(4) *[Repealed by the Act of Sederunt (Sheriff Court Rules) (Miscellaneous Amendments) (No.2) 2010 (SSI 2010/416) r.7 (effective January 1, 2011).]*

(5)[6, 7] Where the address of a person mentioned in paragraph (1)(b), (d), (e), (f), (h), (i), (j), (k), (l), (m) or (p) is not known and cannot reasonably be ascertained, the pursuer shall include a crave in the initial writ to dispense with intimation; and the sheriff may grant that crave or make such other order as he thinks fit.

(6) Where the identity or address of a person to whom intimation of a family action is required becomes known during the course of the action, the party who would have been required to insert a warrant for intimation to that person shall lodge a motion for a warrant for intimation to that person or to dispense with such intimation.

(7) Where a pursuer considers that to order intimation to a child under paragraph (1)(h) is inappropriate, he shall—

(a) include a crave in the initial writ to dispense with intimation to that child, and

(b) include in the initial writ averments setting out the reasons why such intimation is inappropriate;

---

[1] Inserted by the Act of Sederunt (Ordinary Cause Rules) Amendment (No.2) (Pension Sharing on Divorce etc.) 2000 (SSI 2000/408) r.2(2)(b)(ii).

[2] As inserted by the Act of Sederunt (Sheriff Court Rules) (Miscellaneous Amendments) 2011 (SSI 2011/193) r.15 (effective April 6, 2011).

[3] As inserted by the Act of Sederunt (Sheriff Court Rules) (Miscellaneous Amendments) 2011 (SSI 2011/193) r.15 (effective April 6, 2011).

[4] As inserted by the Act of Sederunt (Sheriff Court Rules) (Miscellaneous Amendments) 2012 (SSI 2012/188) para.5 (effective August 1, 2012).

[5] As substituted by the Act of Sederunt (Sheriff Court Rules) (Miscellaneous Amendments) 2012 (SSI 2012/188) para.5 (effective August 1, 2012).

[6] As amended by Act of Sederunt (Ordinary Cause Rules) Amendment (Family Law (Scotland) Act 2006 etc.) 2006 (SSI 2006/207) r.2 (effective May 4, 2006).

[7] As amended by the Act of Sederunt (Sheriff Court Rules) (Miscellaneous Amendments) 2012 (SSI 2012/188) para.5 (effective August 1, 2012).

and the sheriff may dispense with such intimation or make such other order as he thinks fit.

**Intimation where alleged association**[1]

**D1.262**

**33.8.**—(1)[2]  In a family action where the pursuer founds upon an association between the defender and another named person, the pursuer shall, immediately after the expiry of the period of notice, lodge a motion for an order for intimation to that person or to dispense with such intimation.

(2)  In determining a motion under paragraph (1), the sheriff may—

(a)  make such order for intimation as he thinks fit; or

(b)  dispense with intimation; and

(c)  where he dispenses with intimation, order that the name of that person be deleted from the condescendence of the initial writ.

(3)  Where intimation is ordered under paragraph (2), a copy of the initial writ and an intimation in Form F13 shall be intimated to the named person.

(4)[3]  In paragraph (1), "association" means sodomy, incest or any homosexual relationship.

**Productions in action of divorce or where a section 11 order or order for financial provision may be made**

**D1.263**

**33.9.**[4, 5]  Unless the sheriff otherwise directs—

(a)[6]  in an action of divorce or declarator of nullity of marriage, a warrant for citation shall not be granted without there being produced with the initial writ an extract of the relevant entry in the register of marriages or an equivalent document; and

(b)  in an action which includes a crave for a section 11 order, a warrant for citation shall not be granted without there being produced with the initial writ an extract of the relevant entry in the register of births or an equivalent document.

(c)[7]  in an action which includes a crave for an order for financial provision, the pursuer must lodge a completed Form F13A signed by the pursuer with the initial writ or minute of amendment as the case may be.

**Productions in action of divorce on ground of issue of interim gender recognition certificate**

**D1.264**

**33.9A.**—[8](1)  This rule applies where, in an action of divorce, the ground on which decree of divorce may be granted is that an interim gender recognition certificate has, after the date of the marriage, been issued to either party to the marriage.

(2)  Unless the sheriff otherwise directs, a warrant for citation shall not be granted without there being produced with the initial writ—

(a)  where the pursuer is the subject of the interim gender recognition certificate, the interim gender recognition certificate or, failing that, a certified copy of the interim gender recognition certificate; or

(b)  where the pursuer is the spouse of the person who is the subject of the interim gender recognition certificate, a certified copy of the interim gender recognition certificate.

(3)  For the purposes of this rule, a certified copy of an interim gender recognition certificate shall be a copy of that certificate sealed with the seal of the Gender Recognition Panels and certified to be a true copy by an officer authorised by the President of Gender Recognition Panels.

---

[1] As amended by Act of Sederunt (Ordinary Cause Rules) Amendment (Family Law (Scotland) Act 2006 etc.) 2006 (SSI 2006/207) r.2 (effective May 4, 2006).

[2] As amended by Act of Sederunt (Ordinary Cause Rules) Amendment (Family Law (Scotland) Act 2006 etc.) 2006 (SSI 2006/207) r.2 (effective May 4, 2006).

[3] As amended by Act of Sederunt (Ordinary Cause Rules) Amendment (Family Law (Scotland) Act 2006 etc.) 2006 (SSI 2006/207) r.2 (effective May 4, 2006).

[4] As amended by Act of Sederunt (Family Proceedings in the Sheriff Court) 1996 (SI 1996/2167) (effective November 1, 1996).

[5] As amended by the Act of Sederunt (Sheriff Court Rules) (Miscellaneous Amendments) 2012 (SSI 2012/188) para.4 (effective August 1, 2012).

[6] As amended by Act of Sederunt (Ordinary Cause Rules) Amendment (Family Law (Scotland) Act 2006 etc.) 2006 (SSI 2006/207) (effective May 4, 2006).

[7] As amended by the Act of Sederunt (Sheriff Court Rules) (Miscellaneous Amendments) 2012 (SSI 2012/188) para.4 (effective August 1, 2012).

[8] Inserted by the Act of Sederunt (Ordinary Cause Rules) Amendment (Gender Recognition Act 2004) 2005 (SSI 2005/189) r.2 (effective April 4, 2005).

**Application for corrected gender recognition certificate**

**33.9B.**[1]   An application for a corrected gender recognition certificate under section 6 of the Gender Recognition Act 2004 by—

    (a)   the person to whom a full gender recognition certificate has been issued; or

    (b)   the Secretary of State,

shall be made by minute in the process of the action pursuant to which the full gender recognition certificate was issued.

      **D1.265**

**Warrant of citation**

**33.10.**   The warrant of citation in a family action shall be in Form F14.

      **D1.266**

**Form of citation and certificate**

**33.11.**—(1)   Subject to rule 5.6 (service where address of person is not known), citation of a defender shall be in Form F15, which shall be attached to a copy of the initial writ and warrant of citation and shall have appended to it a notice of intention to defend in Form F26.

(2)   The certificate of citation shall be in Form F16 which shall be attached to the initial writ.

      **D1.267**

**Intimation to local authority**

**33.12.**—[2](1)   In any family action where the pursuer craves a residence order in respect of a child, the sheriff may, if the sheriff thinks fit, order intimation to the local authority in which area the pursuer resides; and such intimation shall be in Form F8.

(2)   Where an order for intimation is made under paragraph (1), intimation to that local authority shall be given within 7 days after the date on which an order for intimation has been made.

      **D1.268**

**Service in cases of mental disorder of defender**

**33.13.**—(1)   In a family action where the defender suffers or appears to suffer from mental disorder and is resident in a hospital or other similar institution, citation shall be executed by registered post or the first class recorded delivery service addressed to the medical officer in charge of that hospital or institution; and there shall be included with the copy of the initial writ—

    (a)   a citation in Form F15;

    (b)   any notice required by rule 33.14(1);

    (c)   a request in Form F17;

    (d)   a form of certificate in Form F18 requesting the medical officer to—

        (i)   deliver and explain the initial writ, citation and any notice or form of notice of consent required under rule 33.14(1) personally to the defender; or

        (ii)   certify that such delivery or explanation would be dangerous to the health or mental condition of the defender; and

    (e)   a stamped envelope addressed for return of that certificate to the pursuer or his solicitor, if he has one.

(2)   The medical officer referred to in paragraph (1) shall send the certificate in Form F18 duly completed to the pursuer or his solicitor, as the case may be.

(3)   The certificate mentioned in paragraph (2) shall be attached to the certificate of citation.

(4)   Where such a certificate bears that the initial writ has not been delivered to the defender, the sheriff may, at any time before decree—

    (a)   order such further medical inquiry, and

    (b)   make such order for further service or intimation,

as he thinks fit.

      **D1.269**

**Notices in certain actions of divorce or separation**

**33.14.**—(1)   In the following actions of divorce or separation there shall be attached to the copy of the initial writ served on the defender—

    (a)[3]   in an action relying on section 1(2)(d) of the Act of 1976 (no cohabitation for one year with consent of defender to decree)—

      **D1.270**

---

[1] Inserted by the Act of Sederunt (Ordinary Cause Rules) Amendment (Gender Recognition Act 2004) 2005 (SSI 2005/189) r.2 (effective April 4, 2005).

[2] As substituted by the Act of Sederunt (Sheriff Court Rules) (Miscellaneous Amendments) (No.2) 2010 (SSI 2010/416) r.7 (effective January 1, 2011).

[3] As amended by Act of Sederunt (Ordinary Cause Rules) Amendment (Family Law (Scotland) Act 2006 etc.) 2006 (SSI 2006/207) r.2 (effective May 4, 2006).

      (i)    which is an action of divorce, a notice in Form F19 and a notice of consent in Form F20;

      (ii)   which is an action of separation, a notice in Form F21 and a form of notice of consent in Form F22;

(b)[1]  in an action relying on section 1(2)(e) of the Act of 1976 (no cohabitation for two years)—

      (i)    which is an action of divorce, a notice in Form F23;

      (ii)   which is an action of separation, a notice in Form F24.

(c)[2]  in an action relying on section 1(1)(b) of the Act of 1976 (grounds for divorce: interim gender recognition certificate), a notice in Form F24A

(2)[3]  The certificate of citation of an initial writ in an action mentioned in paragraph (1) shall state which notice or form mentioned in paragraph (1) has been attached to the initial writ.

### Orders for intimation

**D1.271**

**33.15.**—(1)  In any family action, the sheriff may, at any time—

  (a)  subject to paragraph (2), order intimation to be made on such person as he thinks fit;

  (b)  postpone intimation, where he considers that such postponement is appropriate and, in that case, the sheriff shall make such order in respect of postponement of intimation as he thinks fit; or

  (c)  dispense with intimation, where he considers that such dispensation is appropriate.

(2)  Where the sheriff is considering whether to make a section 11 order by virtue of section 12 of the Act of 1995 (restrictions on decrees for divorce, separation or annulment affecting children), he shall, subject to paragraph (1)(c) and without prejudice to paragraph (1)(b) of this rule, order intimation in Form F9 to the child to whom the section 11 order would relate unless—

  (a)  intimation has been given to the child under rule 33.7(1)(h); or

  (b)  the sheriff considers that the child is not of sufficient age or maturity to express his views.

(3)  Where a party makes a crave or averment in a family action which, had it been made in an initial writ, would have required a warrant for intimation under rule 33.7, that party shall include a crave in his writ for a warrant for intimation or to dispense with such intimation; and rule 33.7 shall, with the necessary modifications, apply to a crave for a warrant under this paragraph as it applies to a crave for a warrant under that rule.

### Appointment of curators ad litem to defenders

**D1.272**

**33.16.**—(1)[4, 5]  This rule applies to a family action where it appears to the court that the defender is suffering from a mental disorder.

(2)  In an action to which this rule applies, the sheriff shall—

  (a)  appoint a curator ad litem to the defender;

  (b)[6]  where the facts set out in section 1(2)(d) of the Act of 1976 (no cohabitation for one year with consent of defender to decree) are relied on—

      (i)    make an order for intimation of the ground of the action to the Mental Welfare Commission for Scotland; and

      (ii)   include in such an order a requirement that the Commission sends to the sheriff clerk a report indicating whether in its opinion the defender is capable of deciding whether or not to give consent to the granting of decree.

(3)[7]  Within 7 days after the appointment of a curator ad litem under paragraph (2)(a), the pursuer shall send to him—

  (a)  a copy of the initial writ and any defences (including any adjustments and amendments) lodged; and

  (b)  a copy of any notice in Form G5 sent to him by the sheriff clerk.

---

[1] As amended by Act of Sederunt (Ordinary Cause Rules) Amendment (Family Law (Scotland) Act 2006 etc.) 2006 (SSI 2006/207) r.2 (effective May 4, 2006).

[2] Inserted or substituted by Act of Sederunt (Ordinary Cause Rules) Amendment (Family Law (Scotland) Act 2006 etc.) 2006 (SSI 2006/207) r.2 (effective May 4, 2006).

[3] As amended by SI 1996/2445 (effective November 1, 1996).

[4] As amended by Act of Sederunt (Ordinary Cause Rules) Amendment (Family Law (Scotland) Act 2006 etc.) 2006 (SSI 2006/207) r.2 (effective May 4, 2006).

[5] As amended by the Act of Sederunt (Sheriff Court Rules) (Miscellaneous Amendments) 2012 (SSI 2012/188) para.5 (effective August 1, 2012).

[6] As amended by Act of Sederunt (Ordinary Cause Rules) Amendment (Family Law (Scotland) Act 2006 etc.) 2006 (SSI 2006/207) r.2 (effective May 4, 2006).

[7] As amended by SI 1996/2445 (effective November 1, 1996).

(4)   On receipt of a report required under paragraph (2)(b)(ii), the sheriff clerk shall—

    (a)   lodge the report in process; and

    (b)   intimate that this has been done to—

        (i)   the pursuer;

        (ii)   the solicitor for the defender, if known; and

        (iii)   the curator ad litem.

(5)   The curator ad litem shall lodge in process one of the writs mentioned in paragraph (6)—

    (a)   within 14 days after the report required under paragraph (2)(b)(ii) has been lodged in process; or

    (b)   where no such report is required, within 21 days after the date of his appointment under paragraph (2)(a).

(6)   The writs referred to in paragraph (5) are—

    (a)   a notice of intention to defend;

    (b)   defences to the action;

    (c)   a minute adopting defences already lodged; and

    (d)   a minute stating that the curator ad litem does not intend to lodge defences.

(7)   Notwithstanding that he has lodged a minute stating that he does not intend to lodge defences, a curator ad litem may appear at any stage of the action to protect the interests of the defender.

(8)   If, at any time, it appears to the curator ad litem that the defender is not suffering from mental disorder, he may report that fact to the court and seek his own discharge.

(9)   The pursuer shall be responsible, in the first instance, for payment of the fees and outlays of the curator ad litem incurred during the period from his appointment until—

    (a)   he lodges a minute stating that he does not intend to lodge defences;

    (b)   he decides to instruct the lodging of defences or a minute adopting defences already lodged; or

    (c)   being satisfied after investigation that the defender is not suffering from mental disorder, he is discharged.

### Applications for sist

**33.17.**   An application for a sist, or the recall of a sist, under Schedule 3 to the Domicile and Matrimonial Proceedings Act 1973 shall be made by written motion.

                                                         **D1.273**

### Notices of consent to divorce or separation

**33.18.**—(1)[1]   Where, in an action of divorce or separation in which the facts in section 1(2)(d) of the Act of 1976 (no cohabitation for one year with consent of defender to decree) are relied on, the defender wishes to consent to the grant of decree of divorce or separation he shall do so by giving notice in writing in Form F20 (divorce) or Form F22 (separation), as the case may be, to the sheriff clerk.

                                                         **D1.274**

(2)   The evidence of one witness shall be sufficient for the purpose of establishing that the signature on a notice of consent under paragraph (1) is that of the defender.

(3)   In an action of divorce or separation where the initial writ includes, for the purposes of section 1(2)(d) of the Act of 1976, an averment that the defender consents to the grant of decree, the defender may give notice by letter sent to the sheriff clerk stating that he has not so consented or that he withdraws any consent which he has already given.

(4)   On receipt of a letter under paragraph (3), the sheriff clerk shall intimate the terms of the letter to the pursuer.

(5)   On receipt of any intimation under paragraph (4), the pursuer may, within 14 days after the date of the intimation, if none of the other facts mentioned in section 1(2) of the Act of 1976 is averred in the initial writ, lodge a motion for the action to be sisted.

(6)   If no such motion is lodged, the pursuer shall be deemed to have abandoned the action and the action shall be dismissed.

(7)   If a motion under paragraph (5) is granted and the sist is not recalled or renewed within a period of 6 months from the date of the interlocutor granting the sist, the pursuer shall be deemed to have abandoned the action and the action shall be dismissed.

### Procedure in respect of children

**33.19.**—[2](1)   In a family action, in relation to any matter affecting a child, where that child has—

    (a)   returned to the sheriff clerk Form F9, or

                                                          **D1.275**

---

[1] As amended by Act of Sederunt (Ordinary Cause Rules) Amendment (Family Law (Scotland) Act 2006 etc.) 2006 (SSI 2006/207) r.2 (effective May 4, 2006).

[2] As substituted by SI 1996/2167 (effective November 1, 1996).

(b)    otherwise indicated to the court a wish to express views on a matter affecting him,

the sheriff shall not grant any order unless an opportunity has been given for the views of that child to be obtained or heard.

(2)    Where a child has indicated his wish to express his views, the sheriff shall order such steps to be taken as he considers appropriate to ascertain the views of that child.

(3)    The sheriff shall not grant an order in a family action, in relation to any matter affecting a child who has indicated his wish to express his views, unless due weight has been given by the sheriff to the views expressed by that child, having due regard to his age and maturity.

### Recording of views of the child

**D1.276**    33.20—[1](1)    This rule applies where a child expresses a view on a matter affecting him whether expressed personally to the sheriff or to a person appointed by the sheriff for that purpose or provided by the child in writing.

(2)    The sheriff, or the person appointed by the sheriff, shall record the views of the child in writing; and the sheriff may direct that such views, and any written views, given by a child shall—

(a)    be sealed in an envelope marked "Views of the child—confidential";

(b)    be kept in the court process without being recorded in the inventory of process;

(c)    be available to a sheriff only;

(d)    not be opened by any person other than a sheriff; and

(e)    not form a borrowable part of the process.

### Appointment of local authority or reporter to report on a child

**D1.277**    33.21.—[2](1)    This rule applies where, at any stage of a family action, the sheriff appoints—

(a)    a local authority under section 11(1) of the Matrimonial Proceedings (Children) Act 1958 (reports as to arrangements for future care and upbringing of children) or otherwise, or

(b)    another person (referred to in this rule as a "reporter"), whether under a provision mentioned in sub-paragraph (a) or otherwise,

to investigate and report to the court on the circumstances of a child and on proposed arrangements for the care and upbringing of the child.

(2)    On making an appointment referred to in paragraph (1), the sheriff shall direct that the party who sought the appointment or, where the court makes the appointment of its own motion, the pursuer or minuter, as the case may be, shall—

(a)    instruct the local authority or reporter; and

(b)    be responsible, in the first instance, for the fees and outlays of the local authority or reporter appointed.

(3)    Where a local authority or reporter is appointed—

(a)    the party who sought the appointment, or

(b)    where the sheriff makes the appointment of his own motion, the pursuer or minuter, as the case may be,

shall, within 7 days after the date of the appointment, intimate the name and address of the local authority or reporter to any local authority to which intimation of the family action has been made.

(4)    On completion of a report referred to in paragraph (1), the local authority or reporter, as the case may be, shall send the report, with a copy of it for each party, to the sheriff clerk.

(5)    On receipt of such a report, the sheriff clerk shall send a copy of the report to each party.

(6)    Where a local authority or reporter has been appointed to investigate and report in respect of a child, an application for a section 11 order in respect of that child shall not be determined until the report of the local authority or reporter, as the case may be, has been lodged.

### Referral to family mediation

**D1.278**    33.22.[3]    In any family action in which an order in relation to parental responsibilities or parental rights is in issue, the sheriff may, at any stage of the action, where he considers it appropriate to do so, refer that issue to a mediator accredited to a specified family mediation organisation.

---

[1] As substituted by SI 1996/2167 (effective November 1, 1996).

[2] As amended by Act of Sederunt (Family Proceedings in the Sheriff Court) 1996 (SI 1996/2167) (effective November 1, 1996).

[3] As substituted by SI 1996/2167 (effective November 1, 1996).

**Child Welfare Hearing**

**33.22A.**—[1](1)   Where—

    (a)    on the lodging of a notice of intention to defend in a family action in which the initial writ seeks or includes a crave for a section 11 order, a defender wishes to oppose any such crave or order, or seeks the same order as that craved by the pursuer,

    (b)    on the lodging of a notice of intention to defend in a family action, the defender seeks a section 11 order which is not craved by the pursuer, or

    (c)    in any other circumstances in a family action, the sheriff considers that a Child Welfare Hearing should be fixed and makes an order (whether at his own instance or on the motion of a party) that such a hearing shall be fixed,

the sheriff clerk shall fix a date and time for a Child Welfare Hearing on the first suitable court date occurring not sooner than 21 days after the lodging of such notice of intention to defend, unless the sheriff directs the hearing to be held on an earlier date.

(2)   On fixing the date for the Child Welfare Hearing, the sheriff clerk shall intimate the date of the Child Welfare Hearing to the parties in Form F41.

(3)   The fixing of the date of the Child Welfare Hearing shall not affect the right of a party to make any other application to the court whether by motion or otherwise.

(4)[2]   At the Child Welfare Hearing (which may be held in private), the sheriff shall seek to secure the expeditious resolution of disputes in relation to the child by ascertaining from the parties the matters in dispute and any information relevant to that dispute, and may—

    (a)    order such steps to be taken, make such order, if any, or order further procedure, as he thinks fit, and

    (b)    ascertain whether there is or is likely to be a vulnerable witness within the meaning of section 11(1) of the Act of 2004 who is to give evidence at any proof or hearing and whether any order under section 12(1) of the Act of 2004 requires to be made.

(5)   All parties (including a child who has indicated his wish to attend) shall, except on cause shown, attend the Child Welfare Hearing personally.

(6)   It shall be the duty of the parties to provide the sheriff with sufficient information to enable him to conduct the Child Welfare Hearing.

**Applications for orders to disclose whereabouts of children**

**33.23.**—(1)   An application for an order under section 33(1) of the Family Law Act 1986 (which relates to the disclosure of the whereabouts of a child) shall be made by motion.

(2)   Where the sheriff makes an order under section 33(1) of the Family Law Act 1986, he may ordain the person against whom the order has been made to appear before him or to lodge an affidavit.

**Applications in relation to removal of children**

**33.24.**—[3](1)   An application for leave under section 51(1) of the Act of 1975 (authority to remove a child from the care and possession of the applicant for a residence order) or for an order under section 35(3) of the Family Law Act 1986 (application for interdict or interim interdict prohibiting removal of child from jurisdiction) shall be made—

    (a)    by a party to the action, by motion; or

    (b)    by a person who is not a party to the action, by minute.

(2)   An application under section 35(3) of the Family Law Act 1986 need not be served or intimated.

(3)   An application under section 23(2) of the Child Abduction and Custody Act 1985 (declarator that removal of child from United Kingdom was unlawful) shall be made—

    (a)    in an action depending before the sheriff—

        (i)    by a party, in the initial writ, defences or minute, as the case may be, or by motion; or

        (ii)    by any other person, by minute; or

    (b)    after final decree, by minute in the process of the action to which the application relates.

**D1.279**

**D1.280**

**D1.281**

---

[1] As inserted by the Act of Sederunt (Family Proceedings in the Sheriff Court) 1996 (SI 1996/2167) (effective November 1, 1996).

[2] As substituted by the Act of Sederunt (Ordinary Cause, Summary Application, Summary Cause and Small Claim Rules) Amendment (Vulnerable Witnesses (Scotland) Act 2004) 2007 (SSI 2007/463) r.2(9) (effective November 1, 2007).

[3] As amended by Act of Sederunt (Family Proceedings in the Sheriff Court) 1996 (SI 1996/2167) (effective November 1, 1996).

**Intimation to local authority before supervised contact order**

**D1.282**

**33.25.** Where the sheriff, at his own instance or on the motion of a party, is considering making a contact order or an interim contact order subject to supervision by the social work department of a local authority, he shall ordain the party moving for such an order to intimate to the Chief Executive of that local authority (where not already a party to the action and represented at the hearing at which the issue arises)—

    (a)   the terms of any relevant motion;

    (b)   the intention of the sheriff to order that the contact order be supervised by the social work department of that local authority; and

    (c)   that the local authority shall, within such period as the sheriff has determined—

        (i)   notify the sheriff clerk whether it intends to make representations to the sheriff; and

        (ii)[1]   where it intends to make representations in writing, do so within that period.

NOTES

[1] As amended by the Act of Sederunt (Family Proceedings in the Sheriff Court) 1996 (SI 1996/2167) (effective November 1, 1996).

**Joint minutes**

**D1.283**

**33.26.**[2] Where any parties have reached agreement in relation to—

    (a)   a section 11 order,

    (b)   aliment for a child,

    (c)   an order for financial provision, or

    (d)[3]   an order under section 28 or 29 of the Act of 2006

a joint minute may be entered into expressing that agreement; and, subject to rule 33.19(3) (no order before views of child expressed), the sheriff may grant decree in respect of those parts of the joint minute in relation to which he could otherwise make an order, whether or not such a decree would include a matter for which there was no crave.

**Affidavits**

**D1.284**

**33.27.** The sheriff may accept evidence by affidavit at any hearing for an order or interim order.

**Applications for postponement of decree under section 3A of the Act of 1976**

**D1.285**

**33.27A.**[4] An application under section 3A(1) (application for postponement of decree where impediment to religious marriage exists) or section 3A(4) (application for recall of postponement) of the Act of 1976 shall be made by minute in the process of the action to which the application relates.

Part II

Undefended Family Actions

**Evidence in certain undefended family actions**

**D1.286**

**33.28.**—[5](1)  This rule—

    (a)   subject to sub-paragraph (b), applies to all family actions in which no notice of intention to defend has been lodged, other than a family action—

        (i)   for a section 11 order or for aliment;

        (ii)   of affiliation and aliment;

        (iii)   for financial provision after an overseas divorce or annulment within the meaning of Part IV of the Matrimonial and Family Proceedings Act 1984; or

        (iv)   for an order under the Act of 1981;

---

[1] As amended by Act of Sederunt (Ordinary Cause Rules) Amendment (Family Law (Scotland) Act 2006 etc.) 2006 (SSI 2006/207) r.2 (effective May 4, 2006).

[2] As amended by Act of Sederunt (Family Proceedings in the Sheriff Court) 1996 (SI 1996/2167) (effective November 1, 1996).

[3] As inserted by the Act of Sederunt (Sheriff Court Rules) (Miscellaneous Amendments) 2012 (SSI 2012/188) para.5 (effective August 1, 2012).

[4] Substituted by Act of Sederunt (Ordinary Cause Rules) Amendment (Family Law (Scotland) Act 2006 etc.) 2006 (SSI 2006/207) r.2 (effective May 4, 2006) and amended by the Act of Sederunt (Ordinary Cause, Summary Application, Summary Cause and Small Claim Rules) Amendment (Miscellaneous) 2007 (SSI 2007/6) r.2(14) (effective February 26, 2007).

[5] As amended by Act of Sederunt (Family Proceedings in the Sheriff Court) 1996 (SI 1996/2167) (effective November 1, 1996).

      (v)[1]   for declarator of recognition, or non-recognition, of a relevant foreign decree within the meaning of section 7(9) of the Domicile and Matrimonial Proceedings Act 1973;

      (vi)[2]  for an order under section 28 or 29 of the Act of 2006;

  (b)  applies to a family action in which a curator ad litem has been appointed under rule 33.16 where the curator ad litem to the defender has lodged a minute intimating that he does not intend to lodge defences;

  (c)  applies to any family action which proceeds at any stage as undefended where the sheriff so directs;

  (d)  applies to the merits of a family action which is undefended on the merits where the sheriff so directs, notwithstanding that the action is defended on an ancillary matter.

(2)   Unless the sheriff otherwise directs, evidence shall be given by affidavits.

(3)   Unless the sheriff otherwise directs, evidence relating to the welfare of a child shall be given by affidavit, at least one affidavit being emitted by a person other than a parent or party to the action.

(4)   Evidence in the form of a written statement bearing to be the professional opinion of a duly qualified medical practitioner, which has been signed by him and lodged in process, shall be admissible in place of parole evidence by him.

### Procedure for decree in actions under rule 33.28

**33.29.**—(1)  In an action to which rule 33.28 (evidence in certain undefended family actions) applies, the pursuer shall at any time after the expiry of the period for lodging a notice of intention to defend—

  (a)  lodge in process the affidavit evidence; and

  (b)  endorse a minute in Form F27 on the initial writ.

(2)   The sheriff may, at any time after the pursuer has complied with paragraph (1), without requiring the appearance of parties—

  (a)  grant decree in terms of the motion for decree; or

  (b)  remit the cause for such further procedure, if any, including proof by parole evidence, as the sheriff thinks fit.

D1.287

### Extracts of undefended decree

**33.30.**[3]  In an action to which rule 33.28 (evidence in certain undefended family actions) applies, the sheriff clerk shall, after the expiry of 14 days after the grant of decree under rule 33.29 (procedure for decree in cases under rule 33.28), issue to the pursuer and the defender an extract decree.

D1.288

### Procedure in undefended family action for section 11 order

**33.31.**—[4](1)  Where no notice of intention to defend has been lodged in a family action for a section 11 order, any proceedings in the cause shall be dealt with by the sheriff in chambers.

(2)   In an action to which paragraph (1) applies, decree may be pronounced after such inquiry as the sheriff thinks fit.

D1.289

### No recording of evidence

**33.32.**  It shall not be necessary to record the evidence in any proof in a family action which is not defended.

D1.290

### Disapplication of Chapter 15

**33.33.**[5]  Other than rule 15.1(1), Chapter 15 (motions) shall not apply to a family action in which no notice of intention to defend has been lodged, or to a family action in so far as it proceeds as undefended.

D1.291

---

[1] As inserted by the Act of Sederunt (Sheriff Court Rules) (Miscellaneous Amendments) (No.2) 2010 (SSI 2010/416) r.8 (effective January 1, 2011).

[2] As inserted by the Act of Sederunt (Sheriff Court Rules) (Miscellaneous Amendments) 2012 (SSI 2012/188) para.5 (effective August 1, 2012).

[3] As amended by Act of Sederunt (Ordinary Cause Rules) Amendment (Family Law (Scotland) Act 2006 etc.) 2006 (SSI 2006/207) r.2 (effective May 4, 2006).

[4] As amended by Act of Sederunt (Family Proceedings in the Sheriff Court) 1996 (SI 1996/2167) (effective November 1, 1996).

[5] As amended by SI 1996/2445 (effective November 1, 1996).

**Late appearance and application for recall by defenders**

**D1.292**

**33.33A.**—[1](1)[23]   In a cause mentioned in rule 33.1(a) to (h) or (n) to (q), the sheriff may, at any stage of the action before the granting of final decree, make an order with such conditions, if any, as he thinks fit—

    (a)   directing that a defender who has not lodged a notice of intention to defend be treated as if he had lodged such a notice and the period of notice had expired on the date on which the order was made; or

    (b)   allowing a defender who has not lodged a notice of intention to defend to appear and be heard at a diet of proof although he has not lodged defences, but he shall not, in that event, be allowed to lead evidence without the pursuer's consent.

(2)   Where the sheriff makes an order under paragraph (1), the pursuer may recall a witness already examined or lead other evidence whether or not he closed his proof before that order was made.

(3)   Where no order under paragraph (1) has been sought by a defender who has not lodged a notice of intention to defend and decree is granted against him, the sheriff may, on an application made within 14 days of the date of the decree, and with such conditions, if any, as he thinks fit, make an order recalling the decree.

(4)   Where the sheriff makes an order under paragraph (3), the cause shall thereafter proceed as if the defender had lodged a notice of intention to defend and the period of notice had expired on the date on which the decree was recalled.

(5)   An application under paragraph (1) or (3) shall be made by note setting out the proposed defence and explaining the defender's failure to appear.

(6)   An application under paragraph (1) or (3) shall not affect any right of appeal the defender may otherwise have.

(7)   A note lodged in an application under paragraph (1) or (3) shall be served on the pursuer and any other party.

Part III

Defended Family Actions

**Notice of intention to defend and defences etc.[4]**

**D1.293**

**33.34.**—[5](1)   This rule applies where the defender in a family action seeks—

    (a)   to oppose any crave in the initial writ;

    (b)   to make a claim for—

        (i)   aliment;

        (ii)   an order for financial provision within the meaning of section 8(3) of the Act of 1985;

        (iii)   a section 11 order;

        (iv)[6]   an order for financial provision under section 28 or 29 of the Family Law (Scotland) Act 2006; or

    (c)   an order—

        (i)   under section 16(1)(b) or (3) of the Act of 1985 (setting aside or varying agreement as to financial provision);

        (ii)   under section 18 of the Act of 1985 (which relates to avoidance transactions); or

        (iii)   under the Act of 1981; or

    (d)   to challenge the jurisdiction of the court.

(2)   In an action to which this rule applies, the defender shall—

    (a)   lodge a notice of intention to defend in Form F26 before the expiry of the period of notice; and

---

[1] As inserted by the Act of Sederunt (Sheriff Court Rules) (Miscellaneous Amendments) 2008 (SSI 2008/223) r.2(2) (effective July 1, 2008).

[2] As amended by the Act of Sederunt (Sheriff Court Rules) (Miscellaneous Amendments) (No.2) 2010 (SSI 2010/416) r.8 (effective January 1, 2011).

[3] As amended by the Act of Sederunt (Sheriff Court Rules) (Miscellaneous Amendments) 2012 (SSI 2012/188) para.5 (effective August 1, 2012).

[4] As amended by the Act of Sederunt (Sheriff Court Rules) (Miscellaneous Amendments) 2012 (SSI 2012/188) para.5 (effective August 1, 2012).

[5] As amended by Act of Sederunt (Family Proceedings in the Sheriff Court) 1996 (SI 1996/2167) (effective November 1, 1996).

[6] As inserted by the Act of Sederunt (Sheriff Court Rules) (Miscellaneous Amendments) 2012 (SSI 2012/188) para.4,5 (effective August 1, 2012).

    (b)    make any claim or seek any order referred to in paragraph (1), as the case may be, in those defences by setting out in his defences—
          (i)    craves;
          (ii)    averments in the answers to the condescendence in support of those craves; and
          (iii)    appropriate pleas-in-law.

(3)    Where a defender intends to make an application for a section 11 order which, had it been made in an initial writ, would have required a warrant for intimation under rule 33.7, the defender shall include a crave in his notice of intention to defend for a warrant for intimation or to dispense with such intimation; and rule 33.7 shall, with the necessary modifications, apply to a crave for a warrant under this paragraph as it applies to a crave for a warrant under that rule.

(4)[1, 2]    Where a defender opposes a crave for an order for financial provision or makes a claim in accordance with paragraph (1)(b)(ii), the defender must lodge a completed Form F13A signed by the defender with the defences, minute of amendment or answers as the case may be.

### Abandonment by pursuer

**33.35.**    Notwithstanding abandonment by a pursuer, the court may allow a defender to pursue an order or claim sought in his defences; and the proceedings in relation to that order or claim shall continue in dependence as if a separate cause.    **D1.294**

### Attendance of parties at Options Hearing

**33.36.**    All parties shall, except on cause shown, attend personally the hearing under rule 9.12 (Options Hearing).    **D1.295**

### Decree by default

**33.37.**—(1)[3]    In a family action in which the defender has lodged a notice of intention to defend, where a party fails—    **D1.296**
    (a)    to lodge, or intimate the lodging of, any production or part of process,
    (b)    to implement an order of the sheriff within a specified period,
    (c)    to appear or be represented at any diet, or
    (d)[4]    otherwise to comply with any requirement imposed upon that party by these Rules;
that party shall be in default.

(2)[5]    Where a party is in default under paragraph (1), the sheriff may—
    (a)[6]    where the family action is one mentioned in rule 33.1(a) to (h) or (n) to (p) allow the cause to proceed as undefended under Part II of this Chapter; or
    (b)[7]    where the family action is one mentioned in rule 33.1(1)(i) to (m) or (q), grant decree as craved; or
    (c)    grant decree of absolvitor; or
    (d)    dismiss the family action or any claim made or order sought; or
    (da)    make such other order as he thinks fit to secure the expeditious progress of the cause; and
    (e)    award expenses.

(3)    Where no party appears at a diet in a family action, the sheriff may dismiss that action.

---

[1] As inserted by the Act of Sederunt (Sheriff Court Rules) (Miscellaneous Amendments) 2012 (SSI 2012/188) para.4,5 (effective August 1, 2012).

[2] As amended by the Act of Sederunt (Sheriff Court Rules) (Miscellaneous Amendments) (No.2) 2012 (SSI 2012/221) para.2 (effective July 31, 2012).

[3] As amended by Act of Sederunt (Sheriff Court Ordinary Cause Rules Amendment) (Miscellaneous) 1996 (SI 1996/2445) (effective November 1, 1996) (clerical error).

[4] As inserted by the Act of Sederunt (Ordinary Cause and Summary Application Rules) Amendment (Miscellaneous) 2006 (SSI 2006/410) (effective August 18, 2006).

[5] As amended by Act of Sederunt (Ordinary Cause Rules) Amendment (Family Law (Scotland) Act 2006 etc.) 2006, para.2 (SSI 2006/207) (effective May 4, 2006) and the Act of Sederunt (Ordinary Cause and Summary Application Rules) Amendment (Miscellaneous) 2006 (SSI 2006/410) (effective August 18, 2006).

[6] As amended by the Act of Sederunt (Sheriff Court Rules) (Miscellaneous Amendments) (No.2) 2010 (SSI 2010/416) r.8 (effective January 1, 2011).

[7] As amended by the Act of Sederunt (Sheriff Court Rules) (Miscellaneous Amendments) 2012 (SSI 2012/188) para.5 (effective August 1, 2012).

(4) In a family action, the sheriff may, on cause shown, prorogate the time for lodging any production or part of process, or for intimating or implementing any order.

Part IV

Applications and Orders Relating to Children in Certain Actions

**Application and interpretation of this Part**

D1.297

**33.38.**[1, 2] This Part applies to an action of divorce, separation or declarator of nullity of marriage.

**Applications in actions to which this Part applies**

D1.298

**33.39.**—[3](1) An application for an order mentioned in paragraph (2) shall be made—
   (a) by a crave in the initial writ or defences, as the case may be, in an action to which this Part applies; or
   (b) where the application is made by a person other than the pursuer or defender, by minute in that action.
(2) The orders referred to in paragraph (1) are—
   (a) an order for a section 11 order; and
   (b) an order for aliment for a child.
**33.40.** [Repealed by the Act of Sederunt (Family Proceedings in the Sheriff Court) 1996 (SI 1996/2167) (effective November 1, 1996).]
**33.41.** [Repealed by the Act of Sederunt (Family Proceedings in the Sheriff Court) 1996 (SI 1996/2167) (effective November 1, 1996).]
**33.42.** [Repealed by the Act of Sederunt (Family Proceedings in the Sheriff Court) 1996 (SI 1996/2167) (effective November 1, 1996).]

**Applications in depending actions by motion**

D1.299

**33.43.**[4] An application by a party in an action depending before the court to which this Part applies for, or for variation of, an order for—
   (a) interim aliment for a child under the age of 18, or
   (b) a residence order or a contact order,
shall be made by motion.

**Applications after decree relating to a section 11 order**

D1.300

**33.44.**—[5](1)[6] An application after final decree for, or for the variation or recall of, a section 11 order or in relation to the enforcement of such an order shall be made by minute in the process of the action to which the application relates.
(2) Where a minute has been lodged under paragraph (1), any party may apply by motion for any interim order which may be made pending the determination of the application.

**Applications after decree relating to aliment**

D1.301

**33.45.**—(1) An application after final decree for, or for the variation or recall of, an order for aliment for a child shall be made by minute in the process of the action to which the application relates.
(2) Where a minute has been lodged under paragraph (1), any party may lodge a motion for any interim order which may be made pending the determination of the application.

**Applications after decree by persons over 18 years for aliment**

D1.302

**33.46.**—(1) A person—
   (a) to whom an obligation of aliment is owed under section 1 of the Act of 1985,
   (b) in whose favour an order for aliment while under the age of 18 years was made in an action to which this Part applies, and
   (c) who seeks, after attaining that age, an order for aliment against the person in that action

---

[1] As amended by Act of Sederunt (Family Proceedings in the Sheriff Court) 1996 (SI 1996/2167) (effective November 1, 1996).
[2] As amended by Act of Sederunt (Ordinary Cause Rules) Amendment (Family Law (Scotland) Act 2006 etc.) 2006, para.2 (SSI 2006/207) (effective May 4, 2006).
[3] As amended by Act of Sederunt (Family Proceedings in the Sheriff Court) 1996 (SI 1996/2167) (effective November 1, 1996).
[4] As amended by Act of Sederunt (Family Proceedings in the Sheriff Court) 1996 (SI 1996/2167) (effective November 1, 1996).
[5] As amended by Act of Sederunt (Family Proceedings in the Sheriff Court) 1996 (SI 1996/2167) (effective November 1, 1996).
[6] As amended by SSI 2000/239 (effective October 2, 2000).

against whom the order for aliment in his favour was made,
shall apply by minute in the process of that action.

(2)　An application for interim aliment pending the determination of an application under paragraph (1) shall be made by motion.

(3)　Where a decree has been pronounced in an application under paragraph (1) or (2), any application for variation or recall of any such decree shall be made by minute in the process of the action to which the application relates.

### Part V

### Orders Relating to Financial Provision

**Application and interpretation of this Part**

**33.47.**—(1)　This Part applies to an action of divorce.　　　　　　　　　　　　　　　　**D1.303**

(2)　In this Part, "incidental order" has the meaning assigned in section 14(2) of the Act of 1985.

**Applications in actions to which this Part applies**

**33.48.**—(1)　An application for an order mentioned in paragraph (2) shall be made—　　　**D1.304**

    (a)　by a crave in the initial writ or defences, as the case may be, in an action to which this Part applies; or

    (b)　where the application is made by a person other than the pursuer or defender, by minute in that action.

(2)　The orders referred to in paragraph (1) are—

    (a)　an order for financial provision within the meaning of section 8(3) of the Act of 1985;

    (b)　an order under section 16(1)(b) or (3) of the Act of 1985 (setting aside or varying agreement as to financial provision);

    (c)　an order under section 18 of the Act of 1985 (which relates to avoidance transactions); and

    (d)　an order under section 13 of the Act of 1981 (transfer or vesting of tenancy).

**Applications in depending actions relating to incidental orders**

**33.49.**—(1)　In an action depending before the sheriff to which this Part applies—　　　**D1.305**

    (a)　the pursuer, notwithstanding rules 33.34(2) (application by defender for order for financial provision) and 33.48(1)(a) (application for order for financial provision in initial writ or defences), may apply by motion for an incidental order; and

    (b)　the sheriff shall not be bound to determine such a motion if he considers that the application should properly be by a crave in the initial writ or defences, as the case may be.

(2)　In an action depending before the sheriff to which this Part applies, an application under section 14(4) of the Act of 1985 for the variation or recall of an incidental order shall be made by minute in the process of the action to which the application relates.

**Applications relating to interim aliment**

**33.50.**　An application for, or for the variation or recall of, an order for interim aliment for the　**D1.306**
pursuer or the defender shall be made by motion.

**Applications relating to orders for financial provision**

**33.51.**—(1)　An application—　　　　　　　　　　　　　　　　　　　　　　　　　　**D1.307**

    (a)　after final decree under any of the following provisions of the Act of 1985—

        (i)　section 8(1) for periodical allowance,

        (ii)　section 12(1)(b) (payment of capital sum or transfer of property),

        (iii)　section 12(4) (variation of date or method of payment of capital sum or date of transfer of property), or

        (iv)　section 13(4) (variation, recall, backdating or conversion of periodical allowance), or

        (v)[1]　section 14(1) (incidental orders), or

    (b)　after the grant or refusal of an application under—

        (i)　section 8(1) or 14(3) for an incidental order, or

        (ii)　section 14(4) (variation or recall of incidental order),

shall be made by minute in the process of the action to which the application relates.

---

[1] As inserted by the Act of Sederunt (Sheriff Court Rules) (Miscellaneous Amendments) (No.3) 2011 (SSI 2011/386) para.2 (effective November 28, 2011).

(2) Where a minute is lodged under paragraph (1), any party may lodge a motion for any interim order which may be made pending the determination of the application.

(3)[1] An application under—

    (a) paragraph (5) of section 12A of the Act of 1985 (recall or variation of order in respect of a pension lump sum),

    (b) paragraph (7) of that section (variation of order in respect of pension lump sum to substitute trustees or managers),

    (ba)[2] section 12B(4) of the Act of 1985 (recall or variation of a capital sum order), or

    (c) section 28(10) or 48(9) of the Welfare Reform and Pensions Act 1999,

shall be made by minute in the process of the action to which the application relates.

**Pension Protection Fund notification**

**D1.308**

33.51A.—[3](1) In this rule—

"assessment period" shall be construed in accordance with section 132 of the Pensions Act 2004;

"pension arrangement" shall be construed in accordance with the definition in section 27 of the Act of 1985; and

"valuation summary" shall be construed in accordance with the definition in Schedule 2 to the Pension Protection Fund (Provision of Information) Regulations 2005.

(2) This rule applies where a party at any stage in the proceedings applies for an order under section 8 or section 16 of the Act of 1985.

(3) Where the party against whom an order referred to in paragraph (2) is sought has received notification in compliance with the Pension Protection Fund (Provision of Information) Regulations 2005 or does so after the order is sought—

    (a) that there is an assessment period in relation to his pension arrangement; or

    (b) that the Board of the Pension Protection Fund has assumed responsibility for all or part of his pension arrangement,

    he shall comply with paragraph (4).

(4) The party shall—

    (a) lodge the notification; and

    (b) obtain and lodge as soon as reasonably practicable thereafter–

        (i) a valuation summary; and

        (ii) a forecast of his compensation entitlement.

(5) Subject to paragraph (6), the notification referred to in paragraph (4)(a) requires to be lodged—

    (a) where the notification is received before the order is sought, within 7 days of the order being sought;

    (b) where the notification is received after the order is sought, within 7 days of receiving the notification.

(6) Where an order is sought against the defender before the defences are lodged, and the notification is received before that step occurs, the notification shall be lodged with the defences.

(7) At the same time as lodging documents under paragraph (4), copies shall be sent to the other party to the proceedings.

**Applications after decree relating to agreements and avoidance transactions**

**D1.309**

33.52. An application for an order—

    (a) under section 16(1)(a) or (3) of the Act of 1985 (setting aside or varying agreement as to financial provision), or

---

[1] As inserted by SI 1996/2445 (effective November 1, 1996) and as amended by the Act of Sederunt (Ordinary Cause, Summary Application, Summary Cause and Small Claim Rules) Amendment (Miscellaneous) 2003 (SSI 2003/26), para.2(9) (effective January 24, 2003).

[2] As inserted by the Act of Sederunt (Sheriff Court Rules) (Miscellaneous Amendments) 2011 (SSI 2011/193) r.15 (effective April 6, 2011).

[3] As inserted by the Act of Sederunt (Sheriff Court Rules) (Miscellaneous Amendments) 2008 (SSI 2008/223) para.3(2) (effective July 1, 2008).

(b)    under section 18 of the Act of 1985 (which relates to avoidance transactions),
made after final decree shall be made by minute in the process of the action to which the application relates.

## Part VI

## Applications Relating to Avoidance Transactions

### Form of applications

**33.53.**—(1)    An application for an order under section 18 of the Act of 1985 (which relates to avoidance transactions) by a party to an action shall be made by including in the initial writ, defences or minute, as the case may be, appropriate craves, averments and pleas-in-law.

**D1.310**

(2)    An application for an order under section 18 of the Act of 1985 after final decree in an action, shall be made by minute in the process of the action to which the application relates.

## Part VII

## Financial Provision after Overseas Divorce or Annulment

### Interpretation of this Part

**33.54.**    In this Part—

**D1.311**

"the Act of 1984" means the Matrimonial and Family Proceedings Act 1984;
"order for financial provision" has the meaning assigned in section 30(1) of the Act of 1984;
"overseas country" has the meaning assigned in section 30(1) of the Act of 1984.

### Applications for financial provision after overseas divorce or annulment

**33.55.**—[1](1)    An application under section 28 of the Act of 1984 for an order for financial provision after a divorce or annulment in an overseas country shall be made by initial writ.

**D1.312**

(2)    An application for an order in an action to which paragraph (1) applies made before final decree under—

    (a)    section 13 of the Act of 1981 (transfer of tenancy of matrimonial home),
    (b)    section 29(4) of the Act of 1984 for interim periodical allowance, or
    (c)    section 14(4) of the Act of 1985 (variation or recall of incidental order),
shall be made by motion.

(3)    An application for an order in an action to which paragraph (1) applies made after final decree under—

    (a)    section 12(4) of the Act of 1985 (variation of date or method of payment of capital sum or date of transfer of property),
    (b)    section 13(4) of the Act of 1985 (variation, recall, backdating or conversion of periodical allowance), or
    (c)    section 14(4) of the Act of 1985 (variation or recall of incidental order),
shall be made by minute in the process of the action to which the application relates.

(4)[2]    An application under—

    (a)    paragraph (5) of section 12A of the Act of 1985 (recall or variation of order in respect of a pension lump sum), or
    (b)    paragraph (7) of that section (variation of order in respect of pension lump sum to substitute trustees or managers),
shall be made by minute in the process of the action to which the application relates.

---

[1] Heading amended by SI 1996/2445 (effective November 1, 1996).
[2] Inserted by SI 1996/2445 (effective November 1, 1996).

(5) Where a minute has been lodged under paragraph (3), any party may apply by motion for an interim order pending the determination of the application.

## Part VIII

### Actions of Aliment

**Interpretation of this Part**

**D1.313**

**33.56.** In this Part, "action of aliment" means a claim for aliment under section 2(1) of the Act of 1985.

**Undefended actions of aliment**

**D1.314**

**33.57.**—(1) Where a motion for decree in absence under Chapter 7 (undefended causes) is lodged in an action of aliment, the pursuer shall, on lodging the motion, lodge all documentary evidence of the means of the parties available to him in support of the amount of aliment sought.

(2) Where the sheriff requires the appearance of parties, the sheriff clerk shall fix a hearing.

**Applications relating to aliment**

**D1.315**

**33.58.**—(1) An application for, or for variation of, an order for interim aliment in a depending action of aliment shall be made by motion.

(2) An application after final decree for the variation or recall of an order for aliment in an action of aliment shall be made by minute in the process of the action to which the application relates.

(3) A person—

    (a) to whom an obligation of aliment is owed under section 1 of the Act of 1985,

    (b) in whose favour an order for aliment while under the age of 18 years was made in an action of aliment, or

    (c) who seeks, after attaining that age, an order for aliment against the person in that action against whom the order for aliment in his favour was made,

shall apply by minute in the process of that action.

(4) An application for interim aliment pending the determination of an application under paragraph (2) or (3) shall be made by motion.

(5) Where a decree has been pronounced in an application under paragraph (2) or (3), any application for variation or recall of any such decree shall be made by minute in the process of the action to which the application relates.

**Applications relating to agreements on aliment**

**D1.316**

**33.59.**—[1](1) Subject to paragraph (2) and rule 33A.53, an application under section 7(2) of the Act of 1985 (variation or termination of agreement on aliment) shall be made by summary application.

(2) In a family action in which a crave for aliment may be made, an application under section 7(2) of the Act of 1985 shall be made by a crave in the initial writ or in defences, as the case may be.

## Part IX

### Applications for Orders under Section II of the Children (Scotland) Act 1995

**Application of this Part**

**D1.317**

**33.60.**[23] This Part applies to an application for a section 11 order in a family action other than in an action of divorce, separation or declarator of nullity of marriage.

**Form of applications**

**D1.318**

**33.61.**[4] Subject to any other provision in this Chapter, an application for a section 11 order shall be made—

    (a) by an action for a section 11 order;

    (b) by a crave in the initial writ or defences, as the case may be, in any other family action to which this Part applies; or

    (c) where the application is made by a person other than a party to an action mentioned in paragraph (a) or (b), by minute in that action.

---

[1] As amended by Act of Sederunt (Ordinary Cause Rules) Amendment (Family Law (Scotland) Act 2006 etc.) 2006, para.2 (SSI 2006/207) (effective May 4, 2006).

[2] Substituted by SI 1996/2167 (effective November 1, 1996).

[3] As amended by Act of Sederunt (Ordinary Cause Rules) Amendment (Family Law (Scotland) Act 2006 etc.) 2006, para.2 (SSI 2006/207) (effective May 4, 2006).

[4] As amended by Act of Sederunt (Family Proceedings in the Sheriff Court) 1996 (SI 1996/2167) (effective November 1, 1996).

**Defenders in action for a section 11 order**

**33.62.**[1]  In an action for a section 11 order, the pursuer shall call as a defender—

    (a)   the parents or other parent of the child in respect of whom the order is sought;

    (b)   any guardian of the child;

    (c)   any person who has treated the child as a child of his family;

    (d)   any person who in fact exercises care or control in respect of the child; and

    (e)   *[Repealed by SSI 2000/239 (effective October 2, 2000).]*

**D1.319**

**Applications relating to interim orders in depending actions**

**33.63.**[2, 3]  An application, in an action depending before the sheriff to which this Part applies, for, or for the variation or recall of, an interim residence order or an interim contact order shall be made—

    (a)   by a party to the action, by motion; or

    (b)   by a person who is not a party to the action, by minute.

**33.64.**  [Repealed by SI 1996/2167 (effective November 1, 1996).]

**D1.320**

**Applications after decree**

**33.65.**—[4](1)  An application after final decree for variation or recall of a section 11 order shall be made by minute in the process of the action to which the application relates.

(2)  Where a minute has been lodged under paragraph (1), any party may apply by motion for an interim order pending the determination of the application.

**D1.321**

**Application for leave**

**33.65A.**—[5](1)  Where leave of the court is required under section 11(3)(aa) of the Act of 1995 for the making of an application for a contact order under that section, the applicant must lodge along with the initial writ a written application in the form of a letter addressed to the sheriff clerk stating—

    (a)   the grounds on which leave is sought;

    (b)   whether or not the applicant has applied for legal aid.

(2)  Where the applicant has applied for legal aid he must also lodge along with the initial writ written confirmation from the Scottish Legal Aid Board that it has determined, under regulation 7(2)(b) of the Civil Legal Aid (Scotland) Regulations 2002, that notification of the application should be dispensed with or postponed pending the making by the sheriff of an order for intimation under paragraph (4)(b).

(3)  Subject to paragraph (4)(b), an application under paragraph (1) shall not be served or intimated to any party.

(4)  The sheriff shall consider an application under paragraph (1) without hearing the applicant and may—

    (a)   refuse the application and pronounce an interlocutor accordingly; or

    (b)   if he is minded to grant the application order the applicant—

        (i)   to intimate the application to such persons as the sheriff considers appropriate; and

        (ii)   to lodge a certificate of intimation in, as near as may be, Form G8.

(5)  If any person who receives intimation of an application under paragraph (4)(b) wishes to be heard he shall notify the sheriff clerk in writing within 14 days of receipt of intimation of the application.

(6)  On receipt of any notification under paragraph (5) the sheriff clerk shall fix a hearing and intimate the date of the hearing to the parties.

**D1.322**

---

[1]  Substituted by SI 1996/2167 (effective November 1, 1996). Clerical error corrected by SI 1996/2445 (effective November 1, 1996).

[2]  As amended by Act of Sederunt (Family Proceedings in the Sheriff Court) 1996 (SI 1996/2167) (effective November 1, 1996).

[3]  As amended by Act of Sederunt (Ordinary Cause Rules) Amendment (Family Law (Scotland) Act 2006 etc.) 2006, para.2 (SSI 2006/207) (effective May 4, 2006).

[4]  As amended by Act of Sederunt (Family Proceedings in the Sheriff Court) 1996 (SI 1996/2167) (effective November 1, 1996).

[5]  As inserted by the Act of Sederunt (Sheriff Court Rules Amendment) (Adoption and Children (Scotland) Act 2007) 2009 (SSI 2009/284) (effective September 28, 2009).

(7)    Where an application under paragraph (1) is granted, a copy of the sheriffs interlocutor must be served on the defender along with the warrant of citation.

Part X

Actions under the Matrimonial Homes (Family Protection) (Scotland) Act 1981

**Interpretation of this Part**

**D1.323**

**33.66.**    Unless the context otherwise requires, words and expressions used in this Part which are also used in the Act of 1981 have the same meaning as in that Act.

**Form of applications**

**D1.324**

**33.67.**—(1)    Subject to any other provision in this Chapter, an application for an order under the Act of 1981 shall be made—

   (a)    by an action for such an order;

   (b)    by a crave in the initial writ or in defences, as the case may be, in any other family action; or

   (c)    where the application is made by a person other than a party to any action mentioned in paragraph (a) or (b), by minute in that action.

   (2)[1]    An application under section 7(1) (dispensing with consent of non-entitled spouse to a dealing) or section 11 (application in relation to attachment) shall, unless made in a depending family action, be made by summary application.

**Defenders**

**D1.325**

**33.68.**    The applicant for an order under the Act of 1981 shall call as a defender—

   (a)    where he is seeking an order as a spouse, the other spouse;

   (b)[2]    where he is a third party making an application under section 7(1) dispensing with consent of non-entitled spouse to a dealing), or 8(1) (payment from non-entitled spouse in respect of loan), of the Act of 1981, both spouses;

   (c)    where the application is made under section 18 of the Act of 1981 (occupancy rights of cohabiting couples), or is one to which that section applies, the other partner; and

   (d)[3]    where the application is made under section 18A of the Act of 1981 (application for domestic interdict), the other partner.

**Applications by motion**

**D1.326**

**33.69.**—(1)    An application under any of the following provisions of the Act of 1981 shall be made by motion in the process of the depending action to which the application relates:—

   (a)    section 3(4) (interim order for regulation of rights of occupancy, etc.);

   (b)    section 4(6) (interim order suspending occupancy rights);

   (c)    section 7(1) (dispensing with consent of non-entitled spouse to a dealing);

   (d)    [Omitted by Act of Sederunt (Ordinary Cause Rules) Amendment (Family Law (Scotland) Act 2006 etc.) 2006, para.2 (SSI 2006/207) (effective May 4, 2006).]; and

   (e)    the proviso to section 18(1) (extension of period of occupancy rights).

   (2)    Intimation of a motion under paragraph (1) shall be given—

   (a)    to the other spouse or partner, as the case may be;

   (b)    where the motion is under paragraph (1)(a), (b) or (e) and the entitled spouse or partner is a tenant or occupies the matrimonial home by the permission of a third party, to the landlord or third party, as the case may be; and

   (c)    to any other person to whom intimation of the application was or is to be made by virtue of rule 33.7(1)(k) (warrant for intimation to certain persons in actions for orders under the Act of 1981) or 33.15 (order for intimation by sheriff).

**Applications by minute**

**D1.327**

**33.70.**—(1)    An application for an order under—

   (a)    section 5 of the Act of 1981 (variation and recall of orders regulating occupancy rights and of exclusion order), or

   (b)    [Omitted by Act of Sederunt (Ordinary Cause Rules) Amendment (Family Law

---

[1] As amended by the Act of Sederunt (Debt Arrangement and Attachment (Scotland) Act 2002) 2002 (SSI 2002/560), art.4, Sch.3 (effective December 30, 2002).

[2] As amended by Act of Sederunt (Ordinary Cause Rules) Amendment (Family Law (Scotland) Act 2006 etc.) 2006, para.2 (SSI 2006/207) (effective May 4, 2006).

[3] Inserted by Act of Sederunt (Ordinary Cause Rules) Amendment (Family Law (Scotland) Act 2006 etc.) 2006, para.2 (SSI 2006/207) (effective May 4, 2006).

(Scotland) Act 2006 etc.) 2006, para.2 (SSI 2006/207) (effective May 4, 2006).]
shall be made by minute.

(2)   A minute under paragraph (1) shall be intimated—

     (a)    to the other spouse or partner, as the case may be;

     (b)    where the entitled spouse or partner is a tenant or occupies the matrimonial home by the permission of a third party, to the landlord or third party, as the case may be; and

     (c)    to any other person to whom intimation of the application was or is to be made by virtue of rule 33.7(1)(k) (warrant for intimation to certain persons in actions for orders under the Act of 1981) or 33.15 (order for intimation by sheriff).

### Sist of actions to enforce occupancy rights

**33.71.**   Unless the sheriff otherwise directs, the sist of an action by virtue of section 7(4) of the Act of 1981 (where action raised by non-entitled spouse to enforce occupancy rights) shall apply only to such part of the action as relates to the enforcement of occupancy rights by a non-entitled spouse.

D1.328

### Certificates of delivery of documents to chief constable

**33.72.**   [Omitted by Act of Sederunt (Ordinary Cause Rules) Amendment (Family Law (Scotland) Act 2006 etc.) 2006, para.2 (SSI 2006/207) (effective May 4, 2006).]

Part XI

Simplified Divorce Applications

### Application and interpretation of this Part

**33.73.**—(1)[1]   This Part applies to an application for divorce by a party to a marriage made in the manner prescribed in rule 33.74 (form of applications) if, but only if—

D1.329

     (a)    that party relies on the facts set out in section 1(2)(d) (no cohabitation for one year with consent of defender to decree), or section 1(2)(e) (no cohabitation for two years), or section 1(1)(b) (issue of interim gender recognition certificate) of the Act of 1976;

     (b)    in an application under section 1(2)(d) of the Act of 1976, the other party consents to decree of divorce being granted;

     (c)    no other proceedings are pending in any court which could have the effect of bringing the marriage to an end;

     (d)    there are no children of the marriage under the age of 16 years;

     (e)    neither party to the marriage applies for an order for financial provision on divorce;

     (f)    neither party to the marriage suffers from mental disorder; and

     (g)[2]    neither party to the marriage applies for postponement of decree under section 3A of the Act of 1976 (postponement of decree where impediment to religious marriage exists).

(2)   If an application ceases to be one to which this Part applies at any time before final decree, it shall be deemed to be abandoned and shall be dismissed.

(3)   In this Part "simplified divorce application" means an application mentioned in paragraph (1).

### Form of applications

**33.74.**—[3](1)[4]   A simplified divorce application in which the facts set out in section 1(2)(d) of the Act of 1976 (no cohabitation for one year with consent of defender to decree) are relied on shall be made in Form F31 and shall only be of effect if—

D1.330

     (a)    it is signed by the applicant; and

     (b)    the form of consent in Part 2 of Form F31 is signed by the party to the marriage giving consent.

(2)   A simplified divorce application in which the facts set out in section 1(2)(e) of the Act of 1976 (no cohabitation for two years) are relied on shall be made in Form F33 and shall only be of effect if it is signed by the applicant.

---

[1] As amended by Act of Sederunt (Ordinary Cause Rules) Amendment (Family Law (Scotland) Act 2006 etc.) 2006, para.2 (SSI 2006/207) (effective May 4, 2006).

[2] Inserted by Act of Sederunt (Ordinary Cause Rules) Amendment (Family Law (Scotland) Act 2006 etc.) 2006, para.2 (SSI 2006/207) (effective May 4, 2006) and substituted by the Act of Sederunt (Ordinary Cause, Summary Application, Summary Cause and Small Claim Rules) Amendment (Miscellaneous) 2007 (SSI 2007/6), para.2(15) (effective February 26, 2007).

[3] —As amended by Act of Sederunt (Ordinary Cause Rules) Amendment (Family Law (Scotland) Act 2006 etc.) 2006, para.2 (SSI 2006/207) (effective May 4, 2006).

[4] As amended by Act of Sederunt (Sheriff Court Ordinary Cause Rules Amendment) (Miscellaneous) 1996 (SI 1996/2445) (effective November 1, 1996) (clerical error).

(3)[1]   A simplified divorce application in which the facts set out in section 1(1)(b) of the Act of 1976 (grounds of divorce: interim gender recognition certificate) are relied on shall be made in Form F33A and shall only be of effect if signed by the applicant.

**Lodging of applications**

**D1.331**

**33.75.**[2]   The applicant shall send a simplified divorce application to the sheriff clerk with—
  (a)   an extract or certified copy of the marriage certificate;
  (b)   the appropriate fee; and
  (c)[3]   in an application under section 1(1)(b) of the Act of 1976 (grounds of divorce: interim gender recognition certificate), the interim gender recognition certificate or a certified copy within the meaning of rule 33.9A(3).

**Citation and intimation**

**D1.332**

**33.76.**—(1)   This rule is subject to rule 33.77 (citation where address not known).
  (2)   It shall be the duty of the sheriff clerk to cite any person or intimate any document in connection with a simplified divorce application.
  (3)   The form of citation—
  (a)[4]   in an application relying on the facts in section 1(2)(d) of the Act of 1976 shall be in Form F34;
  (b)   in an application relying on the facts in section 1(2)(e) of the Act of 1976 shall be in Form F35; and
  (c)[5]   in an application relying on the facts in section 1(1)(b) of the Act of 1976 shall be in Form F35A.
  (4)[6]   The citation or intimation required by paragraph (2) shall be made—
  (a)   by the sheriff clerk by registered post or the first class recorded delivery service in accordance with rule 5.3 (postal service or intimation);
  (b)[7]   on payment of an additional fee, by a sheriff officer in accordance with rule 5.4(1) to (4) (service within Scotland by sheriff officer); or
  (c)   where necessary, by the sheriff clerk in accordance with rule 5.5 (service on persons furth of Scotland).
  (5)[8]   Where citation or intimation is made in accordance with paragraph (4)(c), the translation into an official language of the country in which service is to be executed required by rule 5.5(6) shall be provided by the party lodging the simplified divorce application.

**Citation where address not known**

**D1.333**

**33.77.**—(1)[9]   In a simplified divorce application in which the facts in section 1(2)(e) of the Act of 1976 (no cohabitation for two years) or section 1(1)(b) of the Act of 1976 (grounds of divorce: issue of interim gender recognition certificate) are relied on and the address of the other party to the marriage is not known and cannot reasonably be ascertained—
  (a)   citation shall be executed by displaying a copy of the application and a notice in Form F36 on the walls of court on a period of notice of 21 days; and
  (b)   intimation shall be made to—
    (i)   every child of the marriage between the parties who has reached the age of 16 years, and

---

[1] Inserted by Act of Sederunt (Ordinary Cause Rules) Amendment (Family Law (Scotland) Act etc.) 2006, para.2 (SSI 2006/207) (effective May 4, 2006).
[2] As amended by Act of Sederunt (Ordinary Cause Rules) Amendment (Family Law (Scotland) Act 2006 etc.) 2006, para.2 (SSI 2006/207) (effective May 4, 2006).
[3] Inserted by Act of Sederunt (Ordinary Cause Rules) Amendment (Family Law (Scotland) Act 2006 etc.) 2006, para.2 (SSI 2006/207) (effective May 4, 2006).
[4] As amended by Act of Sederunt (Ordinary Cause Rules) Amendment (Family Law (Scotland) Act 2006 etc.) 2006, para.2 (SSI 2006/207) (effective May 4, 2006).
[5] Inserted by Act of Sederunt (Ordinary Cause Rules) Amendment (Family Law (Scotland) Act 2006 etc.) 2006, para.2 (SSI 2006/207) (effective May 4, 2006).
[6] Substituted by SSI 2000/239 (effective October 2, 2000).
[7] As substituted by the Act of Sederunt (Sheriff Court Rules) (Miscellaneous Amendments) 2010 (SSI 2010/279) r.2 (effective July 29, 2010).
[8] Inserted by SSI 2000/239 (effective October 2, 2000).
[9] As amended by Act of Sederunt (Ordinary Cause Rules) Amendment (Family Law (Scotland) Act 2006 etc.) 2006, para.2 (SSI 2006/207) (effective May 4, 2006).

(ii) one of the next of kin of the other party to the marriage who has reached that age, unless the address of such person is not known and cannot reasonably be ascertained.

(2) Intimation to a person referred to in paragraph (1)(b) shall be given by intimating a copy of the application and a notice of intimation in Form F37.

### Opposition to applications

**33.78.**—(1) Any person on whom service or intimation of a simplified divorce application has been made may give notice by letter sent to the sheriff clerk that he challenges the jurisdiction of the court or opposes the grant of decree of divorce and giving the reasons for his opposition to the application.

(2) Where opposition to a simplified divorce application is made under paragraph (1), the sheriff shall dismiss the application unless he is satisfied that the reasons given for the opposition are frivolous.

(3) The sheriff clerk shall intimate the decision under paragraph (2) to the applicant and the respondent.

(4) The sending of a letter under paragraph (1) shall not imply acceptance of the jurisdiction of the court.

**D1.334**

### Evidence

**33.79.** Parole evidence shall not be given in a simplified divorce application.

**D1.335**

### Decree

**33.80.**—(1) The sheriff may grant decree in terms of the simplified divorce application on the expiry of the period of notice if such application has been properly served provided that, when the application has been served in a country to which the Hague Convention on the Service Abroad of Judicial and Extra-Judicial Documents in Civil and Commercial Matters dated November 15, 1965 applies, decree shall not be granted until it is established to the satisfaction of the sheriff that the requirements of Article 15 of that Convention have been complied with.

(2) The sheriff clerk shall, not sooner than 14 days after the granting of decree in terms of paragraph (1), issue to each party to the marriage an extract of the decree of divorce in Form F38.

**D1.336**

### Appeals

**33.81.** Any appeal against an interlocutor granting decree of divorce under rule 33.80 (decree) may be made, within 14 days after the date of decree, by sending a letter to the court giving reasons for the appeal.

**D1.337**

### Applications after decree

**33.82.** Any application to the court after decree of divorce has been granted in a simplified divorce application which could have been made if it had been made in an action of divorce shall be made by minute.

**D1.338**

Part XII

Variation of Court of Session Decrees

### Application and interpretation of this Part

**33.83.**—(1) This Part applies to an application to the sheriff for variation or recall of any order to which section 8 of the Act of 1966 (variation of certain Court of Session orders) applies.

(2) In this Part, the "Act of 1966" means the Law Reform (Miscellaneous Provisions) (Scotland) Act 1966.

**D1.339**

### Form of application and intimation to Court of Session

**33.84.**—(1) An application to which this Part applies shall be made by initial writ.

(2) In such an application there shall be lodged with the initial writ a copy of the interlocutor, certified by a clerk of the Court of Session, which it is sought to vary.

(3) Before lodging the initial writ, a copy of the initial writ certified by the pursuer or his solicitor shall be lodged, or sent by first class recorded delivery post to the Deputy Principal Clerk of Session to be lodged in the process of the cause in the Court of Session in which the original order was made.

(4) The pursuer or his solicitor shall attach a certificate to the initial writ stating that paragraph (3) has been complied with.

(5)[1] The sheriff may, on cause shown, prorogate the time for lodging the certified copy of the interlocutor required under paragraph (2).

**D1.340**

---

[1] As amended by Act of Sederunt (Sheriff Court Ordinary Cause Rules Amendment) (Miscellaneous) 1996 (SI 1996/2445) (effective November 1, 1996) (clerical error).

**Defended actions**

D1.341

33.85.—(1) Where a notice of intention to defend has been lodged and no request is made under rule 33.87 (remit of application to Court of Session), the pursuer shall within 14 days after the date of the lodging of a notice of intention to defend or within such other period as the sheriff may order, lodge in process the following documents (or copies) from the process in the cause in the Court of Session in which the original order was made:—

    (a)   the pleadings;

    (b)   the interlocutor sheets;

    (c)   any opinion of the court; and

    (d)   any productions on which he seeks to found.

(2) The sheriff may, on the joint motion of parties made at any time after the lodging of the documents mentioned in paragraph (1)—

    (a)   dispense with proof;

    (b)   whether defences have been lodged or not, hear the parties; and

    (c)   thereafter, grant decree or otherwise dispose of the cause as he thinks fit.

**Transmission of process to Court of Session**

D1.342

33.86.—(1) Where decree has been granted or the cause otherwise disposed of—

    (a)   and the period for marking an appeal has elapsed without an appeal being marked, or

    (b)   after the determination of the cause on any appeal,

the sheriff clerk shall transmit to the Court of Session the sheriff court process and the documents from the process of the cause in the Court of Session which have been lodged in the sheriff court process.

(2) A sheriff court process transmitted under paragraph (1) shall form part of the process of the cause in the Court of Session in which the original order was made.

**Remit of application to Court of Session**

D1.343

33.87.—(1) A request for a remit to the Court of Session under section 8(3) of the Act of 1966 shall be made by motion.

(2) The sheriff shall, in respect of any such motion, order that the cause be remitted to the Court of Session; and, within 4 days after the date of such order, the sheriff clerk shall transmit the whole sheriff court process to the Court of Session.

(3) A cause remitted to the Court of Session under paragraph (2) shall form part of the process of the cause in the Court of Session in which the original order was made.

Part XIII

Child Support Act 1991

**Interpretation of this Part**

D1.344

33.88.[1] In this Part—

"the Act of 1991" means the Child Support Act 1991;

"child" has the meaning assigned in section 55 of the Act of 1991;

"maintenance calculation" has the meaning assigned in section 54 of the Act of 1991.

**Restriction of expenses**

D1.345

33.89. Where the Secretary of State is named as a defender in an action for declarator of non-parentage or illegitimacy, and the Secretary of State does not defend the action, no expenses shall be awarded against the Secretary of State.

**Effect of maintenance calculations**

D1.346

33.90.—(1)[2] The sheriff clerk shall, on receiving notification that a maintenance calculation has been made, cancelled or has ceased to have effect so as to affect an order of a kind prescribed for the purposes of section 10 of the Act of 1991, endorse on the interlocutor sheet relating to that order a certificate, in Form F39 or F40, as the case may be.

---

[1] As amended by SI 1996/2445 (effective November 1, 1996) and the Act of Sederunt (Ordinary Cause, Summary Application, Summary Cause and Small Claim Rules) Amendment (Miscellaneous) 2003 (SSI 2003/26), para.2(10) (effective January 24, 2003).

[2] As amended by the Act of Sederunt (Ordinary Cause, Summary Application, Summary Cause and Small Claim Rules) Amendment (Miscellaneous) 2003 (SSI 2003/26), para.2(11) (effective January 24, 2003).

**Effect of maintenance calculations on extracts relating to aliment**

**33.91.**—(1)[1]  Where an order relating to aliment is affected by a maintenance calculation, any extract of that order issued by the sheriff clerk shall be endorsed with the following certificate:—

**D1.347**

"A maintenance calculation having been made under the Child Support Act 1991 on (*insert date*), this order, in so far as it relates to the making or securing of periodical payments to or for the benefit of (*insert name(s) of child/children*), ceases to have effect from (*insert date 2 days after the date on which the maintenance calculation was made*)."

(2)  Where an order relating to aliment has ceased to have effect on the making of a maintenance calculation, and that maintenance calculation is later cancelled or ceases to have effect, any extract of that order issued by the sheriff clerk shall be endorsed also with the following certificate:—

"The jurisdiction of the child support officer under the Child Support Act 1991 having terminated on (*insert date*), this order, in so far as it relates to (*insert name(s) of child/children*), again shall have effect as from (*insert date of termination of child support officer's jurisdiction*).".

**Applications to recall or vary an interdict**

**33.91A.**[2]  An application under section 32L(11)(b) of the Act of 1991 (orders preventing avoidance) for the variation or recall of an order for interdict is to be made by minute in the process of the action to which the application relates.

**D1.348**

Part XIV

Referrals to Principal Reporter

**33.92.–33.94.**  *[Repealed by the Act of Sederunt (Children's Hearings (Scotland) Act 2011) (Miscellaneous Amendments) 2013 (SI 2013/172) para.5 (effective June 24, 2013).]*

Part XV

Management of Money Payable to Children

**33.95.**  Where the sheriff has made an order under section 13 of the Act of 1995 (awards of damages to children), an application by a person for an order by virtue of section 11(1)(d) of that Act (administration of child's property) may be made in the process of the cause in which the order under section 13 of that Act was made.

**D1.349**

Part XVI[3]

Action of Declarator of Recognition or Non-recognition of a Foreign Decree

**Action of declarator in relation to certain foreign decrees**

**33.96.**—(1)  This rule applies to an action for declarator of recognition, or non-recognition, of a decree of divorce, nullity or separation granted outwith a member state of the European Union.

**D1.350**

(2)  In an action to which this rule applies, the pursuer shall state in the condescendence of the initial writ—

    (a)    the court, tribunal or other authority which granted the decree;

    (b)    the date of the decree of divorce, annulment or separation to which the action relates;

    (c)    the date and place of the marriage to which the decree of divorce, nullity or separation relates;

    (d)    the basis on which the court has jurisdiction to entertain the action;

    (e)    whether to the pursuer's knowledge any other proceedings whether in Scotland or in any other country are continuing in respect of the marriage to which the action relates or are capable of affecting its validity or subsistence; and

    (f)    where such proceedings are continuing—

        (i)    the court, tribunal or authority before which the proceedings have been commenced;

        (ii)    the date of commencement;

---

[1] As amended by the Act of Sederunt (Ordinary Cause, Summary Application, Summary Cause and Small Claim Rules) Amendment (Miscellaneous) 2003 (SSI 2003/26), para.2(12) (effective January 24, 2003).

[2] As inserted by the Act of Sederunt (Ordinary Cause Rules) Amendment (Child Maintenance and Other Payments Act 2008) 2010 (SSI 2010/120) r.2 (effective April 6, 2010).

[3] As inserted by the Act of Sederunt (Sheriff Court Rules) (Miscellaneous Amendments) (No.2) 2010 (SSI 2010/416) r.8 (effective January 1, 2011).

      (iii)    the names of the parties; and

      (iv)    the date, or expected date of any proof (or its equivalent), in the proceedings.

(3)   Where—

    (a)   such proceedings are continuing;

    (b)   the action before the sheriff is defended; and

    (c)   either—

      (i)    the initial writ does not contain the statement referred to in paragraph (2)(e), or

      (ii)   the particulars mentioned in paragraph (2)(f) as set out in the initial writ are incomplete or incorrect,

any defences or minute, as the case may be, lodged by any person to the action shall include that statement and, where appropriate, the further or correct particulars mentioned in paragraph (2)(f).

(4)   Unless the sheriff otherwise directs, a declarator of recognition, or non-recognition, of a decree under this rule shall not be granted without there being produced with the initial writ—

    (a)   the decree in question or a certified copy of the decree;

    (b)   the marriage extract or equivalent document to which the action relates.

(5)   Where a document produced under paragraph (4)(a) or (b) is not in English it shall, unless the sheriff otherwise directs, be accompanied by a translation certified by a notary public or authenticated by affidavit.

(6)   For the purposes of this rule, proceedings are continuing at any time after they have commenced and before they are finally disposed of.

CHAPTER 33A[1]

CIVIL PARTNERSHIP ACTIONS

Part I

General Provisions

**Interpretation of this Chapter**

**D1.351**

**33A.1.**—(1)   In this Chapter, "civil partnership action" means—

    (a)   an action of dissolution of civil partnership;

    (b)   an action of separation of civil partners;

    (c)   an action or application for an order under Chapter 3 or Chapter 4 of Part 3 of the Act of 2004;

    (d)   an application for a declarator or other order under section 127 of the Act of 2004;

    (e)   an action or application for financial provision after overseas proceedings as provided for in Schedule 11 to the Act of 2004;

    (f)[2]  an action for declarator of nullity of civil partnership.

(2)   In this Chapter, unless the context otherwise requires—

"the Act of 1985" means the Family Law (Scotland) Act 1985;

"the Act of 1995" means the Children (Scotland) Act 1995;

"the Act of 2004" means the Civil Partnership Act 2004;

"civil partnership" has the meaning assigned in section 1(1) of the Act of 2004;

"contact order" has the meaning assigned in section 11(2)(d) of the Act of 1995;

"Gender Recognition Panel" is to be construed in accordance with Schedule 1 to the Gender Recognition Act 2004;

"interim gender recognition certificate" means the certificate issued under section 4 of the Gender Recognition Act 2004;

"local authority" means a council constituted under section 2 of the Local Government etc. (Scotland) Act 1994;

"mental disorder" has the meaning assigned in section 328 of the Mental Health (Care and Treatment) (Scotland) Act 2003;

"order for financial provision" means, except in Part VII of this Chapter (financial provision after overseas proceedings as provided for in Schedule 11 to the Act of 2004), an order mentioned in section 8(1) of the Act of 1985;

"parental responsibilities" has the meaning assigned in section 1(3) of the Act of 1995;

---

[1] Inserted by Act of Sederunt (Ordinary Cause Rules) Amendment (Civil Partnership Act 2004) 2005 (SSI 2005/638), para.2 (effective December 8, 2005).

[2] Inserted by Act of Sederunt (Ordinary Cause Rules) Amendment (Family Law (Scotland) Act 2006 etc.) 2006, para.2 (SSI 2006/207) (effective May 4, 2006).

"parental rights" has the meaning assigned in section 2(4) of the Act of 1995;

"relevant interdict" has the meaning assigned in section 113(2) of the Act of 2004;

"residence order" has the meaning assigned in section 11(2)(c) of the Act of 1995;

"section 11 order" means an order under section 11 of the Act of 1995.

(3)　For the purposes of rules 33A.2 (averments in actions of dissolution of civil partnership or separation of civil partners about other proceedings) and 33A.3 (averments where section 11 order sought) and, in relation to proceedings in another jurisdiction, Part XIII of this Chapter (sisting of civil partnership actions in Scotland), proceedings are continuing at any time after they have commenced and before they are finally disposed of.

**Averments in certain civil partnership actions about other proceedings**[1]

**33A.2.**—(1)[2]　This rule applies to an action of dissolution or declarator of nullity of civil partnership or separation of civil partners.

**D1.352**

(2)　In an action to which this rule applies, the pursuer shall state in the condescendence of the initial writ—

(a)　whether to his knowledge any proceedings are continuing in Scotland or in any other country in respect of the civil partnership to which the initial writ relates or are capable of affecting its validity or subsistence; and

(b)　where such proceedings are continuing—

(i)　the court, tribunal or authority before which the proceedings have been commenced;

(ii)　the date of commencement;

(iii)　the names of the parties;

(iv)　the date, or expected date of any proof (or its equivalent) in the proceedings; and

(v)　such other facts as may be relevant to the question of whether or not the action before the sheriff should be sisted under Part XIII of this Chapter.

(3)　Where—

(a)　such proceedings are continuing;

(b)　the action before the sheriff is defended; and

(c)　either—

(i)　the initial writ does not contain the statement referred to in paragraph (2)(a); or

(ii)　the particulars mentioned in paragraph (2)(b) as set out in the initial writ are incomplete or incorrect,

any defences or minute, as the case may be, lodged by any person to the action shall include that statement and, where appropriate, the further or correct particulars mentioned in paragraph (2)(b).

**Averments where section 11 order sought**

**33A.3.**—(1)　A party to a civil partnership action who makes an application in that action for a section 11 order in respect of a child shall include in his pleadings—

**D1.353**

(a)[3]　where that action is an action of dissolution or declarator of nullity of civil partnership or separation of civil partners, averments giving particulars of any other proceedings known to him, whether in Scotland or elsewhere and whether concluded or not, which relate to the child in respect of whom the section 11 order is sought;

(b)　(b) in any other civil partnership action—

(i)　the averments mentioned in paragraph (a); and

(ii)　averments giving particulars of any proceedings known to him which are continuing, whether in Scotland or elsewhere, and which relate to the civil partnership of either of the parents of that child.

(c)[4]　where the party seeks an order such as is mentioned in any of paragraphs (a) to (e) of subsection (2) of that section, an averment that no permanence order (as defined in section 80(2) of the Adoption and Children (Scotland) Act 2007) is in force in respect of the child.

(2)　Where such other proceedings are continuing or have taken place and the averments of the applicant for such a section 11 order—

---

[1] As amended by Act of Sederunt (Ordinary Cause Rules) Amendment (Family Law (Scotland) Act 2006 etc.) 2006, para.2 (SSI 2006/207) (effective May 4, 2006).

[2] As amended by Act of Sederunt (Ordinary Cause Rules) Amendment (Family Law (Scotland) Act 2006 etc.) 2006, para.2 (SSI 2006/207) (effective May 4, 2006).

[3] As amended by Act of Sederunt (Ordinary Cause Rules) Amendment (Family Law (Scotland) Act 2006 etc.) 2006, para.2 (SSI 2006/207) (effective May 4, 2006).

[4] As inserted by the Act of Sederunt (Sheriff Court Rules Amendment) (Adoption and Children (Scotland) Act 2007) 2009 (SSI 2009/284) (effective September 28, 2009).

(a)    do not contain particulars of the other proceedings, or

(b)    contain particulars which are incomplete or incorrect,

any defences or minute, as the case may be, lodged by any party to the civil partnership action shall include such particulars or such further or correct particulars as are known to him.

(3)    In paragraph 1(b)(ii), "child" includes a child of the family within the meaning assigned in section 101(7) of the Act of 2004.

### Averments where identity or address of person not known

**D1.354**

**33A.4.**    In a civil partnership action, where the identity or address of any person referred to in rule 33A.7 as a person in respect of whom a warrant for intimation requires to be applied for is not known and cannot reasonably be ascertained, the party required to apply for the warrant shall include in his pleadings an averment of that fact and averments setting out what steps have been taken to ascertain the identity or address, as the case may be, of that person.

### Averments about maintenance orders

**D1.355**

**33A.5.**    In a civil partnership action in which an order for aliment or periodical allowance is sought, or is sought to be varied or recalled, by any party, the pleadings of that party shall contain an averment stating whether and, if so, when and by whom, a maintenance order (within the meaning of section 106 of the Debtors (Scotland) Act 1987) has been granted in favour of or against that party or of any other person in respect of whom the order is sought.

### Averments where aliment or financial provision sought

**D1.356**

**33A.6.**—(1)    In this rule—

"the Act of 1991" means the Child Support Act 1991;
"child" has the meaning assigned in section 55 of the Act of 1991;
"crave relating to aliment" means—

(a)    for the purposes of paragraph (2), a crave for decree of aliment in relation to a child or for recall or variation of such a decree; and

(b)    for the purposes of paragraph (3), a crave for decree of aliment in relation to a child or for recall or variation of such a decree or for the variation or termination of an agreement on aliment in relation to a child;

"maintenance calculation" has the meaning assigned in section 54 of the Act of 1991.

(2)    A civil partnership action containing a crave relating to aliment and to which section 8(6), (7), (8), or (10) of the Act of 1991 (top up maintenance orders) applies shall—

(a)    include averments stating, where appropriate—

(i)    that a maintenance calculation under section 11 of that Act (maintenance calculations) is in force;

(ii)    the date of the maintenance calculation;

(iii)    the amount and frequency of periodical payments of child support maintenance fixed by the maintenance calculation; and

(iv)    the grounds on which the sheriff retains jurisdiction under section 8(6), (7), (8) or (10) of that Act; and

(b)    unless the sheriff on cause shown otherwise directs, be accompanied by any document issued by the Secretary of State to the party intimating the making of the maintenance calculation referred to in sub paragraph (a).

(3)    A civil partnership action containing a crave relating to aliment, and to which section 8(6), (7), (8) or (10) of the Act of 1991 does not apply, shall include averments stating—

(a)    that the habitual residence of the absent parent, person with care or qualifying child, within the meaning of section 3 of that Act, is furth of the United Kingdom; or

(b)    that the child is not a child within the meaning of section 55 of that Act.

(4)    A civil partnership action involving parties in respect of whom a decision has been made in any application, review or appeal under the Act of 1991 relating to any child of those parties, shall—

(a)    include averments stating that such a decision has been made and giving details of that decision; and

(b)    unless the sheriff on cause shown otherwise directs, be accompanied by any document issued by the Secretary of State to the parties intimating that decision.

**Warrants and forms for intimation**

33A.7.—(1)  Subject to paragraphs (5) and (7), in the initial writ in a civil partnership action, the pursuer shall include a crave for a warrant for intimation—

**D1.357**

(a)  in an action where the address of the defender is not known to the pursuer and cannot reasonably be ascertained, to—

    (i)  every person who was a child of the family (within the meaning of section 101(7) of the Act of 2004) and who has reached the age of 16 years, and

    (ii)  one of the next of kin of the defender who has reached that age,

unless the address of such a person is not known to the pursuer and cannot reasonably be ascertained, and a notice of intimation in Form CP1 shall be attached to the copy of the initial writ intimated to any such person;

(b)  in an action where the defender is a person who is suffering from a mental disorder, to—

    (i)  those persons mentioned in sub paragraph (a)(i) and (ii), unless the address of such person is not known to the pursuer and cannot reasonably be ascertained; and

    (ii)  any person who holds the office of guardian, or continuing or welfare attorney to the defender under or by virtue of the Adults with Incapacity (Scotland) Act 2000,

and a notice of intimation in Form CP2 shall be attached to the copy of the initial writ intimated to any such person;

(c)[1]  in an action of dissolution or declarator of nullity of civil partnership or separation of civil partners where the sheriff may make a section 11 order in respect of a child—

    (i)  who is in the care of a local authority, to that authority and a notice of intimation in Form CP3 shall be attached to the initial writ intimated to that authority;

    (ii)  who, being a child of one party to the civil partnership, has been accepted as a child of the family by the other party to the civil partnership and who is liable to be maintained by a third party, to that third party, and a notice of intimation in Form CP3 shall be attached to the initial writ intimated to that third party; or

    (iii)  in respect of whom a third party in fact exercises care or control, to that third party, and a notice of intimation in Form CP4 shall be attached to the initial writ intimated to that third party;

(d)  in an action where the pursuer craves a section 11 order, to any parent or guardian of the child who is not a party to the action, and a notice of intimation in Form CP5 shall be attached to the initial writ intimated to any such parent or guardian;

(e)  [Repealed by the Act of Sederunt (Sheriff Court Rules) (Miscellaneous Amendments) (No.2) 2010 (SSI 2010/416) r.7 (effective January 1, 2011).]

(f)  in an action which includes a crave for a section 11 order, to the child to whom such an order would relate if not a party to the action, and a notice of intimation in Form CP7 shall be intimated to that child;

(g)  in an action where the pursuer makes an application for an order under section 8(aa) of the Act of 1985 (transfer of property) and—

    (i)  the consent of a third party to such a transfer is necessary by virtue of an obligation, enactment or rule of law, or

    (ii)  the property is subject to a security,

to the third party or creditor, as the case may be, and a notice of intimation in Form CP8 shall be attached to the initial writ intimated to any such person;

(h)  in an action where the pursuer makes an application for an order under section 18 of the Act of 1985 (which relates to avoidance transactions), to—

    (i)  any third party in whose favour the transfer of, or transaction involving, the property is to be or was made, and

    (ii)  any other person having an interest in the transfer of, or transaction involving, the property,

and a notice of intimation in Form CP9 shall be attached to the initial writ intimated to any such person;

(i)  in an action where the pursuer makes an application for an order under Chapter 3 of Part 3 of the Act of 2004, where the application is under section 102(e), 102(4)(a), 103(1), 103(2), 104, 107 or 112 of that Act, and the entitled civil partner is a tenant or occupies the family home by permission of a third party, to the landlord or the third party, as the case may be and a notice of intimation in Form CP10 shall be attached to the initial writ intimated to any such person;

---

[1]  As amended by Act of Sederunt (Ordinary Cause Rules) Amendment (Family Law (Scotland) Act 2006 etc.) 2006, para.2 (SSI 2006/207) (effective May 4, 2006).

(j)  in an action where the pursuer makes an application for an order under section 8(ba) of the Act of 1985 (orders under section 12A of the Act of 1985 for pension lump sum), to the person responsible for the pension arrangement, and a notice of intimation in Form CP11 shall be attached to the initial writ intimated to any such person;

(k)  in an action where a pursuer makes an application for an order under section 8(baa) of the Act of 1985 (pension sharing orders), to the person responsible for the pension arrangement and a notice of intimation in Form CP12 shall be attached to the initial writ intimated to any such person.

(l)[1]  in an action where a pursuer makes an application for an order under section 8(1)(bab) of the Act of 1985 (pension compensation sharing order), to the Board of the Pension Protection Fund, and a notice of intimation in Form CP12A shall be attached to the initial writ intimated to that Board; and

(m)[2]  in an action where a pursuer makes an application for an order under section 8(1)(bb) of the Act of 1985 (an order under section 12B(2) of the Act of 1985 for pension compensation), to the Board of the Pension Protection Fund and a notice of intimation in Form CP12B shall be attached to the initial writ intimated to that Board.

(2)  Expressions used in paragraph (1)(i) which are also used in Chapter 3 of Part 3 of the Act of 2004 have the same meaning as in that Chapter.

(3)  A notice of intimation under paragraph (1) shall be on a period of notice of 21 days unless the sheriff otherwise orders; but the sheriff shall not order a period of notice of less than 2 days.

(4)  *[Repealed by the Act of Sederunt (Sheriff Court Rules) (Miscellaneous Amendments) (No.2) 2010 (SSI 2010/416) r.7 (effective January 1, 2011).]*

(5)  Where the address of a person mentioned in paragraph (1)(c), (d), (f), (g), (h), (i), (j) or (k) is not known and cannot reasonably be ascertained, the pursuer shall include a crave in the initial writ to dispense with intimation; and the sheriff may grant that crave or make such other order as he thinks fit.

(6)  Where the identity or address of a person to whom intimation of a civil partnership action is required becomes known during the course of the action, the party who would have been required to insert a warrant for intimation to that person shall lodge a motion for a warrant for intimation to that person or to dispense with such intimation.

(7)  Where a pursuer considers that to order intimation to a child under paragraph (1)(f) is inappropriate, he shall—

(a)  include a crave in the initial writ to dispense with intimation to that child; and

(b)  include in the initial writ averments setting out the reasons why such intimation is inappropriate;

and the sheriff may dispense with such intimation or make such other order as he thinks fit.

**Intimation where alleged association**

**D1.358**

33A.8.—(1)  In a civil partnership action where the pursuer founds upon an alleged association between the defender and another named person, the pursuer shall, immediately after the expiry of the period of notice, lodge a motion for an order for intimation to that person or to dispense with such intimation.

(2)  In determining a motion under paragraph (1), the sheriff may—

(a)  make such order for intimation as he thinks fit; or

(b)  dispense with intimation; and

(c)  where he dispenses with intimation, order that the name of that person be deleted from the condescendence of the initial writ.

(3)  Where intimation is ordered under paragraph (2), a copy of the initial writ and an intimation in Form CP13 shall be intimated to the named person.

(4)  In paragraph (1), "association" means sodomy, incest, or any homosexual or heterosexual relationship.

**Productions in action of dissolution of civil partnership or where a section 11 order or order for financial provision may be made[3]**

**D1.359**

33A.9.—(1)  This rule applies unless the sheriff directs otherwise.

---

[1] As inserted by the Act of Sederunt (Sheriff Court Rules) (Miscellaneous Amendments) 2011 (SSI 2011/193) r.15 (effective April 6, 2011).
[2] As inserted by the Act of Sederunt (Sheriff Court Rules) (Miscellaneous Amendments) 2011 (SSI 2011/193) r.15 (effective April 6, 2011).
[3] As amended by the Act of Sederunt (Sheriff Court Rules) (Miscellaneous Amendments) 2012 (SSI 2012/188) para.4 (effective August 1, 2012).

(2)[1]  In an action of dissolution or declarator of nullity of civil partnership, a warrant for citation shall not be granted without there being produced with the initial writ—

    (a)   an extract of the relevant entry in the civil partnership register or an equivalent document; and

    (b)   where the ground of action is that an interim gender recognition certificate has, after the date of registration of the civil partnership, been issued to either of the civil partners—

        (i)   where the pursuer is the subject of the interim gender recognition certificate, the interim gender recognition certificate or, failing that, a certified copy of the interim gender recognition certificate; or

        (ii)   where the defender is the subject of the interim gender recognition certificate, a certified copy of the interim gender recognition certificate.

(3)  In a civil partnership action which includes a crave for a section 11 order, a warrant for citation shall not be granted without there being produced with the initial writ an extract of the relevant entry in the register of births or an equivalent document.

(4)  For the purposes of this rule, a certified copy of an interim gender recognition certificate shall be a copy of that certificate sealed with the seal of the Gender Recognition Panels and certified to be a true copy by an officer authorised by the President of Gender Recognition Panels.

(5)[2]  In a civil partnership action which includes a crave for an order for financial provision, the pursuer must lodge a completed Form CP13A signed by the pursuer with the initial writ or minute of amendment as the case may be.

**Warrant of citation**

**33A.10.**  The warrant of citation in a civil partnership action shall be in Form CP14.      **D1.360**

**Form of citation and certificate**

**33A.11.**—(1)  Subject to rule 5.6 (service where address of person is not known), citation of a     **D1.361** defender shall be in Form CP15, which shall be attached to a copy of the initial writ and warrant of citation and shall have appended to it a notice of intention to defend in Form CP16.

(2)  The certificate of citation shall be in Form CP17 which shall be attached to the initial writ.

**Intimation to local authority**

**33A.12.**—(1)  In any civil partnership action where the pursuer craves a residence order in respect of     **D1.362** a child, the sheriff may, if the sheriff thinks fit, order intimation to the local authority in which area the pursuer resides; and such intimation shall be in Form CP6.

(2)  Where an order for intimation is made under paragraph (1), intimation to that local authority shall be given within 7 days after the date on which an order for intimation has been made.

**Service in cases of mental disorder of defender**

**33A.13.**—(1)  In a civil partnership action where the defender suffers or appears to suffer from     **D1.363** mental disorder and is resident in a hospital or other similar institution, citation shall be executed by registered post or the first class recorded delivery service addressed to the medical officer in charge of that hospital or institution; and there shall be included with the copy of the initial writ—

    (a)   a citation in Form CP15;

    (b)   any notice required by rule 33A.14(1);

    (c)   a request in Form CP18;

    (d)   a form of certificate in Form CP19 requesting the medical officer to—

        (i)   deliver and explain the initial writ, citation and any notice or form of notice of consent required under rule 33A.14(1) personally to the defender; or

        (ii)   certify that such delivery or explanation would be dangerous to the health or mental condition of the defender; and

    (e)   a stamped envelope addressed for return of that certificate to the pursuer or his solicitor, if he has one.

(2)  The medical officer referred to in paragraph (1) shall send the certificate in Form CP19 duly completed to the pursuer or his solicitor, as the case may be.

(3)  The certificate mentioned in paragraph (2) shall be attached to the certificate of citation.

---

[1] As amended by Act of Sederunt (Ordinary Cause Rules) Amendment (Family Law (Scotland) Act 2006 etc.) 2006, para.2 (SSI 2006/207) (effective May 4, 2006).

[2] As inserted by the Act of Sederunt (Sheriff Court Rules) (Miscellaneous Amendments) 2012 (SSI 2012/188) para.4 (effective August 1, 2012).

(4)   Where such a certificate bears that the initial writ has not been delivered to the defender, the sheriff may, at any time before decree—

    (a)   order such further medical inquiry, and

    (b)   make such order for further service or intimation,

as he thinks fit.

### Notices in certain actions of dissolution of civil partnership or separation of civil partners

**D1.364**

**33A.14.**—(1)   In the following actions of dissolution of civil partnership or separation of civil partners there shall be attached to the copy of the initial writ served on the defender—

    (a)[1]   in an action relying on section 117(3)(c) of the Act of 2004 (no cohabitation for one year with consent of defender to decree)—

        (i)   which is an action of dissolution of civil partnership, a notice in Form CP20 and a notice of consent in Form CP21;

        (ii)   which is an action of separation of civil partners, a notice in Form CP22 and a form of notice of consent in Form CP23;

    (b)[2]   in an action relying on section 117(3)(d) of the Act of 2004 (no cohabitation for two years)—

        (i)   which is an action of dissolution of civil partnership, a notice in Form CP24;

        (ii)   which is an action of separation of civil partners, a notice in Form CP25.

    (c)[3]   in an action relying on section 117(2)(b) of the Act of 2004 (grounds of dissolution: interim gender recognition certificate), a notice in Form CP25A.

(2)   The certificate of citation of an initial writ in an action mentioned in paragraph (1) shall state which notice or form mentioned in paragraph (1) has been attached to the initial writ.

### Orders for intimation

**D1.365**

**33A.15.**—(1)   In any civil partnership action, the sheriff may, at any time—

    (a)   subject to paragraph (2), order intimation to be made on such person as he thinks fit;

    (b)   postpone intimation, where he considers that such postponement is appropriate and, in that case, the sheriff shall make such order in respect of postponement of intimation as he thinks fit; or

    (c)   dispense with intimation, where he considers that such dispensation is appropriate.

(2)   Where the sheriff is considering whether to make a section 11 order by virtue of section 12 of the Act of 1995 (restrictions on decrees for dissolution of civil partnership, separation or annulment affecting children), he shall, subject to paragraph (1)(c) and without prejudice to paragraph (1)(b) of this rule, order intimation in Form CP7 to the child to whom the section 11 order would relate unless—

    (a)   intimation has been given to the child under rule 33A.7(1)(f); or

    (b)   the sheriff considers that the child is not of sufficient age or maturity to express his views.

(3)   Where a party makes a crave or averment in a civil partnership action which, had it been made in an initial writ, would have required a warrant for intimation under rule 33.7, that party shall include a crave in his writ for a warrant for intimation or to dispense with such intimation; and rule 33A.7 shall, with the necessary modifications, apply to a crave for a warrant under this paragraph as it applies to a crave for a warrant under that rule.

### Appointment of curators ad litem to defenders

**D1.366**

**33A.16.**—(1)[4, 5]   This rule applies to a civil partnership action where it appears to the court that the defender is suffering from a mental disorder.

(2)   In an action to which this rule applies, the sheriff shall—

    (a)   appoint a curator ad litem to the defender;

---

[1] As amended by Act of Sederunt (Ordinary Cause Rules) Amendment (Family Law (Scotland) Act 2006 etc.) 2006, para.2 (SSI 2006/207) (effective May 4, 2006).

[2] As amended by Act of Sederunt (Ordinary Cause Rules) Amendment (Family Law (Scotland) Act 2006 etc.) 2006, para.2 (SSI 2006/207) (effective May 4, 2006).

[3] Inserted by Act of Sederunt (Ordinary Cause Rules) Amendment (Family Law (Scotland) Act 2006 etc.) 2006, para.2 (SSI 2006/207) (effective May 4, 2006).

[4] As amended by Act of Sederunt (Ordinary Cause Rules) Amendment (Family Law (Scotland) Act 2006 etc.) 2006, para.2 (SSI 2006/207) (effective May 4, 2006).

[5] As amended by the Act of Sederunt (Sheriff Court Rules) (Miscellaneous Amendments) 2012 (SSI 2012/188) para.6 (effective August 1, 2012).

(b)[1]   where the facts set out in section 117(3)(c) of the Act of 2004 (no cohabitation for one year with consent of defender to decree) are relied on—

    (i)   make an order for intimation of the ground of the action to the Mental Welfare Commission for Scotland; and

    (ii)   include in such an order a requirement that the Commission sends to the sheriff clerk a report indicating whether in its opinion the defender is capable of deciding whether or not to give consent to the granting of decree.

(3)   Within 7 days after the appointment of a curator ad litem under paragraph (2)(a), the pursuer shall send to him—

(a)   a copy of the initial writ and any defences (including any adjustments and amendments) lodged; and

(b)   a copy of any notice in Form G5 sent to him by the sheriff clerk.

(4)   On receipt of a report required under paragraph (2)(b)(ii), the sheriff clerk shall—

(a)   lodge the report in process; and

(b)   intimate that this has been done to—

    (i)   the pursuer;

    (ii)   the solicitor for the defender, if known; and

    (iii)   the curator ad litem.

(5)   The curator ad litem shall lodge in process one of the writs mentioned in paragraph (6)—

(a)   within 14 days after the report required under paragraph (2)(b)(ii) has been lodged in process; or

(b)   where no such report is required, within 21 days after the date of his appointment under paragraph (2)(a).

(6)   The writs referred to in paragraph (5) are—

(a)   a notice of intention to defend;

(b)   defences to the action;

(c)   a minute adopting defences already lodged; and

(d)   a minute stating that the curator ad litem does not intend to lodge defences.

(7)   Notwithstanding that he has lodged a minute stating that he does not intend to lodge defences, a curator ad litem may appear at any stage of the action to protect the interests of the defender.

(8)   If, at any time, it appears to the curator ad litem that the defender is not suffering from mental disorder, he may report that fact to the court and seek his own discharge.

(9)   The pursuer shall be responsible, in the first instance, for payment of the fees and outlays of the curator ad litem incurred during the period from his appointment until—

(a)   he lodges a minute stating that he does not intend to lodge defences;

(b)   he decides to instruct the lodging of defences or a minute adopting defences already lodged; or

(c)   being satisfied after investigation that the defender is not suffering from mental disorder, he is discharged.

**Applications for sist**

**33A.17.**   An application for a sist, or the recall of a sist, under Part XIII of this Chapter shall be made by written motion.

**D1.367**

**Notices of consent to dissolution of civil partnership or separation of civil partners**

**33A.18.**—(1)[2]   Where, in an action of dissolution of civil partnership or separation of civil partners in which the facts in section 117(3)(c) of the Act of 2004 (no cohabitation for one year with consent of defender to decree) are relied on, the defender wishes to consent to the grant of decree of dissolution of civil partnership or separation of civil partners he shall do so by giving notice in writing in Form CP21 (dissolution) or Form CP23 (separation), as the case may be, to the sheriff clerk.

**D1.368**

(2)   The evidence of one witness shall be sufficient for the purpose of establishing that the signature on a notice of consent under paragraph (1) is that of the defender.

(3)   In an action of dissolution of civil partnership or separation of civil partners where the initial writ includes, for the purposes of section 117(3)(c) of the Act of 2004, an averment that the defender consents to the grant of decree, the defender may give notice by letter sent to the sheriff clerk stating that he has not so consented or that he withdraws any consent which he has already given.

---

[1] As amended by Act of Sederunt (Ordinary Cause Rules) Amendment (Family Law (Scotland) Act 2006 etc.) 2006, para.2 (SSI 2006/207) (effective May 4, 2006).

[2] As amended by Act of Sederunt (Ordinary Cause Rules) Amendment (Family Law (Scotland) Act 2006 etc.) 2006, para.2 (SSI 2006/207) (effective May 4, 2006).

(4)  On receipt of a letter under paragraph (3), the sheriff clerk shall intimate the terms of the letter to the pursuer.

(5)  On receipt of any intimation under paragraph (4), the pursuer may, within 14 days after the date of the intimation, if none of the other facts mentioned in section 117(3) of the Act of 2004 is averred in the initial writ, lodge a motion for the action to be sisted.

(6)  If no such motion is lodged, the pursuer shall be deemed to have abandoned the action and the action shall be dismissed.

(7)  If a motion under paragraph (5) is granted and the sist is not recalled or renewed within a period of 6 months from the date of the interlocutor granting the sist, the pursuer shall be deemed to have abandoned the action and the action shall be dismissed.

### Procedure in respect of children

**D1.369**

**33A.19.**—(1)  In a civil partnership action, in relation to any matter affecting a child, where that child has—

  (a)  returned to the sheriff clerk Form CP7, or

  (b)  otherwise indicated to the court a wish to express views on a matter affecting him, the sheriff shall not grant any order unless an opportunity has been given for the views of that child to be obtained or heard.

(2)  Where a child has indicated his wish to express his views, the sheriff shall order such steps to be taken as he considers appropriate to ascertain the views of that child.

(3)  The sheriff shall not grant an order in a civil partnership action, in relation to any matter affecting a child who has indicated his wish to express his views, unless due weight has been given by the sheriff to the views expressed by that child, having due regard to his age and maturity.

### Recording of views of the child

**D1.370**

**33A.20.**—(1)  This rule applies where a child expresses a view on a matter affecting him whether expressed personally to the sheriff or to a person appointed by the sheriff for that purpose or provided by the child in writing.

(2)  The sheriff, or the person appointed by the sheriff, shall record the views of the child in writing; and the sheriff may direct that such views, and any written views, given by a child shall—

  (a)  be sealed in an envelope marked "Views of the child confidential";

  (b)  be kept in the court process without being recorded in the inventory of process;

  (c)  be available to a sheriff only;

  (d)  not be opened by any person other than a sheriff; and

  (e)  not form a borrowable part of the process.

### Appointment of local authority or reporter to report on a child

**D1.371**

**33A.21.**—(1)  This rule applies where, at any stage of a civil partnership action, the sheriff appoints—

  (a)  a local authority, whether under section 11(1) of the Matrimonial Proceedings (Children) Act 1958 (reports as to arrangements for future care and upbringing of children) or otherwise, or

  (b)  another person (referred to in this rule as a "reporter"), whether under a provision mentioned in sub paragraph (a) or otherwise,

to investigate and report to the court on the circumstances of a child and on proposed arrangements for the care and upbringing of the child.

(2)  On making an appointment referred to in paragraph (1), the sheriff shall direct that the party who sought the appointment or, where the court makes the appointment of its own motion, the pursuer or minuter, as the case may be, shall—

  (a)  instruct the local authority or reporter; and

  (b)  be responsible, in the first instance, for the fees and outlays of the local authority or reporter appointed.

(3)  Where a local authority or reporter is appointed—

  (a)  the party who sought the appointment, or

  (b)  where the sheriff makes the appointment of his own motion, the pursuer or minuter, as the case may be,

shall, within 7 days after the date of the appointment, intimate the name and address of the local authority or reporter to any local authority to which intimation of the family action has been made.

(4)  On completion of a report referred to in paragraph (1), the local authority or reporter, as the case may be, shall send the report, with a copy of it for each party, to the sheriff clerk.

(5)  On receipt of such a report, the sheriff clerk shall send a copy of the report to each party.

(6)   Where a local authority or reporter has been appointed to investigate and report in respect of a child, an application for a section 11 order in respect of that child shall not be determined until the report of the local authority or reporter, as the case may be, has been lodged.

### Referral to family mediation

**33A.22.**   In any civil partnership action in which an order in relation to parental responsibilities or parental rights is in issue, the sheriff may, at any stage of the action, where he considers it appropriate to do so, refer that issue to a mediator accredited to a specified family mediation organisation.

**D1.372**

### Child Welfare Hearing

**33A.23.**—(1)   Where—

**D1.373**

(a)   on the lodging of a notice of intention to defend in a civil partnership action in which the initial writ seeks or includes a crave for a section 11 order, a defender wishes to oppose any such crave or order, or seeks the same order as that craved by the pursuer,

(b)   on the lodging of a notice of intention to defend in a civil partnership action, the defender seeks a section 11 order which is not craved by the pursuer, or

(c)   in any other circumstances in a civil partnership action, the sheriff considers that a Child Welfare Hearing should be fixed and makes an order (whether at his own instance or on the motion of a party) that such a hearing shall be fixed,

the sheriff clerk shall fix a date and time for a Child Welfare Hearing on the first suitable court date occurring not sooner than 21 days after the lodging of such notice of intention to defend, unless the sheriff directs the hearing to be held on an earlier date.

(2)   On fixing the date for the Child Welfare Hearing, the sheriff clerk shall intimate the date of the Child Welfare Hearing to the parties in Form CP26.

(3)   The fixing of the date of the Child Welfare Hearing shall not affect the right of a party to make any other application to the court whether by motion or otherwise.

(4)[1]   At the Child Welfare Hearing (which may be held in private), the sheriff shall seek to secure the expeditious resolution of disputes in relation to the child by ascertaining from the parties the matters in dispute and any information relevant to that dispute, and may—

(a)   order such steps to be taken, make such order, if any, or order further procedure, as he thinks fit, and

(b)   ascertain whether there is or is likely to be a vulnerable witness within the meaning of section 11(1) of the Act of 2004 who is to give evidence at any proof or hearing and whether any order under section 12(1) of the Act of 2004 requires to be made.

(5)   All parties (including a child who has indicated his wish to attend) shall, except on cause shown, attend the Child Welfare Hearing personally.

(6)   It shall be the duty of the parties to provide the sheriff with sufficient information to enable him to conduct the Child Welfare Hearing.

### Applications for orders to disclose whereabouts of children

**33A.24.**—(1)   An application in a civil partnership action for an order under section 33(1) of the Family Law Act 1986 (which relates to the disclosure of the whereabouts of a child) shall be made by motion.

**D1.374**

(2)   Where the sheriff makes an order under section 33(1) of the Family Law Act 1986, he may ordain the person against whom the order has been made to appear before him or to lodge an affidavit.

### Applications in relation to removal of children

**33A.25.**—(1)   An application in a civil partnership action for leave under section 51(1) of the Children Act 1975 (authority to remove a child from the care and possession of the applicant for a residence order) or for an order under section 35(3) of the Family Law Act 1986 (application for interdict or interim interdict prohibiting removal of child from jurisdiction) shall be made—

**D1.375**

(a)   by a party to the action, by motion; or

(b)   by a person who is not a party to the action, by minute.

(2)   An application under section 35(3) of the Family Law Act 1986 need not be served or intimated.

(3)   An application in a civil partnership action under section 23(2) of the Child Abduction and Custody Act 1985 (declarator that removal of child from United Kingdom was unlawful) shall be made—

(a)   in an action depending before the sheriff—

---

[1] As substituted by the Act of Sederunt (Ordinary Cause, Summary Application, Summary Cause and Small Claim Rules) Amendment (Vulnerable Witnesses (Scotland) Act 2004) 2007, r.2(10) (effective November 1, 2007).

      (i)   by a party, in the initial writ, defences or minute, as the case may be, or by motion; or

      (ii)  by any other person, by minute; or

  (b)   after final decree, by minute in the process of the action to which the application relates.

### Intimation to local authority before supervised contact order

**D1.376**

**33A.26.** Where in a civil partnership action the sheriff, at his own instance or on the motion of a party, is considering making a contact order or an interim contact order subject to supervision by the social work department of a local authority, he shall ordain the party moving for such an order to intimate to the chief executive of that local authority (where not already a party to the action and represented at the hearing at which the issue arises)—

  (a)   the terms of any relevant motion;

  (b)   the intention of the sheriff to order that the contact order be supervised by the social work department of that local authority; and

  (c)   that the local authority shall, within such period as the sheriff has determined—

      (i)   notify the sheriff clerk whether it intends to make representations to the sheriff; and

      (ii)  where it intends to make representations in writing, do so within that period.

### Joint minutes

**D1.377**

**33A.27.** Where any parties in a civil partnership action have reached agreement in relation to—

  (a)   a section 11 order;

  (b)   aliment for a child; or

  (c)   an order for financial provision,

a joint minute may be entered into expressing that agreement; and, subject to rule 33A.19(3) (no order before views of child expressed), the sheriff may grant decree in respect of those parts of the joint minute in relation to which he could otherwise make an order, whether or not such a decree would include a matter for which there was no crave.

### Affidavits

**D1.378**

**33A.28.** The sheriff in a civil partnership action may accept evidence by affidavit at any hearing for an order or interim order.

Part II

Undefended Civil Partnership Actions

### Evidence in certain undefended civil partnership actions

**D1.379**

**33A.29.**—(1) This rule—

  (a)   subject to sub paragraph (b), applies to all civil partnership actions in which no notice of intention to defend has been lodged, other than a civil partnership action—

      (i)   for financial provision after overseas proceedings as provided for in Schedule 11 to the Act of 2004; or

      (ii)  for an order under Chapter 3 or Chapter 4 of Part 3 or section 127 of the Act of 2004;

  (b)   applies to a civil partnership action in which a curator ad litem has been appointed under rule 33A.16 where the curator ad litem to the defender has lodged a minute intimating that he does not intend to lodge defences;

  (c)   applies to any civil partnership action which proceeds at any stage as undefended where the sheriff so directs;

  (d)   applies to the merits of a civil partnership action which is undefended on the merits where the sheriff so directs, notwithstanding that the action is defended on an ancillary matter.

(2)   Unless the sheriff otherwise directs, evidence shall be given by affidavits.

(3)   Unless the sheriff otherwise directs, evidence relating to the welfare of a child shall be given by affidavit, at least one affidavit being emitted by a person other than a parent or party to the action.

(4)   Evidence in the form of a written statement bearing to be the professional opinion of a duly qualified medical practitioner, which has been signed by him and lodged in process, shall be admissible in place of parole evidence by him.

### Procedure for decree in actions under rule 33A.29

**D1.380**

**33A.30.**—(1) In an action to which rule 33A.29 (evidence in certain undefended civil partnership actions) applies, the pursuer shall at any time after the expiry of the period for lodging a notice of intention to defend—

  (a)   lodge in process the affidavit evidence; and

  (b)   endorse a minute in Form CP27 on the initial writ.

(2)    The sheriff may, at any time after the pursuer has complied with paragraph (1), without requiring the appearance of parties—

    (a)    grant decree in terms of the motion for decree; or

    (b)    remit the cause for such further procedure, if any, including proof by parole evidence, as the sheriff thinks fit.

### Extracts of undefended decree

**33A.31**    In an action to which rule 33A.29 (evidence in certain undefended civil partnership actions) applies, the sheriff clerk shall, after the expiry of 14 days after the grant of decree under rule 33A.30 (procedure for decree in actions under rule 33A.29), issue to the pursuer and the defender an extract decree.

        **D1.381**

### No recording of evidence

**33A.32.**    It shall not be necessary to record the evidence in any proof in a civil partnership action which is not defended.

        **D1.382**

### Disapplication of Chapter 15

**33A.33.**    Other than rule 15.1(1), Chapter 15 (motions) shall not apply to a civil partnership action in which no notice of intention to defend has been lodged, or to a civil partnership action in so far as it proceeds as undefended.

        **D1.383**

### Late appearance and application for recall by defenders

**33A.33A.**—[1](1)    In a cause mentioned in rule 33A.1(a), (b) or (f), the sheriff may, at any stage of the action before the granting of final decree, make an order with such conditions, if any, as he thinks fit—

        **D1.384**

    (a)    directing that a defender who has not lodged a notice of intention to defend be treated as if he had lodged such a notice and the period of notice had expired on the date on which the order was made; or

    (b)    allowing a defender who has not lodged a notice of intention to defend to appear and be heard at a diet of proof although he has not lodged defences, but he shall not, in that event, be allowed to lead evidence without the pursuer's consent.

(2)    Where the sheriff makes an order under paragraph (1), the pursuer may recall a witness already examined or lead other evidence whether or not he closed his proof before that order was made.

(3)    Where no order under paragraph (1) has been sought by a defender who has not lodged a notice of intention to defend and decree is granted against him, the sheriff may, on an application made within 14 days of the date of the decree, and with such conditions, if any, as he thinks fit, make an order recalling the decree.

(4)    Where the sheriff makes an order under paragraph (3), the cause shall thereafter proceed as if the defender had lodged a notice of intention to defend and the period of notice had expired on the date on which the decree was recalled.

(5)    An application under paragraph (1) or (3) shall be made by note setting out the proposed defence and explaining the defender's failure to appear.

(6)    An application under paragraph (1) or (3) shall not affect any right of appeal the defender may otherwise have.

(7)    A note lodged in an application under paragraph (1) or (3) shall be served on the pursuer and any other party.

Part III

Defended Civil Partnership Actions

### Notice of intention to defend and defences[2]

**33A.34.**—(1)    This rule applies where the defender in a civil partnership action seeks—

        **D1.385**

    (a)    to oppose any crave in the initial writ;

    (b)    to make a claim for—

        (i)    aliment;

        (ii)    an order for financial provision within the meaning of section 8(3) of the Act of 1985; or

        (iii)    a section 11 order; or

---

[1] As inserted by the Act of Sederunt (Sheriff Court Rules) (Miscellaneous Amendments) 2008 (SSI 2008/223) para.2(3) (effective July 1, 2008).

[2] As inserted by the Act of Sederunt (Sheriff Court Rules) (Miscellaneous Amendments) 2012 (SSI 2012/188) para.4 (effective August 1, 2012).

(c)   an order—
     (i)   under section 16(1)(b) or (3) of the Act of 1985 (setting aside or varying agreement as to financial provision);
     (ii)   under section 18 of the Act of 1985 (which relates to avoidance transactions); or
     (iii)   under Chapter 3 or Chapter 4 of Part 3 or section 127 of the Act of 2004; or
(d)   to challenge the jurisdiction of the court.

(2)   In an action to which this rule applies, the defender shall—
(a)   lodge a notice of intention to defend in Form CP16 before the expiry of the period of notice; and
(b)   make any claim or seek any order referred to in paragraph (1), as the case may be, in those defences by setting out in his defences—
     (i)   craves;
     (ii)   averments in the answers to the condescendence in support of those craves; and
     (iii)   appropriate pleas-in-law.

(3)   Where a defender intends to make an application for a section 11 order which, had it been made in an initial writ, would have required a warrant for intimation under rule 33A.7, the defender shall include a crave in his notice of intention to defend for a warrant for intimation or to dispense with such intimation; and rule 33A.7 shall, with the necessary modifications, apply to a crave for a warrant under this paragraph as it applies to a crave for a warrant under that rule.

(4)[1, 2]   Where a defender opposes a crave for an order for financial provision or makes a claim in accordance with paragraph (1)(b)(ii), the defender must lodge a completed Form CP13A signed by the defender with the defences, minute of amendment or answers as the case may be.

**Abandonment by pursuer**

**D1.386**

**33A.35.**   Notwithstanding abandonment by a pursuer of a civil partnership action, the court may allow a defender to pursue an order or claim sought in his defences; and the proceedings in relation to that order or claim shall continue in dependence as if a separate cause.

**Attendance of parties at Options Hearing**

**D1.387**

**33A.36.**   All parties to a civil partnership action shall, except on cause shown, attend personally the hearing under rule 9.12 (Options Hearing).

**Decree by default**

**D1.388**

**33A.37.**—(1)   In a civil partnership action in which the defender has lodged a notice of intention to defend, where a party fails—
(a)   to lodge, or intimate the lodging of, any production or part of process;
(b)   to implement an order of the sheriff within a specified period; or
(c)   to appear or be represented at any diet,
that party shall be in default.

(2)   Where a party is in default under paragraph (1), the sheriff may—
(a)[3]   where the civil partnership action is one mentioned in rule 33A.1(1)(a), (b) or (f) allow that action to proceed as undefended under Part II of this Chapter; or
(b)   where the civil partnership action is one mentioned in rule 33A.1(1)(c) to (e), grant decree as craved; or
(c)   grant decree of absolvitor; or
(d)   dismiss the civil partnership action or any claim made or order sought; and
(e)   award expenses.

(3)   Where no party appears at a diet in a civil partnership action, the sheriff may dismiss that action.

---

[1] As inserted by the Act of Sederunt (Sheriff Court Rules) (Miscellaneous Amendments) 2012 (SSI 2012/188) para.4 (effective August 1, 2012).

[2] As amended by the Act of Sederunt (Sheriff Court Rules) (Miscellaneous Amendments) (No.2) 2012 (SSI 2012/221) para.2 (effective July 31, 2012).

[3] As amended by Act of Sederunt (Ordinary Cause Rules) Amendment (Family Law (Scotland) Act 2006 etc.) 2006, para.2 (SSI 2006/207) (effective May 4, 2006).

(4)   In a civil partnership action, the sheriff may, on cause shown, prorogate the time for lodging any production or part of process, or for intimating or implementing any order.

Part IV

Applications And Orders Relating To Children In Certain Actions

**Application and interpretation of this Part**

**33A.38.**[1]   This Part applies to an action of dissolution or declarator of nullity of civil partnership or separation of civil partners.

D1.389

**Applications in actions to which this Part applies**

**33A.39.**—(1)   An application for an order mentioned in paragraph (2) shall be made—

D1.390

   (a)   by a crave in the initial writ or defences, as the case may be, in an action to which this Part applies; or

   (b)   where the application is made by a person other than the pursuer or defender, by minute in that action.

(2)   The orders referred to in paragraph (1) are:—

   (a)   an order for a section 11 order; and

   (b)   an order for aliment for a child.

**Applications in depending actions by motion**

**33A.40.**   An application by a party in an action depending before the court to which this Part applies for, or for variation of, an order for—

D1.391

   (a)   interim aliment for a child under the age of 18; or

   (b)   a residence order or a contact order,

shall be made by motion.

**Applications after decree relating to a section 11 order**

**33A.41.**—(1)   An application after final decree for, or for the variation or recall of, a section 11 order or in relation to the enforcement of such an order shall be made by minute in the process of the action to which the application relates.

D1.392

(2)   Where a minute has been lodged under paragraph (1), any party may apply by motion for any interim order which may be made pending the determination of the application.

**Applications after decree relating to aliment**

**33A.42.**—(1)   An application after final decree for, or for the variation or recall of, an order for aliment for a child shall be made by minute in the process of the action to which the application relates.

D1.393

(2)   Where a minute has been lodged under paragraph (1), any party may lodge a motion for any interim order which may be made pending the determination of the application.

**Applications after decree by persons over 18 years for aliment**

**33A.43**—(1)   A person—

D1.394

   (a)   to whom an obligation of aliment is owed under section 1 of the Act of 1985;

   (b)   in whose favour an order for aliment while under the age of 18 years was made in an action to which this Part applies, and

   (c)   who seeks, after attaining that age, an order for aliment against the person in that action against whom the order for aliment in his favour was made,

shall apply by minute in the process of that action.

(2)   An application for interim aliment pending the determination of an application under paragraph (1) shall be made by motion.

---

[1] As amended by Act of Sederunt (Ordinary Cause Rules) Amendment (Family Law (Scotland) Act 2006 etc.) 2006, para.2 (SSI 2006/207) (effective May 4, 2006).

(3)   Where a decree has been pronounced in an application under paragraph (1) or (2), any application for variation or recall of any such decree shall be made by minute in the process of the action to which the application relates.

## Part V

### Orders Relating To Financial Provisions

**Application and interpretation of this Part**

**D1.395**

**33A.44.**—[1](1)   This Part applies to an action of dissolution or declarator of nullity of civil partnership.

(2)   In this Part, "incidental order" has the meaning assigned in section 14(2) of the Act of 1985.

**Applications in actions to which this Part applies**

**D1.396**

**33A.45.**—(1)   An application for an order mentioned in paragraph (2) shall be made—

(a)   by a crave in the initial writ or defences, as the case may be, in an action to which this Part applies; or

(b)   where the application is made by a person other than the pursuer or defender, by minute in that action.

(2)   The orders referred to in paragraph (1) are:—

(a)   an order for financial provision within the meaning of section 8(3) of the Act of 1985;

(b)   an order under section 16(1)(b) or (3) of the Act of 1985 (setting aside or varying agreement as to financial provision);

(c)   an order under section 18 of the Act of 1985 (which relates to avoidance transactions); and

(d)   an order under section 112 of the Act of 2004 (transfer of tenancy).

**Applications in depending actions relating to incidental orders**

**D1.397**

**33A.46.**—(1)   In an action depending before the sheriff to which this Part applies—

(a)   the pursuer or defender, notwithstanding rules 33A.34(2) (application by defender for order for financial provision) and 33A.45(1)(a) (application for order for financial provision in initial writ or defences), may apply by motion for an incidental order; and

(b)   the sheriff shall not be bound to determine such a motion if he considers that the application should properly be by a crave in the initial writ or defences, as the case may be.

(2)   In an action depending before the sheriff to which this Part applies, an application under section 14(4) of the Act of 1985 for the variation or recall of an incidental order shall be made by minute in the process of the action to which the application relates.

**Applications relating to interim aliment**

**D1.398**

**33A.47.**   An application for, or for the variation or recall of, an order for interim aliment for the pursuer or defender shall be made by motion.

**Applications relating to orders for financial provision**

**D1.399**

**33A.48.**—(1)   An application—

(a)   after final decree under any of the following provisions of the Act of 1985—

(i)   section 8(1) for periodical allowance;

(ii)   section 12(1)(b) (payment of capital sum or transfer of property);

(iii)   section 12(4) (variation of date or method of payment of capital sum or date of transfer of property); or

(iv)   section 13(4) (variation, recall, backdating or conversion of periodical allowance); or

(v)[2]   section 14(1) (incidental orders), or

(b)   after the grant or refusal of an application under—

(i)   section 8(1) or 14(3) for an incidental order; or

(ii)   section 14(4) (variation or recall of incidental order),

shall be made by minute in the process of the action to which the application relates.

(2)   Where a minute is lodged under paragraph (1), any party may lodge a motion for any interim order which may be made pending the determination of the application.

(3)   An application under—

---

[1] As amended by Act of Sederunt (Ordinary Cause Rules) Amendment (Family Law (Scotland) Act 2006 etc.) 2006, para.2 (SSI 2006/207) (effective May 4, 2006).

[2] As inserted by the Act of Sederunt (Sheriff Court Rules) (Miscellaneous Amendments) (No.3) 2011 (SSI 2011/386) para.2 (effective November 28, 2011).

(a) paragraph (5) of section 12A of the Act of 1985 (recall or variation of order in respect of a pension lump sum);

(b) paragraph (7) of that section (variation of order in respect of pension lump sum to substitute trustees or managers);

(ba)[1] section 12B(4) of the Act of 1985 (recall or variation of a capital sum order); or

(c) section 28(10) or 48(9) of the Welfare Reform and Pensions Act 1999,

shall be made by minute in the process of the action to which the application relates.

### Pension Protection Fund notification

**33A.48A.**—[2](1)  In this rule—

**D1.400**

"assessment period" shall be construed in accordance with section 132 of the Pensions Act 2004;

"pension arrangement" shall be construed in accordance with the definition in section 27 of the Act of 1985; and

"valuation summary" shall be construed in accordance with the definition in Schedule 2 to the Pension Protection Fund (Provision of Information) Regulations 2005.

(2)  This rule applies where a party at any stage in the proceedings applies for an order under section 8 or section 16 of the Act of 1985.

(3)  Where the party against whom an order referred to in paragraph (2) is sought has received notification in compliance with the Pension Protection Fund (Provision of Information) Regulations 2005 or does so after the order is sought—

(a) that there is an assessment period in relation to his pension arrangement; or

(b) that the Board of the Pension Protection Fund has assumed responsibility for all or part of his pension arrangement, he shall comply with paragraph (4).

(4)  The party shall—

(a) lodge the notification; and

(b) obtain and lodge as soon as reasonably practicable thereafter—

(i) a valuation summary; and

(ii) a forecast of his compensation entitlement.

(5)  Subject to paragraph (6), the notification referred to in paragraph (4)(a) requires to be lodged—

(a) where the notification is received before the order is sought, within 7 days of the order being sought;

(b) where the notification is received after the order is sought, within 7 days of receiving the notification.

(6)  Where an order is sought against the defender before the defences are lodged, and the notification is received before that step occurs, the notification shall be lodged with the defences.

(7)  At the same time as lodging documents under paragraph (4), copies shall be sent to the other party to the proceedings.

### Applications after decree relating to agreements and avoidance transactions

**33A.49.**  An application for an order—

**D1.401**

(a) under section 16(1)(a) or (3) of the Act of 1985 (setting aside or varying agreements as to financial provision), or

(b) under section 18 of the Act of 1985 (which relates to avoidance transactions), made after final decree shall be made by minute in the process of the action to which the application relates.

Part VI

Applications Relating To Avoidance Transactions

### Form of applications

**33A.50.**—(1)  An application for an order under section 18 of the Act of 1985 (which relates to avoidance transactions) by a party to a civil partnership action shall be made by including in the initial writ, defences or minute, as the case may be, appropriate craves, averments and pleas in law.

**D1.402**

---

[1] As inserted by the Act of Sederunt (Sheriff Court Rules) (Miscellaneous Amendments) 2011 (SSI 2011/193) r.15 (effective April 6, 2011).

[2] As inserted by the Act of Sederunt (Sheriff Court Rules) (Miscellaneous Amendments) 2008 (SSI 2008/223) r.3(3) (effective July 1, 2008).

(2) An application for an order under section 18 of the Act of 1985 after final decree in a civil partnership action shall be made by minute in the process of the action to which the application relates.

## Part VII

### Financial Provision After Overseas Proceedings

**Interpretation of this Part**

D1.403

**33A.51.** In this Part—

"order for financial provision" has the meaning assigned in paragraph 4 of Schedule 11 to the Act of 2004;

"overseas proceedings" has the meaning assigned in paragraph 1(1)(a) of Schedule 11 to the Act of 2004.

**Applications for financial provision after overseas proceedings**

D1.404

**33A.52.**—(1) An application under paragraph 2(1) of Schedule 11 to the Act of 2004 for an order for financial provision after overseas proceedings shall be made by initial writ.

(2) An application for an order in an action to which paragraph (1) applies made before final decree under—

    (a)    section 112 of the Act of 2004 (transfer of tenancy of family home);

    (b)    paragraph 3(4) of Schedule 11 to the Act of 2004 for interim periodical allowance; or

    (c)    section 14(4) of the Act of 1985 (variation or recall of incidental order), shall be made by motion.

(3) An application for an order in an action to which paragraph (1) applies made after final decree under—

    (a)    section 12(4) of the Act of 1985 (variation of date or method of payment of capital sum or date of transfer of property);

    (b)    section 13(4) of the Act of 1985 (variation, recall, backdating or conversion of periodical allowance); or

    (c)    section 14(4) of the Act of 1985 (variation or recall of incidental order),

shall be made by minute in the process of the action to which it relates.

(4) An application under—

    (a)    paragraph (5) of section 12A of the Act of 1985 (recall or variation of order in respect of a pension lump sum); or

    (b)    paragraph (7) of that section (variation of order in respect of pension lump sum to substitute trustees or managers),

shall be made by minute in the process of the action to which the application relates.

(5) Where a minute has been lodged under paragraph (3), any party may apply by motion for an interim order pending the determination of the application.

## Part VIII

### Actions In Respect Of Aliment

**Applications relating to agreements on aliment**

D1.405

**33A.53.** In a civil partnership action in which a crave for aliment may be made, an application under section 7(2) of the Act of 1985 shall be made by a crave in the initial writ or in defences, as the case may be.

## Part IX

### Applications For Orders Under Section it Of The Children (Scotland) Act 1995

**Application of this Part**

D1.406

**33A.54**[1] This Part applies to an application for a section 11 order in a civil partnership action other than in an action of dissolution or declarator of nullity of civil partnership or separation of civil partners.

---

[1] As amended by Act of Sederunt (Ordinary Cause Rules) Amendment (Family Law (Scotland) Act 2006 etc.) 2006, para.2 (SSI 2006/207) (effective May 4, 2006).

**Form of applications**

**33A.55.** Subject to any other provision in this Chapter, an application for a section 11 order shall be made—

    (a)    by a crave in the initial writ or defences, as the case may be, in a civil partnership action to which this Part applies; or

    (b)    where the application is made by a person other than a party to an action mentioned in paragraph (a), by minute in that action.

**D1.407**

**Applications relating to interim orders in depending actions**

**33A.56.** An application, in an action depending before the sheriff to which this Part applies, for, or for the variation or recall of, an interim residence order or an interim contact order shall be made—

    (a)    by a party to the action, by motion; or

    (b)    by a person who is not a party to the action, by minute.

**D1.408**

**Applications after decree**

**33A.57.**—(1) An application after final decree for variation or recall of a section 11 order shall be made by minute in the process of the action to which the application relates.

(2) Where a minute has been lodged under paragraph (1), any party may apply by motion for an interim order pending the determination of the application.

**D1.409**

**Application for leave**

**33A.57A.**—[1](1) Where leave of the court is required under section 11(3)(aa) of the Act of 1995 for the making of an application for a contact order under that section, the applicant must lodge along with the initial writ a written application in the form of a letter addressed to the sheriff clerk stating—

    (a)    the grounds of which leave is sought; and

    (b)    whether or not the applicant has applied for legal aid.

(2) Where the applicant has applied for legal aid he must also lodge along with the initial writ written confirmation from the Scottish Legal Aid Board that it has determined, under regulation 7(2)(b) of the Civil Legal Aid (Scotland) Regulations 2002, that notification of the application for legal aid should be dispensed with or postponed pending the making by the sheriff of an order for intimation under paragraph (4)(b).

(3) Subject to paragraph (4)(b) an application under paragraph (1) shall not be served or intimated to any party.

(4) The sheriff shall consider an application under paragraph (1) without hearing the applicant and may—

    (a)    refuse the application and pronounce an interlocutor accordingly; or

    (b)    if he is minded to grant the application order the applicant—

        (i)    to intimate the application to such persons as the sheriff considers appropriate; and

        (ii)    to lodge a certificate of intimation in, as near as may be, Form G8.

(5) If any person who receives intimation of an application under paragraph (4)(b) wishes to be heard he shall notify the sheriff clerk in writing within 14 days of receipt of intimation of the application.

(6) On receipt of any notification under paragraph (5) the sheriff clerk shall fix a hearing and intimate the date of the hearing to the parties.

**D1.410**

---

[1] As inserted by the Act of Sederunt (Sheriff Court Rules Amendment) (Adoption and Children (Scotland) Act 2007) 2009 (SSI 2009/284) (effective September 28, 2009).

(7)   Where an application under paragraph (1) is granted, a copy of the sheriff's interlocutor must be served on the defender along with the warrant of citation.

Part X

Actions Relating To Occupancy Rights And Tenancies

**Application of this Part**

**D1.411**   **33A.58.**   This Part applies to an action or application for an order under Chapter 3 or Chapter 4 of Part 3 or section 127 of the Act of 2004.

**Interpretation of this Part**

**D1.412**   **33A.59.**   Unless the context otherwise requires, words and expressions used in this Part which are also used in Chapter 3 or Chapter 4 of Part 3 of the Act of 2004 have the same meaning as in Chapter 3 or Chapter 4, as the case may be.

**Form of application**

**D1.413**   **33A.60.**—(1)   Subject to any other provision in this Chapter, an application for an order under this Part shall be made—
    (a)   by an action for such an order;
    (b)   by a crave in the initial writ or defences, as the case may be, in any other civil partnership action;
    (c)   where the application is made by a person other than a party to any action mentioned in paragraph (a) or (b), by minute in that action.

(2)   An application under section 107(1) (dispensation with civil partner's consent to dealing) or section 127 (application in relation to attachment) of the Act of 2004 shall, unless made in a depending civil partnership action, be made by summary application.

**Defenders**

**D1.414**   **33A.61.**   The applicant for an order under this Part shall call as a defender—
    (a)   where he is seeking an order as a civil partner, the other civil partner; and
    (b)   where he is a third party making an application under section 107(1) (dispensation with civil partner's consent to dealing), or 108(1) (payment from non-entitled civil partner in respect of loan) of the Act of 2004, both civil partners.

**Applications by motion**

**D1.415**   **33A.62.**—(1)   An application under any of the following provisions of the Act of 2004 shall be made by motion in the process of the depending action to which the application relates—
    (a)   section 103(4) (interim order for regulation of rights of occupancy, etc.);
    (b)   section 104(6) (interim order suspending occupancy rights);
    (c)   section 107(1) (dispensation with civil partner's consent to dealing); and
    (d)   *[Omitted by Act of Sederunt (Ordinary Cause Rules) Amendment (Family Law (Scotland) Act 2006 etc.) 2006, para.2 (SSI 2006/207) (effective May 4, 2006).]*
(2)   Intimation of a motion under paragraph (1) shall be given—
    (a)   to the other civil partner;
    (b)   where the motion is under paragraph (1)(a) or (b) and the entitled civil partner is a tenant or occupies the family home by the permission of a third party, to the landlord or third party, as the case may be; and
    (c)   to any other person to whom intimation of the application was or is to be made by virtue of rule 33A.7(1)(i) (warrant for intimation to certain persons in actions for orders under Chapter 3 of Part 3 of the Act of 2004) or rule 33A.15 (order for intimation by sheriff).

**Applications by minute**

**D1.416**   **33A.63.**—(1)   An application for an order under section 105 of the Act of 2004 (variation and recall of orders made under section 103 or section 104 of the Act of 2004) shall be made by minute.
(2)   A minute under paragraph (1) shall be intimated—
    (a)   to the other civil partner;
    (b)   where the entitled civil partner is a tenant or occupies the family home by the permission of a third party, to the landlord or third party, as the case may be; and
    (c)   to any other person to whom intimation of the application was or is to be made by virtue of rule 33A.7(1)(i) (warrant for intimation to certain persons in actions for orders under Chapter 3 of Part 3 of the Act of 2004) or rule 33A.15 (order for intimation by sheriff).

**Sist of actions to enforce occupancy rights**

**33A.64.** Unless the sheriff otherwise directs, the sist of an action by virtue of section 107(4) of the Act of 2004 (where action raised by non entitled civil partner to enforce occupancy rights) shall apply only to such part of the action as relates to the enforcement of occupancy rights by a non entitled civil partner.

**D1.417**

**Certificates of delivery of documents to chief constable**

**33A.65.** *[Omitted by Act of Sederunt (Ordinary Cause Rules) Amendment (Family Law (Scotland) Act 2006 etc.) 2006, para.2 (SSI 2006/207) (effective May 4, 2006).]*

Part XI

Simplified Dissolution Of Civil Partnership Applications

**Application and interpretation of this Part**

**33A.66.**—(1) This Part applies to an application for dissolution of civil partnership by a party to a civil partnership made in the manner prescribed in rule 33A.67 (form of applications) if, but only if—

    (a)[1] that party relies on the facts set out in section 117(3)(c) (no cohabitation for one year with consent of defender to decree), section 117(3)(d) (no cohabitation for two years), or section 117(2)(b) (issue of interim gender recognition certificate) of the Act of 2004;

    (b) in an application under section 117(3)(c) of the Act of 2004, the other party consents to decree of dissolution of civil partnership being granted;

    (c) no other proceedings are pending in any court which could have the effect of bringing the civil partnership to an end;

    (d)[2] there is no child of the family (as defined in section 12(4)(b) of the Act of 1995) under the age of 16 years;

    (e) neither party to the civil partnership applies for an order for financial provision on dissolution of civil partnership; and

    (f) neither party to the civil partnership suffers from mental disorder.

(2) If an application ceases to be one to which this Part applies at any time before final decree, it shall be deemed to be abandoned and shall be dismissed.

(3) In this Part "simplified dissolution of civil partnership application" means an application mentioned in paragraph (1).

**D1.418**

**Form of applications**

**33A.67.**—(1) A simplified dissolution of civil partnership application in which the facts set out in section 117(3)(c) of the Act of 2004 (no cohabitation for two years with consent of defender to decree) are relied on shall be made in Form CP29 and shall only be of effect if—

    (a) it is signed by the applicant; and

    (b) the form of consent in Part 2 of Form CP29 is signed by the party to the civil partnership giving consent.

(2) A simplified dissolution of civil partnership application in which the facts set out in section 117(3)(d) of the Act of 2004 (no cohabitation for five years) are relied on shall be made in Form CP30 and shall only be of effect if it is signed by the applicant.

(3) A simplified dissolution of civil partnership application in which the facts set out in section 117(2)(b) of the Act of 2004 (issue of interim gender recognition certificate) are relied on shall be made in Form CP31 and shall only be of effect if it is signed by the applicant.

**D1.419**

**Lodging of applications**

**33A.68.** The applicant shall send a simplified dissolution of civil partnership application to the sheriff clerk with—

    (a) an extract or certified copy of the civil partnership certificate;

    (b) the appropriate fee; and

    (c) in an application under section 117(2)(b) of the Act of 2004, the interim gender recognition certificate or a certified copy, within the meaning of rule 33A.9(4).

**D1.420**

**Citation and intimation**

**33A.69.**—(1) This rule is subject to rule 33A.70 (citation where address not known).

**D1.421**

---

[1] As amended by Act of Sederunt (Ordinary Cause Rules) Amendment (Family Law (Scotland) Act 2006 etc.) 2006, para.2 (SSI 2006/207) (effective May 4, 2006).

[2] As amended by the Act of Sederunt (Sheriff Court Rules) (Miscellaneous Amendments) 2012 (SSI 2012/188) para.9 (effective August 1, 2012).

(2) It shall be the duty of the sheriff clerk to cite any person or intimate any document in connection with a simplified dissolution of civil partnership application.

(3) The form of citation—

(a) in an application relying on the facts in section 117(3)(c) of the Act of 2004 shall be in Form CP32;

(b) in an application relying on the facts in section 117(3)(d) of the Act of 2004 shall be in Form CP33; and

(c) in an application relying on the facts in section 117(2)(b) of the Act of 2004 shall be in Form CP34.

(4) The citation or intimation required by paragraph (2) shall be made—

(a) by the sheriff clerk by registered post or the first class recorded delivery service in accordance with rule 5.3 (postal service or intimation);

(b)[1] on payment of an additional fee, by a sheriff officer in accordance with rule 5.4(1) to (4) (service within Scotland by sheriff officer); or

(c) where necessary, by the sheriff clerk in accordance with rule 5.5 (service on persons furth of Scotland).

(5) Where citation or intimation is made in accordance with paragraph (4)(c), the translation into an official language of the country in which service is to be executed required by rule 5.5(6) shall be provided by the party lodging the simplified dissolution of civil partnership application.

### Citation where address not known

D1.422

**33A.70.**—(1)[2] In a simplified dissolution of civil partnership application in which the facts in section 117(3)(d) (no cohabitation for two years) or section 117(2)(b) (issue of interim gender recognition certificate) of the Act of 2004 are relied on and the address of the other party to the civil partnership is not known and cannot reasonably be ascertained—

(a) citation shall be executed by displaying a copy of the application and a notice in Form CP35 on the walls of court on a period of notice of 21 days; and

(b) intimation shall be made to—

(i)[3] every person who was a child of the family (within the meaning of section 101(7) of the Act of 2004) who has reached the age of 16 years, and

(ii) one of the next of kin of the other party to the civil partnership who has reached that age, unless the address of such person is not known and cannot reasonably be ascertained.

(2) Intimation to a person referred to in paragraph (1)(b) shall be given by intimating a copy of the application and a notice of intimation in Form CP36.

### Opposition to applications

D1.423

**33A.71.**—(1) Any person on whom service or intimation of a simplified dissolution of civil partnership application has been made may give notice by letter sent to the sheriff clerk that he challenges the jurisdiction of the court or opposes the grant of decree of dissolution of civil partnership and giving the reasons for his opposition to the application.

(2) Where opposition to a simplified dissolution of civil partnership application is made under paragraph (1), the sheriff shall dismiss the application unless he is satisfied that the reasons given for the opposition are frivolous.

(3) The sheriff clerk shall intimate the decision under paragraph (2) to the applicant and the respondent.

(4) The sending of a letter under paragraph (1) shall not imply acceptance of the jurisdiction of the court.

---

[1] As substituted by the Act of Sederunt (Sheriff Court Rules) (Miscellaneous Amendments) 2010 (SSI 2010/279) r.3 (effective July 29, 2010).

[2] As amended by Act of Sederunt (Ordinary Cause Rules) Amendment (Family Law (Scotland) Act 2006 etc.) 2006, para.2 (SSI 2006/207) (effective May 4, 2006).

[3] As amended by the Act of Sederunt (Sheriff Court Rules) (Miscellaneous Amendments) 2012 (SSI 2012/188) para.9 (effective August 1, 2012).

**Evidence**

**33A.72.**   Parole evidence shall not be given in a simplified dissolution of civil partnership application.   **D1.424**

**Decree**

**33A.73.**—(1)   The sheriff may grant decree in terms of the simplified dissolution of civil partnership   **D1.425**
application on the expiry of the period of notice if such application has been properly served provided
that, when the application has been served in a country to which the Hague Convention on the Service
Abroad of Judicial and Extra Judicial Documents in Civil or Commercial Matters dated 15 November
1965 applies, decree shall not be granted until it is established to the satisfaction of the sheriff that the
requirements of article 15 of that Convention have been complied with.

(2)   The sheriff clerk shall, not sooner than 14 days after the granting of decree in terms of paragraph
(1), issue to each party to the civil partnership an extract of the decree of dissolution of civil partnership
in Form CP37.

**Appeals**

**33A.74.**   Any appeal against an interlocutor granting decree of dissolution of civil partnership under   **D1.426**
rule 33A.73 (decree) may be made, within 14 days after the date of decree, by sending a letter to the court
giving reasons for the appeal.

**Applications after decree**

**33A.75.**   Any application to the court after decree of dissolution of civil partnership has been granted   **D1.427**
in a simplified dissolution of civil partnership application which could have been made if it had been
made in an action of dissolution of civil partnership shall be made by minute.

Part XII

Referrals To Principal Reporter

**33A.76.–33A.78.**   *[Repealed by the Act of Sederunt (Children's Hearings (Scotland) Act 2011)*
*(Miscellaneous Amendments) 2013 (SI 2013/172) para.5 (effective June 24, 2013).]*

Part XIII

Sisting Of Civil Partnership Actions

**Application and interpretation of this Part**

**33A.79.**—(1)   This Part applies to any action for—   **D1.428**
dissolution of civil partnership;
separation of civil partners.

(2)   In this Part—

"another jurisdiction" means any country outside Scotland.
"related jurisdiction" means any of the following countries, namely, England and Wales, Northern
    Ireland, Jersey, Guernsey and the Isle of Man (the reference to Guernsey being treated as includ-
    ing Alderney and Sark).

(3)   For the purposes of this Part—

(a)   neither the taking of evidence on commission nor a separate proof relating to any preliminary
        plea shall be regarded as part of the proof in the action; and
(b)   an action is continuing if it is pending and not sisted.

(4)   Any reference in this Part to proceedings in another jurisdiction is to proceedings in a court or
before an administrative authority of that jurisdiction.

**Duty to furnish particulars of concurrent proceedings**

**33A.80.**   While any action to which this Part applies is pending in a sheriff court and proof in that ac-   **D1.429**
tion has not begun, it shall be the duty of the pursuer, and of any other person who has entered appearance in the action, to furnish, in such manner and to such persons and on such occasions as may be
prescribed, such particulars as may be so prescribed of any proceedings which—

(a)   he knows to be continuing in another jurisdiction; and
(b)   are in respect of that civil partnership or capable of affecting its validity.

**Mandatory sists**

**33A.81.**   Where before the beginning of the proof in any action for dissolution of civil partnership it   **D1.430**
appears to the sheriff on the application of a party to the civil partnership—

(a)   that in respect of the same civil partnership proceedings for dissolution or nullity of civil
        partnership are continuing in a related jurisdiction; and

(b)    that the parties to the civil partnership have resided together after the civil partnership was formed or treated as having been formed within the meaning of section 1(1) of the Act of 2004; and

(c)    that the place where they resided together when the action was begun or, if they did not then reside together, where they last resided together before the date on which that action was begun is in that jurisdiction; and

(d)    that either of the said parties was habitually resident in that jurisdiction throughout the year ending with the date on which they last resided together before the date on which that action was begun;

it shall be the duty of the sheriff, subject to rule 33A.83(2) below, to sist the action before him.

### Discretionary sists

**D1.431**

**33A.82.**—(1)  Where before the beginning of the proof in any action to which this Part applies, it appears to the sheriff—

(a)    that any other proceedings in respect of the civil partnership in question or capable of affecting its validity are continuing in another jurisdiction, and

(b)    that the balance of fairness (including convenience) as between the parties to the civil partnership is such that it is appropriate for those other proceedings to be disposed of before further steps are taken in the action,

the sheriff may then if he thinks fit sist that action.

(2)  In considering the balance of fairness and convenience for the purposes of paragraph (1)(b), the sheriff shall have regard to all factors appearing to be relevant, including the convenience of witnesses and any delay or expense which may result from the proceedings being sisted, or not being sisted.

(3)  Paragraph (1) is without prejudice to the duty imposed by rule 33A.81 above.

(4)  If, at any time after the beginning of the proof in any action to which this Part applies, the sheriff is satisfied that a person has failed to perform the duty imposed on him in respect of the action and any such other proceedings as aforesaid by rule 33A.80, paragraph (1) shall have effect in relation to that action and to the other proceedings as if the words "before the beginning of the proof" were omitted; but no action in respect of the failure of a person to perform such a duty shall be competent.

### Recall of sists

**D1.432**

**33A.83.**—(1)  Where an action is sisted in pursuance of rule 33A.81 or 33A.82, the sheriff may if he thinks fit, on the application of a party to the action, recall the sist if it appears to him that the other proceedings by reference to which the action was sisted are sisted or concluded or that a party to those other proceedings has delayed unreasonably in prosecuting those other proceedings.

(2)  Where an action has been sisted in pursuance of rule 33A.82 by reference to some other proceedings, and the sheriff recalls the sist in pursuance of the preceding paragraph, the sheriff shall not again sist the action in pursuance of the said rule 33A.82.

### Orders in sisted actions

**D1.433**

**33A.84.**—(1)  The provisions of paragraphs (2) and (3) shall apply where an action to which this Part applies is sisted by reference to proceedings in a related jurisdiction for any of those remedies; and in this rule—

"the other proceedings", in relation to any sisted action, means the proceedings in another jurisdiction by reference to which the action was sisted;

"relevant order" means an interim order relating to aliment or children; and

"sisted" means sisted in pursuance of this Part.

(2)  Where an action such as is mentioned in paragraph (1) is sisted, then, without prejudice to the effect of the sist apart from this paragraph—

(a)    the sheriff shall not have power to make a relevant order in connection with the sisted action except in pursuance of sub paragraph (c); and

(b)    subject to the said sub paragraph (c), any relevant order made in connection with the sisted action shall (unless the sist or the relevant order has been previously recalled) cease to have effect on the expiration of the period of three months beginning with the date on which the sist comes into operation; but

(c)    if the sheriff considers that as a matter of necessity and urgency it is necessary during or after that period to make a relevant order in connection with the sisted action or to extend or further extend the duration of a relevant order made in connection with the sisted action, the sheriff may do so, and the order shall not cease to have effect by virtue of sub paragraph (b).

(3)  Where any action such as is mentioned in paragraph (1) is sisted and at the time when the sist comes into operation, an order is in force, or at a subsequent time an order comes into force, being an order made in connection with the other proceedings and providing for any of the following matters,

namely periodical payments for a party to the civil partnership in question, periodical payments for a child, the arrangements to be made as to with whom a child is to live, contact with a child, and any other matter relating to parental responsibilities or parental rights, then, as from the time when the sist comes into operation (in a case where the order is in force at that time) or (in any other case) on the coming into force of the order—

(a) any relevant order made in connection with the sisted action shall cease to have effect in so far as it makes for a civil partner or child any provision for any of the said matters as respects which the same or different provision for that civil partner or child is made by the other order; and

(b) the sheriff shall not have power in connection with the sisted action to make a relevant order containing for a civil partner or child provision for any of the matters aforesaid as respects which any provision for that civil partner or child is made by the other order.

(4) Nothing in this paragraph affects any power of a sheriff—

(a) to vary or recall a relevant order in so far as the order is for the time being in force; or

(b) to enforce a relevant order as respects any period when it is or was in force; or

(c) to make a relevant order in connection with an action which was, but is no longer, sisted.

CHAPTER 33AA[1]

EXPEDITIOUS RESOLUTION OF CERTAIN CAUSES

**Application of Chapter**

**33AA.1.** This Chapter applies where a cause is proceeding to proof or proof before answer in respect of a crave for an order under section 11 of the Children (Scotland) Act 1995 (court orders relating to parental responsibilities etc.).

**D1.434**

**Fixing date for Case Management Hearing**

**33AA.2.**—(1) The sheriff shall fix a date for a case management hearing—

(a) at the Options Hearing in accordance with rule 9.12(3)(f);

(b) at the Procedural Hearing in accordance with rule 10.6(3)(f);

(c) on the motion of any party; or

(d) on the sheriff's own motion.

(2) Except on cause shown, the date and time to be fixed under paragraph (1) shall be not less than 14 days and not more than 28 days after the interlocutor appointing the cause to a proof or proof before answer.

**D1.435**

**Pre-hearing conference**

**33AA.3.**—(1) In advance of the case management hearing the parties shall hold a prehearing conference, at which parties must—

(a) discuss settlement of the action;

(b) agree, so far as is possible, the matters which are not in dispute between them;

(c) discuss the information referred to in rule 33AA.4(1).

(2) Prior to the case management hearing the pursuer shall lodge with the court a joint minute of the pre-hearing conference or explain to the sheriff why such a minute has not been lodged.

(3) If a party is not present during the pre-hearing conference, that party's representative must be able to contact the party during the conference, and be in full possession of all relevant facts.

**D1.436**

**Case Management Hearing**

**33AA.4.**—(1) At the case management hearing the parties must provide the sheriff with sufficient information to enable the sheriff to ascertain—

(a) the nature of the issues in dispute, including any questions of admissibility of evidence or any other legal issues;

(b) the state of the pleadings and whether amendment will be required;

(c) the state of preparation of the parties;

(d) the scope for agreement of facts, questions of law and matters of evidence;

(e) the scope for use of affidavits and other documents in place of oral evidence;

(f) the scope for joint instruction of a single expert;

(g) the number and availability of witnesses;

(h) the nature of productions;

(i) whether sanction is sought for the employment of counsel;

**D1.437**

---

[1] As inserted by the Act of Sederunt (Sheriff Court Rules)(Miscellaneous Amendments) (No.2) 2013 (SI 2013/139) para.2 (effective June 3, 2013).

        (j)   the reasonable estimate of time needed by each party for examination-in-chief, cross-examination and submissions.

(2)   Subject to paragraph (4), at the case management hearing the sheriff will fix—

        (a)   a diet for proof or a proof before answer;
        (b)   a pre-proof hearing in accordance with Chapter 28A.

(3)   The diet fixed under paragraph (2)(a)—

        (a)   shall be assigned for the appropriate number of days for resolution of the issues with reference to the information provided under paragraph (1) and subject to paragraph (4);
        (b)   may only be extended or varied on exceptional cause shown and subject to such orders (including awards of expenses) as the sheriff considers appropriate.

(4)   The sheriff may make such orders as thought fit to ensure compliance with this rule and the expeditious resolution of the issues in dispute, including—

        (a)   restricting the issues for proof;
        (b)   excluding specified documents, reports and/or witnesses from proof;
        (c)   fixing other hearings and awarding expenses.

(5)   A case management hearing may, on cause shown, be continued to a further case management hearing.

(6)   For the purposes of rules 16.2 (decrees where party in default), 33.37 (decree by default in family action) and 33A.37 (decree by default in civil partnership action), a case management hearing shall be a diet in accordance with those rules.

## CHAPTER 33B

### FINANCIAL PROVISION FOR FORMER COHABITANTS

**Interpretation of this Chapter**

**33B.**   *[Omitted by the Act of Sederunt (Sheriff Court Rules) (Miscellaneous Amendments) 2012 (SSI 2012/188) para.7 (effective August 1, 2012).]*

## CHAPTER 33C[1]

### REFERRALS TO PRINCIPAL REPORTER

**Application and interpretation of this Part**

**D1.438**

**33C.1.**—(1)   In this Chapter—

"2011 Act" means the Children's Hearings (Scotland) Act 2011;

"relevant proceedings" means those proceedings referred to in section 62(5)(a) to (j) and (m) of the 2011 Act, ;

"section 62 statement" has the meaning given in section 62(4) of the 2011 Act;

"Principal Reporter" is the person referred to in section 14 of the 2011 Act or any person carrying out the functions of the Principal Reporter by virtue of paragraph 10(1) of schedule 3 to that Act.

(2)   This Chapter applies where a sheriff, in relevant proceedings, makes a referral to the Principal Reporter under section 62(2) of the 2011 Act ("a referral").

**Intimation to Principal Reporter**

**D1.439**

**33C.2.**   Where a referral is made, there shall be attached to the interlocutor a section 62 statement, which shall be intimated forthwith by the sheriff clerk to the Principal Reporter.

**Intimation of decision by Principal Reporter**

**D1.440**

**33C.3.**—(1)   Where a referral is made and the Principal Reporter considers that it is necessary for a compulsory supervision order to be made in respect of the child and arranges a children's hearing under section 69(2) of the 2011 Act, the Principal Reporter shall intimate to the court which issued the section 62 statement the matters referred to in paragraph (2).

(2)   The matters referred to in paragraph (1) are—

        (a)   the decision to arrange such a hearing;
        (b)   where no appeal is made against the decision of that children's hearing prior to the period for appeal expiring, the outcome of the children's hearing; and
        (c)   where such an appeal has been made, that an appeal has been made and, once determined, the outcome of that appeal.

---

[1] As inserted by the Act of Sederunt (Children's Hearings (Scotland) Act 2011) (Miscellaneous Amendments) 2013 (SI 2013/172) para.5 (effective June 24, 2013).

(3)    Where a referral has been made and the Principal Reporter determines that—

    (a)    none of the section 67 grounds apply in relation to the child; or

    (b)    it is not necessary for a compulsory supervision order to be made in respect of the child

the Principal Reporter shall intimate that decision to the court which issued the section 62 statement.

CHAPTER 34

ACTIONS RELATING TO HERITABLE PROPERTY

Part I

Sequestration for Rent

[Revoked by the Act of Sederunt (Sheriff Court Rules Amendment) (Diligence) 2008 (SSI 2008/121) r.2(1)(a) (effective April 1, 2008).]

Part II

Removing

**Action of removing where fixed term of removal**

**D1.441**

**34.5.**—(1)    Subject to section 21 of the Agricultural Holdings (Scotland) Act 1991 (notice to quit and notice of intention to quit)—

    (a)    where the tenant has bound himself to remove by writing, dated and signed—

        (i)    within 12 months after the term of removal; or

        (ii)    where there is more than one ish, after the ish first in date to remove;

    an action of removing may be raised at any time; and

    (b)    where the tenant has not bound himself, an action of removing may be raised at any time, but—

        (i)    in the case of a lease of lands exceeding two acres in extent for three years and upwards, an interval of not less than one year nor more than two years shall elapse between the date of notice of removal and the term of removal first in date;

        (ii)    in the case of a lease of lands exceeding two acres in extent, whether written or verbal, held from year to year or under tacit relocation, or for any other period less than three years, an interval of not less than six months shall elapse between the date of notice of removal and the term of removal first in date; and

        (iii)    in the case of a house let with or without land attached not exceeding two acres in extent, as also of land not exceeding two acres in extent without houses, as also of mills, fishings, shootings, and all other heritable subjects excepting land exceeding two acres in extent, and let for a year or more, 40 days at least shall elapse between the date of notice of removal and the term of removal first in date.

(2)    In any defended action of removing the sheriff may order the defender to find caution for violent profits.

(3)    In an action for declarator of irritancy and removing by a superior against a vassal, the pursuer shall call as parties the last entered vassal and such heritable creditors and holders of postponed ground burdens as are disclosed by a search for 20 years before the raising of the action, and the expense of the search shall form part of the pursuer's expenses of process.

**Form of notice of removal**

**D1.442**

**34.6.**—(1)[1]    A notice under the following sections of the Sheriff Courts (Scotland) Act 1907 shall be in Form H2:—

    (a)    section 34 (notice in writing to remove where lands exceeding two acres held on probative lease),

    (b)    section 35 (letter of removal where tenant in possession of lands exceeding two acres), and

    (c)    section 36 (notice of removal where lands exceeding two acres occupied by tenant without written lease).

(2)    A letter of removal shall be in Form H3.

**Form of notice under section 37 of the Act of 1907**

**D1.443**

**34.7.**[2]    A notice under section 37 of the Sheriff Courts (Scotland) Act 1907 (notice of termination of tenancy) shall be in Form H4.

---

[1] As amended by SI 1996/2445 (effective November 1, 1996).
[2] As amended by SI 1996/2445 (effective November 1, 1996).

**Giving notice of removal**

**D1.444**

**34.8—**[1](1)   A notice under section 34, 35, 36, 37 or 38 of the Sheriff Courts (Scotland) Act 1907 (which relate to notices of removal) may be given by—

(a)   a sheriff officer

(b)   the person entitled to give such notice, or

(c)   the solicitor or factor of such person,

posting the notice by registered post or the first class recorded delivery service at any post office within the United Kingdom in time for it to be delivered at the address on the notice before the last date on which by law such notice must be given, addressed to the person entitled to receive such notice, and bearing the address of that person at the time, if known, or, if not known, to the last known address of that person.

(2)   A sheriff officer may also give notice under a section of the Sheriff Courts (Scotland) Act 1907 mentioned in paragraph (1) in any manner in which he may serve an initial writ; and, accordingly, rule 5.4 (service within Scotland by sheriff officer) shall, with the necessary modifications, apply to the giving of notice under this paragraph as it applies to service of an initial writ.

**Evidence of notice to remove**

**D1.445**

**34.9.—**(1)   A certificate of the sending of notice under rule 34.8 dated and endorsed on the lease or an extract of it, or on the letter of removal, signed by the sheriff officer or the person sending the notice, his solicitor or factor, or an acknowledgement of the notice endorsed on the lease or an extract of it, or on the letter of removal, by the party in possession or his agent, shall be sufficient evidence that notice has been given.

(2)   Where there is no lease, a certificate of the sending of such notice shall be endorsed on a copy of the notice or letter of removal.

**Disposal of applications under Part II of the Conveyancing and Feudal Reform (Scotland) Act 1970 for non-residential purposes**

**D1.446**

**34.10.—**[2](1)   This rule applies to an application or counter-application made by virtue of paragraph 3(2)(a) of the Act of Sederunt (Sheriff Court Rules) (Enforcement of Securities over Heritable Property) 2010.

(2)   An interlocutor of the sheriff disposing of an application or counter-application is final and not subject to appeal except as to a question of title or as to any other remedy granted.

**Service on unnamed occupiers**

**D1.447**

**34.11.—**[3](1)   Subject to paragraph (2), this rule applies only to a crave for removing in an action of removing against a person or persons in possession of heritable property without right or title to possess the property.

(2)   This rule shall not apply with respect to a person who has or had a title or other right to occupy the heritable property and who has been in continuous occupation since that title or right is alleged to have come to an end.

(3)   Where this rule applies, the pursuer may apply by motion to shorten or dispense with the period of notice or other period of time in these Rules relating to the conduct of the action or the extracting of any decree.

(4)   Where the name of a person in occupation of the heritable property is not known and cannot reasonably be ascertained, the pursuer shall call that person as a defender by naming him as an "occupier".

(5)   Where the name of a person in occupation of the heritable property is not known and cannot reasonably be ascertained, the initial writ shall be served (whether or not it is also served on a named person), unless the court otherwise directs, by a sheriff officer—

(a)   affixing a copy of the initial writ and a citation in Form H5 addressed to "the occupiers" to the main door or other conspicuous part of the premises, and if practicable, depositing a copy of each of those documents in the premises; or

(b)   in the case of land only, inserting stakes in the ground at conspicuous parts of the occupied land to each of which is attached a sealed transparent envelope containing a copy of the initial writ and a citation in Form H5 addressed to "the occupiers".

---

[1] As amended by SI 1996/2445 (effective November 1, 1996).

[2] As substituted by the Act of Sederunt (Sheriff Court Rules) (Enforcement of Securities over Heritable Property) 2010 (SSI 2010/324) para.3 (effective September 30, 2010).

[3] Inserted by the Act of Sederunt (Sheriff Court Ordinary Cause Rules Amendment) (Miscellaneous) 2000 (SSI 2000/239) (effective October 2, 2000).

## Applications under the Mortgage Rights (Scotland) Act 2001

**34.12.** *[Repealed by the Act of Sederunt (Sheriff Court Rules) (Enforcement of Securities over Heritable Property) 2010 (SSI 2010/324) para.2 (effective September 30, 2010).]*

### CHAPTER 35

### ACTIONS OF MULTIPLEPOINDING

*Annotations to Chapter 35 are by Tim Edward, Partner, Maclay Murray and Spens W.S.*

GENERAL NOTE

An action of multiplepoinding is used where any number of parties have claims on money or an item **D1.448** of property, whether heritable or moveable, which is held by another party. The purpose of the action is to decide which claimant is entitled to the property or in what proportions it should be divided between claimants. It also enables the holder of the property to part with it in a legally authorised manner. The subject of the action is known as the "fund *in medio*".

Originally, an action of multiplepoinding was competent only where there was double distress, where two or more arrestments of the fund had been lodged in the hands of the holder, but this rule has gradually been relaxed, and multiplepoindings are now competent wherever there are competing claims to one fund.

The court is generally more liberal towards the competency of a claim by the holder of the fund *in medio* than by a claimant, on the principle that the holder cannot raise a direct action, and should not be bound to remain a holder until the day of his death, or until the competing parties settle their claims. A holder has often been held entitled to bring a multiplepoinding even where a claim is obviously bad, since otherwise he would be liable to have to defend an unfounded action by that claimant.

An action of multiplepoinding may involve a succession of separate actions to determine (i) objections to the raising of the action, (ii) the extent and identity of the fund *in medio*, and (iii) the claims of the respective claimants in a competition on that fund.

*Jurisdiction*

This is regulated by Schedule 8 to the Civil Jurisdiction and Judgments Act 1982 as substituted by SI 2001/3929, Sch.2, para.7. Rule 2(i) of that act, which refers to "proceedings which are brought to assert, declare or determine proprietary or possessory rights, ...in or over moveable property, or to obtain authority to dispose of moveable property", is deemed wide enough to include actions of multiplepoinding (Anton and Beaumont, *Civil Jurisdiction in Scotland*, 1995, para.10.42(2)). In such proceedings, the courts where the property is situated have jurisdiction. If the fund *in medio* consists of or includes immoveable property situated in Scotland, rule 5(1)(a) of Sch.8 to the C.J.J.A 1982 confers jurisdiction on the Sheriff Court of the place where it is situated, even if the defender's domicile is outwith the UK (rule 2(h)(ii)). Also, if any one of the defenders in an action of multiplepoinding is domiciled in Scotland, then the Sheriff Court of the place where that defender is domiciled has jurisdiction. (CJJA 1982, Sch.8, rule 2(o)(i)).

### Application of this Chapter

**35.1.**—(1)   This Chapter applies to an action of multiplepoinding.

**D1.449**

### Application of Chapters 9 and 10

**35.2.**   Chapter 10 (additional procedure) and the following rules in Chapter 9 (standard procedure in **D1.450** defended causes) shall not apply to an action of multiplepoinding:—

rule 9.1 (notice of intention to defend),

rule 9.2 (fixing date for Options Hearing),

rule 9.4 (lodging of pleadings before Options Hearing),

rule 9.8 (adjustment of pleadings),

rule 9.9 (effect of sist on adjustment),

rule 9.10 (open record),

rule 9.11 (record for Options Hearing),

rule 9.12 (Options Hearing),

rule 9.15 (applications for time to pay directions).

An action of multiplepoinding has its own procedure, to which many general rules governing ordinary causes do not apply. Rule 35.2 lists these rules; they include the rule on notices of intention to defend and the rules on Options Hearings and related procedure.

**Parties**

**D1.451**

**35.3.**—(1)  An action of multiplepoinding may be brought by any person holding, or having an interest in, or claim on, the fund *in medio*, in his own name.

(2)  The pursuer shall call as defenders to such an action—

(a)  all persons so far as known to him as having an interest in the fund *in medio*; and

(b)  where he is not the holder of the fund, the holder of that fund.

"ANY PERSON HOLDING, OR HAVING AN INTEREST IN, OR CLAIM ON, THE FUND"

The pursuer is the person who raises the action, whether he is the holder of the fund, or someone with an interest in or a claim on the fund. It is raised in his own name. If the holder of the fund raises the action he is known as the "pursuer and real raiser". Any other party raising the action is known as the 'pursuer and nominal raiser'. If the pursuer is not the holder of the fund, he must call the holder as a defender, and must also call as a defender any person whom he knows to have an interest in the fund. If there are heirs and beneficiaries whose identities are not known, the Lord Advocate should be called as representing the Crown as *ultimus haeres*.

Where the pursuer is the holder, the crave will be in the form:

"(1)  To find that the Pursuer is the holder of [specific description of fund *in medio*], which is claimed by the defenders, and that he is only liable in once and single payment thereof, and is entitled on payment, or consignation, to be exonerated thereof, and to obtain payment of his expenses;

(2)  To grant decree in favour of the party or parties who shall be found to have the best right to the fund *in medio*."

"FUND IN MEDIO"

This is the property in dispute in an action of multiplepoinding. There must be a fund *in medio*; an action is incompetent if there is no debt which the holder is obliged to pay to someone. Therefore, it is incompetent to raise an action of multiplepoinding in respect of a right to future rents (*Pentland v Royal Exchange Assce. Co.* (1830) 9 S. 164), or a fund only in expectation (*Provan v Provan* (1840) 2 D. 298), or not yet received (*Anderson v Cameron's Trs* (1844) 17 Sc.Jur. 42). However, the amount or value of the fund need not be definitely ascertained, so long as there is a fund (*Highland Railway Co. v British Linen Co.* (1901) 38 S.L.R. 584).

The fund can consist of heritable property (e.g. *Edinburgh Merchant Maiden's Hospital v Greig's Exrs* (1902) 10 S.L.T. 317; *Boyd's Trs v Boyd* (1906) 13 S.L.T. 878) or moveable property (including right to title deeds: *Baillie v Baillie* (1830) 8 S. 318), or a combination of both heritable and moveable property (*Logan v Byres* (1895) 2 S.L.T. 445).

In the course of a multiplepoinding action the court may have to decide whether the property in dispute falls under the category of heritable or moveable property, for example where rights of succession to that property require to be determined: *Cowan v Cowan* (1887) 14 R. 670.

The fund *in medio* should include only what is in dispute and no other property: *McNab v Waddell* (1894) 21 R. 827; *MacGillvray's Trs v Dallas* (1905) 7 F. 733. If other property is included, then the court may dismiss the action as incompetent (as in *McNab*), or allow the holder to amend the condescendence of the fund (*MacGillvray's Trs*). If, before the conclusion of the action of multiplepoinding, the holder loses title to property in the fund *in medio*, (i.e. by reduction of that title in a separate action), that property to which the holder no longer has title should be excluded from the condescendence of the fund: *Dunn's Trs v Barstow* (1870) 9 M. 281.

"DEFENDERS"

There must be at least two parties called as defenders, otherwise the action must be a direct action and not a multiplepoinding. (See note to rule 35.8.)

"HAVING AN INTEREST IN"

The purpose of an action of multiplepoinding is to dispose of all competing claims to the fund *in medio* and free the holder from any future responsibility towards possible claimants, so all persons who are believed to have some claim on the fund must be called as defenders. Persons not called may be allowed to lodge a claim at a later stage than they would be in most ordinary cause actions: *Morgan v Morris* (1856) 18 D. 797; aff'd. sub. nom. *Young v Morris* (1858) 20 D. (HL)12. Hence the provision for advertisement at rule 35.7.

**Condescendence of fund in medio**

**35.4.**—(1) Where the pursuer is the holder of the fund *in medio*, he shall include a detailed statement of the fund in the condescendence in the initial writ.

(2) Where the pursuer is not the holder of the fund *in medio*, the holder shall, before the expiry of the period of notice—

    (a) lodge in process—

        (i) a condescendence of the fund *in medio*, stating any claim or lien which he may profess to have on that fund;

        (ii) a list of all persons known to him as having an interest in the fund; and

    (b) intimate a copy of the condescendence and list to any other party.

"CONDESCENDENCE OF THE FUND IN MEDIO"

There must be a condescendence: *Carmichael v Todd* (1853) 15 D. 473. It is essential that the court be able to establish the extent of the fund *in medio*, otherwise it cannot go on to assess the various claims upon the fund. The condescendence should specify the grounds on which each defender is called, and state the facts which justify the raising of the action.

Where a party's case is founded on a document, that document must be produced and specifically described, either by quoting its critical provisions in the averments, or expressly incorporating the document and holding its provisions as repeated in the averments by reference *brevitatis causa*.

"DETAILED STATEMENT OF THE FUND"

It should be sufficient to identify the property comprising the fund.

"INITIAL WRIT"

This is in Form G1 in Appendix 1 to the Ordinary Cause Rules.

"WHERE THE PURSUER IS NOT THE HOLDER…"

In this case the holder must lodge in process a statement of the property comprising the fund *in medio*, and state any claim or lien which he himself has on the fund as well as a list of all the persons he knows to have an interest in the fund. His failure to state his own claim at this point may not bar the claim, if the claim is stateable by way of retention or compensation, when objections to the condescendence of the fund *in medio* are determined: *Ramsay's JF v British Linen Bank*, 1912 S.C. 206, 208. Trustees holding a fund for administration are obliged to lodge a claim, as trustees, for the whole fund for the purpose of administration: *Hall's Trs v McDonald* (1892)19 R. 567, 577 per Lord Kinnear.

"PERIOD OF NOTICE"

This is determined by reference to rule 3.6.

"INTIMATE"

For methods, see rule 5.3.

"WARRANT OF CITATION IN MULTIPLEPOINDINGS"

35.5. The warrant of citation of the initial writ in an action of multiplepoinding shall be in Form M1.

"WARRANT OF CITATION"

The writ is served on all defenders, including, where the pursuer is not the holder of the fund in medio, the holder of that fund. The warrant of citation is in the Form M1 in Appendix 1 to the Rules. The defender is ordained to intimate if he or she intends to lodge (a) defences challenging the jurisdiction of the court or the competence of the action; (b) objections to the condescendence of the fund in medio; or (c) a claim on the fund; or any combination of these.

**Citation**

**35.6.**—(1) Subject to rule 5.6 (service where address of person is not known), citation of any person in an action of multiplepoinding shall be in Form M2 which shall be attached to a copy of the initial writ and warrant of citation and shall have appended to it a notice of appearance in Form M4.

(2) The certificate of citation shall be in Form M3 and shall be attached to the initial writ.

"RULE 5.6"

This rule provides for service upon a person whose address is unknown by the publication of an advertisement in a specified newspaper circulating in the area of the last known address of that person, or by displaying on the walls of court a copy of the instance and crave of the initial writ, the warrant of citation, and a notice in Form G4.

"NOTICE OF APPEARANCE"

See rule 35.8.

**D1.454**

**Advertisement**

**35.7.** The sheriff may make an order for advertisement of the action in such newspapers as he thinks fit.

"ADVERTISEMENT"

Intimation of the raising of an action of multiplepoinding ensures that all persons entitled to make a claim have an opportunity to do so. Lord Neaves described it as "an essential prerequisite to any judgement in [a] competition": *Connell v Ferguson* (1861) 23 D. 683, at 687.

Further, rule 35.16 states that the sheriff may at any time during the action, either *ex proprio motu* or on the motion of any party, order further service on any person, or advertisement or further advertisement of the action.

**D1.455**

**Lodging of notice of appearance**

**35.8.** Where a party intends to lodge—

    (a)   defences to challenge the jurisdiction of the court or the competency of the action,

    (b)   objections to the condescendence of the fund *in medio*, or

    (c)   a claim on the fund,

he shall, before the expiry of the period of notice, lodge a notice of appearance in Form M4.

"DEFENCES TO CHALLENGE THE JURISDICTION... OR THE COMPETENCY..."

N.B. rule 35.12(2): defences must be disposed of before any further procedure in the action, unless the sheriff directs otherwise.

A party may wish to lodge defences on grounds such as lack of jurisdiction (see General Note at rule 35.1), or forum non conveniens (e.g. *Provan v Provan* (1840) 2 D. 298).

Also, an action of multiplepoinding is incompetent in a situation where a direct action is available to the claimant. Greater latitude is allowed, however, where the action is raised by the holder of the fund rather than a claimant. The holder of the fund 'is entitled to be relieved by means of an action of multiplepoinding ... and accordingly it is sufficient justification of the institution of the action, and is the criterion of its competency, that the claims intimated make it impossible for the depositary to pay to one of the parties without running the risk of an action at the instance of the other.': *Winchester v Blakey* (1890) 17 R. 1046, 1050 per Lord MacLaren. Accordingly, it is enough to show that there are competing claims which the holder of the fund is unable to meet. So, for example, actions of multiplepoinding which would otherwise have been dismissed as incompetent, because they raised an issue between two claimants which would have been triable by direct action, were nonetheless allowed when raised by the holders: *Royal Bank of Scotland v Price* (1893) 20 R. 290; *Commercial Bank of Scotland v Muir* (1897 ) 25 R. 219.

An action of multiplepoinding should not be used by trustees, executors, or those who hold property on behalf of others simply as a means of dealing with disputes over the property, if there is no genuine double distress. For example, an action of multiplepoinding raised by trustees was held to be incompetent where the only dispute was between a beneficiary and a creditor on the estate (*Glen's Trs v Miller* , 1911 S.C. 1178; cf. *Ogilvy's Trs v Chevallier* (1874)1 R. 693 (where a multiplepoinding by testamentary trustees was only reluctantly allowed where the only dispute was between the sole beneficiary and her creditor)) or where a solicitor was called upon to pay over the confirmed estate to the confirmed executor and another party claimed a right to those funds (*Adam Cochran & Co. v Conn* , 1989 S.L.T. (Sh. Ct.) 27).

Executors and trustees should not resort to a multiplepoinding to obtain exoneration and discharge where there is no difficulty obtaining this by the usual means (*Mackenzie's Trs v Gray* (1895) 2 S.L.T. 422); however, it is competent for those holding monies in a fiduciary capacity, such as executors and trustees, to raise an action of multiplepoinding in order to obtain exoneration and discharge if those who have the power to grant this refuse to do so (*Fraser's Exr v Wallace's Trs* (1893) 20 R. 374, 379 per Lord Maclaren), or where they are otherwise unable to grant sufficient exoneration (*Davidson v Ewen* (1895) 3 S.L.T. 162), or where, because of doubts as to the meaning of testamentary bequests it is unclear who is entitled to the fund and able to give valid discharge (*McClement's Trs v Lord Advocate* , 1949 S.L.T. (Notes) 59).

A judicial factor cannot obtain his exoneration and discharge through an action of multiplepoinding; he is appointed by the court in the exercise of its nobile officium and must likewise be discharged through the exercise of those powers: *Campbell v Grant* (1869) 7 M. 227, 233 per Lord Deas.

"OBJECTIONS TO THE CONDESCENDENCE OF THE FUND"

A party may wish to lodge objections to the existence or composition of the fund *in medio*. In *Provan v Provan* (1840) 23 D. 298, the Lord Ordinary himself raised an objection to the competency of the action on the ground that there was no fund *in medio*. A common objection is that there is some property which should be excluded from the condescendence of the fund: e.g. *Walker's Trs v Walker* (1878) 5 R. 678; *Donaldson's Trs v Beattie* 1914 1 S.L.T. 170. However, objections that the fund in medio includes property which is clearly not in dispute, appear to be treated rather as defences challenging the competency of the action itself, and dealt with at the initial stage of disposal of defences under rule 35.12(2): eg *McNab v Waddell* (1894) 21 R. 827. Likewise, an objection that the pursuer is not entitled to the fund is not an objection to the competency of the action, but one which affects the merits: *Greenshields' Trs v Greenshields* , 1915 2 S.L.T. 189.

"CLAIM ON THE FUND"

This is a short sentence in which the claimant claims to be ranked and preferred to the fund *in medio*, or to a particular portion of that fund. A holder's claim may include a right of retention or compensation.

In some circumstances, a claimant has what is known as a "riding claim", where he is ranked on the fund in medio by virtue of his debtor's claim in the multiplepoinding. However, that debtor's claim must be a direct one, and not a riding claim itself: *Gill's Trs v Patrick* (1889) 16 R. 403. A riding claim must be constituted (*Royal Bank of Scotland v Stevenson* (1849) 12 D. 250) and liquid (*Home's Trs v Ralston's Trs.* (1833) 12 S. 727; *Wilson v Young* (1851) 13 D. 1366). The riding claim must be lodged before decree for payment is pronounced in favour of the original claimant (i.e. the debtor): *Anglo-Foreign Banking Co.* (1879) 16 S.L.R. 731. There are no reported decisions to confirm it, but it would appear to be competent for more than one riding claim to be ranked on a principal claim, leading to a separate competition in respect of those riding claims on the principal claimant's share of the fund: Thomson & Middleton, *Manual of Court of Session Practice*, p.124.

"PERIOD OF NOTICE"

This is determined by reference to rule 3.6.

"NOTICE OF APPEARANCE"

The party lodging notice of appearance must specify in the notice the purpose of his intended appearance. The notice, in Form M4, is signed by the party or his solicitor. It is improper for parties with conflicting interests to be represented by the same firm of solicitors: *Dunlop's Trs v Farquharson* , 1956 S.L.T. 16.

If no notice of appearance is lodged, the sheriff may decide to order advertisement, or further advertisement, of the action, in accordance with rule 35.16.

**Fixing date for first hearing**                                                                                                  D1.456

**35.9.** Where a notice of appearance, or a condescendence on the fund *in medio* and list under rule 35.4(2)(a) has been lodged, the sheriff clerk shall—

    (a)   fix a date and time for the first hearing, which date shall be the first suitable court day occurring not sooner than 4 weeks after the expiry of the period of notice;

    (b)   on fixing the date for the first hearing forthwith intimate that date in Form M5 to each party; and

    (c)   prepare and sign an interlocutor recording the date of the first hearing.

"INTIMATE"

For methods, see rule 5.3.

"INTERLOCUTOR"

For rules relating to interlocutors, see rule 12.1.

**Hearings**                                                                                                                        D1.457

**35.10.**—(1)   The sheriff shall conduct the first, and any subsequent hearing, with a view to securing the expeditious progress of the cause by ascertaining from parties the matters in dispute.

(2)[1]   The parties shall provide the sheriff with sufficient information to enable him to—

    (a)   conduct the hearing as provided for in this Chapter,

---

[1] As substituted by the Act of Sederunt (Ordinary Cause, Summary Application, Summary Cause and Small Claim Rules) Amendment (Vulnerable Witnesses (Scotland) Act 2004) 2007, r.2(11) (effective November 1, 2007).

(b) consider any child witness notice or vulnerable witness application that has been lodged where no order has been made, or

(c) ascertain whether there is or is likely to be a vulnerable witness within the meaning of section 11(1) of the Act of 2004 who is to give evidence at any proof or hearing and whether any order under section 12(1) of the Act of 2004 requires to be made.

(3) At the first, or any subsequent hearing, the sheriff shall fix a period within which defences, objections or claims shall be lodged, and appoint a date for a second hearing.

(4) Where the list lodged under rule 35.4(2)(a) contains any person who is not a party to the action, the sheriff shall order—

(a) the initial writ to be amended to add that person as a defender;

(b) service of the pleadings so amended to be made on that person, with a citation in Form M6; and

(c) intimation to that person of any condescendence of the fund *in medio* lodged by a holder of the fund who is not the pursuer.

(5) Where a person to whom service has been made under paragraph (4) lodges a notice of appearance under rule 35.8, the sheriff clerk shall intimate to him in Form M5 the date of the next hearing fixed in the action.

GENERAL NOTE

Rule 35.10 focuses on the need for efficiency throughout the course of an action of multiplepoinding, so that the case may be disposed of as quickly and satisfactorily as possible. These provisions are similar to the rules for the conduct of options hearings and procedural hearings in other ordinary causes. (See for example OCR rules 9.12(1), (2) and 10.6(1), (2).)

**D1.458**

**Lodging defences, objections and claims**

**35.11.**—(1) Defences, objections and claims by a party shall be lodged with the sheriff clerk in a single document under separate headings.

(2) Each claimant shall lodge with his claim any documents founded on in his claim, so far as they are within his custody or power.

"A SINGLE DOCUMENT"

This is the equivalent of lodging defences in a normal ordinary cause action. Each party must lodge a single document which, under separate headings, deals with defences, objections and claims. Where a party wishes to state defences to the competency of the action, he lodges defences in the usual form, with any objections or claim by the defender following the pleas-in-law under separate headings.

If a party does not wish to lodge defences to the competency of the action, but wishes to lodge objections, his writ is headed: "OBJECTIONS/for/A.B. [*designed*]/to/Condescendence of the fund *in medio*/ in/Action of Multiplepoinding/[*names and designations of parties as in the instance*]." Objections are specifically stated in numbered paragraphs and are followed by appropriate pleas-in-law.

If a party simply wishes to lodge a claim, it is headed: "CONDESCENDENCE AND CLAIM/for/ A.B. [*designed*], Claimant/in/Action of Multiplepoinding [etc., *as above*]."

A claim consists of a condescendence, claim, and pleas-in-law. The condescendence is headed "Condescendence" and sets out in numbered paragraphs the facts on which the claimant bases his claim. The claim is headed "Claim" and must set out specifically what is claimed. This is an essential part of the writ: *Connell v Ferguson* (1861) 23 D. 683, per Lord Neaves at 686. In a riding claim, the claimant is described as a riding claimant.

The plea in the pleas-in-law is that the claimant is entitled to be ranked and preferred to the fund *in medio* in terms of his claim.

"DOCUMENTS"

When a document is founded upon or adopted in defences, objections, or claims, it must, so far as in the possession or within the control of the party founding upon it or adopting it, be lodged in process by that party. If the document is not produced, it cannot be considered by the court: *Hayes v Robinson* , 1984 S.L.T. 300, per Lord Ross at 301. Under rule 21.1, the sheriff has power to order the production of any document or grant a commission and diligence for recovery of it.

**D1.459**

**Disposal of defences**

**35.12.**—(1) Where defences have been lodged, the sheriff may order the initial writ and defences to be adjusted and thereafter close the record and regulate further procedure.

(2) Unless the sheriff otherwise directs, defences shall be disposed of before any further procedure in the action.

The rules set out consecutive procedural stages by which defences, objections and claims are successively disposed of. Unless the sheriff otherwise directs, defences challenging the jurisdiction or competency of an action are dealt with first, before any further procedure. After defences have been lodged, the sheriff may order the initial writ and defences to be adjusted. He then closes the record and regulates further procedure, usually by appointing parties to debate. If the sheriff sustains the objections to jurisdiction or to the competency of the action, the case comes to an end here. If he rejects them, the case will continue to a new hearing at which further procedure will be determined.

### Objections to fund in medio

**35.13.**—(1)  Where objections to the fund *in medio* have been lodged, the sheriff may, after disposal of any defences, order the condescendence of the fund and objections to be adjusted, and thereafter close the record and regulate further procedure.

(2)  If no objections to the fund *in medio* have been lodged, or if objections have been lodged and disposed of, the sheriff may, on the motion of the holder of the fund, and without ordering intimation to any party approve the condescendence of the fund and find the holder liable only in one single payment.

*"objections to the fund in medio"*

Objections to the condescendence of the fund are dealt with next, after disposal of defences. The sheriff may order the condescendence and objections to be adjusted, after which he again closes the record and regulates further procedure. He will usually order a debate or proof, and then dispose of objections and fix a further hearing. The interlocutor disposing of the objections may be appealed without leave: *Walker's Trs v Walker* (1878) 5 R. 678; *Harris School Board v Davidson* (1881) 9 R. 371.

*"approve the condescendence of the fund"*

This is a final interlocutor, which, again, may be appealed without leave: *Harris School Board v Davidson* (1881) 9 R. 371.

The court's approval of the fund is essential, as the interlocutor determines the amount for which the holder is liable to account.

*"find the holder liable only in one single payment"*

This is a judicial determination that the action is competent.

(The motion in respect of this finding and the approval of the condescendence may be made at an earlier hearing on objections, so that the interlocutor disposing of objections may at the same time approve the condescendence and find the holder liable in one single payment.)

The purpose of this finding, once the objections (if any) are disposed of and the fund is approved, is to enable the holder to make payment (usually by consigning the fund into court) and effectively drop out of the action; that is, unless the holder also wishes to assert a claim on the fund.

### Preliminary pleas in multiplepoindings

**D1.460**

**35.14.**—(1)  A party intending to insist on a preliminary plea shall, not later than 3 days before any hearing to determine further procedure following the lodging of defences, objections or claims, lodge with the sheriff clerk a note of the basis of the plea.

(2)  Where a party fails to comply with the provisions of paragraph (1), he shall be deemed to be no longer insisting on the plea and the plea shall be repelled by the sheriff at the hearing referred to in paragraph (1).

(3)  If satisfied that there is a preliminary matter of law which justifies a debate, the sheriff shall, after having heard parties and considered the note lodged under this rule, appoint the action to debate.

"PRELIMINARY PLEAS"

The provisions relating to preliminary pleas in actions of multiplepoinding are similar to those for other ordinary causes (cf. rule 22.1).

### Consignation of the fund and discharge of holder

**D1.461**

**35.15.**—(1)  At any time after the condescendence of the fund *in medio* has been approved, the sheriff may order the whole or any part of the fund to be sold and the proceeds of the sale consigned into court.

(2)  After such consignation the holder of the fund *in medio* may apply for his exoneration and discharge.

(3)  The sheriff may allow the holder of the fund *in medio*, on his exoneration and discharge, his expenses out of the fund as a first charge on the fund.

The amount consigned is the balance in the hands of the holder after deduction of the holder's taxed expenses (if any).

Unlike the 1983 Ordinary Cause Rules, the current rules make no specific provision for consignation into court where no sale takes place. However, consignation is still probably the appropriate step to take even where there is no sale.

The form of the fund, or part of it, may make consignation difficult. There may be a problem if the fund *in medio* consists of a bulky or valuable object which the parties do not wish to be sold. The only way for the sheriff clerk to keep such an object would be to arrange for it to be commercially stored, incurring costs which may significantly reduce the value of the fund *in medio*. In this situation, therefore, the court may ask the holder to retain it, or ask the parties to agree an arrangement for its safekeeping pending the outcome of the action.

For procedure where the fund *in medio* consists of or includes a heritable security, see *Currie's Trs v. Bothwell* , 1954 S.L.T. (Sh. Ct.) 87.

"EXONERATION AND DISCHARGE"

This allows the holder of the fund *in medio* legally to dispose of the property of which he has been in possession, and free him from the possibility of any future claims by any person: see e.g. *Farquhar v. Farquhar* (1896) 13 R. 596. This will be the end of his involvement in the action.

"HIS EXPENSES OUT OF THE FUND"

If the holder of the fund *in medio* is not the pursuer, he will be entitled to the expenses of the condescendence of the fund out of that fund. If the holder is the pursuer and the action was justified, he will usually be entitled to expenses out of the fund. However, if trustees raise an action of multiplepoinding which is subsequently found to be unjustified, they may be found personally liable in expenses: *MacKenzie's Trs v. Sutherland* (1894) 22 R. 233; *Paterson's Trs v. Paterson* (1897) 7 S.L.T. 134; cf. *Gens Trs v. Miller* , 1911 S.C. 1178.

In practice, the steps laid out in rules 35.13(2), and 35.15(2) and (3) are normally combined in a single interlocutor, in which the sheriff: (1) holds the fund *in medio* to be correctly stated in the initial writ or other pleading at the sum therein specified; (2) finds the holder liable in one single payment; (3) finds the holder entitled to payment of his expenses out of the fund *in medio* and allows an account of those expenses to be given in and remits the account, when lodged, to the auditor of court to tax and to report; (4) ordains the holder to lodge the fund *in medio*, with his expenses deducted, in the hands of the sheriff clerk; and (5) upon consignation being made exoners and discharges him of the fund *in medio* and of his whole actings and intromissions therewith. Once this has been done, the holder has no further involvement in the action.

Where the holder is to retain possession of the fund in the circumstances outlined above (in the notes for "*consignation of the fund*"), he cannot yet be exonered and discharged, but he may not wish to be further involved in the litigation. In this situation, the sheriff approves the condescendence of the fund, finds the holder liable only in one single payment, finds him entitled to expenses and has these taxed and approved. Thereafter the holder takes no part in the proceedings. The final interlocutor, as well as ranking and preferring the claimants, ordains delivery on payment of the holder's expenses, and on delivery being made exoners and discharges the holder.

**D1.462**

**Further service or advertisement**

**35.16.** The sheriff may at any time, of his own motion or on the motion of any party, order further service on any person or advertisement.

"FURTHER SERVICE ON ANY PERSON OR ADVERTISEMENT"

See under "*advertisement*" at notes for rule 35.7.

**D1.463**

**Ranking of claims**

**35.17.**—(1) After disposal of any defences, and approval of the condescendence of the fund *in medio*, the sheriff may, where there is no competition on the fund, rank and prefer the claimants and grant decree in terms of that ranking.

(2) Where there is competition on the fund, the sheriff may order claims to be adjusted and thereafter close the record and regulate further procedure.

"NO COMPETITION"

If there is no competition, the parties may agree in a joint minute to a ranking of their respective claims, though it is not necessary to do this. The sheriff grants decree, and directs the sheriff clerk to make payment to the claimants out of the consigned fund on the lodging of any necessary clearance certificate, and to require receipts. A decree of ranking and preference may be granted without proof (*Union Bank v. Grade* (1887) 25 S.L.R. 61), although the court may refuse to grant the decree, even where there is no competition, if it appears ex facie of a claimant's claim that he has no right to that part of the fund which he claims: *Clark's Exr v. Clark*, 1953 S.L.T. (Notes) 58.

Once a decree of ranking and preference has been pronounced, it can only be brought under review by a person called as defender in the multiplepoinding, by an action of reduction (*Stodart v. Bell* (1860) 22 D. 1092, 1093 per Lord Cowan); and where payment has been made, the only remedy is an action against the party who has received payment, the holder of the fund being no longer liable (*Geikie v. Morris* (1858) 3 Macq. 353).

The rule that payment must not be made until any necessary clearance certificate has been lodged (see rule 30.2(1)) must be strictly observed: *Simpson's Trs v. Fox*, 1954 S.L.T. (Notes) 12. If any payments are made out of the fund before all government duties have been paid, the court may not grant the holder of the fund exoneration and discharge: *Simpson's Trs v. Fox*, 1954 S.L.T. (Notes) 12. (But note the exception to this rule, at rule 30.2(2), which applies only to multiplepoindings: decree may be granted even though not all of the taxes or duties payable on the estate of a deceased claimant have yet been paid or satisfied.)

It is essential that the interlocutor disposing of an action of multiplepoinding be clearly expressed. Likewise, any joint minute should specify in detail the steps which the court is asked to take when pronouncing decree. In particular, the agreement contained in the joint minute should: (1) ensure that the total fund will be disposed of, and that provision will be made for such matters as the assignation of life policies or the delivery of goods; (2) wherever possible, specify the payments to be made in precise figures or in specific fractions of the total, rather than by reference to any formula; (3) deal clearly with any accrued interest; and (4) deal with expenses.

"COMPETITION"

A competition arises where the claims amount to more than the value of the fund, or where the claims are competing in respect of a particular part of the fund. The sheriff may order claims to be adjusted and then close the record and regulate further procedure. Here, as at any earlier closings of the record, the case may be heard by debate (provided that a note of the basis of the preliminary plea has been lodged as set out in rule 35.14), or by proof if there is a dispute as to fact. In the interlocutor disposing of the competition, the sheriff will rank and prefer the successful claimant or claimants and repel the claims of the unsuccessful. If the interlocutor deals with expenses it may be appealed without leave by the unsuccessful claimant (*Glasgow Corporation v. General Accident Fire and Life Assurance Corporation Ltd*, 1914 S.C. 835). The sheriff may make an order for payment in the same interlocutor, or he may delay dealing with this, in which case the interlocutor will make findings in fact and in law determining the principles on which division of the fund is to proceed, and grant leave to appeal.

The interlocutor ordering payment or transference of the fund in medio to the successful claimants protects the holder, after payment or transference, from any further claims at the instance of any person (Stair, IV, xvi, 3; Erskine, IV, iii, 23). It constitutes res judicata as against all the parties in the process: *McCaig v. Maitland* (1887) 14 R. 295; *Elder's Trs v. Elder* (1895) 22 R. 505.

### Remit to reporter

**D1.464**

**35.18.**—(1)  Where several claims have been lodged, the sheriff may remit to a reporter to prepare a scheme of division and report.

(2)  The expenses of such remit, when approved by the sheriff, shall be made a charge on the fund, to be deducted before division.

"REPORTER"

In practice, it is rarely necessary for the sheriff to remit to a reporter. If he does, the scheme prepared by the reporter will show the amounts which the decree of ranking and preference determines to be payable to each of the successful claimants.

**D1.465**

CHAPTER 36

ACTIONS OF DAMAGES

Part AI[1]

Special Procedure for Actions for, or Arising from Personal Injuries

*Application and interpretation*

**Application and interpretation of this Part**

**D1.466**

**36.A1.**—(1)  This Part applies to a personal injuries action.

(2)  In this Part—

"personal injuries action" means an action of damages for, or arising from, personal injuries or death of a person from personal injuries; and

"personal injuries procedure" means the procedure established by rules 36.G1 to 36.L1.

(3)  In the definition of "personal injuries action", "personal injuries" includes any disease or impairment, whether physical or mental.

*Raising a personal injuries action*

**Form of initial writ**

**D1.467**

**36.B1.**—(1)  Subject to rule 36.C1, the initial writ in a personal injuries action shall be in Form P11 and there shall be annexed to it a brief statement containing—

(a)  averments in numbered paragraphs relating only to those facts necessary to establish the claim;

(b)  the names of every medical practitioner from whom, and every hospital or other institution in which, the pursuer or, in an action in respect of the death of a person,

the deceased received treatment for the personal injuries.

(2)  An initial writ may include—

(a)  warrants for intimation so far as permitted under these Rules, and

(b)  a specification of documents in Form PI2.

**Actions based on clinical negligence**

**D1.468**

**36.C1.**—(1)  An initial writ in a personal injuries action may include a draft interlocutor in Form PI4.

(2)  At the same time as an initial writ which includes a draft interlocutor in Form PI4 is presented for warranting, the pursuer may lodge a written application in the form of a letter addressed to the sheriff clerk for authority to raise the action, where it is based on alleged clinical negligence, as an ordinary cause.

(3)  On the making of an application under paragraph (2), the initial writ shall be placed before a sheriff in chambers and in the absence of the parties.

(4)  On consideration of the initial writ in accordance with paragraph (3), the sheriff may—

(a)  if he considers that there are exceptional reasons for not following personal injuries procedure such as would justify the granting of a motion under rule 36.F1, grant authority for the cause to proceed as an ordinary cause by signing the draft interlocutor in the initial writ; or

(b)  fix a hearing.

(5)  The sheriff clerk shall notify the parties of the date and time of any hearing under paragraph (4)(b).

(6)  At a hearing under paragraph (4)(b), the sheriff may refuse the application or, if he considers that there are exceptional reasons for not following personal injuries procedure such as would justify the granting of a motion under rule 36.F1, grant authority for the cause to proceed as an ordinary cause by signing the draft interlocutor in the initial writ.

---

[1] As inserted by the Act of Sederunt (Ordinary Cause Rules Amendment) (Personal Injuries Actions) 2009 (SSI 2009/285) r.2 (effective November 2, 2009).

(7)    Where the sheriff grants authority for the cause to proceed as an ordinary cause under paragraph (4)(a) or (6)—

    (a)    the sheriff or, as the case may be, the sheriff clerk shall sign a warrant in accordance with rule 5.1 (signature of warrants);

    (b)    the cause shall thereafter proceed in accordance with Chapter 9 (standard procedure in defended causes) rather than in accordance with personal injuries procedure.

(8)    In this rule—

"clinical negligence" means a breach of a duty of care by a health care professional in connection with that person's diagnosis or the care and treatment of any person, by act or omission, whilst the health care professional was acting in his professional capacity; and

"health care professional" includes a doctor, dentist, nurse, midwife, health visitor, pharmacy practitioner, registered ophthalmic practitioner, registered dispensing optician, member of Professions Allied to Medicine, member of the Allied Health Professions, a person who is a member of ambulance personnel, a member of laboratory staff or a relevant technician.

### Inspection and recovery of documents

**36.D1.**—(1)    This rule applies where the initial writ in a personal injuries action contains a specification of documents by virtue of rule 36.B1(2)(b).

**D1.469**

(2)    On the granting of a warrant for citation, an order granting commission and diligence for the production and recovery of the documents mentioned in the specification shall be deemed to have been granted and the sheriff clerk shall certify Form PI2 to that effect by attaching thereto a docquet in Form PI3.

(3)    An order which is deemed to have been made under paragraph (2) shall be treated for all purposes as an interlocutor granting commission and diligence signed by the sheriff.

(4)    The pursuer may serve an order under paragraph (2) and the provisions of Chapter 28 (recovery of evidence) shall thereafter apply, subject to any necessary modifications, as if the order were an order obtained on an application under rule 28.2 (applications for commission and diligence for recovery of documents etc.).

(5)    Nothing in this rule shall affect the right of a party to apply under rule 28.2 for a commission and diligence for recovery of documents or for an order under section 1 of the Administration of Justice (Scotland) Act 1972 in respect of any document or other property whether or not mentioned in the specification annexed to the initial writ.

*Personal injuries action: application of other rules and withdrawal from personal injuries procedure*

### Application of other rules

**36.E1.**—(1)    Subject to rule 36.F1, a defended personal injuries action shall, instead of proceeding in accordance with Chapter 9 (standard procedure in defended causes), proceed in accordance with personal injuries procedure.

**D1.470**

(2)    Paragraph (1) does not apply to a personal injuries action in respect of which the sheriff has granted an application under rule 36.C1(2).

(3)    Paragraphs (4) to (14) apply to a personal injuries action proceeding in accordance with personal injuries procedure.

(4)    Despite paragraph (1), the following rules of Chapter 9 apply—

    (a)    rule 9.1 (notice of intention to defend);

    (b)    rule 9.3 (return of initial writ);

    (c)    rule 9.5 (process folder);

    (d)    rule 9.6 (defences); and

    (e)    rule 9.7 (implied admissions).

(5)    But the defences shall not include a note of pleas-in-law.

(6)    In the application of rule 18.3(1) (applications to amend), a minute of amendment lodged in process shall include, where appropriate, confirmation as to whether any warrants are sought under rule 36.B1(2)(a) or whether a specification of documents is sought under rule 36.B1(2)(b).

(7)    In the application of rule 18.5(1)(a) (service of amended pleadings), the sheriff shall order any timetable issued in terms of rule 36.G1 to be served together with a copy of the initial writ or record.

(8)    Rule 18.5(3) (fixing of hearing following service of amended pleadings and lodging of notice of intention to defend) shall not apply.

(9)    In the application of rule 19.1 (counterclaims) a counterclaim may also include—

    (a)    warrants for intimation so far as permitted under these Rules; and

    (b)    a specification of documents in Form PI2.

(10)    In rule 19.4 (disposal of counterclaims), paragraph (b) shall not apply.

(11)  In the application of rule 20.4(3) (service on third party), any timetable already issued in terms of rule 36.G1 shall also be served with a third party notice.

(12)  In the application of rule 20.6 (procedure following answers)—

(a)  paragraphs (1) and (2) shall not apply; and

(b)  where a third party lodges answers, any timetable already issued under rule 36.G1 shall apply to the third party.

(13)  Chapters 22 (preliminary pleas) and 28A (pre-proof hearing) shall not apply.

(14)  In relation to an action proceeding in accordance with personal injuries procedure—

(a)  references elsewhere in these Rules to the condescendence of an initial writ or to the articles of the condescendence shall be construed as references to the statement required under rule 36.B1(1) and the numbered paragraphs of that statement;

(b)  references elsewhere in these Rules to pleas-in-law, an open record, a closed record or a record for an Options Hearing shall be ignored;

(c)  references elsewhere in these Rules to any action carried out before or after the closing of the record shall be construed as references to that action being carried out before, or as the case may be, after, the date fixed for completion of adjustment under rule 36.G1(1)(b)(iii).

### Disapplication of personal injuries procedure

**D1.471**

**36.F1.**—(1)  Any party to a personal injuries action proceeding in accordance with personal injuries procedure may, within 28 days of the lodging of defences (or, where there is more than one defender the first lodging of defences), by motion apply to have the action withdrawn from personal injuries procedure and to be appointed to proceed as an ordinary cause.

(2)  No motion under paragraph (1) shall be granted unless the sheriff is satisfied that there are exceptional reasons for not following personal injuries procedure.

(3)  In determining whether there are exceptional reasons justifying the granting of a motion made under paragraph (1), the sheriff shall have regard to—

(a)  the likely need for detailed pleadings;

(b)  the length of time required for preparation of the action; and

(c)  any other relevant circumstances.

(4)  Where the sheriff appoints the cause to proceed as an ordinary cause under paragraph (1)—

(a)  the sheriff clerk shall fix a date and time for an Options Hearing;

(b)  the cause shall thereafter proceed in accordance with Chapter 9 rather than in accordance with personal injuries procedure;

(c)  the pursuer shall within 14 days thereof lodge a revised initial writ as nearly as may be in Form G1; and

(d)  the defender shall thereafter adjust his defences so as to comply with rule 9.6(2).

*Personal injuries procedure*

### Allocation of diets and timetables

**D1.472**

**36.G1.**—[1](1)  The sheriff clerk shall, on the lodging of defences in the action or, where there is more than one defender, the first lodging of defences—

(a)  allocate a diet of proof of the action, which shall be no earlier than 4 months (unless the sheriff on cause shown directs an earlier diet to be fixed) and no later than 9 months from the date of the first lodging of defences; and

(b)  issue a timetable stating—

(i)  the date of the diet mentioned in subparagraph (a); and

(ii)  the dates no later than which the procedural steps mentioned in paragraph (1A) are to take place.

(1A)  Those procedural steps are—

(a)  application for a third party notice under rule 20.1;

(b)[2]  the pursuer serving a commission for recovery of documents under rule 36.D1;

(c)  the parties adjusting their pleadings;

(d)  the pursuer lodging a statement of valuation of claim in process;

(e)  the pursuer lodging a record;

---

[1] As amended by the Act of Sederunt (Sheriff Court Rules) (Miscellaneous Amendments) 2010 (SSI 2010/279) r.4 (effective July 29, 2010).

[2] As amended by the Act of Sederunt (Sheriff Court Rules) (Miscellaneous Amendments) (No.3) 2011 (SSI 2011/386) para.4 (effective November 28, 2011).

(f)    the defender (and any third party to the action) lodging a statement of valuation of claim in process;

(g)    the parties each lodging in process a list of witnesses together with any productions upon which they wish to rely; and

(h)    the pursuer lodging in process the minute of the pre-proof conference.

(1B)    The dates mentioned in paragraph (1)(b)(ii) are to be calculated by reference to periods specified in Appendix 3, which, with the exception of the period specified in rule 36.K1(2), the sheriff principal may vary for his sheriffdom or for any court within his sheriffdom.;

(2)    A timetable issued under paragraph (1)(b) shall be in Form PI5 and shall be treated for all purposes as an interlocutor signed by the sheriff; and so far as the timetable is inconsistent with any provision in these Rules which relates to a matter to which the timetable relates, the timetable shall prevail.

(3)    Where a party fails to comply with any requirement of a timetable other than that referred to in paragraph (8) or rule 36.K1(3), the sheriff clerk may fix a date and time for the parties to be heard by the sheriff.

(4)    The pursuer shall lodge a certified copy of the record, which shall consist of the pleadings of the parties, in process by the date specified in the timetable and shall at the same time send one copy to the defender and any other parties.

(5)    The pursuer shall, on lodging the certified copy of the record as required by paragraph (4), apply by motion to the sheriff, craving the court—

(a)    to allow to parties a preliminary proof on specified matters;

(b)    to allow a proof; or

(c)    to make some other specified order.

(6)    The motion lodged under paragraph (5) shall specify the anticipated length of the preliminary proof, or proof, as the case may be.

(7)    In the event that any party proposes to crave the court to make any order other than an order allowing a proof under paragraph (5)(b), that party shall, on making or opposing (as the case may be) the pursuer's motion, specify the order to be sought and give full notice in the motion or the notice of opposition thereto of the grounds thereof.

(8)    Where the pursuer fails to lodge a record by the date specified in the timetable issued under paragraph (1), the sheriff clerk shall fix a date and time for the parties to be heard by the sheriff.

(8A)    A party who seeks to rely on the evidence of a person not on his or her list lodged in accordance with paragraph (1A)(g) must, if any other party objects to such evidence being admitted, seek leave of the sheriff to admit that evidence whether it is to be given orally or not; and such leave may be granted on such conditions, if any, as the sheriff thinks fit.

(8B)    The list of witnesses intimated in accordance with paragraph (1A)(g) must include the name, occupation (where known) and address of each intended witness and indicate whether the witness is considered to be a vulnerable witness within the meaning of section 11(1) of the Act of 2004 and whether any child witness notice or vulnerable witness application has been lodged in respect of that witness.

(9)    A production which is not lodged in accordance with paragraph (1A)(g) shall not be used or put in evidence at proof unless—

(a)    by consent of parties; or

(b)    with the leave of the sheriff on cause shown and on such conditions, if any, as to expenses or otherwise as the court thinks fit.

(10)    In a cause which is one of a number of causes arising out of the same cause of action, the sheriff may—

(a)    on the motion of a party to that cause; and

(b)    after hearing parties to all those causes,

appoint that cause or any part of those causes to be the leading cause and to sist the other causes pending the determination of the leading cause.

(11)    In this rule, "pursuer" includes additional pursuer or minuter as the case may be.

### Applications for sist or for variation of timetable

**D1.473**

**36.H1.**—[1](1)    The action may be sisted or the timetable varied by the sheriff on an application by any party to the action by motion.

(2)    An application under paragraph (1)—

(a)    shall be placed before the sheriff; and

---

[1] As amended by the Act of Sederunt (Sheriff Court Rules) (Miscellaneous Amendments) 2010 (SSI 2010/279) r.4 (effective July 29, 2010).

(b)    shall be granted only on special cause shown.

(3)    Any sist of an action in terms of this rule shall be for a specific period.

(4)    Where the timetable issued under rule 36.G1 is varied under this rule, the sheriff clerk shall issue a revised timetable in Form PI5.

(5)    A revised timetable issued under paragraph (4) shall have effect as if it were a timetable issued under rule 36.G1 and any reference in this Part to any action being taken in accordance with the timetable shall be construed as a reference to its being taken in accordance with the timetable as varied under this rule.

### Statements of valuation of claim

**D1.474**

**36.J1.**—(1)    Each party to the action shall make a statement of valuation of claim in Form PI6.

(2)    A statement of valuation of claim (which shall include a list of supporting documents) shall be lodged in process.

(3)    Each party shall, on lodging a statement of valuation of claim—
(a)    intimate the list of documents included in the statement of valuation of claim to every other party; and
(b)    lodge each of those documents.

(4)    Nothing in paragraph (3) shall affect—
(a)    the law relating to, or the right of a party to object to, the recovery of a document on the ground of privilege or confidentiality; or
(b)    the right of a party to apply under rule 28.2 for a commission and diligence for recovery of documents or an order under section 1 of the Administration of Justice (Scotland) Act 1972.

(5)    Without prejudice to paragraph (2) of rule 36.L1, where a party has failed to lodge a statement of valuation of claim in accordance with a timetable issued under rule 36.G1, the sheriff may, at any hearing under paragraph (3) of that rule—
(a)    where the party in default is the pursuer, dismiss the action; or
(b)    where the party in default is the defender, grant decree against the defender for an amount not exceeding the pursuer's valuation.

### Pre-proof conferences

**D1.475**

**36.K1.**—(1)    For the purposes of this rule, a pre-proof conference is a conference of the parties, which shall be held not later than four weeks before the date assigned for the proof—
(a)    to discuss settlement of the action; and
(b)    to agree, so far as is possible, the matters which are not in dispute between them.

(2)    Subject to any variation of the timetable in terms of rule 36.H1, a joint minute of a pre-proof conference, made in Form PI7, shall be lodged in process by the pursuer not later than three weeks before the date assigned for proof.

(3)    Where a joint minute in Form PI7 has not been lodged in accordance with paragraph (2) and by the date specified in the timetable the sheriff clerk shall fix a date and time for the parties to be heard by the sheriff.

(4)[1]    If a party is not present during the pre-proof conference, the representative of such party shall have access to the party or another person who has authority to commit the party in settlement of the action.

### Incidental hearings

**D1.476**

**36.L1.**—(1)    Where the sheriff clerk fixes a date and time for a hearing under paragraph (3) or (8) of rule 36.G1 or paragraph (3) of rule 36.K1 he shall—
(a)    fix a date not less than seven days after the date of the notice referred to in subparagraph (b);
(b)    give notice to the parties to the action—
(i)    of the date and time of the hearing; and
(ii)    requiring the party in default to lodge in process a written explanation as to why the timetable has not been complied with and to intimate a copy to all other parties, not less than two clear working days before the date of the hearing.

(2)    At the hearing, the sheriff—
(a)    shall consider any explanation provided by the party in default;
(b)    may award expenses against that party; and

---

[1] As substituted by the Act of Sederunt (Sheriff Court Rules) (Miscellaneous Amendments) 2010 (SSI 2010/279) r.4 (effective July 29, 2010).

(c)  may make any other appropriate order, including decree of dismissal.

Part I

Intimation to Connected Persons in Certain Actions of Damages

### Application and interpretation of this Part

**36.1.**—[1](1)  This Part applies to an action of damages in which, following the death of any person from personal injuries, damages are claimed—

(a)  in respect of the injuries from which the deceased died; or

(b)  in respect of the death of the deceased.

(2)  In this Part—

"connected person" means a person, not being a party to the action, who has title to sue the defender in respect of the personal injuries from which the deceased died or in respect of his death;

**D1.477**

### Averments

**36.2.**  In an action to which this Part applies, the pursuer shall aver in the condescendence, as the case may be—

(a)  that there are no connected persons;

(b)  that there are connected persons, being the persons specified in the crave for intimation;

(c)  that there are connected persons in respect of whom intimation should be dispensed with on the ground that—

    (i)  the names or whereabouts of such persons are not known to, and cannot reasonably be ascertained by, the pursuer; or

    (ii)  such persons are unlikely to be awarded more than £200 each.

**D1.478**

### Warrants for intimation

**36.3.**—(1)  Where the pursuer makes averments under rule 36.2(b) (existence of connected persons), he shall include a crave in the initial writ for intimation to any person who is believed to have title to sue the defender in an action in respect of the death of the deceased or the personal injuries from which the deceased died.

(2)  A notice of intimation in Form D1 shall be attached to the copy of the initial writ where intimation is given on a warrant under paragraph (1).

**D1.479**

### Applications to dispense with intimation

**36.4.**—(1)  Where the pursuer makes averments under rule 36.2(c) (dispensing with intimation to connected persons), he shall apply by crave in the initial writ for an order to dispense with intimation.

(2)  In determining an application under paragraph (1), the sheriff shall have regard to—

(a)  the desirability of avoiding a multiplicity of actions; and

(b)  the expense, inconvenience or difficulty likely to be involved in taking steps to ascertain the name or whereabouts of the connected person.

(3)  Where the sheriff is not satisfied that intimation to a connected person should be dispensed with, he may—

(a)  order intimation to a connected person whose name and whereabouts are known;

(b)  order the pursuer to take such further steps as he may specify in the interlocutor to ascertain the name or whereabouts of any connected person; and

(c)  order advertisement in such manner, place and at such times as he may specify in the interlocutor.

**D1.480**

### Subsequent disclosure of connected persons

**36.5.**  Where the name or whereabouts of a person, in respect of whom the sheriff has dispensed with intimation on a ground specified in rule 36.2(c) (dispensing with intimation to connected persons), subsequently becomes known to the pursuer, the pursuer shall apply to the sheriff by motion for a warrant for intimation to such a person; and such intimation shall be made in accordance with rule 36.3(2).

**D1.481**

### Connected persons entering process

**36.6.**—(1)  A connected person may apply by minute craving leave to be sisted as an additional pursuer to the action.

**D1.482**

---

[1] As amended by the Act of Sederunt (Sheriff Court Rules) (Miscellaneous Amendments) (No.2) 2011 (SSI 2011/289) para.2 (effective July 7, 2011).

(2)    Such a minute shall also crave leave of the sheriff to adopt the existing grounds of action, and to amend the craves, condescendence and pleas-in-law.

(3)    The period within which answers to a minute under this rule may be lodged shall be 14 days from the date of intimation of the minute.

(4)[1]    Rule 14.13 (procedure following grant of minute) shall not apply to a minute to which this rule applies.

**Failure to enter process**

**D1.483**

36.7.    Where a connected person to whom intimation is made in accordance with this Part—

    (a)    does not apply to be sisted as an additional pursuer to the action,

    (b)    subsequently raises a separate action against the same defender in respect of the same personal injuries or death, and

    (c)    would, apart from this rule, be awarded the expenses or part of the expenses of that action,

he shall not be awarded those expenses except on cause shown.

Part II

Interim Payments of Damages

**Application and interpretation of this Part**

**D1.484**

36.8.—(1)    This Part applies to an action of damages for personal injuries or the death of a person in consequence of personal injuries.

(2)    In this Part—

"defender" includes a third party against whom the pursuer has a crave for damages;

"personal injuries" includes any disease or impairment of a physical or mental condition.

**Applications for interim payment of damages**

**D1.485**

36.9.—(1)    In an action to which this Part applies, a pursuer may, at any time after defences have been lodged, apply by motion for an order for interim payment of damages to him by the defender or, where there are two or more of them, by any one or more of them.

(2)    The pursuer shall intimate a motion under paragraph (1) to every other party on a period of notice of 14 days.

(3)    On a motion under paragraph (1), the sheriff may, if satisfied that—

    (a)    the defender has admitted liability to the pursuer in the action, or

    (b)    if the action proceeded to proof, the pursuer would succeed in the action on the question of liability without any substantial finding of contributory negligence on his part, or on the part of any person in respect of whose injury or death the claim of the pursuer arises, and would obtain decree for damages against any defender,

ordain that defender to make an interim payment to the pursuer of such amount as the sheriff thinks fit, not exceeding a reasonable proportion of the damages which, in the opinion of the sheriff, are likely to be recovered by the pursuer.

(4)    Any such payment may be ordered to be made in one lump sum or otherwise as the sheriff thinks fit.

(5)[2]    No order shall be made against a defender under this rule unless it appears to the sheriff that the defender is—

    (a)    a person who is insured in respect of the claim of the pursuer;

    (b)    a public authority;

    (c)    a person whose means and resources are such as to enable him to make the interim payment; or

    (d)    the person's liability will be met by—

        (i)    an insurer under section 151 of the Road Traffic Act 1988; or

        (ii)    an insurer acting under the Motor Insurers Bureau Agreement, or the Motor Insurers Bureau where it is acting itself.

(6)    Notwithstanding the grant or refusal of a motion for an interim payment, a subsequent motion may be made where there has been a change of circumstances.

(7)    Subject to Part IV (management of damages payable to persons under legal disability) an interim payment shall be paid to the pursuer unless the sheriff otherwise directs.

---

[1] As substituted by the Act of Sederunt (Sheriff Court Ordinary Cause Rules Amendment) (Miscellaneous) 1996 (SI 1996/2445) r.3 (effective November 1, 1996).

[2] Amended by the Act of Sederunt (Ordinary Cause, Summary Application and Small Claim Rules) Amendment (Miscellaneous) 2004 (SSI 2004/197) (effective May 21, 2004), para.2(13).

(8) This rule shall, with the necessary modifications, apply to a counterclaim for damages for personal injuries made by a defender as it applies to an action in which the pursuer may apply for an order for interim payment of damages.

**Adjustment on final decree**

**36.10.** Where a defender has made an interim payment under rule 36.9, the sheriff may, when final decree is pronounced, make such order with respect to the interim payment as he thinks fit to give effect to the final liability of that defender to the pursuer; and in particular may order—

**D1.486**

(a) repayment by the pursuer of any sum by which the interim payment exceeds the amount which that defender is liable to pay to the pursuer; or

(b) payment by any other defender or a third party, of any part of the interim payment which the defender who made it is entitled to recover from him by way of contribution or indemnity or in respect of any remedy or relief relating to, or connected with, the claim of the pursuer.

Part III

Provisional Damages for Personal Injuries

**Application and interpretation of this Part**

**36.11.**—(1) This Part applies to an action of damages for personal injuries.

**D1.487**

(2) In this Part—

"the Act of 1982" means the Administration of Justice Act 1982;
"further damages" means the damages referred to in section 12(4)(b) of the Act of 1982;
"provisional damages" means the damages referred to in section 12(4)(a) of the Act of 1982.

**Applications for provisional damages**

**36.12.** An application under section 12(2)(a) of the Act of 1982 for provisional damages for personal injuries shall be made by including in the initial writ—

**D1.488**

(a) a crave for provisional damages;

(b) averments in the condescendence supporting the crave, including averments—

(i) that there is a risk that, at some definite or indefinite time in the future, the pursuer will, as a result of the act or omission which gave rise to the cause of action, develop some serious disease or suffer some serious deterioration of his physical or mental condition; and

(ii) that the defender was, at the time of the act or omission which gave rise to the cause of action, a public authority, public corporation or insured or otherwise indemnified in respect of the claim; and

(c) an appropriate plea-in-law.

**Applications for further damages**

**36.13.**—(1) An application for further damages by a pursuer in respect of whom an order under section 12(2)(b) of the Act of 1982 has been made shall be made by minute in the process of the action to which it relates and shall include—

**D1.489**

(a) a crave for further damages;

(b) averments in the statement of facts supporting that crave; and

(c) appropriate pleas-in-law.

(2) On lodging such a minute in process, the pursuer shall apply by motion for warrant to serve the minute on—

(a) every other party; and

(b) where such other party is insured or otherwise indemnified, his insurer or indemnifier, if known to the pursuer.

(3) Any such party, insurer or indemnifier may lodge answers to such a minute in process within 28 days after the date of service on him.

(4)   Where answers have been lodged under paragraph (3), the sheriff may, on the motion of any party, make such further order as to procedure as he thinks fit.

Part IV

Management of Damages Payable to Persons under Legal Disability

**Orders for payment and management of money**

**D1.490**

**36.14.**—(1)[1]   In an action of damages in which a sum of money becomes payable, by virtue of a decree or an extra-judicial settlement, to or for the benefit of a person under legal disability (other than a person under the age of 18 years), the sheriff shall make such order regarding the payment and management of that sum for the benefit of that person as he thinks fit.

(2)   An order under paragraph (1) shall be made on the granting of decree for payment or of absolvitor.

**Methods of management**

**D1.491**

**36.15.**   In making an order under rule 36.14(1), the sheriff may—

(a)   appoint a judicial factor to apply, invest or otherwise deal with the money for the benefit of the person under legal disability;

(b)   order the money to be paid to—

(i)   the Accountant of Court, or

(ii)   the guardian of the person under legal disability,

as trustee, to be applied, invested or otherwise dealt with and administered under the directions of the sheriff for the benefit of the person under legal disability;

(c)   order the money to be paid to the sheriff clerk of the sheriff court district in which the person under legal disability resides, to be applied, invested or otherwise dealt with and administered, under the directions of the sheriff of that district, for the benefit of the person under legal disability; or

(d)   order the money to be paid directly to the person under legal disability.

**Subsequent orders**

**D1.492**

**36.16.**—(1)   Where the sheriff has made an order under rule 36.14(1), any person having an interest may apply for an appointment or order under rule 36.15, or any other order for the payment or management of the money, by minute in the process of the cause to which the application relates.

(2)   An application for directions under rule 36.15(b) or (c) may be made by any person having an interest by minute in the process of the cause to which the application relates.

**Management of money paid to sheriff clerk**

**D1.493**

**36.17.**—(1)   A receipt in Form D2 by the sheriff clerk shall be a sufficient discharge in respect of the amount paid to him under this Part.

(2)   The sheriff clerk shall, at the request of any competent court, accept custody of any sum of money in an action of damages ordered to be paid to, applied, invested or otherwise dealt with by him, for the benefit of a person under legal disability.

(3)   Any money paid to the sheriff clerk under this Part shall be paid out, applied, invested or otherwise dealt with by the sheriff clerk only after such intimation, service and enquiry as the sheriff may order.

(4)   Any sum of money invested by the sheriff clerk under this Part shall be invested in a manner in which trustees are authorised to invest by virtue of the Trustee Investments Act 1961.

Part IV A[2]

Productions in Certain Actions of Damages

**Application of this Part**

**D1.494**

**36.17A.**[3]   This Part applies to an action of damages for personal injuries or the death of a person in consequence of personal injuries, which, by virtue of rule 36.C1 or rule 36.F1, is to proceed as an ordinary cause.

---

[1] As amended by S.I. 1996 No. 2167 (effective November 1, 1996).

[2] As inserted by the Act of Sederunt (Sheriff Court Ordinary Cause Rules Amendment) (Miscellaneous) 2000 (SSI 2000/239) (effective October 2, 2000).

[3] As amended by the Act of Sederunt (Ordinary Cause Rules Amendment) (Personal Injuries Actions) 2009 (SSI 2009/285) r.2 (effective November 2, 2009).

**Averments of medical treatment**

**36.17B.** The condescendence of the initial writ in an action to which this Part applies shall include averments naming—

    (a)    every general medical practitioner or general medical practice from whom; and

    (b)    every hospital or other institution in which,

the pursuer or, in an action in respect of the death of a person, the deceased received treatment for the injuries sustained, or disease suffered, by him.

**D1.495**

**Lodging of medical reports**

**36.17C.**—(1)    In an action to which this Part applies, the pursuer shall lodge as productions, with the initial writ when it is presented for warranting in accordance with rule 5.1, all medical reports on which he intends, or intends to reserve the right, to rely in the action.

(2)    Where no medical report is lodged as required by paragraph (1), the defender may apply by motion for an order specifying a period within which such a report shall be lodged in process.

**D1.496**

Part V

Sex Discrimination Act 1975

**Causes under section 66 of the Act of 1975**

**36.18.**    *[Omitted by the Act of Sederunt (Ordinary Cause, Summary Application, Summary Cause and Small Claim Rules) Amendment (Equality Act 2006 etc.) 2006 (SSI 2006/509) (effective November 3, 2006).]*

Part VI[1]

Mesothelioma Actions: Special Provisions

**Mesothelioma actions: special provisions**

**36.19.**—(1)As amended by the Act of Sederunt (Sheriff Court Rules) (Miscellaneous Amendments) (No.2) 2011 (SSI 2011/289) para.2 (effective July 7, 2011).    This Part applies where liability to a relative of the pursuer may arise under section 5 of the Damages (Scotland) Act 2011 (discharge of liability to pay damages: exception for mesothelioma).

**D1.497**

(2)    On settlement of the pursuer's claim, the pursuer may apply by motion for all or any of the following—

    (a)    a sist for a specified period;

    (b)    discharge of any diet;

    (c)    where the action is one to which the personal injuries procedure in Part A1 of this Chapter applies, variation of the timetable issued under rule 36.G1.

(3)    Paragraphs (4) to (7) apply where a motion under paragraph (2) has been granted.

(4)    As soon as reasonably practicable after the death of the pursuer, any agent who immediately prior to the death was instructed in a cause by the deceased pursuer shall notify the court of the death.

(5)    The notification under paragraph (4) shall be by letter to the sheriff clerk and shall be accompanied by a certified copy of the death certificate relative to the deceased pursuer.

(6)    A relative of the deceased may apply by motion for the recall of the sist and for an order for further procedure.

(7)    On expiration of the period of any sist pronounced on a motion under paragraph (2), the sheriff clerk may fix a date and time for the parties to be heard by the sheriff.

CHAPTER 37

CAUSES UNDER THE PRESUMPTION OF DEATH (SCOTLAND) ACT 1977

**Interpretation of this Chapter**

**37.1.**    In this Chapter—

**D1.498**

"the Act of 1977" means the Presumption of Death (Scotland) Act 1977;

"action of declarator" means an action under section 1(1) of the Act of 1977;

"missing person" has the meaning assigned in section 1(1) of the Act of 1977.

---

[1] As inserted by the Act of Sederunt (Ordinary Cause Rules Amendment) (Personal Injuries Actions) 2009 (SSI 2009/285) r.2 (effective November 2, 2009).

**Parties to, and service and intimation of, actions of declarator**

**D1.499**

37.2.—(1)[1, 2] In an action of declarator—

    (a)   the missing person shall be named as the defender;

    (b)   subject to paragraph (2), service on that person shall be executed by advertisement in such newspaper or other publication as the sheriff thinks fit of such facts relating to the missing person and set out in the initial writ as the sheriff may specify; and

    (c)   the period of notice shall be 21 days from the date of publication of the advertisement unless the sheriff otherwise directs.

(2)[3] The advertisement mentioned in paragraph (1) shall be in Form P1.

(3) Subject to paragraph (5), in an action of declarator, the pursuer shall include a crave for a warrant for intimation to—

    (a)   the missing person's—

        (i)   spouse, and

        (ii)  children, or, if he has no children, his nearest relative known to the pursuer,

    (b)   any person, including any insurance company, who so far as known to the pursuer has an interest in the action, and

    (c)   the Lord Advocate,

in the following terms:— "For intimation to (*name and address*) as [husband or wife, child *or* nearest relative] [a person having an interest in the presumed death] of (*name and last known address of the missing person*) and to the Lord Advocate.".

(4)[4] A notice of intimation in Form P2 shall be attached to the copy of the initial writ where intimation is given on a warrant under paragraph (3).

(5) The sheriff may, on the motion of the pursuer, dispense with intimation on a person mentioned in paragraph (3)(a) or (b).

(6) An application by minute under section 1(5) of the Act of 1977 (person interested in seeking determination or appointment not sought by pursuer) shall contain a crave for the determination or appointment sought, averments in the answers to the condescendence in support of that crave and an appropriate plea-in-law.

(7) On lodging a minute under paragraph (6), the minuter shall—

    (a)   send a copy of the minute by registered post or the first class recorded delivery service to each person to whom intimation of the action has been made under paragraph (2); and

    (b)   lodge in process the Post Office receipt or certificate of posting of that minute.

**Further advertisement**

**D1.500**

37.3. Where no minute has been lodged indicating knowledge of the present whereabouts of the missing person, at any time before the determination of the action, the sheriff may, of his own motion or on the motion of a party, make such order for further advertisement as he thinks fit.

**Applications for proof**

**D1.501**

37.4.—(1) In an action of declarator where no minute has been lodged, the pursuer shall, after such further advertisement as may be ordered under rule 37.3, apply to the sheriff by motion for an order for proof.

(2) A proof ordered under paragraph (1) shall be by affidavit evidence unless the sheriff otherwise directs.

**Applications for variation or recall of decree**

**D1.502**

37.5.—(1) An application under section 4(1) of the Act of 1977 (variation or recall of decree) shall be made by minute in the process of the action to which it relates.

(2) On the lodging of such a minute, the sheriff shall make an order—

    (a)   for service on the missing person, where his whereabouts have become known;

    (b)   for intimation to those persons mentioned in rule 37.2(3) or to dispense with intimation to a person mentioned in rule 37.2(3)(a) or (b); and

---

[1] As amended by the Act of Sederunt (Sheriff Court Ordinary Cause Rules Amendment) (Miscellaneous) 1996 (SI 1996/2445) (effective November 1, 1996) (clerical error).

[2] Substituted by the Act of Sederunt (Sheriff Court Ordinary Cause Rules Amendment) (Miscellaneous) 2000 (SSI 2000/239) (effective October 2, 2000).

[3] Substituted by the Act of Sederunt (Sheriff Court Ordinary Cause Rules Amendment) (Miscellaneous) 2000 (SSI 2000/239) (effective October 2, 2000).

[4] As amended by the Act of Sederunt (Sheriff Court Ordinary Cause Rules Amendment) (Miscellaneous) 2000 (SSI 2000/239) (effective October 2, 2000).

(c) for any answers to the minute to be lodged in process within such period as the sheriff thinks fit.

(3) An application under section 4(3) of the Act of 1977 (person interested seeking determination or appointment not sought by applicant for variation order) shall be made by lodging answers containing a crave for the determination or appointment sought.

(4) A person lodging answers containing a crave under paragraph (3) shall, as well as sending a copy of the answers to the minuter—

(a) send a copy of the answers by registered post or the first class recorded delivery service to each person on whom service or intimation of the minute was ordered; and

(b) lodge in process the Post Office receipt or certificate of posting of those answers.

### Appointment of judicial factors

**37.6.**—(1) The Act of Sederunt (Judicial Factors Rules) 1992 shall apply to an application for the appointment of a judicial factor under section 2(2)(c) or section 4(2) of the Act of 1977 as it applies to a petition for the appointment of a judicial factor.

**D1.503**

(2) In the application of rule 37.5 (applications for variation or recall of decree) to an application under section 4(1) of the Act of 1977 in a cause in which variation or recall of the appointment of a judicial factor is sought, for reference to a minute there shall be substituted references to a note.

CHAPTER 38

EUROPEAN COURT

### Interpretation of this Chapter

**38.1.**—(1) In this Chapter—

**D1.504**

"appeal" includes an application for leave to appeal;
"the European Court" means the Court of Justice of the European Communities;
"reference" means a reference to the European Court for

(a)[1,2] a preliminary ruling under Article 267 of the Treaty on the Functioning of the European Union, Article 150 of the Euratom Treaty or Article 41 of the E.C.S.C. Treaty; or

(b) a ruling on the interpretation of the Conventions, as defined in section 1(1) of the Civil Jurisdiction and Judgments Act 1982, under Article 3 of Schedule 2 to that Act.

(2)[3] The expressions "Euratom Treaty" and "E.C.S.C. Treaty" have the meanings assigned respectively in Schedule 1 to the European Communities Act 1972.

(3)[4] In paragraph (1), "the Treaty on the Functioning of the European Union" means the treaty referred to in section 1(2)(s) of the European Communities Act 1972.

### Applications for reference

**38.2.**—(1) A reference may be made by the sheriff of his own motion or on the motion of a party.

**D1.505**

(2) *[Repealed by SSI 2000/239 (effective October 2, 2000).]*

### Preparation of case for reference

**38.3.**—(1) Where the sheriff decides that a reference shall be made, he shall continue the cause for that purpose and, within 4 weeks after the date of that continuation, draft a reference.

**D1.506**

(1A)[5] Except in so far as the sheriff may otherwise direct, a reference shall be prepared in accordance with Form E1, having regard to the guidance set out in the Notes for Guidance issued by the Court of Justice of the European Communities.

(2) On the reference being drafted, the sheriff clerk shall send a copy to each party.

---

[1] As amended by the Act of Sederunt (Sheriff Court Ordinary Cause Rules Amendment) (Miscellaneous) 2000 (SSI 2000/239) (effective October 2, 2000).

[2] As amended by the Act of Sederunt (Sheriff Court Rules) (Miscellaneous Amendments) (No.3) 2012 (SSI 2012/271) para.6 (effective November 1, 2012).

[3] As amended by the Act of Sederunt (Sheriff Court Rules) (Miscellaneous Amendments) (No.3) 2012 (SSI 2012/271) para.6 (effective November 1, 2012).

[4] As inserted by the Act of Sederunt (Sheriff Court Rules) (Miscellaneous Amendments) (No.3) 2012 (SSI 2012/271) para.6 (effective November 1, 2012).

[5] Inserted by the Act of Sederunt (Sheriff Court Ordinary Cause Rules Amendment) (Miscellaneous) 2000 (S.S.I 2000 No. 239) (effective October 2, 2000).

(3)   Within 4 weeks after the date on which copies of the draft have been sent to parties, each party may—

    (a)   lodge with the sheriff clerk, and

    (b)   send to every other party,

a note of any adjustments he seeks to have made in the draft reference.

(4)   Within 14 days after the date on which any such note of adjustments may be lodged, the sheriff, after considering any such adjustments, shall make and sign the reference.

(5)   The sheriff clerk shall forthwith intimate the making of the reference to each party.

### Sist of cause

**D1.507**

**38.4.**—(1)   Subject to paragraph (2), on a reference being made, the cause shall, unless the sheriff when making such a reference otherwise orders, be sisted until the European Court has given a preliminary ruling on the question referred to it.

(2)   The sheriff may recall a sist made under paragraph (1) for the purpose of making an interim order which a due regard to the interests of the parties may require.

### Transmission of reference

**D1.508**

**38.5.**—(1)   Subject to paragraph (2), a copy of the reference, certified by the sheriff clerk, shall be transmitted by the sheriff clerk to the Registrar of the European Court.

(2)   Unless the sheriff otherwise directs, a copy of the reference shall not be sent to the Registrar of the European Court where an appeal against the making of the reference is pending.

(3)   For the purpose of paragraph (2), an appeal shall be treated as pending—

    (a)   until the expiry of the time for making that appeal; or

    (b)   where an appeal has been made, until that appeal has been determined.

## CHAPTER 39[1]

### PROVISIONS IN RELATION TO CURATORS AD LITEM

**Fees and outlays of curators ad litem in respect of children**

**D1.509**

**39.1.**—(1)   This rule applies to any civil proceedings whether or not the child is a party to the action.

(2)   In an action where the sheriff appoints a curator ad litem to a child, the pursuer shall in the first instance, unless the court otherwise directs, be responsible for the fees and outlays of the curator ad litem incurred during the period from his appointment until the occurrence of any of the following events:

    (a)   he lodges a minute stating that he does not intend to lodge defences or to enter the process;

    (b)   he decides to instruct the lodging of defences or a minute adopting defences already lodged; or(c)   the discharge, before the occurrence of the events mentioned in sub paragraphs (a) and (b), of the curator.

## CHAPTER 40[2]

### COMMERCIAL ACTIONS

*Annotations by Sheriff James Taylor*

### GENERAL NOTE

In 1994 new rules were introduced to the Court of Session governing commercial actions (RCS, Chapter 47). These were deemed to be a success and provided litigants with a more efficient means of resolving commercial disputes. It was sometimes referred to as a "fast track" procedure but this could be misleading. Undoubtedly some actions can be decided with a minimum of procedure, such as a dispute which turns on the interpretation of a contract, thus rendering the description appropriate. However, it was accepted that there are some actions which require a reasonable amount of time for the appropriate experts to be instructed and report and notice be given to the opponent. The advantage of using Chapter 47 procedure was that there was case management from the bench. This resulted in an efficient procedure.

Sheriff Principal Bowen, Q.C., the sheriff principal of Glasgow and Strathkelvin, decided in 1999 to introduce a similar procedure to Glasgow Sheriff Court. Four sheriffs were designated as commercial sheriffs. There were however no rules equivalent to Chapter 47. One of the essential features of Chapter 47 is the preliminary hearing which must take place before the assigned judge within 14 days of defences

---

[1] Inserted by the Act of Sederunt (Sheriff Court Ordinary Cause Rules Amendment) (Miscellaneous) 2000 (SSI 2000/239) (effective October 2, 2000).

[2] Inserted by the Act of Sederunt (Ordinary Cause Rules) Amendment (Commercial Actions) 2001 (SSI 2001/8).

being lodged. Under the Ordinary Cause Rules of the sheriff court a case would not come before a sheriff until the options hearing. The options hearing requires to be fixed not sooner than 10 weeks after the expiry of the period of notice (OCR, r.9.2). If the advantages of Chapter 47 procedure were to be replicated, the case would need to call before then. To overcome this difficulty the Civil Department of the Sheriff Clerk's Office identified cases which appeared to fit the description of a commercial action using the same definition as in the Practice Note for Commercial Actions in the Court of Session (No. 12 of 1994). After defences had been lodged the solicitors in the case were invited to attend a preliminary hearing. At this hearing the issues in the case were identified and a procedure agreed for resolving the issues. At first, approximately 50 per cent of the cases in which invitations were extended had preliminary hearings, but as the procedure became more familiar that rose to over 90 per cent. Due to the lack of rules the procedure required to be agreed. There was no sanction if one of the parties did not comply. This problem was resolved with the introduction of Chapter 40 to the Ordinary Cause Rules (Act of Sederunt (Ordinary Cause Rules) Amendment (Commercial Actions) 2001 (SSI 2001/8)).

**Application and interpretation of this Chapter**

**D1.511**

**40.1.**—(1)   This Chapter applies to a commercial action.

(2)   In this Chapter—

> (a)   "commercial action" means—an action arising out of, or concerned with, any transaction or dispute of a commercial or business nature including, but not limited to, actions relating to—
>
>> (i)   the construction of a commercial document;
>> (ii)   the sale or hire purchase of goods;
>> (iii)   the export or import of merchandise;
>> (iv)   the carriage of goods by land, air or sea;
>> (v)   insurance;
>> (vi)   banking;
>> (vii)   the provision of services;
>> (viii)   a building, engineering or construction contract; or
>> (ix)   a commercial lease; and
>
> (b)   "commercial action" does not include an action in relation to consumer credit transactions.

(3)   A commercial action may be raised only in a sheriff court where the Sheriff Principal for the sheriffdom has directed that the procedure should be available.

GENERAL NOTE

Before advantage can be taken of this chapter the sheriff principal must direct that these rules will apply to the particular court in the sheriffdom in which the action is raised. The only courts in which there is such a direction are Glasgow, Jedburgh, Selkirk and Duns Sheriff Courts. Jedburgh, Selkirk and Duns are included because the sheriff presently appointed to these courts was one of the original commercial sheriffs in Glasgow.

The definition of a commercial action closely follows the definition under Chapter 47 procedure in the Court of Session.

*"The provision of services"*

The minor differences between the two definitions are that where the Court of Session definition refers to "the provision of financial services", the equivalent description in Chapter 40 is "the provision of services". The sheriff court definition can thus be seen to be broader. The Court of Session definition also refers specifically to actions relating to "mercantile agency" and "mercantile usage or a custom of trade". There is no equivalent in Chapter 40.

*"Arising out of, or concerned with, any transaction or dispute of a commercial or business nature"*

The differences between the Court of Session and Ordinary Cause Rules are of no significance since the examples in both sets of rules are not limiting and the overarching criteria is the same in both, namely that the action should arise out of, or be concerned with, a commercial or business dispute. This phrase is intended to be of broad scope and is habile to include an action by a trustee in sequestration for declarator of vesting of acquirenda, where the issue was one of insolvency and not of succession: *Rankin's Trs v HC Somerville & Russell* , 1999 S.C. 166.

*"Does not include an action in relation to consumer credit transactions"*

This exclusion is self-explanatory.

**D1.512**

**Proceedings before a nominated sheriff**

**40.2.** All proceedings in a commercial action shall be brought before—

    (a) a sheriff of the sheriffdom nominated by the Sheriff Principal; or

    (b) where a nominated sheriff is not available, any other sheriff of the sheriffdom.

GENERAL NOTE

The working party, which consulted before the introduction of Chapter 47 procedures to the Court of Session, recognised a demand for a forum where commercial disputes could be resolved before a judge who had commercial experience. To reflect this expression, there requires to be in the sheriff court where the procedures are available, a sheriff or sheriffs designated by the sheriff principal to deal with commercial business. As a backstop, where a designated commercial sheriff is unavailable another sheriff can deal with proceedings in a commercial action. There are currently three designated commercial sheriffs in Glasgow and one in Jedburgh, Selkirk and Duns.

**D1.513**

**Procedure in commercial actions**

**40.3.**—(1) In a commercial action the sheriff may make such order as he thinks fit for the progress of the case in so far as not inconsistent with the provisions in this Chapter.

(2) Where any hearing is continued, the reason for such continuation shall be recorded in the interlocutor.

GENERAL NOTE

*"May make such order as he thinks fit"*

The intent of the rules is that the sheriff, counsel and solicitors who may be involved in the action should not be constrained by rules of procedure in dealing efficiently with a case. Thus it is deemed that an order is competent unless it is inconsistent with the commercial rules. A specific enabling power is not necessary.

**D1.514**

**Election of procedure for commercial actions**

**40.4.** The pursuer may elect to adopt the procedure in this Chapter by bringing an action in Form G1A.

GENERAL NOTE

In order to distinguish a commercial action from an ordinary action, all that is required is for the pursuer's solicitor to type the words "Commercial Action" above the words "Initial Writ" in the instance of the initial writ. Thus the pursuer has the right to elect for Chapter 40 procedure. The defender is protected, should the election be inappropriate, by the terms of rule 40.6(1). To facilitate communication, Glasgow Sheriff Court request that the initial writ, notice of intention to defend and defences should have marked on them the name of the individual solicitor dealing with the case and that individual's telephone number and e-mail address.

**D1.515**

**Transfer of action to be a commercial action**

**40.5.**—(1) In an action within the meaning of rule 40.1(2) in which the pursuer has not made an election under rule 40.4, any party may apply by motion at any time to have the action appointed to be a commercial action.

(2) An interlocutor granted under paragraph (1) shall include a direction as to further procedure.

GENERAL NOTE

If the pursuer does not elect for the action to be dealt with as a commercial action at the time when the action is raised, it is still open to the pursuer, or any other party, once the action has been warranted, to move that these rules should apply.

Since these rules are applicable in Glasgow, Jedburgh, Selkirk and Duns Sheriff Courts only, there have been motions made in other courts, where the rules are not available, for particular cases to be remitted to one of the four courts. These have usually involved the defender prorogating the jurisdiction of one of the four courts. Glasgow is prepared to accept such remits, but the Borders Courts are not.

**D1.516**

**Appointment of a commercial action as an ordinary cause**

**40.6.**—(1) At any time before, or at the Case Management Conference, the sheriff shall appoint a commercial action to proceed as an ordinary cause—

    (a) on the motion of a party where—

        (i) detailed pleadings are required to enable justice to be done between the parties; or

        (ii) any other circumstances warrant such an order being made; or

    (b) on the joint motion of parties.

(2) If a motion to appoint a commercial action to proceed as an ordinary action is refused, no subsequent motion to appoint the action to proceed as an ordinary cause shall be considered except on a material change of circumstances.

(3) Where the sheriff orders that a commercial action shall proceed as an ordinary cause the interlocutor granting such shall prescribe—

    (a) a period of adjustment, if appropriate; and

    (b) the date, time and place for any options hearing fixed.

(4) In determining what order to make in deciding that a commercial action proceed as an ordinary cause the sheriff shall have regard to the periods prescribed in rule 9.2.

GENERAL NOTE

This rule provides for an action being remitted from the commercial roll to the ordinary roll on the motion of any party or on joint motion.

*"Detailed pleadings are required"*

The only guidance as to when such a motion should be considered, apart from the generality that "circumstances warrant such", is if detailed pleadings are required. It is submitted that this is a strange provision. Several of the commercial actions raised under these rules have involved detailed pleading. There is nothing in the rules which makes the rules unsuitable to regulate actions where detailed pleading is required. No motion to have the case remitted to the ordinary roll has succeeded when reliance has been placed on this specific provision only.

The rule does not give the sheriff power *ex proprio motu* to remit the case to the ordinary role. This was originally the case under Chapter 47 procedure in the Court of Session. That was remedied in the Court of Session by para.2(7) of SSI 2000/66, which gives the commercial judge power, *ex proprio motu*, to remit the case to the ordinary roll

In the event that a motion to remit to the ordinary roll is successful, the interlocutor shall allow a period of adjustment, if appropriate. If the reason for the motion succeeding is that detailed pleadings are required, it would be consistent for there to be a further period allowed for adjustment. One might expect a subsequent motion to seek that the action be dealt with in terms of Chapter 10.

**Special requirements for initial writ in a commercial action**

    **D1.517**

**40.7.**—(1) Where the construction of a document is the only matter in dispute no pleadings or pleas-in-law require to be included in the initial writ.

(2) There shall be appended to an initial writ in Form G1A a list of the documents founded on or adopted as incorporated in the initial writ.

GENERAL NOTE

This provision enables a pursuer who considers that the construction of a document will resolve a dispute to put that clearly in focus in the initial writ. There will still require to be a crave in which it would be open to a pursuer to seek declarator that the provisions of the document in question, properly understood, have a particular meaning. There could still be a secondary crave dealing with the consequences in the event of declarator being granted, e.g. a crave for payment or specific implement. Averments will still be required to establish jurisdiction. It would be appropriate, although not necessary, in such circumstances to set out in outline in the condescendence, the argument to be deployed by the pursuer in submitting that the document should be said to have the construction for which he contends. It might even be thought appropriate to cite any authorities said to support the desired construction.

*"List of the documents founded on"*

Rule 40.7(2) reflects the provisions of rule 47.3(3) of the Court of Session Rules. It would be good practice to send to the defender's solicitor a copy of the documents founded upon as soon as a notice of intention to defend the action is intimated if these have not been served with the initial writ. This will enable the issues to be more easily identified at the case management conference. Absent any specific order of the Court in terms of rule 40.12, all productions will require to be lodged not later than 14 days before the diet of proof (rule 29.11(1)).

**Notice of Intention to Defend**

    **D1.518**

**40.8.**—(1) Where the defender intends to—

    (a) challenge the jurisdiction of the court;

    (b) state a defence; or

    (c) make a counterclaim,

he shall, before the expiry of the period of notice lodge with the sheriff clerk a notice of intention to defend in Form O7 and shall, at the same time, send a copy to the pursuer.

(2)   The lodging of a notice of intention to defend shall not imply acceptance of the jurisdiction of the court.

GENERAL NOTE

A defender who wishes to defend a commercial action requires to lodge a notice of intention to defend in the same way and within the same period of notice as he would were the action an ordinary action. As for ordinary actions, the rules specifically provide that the defender can lodge a notice of intention to defend and still challenge the jurisdiction of the court to hear the case.

**D1.519**

**Defences**

**40.9.**—(1)   Where a notice of intention to defend has been lodged, the defender shall lodge defences within 7 days after the expiry of the period of notice.

(2)   There shall be appended to the defences a list of the documents founded on or adopted as incorporated in the defences.

(3)   Subject to the requirement that each article of condescendence in the initial writ need not be admitted or denied, defences shall be in the form of answers that allow the extent of the dispute to be identified and shall have appended a note of the pleas in law of the defender.

GENERAL NOTE

In a commercial action the defender has only seven days from the expiry of the period of notice in which to lodge defences as opposed to 14 days in an ordinary action (rule 9.6(1)). Unlike an ordinary action there will be no intimation from the sheriff clerk specifying the date by which defences require to be lodged. As a pursuer has to append a list of documents to the initial writ, so a defender has to append a list of the documents upon which he founds, or which have been incorporated into the pleadings, to the defences. It is considered good practice for the documents to be lodged in process before the first case management conference. The defences should contain the name of the solicitor dealing with the case together with the telephone number and e-mail address.

*"Each article of condescendence in the initial writ need not be admitted or denied"*

The defences do not require to be in traditional form where the defender repeats *ad longum* which of the pursuer's averments are admitted. It has never been good practice to adopt such an approach with regard to denials. It would appear therefore that the reference to each article of condescendence not requiring to be denied is meant to convey that a defender will no longer be deemed to have admitted a fact which is subject to an averment by the pursuer and which is within the defender's knowledge but which is not covered by a general denial.

*"Answers that allow the extent of the dispute to be identified"*

The guiding principle is always whether fair notice is given to the other side to enable them to know the case which they require to meet and to be able to properly prepare for proof. The means of achieving that can take a number of forms. Lengthy narrative is discouraged. Parties regularly use spreadsheets or schedules to set out their position with regard to particular issues. The sheriffs welcome this. It is a cardinal feature of commercial actions that parties make full and frank disclosure. Some guidance as to the degree of specification required can be found in *Kaur v Singh* , 1998 S.C. 233 at 237C, per Lord Hamilton, and *Johnston v WH Brown Construction (Dundee) Ltd* , 2000 S.L.T. 223.

*"Shall have appended a note of the pleas-in-law"*

It is worth noting that the defences require that there be pleas-in-law appended to them. There is no dispensation for defences as there is with an initial writ when the only matter in dispute is the construction of a document as one finds in rule 40.7(1).

**D1.520**

**Fixing date for Case Management Conference**

**40.10.**—(1)   On the lodging of defences, the sheriff clerk shall fix a date and time for a Case Management Conference, which date shall be on the first suitable court day occurring not sooner than 14 days, nor later than 28 days after the date of expiry of the period of notice.

(2)   On fixing the date for the Case Management Conference, the sheriff clerk shall—

    (a)   forthwith intimate to the parties the date and time of the Case Management Conference; and

    (b)   prepare and sign an interlocutor recording that information.

(3)   The fixing of the date of the Case Management Conference shall not affect the right of a party to make application by motion, to the court.

GENERAL NOTE

On defences being lodged the process is normally placed before one of the commercial sheriffs who will decide whether the first case management conference will be conducted in court, chambers, or, in Glasgow, by conference call. The majority of case management conferences in Glasgow Sheriff Court are now dealt with by conference call which the sheriff initiates. The introduction of conference call facilities was in response to the profession and litigants being concerned by the inefficiency of having to travel to court and wait for their case to call. If a solicitor does not wish to make use of the conference call facility, he or she is entitled to request a traditional hearing. The date of the case management conference, which must not be sooner than 14 days after the period of notice nor later than 28 days after its expiry, is then intimated to the parties. In Glasgow Sheriff Court this intimation informs the parties of the date and time for the case management conference, whether it will be in court or chambers or whether it can proceed by conference call, the identity of the commercial sheriff allocated to the case and the e-mail address for that particular sheriff. Wherever possible that sheriff will deal with all hearings in the case.

It is important that the solicitor with responsibility for the case is available for the case management conference and it is not uncommon for the initial date and time to be altered to suit solicitors' diaries.

The rules make it clear that the fixing of a case management conference will not preclude a party from enrolling a motion. Very often the motion will be dealt with at the case management conference but where there is a degree of urgency the motion can usually be accommodated in advance of that date.

**Applications for summary decree in a commercial action**                    **D1.521**

**40.11.**   *[Repealed by the Act of Sederunt (Sheriff Court Rules) (Miscellaneous Amendments) 2012 (SSI 2012/188) r.3(3) (effective August 1, 2012: repeal has effect subject to savings specified in SSI 2012/188 r.15).]*

GENERAL NOTE

In an ordinary action should a pursuer, or counterclaiming defender, enrol a motion for summary decree, notice of opposition must be given within seven days (rule 15.3(1)(c)). That period is shortened to 48 hours in a commercial action.

**Case Management Conference**                                                **D1.522**

**40.12.**—(1)   At the Case Management Conference in a commercial action the sheriff shall seek to secure the expeditious resolution of the action.

(2)   Parties shall be prepared to provide such information as the sheriff may require to determine—

    (a)   whether, and to what extent, further specification of the claim and defences is required; and

    (b)   the orders to make to ensure the expeditious resolution of the action; and

    (c)[1]   whether there is or is likely to be a vulnerable witness within the meaning of section 11(1) of the Act of 2004 who is to give evidence at any proof or hearing, consider any child witness notice or vulnerable witness application that has been lodged where no order has been made and consider whether any order under section 12(1) of the Act of 2004 requires to be made.

(3)   The orders the sheriff may make in terms of paragraph 2(b) may include but shall not be limited to—

    (a)   the lodging of written pleadings by any party to the action which may be restricted to particular issues;

    (b)   the lodging of a statement of facts by any party which may be restricted to particular issues;

    (c)   allowing an amendment by a party to his pleadings;

    (d)   disclosure of the identity of witnesses and the existence and nature of documents relating to the action or authority to recover documents either generally or specifically;

    (e)   the lodging of documents constituting, evidencing or relating to the subject matter of the action or any invoices, correspondence or similar documents;

    (f)   the exchanging of lists of witnesses;

    (g)   the lodging of reports of skilled persons or witness statements;

    (h)   the lodging of affidavits concerned with any of the issues in the action;

    (i)   the lodging of notes of arguments setting out the basis of any preliminary plea;

---

[1] As inserted by the Act of Sederunt (Ordinary Cause, Summary Application, Summary Cause and Small Claim Rules) Amendment (Vulnerable Witnesses (Scotland) Act 2004) 2007, r.2(12) (effective November 1, 2007).

(j)    fixing a debate or proof, with or without any further preliminary procedure, to determine the action or any particular aspect thereof;

(k)    the lodging of joint minutes of admission or agreement;

(l)    recording admissions made on the basis of information produced; or

(m)    any order which the sheriff thinks will result in the speedy resolution of the action (including the use of alternative dispute resolution), or requiring the attendance of parties in person at any subsequent hearing.

(4)   In making any order in terms of paragraph (3) the sheriff may fix a period within which such order shall be complied with.

(5)   The sheriff may continue the Case Management Conference to a specified date where he considers it necessary to do so—

(a)    to allow any order made in terms of paragraph (3) to be complied with; or

(b)    to advance the possibility of resolution of the action.

(6)   Where the sheriff makes an order in terms of paragraph (3) he may ordain the pursuer to—

(a)    make up a record; and

(b)    lodge that record in process,

within such period as he thinks fit.

### GENERAL NOTE

The Ordinary Cause Rules did not follow the Court of Session model and avoided having both a preliminary and procedural hearing. Instead there is a case management conference which serves the purpose of both. If the action involves the interpretation of a contract it can be sent straight to a debate. The only further procedure in such a case might be the preparation of notes of argument and lists of authorities. Otherwise the purpose of the case management conference is to identify the issues and agree upon a framework for their resolution. For example, it is quite common to restrict the first stage to identifying the contractual terms regulating the relationship between the parties, should these be in issue. Sometimes liability is determined first leaving quantum for a later stage. Further factual information may well be required to properly identify the issues. The case management conference can be continued for this purpose. There is often a time frame agreed within which the information is to be obtained and exchanged.

### Form of the case management conference

In Glasgow Sheriff Court the case management conference will often be conducted by telephone conference call which is initiated by the sheriff. If there is a hearing, wigs and gowns are not worn and parties remain seated. It is intended that the hearing be conducted as a business meeting. One of the advantages of conference calls is that the principal solicitor is able to conduct the hearing regardless of where his office is located. Conference call facilities are not presently available in the Borders Courts. If the principal solicitor is unable to appear at the case management conference, it is vital that the solicitor instructed to appear is properly briefed and able to contribute fully to the discussion.

### Written pleadings

Although written pleadings remain the most common vehicle for focusing issues, spreadsheets, schedules and similar forms are increasingly used. Intimation of pleadings, etc. is usually given in electronic form both between solicitors and to the sheriff. If there are issues with regard to a lack of specification, these are normally discussed and resolved at a case management conference and should not thereafter be the focus for a debate. Any adjustment to the initial writ and defences should be achieved by red lining, striking out or similar. The court will not welcome receipt of a traditional "note of adjustment".

### Recovery and disclosure of documents

The procedures in Chapter 28 for recovery of evidence are still available to the parties. However, recourse to this provision is not usually required when the documents, the production of which is sought, are in the hands of the parties to the litigation. It is normally agreed that such documents should be produced and the timescale for achieving this.

### Exchange of lists of witnesses

Unlike Chapter 47 procedure in the Court of Session, lists of witnesses are not normally required in advance of proof being allowed. However, parties are required to know how many witnesses they will be leading in evidence in order that the appropriate number of days can be allowed for the proof. A list of witnesses is normally required at least 28 days before the diet of proof.

*Reports of skilled persons and witness statements*

If parties have retained expert witnesses it is customary for their reports to be lodged and exchanged before proof is allowed. If this is not done voluntarily it is unlikely that a party will be able to resist a motion that their expert's report should be lodged as a production. Little recourse is made to the production of witness statements.

*Affidavits*

As for witness statements, parties are not usually put to the expense of preparing affidavits. The exception to this is when there is a motion for summary decree. On such occasions the commercial sheriff may require that an affidavit be produced, usually by the defender, covering a particularly critical averment.

*Notes of argument*

If there has been a full discussion of the basis of a preliminary plea at a case management conference, the lodging of a note of argument might be dispensed with. However, it is more than likely that the commercial sheriff will require a note of argument in advance of the debate being allowed. Although there is no specific provision in the rules for producing a note on further procedure, this is sometimes ordered at the same time as is the note of argument. The two documents then assist the sheriff in deciding whether there should be some form of enquiry into the facts or whether the case should go to debate. In advance of any debate the commercial sheriff will normally require that lists of authorities be exchanged. The commercial sheriff is not obliged to send a case to debate only because one of the parties has tabled a preliminary plea.

*"Speedy resolution"*

Perhaps this is an unfortunate expression as it might give the impression that thoroughness and fairness will be sacrificed at the altar of speed. A more balanced expression might be "efficient resolution".

*Record*

It should be noted that unless ordained so to do the pursuer does not require to lodge a record. The initial writ and defences, as these have been adjusted, are often sufficient for the purposes of the commercial sheriff and the parties.

**Lodging of productions**                                                                                    D1.523

**40.13**    Prior to any proof or other hearing at which the documents listed in terms of rules 40.7(2) and 40.9(2) are to be referred to parties shall, in addition to lodging the productions in terms of rule 21.1, prepare, for the use of the sheriff, a working bundle in which the documents are arranged chronologically or in another appropriate order.

GENERAL NOTE

This rule reflects the terms of para.14 of Court of Session Practice Note No. 12 of 1994. In practice it is not always insisted upon by the commercial sheriff. In advance of the hearing solicitors should ascertain from the sheriff if the terms of this rule can be dispensed with.

**Hearing for further procedure**                                                                             D1.524

**40.14.**    At any time before final judgement, the sheriff may—
    (a)    of his own motion or on the motion of any party, fix a hearing for further procedure; and
    (b)    make such other order as he thinks fit.

GENERAL NOTE

The main thrust of Chapter 40 rules is that the commercial sheriff should be involved in managing all procedural aspects of the case. This rule enables the sheriff to put a case out for a by order hearing at any time before final judgment when the sheriff would, in any event, be functus. It is sometimes used by the sheriff to convene a pre-proof hearing to ascertain how preparations for the proof are proceeding and if there is likely to be a settlement. It is also used after there has been a debate or preliminary proof to discuss what further procedure there should be once the decision on the debate or preliminary point is known.

**Failure to comply with rule or order of sheriff**                                                           D1.525

**40.15**    Any failure by a party to comply timeously with a provision in this Chapter or any order made by the sheriff in a commercial action shall entitle the sheriff, of his own motion—
    (a)    to refuse to extend any period for compliance with a provision in these Rules or an order of the court;
    (b)    to dismiss the action or counterclaim, as the case may be, in whole or in part;

(c) to grant decree in respect of all or any of the craves of the initial writ or counterclaim, as the case may be; or

(d) to make an award of expenses,

as he thinks fit.

GENERAL NOTE

This rule provides the commercial sheriff with the necessary sanctions to attain the aim of achieving an efficient determination of commercial actions.

**D1.526**

**Determination of action**

**40.16.** It shall be open to the sheriff, at the end of any hearing, to restrict any interlocutor to a finding.

GENERAL NOTE

This provision may be thought to dispense with the requirement to make findings in fact at the conclusion of a diet of proof or proof before answer. Such dispensation would be consistent with the stated desire to achieve a speedy decision.

**D1.527**

**Parts of Process**

**40.17.** All parts of process lodged in a commercial action shall be clearly marked "Commercial Action".

GENERAL NOTE

Not only should the initial writ bear the expression "Commercial Action" but all steps in the process should also be so distinguished.

**D1.528**

Chapter 41[1]

Protection from Abuse (Scotland) Act 2001

**Interpretation**

**41.1.**—(1) In this Chapter a section referred to by number means the section so numbered in the Protection from Abuse (Scotland) Act 2001.

(2) Words and expressions used in this Chapter which are also used in the Protection from Abuse (Scotland) Act 2001 have the same meaning as in that Act.

**Attachment of power of arrest to interdict**

**D1.529**

**41.2.**—[2](1) An application under section 1(1) (application for attachment of power of arrest to interdict)—

(a) shall be made in the crave in the initial writ, defences or counterclaim in which the interdict to which it relates is applied for, or, if made after the application for interdict, by motion in the process of the action in which the interdict was sought, or by minute, with answers if appropriate, should the sheriff so order; and

(b) shall be intimated to the person against whom the interdict is sought or was obtained.

(2)[3] Where the sheriff attaches a power of arrest under section 1(2) or (1A) (order attaching power of arrest) the following documents shall be served along with the power of arrest in accordance with section 2(1) (documents to be served along with power of arrest)—

(a) a copy of the application for interdict;

(b) a copy of the interlocutor granting interdict; and

(c) where the application to attach the power of arrest was made after the interdict was granted, a copy of the certificate of service of the interdict.

(3) After the power of arrest has been served, the following documents shall be delivered by the person who obtained the power to the chief constable in accordance with section 3(1) (notification to police)—

(a) a copy of the application for interdict;

(b) a copy of the interlocutor granting interdict;

---

[1] Inserted by the Act of Sederunt (Ordinary Cause Rules) Amendment (Applications under the Protection from Abuse (Scotland) Act 2001) 2002 (SSI 2002/128), para.2.

[2] As amended by the Act of Sederunt (Ordinary Cause, Summary Application, Summary Cause and Small Claim Rules) Amendment (Miscellaneous) 2003 (SSI 2003/26), para.2(13) (effective January 24, 2003).

[3] As amended by Act of Sederunt (Ordinary Cause Rules) Amendment (Family Law (Scotland) Act 2006 etc.) 2006, para.2 (SSI 2006/207) (effective May 4, 2006).

    (c)    a copy of the certificate of service of the interdict; and

    (d)    where the application to attach the power of arrest was made after the interdict was granted—

        (i)    a copy of the application for the power of arrest;

        (ii)    a copy of the interlocutor granting it; and

        (iii)    a copy of the certificate of service of the power of arrest and the documents that required to be served along with it in accordance with section 2(1).

    (e)[1]    where a determination has previously been made in respect of such interdict under section 3(1) of the Domestic Abuse (Scotland) Act 2011, a copy of the interlocutor in Form DA1.

### Extension or recall of power of arrest

**41.3.**—(1)   An application under either of the following provisions shall be made by minute in the process of the action in which the power of arrest was attached—

    (a)    section 2(3) (extension of duration of power of arrest);

    (b)    section 2(7) (recall of power of arrest).

(2)   Where the sheriff extends the duration of, or recalls, a power of arrest, the person who obtained the extension or recall must deliver a copy of the interlocutor granting the extension or recall in accordance with section 3(1).

**D1.530**

### Documents to be delivered to chief constable in relation to recall or variation of interdict

**41.4.**   Where an interdict to which a power of arrest has been attached under section 1(2) is varied or recalled, the person who obtained the variation or recall must deliver a copy of the interlocutor varying or recalling the interdict in accordance with section 3(1).

**D1.531**

### Certificate of delivery of documents to chief constable

**41.5.**   Where a person is in any circumstances required to comply with section 3(1) he shall, after such compliance, lodge in process a certificate of delivery in Form PA1.

**D1.532**

Chapter 41A[2]

Domestic Abuse (Scotland) Act 2011

### Interpretation and application of this Chapter

**41A.1.**—(1)   In this Chapter—

**D1.533**

"the 2011 Act" means the Domestic Abuse (Scotland) Act 2011;
"interdict" includes interim interdict.

(2)   This Chapter applies to an application for a determination under section 3(1) of the 2011 Act that an interdict is a domestic abuse interdict.

### Applications for a determination that an interdict is a domestic abuse interdict

**41A.2.**—(1)   An application made before the interdict is obtained must be made by crave in the initial writ, defences or counterclaim in which the interdict is sought.

**D1.534**

(2)   An application made after the interdict is obtained must be made by minute.

(3)   Where a determination is made under section 3(1) of the 2011 Act, the interlocutor shall be in Form DA1.

(4)   In pursuance of section 3(4) of the 2011 Act, the applicant must serve a copy of the interlocutor in Form DA1 on the person against whom the interdict has been granted and lodge in process a certificate of service in Form DA2.

(5)   Where a determination is recalled under section 3(5)(b) of the 2011 Act, the interlocutor shall be in Form DA3.

(6)   Paragraph (7) applies where, in respect of the same interdict—

    (a)    a power of arrest under section 1 of the Protection from Abuse (Scotland) Act 2001 is in effect; and

    (b)    a determination under section 3(1) of the 2011 Act is made.

---

[1] As inserted by the Act of Sederunt (Sheriff Court Rules) (Miscellaneous Amendments) (No.2) 2011 (SSI 2011/289) para.2 (effective July 20, 2011).

[2] As inserted by the Act of Sederunt (Sheriff Court Rules) (Miscellaneous Amendments) (No.2) 2011 (SSI 2011/289) para.5 (effective July 20, 2011).

(7)[1]  Where a determination is made or where such determination is recalled, the sheriff must appoint a person to send forthwith to the chief constable of the Police Service of Scotland a copy of—

    (a)   the interlocutor in Form DA1 and the certificate of service in Form DA2; or

    (b)   the interlocutor in Form DA3,

as the case may be.

(8)[2]  Where a person is required by virtue of this Chapter to send documents to the chief constable, such person must, after each such compliance, lodge in process a certificate of sending in Form DA4.

Chapter 42[3]

Competition Appeal Tribunal

**Interpretation**

**D1.535**

**42.1.**  In this Chapter—

"the 1998 Act" means the Competition Act 1998; and

"the Tribunal" means the Competition Appeal Tribunal established by section 12 of the Enterprise Act 2002.

**Transfer of proceedings to the Tribunal**

**D1.536**

**42.2.**—(1)  A party in proceedings for a monetary claim to which section 47A of the 1998 Act applies may apply by motion to the sheriff for an order transferring the proceedings, or any part of them, to the Tribunal.

(2)  Where the sheriff orders that such proceedings (or any part of them) are transferred to the Tribunal, the sheriff clerk shall, within 7 days from the date of such order—

    (a)   transmit the process (or the appropriate part) to the clerk of the Tribunal;

    (b)   notify each party to the proceedings in writing of the transmission under sub paragraph (a); and

    (c)   certify, by making an appropriate entry on the interlocutor sheet, that he has made all notifications required under sub paragraph (b).

(3)  Transmission of the process under paragraph (2)(a) shall be valid notwithstanding any failure by the sheriff clerk to comply with paragraph (2)(b) and (c).

Chapter 43[4]

Causes Relating to Articles 101 and 102 of the Treaty Establishing the European Community

**Intimation of actions to the Office of Fair Trading**

**D1.537**

**43.1**—(1)  In this rule—

"the Treaty" means Treaty on the Functioning of the European Union, as referred to in section 1(2)(s) of the European Communities Act 1972; and

"the OFT" means the Office of Fair Trading.

(2)  In an action where an issue under Article 101 or 102 of the Treaty is raised—

    (a)   by the pursuer in the initial writ;

    (b)   by the defender in the defences;

    (c)   by any party in the pleadings;

intimation of the action shall be given to the OFT by the party raising the issue by a notice of intimation in Form OFT1.

(3)  The initial writ, defences or pleadings in which the issue under Article 81 or 82 of the Treaty is raised shall include a crave for warrant for intimation to the OFT.

(4)  A certified copy of an interlocutor granting a warrant under paragraph (3) shall be sufficient authority for the party to intimate by notice in Form OFT1.

---

[1] As amended by the Act of Sederunt (Sheriff Court Rules)(Miscellaneous Amendments) 2013 (SSI 2013/135) para.4 (effective May 27, 2013).

[2] As amended by the Act of Sederunt (Sheriff Court Rules)(Miscellaneous Amendments) 2013 (SSI 2013/135) para.4 (effective May 27, 2013).

[3] Inserted by the Act of Sederunt (Ordinary Cause Rules) Amendment (Competition Appeal Tribunal) 2004 (SSI 2004/350), para.2 (effective August 20, 2004).

[4] Inserted by Act of Sederunt (Ordinary Cause Rules) Amendment (Causes Relating to Articles 81 and 82 of the Treaty Establishing the European Community) 2006 (SSI 2006/293) (effective June 16, 2006) and amended by the Act of Sederunt (Sheriff Court Rules) (Miscellaneous Amendments) (No.3) 2012 (SSI 2012/271) para.6 (effective November 1, 2012).

(5)  A notice of intimation under paragraph (2) shall be on a period of notice of 21 days unless the sheriff otherwise orders; but the sheriff shall not order a period of notice of less than 2 days.

(6)  There shall be attached to the notice of intimation—

    (a)  a copy of the initial writ, defences or pleadings (including any adjustments and amendments), as the case may be;

    (b)  a copy of the interlocutor allowing intimation of the notice; and

    (c)  where the pleadings have not been amended in accordance with any minute of amendment, a copy of that minute.

Chapter 44[1]

The Equality Act 2010

### Interpretation and application

**44.1.**—[2](1)  In this Chapter—  **D1.538**

"the Commission" means the Commis sion for Equality and Human Rights; and
"the 2010 Act" means the Equality Act 2010.

(2)  This Chapter applies to claims made by virtue of section 114(1) of the 2010 Act including a claim for damages.

### Intimation to Commission

**44.2.**[3]  The pursuer shall send a copy of the initial writ to the Commission by registered or recorded  **D1.539**
delivery post.

### Assessor

**44.3.**—(1)  The sheriff may, of his own motion or on the motion of any party, appoint an assessor.  **D1.540**

(2)  The assessor shall be a person who the sheriff considers has special qualifications to be of assistance in determining the cause.

### Taxation of Commission expenses

**44.4.**  *[Omitted by the Act of Sederunt (Sheriff Court Rules) (Miscellaneous Amendments) 2008 (SSI 2008/223) para.4(3)(c) (effective July 1, 2008).]*

### National security

**44.5.**—[4](1)  Where, on a motion under paragraph (3) or of the sheriff's own motion, the sheriff  **D1.541**
considers it expedient in the interests of national security, the sheriff may—

    (a)  exclude from all or part of the proceedings—

        (i)  the pursuer;

        (ii)  the pursuer's representatives;

        (iii)  any assessors;

    (b)  permit a pursuer or representative who has been excluded to make a statement to the court before the commencement of the proceedings or the part of the proceedings, from which he or she is excluded;

    (c)  take steps to keep secret all or part of the reasons for his or her decision in the proceedings.

(2)  The sheriff clerk shall, on the making of an order under paragraph (1) excluding the pursuer or the pursuer's representatives, notify the Advocate General for Scotland of that order.

(3)  A party may apply by motion for an order under paragraph (1).

(4)  The steps referred to in paragraph (1)(c) may include the following—

    (a)  directions to the sheriff clerk; and

    (b)  orders requiring any person appointed to represent the interests of the pursuer in proceedings from which the pursuer or the pursuer's representatives are excluded not to communicate (directly or indirectly) with any persons (including the excluded pursuer)—

---

[1] As inserted by the Act of Sederunt (Ordinary Cause, Summary Application, Summary Cause and Small Claim Rules) Amendment (Equality Act 2006 etc.) 2006 (SSI 2006/509), (effective November 3, 2006). Chapter title amended by the Act of Sederunt (Sheriff Court Rules) (Equality Act 2010) 2010 (SSI 2010/340) para.2 (effective October 1, 2010).

[2] As substituted by the Act of Sederunt (Sheriff Court Rules) (Equality Act 2010) 2010 (SSI 2010/340) para.2 (effective October 1, 2010).

[3] As inserted by the Act of Sederunt (Sheriff Court Rules) (Miscellaneous Amendments) 2008 (SSI 2008/223) para.4(3)(b) (effective July 1, 2008).

[4] As substituted by the Act of Sederunt (Sheriff Court Rules) (Equality Act 2010) 2010 (SSI 2010/340) para.2 (effective October 1, 2010).

(i) on any matter discussed or referred to;

(ii) with regard to any material disclosed,

during or with reference to any part of the proceedings from which the pursuer or the pursuer's representatives are excluded.

(5) Where the sheriff has made an order under paragraph (4)(b), the person appointed to represent the interests of the pursuer may apply by motion for authority to seek instructions from or otherwise communicate with an excluded person.

### Transfer to Employment Tribunal

**D1.542**

**44.6.**—[1](1) On transferring proceedings to an employment tribunal under section 140(2) of the 2010 Act, the sheriff—

    (a) shall state his or her reasons for doing so in the interlocutor; and

    (b) may make the order on such conditions as to expenses or otherwise as he or she thinks fit.

(2) The sheriff clerk must, within 7 days from the date of such order—

    (a) transmit the process to the Secretary of the Employment Tribunals (Scotland);

    (b) notify each party to the proceedings in writing of the transmission under subparagraph (a); and

    (c) certify, by making an appropriate entry on the interlocutor sheet, that he or she has made all notifications required under subparagraph (b).

(3) Transmission of the process under paragraph (2)(a) will be valid notwithstanding any failure by the sheriff clerk to comply with paragraph (2)(b) and (c).

### Transfer from Employment Tribunal

**D1.543**

**44.7.**—[2](1) On receipt of the documentation in proceedings which have been remitted from an employment tribunal under section 140(3) of the 2010 Act, the sheriff clerk must—

    (a) record the date of receipt on the first page of the documentation;

    (b) fix a hearing to determine further procedure not less than 14 days after the date of receipt of the process; and

    (c) forthwith send written notice of the date of the hearing fixed under subparagraph (b) to each party.

(2) At the hearing fixed under paragraph (1)(b) the sheriff may make such order as he or she thinks fit to secure so far as practicable that the cause thereafter proceeds in accordance with these Rules.

Chapter 45[3]

Vulnerable Witnesses (Scotland) Act 2004

### Interpretation

**D1.544**

**45.1.** In this Chapter—

"child witness notice" has the meaning given in section 12(2) of the Act of 2004;

"review application" means an application for review of arrangements for vulnerable witnesses pursuant to section 13 of the Act of 2004;

"vulnerable witness application" has the meaning given in section 12(6) of the Act of 2004.

---

[1] As inserted by the Act of Sederunt (Sheriff Court Rules) (Equality Act 2010) 2010 (SSI 2010/340) para.2 (effective October 1, 2010).

[2] As inserted by the Act of Sederunt (Sheriff Court Rules) (Equality Act 2010) 2010 (SSI 2010/340) para.2 (effective October 1, 2010).

[3] As inserted by the Act of Sederunt (Ordinary Cause, Summary Application, Summary Cause and Small Claim Rules) Amendment (Vulnerable Witnesses (Scotland) Act 2004) 2007, r.2(13) (effective November 1, 2007).

**Child Witness Notice**

**45.2.** A child witness notice lodged in accordance with section 12(2) of the Act of 2004 shall be in Form G19.

**D1.545**

**Vulnerable Witness Application**

**45.3.** A vulnerable witness application lodged in accordance with section 12(6) of the Act of 2004 shall be in Form G20.

**D1.546**

**Intimation**

**45.4.**—(1) The party lodging a child witness notice or vulnerable witness application shall intimate a copy of the child witness notice or vulnerable witness application to all the other parties to the proceedings and complete a certificate of intimation.

**D1.547**

(2) A certificate of intimation referred to in paragraph (1) shall be in Form G21 and shall be lodged with the child witness notice or vulnerable witness application.

**Procedure on lodging child witness notice or vulnerable witness application**

**45.5.**—(1) On receipt of a child witness notice or vulnerable witness application, the sheriff may—

**D1.548**

    (a) make an order under section 12(1) or (6) of the Act of 2004 without holding a hearing;

    (b) require further information from any of the parties before making any further order;

    (c) fix a date for a hearing of the child witness notice or vulnerable witness application.

(2) The sheriff may, subject to any statutory time limits, make an order altering the date of the proof or other hearing at which the child or vulnerable witness is to give evidence and make such provision for intimation of such alteration to all parties concerned as he deems appropriate.

(3) An order fixing a hearing for a child witness notice or vulnerable witness application shall be intimated by the sheriff clerk—

    (a) on the day the order is made; and

    (b) in such manner as may be prescribed by the sheriff,

to all parties to the proceedings and such other persons as are named in the order where such parties or persons are not present at the time the order is made.

**Review of arrangements for vulnerable witnesses**

**45.6.**—(1) A review application shall be in Form G22.

**D1.549**

(2) Where the review application is made orally, the sheriff may dispense with the requirements of paragraph (1).

**Intimation of review application**

**45.7.**—(1) Where a review application is lodged, the applicant shall intimate a copy of the review application to all other parties to the proceedings and complete a certificate of intimation.

**D1.550**

(2) A certificate of intimation referred to in paragraph (1) shall be in Form G23 and shall be lodged together with the review application.

**Procedure on lodging a review application**

**45.8.**—(1) On receipt of a review application, the sheriff may—

**D1.551**

    (a) if he is satisfied that he may properly do so, make an order under section 13(2) of the Act of 2004 without holding a hearing or, if he is not so satisfied, make such an order after giving the parties an opportunity to be heard;

    (b) require of any of the parties further information before making any further order;

    (c) fix a date for a hearing of the review application.

(2) The sheriff may, subject to any statutory time limits, make an order altering the date of the proof or other hearing at which the child or vulnerable witness is to give evidence and make such provision for intimation of such alteration to all parties concerned as he deems appropriate.

(3) An order fixing a hearing for a review application shall be intimated by the sheriff clerk—

    (a) on the day the order is made; and

    (b) in such manner as may be prescribed by the sheriff,

to all parties to the proceedings and such other persons as are named in the order where such parties or persons are not present at the time the order is made.

**D1.552**

### Determination of special measures

**45.9.** When making an order under section 12(1) or (6) or 13(2) of the Act of 2004 the sheriff may, in light thereof, make such further orders as he deems appropriate in all the circumstances.

**D1.553**

### Intimation of an order under section 12(1) or (6) or 13(2)

**45.10.** An order under section 12(1) or (6) or 13(2) of the Act of 2004 shall be intimated by the sheriff clerk—

    (a)  on the day the order is made; and

    (b)  in such manner as may be prescribed by the sheriff,

to all parties to the proceedings and such other persons as are named in the order where such parties or persons are not present at the time the order is made.

**D1.554**

### Taking of evidence by commissioner

**45.11.**—(1) An interlocutor authorising the special measure of taking evidence by a commissioner shall be sufficient authority for the citing the witness to appear before the commissioner.

    (2)  At the commission the commissioner shall—

        (a)  administer the oath *de fideli administratione* to any clerk appointed for the commission; and

        (b)  administer to the witness the oath in Form G14, or where the witness elects to affirm, the affirmation in Form G15.

    (3)  The commission shall proceed without interrogatories unless, on cause shown, the sheriff otherwise directs.

**D1.555**

### Commission on interrogatories

**45.12.**—(1) Where interrogatories have not been dispensed with, the party citing or intending to cite the vulnerable witness shall lodge draft interrogatories in process.

    (2)  Any other party may lodge cross-interrogatories.

    (3)  The interrogatories and cross-interrogatories, when adjusted, shall be extended and returned to the sheriff clerk for approval and the settlement of any dispute as to their contents by the sheriff.

    (4)  The party who cited the vulnerable witness shall—

        (a)  provide the commissioner with a copy of the pleadings (including any adjustments and amendments), the approved interrogatories and any cross-interrogatories and a certified copy of the interlocutor of his appointment;

        (b)  instruct the clerk; and

        (c)  be responsible in the first instance for the fee of the commissioner and his clerk.

    (5)  The commissioner shall, in consultation with the parties, fix a diet for the execution of the commission to examine the witness.

**D1.556**

### Commission without interrogatories

**45.13.** Where interrogatories have been dispensed with, the party citing or intending to cite the vulnerable witness shall—

    (a)  provide the commissioner with a copy of the pleadings (including any adjustments and amendments) and a certified copy of the interlocutor of his appointment;

    (b)  fix a diet for the execution of the commission in consultation with the commissioner and every other party;

    (c)  instruct the clerk; and

    (d)  be responsible in the first instance for the fees of the commissioner and his clerk.

**D1.557**

### Lodging of video record and documents

**45.14.**—(1) Where evidence is taken on commission pursuant to an order made under section 12(1) or (6) or 13(2) of the Act of 2004 the commissioner shall lodge the video record of the commission and relevant documents with the sheriff clerk.

    (2)  On the video record and any documents being lodged the sheriff clerk shall—

        (a)  note—

            (i)  the documents lodged;

            (ii)  by whom they were lodged; and

            (iii)  the date on which they were lodged, and

        (b)  intimate what he has noted to all parties concerned.

**D1.558**

### Custody of video record and documents

**45.15.**—(1) The video record and documents referred to in rule 45.14 shall, subject to paragraph (2), be kept in the custody of the sheriff clerk.

(2) Where the video record of the evidence of a witness is in the custody of the sheriff clerk under this rule and where intimation has been given to that effect under rule 45.14(2), the name and address of that witness and the record of his evidence shall be treated as being in the knowledge of the parties; and no party shall be required, notwithstanding any enactment to the contrary—

    (a)   to include the name of that witness in any list of witnesses; or

    (b)   to include the record of his evidence in any list of productions.

### Application for leave for party to be present at the commission

**45.16.** An application for leave for a party to be present in the room where the commission proceedings are taking place shall be by motion..          **D1.559**

   (1) In Appendix 1—

    (a)   for Form G13 there shall be substituted the form set out in Part 1 of Schedule 1 to this Act of Sederunt; and

    (b)   after Form G18 there shall be inserted the forms set out in Part 2 of Schedule 1 to this Act of Sederunt.

Chapter 46[1]

Companies Act 2006

### Leave to raise derivative proceedings

**46.1.**—(1) Where leave of the court is required under section 266(1) (derivative proceedings: requirement for leave and notice) of the Companies Act 2006 (the "2006 Act"), the applicant must lodge, along with the initial writ, a written application in the form of a letter addressed to the sheriff clerk stating the grounds on which leave is sought.       **D1.560**

   (2) Subject to paragraph (4), an application under paragraph (1) is not to be served on, or intimated to, any party.

   (3) The application is to be placed before the sheriff, who shall consider it for the purposes of section 266(3) of the 2006 Act without hearing the applicant.

   (4) Service under section 266(4)(a) of the 2006 Act may be given by any of the methods provided for in Chapter 5 (citation, service and intimation) and a certificate of service must be lodged.

   (5) If the company wishes to be heard it must, within 21 days after the date of service of the application, lodge written submissions setting out its position in relation to the application.

   (6) Subject to section 266(4)(b) of the 2006 Act, the next stage in the proceedings is a hearing at which the applicant and the company may be heard.

   (7) The sheriff clerk is to fix the hearing and intimate its date to the applicant and the company.

   (8) Where an application under paragraph (1) is granted, a copy of the sheriff's interlocutor must be served on the defender along with the warrant of citation.

### Application to continue proceedings as derivative proceedings

**46.2.** An application under section 267(2) (application to continue proceedings as derivative proceedings) of the 2006 Act is to be in the form of a minute and Chapter 14 (applications by minute) applies with the necessary modifications.      **D1.561**

Chapter 47[2]

Actions of Division and Sale and Orders for Division and/or Sale of Property

### Remit to reporter to examine heritable property

**47.1.**—(1) In an action of division and sale of heritable property, the sheriff may, in accordance with paragraph (2), remit to a reporter to examine the property and to report to the sheriff—      **D1.562**

    (a)   whether the property is capable of division in a manner equitable to the interests of the *pro indiviso* proprietors and, if so, how such division may be effected; and

    (b)   in the event that the property is to be sold—

        (i)   whether the property should be sold as a whole or in lots and, if in lots, what those lots should be;

        (ii)   whether the property should be exposed for sale by public roup or private bargain;

---

[1] As inserted by the Act of Sederunt (Sheriff Court Rules) (Miscellaneous Amendments) 2010 (SSI 2010/279) r.5 (effective July 29, 2010).

[2] As inserted by the Act of Sederunt (Sheriff Court Rules) (Miscellaneous Amendments) (No.3) 2011 (SSI 2011/386) para.2 (effective November 28, 2011).

    (iii)    whether the sale should be subject to any upset or minimum price and, if so, the amount;

    (iv)    the manner and extent to which the property should be advertised for sale; and

    (v)    any other matter which the reporter considers pertinent to a sale of the property.

(2)    A remit under paragraph (1) shall be made—

    (a)    where the action is undefended, on the motion of the pursuer at any time after the expiry of the period of notice;

    (b)    where the action is defended—

        (i)    at the options hearing, on the motion of any party to the action;

        (ii)    on the sheriff finding, after a debate or proof, that the pursuer is entitled to bring and insist in the action of division and sale; or

        (iii)    at such other time as the sheriff thinks fit.

(3)    On completion of a report made under paragraph (1), the reporter shall send the report, with a copy for each party, to the sheriff clerk.

(4)    On receipt of such report, the sheriff clerk must—

    (a)    lodge the report in process; and

    (b)    give written intimation to each party that this has been done and that parties may uplift a copy of the report from the process.

(5)    After the lodging of such a report, any party may apply by motion for further procedure or for approval of the report.

(6)    At the hearing of a motion under paragraph (5), the sheriff may—

    (a)    in the event of a challenge to any part of the report, order parties to state their objections to the report and answers to such objections and lodge them within such period as the sheriff thinks fit; or

    (b)    in the absence of such challenge, order that the property be divided or sold, as the case may be, in accordance with the recommendations of the reporter, subject to such modification, if any, as the sheriff thinks fit.

(7)    Where, in accordance with paragraph (6)(a), the lodging of objections and answers has been ordered, the sheriff clerk will fix a date and time for the parties to be heard by the sheriff; and the sheriff may make such order for further procedure as he or she thinks fit.

### Division and/or sale of property

**D1.563**

**47.2.**—(1)    Where the sheriff orders the division and/or sale of property, heritable or otherwise, the sheriff shall direct that the division and/or sale, as the case may be, shall be conducted under the oversight and direction of the sheriff clerk or any other fit person whom the sheriff may appoint for that purpose.

(2)    The sheriff clerk or person appointed under paragraph (1), as the case may be, may report any matter of difficulty arising in the course of the division and/or sale to the sheriff.

(3)    At a hearing on a report made under paragraph (2), the sheriff may give such directions as the sheriff thinks fit, including authority to the sheriff clerk to sign, on behalf of any proprietor, a disposition of his or her interest in the property.

(4)    On the conclusion of a sale of property—

    (a)    the proceeds of the sale, under deduction of the expenses of the sale, shall be consigned into court; and

    (b)    the sheriff clerk or the person appointed under paragraph (1), as the case may be, shall lodge in process a report of the sale and a proposed scheme of division of the proceeds of sale.

(5)    At the hearing of a motion for approval of a report of the sale of property lodged under paragraph (4) and the proposed scheme of division, the sheriff may—

    (a)    approve the report and scheme of division, and direct that payment of the proceeds of sale be made in terms of the report;

    (b)    deal with any question as to the expenses of process or of sale; and

    (c)    make such other order as the sheriff thinks fit.

Chapter 48[1]

Reporting Restrictions under the Contempt of Court Act 1981

**Interpretation and application of this Chapter**

**48.1.** In this Chapter "the 1981 Act" means the Contempt of Court Act 1981.

**D1.564**

**Notification of reporting restrictions etc.**

**48.2.**—(1) Paragraph (2) applies where the sheriff makes an order under section 4(2) of the 1981 Act (order postponing publication of report of legal proceedings).

**D1.565**

(2) The sheriff clerk shall immediately arrange—
- (a) for a copy of the order to be sent to those persons who have asked to see any such order made by the sheriff and whose names are on the list kept by the Lord President for that purpose;
- (b) for the publication of the making of the order on the website used to provide official information about the Scottish courts.

**Applications for variation or revocation**

**48.3.**—(1) A person aggrieved by the terms of an order made under section 4(2) of the 1981 Act may apply to the sheriff for its variation or revocation.

**D1.566**

(2) An application shall be made by letter addressed to the sheriff clerk.

(3) On an application being made the sheriff shall—
- (a) appoint the application for a hearing;
- (b) order written intimation of the date and time of the hearing, together with a copy of the application, to the parties to the proceedings.

(4) The hearing shall—
- (a) unless there are exceptional circumstances or a later date is requested by the applicant, take place within 48 hours of receipt of the application by the sheriff clerk;
- (b) so far as reasonably practicable, be before the sheriff who made the order.

(5) The decision of the sheriff is final.

Chapter 49[2]

Admiralty Actions

**Interpretation of this Chapter**

**49.1.** In this Chapter—

**D1.567**

"Admiralty action" means an action having a crave appropriate for the enforcement of a claim to which section 47(2) of the Administration of Justice Act 1956 applies;

"ship" has the meaning assigned in section 48(f) of that Act.

**Forms of action**

**49.2.**—(1) An Admiralty action against the owners or demise charterers of, or other parties interested in, a ship or the owners of the cargo may be brought—

**D1.568**

- (a) in rem, where the crave of the initial writ is directed to recovery in respect of a maritime lien against the ship or cargo or the proceeds of it as sold under order of the sheriff or where arrestment in rem may be made under section 47(3) of the Administration of Justice Act 1956;
- (b) in personam, where the crave of the initial writ is directed to a decree against the defender; or
- (c) both in rem and in personam, where sub-paragraphs (a) and (b) apply.

(2) When bringing an Admiralty action, the pursuer shall use Form G1 (initial writ) and insert the words "Admiralty Action in rem", "Admiralty Action in personam" or "Admiralty Action in rem and in personam", as the case may be, immediately below where the Sheriffdom and court are designed, above the instance.

---

[1] As inserted by the Act of Sederunt (Sheriff Court Rules) (Miscellaneous Amendments) (No.3) 2011 (SSI 2011/386) para.3 (effective November 28, 2011).

[2] As inserted by the Act of Sederunt (Sheriff Court Rules) (Miscellaneous Amendments) 2012 (SSI 2012/188) para.10 (effective August 1, 2012).

**Actions in rem**

**D1.569**

49.3.—(1)  In an Admiralty action in rem—

    (a)  where the owners or demise charterers of, or other parties interested in, the ship or the owners of the cargo against which the action is directed are known to the pursuer, they shall be called as defenders by name;

    (b)  where such owners or demise charterers or other parties are unknown to the pursuer—

        (i)  the pursuer may call them as defenders as "the owners of or parties interested in the ship (*name and identify by its port of registry*) or the owners of the cargo"; and

        (ii)  the master, if known, shall also be called as a defender representing the owners or demise charterers.

(2)  In an Admiralty action in rem, the ship or cargo shall be arrested in rem and a warrant for such arrestment may include warrant to dismantle where craved in the initial writ.

**Actions in personam**

**D1.570**

49.4.—(1)  In an Admiralty action in personam directed against the owners or demise charterers, or other parties, interested in a ship, or the owners of cargo, the defenders shall, if known to the pursuer, be called as defenders by name.

(2)  In such an action, where—

    (a)  the vessel is not a British ship, and

    (b)  the names of the owners or demise charterers are not known to the pursuer,

the master of the ship may be called as the defender representing the owners or demise charterers.

(3)  In an action to which paragraph (2) applies, any warrant to arrest to found jurisdiction shall be executed against the master of the ship in his or her representative capacity.

(4)  In an action to which paragraph (2) applies, any decree shall be pronounced against the master in his or her representative capacity.

(5)  A decree in an Admiralty action in personam may be pronounced against an owner or demise charterer of, or other party interested in, the ship or the owner of the cargo only where that owner or demise charterer or other party interested, as the case may be, has been called or added as a defender.

**Sale of ship or cargo**

**D1.571**

49.5.—(1)  This rule shall not apply to the sale of a cargo arrested on the dependence of an Admiralty action in personam.

(2)  Where, in an Admiralty action or an action of declarator and sale of a ship—

    (a)  the sheriff makes a finding that the pursuer has a claim which falls to be satisfied out of an arrested ship or cargo, or

    (b)  a decree for a sum of money has been granted in an action in which a ship has been arrested on the dependence,

the pursuer may apply by motion for an order for the sale of that ship or a share in it, or the cargo, as the case may be, by public auction or private bargain.

(3)  Before making such an order, the sheriff shall remit to a reporter for the purpose of obtaining—

    (a)  an inventory of,

    (b)  a valuation and recommendation upset price for, and

    (c)  any recommendation as to the appropriate advertisement for the sale of, the ship, share or cargo.

(4)  Where a remit is made under paragraph (3), the pursuer shall instruct the reporter within 14 days after the date of the interlocutor making the remit and be responsible, in the first instance, for payment of his or her fee.

(5)  On completion of a report following a remit under paragraph (3), the reporter shall send the report and a copy for each party to the sheriff clerk.

(6)  On receipt of such a report, the sheriff clerk shall—

    (a)  give written intimation to each party of receipt of the report;

    (b)  request the pursuer to show to him or her a discharge in respect of the fee for which the pursuer is responsible under paragraph (4); and

    (c)  after sight of such a discharge—

        (i)  lodge the report in process;

        (ii)  give written intimation to each party that this has been done and that he or she may uplift a copy of the report from process; and

        (iii)  cause the action to call for a procedural hearing.

(7)  Where the sheriff orders the sale of a ship, share or cargo, the conduct of the sale, including any advertisement of it, shall be under the direction of the sheriff clerk.

(8)   Where such a sale is the sale of a ship or a share in it, the interlocutor ordering the sale shall include a declaration that the right to transfer the ship or share to the purchaser is vested in the sheriff clerk.

(9)   Where, in such a sale, no offer to purchase the ship, share or cargo, as the case may be, has reached the upset price, the pursuer may apply by motion for authority to expose such ship, share or cargo for sale at a reduced upset price.

(10)   The proceeds of such a sale shall be consigned into court, under deduction of all dues to the date the sheriff adjudges the ship, share or cargo to belong to the purchaser under paragraph (11)(a), payable to Her Majesty's Revenue and Customs or to the port or harbour authority within the jurisdiction of which the ship or cargo lies and in respect of which such port or harbour authority has statutory power to detain the ship or cargo.

(11)   On consignation being made under paragraph (10), the sheriff shall—

    (a)    adjudge the ship, share or cargo, as the case may be, declaring the same to belong to the purchaser, freed and disburdened of all bonds, mortgages, liens, rights of retention and other incumbrances affecting it and ordering such ship, share or cargo to be delivered to the purchaser on production of a certified copy of the interlocutor pronounced under this subparagraph; and

    (b)    order such intimation and advertisement, if any, for claims on the consigned fund as the sheriff thinks fit.

(12)   The sheriff shall, after such hearing or inquiry as the sheriff thinks fit—

    (a)    determine all questions of expenses;

    (b)    rank and prefer any claimants in order of preference; and

    (c)    make such other order, if any, as the sheriff thinks fit.

### Ship collisions and preliminary acts

**49.6.**—(1)   Subject to rule 49.7 (applications to dispense with preliminary acts), this rule applies to an Admiralty action of damages arising out of a collision between ships at sea.

**D1.572**

(2)   An action to which this rule applies may be brought in rem, in personam or in rem and in personam.

(3)   An initial writ in such an action shall not contain a condescendence or pleas-in-law.

(4)   Where such an action is brought in personam, the crave of the initial writ shall contain sufficient detail to enable the defender to identify the date and place of and the ships involved in the collision.

(5)   Where a notice of intention to defend has been lodged Rule 9.2 shall, subject to paragraph 11 of this rule, not apply.

(6)   Within 7 days after the expiry of the period of notice, the pursuer shall lodge in process a sealed envelope containing—

    (a)    a preliminary act in Form 49.6; and

    (b)    a brief condescendence and appropriate pleas-in-law.

(7)   Within 28 days after the preliminary act for the pursuer has been lodged under paragraph (6), the defender shall lodge in process a sealed envelope containing a preliminary act in Form 49.6.

(8)   A party who lodges a preliminary act under paragraph (6) or (7) shall not send a copy of it to any other party.

(9)   On the lodging of a preliminary act by the defender under paragraph (7) the sheriff clerk shall—

    (a)    open both sealed envelopes;

    (b)    mark the contents of those envelopes with appropriate numbers of process; and

    (c)    give written intimation to each party that subparagraphs (a) and (b) have been complied with.

(10)   On receipt of the written intimation under paragraph (9)(c), the pursuer and defender shall exchange copies of the contents of their respective envelopes.

(11)   Within 7 days after the sealed envelopes have been opened up under paragraph (9), the sheriff clerk shall fix a date and time for an Options Hearing and send parties Form G5 in terms of Rule 9.2.

(12)   When the pursuer lodges a record in terms of Rule 9.11 he or she shall do so with a copy of each of the preliminary acts appended to it.

(13)   No amendment, adjustment or alteration may be made to a preliminary act except by order of the sheriff.

### Applications to dispense with preliminary acts

**49.7.**—(1)   Within 7 days after the expiry of the period of notice, any party may apply for an order to dispense with preliminary acts in an action to which rule 49.6 applies.

**D1.573**

(2)   An application under paragraph (1) shall be made by minute craving the sheriff to dispense with preliminary acts and setting out the grounds on which the application is made.

(3)   Before lodging such a minute in process, the party making the application shall intimate a copy of the minute, and the date on which it will be lodged, to every other party.

(4)   Any other party may lodge in process answers to such a minute within 14 days after such a minute has been lodged.

(5)   After the expiry of the period mentioned in paragraph (4), the sheriff may, on the motion of any party, after such further procedure, if any, as the sheriff thinks fit, dispense with preliminary acts.

(6)   Where the sheriff dispenses with preliminary acts, the pursuer shall lodge a condescendence with appropriate pleas-in-law within such period as the sheriff thinks fit; and the action shall thereafter proceed in the same way as an ordinary action.

(7)   Where the sheriff refuses to dispense with preliminary acts, the sheriff shall ordain a party or parties, as the case may be, to lodge preliminary acts under rule 49.6 within such period as the sheriff thinks fit.

(8)   An interlocutor dispensing or refusing to dispense with preliminary acts shall be final and not subject to review.

**Ship collision and salvage actions**

**D1.574**

**49.8.**—(1)   Without prejudice to rule 29.11 (lodging productions), in an Admiralty action arising out of a collision between ships at sea or salvage, the parties shall—
    (a)   within 4 days after the interlocutor allowing proof,
    (b)   within 4 days before the taking of evidence on commission, or
    (c)   on or before such other date as the sheriff, on special cause shown, shall determine,
lodge in process the documents, if any, mentioned in paragraph (2).

(2)   The documents to be lodged under paragraph (1) are—
    (a)   the log books, including scrap log books, of the ships concerned;
    (b)   all *de recenti* written reports in connection with the collision or salvage, as the case may be, by the masters or mates of the vessels concerned to their respective owners; and
    (c)   reports of any surveys of the ship in respect of which damage or salvage is claimed.

**Arrestment of ships and arrestment in rem of cargo on board ship**

**D1.575**

**49.9.**—(1)   An arrestment of a ship in rem or on the dependence, or an arrestment in rem of cargo on board ship, may be executed on any day by a sheriff officer who shall affix the schedule of arrestment—
    (a)   to the mainmast of the ship;
    (b)   to the single mast of the ship; or
    (c)   where there is no mast, to some prominent part of the ship.

(2)   In the execution of an arrestment of a ship on the dependence, the sheriff officer shall, in addition to complying with paragraph (1), mark the initials "ER" above the place where the schedule of arrestment is fixed.

(3)   On executing an arrestment under paragraph (1), the sheriff officer shall deliver a copy of the schedule of arrestment and a copy of the certificate of execution of it to the master of the ship, or other person on board in charge of the ship or cargo, as the case may be, as representing the owners or demise charterers of, or parties interested in, the ship or the owners of the cargo, as the case may be.

(4)   Where the schedule of arrestment and the copy of the certificate of execution of it cannot be delivered as required under paragraph (3)—
    (a)   the certificate of execution shall state that fact; and
    (b)   either—
        (i)    the arrestment shall be executed by serving it on the harbour master of the port where the ship lies; or
        (ii)   where there is no harbour master, or the ship is not in a harbour, the pursuer shall enrol a motion for such further order as to intimation and advertisement, if any, as may be necessary.

(5)   A copy of the schedule of arrestment and a copy of the certificate of execution of it shall be delivered by the sheriff officer to the harbour master, if any, of any port where the ship lies.

**Arrestment of cargo**

**D1.576**

**49.10.**—(1)   An arrestment of cargo on board a ship shall be executed by a sheriff officer who shall serve the schedule of arrestment on—
    (a)   the master of the ship;
    (b)   any other person in charge of the ship or cargo; or
    (c)   other proper arrestee.

(2)   Where the schedule of arrestment cannot be executed in accordance with paragraph (1), the arrestment may be executed as provided for in rule 49.9(4) and (5).

**Forms for diligence in admiralty actions**

**49.11.**—(1)   In the execution of diligence in an Admiralty action, the following forms shall be used—

**D1.577**

- (a)   in the case of—
    - (i)   an arrestment to found jurisdiction (other than the arrestment of a ship), a schedule in Form 49.11-A and a certificate of execution in Form 49.11-E;
    - (ii)   an arrestment of a ship to found jurisdiction, a schedule in Form 49.11-AA and a certificate of execution in Form 49.11-F;
- (b)   subject to subparagraph (e), in the case of an arrestment on the dependence, a schedule in Form G4B and a certificate of execution in Form 49.11-E;
- (c)   in the case of an arrestment in rem of a ship, cargo or other maritime *res* to enforce a maritime hypothec or lien, a schedule in Form 49.11-B and a certificate of execution in Form 49.11-G;
- (d)   in the case of an arrestment in rem of a ship to enforce a non-pecuniary claim, a schedule in Form 49.11-C and a certificate of execution in Form 49.11-G;
- (e)   in the case of an arrestment on the dependence of—
    - (i)   a cargo on board a ship, a schedule in Form G4B;
    - (ii)   a ship, a schedule in Form 49.11-D,

and a certificate of execution in Form 49.11-H.

(2)   Where two or more of the arrestments mentioned in paragraph (1)(a), (b) and (c) are to be executed, they may be combined in one schedule of arrestment.

**Movement of arrested property**

**49.12.**(1)   Any person who has an interest in a ship or cargo which is the subject of an arrestment under this Chapter may apply by motion for a warrant authorising the movement of the ship or cargo.

**D1.578**

(2)   Where the sheriff grants a warrant sought under paragraph (1), the sheriff may make such further order as the sheriff thinks fit to give effect to that warrant.

**Arrestment before service**

**49.13.**   Before the service of an Admiralty action, where it is craved in the initial writ, the pursuer may apply by motion for warrant for arrestment of any of the types of arrestment mentioned in this Chapter.

**D1.579**

Chapter 50[1]

Lodging Audio or Audio-visual Recordings of Children

**Interpretation**

**50.1.**   In this Chapter "child" is a person under the age of 16 on the date of commencement of the proceedings and "children" shall be construed accordingly.

**D1.580**

**Lodging an audio or audio-visual recording of a child**

**50.2.**—(1)   Where a party seeks to lodge an audio or audio-visual recording of a child as a production, such party must—

**D1.581**

- (a)   ensure that the recording is in a format that can be heard or viewed by means of equipment available in court;
- (b)   place the recording together with a copy of the relevant inventory of productions in a sealed envelope marked with—
    - (i)   the names of the parties to the court action;
    - (ii)   the case reference number;
    - (iii)   (where available) the date and time of commencement and of termination of the recording; and
    - (iv)   "recording of a child - confidential".

(2)   The sealed envelope must be lodged with the sheriff clerk.

(3)   In the remainder of this Chapter a "recording of a child" means any such recording lodged under this rule.

**Separate inventory of productions**

**50.3.**—(1)   On each occasion that a recording of a child is lodged, a separate inventory of productions shall be lodged in process.

**D1.582**

---

[1] As inserted by the Act of Sederunt (Sheriff Court Rules) (Miscellaneous Amendments) (No.3) 2012 (SSI 2012/271) para.2 (effective November 1, 2012).

(2)   The sheriff clerk will mark the date of receipt and the number of process on the sealed envelope containing a recording of a child.

**Custody of a recording of a child**

**D1.583**

**50.4.**—(1)   A recording of a child—

    (a)   must be kept in the safe custody of the sheriff clerk;

    (b)   subject to rule 50.5, will not form a borrowable part of the process.

(2)   The seal of the envelope containing a recording of a child shall be broken only with the authority of the sheriff and on such conditions as the sheriff thinks fit (which conditions may relate to listening to or viewing the recording).

**Access to a recording of a child**

**D1.584**

**50.5.**—(1)   A party may lodge a written motion to gain access to and listen to or view a recording of a child.

(2)   The sheriff may refuse a motion or grant it on such conditions as the sheriff thinks fit, including—

    (a)   allowing only such persons as the sheriff may specify to listen to or view the recording;

    (b)   specifying the location where such listening or viewing is to take place;

    (c)   specifying the date and time when such listening or viewing is to take place;

    (d)   allowing a copy of the recording to be made (in the same or different format) and arrangements for the safe-keeping and disposal of such copy;

    (e)   arrangements for the return of the recording and re-sealing the envelope.

**Incidental appeal against rulings on access to a recording of a child**

**D1.585**

**50.6.**—(1)   Where a party is dissatisfied with the ruling of the sheriff under rule 50.5, such party may express immediately his or her formal dissatisfaction with the ruling and, with leave of the sheriff, appeal to the sheriff principal.

(2)   The sheriff principal must dispose of an appeal under paragraph (1) with the least possible delay.

**Exceptions**

**D1.586**

**50.7.**—(1)   The sheriff may, on the application of a party and on cause shown, disapply the provisions of this Chapter.

(2)   An application under paragraph (1) shall be made—

    (a)   at the time of presenting the recording for lodging;

    (b)   by letter addressed to the sheriff clerk stating the grounds on which the application is made.

**Application of other rules**

**D1.587**

**50.8.**—(1)   The following rules do not apply to a recording of a child—

    (a)   rule 9A.2(2) (inspection of documents);

    (b)   rule 11.6(1) (intimation of parts of process and adjustments), in so far as it would otherwise require a party to deliver a copy of a recording of a child to every other party;

    (c)   rule 29.12(1) (copy productions).

**Appendix 1**

**FORMS**

**Rule 1.4**

**D1.588**

Form 1A.2[1]

Rule 1A.2(2)(b)

Statement by prospective lay representative for Pursuer/Defender*

Case Ref. No.:

in the cause

SHERIFFDOM OF (*insert name of sheriffdom*)

AT (*insert place of sheriff court*)

[A.B.], (*insert designation and address*), Pursuer

---

[1] As inserted by the Act of Sederunt (Sheriff Court Rules) (Lay Representation) 2013 (SSI 2013/91) r.2 (effective April 4, 2013).

against

[C.D.], (*insert designation and address*), Defender

Court ref. no:

| | |
|---|---|
| Name and address of prospective lay representative who requests to make oral submissions on behalf of party litigant: | |
| Identify hearing(s) in respect of which permission for lay representation is sought: | |
| The prospective lay representative declares that: | |
| (a) | I have no financial interest in the outcome of the case or I have the following financial interest in it:* |
| (b) | I am not receiving remuneration or other reward directly or indirectly from the litigant for my assistance and will not receive directly or indirectly such remuneration or other reward from the litigant. |
| (c) | I accept that documents and information are provided to me by the litigant on a confidential basis and I undertake to keep them confidential. |
| (d) | I have no previous convictions *or* I have the following convictions: (list convictions)* |
| (e) | I have not been declared a vexatious litigant under the Vexatious Actions (Scotland) Act 1898 *or* I was declared a vexatious litigant under the Vexatious Actions (Scotland) Act 1898 on [insert date].* |

*(Signed)*

[Name of prospective lay representative]

[Date]

*(Insert Place/Date)*

The Sheriff grants/refuses* the application.

*[Signed]*

Sheriff Clerk

[Date]

*(*delete as appropriate)*

### Form G1
### Form of initial writ

Rule 3.1(1)(a)

#### INITIAL WRIT

SHERIFFDOM OF (*insert name of sheriffdom*)

AT (*insert place of sheriff court*)

[A.B.] (*design and state any special capacity in which the pursuer is suing*). Pursuer.

#### Against

[C.D.] (*design and state any special capacity in which the defender is being sued*). Defender.

The Pursuer craves the court (*here state the specific decree, warrant or order sought*).

#### CONDESCENDENCE

*(State in numbered paragraphs the facts which form the ground of action)*

#### PLEAS-IN-LAW

*(State in numbered sentences)*

Signed

[A.B.], Pursuer.

or [X.Y.], Solicitor for the pursuer (*state designation and business address*)

#### [1]FORM G1A
#### Form of initial writ in a commercial action

Rule 3.1(1)(b) and 40.4

SHERIFFDOM OF (*insert name of sheriffdom*)

AT (*insert place of sheriff court*)

#### COMMERCIAL ACTION

[A.B.] (*design and state any special capacity in which the pursuer is being sued*). Pursuer.

---

[1] Inserted by the Act of Sederunt (Ordinary Cause Rules) Amendment (Commercial Actions) Rules 2001 (SSI 2001/8) (effective March 1, 2001).

Against

[C.D.] (*design and state any special capacity in which the defender is being sued*). Defender.

[A.B.] for the Pursuer craves the court (*specify the orders sought*)

CONDESCENDENCE

(*provide the following, in numbered paragraphs—*

*information sufficient to identify the transaction or dispute from which the action arises; a summary of the circumstances which have resulted in the action being raised; and details setting out the grounds on which the action proceeds.*)

Note: *Where damages are sought, the claim may be summarised in the pleadings— in the form of a statement of damages; or*

*by lodging with the initial writ a schedule detailing the claim.*

PLEAS-IN-LAW

(*state in numbered sentences*)

Signed

[A.B.], Pursuer

*or* [X.Y.], Solicitor for the Pursuer (*state designation and business address*)

FORM G2

Rule 4.2(1)

[*Omitted by* Act of Sederunt (Sheriff Court Caveat Rules) 2006 (SI 2006/198), *effective April 28, 2006*]

FORM G3

Form of advertisement

Rule 5.6(1)(a)

NOTICE TO [C.D.]............... Court ref. no...........

An action has been raised in..........Sheriff Court by [A.B.], Pursuer, calling as a Defender [C.D.] whose last known address was (*insert last known address of defender*). If [C.D.] wishes to defend the action [*where notice is given in a family action*] or make any claim or seek any order] he [*or* she] should immediately contact the sheriff clerk at (*insert address*) from whom the service copy initial writ may be obtained. If he [*or* she] fails to do so decree may be granted against him [*or* her].

Signed

[X.Y.], (*add designation and business address*)

Solicitor for the pursuer *or* [P.Q.], (*add business address*)

Sheriff officer

FORM G4

Form of notice for walls of court

Rule 5.6(1)(b)

NOTICE TO [C.D.]............... Court ref. no...........

An action has been raised in..........Sheriff Court by [A.B.], Pursuer, calling as a Defender [C.D.] whose last known address was (*insert last known address of defender*). If [C.D.] wishes to defend the action [*where notice is to be given in a family action add*: or make any claim or seek any order] he [*or* she] should immediately contact the sheriff clerk at (*insert address*) from whom the service copy initial writ may be obtained. If he [*or* she] fails to do so decree may be granted against him [*or* her].

Date (*insert date*)...............(*Signed*)

Sheriff clerk (depute)

Telephone no. (*insert telephone number of sheriff clerk's office*)

[1]FORM G4A

Rule 6.A2(2)

Statement to accompany application for interim diligence

DEBTORS (SCOTLAND) ACT 1987 Section 15D [or DEBT ARRANGEMENT AND ATTACHMENT (SCOTLAND) ACT 2002 Section 9C]

Sheriff Court.........

In the Cause (Cause Reference No.)

[A.B.] (*designation and address*)

Pursuer

---

[1] As inserted by the Act of Sederunt (Sheriff Court Rules Amendment) (Diligence) (SSI 2008/121) r.5(7) (effective April 1, 2008).

against

[C.D.] (*designation and address*)

Defender

Statement

1. The applicant is the pursuer [*or* defender] in the action by [A.B] (*design*) against [C.D.] (*design*).
2. [The following persons have an interest (*specify names and addresses*)].
3. The applicant is [*or* is not] seeking the grant under section 15E(1) of the 1987 Act of warrant for diligence [*or* section 9D(1) of the 2002 Act of interim attachment] in advance of a hearing on the application.
4. [*Here provide such other information as may he prescribed by regulations made by the Scottish Ministers under* section 15D(2)(d) of the 1987 Act or 9C(2)(d) of the 2002 Act]

(*Signed*)

Solicitor [*or* Agent] for A.B. [*or* C.D.]

(include full designation)

¹FORM G4B

Rule 6.A8

Form of schedule of arrestment on the dependence

*Schedule of Arrestment On the Dependence*

Date: (*date of execution*)

Time: (*time arrestment executed*)

To: (*name and address of arrestee*)

IN HER MAJESTY'S NAME AND AUTHORITY AND IN NAME AND AUTHORITY OF THE SHERIFF, I, (*name*), Sheriff Officer, by virtue of:

- an initial writ containing warrant which has been granted for arrestment on the dependence of the action at the instance of (*name and address of pursuer*) against (*name and address of defender*) and dated (*date*);
- a counterclaim containing a warrant which has been granted for arrestment on the dependence of the claim by (*name and address of creditor*) against (*name and address of debtor*) and dated (*date of warrant*);
- an order of the Sheriff at (*place*) dated (*date of order*) granting warrant [for arrestment on the dependence of the action raised at the instance of (*name and address of pursuer*) against (*name and address of defender*)] [*or* for arrestment on the dependence of the claim in the counterclaim [*or* third party notice] by (*name and address of creditor*) against (*name and address or debtor*)],

arrest in your hands (i) the sum of (*amount*), in excess of the Protected Minimum Balance, where applicable (*see Note 1*), more or less, due by you to (*defender's name*) [*or* name and address of common debtor if common debtor is not the defender*] or to any other person on his [*or* her] [*or* its] [*or* their] behalf; and (ii) all moveable things in your hands belonging or pertaining to the said (*name of common debtor*), to remain in your hands under arrestment until they are made forthcoming to (*name of pursuer*) [*or* name and address of creditor if he is not the pursuer*] or until further order of the court.

This I do in the presence of (*name, occupation and address of witness*).

(*Signed*)

Sheriff Officer

(*Address*)

NOTE

1. This Schedule arrests in your hands (i) funds due by you to (*name of common debtor*) and (ii) goods or other moveables held by you for him. **You should not pay any funds to him or hand over any goods or other moveables to him without taking legal advice.**
2. This Schedule may be used to arrest a ship or cargo. If it is, you should consult your legal adviser about the effect of it.
3. The Protected Minimum Balance is the sum referred to in section 73F(4) of the Debtors (Scotland) Act 1987. This sum is currently set at [*insert current sum*]. The Protected Minimum Balance applies where the arrestment attaches funds standing to the credit of a debtor in an account held by a bank or other financial institution and the debtor is an individual. The Protected Minimum Balance does not apply where the account is held in the name of a company, a limited liability partnership, a partnership or an unincorporated association or where the account is operated by the debtor as a trading account.

---

¹ As inserted by the Act of Sederunt (Sheriff Court Rules Amendment) (Diligence) 2008 (SSI 2008/121) r.5(7) (effective April 1, 2008) and substituted by the Act of Sederunt (Sheriff Court Rules Amendment) (Diligence) 2009 (SSI 2009/107) (effective April 22, 2009).

4. Under section 73G of the Debtors (Scotland) Act 1987 you must also, within the period of 3 weeks beginning with the day on which the arrestment is executed, disclose to the creditor the nature and value of the funds and/or moveable property which have been attached. This disclosure must be in the form set out in Schedule 8 to the Diligence (Scotland) Regulations 2009. Failure to comply may lead to a financial penalty under section 73G of the Debtors (Scotland) Act 1987 and may also be dealt with as a contempt of court. You must, at the same time, send a copy of the disclosure to the debtor and to any person known to you who owns (or claims to own) attached property and to any person to whom attached funds are (or are claimed to be due), solely or in common with the debtor.

**IF YOU WISH FURTHER ADVICE CONTACT ANY CITIZENS ADVICE BUREAU/LOCAL ADVICE CENTRE/SHERIFF CLERK OR SOLICITOR**

[1]FORM G4C

Form of certificate of execution of arrestment on the dependence

Rule 6.A8

CERTIFICATE OF EXECUTION

I, (*name*), Sheriff Officer, certify that I executed an arrestment on the dependence, by virtue of an interlocutor of the Sheriff at (*place*) on (*date*) obtained at the instance of (*name and address of party arresting*) against (*name and address of defender*) on (name of arrestee)—

* by delivering the schedule of arrestment to (*name of arrestee or other person*) at (*place*) personally on (*date*).
* by leaving the schedule of arrestment with (*name and occupation of person with whom left*) at (*place*) on (*date*) [and by posting a copy of the schedule to the arrestee by registered post or first class recorded delivery to the address specified on the receipt annexed to this certificate].
* by depositing the schedule of arrestment in (*place*) on (*date*). (*Specify that enquiry made and reasonable grounds exist for believing that the person on whom service is to be made resides at the place but is not available*) [and by posting a copy of the schedule to the arrestee by registered post or first class recorded delivery to the address specified on the receipt annexed to this certificate].
* by affixing the schedule of arrestment to the door at (*place*) on (*date*). (*Specify that enquiry-made and that reasonable grounds exist for believing that the person on whom service is to be made resides at the place but is not available*) [and by posting a copy of the schedule to the arrestee by registered post or first class recorded delivery to the address specified on the receipt annexed to this certificate].
* by leaving the schedule of arrestment with (*name and occupation of person with whom left*) at (*place of business*) on (*date*) [and by posting a copy of the schedule to the arrestee by registered post or first class recorded delivery to the address specified on the receipt annexed to this certificate].
* by depositing the schedule of arrestment at (*place of business*) on (*date*). (*Specify that enquiry made and that reasonable grounds exist for believing that the person on whom service is to be made carries on business at that place*) [and by posting a copy of the schedule to the arrestee by registered post or first class recorded delivery to the address specified on the receipt annexed to this certificate].
* by affixing the schedule of arrestment to the door at (*place of business*) on (*date*). (*Specify that enquiry made and that reasonable grounds exist for believing that the person on whom service is to be made carries on business at that place.*) [and by posting a copy of the schedule to the arrestee by registered post or first class recorded delivery to the address specified on the receipt annexed to this certificate].
* by leaving the schedule of arrestment at (*registered office*) on (*date*), in the hands of (*name of person*) [and by posting a copy of the schedule to the arrestee by registered post or first class recorded delivery to the address specified on the receipt annexed to this certificate].
* by depositing the schedule of arrestment at (*registered office*) on (*date*) [and by posting a copy of the schedule to the arrestee by registered post or first class recorded delivery to the address specified on the receipt annexed to this certificate].
* by affixing the schedule of arrestment to the door at (*registered office*) on (*date*) [and by posting a copy of the schedule to the arrestee by registered post or first class recorded delivery to the address specified on the receipt annexed to this certificate].

I did this in the presence of (*name, occupation and address of witness*).

---

[1] As inserted by the Act of Sederunt (Sheriff Court Rules Amendment) (Diligence) 2008 (SSI 2008/121) r.5(7) (effective April 1, 2008) and substituted by the Act of Sederunt (Sheriff Court Rules Amendment) (Diligence) 2009 (SSI 2009/107) (effective April 22, 2009).

(*Signed*)
Sheriff Officer
(*Address*)
(*Signed*)
(*Witness*)

*Delete where not applicable
**NOTE**
**A copy of the Schedule of arrestment on the dependence is to be attached to this certificate.**

[1]FORM G5
Form of intimation of Options Hearing
Rules 9.2(2)(a) and 33.16(3)(b)
Sheriff Court (insert address and telephone number).............. Court ref. no..........
[A.B.] (design) Pursuer against [C.D.] (*design*) Defender
You are given notice that in this action:—

| | |
|---|---|
| (insert date) | is the last day for lodging defences; |
| (insert date) | is the last day for making adjustments to the writ or defences; |
| (insert date, time and place) | is the date, time and place for the Options Hearing. |

Date (insert date).............. (Signed)..........

Sheriff clerk (depute)

NOTE:
If you fail to comply with the terms of this notice or with any of the rules 9.3, 9.4, 9.6, 9.10 and 9.11 of the Standard Procedure of the Ordinary Cause Rules of the Sheriff Court or, where applicable, rule 33.37 (decree by default in a family action), decree by default may be granted in terms of rule 16.2(2) of those Rules.
NOTE TO BE ADDED WHERE PARTY UNREPRESENTED

---

**Note**

**IF YOU ARE UNCERTAIN WHAT ACTION TO TAKE** you should consult a solicitor. You may be eligible for legal aid depending on your income, and you can get information from any Citizens Advice Bureau or other advice agency.

---

FORM G6
Form of motion
Rule 15.1(1)(b)
SHERIFFDOM OF (*insert name of sheriffdom*).............. Court ref. no..........
AT (*insert place of sheriff court*)
MOTION FOR THE PURSUER [or DEFENDER]
in the cause
[A.B.] (*insert designation and address*)

Pursuer

against
[C.D.] (*insert designation and address*)

Defender

The (*insert description of party*) moves the court to (*insert details of motion and, where appropriate, the reason (s) for seeking the order*).
List the documents or parts of process lodged with the motion:—
(*Insert description of document or name part of process*)
Date (insert date).............. (Signed)..........

Party (insert name and description of party)
or Solicitor for party (insert designation and business address)

---

[1] As amended by S.I. 1996 No. 2445 (effective November 1, 1996)

[1]FORM G7

Form of intimation of motion

Rule 15.2(1) Cause Rules 1993

SHERIFFDOM OF (insert name of sheriffdom)............... Court ref. no...........

AT (insert place of sheriff court)

in the cause

[A.B.] (insert name and address)

Pursuer

against

[C.D.] (insert name and address)

Defender

| LAST DATE FOR LODGING NOTICE OF OPPOSITION: |
| --- |

APPLICATION IS MADE BY MOTION FOR THE ORDER(S) SOUGHT IN THE ATTACHED FORM (attach a copy of the motion in Form G6)

\* A copy of the document(s) or part(s) of process referred to in Form G6 is/are attached.

OPPOSITION TO THE MOTION MAY BE MADE by completing Form G9 (notice of opposition to motion) and lodging it with the sheriff clerk at (insert address) on or before the last date for lodging notice of opposition. A copy of the notice of opposition must be sent immediately to any other party in the action.

IN THE EVENT OF A NOTICE OF OPPOSITION BEING LODGED the sheriff clerk will assign a date, time and place for hearing parties on the motion. Intimation of this hearing will be sent to parties by the sheriff clerk.

IF NO NOTICE OF OPPOSITION IS LODGED, the motion may be considered by the sheriff without the attendance of parties.

Date (insert date)................... (Signed)

Pursuer (or as the case may be)

[or Solicitor for pursuer [or as the case may be]

(insert name and business address)]

Explanatory Note to Be Added Where Party to Whom Intimation is Made is Not Legally Represented

| **IF YOU ARE UNCERTAIN WHAT ACTION TO TAKE** you should consult a solicitor. You may also obtain advice from a Citizens Advice Bureau or other advice agency. |
| --- |

NOTE: If YOU intend to oppose the motion you must appear or be represented on the date of the hearing. If you return Form G9 (notice of opposition to motion) and then fail to attend or be represented at the court hearing, the court may consider the motion in your absence and may grant the order(s) sought.

\* Delete if not applicable

[2]FORM G7A

Form of intimation of minute (answers lodged)

Rule 14.4(1)(a)

SHERIFFDOM OF (insert name of sheriffdom)............... Court ref. no.

AT (insert place of sheriff court)

in the cause

[A.B.] (insert name and address)

Pursuer

against

[C.D.] (insert name and address)

Defender

| LAST DATE FOR LODGING ANSWERS: |
| --- |

---

[1] Substituted by S.I. 1996 No. 2445 (effective November 1, 1996).
[2] Inserted by S.I. 1996 No. 2445 (effective November 1, 1996).

APPLICATION IS MADE BY MOTION FOR THE ORDER(S) SOUGHT IN THE MINUTE AT-TACHED (attach a copy of minute and interlocutor)

* A copy of the document(s) or part(s) of process referred to in the minute is/are attached.

IN THE EVENT OF ANSWERS BEING LODGED the sheriff clerk will assign a date, time and place for hearing parties on the minute and answers. Intimation of this hearing will be sent to parties by the sheriff clerk.

IF NO ANSWERS ARE LODGED, the motion may be considered by the sheriff without the attendance of parties.

Date (insert date)............... (Signed)

Pursuer (or as the case may be)

[or Solicitor for pursuer [or as the case may he]

(Add name and business address)]

Explanatory Note to Be Added Where Party to Whom Intimation is Made is Not Legally Represented

---

**IF YOU ARE UNCERTAIN WHAT ACTION TO TAKE** you should consult a solicitor. You may also obtain advice from a Citizens Advice Bureau or other advice agency.

---

NOTE: If you intend to oppose the minute you must appear or be represented on the date of the hearing. If you return Form G9 (notice of opposition to minute) and then fail to attend or be represented at the court hearing, the court may consider the minute in your absence and may grant the order(s) sought.

---

* Delete if not applicable

[1]FORM G7B

Form of intimation of minute (no order for answers or no hearing fixed)

Rule 14.4(1)(a)

SHERIFFDOM OF (insert name of sheriffdom)............... Court ref. no.

AT (insert place of sheriff court)

in the cause

[A.B.] (insert name and address)

Pursuer

against

[C.D.] (insert name and address)

Defender

---

LAST DATE FOR LODGING NOTICE OF OPPOSITION:

---

APPLICATION IS MADE BY MINUTE FOR THE ORDER(S) SOUGHT IN THE MINUTE AT-TACHED (*attach a copy of minute and interlocutor*)

* A copy of the document(s) or part(s) of process referred to in the minute is/are attached.

OPPOSITION TO THE MOTION MAY BE MADE by completing Form G9 (notice of opposition to motion) and lodging it with the sheriff clerk at (*insert address*) on or before the last date for lodging notice of opposition. A copy of the notice of opposition must be sent immediately to any other party in the action.

IN THE EVENT OF A NOTICE OF OPPOSITION BEING LODGED the sheriff clerk will

assign a date, time and place for hearing parties on the minute. Intimation of this hearing will be sent to parties by the sheriff clerk.

IF NO NOTICE OF OPPOSITION IS LODGED, the minute may be considered by the sheriff without the attendance of parties.

Date (*insert date*)...............(*Signed*)

Pursuer (or as the case may be)

[or Solicitor for pursuer [or as the case may be]

(Add name and business address)]

Explanatory Note to Be Added Where Party to Whom Intimation is Made is Not Legally Represented

---

**IF YOU ARE UNCERTAIN WHAT ACTION TO TAKE** you should consult a solicitor. You may also obtain advice from a Citizens Advice Bureau or other advice agency.

---

[1] Inserted by S.I. 1996 No. 2445 (effective November 1, 1996).

> NOTE: If YOU intend to oppose the minute you must appear or be represented on the date of the hearing. If you return Form G9 (notice of opposition to minute) and then fail to attend or be represented at the court hearing, the court may consider the motion in your absence and may grant the order(s) sought.

* Delete if not applicable

[1]FORM G7C

Form of intimation of minute (hearing fixed)

Rule 14.4(1)(a)

SHERIFFDOM OF (*insert name of sheriffdom*)............... Court ref. no.

AT (*insert place of sheriff court*)

in the cause

[A.B.] (*insert name and address*)

Pursuer

against

[C.D.] (*insert name and address*)

Defender

---

DATE AND TIME FOR HEARING MINUTE:

---

*DATE FOR LODGING ANSWERS OR AFFIDAVIT EVIDENCE:

---

APPLICATION IS MADE FOR THE ORDER(S) SOUGHT IN THE MINUTE ATTACHED (*attach a copy of minute and interlocutor*)

* A copy of the document(s) or part(s) of process referred to in the minute is/are attached.

IF YOU WISH TO OPPOSE THE MINUTE OR MAKE ANY REPRESENTATIONS you must attend or be represented at (insert name and address of court) on the date and time referred to above.

* If an order has been made for you to lodge answers or affidavit evidence these must be lodged with the sheriff clerk (insert address) on or before the above date.

IF YOU FAIL TO ATTEND OR BE REPRESENTED the minute may be determined in your absence.

Date (*insert date*)............... (*Signed*)

Pursuer (*or as the case may be*)

[*or* Solicitor for pursuer [*or as the case may be*]

(*Add name and business address*)]

Explanatory Note to Be Added Where Party to Whom Intimation is Made is Not Legally Represented

**IF YOU ARE UNCERTAIN WHAT ACTION TO TAKE** you should consult a solicitor. You may also obtain advice from a Citizens Advice Bureau or other advice agency.

NOTE: If you intend to oppose the minute you must appear or be represented on the date of the hearing. If you return Form G9 (notice of opposition to minute) and then fail to attend or be represented at the court hearing, the court may consider the minute in your absence and may grant the order(s) sought.

* Delete if not applicable

Rules 14.6 and 15.1(2)

[2]FORM G8

Form of certificate of intimation of motion or minute

CERTIFICATE OF INTIMATION OF MOTION [*or* MINUTE]

I certify that intimation of the motion [*or* minute] was made to (*insert names of parties or solicitors for the parties, as appropriate*) by (*insert method of intimation; where intimation is by facsimile transmission, insert fax number to which Intimation sent*) on (*insert date of intimation*).

Date (*insert date*)

(*Signed*)

Solicitor [*or* Sheriff Officer]

(*Add name and business address*)

Rules 14.7(1)(a) and 15.3(1)(a)

---

[1] Inserted by SI 1996/2445 (effective November 1, 1996).
[2] Substituted by SI 1996/2445 (effective November 1, 1996).

[1]FORM G9

Form of notice of opposition to motion or minute

NOTICE OF OPPOSITION TO MOTION [*or* MINUTE]

SHERIFFDOM OF (*insert name of sheriffdom*)

Court ref. no.:

AT (*insert place of sheriff court*)

in the cause

[A.B.] (*insert name and address*)

Pursuer

against

[C.D.] (*insert name and address*)

Defender

Notice of opposition to motion [*or* minute] given by (*insert name of party opposing motion*) to (*insert names of all other parties, or solicitors for the parties, to the action*) by (*insert method of intimation; where intimation is made by facsimile transmission, Insert fax number to which notice of opposition sent*) on (*insert date of intimation*).

Date (*insert date*)

(*Signed*)

Pursuer (*or as the case may be*)

(*insert name and address of party*)
[*or* Solicitor for Pursuer [*or as the case may be*]
(*Add name and business address*)]

Rule 24.2(3)

[2]FORM G10

Form of intimation to a party whose solicitor has withdrawn

SHERIFFDOM OF (*insert name of sheriffdom*) AT (*insert place of sheriff court*)

in the cause

[A.B.] (*insert designation*)

Pursuer

against

[C.D.] (*insert designation*)

Defender

Court ref. no.

The court has been informed that your solicitors have ceased to act for you.

As a result the sheriff has ordered that you appear or be represented on (insert date and time) within the Sheriff Court at the above address. A copy of the order is attached.

When you appear you will be asked by the sheriff to state whether you intend to proceed with your action [or defences or answers].

**NOTE:**

**IF YOU ARE UNCERTAIN WHAT ACTION TO TAKE** you should consult a solicitor. You may also obtain advice from a Citizens Advice Bureau or other advice agency.

Rule 28.3(1)

[3]FORM G11

Form of notice in optional procedure for commission and diligence

Court ref. no.

Order by the Sheriff Court at (*insert address*)

In the cause

[A.B.] (*design*) Pursuer

Against

[C.D.] (*design*) Defender

To (*insert name and designation of party or parties or haver, from whom documents are sought to be recovered*)

---

[1] Substituted by SI 1996/2445 (effective November 1, 1996).
[2] As amended by SI 1996/2445 (effective November 1, 1996).
[3] Substituted by Act of Sederunt (Ordinary Cause, Summary Application, Summary Cause and Small Claim Rules) Amendment (Miscellaneous) 2005 (SSI 2005/648), para.2 (effective January 2, 2006).

You are given notice that you are required to produce to the sheriff clerk at the above address within seven days of (*insert date on which service was executed. N.B.* Rule 5.3(2) *relating to postal service or intimation*):

(1) this order; which must be produced intact;
(2) a certificate signed and completed in terms of the form appended to this notice; and
(3) all documents in your possession falling within the enclosed specification, with an inventory of such documents signed by you relating to this order and your certificate.

Production may be made by lodging the documents with the sheriff clerk at the above address, by posting them by registered post or the first class recorded delivery service addressed to the sheriff clerk at the above address.

Date (*insert date*)

Signed

Solicitor for party (*add designation and business address of the solicitor for the party in whose favour commission and diligence granted*)

Note

If you claim confidentiality for any of the documents produced by you, such documents must nevertheless be produced, but may be placed in a special sealed packet by themselves, marked "confidential".

Claims for necessary outlays within certain specified limits may be paid. Claims should be made in writing to the person who has obtained the order that you produce the documents.

CERTIFICATE

I hereby certify with reference to the order of the Sheriff Court at (*insert place of sheriff court*) in the cause (*insert court ref. no*) and the relative specification of documents, served upon me and marked respectively X and Y:

(1) that the documents which are produced and which are numbered in the inventory signed by me and marked Z, are the whole documents in my possession falling under the specification [*or* that I have no documents in my possession falling within the specification];
(2) that, to the best of my knowledge and belief, there are in existence other documents falling within the specification, but not in my possession, namely (*describe them by reference to one or more of the descriptions of documents in the specification*), which were last seen by me on or about (*insert date*), at (*insert place*), in the hands of (*insert name and address of the person*) [*or* that I know of the existence of no documents in the possession of any person, other than myself, which fall within the specification*].

Signed

Rules 28.4(4) and 29.7(4)

FORM G12

Form of certificate of citation of witness or haver

I certify that on (*insert date of citation*).......... I duly cited [K.L.], (*design*) to attend at (*insert name of sheriff court*) Sheriff Court on (*insert date*) at (*insert time*) as a witness for the pursuer [*or* defender] in the action at the instance of [A.B.] (*design*), Pursuer, against [C.D.] (*design*), Defender, [and I required him [*or* her] to bring with him [*or* her] (*specify documents*)]. This I did by (*state mode of citation*).

Date (insert date)

(*Signed*)
[P.Q.], Sheriff officer;
*or* [X.Y.], (*add designation and business address*)
Solicitor for the pursuer [*or* defender]

[1]FORM G13

Form of citation of witness or haver

Rule 28.4(4) and 29.7(4)

(*date*)

Citation
SHERIFFDOM OF (*insert name of sheriffdom*)
AT (*insert place of sheriff court*)

---

[1] As substituted by SSI 2007/463 (effective November 1, 2007).

To [A.B.] (*design*)

(*Name*) who is pursuing/defending a case against (*name*) [or is a (*specify*) in the case of (*name*) against (*name*) has asked you to be a witness. You must attend the above sheriff court on (*insert date*) at (*insert time*) for that purpose, [and to bring with you (*specify documents*)].

If you would like to know more about being a witness

are a child under the age of 16

think you may be a vulnerable witness within the meaning of section 11(1) of the Vulnerable Witnesses (Scotland) Act 2004 (that is someone the court considers may be less able to give their evidence due to mental disorder or fear or distress connected to giving your evidence at the court hearings)

you should contact (*specify the solicitor acting for the party or the litigant citing the witness*) for further information.

If you are a vulnerable witness (including a child under the age of 16), then you should be able to use a special measure (such measures include the use of a screen, a live TV link or a supporter, or a commissioner) to help you give evidence.

*Expenses*

You may claim back money which you have to spend and any earnings you have lost within certain specified limits, because you have to come to court on the above date. These may be paid to you if you claim within specified time limits. Claims should be made to the person who has asked you to attend court. Proof of any loss of earnings should be given to that person.

If you wish your travelling expenses to be paid before you go to court, you should apply for payment to the person who has asked you to attend court.

*Failure to attend*

*It is very important that you attend court and you should note that failure to do so may result in a warrant being granted for your arrest. In addition, if you fail to attend without any good reason, having requested and been paid your travelling expenses, you may be ordered to pay a penalty not exceeding £250.*

If you have any questions about anything in this citation, please contact (*specify the solicitor acting for the party or the party litigant citing the witness*) for further information.

Signed

[P.Q.], Sheriff Officer,

or [X.Y.], (*add designation and business address*)

Solicitor for the pursuer [*or defender*] [*or specify*]

Rules 28.4(6)(b), 28.10(4)(b) and 29.16

### FORM G14

Form of oath for witness

The witness to raise his right hand and repeat after the sheriff [*or* commissioner]: "I swear by Almighty God that I will tell the truth, the whole truth and nothing but the truth".

Rules 28.4(6)(b), 28.10(4)(b) and 29.16

### FORM G15

Form of affirmation for witness

The witness to repeat after the sheriff [*or* commissioner]: "I solemnly, sincerely and truly declare and affirm that I will tell the truth, the whole truth and nothing but the truth".

### [1]FORM G16

Rules 28.14(3) and 28.14A(2)

Form of minute for [letter of request] [taking of evidence in the European Community]*

SHERIFFDOM OF (*insert name of sheriffdom*)

AT (*insert place of sheriff court*)

MINUTE FOR PURSUER [DEFENDER]*

in the cause

[A.B.] (*insert designation and address*)

Pursuer

against

[C.D.] (*insert designation and addres*)

Defender

Court ref. no.

---

[1] As substituted by the Act of Sederunt (Taking of Evidence in the European Community) 2003 (SSI 2003/601).

The Minuter states that the evidence specified in the attached [letter of request] [Form A] [Form I]* is required for the purpose of these proceedings and craves the court to issue [a letter of request] [that Form]* to (*specify in the case of a letter of request the central or other appropriate authority of the country or territory in which the evidence is to he obtained, and in the case of Form A or I the applicable court, tribunal, central body or competent authority*) to obtain the evidence specified.

Date (*insert date*)

Signed

(*insert designation and address*)

\* *delete as applicable*

FORM G17

Rule 28.14(3)

Form of letter of request

**Letter of Request**

1. Sender (insert name and address)

2. Central authority of the requested state (insert name and address)

3. Person to whom the executed request is to be returned (insert name and address)

4. The undersigned applicant has the honour to submit the following request:

5. a. Requesting judicial authority (insert name and address)

b. To the competent authority (insert name of requested state)

6. Names and addresses of the parties and their representatives

a. Pursuer

b. Defender

c. Other parties

7. Nature and purpose of the proceedings and summary of facts

8. Evidence to be obtained or other judicial act to be performed

(Items to be completed where applicable)

9. Identity and address of any person to be examined

10. Questions to be put to the persons to be examined or (or see attached list) statement of the subject-matter about which they are to be examined

11. Documents or other property to be inspected (specify whether it is to he produced, copied, valued, etc.)

12. Any requirement that the evidence be given on oath (in the event that the evidence cannot be taken or affirmation and any special form to be used in the manner requested, specify whether it is to be taken in such manner as provided by local law for the formal taking of evidence)

13. Special methods or procedure to be followed

14. Request for notification of the time and place for the execution of the request and identity and address of any person to be notified

15. Request for attendance or participation of judicial personnel of the requesting authority at the execution of the letter of request

16. Specification of privilege or duty to refuse to give evidence under the law of the state of origin

17. The fees and expenses (costs) incurred will be borne (insert name and address) by

(Items to be included in all letters of request)

18. Date of request

19. Signature and seal of the requesting authority

FORM G18

Form of certificate of rate of exchange

Certificate of Rate of Exchange

I (insert designation and address) certify that the rates current in London for the purchase of (state the unit of currency in which the decree is expressed) on (insert date) was (state rate of exchange) to the £ sterling and at this rate the sum of (state the amount of the sum in the decree) amounts to (insert sterling equivalent).

Date (Insert date)

Signed

For and on behalf of the bank manager or other official

[1]FORM G19

Form of child witness notice

Rule 45.2

VULNERABLE WITNESSES (SCOTLAND) ACT 2004 Section 12

Received the day of 20

(Date of receipt of this notice)

..........(signed)

Sheriff Clerk

Child Witness Notice

Sheriff Court..........

..........20..........

Court Ref. No.

1. The applicant is the pursuer [or defender] in the action by [A.B.] (design) against [C.D.] (design).

2. The applicant has cited [or intends to cite] [E.F.] (date of birth) as a witness.

3. [E.F.] is a child witnesses under section 11 of the Vulnerable Witnesses (Scotland) Act 2004 [and was under the age of sixteen on the date of the commencement of proceedings].

4. The applicant considers that the following special measure[s] is [are] the most appropriate for the purpose of taking the evidence of [E.F.][or that [E.F.] should give evidence without the benefit of any special measure]:—

(delete as appropriate and specify any special measure(s) sought).

5. [(a) The reason[s] this [these] special measure[s] is [are] considered the most appropriate is [are] as follows:—

(here specify the reason(s) for the special measure(s) sought)].

OR

[(b) The reason[s] it is considered that [E.F.] should give evidence without the benefit of any special measure is [are]:—

(here explain why it is felt that no special measures are required)].

6. [E.F.] and the parent[s] of [or person[s] with parental responsibility for] [E.F.] has [have] expressed the following view[s] on the special measure[s] that is [are] considered most appropriate [or [the appropriateness of [E.F.] giving evidence without the benefit of any special measure]:—

(delete as appropriate and set out the views(s) expressed and how they were obtained)

7. Other information considered relevant to this application is as follows:—

(here set out any other information relevant to the child witness notice).

8. The applicant asks the court to —

(a)   consider this child witness notice;

(b)   make an order authorising the special measure[s] sought; or

(c)   make an order authorising the giving of evidence by [E.F.] without the benefit of special measures.

(delete as appropriate)

(Signed)

[A.B. or CD]

[or Legal representative of A.B. [or C.D.]] (include full designation)

NOTE: This form should be suitably adapted where section 16 of the Act of 2004 applies.

---

[1] As inserted by the Act of Sederunt (Ordinary Cause, Summary Application, Summary Cause and Small Claim Rules) Amendment (Vulnerable Witnesses (Scotland) Act 2004) 2007 (SSI 2007/463) (effective November 1, 2007).

[1]FORM G20

Form of vulnerable witness application

Rule 45.3

VULNERABLE WITNESSES (SCOTLAND) ACT 2004 Section 12

Received the..........day of..........20..........

(*Date of receipt of this notice*)

..........(*signed*)

Sheriff Clerk

VULNERABLE WITNESS APPLICATION

Sheriff Court....................

..........20..........

Court Ref. No.

1. The applicant is the pursuer [*or* defender] in the action by [A.B] (*design*) against [C.D.] (*design*).

2. The applicant has cited [*or* intends to cite] [E.F.] (*date of birth*) as a witness.

3. The applicant considers that [E.F.] is a vulnerable witness under section 11(1)(b) of the Vulnerable Witnesses (Scotland) Act 2004 for the following reasons:—

(*here specify reasons witness is considered to be a vulnerable witness*).

4. The applicant considers that the following special measure[s] is [are] the most appropriate for the purpose of taking the evidence of [E.F.]:—

(*specify any special measure(s) sought*).

5. The reason[s] this [these] special measure[s] is [are] considered the most appropriate is [are] as follows:—

(*here specify the reason(s) for the special measures(s) sought*).

6. [E.F.] has expressed the following view[s] on the special measure[s] that is [are] considered most appropriate:—

(*set out the views expressed and how they were obtained*).

7. Other information considered relevant to this application is as follows:—

(*here set out any other information relevant to the vulnerable witness application*).

8. The applicant asks the court to—

(a)    consider this vulnerable witness application;

(b)    make an order authorising the special measure[s] sought.

................(*Signed*)

[A.B. *or* C.D.]

[*or* Legal representative of A.B. [*or* C.D.]] (*include full designation*)

NOTE: *This form should be suitably adapted where* section 16 of the Act of 2004 *applies*.

[2]FORM G21

Form of certificate of intimation

Rule 45.4(1)

VULNERABLE WITNESSES (SCOTLAND) ACT 2004 Section 12

CERTIFICATE OF INTIMATION

Sheriff Court..........

..........20..........

Court Ref. No.

I certify that intimation of the child witness notice [*or* vulnerable witness application] relating to (*insert name of witness*) was made to (*insert names of parties or solicitors for parties, as appropriate*) by (*insert method of intimation; where intimation is by facsimile transmission, insert fax number to which intimation sent*) on (*insert date of intimation*).

Date:..........

..........(*Signed*)

Solicitor [*or* Sheriff Officer]

---

[1] As inserted by the Act of Sederunt (Ordinary Cause, Summary Application, Summary Cause and Small Claim Rules) Amendment (Vulnerable Witnesses (Scotland) Act 2004) 2007 (SSI 2007/463) (effective November 1, 2007).

[2] As inserted by the Act of Sederunt (Ordinary Cause, Summary Application, Summary Cause and Small Claim Rules) Amendment (Vulnerable Witnesses (Scotland) Act 2004) 2007 (SSI 2007/463) (effective November 1, 2007).

*(include full business designation)*

### [1]FORM G22
### Form of application for review

Rule 45.6

VULNERABLE WITNESSES (SCOTLAND) ACT 2004 Section 13

Received the..........day of..........20..........

*(date of receipt of this notice)*

...............*(signed)*

Sheriff Clerk

APPLICATION FOR REVIEW OF ARRANGEMENTS FOR VULNERABLE WITNESS

Sheriff Court...............

..........20..........

Court Ref. No.

1. The applicant is the pursuer [*or* defender] in the action by [A.B.] (*design*) against [C.D.] (*design*).

2. A proof [*or* hearing] is fixed for (*date*) at (*time*).

3. [E.F.] is a witness who is to give evidence at, or for the purposes of, the proof [*or* hearing ]. [E.F.] is a child witness [*or* vulnerable witness] under section 11 of the Vulnerable Witnesses (Scotland) Act 2004.

4. The current arrangements for taking the evidence of [E.F.] are (*here specify current arrangements*).

5. The current arrangements should be reviewed as (*here specify reasons for review*).

6. [E.F.] [and the parent[s] of [*or* person[s] with parental responsibility for] [E.F.]] has [have] expressed the following view[s] on [the special measure[s] that is [are] considered most appropriate] [*or* the appropriateness of [E.F.] giving evidence without the benefit of any special measure]:—

*(delete as appropriate and set out the view(s) expressed and how they were obtained).*

7. The applicant seeks (here specify the order sought).

*(Signed)*

[A.B. *or* C.D.]

[*or* Legal representative of A.B. [*or* C.D.]] (*include full designation*)

*NOTE: This form should be suitably adapted where* section 16 of the Act of 2004 *applies.*

### [2]FORM G23
### Form of certificate of intimation

Rule 45.7(2)

VULNERABLE WITNESSES (SCOTLAND) ACT 2004 Section 13

CERTIFICATE OF INTIMATION

Sheriff Court..........

..........20..........

Court Ref. No.

I certify that intimation of the review application relating to (*insert name of witness*) was made to (*insert names of parties or solicitors for parties, as appropriate*) by (*insert method of intimation; where intimation is by facsimile transmission, insert fax number to which intimation sent*) on (*insert date of intimation*).

Date:..........

*(Signed)*

Solicitor [*or* Sheriff Officer]

*(include full business designation)*

FORM O1                                   Rule 3.3(1)

### Form of warrant of citation

(*Insert place and date*) Grants warrant to cite the defender (*insert name and address*) by serving upon him [*or* her] a copy of the writ and warrant on a period of notice of (*insert period of notice*) days, and

---

[1] As inserted by the Act of Sederunt (Ordinary Cause, Summary Application, Summary Cause and Small Claim Rules) Amendment (Vulnerable Witnesses (Scotland) Act 2004) 2007 (SSI 2007/463) (effective November 1, 2007).

[2] As inserted by the Act of Sederunt (Ordinary Cause, Summary Application, Summary Cause and Small Claim Rules) Amendment (Vulnerable Witnesses (Scotland) Act 2004) 2007 (SSI 2007/463) (effective November 1, 2007).

ordains him [*or* her], if he [*or* she] intends to defend the action or make any claim, to lodge a notice of intention to defend with the sheriff clerk at (*insert place of sheriff court*) within the said period of notice after such service [and grants warrant to arrest on the dependence].

[Meantime grants interim interdict; *or* grants warrant to arrest to found jurisdiction; *or* sequestrates and grants warrant to inventory; *or otherwise, as the case may be.*]

Signed

Sheriff [*or* sheriff clerk]

[1] FORM O2                                      Rule 3.3(2)

Form of warrant of citation where time to pay direction or time order may be applied for

(*Insert place and date*) Grants warrant to cite the defender (*insert name and address*) by serving a copy of the writ and warrant, with Form O3, on a period of notice of (*insert period of notice*) days and ordains him [*or* her] if he [*or* she]—

(a)    intends to defend the action or make any claim, to lodge a notice of intention to defend; or

(b)    admits the claim and intends to apply for a time to pay direction [*or* time order] [and apply for recall or restriction of an arrestment] to lodge the appropriate part of Form O3 duly completed;

with the sheriff clerk at (*insert place of sheriff court*) within the said period of notice after such service [and grants warrant to arrest on the dependence].

[Meantime grants interim interdict, or grants warrant to arrest to found jurisdiction; *or* sequestrates and grants warrant to inventory; *or otherwise, as the case may be.*]

Signed

Sheriff [*or* sheriff clerk]

Form O2A

Form of warrant in an action to which rule 3.2(3) applies

[*Repealed by the* Act of Sederunt (Sheriff Court Rules) (Enforcement of Securities over Heritable Property) 2010 (SSI 2010/324) para.2 (*effective September 30, 2010*).]

[2, 3]FORM O3

Form of notice to be served on defender in ordinary action where time to pay direction or time order may be applied for

Rule 3.3(3), 7.3(2) and 18.5(1)(a)

ACTION RAISED BY

..........PURSUER..........DEFENDER

AT...............SHERIFF COURT

(Including address)

COURT REF. NO.

DATE OF EXPIRY OF

PERIOD OF NOTICE

**THIS SECTION MUST BE COMPLETED BY THE PURSUER BEFORE SERVICE**

(1) Time to pay directions

The Debtors (Scotland) Act 1987 gives you the right to apply to the court for a "time to pay direction" which is an order permitting you to pay any sum of money you are ordered to pay to the pursuer (which may include interest and court expenses) either by way of instalments or deferred lump sum. A deferred lump sum means that you must pay all the amount at one time within a period specified by the court.

When making a time to pay direction the court may recall or restrict an arrestment made on your property by the pursuer in connection with the action or debt (for example, your bank account may have been frozen).

(2) Time Orders

The Consumer Credit Act 1974 allows you to apply to the court for a "time order" during a court action, to ask the court to give you more time to pay a loan agreement. **A time order is similar to a time to**

---

[1] As amended by the Act of Sederunt (Ordinary Cause, Summary Application, Summary Cause and Small Claim Rules) Amendment (Miscellaneous) 2007 (SSI 2007/6), para.2(16) (effective January 29, 2007).

[2] As amended by SSI 2007/6 (effective January 29, 2007) and substituted by the Act of Sederunt (Sheriff Court Rules) (Miscellaneous Amendments) 2009 (SSI 2009/294) r.2 (effective December 1, 2009).

[3] As amended by the Act of Sederunt (Sheriff Court Rules) (Miscellaneous Amendments) 2011 (SSI 2011/193) r.9 (effective April 4, 2011).

**pay direction, but can only be applied for where the court action is about a credit agreement regulated by the Consumer Credit Act.** The court has power to grant a time order in respect of a regulated agreement to reschedule payment of the sum owed. This means that a time order can change:

- the amount you have to pay each month
- how long the loan will last
- in some cases, the interest rate payable

A time order can also stop the creditor taking away any item bought by you on hire purchase or conditional sale under the regulated agreement, so long as you continue to pay the instalments agreed.

### HOW TO APPLY FOR A TIME TO PAY DIRECTION OR TIME ORDER WHERE YOU ADMIT THE CLAIM AND YOU DO NOT WANT TO DEFEND THE ACTION

1. The appropriate application forms are attached to this notice. If you want to make an application you should lodge the completed application with the sheriff clerk at the above address before the expiry of the period of notice, the date of which is given above. No court fee is payable when lodging the application.

2. Before completing the application please read carefully the notes on how to complete the application. In the event of difficulty you may contact the court's civil department at the address above or any sheriff clerk's office, solicitor, Citizens Advice Bureau or other advice agency. Written guidance can also be obtained from the Scottish Court Service website (www.scotcourts.gov.uk).

NOTE

Where this form is being served on a defender along with Form O9 (notice to additional defender) the reference to "date of expiry of period of notice" should be amended to "date for lodging of defences or an application for a time to pay direction or time order" and the reference to "before the expiry of the period of notice" should be amended to "on or before the date for lodging of defences or an application for a time to pay direction or time order".

### WHAT WILL HAPPEN NEXT

If the pursuer objects to your application, a hearing will be fixed and the court will advise you in writing of the date and time.

If the pursuer does not object to your application, a copy of the court order for payment (called an extract decree) will be served on you by the pursuer's solicitor advising when instalment payments should commence or deferred payment be made.

Court ref. no.

### APPLICATION FOR A TIME TO PAY DIRECTION UNDER THE DEBTORS (SCOTLAND) ACT 1987

**\*PART A**

By

**\*(This section must be completed by pursuer before service)**

DEFENDER

**In an action raised by**

PURSUER

### HOW TO COMPLETE THE APPLICATION

PLEASE WRITE IN INK USING BLOCK CAPITALS

**PART A** of the application will have been completed in advance by the pursuer and gives details of the pursuer and you as the defender.

**PART B** If you wish to apply to pay by instalments enter the amount and tick the appropriate box at B3(1). If you wish to apply to pay the full sum due in one deferred payment enter the period of deferment you propose at B3(2).

**PART C** Give full details of your financial position in the space provided.

**PART D** If you wish the court, when making the time to pay direction, to recall or restrict an arrestment made in connection with the action, enter the appropriate details about what has been arrested and the place and date of the arrestment at D5, and attach the schedule of arrestment or copy.

Sign the application where indicated. Retain the copy initial writ and the form of notice which accompanied this application form as you may need them at a later stage. You should ensure that your application arrives at the court before the expiry of the period of notice.

**Part B**

1. The applicant is a defender in the action brought by the above named pursuer.
2. The defender admits the claim and applies to the court for a time to pay direction.
3. The defender applies

(1) To pay by instalments of £

(Tick one box only)

| EACH WEEK | FORTNIGHT | MONTH |
|---|---|---|
| | OR | |

(2) To pay the sum ordered in one payment within
WEEKS/MONTHS

Please state in this box why you say a time to pay direction should be made. In doing so, please consider the Note below.

**NOTE**

Under the 1987 Act , the court is required to make a time to pay direction if satisfied that it is reasonable in the circumstances to do so, and having regard in particular to the following matters—

The nature of and reasons for the debt in relation to which decree is granted or the order is sought

Any action taken by the creditor to assist the debtor in paying the debt

The debtor's financial position

The reasonableness of any proposal by the debtor to pay that debt

The reasonableness of any refusal or objection by the creditor to any proposal or offer by the debtor to pay the debt.

PART C

4. **Defender's financial position**

I am employed /self employed / unemployed

| My net income is: | weekly, fortnightly or monthly | My outgoings are: | weekly, fortnightly or monthly |
|---|---|---|---|
| Wages | £ | Mortgage/rent | £ |
| State benefits | £ | Council tax | £ |
| Tax credits | £ | Gas/electricity etc | £ |
| Other | £ | Food | £ |
| | | Credit and loans | £ |
| | | Phone | £ |
| | | Other | £ |
| Total | £ | Total | £ |

People who rely on your income (e.g. spouse/civil partner/partner/children) — how many

Here list all assets (if any) e.g. value of house; amounts in bank or building society accounts; shares or other investments:

Here list any outstanding debts:

**Part D**

5. The defender seeks to recall or restrict an arrestment of which the details are as follows (*please state, and attach the schedule of arrestment or copy*).

6. This application is made under sections 1(1) and 2(3) of the Debtors (Scotland) Act 1987.

Therefore the defender asks the court

*to make a time to pay direction

*to recall the above arrestment

*to restrict the above arrestment (*in which case state restriction wanted*)

Date (*insert date*)

Signed

Defender

Court ref. no.

**APPLICATION FOR A TIME ORDER UNDER THE** CONSUMER CREDIT ACT 1974

**\*PART A**

By

**\*(This section must be completed by pursuer before service)**

DEFENDER

**In an action raised by**

PURSUER

**HOW TO COMPLETE THE APPLICATION**

PLEASE WRITE IN INK USING BLOCK CAPITALS

**PART A** of the application will have been completed in advance by the pursuer and gives details of the pursuer and you as the defender.

**PART B** If you wish to apply to pay by instalments enter the amount and tick the appropriate box at B3. If you wish the court to make any additional orders, please give details at B4. Please give details of the regulated agreement at B5.

**PART C** Give full details of your financial position in the space provided.

Sign the application where indicated. Retain the copy initial writ and the form of notice which accompanied this application form as you may need them at a later stage. You should ensure that your application arrives at the court before the expiry of the period of notice.

### Part B

1. The Applicant is a defender in the action brought by the above named pursuer.

**I/WE WISH TO APPLY FOR A TIME ORDER under the** Consumer Credit Act 1974

### 2. Details of order(s) sought

The defender wishes to apply for a time order under section 129 of the Consumer Credit Act 1974

The defender wishes to apply for an order in terms of section..........of the Consumer Credit Act 1974

### 3. Proposals for payment

I admit the claim and apply to pay the arrears and future instalments as follows:

By instalments of £ .......... per *week/fortnight/month

No time to pay direction or time to pay order has been made in relation to this debt.

### 4. Additional orders sought

The following additional order(s) is (are) sought: (*specify*)

The order(s) sought in addition to the time order is (are) sought for the following reasons:

### 5. Details of regulated agreement

(*Please attach a copy of the agreement if you have retained it and insert details of the agreement where known*)

  (a)   Date of agreement
  (b)   Reference number of agreement
  (c)   Names and addresses of other parties to agreement
  (d)   Name and address of person (if any) who acted as surety (guarantor) to the agreement
  (e)   Place where agreement signed (e.g. the shop where agreement signed, including name and address)
  (f)   Details of payment arrangements
      i.   The agreement is to pay instalments of £..........per week/month
     ii.   The unpaid balance is £........../ I do not know the amount of arrears
   iii.   I am £..........in arrears / I do not know the amount of arrears

### Part C

4. Defender's financial position

I am employed /self employed / unemployed

| My net income is: | weekly, nightly monthly | fort- or | My outgoings are: | weekly, nightly monthly | fort- or |
|---|---|---|---|---|---|
| Wages | £ | | Mortgage/rent | £ | |
| State benefits | £ | | Council tax | £ | |
| Tax credits | £ | | Gas/electricity etc | £ | |
| Other | £ | | Food | £ | |
| Credit and loans | £ | | Phone | £ | |
| | | | Other | £ | |
| Total | £ | | Total | £ | |

People who rely on your income (e.g. spouse/civil partner/partner/children) — how many

Here list all assets (if any) e.g. value of house; amounts in bank or building society accounts; shares or other investments:

Here list any outstanding debts:

Therefore the defender asks the court to make a time order

Date...............Signed..........

...............Defender..........

Rule 7.3(4)

[1] FORM O3A

Form of pursuer's response objecting to application for time to pay direction or time order

**Court ref no:**

SHERIFFDOM OF (*insert name of sheriffdom*)

AT (*insert place of sheriff court*)

PURSUER'S RESPONSE OBJECTING TO APPLICATION FOR TIME TO PAY DIRECTION OR TIME ORDER

in the cause

[A.B.], (*insert designation and address*), Pursuer

against

[C.D.], (*insert designation and address*), Defender

1. The pursuer received a copy application for a time to pay direction or time order lodged by the defender on (*date*).

2. The pursuer does not accept the offer.

3. The debt is (*please specify the nature of the debt*).

4. The debt was incurred on (*specify date*) and the pursuer has contacted the defender in relation to the debt on (*specify date(s)*).

*5. The contractual payments were (*specify amount*).

*6. (*Specify any action taken by the pursuer to assist the defender to pay the debt*).

*7. The defender has made payment(s) towards the debt of (*specify amount(s)*) on (*specify date(s)*).

*8. The debtor has made offers to pay (*specify amount(s)*) on (*specify date(s)*) which offer(s) was [were] accepted [*or* rejected] and (*specify amount*) was paid on (*specify date(s)*).

9. (*Here set out any information you consider relevant to the court's determination of the application*).

* delete as appropriate

Minute for decree

(*Signed*)

Pursuer *or* Solicitor for pursuer

(*Date*)

Rule 5.2(1)

[2, 3] FORM 04

Form of Citation

CITATION

SHERIFFDOM OF (*insert name of Sheriffdom*)

AT (*insert place of sheriff court*)

[A.B.], (*insert designation and address*), Pursuer, against [C.D.], (*insert designation and address*), Defender

Court Ref No:

(*Insert place and date*). You [C.D.], are hereby served with this copy writ and warrant, with Form 07 (notice of intention to defend).

---

**Form 07** is served on you for use should you wish to intimate an intention to defend this action.

*IF YOU WISH TO DEFEND THIS ACTION* you should consult a solicitor with a view to lodging a notice of intention to defend (Form 07). The notice of intention to defend, together with the court fee of £ (*insert amount*) must be lodged with the Sheriff Clerk at the above address within 21 days (*or insert the appropriate period of notice*) of (*insert the date on which service was executed NB. Rule 5.3(2) relating to postal service*).

---

**A copy of any notice of intention to defend should be sent to the Solicitor for the pursuer at the same time as your notice of intention to defend is lodged with the Sheriff Clerk.**

---

[1] As inserted by Act of Sederunt (Sheriff Court Rules) (Miscellaneous Amendments) 2009 (SSI 2009/294) r.2 (effective December 1, 2009).

[2] As substituted by the Act of Sederunt (Sheriff Court Ordinary Cause Rules Amendment) (Miscellaneous) 2000 (SSI 2000/239) (effective October 2, 2000).

[3] As amended by the Act of Sederunt (Sheriff Court Rules) (Miscellaneous Amendments) (No.2) 2008 (SSI 2008/365) para.2 (effective December 1, 2008).

**IF THE WORDS "COMMERCIAL ACTION" APPEAR AT THE HEAD OF THIS INITIAL WRIT** then you should note that this action is a commercial action governed by Chapter 40 of the Ordinary Cause Rules 1993. You should also note in particular that if you lodge a notice of intention to defend you must then lodge defences within 7 days of the expiry of the period of notice. You will receive no further notification of this requirement from the court.

**IF YOU ARE UNCERTAIN WHAT ACTION TO TAKE** you should consult a solicitor. You may be eligible for legal aid depending on your income, and you can get information about legal aid from a solicitor. You may also obtain advice from any Citizens' Advice Bureau or other advice agency.

**PLEASE NOTE THAT IF YOU DO NOTHING IN ANSWER TO THIS DOCUMENT** the court may regard you as admitting the claim made against you and the pursuer may obtain decree against you in your absence.

Signed

[P.Q.], Sheriff Officer

*or* [X.Y.] (*add designation and business address*)

Solicitor for the Pursuer

Rule 5.2(2)                                     [1, 2] FORM 05

Form of citation where time to pay direction or time order may be applied for

CITATION

SHERIFFDOM OF (*insert name of Sheriffdom*)

AT (*insert place of Sheriff Court*)

[A.B.], (*insert designation and address*) Pursuer against [C.D.], (*insert designation and address*) Defender

Court Ref No:

(*insert place and date*). You [C.D.], are hereby served with this copy writ and warrant, together with the following forms—

Form 03 (application for time to pay direction or time order); and

Form 07 (notice of intention to defend).

**Form 03** is served on you because it is considered that you may be entitled to apply for a time to pay direction or time order [and for the recall or restriction of an arrestment used on the dependence of the action or in security of the debt referred to in the copy writ]. See Form 03 for further details.

**IF YOU ADMIT THE CLAIM AND WISH TO APPLY FOR A TIME TO PAY DIRECTION OR TIME ORDER**, you must complete Form 03 and return it to the Sheriff Clerk at (*insert address*) within 21 days (*or insert the appropriate period of notice*) of (*insert the date on which service was executed. NB Rule 5.3 (2) relating to postal service*).

**IF YOU ADMIT THE CLAIM AND WISH TO AVOID A COURT ORDER BEING MADE AGAINST YOU**, the whole sum claimed including interest and any expense due should be paid to the pursuer or his solicitor in good time before the expiry of the period of notice.

**Form 07** is served on you for use should you wish to intimate an intention to defend the action.

**IF YOU WISH TO DEFEND THIS ACTION** you should consult a solicitor with a view to lodging a notice of intention to defend (Form 07). The notice of intention to defend, together with the court fee of £ (*insert amount*) must be lodged with the Sheriff Clerk at the above address within 21 days (*or insert the appropriate period of notice*) of (*insert the date on which service was executed. NB Rule 5.3(2) relating to postal service*).

**A copy of any notice of intention to defend should be sent to the Solicitor for the pursuer at the same time as your notice of intention to defend is lodged with the Sheriff Clerk.**

---

[1] As substituted by the Act of Sederunt (Sheriff Court Ordinary Cause Rules Amendment) (Miscellaneous) 2000 (SSI 2000/239) (effective October 2, 2000) and amended by the Act of Sederunt (Ordinary Cause, Summary Application, Summary Cause and Small Claim Rules) Amendment (Miscellaneous) 2007 (SSI 2007/6), para.2(16) (effective January 29, 2007).

[2] As amended by the Act of Sederunt (Sheriff Court Rules) (Miscellaneous Amendments) (No.2) 2008 (SSI 2008/365) para.2 (effective December 1, 2008).

> **IF THE WORDS "COMMERCIAL ACTION" APPEAR AT THE HEAD OF THIS INITIAL WRIT** then you should note that this action is a commercial action governed by Chapter 40 of the Ordinary Cause Rules 1993. You should also note in particular that if you lodge a notice of intention to defend you must then lodge defences within 7 days of the expiry of the period of notice. You will receive no further notification of this requirement from the court.
>
> **IF YOU ARE UNCERTAIN WHAT ACTION TO TAKE** you should consult a solicitor. You may be eligible for legal aid depending on your income, and you can get information about legal aid from a solicitor. You may also obtain advice from any Citizens' Advice Bureau or other advice agency.
>
> **PLEASE NOTE THAT IF YOU DO NOTHING IN ANSWER TO THIS DOCUMENT** the court may regard you as admitting the claim made against you and the pursuer may obtain decree against you in your absence.

Signed

[P.Q.], Sheriff Officer

*or* [X.Y.] (*add designation and business address*)

Solicitor for the Pursuer

Form O5A

Form of citation in an action to which rule 3.2(3) applies

[*Repealed by the* Act of Sederunt (Sheriff Court Rules) (Enforcement of Securities over Heritable Property) 2010 (SSI 2010/324) para.2 (*effective September 30. 2010*).]

Rule 5.2(3)                      [1] FORM O6

Form of certificate of citation

CERTIFICATE OF CITATION

(*Insert place and date*) I, hereby certify that upon the day of I duly cited [C.D.], Defender, to answer to the foregoing writ. This I did by (*state method of service; if by officer and not by post, add*: in presence of [L.M.], (*insert designation*), witness hereto with me subscribing; *and where service executed by post state whether by registered post or the first class recorded delivery service*).

(*In actions in which a time to pay direction may be applied for, state whether Form O2 and Form O3 were sent in accordance with* rule 3.3).

Signed

[P.Q.], Sheriff officer

[L.M.], witness

*or* [X.Y.]. (*add designation and business address*)

Solicitor for the pursuer

Rules 5.2(1) and 9.1(1)                [2] FORM O7

Form of notice of intention to defend

**NOTICE OF INTENTION TO DEFEND**

*PART A              in an action raised at           Sheriff Court

Court Ref No

| | |
|---|---|
| (Insert name and business address of solicitor for the Pursuer) | |
| | **Pursuer** |

Solicitor for the pursuer

---

[1] As substituted by the Act of Sederunt (Amendment of Ordinary Cause Rules and Summary Applications, Statutory Applications and Appeals etc. Rules) (Applications under the Mortgage Rights (Scotland) Act 2001) 2002 (SSI 2002 No.7), para.2(6) and amended by the Act of Sederunt (Sheriff Court Rules) (Enforcement of Securities over Heritable Property) 2010 (SSI 2010/324) para.2 (effective September 30, 2010).

[2] As substituted by the Act of Sederunt (Sheriff Court Ordinary Cause Rules Amendment) (Miscellaneous) 2000 (SSI 2000/239) (effective October 2, 2000).

Defender

**\*(This section to be completed by the Pursuer before service)**

DATE        OF        DATE OF EXPIRY OF PERIOD OF NOTICE:
SERVICE:

Part B

**(This section to be completed by the defender or defender's solicitors, and both parts of this form to be returned to the Sheriff Clerk (insert address of Sheriff Clerk) on or before the date of expiry of the period of notice referred to in PART A above. At the same time a copy of the form should be sent to the Solicitor for the Pursuer).**

(*Insert place and date*)

[C.D.], (*insert designation and address*), Defender, intends to defend the action raised by [A.B.], (*insert designation and address*), Pursuer, against him (and others).

Signed

[C.D.], Defender

or [X.Y.], (*add designation and business address*)

Solicitor for the defender

Paragraph 4(4)

[1]Form 07A

Rule 13A.3(1)

Form of minute of intervention by the Commission for Equality and Human Rights

SHERIFFDOM OF (*insert name of sheriffdom*)

Court ref. no.

AT (*insert place of sheriff court*)

Application for Leave to Intervene by the Commission for Equality And Human Rights

in the cause

[A.B.] (*designation and address*), Pursuer

against

[C.D.] (*designation and address*), Defender

[*Here set out briefly:*

(a)    the Commission's reasons for believing that the proceedings are relevant to a matter in connection with which the Commission has a function;

(b)    the issue in the proceedings which the Commission wishes to address; and

(c)    the propositions to be advanced by the Commission and the Commission's reasons for believing that they are relevant to the proceedings and that they will assist the court.]

[2]Form 07B

Rule 13B.2(1)

Form of minute of intervention by the Scottish Commission for Human Rights

SHERIFFDOM OF (*insert name of sheriffdom*)

Court ref. no.

AT (*insert place of sheriff court*)

APPLICATION FOR LEAVE TO INTERVENE BY THE SCOTTISH COMMISSION FOR HUMAN RIGHTS

in the cause

[A.B.] (*designation and address*), Pursuer

against

[C.D.] (*designation and address*), Defender

[*Here set out briefly:*

(a)    the issue in the proceedings which the Commission intends to address;

(b)    a summary of the submission the Commission intends to make.]

---

[1] As inserted by the Act of Sederunt (Sheriff Court Rules) (Miscellaneous Amendments) 2008 (SSI 2008/223) para.4(4) (effective July 1, 2008).

[2] As inserted by the Act of Sederunt (Sheriff Court Rules) (Miscellaneous Amendments) 2008 (SSI 2008/223) para.4(4) (effective July 1, 2008).

[1]Form 07C

Rule 13B.3(1)

Invitation to the Scottish Commission for Human Rights to intervene

SHERIFFDOM OF *(insert name of sheriffdom)*

Court ref. no.

AT *(insert place of sheriff court)*

INVITATION TO THE SCOTTISH COMMISSION FOR HUMAN RIGHTS TO INTERVENE

in the cause

[A.B.] *(designation and address)*, Pursuer

against

[C.D.] *(designation and address)*, Defender

[*Here set out briefly:*
*(a)* the facts, procedural history and issues in the proceedings;
*(b)* the issue in the proceedings on which the court seeks a submission.]

[2]FORM 08

Rule 18.5(1)(a)(i)

Form of notice to additional or substitute defender where time to pay direction or time order may be applied for

SHERIFFDOM OF *(insert name of sheriffdom)*

AT *(insert place of sheriff court)*

To [E.F.] *(insert designation and address of additional* [or *substitute*] defender) Court ref. no.

You [E.F.] are given notice that in this action in which [A.B.] is the pursuer and [C.D.] is the defender, your name has, by order of the court dated *(insert date of court order)* been added [*or* substituted] as a defender to the said action; and the action, originally against [C.D.] is now [*or* also] directed against you.

Enclosed with this notice are the following documents—

Copies of the [*insert as appropriate*, pleadings as adjusted *or* closed record];

Form 03 (application for a time to pay direction or time order); and

Form 07 (notice of intention to defend).

**Form 03** is served on you because it is considered that you may be entitled to apply for a time to pay direction or time order [and for the recall or restriction of an arrestment used on the dependence of the action or in security of the debt referred to in the copy writ]. See Form 03 for further details.

**IF YOU ADMIT THE CLAIM AND WISH TO APPLY FOR A TIME TO PAY DIRECTION OR TIME ORDER,** you must complete Form 03 and return it to the sheriff clerk at *(insert address)* within 21 days *(or insert the appropriate period of notice)* of *(Insert the date on which service was executed. N.B. Rule 5.3(2) relating to postal citation)*.

**IF YOU ADMIT THE CLAIM AND WISH TO AVOID A COURT ORDER BEING MADE AGAINST YOU,** the whole sum claimed including interest and any expenses due should be paid to the pursuer or his solicitor in good time before the expiry of the period of notice.

**Form 07** is served on you for use should you wish to intimate an intention to defend the action.

**IF YOU WISH TO DEFEND THIS ACTION** you should consult a solicitor with a view to lodging a notice of intention to defend (Form 07). The notice of intention to defend, together with the court fee of £ *(insert amount)* must be lodged with the sheriff clerk at the above address within 21 days *(or insert the appropriate period of notice)* of *(insert the date on which service was executed. N.B. See Rule 5.3(2) relating to postal service)*.

**IF YOU ARE UNCERTAIN WHAT ACTION TO TAKE** you should consult a solicitor. You may be eligible for legal aid depending on your income, and you can get information about legal aid from a solicitor. You may also obtain advice from any Citizens Advice Bureau or other advice agency.

**PLEASE NOTE THAT IF YOU DO NOTHING IN ANSWER TO THIS DOCUMENT** the court may regard you as admitting the claim made against you and the pursuer may obtain decree against you in your absence.

Signed

[P.Q.], Sheriff officer

---

[1] As inserted by the Act of Sederunt (Sheriff Court Rules) (Miscellaneous Amendments) 2008 (SSI 2008/223) para.4(4) (effective July 1, 2008).

[2] As amended by the Act of Sederunt (Ordinary Cause, Summary Application, Summary Cause and Small Claim Rules) Amendment (Miscellaneous) 2007 (SSI 2007/6), para.2(16) (effective January 29, 2007).

or [X.Y.] (*add designation and business address*)
Solicitor for the pursuer [or defender]

FORM 09

Rule 18.5(1)(a)(ii)

Form of notice to additional or substitute defender

SHERIFFDOM OF (*insert name of sheriffdom*)

AT (*insert place of sheriff court*)

To [E.F.] (*insert designation and address of additional* [or *substitute*] defender) Court ref. no.

You [E.F.] are given notice that in this action in which [A.B.] is the pursuer and [C.D.] is the defender, your name has, by order of the court dated (*insert date of court order*) been added [*or* substituted] as a defender to the said action; and the action, originally against the said [C.D.] is now [*or* also] directed against you.

Enclosed with this notice are the following documents—

Copies of the [*insert as appropriate* pleadings as adjusted *or* closed record]; and

Form 07 (notice of intention to defend).

**Form 07** is served on you for use should you wish to intimate an intention to defend the action.

**IF YOU WISH TO DEFEND THIS ACTION** you should consult a solicitor with a view to lodging a notice of intention to defend (Form 07). The notice of intention to defend, together with the court fee of £ (insert amount) must be lodged with the sheriff clerk at the above address with 28 days (*or insert the appropriate period of notice*) of (*insert the date on which service was executed. N.B.* Rule 5.3(2) *relating to postal service*).

**IF YOU ARE UNDERTAIN WHAT ACTION TO TAKE** you should consult a solicitor. You may be eligible for legal aid depending on your income, and you can get information about legal aid from a solicitor. You may also obtain advice from any Citizens Advice Bureau or other advice agency.

**PLEASE NOTE THAT IF YOU DO NOTHING IN ANSWER TO THIS DOCUMENT** the court may regard you as admitting the claim made against you and the pursuer may obtain decree against you in your absence.

Signed
[P.Q.], Sheriff officer
or [X.Y.] (*add designation and business address*)
Solicitor for the pursuer [or defender]

[1]FORM O10

Rule 20.1

Form of third party notice

SHERIFFDOM OF (*insert name of sheriffdom*)

Court ref. no.

AT (*insert place of sheriff court*)...............

THIRD PARTY NOTICE
in the cause
[A.B.], (*insert designation and address*), Pursuer
against
[C.D.], (*insert designation and address*), Defender

To [E.F.]

You are given notice by [C.D.] of an order granted by Sheriff (*insert name of sheriff*) in this action in which [A.B.] is the pursuer and [C.D.] the defender. In the action the pursuer claims against the defender the sum of £ as damages in respect of (*insert brief account of the circumstances of the claim*) as more fully appears in the [*insert as appropriate*, pleadings as adjusted *or* amended *or* closed record] enclosed.

*The defender admits [*or* denies] liability to the pursuer but claims that, if he [*or* she] is liable to the pursuer, you are liable to relieve him [*or* her] wholly [*or* partially] of his [*or* her] liability because (*set forth contract or other right of contribution, relief, or indemnity*) as more fully appears from the defences lodged by him [*or* her] in the action,

or

*Delete as appropriate.    *The defender denies liability for the injury claimed to have been suffered by the pursuer and maintains that liability, if any, to the pursuer rests solely

---

[1] As amended by SI 1996/2445 (effective November 1,1996) (clerical error).

on you [along with (*insert names of any other person whom defender maintains is liable to him [or her] by way of contribution, relief or indemnity)*] as more fully appears from the defences lodged by him [*or* her] in the action.

or

*The defender denies liability for the injury said to have been suffered by the pursuer but maintains that if there is any liability he [*or* she] shares that with you, as more fully appears from the defences lodged by him [*or* her] in the action.

or

*The defender admits liability in part for the injury suffered by the pursuer but disputes the amount of damages and maintains that liability falls to be shared by you, as more fully appears from the defences lodged by him [*or* her] in the action.

or

*The defender admits liability in part for the injury suffered by the pursuer and for the damages claimed but maintains that liability falls to be shared by you, as more fully appears from the defences lodged by him [*or* her] in the action.

or

*(*Otherwise as the case may be*)

IF YOU WISH TO resist either the claim of the pursuer against the defender, or the claim of the defender against you, you must lodge answers with the sheriff clerk at the above address within 28 days of (*insert the date on which service was executed. N.B. Rule 5.3(2) relating to postal service*). You must also pay the court fee of £ (*insert amount*).

Date (*insert date*)...............(*Signed*)

Solicitor for the defender.

Rule 31.4(1)

[1]FORM A1

Form of note of appeal to the sheriff principal

SHERIFFDOM OF (*insert name of sheriffdom*)

AT (*insert name of sheriff court*)

Court ref. no.

in the cause

[A.B.] (*insert name and address*)

Pursuer [*or as the case may be*]

against

[C.D.] (*insert name and address*)

Defender [*or as the case may be*]

The pursuer (*or* defender *or as the case may be*) appeals to the sheriff principal on the following grounds:—

(*state grounds on which appeal is to proceed*)

[and requests the sheriff to write a note].

Date (*insert date*)

(*Signed*)

[*or* Solicitor for pursuer [*or as the case may be*]

(*add name and business address*)]

Rule 33.7(1)(a)

FORM F1

Form of intimation to children and next-of-kin in an action of divorce or separation where the defender's address is not known

Court ref. no.

To (*insert name and address as in warrant*)

---

[1] Inserted by SI 1996/2445 (effective November 1,1996).

You are given NOTICE that an action of divorce [*or* separation] has been raised against (*insert name*) your (*insert relationship, e.g. father, mother, brother or other relative as the case may be*). If you know of his [*or* her] present address, you are requested to inform the sheriff clerk (*insert address of sheriff clerk*) in writing immediately. If you wish to appear as a party you must lodge a minute with the sheriff clerk for leave to do so. Your minute must be lodged within 21 days of (*insert date on which intimation was given. N.B.* Rule 5.3(2) *relating to postal service or intimation*).

Date (*insert date*)

(Signed)<br>
Solicitor for the pursuer (add designation and business address)

**NOTE**

If you decide to lodge a minute it may be in your best interest to consult a solicitor. The minute should be lodged with the sheriff clerk together with the appropriate fee of (*insert amount*) and a copy of this intimation.

**IF YOU ARE UNCERTAIN WHAT ACTION TO TAKE** you should consult a solicitor. You may be entitled to legal aid depending on your financial circumstances, and you can get information about legal aid from a solicitor. You may also obtain advice from any Citizens Advice Bureau or other advice agency.

Rule 33.7(1)(b)

FORM F2

Form of intimation to alleged adulterer in action of divorce or separation

To (*insert name and address as in warrant*)

Court ref. no.

You are given NOTICE that in this action, you are alleged to have committed adultery. A copy of the initial writ is attached. If you wish to dispute the truth of the allegation made against you, you must lodge a minute with the sheriff clerk (*insert address of sheriff clerk*) for leave to appear as a party. Your minute must be lodged within 21 days of (*insert date on which intimation was given. N.B.* Rule 5.3(2) *relating to postal service or intimation*).

Date (*insert date*)

(Signed)<br>
Solicitor for the pursuer

**NOTE**

If you decide to lodge a minute it may be in your best interest to consult a solicitor. The minute should be lodged with the sheriff clerk together with the appropriate fee of (*insert amount*) and a copy of this intimation.

**IF YOU ARE UNCERTAIN WHAT ACTION TO TAKE** you should consult a solicitor. You may be entitled to legal aid depending on your financial circumstances, and you can get information about legal aid from a solicitor. You may also obtain advice from any Citizens Advice Bureau or other advice agency.

Rule 33.7(1)(c)

FORM F3

Form of intimation to children, next-of-kin and curator bonis in an action of divorce or separation<br>
where the defender suffers from a mental disorder

To (*insert name and address as in warrant*)

Court ref. no.

You are given NOTICE that an action of divorce [*or* separation] has been raised against (*insert name and designation*) your (*insert relationship, e.g. father, mother, brother or other relative, or ward, as the case may be*). A copy of the initial writ is enclosed. If you wish to appear as a party, you must lodge a minute with the sheriff clerk (*insert address of sheriff clerk*), for leave to do so. Your minute must be lodged within 21 days of (*insert date on which intimation was given. N.B.* Rule 5.3(2) *relating to postal service or intimation*).

Date (*insert date*)

(Signed)<br>
Solicitor for the pursuer (insert designation and business address)

**NOTE**

If you decide to lodge a minute it may be in your best interest to consult a solicitor. The minute should be lodged with the sheriff clerk together with the appropriate fee of (*insert amount*) and a copy of this intimation.

**IF YOU ARE UNCERTAIN WHAT ACTION TO TAKE** you should consult a solicitor. You may be entitled to legal aid depending on your financial circumstances, and you can get information about legal aid from a solicitor. You may also obtain advice from any Citizens Advice Bureau or other advice agency.

**IF YOU ARE UNCERTAIN WHAT ACTION TO TAKE** you should consult a solicitor. You may be entitled to legal aid depending on your financial circumstances, and you can get information about legal aid from a solicitor. You may also obtain advice from any Citizens Advice Bureau or other advice agency.

Rule 33.7(1)(d)

## FORM F4

Form of intimation to additional spouse of either party in proceedings relating to a polygamous marriage

To (*name and address as in warrant*)

Court ref. no.

You are given NOTICE that this action for divorce [*or* separation], involves (*insert name and designation*) your spouse. A copy of the initial writ is attached. If you wish to appear as a party, you must lodge a minute with the sheriff clerk (*insert address of sheriff clerk*) for leave to do so. Your minute must be lodged within 21 days of (*insert date on which intimation was given. N.B.* Rule 5.3(2) *relating to postal service or intimation*).

Date (*insert date*)

(Signed)<br>Solicitor for the pursuer

**NOTE**

If you decide to lodge a minute it may be in your best interest to consult a solicitor. The minute should be lodged with the sheriff clerk together with the appropriate fee of (*insert amount*) and a copy of this intimation.

**IF YOU ARE UNCERTAIN WHAT ACTION TO TAKE** you should consult a solicitor. You may be entitled to legal aid depending on your financial circumstances, and you can get information about legal aid from a solicitor. You may also obtain advice from any Citizens Advice Bureau or other advice agency.

Rule 33.7(1)(e)(i) and (ii)

## [1]FORM F5

Form of intimation to a local authority or third party who may be liable to maintain a child

To (*insert name and address as in warrant*)

Court ref. no.

YOU ARE GIVEN NOTICE that in this action, the court may make an order under section 11 of the Children (Scotland) Act 1995 in respect of (*insert name and address*), a child in your care [or liable to be maintained by you]. A copy of the initial writ is attached. If you wish to appear as a party, you must lodge a minute with the sheriff clerk (*insert address of sheriff clerk*) for leave to do so. Your minute must be lodged within 21 days of (*insert date on which intimation was given. N.B.* Rule 5.3(2) *relating to postal service or intimation*).

Date (*insert date*)

(*Signed*)

Solicitor for the pursuer

**NOTE**

If you decide to lodge a minute it may be in your best interests to consult a solicitor. The minute should be lodged with the sheriff clerk together with the appropriate fee of (*insert amount*) and a copy of this intimation.

**IF YOU ARE UNCERTAIN WHAT ACTION TO TAKE** you should consult a solicitor. You may be entitled to legal aid depending on your financial circumstances, and you can get information about legal aid from a solicitor. You may also obtain advice from any Citizens Advice Bureau or other advice agency.

Rule 33.7(1)(e)(iii)

## [2]FORM F6

Form of intimation to person who in fact exercises care or control of a child

To (*insert name and address as in warrant*)

---

[1] Substituted by SI 1996/216 (effective November 1, 1996).
[2] Substituted by SI 1996/2167 (effective November 1, 1996).

Court ref. no.

YOU ARE GIVEN NOTICE that in this action, the court may make an order under section 11 of the Children (Scotland) Act 1995 in respect of (*insert name and address*) a child at present in your care or control. A copy of the initial writ is attached. If you wish to appear as a party, you must lodge a minute with the sheriff clerk (*insert address of sheriff clerk*) for leave to do so. Your minute must be lodged within 21 days of (*insert date on which intimation was given. N.B.* Rule 5.3(2) *relating to postal service or intimation*).

Date (*insert date*)...............(*Signed*)

Solicitor for the pursuer

**NOTE**

If you decide to lodge a minute it may be in your best interests to consult a solicitor. The minute should be lodged with the sheriff clerk together with the appropriate fee of (*insert amount*) and a copy of this intimation.

**IF YOU ARE UNCERTAIN WHAT ACTION TO TAKE** you should consult a solicitor. You may be entitled to legal aid depending on your financial circumstances, and you can get information about legal aid from a solicitor. You may also obtain advice from any Citizens Advice Bureau or other advice agency.

Rule 33.7(1)(f)

[1]FORM F7

Form of notice to parent or guardian in action for a section 11 order in respect of a child

1. YOU ARE GIVEN NOTICE that in this action, the pursuer is applying for an order under section 11 of the Children (Scotland) Act 1995 in respect of the child (*insert name of child*). A copy of the initial writ is served on you and is attached to this notice.

2. If you wish to oppose this action, or oppose the granting of any order applied for by the pursuer in respect of the child, you must lodge a notice of intention to defend (Form F26). See Form F26 attached for further details.

Date (*insert date*)

(*Signed*)

Pursuer

*or* Solicitor for the pursuer (*add designation and business address*)

**NOTE: IF YOU ARE UNCERTAIN WHAT ACTION TO TAKE** you should consult a solicitor. You may be entitled to legal aid depending on your financial circumstances, and you can get information about legal aid from a solicitor. You may also obtain advice from any Citizens Advice Bureau or other advice agency.

Rules 33.7(1)(g), 33.7(4) and 33.12(2) and (3)

[2]FORM F8

Form of notice to local authority

To (insert name and address)

Court ref. no.

1. YOU ARE GIVEN NOTICE that in an action in the Sheriff Court at (*insert address*) the pursuer has applied for a residence order in respect of the child (*insert name of child*). A copy of the initial writ is enclosed.

2. If you wish to oppose this action, or oppose the granting of any order applied for by the pursuer in respect of the child, you must lodge a notice of intention to defend (Form F26). See Form F26 attached for further details.

Date (*insert date*)

(*Signed*)

Solicitor for the pursuer (*add designation and business address*)

Rule 33.7(1)(h)

[3]FORM F9

Form of intimation in an action which includes a crave for a section 11 order

PART A

---

[1] Substituted by S.I. 1996 No. 2167 (effective November 1, 1996).

[2] Substituted by SI 1996/2167 (effective November 1, 1996) and SSI 2010/416 (effective January 1, 2011).

[3] Substituted by SI 1996/2167 (effective November 1, 1996) and amended by SSI 2003/26 (effective January 24, 2003).

Court ref. No.

---

| This part must be completed by the Pursuer's solicitor in language a child is capable of understanding. |
|---|

To (1)

The Sheriff (the person who has to decide about your future) has been asked by (2)..........to decide:—

(a)   (3) and (4)

(b)   (5)

(c)   (6)

If you want to tell the Sheriff what you think about the things your (2).......... has asked the Sheriff to decide about your future you should complete Part B of this form and send it to the Sheriff Clerk at (7) by (8)........... An envelope which does not need a postage stamp is enclosed for you to use to return the form.

**IF YOU DO NOT UNDERSTAND THIS FORM OR IF YOU WANT HELP TO COMPLETE IT you may get help from a SOLICITOR or contact the SCOTTISH CHILD LAW CENTRE ON the FREE ADVICE TELEPHONE LINE ON 0800 328 8970.**

If you return the form it will be given to the Sheriff. The Sheriff may wish to speak with you and may ask you to come and see him or her.

### Notes for Completion

| | |
|---|---|
| (1) Insert name and address of child. | (2) Insert relationship to the child of party making the application to court. |
| (3) Insert appropriate wording for residence order sought. | (4) Insert address. |
| (5) Insert appropriate wording for contact order sought. | (6) Insert appropriate wording for any other order sought. |
| (7) Insert address of sheriff clerk. | (8) Insert the date occurring 21 days after the date on which intimation is given. N.B. Rule 5.3(2) relating to intimation and service. |
| (9) Insert court reference number. | (10) Insert name and address of parties to the action. |

Part B

IF YOU WISH THE SHERIFF TO KNOW YOUR VIEWS ABOUT YOUR FUTURE YOU SHOULD COMPLETE THIS PART OF THE FORM

To the Sheriff Clerk, (7)

Court Ref. No. (9)

(10).................................................

QUESTION (1): DO YOU WISH THE SHERIFF TO KNOW WHAT YOUR VIEWS ARE ABOUT YOUR FUTURE?

(PLEASE TICK BOX)

| | |
|---|---|
| Yes | |
| No | |

If you have ticked YES please also answer Question (2) *or* (3)

QUESTION (2): WOULD YOU LIKE A FRIEND, RELATIVE OR OTHER PERSON TO TELL THE SHERIFF YOUR VIEWS ABOUT YOUR FUTURE?

(PLEASE TICK BOX)

| | |
|---|---|
| Yes | |
| No | |

If you have ticked YES please write the name and address of the person you wish to tell the Sheriff your views in Box (A) below. You should also tell that person what your views are about your future.

| BOX A: | (NAME)........................................ |
|---|---|
| | (ADDRESS)........................................ |
| | .................................................... |
| | Is  this A friend? ☐        A rela- ☐ person:—                        tive? |

| | |
|---|---|
| A teacher? ☐ | Other? ☐ |

OR

QUESTION (3): WOULD YOU LIKE TO WRITE TO THE SHERIFF AND TELL HIM WHAT YOUR VIEWS ARE ABOUT YOUR FUTURE?

(PLEASE TICK BOX)

| | |
|---|---|
| Yes | |
| No | |

If you decide that you wish to write to the Sheriff you can write what your views are about your future in Box (B) below or on a separate piece of paper. If you decide to write your views on a separate piece of paper you should send it along with this form to the Sheriff Clerk in the envelope provided.

BOX B:       WHAT I HAVE TO SAY ABOUT MY FUTURE:—

NAME: .......................................
ADDRESS: .......................................
DATE: .......................................
Rule 33.7(1)(a)

FORM F10

Form of intimation to creditor in application for order for the transfer of property under section 8 of the Family Law (Scotland) Act 1985

To (*insert name and address as in warrant*)

Court ref. no.

You are given NOTICE that in this action an order is sought for the transfer of property (*specify the order*), over which you hold a security. A copy of the initial writ is attached. If you wish to appear as a party, you must lodge a minute with the sheriff clerk (*insert address of sheriff clerk*) for leave to do so. Your minute must be lodged within 21 days of (*insert date on which intimation was given. N.B. Rule 5.3(2) relating to postal service or intimation*).

Date (*insert date*)

(*Signed*)
Solicitor for the pursuer

**NOTE**

If you decide to lodge a minute it may be in your best interests to consult a solicitor. The minute should be lodged with the sheriff clerk together with the appropriate fee of (*insert amount*) and a copy of this intimation.

**IF YOU ARE UNCERTAIN WHAT ACTION TO TAKE** you should consult a solicitor. You may be entitled to legal aid depending on your financial circumstances, and you can get information about legal aid from a solicitor. You may also obtain advice from any Citizens Advice Bureau or other advice agency.

Rule 33.7(1)(j)

FORM F11

Form of intimation in an action where the pursuer makes an application for an order under section 18 of the Family Law (Scotland) Act 1985

To (*insert name and address as in warrant*)

Court ref. no.

You are given NOTICE that in this action, the pursuer craves the court to make an order under section 18 of the Family Law (Scotland) Act 1985. A copy of the initial writ is attached. If you wish to appear as a party, you must lodge a minute with the sheriff clerk (*insert address of sheriff clerk*) for leave to do so. Your minute must be lodged within 21 days of (*insert date on which intimation was given. N.B. Rule 5.3(2) relating to postal service or intimation*).

Date (*insert date*)
(*Signed*)
Solicitor for the pursuer

**NOTE**

If you decide to lodge a minute it may be in your best interests to consult a solicitor. The minute should be lodged with the sheriff clerk together with the appropriate fee of (*insert amount*) and a copy of this intimation.

**IF YOU ARE UNCERTAIN WHAT ACTION TO TAKE** you should consult a solicitor. You may be entitled to legal aid depending on your financial circumstances, and you can get information about legal aid from a solicitor. You may also obtain advice from any Citizens Advice Bureau or other advice agency.

Rule 33.7(1)(k)

FORM F12

Form of intimation in an action where a non-entitled pursuer makes an application for an order under the Matrimonial Homes (Family Protection) (Scotland) Act 1981

To (*insert name and address as in warrant*)

Court ref. no.

You are given NOTICE that in this action, the pursuer craves the court to make an order under section (*insert the section under which the order(s) is sought*) of the Matrimonial Homes (Family Protection) (Scotland) Act 1981. A copy of the initial writ is attached. If you wish to appear as a party, you must may lodge a minute with the sheriff clerk (*insert address of sheriff clerk*) for leave to do so. Your minute must be lodged within 21 days of (*insert date on which intimation was given. N.B.* Rule 5.3(2) *relating to postal service or intimation*).

Date (*insert date*)

(Signed)<br>Solicitor for the pursuer

**NOTE**

If you decide to lodge a minute it may be in your best interests to consult a solicitor. The minute should be lodged with the sheriff clerk together with the appropriate fee of (*insert amount*) and a copy of this intimation.

**IF YOU ARE UNCERTAIN WHAT ACTION TO TAKE** you should consult a solicitor. You may be entitled to legal aid depending on your financial circumstances, and you can get information about legal aid from a solicitor. You may also obtain advice from any Citizens Advice Bureau or other advice agency.

Rule 33.7(1)(1)

[1]FORM F12A

Form of intimation to person responsible for pension arrangement in relation to order for payment in respect of pension lump sum under section 12A of the Family Law (Scotland) Act 1985

To (*insert name and address as in warrant*)

Court ref. no.

You are given NOTICE that in this action the pursuer has applied for an order under section 8 of the Family Law (Scotland) Act 1985 for a capital sum in circumstances where the matrimonial property includes rights in a pension scheme under which a lump sum is payable. The relevant pension scheme is (*give brief details, including number, if known*). If you wish to apply to appear as a party, you must lodge a minute with the sheriff clerk (*insert address of sheriff clerk*) for leave to do so. Your minute must be lodged within 21 days of (*insert date on which intimation was given. N.B.* rule 5.3(2) *relating to postal service or intimation.*)

Date (*insert date*)

(Signed)<br>Solicitor for the pursuer<br>(add designation and business address)

**NOTE**

If you decide to lodge a minute it may be in your best interests to consult a solicitor. The minute should be lodged with the sheriff clerk together with the appropriate fee of (*insert amount*) and a copy of this intimation.

**IF YOU ARE UNCERTAIN WHAT ACTION TO TAKE** you should consult a solicitor. You may be entitled to legal aid depending on your financial circumstances, and you can get information about legal aid from a solicitor. You may also obtain advice from any Citizens Advice Bureau or other advice agency.

---

[1] Inserted by S.I. 1996 No. 2445 (effective November 1, 1996) and amended by the Act of Sederunt (Ordinary Cause Rules) Amendment (No.2)(Pension Sharing on Divorce etc.) 2000 (S.S.I. 2000 No. 408) para. 2(3)(a).

Rule 33.7(1)(m)

### [1]FORM F12B

Form of intimation to person responsible for the pension arrangement in relation to pension sharing order under section 8(1)(baa) of the Family Law (Scotland) Act 1985.

Court ref. no.

To (*insert name and address as in warrant*)

You are given NOTICE that in this action the pursuer has applied under section 8 of the Family Law (Scotland) Act 1985 for a pension sharing order in circumstances where the matrimonial property includes rights in a pension scheme. The relevant pension scheme is (give brief details, including number, if known). If you wish to apply to appear as a party, you must lodge a minute with the sheriff clerk (insert address of sheriff clerk) for leave to do so. Your minute must be lodged within 21 days of (*insert date on which intimation was given, N.B.* rule 5.3(2) *relating to postal service or intimation.*)

Date (*insert date*)

(*Signed*)

Solicitor for the pursuer

(*add designation and business address*)

**NOTE**

If you decide to lodge a minute it may be in your best interests to consult a solicitor. The minute should be lodged with the sheriff clerk together with the appropriate fee of (insert amount) and a copy of this intimation.

**IF YOU ARE UNCERTAIN WHAT ACTION TO TAKE** you should consult a solicitor. You may be entitled to legal aid depending on your financial circumstances, and you can get information about legal aid from a solicitor. You may also obtain advice from any Citizens Advice Bureau or other advice agency.

Rule 33.7(1)(n)

### [2]FORM F12C

Form of intimation to Board of the Pension Protection Fund in relation to pension compensation sharing order under section 8(1)(bab) of the Family Law (Scotland) Act 1985

Court ref. no.

To (*insert name and address as in warrant*)

You are given NOTICE that in this action the pursuer has applied under section 8(1)(bab) of the Family Law (Scotland) Act 1985 for a pension compensation sharing order in circumstances where the matrimonial property includes rights to Pension Protection Fund compensation. The relevant pension arrangement is (*give brief details, including number, if known*). If you wish to appear as a party, you must lodge a minute with the sheriff clerk (*insert address of sheriff clerk*), for leave to do so. Your minute must be lodged within 21 days of (*insert date on which intimation was given. N.B.* Rule 5.3(2) *relating to postal service or intimation*).

Date (*insert date*)

(*Signed*)

Solicitor for the pursuer

(*insert designation and business address*)

Rule 33.7(1)(o)

### [3]FORM F12D

Form of intimation to Board of the Pension Protection Fund in relation to an order under section 12B(2) of the Family Law (Scotland) Act 1985

Court ref. no.

To (*insert name and address as in warrant*)

You are given NOTICE that in this action the pursuer has applied under section 8(1)(bb) of the Family Law (Scotland) Act 1985 for an order under section 12B(2) of the Act in circumstances where the matrimonial property includes rights to Pension Protection Fund compensation. The relevant pension arrangement is (*give brief details, including number, if known*). If you wish to appear as a party, you must lodge a minute with the sheriff clerk (*insert address of sheriff clerk*), for leave to do so. Your minute must

---

[1] Inserted by the Act of Sederunt (Ordinary Cause Rules) Amendment (No.2)(Pension Sharing on Divorce etc.) 2000 (S.S.I. 2000 No. 408) para. 2(3)(b).

[2] As inserted by the Act of Sederunt (Sheriff Court Rules) (Miscellaneous Amendments) 2011 (SSI 2011/193) r.15 (effective April 6, 2011).

[3] As inserted by the Act of Sederunt (Sheriff Court Rules) (Miscellaneous Amendments) 2011 (SSI 2011/193) r.15 (effective April 6, 2011).

be lodged within 21 days of (*insert date on which intimation was given. N.B.* Rule 5.3(2) *relating to postal service or intimation*).

Date (*insert date*)

(*Signed*)

Solicitor for the pursuer

(*insert designation and business address*)

Rule 33.7(1)(p)                              [1, 2]FORM F12E

Form of intimation of application for financial provision on intestacy under section 29(2) of the Family Law (Scotland) Act 2006

To: (insert name and address as in warrant)          Court ref no.

You are given NOTICE that the pursuer has applied for an order for financial provision on intestacy under section 29(2) of the Family Law (Scotland) Act 2006. A copy of the initial writ is attached. If you wish to appear as a party, you must lodge a minute with the sheriff clerk (*insert address of sheriff clerk*) for leave to do so. Your minute must be lodged within 21 days of (*insert date on which intimation is given. N.B.* rule 5.3(2) *relating to postal service or intimation*).

Date (insert date)                            (signed)

Solicitor for the pursuer

> **NOTE**
> If you decide to lodge a minute it may be in your best interests to consult a solicitor. The minute should be lodged with the sheriff clerk together with the appropriate fee of (*insert amount*) and a copy of this intimation.

> **IF YOU ARE UNCERTAIN WHAT ACTION TO TAKE** you should consult a solicitor. You may be entitled to legal aid depending on your financial circumstances, and you can get information about legal aid from a solicitor. You may also obtain advice from any Citizens Advice Bureau or other advice agency.

Rule 33.8(3)                                  FORM F13

Form of intimation to person with whom an improper association is alleged to have occurred

To (*insert name and address as in warrant*)          Court ref. no.

You are given NOTICE that in this action, the defender is alleged to have had an improper association with you. A copy of the initial writ is attached. If you wish to dispute the truth of the allegation made against you, you must lodge a minute with the sheriff clerk (*insert address of sheriff clerk*) for leave to appear as a party. Your minute must be lodged within 21 days of (*insert date on which intimation was given. N.B.* Rule 5.3(2) *relating to postal service or intimation*).

Date (*insert date*)                          (*Signed*)

Solicitor for the pursuer

> **NOTE**
> If you decide to lodge a minute it may be in your best interests to consult a solicitor. The minute should be lodged with the sheriff clerk together with the appropriate fee of (*insert amount*) and a copy of this intimation.

> **IF YOU ARE UNCERTAIN WHAT ACTION TO TAKE** you should consult a solicitor. You may be entitled to legal aid depending on your financial circumstances, and you can get information about legal aid from a solicitor. You may also obtain advice from any Citizens Advice Bureau or other advice agency.

---

[1] Inserted by Act of Sederunt (Ordinary Cause Rules) Amendment (Family Law (Scotland) Act 2006 etc.) 2006, para.2 (SSI 2006/207) (effective May 4, 2006).

[2] As amended and renumbered by the Act of Sederunt (Sheriff Court Rules) (Miscellaneous Amendments) 2012 (SSI 2012/188) para.8 (effective August 1, 2012).

Rules 33.9(c) and 33.34(4)

[1]FORM F13A

Form of statement of matrimonial property in the cause

SHERIFFDOM OF (*insert name of sheriffdom*)

AT (*insert place of sheriff court*)

[A.B.], (*insert designation and address*, Pursuer against

[C.D..], (*insert designation and address*, Defender

Court ref. no:

| The [Pursuer] [Defender]rsquo;s* financial position at ( *insert date* ), being the relevant date as defined in section 10(3) of the Family Law (Scotland) Act 1985 |
| --- |
| Here list all assets owned by you, including assets which are jointly owned (if any) e.g. bank or building society accounts; shares or other investments; houses; land; pension entitlement; and life policies: |
| Here list your outstanding debts including joint debts with the other party: |
| Date (*insert date*) |
| I certify that this information is correct to the best of my knowledge and belief. |
| (*Signed*) |
| [Pursuer][Defender]* |

(*delete as applicable)

Rule 33.10 FORM F14

Form of warrant of citation in family action

(*Insert place and date*)

Grants warrant to cite the defender (*insert name and address of defender*) by serving upon him [*or* her] a copy of the writ and warrant upon a period of notice of (*insert period of notice*) days, and ordains the defender to lodge a notice of intention to defend with the sheriff clerk at (*insert address of sheriff court*) if he [*or* she] wishes to:

    (a)    challenge the jurisdiction of the court;

    (b)    oppose any claim made or order sought;

    (c)    make any claim or seek any order.

[Meantime grants interim interdict, *or* warrant to arrest on the dependence].

Rules 33.11(1) and 33.13(1)(a) FORM F15

Form of citation in family action

CITATION

SHERIFFDOM OF (*insert name of sheriffdom*)

AT (*insert place of sheriff court*)

[A.B.], (*insert designation and address*), Pursuer, against [C.D.], (*insert designation and address*), Defender.

(*Insert place and date*) Court ref. no.

You [C.D.], are hereby served with this copy writ and warrant, with Form F26 (notice of intention to defend) [and (*insert details of any other form of notice served, e.g. any of the forms served in accordance with* rule 33.14.)].

| **Form F26** is served on you for use should you wish to intimate an intention to defend the action. |
| --- |
| **IF YOU WISH TO—** |
|     (a)    challenge the jurisdiction of the court; |
|     (b)    oppose any claim made or order sought; |
|     (c)    make any claim or seek any order; or |
|     (d)    seek any order; |

---

[1] As inserted by the Act of Sederunt (Sheriff Court Rules) (Miscellaneous Amendments) 2012 (SSI 2012/188) para.4 (effective August 1, 2012).

you should consult a solicitor with a view to lodging a notice of intention to defend (Form F26). The notice of intention to defend, together with the court fee of £ (*insert amount*) must be lodged with the sheriff clerk at the above address within 21 days (*or insert appropriate period of notice) of (insert the date on which service was executed. N.B.* Rule 5.3(2) *relating to postal service or intimation).*

**IF YOU ARE UNCERTAIN WHAT ACTION TO TAKE** you should consult a solicitor. You may be entitled to legal aid depending on your financial circumstances, and you can get information about legal aid from a solicitor. You may also obtain advice from any Citizens Advice Bureau or other advice agency.

**PLEASE NOTE THAT IF YOU DO NOTHING IN ANSWER TO THIS DOCUMENT** the court may regard you as admitting the claim made against you and the pursuer may obtain decree against you in your absence.

Signed
[P.Q.], Sheriff officer
*or*
[X.Y.], (*add designation and business address*)
Solicitor for the pursuer

Rule 33.11(2)                              FORM F16

Form of certificate of citation in family action
CERTIFICATE OF CITATION

(*Insert place and date*) I, ......... hereby certify that upon the .......... day of .......... I duly cited [C.D.], Defender, to answer to the foregoing writ. This I did by (*state method of service; if by officer and not by post, add*: in presence of [L.M.], (*insert designation*), witness hereto with me subscribing; *and (insert details of any forms of intimation or notice sent including details of the person to whom intimation sent and the method of service).*

Signed
[P.Q.], Sheriff officer
[L.M.], witness
*or*
[X.Y.] (*add designation and business address*)
Solicitor for the pursuer

**FORM F17**

Rule 33.13(1)(c)

Form of request to medical officer of hospital or similar institution

To (*insert name and address of medical officer*)

In terms of rule 33.13(1)(c) of the Ordinary Cause Rules of the Sheriff Court a copy of the initial writ at the instance of (*insert name and address of pursuer*), Pursuer, against (*insert name and address of defender*), Defender, is enclosed and you are requested to

    (a)   deliver it personally to (*insert name of defender*), and

    (b)   explain the contents to him or her,

unless you are satisfied that such delivery or explanation would be dangerous to his or her health or mental condition. You are further requested to complete and return to me in the enclosed stamped addressed envelope the certificate appended hereto, making necessary deletions.

Date (*insert date*)

(*Signed*)
Solicitor for the pursuer (*add designation and business address*)

**FORM F18**

Rules 33.13(1)(d) and 33.13(2)

Form of certificate by medical officer of hospital or similar institution

Court ref. no.

I (*insert name and designation*) certify that I have received a copy initial writ in an action of (*type of family action to be inserted by the party requesting service*) at the instance of (*insert name and designation*), Pursuer, against (*insert name and designation*), Defender, and that

    * I have on the.......... day of.......... personally delivered a copy thereof to the said defender who is under my care at (*insert address*) and I have explained the contents or purport thereof to him or her, *or*

    * I have not delivered a copy thereof to the said defender who is under my care at (*insert address*) and I have not explained the contents or purport thereof to him or her because (*state reasons*).

Date (*insert date*)

(*Signed*)
Medical officer (*add designation and address*)

\* Delete as appropriate.

[1]FORM F19

Rule 33.14(1)(a)(i)

Form of notice to defender where it is stated that defender consents to the granting of decree of divorce

YOU ARE GIVEN NOTICE that the copy initial writ served on you with this notice states that you consent to the grant of decree of divorce.

1. If you do so consent the consequences for you are that:—

[2](a)    provided the pursuer establishes the fact that he [or she] has not cohabited with you at any time during a continuous period of one year after the date of your marriage and immediately preceding the bringing of this action and that you consent, a decree of divorce will be granted;

(b)    on the grant of a decree of divorce you may lose your rights of succession to the pursuer's estate; and

(c)    decree of divorce will end the marriage thereby affecting any right to such pension as may depend on the marriage continuing, or, on your being left a widow the state widow's pension will not be payable to you when the pursuer dies.

Apart from these, there may be other consequences for you depending upon your particular circumstances.

2. You are entitled, whether or not you consent to the grant of decree of divorce in this action, to apply to the sheriff in this action—

(a)    to make financial or other provision for you under the Family Law (Scotland) Act 1985;

(b)    for an order under section 11 of the Children (Scotland) Act 1995 in respect of any child of the marriage, or any child accepted as such, who is under 16 years of age; or

(c)    for any other competent order.

3. IF YOU WISH TO APPLY FOR ANY OF THE ABOVE ORDERS you should consult a solicitor with a view to lodging a notice of intention to defend (Form F26).

4. If, after consideration, you wish to consent to the grant of decree of divorce in this action, you should complete and sign the attached notice of consent (Form F20) and send it to the sheriff clerk at the sheriff court referred to in the initial writ within 21 days of (*insert the date on which service was executed. N.B.* Rule 5.3(2) *relating to postal service*).

5. If at a later stage, you wish to withdraw your consent to decree being granted against you in this action, you must inform the sheriff clerk immediately in writing.

Date (*insert date*)

(*Signed*)
Solicitor for the pursuer (*add designation and business address*)

FORM F20

Rules 33.14(1)(a)(i) and 33.18(1)

Form of notice of consent in actions of divorce under section 1(2)(d) of the Divorce (Scotland) Act 1976

Court ref. no.

[A.B.], (*insert designation and address*), Pursuer, against [C.D.], (*insert designation and address*), Defender.

I (*full name and address of the defender to be inserted by pursuer or pursuer's solicitor before sending notice*) have received a copy of the initial writ in the action against me at the instance of (*full name and address of pursuer to be inserted by pursuer or pursuer's solicitor before sending notice*). I understand that it states that I consent to the grant of decree of divorce in this action. I have considered the consequences for me mentioned in the notice (Form F19) sent to me with this notice. I consent to the grant of decree of divorce in this action.

Date (*insert date*)

(*Signed*)
Defender

[3]FORM F21

Rule 33.14(1)(a)(ii)

---

[1] Substituted by SI 1996/2167 (effective November 1, 1996).

[2] As amended by Act of Sederunt (Ordinary Cause Rules) Amendment (Family Law (Scotland) Act 2006 etc.) 2006, para.2 (SSI 2006/207) (effective May 4, 2006).

[3] Substituted by SI 1996/2167 (effective November 1, 1996).

Form of notice to defender where it is stated that defender consents to the granting of decree of separation

YOU ARE GIVEN NOTICE that the copy initial writ served on you with this notice states that you consent to the grant of decree of separation.

1.   If you do so consent the consequences for you are that—

      [1](a)   provided the pursuer establishes the fact that he [or she] has not cohabited with you at any time during a continuous period of one year after the date of your marriage and immediately preceding the bringing of this action and that you consent, a decree of separation will be granted;

      (b)   on the grant of a decree of separation you will be obliged to live apart from the pursuer but the marriage will continue to subsist; you will continue to have a legal obligation to support your wife [or husband] and children;

Apart from these, there may be other consequences for you depending upon your particular circumstances.

2.   You are entitled, whether or not you consent to the grant of decree of separation in this action, to apply to the sheriff in this action—

      (a)   to make financial or other provision for you under the Family Law (Scotland) Act 1985;

      (b)   for an order under Section 11 of the Children (Scotland) Act 1995 in respect of any child of the marriage, or any child accepted as such, who is under 16 years of age; or

      (c)   for any other competent order.

3.   IF YOU WISH TO APPLY FOR ANY OF THE ABOVE ORDERS you should consult a solicitor with a view to lodging a notice of intention to defend (Form F26).

4.   If, after consideration, you wish to consent to the grant of decree of separation in this action, you should complete and sign the attached notice of consent (Form F22) and send it to the sheriff clerk at the sheriff court referred to in the initial writ and other papers within 21 days of (*insert the date on which service was executed. N.B. Rule 5.3(2) relating to postal service or intimation*).

5.   If at a later stage you wish to withdraw your consent to decree being granted against you in this action, you must inform the sheriff clerk immediately in writing.

Date (*insert date*)

(*Signed*)

Solicitor for the pursuer (*add designation and business address*)

FORM F22

Rules 33.14(1)(a)(ii) and 33.18(1)

Form of notice of consent in actions of separation under section 1 (2)(d) of the Divorce (Scotland) Act 1976

Court ref. no.

[A.B.], (*insert designation and address*), Pursuer against [C.D.], (*insert designation and address*), Defender.

I (*full name and address of the defender to be inserted by pursuer or pursuer's solicitor before sending notice*) confirm that I have received a copy of the initial writ in the action against me at the instance of (*full name and address of pursuer to be Inserted by pursuer or pursuer's solicitor before sending notice*). I understand that it states that I consent to the grant of decree of separation in this action. I have considered the consequences for me mentioned in the notice (Form F21) sent together with this notice. I consent to the grant of decree of separation in this action.

Date (*insert date*)

(*Signed*)

Defender

[2]FORM F23

Rule 33.14(1)(b)(i)

[3]Form of notice to defender in an action of divorce where it is stated there has been two years' non-cohabitation

YOU ARE GIVEN NOTICE that—

---

[1] As amended by Act of Sederunt (Ordinary Cause Rules) Amendment (Family Law (Scotland) Act 2006 etc.) 2006, para.2 (SSI 2006/207) (effective May 4, 2006).

[2] Substituted by SI 1996/2167 (effective November 1, 1996).

[3] As amended by Act of Sederunt (Ordinary Cause Rules) Amendment (Family Law (Scotland) Act 2006 etc.) 2006, para.2 (SSI 2006/207) (effective May 4, 2006).

[1]1. The copy initial writ served on you with this notice states that there has been no cohabitation between you and the pursuer at any time during a continuous period of two years after the date of the marriage and immediately preceding the commencement of this action. If the pursuer establishes this as a fact and the sheriff is satisfied that the marriage has broken down irretrievably, a decree will be granted.

2. Decree of divorce will end the marriage thereby affecting any right to such pension as may depend on the marriage continuing, or, on your being left a widow the state widow's pension will not be payable to you when the pursuer dies. You may also lose your rights of succession to the pursuer's estate.

[2]3. You are entitled, whether or not you dispute that there has been no such cohabitation during that two year period, to apply to the sheriff in this action—

    (a) to make financial or other provision for you under the Family Law (Scotland) Act 1985;

    (b) for an order under section 11 of the Children (Scotland) Act 1995 in respect of any child of the marriage, or any child accepted as such, who is under 16 years of age; or

    (c) for any other competent order.

4. IF YOU WISH TO APPLY FOR ANY OF THE ABOVE ORDERS you should consult a solicitor with a view to lodging a notice of intention to defend (Form F26).

Date (*insert date*)

    (*Signed*)

Solicitor for the pursuer (*add designation and business address*)
**NOTE**

[3]FORM F24

Rule 33.14(1)(b)(ii)

[4]Form of notice to defender in an action of separation where it is stated there has been two years' non-cohabitation

YOU ARE GIVEN NOTICE that—

[5]1. The copy initial writ served on you together with this notice states that there has been no cohabitation between you and the pursuer at any time during a continuous period of two years after the date of the marriage and immediately preceding the commencement of this action and that if the pursuer establishes this as a fact, and the sheriff is satisfied that there are grounds justifying decree of separation, a decree will be granted.

2. On the granting of decree of separation you will be obliged to live apart from the pursuer but the marriage will continue to subsist. You will continue to have a legal obligation to support your wife [or husband] and children.

[6]3. You are entitled, whether or not you dispute that there has been no such cohabitation during that two year period, to apply to the sheriff in this action—

    (a) to make provision under the Family Law (Scotland) Act 1985;

    (b) for an order under section 11 of the Children (Scotland) Act 1995 in respect of any child of the marriage, or any child accepted as such, who is under 16 years of age; or

    (c) for any other competent order.

4. **IF YOU WISH TO APPLY FOR ANY OF THE ABOVE ORDERS** you should consult a solicitor with a view to lodging a notice of intention to defend (Form F26).

Date (*insert date*)

    (*Signed*)

Solicitor for the pursuer (*add designation and business address*)

---

[1] As amended by Act of Sederunt (Ordinary Cause Rules) Amendment (Family Law (Scotland) Act 2006 etc.) 2006, para.2 (SSI 2006/207) (effective May 4, 2006).

[2] As amended by Act of Sederunt (Ordinary Cause Rules) Amendment (Family Law (Scotland) Act 2006 etc.) 2006, para.2 (SSI 2006/207) (effective May 4, 2006).

[3] Substituted by SI 1996/2167 (effective November 1, 1996).

[4] As amended by Act of Sederunt (Ordinary Cause Rules) Amendment (Family Law (Scotland) Act 2006 etc.) 2006, para.2 (SSI 2006/207) (effective May 4, 2006).

[5] As amended by Act of Sederunt (Ordinary Cause Rules) Amendment (Family Law (Scotland) Act 2006 etc.) 2006, para.2 (SSI 2006/207) (effective May 4, 2006).

[6] As amended by Act of Sederunt (Ordinary Cause Rules) Amendment (Family Law (Scotland) Act 2006 etc.) 2006, para.2 (SSI 2006/207) (effective May 4, 2006).

[1]FORM F24A

Rule 33.14(1)(c)

Form of notice to defender in action of divorce where an interim gender recognition certificate has been issued

YOU ARE GIVEN NOTICE that—

1. The copy initial writ served on you together with this notice states that an interim gender recognition certificate has been issued to you [or the pursuer]. If the pursuer establishes this as a fact, decree will be granted.

2. Decree of divorce will end the marriage thereby affecting any right to such pension as may depend on the marriage continuing, or, on your being left a widow the state widow's pension will not be payable to you when the pursuer dies. You may also lose your rights of succession to the pursuer's estate.

3. If the pursuer is entitled to a decree of divorce, you are nevertheless entitled to apply to the sheriff in this action—

   (a)  to make financial or other provision for you under the Family Law (Scotland) Act 1985;

   (b)  for an order under section 11 of the Children (Scotland) Act 1995 in respect of any child of the marriage, or any child accepted as such, who is under 16 years of age; or

   (c)  for any competent order.

4. IF YOU WISH TO APPLY FOR ANY OF THE ABOVE ORDERS you should consult a solicitor with a view to lodging a notice of intention to defend (Form F26).

Date (*insert date*)

(*Signed*)

Solicitor for the pursuer (*add designation and business address*)

FORM F25

[Removed by SI 1996/2167 (effective November 1, 1996).]

[2] FORM F26

Rules 33.11(1) and 33.34(2)(a)

Form of notice of intention to defend in family action

**NOTICE OF INTENTION TO DEFEND**

**PART A**

| PART A(This section to be completed by the pursuer's solicitor before service.) [Insert name and business address of solicitor for the pursuer] | Court ref. No.In an action brought in Sheriff Court | Date of expiry of period of notice |
|---|---|---|
| | Pursuer | |
| | Defender Date of service: | |

**PART B**

**(This section to be completed by the defender or defender's solicitor, and both parts of the form to be returned to the Sheriff Clerk at the above Sheriff Court on or before the date of expiry of the period of notice referred to in Part A above.)**

(*Insert place and date*)

[C.D.] (Insert designation and address), Defender, intends to

(a)  challenge the jurisdiction of the court;

(b)  oppose a crave in the initial writ;

(c)  make a claim;

(d)  seek an order;

in the action against him [or her] raised by [A.B.], (insert designation and address), Pursuer.

**PART C**

**(This section to be completed by the defender or the defender's solicitor where an order under section 11 of the Children (Scotland) Act 1995 in respect of a child is opposed by the defender).**

---

[1] Inserted by Act of Sederunt (Ordinary Cause Rules) Amendment (Family Law (Scotland) Act 2006 etc.) 2006, para.2 (SSI 2006/207) (effective May 4, 2006).

[2] Substituted by Act of Sederunt (Ordinary Cause, Summary Application, Summary Cause and Small Claim Rules) Amendment (Miscellaneous) 2005 (SSI 2005/648), para.2 (effective January 2, 2006).

**DO YOU WISH TO OPPOSE THE MAKING OF ANY ORDER CRAVED BY THE PURSUER IN RESPECT OF A CHILD?**

YES/NO*

*delete as appropriate

If you answered YES to the above question, please state here the order(s) which you wish to oppose and the reasons why the court should not make such order(s).

**PART D**

**(This section to be completed by the defender or the defender's solicitor where an order under section 11 of the Children (Scotland) Act 1995 in respect of a child is sought by the defender).**

DO YOU WISH THE COURT TO MAKE ANY ORDER UNDER SECTION 11 OF THE CHILDREN (SCOTLAND) ACT 1995 IN RESPECT OF A CHILD?

YES/NO*

*delete as appropriate

If you answered YES to the above question, please state here the order(s) which you wish the court to make and the reasons why the court should make such order(s).

**PART E**

IF YOU HAVE COMPLETED PART D OF THIS FORM YOU MUST INCLUDE EITHER CRAVE (1) OR (2) BELOW (*delete as appropriate)

(1) * Warrant for intimation of notice in terms of Form F9 on the child(ren) (insert full name(s) and date (s) of birth) is sought.

(2) * I seek to dispense with intimation on the child(ren) (insert full name(s) and date(s) of birth) for the following reasons:—

Signed

[C.D.] Defender [or [X.Y.] (add designation and business address) Solicitor for Defender]

FORM F27

**Rule 33.29(1)(b)**

Form of minute for decree in family action to which rule 33.28 applies

(*Insert name of solicitor for the pursuer*) having considered the evidence contained in the affidavits and the other documents all as specified in the schedule hereto, and being satisfied that upon the evidence a motion for decree (in terms of the crave of the initial writ) [*or in such restricted terms as may be appropriate*] may properly be made, moves the court accordingly.

In respect whereof

Signed

Solicitor for the Pursuer (*add designation and business address*)

Schedule

(*Number and specify documents considered*)

FORM F28

**Rules 33.40(c) and 33.64(1)(c)**

Form of notice of intimation to local authority or third party to whom care of a child is to be given

To (*name and address as in warrant*)

Court ref. no.

You are given NOTICE that in this action, the sheriff proposes to commit to your care the child (*insert name and address*). A copy of the initial writ is attached. If you wish to appear as a party, you must lodge a minute with the sheriff clerk (*insert address of sheriff clerk*) for leave to do so. Your minute must be lodged within 21 days of (*insert date on which intimation was given. N.B.* Rule 53(2) *relating to postal service or intimation*).

Date (*insert date*)

(*Signed*)

Solicitor for the pursuer

**NOTE**

If you decide to lodge a minute it may be in your best interest to consult a solicitor. The minute should be lodged with the sheriff clerk together with the appropriate fee of (*insert amount*) and a copy of this intimation.

**IF YOU ARE UNCERTAIN WHAT ACTION TO TAKE** you should consult a solicitor. You may be entitled to legal aid depending on your financial circumstances, and you can get information about legal aid from a solicitor. You may also obtain advice from any Citizens Advice Bureau or other advice agency.

FORM F29

**Rules 33.41 and 33.64(2)**

Form of notice of intimation to local authority of supervision order

[A.B.], (*insert designation and address*), Pursuer, against [C.D.], (*Insert designation and address*), Defender.

To (*insert name and address of local authority*)

Court ref. no.

You are given NOTICE that on (*insert date*) in the Sheriff Court at (*insert place*) the sheriff made a supervision order under section 12 of the Matrimonial Proceedings (Children) Act 1958 [*or* section 1 l(1)(b) of the Guardianship Act 1973] placing the child (*insert name and address of child*) under your supervision. A certified copy of the sheriffs interlocutor is attached.

Date (*Insert date*)

(*Signed*)

Sheriff clerk (depute)

FORM F30

**Rules 33.72(1) and 33.72(2)**

[*Omitted by Act of Sederunt (Ordinary Cause Rules) Amendment (Family Law (Scotland) Act 2006 etc.) 2006, para.2 (SSI 2006/207) (effective May 4, 2006).*]

[1, 2, 3]FORM F31

**Rule 33.74(1)**

Form of simplified divorce application under section 1 (2)(d) of the Divorce (Scotland) Act 1976

Sheriff Clerk

Sheriff Court House

....................

....................

(Telephone) ...............

APPLICATION FOR DIVORCE WITH CONSENT OF OTHER PARTY TO THE MARRIAGE (HUSBAND AND WIFE HAVING LIVED APART FOR AT LEAST ONE YEAR)

Before completing this form, you should have read the leaflet entitled "Do it yourself Divorce", which explains the circumstances in which a divorce may be sought by this method. If simplified procedure appears to suit your circumstances, you may use this form to apply for divorce. Below you will find directions designed to assist you with your application. Please follow them carefully. In the event of difficulty, you may contact any sheriff clerk's office or Citizens Advice Bureau.

**Directions for making application**

WRITE IN INK, USING BLOCK CAPITALS

| | |
|---|---|
| Application (Part 1) | 1. Complete and sign Part 1 of the form (pages 3–7), paying particular attention to the notes opposite each section. |
| Consent of husband/wife (Part 2) | 2. When you have completed Part 1 of the form, attach the (blue) instruction sheet SP3 to it and send both documents to your spouse for completion of (Part 2) the consent at (page 9). |
| | **NOTE:** If your spouse does NOT complete and sign the form of consent, your application cannot proceed further under the simplified procedure. In that event, if you still wish to obtain a divorce, you should consult a solicitor. |
| Affidavit (Part 3) | 3. When the application has been returned to you with the consent (Part 2) duly completed and signed, you should take the form to a Justice of the Peace, Notary Public, Commissioner for Oaths or other duly authorised person so that your affidavit at Part 3 (page 10) may be completed and sworn. |
| Returning completed application form to court | 4. When directions 1–3 above have been complied with, your application is now ready to be sent to the sheriff clerk at the above address. With it you must enclose: (i)   your marriage certificate (the document headed "Extract of an entry in a |

---

[1] As amended by SI 1996/2445 (effective November 1, 1996) and the Act of Sederunt (Ordinary Cause Rules) Amendment (Form of Simplified Divorce Application) 2003 (SSI 2003/ 25), para.2(2)(a) (effective January 31, 2003).

[2] As amended by Act of Sederunt (Ordinary Cause Rules) Amendment (Family Law (Scotland) Act 2006 etc.) 2006, para.2 (SSI 2006/207) (effective May 4, 2006).

[3] As amended by the Act of Sederunt (Ordinary Cause, Summary Application, Summary Cause and Small Claim Rules) Amendment (Miscellaneous) 2007 (SSI 2007/6), para.2(16)(f) (effective February 26, 2007).

Register of Marriages", which will be returned to you in due course), and

(ii) either a cheque or postal order in respect of the court fee, crossed and made payable to "the Scottish Court Service" or a completed fee exemption form,

or a completed form SP15, claiming exemption from the court fee.

5. Receipt of your application will be promptly acknowledged. Should you wish to withdraw the application for any reason, please contact the sheriff clerk immediately.

## PART 1

**WRITE IN INK, USING BLOCK CAPITALS**

1. NAME AND ADDRESS OF APPLICANT

Surname ...............

Other name(s) in full ...............

...................

Present address ...............

...................

Daytime telephone number (if any)

...................

2. NAME AND ADDRESS OF SPOUSE

Surname ...............

Other name(s) in full ...............

...................

Present address ...............

...................

Daytime telephone number (if any) ...............

3. JURISDICTION

Please indicate with a tick (✔) in the appropriate box or boxes which of the following apply:

PART A

(i) My spouse and I are habitually resident in Scotland ☐

(ii) My spouse and I were last habitually resident in Scotland, and one of ☐ us still resides there

(iii) My spouse is habitually resident in Scotland ☐

(iv) I am habitually resident in Scotland having resided there for at least a ☐ year immediately before this application was made

(v) I am habitually resident in Scotland having resided there for at least ☐ six months immediately before this application was made and am domiciled in Scotland

(vi) My spouse and I are domiciled in Scotland ☐

**If you have ticked one or more of the boxes in Part A, you should go direct to Part C. You should only complete Part B if you have not ticked any boxes in Part A**

PART B

(i) I am domiciled in Scotland ☐

(ii) My spouse is domiciled in Scotland ☐

AND

(iii) No court of a Contracting State has jurisdiction under the Council ☐ Regulation (E.C.) No. 2201/2003 of 27th November 2003 concerning jurisdiction and the recognition and enforcement of judgments in matrimonial matters and in matters of Parental Responsibility (O.J. No L.338, 23.12.2003, p.1)

PART C

(i)       I have lived at the address shown above for at least 40 days im- ☐
mediately before the date I signed this application

(ii)     My spouse has lived at the address shown above for at least 40 days ☐
immediately before the date I signed this application

(iii)    I lived at the address shown above for a period of at least 40 days ☐
ending not more than 40 days before the date I signed this application
and have no known residence in Scotland at that date

(iv)   My spouse lived at the address shown above for a period of at least 40 ☐
days ending not more than 40 days before the date I signed this application and has no known residence in Scotland at that date

## 4. DETAILS OF PRESENT MARRIAGE

Place of Marriage............... (Registration District)

Date of Marriage: Day .......... month .......... year ..........

### 5. Period of Separation

(i)      Please the date on which you ceased to live with your spouse. (If
more than 1 year, just give the month and year)

Day .......... Month .......... Year ..........

(ii)     Have you lived with your spouse since that date?          *[YES/NO]

(iii)    If yes, for how long in total did you live together before finally
separating again?

.............. months

## 6. RECONCILIATION

Is there any reasonable prospect of reconciliation with your spouse?     *[YES/NO]

Do you consider that the marriage has broken down irretrievably?     *[YES/NO]

## 7. CONSENT

Does your spouse consent to a divorce being granted?     *[YES/NO]

## 8. MENTAL DISORDER

Does your spouse have any mental disorder (whether mental illness,     *[YES/NO]
personality disorder or learning disability)?..........(if yes, give details)

## 9. CHILDREN

Are there any children of the marriage under the age of 16?     *[YES/NO]

## 10. OTHER COURT ACTIONS

Are you aware of any court actions currently proceeding in any     *[YES/NO]
country (including Scotland) which may affect your
marriage?..........(If yes, give details)                   *Delete as appropriate

## 11. DECLARATION AND REQUEST FOR DIVORCE

I confirm that the facts stated in paragraphs 1–10 above apply to my marriage.

I do NOT ask the sheriff to make any financial provision in connection with this application.

I do NOT ask the court to postpone the grant of decree under section 3A of the Divorce (Scotland) Act
1976.

I request the sheriff to grant decree of divorce from my spouse.

Date .......... Signature of applicant's spouse ...............

**IMPORTANT**

Part 1 MUST be completed, signed and dated before sending the application form to your spouse.

PART 2

NOTICE TO CONSENTING SPOUSE

*(Insert name and address of consenting spouse)*

CONSENT TO APPLICATION FOR DIVORCE (HUSBAND AND WIFE HAVING LIVED APART FOR AT LEAST ONE YEAR)

In Part 1 of the enclosed application form your spouse is applying for divorce on the ground that the marriage has broken down irretrievably because you and he [or she] have lived apart for at least one year and you consent to the divorce being granted.

Such consent must be given formally in writing at Part 2 of the application form. BEFORE completing that part, you are requested to read it over carefully so that you understand the effect of consenting to divorce. Thereafter if you wish to consent—

(a)   check the details given by the Applicant at Part 1 of the form to ensure that they are correct to the best of your knowledge;

(b)   complete Part 2 (Consent by Applicant's spouse to divorce) by entering your name and address at the appropriate place and adding your signature and the date; and

(c)   return the whole application form to your spouse at the address given in Part 1.

Once your husband or wife has completed the remainder of the form and has submitted it to the court, a copy of the whole application (including your consent) will later be served upon you formally by the sheriff clerk.

In the event of the divorce being granted, you will automatically be sent a copy of the extract decree. (Should you change your address before receiving the copy extract decree, please notify the sheriff clerk immediately.)

If you do NOT wish to consent please return the application form, with Part 2 uncompleted, to your spouse and advise him or her of your decision.

The sheriff will NOT grant a divorce on this application if Part 2 of the form is not completed by you.

Sheriff clerk (depute)
Sheriff Court (*insert address*)

CONSENT BY APPLICANT'S SPOUSE TO DIVORCE

NOTE: Before completing this part of the form, please read the notes opposite (page 8)

**I,** ....................

(*Insert full name, in BLOCK letters, of Applicant's spouse*)

residing at

....................

(*Insert address, also in BLOCK letters*)

....................

....................

HEREBY STATE THAT

(a)   I have read Part 1 of this application;

(b)   the Applicant has lived apart from me for a continuous period of one year immediately preceding the date of the application (paragraph 11 of Part 1);

(c)   I do not ask the sheriff to make any financial provision for me including—

(i)    the payment by the Applicant of a periodical allowance (i.e. a regular payment of money weekly or monthly, etc. for maintenance);

(ii)   the payment by the Applicant of a capital sum (i.e. a lump sum payment);

(d)   I understand that divorce may result in the loss to me of property rights;

(e)   I do not ask the court to postpone the grant of decree under section 3A of the Divorce (Scotland) Act 1976; and

(f)    I CONSENT TO DECREE OF DIVORCE BEING GRANTED IN RESPECT OF THIS APPLICATION.

Date .......... Signature ..............

NOTE: You may withdraw your consent, even after giving it, at any time before divorce is granted by the sheriff. Should you wish to do so, please contact the sheriff clerk immediately.

PART 3

APPLICANT'S AFFIDAVIT

To be completed by the Applicant only after Parts 1 and 2 have been signed and dated.

**I,** (*insert Applicant's full name*) ..............

residing at (*insert Applicant's present home address*) ..........

....................

....................

SWEAR that to the best of my knowledge and belief:

(1)   the facts stated in Part 1 of this Application are true; and

(2)   the signature in Part 2 of this Application is that of my *husband/wife.

Signature of Applicant..............

253

| To be completed by Justice of the Peace, Notary Public or Commissioner for Oaths | SWORN at (insert place) ...............<br><br>this .......... day of ..........19......... before me (*insert full name*) ............... (*insert full address*).............. ..................... |
|---|---|

..................

Signature ...............

*Justice of the Peace/Notary Public/Commissioner for Oaths

*Delete as appropriate

[1]FORM F32

[1, 3, 4]FORM F33

Rule 33.74(2)

Form of simplified divorce application under section 1(2)(e) of the Divorce (Scotland) Act 1976

Sheriff Clerk

Sheriff Court House

..................

..................

(Telephone)...............

APPLICATION FOR DIVORCE (HUSBAND AND WIFE HAVING LIVED APART FOR AT LEAST TWO YEARS)

Before completing this form, you should have read the leaflet entitled "Do it yourself Divorce", which explains the circumstances in which a divorce may be sought by this method. If the simplified procedure appears to suit your circumstances, you may use this form to apply for divorce.

Below you will find directions to assist you with your application. Please follow them carefully. In the event of difficulty, you may contact any sheriff clerk's office or Citizens Advice Bureau.

**Directions for making application**

WRITE IN INK, USING BLOCK CAPITALS

| Application- (Part 1) | 1. Complete and sign Part 1 of the form (pages 3-7), paying particular attention to the notes opposite each section. |
|---|---|
| Affidavits(Part 2) | 2. When you have completed Part 1, you should take the form to a Justice of the Peace, Notary Public, Commissioner for Oaths or other duly authorised person in order that your affidavit in Part 2 (page 8) may be completed and sworn. |
| Returning completed application form to court | 3. When directions 1 and 2 above have been complied with, your is now ready to be sent to the sheriff clerk at the above address. With it you application must enclose: |

    (i)    your marriage certificate (the document headed "Extract of an entry in a Register of Marriages", which will be returned to you in due course). Check the notes on page 2 to see if you need to obtain a letter from the General Register Office stating that there is no record of your spouse having divorced you, and

    (ii)    either a cheque or postal order in respect of the court fee, crossed and made out to "the Scottish Court Service" or a completed fee exemption form.

4. Receipt of your application will be promptly acknowledged. Should you wish to withdraw the application for any reason, please contact the sheriff clerk immediately.

PART 1

**WRITE IN INK, USING BLOCK CAPITALS**

1. NAME AND ADDRESS OF APPLICANT

Surname ...............

---

[1] [Repealed by SI 1996/2445 (effective November 1, 1996).]

Other name(s) in full ...............
Present address ...............
....................
....................
Daytime telephone number (if any) ...............
2. NAME OF SPOUSE
Surname ...............
Other name(s) in full ...............
3. ADDRESS OF SPOUSE (if the address of your spouse is not known, please enter "not known" in this paragraph and proceed to paragraph 4)
Present address ...............
....................
....................
Daytime telephone (if any) ...............
4. Only complete this paragraph if you do not know the present address of your spouse
NEXT-OF-KIN
Name ...............
Address ...............
....................
....................
Relationship to your spouse ...............
CHILDREN OF THE MARRIAGE

Names and dates of   Addresses
birth

....................          ....................

                             ....................

....................          ....................

                             ....................

....................          ....................

                             ....................

If insufficient space is available to list all the children of the marriage, please continue on a separate sheet and attach to this form.
5. JURISDICTION
Please indicate with a tick ( ✔ ) in the appropriate box or boxes which of the following apply:
PART A

| (i) | My spouse and I are habitually resident in Scotland | ☐ |
|---|---|---|
| (ii) | My spouse and I were last habitually resident in Scotland, and one of us still resides there | ☐ |
| (iii) | My spouse is habitually resident in Scotland | ☐ |
| (iv) | I am habitually resident in Scotland having resided there for at least a year immediately before this application was made | ☐ |
| (v) | I am habitually resident in Scotland having resided there for at least six months immediately before this application was made and am domiciled in Scotland | ☐ |
| (vi) | My spouse and I are domiciled in Scotland | ☐ |

**If you have ticked one or more of the boxes in Part A, you should go direct to Part C. You should only complete Part B if you have not ticked any boxes in Part A**
PART B

(i)      I am domiciled in Scotland       ☐

(ii)     My spouse is domiciled in Scotland      ☐

AND

(iii)    No court of a Contracting State has jurisdiction under the Council Regula- ☐
tion (E.C.) No. 2201/2003 of 27th November 2003 concerning jurisdiction
and the recognition and enforcement of judgments in matrimonial matters
and in matters of Parental Responsibility (O.J. No L.338, 23.12.2003, p.1)

PART C

(i)      I have lived at the address shown above for at least 40 days immediately ☐
before the date I signed this application

(ii)     My spouse has lived at the address shown above for at least 40 days im- ☐
mediately before the date I signed this application

(iii)    I lived at the address shown above for a period of at least 40 days ending ☐
not more than 40 days before the date I signed this application and have no
known residence in Scotland at that date

(iv)    My spouse lived at the address shown above for a period of at least 40 ☐
days ending not more than 40 days before the date I signed this application
and has no known residence in Scotland at that date

## 6. DETAILS OF PRESENT MARRIAGE

Place of Marriage ............... (Registration District)

Date of Marriage: Day .......... month .......... year ..........

## 7. PERIOD OF SEPARATION

(i)      Please state the date on which you ceased to live with your spouse. (If
more than 2 years, just give the month and year) Day .......... Month
.......... Year ..........

(ii)     Have you lived with your spouse since that date?       *[YES/NO]

(iii)    If yes, for how long in total did you live together before finally
separating again?

                                      ............... months

## 8. RECONCILIATION

Is there any reasonable prospect of reconciliation with your spouse?   *[YES/NO]

Do you consider that the marriage has broken down irretrievably?   *[YES/NO]

## 9. MENTAL DISORDER

Does your spouse have any mental disorder (whether mental illness, personality *[YES/NO]
disorder or learning disability)?..........(If yes, give details)

## 10. CHILDREN

Are there any children of the marriage under the age of 16?      *[YES/NO]

## 11. Other Court Actions

Are you aware of any court actions currently proceeding in any country (includ- *[YES/NO]
ing Scotland) which may affect your marriage?

(If yes, give details)                              *Delete as appropriate

## 12. DECLARATION AND REQUEST FOR DIVORCE

I confirm that the facts stated in paragraphs 1–12 above apply to my marriage.

I do NOT ask the sheriff to make any financial provision in connection with this application.

I do NOT ask the court to postpone the grant of decree under section 3A of the Divorce (Scotland) Act
1976.

I request the sheriff to grant decree of divorce from my husband or wife.

Date ..............

Signature of Applicant ..............

PART 2

APPLICANT'S AFFIDAVIT

(To be completed by the Applicant only after Part 1 has been signed and dated.)

I, (*insert full name*) ..............

residing at (*insert present home address*) ..........

....................

SWEAR that to the best of my knowledge and belief the facts stated in Part 1 of this Application are true.

Signature of Applicant ..............

SWORN at (*insert place*)

| | |
|---|---|
| To be completed by Justice of the Peace, Notary Public or Commissioner for Oaths | this .......... day of .......... 19.......... before me (*insert full name*) .............. of (insert full address) .............. |

....................

....................

Signature ..............

*Justice of the Peace/Notary Public/Commissioner for Oaths

*Delete as appropriate

[1,2]FORM F33A

**Rule 33.74(1)(3)**

Form of simplified divorce application under section 1(1)(b) of the Divorce (Scotland) Act 1976

Sheriff Clerk

Sheriff Court House

....................

....................

(Telephone) ..............

APPLICATION FOR DIVORCE (INTERIM GENDER RECOGNITION CERTIFICATE ISSUED TO ONE OF THE PARTIES AFTER THE MARRIAGE

Before completing this form, you should have read the leaflet entitled "Do it yourself Divorce", which explains the circumstances in which a divorce may be sought by this method. If the simplified procedure appears to suit your circumstances, you may use this form to apply for divorce. Below you will find directions designed to assist you with your application. Please follow them carefully. In the event of difficulty, you may contact any sheriff clerk's office or Citizen's Advice Bureau.

**Directions for making application**

WRITE IN INK, USING BLOCK CAPITALS

| | |
|---|---|
| Application (Part 1) | 1. Complete and sign Part 1 of the form (pages 3-7), paying particular attention to the notes opposite each section. |
| Affidavits (Part 2) | 2. When you have completed Part 1, you should take the form to a Justice of the Peace, Notary Public, Commissioner for Oaths or other duly authorised person so that your affidavit at Part 2 (page 8) may be completed and sworn. |
| Returning completed application form to court | 3. When directions 1-2 above have been complied with, your application is now ready to be sent to the sheriff clerk at the above address. With it you must enclose:<br>(i) your marriage certificate (the document headed "Extract of an entry in a Register of Marriages, which will be returned to you in due course). Check the notes on page 2 to see if you also need to obtain a letter from |

---

[1] Inserted by Act of Sederunt (Ordinary Cause Rules) Amendment (Family Law (Scotland) Act 2006 etc.) 2006, para.2 (SSI 2006/207) (effective May 4, 2006).

[2] As amended by the Act of Sederunt (Ordinary Cause, Summary Application, Summary Cause and Small Claim Rules) Amendment (Miscellaneous) 2007 (SSI 2007/6), para.2(16)(h) (effective February 26, 2007).

the General Register Office stating that there is no record that your spouse has divorced you, and,

(ii) either a cheque or postal order in respect of the court fee, crossed and made payable to "Scottish Court Service or a completed fee exemption form, and

(iii) the interim gender recognition certificate or a copy sealed with the seal of the Gender Recognition Panels and certified to be a true copy by an officer authorised by the President of Gender Recognition Panels.

4. Receipt of your application will be promptly acknowledged. Should you wish to withdraw the application for any reason, please contact the sheriff clerk immediately.

Part 1

**WRITE IN INK, USING BLOCK CAPITALS**

1. NAME AND ADDRESS OF APPLICANT

Surname...............

Other name(s) in full...............

...............

Present address...............

........................

Daytime telephone number (if any)...............

2. NAME OF SPOUSE

Surname...............

Other name(s) in full...............

3. ADDRESS OF SPOUSE (if the address of your spouse is not known, please enter "not known" in this paragraph and proceed to paragraph 4)

Present address...............

....................

....................

Daytime telephone (if any)...............

4. Only complete this paragraph if you do not know the present address of your spouse

NEXT-OF-KIN

Name...............

Address...............

....................

....................

Relationship to your spouse...............

CHILDREN OF THE MARRIAGE

| **Names and dates of birth** | **Addresses** |
|---|---|
| ............... | ............... |
| | ............... |
| ............... | ............... |
| | ............... |
| ............... | ............... |
| | ............... |

If insufficient space is available to list all the children of the marriage, please continue on a separate sheet and attach to this form.

5. JURISDICTION

Please indicate with a tick (✔) in the appropriate box or boxes which of the following apply:

PART A

(i) My spouse and I are habitually resident in Scotland ☐

(ii) My spouse and I were last habitually resident in Scotland, and one of us still resides there ☐

(iii) My spouse is habitually resident in Scotland ☐

(iv)   I am habitually resident in Scotland having resided there for at least a year im- ☐
       mediately before this application was made

(v)    I am habitually resident in Scotland having resided there for at least six months im- ☐
       mediately before this application was made and am domiciled in Scotland

(vi)   My spouse and I are domiciled in Scotland                                          ☐

**If you have ticked one or more of the boxes in Part A, you should go direct to Part C. You should only complete Part B if you have not ticked any boxes in Part A**

Part B

(i)                              I am domiciled in Scotland              ☐

(ii)                             My spouse is domiciled in Scotland      ☐

AND

(iii)                            No court of a Contracting  ☐
                                 State has jurisdiction under
                                 Council Regulation (E.C.)
                                 No. 2201/2003 of 27th No-
                                 vember 2003 concerning ju-
                                 risdiction and the recognition
                                 and enforcement of judg-
                                 ments in matrimonial matters
                                 and matters of parental re-
                                 sponsibility (O.J. No. L. 338,
                                 23.12.2003, p.1.)

Part C

(i)                              I have lived at the address  ☐
                                 shown above for at least 40
                                 days immediately before the
                                 date I signed this application

(ii)                             My spouse has lived at the ad-  ☐
                                 dress shown above for at least
                                 40 days immediately before
                                 the date I signed this applica-
                                 tion

(iii)                            I lived at the address shown  ☐
                                 above for a period of at least
                                 40 days ending not more than
                                 40 days before the date I
                                 signed this application and
                                 have no known residence in
                                 Scotland at that date

(iv)                             My spouse lived at the ad-  ☐
                                 dress shown above for a pe-
                                 riod of at least 40 days end-
                                 ing not more than 40 days
                                 before the date I signed this
                                 application and has no known
                                 residence in Scotland at that
                                 date

6. DETAILS OF PRESENT MARRIAGE

   Place of Marriage.......... (Registration District)

   Date of Marriage: Day.......... month.......... year..........

   7. DETAILS OF ISSUE OF INTERIM GENDER RECOGNITION CERTIFICATE

   (i) Please state whether the interim gender recognition certificate has been issued to you or your spouse

   (ii) Please state the date the interim gender recognition certificate was issued Day.......... Month..........
Year..........

### 8. MENTAL DISORDER

Does your spouse have any mental disorder (whether mental illness, personality
disorder or learning disability)? (If yes, give details) \*[YES/NO]

### 9. CHILDREN

Are there any children of the marriage under the age of 16? \*[YES/NO]

### 10. OTHER COURT ACTIONS

Are you aware of any court actions currently proceeding in any country (including
Scotland) which may affect your marriage? (If yes, give details) \*[YES/NO]

* Delete as appropriate

### 11. DECLARATION AND REQUEST FOR DIVORCE

I confirm that the facts stated in paragraphs 1–10 above apply to my marriage.

I do NOT ask the sheriff to make any financial provision in connection with this application.

I do NOT ask the court to postpone the grant of decree under section 3A of the Divorce (Scotland) Act 1976.

I request the sheriff to grant decree of divorce from my husband or wife.

Date............... Signature of Applicant...............

PART 2

APPLICANT'S AFFIDAVIT

To be completed by the Applicant only after Part 1 has been signed and dated.

I, (*Insert Applicant's full name*)...............

residing at (insert Applicant's present home address)...............

....................

....................

SWEAR that to the best of my knowledge and belief the facts stated in Part 1 of this Application are true.

Signature of Applicant....................

| To be completed by Justice of the Peace, Notary Public or Commissioner for Oaths | SWORN at (*insert place*)............... this.......... day of.......... 20.......... before me (*insert full name*)...............of (*insert full address*).................... |
|---|---|
| | Signature............... |
| | *Justice of the Peace/Notary Public/Commissioner for Oaths |
| | *Delete as appropriate |

### [1,2]FORM F34

**Rule 33.76(3)(a)**

Form of citation in application relying on the facts in section 1(2)(d) of the Divorce (Scotland) Act 1976

(*Insert name and address of non-applicant spouse*)

APPLICATION FOR DIVORCE (HUSBAND AND WIFE HAVING LIVED APART FOR AT LEAST ONE YEAR WITH CONSENT OF OTHER PARTY)

Your spouse has applied to the sheriff for divorce on the ground that the marriage has broken down irretrievably because you and he or she have lived apart for a period of at least one year and you consent to divorce being granted.

A copy of the application is hereby served upon you.

1. Please note:

---

[1] As amended by Act of Sederunt (Ordinary Cause Rules) Amendment (Family Law (Scotland) Act 2006 etc.) 2006, para.2 (SSI 2006/207) (effective May 4, 2006).

[2] As amended by the Act of Sederunt (Ordinary Cause, Summary Application, Summary Cause and Small Claim Rules) Amendment (Miscellaneous) 2007 (SSI 2007/6), para.2(16)(i) (effective February 26, 2007).

(a)  that the sheriff may not make financial provision under this procedure and that your spouse is making no claim for—

    (i)  the payment by you of a periodical allowance (i.e. a regular payment of money weekly or monthly, etc. for maintenance);

    (ii)  the payment by you of a capital sum (i.e. a lump sum payment);

(b)  that no application may be made under this procedure for postponement of decree under section 3A of the Divorce (Scotland) Act 1976 (postponement of decree where impediment to religious marriage exists).

2. Divorce may result in the loss to you of property rights (e.g. the right to succeed to the Applicant's estate on his or her death) or the right, where appropriate, to a widow's pension.

3. If you wish to oppose the granting of a divorce, you should put your reasons in writing and send your letter to the address shown below. Your letter must reach the sheriff clerk before (insert date).

4. In the event of the divorce being granted, you will be sent a copy of the extract decree. Should you change your address before receiving the copy extract decree, please notify the sheriff clerk immediately.

Signed

Sheriff clerk (depute)

(insert address and telephone number of the sheriff clerk) or Sheriff officer

NOTE: If you wish to exercise your right to make a claim for financial provision, or if you wish to apply for postponement of decree under section 3A of the Divorce (Scotland) Act 1976 (postponement of decree where impediment to religious marriage exists), you should immediately advise the sheriff clerk that you oppose the application for that reason, and thereafter consult a solicitor.

[1,2]FORM F35

**Rule 33.76(3)(b)**

Form of citation in application relying on the facts in section 1 (2)(e) of the Divorce (Scotland) Act 1976

(Insert name and address of non-applicant spouse)

APPLICATION FOR DIVORCE (HUSBAND AND WIFE HAVING LIVED APART FOR AT LEAST TWO YEARS)

Your spouse has applied to the sheriff for divorce on the ground that the marriage has broken down irretrievably because you and he or she have lived apart for a period of at least two years.

A copy of the application is hereby served upon you.

1. Please note:

(a)  that the sheriff may not make financial provision under this procedure and that your spouse is making no claim for—

    (i)  the payment by you of a periodical allowance (i.e. a regular payment of money weekly or monthly, etc., for maintenance);

    (ii)  the payment by you of a capital sum (i.e. a lump sum payment);

(b)  that no application may be made under this procedure for postponement of decree under section 3A of the Divorce (Scotland) Act 1976 (postponement of decree where impediment to religious marriage exists).

2. Divorce may result in the loss to you of property rights (e.g. the right to succeed to the Applicant's estate on his or her death) or the right, where appropriate, to a widow's pension.

3. If you wish to oppose the granting of a divorce, you should put your reasons in writing and send your letter to the address shown below. Your letter must reach the sheriff clerk before (insert date).

4. In the event of the divorce being granted, you will be sent a copy of the extract decree. Should you change your address before receiving the copy extract decree, please notify the sheriff clerk immediately.

Signed..........

Sheriff clerk (depute)

(insert the address and telephone number of the sheriff court)

or Sheriff officer

NOTE: If you wish to exercise your right to make a claim for financial provision, or if you wish to apply for postponement of decree under section 3A of the Divorce (Scotland) Act 1976 (postponement of

---

[1] As amended by Act of Sederunt (Ordinary Cause Rules) Amendment (Family Law (Scotland) Act 2006 etc.) 2006, para.2 (SSI 2006/207) (effective May 4, 2006).

[2] As amended by the Act of Sederunt (Ordinary Cause, Summary Application, Summary Cause and Small Claim Rules) Amendment (Miscellaneous) 2007 (SSI 2007/6), para.2(16)G) (effective February 26, 2007).

decree where impediment to religious marriage exists), you should immediately advise the sheriff clerk that you oppose the application for that reason, and thereafter consult a solicitor.

[1,2]FORM 35A

Rule 33.76(3)(c)

Form of citation in application on grounds under section 1(1)(b) of the Divorce (Scotland) Act 1976

(*Insert name and address of non-applicant spouse*)

APPLICATION FOR DIVORCE (INTERIM GENDER RECOGNITION CERTIFICATE ISSUED TO ONE OF THE PARTIES AFTER THE MARRIAGE)

Your spouse has applied to the sheriff for divorce on the ground that an interim gender recognition certificate has been issued to you or your spouse after your marriage.

A copy of the application is hereby served upon you.

1. Please note that the sheriff may not make financial provision under this procedure and that your spouse is making no claim for—
   (a) the payment by you of a periodical allowance (i.e. a regular payment of money weekly or monthly, etc. for maintenance);
   (b) the payment by you of a capital sum (i.e. a lump sum payment).

2. Divorce may result in the loss to you of property rights (e.g. the right to succeed to the Applicant's estate on his or her death) or the right, where appropriate, to a pension.

2A. Please note that no application may be made under this procedure for postponement of decree under section 3A of the Divorce (Scotland) Act 1976 (postponement of decree where impediment to religious marriage exists).

3. If you wish to oppose the granting of a decree of divorce, you should put your reasons in writing and send your letter to the address shown below. Your letter must reach the sheriff clerk before (*insert date*).

4. In the event of the decree of divorce being granted, you will be sent a copy of the extract decree. Should you change your address before receiving the copy extract decree, please notify the sheriff clerk immediately.

(*Signed*)

Sheriff clerk (depute) (*insert address and telephone number of the sheriff clerk*) [*or* Sheriff officer]

NOTE: If you wish to exercise your right to make a claim for financial provision, or if you wish to apply for postponement of decree under section 3A of the Divorce (Scotland) Act 1976 (postponement of decree where impediment to religious marriage exists), you should immediately advise the sheriff clerk that you oppose the application for that reason, and thereafter consult a solicitor.

FORM F36

**Rule 33.77(1)(a)**

Form of intimation of simplified divorce application for display on the walls of court

Court ref. no.

An application for divorce has been made in this sheriff court by [A.B.], (*insert designation and address*), Applicant, naming [C.D.], (*insert designation and address*) as Respondent.

If [C.D.] wishes to oppose the granting of decree of divorce he [*or* she] should immediately contact the sheriff clerk from whom he [*or* she] may obtain a copy of the application.

Date (*insert date*)

Signed

Sheriff clerk (depute)

FORM F37

**Rule 33.77(2)**

Form of intimation to children and next-of-kin in simplified divorce application

To (*insert name and address*)

Court ref. no.

You are hereby given NOTICE that an application for divorce has been made against (*insert name of respondent*) your (*insert relationship e.g. father, mother, brother or other relative as the case may be*). A copy of this application is attached.

---

[1] As inserted by Act of Sederunt (Ordinary Cause Rules) Amendment (Family Law (Scotland) Act 2006 etc.) 2006, para.2 (SSI 2006/207) (effective May 4, 2006).

[2] As amended by the Act of Sederunt (Ordinary Cause, Summary Application, Summary Cause and Small Claim Rules) Amendment (Miscellaneous) 2007 (SSI 2007/6), para.2(16)(k) (effective February 26, 2007).

If you know of his or her present address, you are requested to inform the sheriff clerk (*insert address of sheriff clerk*) in writing immediately. You may also, if you wish, oppose the granting of decree of divorce by sending a letter to the court giving your reasons for your opposition to the application. Your letter must be sent to the sheriff clerk within 21 days of (*insert date on which intimation was given. N.B. Rule 53(2) relating to postal service or intimation*).

Date (*insert date*)

Signed

Sheriff clerk (depute)

**NOTE**

**IF YOU ARE UNCERTAIN WHAT ACTION TO TAKE** you should consult a solicitor. You may be entitled to legal aid depending on your financial circumstances, and you can get information about legal aid from a solicitor. You may also obtain advice from any Citizens Advice Bureau or other advice agency.

Rule 33.80(2)

FORM F38

Form of extract decree of divorce in simplified divorce application

At (*insert place and date*)

in an action in the Sheriff Court of the Sheriffdom of (*insert name of sheriffdom*) at (*insert place of sheriff court*)

at the instance of [A.B.], (*insert full name of applicant*), Applicant,

against (*insert full name of respondent*), Respondent,

who were married at (*insert place*) on (*insert date*),

the sheriff pronounced decree divorcing the Respondent from the Applicant. Extracted at (*insert place and date*)

by me, sheriff clerk of the Sheriffdom of (*insert name of sheriffdom*).

Signed

Sheriff clerk (depute)

Rule 33.90

FORM F39

Form of certificate relating to the making of a maintenance assessment under the Child Support Act 1991

Sheriff Court (*insert address*)

Date (*insert date*)

I certify that notification has been received from the Secretary of State under section 10 of the Child Support Act 1991 of the making of a maintenance assessment under that Act which supersedes the decree or order granted on (*insert date*) in relation to aliment for (*insert the name(s) of child(ren)*) with effect from (*insert date*).

Signed

Sheriff clerk (depute)

Rule 33.90

FORM F40

Form of certificate relating to the cancellation or ceasing to have effect of a maintenance assessment under the Child Support Act 1991

Sheriff Court (*insert address*) Date (*insert date*)

I certify that notification has been received from the Secretary of State under section 10 of the Child Support Act 1991 that the maintenance assessment made on (*insert date*) has been cancelled [*or* ceased to have effect] on (*insert date*).

Signed

Sheriff clerk (depute)

Rule 33.22A(2)

[1]FORM F41

Form of intimation to parties of a Child Welfare Hearing

Sheriff Court (*insert address and telephone number*)

Court Ref No:

In the action [A.B.], (*design*), Pursuer against [C.D.], (*design*), Defender

---

[1] Substituted by SSI 2000/239 (effective October 2, 2000).

YOU ARE GIVEN NOTICE that a Child Welfare Hearing has been fixed for (*insert time*) on (*insert date*) at (*insert place*).

Date (*insert date*)

Signed..............
Sheriff Clerk (Depute)

**NOTE**

**Please note that in terms of** Rule 33.22A(5) **parties to the action must attend personally**

\* *IF YOU ARE UNCERTAIN WHAT ACTION TO TAKE* you should consult a solicitor. You may be eligible for legal aid depending on your financial circumstances, and you can get information about legal aid from a solicitor. You may also obtain information from any Citizens' Advice Bureau or other advice agency.

\* This section to be deleted where service is to be made on a solicitor.

Rule 33.27A(1)

[1]FORM F42

Form of Certificate under Article 32 of Council Regulation (EC) No. 1347/2000 of 29th May 2000 on jurisdiction and the recognition and enforcement of judgments in matrimonial matters and in matters of parental responsibility for children of both spouses

**Matrimonial matters**

Sheriffdom of (*insert name of sheriffdom*)

at (*insert place of Sheriff Court*)

I hereby certify, pursuant to Article 32 of Council Regulation (EC) No. 1347/2000 of 29th May 2000 on jurisdiction and the recognition and enforcement of judgments in matrimonial matters and in matters of parental responsibility for children of both spouses, concerning judgments in matrimonial matters, the following:

**1.** Member State of origin: (*insert country*)

**2.** Court or authority issuing the certificate:

2.1 Name: Sheriff Court of (*insert name*)

2.2 Address: (*insert address of sheriff court*)

2.3 Tel/Fax/E-mail: (*insert Tel/Fax/E-mail*)

**3.** Marriage:

3.1   Wife:

    3.1.1   Full Name: (*insert name*)

    3.1.2   Country and place of birth: (*insert country and place*)

    3.1.3   Date of birth: (*insert date*)

3.2   Husband:

    3.2.1   Full Name: (*insert name*)

    3.2.2   Country and place of birth: (*insert country and place*)

    3.2.3   Date of birth: (*insert date*)

3.3   Country, place (where available ) and date of marriage

    3.3.1   Country of marriage : (*insert country*)

    3.3.2   Place of marriage (where available): (*insert place*)

    3.3.3   Date of marriage: (*insert date*)

**4.** Court which delivered the judgment:

4.1 Name of Court: (*insert name*)

4.2 Place of Court: (*insert place*)

**5.** Judgment:

5.1 Date: (*insert date*)

5.2 Case reference number: (*insert reference number*)

5.3 Type of judgment:

| | | |
|---|---|---|
| 5.3.1 | Divorce | ☐ |
| 5.3.3 | Legal separation | ☐ |

5.4 Was the Judgment given in default of appearance ?

---

[1] Inserted by Act of Sederunt (Ordinary Cause Rules) Amendment (European Matrimonial and Parental Responsibility Jurisdiction and Judgments) 2001 (SSI 2001/144), para.4 (effective April 2, 2001).

| | | |
|---|---|---|
| 5.4.1 | No | ☐ |
| 5.4.2 | Yes | ☐ |

**6.** Name of parties to whom legal aid has been granted: *(insert names)*

**7.** Is the judgment subject to further appeal under the law of the Member State of origin?

| | | |
|---|---|---|
| 7.1 | No | ☐ |
| 7.2 | Yes | ☐ |

**8.** Date of legal effect in the Member State where the judgment was given:

8.1 of divorce: *(insert date)*

8.2 of separation: *(insert date)*

*(Signed)*

Sheriff Clerk

*(Place and date)*

Rule 33.27A(1)

[1]FORM F43

Form of Certificate under Article 32 of Council Regulation (EC) No. 1347/2000 of 29th May 2000 on jurisdiction and the recognition and enforcement of judgments in matrimonial matters and in matters of parental responsibility for children of both spouses

**Parental Responsibility**

Sheriffdom of *(insert name of sheriffdom)*

at *(insert place of Sheriff Court)*

I hereby certify, pursuant to Article 32 of Council Regulation (EC) No. 1347/2000 of 29th May 2000 on jurisdiction and the recognition and enforcement of judgments in Matrimonial matters and in matters of parental responsibility for children of both spouses, concerning judgments in matters of parental responsibility, the following:

**1.** Member State of origin: *(insert country)*

**2.** Court or authority issuing the certificate:

2.1 Name: Sheriff Court of *(insert name)*

2.2 Address: *(insert address of sheriff court)*

2.3 Tel/Fax/E-mail: *(insert tel/fax/e-mail)*

**3.** Parents:

3.1   Mother:

    3.1.1   Full Name: *(insert name)*

    3.1.2   Date and place of birth: *(insert date and place)*

3.2   Father:

    3.2.1   Full Name: *(insert name)*

    3.2.2   Date and place of birth: *(insert date and place)*

**4.** Court which delivered Judgment:

4.1 Name of Court: *(insert name)*

4.2 Place of Court; *(insert place)*

5. Judgment:

5.1 Date: *(insert date)*

5.2 Case Reference number: *(insert reference number)*

5.3 Was the Judgment given in default of appearance?

| | | |
|---|---|---|
| 5.3.1 | No | ☐ |
| 5.3.2 | Yes | ☐ |

**6.** Children who are covered by the judgment:

6.1 Full Name and date of birth: *(insert name and date of birth)*

6.2 Full Name and date of birth: *(insert name and date of birth)*

6.3 Full Name and date of birth: *(insert name and date of birth)*

6.4 Full Name and date of birth: *(insert name and date of birth)*

---

[1] Inserted by Act of Sederunt (Ordinary Cause Rules) Amendment (European Matrimonial and Parental Responsibility Jurisdiction and Judgments) 2001 (SSI 2001/144), para.4 (effective April 2, 2001).

**7.** Names of parties to whom legal aid has been granted: *(insert names)*

**8.** Attestation of enforceability and service

8.1 Is the judgment enforceable according to the law of the Member State of origin?

| | | |
|---|---|---|
| 8.1.1 | No | ☐ |
| 8.1.2 | Yes | ☐ |

8.2 Has the judgment been served on the party against whom enforcement is sought?

| | | |
|---|---|---|
| 8.2.1 | Yes | ☐ |

8.2.1.1 Full name of party: *(insert name)*

   8.2.1.2 Date of service: *(insert date)*

| | | |
|---|---|---|
| 8.2.2 | No | ☐ |

(Place and date)

*(Signed)*

Sheriff Clerk

### [1]FORM CP1

Rule 33A.7(1)(a)

Form of intimation to children and next-of-kin in an action of dissolution of civil partnership or separation of civil partners where defender's address is not known

Court ref. no.

To *(insert name and address as in warrant)*

You are given NOTICE that an action of dissolution of a civil partnership [or separation of civil partners] has been raised against *(insert name)* your *(insert relationship, e.g. father, mother, brother or other relative as the case may be)*. If you know of his [or her] present address, you are requested to inform the sheriff clerk *(insert address of sheriff clerk)* in writing immediately. If you wish to appear as a party you must lodge a minute with the sheriff clerk for leave to do so. Your minute must be lodged within 21 days of *(insert date on which intimation was given. N.B. Rule 5.3(2) relating to postal service or intimation)*.

Date *(insert date)*

*(Signed)*

Solicitor for the pursuer

*(insert designation and business address)*

**NOTE**

If you decide to lodge a minute it may be in your best interests to consult a solicitor. The minute should be lodged with the sheriff clerk together with the appropriate fee of *(insert amount)* and a copy of this intimation.

**IF YOU ARE UNCERTAIN WHAT ACTION TO TAKE** you should consult a solicitor. You may be entitled to legal aid depending on your financial circumstances, and you can get information about legal aid from a solicitor. You may also obtain advice from any Citizens Advice Bureau or other advice agency.

### [2]FORM CP2

Rule 33A.7(1)(b)

Form of intimation to children, next-of-kin, guardian and attorney in action of dissolution of civil partnership or separation of civil partners where defender suffers from a mental disorder

Court ref. no.

To *(insert name and address as in warrant)*

You are given NOTICE that an action of dissolution of a civil partnership [or separation of civil partners] has been raised against *(insert name)* your *(insert relationship, e.g. father, mother, brother or other relative, ward or granter of a power of attorney as the case may be)*. A copy of the initial writ is enclosed. If you wish to appear as a party, you must lodge a minute with the sheriff clerk *(insert address*

---

[1] Inserted by Act of Sederunt (Ordinary Cause Rules) Amendment (Civil Partnership Act 2004) 2005 (SSI 2005/638), para.3 (effective December 8, 2005).

[2] Inserted by Act of Sederunt (Ordinary Cause Rules) Amendment (Civil Partnership Act 2004) 2005 (SSI 2005/638), para.3 (effective December 8, 2005).

*of sheriff clerk),* for leave to do so. Your minute must be lodged within 21 days of *(insert date on which intimation was given.* N.B. Rule 5.3(2) *relating to postal service or intimation).*

Date *(insert date)*

*(Signed)*
Solicitor for the pursuer
*(insert designation and business address)*

**NOTE**

If you decide to lodge a minute it may be in your best interests to consult a solicitor. The minute should be lodged with the sheriff clerk together with the appropriate fee of *(insert amount)* and a copy of this intimation.

**IF YOU ARE UNCERTAIN WHAT ACTION TO TAKE** you should consult a solicitor. You may be entitled to legal aid depending on your financial circumstances, and you can get information about legal aid from a solicitor. You may also obtain advice from any Citizens Advice Bureau or other advice agency.

[1]FORM CP3

Rule 33A.7(1)(c)(i) and (ii)

Form of intimation to a local authority or third party who may be liable to maintain a child in a civil partnership action

Court ref. no.

To *(insert name and address as in warrant)*

YOU ARE GIVEN NOTICE that in this action, the court may make an order under section 11 of the Children (Scotland) Act 1995 in respect of *(insert name and address),* a child in your care *[or liable to be maintained by you].* A copy of the initial writ is attached. If you wish to appear as a party, you must lodge a minute with the sheriff clerk *(insert address of sheriff clerk),* for leave to do so. Your minute must be lodged within 21 days of *(insert date on which intimation was given.* N.B. Rule 5.3(2) *relating to postal service or intimation).*

Date *(insert date)*

*(Signed)*
Solicitor for the pursuer
*(insert designation and business address)*

**NOTE**

If you decide to lodge a minute it may be in your best interests to consult a solicitor. The minute should be lodged with the sheriff clerk together with the appropriate fee of *(insert amount)* and a copy of this intimation.

**IF YOU ARE UNCERTAIN WHAT ACTION TO TAKE** you should consult a solicitor. You may be entitled to legal aid depending on your financial circumstances, and you can get information about legal aid from a solicitor. You may also obtain advice from any Citizens

[2]FORM CP4

Rule 33A.7(1)(c)(iii)

Form of intimation to person who in fact exercises care or control of a child in a civil partnership action

Court ref. no.

To *(insert name and address as in warrant)*

YOU ARE GIVEN NOTICE that in this action, the court may make an order under section 11 of the Children (Scotland) Act 1995 in respect of *(insert name and address),* a child at present in your care or control. A copy of the initial writ is attached. If you wish to appear as a party, you must lodge a minute with the sheriff clerk *(insert address of sheriff clerk),* for leave to do so. Your minute must be lodged within 21 days of *(insert date on which Intimation was given.* N.B. Rule 5.3(2) *relating to postal service or intimation).*

Date *(insert date)*

*(Signed)*
Solicitor for the pursuer
*(insert designation and business address)*

**NOTE**

---

[1] Inserted by Act of Sederunt (Ordinary Cause Rules) Amendment (Civil Partnership Act 2004) 2005 (SSI 2005/638), para.3 (effective December 8, 2005).
[2] Inserted by Act of Sederunt (Ordinary Cause Rules) Amendment (Civil Partnership Act 2004) 2005 (SSI 2005/638), para.3 (effective December 8, 2005).

If you decide to lodge a minute it may be in your best interests to consult a solicitor. The minute should be lodged with the sheriff clerk together with the appropriate fee of (*insert amount*) and a copy of this intimation.

**IF YOU ARE UNCERTAIN WHAT ACTION TO TAKE** you should consult a solicitor. You may be entitled to legal aid depending on your financial circumstances, and you can get information about legal aid from a solicitor. You may also obtain advice from any Citizens Advice Bureau or other advice agency.

[1]FORM CP5

Rule 33A.7(1)(d)

Form of notice to parent or guardian in a civil partnership action which includes a crave for a section 11 order in respect of a child

Court ref. no.

1. YOU ARE GIVEN NOTICE that in this action, the pursuer is applying for an order under section 11 of the Children (Scotland) Act 1995 in respect of the child (*insert name of child*). A copy of the initial writ is served on you and is attached to this notice.

2. If you wish to oppose this action, or oppose the granting of any order applied for by the pursuer in respect of the child, you must lodge a notice of intention to defend (Form CP16). See Form CP16 attached for further details.

Date (*insert date*)

(*Signed*)
Pursuer
[*or* Solicitor for the pursuer]
(*insert designation and business address*)

**NOTE: IF YOU ARE UNCERTAIN WHAT ACTION TO TAKE** you should consult a solicitor. You may be entitled to legal aid depending on your financial circumstances, and you can get information about legal aid from a solicitor. You may also obtain advice from any Citizens Advice Bureau or other advice agency.

[2]FORM CP6

Rule 33A.7(1)(e), 33A.7(4) and 33A.12(2) and (3)

Form of notice to local authority

Court ref. no.

To (*insert name and address*)

1. YOU ARE GIVEN NOTICE that in an action in the Sheriff Court at (*insert address*) the pursuer has applied for a residence order in respect of the child (*insert name of child*). A copy of the initial writ is enclosed.

2. If you wish to oppose this action, or oppose the granting of any order applied for by the pursuer in respect of the child, you must lodge a notice of intention to defend (Form CP16). See Form CP16 attached for further details.

Date (*insert date*)

(*Signed*)
Solicitor for the pursuer
(*insert designation and business address*)

[3]FORM CP7

Rule 33A.7(1)(f), 33A.15(2) and 33A.19(1)(a)

Form of intimation in a civil partnership action which includes a crave for a section 11 order

Court ref. no.

Part A

This part must be completed by the Pursuer's solicitor in language a child is capable of understanding.

To (1)

---

[1] Inserted by Act of Sederunt (Ordinary Cause Rules) Amendment (Civil Partnership Act 2004) 2005 (SSI 2005/638), para.3 (effective December 8, 2005).

[2] Inserted by Act of Sederunt (Ordinary Cause Rules) Amendment (Civil Partnership Act 2004) 2005 (SSI 2005/638), para.3 (effective December 8, 2005) and substituted by the Act of Sederunt (Sheriff Court Rules) (Miscellaneous Amendments) (No.2) 2010 (SSI 2010/416) r.7 (effective January 1, 2011).

[3] Inserted by Act of Sederunt (Ordinary Cause Rules) Amendment (Civil Partnership Act 2004) 2005 (SSI 2005/638), para.3 (effective December 8, 2005).

The Sheriff (the person who has to decide about your future) has been asked by (2) to decide:—

(a) (3) and (4)

(b) (5)

(c) (6)

If you want to tell the Sheriff what you think about the things your (2) .......... has asked the Sheriff to decide about your future you should complete Part B of this form and send it to the Sheriff Clerk at (7) by (8) .......... . An envelope which does not need a postage stamp is enclosed for you to use to return the form.

**IF YOU DO NOT UNDERSTAND THIS FORM OR IF YOU WANT HELP TO COMPLETE IT you may get help from a SOLICITOR or contact the SCOTTISH CHILD LAW CENTRE on the FREE ADVICE TELEPHONE LINE ON 0800 328 8970.**

If you return the form it will be given to the Sheriff. The Sheriff may wish to speak with you and ask you to come and see him or her.

## NOTES FOR COMPLETION

| | |
|---|---|
| (1) Insert name and address of child | (2) Insert relationship to the child of party making the application to court. |
| (3) Insert appropriate wording for residence | (4) Insert address |
| (5) Insert appropriate wording for contact order sought. | (6) Insert appropriate wording for any other order sought. |
| (7) Insert address of sheriff clerk. | (8) Insert the date occurring 21 days after the date on which intimation is given. N.B. Rule 5.3(2) relating to intimation and service. |
| (9) Insert court reference number. | (10) Insert name and address of parties to the action. |

PART B

IF YOU WISH THE SHERIFF TO KNOW YOUR VIEWS ABOUT YOUR FUTURE YOU SHOULD COMPLETE THIS PART OF THE FORM

To the Sheriff Clerk, (7)

Court Ref. No. (9)

(10)....................

QUESTION (1): DO YOU WISH THE SHERIFF TO KNOW WHAT YOUR VIEWS ARE ABOUT YOUR FUTURE?

(PLEASE TICK BOX)

| | |
|---|---|
| Yes | |
| No | |

If you have ticked YES please also answer Question (2) *or* (3)

QUESTION (2): WOULD YOU LIKE A FRIEND, RELATIVE OR OTHER PERSON TO TELL THE SHERIFF YOUR VIEWS ABOUT YOUR FUTURE?

(PLEASE TICK BOX)

| | |
|---|---|
| Yes | |
| No | |

If you have ticked YES please write the name and address of the person you wish to tell the Sheriff your views in Box (A) below. You should also tell that person what your views are about your future.

| | |
|---|---|
| BOX A: | (NAME)............................ |

```
┌─────────────────────────────────────────────────────────────────┐
│          (ADDRESS)..............................                  │
│          ....................                                     │
│                                                                   │
│      Is   this    A                □      A rela-      □          │
│      person:      friend?                 tive?                   │
│                                                                   │
│                   A                □      Other?       □          │
│                   teacher?                                        │
└─────────────────────────────────────────────────────────────────┘
```

OR

QUESTION (3): WOULD YOU LIKE TO WRITE TO THE SHERIFF AND TELL HIM WHAT YOUR VIEWS ARE ABOUT YOUR FUTURE?

(PLEASE TICK BOX)

| | |
|---|---|
| Yes | |
| No | |

If you decide that you wish to write to the Sheriff you can write what your views are about your future in Box (B) below or on a separate piece of paper. If you decide to write your views on a separate piece of paper you should send it along with this form to the Sheriff Clerk in the envelope provided.

BOX B: WHAT I HAVE TO SAY ABOUT MY FUTURE:-

NAME: ...................

ADDRESS: ....................

DATE: ....................

[1]FORM CP8

Rule 33A.7(1)(g)

Form of intimation to creditor in application for order for the transfer of property under section 8 of the Family Law (Scotland) Act 1985 in a civil partnership action

Court ref. no.

To (*insert name and address as in warrant*)

You are given NOTICE that in this action, an order is sought for the transfer of property (*specify the order*), over which you hold a security. A copy of the initial writ is attached. If you wish to appear as a party, you must lodge a minute with the sheriff clerk (*insert address of sheriff clerk*), for leave to do so. Your minute must be lodged within 21 days of (*insert date on which intimation was given.* N.B. Rule 5.3(2) *relating to postal service or intimation*).

Date (*insert date*)

(*Signed*)
Solicitor for the pursuer
(*insert designation and business address*)

**NOTE**

If you decide to lodge a minute it may be in your best interests to consult a solicitor. The minute should be lodged with the sheriff clerk together with the appropriate fee of (*insert amount*) and a copy of this intimation.

**IF YOU ARE UNCERTAIN WHAT ACTION TO TAKE** you should consult a solicitor. You may be entitled to legal aid depending on your financial circumstances, and you can get information about legal aid from a solicitor. You may also obtain advice from any Citizens Advice Bureau or other advice agency.

[2]FORM CP9

Rule 33A.7(1)(h)

---

[1] Inserted by Act of Sederunt (Ordinary Cause Rules) Amendment (Civil Partnership Act 2004) 2005 (SSI 2005/638), para.3 (effective December 8, 2005).
[2] Inserted by Act of Sederunt (Ordinary Cause Rules) Amendment (Civil Partnership Act 2004) 2005 (SSI 2005/638), para.3 (effective December 8, 2005).

Form of intimation in a civil partnership action where the pursuer makes an application for an order under section 18 of the Family Law (Scotland) Act 1985

Court ref. no.

To (*insert name and address as in warrant*)

You are given NOTICE that in this action, the pursuer craves the court to make an order under section 18 of the Family Law (Scotland) Act 1985. A copy of the initial writ is attached. If you wish to appear as a party, you must lodge a minute with the sheriff clerk (*insert address of sheriff clerk*), for leave to do so. Your minute must be lodged within 21 days of (*insert date on which intimation was given. N.B. Rule 5.3(2) relating to postal service or intimation*).

Date (*insert date*)

(*Signed*)

Solicitor for the pursuer

(*insert designation and business address*)

**NOTE**

If you decide to lodge a minute it may be in your best interests to consult a solicitor. The minute should be lodged with the sheriff clerk together with the appropriate fee of (*insert amount*) and a copy of this intimation.

**IF YOU ARE UNCERTAIN WHAT ACTION TO TAKE** you should consult a solicitor. You may be entitled to legal aid depending on your financial circumstances, and you can get information about legal aid from a solicitor. You may also obtain advice from any Citizens Advice Bureau or other advice agency.

[1]FORM CP10

Rule 33A.7(1)(i)

Form of intimation in an action where an application is made under Chapter 3 of Part 3 of the Civil Partnership Act 2004

Court ref. no

To (*insert name and address as in warrant*)

You are given NOTICE that in this action the pursuer craves the court to make an order under Section (*insert the section under which the order(s) is sought*) of Chapter 3 of Part 3 of the Civil Partnership Act 2004. A copy of the initial writ is attached. If you wish to appear as a party, you must lodge a minute with the sheriff clerk (*insert address of sheriff clerk*), for leave to do so. Your minute must be lodged within 21 days of (*insert date on which intimation was given. N.B. Rule 5.3(2) relating to postal service or intimation*).

Date (*insert date*)

(*Signed*)

Solicitor for the pursuer

(*insert designation and business address*)

**NOTE**

If you decide to lodge a minute it may be in your best interests to consult a solicitor. The minute should be lodged with the sheriff clerk together with the appropriate fee of (*insert amount*) and a copy of this intimation.

**IF YOU ARE UNCERTAIN WHAT ACTION TO TAKE** you should consult a solicitor. You may be entitled to legal aid depending on your financial circumstances, and you can get information about legal aid from a solicitor. You may also obtain advice from any Citizens Advice Bureau or other advice agency.

[2]FORM CP11

Rule 33A.7(1)(j)

Form of intimation to person responsible for pension arrangement in relation to an order for payment in respect of pension lump sum under section 12A of the Family Law (Scotland) Act 1985 in a civil partnership action

Court ref. no.

To (*insert name and address as in warrant*)

You are given NOTICE that in this action, the pursuer has applied for an order under section 8 of the Family Law (Scotland) Act 1985 for a capital sum in circumstances where the family property includes

---

[1] Inserted by Act of Sederunt (Ordinary Cause Rules) Amendment (Civil Partnership Act 2004) 2005 (SSI 2005/638), para.3 (effective December 8, 2005).

[2] Inserted by Act of Sederunt (Ordinary Cause Rules) Amendment (Civil Partnership Act 2004) 2005 (SSI 2005/638), para.3 (effective December 8, 2005).

rights in a pension arrangement under which a lump sum is payable. The relevant pension arrangement is (*give brief details, including number, if known*). If you wish to appear as a party, you must lodge a minute with the sheriff clerk (*insert address of sheriff clerk*), for leave to do so. Your minute must be lodged within 21 days of (*insert date on which intimation was given. N.B. Rule 5.3(2) relating to postal service or intimation*).

Date (*insert date*)

(*Signed*)

Solicitor for the pursuer

(*insert designation and business address*)

**NOTE**

If you decide to lodge a minute it may be in your best interests to consult a solicitor. The minute should be lodged with the sheriff clerk together with the appropriate fee of (*insert amount*) and a copy of this intimation.

**IF YOU ARE UNCERTAIN WHAT ACTION TO TAKE** you should consult a solicitor. You may be entitled to legal aid depending on your financial circumstances, and you can get information about legal aid from a solicitor. You may also obtain advice from any Citizens Advice Bureau or other advice agency.

[1]FORM CP12

Rule 33A.7(1)(k)

Form of intimation to person responsible for pension arrangement in relation to pension sharing order under section 8(1)(baa) of the Family Law (Scotland) Act 1985 in a civil partnership action

Court ref. no.

To (*insert name and address as in warrant*)

You are given NOTICE that in this action, the pursuer has applied under section 8 of the Family Law (Scotland) Act 1985 for a pension sharing order in circumstances where the family property includes rights in a pension arrangement. The relevant pension arrangement is (*give brief details, including number, if known*). If you wish to appear as a party, you must lodge a minute with the sheriff clerk (*insert address of sheriff clerk*), for leave to do so. Your minute must be lodged within 21 days of (*insert date on which intimation was given. N.B. Rule 5.3(2) relating to postal service or intimation*).

Date (*insert date*)

(*Signed*)

Solicitor for the pursuer

(*insert designation and business address*)

**NOTE**

If you decide to lodge a minute it may be in your best interests to consult a solicitor. The minute should be lodged with the sheriff clerk together with the appropriate fee of (*insert amount*) and a copy of this intimation.

**IF YOU ARE UNCERTAIN WHAT ACTION TO TAKE** you should consult a solicitor. You may be entitled to legal aid depending on your financial circumstances, and you can get information about legal aid from a solicitor. You may also obtain advice from any Citizens Advice Bureau or other advice agency.

[2]FORM CP12A

Rule 33A.7(1)(l)

Form of intimation to Board of the Pension Protection Fund in relation to pension compensation sharing order under section 8(1)(bab) of the Family Law (Scotland) Act 1985 in a civil partnership action

Court ref. no.

To (*insert name and address as in warrant*)

You are given NOTICE that in this action the pursuer has applied under section 8(1)(bab) of the Family Law (Scotland) Act 1985 for a pension compensation sharing order in circumstances where the family property includes rights to Pension Protection Fund compensation. The relevant pension arrangement is (*give brief details, including number, if known*). If you wish to appear as a party, you must lodge a minute with the sheriff clerk (*insert address of sheriff clerk*), for leave to do so. Your minute must be lodged within 21 days of (*insert date on which intimation was given. N.B. Rule 5.3(2) relating to postal service or intimation*).

---

[1] Inserted by Act of Sederunt (Ordinary Cause Rules) Amendment (Civil Partnership Act 2004) 2005 (SSI 2005/638), para.3 (effective December 8, 2005).

[2] As inserted by the Act of Sederunt (Sheriff Court Rules) (Miscellaneous Amendments) 2011 (SSI 2011/193) r.15 (effective April 6, 2011).

Date (*insert date*)

(*Signed*)
Solicitor for the pursuer
(*insert designation and business address*)

### [1]FORM CP12B

Rule 33.7(1)(m)

Form of intimation to Board of the Pension Protection Fund in relation to an order under section 12B(2) of the Family Law (Scotland) Act 1985 in a civil partnership action

Court ref. no.

To (*insert name and address as in warrant*)

You arc given NOTICE that in this action the pursuer has applied under section 8(1)(bb) of the Family Law (Scotland) Act 1985 for an order under section 12B(2) of the Act in circumstances where the family property includes rights to Pension Protection Fund compensation. The relevant pension arrangement is (*give brief details, including number, if known*). If you wish to appear as a party, you must lodge a minute with the sheriff clerk (*insert address of sheriff clerk*), for leave to do so. Your minute must be lodged within 21 days of (*insert date on which intimation was given. N.B. Rule 5.3(2) relating to postal service or intimation*).

Date (*insert date*)

(*Signed*)
Solicitor for the pursuer
(*insert designation and business address*)

### [2]FORM CP13

Rule 33A.8(3)

Form of intimation to person with whom an association is alleged to have occurred in a civil partnership action

Court ref. no.

To (*insert name and address as in warrant*)

You are given NOTICE that in this action, the defender is alleged to have had an association with you. A copy of the initial writ is attached. If you wish to dispute the truth of the allegation made against you, you must lodge a minute with the sheriff clerk (*insert address of sheriff clerk*), for leave to appear as a party. Your minute must be lodged within 21 days of (*insert date on which intimation was given. N.B. Rule 5.3(2) relating to postal service or intimation*).

Date (*insert date*)

(*Signed*)
Solicitor for the pursuer
(*insert designation and business address*)

**NOTE**

If you decide to lodge a minute it may be in your best interests to consult a solicitor. The minute should be lodged with the sheriff clerk together with the appropriate fee of (*insert amount*) and a copy of this intimation.

**IF YOU ARE UNCERTAIN WHAT ACTION TO TAKE** you should consult a solicitor. You may be entitled to legal aid depending on your financial circumstances, and you can get information about legal aid from a solicitor. You may also obtain advice from any Citizens Advice Bureau or other advice agency.

Rules 33A.9(5) and 33A.34(4)                [3] FORM CP13A

Form of statement of civil partnership property in the cause

SHERIFFDOM OF (*insert name of sheriffdom*)

AT (*insert place of sheriff court*)

[A.B.], (*insert designation and address*, Pursuer against

[C.D..], (*insert designation and address*, Defender Court ref. no:

---

[1] As inserted by the Act of Sederunt (Sheriff Court Rules) (Miscellaneous Amendments) 2011 (SSI 2011/193) r.15 (effective April 6, 2011).

[2] Inserted by Act of Sederunt (Ordinary Cause Rules) Amendment (Civil Partnership Act 2004) 2005 (SSI 2005/638), para.3(effective December 8, 2005).

[3] As inserted by the Act of Sederunt (Sheriff Court Rules) (Miscellaneous Amendments) 2012 (SSI 2012/188) para.4 (effective August 1, 2012).

| |
|---|
| **The [Pursuer] [Defender]'s\* financial position at ( *insert date* ), being the relevant date as defined in section 10(3) of the Family Law (Scotland) Act 1985** |
| Here list all assets owned by you, including assets which are jointly owned (if any) e.g. bank or building society accounts; shares or other investments; houses; land; pension entitlement; and life policies: |
| Here list your outstanding debts including joint debts with the other party: |
| Date (*insert date*) |
| I certify that this information is correct to the best of my knowledge and belief. *(Signed)* |
| [Pursuer][Defender]\* |

(\*delete as applicable)

Rule 33A.10                                    [1]FORM CP14

Form of warrant of citation in a civil partnership action

Court ref. no.

(*Insert place and date*)

Grants warrant to cite the defender (*insert name and address of defender*) by serving upon him [*or* her*] a copy of the writ and warrant upon a period of notice of (*insert period of notice*) days, and ordains the defender to lodge a notice of intention to defend with the sheriff clerk at (*insert address of sheriff court*), if he [*or* she] wishes to:

(a)    challenge the jurisdiction of the court;
(b)    oppose any claim made or order sought;
(c)    make any claim or seek any order.

[Meantime grants interim interdict, or warrant to arrest on the dependence].

Rule 33A.11(1) and 33A.13(1)(a)                [2]FORM CP15

Form of citation in a civil partnership action

CITATION

SHERIFFDOM OF (*insert name of sheriffdom*)

AT (*insert place of sheriff court*)

[A.B.], (*insert designation and address*), Pursuer, against [C.D.], (*insert designation and address*), Defender.

(*Insert place and date*)

Court ref. no.

You [C.D.], are hereby served with this copy writ and warrant, with Form CP16 (notice of intention to defend) [and (*insert details of any other form of notice served, e.g. any of the forms served in accordance with* rule 33A.14.)].

Form CP16 is served on you for use should you wish to intimate an intention to defend the action.

**IF YOU WISH TO—**

(a)    challenge the jurisdiction of the court;
(b)    oppose any claim made or order sought;
(c)    make any claim; or
(d)    seek any order;

you should consult a solicitor with a view to lodging a notice of intention to defend (Form CP16). The notice of intention to defend, together with the court fee of £ (*insert amount*) must be lodged with the sheriff clerk at the above address within 21 days (*or insert appropriate period of notice*) of (*insert the date on which service was executed. N.B. Rule 5.3(2) relating to postal service or intimation*).

---

[1] Inserted by Act of Sederunt (Ordinary Cause Rules) Amendment (Civil Partnership Act 2004) 2005 (SSI 2005/638), para.3 (effective December 8, 2005).
[2] Inserted by Act of Sederunt (Ordinary Cause Rules) Amendment (Civil Partnership Act 2004) 2005 (SSI 2005/638), para.3 (effective December 8, 2005).

**IF YOU ARE UNCERTAIN WHAT ACTION TO TAKE** you should consult a solicitor. You may be entitled to legal aid depending on your financial circumstances, and you can get information about legal aid from a solicitor. You may also obtain advice from any Citizens Advice Bureau or other advice agency.

**PLEASE NOTE THAT IF YOU DO NOTHING IN ANSWER TO THIS DOCUMENT** the court may regard you as admitting the claim made against you and the pursuer may obtain decree against you in your absence.

(*Signed*)

[P.Q.], Sheriff officer

[*or*

[X.Y.], (*insert designation and business address*)

Solicitor for the pursuer]

Rules 33A.11(1) and 33A.34(2)(a)        [1]FORM CP 16

Form of notice of intention to defend in a civil partnership action

**Notice of Intention to Defend**

**Part A**

PART A        Court ref. No.        Date of expiry of period of notice

(This section to be completed by the pursuer's solicitor before service.)

In an action brought in Sheriff Court

[*Insert name and business address of solicitor for the pursuer*]    Pursuer

Defender

Date of service

**Part B**

**(This section to be completed by the defender or defender's solicitor, and both parts of the form to be returned to the Sheriff Clerk at the above Sheriff Court on or before the date of expiry of the period of notice referred to in Part A above.)**

(*Insert place and date*)

[C.D.] (*Insert designation and address*), Defender, intends to

(a)    challenge the jurisdiction of the court;

(b)    oppose a crave in the initial writ;

(c)    make a claim;

(d)    seek an order;

in the action against him [*or* her] raised by [A.B.], (*insert designation and address*), Pursuer.

**Part C**

**(This section to be completed by the defender or the defender's solicitor where an order under** section 11 of the Children (Scotland) Act 1995 **in respect of a child is opposed by the defender).**

DO YOU WISH TO OPPOSE THE MAKING OF ANY ORDER CRAVED BY THE PURSUER IN RESPECT OF A CHILD?

YES/NO*

*delete as appropriate

If you answered YES to the above question, please state here the order(s) which you wish to oppose and the reasons why the court should not make such order(s).

**Part D**

**(This section to be completed by the defender or the defender's solicitor where an order under** section 11 of the Children (Scotland) Act 1995 **in respect of a child is sought by the defender).**

DO YOU WISH THE COURT TO MAKE ANY ORDER UNDER SECTION 11 OF THE CHILDREN (SCOTLAND) ACT 1995 IN RESPECT OF A CHILD?

---

[1] Inserted by Act of Sederunt (Ordinary Cause Rules) Amendment (Civil Partnership Act 2004) 2005 (SSI 2005/638), para.3 (effective December 8, 2005).

YES/NO*

*delete as appropriate

If you answered YES to the above question, please state here the order(s) which you wish the court to make and the reasons why the court should make such order(s).

Part E

IF YOU HAVE COMPLETED PART D OF THIS FORM YOU MUST INCLUDE EITHER CRAVE (1) OR (2) BELOW (*delete as appropriate)

(1)  * Warrant for intimation of notice in terms of Form CP7 on the child(ren) (*insert full name(s) and date(s) of birth*) is sought.

(2)  * I seek to dispense with intimation on the child(ren) (*insert full name(s) and date(s) of birth*) for the following reasons:—

Signed

[C.D.] Defender [or [X.Y.]

(*add designation and business address*)

Solicitor for Defender]

Rule 33A.11(2)                                             [1](FORM CP17

Form of certificate of citation in a civil partnership action

Certificate of Citation

(*Insert place and date*) I,.......... hereby certify that upon the.......... day of.......... I duly cited [C.D.], Defender, to answer to the foregoing writ. This I did by (*state method of service; if by-officer and not by post, add*: in the presence of [L.M.], (*insert designation*), witness hereto with me subscribing; *and insert details of any forms of intimation or notice sent including details of the person to whom intimation sent and the method of service*).

(*Signed*)

[P.Q.], Sheriff officer

[L.M.], witness

[*or*

[X.Y.] (*add designation and business address*)

Solicitor for the pursuer]

Rule 33A.13(1)(c)                                          [2]FORM CP18

Form of request to medical officer of hospital or similar institution in a civil partnership action

To (*insert name and address of medical officer*)

In terms of rule 33A.13(1)(c) of the Ordinary Cause Rules of the Sheriff Court a copy of the initial writ at the instance of (*insert name and address of pursuer*), Pursuer, against (*insert name and address of defender*), Defender, is enclosed and you are requested to

(a)  deliver it personally to (*insert name of defender*), and

(b)  explain the contents to him or her,

unless you are satisfied that such delivery or explanation would be dangerous to his or her health or mental condition. You are further requested to complete and return to me in the enclosed stamped addressed envelope the certificate appended hereto, making necessary deletions.

Date (insert date).........

(*Signed*).........

Solicitor for the pursuer

(*insert designation and business address*)

Rule 33A.13(1)(d) and 33A.13(2)                            [3]FORM CP19

Form of certificate by medical officer of hospital or similar institution in a civil partnership action

Court ref. no.

---

[1] Inserted by Act of Sederunt (Ordinary Cause Rules) Amendment (Civil Partnership Act 2004) 2005 (SSI 2005/638), para.3 (effective December 8, 2005).

[2] Inserted by Act of Sederunt (Ordinary Cause Rules) Amendment (Civil Partnership Act 2004) 2005 (SSI 2005/638), para.3 (effective December 8, 2005).

[3] Inserted by Act of Sederunt (Ordinary Cause Rules) Amendment (Civil Partnership Act 2004) 2005 (SSI 2005/638), para.3 (effective December 8, 2005).

I (*insert name and designation*) certify that I have received a copy initial writ in an action of (*type of civil partnership action to be inserted by the party requesting service*) at the instance of (*insert name and designation*), Pursuer, against (*insert name and designation*), Defender, and that

\* I have on the.......... day of.......... personally delivered a copy thereof to the said defender who is under my care at (*insert address*) and I have explained the contents or purport thereof to him or her, *or*

\* I have not delivered a copy thereof to the said defender who is under my care at (*insert address*) and I have not explained the contents thereof to him or her because (*state reasons*).

Date (*insert date*)

(*Signed*)

Medical officer (*add designation and address*)
\* Delete as appropriate.

Rule 33A.14(1)(a)(i)          [1]FORM CP20

Form of notice to defender where it is stated that defender consents to granting decree of dissolution of a civil partnership

YOU ARE GIVEN NOTICE that the copy initial writ served on you with this notice states that you consent to the grant of decree of dissolution of your civil partnership.

    1.    If you do so consent the consequences for you are that—

        [2](a)    provided the pursuer establishes the fact that he [*or* she] has not cohabited with you at any time during a continuous period of one year after the date of registration of your civil partnership and immediately preceding the bringing of this action and that you consent, a decree of dissolution of your civil partnership will be granted;

        (b)    on the grant of a decree of dissolution of your civil partnership you may lose your rights of succession to the pursuer's estate; and

        (c)    decree of dissolution will end your civil partnership thereby affecting any right to such pension as may depend on the civil partnership continuing, or, your right to any state pension that may have been payable to you on the death of your civil partner.

Apart from these, there may be other consequences for you depending upon your particular circumstances.

    2.    You are entitled, whether or not you consent to the grant of decree of dissolution of your civil partnership, to apply to the sheriff in this action—

        (a)    to make financial or other provision for you under the Family Law (Scotland) Act 1985;

        (b)    for an order under section 11 of the Children (Scotland) Act 1995 in respect of any child of the family within the meaning of section 101(7) of the Civil Partnership Act 2004; or

        (c)    for any other competent order.

    3.    IF YOU WISH TO APPLY FOR ANY OF THE ABOVE ORDERS you should consult a solicitor with a view to lodging a notice of intention to defend (Form CP16).

    4.    If, after consideration, you wish to consent to the grant of decree of dissolution of your civil partnership in this action, you should complete and sign the attached notice of consent (Form CP21) and send it to the sheriff clerk at the sheriff court referred to in the initial writ within 21 days of (*insert the date on which service was executed N.B. Rule 5.3(2) relating to postal service*).

    5.    If, at a later stage, you wish to withdraw your consent to decree being granted against you in this action, you must inform the sheriff clerk immediately in writing.

Date (*insert date*)

(*Signed*)
Solicitor for the pursuer
(*insert designation and business address*)

Rules 33A.14(1)(a)(i) and 33A.18(1)          [3]FORM CP21

---

[1] Inserted by Act of Sederunt (Ordinary Cause Rules) Amendment (Civil Partnership Act 2004) 2005 (SSI 2005/638), para.3 (effective December 8, 2005).

[2] As amended by Act of Sederunt (Ordinary Cause Rules) Amendment (Family Law (Scotland) Act 2006 etc.) 2006, para.2 (SSI 2006/207) (effective May 4, 2006).

[3] Inserted by Act of Sederunt (Ordinary Cause Rules) Amendment (Civil Partnership Act 2004) 2005 (SSI 2005/638), para.3 (effective December 8, 2005).

Form of notice of consent in actions of dissolution of a civil partnership under section 117(3)(c) of the Civil Partnership Act 2004

Court ref. no.

[A.B.], (*insert designation and address*), Pursuer, against [C.D.], (*insert designation and address*), Defender.

I, (*full name and address of the defender to be inserted by pursuer or pursuer's solicitor before sending notice*) have received a copy of the initial writ in the action against me at the instance of (*full name and address of pursuer to be inserted by pursuer or pursuer's solicitor before sending notice*). I understand that it states that I consent to the grant of decree of dissolution of the civil partnership in this action. I have considered the consequences for me mentioned in the notice (Form CP20) sent to me with this notice. I consent to the grant of decree of dissolution of the civil partnership in this action.

Date (insert date).........

(Signed)

Defender

Rule 33A.14(1)(a)(ii)                    [1]FORM CP22

Form of notice to defender where it is stated that defender consents to the granting of decree of separation of civil partners

YOU ARE GIVEN NOTICE that the copy initial writ served on you with this notice states that you consent to the grant of decree of separation of you and your civil partner.

1.    If you do so consent the consequences for you are that—

[2](a)    provided the pursuer establishes the fact that he [*or* she] has not cohabited with you at any time during a continuous period of one year after the date of registration of your civil partnership and immediately preceding the bringing of this action and that you consent, a decree of separation of civil partners will be granted;

(b)    on the grant of a decree of separation of civil partners you will be obliged to live apart from the pursuer but the civil partnership will continue to subsist; you will continue to have a legal obligation to support your civil partner and any child of the family within the meaning of section 101(7) of the Civil Partnership Act 2004; and

Apart from these, there may be other consequences for you depending upon your particular circumstances.

2.    You are entitled, whether or not you consent to the grant of decree of separation of civil partners, to apply to the sheriff in this action—

(a)    to make financial or other provision for you under the Family Law (Scotland) Act 1985;

(b)    for an order under section 11 of the Children (Scotland) Act 1995 in respect of any child of the family within the meaning of section 101(7) of the Civil Partnership Act 2004; or

(c)    for any other competent order.

3.    IF YOU WISH TO APPLY FOR ANY OF THE ABOVE ORDERS you should consult a solicitor with a view to lodging a notice of intention to defend (Form CP16).

4.    If, after consideration, you wish to consent to the grant of decree of separation of civil partners in this action, you should complete and sign the attached notice of consent (Form CP23) and send it to the sheriff clerk at the sheriff court referred to in the initial writ and other papers within 21 days of (*insert the date on which service was executed. N.B. Rule 5.3(2) relating to postal service or intimation*).

5.    If, at a later stage, you wish to withdraw your consent to decree being granted against you in this action, you must inform the sheriff clerk immediately in writing.

Date (*insert date*)                    (*Signed*)

Solicitor for the pursuer (*add designation and business address*)

Rules 33A.14(1)(a)(ii) and 33A.18(1)                    [3]FORM CP23

---

[1] Inserted by Act of Sederunt (Ordinary Cause Rules) Amendment (Civil Partnership Act 2004) 2005 (SSI 2005/638), para.3 (effective December 8, 2005).

[2] As amended by Act of Sederunt (Ordinary Cause Rules) Amendment (Family Law (Scotland) Act 2006 etc.) 2006, para.2 (SSI 2006/207) (effective May 4, 2006).

[3] Inserted by Act of Sederunt (Ordinary Cause Rules) Amendment (Civil Partnership Act 2004) 2005 (SSI 2005/638), para.3 (effective December 8, 2005).

Form of notice of consent in actions of separation of civil partners under section 120 of the Civil Partnership Act 2004

Court ref. no

[A.B.], (*insert designation and address*), Pursuer against [C.D.], (*insert designation and address*), Defender.

I, (*full name and address of the defender to be inserted by pursuer or pursuer's solicitor before sending notice*) confirm that I have received a copy of the initial writ in the action against me at the instance of (*full name and address of pursuer to be inserted by pursuer or pursuer's solicitor before sending notice*). I understand that it states that I consent to the grant of decree of separation of civil partners in this action. I have considered the consequences for me mentioned in the notice (Form CP22) sent together with this notice. I consent to the grant of decree of separation of civil partners in this action.

Date (*insert date*)

(*Signed*)
Defender

Rule 33A.14(1)(b)(i)         [1] [2]FORM CP24

Form of notice to defender in an action for dissolution of a civil partnership where it is stated there has been two years' non-cohabitation

YOU ARE GIVEN NOTICE that—

1. The copy initial writ served on you with this notice states that there has been no cohabitation between you and the pursuer at any time during a continuous period of two years after the date of registration of the civil partnership and immediately preceding the commencement of this action. If the pursuer establishes this as a fact and the sheriff is satisfied that the civil partnership has broken down irretrievably, a decree will be granted.
2. Decree of dissolution will end the civil partnership thereby affecting any right to such pension as may depend on the civil partnership continuing or your right to any state pension that may have been payable to you on the death of your civil partner. You may also lose your rights of succession to the pursuer's estate.
3. You are entitled, whether or not you dispute that there has been no such cohabitation during that five year period, to apply to the sheriff in this action—
    (a) to make financial or other provision for you under the Family Law (Scotland) Act
    (b) for an order under section 11 of the Children (Scotland) Act 1995 in respect of any child of the family within the meaning of section 101(7) of the Civil Partnership Act 2004; or
    (c) for any other competent order.
4. IF YOU WISH TO APPLY FOR ANY OF THE ABOVE ORDERS you should consult a solicitor with a view to lodging a notice of intention to defend (Form CP16).

Date (*insert date*)

(*Signed*)
Solicitor for the pursuer (*add designation and business address*)

**Rule 33A.14(1)(b)(ii)**         [3, 4]FORM CP25

Form of notice to defender in an action for separation of civil partners where it is stated there has been two years' non-cohabitation

YOU ARE GIVEN NOTICE that—

1. The copy initial writ served on you with this notice states that there has been no cohabitation between you and the pursuer at any time during a continuous period of five years after the date of registration of the civil partnership and immediately preceding the commencement of this action. If the pursuer establishes this as a fact and the sheriff is satisfied that there are grounds justifying a decree of separation of civil partners, a decree will be granted.
2. On the granting of decree of separation you will be obliged to live apart from the pursuer but the

---

[1] Inserted by Act of Sederunt (Ordinary Cause Rules) Amendment (Civil Partnership Act 2004) 2005 (SSI 2005/638), para.3 (effective December 8, 2005).
[2] As amended by Act of Sederunt (Ordinary Cause Rules) Amendment (Family Law (Scotland) Act 2006 etc.) 2006, para.2 (SSI 2006/207) (effective May 4, 2006).
[3] Inserted by Act of Sederunt (Ordinary Cause Rules) Amendment (Civil Partnership Act 2004) 2005 (SSI 2005/638), para.3 (effective December 8, 2005).
[4] As amended by Act of Sederunt (Ordinary Cause Rules) Amendment (Family Law (Scotland) Act 2006 etc.) 2006, para.2 (SSI 2006/207) (effective May 4, 2006).

civil partnership will continue to subsist. You will continue to have a legal obligation to support your civil partner and any child of the family within the meaning of section 101(7) of the Civil Partnership Act 2004.

3.    You are entitled, whether or not you dispute that there has been no such cohabitation during that two year period, to apply to the sheriff in this action—

(a)   to make provision under the Family Law (Scotland) Act 1985;

(b)   for an order under section 11 of the Children (Scotland) Act 1995 in respect of any child of the family within the meaning of section 101(7) of the Civil Partnership Act 2004; or

(c)   for any other competent order.

4.    IF YOU WISH TO APPLY FOR ANY OF THE ABOVE ORDERS you should consult a solicitor with a view to lodging a notice of intention to defend (Form CP16).

Date (*insert date*)

(*Signed*)

Solicitor for the pursuer (*add designation and business address*)

**Rule 33A.14(1)(c)**                                          [1] FORM CP25A

Form of notice to defender in action of dissolution of civil partnership where an interim gender recognition certificate has been issued

YOU ARE GIVEN NOTICE that—

1.    The copy initial writ served on you together with this notice states that an interim gender recognition certificate has been issued to you [*or* the pursuer]. If the pursuer establishes this as a fact, decree will be granted.

2.    Decree of dissolution will end the civil partnership thereby affecting any right to such pension as may depend on the civil partnership continuing or your right to any state pension that may have been payable to you on the death of your civil partner. You may also lose your rights of succession to the pursuer's estate.

3.    If the pursuer is entitled to decree of dissolution you are nevertheless entitled to apply to the sheriff in this action—

(a)   to make financial or other provision for you under the Family Law (Scotland) Act 1985;

(b)   for an order under section 11 of the Children (Scotland) Act 1995 in respect of any child of the family within the meaning of section 101(7) of the Civil Partnership Act 2004; or

(c)   for any other competent order.

4.    IF YOU WISH TO APPLY FOR ANY OF THE ABOVE ORDERS you should consult a solicitor with a view to lodging a notice of intention to defend (Form CP16).

Date (*insert date*)                                          (*Signed*)

Solicitor for the pursuer (*add designation and business address*)

Rule 33A.23(2)                                          [2] FORM CP26

Form of intimation to parties of a Child Welfare Hearing in a civil partnership action

Sheriff court (*insert address and telephone number*).......... Court ref. no.

In this action [A.B.], (*design*), Pursuer, against [C.D.] (*design*), Defender

YOU ARE GIVEN NOTICE that a Child Welfare Hearing has been fixed for (*insert time*) on (*insert date*) at (*insert place*).

Date (*insert date*)                                          Signed...................

Sheriff Clerk (Depute)

---

[1] Inserted by Act of Sederunt (Ordinary Cause Rules) Amendment (Family Law (Scotland) Act 2006 etc.) 2006, para.2 (SSI 2006/207) (effective May 4, 2006).

[2] Inserted by Act of Sederunt (Ordinary Cause Rules) Amendment (Civil Partnership Act 2004) 2005 (SSI 2005/638), para.3 (effective December 8, 2005).

**Rule 33A.30(1)(b)** <sup>1</sup> FORM CP27

Form of minute for decree in a civil partnership action to which rule 33A.29 applies

(*Insert name of solicitor for the pursuer*) having considered the evidence contained in the affidavits and the other documents all as specified in the schedule hereto, and being satisfied that upon the evidence a motion for decree (in terms of the crave of initial writ) [*or in such restricted terms as may he appropriate*] may be properly be made, moves the court accordingly.

In respect whereof

Signed

Solicitor for the Pursuer (*add designation and business address*)

Schedule

(*Number and specify documents considered*)

**Rules 33A.65(1) and 33A.65(2)** <sup>2, 3</sup> FORM CP28

Form of certificate of delivery of documents to chief constable in a civil partnership action

[*Omitted by* Act of Sederunt (Ordinary Cause Rules) Amendment (Family Law (Scotland) Act 2006 etc.) 2006, para.2 (SSI 2006/207) (*effective May 4, 2006).*]

**Rule 33A.67(1)** <sup>4, 5</sup>FORM CP29

Form of simplified dissolution of civil partnership application under section 117(3)(c) of the Civil Partnership Act 2004

Sheriff Clerk

Sheriff Court House

...............

...............

(Telephone)...............

APPLICATION FOR DISSOLUTION OF A CIVIL PARTNERSHIP WITH CONSENT OF OTHER PARTY TO THE CIVIL PARTNERSHIP (CIVIL PARTNERS HAVING LIVED APART FOR AT LEAST ONE YEAR)

Before completing this form, you should have read the leaflet entitled "Do it yourself Dissolution", which explains the circumstances in which a dissolution of a civil partnership may be sought by this method. If the simplified procedure appears to suit your circumstances, you may use this form to apply for dissolution of your civil partnership. Below you will find directions designed to assist you with your application. Please follow them carefully. In the event of difficulty, you may contact any sheriff clerk's office or Citizen Advice Bureau.

**Directions for making application**

Write In Ink, Using Block Capitals

| | |
|---|---|
| Application (Part 1) | 1. Complete and sign Part 1 of the form (pages 3-7), paying particular attention to the notes opposite each section. |
| Consent of civil partner (Part 2) | 2. When you have completed Part 1 of the form, attach the (blue) instruction civil partner sheet SP3 to it and send both documents to your for completion of the consent at Part 2 (page 9). |
| | **NOTE:** If your civil partner does **NOT** complete and sign the form of consent, your application cannot proceed further under the simplified procedure. |

---

<sup>1</sup> Inserted by Act of Sederunt (Ordinary Cause Rules) Amendment (Civil Partnership Act 2004) 2005 (SSI 2005/638), para.3 (effective December 8, 2005).

<sup>2</sup> Inserted by Act of Sederunt (Ordinary Cause Rules) Amendment (Civil Partnership Act 2004) 2005 (SSI 2005/638), para.3 (effective December 8, 2005).

<sup>3</sup> As amended by Act of Sederunt (Ordinary Cause Rules) Amendment (Family Law (Scotland) Act 2006 etc.) 2006, para.2 (SSI 2006/207) (effective May 4, 2006).

<sup>4</sup> Inserted by Act of SEderunt (Ordinary Cause Rules) Amendment (Civil Partnership Act 2004) 2005 (SSI 2005/638), para.3 (effective December 8, 2005),

<sup>5</sup> As amended by Act of Sederunt (Ordinary Cause Rules) Amendment (Family Law (Scotland) Act 2006 etc.) 2006, para.2 (SSI 2006/207) (effective May 4, 2006).

Affidavit (Part 3)

Returning completed application form to court

In that event, if you still wish to obtain a dissolution of your civil partnership, you should consult a solicitor.

3. When the application has been returned to you with the consent (Part 2) duly completed and signed, you should take the form to a Justice of the Peace, Notary Public, Commissioner for Oaths or other duly authorised person so that your affidavit at Part 3 (page 10) may be completed and sworn.

4. When directions 1–3 above have been complied with, your application is now ready to be sent to the sheriff clerk at the above address. With it you must enclose:

(i) an extract of the registration of your civil partnership in the civil partnership register (the document headed "Extract of an entry in the Register of Civil Partnerships", which will be returned to you in due course), or an equivalent document, and

(ii) either a cheque or postal order in respect of the court fee, crossed and made payable to "the Scottish Court Service",

or a completed form SP15, claiming exemption from the court fee.

5. Receipt of your application will be promptly acknowledged. Should you wish to withdraw the application for any reason, please contact the sheriff clerk immediately.

## PART 1

**WRITE IN INK, USING BLOCK CAPITALS**

1. NAME AND ADDRESS OF APPLICANT

Surname ...............

Other name(s) in full ...............

....................

Present address ....................

....................

Daytime telephone number (if any) ...............

2. NAME AND ADDRESS OF CIVIL PARTNER

Surname ...............

Other name(s) in full ...............

....................

Present address ...............

....................

Daytime telephone number (if any) ...............

3. JURISDICTION Please indicate with a tick () in the appropriate box or boxes which of the following apply:

PART A

| | | |
|---|---|---|
| (i) | My civil partner and I are habitually resident in Scotland | ☐ |
| (ii) | My civil partner and I were last habitually resident in Scotland, and one of us still resides there | ☐ |
| (iii) | My civil partner is habitually resident in Scotland | ☐ |
| (iv) | I am habitually resident in Scotland having resided there for at least a year immediately before this application was made | ☐ |
| (v) | I am habitually resident in Scotland having resided there for at least six months immediately before this application was made and am domiciled in Scotland | ☐ |

**If you have ticked one or more of the boxes in Part A, you should go direct to Part C. You should only complete Part B if you have not ticked any of the boxes in Part A**

PART B

(i)       I am domiciled in Scotland ☐

(ii)     My civil partner is domiciled in Scotland ☐

(iii)    No court has, or is recognised as having, jurisdiction under regula- ☐ tions made under section 219 of the Civil Partnership Act 2004

PART C

(i)       I have lived at the address shown above for at least 40 days im- ☐ mediately before the date I signed this application

(ii)     My civil partner has lived at the address shown above for at least 40 ☐ days immediately before the date I signed this application

(iii)    I lived at the address shown above for a period of at least 40 days ☐ ending not more than 40 days before the date I signed this application and have no known residence in Scotland at that date

(iv)   My civil partner lived at the address shown above for a period of at ☐ least 40 days ending not more than 40 days before the date I signed this application and has no known residence in Scotland at that date

4. DETAILS OF PRESENT CIVIL PARTNERSHIP

Place of Registration of Civil Partnership...............(Registration District)

Date of Registration of Civil Partnership: Day..........month..........year..........

5. PERIOD OF SEPARATION

(i)       Please state the date on which you ceased to live with your civil partner. (If more than 1 year, just give the month and year)

Day..........Month..........Year..........

(ii)     Have you lived with your civil partner since that date?            *[YES/NO]

(iii)    If yes, for how long in total did you live together before finally separating again?

..........months

6. RECONCILIATION

Is there any reasonable prospect of reconciliation with your civil partner?    *[YES/NO]

Do you consider that the civil partnership has broken down irretrievably?    *[YES/NO]

7. CONSENT

Does your civil partner consent to a dissolution of the civil partnership granted?    *[YES/NO] being

8. MENTAL DISORDER

Does your civil partner have any mental disorder (whether mental illness,    *[YES/NO] personality disorder or learning disability)?

Is your civil partner suffering from any mental disorder    *[YES/NO]

(whether illness or handicap)?(If yes, give details)

9. CHILDREN

Are there any children of the family under the age of 16?    *[YES/NO]

10. Other Court Actions

Are you aware of any court actions currently proceeding in any country (includ-    *[YES/NO] ing Scotland) which may affect your civil partnership?

(If yes, give details)

* Delete as appropriate

11. REQUEST FOR DISSOLUTION OF THE CIVIL PARTNERSHIP AND DISCLAIMER OF FINANCIAL PROVISION

I confirm that the facts stated in paragraphs 1–10 above apply to my civil partnership.

I do NOT ask the sheriff to make any financial provision in connection with this application.

I request the sheriff to grant decree of dissolution of my civil partnership.

Date ..........          Signature of Applicant ..............

**IMPORTANT**

Part 1 MUST be completed, signed and dated before sending the application form to your civil partner.

Part 2

Notice to Consenting Civil Partner

*(Insert name and address of consenting civil partner)*

CONSENT TO APPLICATION FOR DISSOLUTION OF A CIVIL PARTNERSHIP (CIVIL PARTNERS HAVING LIVED APART FOR AT LEAST ONE YEAR)

In Part 1 of the enclosed application form your civil partner is applying for dissolution of your civil partnership on the ground the civil partnership has broken down irretrievably because you and he [*or* she] have lived apart for at least one year and you consent to the dissolution being granted.

Such consent must be given formally in writing at Part 2 of the application form. BEFORE completing that part, you are requested to read it over carefully so that you understand the effect of consenting to the dissolution of the civil partnership. Thereafter if you wish to consent—

(a) check the details given by the Applicant at Part 1 of the form to ensure that they are correct to the best of your knowledge;

(b) complete Part 2 (Consent by Applicant's civil partner to dissolution) by entering your name and address at the appropriate place and adding your signature and the date; and

(c) return the whole application form to your civil partner at the address given in Part 1.

Once your civil partner has completed the remainder of the form and has submitted it to the court, a copy of the whole application (including your consent) will later be served upon you formally by the sheriff clerk.

In the event of the dissolution of the civil partnership being granted, you will automatically be sent a copy of the extract decree. (Should you change your address before receiving the copy extract decree, please notify the sheriff clerk immediately.)

If you do NOT wish to consent please return the application form, with Part 2 uncompleted, to your civil partner and advise him or her of your decision.

The sheriff will NOT grant a dissolution of your civil partnership on this application if Part 2 of the form is not completed by you.

CONSENT BY APPLICANT'S CIVIL PARTNER TO DISSOLUTION OF CIVIL PARTNERSHIP

NOTE: Before completing this part of the form, please read the notes opposite (page 8)

I, ....................

*(Insert full name, in BLOCK letters, of Applicant's civil partner)*

residing at ....................

....................

....................

*(Insert address, also in BLOCK letters)*

HEREBY STATE THAT

(a) I have read Part 1 of this application;

(b) the Applicant has lived apart from me for a continuous period of one year immediately preceding the date of the application (paragraph 11 of Part 1);

(c) I do not ask the sheriff to make any financial provision for me including—

    (i) the payment by the Applicant of a periodical allowance (i.e. a regular payment of money weekly or monthly, etc. for maintenance);

    (ii) the payment by the Applicant of a capital sum (i.e. a lump sum payment);

(d) I understand that dissolution of my civil partnership may result in the loss to me of property rights; and

(e) I CONSENT TO DECREE OF DISSOLUTION BEING GRANTED IN RESPECT OF THIS APPLICATION

Date ..........          Signature ..............

NOTE: You may withdraw your consent, even after giving it, at any time before the dissolution of the civil partnership is granted by the sheriff. Should you wish to do so, please contact the sheriff clerk immediately.

Part 3

APPLICANT'S AFFIDAVIT

To be completed by the Applicant only after Parts 1 and 2 have been signed and dated.

I, (*Insert Applicant's full name*) ...................

residing at (*insert Applicant's present home address*) ...............

...................

...................

SWEAR that to the best of my knowledge and belief:

(1)   the facts stated in Part 1 of this Application are true; and

(2)   the signature in Part 2 of this Application is that of my civil partner.

Signature of Applicant ...................

SWORN at (*insert place*) ...............

To be completed by   this..........day of..........20..........
Justice of the Peace,

Notary Public or   before me (*insert full name*) ...............
Commissioner for

Oaths           (*insert full address*) ...................

           ...................

           ...................

           Signature ...................

           *Justice of the Peace/ Notary Public/Commissioner for Oaths

           * Delete as appropriate

**Rule 33A.67(2)**

[1,2]FORM CP30

Form of simplified dissolution of civil partnership application under section 117(3)(d) of the Civil Partnership Act 2004

Sheriff Clerk

Sheriff Court House

...............

...............

(Telephone)...............

APPLICATION FOR DISSOLUTION OF A CIVIL PARTNERSHIP (CIVIL PARTNERS HAVING LIVED APART FOR AT LEAST TWO YEARS)

Before completing this form, you should have read the leaflet entitled "Do it yourself Dissolution", which explains the circumstances in which a dissolution of a civil partnership may be sought by this method. If the simplified procedure appears to suit your circumstances, you may use this form to apply for dissolution of your civil partnership. Below you will find directions designed to assist you with your application. Please follow them carefully. In the event of difficulty, you may contact any sheriff clerk's office or Citizen Advice Bureau.

**Directions for making application**

WRITE IN INK, USING BLOCK CAPITALS

| | |
|---|---|
| Application (Part 1) | 1. Complete and sign Part 1 of the form (pages 3–7), paying particular attention to the notes opposite each section. |
| Affidavits (Part 2) | 2. When you have completed Part 1, you should take the form to a Justice of the Peace, Notary Public, Commissioner for Oaths or other duly authorised person so that your affidavit at Part 2 (page 8) may be completed and sworn. |
| Returning completed application form to court | 3. When directions 1–2 above have been complied with, your application now ready to be sent to the sheriff clerk at the above address. With it you must enclose: |

---

[1] Inserted by Act of Sederunt (Ordinary Cause Rules) Amendment (Civil Partnership Act 2004) 2005 (SSI 2005/638), para.3 (effective December 8, 2005).

[2] As amended by Act of Sederunt (Ordinary Cause Rules) Amendment (Family Law (Scotland) Act 2006 etc.) 2006, para.2 (SSI 2006/207) (effective May 4, 2006).

(i) an extract of the registration of your civil partnership in the civil partnership register (the document headed "Extract of an entry in the Register of Civil Partnerships", which will be returned to you in due course), or an equivalent document. Check the notes on page 2 to see if you need to obtain a letter from the General Register Office stating that there is no record of your civil partner having dissolved the civil partnership, and

(ii) either a cheque or postal order in respect of the court fee, crossed and made payable to "the Scottish Court Service",

or a completed fee exemption form.

4. Receipt of your application will be promptly acknowledged. Should you wish to withdraw the application for any reason, please contact the sheriff clerk immediately.

## PART 1

WRITE IN INK, USING BLOCK CAPITALS

1. NAME AND ADDRESS OF APPLICANT

Surname ...............

Other name(s) in full..............

....................

Present address...............

....................

Daytime telephone number (if any)...............

2. NAME OF CIVIL PARTNER

Surname ...............

Other name(s) in full ...............

3. ADDRESS OF CIVIL PARTNER (If the address of your civil partner is not known, please enter "not known" in this paragraph and proceed to paragraph 4)

Present address ...............

....................

....................

Daytime telephone number (if any) ...............

4. Only complete this paragraph if you do not know the present address of your civil partner

NEXT-OF-KIN Name...............

Address ....................

....................

....................

Relationship to your civil partner ...............

CHILDREN OF THE FAMILY

**Names and dates of birth**                          Addresses

...............                                        ...............

                                                       ...............

...............                                        ...............

                                                       ...............

If insufficient space is available to list all the children of the family, please continue on a separate sheet and attach to this form.

5. JURISDICTION

Please indicate with a tick () in the appropriate box or boxes which of the following apply:

PART A

| | | |
|---|---|---|
| (i) | My civil partner and I are habitually resident in Scotland | ☐ |
| (ii) | My civil partner and I were last habitually resident in Scotland, and one of us still resides there | ☐ |
| (iii) | My civil partner is habitually resident in Scotland | ☐ |
| (iv) | I am habitually resident in Scotland having resided there for at least a year immediately before this application was made | ☐ |

286

(v)       I am habitually resident in Scotland having resided there for at least ☐
six months immediately before this application was made and am
domiciled in Scotland

**If you have ticked one or more of the boxes in Part A, you should go direct to Part C. You should only complete Part B if you have not ticked any of the boxes in Part A.**

PART B

(i)       I am domiciled in Scotland ☐

(ii)      My civil partner is domiciled in Scotland ☐

(iii)    No court has, or is recognised as having, jurisdiction under regula- ☐
tions made under section 219 of the Civil Partnership Act 2004

PART C

(i)       I have lived at the address shown above for at least 40 days im- ☐
mediately before the date I signed this application

(ii)      My civil partner has lived at the address shown above for at least 40 ☐
days immediately before the date I signed this application

(iii)    I lived at the address shown above for a period of at least 40 days ☐
ending not more than 40 days before the date I signed this application
and have no known residence in Scotland at that date

(iv)    My civil partner lived at the address shown above for a period of at ☐
least 40 days ending not more than 40 days before the date I signed
this application and has no known residence in Scotland at that date

6. DETAILS OF PRESENT CIVIL PARTNERSHIP

Place of Registration of Civil Partnership...............(Registration District)

Date of Registration of Civil Partnership: Day..........month..........year...............

7. PERIOD OF SEPARATION

(i)       Please state the date on which you ceased to live with your civil partner. (If more than 2
years, just give the month and year)

Day..........Month..........Year..........

(ii)      Have you lived with your civil partner since that date?      *[YES/NO]

(iii)    If yes, for how long in total did you live together before finally separating again?

..........months

8. RECONCILIATION

Is there any reasonable prospect of reconciliation with your civil partner?    *[YES/NO]

Do you consider that the civil partnership has broken down irretrievably?    *[YES/NO]

9. MENTAL DISORDER

Does your civil partner have any mental disorder (whether mental illness,  *[YES/NO]
personality disorder or learning disability)?

(If yes, give details)

10. CHILDREN

Are there any children of the family under the age of 16?    *[YES/NO]

11. OTHER COURT ACTIONS

Are you aware of any court actions currently proceeding in any country (includ-  *[YES/NO]
ing Scotland) which may affect your civil partnership?

(If yes, give details)        * Delete as appropriate

12. DECLARATION AND REQUEST FOR DISSOLUTION OF THE CIVIL PARTNERSHIP

I confirm that the facts stated in paragraphs 1–11 above apply to my civil partnership.

287

I do NOT ask the sheriff to make any financial provision in connection with this application.

I request the sheriff to grant decree of dissolution of my civil partnership.

Date............... Signature of Applicant...............

PART 2

APPLICANT'S AFFIDAVIT

To be completed by the Applicant only after Part 1 has been signed and dated.

I, (*Insert Applicant's full name*) ...................

residing at (*insert Applicant's present home address*) ...............

...................

...................

SWEAR that to the best of my knowledge and belief the facts stated in Part 1 of this Application are true.

Signature of Applicant...................

|   |   |
|---|---|
| | SWORN at (*insert place*)................... |
| To be completed by Justice of the Peace, | this..........day of..........20 ......... |
| Notary Public or Commissioner for | before me (*insert full name*)............... |
| Oaths | (*insert full address*)............... |
| | ................... |
| | ................... |
| | Signature................... |
| | *Justice of the Peace/ Notary Public/Commissioner for Oaths |
| | * Delete as appropriate |

Rule 33A.67(3)

[1, 2]FORM CP31

Form of simplified dissolution of a civil partnership application on grounds under section 117(2)(b) of the Civil Partnership Act 2004

Sheriff Clerk

Sheriff Court House

...................

...................

(Telephone) ...................

APPLICATION FOR DISSOLUTION OF A CIVIL PARTNERSHIP (INTERIM GENDER RECOGNITION CERTIFICATE ISSUED TO ONE OF THE CIVIL PARTNERS AFTER REGISTRATION OF THE CIVIL PARTNERSHIP)

Before completing this form, you should have read the leaflet entitled "Do it yourself Dissolution", which explains the circumstances in which a dissolution of a civil partnership may be sought by this method. If the simplified procedure appears to suit your circumstances, you may use this form to apply for dissolution of your civil partnership. Below you will find directions designed to assist you with your application. Please follow them carefully. In the event of difficulty, you may contact any sheriff clerk's office or Citizen Advice Bureau.

**Directions for making application**

WRITE IN INK, USING BLOCK CAPITALS

| | |
|---|---|
| Application (Part 1) | 1. Complete and sign Part 1 of the form (pages 3–7), paying particular attention to the notes opposite each section |
| Affidavits (Part 2) | 2. When you have completed Part 1, you should take the form to a Justice of the Peace, Notary Public, Commissioner for Oaths or other duly authorised person so that your affidavit at Part 2 (page 8) may be completed and sworn. |

---

[1] Inserted by Act of Sederunt (Ordinary Cause Rules) Amendment (Civil Partnership Act 2004) 2005 (SSI 2005/638), para.3 (effective December 8, 2005).

[2] As amended by Act of Sederunt (Ordinary Cause Rules) Amendment (Family Law (Scotland) Act 2006 etc.) 2006, para.2 (SSI 2006/207) (effective May 4, 2006).

Returning Completed Application form to court

3. When directions 1–2 above have been complied with, your application is now ready to be sent to the sheriff clerk at the above address. With it you must enclose: form to court

(i) an extract of the registration of your civil partnership in the civil partnership register (the document headed "Extract of an entry in the Register of Civil Partnerships", which will be returned to you in due course), or an equivalent document. Check the notes on page 2 to see if you need to obtain a letter from the General Register Office stating that there is no record of your civil partner having dissolved the civil partnership,

(ii) either a cheque or postal order in respect of the court fee, crossed and made payable to "the Scottish Court Service" or a completed fee exemption form, and

(iii) the interim gender recognition certificate or a copy sealed with the seal of the Gender Recognition Panels and certified to be a true copy by an officer authorised by the President of Gender Recognition Panels.

4. Receipt of your application will be promptly acknowledged. Should you wish to withdraw the application for any reason, please contact the sheriff clerk immediately.

**PART 1**

**WRITE IN INK, USING BLOCK CAPITALS**

1. NAME AND ADDRESS OF APPLICANT

Surname ....................

Other name(s) in full ....................

....................

Present address ....................

....................

Daytime telephone number (if any) ....................

2. NAME OF CIVIL PARTNER

Surname ....................

Other name(s) in full ....................

3. ADDRESS OF CIVIL PARTNER (If the address of your civil partner is not known, please enter "not known" in this paragraph and proceed to paragraph 4)

Present address ....................

....................

....................

Daytime telephone number (if any) ...............

4. Only complete this paragraph if you do not know the present address of your civil partner

NEXT-OF-KIN

Name ...............

Address ...............

....................

....................

Relationship to your civil partner ..........

CHILDREN OF THE FAMILY

| Names and dates of birth | Addresses |
| --- | --- |
| .......... | .......... |
| | .......... |
| | .......... |
| .......... | .......... |
| | .......... |

If insufficient space is available to list all the children of the family, please continue on a separate sheet and attach to this form.

5. JURISDICTION

Please indicate with a tick () in the appropriate box or boxes which of the following apply:

PART A

(i)      My civil partner and I are habitually resident in Scotland       ☐

(ii)     My civil partner and I were last habitually resident in Scotland, and   ☐
one of us still resides there

(iii)     My civil partner is habitually resident in Scotland      ☐

(iv)     I am habitually resident in Scotland having resided there for at least a   ☐
year immediately before this application was made

(v)     I am habitually resident in Scotland having resided there for at least   ☐
six months immediately before this application was made and am
domiciled in Scotland

If you have ticked one or more of the boxes in Part A, you should go direct to Part C. You should only
complete Part B if you have not ticked any of the boxes in Part A

     PART B

(i)     I am domiciled in Scotland      ☐

(ii)     My civil partner is domiciled in Scotland      ☐

(iii)     No court has, or is recognised as having, jurisdiction under regula-   ☐
tions made under section 219 of the Civil Partnership Act 2004

PART C

(i)     I have lived at the address shown above for at least 40 days im-   ☐
mediately before the date I signed this application

(ii)     My civil partner has lived at the address shown above for at least 40   ☐
days immediately before the date I signed this application

(iii)     I lived at the address shown above for a period of at least 40 days   ☐
ending not more than 40 days before the date I signed this application
and have no known residence in Scotland at that date

(iv)     My civil partner lived at the address shown above for a period of at   ☐
least 40 days ending not more than 40 days before the date I signed
this application and has no known residence in Scotland at that date

6. DETAILS OF PRESENT CIVIL PARTNERSHIP

Place of Registration of Civil Partnership ...............(Registration District)

Date of Registration of Civil Partnership: Day..........month..........year..........

7. DETAILS OF ISSUE OF INTERIM GENDER RECOGNITION CERTIFICATE

(i)      Please state whether the interim gender recognition certificate has been issued to
you or your civil partner

(ii)      Please state the date the interim gender recognition certificate was issued
Day..........Month...........Year..........

8. MENTAL DISORDER

Does your civil partner have any mental disorder (whether mental illness,      *[YES/NO]
personality disorder or learning disability)?

(If yes, give details)

9. CHILDREN Are there any children of the family under the age of 16?      *[YES/NO]

10. OTHER COURT ACTIONS

Are you aware of any court actions currently proceeding in any country (includ-      *[YES/NO]
ing Scotland) which may affect your civil partnership?

(If yes, give details)      * Delete as appropriate

11. DECLARATION AND REQUEST FOR DISSOLUTION OF THE CIVIL PARTNERSHIP

I confirm that the facts stated in paragraphs 1-10 above apply to my civil partnership.

I do NOT ask the sheriff to make any financial provision in connection with this application.

I request the sheriff to grant decree of dissolution of my civil partnership.

Date.......... Signature of Applicant................

PART 2

APPLICANT'S AFFIDAVIT

To be completed by the Applicant only after Part 1 has been signed and dated.

I, (*Insert Applicant's full name*) ...............

residing at (*insert Applicant's present home address*) ..........

....................

....................

SWEAR that to the best of my knowledge and belief the facts stated in Part 1 of this Application are true.

Signature of Applicant ...............

SWORN at (*insert place*) ...............

To be completed by Justice of   this..........day of..........20 ..........
the Peace,

Notary Public or Commis-   before me (*insert full name*) ...............
sioner for

Oaths   (*insert full address*) ...............

....................

....................

Signature ...............

*Justice of the Peace/ Notary Public/Commissioner for Oaths

* Delete as appropriate

**Rule 33A.69(3)(a)**

[1,2] FORM CP32

Form of citation in application relying on facts in section 117(3)(c) of the Civil Partnership Act 2004
(*Insert name and address of non-applicant civil partner*)

APPLICATION FOR DISSOLUTION OF A CIVIL PARTNERSHIP (CIVIL PARTNERS HAVING LIVED APART FOR AT LEAST ONE YEAR WITH THE CONSENT OF THE OTHER CIVIL PARTNER)

Your civil partner has applied to the sheriff for dissolution of your civil partnership on the ground that the civil partnership has broken down irretrievably because you and he or she have lived apart for a period of at least one year and you consent to decree of dissolution being granted.

A copy of the application is hereby served upon you.

1. Please note that the sheriff may not make financial provision under this procedure and that your civil partner is making no claim for—

   (a)   the payment by you of a periodical allowance (i.e. a regular payment of money weekly or monthly, etc. for maintenance);

   (b)   the payment by you of a capital sum (i.e. a lump sum payment).

2. Dissolution of your civil partnership may result in the loss to you of property rights (e.g. the right to succeed to the Applicant's estate on his or her death) or the right, where appropriate, to a pension.

3. If you wish to oppose the granting of a decree of dissolution of your civil partnership, you should put your reasons in writing and send your letter to the address shown below. Your letter must reach the sheriff clerk before (*insert date*).

4. In the event of the decree of dissolution of your civil partnership being granted, you will be sent a copy of the extract decree. Should you change your address before receiving the copy extract decree, please notify the sheriff clerk immediately.

Signed

Sheriff clerk (depute)

(*insert address and telephone number of the sheriff clerk*)

[*or* Sheriff officer]

NOTE: If you wish to exercise your right to make a claim for financial provision you should immediately advise the sheriff clerk that you oppose the application for that reason, and thereafter consult a solicitor.

**Rule 33A.69(3)(b)**

---

[1] Inserted by Act of Sederunt (Ordinary Cause Rules) Amendment (Civil Partnership Act 2004) 2005 (SSI 2005/638), para.3 (effective December 8, 2005).

[2] As amended by Act of Sederunt (Ordinary Cause Rules) Amendment (Family Law (Scotland) Act 2006 etc.) 2006, para.2 (SSI 2006/207) (effective May 4, 2006).

[1, 2] FORM CP33

Form of citation in application relying on facts in section 117(3)(d) of the Civil Partnership Act 2004

(*Insert name and address of non-applicant civil partner*)

APPLICATION FOR DISSOLUTION OF A CIVIL PARTNERSHIP (CIVIL PARTNERS HAVING LIVED APART FOR AT LEAST TWO YEARS)

Your civil partner has applied to the sheriff for dissolution of your civil partnership on the ground that the civil partnership has broken down irretrievably because you and he or she have lived apart for a period of at least two years.

A copy of the application is hereby served upon you.

1. Please note:

(a) that the sheriff may not make financial provision under this procedure and that your civil partner is making no claim for—

(i) the payment by you of a periodical allowance (i.e. a regular payment of money weekly or monthly, etc. for maintenance);

(ii) the payment by you of a capital sum (i.e. a lump sum payment);

(b) *[Omitted by Act of Sederunt (Ordinary Cause Rules) Amendment (Family Law (Scotland) Act 2006 etc.) 2006, para.2 (SSI 2006/207) (effective May 4, 2006).]*

2. Dissolution of your civil partnership may result in the loss to you of property rights (e.g. the right to succeed to the Applicant's estate on his or her death) or the right, where appropriate, to a pension.

3. If you wish to oppose the granting of a decree of dissolution of your civil partnership, you should put your reasons in writing and send your letter to the address shown below. Your letter must reach the sheriff clerk before (*insert date*).

4. In the event of the decree of dissolution of your civil partnership being granted, you will be sent a copy of the extract decree. Should you change your address before receiving the copy extract decree, please notify the sheriff clerk immediately.

Signed

Sheriff clerk (depute)

(*insert address and telephone number of the sheriff clerk*)

[*or* Sheriff officer]

NOTE: If you wish to exercise your right to make a claim for financial provision you should immediately advise the sheriff clerk that you oppose the application for that reason, and thereafter consult a solicitor.

**Rule 33A.69(3)(c)**

[3]FORM CP34

Form of citation in application on grounds under section 117(2)(b) of the Civil Partnership Act 2004

(*Insert name and address of non-applicant civil partner*)

APPLICATION FOR DISSOLUTION OF A CIVIL PARTNERSHIP (INTERIM GENDER RECOGNITION CERTIFICATE ISSUED TO ONE OF THE CIVIL PARTNERS AFTER THE REGISTRATION OF THE CIVIL PARTNERSHIP)

Your civil partner has applied to the sheriff for dissolution of your civil partnership on the ground that an interim gender recognition certificate has been issued to you or your civil partner after your civil partnership was registered.

A copy of the application is hereby served upon you.

1. Please note that the sheriff may not make financial provision under this procedure and that your civil partner is making no claim for—

(a)  the payment by you of a periodical allowance (i.e. a regular payment of money weekly or monthly, etc. for maintenance);

(b)  the payment by you of a capital sum (i.e. a lump sum payment).

2. Dissolution of your civil partnership may result in the loss to you of property rights (e.g. the right to succeed to the Applicant's estate on his or her death) or the right, where appropriate, to a pension.

---

[1] Inserted by Act of Sederunt (Ordinary Cause Rules) Amendment (Civil Partnership Act 2004) 2005 (SSI 2005/638), para.3 (effective December 8, 2005).

[2] As amended by Act of Sederunt (Ordinary Cause Rules) Amendment (Family Law (Scotland) Act 2006 etc.) 2006, para.2 (SSI 2006/207) (effective May 4, 2006).

[3] Inserted by Act of Sederunt (Ordinary Cause Rules) Amendment (Civil Partnership Act 2004) 2005 (SSI 2005/638), para.3 (effective December 8, 2005).

3. If you wish to oppose the granting of a decree of dissolution of your civil partnership, you should put your reasons in writing and send your letter to the address shown below. Your letter must reach the sheriff clerk before (*insert date*).

4. In the event of the decree of dissolution of your civil partnership being granted, you will be sent a copy of the extract decree. Should you change your address before receiving the copy extract decree, please notify the sheriff clerk immediately.

Signed

Sheriff clerk (depute)

(*insert address and telephone number of the sheriff clerk*)

[*or* Sheriff officer]

NOTE: If you wish to exercise your right to make a claim for financial provision you should immediately advise the sheriff clerk that you oppose the application for that reason, and thereafter consult a solicitor.

Rule 33A.70(1)(a)

[1]FORM CP35

Form of intimation of simplified dissolution of a civil partnership application for display on the walls of court

Court ref. no.

An application for dissolution of a civil partnership has been made in this sheriff court by [A.B.], (*insert designation and address*), Applicant, naming [C.D.], (*insert designation and address*) as Respondent.

If [C.D.] wishes to oppose the granting of decree of dissolution of the civil partnership he [*or* she] should immediately contact the sheriff clerk from whom he [or she] may obtain a copy of the application.

Date (*insert date*)

Signed

Sheriff clerk (depute)

Rule 33A.70(2)

[2]FORM CP36

Form of intimation to children of the family and next-of-kin in a simplified dissolution of a civil partnership application

Court ref. no.

To (*insert name and address*)

You are hereby given NOTICE that an application for dissolution of a civil partnership has been made against (*insert name of respondent*) your (*insert relationship e.g. father, mother, brother or other relative as the case may be*). A copy of this application is attached.

If you know of his or her present address, you are requested to inform the sheriff clerk (*insert address of sheriff clerk*) in writing immediately. You may also, if you wish, oppose the granting of the decree of dissolution by sending a letter to the court giving your reasons for your opposition to the application. Your letter must be sent to the sheriff clerk within 21 days of (*insert date on which intimation was given*). *N.B.* Rule 5.3(2) *relating to postal service or intimation*).

Date (*insert date*)

Signed

Sheriff clerk (depute)

**IF YOU ARE UNCERTAIN WHAT ACTION TO TAKE** you should consult a solicitor. You may be entitled to legal aid depending on your financial circumstances, and you can get information about legal aid from a solicitor. You may also obtain advice from any Citizens Advice Bureau or other advice agency.

Rule 33A.73(2)

[3]FORM CP37

---

[1] Inserted by Act of Sederunt (Ordinary Cause Rules) Amendment (Civil Partnership Act 2004) 2005 (SSI 2005/638), para.3 (effective December 8, 2005).

[2] Inserted by Act of Sederunt (Ordinary Cause Rules) Amendment (Civil Partnership Act 2004) 2005 (SSI 2005/638), para.3 (effective December 8, 2005).

[3] Inserted by Act of Sederunt (Ordinary Cause Rules) Amendment (Civil Partnership Act 2004) 2005 (SSI 2005/638), para.3 (effective December 8, 2005).

Form of extract decree of dissolution of a civil partnership in an application for a simplified dissolution of a civil partnership

At (*insert place and date*)

in an action in the Sheriff Court of the Sheriffdom of (*insert name of sheriffdom*) at (*insert place of sheriff court*)

at the instance of (*insert full name of applicant*), Applicant,

against (*insert full name of respondent*), Respondent,

whose civil partnership was registered at (*insert place*) on (*insert date*),

the sheriff pronounced decree dissolving the civil partnership of the Applicant and the Respondent.

Extracted at (*insert place and date*)

by me, sheriff clerk of the Sheriffdom of (*insert name of sheriffdom*).

Signed

Sheriff clerk (depute)

Rule 34.1(2)

[1]FORM H1

Form of notice informing defender of right to apply for certain orders under the Debtors (Scotland) Act 1987 on sequestration for rent

Rule 34.6(1)

FORM H2
Form of notice of removal

To (*insert name, designation, and address of party in possession*). You are required to remove from (*describe subjects*) at the term of (*or if different terms, state them and the subjects to which they apply*), in terms of lease (*describe it*) [or in terms of your letter of removal dated (*insert date*)] [or otherwise as the case may be].

Date (*insert date*)

Signed

(*add designation and address*)

Rule 34.6(2)

FORM H3
Form of letter of removal

To (*insert name and designation of addressee*)

(*Insert place and date*) I am to remove from (*state subjects by usual name or short description sufficient for identification*) at the term of (*insert term and date*)

[K.L.] (*add designation and address*).

(*If not holograph, to be attested thus—*)

[M.N.] (*add designation and address*), witness.)

Rule 34.7

FORM H4

Form of notice of removal under section 37 of the 1907 Act

NOTICE OF REMOVAL UNDER SECTION 37 OF THE SHERIFF COURTS (SCOTLAND) ACT 1907

To (*insert designation and address*).

You are required to remove from (*insert description of heritable subjects, land, ground, etc.*) at the term of [Whitsunday or Martinmas], (*insert date*)

Date (*insert date*)

Signed

(*add designation and address*)

[2]FORM H5

Rule 34.11(4)

Form of citation of unnamed occupiers

CITATION

SHERIFFDOM OF (*insert name of sheriffdom*)

---

[1] Revoked by the Act of Sederunt (Sheriff Court Rules Amendment) (Diligence) 2008 (SSI 2008/121) r.2(1)(a) (effective April 1, 2008).

[2] Inserted by SSI 2000/239 (effective October 2, 2000).

AT (*insert place of sheriff court*)

[A.B.] (*insert designation and address*)

Pursuer

against

The Occupier[s] of (*address*)

Defender

An action has been brought in the above Sheriff Court by [A.B.]. [A.B.] calls as a defender the occupier[s] of the property at (*insert address*). If the occupier[s] [or any of them] wish[es] to challenge the jurisdiction of the court or to defend the action, he [or she [or it] [or they]] should contact the sheriff clerk at (*insert address of sheriff court*) immediately and in any event by (*date on which period of notice expires*).

Signed

Sheriff [or Sheriff Clerk]

FORM M1

Rule 35.5

Form of warrant of citation in an action of multiplepoinding

(*Insert place and date*) Grants warrant to cite the defender (*insert name and address*) by serving a copy of the writ and warrant upon a period of notice of (*insert period of notice*) days, and ordains him [*or her*], if he [*or she*] intends to lodge:—

(a) defences challenging the jurisdiction of the court or the competence of the action; or

(b) objections to the condescendence on the fund *in medio*; or

(c) a claim on the fund;

to lodge a notice of appearance with the sheriff clerk at (*insert name and address of sheriff court*) within the said period of notice after such service [and grants warrant to arrest on the dependence].

[*Where the holder of the fund in medio is a defender, insert:* Appoints the holder of the fund in medio to

(a) lodge with the sheriff clerk at (*insert place of sheriff court*) within the said period of notice after such service

(i) a detailed condescendence on the fund in medio; and

(ii) a list of parties having an interest in the fund; and

(b) intimate to all parties to the action a copy of the condescendence and list.]

FORM M2

Rule 35.6(1)

Form of citation in an action of multiplepoinding

Citation

SHERIFFDOM OF (*insert name of sheriffdom*) ............... Court ref. no. ..........

AT (*insert place of sheriff court*) ..............

[A.B.]. (*insert designation and address*). Pursuer, against [C.D.], (*insert designation and address*). Defender.

(*Insert place and date*) You [C.D.] are hereby served with this copy writ and warrant, together with Form M4 (notice of appearance).

[*Where the defender is the holder of the fund in medio. insert the following paragraph:*— As holder of the fund in medio you must lodge with the sheriff clerk at the above address within (*insert period of notice*) days of (insert date on which service was executed. N. B. Rule 5.3(2) relating to postal service)—

(a) a detailed condescendence on the fund in medio: and

(b) a list of parties having an interest in the fund.

You must at the same time intimate to all other parties to the action a copy of

(a) the detailed condescendence on the fund; and

(b) the list of parties having an interest in the fund.]

---

**Form M4** is served on you for use should you wish to intimate that you intend to lodge:—

(a) defences challenging the jurisdiction of the court or the competence of the action; or(b) objections to the condescendence on the fund in medio: or(c) a claim on the fund.

**IF YOU WISH TO APPEAR IN THIS ACTION** you should consult a solicitor with a view to lodging a notice of appearance (Form M4). The notice of appearance, together with the court fee of £(*insert amount*) must be lodged with the sheriff clerk at the above address within (*insert the appropriat period of notice*) days of (*insert the date on which service was executed. N. B. Rule 5.3(2)* **relating to postal service**).

---

**IF YOU ARE UNCERTAIN WHAT ACTION TO TAKE** you should consult a solicitor. You may be eligible for legal aid depending on your income. You can get information about legal aid from a solicitor. You may also obtain advice from any Citizens Advice Bureau or other advice agency.

**PLEASE NOTE THAT IF YOU DO NOTHING IN ANSWER TO THIS DOCUMENT** the court may regard you as having no interest in the fund in medio and will proceed accordingly.

Signed

[P.O.], Sheriff officer,

*or* [X.Y.] (*add designation and business address*)

Solicitor for the pursuer

FORM M3

Rule 35.6(2)

Form of certificate of citation in an action of multiplepoinding

Certificate of Citation

(*Insert place and date*) I,.......... hereby certify that upon the..........day of..........

I duly cited [C.D.]. Defender, to answer to the foregoing writ. This I did by (*state method of service; if by officer and not by post, add:* in presence of [L.M.], (*insert designation*), witness hereto with me subscribing *and where service is executed by post state whether made by registered post of the first class recorded delivery service*):

Signed

[P.O.]. Sheriff officer [L.M.], witness

*or* [X.Y.] (*add designation and business address*)

Solicitor for the pursuer

FORM M4

Rules 35.6(1) and 35.8

Form of notice of appearance in an action of multiplepoinding

NOTICE OF APPEARANCE (MULTIPLEPOINDING)

*PART A Court Ref. No.

(Insert name and business address of solicitor for the pursuer) 　　　　　　　In an action raised at Sheriff Court

Pursuer

Solicitor for the pursuer 　　　　　　　　　　　　Defender

*(This part to be completed by the pursuer before service)

DATE OF SERVICE: DATE OF EXPIRY OF PERIOD OF NOTICE:

....................

*PART B

**\* (This section to be completed by the defender or the defender's solicitor and both parts of this form returned to the sheriff clerk at (insert address of sheriff clerk) on or before the expiry of the period of notice referred to in PART A above)**

(*Insert place and date*)

[C.D.] (design), Defender, intends to lodge:

|  |  |  |
|---|---|---|
|  | ☐ | defences challenging the jurisdiction of the court or the competence of the action. |
| Tick the appropriate box(es) | ☐ | objections to the condescendence on the fund *in medio* |
|  | ☐ | a claim on the fund *in medio*. |

Signed

[C.D.] Defender,

*or* [X.Y.] (*add designation and business address*)

Solicitor for the defender

FORM M5

Rules 35.9(b) and 35.10(5)

Form of intimation of first hearing in an action of multiplepoinding

SHERIFFDOM OF (*insert name of sheriffdom*)............... Court ref. no. ..........

AT (*insert place of sheriff court*)

[A.B.] (*insert designation and address*). Pursuer, against [C.D.] (*insert designation and address*), Defender.

You are given notice that in this action of multiplepoinding

| |
|---|
| *Insert date, time and place)* |

is the date, time and place for the first hearing.

Date (*Insert date*)

Signed

Sheriff clerk (dispute)

**Note**

If the pursuer fails to return the writ in terms of rule 9.3 of the Ordinary Cause Rules of the Sheriff Court or any party fails to comply with the terms of this notice or to provide the sheriff at the hearing with sufficient information to enable it to be conducted it in terms of rule 35.10 of these rules, the sheriff may make such order or finding against that party so failing as he thinks fit.

NOTE TO BE ADDED WHERE PARTY UNREPRESENTED

**Note**

**IF YOU ARE UNCERTAIN WHAT ACTION TO TAKE** you should consult a solicitor. You may be eligible for legal aid depending on your income. You can get information about legal aid from a solicitor. You may also obtain advice from any Citizens Advice Bureau or other advice agency.

FORM M6

Rule 35.10(4)(b)

Form of citation of person having an interest in the fund in an action of multiplepoinding

CITATION

SHERIFFDOM OF (*insert name of sheriffdom*)...............Court ref. no. AT (*insert place of sheriff court*)

[A.B.], (*insert designation and address*), Pursuer, against [C.D.], (*insert designation and address*), Defender.

(*Insert place and date*) In the above action the court has been advised that you (*insert name and address*) have an interest in (*insert details of the fund in medio*). You are hereby served with a copy of the pleadings in this action, together with Form M4 (notice of appearance).

Form M4 is served on you for use should you wish to intimate that you intend to lodge:

(a)  defences challenging the jurisdiction of the court or the competence of the action; or

(b)  objections to the condescendence on the fund *in medio*; or

(c)  a claim on the fund.

**IF YOU WISH TO APPEAR IN THIS ACTION** you should consult a solicitor with a view to lodging a notice of appearance (Form M4). The notice of appearance, together with the court fee of £ (insert amount) must be lodged with the sheriff clerk at the above address within.......... days of (*insert date on which service was executed N.B.* Rule 5.3(2) *relating to postal service*).

NOTE:

**IF YOU ARE UNCERTAIN WHAT ACTION TO TAKE** you should consult a solicitor. You may be eligible for legal aid depending on your income. You can get information about legal aid from a solicitor. You may also obtain advice from any Citizens Advice Bureau or other advice agency.

*PLEASE NOTE THAT IF YOU DO NOTHING IN ANSWER TO THIS DOCUMENT* the court may regard you as having no interest in the fund *in medio* and will proceed accordingly.

Signed

[P.Q.], Sheriff officer,

*or* [X.Y.] (*add designation and business address*)

Solicitor for the pursuer

[1]FORM PI1

**Rule 36.B1**

Form of initial writ in a personal injuries action

---

[1]  As inserted by the Act of Sederunt (Ordinary Cause Rules Amendment) (Personal Injuries Actions) 2009 (SSI 2009/285) r.2 (effective November 2, 2009).

INITIAL WRIT
(Personal Injuries Action)
SHERIFFDOM OF (*insert name of sheriffdom*)
AT (*insert place of sheriff court*) [A.B.] (*design and state any special capacity in which pursuer is suing*), Pursuer
against
[C.D.] (*design and state any special capacity in which defender is being sued*), Defender

The pursuer craves the court to grant decree—
(a) for payment by the defender to the pursuer of the sum of (*amount of sum in words and figures*);
(b) (*enter only if a claim for provisional damages is sought in terms of* rule 36.12) for payment by the defender to the pursuer of (*enter amount in words and figures*) of provisional damages; and
(c) for the expenses of the action.

Statement of Claim
1. The pursuer is (*state designation, address, occupation and date of birth of pursuer*). (In an action arising out of the death of a relative state designation of the deceased and relation to the pursuer).
2. The defender is (*state designation, address and occupation of the defender*).
3. The court has jurisdiction to hear this claim against the defender because (*state briefly ground of jurisdiction*).
4. (*State briefly the facts necessary to establish the claim*).
5. (*State briefly the personal injuries suffered and the heads of claim. Give names and addresses of medical practitioners and hospitals or other institutions in which the person injured received treatment*).
6. (*State whether claim based on fault at common law or breach of statutory duty; If breach of statutory duty, state provision of enactment*).

(*Signed*)
[A.B.], Pursuer
or [X.Y.], Solicitor for the pursuer (*insert designation and business address*)
[1]FORM PI2

Rule 36.B1
Form of order of court for recovery of documents in personal injuries action

Court ref. no.

SHERIFFDOM OF (*insert name of sheriffdom*)
AT (*insert place of sheriff court*)
SPECIFICATION OF DOCUMENTS
*in the cause*
[A.B.] (*designation and address*), Pursuer against
[C.D.] (*designation and address*), Defender

Date: (*date of posting or other method of service*)
To: (*name and address of party or parties from whom the following documents are sought to be recovered*)

You are hereby required to produce to the agent for the pursuer within seven days of the service on you of this Order:
[*Insert such of the following calls as are required*].
1. All books, medical records, reports, charts, X-rays, notes and other documents of (*specify the name of each medical practitioner or general practitioner practice named in initial writ in accordance with* rule 36.B1 (1)(b)), and relating to the pursuer [*or, as the case may be, the deceased*] from (*insert date*), in order that excerpts may be taken therefrom at the sight of the Commissioner of all entries showing or tending to show the nature, extent and cause of the pursuer's [*or, as the case may be, the deceased's*] injuries when he attended his doctor on or after (*specify date*) and the treatment received by him since that date.
2. All books, medical records, reports, charts, X-rays, notes and other documents of (*specify, in separate calls, the name of each hospital or other institution named in initial writ in accordance with* rule 36.B1 (1)(b)), and relating to the pursuer [*or, as the case may be, the deceased*] from (*insert date*), in order that excerpts may be taken therefrom at the sight of the Commissioner of all entries showing or tending to show the nature, extent and cause of the pursuer's

---

[1] As inserted by the Act of Sederunt (Ordinary Cause Rules Amendment) (Personal Injuries Actions) 2009 (SSI 2009/285) r.2 (effective November 2, 2009).

[*or, as the case may be, the deceased's*] injuries when he was admitted to that institution on or about (*specify date*), the treatment received by him since that date and his certificate of discharge, if any.

3. The medical records and capability assessments held by the defender's occupational health department relating to the pursuer [*or, as the case may be, the deceased*], except insofar as prepared for or in contemplation of litigation, in order that excerpts may be taken therefrom at the sight of the Commissioner of all entries showing or tending to show the nature and extent of any injuries, symptoms and conditions from which the pursuer [*or, as the case may he, the deceased*] was suffering and the nature of any assessment and diagnosis made thereof on or subsequent to (*specify date*).

4. All wage books, cash books, wage sheets, computer records and other earnings information relating to the pursuer [*or, as the case may he, the deceased*] (N.I. number (*specify number*)) held by or on behalf of (*specify employer*), for the period (*specify dates commencing not earlier than 26 weeks prior to the date of the accident or the first date of relevant absence, as the case may be*) in order that excerpts may be taken therefrom at the sight of the Commissioner of all entries showing or tending to show—

    (a) the pursuer's [*or, as the case may be, the deceased's*] earnings, both gross and net of income tax and employee National Insurance Contributions, over the said period;

    (b) the period or periods of the pursuer's [*or, as the case may be, the deceased's*] absence from employment over the said period and the reason for absence;

    (c) details of any increases in the rate paid over the period (*specify dates*) and the dates on which any such increases took effect;

    (d) the effective date of, the reasons for and the terms (including any terms relative to any pension entitlement) of the termination of the pursuer's [*or, as the case may be, the deceased's*] employment;

    (e) the nature and extent of contributions (if any) to any occupational pension scheme made by the pursuer [*or, as the case may be, the deceased*] and his employer;

    (f) the pursuer's present entitlement (if any) to any occupational pension and the manner in which said entitlement is calculated.

5. All accident reports, memoranda or other written communications made to the defender or anyone on his behalf by an employee of the defender who was present at or about the time at which the pursuer [*or, as the case may be, the deceased*] sustained the injuries in respect of which the initial writ in this cause was issued and relevant to the matters contained in the statement of claim.

6. Any assessment current at the time of the accident referred to in the initial writ or at the time of the circumstances referred to in the initial writ giving rise to the cause of action (as the case may be) undertaken by or on behalf of the defender for the purpose of regulation 3 of the Management of Health and Safety at Work Regulations 1992 and subsequently regulation 3 of the Management of Health and Safety at Work Regulations 1999 [*or (specify the regulations or other legislative provision under which the risk assessment is required)*] in order that excerpts may be taken therefrom at the sight of the Commissioner of all entries relating to the risks posed to workers [*or (specify the matters set out in the statement of claim to which the risk assessment relates)*].

7. Failing principals, drafts, copies or duplicates of the above or any of them.

(Signature, name and business address of the agent for the pursuer)

*NOTES:*

1. The documents recovered will be considered by the parties to the action and they may or may not be lodged in the court process. A written receipt will be given or sent to you by the pursuer, who may thereafter allow them to be inspected by the other parties. The party in whose possession the documents are will be responsible for their safekeeping.

2. Payment may be made, within certain limits, in respect of claims for outlays incurred in relation to the production of documents. Claims should be made in writing to the person who has obtained an order that you produce the documents.

3. If you claim that any of the documents produced by you is **confidential** you must still produce such documents but may place them in a separate sealed packet by themselves, marked "CONFIDENTIAL". In that event they must be delivered or sent by post to the sheriff clerk. Any party who wishes to open the sealed packet must apply to the sheriff by motion. A party who makes such an application must intimate the motion to you.

4. Subject to paragraph 3 above, you may produce these documents by sending them by registered post or by the first class recorded delivery service or registered postal packet, or by hand to (*name and address of the agent for the pursuer*).

**CERTIFICATE**

(*Date*)

I hereby certify with reference to the above order in the cause (*cause reference number*) and the enclosed specification of documents, served on me and marked respectively X and Y—

1. That the documents which are produced and which are listed in the enclosed inventory signed by me and marked Z, are all the documents in my possession falling within the specification. OR That I have no documents in my possession falling within the specification.

2. That, to the best of my knowledge and belief, there are in existence other documents falling within the specification, but not in my possession. These documents are as follows: (*describe them by reference to the descriptions of documents in the specification*). They were last seen by me on or about (*date*), at (*place*), in the hands of (*name and address of the person*). OR That I know of the existence of no documents in the possession of any person, other than me, which fall within the specification.

(Signed)
(Name and address)

### [1]FORM PI3

Rule 36.D1

Form of docquet for deemed grant of recovery of documents in a personal injuries action

Court (*insert court*)

Date (*insert date*)

Commission and diligence for the production and recovery of the documents called for in this specification of documents is deemed to have been granted.

(Signed)

Sheriff Clerk (depute)

### [2]FORM PI4

Rule 36.C1

Form of interlocutor granting authority to raise action based on clinical negligence as an ordinary cause

(*To be inserted on the first page of the initial writ, above the crave(s)*)

Authority

The sheriff, having considered the application of the pursuer [and having heard agents thereon], being satisfied that, although this is a personal injuries action, there are exceptional reasons for not following the personal injuries procedure in Part A1 of Chapter 36 of the Ordinary Cause Rules 1993 such as would justify the granting of a motion under rule 36.F1, grants authority for the cause to proceed as an ordinary cause.

(*Signed*)

Sheriff

Date (*date*)

### [3]FORM PI5

**Rule 36.G1**

Form of timetable
TIMETABLE

Court ref. no.

In the cause [A.B.], Pursuer
Against
[C.D.], Defender

This timetable has effect as if it were an interlocutor of the sheriff

1. The diet allocated for the proof in this action will begin on (*date*). Subject to any variation under rule 36.H1, this order requires the parties to undertake the conduct of this action within the periods specified in paragraphs 2 to 9 below.

2. Any motion under rule 20.1 (third party notice) shall be made by (*date*).

3. Where the pursuer has obtained a commission and diligence for the recovery of documents by virtue of rule 36.D1, the pursuer shall serve an order under rule 28.3 not later than (*date*).

---

[1] As inserted by the Act of Sederunt (Ordinary Cause Rules Amendment) (Personal Injuries Actions) 2009 (SSI 2009/285) r.2 (effective November 2, 2009).

[2] As inserted by the Act of Sederunt (Ordinary Cause Rules Amendment) (Personal Injuries Actions) 2009 (SSI 2009/285) r.2 (effective November 2, 2009).

[3] As inserted by the Act of Sederunt (Ordinary Cause Rules Amendment) (Personal Injuries Actions) 2009 (SSI 2009/285) r.2 (effective November 2, 2009).

4.  The pursuer shall lodge a statement of valuation of claim under rule 36.J1 not later than (*date*).
5.  For the purposes of rule 36.G1, the adjustment period shall end on (*date*).
6.  The pursuer shall lodge a record not later than (*date*).
7.  The defender and any third party convened in the action shall lodge a statement of valuation of claim under rule 36.J1 not later than (*date*).
8.  Not later than (*date*) parties shall lodge lists of witnesses and productions.
9.  Not later than (*date*) the pursuer shall lodge a pre-proof minute under rule 36.K1.

[1]FORM PI6

Rule 36.J1

Form of statement of valuation of claim

| Head of claim | Components | Valuation |
|---|---|---|
| Solatium | Past | £x |
| | Future | £x |
| Interest on past solatium | Percentage applied to past solatium (state percentage rate) | £x |
| Past wage loss | Date from which wage loss claimed: (date) | £x |
| | Date to which wage loss claimed: (date) | |
| | Rate of net wage loss (per week, per month or per annum) | |
| Interest on past wage loss | Percentage applied to pas wage loss: (state percentage rate) | £x |
| Future wage loss | Multiplier: (state multiplier) | £x |
| | Multiplicand: (state multiplicand and show how calculated) | |
| | Discount factor applied (if appropriate): (state factor) | |
| | Or specify any other method of calculation | |
| Past services | Date from which services claimed: (date) | £x |
| | Date to which services claimed: (date) | |
| | Nature of services:(..........) | |
| | Person by whom services provided: (..........) | |
| | Hours per week services provided: (..........) | |
| | Net hourly rate claimed: (..........) | |
| | Total amount claimed: (..........) | |
| | Interest | |
| Future loss of capacity to provide personal service | Multiplier: (insert multiplier) | £x |

[1] As inserted by the Act of Sederunt (Ordinary Cause Rules Amendment) (Personal Injuries Actions) 2009 (SSI 2009/285) r.2 (effective November 2, 2009).

| Head of claim | Components | Valuation |
|---|---|---|
| | Multiplicand: (insert multiplicand, showing how calculated) | |
| Needs and other expenses | One off<br>Multiplier: (insert multiplier)<br>Multiplicand: (insert multiplicand)<br>Interest | £x |
| Any other heads as appropriate (specify) | | |

[1]FORM PI7

Rule 36.K1

Minute of pre-proof conference

SHERIFFDOM OF (*insert sheriffdom*) AT (*insert place*)

Joint minute of pre-proof conference

in the cause

[A.B], Pursuer

Against

[CD], Defender

[E.F.] for the pursuer and

[G.H.] for the defender hereby state to the court:

1. That the pre-proof conference was held in this case [*at (place)* **or** *by (telephone conference or video conference or other remote means)*] on [*date*].
2. That the following persons were present—

(*State names and designations of persons attending conference*)

3. That the following persons were available to provide instructions by telephone or video conference—

(*State names and designations or persons available to provide instructions by telephone or video conference*)

4. That the persons participating in the conference discussed settlement of the action.
5. That the following questions were addressed—

### Section 1

| | | Yes | No |
|---|---|---|---|
| 1. | Is the diet of proof still required? | | |
| 2. | If the answer to question 1 is "yes", does the defender admit liability? (If "no", complete section 2)<br>If yes, does the defender plead contributory negligence?<br>If yes, is the degree of contributory negligence agreed?<br>If yes, state % degree of fault attributed to the pursuer. | | |
| 3. | If the answer to question 1 is "yes", is the quantum of damages agreed? (If "no", complete section 3) | | |

### Section 2

[To be inserted only if the proof is still required]

It is estimated that the hearing will last days

*NB. If the estimate is more than 2 days then this should be brought to the attention of the sheriff clerk. This may affect prioritisation of the case.*

During the course of the pre-proof conference, the pursuer called on the defender to agree certain facts, questions of law and matters of evidence.

Those calls, and the defender's responses, are as follows—

---

[1] As inserted by the Act of Sederunt (Ordinary Cause Rules Amendment) (Personal Injuries Actions) 2009 (SSI 2009/285) r.2 (effective November 2, 2009).

| Call | Response | |
|------|----------|-------|
| | Admitted | Denied |
| 1. | | |
| 2. | | |
| 3. | | |
| 4. | | |

During the course of the pre-proof conference, the defender called on the pursuer to agree certain facts, questions of law and matters of evidence.

Those calls, and the pursuer's responses, are as follows—

| Call | Response | |
|------|----------|-------|
| | Admitted | Denied |
| 1. | | |
| 2. | | |
| 3. | | |
| 4. | | |

**Section 3**

Quantum of damages

Please indicate where agreement has been reached on an element of damages.

| Head of claim | Components | Not agreed | Agreed at |
|---------------|-----------|------------|-----------|
| Solatium | Past | | |
| | Future | | |
| Interest on past solatium | Percentage applied to past solatium (state percentage) | | |
| Past wage loss | Date from which wage lost claimed | | |
| | Date to which wage loss claimed | | |
| | Rate of net wage loss (per week, per month or per annum) | | |
| Interest on past wage loss | | | |
| Future wage loss | Multiplier | | |
| | Multiplicand (showing how calculated) | | |
| Past necessary services | Date from which services claimed | | |
| | Date to which services claimed | | |
| | Hours per week services provided | | |
| | Net hourly rate claimed | | |
| Past personal services | Date from which services claimedDate to which services claimedHours per week services providedNet hourly rate claimed | | |
| Interest on past services | | | |
| Future necessary services | MultiplierMultiplicand (showing how calculated) | | |

| Head of claim | Components | Not agreed | Agreed at |
|---|---|---|---|
| Future personal services | MultiplierMultiplicand (showing how calculated) | | |
| Needs and other expenses | One offMultiplierMultiplicand (showing how calculated) | | |
| Any other heads as appropriate (specify) | | | |

<u>(Signed by agent for each party)</u>

FORM D1

Rule 36.3(2)

Form of intimation to connected person in damages action

SHERIFFDOM OF *(insert name of sheriffdom)* ............... Court ref.no. ..........

AT *(insert place of sheriff court)* ...............

You are given NOTICE that an action has been raised in the above sheriff court by *(insert name and designation of pursuer)* against *(insert name and designation of defender)*. A copy of the initial writ is attached.

It is believed that you may have a title or interest to sue the said *(insert name of defender)* in an action based upon [the injuries from which the late *(insert name and designation)* died] [or the death of the late *(insert name and designation)*]. You may therefore be entitled to enter this action as an additional pursuer. If you wish to do so, you may apply by lodging a minute with the sheriff clerk at the above address to be sisted as an additional pursuer within *(insert the appropriate period of notice)* days of *(insert the date on which service was executed N.B.* Rule 5.3(2) *relating to postal service)*.

Signed...............

Solicitor for the pursuer..........

---

NOTE

The minute must be lodged with the sheriff clerk with the court fee of *(insert amount)* and a motion seeking leave for the minute to be received and for answers to be lodged. When lodging the minute you must present to the sheriff clerk a copy of the initial writ and this intimation.

---

**IF YOU ARE UNCERTAIN WHAT ACTION TO TAKE** you should consult a solicitor. You may be eligible for legal aid depending on your income, and you can obtain information about legal aid from any solicitor. You may also obtain advice from any Citizens Advice Bureau or other advice agency.

---

FORM D2

Rule 36.17(1)

Form of receipt for payment into court
RECEIPT

In the Sheriff Court of *(insert name of sheriffdom)* at *(insert place of sheriff court)* in the cause, *(state names of parties or other appropriate description)* [A.B.] *(insert designation)* has this day paid into court the sum of *(insert sum concerned)* being a payment into court in terms of rule 36.14 of the Ordinary Cause Rules of the Sheriff Court of money which in an action of damages, has become payable to a person under legal disability.

*[If the payment is made under* rule 36.15(c) *add*: [the custody of which money has been accepted at the request of *(insert name of court making request)*.]

Date *(insert date)*...............Signed

Sheriff clerk (depute)

[1]FORM P1

Rule 37.2(2)

Form of advertisement in an action of declarator under section 1(1) of the Presumption of Death (Scotland) Act 1977

(insert such facts relating to the missing person as set out in the initial writ as the sheriff may specify).

---

[1] As amended by the Act of Sederunt (Sheriff Court Ordinary Cause Rules Amendment) (Miscellaneous) 2000 (SSI 2000/239) (effective October 2, 2000).

Sheriff Court *(insert address)*...............Court ref. no. ..........

An action has been raised in *(insert name of sheriff court)* by [A.B.], Pursuer, to declare that [C.D.], Defender, whose last known address was *(insert last known address of [C.D.])* is dead.

Any person wishing to defend the action must apply to do so by *(insert date, being [21] days after the date of the advertisement)* by lodging a minute seeking to be sisted a a party to the action with the sheriff clerk at the above address.

A copy of the initial writ may be obtained from the sheriff clerk at the above address.

Date *(insert date)*...............Signed...............

[X.Y.] *(add designation and business address)* Solicitor for the pursuer *or* [P.Q.] Sheriff officer

FORM P2

Rule 37.2(4)

Form of intimation to missing person's spouse and children or nearest known relative

To *(insert name and address as in warrant)*...............Court ref. no. ..........

You are given notice that in this action the pursuer craves the court to declare that *(insert the name and last known address of missing person)* is dead. A copy of the initial writ is enclosed.

If you wish to appear as a party, and make an application under section 1 (5) of the Presumption of Death (Scotland) Act 1977 craving the court to make any determination or appointment not sought by the pursuer, you must lodge a minute with the sheriff clerk at *(insert address of sheriff clerk)*.

Your minute must be lodged within [..........] days of *(insert the date on which intimation was given N.B. Rule 5.3(2) relating to postal service or intimation)*.

Date *(insert date)*...............Signed..........

Solicitor for the pursuer
*(add designation and business address)*

---

NOTE

The minute must be lodged with the sheriff clerk with the court fee of *(insert amount)* and a motion seeking leave for the minute to be received and for answers to be lodged. When lodging the minute you must present to the sheriff clerk a copy of the initial writ and this intimation.

---

**IF YOU ARE UNCERTAIN WHAT ACTION TO TAKE** you should consult a solicitor. You may be eligible for legal aid depending on your income, and you can obtain information about legal aid from any solicitor. You may also obtain advice from any Citizens Advice Bureau or other advice agency.

[1]FORM E1

Rule 38.3(1A)

Form of reference to the European Court

REQUEST

for

PRELIMINARY RULING

of

THE COURT OF JUSTICE OF THE EUROPEAN COMMUNITIES

from

THE SHERIFFDOM OF *insert name of sheriffdom)* at *(insert place of court)*

in the cause

[A.B.] *(insert designation and address)*, Pursuer

against

[C.D.] *(insert designation and address)*, Defender

[Here set out a clear and succinct statement of the case giving rise to the request for the ruling of the European Court in order to enable the European Court to consider and understand the issues of Community law raised and to enable governments of Member States and other interested parties to submit observations. The statement of the case should include:

(a)   particulars of the parties;

(b)   the history of the dispute between the parties;

(c)   the history of the proceedings;

---

[1] As substituted by the Act of Sederunt (Sheriff Court Ordinary Cause Rules Amendment) (Miscellaneous) 2000 (SSI 2000/239) (effective October 2, 2000).

(d)    the relevant facts as agreed by the parties or found by the court or, failing such agreement or finding, the contentions of the parties on such facts;

(e)    the nature of the issues of law and fact between the parties;

(f)    the Scots law, so far as relevant;

(g)    the Treaty provisions or other acts, instruments or rules of Community law concerned; and

(h)    an explanation of why the reference is being made.]

The preliminary ruling of the Court of Justice of the European Communities is accordingly requested on the following questions:

1, 2, etc. [Here set out the question on which the ruling is sought, identifying the Treaty provisions or other acts, instruments or rules of Community law concerned.] Dated the day of 20 .

**Rule 41.5**

FORM PA1[1] [2]

Form of certificate of delivery of documents to chief constable

*(Insert place and date)* I, hereby certify that upon the day of I duly delivered to the chief constable of the Police Service of Scotland *(insert details of the documents delivered)*. This I did by *(state method of delivery)*.

Signed

Solicitor/sheriff officer

*(add designation and business address)*

**Rule 41A.2(3)**

FORM DA1[3] [4]

Form of interlocutor for a determination of a domestic abuse interdict

Court ref no.

SHERIFFDOM OF *(insert name of sheriffdom)*

AT *(insert place of sheriff court)*

[A.B.], *(insert designation and address)*, Pursuer
against

[C.D.], *(insert designation and address)*, Defender

*(Date)*

The sheriff, in pursuance of section 3(1) of the Domestic Abuse (Scotland) Act 2011, makes a determination that the [interim*] interdict dated *(insert date)* [and to which a power of arrest was attached by interlocutor dated *(insert date)*\*] is a domestic abuse interdict. [The sheriff appoints *(insert name of person)*] to send forthwith a copy of this interlocutor and a copy of the certificate of service in Form DA2 to the chief constable of the Police Service of Scotland].

*(\*delete as appropriate)*

*(Sheriff)*..........

**Rule 41A.2(4)**

[5]FORM DA2

Form of certificate of service

Court ref no.

SHERIFFDOM OF (insert name of sheriffdom)*(insert name of sheriffdom)*
AT *(insert place of sheriff court)*
[A.B.], *(insert designation and address)*, Pursuer
against
[C.D.], *(insert designation and address)*, Defender

*(Insert place and date)*

---

[1] As inserted by the Act of Sederunt (Ordinary Cause Rules) (Applications under the Protection from Abuse (Scotland) Act 2001) 2002 (SSI 2002/128), para. 2(3) and Sched.

[2] As amended by the Act of Sederunt (Sheriff Court Rules)(Miscellaneous Amendments) 2013 (SSI 2013/135) para.4 (effective May 27, 2013).

[3] As inserted by the Act of Sederunt (Sheriff Court Rules) (Miscellaneous Amendments) (No.2) 2011 (SSI 2011/289) para.5 (effective July 20, 2011).

[4] As amended by the Act of Sederunt (Sheriff Court Rules)(Miscellaneous Amendments) 2013 (SSI 2013/135) para.4 (effective May 27, 2013).

[5] As inserted by the Act of Sederunt (Sheriff Court Rules) (Miscellaneous Amendments) (No.2) 2011 (SSI 2011/289) para.5 (effective July 20, 2011).

I hereby certify that on *(insert date)* I duly served on *(insert name and address of person subject to the interdict)* a copy of Form DA1. This I did by *(state method of service)*.

*(Signed)*

(Solicitor/sheriff officer)

*(add designation and business address)*

**Rule 41A.2(5)**

[1] [2]FORM DA3

Form of interlocutor for recall of a determination of a domestic abuse interdict

Court ref no.

SHERIFFDOM OF *(insert name of sheriffdom)*

AT *(insert place of sheriff court)*

[A.B.]. *(insert designation and address)*, Pursuer

against

[C.D.], *(insert designation and address)*, Defender

(Date)

The sheriff, in pursuance of section 3(5)(b) of the Domestic Abuse (Scotland) Act 2011, recalls the determination that the [interim*] interdict dated *(insert date)* is a domestic abuse interdict. [The sheriff appoints *(insert name of person)*] to send forthwith a copy of this interlocutor to the chief constable of the Police Service of Scotland]. *(\*delete as appropriate)*

*(Sheriff)*

FORM DA4[3] [4]

**Rule 41A.2(8)**

Form of certificate of sending documents to the chief constable

Court ref no.

SHERIFFDOM OF *(insert name of sheriffdom)*

AT *(insert place of sheriff court)*

[A.B.], *(insert designation and address)*, Pursuer

against

[C.D.], *(insert designation and address)*, Defender

*(Insert place and date)*

I hereby certify that on *(insert date)* I duly sent to the chief constable of the Police Service of Scotland a copy of [the interlocutor in Form DA1 and the certificate of service in Form DA2*] [the interlocutor in Form DA3*]. This I did by *(state method of sending)*. *\*delete as appropriate)*

*(Signed)*

(Solicitor/sheriff officer)

*(add designation and business address)*

[5]FORM OFT1

**Rule 43.1(2)**

Form of notice of intimation to the Office of Fair Trading

Date: *(date of posting or other method of intimation)*

To: The Office of Fair Trading

TAKE NOTICE

---

[1] As inserted by the Act of Sederunt (Sheriff Court Rules) (Miscellaneous Amendments) (No.2) 2011 (SSI 2011/289) para.5 (effective July 20, 2011).

[2] As amended by the Act of Sederunt (Sheriff Court Rules)(Miscellaneous Amendments) 2013 (SSI 2013/135) para.4 (effective May 27, 2013).

[3] As inserted by the Act of Sederunt (Sheriff Court Rules) (Miscellaneous Amendments) (No.2) 2011 (SSI 2011/289) para.5 (effective July 20, 2011).

[4] As amended by the Act of Sederunt (Sheriff Court Rules)(Miscellaneous Amendments) 2013 (SSI 2013/135) para.4 (effective May 27, 2013).

[5] As inserted by Act of Sederunt (Ordinary Cause Rules) Amendment (Causes Relating to Articles 81 and 82 of the Treaty Establishing the European Community) 2006 (SSI 2006/293) (effective June 16, 2006) and amended by the Act of Sederunt (Sheriff Court Rules) (Miscellaneous Amendments) (No.3) 2012 (SSI 2012/271) para.6 (effective November 1, 2012).

307

(*Name and address of pursuer or defender*) has brought an action against [*or* has defended an action brought by] (*name and address of defender or pursuer*). The action raises an issue under Article 101 or 102 of the Treaty on the Functioning of the European Union. A copy of the initial writ is [*or* pleadings and interlocutor allowing intimation are*] attached.

If you wish to submit written observations to the court, these should be addressed to the sheriff clerk (*insert address of sheriff clerk*) and must be lodged within 21 days of (*insert date on which intimation was given. N.B.* rule 5.3(2) *relating to postal service or intimation*).

If you wish to submit oral observations to the court, you must lodge a minute with the sheriff clerk (*insert address of sheriff clerk*) for leave to do so. Your minute must be lodged within 21 days of (*insert date on which intimation was given. N.B.* rule 5.3(2) *relating to postal service or intimation*).

Date (*insert date*)..........(*Signed*)

Solicitor for pursuer/defender

[1]FORM 49.6

**Rule 49.6(6)** and (7)

Form of preliminary act in ship collision action

In the action in which ............... is Pursuer

.......... and ..........

.............. is Defender

Preliminary Act

for

Pursuer [*or* Defender]

Court Ref. No:...............

(1) (*State the names of the vessels which came into collision, their ports or registry, and the names of their masters.*)

(2) (*State the date and time of the collision.*)

(3) (*State the place of the collision.*)

(4) (*State the direction and force of the wind.*)

(5) (*State the state of the weather.*)

(6) (*State the state, direction and force of the tidal or other current.*)

(7) (*State the magnetic course steered and speed through the water of the vessel when the other vessel was first seen or immediately before any measures were taken with reference to her presence, whichever was the earlier.*)

(8) (*State the lights (if any) carried by the vessel.*)

(9) (*State the distance and bearing of the other vessel if and when her echo was first observed by radar.*)

(10) (*State the distance, bearing and approximate heading of the other vessel when first seen.*)

(11) (*State what light or combination of lights (if any) of the other vessel when first seen.*)

(12) (*State what other lights or combinations of lights (if any) of the other vessel were subsequently seen, before the collision, and when.*)

(13) (*State what alterations (if any) were made to the course and speed of the vessel after the earlier of the two times referred to in paragraph (7) up to the time of the collision, and when, and what measures (if any), other than alterations of course and speed, were taken to avoid the collision and when.*)

(14) (*State the parts of each vessel which first came into contact and the approximate angle between the two vessels at the moment of contact.*)

(15) (*State what sound signals (if any) were given, and when.*)

(16) (*State what sound signals (if any) were heard from the other vessel and when.*)

(*Signed by solicitor or Agent*)

(*Name*)

(*Address*)

(*Telephone number*)

(*Date*)

[2]FORM 49.11-A

Rule 49.11(1)(a)(i)

---

[1] As inserted by the Act of Sederunt (Sheriff Court Rules) (Miscellaneous Amendments) 2012 (SSI 2012/188) para.10 (effective August 1, 2012).

[2] As inserted by the Act of Sederunt (Sheriff Court Rules) (Miscellaneous Amendments) 2012 (SSI 2012/188) para.10 (effective August 1, 2012).

Form of schedule of arrestment of found jurisdiction

Court:...............

Court Ref. No:...............

## SCHEDULE OF ARRESTMENT TO FOUND JURISDICTION

Date: (*date of execution*)

Time: (*time arrestment executed*)

To: (*name and address of arrestee*)

I, (*name*), Sheriff Officer, by virtue of an interlocutor of the Sheriff at (*place*) on (*date*) containing a warrant for arrestment to found jurisdiction, at the instance of (*name and address of pursuer*) against (*name and address of defender*), arrest to found jurisdiction against (*name of defender*) in your hands: (i) the sum of (*amount*), more or less, due by you to (*name of defender*) or to any other person on his [*or* her] [*or* its] [*or* their] behalf; and (ii) all moveable subjects in your hands and belonging or pertaining to (*name of defender*).

This I do in the presence of (*name, occupation and address of witness*).

(*Signed*)

Sheriff Officer

(*Address*)

### NOTE

(*Do not use this note where arrestment to found jurisdiction is combined with arrestment on the dependence in one schedule.*)

(The name, address and twenty-four hour contact telephone number of the agent for the party on whose behalf the arrestment was executed are to be inserted here.)

(*Name of agent*)

(*Address*)

(*Telephone number*)

[1]FORM 49.11-AA

Rule 49.11(1)(a)(ii)

Form of schedule of arrestment of ship to found jurisdiction

Court:...............

Court Ref. No:...............

### SCHEDULE OF ARRESTMENT OF SHIP TO FOUND JURISDICTION

Date: (*date of execution*)

Time: (*time arrestment executed*)

I, (*name*), Sheriff Officer, by virtue of an interlocutor of the Sheriff at (*place*) on (*date*) containing a warrant for arrestment to found jurisdiction, at the instance of (*name and address of pursuer*) against (*name and address of defender*), arrest to found jurisdiction against (*name of defender*) the ship (*name*) presently lying in (*describe location*) and belonging to the defender.

This I do in the presence of (*name, occupation and address of witness*).

(*Signed*)

Sheriff Officer

(*Address*)

### NOTE

You should consult your legal adviser about the effect of this arrestment.

(The name, address and twenty-four hour contact telephone number of the agent for the party on whose behalf the arrestment was executed are to be inserted here.)

(*Name of agent*)

(*Address*)

(*Telephone number*)

[2] FORM 49.11-B

Rule 49.11(1)(c)

Form of schedule of arrestment in rem of ship, cargo or other maritime res to enforce maritime hypothec or lien

---

[1] As inserted by the Act of Sederunt (Sheriff Court Rules) (Miscellaneous Amendments) 2012 (SSI 2012/188) para.10 (effective August 1, 2012).

[2] As inserted by the Act of Sederunt (Sheriff Court Rules) (Miscellaneous Amendments) 2012 (SSI 2012/188) para.10 (effective August 1, 2012).

Court:...............
Court Ref. No:...............

### SCHEDULE OF ARRESTMENT IN REM IN ADMIRALTY ACTION IN REM

Date: (*date of execution*)

Time: (*time arrestment executed*)

I, (*name*), Sheriff Officer, by virtue of an interlocutor of the Sheriff at (*place*) on (*date*) containing a warrant for arrestment in rem of the ship (*name of ship*) [*or* cargo (*describe*)] [*or other maritime res* (*describe*)]] in an Admiralty action in rem at the instance of (*name and address of pursuer*) against (*name and address of defender*), arrest the ship (*name*) presently lying in (*describe current location e.g. the port of X*) with her float, boats, furniture, appurtenances and apparelling [*or* cargo] [*or other maritime res*] (*describe location*)], to remain in that (*specify more precisely if required*) under arrest in rem until they are sold or until this arrestment is recalled or other order of the sheriff.

This I do in the presence of (*name, occupation and address of witness*).

(*Signed*)
Sheriff Officer
(*Address*)

### NOTE

You should consult your legal adviser about the effect of this arrestment.

(The name, address and twenty-four hour contact telephone number of the agent for the party on whose behalf the arrestment was executed are to be inserted here.)

(*Name of agent*)
(*Address*)
(*Telephone number*)

### [1] FORM 49.11-C

Rule 49.11(1)(d)

Form of schedule of arrestment in rem of ship to enforce non-pecuniary claim

Court:...............
Court Ref. No:...............

### SCHEDULE OF ARRESTMENT IN REM OF SHIP UNDER THE ADMINISTRATION OF JUSTICE ACT 1956, SECTION 47(3)(b)

Date: (*date of execution*)

Time: (*time arrestment executed*)

I, (*name*), Sheriff Officer, by virtue of —

*an interlocutor of the Sheriff at (*place*) on (*date*) granting warrant for arrestment in rem under section 47(3)(b) of the Administration of Justice Act 1956 of the ship (*name of ship*) in an action,

*an interlocutor of the Sheriff at (*place*) on (*date*) containing a warrant for arrestment in rem under section 47(3)(b) of the Administration of Justice Act 1956 of the ship (*name of ship*), at the instance of (*name and address of pursuer*) against (*name and address of defender*), arrest the ship [*or vessel*] (*name*) presently lying in (*describe current location e.g. the port of X*) with her float, boats, furniture, appurtenances and apparelling to remain in that (*specify more precisely if required*) under arrestment in rem until this arrestment is recalled or other order of the sheriff.

This I do in the presence of (*name, occupation and address of witness*).

(*Signed*)
Sheriff Officer
(*Address*)

### NOTE

You should consult your legal adviser about the effect of this arrestment.

(The name, address and twenty-four hour contact telephone number of the agent for the party on whose behalf the arrestment was executed are to be inserted here.)

(*Name of agent*)
(*Address*)
(*Telephone number*)

* Delete where not applicable.

---

[1] As inserted by the Act of Sederunt (Sheriff Court Rules) (Miscellaneous Amendments) 2012 (SSI 2012/188) para.10 (effective August 1, 2012).

[1]FORM 49.11-D

Rule 49.11(1)(e)(ii)

Court:...............

Court Ref. No:...............

Form of schedule of arrestment of ship on the dependence

Court: (*date of execution*)

Time: (*time arrestment executed*)

I, (*name*), Sheriff Officer, by virtue of —

*an interlocutor of the Sheriff at (*place*) on (*date*) granting warrant for arrestment on the dependence of the action at the instance of (*name and address of pursuer*) against (*name and address of defender*),

*a counterclaim containing a warrant which has been granted for arrestment on the dependence of the claim by (*name and address of creditor*) against (*name and address of debtor*) and dated (*date of warrant*),

*an interlocutor dated (*date*) granting warrant [for arrestment on the dependence of the action raised at the instance of (*name and address of pursuer*) against (*name and address of defender*)] [or for arrestment on the dependence of the claim in the counterclaim [*or* third party notice] by (*name and address of creditor*) against (*name and address of debtor*) [*or* to arrest in the cause of (*name and address of petitioner*) against (*name and address of respondent*)].

arrest the ship (*name of ship*) presently lying in (*describe current location e.g. the port of X*) to remain in that (*more precisely if required*) under arrestment on the dependence of the action [*or* claim] until further interlocutor of the sheriff.

This I do in the presence of (*name, occupation and address of witness*).

(*Signed*)

Sheriff Officer

(*Address*)

### NOTE

You should consult your legal adviser about the effect of this arrestment.

(The name, address and twenty-four hour contact telephone number of the agent for the party on whose behalf the arrestment was executed are to be inserted here.)

(*Name of agent*)

(*Address*)

(*Telephone number*)

* Delete where not applicable.

[2] FORM 49.11-E

Rule 49.11(1)(a)(i) and (b)

Form of certificate of execution of arrestment

CERTIFICATE OF EXECUTION

I, (*name*), Sheriff Officer, certify that I executed (*specify the kind of arrestment, whether on the dependence of an action, counterclaim or third party notice, whether on the authority of an interlocutor (specify), or in execution of a decree (specify)*), [obtained] at the instance of (*name and address of party arresting*) against (*name and address of common debtor*) on (*name of person on whom executed*)—

* by leaving the schedule of [arrestment] with (*name of defender or other person*) at (*place*) on (*date*).

* by leaving the schedule of [arrestment] with (*name and occupation of person with whom left*) at (*place*) on (*date*). (*Specify that enquiry made and that reasonable grounds exist for believing that the person on whom service is to be made resides at the place but is not available.*)

* by depositing the schedule of [arrestment] in (*place*) on (*date*). (*Specify that enquiry made and that reasonable grounds exist for believing that the person on whom service is to be made resides at the place but is not available.*)

* by leaving the schedule of [arrestment] with (*name and occupation of person with whom left*) at (*place of business*) on (*date*). (*Specify that enquiry made and that reasonable grounds exist for believing that the person on whom service is to be made carries on business at the place.*)

---

[1] As inserted by the Act of Sederunt (Sheriff Court Rules) (Miscellaneous Amendments) 2012 (SSI 2012/188) para.10 (effective August 1, 2012).

[2] As inserted by the Act of Sederunt (Sheriff Court Rules) (Miscellaneous Amendments) 2012 (SSI 2012/188) para.10 (effective August 1, 2012).

* by depositing the schedule of [arrestment] at (*place of business*) on (*date*). (*Specify that enquiry made and that reasonable grounds exist for believing that the person on whom service is to be made carries on business at that place.*)

* by leaving the schedule of [arrestment] with (*registered office or place of business*) on (*date*), in the hands of (*name of person*).

* by leaving [*or* depositing] the schedule of [arrestment] at (*registered office, official address or place of business*) on (*date*) in such a way that it was likely to come to the attention of (*name of defender or other person on whom served*). (*Specify how left.*)

* by leaving the schedule of [arrestment] with (*name and occupation of person with whom left*) at the office of the sheriff clerk at (*place*) on (*date*) and sending a copy of the schedule by first class post (*defender's last known address*) on (*date*).

I did this in the presence of (*name, occupation and address of witness*).

(*Signed*)
Sheriff Officer
(*Address*)
(*Signed*)
Witness

*Delete where not applicable.

[1] FORM 49.11-F

Rule 49.11(1)(a)(ii)

Form of certificate of arrestment of ship to found jurisdiction
CERTIFICATE OF EXECUTION OF ARRESTMENT OF SHIP TO FOUND JURISDICTION

I, (*name*), Sheriff Officer, certify that I, by virtue of an interlocutor of the Sheriff at (*place*) on (*date*) containing a warrant for arrestment to found jurisdiction, executed an arrestment of the ship (*name*) at the instance of (*name and address of pursuer*) against (*name and address of defender*) by affixing the schedule of arrestment to the mainmast [*or as the case may be*] of the ship (*name*) and marked the initials ER above that affixed schedule at (*place*) on (*date*).

I did this in the presence of (*name, occupation and address of witness*).

(*Signed*)
Sheriff Officer
(*Address*)
(*Signed*)
Witness

[2] FORM 49.11-G

Rule 49.11(1)(c) and (d)

Form of certificate of execution of arrestment of ship or cargo in rem
CERTIFICATE OF EXECUTION OF ARRESTMENT OF SHIP [*OR* CARGO] IN REM

I, (*name*), Sheriff Officer, certify that I executed an arrestment in rem of the ship [*or* vessel] (*name*) [*or* cargo (*describe*)] by virtue of an interlocutor of the Sheriff at (*place*) on (*date*) at the instance of (*name and address of pursuer*) against (*name and address of defender*) by affixing the schedule of arrestment to the mainmast [*or as the case may be*] of the ship [*or* vessel] [*or in the case of cargo landed or transhipped on* (*name*) as custodian for the time being of the cargo [*or as harbourmaster of the harbour where the cargo lies*]] [and delivering a copy of the schedule of arrestment and of this certificate to (*name*) the master of the ship [*or as the case may be*] at (*place*) on (*date*).

I did this in the presence of (*name, occupation and address of witness*).

(*Signed*)
Sheriff Officer
(*Address*)
(*Signed*)
Witness

[3] FORM 49.11-H

---

[1] As inserted by the Act of Sederunt (Sheriff Court Rules) (Miscellaneous Amendments) 2012 (SSI 2012/188) para.10 (effective August 1, 2012).

[2] As inserted by the Act of Sederunt (Sheriff Court Rules) (Miscellaneous Amendments) 2012 (SSI 2012/188) para.10 (effective August 1, 2012).

[3] As inserted by the Act of Sederunt (Sheriff Court Rules) (Miscellaneous Amendments) 2012 (SSI 2012/188) para.10(effective August 1, 2012).

Rule 49.11(1)(e)

Form of certificate of execution of arrestment of ship or cargo on the dependence

CERTIFICATE OF EXECUTION OF ARRESTMENT OF SHIP [*OR* CARGO] ON THE DEPEND-
ENCE

I, (*name*), Sheriff Officer, certify that I executed an arrestment on the dependence of the ship [*or vessel*] (*name*) [*or* cargo (*describe*)] by virtue of an interlocutor of the Sheriff at (*place*) on (*date*) at the instance of (*name and address of pursuer*) against (*name and address of defender*) by affixing the schedule of arrestment to the mainmast [*or as the case may be*] of the ship [*or vessel*] (*name*) and marked the initials ER above the same [*or by* (*state method of service*)] at (*place*) on (*date*).

I did this in the presence of (*name, occupation and address of witness*).

(*Signed*)
Sheriff Officer
(*Address*)
(*Signed*)
Witness

## APPENDIX 2

Rule 30.6(1)

FORMS FOR EXTRACT DECREES
FORM 1
Form of extract decree for payment
EXTRACT DECREE FOR PAYMENT

| Sheriff Court | Court ref. no. |
|---|---|
| Date of decree | * In absence |
| Pursuer(s) | Defender(s) |

The sheriff granted decree against the .......... for payment to the .......... of the undernoted sums.

Sum decerned for £ .......... with interest at .......... per cent a year from .......... until payment and expenses against the .......... of £ ..........

* A time to pay direction was made under section 1(1) of the Debtors (Scotland) Act 1987.

* The amount is payable by instalments of £ .......... per .......... commencing within .......... of intimation of this extract decree.

* The amount is payable by lump sum within .......... of intimation of this extract decree.

This extract is warrant for all lawful execution hereon.

Date .............. Sheriff clerk (depute)

* Delete as appropriate.

FORM 2
Form of extract decree ad factum praestandum
EXTRACT DECREE *AD FACTUM PRAESTANDUM*

| Sheriff Court | Court ref. no. |
|---|---|
| Date of decree | * In absence |
| Pursuer(s) | Defender(s) |

The sheriff ordained the defender(s)...............and granted decree against the.......... for payment of expenses of £..........

This extract is warrant for all lawful execution hereon.

Date

Sheriff clerk (depute)

* Delete as appropriate.

FORM 3
Form of extract decree of removing
EXTRACT DECREE OF REMOVING

| Sheriff Court | Court ref. no. |
|---|---|
| Date of decree | * In absence |
| Pursuer(s) | Defender(s) |

The sheriff ordained the defender(s) to remove* himself/herself/themselves and his/her/their sub-tenants, dependents and others, and all effects from the premises at the undernoted address and to leave those premises vacant** [and that after a charge of.......... days].

In the event that the defender(s) fail(s) to remove the sheriff granted warrant to sheriff officers to eject the defender(s), sub-tenants, dependents and others, with all effects, from those premises so as to leave them vacant.

The Sheriff granted decree against the.......... for payment of expenses of £..........

Full address of premises:—

This extract is warrant for all lawful execution hereon.

Date

Sheriff clerk (depute)

** Delete as appropriate.
** Delete if period of charge is not specified in the decree.

FORM 4
Form of extract decree of declarator
EXTRACT DECREE OF DECLARATOR

Sheriff Court                                   Court ref. no.
Date of decree                                  * In absence
Pursuer(s)                                      Defender(s)

The sheriff found and declared that...............and granted decree against the...............for payment of expenses of £..........

This extract is warrant for all lawful execution hereon.

Date

Sheriff clerk (depute)

* Delete as appropriate.

FORM 5
Form of extract decree of forthcoming
EXTRACT DECREE OF FURTHCOMING

Sheriff Court                                   Court ref. no.
Date of decree                                  * In absence
Date of original decree
Pursuer(s)                                      Defender(s)/Arrestee(s)
                                                Common Debtor(s)

The sheriff granted against the arrestee(s) for payment of the undernoted sums.

Sum decerned for £.......... or such other sum(s) as may be owing by the arrestee(s) to the common debtor(s) by virtue of the original decree dated above in favour of the pursuer(s) against the common debtor(s).

Expenses of £.......... * payable out of the arrested fund / payable by the common debtor(s).

This extract is warrant for all lawful execution hereon.

Date

Sheriff clerk (depute)

* Delete as appropriate.

FORM 6
Form of extract decree of absolvitor
EXTRACT DECREE OF ABSOLVITOR

Sheriff Court                                   Court ref. no.
Date of first warrant                           Date of decree
Pursuer(s)                                      Defender(s)

*(Insert the nature of crave(s) in the above action)*

The sheriff absolved............... the defender(s) and granted decree against the.......... for payment of expenses of £..........

This extract is warrant for all lawful execution hereon.

Date

Sheriff clerk (depute)

FORM 7
Form of extract decree of dismissal
EXTRACT DECREE OF DISMISSAL

| Sheriff Court | Court ref. no. |
| Date of first warrant | Date of decree |
| Pursuer(s) | Defender(s) |

The sheriff dismissed the action against the.............. defender(s) and granted decree against the..............
for payment of expenses of £..........
   * This extract is warrant for all lawful execution hereon.
   Date

Sheriff clerk (depute)

   * Delete as appropriate.

FORM 8
[Repealed by the Act of Sederunt (Sheriff Court Ordinary Cause Rules Amendment) (Miscellaneous) 1996 (S.I. 1996 No. 2445) (effective November 1, 1996).]

FORM 9
Form of extract decree
EXTRACT DECREE

| Sheriff Court | Court ref. no. |
| Date of decree | *In absence |
| Pursuer(s) | Defender(s) |

The sheriff and granted decree against the.............. for payment of expenses of £..........
This extract is warrant for all lawful execution hereon.
   Date

Sheriff clerk (depute)

   *Delete as appropriate.

[1]FORM 10
Form of extract decree of divorce
EXTRACT DECREE OF DIVORCE

| Sheriff Court | Court Ref No |
| Date of Decree | *In absence |
| Pursuer | Defender |

Date of parties marriage...............Place of parties marriage
   The sheriff granted decree
   (1) divorcing the defender from the Pursuer;
   *(2) ordering that the following child(ren):
   ..........Full name(s)...............Date(s) of birth
   Reside with the *pursuer/defender and finding the *pursuer/defender entitled to be in contact with the following child(ren): as follows:
   All in terms of the Children (Scotland) Act 1995.
   *(3) ordaining payment
  *(a)   by the to the of a periodical allowance of £ per
  *(b)   by the.......... to the.......... of a capital sum of £
  *(c)   by the.......... to the.......... of £ per.......... as aliment for each child until that child attains years of age, said sum payable in advance and beginning at the date of this decree with interest thereon at the rate of per cent a year until payment;
  *(d)   by the.......... to the.......... of £ of expenses;
  *(4) finding the.......... liable to the.......... in expenses as the same may be subsequently taxed.

---

[1] As substituted by the Act of Sederunt (Sheriff Court Ordinary Cause Rules Amendment) (Miscellaneous) 2000 (S.S.I. 2000 No. 239)(effective October 2, 2000).

This extract is warrant for all lawful execution hereon.

Date: *(insert date)*

Sheriff Clerk (depute)

* Delete as appropriate.

[1]FORM 11

Form of extract decree of separation and aliment

### EXTRACT DECREE OF SEPARATION AND ALIMENT

| | |
|---|---|
| Sheriff Court | Court Ref No |
| Date of Decree | *In absence |
| Pursuer | Defender |

The sheriff found and declared that the pursuer is entitled to live separately from the defender from the date of decree and for all time thereafter.

The Sheriff ordered that the following child(ren):

..........Full name(s)...............Date(s) of birth

Reside with the *pursuer/defender

And found the *pursuer/defender entitled to be in contact with the following child(ren):

as follows:

All in terms of the Children (Scotland) Act 1995.

* The sheriff ordained payment by the .......... to the .......... of £.......... per .......... as aliment for the .........., said sum payable in advance and beginning at the date of this decree with interest thereon at .......... per cent a year until payment.

* The sheriff ordained payment by the .......... to the .......... of £.......... per .......... as aliment for each child, until that child attains .......... years of age, said sum payable in advance and beginning at the date of this decree with interest thereon at .......... per cent a year until payment; and granted decree against the .......... for payment of £..........

This extract is warrant for all lawful execution hereon.

Date: *(insert date)*

Sheriff Clerk (Depute) *Delete as appropriate.

[2]FORM 12

Form of extract decree: Residence Order/Contact Order and aliment

### EXTRACT DECREE OF RESIDENCE ORDER/CONTACT ORDER AND ALIMENT

| | |
|---|---|
| Sheriff Court | Court Ref No |
| Date of Decree | *In absence |
| Pursuer | Defender |

The Sheriff granted decree against the *pursuer/defender.

The Sheriff ordered that the following child(ren):

..........Full name(s)...............Date(s) of birth

reside with the *pursuer/defender and found the *pursuer/defender entitled to be in contact with the following child(ren):

as follows:

All in terms of the Children (Scotland) Act 1995.

*The sheriff ordained payment by the .......... to the of £.......... per .......... as aliment for each child, until that child attains .......... years of age, said sum payable in advance and beginning at the date of this decree with interest thereon at .......... per cent a year until payment;

and granted decree with interest thereon at per cent a year until payment;and granted decree against the for payment of expenses of £..........

This extract is warrant for all lawful execution hereon.

Date: *(insert date)*

Sheriff Clerk (Depute)

---

[1] As substituted by the Act of Sederunt (Sheriff Court Ordinary Cause Rules Amendment) (Miscellaneous) 2000 (S.S.I. 2000 No. 239)(effective October 2, 2000).
[2] As substituted by the Act of Sederunt (Sheriff Court Ordinary Cause Rules Amendment) (Miscellaneous) 2000 (S.S.I. 2000 No. 239)(effective October 2, 2000).

* Delete as appropriate.
**Rule 36.G1(1B)**

[1]APPENDIX 3

## Schedule of Timetable Under Personal Injuries Procedure

| Steps referred to under rule 36.G1 (1A) | Period of time within which action must be carried out* |
|---|---|
| Application for a third party notice under rule 20.1 (rule 36.G1 (1A)(a)) | Not later than 28 days after defences have been lodged |
| Pursuer executing a commission for recovery of documents under rule 36.D1 (rule 36.G1(1A)(b)) | Not later than 28 days after defences have been lodged |
| Parties adjusting their pleadings (rule 36.G1(1A)(c)) | Not later than 8 weeks after defences have been lodged |
| Pursuer lodging a statement of valuation of claim in process (rule 36.G1(1A)(d)) | Not later than 8 weeks after defences have been lodged |
| Pursuer lodging a record (rule 36 G1(1A)(e)) | Not later than 10 weeks after defences have been lodged |
| Defender (and any third party to the action) lodging a statement of valuation of claim in process (rule 36.G1(1A)(f)) | Not later than 12 weeks after defences have been lodged |
| Parties lodging in process a list of witnesses together with any productions upon which they wish to rely (rule 36.G1(1A)(g)) | Not later than 8 weeks before the date assigned for the proof |
| Pursuer lodging in process the minute of the pre-proof conference (rule 36.G1(1A)(h)) | Not later than 21 days before the date assigned for the proof |
| *NOTE: Where there is more than one defender in an action, references in the above table to defences having been lodged should be read as references to the first lodging of defences. | |

---

[1] As substituted by the Act of Sederunt (Sheriff Court Rules) (Miscellaneous Amendments) 2010 (SSI 2010/279) Sch.1 App.001 para.1 (effective July 29, 2010) and amended by the Act of Sederunt (Sheriff Court Rules) (Miscellaneous Amendments) (No.3) 2011 (SSI 2011/386) para.5 (effective November 28, 2011).

317

## RESERVE AND AUXILIARY FORCES (PROTECTION OF CIVIL INTERESTS) ACT 1951

(14 & 15 Geo. 6 c. 65)

**D1.589**

An Act to provide for protecting the interests of persons called up or volunteering for certain naval, military or air force service, or doing work or training under the National Service Act 1948, by virtue of being conditionally registered under that Act as conscientious objectors, and of other persons consequentially affected, in respect of civil rights and liabilities of theirs.[1]

[August 1, 1951]

Part I – Protection against certain Legal Remedies

*Provisions as to Scotland*

**Application of sections 8 to 12**

**7.** The five next following sections shall apply to Scotland only.

**D1.590**

**General restrictions on execution and other remedies**

**8.**—(1) In the cases mentioned in the next following section no person shall be entitled, subject to the provisions of this Part of this Act, to enforce, except with the leave of the appropriate court, a decree of any court (whether pronounced before or after the commencement of this Act) for the payment of a sum of money or for the recovery of possession of land:

Provided that nothing in this subsection shall apply to—

    (a) any decree for damages in respect of loss or damage arising from any wrongful act or omission;

    (b) any decree based upon a contract made after the relevant date;

    (c) any decree for expenses;

    (d)[2] any decree for aliment or any decree or order enforceable by virtue of any enactment in like manner as a decree for aliment; or

    (e) any order made in criminal proceedings, or an order for the recovery of a penalty due in respect of a contravention of, or failure to comply with, any Act.

(2) In the cases mentioned in the next following section no person shall be entitled, subject to the provisions of this Part of this Act, except with the leave of the appropriate court—

    (a) to do any diligence (not being diligence used only on the dependence of an action or *ad fundandam jurisdictionem*);

    (b) to enforce any irritancy, legal or conventional;

    (c) to realise any security or forfeit any deposits;

    (d) to exercise any power of sale conferred by a heritable security;

---

[1] Applied by the Post Office Act 1969 (c.48) Sched. 4, para. 93; the Civil Aviation Act 1971 (c.75) Sched. 5, para. 5(h); the Reserve Forces Act 1980 (c.9) s.146(1); the British Telecommunications Act 1981 (c. 38) Sched. 3; the Civil Aviation Act 1982 (c. 16) Sched. 2, para. 4; the Gas Act 1986 (c. 44) Sched. 7, para. 2(1) and Sched. 8, para. 33; the Merchant Shipping Act 1988 (c. 12) s.29(4); the Electricity Act 1989 (c. 29) Sched. 16, para. 1(1); and the Gas Act 1995 (c. 41) Sched. 4, para. 2(1).

[2] As amended by the Guardianship Act 1973 (c. 29), Sched. 5 and the Children (Scotland) Act 1995 (c. 36), Sched. 5, infra, Division *K* (effective November 1, 1996: S.I. 1996 No. 2203).

(e) to institute an action of maills and duties; or

(f) to take or resume possession of any property by reason of any default by any person in the payment of money or the performance of any obligation:

Provided that this subsection shall not apply to any remedy or proceedings available in consequence of any default in the payment of a debt arising by virtue of a contract made after the relevant date or the performance of an obligation so arising, and nothing in this subsection shall affect—

(i) any right or power of pawnbrokers to deal with pledges; or

(ii) any remedy competent to a heritable creditor in possession of the security subjects at the relevant date;

(iii) any right or power of a person to sell goods in his custody arising by reason of default in the payment of a debt.

(3) If on any application for such leave as is required under this section for the enforcement of any decree or the exercise of any right or remedy mentioned in the foregoing provisions of this section, the appropriate court is of opinion that the person liable to implement such decree or perform the obligation in respect of which such right or remedy arises, is unable immediately to do so by reason of circumstances directly or indirectly attributable to his or someone else's performing or having performed a period of relevant service, the court may, subject to the provisions of this Part of this Act, refuse leave to enforce the decree or to exercise the right or remedy or give leave therefor subject to such restrictions and conditions as the court thinks proper.

Any order pronounced under this subsection may be suspended, rescinded or varied by a subsequent order.

(4) The appropriate court, in determining for the purpose of the last foregoing subsection whether a person is unable immediately to implement the decree or perform the obligation in question by reason of any such circumstances as are mentioned in that subsection, or in determining the restrictions and conditions (if any) subject to which leave is to be given under that subsection, may take account of other liabilities, whether present or future, of that person.

(5) Where—

(a) a petition for sequestration has been presented against any debtor, and it is shown to the satisfaction of the court before which such petition depends that his inability to pay his debts is due to circumstances directly or indirectly attributable to his or someone else's performing or having performed a period of relevant service; or

(b) a winding-up petition has been presented against an exempt private company on the ground that it is unable to pay its debts, and it is shown to the satisfaction of the court before which such petition depends that its inability to pay its debts is due to circumstances directly or indirectly attributable to any person's performing or having performed a period of relevant service;

the court may sist the proceedings in the petition for such time and subject to such conditions as the court thinks fit.

In this subsection the expression "an exempt private company" shall be construed in accordance with subsection (4) of section 129 of the Companies Act 1948.

### Scope of protection

**9.**—(1)  Subject to the following provisions of this section, the provisions of subsection (1) or (2) of the last foregoing section shall apply to the exercise of any right or remedy in the following cases and in the following cases only, that is to say:—

    (a)  they shall apply (by virtue of this paragraph) where the person liable to implement the decree or to perform the obligation in question is for the time being performing a period of relevant service;

    (b)  they shall apply (by virtue of this paragraph but subject to any order of the appropriate court directing that they shall not so apply or shall cease so to apply) where the person liable as aforesaid has been performing a period of relevant service and while he was so doing an application was made to the appropriate court for leave under the last foregoing section to exercise the right or remedy;

    (c)  they shall apply in any case where—

        (i)  the appropriate court by order so directs, on the application of the person liable as aforesaid and on being satisfied that he is unable immediately to implement the decree or to perform the obligation in question by reason of circumstances directly or indirectly attributable to his or someone else's performing or having performed a period of relevant service; or

        (ii)  the person liable as aforesaid has made to the appropriate court an application for an order under this paragraph, and the application has not been disposed of, or not having made such an application has given to the proper person written notice of his intention to do so.

D1.591

(2)  A notice given for the purpose of paragraph (c) of the foregoing subsection shall expire at the expiration of fourteen days (or, if given in a class of case as to which a longer period is prescribed for the purposes of this subsection, at the expiration of that period) from the date on which it was given, and where the person giving a notice for that purpose has given a previous notice to the like effect the later notice shall have no operation unless the previous notice was withdrawn with the consent of the proper person before it expired.

(3)  For the purpose of the foregoing subsections, the expression "the proper person" means the person seeking to exercise the right or remedy in question, but a notice shall be deemed to be given to the proper person if given to any person (whether the proper person or his agent or not) proceeding to enforce that right or remedy.

(4)  Where the appropriate court makes an order under paragraph (c) of subsection (1) of this section with respect to the exercise of any right or remedy the powers of the court under the last foregoing section shall thereupon be exercisable as if an application for leave to exercise the right or remedy in question had been made under that section.

(5)  The appropriate court, in determining for the purpose of the said paragraph (c) whether the applicant is unable immediately to implement the decree or to perform the obligation in question by reason of any such circumstances as are mentioned in that paragraph, may take account of other liabilities, whether present or future, of his.

(6)  Any reference in subsection (3) of the last foregoing section or subsection (1) of this section to the person liable to implement the decree or to perform the obligation in question shall in a case where it is sought to exercise a right or remedy

against one such person separately from any others who are also so liable, be construed as referring to him only and not including any such other person but, in a case where it is sought to exercise it against two or more such persons jointly, shall be construed as referring to all or any of the persons against whom it is sought to exercise the right or remedy; and in this subsection references to exercising a right or a remedy against a person shall include references to exercising it against property in which he has an interest or of which he is in possession.

(7) For the purposes of the last foregoing section, a person in right of a decree who presents a petition for sequestration or a winding up petition founded on the non-payment of money due under the decree shall be deemed to be enforcing the decree.

(8) For the purposes of the last foregoing section, the expression "the relevant date" means the date on which the service man in question began to perform the period of relevant service:

Provided that—

   (a) For the purposes of any reference in that section to a contract made after the relevant date where a service man performs two or more periods of relevant service the said expression means the date on which he began the later or latest of those periods of service; and

   (b) for the purposes of the proviso to subsection (2) of that section—

       (i) where the said date was before the commencement of this Act, then subject to sub-paragraph (ii) of this paragraph the said expression means the date of that commencement; and

       (ii) in a case to which the last foregoing section applies by virtue of paragraph (c) of subsection (1) of this section, the said expression means the date on which that section began so to apply.

**Property in goods subject to hire-purchase agreement**

D1.592

**10.**—[1](1) Where the appropriate court refuses leave under section 8 (3) of this Act to take or resume possession of goods subject to a hire-purchase agreement or a conditional sale agreement or to do diligence on any decree for the delivery of such goods, or gives leave subject to restrictions and conditions, and the person to whom they are hired, or, as the case may be, the buyer before possession is taken or resumed or diligence is done, pays the total price, the creditors' title to the goods shall, notwithstanding any failure to pay the total price at the time required by the agreement, vest in that person.

(2) Where the creditor under a hire-purchase agreement or a conditional sale agreement has taken possession of the goods hired or agreed to be sold under it, the appropriate court on an application under section 9(1)(c) of this Act may, if it thinks fit, deal with the case as if the creditor were proceeding to take possession of the goods and, if it makes an order under that paragraph, may direct accordingly that the goods be restored to the person to whom they were hired or, as the case may be, the buyer: and if, after the creditor has taken possession of the goods, notice is given under that paragraph with respect to them, he shall not, so long as the notice is in force or any application in pursuance of the notice is undisposed of, deal with the goods in such a way as to prejudice the powers of the appropriate court under this subsection.

---

[1] As substituted by the Consumer Credit Act 1974, (c.39) Sch.4.

### Appropriate courts and procedure

**11.**—[1](1)  The appropriate court for the purposes of any of the provisions of this Part of this Act applying to Scotland shall be such court as the Court of Session may by Act of Sederunt designate, and different courts may be designated in relation to different classes of proceedings.

**D1.593**

(2)  The Court of Session may by Act of Sederunt make provision for requiring, or dispensing with, service of notice of any application under this Part of this Act upon persons who may be affected, whether by virtue of subsection (4) of section 8 or subsection (5) of section 9 of this Act or otherwise, and for enabling any such persons to be heard at the hearing, and may also make provision for the making of applications ex parte in such cases as may be prescribed by the Act of Sederunt.

(3)  [Repealed by the Law Reform (Miscellaneous Provisions) (Scotland) Act 1966 (c.19), Sch. Pt I.]

### Interpretation of sections 8 to 11

**12.**  For the purposes of sections 8 to 11 of this Act the expression "heritable security" includes a security constituted by *ex facie* absolute disposition.

**D1.594**

*Effect of failure to observe restrictions under Part I*

### Effect of failure to observe restrictions under Part I

**13.**—[2](1)  Omission to obtain leave required under section [8] of this Act, failure to observe a restriction or condition subject to which leave so required was given, or contravention of the prohibition in subsection [(2)] of section [10] of this Act against dealing with goods, shall not render invalid, or alter the effect of—

**D1.595**

    (a)  anything which would have operated as a transfer of the title to any property or of the possession of any property if leave had not been required or the restriction, condition or prohibition had not been imposed;

    (b)  any payment, receipt, appointment or other transaction; or

    (c)  any legal proceedings.

(2)  In any action for damages for conversion or other proceedings which lie by virtue of any such omission, failure or contravention, the court may take account of the conduct of the [defender] with a view, if the court thinks fit, to awarding exemplary damages in respect of the wrong sustained by the [pursuer].

(3)  If in any action or proceedings which lie by virtue of any such omission, failure or contravention the court is satisfied that the [defender] acted honestly and reasonably, and ought fairly to be excused for it, the court may relieve the [defender] from liability in respect thereof.

(4)  In so far as it appears to the appropriate court to be practicable to remedy the results of any such omission, failure or contravention as aforesaid specifically without prejudice to the interests of third parties, the court may give any such directions for restoration of property, repayment of money or other measures as may appear to the court to be requisite for that purpose.

In this subsection the expression "third parties" means persons other than—

    (a)  in the case of such an omission or failure in connection with the enforce-

---

[1] See SI 1952/117.
[2] As applicable to Scotland by virtue of subs.(6).

ment of a judgment, [decree] or order or the exercise of a remedy, the person proceeding thereto and any person acting in relation thereto on his behalf;

(c) in the case of a contravention of the prohibition in subsection [(2)] of section [10] of this Act, the owner of the goods; and

(d) in any of the cases aforesaid, any person taking a transfer of the title to or possession of any property under a transaction in connection with which the omission, failure or contravention took place, if he took with knowledge of the circumstances which rendered what was done such an omission, failure or contravention.

(5) In relation to an action or other proceedings tried by a judge and jury—

(a) the references to the court in subsections (2) and (3) of this section shall be construed as references to the jury, but without prejudice to the power of the judge to give to the jury directions whether there is any evidence of facts justifying an award of exemplary damages on the one hand or the granting of relief on the other hand, or to give them advice as to the making of such an award or grant;

(b) the references to the court in subsection (4) of this section shall be construed as references to the judge alone.

PART II[1] – PROTECTION AGAINST INSECURITY OF TENURE OF PLACE OF RESIDENCE

*Protection during service other than short period of training*

**Period of residence protection, and scope of three succeeding sections (protection of tenure under lettings at a rent)**

D1.596

**14.**—[2](1) The three next succeeding sections shall have effect, subject to subsection (2) of this section, in the case of a service man who performs a period of relevant service, other than a short period of training, either wholly after the commencement of this Act or partly theretofore and partly thereafter, for giving, during that period of service, or the residue of it if it began before the commencement of this Act, and four months from the date of the ending of it (in this Part of this Act referred to, in relation to such a service man, as his "period of residence protection"), security of tenure of premises which at any time during the period of protection are a rented family residence of his.

For the purposes of the operation of this Part of this Act at any time during a service man's period of residence protection—

(a) the expression "rented family residence" means premises in which (or in part of which) the service man was living immediately before the beginning of his period of service with a dependant or dependants of his in right of a tenancy at a rent of those premises being a tenancy vested in him or in that dependant or any of those dependants, and in which (or in part of which) at the time in question during the period of protection a dependant or dependants of his is or are living, whether with or without him, in right of such a tenancy of those premises being a tenancy vested in him or in that dependant or any of those dependants; and

(b) the expression "tenancy qualifying for protection" means the tenancy

---

[1] As applied to Scotland and updated. See s.24 infra.
[2] As amended by the Rent (Scotland) Act 1971 (c.28), Sch.18.

of a rented family residence of the service man in right of which a dependant or dependants of his is or are living therein or in part thereof at the time in question.

(2)    The three next succeeding sections shall not have effect if and so long as the rented family residence—

(a)[1]    is a dwelling-house which consists of or comprises premises licensed for the sale of exciseable liquor on the premises which, by virtue of a premises licence issued under the Licensing (Scotland) Act 2005, are licensed for the sale of alcohol (within the meaning of section 2 of that Act) for consumption on the premises; or

(b)    is bona fide let at a rent which includes payments in respect of board.

## Protection of tenure of furnished, and certain other, rented premises, by extension of the Furnished Houses (Rent Control) Act

**15.**—[2](1)[3]    Subject to subsection (2) of the last preceding section where at any time during a service man's period of residence protection—

(a)    the rented family residence is let under the tenancy qualifying for protection either on such terms as are mentioned in section 63(1) of the Rent (Scotland) Act 1984 (which relates to premises let in consideration of a rent which includes payment for the use of furniture or for services) or on terms of sharing with the lessor, and

(b)    a notice to quit has been served by the lessor on the lessee (whether after or before the beginning of the period of protection) and the notice has not expired, but

(c)    the condition specified in subsection (1)(b) of section 72 of the Rent (Scotland) Act 1984 is not fulfilled,

the said section 72 shall apply in relation to the notice to quit as if that condition had been fulfilled as to the contract under which that tenancy subsists.

(1A)[4]    This section does not apply in relation to any tenancy entered into on or after 1st December 1980.

(2)    The reference in paragraph (*a*) of the preceding subsection to a letting on terms of sharing with the lessor is a reference to a letting under which—

(a)    the lessee has the exclusive occupation of some accommodation (in this subsection referred to as "the separate accommodation");

(b)    he has the use of other accommodation in common with the lessor or with the lessor and other persons; and

(c)    the accommodation mentioned in the last preceding paragraph is or includes accommodation of such a nature that the circumstance specified in that paragraph is sufficient to prevent the separate accommodation from being a dwelling-house subject to a statutory tenancy within the meaning of the Rent (Scotland) Act 1984, whether apart from that circumstance it would be such a dwelling-house or not.

D1.597

---

[1] As amended by the Licensing (Scotland) Act 2005 (Consequential Provisions) Order 2009 (SSI 2009/248) Sch. 1, para. 1(2), (effective September 1, 2009 at 05.00).

[2] As amended by the Rent (Scotland) Act 1971 (c.28), Sch.18 and the Rent (Scotland) Act 1984 (c.58), Sch.8, Pt II.

[3] As amended by the Rent (Scotland) Act 1984 (c.58), Sch.8, Pt II.

[4] Added by the Tenants' Rights, Etc. (Scotland) Act 1980 (c.52), s.39(2), and as amended by the Rent (Scotland) Act 1984 (c.58), Sch.8, Pt II.

(3)[1]   The subsistence of a Crown interest in premises shall not affect the operation of this section if the interest of the immediate landlord of the tenant under the tenancy in question is not a Crown interest; but nothing in this subsection shall be construed as excluding the operation of this Part of this Act in cases where there subsists a Crown interest not being the interest of the immediate landlord of the tenant under the tenancy in question.

(4)[2]   References in the said section 72 to that section shall be construed as including references to the preceding provisions of this section and to the said section 72 as extended by those provisions.

(5)   [Repealed by the Rent (Scotland) Act 1971, Sched. 20.]

### Protection of tenure of certain rented premises by extension of Housing (Scotland) Act 1988

**D1.598**

16.—[3](1)   Subject to subsection (2) of section 14 of this Act and subsection (3) below, if at any time during a service man's period of residence protection—

    (a)   a tenancy qualifying for protection ends without being continued or renewed by agreement (whether on the same or different terms and conditions), and

    (b)   by reason only of such circumstances as are mentioned in subsection (4) below, on the ending of that tenancy no statutory tenancy of the rented family residence would arise, apart from the provisions of this section,

sections 12 to 31 of the Housing (Scotland) Act 1988 shall, during the remainder of the period of protection, apply in relation to the rented family residence as if those circumstances did not exist and had not existed immediately before the ending of that tenancy and, accordingly, as if on the ending of that tenancy there arose a statutory assured tenancy during the remainder of that period.

(2)   Subject to subsection (2) of section 14 of this Act and subsection (3) below, if at any time during a service man's period of residence protection—

    (a)   a tenancy qualifying for protection would come to an end, apart from the provisions of this section,

    (b)   by reason only of such circumstances as are mentioned in subsection (4) below that tenancy is not an assured tenancy, and

    (c)   if that tenancy had been an assured tenancy, it would not have come to an end at that time,

sections 12 to 31 of the Housing (Scotland) Act 1988 shall, during the remainder of the period of protection, apply in relation to the rented family residence as if those circumstances did not exist and, accordingly, as if the tenancy had become an assured tenancy immediately before it would otherwise have come to an end.

(3)   Neither subsection (1) nor subsection (2) above applies if, on the ending of the tenancy qualifying for protection, a statutory tenancy arises.

(4)   The circumstances referred to in subsections (1) and (2) above are one or more of the following, that is to say—

    (a)   that the circumstances mentioned in paragraph 2 of Schedule 4 to the Housing (Scotland) Act 1988 applied with respect to the tenancy qualifying for protection;

---

[1] As substituted by the Rent (Scotland) Act 1971 (c.28), Sch.18.
[2] As amended by the Rent (Scotland) Act 1971 (c.28), Sch.18, the Tenants' Rights, Etc. (Scotland) Act 1980 (c.52), Sch.5, and by the Rent (Scotland) Act 1984 (c.58), Sch.8, Pt II.
[3] Substituted by the Housing Act 1988 (c.50), Sch.17, para.3.

(b) that the circumstances mentioned in paragraph 5 of that Schedule applied with respect to the tenancy qualifying for protection; and

(c)[1] that the reversion immediately expectant on the tenancy qualifying for protection belongs to any of the bodies specified in paragraph 11 of that Schedule.

### Provisions supplementary to section 16 in case of rented premises which include accommodation shared otherwise than with the landlord

17.—(1)[2]  Where at any time during a service man's period of residence protection a tenancy qualifying for protection ends as mentioned in paragraph (a) of subsection (1) of the last preceding section, and immediately before the ending of the tenancy—

**D1.599**

(a) the tenant under the terms of the tenancy had the exclusive occupation of some accommodation (in this section referred to as "the separate accommodation") and had the use of other accommodation in common with another person or other persons, not being or including the landlord, but

(b) by reason only of such circumstances as are mentioned in section 16(4) above, subsection (1) of section 14 of the Housing (Scotland) Act 1988 did not have effect as respects the separate accommodation,

then subject to the next succeeding subsection the said section 14 shall during the remainder of the period of protection apply in relation to the separate accommodation as if the circumstances referred to in paragraph (b) of this subsection did not exist, and had not existed immediately before the ending of the tenancy and, accordingly, as if on the ending of the tenancy there arose a statutory assured tenancy during the remainder of that period.

(2)[3]  Where, at any time during a service man's period of residence protection—

(a) a tenancy qualifying for protection would come to an end, apart from the provisions of this section and section 16 above, and

(b) paragraphs (a) and (b) of subsection (1) above apply,

section 14 of the Housing (Scotland) Act 1988 shall, during the remainder of the period of protection, apply in relation to the separate accommodation as if the circumstances in subsection (1)(b) above did not exist and, accordingly, as if the tenancy had become an assured tenancy immediately before it would otherwise come to an end.

(3)[4]  Neither subsection (1) nor subsection (2) above applies if, on the ending of the tenancy qualifying for protection, a statutory tenancy arises.

### Protection of tenure, in connection with employment, under a licence or a rent-free letting, by extension of the Rent Acts

18.—[5](1)[6]  Where—

**D1.600**

(a) a service man begins a period of relevant service, other than a short

---

[1] See s.24(f) infra.

[2] As amended by the Rent (Scotland) Act 1971 (c.28), Sch.18, the Tenants' Rights etc. (Scotland) Act 1980 (c.52), s.39, and Sch.5, the Rent (Scotland) Act 1984 (c.58), Sch.8, Pt II and the Housing Act 1988 (c.50), Sch.17, para.5.

[3] As substituted by the Housing Act 1988 (c.50), Sch.17, para.5.

[4] As substituted by the Housing Act 1988 (c.50), Sch.17, para.5.

[5] As applied to Scotland by s.24 infra.

[6] As amended by the Housing Act 1988 (c.50), Sch.17, para.6.

period of training, after the commencement of this Act, and immediately before beginning it he was living, together with a dependant or dependants of his, in any premises by virtue of a right or permission derived otherwise than under a lease granted to him by his employer in consequence of his employment, or by virtue of a tenancy so granted otherwise than at a rent (in this section referred to as a "rent-free tenancy"), or

(b)   a service man is performing a period of relevant service, other than a short period of training, at the commencement of this Act, and immediately before beginning it he was living as aforesaid, and a dependant or dependants of his is or are living in the premises or in part thereof, otherwise than in right of a tenancy at a rent, at the commencement of this Act,

then during the service man's period of residence protection as defined in section 14 of this Act sections 12 to 31 of the Housing (Scotland) Act 1988 shall, subject to the provisions of this section, apply in relation to those premises as if instead of the right or permission derived otherwise than under a lease, or of the rent-free tenancy, as the case may be, there had been granted to the service man a tenancy at a rent—

(i)   a term of years certain expiring at the beginning of the period of service, or at the commencement of this Act if the period of service began theretofore, and

(ii)   in other respects on the same terms and conditions (excluding any terms or conditions relating to the employment) as those on which the right or permission derived otherwise than under a lease, or the rent-free tenancy, as the case may be, was granted;

and those premises shall be deemed to be during the period of protection a dwelling-house let on a statutory assured tenancy if apart from this section they would not have been so.

(2)   *[Repealed by the Housing Act 1988 (c.50) Sch.17 para.6(3).]*

(3)   Subsection (1) of this section shall not have effect—

(a)[1]   where the licence, or the rent-free tenancy, as the case may be, was granted in connection with the management of premises which, by virtue of a premises licence issued under the Licensing (Scotland) Act 2005, are licensed for the sale of alcohol (within the meaning of section 2 of that Act) for consumption on the premises, or

(b)   where the right or permission derived otherwise than under a lease, or the rent-free tenancy, as the case may be, was granted pursuant to a contract which imposed on the grantor thereof an obligation to provide board for the service man and the dependant or dependants.

(4)   As regards the assumption of the granting of a tenancy which is to be made for the purposes of subsection (1) of this section in a case where the grant in question was of a right or permission derived otherwise than under a lease, if the granting of such a tenancy would have been a subletting of the premises it shall not be treated for any purpose as constituting a breach of any covenant or agreement prohibiting or restricting subletting.

---

[1] As amended by the Licensing Act 2003 (c.17), Sch.6, para.23 (effective November 24, 2005) and by the Licensing (Scotland) Act 2005 (Consequential Provisions) Order 2009 (SSI 2009/248) Sch.1 para.1(3) (effective September 1, 2009 at 05.00).

(5)   The subsistence of a Crown interest in the premises shall not affect the application of this section if the interest of the grantor of the right or permission derived otherwise than under a lease, or the rent-free tenancy, as the case may be, is not a Crown interest.

(6)[1]   In relation to a policeman service man this section shall have effect with the substitution of a reference to a grant to him, either by the relevant police authority or by another person under arrangements made by that body or authority with that person, in consequence of the service man's membership of the relevant police force, for the reference in subsection (1) to a grant to a service man by his employer in consequence of his employment.

### Limitation on application of Housing (Scotland) Act 1988 by virtue of sections 16 to 18

**19.**[2]   Where by virtue of sections 16 to 18 above, the operation of sections 12 to 31 of the Housing (Scotland) Act 1988 in relation to any premises is extended or modified, the extension or modification shall not affect—

**D1.601**

(a)   any tenancy of those premises other than the statutory assured tenancy which is deemed to arise or, as the case may be, the tenancy which is for any period deemed to be an assured tenancy by virtue of any of those provisions; or

(b)   any rent payable in respect of a period beginning before the time when that statutory assured tenancy was deemed to arise or, as the case may be, before that tenancy became deemed to be an assured tenancy; or

(c)   anything done or omitted to be done before the time referred to in paragraph (b) above.

### Modifications of Rent Acts as respects occupation by employees

**20.**—[3](1)   Where the carrying out of duties connected with an employment which a service man had before beginning a period of relevant service (or, in the case of a policeman service man, the carrying out of his police duties) constitutes an obligation of a tenancy, and his performing that service prevents his carrying out those duties, the fact that he does not carry them out shall not be treated for the purposes of Case 1 in Schedule 2 to the Rent (Scotland) Act 1984 or Ground 13 in Schedule 5 to the Housing (Scotland) Act 1988 (which relates to recovery of possession where an obligation of a tenancy has been broken or not performed) as a breach or non-performance of the obligation.

**D1.602**

(2)   Case 7 in the said Schedule 2 or, as the case may be, Ground 17 in the said Schedule 5 (which relates to recovery of possession, without proof of suitable alternative accommodation, in circumstances connected with occupation by employees) shall not apply for the purposes of the proceedings on an application for possession of premises made at any time during a service man's period of residence protection (as defined in section 14 of this Act) if either—

(a)   the premises are a rented family residence of his as defined in that section; or

(b)   sections 12 to 31 of the Housing (Scotland) Act 1988 apply in relation

---

[1] As amended by the Police Reform and Social Responsibility Act 2011 (c.13) Sch.16(3) para.70 (effective January 16, 2012).

[2] As substituted by the Housing Act 1988 (c.50), Sch.17, para.8.

[3] As amended by the Rent (Scotland) Act 1971 (c.28), Sch.18, the Rent (Scotland) Act 1984 (c.58), Sch.8, Pt II and the Housing Act 1988 (c.50), Sch.17, para.10. As applied to Scotland by s.24, infra.

to the premises as mentioned in section 18(1) of this Act and a dependant or dependants of the service man is or are living in the premises or
in part thereof in right of the statutory assured tenancy or assured
tenancy referred to in paragraph (a) of section 19 of this Act.

(3) Where the last preceding subsection has effect as to an application for possession, the circumstances specified in the Cases in Part I of the said Schedule 2 or,
as the case may be, Grounds 10 to 17 in Part II of the said Schedule 5 in which the
court has power to make or give an order or judgment for the recovery of possession
without proof of suitable alternative accommodation shall include the circumstances
specified in either of the following paragraphs, that is to say—

(a) that the landlord is a body who are statutory undertakers or a local
authority or development corporation having public utility functions,
and that the premises are required by that body in the public interest for
occupation as a residence for some person who is engaged in their
whole-time employment in connection with their public utility functions or with whom, conditional on housing accommodation being
provided, a contract for such employment has been entered into;

(b)[1] where the last preceding subsection has effect by virtue of paragraph
(b) thereof and the service man in question is a policeman service man,
that the premises are required by the relevant local policing body or
relevant police authority for occupation as a residence by a member of
the police force in question:

Provided that, where the court is satisfied that circumstances exist such as are
specified in paragraph (a) of this subsection, the matters relevant for the court in
determining under section 11(1) of the Rent (Scotland) Act 1984 or, as the case may
be, section 18(4) of the Housing (Scotland) Act 1988 whether it is reasonable to
make or give such an order or judgment shall (without prejudice to the generality of
that subsection) include the question whether the body seeking the order or judgment have at their disposal any vacant accommodation which would be suitable
alternative accommodation for the tenant, or will have such accommodation at their
disposal at or before the time when it is proposed that the order or judgment should
take effect.

(4)[2] In the last preceding subsection the expressions "statutory undertakers" and
"local authority" have the same meanings as in the Town and Country Planning
(Scotland) Act 1947, the expression "development corporation" has the same meaning as in the New Towns Act 1946, and the expression "public utility functions"
means powers or duties conferred or imposed by or under any enactment, being
powers or duties to carry on a statutory undertaking (as defined in the said Act of
1947) or to provide public sewers or provide for the disposal of sewage, or being
powers or duties of a river board or other drainage authority (as defined respectively
in the River Boards Act 1948, and the Land Drainage Act 1930).

---

[1] As amended by the Police Reform and Social Responsibility Act 2011 (c.13) Sch.16(3) para.71 (effective January 16, 2012).
[2] See now the Town and Country Planning (Scotland) Act 1972 (c.52) and the New Towns (Scotland)
Act 1968 (c.16). The River Boards Act 1948 (c.32) and the Land Drainage Act 1930 (c.44) did not
extend to Scotland.

## Modifications of Agricultural Holdings Act 1948, where a tenant is a service man

**21.**—[1](1)   The three next succeeding subsections shall have effect where the tenant of an agricultural holding to which this section applies performs a period of relevant service, other than a short period of training, either wholly after the commencement of this Act or partly theretofore and partly thereafter, and after the commencement of this Act, at a time during his period of residence protection, there is given to him notice to quit the holding, or notice to quit a part of the holding, being a part to which this section applies.

**D1.603**

This section applies to any agricultural holding which comprises a dwelling-house comprised in an agricultural holding and occupied by the person responsible for the control (whether as tenant or as servant or agent of the tenant) of the farming of the holding, and applies to any part of an agricultural holding being a part which consists of or comprises such a dwelling-house.

(2)[2]   Section 22 of the Agricultural Holdings (Scotland) Act 1991 (which restricts the operation of notices to quit) shall apply notwithstanding the existence of any such circumstances as are mentioned in subsection (2) of that section; but where the Land Court is satisfied that such circumstances exist then (subject to the next succeeding subsection) the Land Court shall not be required to withhold its consent to the operation of the notice to quit by reason only that it is not satisfied that circumstances exist such as are mentioned in paragraphs (a) to (e) of subsection (1) of section 24 of that Act.

(3)[3]   In determining whether to give or withhold its consent under the said section 22 the Land Court—

  (a)   if satisfied that circumstances exist such as are mentioned in subsection (2) of the said section 22 or in subsection (1) of the said section 24, shall consider to what extent (if at all) the existence of those circumstances is directly or indirectly attributable to the service man's performing or having performed the period of service in question, and

  (b)   in any case, shall consider to what extent (if at all) the giving of such consent at a time during the period of protection would cause special hardship in view of circumstances directly or indirectly attributable to the service man's performing or having performed that period of service;

and the Land Court shall withhold its consent to the operation of the notice to quit unless in all the circumstances it considers it reasonable to give its consent thereto.

(4)   [Repealed by the Agriculture Act 1958 (c.71), Sch.2, Pt II.]

(5)   Where the tenant of an agricultural holding to which this section applies performs such a period of service as is mentioned in subsection (1) of this section and—

  (a)   a notice to quit the holding or a part thereof to which this section applies was given to him before the commencement of this Act or is given to him thereafter but before the beginning of his period of residence protection, and

---

[1] As applied to Scotland by s.24, infra.
[2] As amended by the Agriculture Act 1958 (c.71), Sch.1, Pt II and Sch.3, and by the Agricultural Holdings (Scotland) Act 1991 (c.55), Sch.11, para.2.
[3] Substituted by the Agriculture Act 1958 (c.71), Sch.1, Pt II. As amended by the Agricultural Holdings (Scotland) Act 1991 (c.55), Sch.11, para.2.

    (b)   the tenant duly serves or has served a counter-notice under subsection (1) of the said section 24, and

    (c)[1]  the Scottish Land Court has not before the beginning of his period of residence protection decided whether to give or withhold consent to the operation of the notice to quit,

the two last preceding subsections shall (with the necessary modifications) apply in relation to the giving or withholding of consent to the operation of the notice to quit as they apply in relation to the giving or withholding of consent to the operation of a notice to quit given in the circumstances mentioned in subsection (1) of this section.

(6)[2]   Section 27 of the said Scottish Act of 1949 (which authorises the Minister to make regulations as to matters arising out of sections 24 and 25 of that Act) shall apply in relation to the provisions of those sections as modified by the preceding provisions of this section as it applies in relation to the provisions of those sections apart from this section.

(7)   [Repealed by the Agriculture Act 1958 (c.71), Sch.2, Pt II.]

(8)[3]   In this section the expression "agricultural holding" has the same meaning as in the Agricultural Holdings (Scotland) Act 1991.

### Facilities for action on behalf of men serving abroad in proceedings as to tenancies

**D1.604**

**22.**—[4](1)[5]   Where in the course of any proceedings brought under the Rent (Scotland) Act 1984 or under Part II of the Housing (Scotland) Act 1988 or of any proceedings consequential upon the making of a reference or application to a rent assessment committee under Part VII of the said Act of 1984 or under Part II of the Housing (Scotland) Act 1988, or under this Part of this Act, it appears to the court or committee—

    (a)   that the proceedings relate to a tenancy or right or permission derived otherwise than under a lease vested in a service man;

    (b)   that a person other than the service man desires to take a step in the proceedings on behalf of the service man at a time when he is serving abroad, or had purported to take a step in the proceedings on his behalf at a time when he was so serving; and

    (c)   that the said person, in seeking or purporting to take that step, is or was acting in good faith in the interests of the service man, and is or was a fit person to take that step on his behalf, but is or was not duly authorised to do so,

the court or committee may direct that the said person shall be deemed to be, or to have been, duly authorised to take that step on behalf of the service man.

(2)   The provisions of the preceding subsection apply in relation to the institution of proceedings before a court as they apply in relation to the taking of a step in such proceedings, and apply in relation to the making of a reference or application

---

[1] Substituted by the Agriculture Act 1958 (c.71), Sch.1, Pt II. As amended by the Agricultural Holdings (Scotland) Act 1991 (c.55), Sch.11, para.2.

[2] See SI 1952/1338. "In subsection (6) the reference to section 27 of the Scottish Act of 1949 shall be construed as a reference to that section as originally enacted and not as amended by this Act": the Agriculture Act 1958, Sch.1, Pt II, para.45(d). See also the Agricultural Holdings (Scotland) Act 1991 (c.55), Sch.12, para.4(b).

[3] As amended by the Agriculture Act 1958 (c.71), Sch.2, Pt II, and by the Agricultural Holdings (Scotland) Act 1991 (c.55), Sch.11, para.2.

[4] As applied to Scotland by s.24, infra. As amended by the Rent (Scotland) Act 1971 (c.28), Sch.18.

[5] As amended by the Housing Act 1988 (c.50), Sch.17, para. 12.

to a rent tribunal as they apply in relation to the taking of a step in proceedings consequential upon the making of such a reference or application; and references in that subsection to proceedings brought or a reference or application made as therein mentioned include references to proceedings which purport to be so brought or to a reference or application which purports to be so made, as the case may be.

(3)   Where in the course of any proceedings a court or tribunal gives a direction under subsection (1) of this section, the person to whom the direction relates shall have the like right of audience in those proceedings as the service man himself would have.

(3A)[1]   In relation to any proceedings before a rent officer or rent assessment committee, within the meaning of the Rent (Scotland) Act 1984, subsections (1) to (3) of this section shall have effect as if the references to the court or tribunal included references to a rent officer or rent assessment committee.

(4)[2]   The Secretary of State may make regulations—

    (a)   for enabling a counter-notice under section 22(1) of the Agricultural Holdings (Scotland) Act 1991, to be served on behalf of a service man at a time when he is serving abroad, in a case where a notice to quit is given to him as mentioned in subsection (1) of section 21 of this Act; and

    (b)   for enabling any act or proceedings consequential upon the service of a counter-notice under subsection (1) of the said section [22] to be performed or conducted on behalf of a service man at a time when he is serving abroad, either in such a case as is mentioned in the preceding paragraph or in a case where subsection (5) of section 21 of this Act applies in relation to the service man.

(5)   Regulations made under the last preceding subsection may contain such incidental and consequential provisions as may appear to the said Minister to be necessary or expedient for the purposes of the regulations.

(6)   The power to make regulations under subsection (4) of this section shall be exercisable by statutory instrument, which shall be subject to annulment in pursuance of a resolution of either House of Parliament.

(7)   References in this section to a time when a service man is serving abroad are references to a time when he is performing a period of relevant service and is outside the United Kingdom.

**Interpretation of Part II**

**D1.605**

23.—(1)[3]   In this Part of this Act, unless the context otherwise requires, the following expressions have the meanings hereby assigned to them respectively, that is to say:—

    "agricultural land" has the same meaning as in section 115(1) of the Rent (Scotland) Act 1984;

    "assured tenancy" and "statutory assured tenancy" have the same meaning as in Part II of the Housing (Scotland) Act 1988;

---

[1] Added by the Rent (Scotland) Act 1971 (c.28), Sch.18, and as amended by the Rent (Scotland) Act 1984 (c.58), Sch.8, Pt.II.

[2] As amended by the Agricultural Holdings (Scotland) Act 1991 (c.55), Sch.11, para.3.

[3] As amended by the Police (Scotland) Act 1967 (c.77), Sch.5, the Rent (Scotland) Act 1971 (c.28), Sch.18, the Rent (Scotland) Act 1984 (c.58), Sch.8, Pt II and the Housing Act 1988 (c.50), Sch.17, para. 14.

"Crown interest" means an interest belonging to His Majesty in right of the Crown or of the Duchy of Lancaster, or to the Duchy of Cornwall, or to a Government department, or held on behalf of His Majesty for the purposes of a Government department;

"dependant",[1] in relation to a service man, means—

    (a)   his spouse or civil partner, and

    (b)   any other member of his family who was wholly or mainly maintained by him immediately before the beginning of the period of service in question;

        in relation to a statutory tenancy or to a provision of the Rent (Scotland) Act 1984 "landlord" and "tenant" have the same meaning as in that Act but, subject to that, those expressions have the same meaning as in Part II of the Housing (Scotland) Act 1988;

"policeman service man" means a service man who, immediately before beginning the period of relevant service in question, was a member of a police force;

"relevant local policing body" or "relevant police authority" means, in relation to a police force, the relevant local policing body or the police authority responsible for the maintenance of that force;[2]

"statutory tenancy" means a right to retain possession of premises after the ending of a tenancy thereof, being a right arising on the ending of that tenancy from the operation of the Rent (Scotland) Act 1984 (or of the Rent (Scotland) Act 1984 as extended by this Part of this Act) in relation to a person as being, or being the surviving spouse or surviving civil partner of or otherwise related to, the former owner of the tenancy, or a right to retain possession of premises arising by virtue of subsection (1) of section 18 of this Act;[3]

"tenancy" includes a statutory tenancy, and, apart from a statutory tenancy, means a tenancy created either immediately or derivatively out of the freehold, whether by a lease or underlease, by an agreement for a lease or underlease or by a tenancy agreement, but does not include any relationship between a mortgagor and a mortgagee as such.

  (1A)   Any reference in this Part of this Act to sections 12 to 31 of the Housing (Scotland) Act 1988 includes a reference to sections 47 to 55 of that Act so far as applicable to those sections.

  (2)   In this Part of this Act—

    (a)   references to the ending of a tenancy are references to the coming to an end thereof however brought about, whether by effluxion of time, notice to quit or otherwise, and in particular, as respects a statutory tenancy, include references to the coming to an end thereof as between the tenant and a landlord who is himself a tenant by reason of the ending of the tenancy of the landlord;

    (b)   references to a tenancy vested in any person include references to a tenancy vested in trustees, or held as part of the estate of a deceased person, where the first-mentioned person has a right or permission to occupy the premises arising by reason of a beneficial interest (whether direct or derivative) under the trusts or, as the case may be, in the estate

---

[1] As amended by the Civil Partnership Act 2004 (c.33), Sch.26, para.21 (effective December 5, 2005).

[2] As substituted by the Police Reform and Social Responsibility Act 2011 (c.13) Sch.16(3) para.72 (effective January 16, 2012).

[3] As amended by the Civil Partnership Act 2004 (c.33), Sch.26, para.21 (effective December 5, 2005).

of the deceased person or under trusts of which the deceased person was trustee.

(3)[1]   In this Part of this Act, and in the Rent (Scotland) Act 1984 or sections 12 to 31 of the Housing (Scotland) Act 1988 as applied by any provision thereof, references to rent shall be construed as including references to any sum in the nature of rent payable in respect of such a right or permission derived otherwise than under a lease as is mentioned in section 18 of this Act.

## Application of Part II to Scotland

**24.**   In the application of the preceding sections of this Part of this Act to Scotland—

D1.606

   (a)   for any reference to the Minister of Local Government and Planning or to the Minister of Agriculture and Fisheries there shall be substituted a reference to the Secretary of State; and for any reference to the county court there shall be substituted a reference to the sheriff[2]

   (b)[3]   and for any reference to such a dwelling-house as is mentioned in paragraph 1 of Schedule 7 to the Agricultural Holdings Act 1948, there shall be substituted a reference to a dwelling-house comprised in an agricultural holding and occupied by the person responsible for the control (whether as tenant or as servant or agent of the tenant) of the farming of the holding;

   (c)   *[Repealed by the Agriculture Act 1958 (c.71), Sch.2, Pt II.]*

   (d)   for any reference to the Town and Country Planning Act 1947, there shall be substituted a reference to the Town and Country Planning (Scotland) Act 1947, and for references to the Furnished Houses (Rent Control) Act 1946, and to section 8 thereof, there shall be respectively substituted references to the Rent of Furnished Houses Control (Scotland) Act 1943, and to section 6 thereof;

   (e)   for any reference to a valuation list there shall be substituted a reference to a valuation roll; for any reference to a hereditament there shall be substituted a reference to lands and heritages; and for any reference to intoxicating liquor there shall be substituted a reference to exciseable liquor;

   (f)   the expression "licence" means a right or permission derived otherwise than under a lease; and any reference to the reversion immediately expectant on a tenancy shall be construed as a reference to the interest of the immediate landlord of the tenant under the tenancy;

   (g)   *[Repealed by the Police (Scotland) Act 1967 (c.77), Sch.5]*

   (h)[4]   section 16 of this Act shall have effect as if for subsection (8) there were substituted the following subsection—

> "(8)   A notice for the purposes of this section may be served in like manner as a notice under section 349 of the Local Government (Scotland) Act 1947."

   (j)[5]   for any reference to the Rent Restrictions Acts there shall be substituted

---

[1] As applied to Scotland by s.24 infra.

[2] For the interpretation of the term "sheriff, see now the Sheriff Courts (Scotland) Act 1971 (c.58), s.4, and the Interpretation Act 1978 (c.30), Sch.1.

[3] As amended by the Agriculture Act 1958 (c.71), Sch.1, Pt II, Sch.2, Pt II and Sch.3, the Police (Scotland) Act 1967 (c.77), Sch.5, Pts I and II, and the Agricultural Holdings (Scotland) Act 1991 (c.55), Sch.13.

[4] S.16 of this Act as enacted was superseded by a substituted section: see notes to s.16, supra.

[5] Added by the Rent (Scotland) Act 1971 (c.28), Sch.18.

a reference to the Rent (Scotland) Act 1971; and for any reference, however expressed, to a dwelling-house to which the Rent Restrictions Acts apply there shall be substituted a reference to a dwelling-house subject to a statutory tenancy within the meaning of the Rent (Scotland) Act 1971.

*Protection during short period of training*

## Protection during short period of training

D1.607

**25.**—(1) Where a service man who has been living with a dependant or dependants of his in any premises in right of a tenancy, or of a licence in that behalf granted by his employer in consequence of his employment, performs a short period of training, then, for so long during that period and within fourteen days from the ending of it as the dependant or dependants and the service man or any of them is or are still living in the premises or any part thereof, no person shall be entitled, except with the leave of the appropriate court, to proceed—

(a) to execution on, or otherwise to the enforcement of, any judgment or order given or made against any of them for the recovery of possession of any part of the premises in which any of them is or are living, or

(b) to exercise against any of them any right to take possession of or to re-enter upon, any such part thereof.

(2) If, on any application for such leave as is required by the preceding subsection, the court is of opinion that, by reason of circumstances directly or indirectly attributable to the service man's performing or having performed the period of service in question, the judgment, order or right ought not to be immediately executed, enforced, or exercised, the court may refuse leave or give leave subject to such restrictions and conditions as the court thinks proper.

(3) References in this section to a judgment or order for the recovery of possession of premises include references to any judgment or order the effect of which is to enable a person to obtain possession of the premises, and in particular includes, in relation to a mortgagee, a judgment or order for the delivery of possession of the premises.

(4) For the purposes of this section a person shall be deemed to be proceeding to execution on, or otherwise to the enforcement of, a judgment or order in the circumstances in which, by virtue of subsection (9) of section 3 of this Act, he would be deemed to be so proceeding for the purposes of section 2 of this Act, and, where a person has, in a case for which leave was not required under this section, taken out any judicial process with a view to, or in the course of, the enforcement of a judgment or order or proceeded to the exercise of a right to take possession of or to re-enter upon premises, he shall be deemed to be proceeding to the enforcement of the judgment or order or to the exercise of the right when any step is taken by him or on his behalf towards its completion.

(5) The references in section 5 and subsection (1) of section 11 of this Act to the provisions of Part I of this Act shall include references to the provisions of this section, and the provisions of section 13 of this Act which relate to omission to obtain leave required under section 2 of this Act shall have effect in relation to omission to obtain leave required under this section.

(6) In this section the expression "dependant", in relation to a service man, means—

    (a)[1]  his spouse or civil partner, and
    (b)  any other member of his family wholly or mainly maintained by him.
(7)  In the application of this section to Scotland—
    (a)  the expression "licence" has the meaning assigned to it by paragraph (f) of section 24 of this Act;
    (b)  a reference to proceeding to execution on or otherwise to the enforcement of a judgment or order shall be construed as a reference to the enforcement of a decree, and any reference to a mortgagee shall be omitted;
    (c)  for the references to section 2 and to subsection (9) of section 3 of this Act there shall be respectively substituted references to section 8 and to subsection (7) of section 9 of this Act.

**26-36.**  [England and Wales.]

Part III – Protection Against Insecurity of Tenure of Business and Professional Premises

*Provisions as to Scotland*

**Application of sections 38 to 40**

**37.**  The three next following sections shall apply to Scotland only.

**Application by service man for renewal of tenancy of business premises**

**38.**—(1)  Where—                                       **D1.608**
    (a)  immediately before beginning (whether before or after the commencement of this Act) a period of relevant service other than a short period of training, a service man was the working proprietor of a business or a professional practice carried on in the premises or part of the premises comprised in a tenancy vested in him, and
    (b)  the landlord gives or has given to the service man notice of termination of tenancy taking effect after the commencement of this Act, and before the date of the ending of that period of service or before the expiration of two months from that date, and
    (c)  at the time when an application for renewal of the tenancy is made in pursuance of the provisions hereinafter contained the service man is still the proprietor of the business or practice and the business or practice is still being carried on in the premises comprised in the tenancy,
the service man may, at any time before the notice of termination of tenancy takes effect and not later than the expiry of twenty-one days after the service of the notice or after the commencement of this Act, whichever is the later, apply to the sheriff for a renewal of his tenancy.

(2)  For the purposes of paragraph (*a*) of the last preceding subsection a service man shall be deemed to have been at any time the working proprietor of a business or professional practice carried on as mentioned in that paragraph if, and only if, he was the proprietor of the business or practice during the whole of the period of one year immediately preceding that time and, during more than one-half of that period, either—

---

[1] As amended by the Civil Partnership Act 2004 (c.33), Sch.26, para.22 (effective December 5, 2005).

    (a)  he worked whole-time in the actual management or conduct of that business or practice, or

    (b)  he worked whole-time in the actual management or conduct of a business or professional practice of which that business or practice was a branch and was mainly engaged in the management or conduct of that branch.

(3)  In the preceding provisions of this section the expression "proprietor" means, in the case of a business or practice carried on by a firm, a partner in the firm on terms and conditions entitling him to not less than one-half of the profits of the firm and, in the case of a business or practice carried on by a company, a person holding shares in the company amounting in nominal value to not less than one-half of the issued share capital of the company; and, in relation to a business or practice carried on by a partnership firm or by a company, references in those provisions to the proprietor of the business or practice include references to a person being one of two such partners in the firm or, as the case may be, being one of two persons each holding such shares in the company, and references to the working proprietor of the business or practice shall be construed accordingly.

(4)  In relation to a business or practice carried on by a firm or by a company, references in the preceding provisions of this section to a tenancy vested in the service man include references to a tenancy vested in one or more partners in the firm, or vested in the company, as the case may be; and for the purposes of those provisions and of this subsection a tenancy shall be treated as having been vested at any time in a person if it was then vested in trustees, or held as part of the estate of a deceased person, and the first-mentioned person then had a right or permission to occupy the premises comprised in the tenancy, or the part of those premises in which the business or practice was being carried on, being a right or permission arising by reason of a beneficial interest (whether direct or derivative) under the trusts or, as the case may be, in the estate of the deceased person or under trusts of which the deceased person was trustee.

(5)[1]  In this section—

    (a)  the expression "profits" in relation to a firm means such profits of the firm as are from time to time distributable among the partners therein;

    (b)[2]  the expression "company" has the meaning given by section 1(1) of the Companies Act 2006;

    (c)  the expression "share" includes stock and the expression "share capital" shall be construed accordingly;

and for the purposes of this section shares held by a person's spouse or civil partner, or held by him jointly with his spouse or civil partner, shall be treated as shares held by that person.

(6)  The foregoing provisions of this section shall not have effect if at the time when an application for renewal of the tenancy might otherwise be made—

    (a)  the premises comprised in the tenancy—

        (i)  are an agricultural holding within the meaning of the Agricultural Holdings (Scotland) Act 1991, or

        (ii)[3]  consist of or comprise premises (other than premises excepted

---

[1] As amended by the Civil Partnership Act 2004 (c.33) Sch.26 para.24 (effective December 5, 2005).

[2] As amended by the Companies Act 2006 (Consequential Amendments, Transitional Provisions and Savings) Order 2009 (SI 2009/1941) Sch.1 para.6(3) (effective October 1, 2009).

[3] As amended by the Licensing (Scotland) Act 2005 (Consequential Provisions) Order 2009 (SSI 2009/248) Sch.1 para.1(4), (effective September 1, 2009 at 05.00).

from this provision) which, by virtue of a premises licence granted under the Licensing (Scotland) Act 2005, are licensed for the sale of alcohol (within the meaning of section 2 of that Act) for consumption on the premises,

(b) [Repealed by the Statute Law Repeals Act 1989 (c.43), Sch.1, Pt I, Group 5.]

In this subsection the reference to premises excepted from the provision as to premises licensed for the sale of exciseable liquor is a reference to premises in respect of which—

(i) the excise licence for the time being in force is a licence the duty in respect of which is the reduced duty payable under section 45 of the Finance (1909–10) Act 1910, or a licence granted in pursuance of regulations under subsection (5) of the said section 45 (which relates to the granting of licences on the provisional payment of reduced duty); or

(ii) the Commissioners of Customs and Excise certify that no application under the said section 45 has been made in respect of the period for which the excise licence for the time being in force was granted, but that if such an application had been made such a licence could properly have been granted as is mentioned in the preceding paragraph.

**Power of sheriff to grant new tenancy**

**39.**—(1)[1]  On any application under subsection (1) of the last foregoing section  **D1.609**
the sheriff may, subject as hereinafter provided, determine that the tenancy shall be renewed for such period, at such rent, and on such terms and conditions as he shall, in all the circumstances, think reasonable, and thereafter the parties shall be deemed to have entered into a new lease of the premises for that period, at that rent and on those terms and conditions.

(2)  The period for which a tenancy may be renewed under the last foregoing subsection shall not extend beyond the expiry of four months from the end of the period of service in consequence of which the application was made.

(3)  Notwithstanding anything in subsection (1) of this section, the sheriff may, if in all the circumstances he thinks it reasonable to do so, dismiss any application under subsection (1) of the last foregoing section, and shall not determine that a tenancy shall be renewed, if he is satisfied—

(a) that the tenant is in breach of any condition of his tenancy which in the opinion of the sheriff is material; or

(b) that the tenant is notour bankrupt or is divested of his estate by virtue of a trust deed for behoof of creditors, or, being a company, is unable to pay its debts; or

(c) that the landlord has offered to sell the premises to the tenant at such price as may, failing agreement, be fixed by a single arbiter agreed on by the parties or appointed, failing such agreement, by the sheriff; or

(d) that the landlord has offered to afford to the tenant, on terms and conditions which in the opinion of the sheriff are reasonable, alternative accommodation which, in the opinion of the sheriff is suitable for the purposes of the business carried on by the tenant in the premises; or

---

[1] For the interpretation of the term "sheriff," see now the Sheriff Courts (Scotland) Act 1971 (c.58), s.4, and the Interpretation Act 1978 (c.30), Sch.1.

(e) that the tenant has given notice of termination of tenancy and in consequence of that notice the landlord has contracted to sell or let the premises or has taken any other steps as a result of which he would in the opinion of the sheriff be seriously prejudiced if he could not obtain possession of the premises; or

(f) that, having regard to all the circumstances of the case, greater hardship would be caused by determining that the tenancy shall be renewed than by refusing so to do.

(4) Where a tenancy has been renewed under subsection (1) of this section, the tenant shall have the like right to apply for further renewals as if the tenancy had been renewed by agreement between the landlord and the tenant, and accordingly the foregoing provisions of this section and the immediately preceding section shall, with any necessary modifications, apply to a tenancy which has been renewed under the said subsection (1) or under this subsection.

(5) If on any application under this section the sheriff is satisfied that it will not be possible to dispose finally of the application before the notice of termination of tenancy takes effect, he may make an interim order authorising the tenant to continue in occupation of the premises at such rent, for such period (which shall not exceed three months) and on such terms and conditions as the sheriff may think fit.

(6)[1] Applications under subsection (1) of the last foregoing section shall be conducted and disposed of in the summary manner in which proceedings are conducted and disposed of under the Small Debt (Scotland) Acts 1837 to 1889, and the decision of the sheriff in any such application shall be final and not subject to review.

### Application to Crown property

D1.610

40.—(1) The last two foregoing sections shall apply to any such premises as are mentioned therein in which the interest of the immediate landlord of the tenant belongs to His Majesty in right of the Crown or to a Government department or is held on behalf of His Majesty for the purposes of a Government department, in like manner as the said section applies to any other such premises.

(2) Where the Minister or Board in charge of any Government department is satisfied that for reasons of national security it is necessary that the use or occupation of any such premises in which the interest aforesaid belongs to a Government department or is held on behalf of His Majesty for the purposes of a Government department should be discontinued or changed, the Minister or Board may certify that this subsection applies to the premises; and where such a certificate is given the sheriff shall not determine that the tenancy shall be renewed.

D1.611

### PART VII – MISCELLANEOUS AND GENERAL

### Evidence as to performance of relevant service

60.—(1)[2] A certificate stating that a person has performed or is performing or is to perform a period of relevant service or of relevant service of any particular description, or the duration or the date of the beginning or ending of such a period,

---

[1] See now the Sheriff Courts (Scotland) Act 1971 (c.58), s.35.
[2] As amended by SI 1964/488, and the Statute Law (Repeals) Act 1977 (c.18), Sch.1, Pt I. Functions of the Minister of Labour and National Service now exercisable by the Secretary of State for Employment: SI 1959/1769, SI 1968/729 and SI 1970/1537.

or whether such a period which has been or is being or is to be performed by any person is or is not a short period of training, being a certificate which is signed by a person authorised in that behalf—

(a)  by the Defence Council

(b)  *[Repealed by the Statute Law (Repeals) Act 1977 (c.18), Sch.1, Pt 1]*

shall in all legal proceedings be sufficient evidence of the facts stated therein for the purposes of this Act except to any extent to which it is shown to be incorrect.

(2)  A certificate signed by a person authorised in that behalf by the Defence Council stating that a person is not performing, and has not within a specified previous time performed, a period of relevant service in a specified force or forces (being a force or forces in respect of which the Defence Council keep records), shall in all legal proceedings be sufficient evidence of the facts stated therein for the purposes of this Act except to any extent to which it is shown to be incorrect.

(3)  A certificate signed by a person authorised in that behalf by the Defence Council referring to an inquiry as to a person therein described and being to the effect that no person answering to that description is identifiable in the relevant records kept by the authority on whose behalf the certificate is signed, shall be sufficient evidence for the purposes of this Act that no such person is so identifiable.

(4)  A certificate signed as aforesaid stating any matter as a matter appearing from records shall be treated for the purposes of subsection (1), and of subsection (2), of this section as stating it as a fact.

(5)  A document purporting to be a certificate signed as aforesaid shall be deemed to be such unless the contrary is proved.

(6)  The Defence Council shall be under obligation to secure that, on inquiry made to them for the purposes of this Act as to a person therein described, if the information appearing from records kept by them is such as to enable a certificate falling within subsection (1) or subsection (2) of this section to be given as to a person appearing to answer that description, or is such as to justify the giving of a certificate falling within subsection (3) of this section, such a certificate shall be given:

Provided that no certificate the giving of which would in the opinion of the authority to whom the inquiry is made be against the interests of national security shall be given.

### Interpretation

D1.612

**64.**—(1)[1]  In this Act, unless the context otherwise requires, the following expressions have the meaning hereby assigned to them respectively, that is to say—

"conditional sale agreement"[2] means an agreement for the sale of goods under which the purchase price or part of it is payable by instalments, and the property in the goods is to remain in the seller (notwithstanding that the buyer is to be in possession of the goods) until such conditions as to the payment of instalments or otherwise as may be specified in the agreement are fulfilled;

"creditor"[3] means the person by whom the goods are bailed or (in Scotland) hired under a hire-purchase agreement or, as the case may be, the seller

---

[1] As amended by the Rent (Scotland) Act 1971 (c.28), Sch.20, and the Statute Law (Repeals) Act 1977 (c.18), Sch.1, Pt I.

[2] Added by the Consumer Credit Act 1974 (c.39), Sch.4, para.14.

[3] Added by the Consumer Credit Act 1974 (c.39), Sch.4, para.14.

under a conditional sale agreement, or the person to whom his rights and duties have passed by assignment or operation of the law;

"hire-purchase agreement"[1] means an agreement, other than a conditional sale agreement, under which—

    (a)    goods are bailed or (in Scotland) hired in return for periodical payments by the person to whom they are bailed or hired, and

    (b)    the property in the goods will pass to that person if the terms of the agreement are complied with and one or more of the following occurs—

        (i)    the exercise of an option to purchase by that person,

        (ii)    the doing of any other specified act by any party to the agreement,

        (iii)    the happening of any other specified event;

"local authority"[2] has the same meaning as in paragraph 6(1) of Schedule 3 to the Pensions (Increase) Act 1971 and any reference in this Act to a local authority shall apply also to the bodies mentioned in paragraph 6(2) of that Schedule;

"local Act scheme"[3] means the superannuation scheme administered by a local authority maintaining a superannuation fund under a local Act;

"relevant service" means service after the 15th day of July 1950 of a description specified in the First Schedule to this Act;

"service" means the discharge of naval, military or air force duties, and includes training for the discharge of such duties;

"service man" means a man who performs a period of relevant service;

"short period of training" means a period of relevant service of a description specified in paragraph 2 of the First Schedule to this Act to which a maximum period of fifteen days is attached, of a description specified in paragraph 6 thereof, or of a description specified in paragraph 7 thereof performed under an obligation or voluntary arrangements under which its continuous duration is limited to less than three months.

"total price"[4] means the total sum payable by the person to whom goods are bailed or hired under a hire-purchase agreement or, as the case may be, the buyer under a conditional sale agreement including any sum payable on the exercise of an option to purchase but excluding any sum payable as a penalty or as compensation or damages for a breach of the agreement.

(2)    [Repealed by the Armed Forces Act 1981 (c.55), Sch.5.]

(3)    [Repealed by the Statute Law (Repeals) Act 1977 (c.18), Sch.1, Pt I.]

(4)    In this Act, unless the context otherwise requires, references to any enactment shall be construed as references to that enactment as amended by or under any other enactment.

---

[1] Added by the Consumer Credit Act 1974 (c.39), Sch.4, para.14.
[2] As substituted by the Superannuation Act 1972 (c. 11), Sch.6.
[3] As substituted by the Superannuation Act 1972 (c. 11), Sch.6.
[4] Added by the Consumer Credit Act 1974 (c.39), Sch.4, para.14.

SCHEDULES

FIRST SCHEDULE

Service relevant for the purposes of this act

*Sections 41 to 44 and sections 52, 63, 64*

**1.**

(i)[1] Service in pursuance of any notice or directions given under any enactment which provides for the calling out on permanent service, or the calling into actual service, or the embodiment, of any reserve or auxiliary force, or members thereof, or for the recall of service pensioners within the meaning of section 1(1) of the Reserve Forces (Safeguard of Employment) Act 1985.

(ii) Service, other than for the purposes of training only, in pursuance of any obligation or undertaking, whether legally enforceable or not, to serve when called upon as a commissioned officer, not being an obligation or undertaking to accept a permanent or short-service commission.

(iii), (iv) *[Repealed by the Statute Law (Repeals) Act 1977 (c.18), Sch.1, Pt 1]*

(v) *[Repealed by the Armed Forces Act 1981 (c.55), Sch.5]*

(vi)–(viii) *[Repealed by the Statute Law (Repeals) Act 1977 (c.18), Sch.1, Pt I.]*

2.–3. *[Repealed by the Statute Law (Repeals) Act 1977 (c.18), Sch.1, Pt I.]*

4. Service for a period of eighteen months for which an officer of any reserve force of the Royal Navy or of the Royal Marines, or an officer of reserve to, or on the retired or emergency list of, or holding a temporary commission in, the Royal Navy or the Royal Marines, volunteers.

5, 6. *[Repealed by the Statute Law (Repeals) Act 1977 (c.18), Sch.1, Pt I]*

7. Service, for the purposes of training only, for a continuous period of seven days or longer performed, whether under an obligation or under voluntary arrangements, by—

(a) an officer or man of any reserve force of the Royal Navy or of the Royal Marines, or an officer of reserve to, or on the retired or emergency list of, or holding a temporary commission in, the Royal Navy or the Royal Marines;

(b) an officer of any army reserve of officers, a man of any army reserve force, an officer or man of the Territorial Army, or an officer of the Territorial Army Reserve of Officers;

(c) an officer of the Royal Air Force Volunteer Reserve or of any air force reserve of officers or on the retired list of the Royal Air Force, a man of any air force reserve force, or an officer or man of the Royal Auxiliary Air Force or the Royal Auxiliary Air Force Reserve;

(d) a member of any reserve of the Women's Royal Naval Service or a member of the Naval Voluntary Aid Detachment Reserve.

not being service of a description specified in any of the preceding paragraphs of this Schedule.

---

[1] As amended by the Reserve Forces (Safeguard of Employment) Act 1985 (c. 17), Sch.4, para.1, and as amended by the Reserve Forces. Act 1996 (Consequential Provisions etc.) Regulations 1998 (SI 1998/3086).

SCHEDULES

FIRST SCHEDULE

Sections 4, 19(4) and (5), 27, 67

(iii) Served in pursuance of any notice or direction given under any enactment upon a man to provide for the fulfilment of his permanent service in the calling out for actual service or the embodiment of any reserve or auxiliary forces of members thereof, or for the recall of service personnel within the meaning of section 1(1) on 1(1) of the Reserve Forces (Safeguard of Employment) Act 1985.

(c) Served (other than for the purpose of attending or, or proceeding to, any of actions of a medical board, whether legally liable or not to be so served, when called upon after completion of his unit being in addition to, or exceeding that, upon completion of his service completed.

(d) Employed by the Admiralty, the Defence Council or by any ...

Service for a period of employment or engagements for an officer or any reserve force of the Royal Navy and the Royal Marine other officers taken up on call-out or ...

For the purposes of this Schedule every period of seven days or longer, performed whole or in ship, training, etc., by a person concerned by—

(a) In officer upon whatever service done of the Royal Navy or of the Royal Marines, or an NCO or man serving by on ...

(b) an officer of any other rank of the Royal Naval Army ...

(c) an officer of the Royal Air Force, or an NCO or man ...

(d) a member of one reserve of the Women's Royal Naval Service or a member of the Royal Auxiliary Air Force ...

not being called up during no attention from the operation of the points of this Schedule

344

# SHERIFF COURTS (CIVIL JURISDICTION AND PROCEDURE) (SCOTLAND) ACT 1963

### (1963 c. 22)

An Act to increase the amount by reference to which actions are classified as summary causes in the sheriff court in Scotland; to increase the amount by reference to which the small debt jurisdiction of the sheriff is limited; to amend the law with regard to the bringing of actions between spouses for interim aliment of small amounts in the sheriff's small debt court and with regard to the jurisdiction of the sheriff in such actions brought as aforesaid; and for purposes connected with the matters aforesaid.

[10th July 1963]

**1, 2.**   *[Repealed by the Sheriff Courts (Scotland) Act 1971, Sched. 2.]*

## Actions for aliment of small amounts

**3.**—(1)[1]   An action under section 2 of the Family Law (Scotland) Act 1985 for aliment only (whether or not expenses are also sought) may be brought before the sheriff as a summary cause if the aliment claimed in the action does not exceed—

(a)   in respect of a child under the age of 18 years, the sum of £35 per week; and

(b)   in any other case, the sum of £70 per week;

and any provision in any enactment limiting the jurisdiction of the sheriff in a summary cause by reference to any amount, or limiting the period for which a decree granted by him shall have effect, shall not apply in relation to such an action.

(2)   *[Repealed by the Civil Jurisdiction and Judgments Act 1982, Sched. 14.]*

(3)[2]   The Secretary of State may by order vary the amounts prescribed in paragraphs (a) and (b) of subsection (1) above.

(4)   The power to make an order under subsection (3) above shall be exercisable by statutory instrument subject to annulment in pursuance of a resolution of either House of Parliament and shall include power to vary or revoke any order made there under.

## Citation, construction and commencement

**4.**—(1)   This Act may be cited as the Sheriff Courts (Civil Jurisdiction and Procedure) (Scotland) Act 1963.

(2)   In this Act the expression "the principal Act" means the Sheriff Courts (Scotland) Act 1907, as amended by any other enactment, and the principal Act and this Act shall be construed together as one.

(3)   This Act shall come into operation on 1st October 1963.

---

[1] Substituted by the Family Law (Scotland) Act 1985, s.23.

[2] As amended by SI 1999 No. 678, Art. 2, Sched. (effective May 19, 1999).

# LAW REFORM (MISCELLANEOUS PROVISIONS) (SCOTLAND) ACT 1966

## (1966 c. 19)

D1.615

An Act to exempt from arrestment on the dependence of an action sums falling to be paid by way of wages, salary or other earnings or by way of pension, to abolish the exemption from arrestment in execution of certain earnings payable by the Crown, and to provide for the variation from time to time of the amount of wages excepted from arrestment under the Wages Arrestment Limitation (Scotland) Act 1870; to amend section 5 of the Adoption Act 1958, and to provide in Scotland for the succession of an adopted person to the estate of his natural parent in certain circumstances; to amend section 5 of the Trusts (Scotland) Act 1961; to provide for the admission in evidence of certain documents in civil proceedings; to confer jurisdiction on the sheriff court to vary or recall certain orders of the Court of Session in respect of maintenance, custody and welfare of children, and to provide for the extension of certain time limits in appeals under the Summary Jurisdiction (Scotland) Act 1954; and to provide that acts of adjournal and acts of sederunt shall be statutory instruments.

[3rd August 1966]

### Wages, pensions, etc., to be exempt from arrestment on the dependence of an action

1.—(1)   After the passing of this Act it shall not be competent to arrest on the dependence of an action any earnings or any pension.

D1.616

(2)

(a)   For the purposes of this and of the next following section "earnings" means any sums payable by way of wages or salary (including any fees, bonus, commission, overtime pay or other emoluments payable in addition to wages or salary by the person paying the wages or salary or payable under a contract of service);

(b)   in this section "pension" includes—

(i)   any annuity in respect of past services, whether or not the services were rendered to the person paying the annuity, and any periodical payments by way of compensation for the loss, abolition or relinquishment, or any diminution in the emoluments, of any office or employment;

(ii)   any pension or allowance payable in respect of disablement or disability.

### Certain earnings payable by the Crown to be arrestable in execution.

2.—(1)   Subject to the provisions of this section, any rule of law which exempts from arrestment in execution earnings falling to be paid by the Crown or a Minister of the Crown or out of the public revenue of the United Kingdom shall cease to have effect, except in relation to earnings payable to a member of the armed forces of the Crown; and accordingly for paragraph (a) of the proviso to section 46 of the Crown Proceedings Act 1947 (provisions as to arrestment in the hands of the Crown), there shall be substituted the following paragraph—

D1.617

"(a)   any earnings payable to any officer of the Crown as such, except as provided by section 2 of the Law Reform (Miscellaneous Provisions) (Scotland) Act 1966;".

(2)   Earnings liable to arrestment by virtue of the last foregoing subsection shall be treated as falling to be paid by the chief officer in Scotland for the time being of the department, office or other body concerned.

(3)[1]   If any question arises, in connection with any proceedings relating to such an arrestment as to who for the purposes of this section is the chief officer in Scotland of the department, office or other body, that question shall be referred to and determined by the Minister for the Civil Service.

(4)[2]   A document purporting to set out a determination of the Minister for the Civil Service under the last foregoing subsection and to be signed by an official of the Minister for the Civil Service shall, in any such proceedings as aforesaid, be sufficient evidence of that determination, and deemed to contain an accurate statement thereof unless the contrary is shown.

(5)   In this section "earnings payable to a member of the armed forces of the Crown" means any sum (other than a pension) the assignation of which is precluded by virtue of section 203 of the Army Act 1955 or of section 203 of the Air Force Act 1955, or any like sum payable to a member of the naval forces of the Crown, or to a member of any women's service administered by the Defence Council.

(6)   The Wages Arrestment Limitation (Scotland) Act 1870 shall apply in relation to earnings arrestable by virtue of this section as it applies to other earnings.

(7)   Nothing in the provisions of this section shall affect the operation of section 163 of the Merchant Shipping Act 1894, which exempts from arrestment wages payable to seamen and apprentices within the meaning of that Act.

**Power to vary amount of wages excepted from arrestment.**

D1.618

3.—(1)   If at any time after the commencement of this Act it appears to Her Majesty in Council that the sum of four pounds specified in section 2 of the Wages Arrestment Limitation (Scotland) Act 1870 (limitation of liability of wages to arrestment) (whether by virtue of the said Act as amended by any other Act, or as previously amended under this section) should be further varied, Her Majesty may by Order in Council direct that the said section shall be further amended so as to substitute, for the sum specified in that section, such other sum as may be specified in the Order.

(2)   No recommendation shall be made to Her Majesty to make an Order in Council under the last preceding subsection unless a draft of the Order has been laid before Parliament and approved by a resolution of each House of Parliament.

(3)   Any Order in Council made under this section may be revoked by a subsequent Order in Council under this section which substitutes another sum for the sum specified in the Order which is thereby revoked.

(4)   An Order in Council made under this section shall come into force on the expiration of a period of not less than one month beginning with the date on which it is made.

4.   *[Repealed by the Children Act 1975 (c.72), Sch.4, Pt IV.]*

5, 6.   [See Division **M**.]

7.   *[Repealed by the Civil Evidence (Scotland) Act 1988 (c.32), Sch.]*

---

[1] As amended by virtue of SI 1968/1656, arts.2(1)(a), 3(2).
[2] As amended by virtue of SI 1968/1656, arts.2(1)(a), 3(2).

### Variation and recall by the sheriff of certain orders made by the Court of Session in respect of maintenance, custody, etc., and amendment of section 2 of the Divorce (Scotland) Act 1938

**8.**—[1](1)    The provisions of this section shall apply to the following orders made          **D1.619**
by the Court of Session, that is to say—

    (a)    an award of aliment,

    (b)    an order for an annual or periodical allowance made under section 2 of the Divorce (Scotland) Act 1938, whether under that section as originally enacted or as amended by any subsequent enactment including this Act,

    (c)[2]    an order for a periodical allowance made under subsection (2) or (3) of section 26 of the Succession (Scotland) Act 1964 or under section 5 of the Divorce (Scotland) Act 1976 or section 29 of the Matrimonial and Family Proceedings Act 1984 or section 8 of the Family Law (Scotland) Act 1985,

    (cc)[3]    an order under section 11 of the Children (Scotland) Act 1995 (orders in respect of parental responsibilities etc.) or under any earlier enactment relating to the custody, care or supervision of a child, or access to a child;

    (d)[4]    an order made by virtue of section 9 of the Conjugal Rights (Scotland) (Amendment) Act 1861, or under Part II of the Matrimonial Proceedings (Children) Act 1958, or by virtue of Part II of the Guardianship Act 1973, and

    (e)    an order varying any such order as aforesaid.

(2)[5]    Where any person has a right to make application for the variation or recall of any order to which the provisions of this section apply, he may make an application in that behalf to the sheriff, and, subject to the provisions of the next following subsection, the sheriff shall have the like powers in relation to the application as the Court of Session.

(3)    Where in any application under this section any other party to the action, not later than the first calling of the application in court, requests that it be remitted to the Court of Session, the sheriff shall so remit, and the Court of Session shall deal with it accordingly.

(4)    Notwithstanding anything in Part I of the Public Records (Scotland) Act 1937 (transmission of court records to and from the Keeper of the Records of Scotland, etc.), the powers of the Court of Session, conferred by sections 16 and 34 respectively of the Administration of Justice (Scotland) Act 1933, to regulate its own procedure and that of the sheriff court, shall include power to provide for the transmission to and from the sheriff court of any process in the action to which an application under this section relates[6]; and for the purposes of the said Act of 1937 and of this section any record of such an application shall be deemed to be a record of the Court of Session.

(5)    *[Repealed by the Divorce (Scotland) Act 1976 (c.39).]*

---

[1] See the Domicile and Matrimonial Proceedings Act 1973 (c.45), s.10(2)(b).
[2] As amended by the Divorce (Scotland) Act 1976 (c.39), Sch.1, the Matrimonial and Family Proceedings Act 1984 (c.42), Sch.1, para.7 and the Family Law (Scotland) Act 1985 (c.37), Sch.1, para.5.
[3] As inserted by the Children (Scotland) Act 1995 (c.36), Sch.4, para.14, infra, Division *K*.
[4] As amended by the Guardianship Act 1973 (c.29), Sch.5.
[5] As amended by the Family Law Act 1986 (c.55), Sch.2.
[6] See SI 1984/667, infra.

(6)[1]  In this section—

"order" includes a provision in a final decree, but does not include an interim order,

"party" means any person having a right to make application for the variation or recall of the order in question, and

"sheriff" means

(a)[2]  in relation to an order under subsection (1)(a), (b), (c), or (cc) above or an order varying any such order the sheriff having jurisdiction over any party on whom the application has to be served, on any of the grounds mentioned in paragraph (a), (b) or (j) of section 6 of the Sheriff Courts (Scotland) Act 1907;

(b)  in relation to an order mentioned in subsection (1)(d) above or an order varying any such order, the sheriff having jurisdiction under section 9, 10 or 12 of the Family Law Act 1986.

9.  *[Repealed by the Criminal Procedure (Scotland) Act 1975 (c.21), Sch.10.]*

## Acts of adjournal and acts of sederunt to be statutory instruments

10.  *[Repealed by the Interpretation and Legislative Reform (Scotland) Act 2010 (asp 10) Pt 2 s.27(5) (effective April 6, 2011).]*

## Interpretation, repeals, citation and extent

**D1.620**

11.—(1)  Any reference in this Act to an enactment shall be construed as a reference to that enactment as amended by any other enactment including this Act.

(2)  *[Repealed by the Statute Law (Repeals) Act 1974 (c.22).]*

(3)  This Act may be cited as the Law Reform (Miscellaneous Provisions) (Scotland) Act 1966, and shall extend to Scotland only.

---

[1] As amended by the Family Law Act 1986 (c.55), Sch.1, para.8.
[2] As amended by the Children (Scotland) Act 1995 (c.36), Sch.4, para.14, infra, Division K.

# SHERIFF COURTS (SCOTLAND) ACT 1971

(1971 c. 58)

An Act to amend the law with respect to sheriff courts in Scotland, and for
purposes connected therewith.

[27th July 1971]

Part I – Constitution, Organisation and Administration

*General duty of the Secretary of State*

## Secretary of State to be responsible for organisation and administration of sheriff courts

**1.** *[Repealed by the Judiciary and Courts (Scotland) Act 2008 (asp 6) Pt 3 s.48
(effective April 1, 2010 subject to transitional provisions and savings specified in
SSI 2010/39 art.6).]*

*Sheriffdoms*

## Power of Secretary of State to alter sheriffdoms

**2.**—(1)  The Secretary of State may by order alter the boundaries of sheriffdoms,
form new sheriffdoms, or provide for the abolition of sheriffdoms existing at the
time of the making of the order.

(2)  An order under subsection (1) above may contain all such provisions as appear to the Secretary of State to be necessary or expedient for rendering the order of
full effect and any incidental, supplemental or consequential provisions which appear to him to be necessary or expedient for the purposes of the order, including, but
without prejudice to the generality of the foregoing words—

    (a)   provision for the abolition of any office,

  (aa)[1]  provision of the kind that may be made by an order under section 3(2)
of this Act;

    (b)   provisions amending, repealing or revoking any enactment (whether
passed or made before or after the commencement of this Act, and
including any enactment contained in or made under this Act).

(2A)[2]  An order under subsection (1) above may be made only with the consent
of—

    (a)   the Lord President of the Court of Session, and

    (b)   where the order includes provision such as is mentioned in subsection
(2)(a) or (aa) above, the Scottish Court Service.

(2B)[3]  Before consenting to the making of such an order, the Scottish Court
Service must consult such persons as it considers appropriate.

(3)  Where an order under subsection (1) above includes, by virtue of subsection
(2)(a) above, provision for the abolition of any office, then—

---

[1] As inserted by the Judiciary and Courts (Scotland) Act 2008 (asp 6) Pt 3 s.50 (effective April 1,
2010).
[2] As inserted by the Judiciary and Courts (Scotland) Act 2008 (asp 6) Pt 3 s.50 (effective April 1,
2010).
[3] As inserted by the Judiciary and Courts (Scotland) Act 2008 (asp 6) Pt 3 s.50 (effective April 1,
2010).

    (a)   that provision shall have effect notwithstanding the provisions of any enactment (including any enactment contained in this Act), or of any instrument in terms of which any person holds that office;

    (b)[1,2]  the Scottish Court Service may, with the concurrence of the Minister for the Civil Service, pay to or in respect of any person who suffers loss of employment, or loss or diminution of emoluments, which is attributable to the said provision such amount by way of compensation as may appear to the Secretary of State to be reasonable in all the circumstances but no payment shall be made under this provision to or in respect of any person who is mentioned in section 51(2) of the Scotland Act 1998.

(4)[3]   The power to make orders under subsection (1) above shall be exercisable by statutory instrument.

(5)[4]   A statutory instrument containing an order under subsection (1) above is subject to annulment in pursuance of a resolution of the Scottish Parliament.

*Sheriff court districts and places where sheriff courts are to be held*

### Sheriff court districts and places where sheriff courts are to be held

**D1.623**

3.—(1)   Subject to any alterations made by an order under section 2(1) of this Act or under subsection (2) below—

    (a)   the sheriff court districts existing immediately before the commencement of this Act shall continue to exist after such commencement, and

    (b)   sheriff courts shall, after such commencement, continue to be held at the places at which they were in use to be held immediately before such commencement.

(2)   The Secretary of State may by order—

    (a)   alter the boundaries of sheriff court districts, form new districts, or provide for the abolition of districts existing at the time of the making of the order;

    (b)   provide that sheriff courts shall be held, or shall cease to be held, at any place.

(2A)[5]   An order under subsection (2) above may be made only with the consent of—

    (a)   the Lord President of the Court of Session, and

    (b)   the Scottish Court Service.

(2B)[6]   Before consenting to the making of such an order, the Scottish Court Service must consult such persons as it considers appropriate.

(3)   An order under subsection (2) above may contain all such provisions as appear to the Secretary of State to be necessary or expedient for rendering the order of

---

[1] As amended by the Scotland Act 1998 (Consequential Modifications) (No.2) Order 1999 (SI 1999/1820) Sch.2(1) para.50(2) (effective July 1, 1999 the principal appointed day for 1998 c.46).

[2] As substituted by the Judiciary and Courts (Scotland) Act 2008 (asp 6) Pt 3 s.50 (effective April 1, 2010).

[3] As amended by the Judiciary and Courts (Scotland) Act 2008 (asp 6) Pt 3 s.50 (effective April 1, 2010).

[4] As inserted by the Judiciary and Courts (Scotland) Act 2008 (asp 6) Pt 3 s.50 (effective April 1, 2010).

[5] As inserted by the Judiciary and Courts (Scotland) Act 2008 (asp 6) Pt 3 s.51 (effective April 1, 2010).

[6] As inserted by the Judiciary and Courts (Scotland) Act 2008 (asp 6) Pt 3 s.51 (effective April 1, 2010).

full effect and any incidental, supplemental or consequential provisions which appear to him to be necessary or expedient for the purposes of the order, including, but without prejudice to the generality of the foregoing words, provisions amending, repealing or revoking any enactment (whether passed or made before or after the commencement of this Act, and including any enactment contained in or made under this Act).

(4)[1, 2]  The Scottish Court Service may, with the concurrence of the Minister for the Civil Service, pay to or in respect of any person who suffers loss of employment, or loss or diminution of emoluments, which is attributable to an order under subsection (2) above such amount by way of compensation as may appear to the Secretary of State to be reasonable in all the circumstances but no payment shall be made under this provision to or in respect of any person who is mentioned in section 51(2) of the Scotland Act 1998.

(5)[3]  The power to make orders under subsection (2) above shall be exercisable by statutory instrument.

(5A)  A statutory instrument containing an order under subsection (2) above is subject to annulment in pursuance of a resolution of the Scottish Parliament.

(6)  Without prejudice to subsection (1) above, any enactment or other instrument in force immediately before the commencement of this Act shall, to the extent that it fixes sheriff court districts or the places at which sheriff courts are to be held, cease to have effect.

*Sheriffs principal and sheriffs*

### Offices of sheriff principal and sheriff

**4.**—(1)  The office of sheriff (that is to say, the office known formerly as the office of sheriff depute, but known immediately before the commencement of this Act as the office of sheriff) shall be known as the office of sheriff principal, the office of sheriff substitute shall be known as the office of sheriff, and the office of honorary sheriff substitute shall be known as the office of honorary sheriff.

**D1.624**

(2)  Accordingly, any enactment or other document in force or having effect at the commencement of this Act which refers whether expressly or by implication, or which falls to be construed as referring, or as including a reference, to the office of sheriff (as defined in subsection (1) above), or to the office of sheriff substitute, or to the holder of any of the said offices, shall be construed in accordance with subsection (1) above.

(3)[4]  Section 28 of the Interpretation Act 1889 shall not apply for the interpretation of this Act.

### Qualification for offices of sheriff principal and sheriff

**5.**—(1)  A person shall not be appointed to the office of sheriff principal or sheriff unless he is, and has been for at least ten years, legally qualified.

**D1.625**

---

[1] As amended by the Scotland Act 1998 (Consequential Modifications) (No.2) Order 1999 (SI 1999/1820) Sch.2(1) para.50(2) (effective July 1, 1999 the principal appointed day for 1998 c.46).

[2] As substituted by the Judiciary and Courts (Scotland) Act 2008 (asp 6) Pt 3 s.51 (effective April 1, 2010).

[3] As inserted by the Judiciary and Courts (Scotland) Act 2008 (asp 6) Pt 3 s.51 (effective April 1, 2010).

[4] As amended by the Interpretation Act 1978 (c.30) Sch.3.

For the purposes of this subsection, a person shall be legally qualified if he is an advocate or a solicitor.

(2)[1] Without prejudice to sections 11(3) and 11A of this Act, in this section "sheriff principal" does not include a temporary sheriff principal and "sheriff" does not include a part-time sheriff or an honorary sheriff.

### Retiring age for sheriff principal and sheriff[2]

D1.626

**5A.**—(1)  A sheriff principal or sheriff shall vacate his office on the day on which he attains the age of 70.

(2)  Subsection (1) above is subject to section 26(4) to (6) of the Judicial Pensions and Retirement Act 1993 (power to authorise continuance in office up to the age of 75).

(3)[3]  Without prejudice to sections 11(4A) and (4B) and 11B(3) of this Act, in this section, "sheriff principal" does not include a temporary sheriff principal and "sheriff" does not include a part-time sheriff.

### Disqualification of sheriffs principal and sheriffs

D1.627

**6.**—(1)  A sheriff principal to whom this subsection applies, or a sheriff, shall not, so long as he holds office as such—

(a)  engage, whether directly or indirectly, in any private practice or business, or be in partnership with or employed by, or act as agent for, any person so engaged;

(b)  *[Repealed by the Law Reform (Miscellaneous Provisions) (Scotland) Act 1985 (c.73) s.20 and Sch.4.]*

(2)  Subsection (1) above shall apply to any person holding the office of sheriff principal who is appointed to that office after the commencement of this Act and on whose appointment the Secretary of State directs that that subsection shall apply to him.

(3)  The sheriff principal of any sheriffdom, not being either a sheriff principal who is restricted by the terms of his appointment from engaging in private practice or a sheriff principal to whom subsection (1) above applies, shall not, so long as he holds office as such, advise, or act as an advocate in any court, in any cause civil or criminal arising within or coming from that sheriffdom.

(4)  Any reference in any enactment passed before the commencement of this Act to a sheriff principal who is restricted by the terms of his appointment from engaging in private practice shall be construed as including a reference to a sheriff principal to whom subsection (1) above applies.

(5)[4]  Without prejudice to the giving of any direction under section 11 (5) of this Act, in this section "sheriff principal" does not include a temporary sheriff principal and "sheriff" does not include a part-time sheriff or an honorary sheriff.

---

[1] As amended by the Bail, Judicial Appointments etc. (Scotland) Act 2000 (asp.9) s.12 and Sch., para.1.

[2] As inserted by the Judicial Pensions and Retirement Act 1993 (c.8) Sch.6 para. 10 (effective March 31, 1995).

[3] As inserted by the Bail, Judicial Appointments etc. (Scotland) Act 2000 (asp 9) s.12 and Sch., para.1 (effective August 9, 2000).

[4] As amended by the Bail, Judicial Appointments etc. (Scotland) Act 2000 (asp 9) s. 12 and Sch., para.1.

## Jurisdiction of sheriff

**7.**—[1](1)   For removal of doubt it is hereby declared that a sheriff by virtue of his appointment as such, has and is entitled to exercise the jurisdiction and powers attaching to the office of sheriff in all parts of the sheriffdom for which he is appointed.

(2)   Without prejudice to section 11A(4) of this Act, in this section, "sheriff" does not include a part-time sheriff.

**D1.628**

## Sheriff may be appointed to assist Secretary of State

**8.**   *[Repealed by the Judiciary and Courts (Scotland) Act 2008 (asp 6) Pt 3 s.52 (effective April 1, 2010).]*

*Functions of Secretary of State in relation to sheriffs principal, sheriffs, etc.*

## Power of Secretary of State to give administrative directions

**9.**   *[Repealed by the Judiciary and Courts (Scotland) Act 2008 (asp 6) Pt 3 s.48 (effective April 1, 2010 subject to transitional provisions and savings specified in SSI 2010/39 art.6).]*

## Scottish Ministers may authorise sheriff principal or direct sheriff to act in another sheriffdom

**10.**—[2](1)[3, 4]   Where a vacancy occurs in the office of sheriff principal of any sheriffdom the Lord President of the Court of Session may, if it appears expedient so to do in order to avoid delay in the administration of justice in that sheriffdom, authorise the sheriff principal of any other sheriffdom to perform the duties of sheriff principal in the first-mentioned sheriffdom (in addition to his own duties) until the Lord President otherwise decides.

**D1.629**

(1A)[5, 6]   Where the sheriff principal of any sheriffdom is unable to perform, or rules that he is precluded from performing, all of, or some part of, his duties as sheriff principal the Lord President may authorise the sheriff principal of any other sheriffdom to perform the duties of sheriff principal, or as the case may be that part of those duties, in the first-mentioned sheriffdom (in addition to his own duties) until the Lord President otherwise decides.

(2)[7]   Where as regards any sheriffdom—

(a)   a sheriff is by reason of illness or otherwise unable to perform his duties as sheriff, or

(b)   a vacancy occurs in the office of sheriff, or

---

[1] Existing text renumbered as s.7(1) and s.7(2) inserted by the Bail, Judicial Appointments etc. (Scotland) Act 2000 (asp 9) s.12 and Sch., para.1.

[2] As substituted by the Judiciary and Courts (Scotland) Act 2008 (asp 6) Pt 3 s.53 (effective April 1, 2010 subject to transitional provisions and savings specified in SSI 2010/39 art.7).

[3] Subss (1) and (1A) substituted for subs. (1) by the Law Reform (Miscellaneous Provisions) (Scotland) Act 1980 s.10(a).

[4] As amended by the Scotland Act 1998 (Consequential Modifications) (No.2) Order 1999 (SI 1999/1820) Sch.2(1) para.50(2) (effective July 1, 1999 the principal appointed day for 1998 c.46).

[5] Subss (1) and (1A) substituted for subs. (1) by the Law Reform (Miscellaneous Provisions) (Scotland) Act 1980 s.10(a).

[6] As amended by the Scotland Act 1998 (Consequential Modifications) (No.2) Order 1999 (SI 1999/1820) Sch.2(1) para.50(2) (effective July 1, 1999 the principal appointed day for 1998 c.46).

[7] As amended by the Scotland Act 1998 (Consequential Modifications) (No.2) Order 1999 (SI 1999/1820) Sch.2(1) para.50(2) (effective July 1, 1999 the principal appointed day for 1998 c.46).

(c)  any other reason it appears to the Scottish Ministers expedient so to do in order to avoid delay in the administration of justice in that sheriffdom,

the Lord President may direct a sheriff appointed for any other sheriffdom to perform, in accordance with the terms of the direction, the duties of sheriff in the first-mentioned sheriffdom (in addition to or in place of his own duties) until otherwise directed by the Lord President, and any sheriff to whom a direction is given under this subsection shall give effect to that direction.

(3)  A sheriff principal authorised, or a sheriff directed, under this section to perform duties in any sheriffdom shall for that purpose, without the necessity of his receiving a commission in that behalf, have and be entitled to exercise the jurisdiction and powers attaching to the office of sheriff principal or, as the case may be, sheriff in that sheriffdom.

(4)[1]  The Scottish Ministers may, pay to a sheriff principal or a sheriff, in respect of any duties performed by that sheriff principal or sheriff (in addition to his own duties) in pursuance of an authority or direction under this section, such remuneration and allowances as may appear to the Secretary of State, with the consent of the Treasury, to be reasonable in all the circumstances.

(5)[2]  In this section "sheriff" does not include an honorary or a part-time sheriff.

### Secretary of State may appoint temporary sheriffs principal and sheriffs

D1.630

**11.**—[3](1)[4]  Where a vacancy occurs in the office of sheriff principal of any sheriffdom the Scottish Ministers must, if the Lord President of the Court of Session so requests, appoint a person to act as sheriff principal of the sheriffdom.

(1ZA)[5]  The Lord President may request the appointment of a person to act as a sheriff principal under subsection (1) only if it appears to him expedient that such an appointment be made in order to avoid delay in the administration of justice in the sheriffdom concerned.

(1A)[6]  Where the sheriff principal of any sheriffdom is unable to perform, or rules that he is precluded from performing, all of, or some part of, his duties as sheriff principal the Scottish Ministers must, if the Lord President so requests, appoint a person to act as sheriff principal of the sheriffdom, or as the case may be to perform that part of the duties of the sheriff principal.

(1B)[7]  A person appointed under subsection (1) or (1A) above shall be known as a temporary sheriff principal.

---

[1] As amended by the Scotland Act 1998 (Consequential Modifications) (No.2) Order 1999 (SI 1999/1820) Sch.2(1) para.50(2) (effective July 1, 1999 the principal appointed day for 1998 c.46).

[2] As amended by the Bail, Judicial Appointments etc. (Scotland) Act 2000 (asp.9) s.12 and Sch., para.1.

[3] As amended by the Judiciary and Courts (Scotland) Act 2008 (asp 6) Pt 2 c.3 s.24 (effective June 1, 2009).

[4] Subsections (1), (1A) and (1B) substituted for subs. (1) by the Law Reform (Miscellaneous Provisions) (Scotland) Act 1980 (c.55), s.10(b). As amended by the Bail, Judicial Appointments etc. (Scotland) Act 2000 (asp.9), s.6, s.12 and Sch., para.1.

[5] As inserted by the Judiciary and Courts (Scotland) Act 2008 (asp 6) Pt 2 c.3 s.24 (effective June 1, 2009).

[6] Subsections (1), (1A) and (1B) substituted for subs. (1) by the Law Reform (Miscellaneous Provisions) (Scotland) Act 1980 (c.55), s.10(b). As amended by the Bail, Judicial Appointments etc. (Scotland) Act 2000 (asp.9), s.6, s.12 and Sch., para.1.

[7] Subsections (1), (1A) and (1B) substituted for subs. (1) by the Law Reform (Miscellaneous Provisions) (Scotland) Act 1980 (c.55), s.10(b). As amended by the Bail, Judicial Appointments etc. (Scotland) Act 2000 (asp.9), s.6, s.12 and Sch., para.1.

(2) *[Repealed by the Bail, Judicial Appointments etc. (Scotland) Act 2000 (asp 9) (Scottish Act), Pt 2 (c.2) s.6(1). Notwithstanding the coming into force of that repeal—*

    (a)   *a temporary sheriff may continue to exercise the jurisdiction and powers of a sheriff for the purposes of any proceedings commenced or other matter which began before such coming into force; and*

    (b)   *a temporary sheriff shall, for those purposes and for the purposes of any further proceedings arising out of the proceedings or other matter referred to in paragraph (a) above, be treated as continuing to be a temporary sheriff.]*

(3)[1]   A person shall not be appointed to be a temporary sheriff principal unless he is legally qualified and has been so qualified—

    (a)   for at least ten years;

For the purposes of this subsection, a person shall be legally qualified if he is an advocate or a solicitor.

(4)[2]   The appointment of a temporary sheriff principal shall subsist until recalled by the Scottish Ministers, at the request of the Lord President.

(4ZA)[3]   The Scottish Ministers must comply with any request made by the Lord President under subsection (4) above.

(4A)[4, 5]   No appointment under this section of a person to be a temporary sheriff principal shall extend beyond the day on which the person reaches the age of 70.

(4B)[6]   Subsection (4A) above is subject to section 26(4) to (6) of the Judicial Pensions and Retirement Act 1993 (power to authorise continuance in office up to the age of 75).

(5)[7]   If the Scottish Ministers, on appointing any person to be a temporary sheriff principal, so direct, the provisions of section 6(1) of this Act shall apply in relation to that person as they apply in relation to a person holding the office of sheriff.

(6)[8]   A person appointed to be temporary sheriff principal of any sheriffdom shall for the purposes of his appointment, without the necessity of his receiving a commission in that behalf, have and be entitled to exercise the jurisdiction and powers attaching to the office of sheriff principal or sheriff in that sheriffdom.

(7)   The appointment of any person holding the office of sheriff to be a temporary sheriff principal shall not affect the commission held by that person as sheriff, but he shall not, while his appointment as a temporary sheriff principal subsists, perform any duties by virtue of the said commission.

(8)[9, 10]   The Scottish Court Service may pay to any person appointed to be a temporary sheriff principal such remuneration and allowances as the Treasury, on the recommendation of the Secretary of State, may determine.

---

[1] As amended by the Bail, Judicial Appointments etc. (Scotland) Act 2000 (asp.9), Sch., para.1.

[2] As amended by the Bail, Judicial Appointments etc. (Scotland) Act 2000 (asp.9), Sch., para.1.

[3] As inserted by the Judiciary and Courts (Scotland) Act 2008 (asp 6) Pt 2 c.3 s.24 (effective June 1, 2009).

[4] As amended by the Bail, Judicial Appointments etc. (Scotland) Act 2000 (asp.9), Sch., para.1.

[5] Inserted by the Judicial Pensions and Retirement Act 1993 (c.8), Sch.6, para.11.

[6] Inserted by the Judicial Pensions and Retirement Act 1993 (c.8), Sch.6, para.11.

[7] As amended by the Bail, Judicial Appointments etc. (Scotland) Act 2000 (asp.9), Sch., para.1.

[8] As amended by the Bail, Judicial Appointments etc. (Scotland) Act 2000 (asp.9), Sch., para.1.

[9] As amended by the Bail, Judicial Appointments etc. (Scotland) Act 2000 (asp.9), Sch., para.1.

[10] As substituted by the Judiciary and Courts (Scotland) Act 2008 (asp 6) Pt 4 s.64 (effective April 1, 2010).

## Appointment of part-time sheriffs

**D1.631**

**11A**—[1](1)   The Scottish Ministers may, under this section, appoint persons to act as sheriffs, and persons so appointed shall be known as "part-time sheriffs".

(2)   *[Repealed by the Judiciary and Courts (Scotland) Act 2008 (asp 6) Sch.5 para.2(2) (effective April 1, 2010 subject to transitional provisions and savings specified in SSI 2010/39 art.3).]*

(3)[2]   A person shall not be appointed a part-time sheriff unless—

   (a)   the person is qualified under section 5(1) of this Act to be appointed to the office of sheriff, and

   (b)   the Scottish Ministers have consulted the Lord President of the Court of Session about the proposed appointment.

(4)   A part-time sheriff shall, without the necessity of receiving a commission in that behalf, be entitled to exercise in every sheriffdom the jurisdiction and powers attaching to the office of sheriff.

(5)[3]   The number of persons holding appointments as part-time sheriffs shall not, at any one time, exceed 80 or such other number as may be fixed in substitution by order made by the Scottish Ministers.

(6)   A part-time sheriff shall be subject to such instructions, arrangements and other provisions as fall to be made under this Act by the sheriff principal of the sheriffdom in which the part-time sheriff is sitting.

(7)   In the performance of their functions under this Act, sheriffs principal shall together have regard to the desirability of securing that every part-time sheriff—

   (a)   is given the opportunity of sitting on not fewer than 20 days; and

   (b)   does not sit for more than 100 days,

in each successive period of 12 months beginning with the day of the part-time sheriffs appointment as such.

(8)[4]   The Scottish Court Service shall pay to part-time sheriffs such remuneration and allowances as the Scottish Ministers determine.

## Limitation, termination etc. of appointment of part-time sheriffs

**D1.632**

**11B.**—[5](1)   An appointment as a part-time sheriff shall, subject to subsections (2) to (4) below, last for 5 years.

(2)   A part-time sheriff may resign at any time by giving notice to that effect to the Scottish Ministers.

(3)   An appointment of a person as a part-time sheriff shall not extend beyond the day when the person reaches the age of 70.

(4)[6]   A part-time sheriffs appointment shall come to an end upon the part-time sheriffs being removed from office under section 12E of this Act.

---

[1] As inserted by the Bail, Judicial Appointments etc. (Scotland) Act 2000 (asp 9) s.7 (effective August 9, 2000).

[2] As amended by the Judiciary and Courts (Scotland) Act 2008 (asp 6) Pt 2 c.3 s.26 (effective June 1, 2009).

[3] As amended by the Maximum Number of Part-Time Sheriffs (Scotland) Order 2006 (SSI 2006/257) (effective May 10, 2006).

[4] As substituted by the Judiciary and Courts (Scotland) Act 2008 (asp 6) Pt 4 s.64 (effective April 1, 2010).

[5] As inserted by the Bail, Judicial Appointments etc. (Scotland) Act 2000 (asp 9) s.7 (effective August 9, 2000).

[6] As amended by the Judiciary and Courts (Scotland) Act 2008 (Consequential Modifications) Order 2009 (SSI 2009/334) art.3(1) (effective April 1, 2010).

(5)   A part-time sheriff whose appointment comes to an end by operation of subsection (1) above may be reappointed and, except in the circumstances set out in subsection (6) below, shall be reappointed.

(6)   The circumstances mentioned in subsection (5) above are that—

   (a)   the part-time sheriff has declined that reappointment;

   (b)   the part-time sheriff is aged 69 or over;

   (c)   a sheriff principal has made a recommendation to the Scottish Ministers against the reappointment;

   (d)   the part-time sheriff has not sat for a total of 50 or more days in the preceding five year period; or

   (e)   the Scottish Ministers have, since the part-time sheriff was last appointed, made an order under section 11A(5) of this Act reducing the number of persons who may hold appointment as part-time sheriffs.

(7)   A part-time sheriff whose appointment comes to an end by resignation under subsection (2) above may be reappointed.

(8)   The provisions of section 11A and this section of this Act apply to a reappointment under subsections (5) and (7) above as they apply to an appointment.

(9)   A part-time sheriff who is a solicitor in practice shall not carry out any function as a part-time sheriff in a sheriff court district in which his or her main place of business as such solicitor is situated.

## Removal of part-time sheriffs from office

**11C.**   *[Repealed by the Judiciary and Courts (Scotland) Act 2008 (asp 6) Sch.5 para.2(3) (effective April 1, 2010 subject to transitional provisions and savings specified in SSI 2010/39 art.3).]*

## Regulations and orders under section 11A

**11D.**—[1,2](1)   Orders under section 11A of this Act shall be made by statutory instrument.

**D1.633**

(2)   No such order shall be made unless laid in draft before, and approved by a resolution of, the Scottish Parliament.

*Consideration of fitness for, and removal from, shrieval office*

## Tribunal to consider fitness for shrieval office

**12A.**—[3](1)   The First Minister—

**D1.634**

   (a)   must, when requested to do so by the Lord President of the Court of Session, and

   (b)   may, in such other circumstances as the First Minister thinks fit,

constitute a tribunal to investigate and report on whether a person holding a shrieval office to which this section applies is unfit to hold the office by reason of inability, neglect of duty or misbehaviour.

(2)   The shrieval offices to which this section applies are—

---

[1]   As inserted by the Bail, Judicial Appointments etc. (Scotland) Act 2000 (asp 9) s.7 (effective August 9, 2000).

[2]   As amended by the Judiciary and Courts (Scotland) Act 2008 (asp 6) Sch.5 para.2(4) (effective April 1, 2010 subject to transitional provisions and savings specified in SSI 2010/39 art.3).

[3]   ss.12A–12F substituted for s.12, and ss.13–14A moved under new heading by Judiciary and Courts (Scotland) Act 2008 (asp 6) Pt 2 c.5 s.40 (effective April 1, 2010: as SSI 2010/39).

    (a)   the office of sheriff principal,

    (b)   the office of sheriff, and

    (c)   the office of part-time sheriff.

(3)   The First Minister may constitute a tribunal under subsection (1)(b) above only if the Lord President has been consulted.

(4)   A tribunal constituted under this section is to consist of—

    (a)   one individual who is a qualifying member of the Judicial Committee of the Privy Council,

    (b)   one individual who holds the relevant shrieval office,

    (c)   one individual who is, and has been for at least 10 years, an advocate or a solicitor, and

    (d)   one individual who is not (and never has been) a qualifying member of the Judicial Committee of the Privy Council, who does not hold (and never has held) a shrieval office to which this section applies and who is not (and never has been) an advocate or solicitor.

(5)   A qualifying member of the Judicial Committee of the Privy Council is someone who is a member of that Committee by virtue of section 1(2)(a) of the Judicial Committee Act 1833 (c.41) (that is, someone who is a member of the Privy Council who holds, or has held, high judicial office).

(6)   The relevant shrieval office is—

    (a)   where the investigation is to be of a person's fitness to hold the office of sheriff principal, that office,

    (b)   where the investigation is to be of a person's fitness to hold the office of sheriff or part-time sheriff, the office of sheriff.

(7)   The selection of persons to be members of a tribunal under this section is to be made by the First Minister, with the agreement of the Lord President of the Court of Session.

(8)   The person mentioned in subsection (4)(a) is to chair the tribunal and has a casting vote.

### Suspension during investigation

**D1.635**

**12B.**—[1](1)   Where the Lord President of the Court of Session has requested that the First Minister constitute a tribunal under section 12A, the Lord President may, at any time before the tribunal reports to the First Minister, suspend the person who is to be, or is, the subject of the investigation, from office.

(2)   Such a suspension lasts until the Lord President orders otherwise.

(3)   A tribunal constituted under section 12A may, at any time before the tribunal reports to the First Minister, recommend to the First Minister that the person who is the subject of the tribunal's investigation be suspended from office.

(4)   Such a recommendation must be in writing.

(5)   The First Minister, on receiving such a recommendation, may suspend the person from office.

(6)   Such a suspension lasts until the First Minister orders otherwise.

(7)   Suspension under this section from the office of sheriff principal or sheriff does not affect remuneration payable to, or in respect of, the office in respect of the period of suspension.

---

[1] ss.12A–12F substituted for s.12, and ss.13–14A moved under new heading by Judiciary and Courts (Scotland) Act 2008 (asp 6) Pt 2 c.5 s.40 (effective April 1, 2010: as SSI 2010/39).

### Further provision about tribunals

**12C.**—[1](1)  A tribunal constituted under section 12A may require any person—

    (a)  to attend its proceedings for the purpose of giving evidence,

    (b)  to produce documents in the person's custody or under the person's control.

**D1.636**

(2)  A person on whom such a requirement is imposed is not obliged to answer any question or produce any document which the person would be entitled to refuse to answer or produce in a court in Scotland.

(3)  Subsection (4) applies where a person on whom a requirement has been imposed under subsection (1)—

    (a)  refuses or fails, without reasonable excuse, to comply with the requirement,

    (b)  refuses or fails, without reasonable excuse, while attending the tribunal proceedings to give evidence, to answer any question, or

    (c)  deliberately alters, conceals or destroys any document which the person is required to produce.

(4)  The Court of Session may, on an application made to it by the tribunal—

    (a)  make such order for enforcing compliance as it sees fit, or

    (b)  deal with the matter as if it were a contempt of the Court.

(5)  The Court of Session may by act of sederunt make provision as to the procedure to be followed by and before tribunals constituted under section 12A.

(6)  The Scottish Ministers may pay such remuneration to, and expenses of, members of tribunals constituted under section 12A as they think fit.

(7)  The Scottish Ministers must pay such expenses as they consider are reasonably required to be incurred to enable a tribunal constituted under section 12A to carry out its functions.

### Report of tribunal

**12D.**—[2](1)  The report of a tribunal constituted under section 12A must—

    (a)  be in writing,

    (b)  contain reasons for its conclusion, and

    (c)  be submitted to the First Minister.

**D1.637**

(2)  The First Minister must lay the report before the Scottish Parliament.

### Removal from office

**12E.**—[3](1)  Where subsection (2) applies, the First Minister may remove a person from the office of sheriff principal, sheriff or part-time sheriff.

**D1.638**

(2)  This subsection applies if—

    (a)  a tribunal constituted under section 12A has reported to the First Minister that the person is unfit to hold that office by reason of inability, neglect of duty or misbehaviour, and

---

[1] ss.12A–12F substituted for s.12, and ss.13–14A moved under new heading by Judiciary and Courts (Scotland) Act 2008 (asp 6) Pt 2 c.5 s.40 (effective February 20, 2010 for the purpose of inserting s.12C(5), as SSI 2010/39; April 1, 2010, subject to savings and transitional provisions specified in SSI 2010/39 art.3 otherwise).

[2] ss.12A–12F substituted for s.12, and ss.13–14A moved under new heading by Judiciary and Courts (Scotland) Act 2008 (asp 6) Pt 2 c.5 s.40 (effective April 1, 2010: as SSI 2010/39).

[3] ss.12A–12F substituted for s.12, and ss.13–14A moved under new heading by Judiciary and Courts (Scotland) Act 2008 (asp 6) Pt 2 c.5 s.40 (effective April 1, 2010: as SSI 2010/39).

(b)   the First Minister has laid the report before the Scottish Parliament.

(3)   The First Minister may remove a sheriff principal or sheriff under subsection (1) only by order made by statutory instrument.

(4)[1]   Such an order—

(a)   is subject to the negative procedure; and

(b)   is not to be made so as to come into effect before the expiry, in relation to the instrument containing the order, of the period of 40 days mentioned in section 28(3) of the Interpretation and Legislative Reform (Scotland) Act 2010 (asp 10).

(5)   Article 10 of that Order applies to such an instrument subject to the following modifications—

(a)   the reference to the period of 21 days in paragraph (2) is to be read as a reference to 40 days, and

(b)   paragraph (3) does not apply.

### Interpretation of sections 12A to 12E

**D1.639**

**12F.**—[2](1)   In sections 12A to 12E "office of part-time sheriff" means an appointment (or reappointment) as a part-time sheriff; and references to removal or suspension from that office are to be construed accordingly.

(2)   In those sections—

(a)   a reference to the office of sheriff principal does not include a reference to an appointment as a temporary sheriff principal,

(b)   a reference to the office of sheriff does not include a reference to the office of honorary sheriff.

### Functions of Secretary of State with respect to residence and leave of absence of sheriffs principal

**D1.640**

**13.**—[3](1)   The Lord President of the Court of Session may require any sheriff principal (being a sheriff principal who is restricted by the terms of his appointment from engaging in private practice or to whom section 6(1) of this Act applies) to reside ordinarily at such place as the Lord President may specify.

(2)   The Lord President may approve such leave of absence for the purpose of holidays for any sheriff principal (being a sheriff principal who is restricted by the terms of his appointment from engaging in private practice or to whom section 6(1) of this Act applies) as appears to the Lord President to be proper, but the amount of leave so approved shall not, unless the Lord President for special reasons otherwise permits, exceed seven weeks in any year.

(3)[4]   The Lord President may approve such leave of absence for any other purpose for any sheriff principal (being a sheriff principal who is restricted by the terms of his appointment from engaging in private practice or to whom section 6(1) of this Act applies) as appears to the Lord President to be proper.

---

[1] As substituted by the Interpretation and Legislative Reform (Scotland) Act 2010 (Consequential, Savings and Transitional Provisions) Order 2011 (SSI 2011/396) art.10 (effective November 11, 2011).

[2] ss.12A–12F substituted for s.12, and ss.13–14A moved under new heading by Judiciary and Courts (Scotland) Act 2008 (asp 6) Pt 2 c.5 s.40 (effective April 1, 2010: as SSI 2010/39).

[3] As amended by the Judiciary and Courts (Scotland) Act 2008 (asp 6) Pt 3 s.54 (effective April 1, 2010).

[4] As inserted by the Judiciary and Courts (Scotland) Act 2008 (asp 6) Pt 3 s.54 (effective April 1, 2010).

### Functions of Secretary of State with respect to number, residence and place of duties of sheriffs

**14.**—[1](1)    *[Repealed by the Judiciary and Courts (Scotland) Act 2008 (asp 6) Pt 3 s.55(2) (effective April 1, 2010 subject to transitional provisions and savings specified in SSI 2010/39 art.8).]*

(2)    The Lord President of the Court of Session may require any sheriff to reside ordinarily at such place as the Lord President may specify.

**D1.641**

(3)    The Lord President—

    (a)    shall, on the appointment of a person to hold the office of sheriff for any sheriffdom,

    (b)    may, at any subsequent time while the said person holds that office,

give to that person a direction designating the sheriff court district or districts in which he is to perform his duties as sheriff:

Provided that a direction given to a sheriff under this subsection shall be subject to any instruction given to that sheriff under section 15 of this Act by the sheriff principal of the sheriffdom, being an instruction given for the purpose of giving effect to any special provision made by the sheriff principal under section 16(1)(b) of this Act.

(4)    If for the purpose of securing the efficient organization and administration of the sheriff courts, the Lord President by order so directs, a person holding the office of sheriff for any sheriffdom shall, on such date as may be specified in the order, cease to hold that office and shall, on and after that date, without the necessity of his receiving a commission in that behalf, hold instead the office of sheriff for such other sheriffdom as may be so specified; and on making an order under this subsection with respect to any person the Lord President shall give to that person a direction under subsection (3) above designating the sheriff court district or districts in which he is to perform his duties as sheriff.

(5)[2]    In this section "sheriff" does not include an honorary or a part-time sheriff.

### Re-employment of retired sheriffs principal and sheriffs

**14A.**—(1)    A sheriff principal may, if it appears to him to be expedient as a temporary measure in order to facilitate the disposal of business in the sheriff courts of the sheriffdom, appoint a qualifying former sheriff principal or sheriff to act as a sheriff of that sheriffdom during such period or on such occasions as the sheriff principal thinks fit.

**D1.642**

(2)    A qualifying former sheriff principal is someone who—

    (a)    ceased to hold that office other than by virtue of an order under section 12E of this Act, and

    (b)    has not reached the age of 75 years.

(3)    A qualifying former sheriff is someone who—

    (a)    ceased to hold that office other than by virtue of an order under section 12E of this Act or by being appointed as a sheriff principal, and

    (b)    has not reached the age of 75 years.

(4)    A person appointed under subsection (1) above is not to be treated as a sheriff for the purposes of any statutory provision or rule of law relating to—

---

[1] As amended by the Judiciary and Courts (Scotland) Act 2008 (asp 6) Pt 3 s.55 (effective April 1, 2010).

[2] As amended by the Bail, Judicial Appointments etc. (Scotland) Act 2000 (asp 9), s.12 and Sched., para.1.

    (a)   the appointment, retirement, removal or disqualification of sheriffs,

    (b)   the tenure of office and oaths to be taken by sheriffs, or

    (c)   the remuneration, allowances or pensions of sheriffs.

(5)   But, otherwise, such a person is to be treated for all purposes as a sheriff of the sheriffdom for which the person is appointed (and so may perform any of the functions of a sheriff of that sheriffdom).

(6)   The Scottish Court Service may pay to, or in respect of, a person appointed under subsection (1) above such remuneration or allowances as the Scottish Ministers may determine.

(7)   Despite subsection (1), the period during which or an occasion on which a person appointed under that subsection may act under that appointment does not extend beyond, or (as the case may be) is not to be after, the date on which the person reaches the age of 75 years.

(8)   Despite the expiry (whether by virtue of subsection (7) above or otherwise) of any period for which a person is appointed under subsection (1) above—

    (a)   the person may attend at a sheriff court for the purpose of continuing to deal with, giving judgment in, or dealing with any matter relating to, any case begun before the person while acting under that appointment, and

    (b)   for that purpose, and for the purpose of any proceedings arising out of any such case or matter, the person is to be treated as acting or, as the case may be, having acted under that appointment.

(9)   In this section—

    "sheriff principal", where it first occurs in subsection (1), includes temporary sheriff principal, and

    "sheriff" does not include part-time sheriff or honorary sheriff.

*Functions of the sheriff principal in relation to sheriffs, etc.*

### Efficient disposal of business in sheriff courts

**D1.643**

**15.**—[1](1)   The sheriff principal of each sheriffdom is responsible for securing the efficient disposal of business in the sheriff courts of that sheriffdom.

(2)   If, in carrying out that responsibility, the sheriff principal gives a direction of an administrative character to a person mentioned in subsection (3), the person must comply with the direction.

(3)   Those persons are—

    (a)   a sheriff authorised by virtue of any enactment to act in that sheriffdom,

    (b)   a member of staff of the Scottish Court Service.

(4)   Subsections (1) and (2) are subject to section 2(2)(a) and (3) of the Judiciary and Courts (Scotland) Act 2008 (asp 6) (which make the Head of the Scottish Judiciary responsible for maintaining arrangements for securing the efficient disposal of business in the Scottish courts and require compliance with directions given in pursuance of that responsibility).

---

[1] As substituted by the Judiciary and Courts (Scotland) Act 2008 (asp 6) Pt 3 s.47(2) (effective April 1, 2010).

### Functions of sheriff principal with respect to duties and leave of absence of sheriffs

**16.**—(1)[1, 2]   The sheriff principal of each sheriffdom shall make such arrangements as appear to him necessary or expedient for the purpose of carrying out the responsibility imposed by section 15(1) of this Act and in particular, but without prejudice to the generality of the foregoing words, may—

D1.644

    (a)    provide for the division of business in the sheriff courts of that sheriffdom between the sheriff principal, the sheriffs appointed for the sheriffdom and any part-time sheriffs, and for the distribution of the business (so far as allocated to the sheriffs) amongst those sheriffs;

    (b)    where any of those sheriffs is by reason of illness or otherwise unable to perform his duties as sheriff, or a vacancy occurs in the office of sheriff in the sheriffdom, or for any other reason it appears to the sheriff principal expedient so to do in order to avoid delay in the administration of justice in the sheriffdom, make special provision of a temporary nature for the disposal of any part of the said business either by the sheriff principal or by any of the sheriffs appointed for the sheriffdom or by any part-time sheriffs, in addition to or in place of the sheriff principal's or, as the case may be, that sheriff's own duties;

so, however, that nothing done under this subsection shall enable a sheriff or part-time sheriff to dispose of business which he does not otherwise have power to dispose of.

(1A)[3]   Subsection (1) is subject to section 2(2)(a) and (3) of the Judiciary and Courts (Scotland) Act 2008 (asp 6) (which make the Head of the Scottish Judiciary responsible for maintaining arrangements for securing the efficient disposal of business in the Scottish courts and require compliance with directions given in pursuance of that responsibility).

(2)[4]   The sheriff principal of any sheriffdom may approve such leave of absence for the purpose of holidays for any sheriff appointed for that sheriffdom as appears to the sheriff principal to be proper, but the amount of leave so approved shall not, unless the Lord President of the Court of Session for special reasons otherwise permits, exceed seven weeks in any year.

(2A)[5]   The sheriff principal of any sheriffdom may approve such leave of absence for any other purpose for any sheriff appointed for that sheriffdom as appears to the sheriff principal to be proper.

(3)[6, 7]   In subsections (2) and (2A) above "sheriff" shall not include a part-time or an honorary sheriff.

---

[1] As amended by the Bail, Judicial Appointments etc. (Scotland) Act 2000 (asp.9), s.12 and Sch., para.1.

[2] As amended by the Judiciary and Courts (Scotland) Act 2008 (asp 6) Pt 3 s.47 (effective April 1, 2010).

[3] As inserted by the Judiciary and Courts (Scotland) Act 2008 (asp 6) Pt 3 s.47 (effective April 1, 2010).

[4] As amended by the Judiciary and Courts (Scotland) Act 2008 (asp 6) Pt 3 s.56 (effective April 1, 2010).

[5] As inserted by the Judiciary and Courts (Scotland) Act 2008 (asp 6) Pt 3 s.56 (effective April 1, 2010).

[6] As amended by the Bail, Judicial Appointments etc. (Scotland) Act 2000 (asp.9), s.12 and Sch., para.1.

[7] As amended by the Judiciary and Courts (Scotland) Act 2008 (asp 6) Pt 3 s.56 (effective April 1, 2010).

**Sheriff principal may fix sittings and business of sheriff courts in sheriffdom, and sessions for civil business**

D1.645

17.—(1)  The sheriff principal of each sheriffdom may by order prescribe—

(a)  the number of sheriff courts to be held at each of the places within that sheriffdom at which a court is required under or by virtue of this Act to be held,

(b)[1]  subject to section 25(2) of this Act, the days on which and the times at which those courts are to be held,

(c)  the descriptions of business to be disposed of at those courts.

(2)  The sheriff principal of each sheriffdom shall by order prescribe the dates of the sessions to be held in the sheriff courts of that sheriffdom for the disposal of civil business, and may prescribe different dates in relation to different courts, so however that—

(a)  there shall be held in the courts of each sheriffdom three sessions in each year for the disposal of civil business, that is to say, a winter session, a spring session and a summer session;

(b)  the dates of the sessions prescribed under this subsection shall not be such as to allow, in any court, a vacation of longer than two weeks at Christmas time, four weeks in the spring and eight weeks in the summer.

(3)  The sheriff principal of each sheriffdom shall, before the end of the spring session in each year, fix in respect of each sheriff court in that sheriffdom at least one day during the vacation immediately following that session for the disposal of civil business in that court, and shall, before the end of the summer session in each year, fix in respect of each court at least two days during the vacation immediately following that session for the said purpose; but civil proceedings in the sheriff courts may proceed during vacation as during session, and interlocutors may competently be pronounced during vacation in any such proceedings.

(4)  A sheriff principal shall give notice of any matter prescribed or fixed by him under the foregoing provisions of this section in such manner as he may think sufficient for bringing that matter to the attention of all persons having an interest therein.

(4A)[2]  Subsections (1) to (4) are subject to section 2(2)(a) and (3) of the Judiciary and Courts (Scotland) Act 2008 (asp 6) (which make the Head of the Scottish Judiciary responsible for maintaining arrangements for securing the efficient disposal of business in the Scottish courts and require compliance with directions given in pursuance of that responsibility).

(5)  Subject to anything done under subsection (1) above, or by an order under section 2(1) or section 3(2) of this Act, after the commencement of this Act—

(a)  there shall be held at each of the places at which a sheriff court was in use to be held immediately before such commencement the same number of courts as was in use to be held there immediately before such commencement;

(b)  the court days and times in use to be observed in any sheriff court im-

---

[1] See the Bail etc. (Scotland) Act 1980 (c.44), s.10(2).

[2] As inserted by the Judiciary and Courts (Scotland) Act 2008 (asp 6) Pt 3 s.47 (effective April 1, 2010).

mediately before such commencement (whether in pursuance of any enactment or other instrument or otherwise) shall continue to be observed in that court;

(c)   the descriptions of business in use to be dealt with on court days in any sheriff court immediately before such commencement shall continue to be dealt with on those days.

(6)   Without prejudice to subsection (5) above, any enactment or other instrument in force immediately before the commencement of this Act shall, to the extent that it contains provisions with respect to any matter which the sheriff principal has power to prescribe under subsection (1) above, cease to have effect.

### Lord President's power to exercise functions in sections 15 to 17

**17A.**—[1](1)   Subsection (2) applies where in any case the Lord President considers that the exercise by the sheriff principal of a sheriffdom of a function conferred by any of sections 15 to 17 of this Act—

**D1.646**

(a)   is prejudicial to the efficient disposal of business in the sheriff courts of that sheriffdom,

(b)   is prejudicial to the efficient organization or administration of those sheriff courts, or

(c)   is otherwise against the interests of the public.

(2)   The Lord President may in that case—

(a)   rescind the sheriff principal's exercise of the function, and

(b)   exercise the function.

(3)   Subsection (2)(b) applies where in any case the Lord President considers that the failure of the sheriff principal of a sheriffdom to exercise a function conferred by any of sections 15 to 17 of this Act—

(a)   is prejudicial to the efficient disposal of business in the sheriff courts of that sheriffdom,

(b)   is prejudicial to the efficient organization or administration of those sheriff courts, or

(c)   is otherwise against the interests of the public.

(4)   The exercise of a function by the Lord President by virtue of subsection (2)(b) is to be treated as if it were the exercise of the function by the sheriff principal.

### Secretary of State may exercise certain functions of sheriff principal in certain circumstances

**18.**   *[Repealed by the Judiciary and Courts (Scotland) Act 2008 (asp 6) Pt 3 s.49(3) (effective April 1, 2010).]*

*Miscellaneous*

### Travelling allowances for sheriffs principal

**19.**[2]   The Scottish Court Service may pay to any sheriff principal such allowances as it may determine in respect of the travelling expenses incurred by the sheriff principal in the performance of the duties of his office.

**D1.647**

---

[1] As inserted by the Judiciary and Courts (Scotland) Act 2008 (asp 6) Pt 3 s.49(2) (effective April 1, 2010).

[2] As amended by the Judiciary and Courts (Scotland) Act 2008 (Consequential Modifications) Order 2009 (SSI 2009/334) art.3(2) (effective April 1, 2010).

**Extension of purposes for which Lord Advocate may give instructions to procurators fiscal**

D1.648

20.[1]   The purposes for which the Lord Advocate may issue instructions to procurators fiscal under section 8(1) of the Sheriff Courts and Legal Officers (Scotland) Act 1927 shall include, in addition to the purpose mentioned in the said section 8(1), the efficient disposal of business in the sheriff courts.

21.   *[Repealed by the House of Commons Disqualification Act 1975 (c.24), Sch.3.]*

**Saving for existing functions**

D1.649

22.   Nothing in the foregoing provisions of this Act shall affect the discharge by any person of any function lawfully held by him immediately before the commencement of this Act, except in so far as the discharge of that function is or would be inconsistent with any of those provisions or anything done thereunder.

Part II – Court Houses, Buildings and Offices

23.–30.   [Not reproduced.]

Part III – Civil Jurisdiction, Procedure and Appeals

*Civil Jurisdiction*

**Upper limit to privative jurisdiction of sheriff court to be £5,000**

D1.650

31.[2]   Section 7 of the Sheriff Courts (Scotland) Act 1907 (which provides that all causes not exceeding £50 in value which are competent in the sheriff court are to be brought in that court only, and are not to be subject to review by the Court of Session) shall have effect as if for the words "£50" there were substituted the words "£5,000".

*Regulation of procedure in civil proceedings*

**Power of Court of Session to regulate civil procedure in sheriff court**

D1.651

32.—[3](1)[4]   Subject to the provisions of this section, the Court of Session may by act of sederunt regulate and prescribe the procedure and practice to be followed in any civil proceedings in the sheriff court (including any matters incidental or relat-

---

[1] As amended by the Judiciary and Courts (Scotland) Act 2008 (asp 6) Pt 3 s.47(5) (effective April 1, 2010).

[2] As substituted subject to savings specified in SSI 2007/507 art.4 by the Sheriff Courts (Scotland) Act 1971 (Privative Jurisdiction and Summary Cause) Order (SSI 2007/507), art.2 (effective January 14, 2008).

[3] See also the Maintenance Orders (Reciprocal Enforcement) Act 1972 (c.18), ss.19 and 31(3) (Division K, infra). Extended: see the Children Act 1975 (c.72), s.66, the Banking Act 1979 (c.37), s.31(7)(b), the Debtors (Scotland) Act 1987 (c.18), s.97 (Division B, supra) and the Child Support Act 1991 (c.48), ss.39(2) and 49 and the Children (Scotland) Act 1995 (c.36), s.91, (effective October 1, 1996: SI 1996/2203), Division K infra. Applied: see the Children Act 1975 (c.72), s.78. See also the Presumption of Death (Scotland) Act 1977 (c.27), s.15(1) (Division M, infra).

[4] As amended by the Law Reform (Miscellaneous Provisions) (Scotland) Act 1985 (c.73), Sch.2, para.12.

ing to any such procedure or practice), and, without prejudice to the generality of the foregoing words, the power conferred on the Court of Session by this section shall extend to—

(a) regulating the procedure to be followed in connection with execution or diligence following on any civil proceedings;

(b) prescribing the manner in which, the time within which, and the conditions on which, an appeal may be taken to the sheriff principal from an interlocutor of a sheriff, or to the Court of Session from an interlocutor of a sheriff principal or a sheriff (including an interlocutor applying the verdict of a jury), or any application may be made to the sheriff court, or anything required or authorised to be done in relation to any civil proceedings shall or may be done;

(c) prescribing the form of any document to be used in, or for the purposes of, any civil proceedings or any execution or diligence following thereon, and the person by whom, and the manner in which, any such document as aforesaid is to be authenticated;

(d) regulating the procedure to be followed in connection with the production and recovery of documents;

(e)[1] providing in respect of any category of civil proceedings for written statements (including affidavits) and reports, admissible under section 2(1)(b) of the Civil Evidence (Scotland) Act 1988, to be received in evidence, on such conditions as may be prescribed, without being spoken to by a witness;

(ea)[2] regulating the procedure to be followed in connection with the making of orders under sections 12(1) and (6) and 13(2) of the Vulnerable Witnesses (Scotland) Act 2004 (asp 3) ("the 2004 Act");

(eb)[3] regulating, so far as not regulated by the 2004 Act, the use of special measures authorised by virtue of that Act to be used;

(f) making such provision as may appear to the Court of Session to be necessary or expedient with respect to the payment, investment or application of any sum of money awarded to or in respect of a person under legal disability in any action in the sheriff court;

(g) regulating the summoning, remuneration and duties of assessors;

(h) making such provision as may appear to the Court of Session to be necessary or expedient for carrying out the provisions of this Act or of any enactment conferring powers or imposing duties on sheriffs principal or sheriffs or relating to proceedings in the sheriff courts;

(i) regulating the expenses which may be awarded by the sheriff to parties in proceedings before him;

---

[1] Substituted by the Civil Evidence (Scotland) Act 1988 (c.32), s.2(4).

[2] As amended by the Vulnerable Witnesses (Scotland) Act 2004 (asp 3), s.14, and brought into force by the Vulnerable Witnesses (Scotland) Act 2004 Commencement Order 2005 (SSI 2005/168) (effective April 1, 2005) but only in respect of proceedings in the sheriff court under Part II of the Children (Scotland) Act 1995 in respect of appeals under section 51(1) and applications under sections 68 and 85 of that Act and only in respect of child witnesses.

[3] As amended by the Vulnerable Witnesses (Scotland) Act 2004 (asp 3), s.14, and brought into force by the Vulnerable Witnesses (Scotland) Act 2004 Commencement Order 2005 (SSI 2005/168) (effective April 1, 2005) but only in respect of proceedings in the sheriff court under Part II of the Children (Scotland) Act 1995 in respect of appeals under section 51(1) and applications under sections 68 and 85 of that Act and only in respect of child witnesses.

(j)[1] permitting a person who is not an advocate or solicitor and is not represented by an advocate or solicitor to transmit, whether orally or in writing, the views of a child to the sheriff for the purposes of any enactment which makes provision (however expressed) for the sheriff to have regard to those views;

(k)[2] prescribing the procedure to be followed in appointing a person under section 3(4) of the Adults with Incapacity (Scotland) Act 2000 (asp 4) and the functions of such a person.

(l)[3] permitting a party to proceedings which relate to an interim attachment, an attachment, a money attachment, a land attachment or a residual attachment to be represented, in such circumstances as may be specified in the act of sederunt, by a person who is neither an advocate nor a solicitor.

(m)[4] permitting a debtor appearing before a sheriff under section 12 of the Bankruptcy (Scotland) Act 1985 (c.66) (award of sequestration) to be represented, in such circumstances as may be specified in the act of sederunt, by a person who is neither an advocate nor a solicitor.

(n)[5] permitting a lay representative, when appearing at a hearing in any category of civil proceedings along with a party to the proceedings, to make oral submissions to the sheriff on the party's behalf.

Provided that nothing contained in an act of sederunt made under this section shall derogate from—

(i) the provisions of sections 35 to 38 of this Act (as amended by the Law Reform (Miscellaneous Provisions) (Scotland) Act 1985) with respect to summary causes, or

(ii) the provisions of subsection (8) of section 20 of the Race Relations Act 1968 with respect to the remuneration to be paid to assessors appointed under subsection (7) of that section.

(2) An act of sederunt under this section may contain such incidental, supplemental or consequential provisions as appear to the Court of Session to be necessary or expedient for the purposes of that act, including, but without prejudice to the generality of the foregoing words, provisions amending, repealing or revoking any enactment (whether passed or made before or after the commencement of this Act) relating to matters with respect to which an act of sederunt may be made under this section.

(3) Before making an act of sederunt under this section with respect to any matter the Court of Session shall (unless that act embodies, with or without modifications, draft rules submitted to them by the Sheriff Court Rules Council under section 34 of this Act) consult the said Council, and shall take into consideration any views expressed by the Council with respect to that matter.

---

[1] Inserted by the Children (Scotland) Act 1995 (c.36), Sch.4, para.18(2) (effective November 1, 1995: SI 1995/2787).

[2] As inserted by the Adults with Incapacity (Scotland) Act 2000 (asp 4), s. 88 and Sch.5, para.13.

[3] As inserted by the Debt Arrangement and Attachment (Scotland) Act 2002 (asp 17) Pt 2 s.43 (effective December 17, 2002) and substituted by the Bankruptcy and Diligence etc. (Scotland) Act 2007 (asp 3) Sch.5 para.10 (effective April 1, 2008 as SSI 2008/115 and November 23, 2009 as SSI 2009/369).

[4] As inserted by the Bankruptcy and Diligence etc. (Scotland) Act 2007 (asp 3) Pt 1 s.33 (effective April 1, 2008).

[5] As inserted by the Legal Services (Scotland) Act 2010 (asp 16) Pt 4 c.3 s.127(a) (effective September 1, 2011).

(4)    Section 34 of the Administration of Justice (Scotland) Act 1933 (power of Court of Session to regulate civil procedure in sheriff court) shall cease to have effect, but any act of sederunt made under or having effect by virtue of that section shall, if and so far as it is in force immediately before the commencement of this Act, continue in force and shall have effect, and be treated, as if it had been made under this section.

### Rules for lay representation

**32A.**—[1](1)    Rules under section 32(1)(n)—

    (a)    are to apply to situations in which the party is not otherwise represented,

    (b)    may specify other conditions by reference to which the rules are to apply.

  (2)    Section 32(1)(n)—

    (a)    does not restrict the operation of section 36(1),

    (b)    is subject to any enactment (apart from section 36(1)) under which special provision may be made for a party to a particular type of case before the Court to be represented by a lay representative.

  (3)    In section 32(1)(n) and this section, a "lay representative" is a person who is not—

    (a)    a solicitor,

    (b)    an advocate, or

    (c)    one having a right to conduct litigation, or a right of audience, by virtue of section 27 of the Law Reform (Miscellaneous Provisions) (Scotland) Act 1990.

**D1.652**

### Sheriff Court Rules Council

**33.**—(1)[2]    There shall be established a body (to be known as the Sheriff Court Rules Council, and hereafter in this section and section 34 called "the Council") which shall have the functions conferred on it by section 34, and which shall consist of—

    (a)    two sheriffs principal, three sheriffs, one advocate, five solicitors and two whole-time sheriff clerks, all appointed by the Lord President of the Court of Session, after consultation with such persons as appear to him to be appropriate;

    (b)    two persons appointed by the Lord President after consultation with the Secretary of State, being persons appearing to the Lord President to have—

      (i)    a knowledge of the working procedures and practices of the civil courts;

      (ii)    a knowledge of consumer affairs; and

      (iii)    an awareness of the interests of litigants in the civil courts; and

    (c)    one person appointed by the Secretary of State, being a person appearing to the Secretary of State to be qualified for such appointment.

**D1.653**

---

[1] As inserted by the Legal Services (Scotland) Act 2010 (asp 16) Pt 4 c.3 s.127(a) (effective September 1, 2011).

[2] As amended by the Law Reform (Miscellaneous Provisions) (Scotland) Act 1990 (c.40), Sch.8, para.26.

(2) The members of the Council shall, so long as they retain the respective qualifications mentioned in subsection (1) above, hold office for three years and be eligible for re-appointment.

(3) Any vacancy in the membership of the Council occurring by reason of death, resignation or other cause before the expiry of the period for which the member whose place is so vacated was appointed shall be filled—

(a)[1] if the member was appointed by the Lord President of the Court of Session, by the appointment by the Lord President, after such consultation as is mentioned in paragraph (a) or, as the case may be, (b) of subsection (1) above, of a person having the same qualifications as that member,

(b) if the member was appointed by the Secretary of State, by the appointment by the Secretary of State of another person appearing to the Secretary of State to have qualifications suitable for such appointment,

and a person so appointed to fill a vacancy shall hold office only until the expiry of the said period.

(4)[2] The Lord President of the Court of Session shall appoint one of the two sheriffs principal who are members of the Council as chairman thereof.

(5) The Council shall have power to regulate the summoning of meetings of the Council and the procedure at such meetings, so however that—

(a) the Council shall meet within one month of its being established and thereafter at intervals of not more than six months, and shall meet at any time on a requisition in that behalf made by the chairman of the Council or any three members thereof, and

(b) at any meeting of the Council six members shall be a quorum.

(6) The Rules Council for the sheriff court established under section 35 of the Administration of Justice (Scotland) Act 1933 is hereby dissolved, and the said section 35 shall cease to have effect.

**Functions of Sheriff Court Rules Council**

D1.654

34.—(1) As soon as practicable after it has been established the Council shall review generally the procedure and practice followed in civil proceedings in the sheriff court (including any matters incidental or relating to that procedure or practice) and, in the light of that review and of the provisions of this Act, shall prepare and submit to the Court of Session draft rules, being rules which—

(a) are designed to regulate and prescribe that procedure and practice (including any such matters as aforesaid), and

(b) are such as the Court of Session have power to make by act of sederunt under section 32 of this Act,

and the Court of Session shall make an act of sederunt under the said section 32 embodying those rules with such modifications, if any, as they think expedient.

(2) After submitting draft rules to the Court of Session under subsection (1) above the Council shall keep under review the procedure and practice followed in civil proceedings in the sheriff court (including any matters incidental or relating to that procedure or practice), and the Council may prepare and submit to the Court of

---

[1] As amended by the Law Reform (Miscellaneous Provisions) (Scotland) Act 1990 (c.40), Sch.8, para.26.

[2] As amended by the Law Reform (Miscellaneous Provisions) (Scotland) Act 1985 (c.73) Sch.2, para. 13 and Sch.4 and by the Judiciary and Courts (Scotland) Act 2008 (asp 6) Sch.5 para.2(6) (effective April 1, 2010 subject to transitional provisions and savings specified in SSI 2010/39 art.3).

Session draft rules designed to deal with any of the matters relating to the sheriff court which the Court of Session have power under section 32 of this Act to regulate or prescribe by act of sederunt, and the Court of Session shall consider any draft rules so submitted and shall, if they approve the rules, make an act of sederunt under the said section 32 embodying those rules with such modifications if any, as they think expedient.

(3)  For the purpose of assisting it in the discharge of its functions under the foregoing provisions of this section the Council may invite representations on any aspect of the procedure or practice in civil proceedings in the sheriff court (including any matters incidental or relating to that procedure or practice), and shall consider any such representations received by it, whether in response to such an invitation as aforesaid or otherwise.

*Summary causes*

## Summary causes

35.—(1)  The definition of "summary cause" contained in paragraph (i) of section 3 of the Sheriff Courts (Scotland) Act 1907 shall cease to have effect, and for the purposes of the procedure and practice in civil proceedings in the sheriff court there shall be a form of process, to be known as a "summary cause", which shall be used for the purposes of all civil proceedings brought in that court, being proceedings of one or other of the following descriptions, namely—

**D1.655**

(a)[1]  actions for payment of money not exceeding £5,000[2] in amount (exclusive of interest and expenses);

(b)[3,4]  actions of multiplepoinding, actions of furthcoming, where the value of the fund *in medio*, or the value of the arrested fund or subject, as the case may be, does not exceed £5,000[5] (exclusive of interest and expenses);

(c)[6]  actions *ad factum praestandum* and actions for the recovery of possession of heritable or moveable property, other than actions in which there is claimed in addition, or as an alternative, to a decree *ad factum praestandum* or for such recovery, as the case may be, a decree for payment of money exceeding £5,000[7] in amount (exclusive of interest and expenses);

(d)  proceedings which, according to the law and practice existing immediately before the commencement of this Act, might competently be brought in the sheriff's small debt court or where required to be

---

[1] As amended by SI 1976/900 and SI 1981/842.

[2] As substituted subject to savings specified in SSI 2007/507 art.4 by the Sheriff Courts (Scotland) Act 1971 (Privative Jurisdiction and Summary Cause) Order (SSI 2007/507), art.3 (effective January 14, 2008).

[3] As amended by SI 1976/900 and SI 1981/842.

[4] As amended by Bankruptcy and Diligence etc. (Scotland) Act 2007 (asp 3) Sch.6(1) para.1 (effective April 1, 2008: as SSI 2008/115).

[5] As substituted subject to savings specified in SSI 2007/507 art.4 by the Sheriff Courts (Scotland) Act 1971 (Privative Jurisdiction and Summary Cause) Order (SSI 2007/507), art.3 (effective January 14, 2008).

[6] As amended by SI 1976/900 and SI 1981/842. Excluded by the Land Tenure Reform (Scotland) Act 1974 (c.38), s.9(6).

[7] As substituted subject to savings specified in SSI 2007/507 art.4 by the Sheriff Courts (Scotland) Act 1971 (Privative Jurisdiction and Summary Cause) Order (SSI 2007/507), art.3 (effective January 14, 2008).

conducted and disposed of in the summary manner in which proceedings were conducted and disposed of under the Small Debt Acts; and any reference in the following provisions of this Act, or in any other enactment (whether passed or made before or after the commencement of this Act) relating to civil procedure in the sheriff court, to a summary cause shall be construed as a reference to a summary cause within the meaning of this subsection.

(1A)[1]  For the avoidance of doubt it is hereby declared that nothing in subsection (1) above shall prevent the Court of Session from making different rules of procedure and practice in relation to different descriptions of summary cause proceedings.

(2)[2, 3]  There shall be a form of summary cause process, to be known as a "small claim", which shall be used for the purposes of such descriptions of summary cause proceedings as are prescribed by the Secretary of State by order.

(3)[4]  No enactment or rule of law relating to admissibility or corroboration of evidence before a court of law shall be binding in a small claim.

(4)[5]  An order under subsection (2) above shall be by statutory instrument but shall not be made unless a draft of it has been approved by a resolution of each House of Parliament.

**Procedure in summary causes**

D1.656

36.—(1)  In relation to summary causes the power conferred on the Court of Session by section 32 of this Act shall extend to the making of rules permitting a party to such a cause, in such circumstances as may be specified in the rules, to be represented by a person who is neither an advocate nor a solicitor.

(2)  A summary cause shall be commenced by a summons in, or as nearly as is practicable in, such form as may be prescribed by rules under the said section 32.

(3)[6]  The evidence, if any, given in a summary cause shall not be recorded.

(4)  *[Repealed by the Debtors (Scotland) Act 1987 (c.18), Sch.8.]*

**Further provisions as to small claims**

D1.657

36A.[7]  Where the pursuer in a small claim is not—

    (a)   a partnership or a body corporate; or

    (b)   acting in a representative capacity,

he may require the sheriff clerk to effect service of the summons on his behalf.

---

[1] As inserted by the Law Reform (Miscellaneous Provisions) (Scotland) Act 1985 (c.73), Sch.2, para.14, with effect from December 30, 1985.

[2] New subss (2)–(4) substituted for subs. (2) by the Law Reform (Miscellaneous Provisions) (Scotland) Act 1985 (c.73), s.18(1).

[3] As amended by SI 1999/678, art.2, Sch.(effective May 19, 1999).

[4] New subss (2)–(4) substituted for subs. (2) by the Law Reform (Miscellaneous Provisions) (Scotland) Act 1985 (c.73), s.18(1).

[5] New subss (2)–(4) substituted for subs. (2) by the Law Reform (Miscellaneous Provisions) (Scotland) Act 1985 (c.73), s.18(1).

[6] Excluded by the Maintenance Orders (Reciprocal Enforcement) Act 1972 (c.18), s.4(4)(b).

[7] As inserted by the Law Reform (Miscellaneous Provisions) (Scotland) Act 1985 (c.73), s.18(2).

**Expenses in small claims**

**36B.**—[1](1)[2]  No award of expenses shall be made in a small claim in which the value of the claim does not exceed such sum as the Secretary of State shall prescribe by order.

**D1.658**

(2)[3]  Any expenses which the sheriff may award in any other small claim shall not exceed such sum as the Secretary of State shall prescribe by order.

(3)  Subsections (1) and (2) above do not apply to a party to a small claim—

    (a)  who being a defender—

        (i)  has not stated a defence; or

        (ii)  having stated a defence, has not proceeded with it; or

        (iii)  having stated and proceeded with a defence, has not acted in good faith as to its merits; or

    (b)  on whose part there has been unreasonable conduct in relation to the proceedings or the claim;

nor do they apply in relation to an appeal to the sheriff principal.

(4)  An order under this section shall be by statutory instrument but shall not be made unless a draft of it has been approved by a resolution of each House of Parliament.

**Remits**

**37.**—[4](1)[5]  In the case of any ordinary cause brought in the sheriff court the sheriff—

**D1.659**

    (a)  shall at any stage, on the joint motion of the parties to the cause, direct that the cause be treated as a summary cause, and in that case the cause shall be treated for all purposes (including appeal) as a summary cause and shall proceed accordingly;

    (b)  may, subject to section 7 of the Sheriff Courts (Scotland) Act 1907, on the motion of any of the parties to the cause, if he is of the opinion that the importance or difficulty of the cause make it appropriate to do so, remit the cause to the Court of Session.

(2)  In the case of any summary cause, the sheriff at any stage—

    (a)  shall, on the joint motion of the parties to the cause, and

    (b)  may, on the motion of any of the parties to the cause, if he is of the opinion that the importance or difficulty of the cause makes it appropriate to do so,

direct that the cause be treated as an ordinary cause, and in that case the cause shall be treated for all purposes (including appeal) as an ordinary cause and shall proceed accordingly:

Provided that a direction under this subsection may, in the case of an action for the recovery of possession of heritable or moveable property, be given by the sheriff of his own accord.

---

[1]  As inserted by the Law Reform (Miscellaneous Provisions) (Scotland) Act 1985 (c.73), s.18(2).

[2]  As amended by SI 1999/678, art.2, Sch. (effective May 19, 1999).

[3]  As amended by SI 1999/678, art.2, Sch. (effective May 19, 1999).

[4]  As inserted by the Agricultural Holdings (Scotland) Act 2003 (asp 11), Pt 7, s.86(1).

[5]  As amended by the Law Reform (Miscellaneous Provisions) (Scotland) Act 1980 (c.55), s.16(a). See the Land Tenure Reform (Scotland) Act 1974 (c.38), s.9(6).

(2A)[1]    In the case of any action in the sheriff court, being an action for divorce or an action in relation to the custody, guardianship or adoption of a child the sheriff may, of his own accord, at any stage remit the action to the Court of Session.

(2B)[2]    In the case of any small claim the sheriff at any stage—

(a)    may, if he is of the opinion that a difficult question of law or a question of fact of exceptional complexity is involved, of his own accord or on the motion of any party to the small claim;

(b)    shall, on the joint motion of the parties to the small claim,

direct that the small claim be treated as a summary cause (not being a small claim) or ordinary cause, and in that case the small claim shall be treated for all purposes (including appeal) as a summary cause (not being a small claim) or ordinary cause as the case may be.

(2C)[3]    In the case of any cause which is not a small claim by reason only of any monetary limit applicable to a small claim or to summary causes, the sheriff at any stage shall, on the joint motion of the parties to the cause, direct that the cause be treated as a small claim and in that case the cause shall be treated for all purposes (including appeal) as a small claim and shall proceed accordingly.

(2D)[4]    In the case of any action in the sheriff court where the matter to which the action relates could competently be determined by the Land Court by virtue of the Agricultural Holdings (Scotland) Act 1991 (c.55) or the Agricultural Holdings (Scotland) Act 2003 (asp 11), the sheriff may (of his own accord or on the motion of any of the parties) at any stage remit the case to the Land Court if he is of the opinion that it is appropriate to do so.

(3)[5]    A decision—

(a)    to remit, or not to remit, under subsection (2A), (2B) or (2C) above; or

(b)    to make, or not to make, a direction by virtue of paragraph (b) of, or the proviso to, subsection (2) above,

shall not be subject to review; but from a decision to remit, or not to remit, under subsection (1)(b) above an appeal shall lie to the Court of Session.

(4)    In this section "sheriff" includes a sheriff principal.

### Appeal in summary causes

D1.660        38.[6]    In the case of—

(a)    any summary cause an appeal shall lie to the sheriff principal on any point of law from the final judgment of the sheriff; and

(b)    any summary cause other than a small claim an appeal shall lie to the Court of Session on any point of law from the final judgment of the sheriff principal, if the sheriff principal certifies the cause as suitable for such an appeal,

---

[1] Added by the Law Reform (Miscellaneous Provisions) (Scotland) Act 1980 (c.55), s.16(b). As amended by the Divorce Jurisdiction, Court Fees and Legal Aid (Scotland) Act 1983 (c.12), Sch.1, para.12, the Law Reform (Parent and Child) (Scotland) Act 1986 (c.9), Sch.1, para.11, the Age of Legal Capacity (Scotland) Act 1991 (c.50), Sch.1, para.35, and the Children (Scotland) Act 1995 (c.36), Sch.4, para. 18(3), infra, Division K (effective April 1, 1997: SI 1996/3201).

[2] Added by the Law Reform (Miscellaneous Provisions) (Scotland) Act 1988, s.18(3).

[3] Added by the Law Reform (Miscellaneous Provisions) (Scotland) Act 1988, s.18(3).

[4] As inserted by the Agricultural Holdings (Scotland) Act 2003 (asp 11), Pt 7, s.86(1).

[5] As substituted by the Law Reform (Miscellaneous Provisions) (Scotland) Act 1980 (c.55), s.16(c). As amended by the Law Reform (Miscellaneous Provisions) (Scotland) Act 1985 (c.73), s.18(3)(b).

[6] As amended by the Law Reform (Miscellaneous Provisions) (Scotland) Act 1985 (c.73), s.18(4). Excluded by the Debtors (Scotland) Act 1987 (c.18), s.103(1).

but save as aforesaid an interlocutor of the sheriff or the sheriff principal in any such cause shall not be subject to review.

### Miscellaneous and supplemental

**39, 40.** *[Repealed by the Law Reform (Miscellaneous Provisions) (Scotland) Act 1980 (c.55), Sch.3.]*

## Power of Her Majesty to vary limit to privative jurisdiction of sheriff court, etc.

**41.**—[1](1)  If it appears to Her Majesty in Council that the sum of £250 specified in any provisions of this Act mentioned in subsection (2) below (or such other sum as may be specified in that provision by virtue of an Order in Council under this section) should be varied, Her Majesty may by Order in Council, specifying the provision and the sum in question, direct that the provision shall be amended so as to substitute for that sum such other sum as may be specified in the Order.

**D1.661**

(2)  The provisions referred to in subsection (1) above are—
section 31,
paragraphs (a), (b) and (c) of section 35.

(3)  An Order in Council under this section may contain such incidental, supplemental or consequential provisions as appear to Her Majesty in Council to be necessary or expedient for the purposes of the Order.

(4)  Any Order in Council made under this section may be revoked by a subsequent Order in Council under this section which substitutes another sum for the sum specified in the Order which is thereby revoked.

(5)  No recommendation shall be made to Her Majesty in Council to make an Order under this section unless a draft of the Order has been laid before Parliament and approved by resolution of each House of Parliament.

## Application of provisions regarding jurisdiction and summary causes

**42.**  The following provisions of this Act, namely—
section 31,
sections 35 to 40,
section 46(2) so far as relating to the enactments mentioned in Part II of Schedule 2,
Schedule 1 (except paragraph 1),
shall not apply in relation to any proceedings commenced before the commencement of this Act.

**D1.662**

### PART IV – MISCELLANEOUS AND GENERAL

## Orders, etc.

**43.**—(1)  Any power conferred by this Act to make an order shall include a power exercisable in the like manner and subject to the like conditions (if any) to vary or revoke the order by a subsequent order.

**D1.663**

(2)  It is hereby declared that any power conferred by this Act to include incidental, consequential or supplemental provisions in any instrument made under this Act includes a power to include transitional provisions in that instrument.

---

[1] As amended by the Law Reform (Miscellaneous Provisions) (Scotland) Act 1980 (c.55), Sch.3.

**Expenses**

D1.664

44.—(1)   There shall be paid out of moneys provided by Parliament any sums payable by the Secretary of State in consequence of the provisions of this Act.

(2)   Any sums payable under or by virtue of this Act to the Secretary of State shall be paid into the Consolidated Fund.

(3)   In the application of section 4(1) of the Local Government (Scotland) Act 1966 (variation of rate support grant orders) to a rate support grant order made before the transfer date appointed under section 30 of this Act for a grant period ending after that date, the Secretary of State shall take into account any relief obtained, or likely to be obtained, by local authorities—

    (a)   which is attributable to the coming into operation of Part II of this Act, and

    (b)   which was not taken into account in making the rate support grant order the variation of which is in question.

The provisions of this subsection are without prejudice to section 4(4) of the said Act of 1966 (under which an order under that section may vary the matters prescribed by a rate support grant order).

**Interpretation**

D1.665

45.—(1)[1]   In this Act, unless the contrary intention appears—

    (a)   references to a sheriff principal include reference to a temporary sheriff principal, and references to the office of sheriff principal include references to an appointment as a temporary sheriff principal;

    (b)   references to a sheriff include references to a part-time sheriff and an honorary sheriff, and references to the office of sheriff include references to an appointment as a part-time sheriff and to the office of honorary sheriff;

    (c)   references to an honorary sheriff are references to a person holding the office of honorary sheriff in his capacity as such.

(2)   In this Act—

    (a)   "enactment" includes an order, regulation, rule or other instrument having effect by virtue of an Act;

    (b)   any references to any enactment shall, unless the contrary intention appears, be construed as a reference to that enactment as amended or extended, and as including a reference thereto as applied, by or under any other enactment (including this Act).

(3)   Subject to the foregoing provisions of this section and to any other express provision of this Act, expressions used in this Act and in the Sheriff Courts (Scotland) Act 1907 shall have the same meanings in this Act as in that Act.

**Amendment and repeal of enactments**

D1.666

46.—(1)   Schedule 1 to this Act (which contains certain minor and consequential amendments of enactments) shall have effect.

(2)   The enactments mentioned in Schedule 2 to this Act are hereby repealed to the extent specified in relation thereto in column 3 of that Schedule.

---

[1] As amended by the Bail, Judicial Appointments etc. (Scotland) Act 2000 (asp 9), s.12 and Sched., para.1.

## Short title, commencement and extent

**47.**—(1)   This Act may be cited as the Sheriff Courts (Scotland) Act 1971.

(2)[1]   This Act shall come into operation on such date as the Secretary of State may appoint by order made by statutory instrument, and different dates may be appointed for different provisions of this Act, or for different purposes.

Any reference in any provision of this Act to the commencement of this Act shall, unless otherwise provided by any such order, be construed as a reference to the date on which that provision comes into operation.

(3)[2]   This Act, except section 4 (offices of sheriff principal and sheriff), shall extend to Scotland only.

**D1.667**

SCHEDULES

**D1.668**

SCHEDULE 1

MINOR AND CONSEQUENTIAL AMENDMENT OF ENACTMENTS

*General*

**1.**   In any enactment passed or made before the commencement of this Act, for any reference to a county, where it appears in relation to a sheriff or a sheriff substitute or in any similar context, there shall, unless the contrary intention appears, be substituted a reference to a sheriffdom.

NOTE

The remaining amendments are shown in the prints in *The Parliament House Book* of the Acts amended.

SCHEDULE 2

**D1.669**

REPEAL OF ENACTMENTS

omitted

NOTE

Repeals of provisions of Acts printed in *The Parliament House Book* are shown in the prints of those Acts.

---

[1] See SI 1971/1582; SI 1973/276 and SI 1976/236. Power fully exercised.
[2] As amended by the House of Commons Disqualification Act 1975 (c.24), Sch.3.

# DISTRICT COURTS (SCOTLAND) ACT 1975

(1975 c. 20)

D1.132

*[Repealed by the Justice of the Peace Courts (Sheriffdom of South Strathclyde, Dumfries and Galloway) etc. Order 2009 (SSI 2009/332) art.7 (effective February 22, 2010).]*

# FATAL ACCIDENTS AND SUDDEN DEATHS INQUIRY (SCOTLAND) ACT 1976

(1976 c.14)

**D1.670**

An Act to make provision for Scotland for the holding of public inquiries in respect of fatal accidents, deaths of persons in legal custody, sudden, suspicious and unexplained deaths and deaths occurring in circumstances giving rise to serious public concern.[1]

[April 13, 1976.]

### Investigation of death and application for public inquiry

**1.**—(1) Subject to the provisions of any enactment specified in Schedule 1 to this Act and subsection (2) below, where—

    (a) in the case of a death to which this paragraph applies—

        (i) it appears that the death has resulted from an accident occurring in Scotland while the person who has died, being an employee, was in the course of his employment or, being an employer or self-employed person, was engaged in his occupation as such; or

        (ii) the person who has died was, at the time of his death, in legal custody; or

    (b) it appears to the Lord Advocate to be expedient in the public interest in the case of a death to which this paragraph applies that an inquiry under this Act should be held into the circumstances of the death on the ground that it was sudden, suspicious or unexplained, or has occurred in circumstances such as to give rise to serious public concern,

the procurator fiscal for the district with which the circumstances of the death appear to be most closely connected shall investigate those circumstances and apply to the sheriff for the holding of an inquiry under this Act into those circumstances.

(2) Paragraph (a) of subsection (1) above applies to a death occurring in Scotland after the commencement of this Act (other than such a death in a case where criminal proceedings have been concluded against any person in respect of the death or any accident from which the death resulted, and the Lord Advocate is satisfied that the circumstances of the death have been sufficiently established in the course of such proceedings), and paragraph (b) of that subsection applies to a death occurring there at any time after the date three years before such commencement.

(3) An application under subsection (1) above—

    (a) shall be made to the sheriff with whose sheriffdom the circumstances of the death appear to be most closely connected;

    (b) shall narrate briefly the circumstances of the death so far as known to the procurator fiscal;

    (c) may, if it appears that more deaths than one have occurred as a result of the same accident or in the same or similar circumstances, relate to both or all such deaths.

(4) For the purposes of subsection (1)(a)(ii) above, a person is in legal custody if—

    (a) he is detained in, or is subject to detention in, a prison, remand centre,

**D1.671**

---

[1] See the Anatomy Act 1984 (c.14), s.4(6).

detention centre, borstal institution, or young offenders institution, all within the meaning of the Prisons (Scotland) Act 1952; or

(b)     he is detained in a police station, police cell, or other similar place; or

(ba)[1]   he is detained in, or is subject to detention in, service custody premises (within the meaning of section 300 of the Armed Forces Act 2006);

(c)     he is being taken—

(i)[2]    to any of the places specified in paragraphs (a) and (b) and (ba) of this subsection to be detained therein; or

(ii)     from any such place in which immediately before such taking he was detained.

### Death of service personnel abroad

**D1.672**

1A.—[3](1)   Subsection (4) applies where—

(a)   the Lord Advocate is notified under section 12(4) or (5) of the Coroners and Justice Act 2009 in relation to a death,

(b)   the death is within subsection (2) or (3), and

(c)   the Lord Advocate—

(i)    decides that it would be appropriate in the public interest for an inquiry under this Act to be held into the circumstances of the death, and

(ii)   does not reverse that decision.

(2)    A death is within this subsection if the person who has died was, at the time of the death, in legal custody (as construed by reference to section 1(4)).

(3)    A death is within this subsection if it appears to the Lord Advocate that the death—

(a)   was sudden, suspicious or unexplained, or

(b)   occurred in circumstances such as to give rise to serious public concern.

(4)    The procurator fiscal for the appropriate district must—

(a)   investigate the circumstances of the death, and

(b)   apply to the sheriff for the holding of an inquiry under this Act into those circumstances.

(5)    But subsection (4) does not extend to a death within subsection (2) if the Lord Advocate is satisfied that the circumstances of the death have been sufficiently established in the course of any criminal proceedings against any person in respect of the death.

(6)    An application under subsection (4)(b)—

(a)   is to be made to the sheriff of the appropriate sheriffdom,

(b)   must narrate briefly the circumstances of the death so far as known to the procurator fiscal,

(c)   may relate to more than one death if the deaths occurred in the same or similar circumstances.

(7)    It is for the Lord Advocate to determine the appropriate district and appropriate sheriffdom for the purposes of subsections (4) and (6)(a).

---

[1] As inserted by the Armed Forces Act 2006 (c.52) Sch.16 para.72 (effective October 31, 2009).

[2] As substituted by the Armed Forces Act 2006 (c.52) Sch.16 para.72 (effective October 31, 2009).

[3] As inserted by the Coroners and Justice Act 2009 (c.25) Pt 1 c.7 s.50(2) (effective September 24, 2012).

## Citation of witnesses for precognition

**2.**—(1)[1]  The procurator fiscal may, for the purpose of carrying out his investigation under section 1(1) or 1A(4) of this Act, cite witnesses for precognition by him, and this section shall be sufficient warrant for such citation.

D1.673

(2)  If any witness cited under subsection (1) above—

    (a)  fails without reasonable excuse and after receiving reasonable notice to attend for precognition by the procurator fiscal at the time and place mentioned in the citation served on him; or

    (b)  refuses when so cited to give information within his knowledge regarding any matter relevant to the investigation in relation to which such precognition is taken,

the procurator fiscal may apply to the sheriff for an order requiring the witness to attend for such precognition or to give such information at a time and place specified in the order; and the sheriff shall, if he considers it expedient to do so, make such an order.

(3)[2]  If the witness fails to comply with the order of the sheriff under subsection (2) above, he shall be liable to be summarily punished forthwith by a fine not exceeding level 3 on the standard scale or by imprisonment for any period not exceeding 20 days.

## Holding of public inquiry

**3.**—(1)[3]  On an application under section 1 or 1A of this Act being made to him, the sheriff shall make an order—

D1.674

    (a)  fixing a time and place for the holding by him of an inquiry under this Act (hereafter in this Act referred to as "the inquiry"), which shall be as soon thereafter as is reasonably practicable in such courthouse or other premises as appear to him to be appropriate, having regard to the apparent circumstances of the death; and

    (b)  granting warrant to cite witnesses and havers to attend at the inquiry at the instance of the procurator fiscal or of any person who may be entitled by virtue of this Act to appear at the inquiry.

(2)  On the making of an order under subsection (1) above, the procurator fiscal shall—

    (a)  intimate the holding of the inquiry and the time and place fixed for it to the wife or husband or the nearest known relative and, in a case where the inquiry is being held in respect of such a death as is referred to in section 1(1)(a)(i) of this Act, to the employer, if any, of the person whose death is the subject of the inquiry, and to such other person or class of persons as may be prescribed in rules made under section 7(1)(g) of this Act; and

    (b)  give public notice of the holding of the inquiry and of the time and place fixed for it.

---

[1] As inserted by the Coroners and Justice Act 2009 (c.25) Pt 1 c.7 s.50(3) (effective September 24, 2012).

[2] As amended by the Criminal Procedure (Consequential Provisions) (Scotland) Act 1995 (c.40) Sch.4, para. 10.

[3] As inserted by the Coroners and Justice Act 2009 (c.25) Pt 1 c.7 s.50(4) (effective September 24, 2012).

(3)[1]   Where an application under section 1 or 1A of this Act relates to more than one death, the order made under subsection (1) above shall so relate; and in this Act references to a death shall include references to both or all deaths or to each death as the case may require, and in subsection (2)(a) above the reference to the person whose death is the subject of the inquiry shall include a reference to each person whose death is the subject of the inquiry.

### Conduct of public inquiry

**D1.675**

4.—(1)   At the inquiry, it shall be the duty of the procurator fiscal to adduce evidence with regard to the circumstances of the death which is the subject of the inquiry.

(2)   The wife or husband, or the nearest known relative, and, in a case where the inquiry is being held in respect of such a death as is referred to in section 1(1)(a)(i) of this Act, the employer, if any, of the person whose death is the subject of the inquiry, an inspector appointed under section 19 of the Health and Safety at Work etc. Act 1974 and any other person who the sheriff is satisfied has an interest in the inquiry may appear and adduce evidence at the inquiry.

(3)   Subject to subsection (4) below, the inquiry shall be open to the public.

(4)   Where a person under the age of 17 is in any way involved in the inquiry, the sheriff may, at his own instance or on an application made to him by any party to the inquiry, make an order providing that—

(a)   no report of the inquiry which is made in a newspaper or other publication or a sound or television broadcast shall reveal the name, address or school, or include any particulars calculated to lead to the identification of that person;

(b)   no picture relating to the inquiry which is or includes a picture of that person shall be published in any newspaper or other publication or televised broadcast.

(5)[2]   Any person who contravenes an order made under subsection (4) above shall be guilty of an offence and shall be liable on summary conviction to a fine not exceeding level 4 on the standard scale in respect of each offence.

(6)   The sheriff may, either at his own instance or at the request of the procurator fiscal or of any party who may be entitled by virtue of this Act to appear at the inquiry, summon any person having special knowledge and being willing to do so, to act as an assessor at the inquiry.

(7)   Subject to the provisions of this Act and any rules made under section 7 of this Act, the rules of evidence, the procedure and the powers of the sheriff to deal with contempt of court and to enforce the attendance of witnesses at the inquiry shall be as nearly as possible those applicable in an ordinary civil cause brought before the sheriff sitting alone.

### Criminal proceedings and compellability of witnesses

**D1.676**

5.—(1)   The examination of a witness or haver at the inquiry shall not be a bar to criminal proceedings being taken against him.

(2)   No witness at the inquiry shall be compellable to answer any question tending to show that he is guilty of any crime or offence.

---

[1] As inserted by the Coroners and Justice Act 2009 (c.25) Pt 1 c.7 s.50(4) (effective September 24, 2012).

[2] As amended by virtue of the Criminal Procedure (Scotland) Act 1975 (c.21), ss.289F and 289G.

**Sheriffs determination, etc.**

**6.**—(1)  At the conclusion of the evidence and any submissions thereon, or as soon as possible thereafter, the sheriff shall make a determination setting out the following circumstances of the death so far as they have been established to his satisfaction—

    (a)  where and when the death and any accident resulting in the death took place;

    (b)  the cause or causes of such death and any accident resulting in the death;

    (c)  the reasonable precautions, if any, whereby the death and any accident resulting in the death might have been avoided;

    (d)  the defects, if any, in any system of working which contributed to the death or any accident resulting in the death; and

    (e)  any other facts which are relevant to the circumstances of the death.

D1.677

(2)  The sheriff shall be entitled to be satisfied that any circumstances referred to in subsection (1) above have been established by evidence, notwithstanding that that evidence is not corroborated.

(3)  The determination of the sheriff shall not be admissible in evidence or be founded on in any judicial proceedings, of whatever nature, arising out of the death or out of any accident from which the death resulted.

(4)  On the conclusion of the inquiry

    (a)  the sheriff clerk shall send to the Lord Advocate a copy of the determination of the sheriff and, on a request being made to him, send to any Minister or Government Department or to the Health and Safety Commission, a copy of

        (i)[1]  the application made under section 1 or 1A of this Act;

        (ii)  the transcript of the evidence;

        (iii)  any report or documentary production used in the inquiry;

        (iv)  the determination of the sheriff, and

    (b)  the procurator fiscal shall send to the Registrar General of Births, Deaths and Marriages for Scotland the name and last known address of the person who has died and the date, place and cause of his death.

(5)  Upon payment of such fee as may be prescribed in rules made under paragraph (i) of section 7(1) of this Act, any person—

    (a)  may obtain a copy of the determination of the sheriff;

    (b)  who has an interest in the inquiry may, within such period as may be prescribed in rules made under paragraph (j) of the said section 7(1), obtain a copy of the transcript of the evidence,

from the sheriff clerk.

**Rules**

**7.**—(1)[2]  The Secretary of State may, by rules, provide in relation to inquiries under this Act—

    (a)  as to the form of any document to be used in or for the purposes of such inquiries;

D1.678

---

[1] As amended by the Coroners and Justice Act 2009 (c.25) Pt 1 c.7 s.50(5) (effective September 24, 2012).
[2] As amended by SI 1999/678, Art.2, Sch. (effective May 19, 1999).

 (b) for the representation, on such conditions as may be specified in the rules, of any person who is entitled by virtue of this Act to appear at the inquiry;

 (c) for the authorisation by the sheriff of the taking and holding in safe custody of anything which it may be considered necessary to produce;

 (d) for the inspection by the sheriff or any person authorised by him of any land, premises, article, or other thing;

 (e) that written statements and reports may, on such conditions as may be specified in the rules, be admissible in lieu of parole evidence;

 (f) as to the duties, remuneration and other conditions of appointment of any assessor summoned under section 4 of this Act, and for keeping of lists of persons willing to act as such;

 (g) as to intimation of the holding of the inquiry;

 (h) as to the payment of fees to solicitors and expenses to witnesses and havers;

 (i) as to the payment of a fee by a person obtaining a copy of the determination of the sheriff or a copy of the transcript of the evidence;

 (j) as to the period within which a person entitled may obtain a copy of the transcript of the evidence at the inquiry;

 (k) as to such other matters relating to procedure as the Lord Advocate thinks appropriate.

(2) The power to make rules conferred by any provision of this Act shall be exercisable by statutory instrument.

(3) Rules made by the Lord Advocate under this Act may contain such incidental, consequential and supplemental provisions as appear to him to be necessary or proper for bringing the rules into operation and giving full effect thereto.

**Minor and consequential amendments and repeals**

 **8.** [Not reprinted.]

**Application to continental shelf**

D1.679

 **9.**[1] For the purposes of this Act a death or any accident from which death has resulted which has occurred—

 (a) in connection with any activity falling within subsection (2) of section 23 of the Oil and Gas (Enterprise) Act 1982; and

 (b) in that area, or any part of that area, in respect of which it is provided by Order in Council under subsection (1) of that section that questions arising out of acts or omissions taking place therein shall be determined in accordance with the law in force in Scotland,

shall be taken to have occurred in Scotland.

---

[1] As amended by the Oil and Gas (Enterprise) Act 1982 (c.23), Sch.3, para.34 and substituted by the Petroleum Act 1998 (c.17), Sch.4 para.9 (effective February 15, 1999).

**Interpretation, transitional, citation, commencement and extent**

**10.**—(1)   Any reference in this Act to any other enactment shall be construed as a reference to that enactment as amended by or under any other enactment including this Act.

(2)–(3)   *[Repealed by the Statute Law (Repeals) Act 1989 (c.43), Sch.1, Pt I.]*

(4)   This Act may be cited as the Fatal Accidents and Sudden Deaths Inquiry (Scotland) Act 1976.

(5)   *[Repealed by the Statute Law (Repeals) Act 1989 (c.43), Sch.1, Pt I.]*

(6)   This Act, other than subsections (4) and (5) of section 4 and section 9 of this Act, extends to Scotland only.

**D1.680**

**Interpretation, transitional, citation, commencement and extent**

U1.698

16.—(1) Any reference in this Act to any other enactment shall be construed as a reference to that enactment as amended by or under any other enactment including this Act.

(2) *Repealed by the Scotland Act (Repeals) No 1972, c. 48, s. 34(3), Pt.II.*

(3) This Act may be cited as the Fatal Accidents and Sudden Deaths Inquiry (Scotland) Act 1976.

(5) *Repealed by the Sheriff Law (Repeals) Act 1985, c. 73, Sch. 4, Pt. I.*

(6) This Act, other than subsections (?) and (5) of section 4 and section 5 of this Act, extends to Scotland only.

# LAW REFORM (MISCELLANEOUS PROVISIONS) (SCOTLAND) ACT 1985[1]

(1985 c.73)

**D1.681**

An Act to amend the law of Scotland in respect of … certain courts and their powers; evidence and procedure; … and to make, as respects Scotland, certain other miscellaneous reforms of the law.

[October 30, 1985]

*Provisions relating to civil jurisdiction and procedure*

**ss.16–18**   [Amendments given effect.]

SCHEDULE 2

**D1.682**

AMENDMENT OF ENACTMENTS

*Sheriff Courts (Scotland) Act 1971 (c.58)*

**12.**   [Amendments to s.32 of the 1971 Act are incorporated in the print of that Act, supra.]

---

[1] Of the provisions noted here, ss.16 and 17 came into force on 30th December 1985, Sch.2, para.12 on 8th December 1986 and s.18 on 30th November 1988. For other provisions of this Act, see Divisions, *B, E, H* and *L*.

## Vulnerable Witnesses (Scotland) Act 2004

D1.683

((ASP 3))

[April 14, 2004]

## PART 2 – CIVIL PROCEEDINGS

*Evidence of children and other vulnerable witnesses: special measures*

### Interpretation of this Part

**11.**—(1) For the purposes of this Part of this Act, a person who is giving or is to give evidence in or for the purposes of any civil proceedings is a vulnerable witness if—

    (a) the person is under the age of 16 on the date of commencement of the proceedings (such a vulnerable witness being referred to in this Part as a "child witness"), or

    (b) where the person is not a child witness, there is a significant risk that the quality of the evidence to be given by the person will be diminished by reason of—

        (i) mental disorder (within the meaning of section 328 of the Mental Health (Care and Treatment) (Scotland) Act 2003 (asp 13)), or

        (ii) fear or distress in connection with giving evidence in the proceedings.

(2) In considering whether a person is a vulnerable witness by virtue of subsection (1)(b) above, the court must take into account—

    (a) the nature and circumstances of the alleged matter to which the proceedings relate,

    (b) the nature of the evidence which the person is likely to give,

D1.684

    (c)   the relationship (if any) between the person and any party to the proceedings,

    (d)   the person's age and maturity,

    (e)   any behaviour towards the person on the part of—

        (i)   any party to the proceedings,

        (ii)   members of the family or associates of any such party,

        (iii)   any other person who is likely to be a party to the proceedings or a witness in the proceedings, and

    (f)   such other matters, including—

        (i)   the social and cultural background and ethnic origins of the person,

        (ii)   the person's sexual orientation,

        (iii)   the domestic and employment circumstances of the person,

        (iv)   any religious beliefs or political opinions of the person, and

        (v)   any physical disability or other physical impairment which the person has,

as appear to the court to be relevant.

(3)   For the purposes of subsection (1)(a) above, proceedings are taken to have commenced when the petition, summons, initial writ or other document initiating the proceedings is served, and, where the document is served on more than one person, the proceedings shall be taken to have commenced when the document is served on the first person on whom it is served.

(4)   In subsection (1)(b), the reference to the quality of evidence is to its quality in terms of completeness, coherence and accuracy.

(5)   In this Part

    "child witness notice" has the meaning given in section 12(2),

    "civil proceedings" includes, in addition to such proceedings in any of the ordinary courts of law, any proceedings to which section 91 (procedural rules in relation to certain applications etc.) of the Children (Scotland) Act 1995 (c. 36) applies,

    "court" is to be construed in accordance with the meaning of "civil proceedings",

    "special measure" means any of the special measures set out in, or prescribed under, section 18,

    "vulnerable witness application" has the meaning given in section 12(6)(a).

### Orders authorising the use of special measures for vulnerable witnesses

**D1.685**

**12.**—(1)   Where a child witness is to give evidence in or for the purposes of any civil proceedings, the court must, before the proof or other hearing at which the child is to give evidence, make an order—

    (a)   authorising the use of such special measure or measures as the court considers to be the most appropriate for the purpose of taking the child witness's evidence, or

    (b)   that the child witness is to give evidence without the benefit of any special measure.

(2)   The party citing or intending to cite a child witness must lodge with the court a notice (referred to in this Part as a "child witness notice")—

    (a)   specifying the special measure or measures which the party considers to be the most appropriate for the purpose of taking the child witness's evidence, or

    (b)   if the party considers that the child witness should give evidence without the benefit of any special measure, stating that fact,

and the court must have regard to the child witness notice in making an order under subsection (1) above.

    (3)   If a child witness notice specifies any of the following special measures, namely—

    (a)   the use of a live television link in accordance with section 20 where the place from which the child witness is to give evidence by means of the link is another part of the court building in which the court-room is located,

    (b)   the use of a screen in accordance with section 21, or

    (c)   the use of a supporter in accordance with section 22 in conjunction with either of the special measures referred to in paragraphs (a) and (b) above,

that special measure is, for the purposes of subsection (1)(a) above, to be taken to be the most appropriate for the purposes of taking the child witness's evidence.

    (4)   The court may make an order under subsection (1)(b) above only if satisfied—

    (a)   that the child witness has expressed a wish to give evidence without the benefit of any special measure and that it is appropriate for the child witness so to give evidence, or

    (b)   that—

        (i)   the use of any special measure for the purpose of taking the evidence of the child witness would give rise to a significant risk of prejudice to the fairness of the proceedings or otherwise to the interests of justice, and

        (ii)   that risk significantly outweighs any risk of prejudice to the interests of the child witness if the order is made.

    (5)   Subsection (6) below applies in relation to a person other than a child witness who is to give evidence in or for the purpose of any civil proceedings (referred to in this section as "the witness").

    (6)   The court may—

    (a)   on an application (referred to in this Part as a "vulnerable witness application") made to it by the party citing or intending to cite the witness, and

    (b)   if satisfied that the witness is a vulnerable witness,

make an order authorising the use of such special measure or measures as the court considers most appropriate for the purpose of taking the witness's evidence.

    (7)   In deciding whether to make an order under subsection (6) above, the court must—

    (a)   have regard to—

        (i)   the possible effect on the witness if required to give evidence without the benefit of any special measure, and

        (ii)   whether it is likely that the witness would be better able to give evidence with the benefit of a special measure, and

    (b)   take into account the matters specified in section 11(2)(a) to (f).

### Review of arrangements for vulnerable witnesses

    **13.**—(1)   In any civil proceedings in which a person who is giving or is to give evidence (referred to in this section as "the witness") appears to the court to be a

                                                  **D1.686**

vulnerable witness, the court may at any stage in the proceedings (whether before or after the commencement of the proof or other hearing at which the witness is giving or is to give evidence or before or after the witness has begun to give evidence)—

    (a)   on the application of the party citing or intending to cite the witness, or

    (b)   of its own motion,

review the current arrangements for taking the witness's evidence and make an order under subsection (2) below.

    (2)   The order which may be made under this subsection is—

    (a)   where the current arrangements for taking the witness's evidence include the use of a special measure or combination of special measures authorised by an order under section 12 or under this subsection (referred to as the "earlier order"), an order varying or revoking the earlier order, or

    (b)   where the current arrangements for taking the witness's evidence do not include any special measure, an order authorising the use of such special measure or measures as the court considers most appropriate for the purpose of taking the witness's evidence.

    (3)   An order under subsection (2)(a) above varying an earlier order may—

    (a)   add to or substitute for any special measure authorised by the earlier order such other special measure as the court considers most appropriate for the purpose of taking the witness's evidence, or

    (b)   where the earlier order authorises the use of a combination of special measures for that purpose, delete any of the special measures so authorised.

    (4)   The court may make an order under subsection (2)(a) above revoking an earlier order only if satisfied that—

    (a)   the witness has expressed a wish to give or, as the case may be, continue to give evidence without the benefit of any special measure and that it is appropriate for the witness so to give evidence, or

    (b)   that—

        (i)   the use, or continued use, of the special measure for the purpose of taking the witness's evidence would give rise to a significant risk of prejudice to the fairness of the proceedings or otherwise to the interests of justice, and

        (ii)   that risk significantly outweighs any risk of prejudice to the interests of the witness if the order is made.

    (5)   Subsection (7) of section 12 applies to the making of an order under subsection (2)(b) of this section as it applies to the making of an order under subsection (6) of that section but as if the references to the witness were to the witness within the meaning of this section.

    (6)   In this section, "current arrangements" means the arrangements in place at the time the review under this section is begun.

### Procedure in connection with orders under sections 12 and 13

D1.687

    **14.**—(1)   In section 5 (power to regulate procedure etc. in the Court of Session by act of sederunt) of the Court of Session Act 1988 (c. 36), after paragraph (d) there is inserted—

> "(da)   to regulate the procedure to be followed in proceedings in the Court in connection with the making of orders under sections 12(1) and (6) and 13(2) of the Vulnerable Witnesses (Scotland) Act 2004 (asp 3) ("the 2004 Act");

(db)   to regulate, so far as not regulated by the 2004 Act, the use in any proceedings in the Court of any special measures authorised by virtue of that Act to be used;".

(2)   In section 32(1) (power of Court of Session to regulate civil procedure in the sheriff court) of the Sheriff Courts (Scotland) Act 1971 (c. 58), after paragraph (e) there is inserted—

    "(ea)   regulating the procedure to be followed in connection with the making of orders under sections 12(1) and (6) and 13(2) of the Vulnerable Witnesses (Scotland) Act 2004 (asp 3) ("the 2004 Act");

    (eb)   regulating, so far as not regulated by the 2004 Act, the use of special measures authorised by virtue of that Act to be used;".

### Vulnerable witnesses: supplementary provision

**15.**—(1)   Subsection (2) below applies where—

   (a)   a party is considering for the purposes of a child witness notice or a vulnerable witness application which of the special measures is or are the most appropriate for the purpose of taking the evidence of the person to whom the notice or application relates, or

   (b)   the court is making an order under section 12(1) or (6) or 13(2).

(2)   The party or, as the case may be, the court must—

   (a)   have regard to the best interests of the witness, and

   (b)   take account of any views expressed by—

      (i)   the witness (having regard, where the witness is a child witness, to the witness's age and maturity), and

      (ii)   where the witness is a child witness, the witness's parent.

(3)   For the purposes of subsection (2)(b) above, where the witness is a child witness—

   (a)   the witness is to be presumed to be of sufficient age and maturity to form a view if aged 12 or older, and

   (b)   in the event that any views expressed by the witness are inconsistent with any views expressed by the witness's parent, the views of the witness are to be given greater weight.

(4)   In this section—

"parent", in relation to a child witness, means any person having parental responsibilities within the meaning of section 1(3) of the Children (Scotland) Act 1995 (c. 36) in relation to the child witness,

"the witness" means—

   (a)   in the case referred to in subsection (1)(a) above, the person to whom the child witness notice or vulnerable witness application relates,

   (b)   in the case referred to in subsection (1)(b) above, the person to whom the order would relate.

### Party to proceedings as a vulnerable witness

**16.**—   Where a child witness or other person who is giving or is to give evidence in or for the purposes of any civil proceedings (referred to in this section as "the witness") is a party to the proceedings—

   (a)   sections 12 and 13 have effect in relation to the witness as if references in those sections to the party citing or intending to cite the witness were references to the witness, and

   (b)   section 15 has effect in relation to the witness as if—

      (i)   in subsection (1), paragraph (a) were omitted, and

D1.688

D1.689

(ii) in subsection (2), the words "The party or, as the case may be," were omitted.

### Relevant proceedings: Principal Reporter's power to act for party to proceedings

D1.690

**16A.**—[1](1) Subsection (2) applies where a child witness or other person who is giving or is to give evidence in or for the purposes of relevant proceedings (referred to in this section as "the party") is a party to the proceedings.

(2) The Principal Reporter may, on the party's behalf—

(a) lodge a child witness notice under section 12(2),

(b) make a vulnerable witness application for an order under section 12(6),

(c) make an application under section 13(1)(a) for review of the current arrangements for taking a witness's evidence.

### Crown application and saving provision

D1.691

**17.**—(1) Sections 11 to 15 of this Act apply to the Crown.

(2) Nothing in section 12 or 13 of this Act affects any power or duty which a court has otherwise than by virtue of those sections to make or authorise any special arrangements for taking the evidence of any person in any civil proceedings.

### The special measures

D1.692

**18.**—(1) The special measures which may be authorised to be used by virtue of section 12 or 13 of this Act for the purpose of taking the evidence of a vulnerable witness are—

(a) taking of evidence by a commissioner in accordance with section 19,

(b) use of a live television link in accordance with section 20,

(c) use of screen in accordance with section 21,

(d) use of a supporter in accordance with section 22, and

(e) such other measures as the Scottish Ministers may, by order made by statutory instrument, prescribe.

(2) An order under subsection (1)(e) above is not to be made unless a draft of the statutory instrument containing the order has been laid before and approved by a resolution of the Scottish Parliament.

### Taking of evidence by a commissioner

D1.693

**19.**—(1) Where the special measure to be used is taking of evidence by a commissioner, the court must appoint a commissioner to take the evidence of the vulnerable witness in respect of whom the special measure is to be used.

(2) Proceedings before a commissioner appointed under subsection (1) above must be recorded by video recorder.

(3) A party to the proceedings—

(a) must not, except by leave of the court, be present in the room where such proceedings are taking place, but

(b) is entitled by such means as seem suitable to the court to watch and hear the proceedings.

---

[1] Prospectively inserted by the Children's Hearings (Scotland) Act 2011 (asp 1) Pt 17 s.176(4) (not yet in force).

(4)   The recording of the proceedings made in pursuance of subsection (2) above is to be received in evidence without being sworn to by witnesses.

## Live television link

**20.**—(1)   Where the special measure to be used is a live television link, the court must make such arrangements as seem to it appropriate for the vulnerable witness in respect of whom the special measure is to be used to give evidence by means of such a link.

(2)   Where—

    (a)   the live television link is to be used in proceedings in a sheriff court, but

    (b)   that court lacks accommodation or equipment necessary for the purpose of receiving such a link,

the sheriff may by order transfer the proceedings to any sheriff court in the same sheriffdom which has such accommodation or equipment available.

(3)   An order may be made under subsection (2) above—

    (a)   at any stage in the proceedings (whether before or after the commencement of the proof or other hearing at which the vulnerable witness is to give evidence), or

    (b)   in relation to a part of the proceedings.

**D1.694**

## Screens

**21.**—(1)   Where the special measure to be used is a screen, the screen must be used to conceal the parties to the proceedings from the sight of the vulnerable witness in respect of whom the special measure is to be used.

(2)   However, the court must make arrangements to ensure that the parties are able to watch and hear the vulnerable witness giving evidence.

(3)   Subsections (2) and (3) of section 20 apply for the purposes of use of a screen under this section as they apply for the purposes of use of a live television link under that section but as if—

    (a)   references to the live television link were references to the screen, and

    (b)   the reference to receiving such a link were a reference to the use of a screen.

**D1.695**

## Supporters

**22.**—(1)   Where the special measure to be used is a supporter, another person ("the supporter") nominated by or on behalf of the vulnerable witness in respect of whom the special measure is to be used may be present alongside the witness for the purpose of providing support whilst the witness is giving evidence.

(2)   Where the person nominated as the supporter is to give evidence in the proceedings, that person may not act as the supporter at any time before giving evidence.

(3)   The supporter must not prompt or otherwise seek to influence the vulnerable witness in the course of giving evidence.

**D1.696**

## Giving evidence in chief in the form of a prior statement

**22A.**—[1](1)   This section applies to proceedings in relation to—

**D1.697**

---

[1] Prospectively inserted by the Children's Hearings (Scotland) Act 2011 (asp 1) Pt 17 s.176(5) (not yet in force).

    (a)   an application made by virtue of section 93 or 94 of the 2011 Act to determine whether the ground mentioned in section 67(2)(j) of that Act is established, or

    (b)   an application under section 110 of that Act for review of a finding that the ground mentioned in section 67(2)(j) of that Act is established.

(2)   The special measures which may be authorised by virtue of section 12 or 13 for the purpose of taking the evidence of a vulnerable witness at a hearing to consider such an application include (in addition to those listed in section 18(1)) the giving of evidence in chief in the form of a prior statement in accordance with subsections (3) to (10).

(3)   Where that special measure is to be used, a statement made by the vulnerable witness (a "prior statement") may be lodged in evidence for the purposes of this section by or on behalf of the party citing the vulnerable witness.

(4)   A prior statement is admissible as the witness's evidence in chief, or as part of the witness's evidence in chief, without the witness being required to adopt or otherwise speak to the statement in giving evidence.

(5)   A prior statement is admissible as evidence of any matter stated in it of which direct oral evidence by the vulnerable witness would be admissible if given at the hearing.

(6)   A prior statement is admissible under this section only if—

    (a)   it is contained in a document, and

    (b)   at the time the statement was made, the vulnerable witness would have been a competent witness for the purposes of the hearing.

(7)   Subsection (6) does not apply to a prior statement—

    (a)   contained in a precognition on oath, or

    (b)   made in other proceedings (whether criminal or civil and whether taking place in the United Kingdom or elsewhere).

(8)   A prior statement of a type mentioned in subsection (7) is not admissible for the purposes of this section unless it is authenticated in such manner as may be prescribed by regulations made by statutory instrument by the Scottish Ministers.

(9)   This section does not affect the admissibility of any statement made by any person which is admissible otherwise than by virtue of this section.

(10)   In this section—

"document" has the meaning given by section 262(3) of the Criminal Procedure (Scotland) Act 1995 (c.46),

"statement"—

    (a)   includes—

        (i)   any representation, however made or expressed, of fact or opinion, and

        (ii)   any part of a statement, but

    (b)   does not include a statement in a precognition other than a precognition on oath.

(11)   For the purposes of this section, a statement is contained in a document where the person who makes it—

    (a)   makes the statement in the document personally,

    (b)   makes a statement which is, with or without the person's knowledge, embodied in a document by whatever means or by any person who has direct personal knowledge of the making of the statement, or

    (c)   approves a document as embodying the statement.

(12)    A statutory instrument containing regulations under subsection (8) is subject to annulment in pursuance of a resolution of the Scottish Parliament.

## Establishment of grounds of referral to children's hearings: restrictions on evidence

**23.**    Establishment of grounds of referral to children's hearings: restrictions on evidence

**D1.698**

After section 68 (application to sheriff to establish grounds of referral) of the Children (Scotland) Act 1995 (c. 36) there is inserted—

### Restrictions on evidence in certain cases involving sexual abuse

"**68A**(1)    This section applies in relation to—

**D1.699**

    (a)    an application under section 65(7) or (9) of this Act in which the ground of referral to be established is a condition mentioned in—

        (i)    paragraph (b) of subsection (2) of section 52 of this Act where that condition is alleged to be satisfied by reference to sexual behaviour engaged in by any person,

        (ii)    paragraph (d), (e) or (f) of that subsection where that condition is alleged to be satisfied by reference to a relevant offence, or

        (iii)    paragraph (g) of that subsection, or

    (b)    an application under section 85 of this Act for a review of a finding that any such ground of referral is established.

(2)    In hearing the application, the sheriff shall not admit, or allow questioning designed to elicit, evidence which shows or tends to show that the child who is the subject of the application or any other witness giving evidence at the hearing (such child or other witness being referred to in this section and section 68B of this Act as "the witness")—

    (a)    is not of good character (whether in relation to sexual matters or otherwise),

    (b)    has, at any time, engaged in sexual behaviour not forming part of the subject matter of the ground of referral,

    (c)    has, at any time (other than shortly before, at the same time as or shortly after the acts which form part of the subject matter of the ground of referral), engaged in such behaviour, not being sexual behaviour, as might found the inference that the witness is not a credible or reliable witness, or

    (d)    has, at any time, been subject to any such condition or predisposition as might found the inference referred to in paragraph (c) above.

(3)    In subsection (1)(a)(ii) above, "relevant offence" means—

    (a)    an offence mentioned in paragraph 1 or 4 of Schedule 1 (offences against children under the age of 17 to which special provisions apply) to the Criminal Procedure (Scotland) Act 1995 (c. 46), or

    (b)    any other offence mentioned in that Schedule where there is a substantial sexual element in the alleged commission of the offence.

(4)    In subsection (2)(b) and (c) above—

    (a)    "the subject matter of the ground of referral" means—

        (i)    in the case of an application in which the ground of referral to be established is the condition referred to in paragraph (a)(i) of subsection (1) above, the sexual behaviour referred to in that paragraph,

        (ii)    in the case of any other application, the acts or behaviour constituting the offence by reference to which the ground of referral is alleged to be established,

    and

    (b)    the reference to engaging in sexual behaviour includes a reference to undergoing or being made subject to any experience of a sexual nature.

### Exceptions to restrictions under section 68A

**68B**(1)    The sheriff hearing an application referred to in subsection (1) of section 68A of this Act may, on an application by any party to the proceedings, admit such evidence or allow such questioning as is referred to in subsection (2) of that section if satisfied that—

**D1.700**

(a)   the evidence or questioning will relate only to a specific occurrence or occurrences of sexual or other behaviour or to specific facts demonstrating—

     (i)   the character of the witness, or

     (ii)   any condition or predisposition to which the witness is or has been subject,

(b)   that occurrence or those occurrences of behaviour or facts are relevant to establishing the ground of referral, and

(c)   the probative value of the evidence sought to be admitted or elicited is significant and is likely to outweigh any risk of prejudice to the proper administration of justice arising from its being admitted or elicited.

(2)   In subsection (1) above—

(a)   the reference to an occurrence or occurrences of sexual behaviour includes a reference to undergoing or being made subject to any experience of a sexual nature,

(b)   "the proper administration of justice" includes—

     (i)   appropriate protection of the witness's dignity and privacy, and

     (ii)   ensuring the facts and circumstances of which the sheriff is made aware are relevant to an issue to be put before the sheriff and commensurate with the importance of that issue to the sheriff's decision on the question whether the ground of referral is established.

(3)   In this section, "the witness" means the child who is the subject of the application referred to in section 68A(1) or other witness in respect of whom the evidence is sought to be admitted or elicited.".

## PART 3 – MISCELLANEOUS AND GENERAL

*Abolition of the competence test*

### Abolition of the competence test for witnesses in criminal and civil proceedings

D1.701     **24.**—(1)   The evidence of any person called as a witness (referred to in this section as "the witness") in criminal or civil proceedings is not inadmissible solely because the witness does not understand—

(a)   the nature of the duty of a witness to give truthful evidence, or

(b)   the difference between truth and lies.

(2)   Accordingly, the court must not, at any time before the witness gives evidence, take any step intended to establish whether the witness understands those matters.

# ACTS OF SEDERUNT, ETC.

*4 June 1913.*

Book L—Sheriff Courts

## Chapter I—

### Nautical Assessors in Sheriff Court (C.A.S. L, I)

**Procedure and number of assessors**

1. In any action or proceeding in the sheriff court to which the Nautical Assessors Act 1894 applies, the number of assessors to be summoned to the assistance of the court at any particular stage of the cause, whether on the initiative of the court or on the application of any party, shall be one in the case of a proof, and one or more than one in the case of a hearing on appeal, as the court shall think fit, provided always (*a*) that intimation of the name or names of the person or persons proposed to be summoned shall be given to the parties by the sheriff clerk at least *eight* days before the proof or the hearing for which the summons is to be issued; (*b*) that if any party intends to object to the person or persons proposed to be summoned he shall state his objection, with the grounds of it, by minute lodged in process within *two* days after receipt of the intimation; (*c*) that the objections, if any, shall be disposed of by the court at least *three* days before the proof or the hearing; (*d*) that if the objection is sustained, the like procedure shall be followed for securing another assessor, and the court shall, if necessary for that purpose, adjourn the proof or the hearing; and (*e*) that it shall be the duty of the sheriff-clerk, if no minute is lodged as aforesaid, or when any objection has been taken and repelled, to arrange for the attendance at the proof or hearing of the person or persons named in the foresaid intimation.

**Remuneration of assessor**

2.[1] The remuneration of every person attending as a nautical assessor under the aforesaid Act of Parliament shall be £3.15 a day for each day on which he so attends, and also for any Sunday over which he is necessarily detained at the seat of court, besides maintenance and travelling expenses. In the case of an assessor resident out of Scotland, he shall be entitled to charge a day for coming and a day for going at the above rate, but other assessors shall not be entitled to a fee for travelling days unless, owing to the distance from the seat of the court at which they reside, it is impossible, with reasonable convenience, to travel on the day or days on which they are required to sit in court.

**Consignation to meet expense**

3. When, on the motion of a party to the cause, an assessor or assessors is or are to be summoned under the provisions of the foresaid Act of Parliament, the motion shall only be granted on condition that the party making it shall consign with the

---

[1] As amended by the Decimal Currency Act 1969, s.10(1).

sheriff clerk such sum to meet the fees and expenses above provided as the court may determine; and when an assessor or assessors is or are to be summoned *ex proprio motu* of the court, such consignation shall be made by the pursuer of the action, unless the court shall otherwise direct.

**D2.2**

Chapter II—

**Letters of Request—(foreign Witnesses) (C.A.S. L, II)**

*[Repealed by the Act of Sederunt (Sheriff Court Ordinary Cause Rules) 1993 (SI 1993/1956) Sch.2 (effective January 1, 1994).]*

**D2.3**

Chapter VII—

**Winding up under the Building Societies Act 1874 (C.A.S., L, VII)**

**Form of application for winding up**

    **1.** All applications presented to the court for the winding up of a society registered under the Building Societies Act 1874, either voluntarily under the supervision of the sheriff court, or by the court, shall be by petition in form as nearly as may be of initial writs under the Act 7 Edw. VII. c. 51 (Sheriff Courts Act 1907), and the court shall order service and advertisement thereof in the *Edinburgh Gazette*, and such further advertisement, if any, as the court may consider necessary, and shall appoint the said petition to be heard on such early day as may be suitable.

**Petition to be printed**

    **2.** The said petition shall be printed, and every shareholder and creditor of the company shall be entitled to receive from the solicitor of the petitioner a copy thereof on demand at his office.

**Procedure on Petition**

    **3.** The court on the day appointed may hear the petitioner's proof in support of the petition, and may also hear any parties interested in support thereof or in opposition thereto, and also any application which may follow thereon in the course of the winding up, either in open court or in chambers, and may order such answers as may be deemed necessary, and may adjourn the hearing; and after such inquiry, by proof or otherwise, as may be deemed necessary, the court may order the society to be wound up, or may dismiss the petition, or may make such other order as may be just.

**Procedure in winding up**

    **4.** The court may, as to all matters relating to the winding up, have regard to the wishes of the creditors or members, as proved by sufficient evidence; and may direct meetings of the creditors or members to be summoned, held, and conducted in such manner as may be directed, for the purpose of ascertaining their wishes, and may appoint a person to act as chairman of any such meeting, and to report the result of such meeting to the court. In the case of creditors regard is to be had to the value of the debt due to each creditor; and in the case of members, to the number of votes conferred on each member by the regulations of the society, or failing such regulations, to the number of shares held by each member.

## Liquidator's appointment

**5.** For the purpose of winding up a society, a liquidator shall be appointed. The shareholders may nominate a liquidator at any meeting held by them, and called in terms of section 32 of the said Building Societies Act, for the purpose of resolving to wind up the society under supervision of the court, and of presenting a petition to the court to that effect; and the court shall confirm the nomination so made, unless sufficient cause to the contrary be shown. If the court do not confirm the nomination, or if no such nomination has been made before the presenting of the petition, the court shall, at the hearing of the said petition, or at any subsequent time, nominate a liquidator, either provisionally or otherwise. In the case of winding up by the court, the liquidator shall be nominated by the court. The court may also determine whether any and what security shall be given by the liquidator; and every appointment of a liquidator shall be advertised in such manner as the court may appoint.

## Liquidator's tenure of office and remuneration

**6.** Any liquidator may resign, or may be removed by the court on due cause shown; and any vacancy in the office of a liquidator shall be filled up by the court. There shall be paid to the liquidator such salary or remuneration by way of percentage or otherwise as the court may direct.

## Special powers

**7.** When in course of winding up the society it shall be necessary to carry on the business thereof for a time, or to make up titles to heritable property, or to compromise claims with contributories, these powers shall only be exercised with the sanction of the court, obtained upon a note presented to the court setting forth the grounds upon which the powers are asked for. The court may, on the presentation of such notes, order such intimation thereof as shall be deemed suitable and expedient in the circumstances. And further, it shall be competent to the liquidator to apply to the court for instruction and direction in regard to any matter wherein, in his judgment, such instruction and direction are necessary.

## Law agents and factors

**8.** The liquidator shall have power to appoint a law agent to assist him in the performance of his duties, and also, with sanction of the court, to appoint a factor for taking charge of or managing any of the properties of the society.

## General meetings of members in voluntary liquidation

**9.** Where a society is being wound up voluntarily under the supervision of the court, the liquidator may from time to time during the continuance of such winding up call general meetings of the members of the society; and in the event of the winding up continuing for more than one year, the liquidator shall call a general meeting of the members at the end of the first year, and of each succeeding year from the commencement of the winding up, or as soon thereafter as may be convenient, and shall lay before such meeting an account showing his acts and dealings, and the manner in which the winding up has been conducted during the preceding year.

## State of liabilities and assets, etc., and objections thereto

**10.** The liquidator shall, as soon as may be after an order is made for winding up a society, make up and lodge in process a state showing—

    (a)  The liabilities and assets of the society in detail.

    (b)  The number of members, and the amounts standing to their credit in the books of the society.

    (c)  The liabilities of members of the society in terms of sections 13 and 14 of the Building Societies Act and of the rules of the society.

    (d)  The claims of depositors and other creditors, and the provision to be made for their payment.

    (e)  The sums to be repaid to the members, if any, after payment of the debts due by the society.

And such state may be objected to by any person having interest, and may be amended from time to time.

And the court may, after such notice or advertisement as may be thought proper, and after hearing any party or parties, sanction and approve of such state, or disapprove thereof; and if the same be sanctioned and approved of, the court may authorise the funds to be distributed in terms of such state; and thereafter, on being satisfied that payment has been made to the creditors of the society and depositors so far as possible, and to the members of the society in terms of the said state, or when any sum or sums payable to any member or members of the society have not been claimed, that such consignation thereof has been made by the liquidator as the court may direct, the court shall declare the winding up of the said society to be at an end and the society dissolved, discharge the liquidator of his whole actings and intromissions, and appoint his bond of caution, if any, to be delivered up.

## Audit of liquidator's accounts

**11.** The accounts of the liquidator shall be audited annually. The audit shall be made by such person as the court may select, whether he be an auditor of court or not, and the auditor shall report to the court the audit so made. If it shall appear to the auditor that any payment by the liquidator should be disallowed, or that any charge has been incurred, as against the estate, which was unnecessary, or that any sum ought to have been, but is not, brought into account, he shall in his report bring the same under the notice of the court, setting forth the grounds of his opinion, and the court shall pronounce judgment upon the matter so reported upon as may seem just.

## Expenses of winding up

**12.** The court may, in the event of the assets being insufficient to satisfy the liabilities, make an order as to the payment out of the estate of the society of the costs, charges, and expenses incurred in winding up the society in such order of priority as may be considered just.

## Liquidator to deposit moneys in bank

**13.** The liquidator shall lodge all money received by him on account of the society in one of the banks in Scotland established by Act of Parliament or Royal Charter, in a separate account or on deposit, in his name as such liquidator, within seven days after the receipt thereof, unless the court has otherwise directed. If the liquidator shall keep in his hands more than £50 of money belonging to the society for more than seven days he shall be charged in his account with a sum at the rate of 20 per cent. per annum on the excess of the said sum of £50 for such time as it shall be in his hands beyond the said seven days, and the court may, in respect of any such retention, disallow the salary or remuneration of such liquidator, or may remove him from his office.

Chapter IX—

**D2.4**

## Inferior Courts Judgments Extension Act 1882 (C.A.S., L, IX)

### Register of English and Irish judgments

**1.** In each county in Scotland, and at each place in such county at which the ordinary courts of the sheriffs-substitute are held, there shall be kept by the sheriff clerk a book, to be called " The Register of English and Irish Judgments ", in which shall be registered *in extenso* all certificates issued in terms of the said Act, from any of the inferior courts of England and Ireland, with the note of presentation appended to such certificate required by said Act.

### Attestation of registration

**2.** After registration as aforesaid, the sheriff clerk shall append to such certificate and note of presentation an attestation, signed by himself, of the registration of the same, in the terms set forth in the annexed Schedule A, which registered certificate, with the attestation thereon by the sheriff clerk, shall be sufficient warrant to officers of court to charge the debtor in the judgment debt to make payment of the whole sums recoverable under such judgment, with the costs of obtaining and registering such certificate, within fifteen days after the date of such charge, and to use any further diligence that may be competent.

### Fees

**3.** For granting any certificate issued in terms of said Act, and for registering any such certificate, with note of presentation as aforesaid, and attesting that such registration has been made, the sheriff clerk shall be entitled to charge the fees set forth in the Schedule B hereto annexed and for preparing and presenting any note of presentation required by said Act and obtaining the registration of any certificate, and the attestation of such registration, law agents shall be entitled to charge the fees also set forth in said Schedule B.

### Sheriff clerk

**4.** The words " sheriff clerk " shall include sheriff clerk depute.

SCHEDULE A

*[Place and date.]*

I hereby declare that the foregoing certificate and note of presentation have been duly registered by me in the " Register of English and Irish Judgments " kept at this place, in terms of the Act 45 & 46 Vict. c. 31 and relative Act of Sederunt, Book L, Chapter IX.

A.B., sheriff clerk (or sheriff clerk depute) of

SCHEDULE B[1]

*2. Law Agents' Fees*

1.  For preparing and presenting any note of presentation as required by said Act, and obtaining registration of certificate issued in terms of said Act, with such note of presentation together with attestation of such registration.

| | |
|---|---|
| In cases where the debt or sum decerned for does not exceed £12 | 7p |
| In cases where the debt or sum decerned for exceeds £12 and does not exceed £50 | 13p |
| In cases where the debt or sum decerned for exceeds £50 and does not exceed £200 | 17p |
| In all other cases | 25p |

Chapter X—

**Proceedings under the Representation of the People Act 1983 (C.A.S., L, X)**
*[Repealed by SI 1999/929 effective July 1, 1999]*

Chapter XI—

**Appeals to the Court under the Pilotage Act 1913 (C.A.S., L, XI)**
*[Repealed by SI 1999/929 effective July 1, 1999]*

D2.5

Chapter XV—

**Removings (C.A.S., L, XV)**

*(Statute 1555, anent Warnings of Tenants)*

1.  Where a tenant is bound by his tack to remove without warning at the issue or determination of his tack, it shall be lawful to the heritor or other setter of the tack, upon such obligation, to obtain letters of homing, and thereupon to charge the tenant with homing forty days preceding the term of Whitsunday in the year in which his tack is to determine, or forty days preceding any other term of Whitsunday thereafter: And upon production of such tack and homing duly executed to the sheriff or sheriff-substitute of the shire where the lands lie, they are hereby authorised and required, within six days after the term of removal appointed by the tack, to eject such tenant, and to deliver the possession void to the setter, or those having right from him.

2.  Where the tenant hath not obliged himself to remove without warning, in such case it shall be lawful to the heritor or other setter of the tack in his option, either to use the order prescribed by the Act of Parliament made in the year 1555, intituled "Act anent the Warning of Tenants", and thereupon pursue a warning and ejection, or to bring his action of removing against the tenant before the Judge Ordinary: And such action being called before the Judge Ordinary at least forty days before the term of Whitsunday, shall be held as equal to a warning execute in terms of the foresaid Act: And the Judge shall thereupon proceed to determine in the removing in the terms of that Act, in the same manner as if a warning had been executed in terms of the foresaid Act of Parliament.

---

[1] As amended by the Decimal Currency Act 1969, s.10(2).

**3.** Where a tack is assigned and the assignation not intimated by an instrument, or where the lands are sublet in whole or in part to sub-tenants, such homing execute as aforesaid, or where process of removing and decreet is obtained, or where warning in terms of the Act 1555 is used against the principal or original tacksman, the same shall be effectual against the assignees or sub-tenants, one or more, and the action of removing against the principal or original tacksman, and decreet of removing following there on, shall be effectual against such assignees and sub-tenants as aforesaid, and shall be sufficient ground of ejecting them, anything in the former practice to the contrary notwithstanding.

**4.** Where a tenant has irritated his tack by suffering two years' rent to be in arrear, it shall be lawful to the setter or heritor to declare the irritancy before the Judge Ordinary, and to insist in a summar removing before him: and it shall be lawful to the sheriff or sheriff-substitute to find the irritancy incurred, and to decem in the removing, any practice to the contrary notwithstanding.

**5.**[1] Where a tenant shall run in arrear of one full year's rent, or shall desert his possession and leave it unlaboured at the usual time of labouring, in these, or either of these cases, it shall be lawful to the heritor or other setter of the lands to bring his action against the tenant before the Judge Ordinary, who is hereby empowered and required to decem and ordain the tenant to find caution for the arrears, and for payment of the rent for the five crops following or during the currency of the tack, if the tack is of shorter endurance than five years, within a certain time to be limited by the judge, and failing thereof, to decem the tenant summarily to remove, and to eject him in the same manner as if the tack were determined and the tenant had been legally warned in terms of the foresaid Act 1555.

**6.** Upon passing of any bill of suspension of a decreet or process of removing, or at least within ten days after the date of the deliverance thereon, the complainer shall be bound to find sufficient caution, not only for implement of what shall be decerned on the suspension upon discussion thereof, but also for damage and expense in case the same shall be found due; and upon the complainers failing to find caution as aforesaid, such bill of suspension shall be held to be refused, and it shall be lawful for the other party to proceed in his action of removing, or in the execution of his decreet, as if no such bill of suspension had been presented or passed.

**7.** In all removings, whether originally brought before this court, or by suspension, they will proceed and determine the same summarily without abridging the course of any roll.

---

[1] Anent removings, s.5 shall not apply in any case where the procedure under s.20 of the Agricultural Holdings (Scotland) Act 1991 is competent.

# CERTAIN FORMS OF PROCEDURE IN THE SHERIFFS ORDINARY AND SMALL DEBT COURTS AND FOR THE CONFIRMATION OF EXECUTORS, AND ANENT THE REGISTERS OR RECORDS TO BE KEPT BY SHERIFF CLERKS OF CONSIGNATIONS, SEQUESTRATIONS FOR RENT, REPORTS OF ARRESTMENT, AND REPORTS OF POINDING AND SALE 1933[1]

(SI 1933/48) **D2.6**

*3 February 1933.*

The Lords of Council and Session, in virtue of the powers conferred on them by section 2 of the Courts of Law Fees (Scotland) Act 1895, and by section 16 of the Sheriff Courts and Legal Oficers (Scotland) Act 1927 with the concurrence of the Treasury, enact and declare as follows:

**1.** Schedule A annexed hereto is hereby substituted for Schedules A and B annexed to C.A.S., Book L, Chapter IV.

**2.** It shall not be necessary to keep, as a separate book, the "Register of Sequestrations for Rent" prescribed by section 7 of the Hypothec Amendment (Scotland) Act 1867. The particulars specified in the Schedule to that Act may be recorded in the Act Book of Court or other suitable register kept by the sheriff clerk.

**3.** The record kept by the sheriff clerk of warrants for arrestment on the dependence, reports thereof, loosings of arrestment, reports of poindings, reports of sales under poindings, and reports of sales following upon sequestrations for rent may be made in the appropriate A or B Register or other suitable register approved by the sheriff.

**7.** In Summary Applications for removing under section 38 of the Sheriff Courts **D2.7** (Scotland) Act 1907, the Book of Causes, containing entries of the sheriffs deliverances, interlocutors, decrees and warrants, with the dates thereof, shall be signed each court day by the sheriff; and the forms contained in Schedule F annexed hereto shall be substituted for Form L annexed to Schedule I of the said Act, shall be signed by the sheriff clerk, shall have the force and effect of extracts, and may be written on the principal complaint, on the copy thereof, or, with necessary modifications separately.

**9.** This Act of Sederunt shall come into operation on the 1st day of March 1933. **D2.8**

---

[1] As amended by S. R. & O. 1936 No. 1410.

SCHEDULE A

REGISTER OF SHERIFF COURT CONSIGNATIONS

| Date of Consignation. | Parties by whom Consignation is made—Cause and Court. | Sum Consigned. | Bank in which Money Lodged. | Date of Lodging in Bank. | Date of Payment. | Deposits withdrawn from Bank. | | | To Whom Paid and Receipts. | Sum Paid. |
|---|---|---|---|---|---|---|---|---|---|---|
| | | | | | | Principal Sums. | Interest Thereon. | Total. | | |
| | | | | | | | | | | |

SCHEDULE F

FORMS OF EXTRACTS OF DECREES IN SUMMARY REMOVING PETITION OR COMPLAINT

(1) EXTRACT OF DECREE AND WARRANT OF EJECTION

At.......... the.......... day of.......... 19.........., the Sheriff.......... of Decerned and hereby Decerns, Granted and hereby Grants Warrant for Ejecting the said.......... Defender, and others mentioned in the Complaint, from the subjects therein specified, such Ejection not being sooner than.......... 19 at Twelve o'clock noon, Found and hereby Finds the said Defender liable to the Pursuer in the sum of.......... of Expenses, and Decerns and Ordains instant Execution by Arrestment, and also Execution to pass hereon by Poinding and Sale for said Expenses, after.......... a of Ten free days.

Sheriff Clerk.

(2) EXTRACT OF DECREE OF ABSOLVITOR

At.......... the.......... day of.......... 19.......... the Sheriff of.......... Assoilzied and hereby Assoilzies the within designed.......... Defender from the foregoing Complaint, and Found and hereby Finds the within designed.......... Pursuer, liable to the.......... Defender in the sum of of Expenses, and Decerns and Ordains instant Execution by Arrestment, and also Execution to pass hereon by Poinding and Sale, after a.......... of Ten free days.

Sheriff Clerk

(3) EXTRACT OF DECREE OF DISMISSAL

At.......... the.......... day of.......... 19.......... the Sheriff of.......... Dismissed and hereby Dismisses the foregoing Complaint, Found and hereby Finds the within designed.......... Pursuer, liable to the.......... Defender in the sum of.......... of Expenses; and Decerns and Ordains instant execution by Arrestment, and also execution to pass hereon by Poinding and Sale after a.......... of Ten free days.

Sheriff Clerk.

*19 December 1935.*

The Lords of Council and Session, in terms of section 16(2) and section 31(5) of the Betting and Lotteries Act 1934 (hereinafter called "the Act") do hereby enact and declare as follows:—

The holder of a license which has been revoked under section 16 of the Act may appeal against such revocation, at any time within fourteen days after receipt by him of the notice of revocation, by initial writ under the Sheriff Courts (Scotland) Acts 1907 and 1913 and such appeal shall be disposed of as a summary application as defined in the said Acts.

# AMEND THE SHERIFF COURTS (SCOTLAND) ACT 1907 AND CODIFY-ING ACT OF SEDERUNT OF 4TH JUNE 1913, 1936[1]

(SR&O 1936/780)

D2.10

*16 July 1936.*

The Lords of Council and Session, under and by virtue of the provisions of the Administration of Justice (Scotland) Act 1933 and of the powers thereby conferred on them do hereby enact and declare:—

**3.**   That section 1 of Chapter III of Book L of the Codifying Act of Sederunt of 4th June 1913 (C.A.S., L, III, 1) is hereby repealed and the following provision substituted therefor:—

  (1)  *Certificate by Officer of Inland Revenue.*

      (1)  No decree, warrant, or order for payment of any consigned money; and (2) no decree, warrant or order for transfer or conveyance to any person of any stocks, shares, or other property, heritable or moveable, in any process for the distribution of the estate of any deceased, pending in the sheriff court, shall issue until there is lodged with the sheriff clerk a certificate by the proper officer in the Department of Inland Revenue that all income tax, estate duty, legacy duty, succession duty, and any other duty payable to the Commissioners of Inland Revenue, have been paid and satisfied to the Department in respect of any such money, stocks, shares, or other property or any part thereof so to be paid, transferred, or conveyed as aforesaid.

**4.**   That this Act of Sederunt shall come into force on 1st October 1936.

---

[1] The amendments made by this Act of Sederunt to the Sheriff Courts (Scotland) Act 1907 have been incorporated in the print of that Act.

**D2.11**

*22 January 1952.*

The Lords of Council and Session in exercise of the powers conferred upon them
by section 11 of the Reserve and Auxiliary Forces (Protection of Civil Interests) Act
1951 and of all other powers enabling them in that behalf, do hereby enact and
declare as follows:

### Citation and commencement

**1.**   This Act of Sederunt may be cited as the Act of Sederunt (Reserve and
Auxiliary Forces (Protection of Civil Interests) 1952, and shall come into operation
on the first day of March 1952.

### Interpretation

**2.**—(1)   In this Act of Sederunt, unless the context otherwise requires, the following expressions have the meanings hereby assigned to them that is to say:

"the Act" means the Reserve and Auxiliary Forces (Protection of Civil
Interests) Act 1951;

"declaratory order" means an order under paragraph (c) of subsection (1) of
section 9 of the Act;

"leave" means leave of the appropriate court under the Act.

(2)   Any reference in this Act of Sederunt to a numbered form shall be construed
as a reference to the form of that number in the Schedule to this Act of Sederunt or a
form to the like effect.

(3)   The Interpretation Act 1889 shall apply to the interpretation of this Act of
Sederunt as it applies to the interpretation of an Act of Parliament.

### Appropriate court

**3.**—(1)   The appropriate court in relation to an application for leave to enforce,
or for a declaratory order relating to, a decree, shall be:

(a)   the court which pronounced the decree; or

(b)   if the judgment has been obtained in a court outside Scotland and is
registered in a court in Scotland for the purpose of enforcement, the
court in which the judgment is registered.

(2)   The appropriate court in relation to an application for leave to exercise any
right or remedy mentioned in subsection (2) of section 8 or in paragraph (b) of
subsection (1) of section 25 of the Act, or for a declaratory order relating to the
exercise of any such right or remedy, shall be any court which according to present
practice has jurisdiction to deal with causes or matters of the nature and value
involved in the application.

(3)   The appropriate court for the giving of directions for restoration of property,
repayment of money or other measures under subsection (4) of section 13 of the Act
shall be:

(a)   where there has been an omission to obtain leave required under section
8 or section 25 of the Act, the court having jurisdiction to give such
leave;

    (b)   where there has been a failure to observe a restriction subject to which leave so required was given, the court which imposed the restriction or condition; and

    (c)   where there has been a contravention of the prohibition in subsection (2) of section 10 of the Act against dealing with the goods, the court having jurisdiction to make a declaratory order in respect of the taking possession of the goods:

Provided that where any proceedings which lie by virtue of any such omission, failure or contravention have been instituted in any court, that court shall have jurisdiction to give such directions as aforesaid.

### Form of, and procedure on, applications

**4.**—(1)   Subject as hereinafter provided an application under the Act shall be initiated by a document (hereinafter referred to as an "application") in the forms, as nearly as may be:

    (a)   in the case of an application for leave to enforce a decree, or to present a petition for sequestration or a winding up petition founded on the non-payment of money due under a decree, of Form 1;

    (b)   in the case of an application for a declaratory order relating to a decree, of Form 2;

    (c)   in the case of an application for leave to exercise any right or remedy mentioned in subsection (2) of section 8 or in paragraph (b) of subsection (1) of section 25 of the Act, of Form 3; and

    (d)   in the case of an application for a declaratory order relating to the exercise of any such right or remedy as aforesaid, of Form 4.

(2)   An application under the foregoing sub-paragraph shall be lodged in the case of an application to the Court of Session, in the Petition Department and, in the case of an application to the sheriff court, with the sheriff clerk. Every such application so lodged shall have attached to it a blank sheet of process paper.

(3)   Upon the lodging of any application as aforesaid the clerk in charge of the Petition Department, or the sheriff clerk, as the case may be, shall appoint a diet for appearance and shall grant a warrant for intimation in Form 5, and a copy of the application, of the warrant for intimation and (except in the case of an application for a declaratory order) of the note set forth in Form 6 or Form 7, as the case may require, shall, not later than two days after the granting of the said warrant, be served upon the person liable to implement the decree or perform the obligation in question, or upon the proper person as defined in subsection (3) of section nine of the Act, as the case may be.

(4)   A certificate of service in Form 8 shall be endorsed by or on behalf of the applicant on the process copy of the application before the date appointed in the warrant for intimation for the diet for appearance.

(5)   At the diet for appearance appointed in the warrant for intimation the appropriate court shall dispose of the application, or appoint such further procedure as it may deem necessary.

### Application for leave to enforce a decree made at the same time as motion for decree

**5.**   An application for leave to enforce a decree may be made by verbal motion at the time when the motion for decree is made, and the appropriate court may, then, if it thinks fit, dispose of the application if:

(a) in the case of a defended action, the court is satisfied that due intimation of the intention so to apply has been made to the defender;

(b) in the case of an undefended action in the Court of Session or an ordinary cause in the sheriff court in which no notice of appearance has been lodged or in which the defender does not answer, a notice as nearly as may be in the form of Form 9 has been sent to the defender at least six clear days before the application is made; and

(c) in the case of a summary cause or small debt action in the sheriff court, there has been sent to the defender, either along with the initial writ or summons or at least six clear days before the application is made, a notice as nearly as may be in the form of Form 10.

### Intimation to persons affected in certain cases

**6.** In the case of an application for leave to enforce a decree or for leave to exercise any right or remedy mentioned in subsection (2) of section 8 or in paragraph (b) of subsection (1) of section 25 of the Act the appropriate court, before considering the application, may order intimation thereof to any person whom the court considers to be interested therein, including the spouse of the person liable to implement the decree or perform the obligation in question, and may give to any person to whom intimation is so made an opportunity to be heard.

### Service of application or notice on representative of service man

**7.** Where any person upon whom an application or notice is to be served under this Act of Sederunt (in this paragraph referred to as " the respondent ") is for the time being performing a period of relevant service, the appropriate court may, if, in view of any special circumstances, it considers it expedient to do so, authorise the application or notice to be served instead on any person (including the spouse of the respondent) who appears to the court to have been entrusted with the management of the respondent's affairs in general or of the premises or property to which the application or notice relates.

### Application by representative on behalf of service man

**8.** Where a person who would be entitled to apply for a declaratory order is for the time being performing a period of relevant service, the appropriate court may, if, in view of any special circumstances, it considers it expedient to do so, treat as an application made by him for a declaratory order an application for that purpose made on his behalf by his spouse or by any other person acting in good faith in his interest.

### Appearance of representative of service man

**9.**—(1) Where an application or notice is served in the manner provided by paragraph 7 of this Act of Sederunt or an application is made in the manner provided by the last foregoing paragraph of this Act of Sederunt, the person on whom the application or notice is served or by whom the application is made, as the case may be (in this paragraph referred to as " the representative "), shall be entitled to attend and be heard at that hearing of the application as if he were the respondent, or the person on whose behalf the application is made, as the case may be.

(2) If the appropriate court is of opinion that the representative has acted unreasonably in opposing, making or presenting the application, the appropriate

court may make an order for payment by him of the expenses of any other party, but save as aforesaid the representative shall not be personally liable for any such expenses.

## Recall or variation of orders

10. Any order made on any application referred to in this Act of Sederunt may, should subsequent circumstances render it just so to do, be recalled, suspended, discharged, or otherwise varied or altered on a motion to the court which made such order, after written intimation to all parties interested of the intention to make such motion.

## Application may be heard and disposed of in Chambers

11. Any application under this Act of Sederunt to the Court of Session or to the sheriff court may be heard and disposed of by a judge or by the sheriff, as the case may be, either in court or in Chambers, whether during session, vacation or recess and any such application may be heard *in camera* if a judge or the sheriff so orders.

## Postal services

12. Where the service of any document is required by this Act of Sederunt to be made, and the service is made by post, the date of making it shall be reckoned as the day after that on which the document was posted.

## Fee fund dues

13. No fee fund dues or court fees shall be payable in proceedings on any application referred to in this Act of Sederunt.

## Expenses

14. The expenses of proceedings on any application referred to in this Act of Sederunt shall be in the discretion of the appropriate court; and the appropriate court, if it thinks fit, may award no expenses or modify the amount thereof.

SCHEDULE

Form 1

Reserve and Auxiliary Forces (Protection of Civil Interests) Act 1951

Unto [specify Court]

Application

for

A.B. [designation]

A.B. applies to the court for leave to enforce a decree of the court dated [date] against the therein designed C.D., a copy of which decree is appended hereto [or otherwise competently produced and referred to] *or* [as the case may be] to present a petition for sequestration of the estate of C.D. [designation] or for the winding up of [specify company].

[Signature of applicant or solicitor or counsel.]

[Place and date.]

Form 2

Reserve and Auxiliary Forces (Protection of Civil Interests) Act 1951

Unto [specify court]

Application

for

A.B. [designation]

A.B. applies to the court for an order under paragraph (c) of subsection (1) of section 9 of the said Act directing that subsection (1) of section 8 of the said Act shall apply in relation to a decree by the court dated [date] against him in favour of the therein designed C.D., a copy of which decree is appended hereto [or otherwise competently produced and referred to].

[Signature of applicant or solicitor or counsel.]

[Place and date.]

## Form 3
Reserve and Auxiliary Forces (Protection of Civil Interests) Act 1951

Unto [specify Court]

Application
for
A.B. [designation]

A.B. applies to the court for leave to exercise the following right [or remedy] that is to say [specify right or remedy by reference to subsection (2) of section 8 or to paragraph (b) of subsection (1) of section 25 of the Act] against CD. [designation] who is under the following obligation to the said A.B. [give brief particulars of obligation in question].

[Signature of applicant or solicitor or counsel.]

[Place and date.]

## Form 4
Reserve and Auxiliary Forces (Protection of Civil Interests) Act 1951

Unto [specify Court]

Application
for
A.B. [designation]

A.B. applies to the court for an order under paragraph (c) of subsection (1) of section 9 of the said Act directing that subsection (2) of section 8 of the said Act shall apply in relation to the following obligation which the said a.b. Is alleged to be liable to perform in favour of cd. [designation] that is to say [give brief particulars of obligation].

[Signature of Applicant Or Solicitor Or Counsel.]

[Place and Date.]

## Form 5
Reserve and Auxiliary Forces (protection of Civil Interests) Act 1951

[Place and date.]

The court grants warrant for intimation and appoints parties to appear on the.......... day of.......... at ..........o'clock in [place].

[Signature of clerk of court.]

Note.—the clerk in fixing the *induciae* shall have regard to the period necessary to enable the respondent to appear and shall, if necessary, consult the court.

## Form 6
Note on the Effect of the Reserve and Auxiliary Forces (Protection of Civil Interests) Act 1951
(For use with an application for leave to enforce a decree.)

The Reserve and Auxiliary Forces (Protection of Civil Interests) Act 1951, prevents the enforcement of the decree to which the application herewith applies if the court is of opinion that you are unable immediately to obey the order of the court contained in the decree by reason of circumstances directly or indirectly attributable to service to which the act applies. If you desire to take advantage of the act you should attend the court by yourself or by your solicitor (or, in the court of session, your counsel) on the date specified in the warrant for intimation, and satisfy the court that your inability to obey the order contained in the decree is due to the circumstances aforesaid. If the application has been served on your wife or other person entrusted with the management of your affairs or of the property to which the decree relates, the court will hear such person on your behalf.

## Form 7
Note on the Effect of the Reserve and Auxiliary Forces (Protection of Civil Interests) Act 1951
(For use with application for leave to exercise any right or remedy of the kind mentioned in subsection (2) of section 8 or in paragraph (b) of subsection (1) of section 25 of the Act.)

The Reserve and Auxiliary Forces (Protection of Civil Interests) Act 1951, prevents the exercise of certain rights including the right specified in the application herewith if the court is of opinion that by reason of circumstances directly or indirectly attributable to service to which the act applies you are unable to perform the obligation in respect of which the aforesaid right arises. If you desire to take advantage of the act you should attend the court by yourself or by your solicitor (or, in the court of session, your counsel) on the date specified in the warrant of intimation, and satisfy the court that your inability to perform your obligation is due to the circumstances aforesaid. If the application has been served on your wife or other person having the management of your affairs in general or of the property to which the right relates, the court will hear such person on your behalf.

## Form 8
### Certificate of Service

I, [name, designation and address], solicitor for the applicant hereby certify that 1 have intimated the foregoing application, in terms of the foregoing warrant for intimation, to [name and designate persons upon whom service has been made] by posting on [date] between the hours of.......... and.......... at the.......... Post Office a copy of the same to him **or** [them], together with a copy of a note in the terms of form 6 (or, as the case may require, form 7), in a registered letter [1] addressed as follows [address] and the post office receipt for the said registered letter accompanies this certificate.

[Signature of Solicitor For Applicant.]

[Date.]

## Form 9
### Reserve and Auxiliary Forces (Protection of Civil Interests) Act 1951

In the Court of Session *or* [Sheriff Court of ..........at ...........]

..........Pursuer

v.

..........Defender

To..........Defender above Designed.

Take note that when decree is granted in the above cause [which will be enrolled in the undefended roll before Hon. Lord..........for the..........day of ..........at 10 A.m. within the Parliament House, Edinburgh]............................ or..............[in the Sheriff Court at.......... before Sheriff.......... on the.......... day of.......... at ..........] the pursuer will make application to the court for leave to enforce the decree immediately in conformity with the above recited Acts and relative Act of Sederunt dated,..........1952.

[Signature of applicant or officer of court or Solicitor.]

[Place and Date.]

Note.—The Reserve and Auxiliary Forces (protection of Civil Interests) Act 1951, prevents the enforcement of the decree if the court is of opinion that you are unable immediately to obey the order of the court contained in the decree by reason of circumstances directly or indirectly attributable to service to which the act applies. If you desire to take advantage of the act you should attend the court by yourself or by your solicitor (or, in the court of session, your counsel) on the date when the motion for decree will be moved, and satisfy the court that your inability to obey the order of the court contained in the decree is due to the circumstances aforesaid. If the notice has been served on your wife or other person entrusted with the management of your affairs in general or of the property to which the action relates, the court will hear such person on your behalf.

## Form 10
### Reserve and Auxiliary Forces (Protection of Civil Interests) Act 1951

Sheriff Court of.......... at...............

..........Pursuer

v

..........Defender

To..........Defender above designed.

Take notice that when the above cause is called at the time and place specified in the [Initial Writ] *or* [summons] served herewith *or* [already served on you] application will be made, in the event of decree being granted, for leave to enforce the decree immediately in conformity with the above recited Acts and relative Act of Sederunt dated.........., 1952.

[Signature of applicant or officer of court or solicitor.]

[Place and date.]

Note.—The Reserve And Auxiliary Forces (Protection of Civil Interests) Act 1951, prevents the enforcement of the decree if the court is of opinion that you are unable immediately to obey the order of the court contained in the decree by reason of circumstances directly or indirectly attributable to service to which the Act applies. If you desire to take advantage of the Act you should attend the court by yourself or by your solicitor on the date when the motion for decree will be moved, and satisfy the court that your inability to obey the order of the court contained in the decree is due to the circumstances aforesaid. If the notice has been served on your wife or other person entrusted with the management of your affairs in general or of the property to which the action relates, the court will hear such person on your behalf.

---

[1] S.I. 1962 No. 1593

(SI 1962/1517)

*17 July 1962.*

The Lords of Council and Session, under and by virtue of the powers conferred upon them by section 34(1) of the Administration of Justice (Scotland) Act 1933 and of all other powers competent to them in that behalf, do hereby enact as follows:—

### Interpretation

1.   In this Act of Sederunt—

"sheriff" includes sheriff-substitute;
"sheriff clerk" includes sheriff clerk depute;
"initial writ" means the statement of claim, petition, note of appeal, or other document by which the action is initiated.

2.[1]   An application for a certified copy of a judgment obtained in a sheriff court, made for the purpose of the enforcement of the judgment in a country other than a country to which Parts I and II of the Civil Jurisdiction and Judgments Act 1982 applies, shall be made in that sheriff court by minute lodged in the process in which the judgment was obtained. There shall be lodged with the minute either an extract decree setting forth the judgment or a copy of the judgment. The sheriff, on being satisfied, by affidavit or by other proper evidence, as to the purpose for which the application is being made, shall pronounce an order ordaining the sheriff clerk to issue a certified copy of the judgment. The certificate shall be in the following terms:—

"I certify that the foregoing is a true copy of a judgment obtained in the.........Sheriff Court and that this certificate is issued for the purpose of the enforcement of the judgment in a country other than a country to which Parts I and II of the Civil Jurisdiction and Judgments Act 1982 applies and in obedience to an order by the Sheriff of.........dated.........

(Signed)
Sheriff Clerk."

3.   There shall be issued along with the foregoing certificate the following further certificate also certified by the sheriff clerk—

A certificate, enumerating and identifying and having annexed to it; (1) a copy of the initial writ by which the proceedings were initiated, showing the manner in which the initial writ was served on the defender or respondent and whether the defender or respondent appeared thereto, and the objections made to the jurisdiction if any; (2) a copy of the pleadings, if any, in the proceedings; (3) a copy of the opinion or note, if any, of the sheriff, and (4) a statement of such other particulars as it may be necessary to give to the foreign tribunal in which it is sought to obtain execution of the judgment. Copies of the foregoing documents shall be supplied where necessary by the person making the application.

4.   This Act of Sederunt may be cited as the Act of Sederunt (Enforcement Abroad of Sheriff Court Judgments) 1962, and shall come into operation on 17th July 1962.

---

[1] As amended by S.I. 1986 No. 1947.

**D2.13**

*18 November 1969.*

The Lords of Council and Session, by virtue of the powers conferred upon them by section 34 of the Administration of Justice (Scotland) Act 1933 and section 15(6) of the Law Reform (Miscellaneous Provisions)(Scotland) Act 1968, do hereby enact and declare as follows:—

**1.** A party to any civil proceedings who wishes to rely on a statement contained in a document produced by a computer shall, not later than the date of closing the record, send to every other party to the proceedings a copy of the statement together with a notice in writing—

(a)  intimating that the party intends to rely on the statement;

(b)  stating that the statement is contained in a document produced by a computer; and

(c)[1]  informing the party to whom it is addressed that he may give a counter-notice in terms of paragraph 3 hereof;

and the party so giving notice may within fourteen days thereafter lodge in process a certificate in terms of section 13(4) of the Law Reform (Miscellaneous Provisions) (Scotland) Act 1968 relating to the document.

**2.** When a certificate in terms of section 13(4) of the Law Reform (Miscellaneous Provisions) (Scotland) Act 1968 shall have been lodged in process, a copy thereof shall be sent to every other party to the proceedings within fourteen days after the date of the notice referred to in paragraph 1 hereof.

**3.** Any party who receives such a notice as is mentioned in paragraph 1 hereof may, within twenty-one days thereafter, by counter-notice in writing addressed to the party who served the notice, require him, within twenty-one days, to furnish him in writing with all or any of the following information—

(a)  any such information as might have been the subject of a certificate under section 13(4) of the Law Reform (Miscellaneous Provisions) (Scotland) Act 1968, except in so far as such information is the subject of a certificate lodged in process as aforesaid;

(b)  the name, occupation, business address and place of residence of a person occupying at the material time a responsible position in relation to each of (i) the operation of the device involved in the production of the document, (ii) the management of the activities for the purposes of which the computer was used to store or process information, (iii) the supply of information to the computer, (iv) the operation of the computer, and (v) the operation of any equipment by means of which the document containing the statement was produced by the computer; and

(c)  the name, occupation, business address and place of residence of the person who signed any certificate lodged in process in terms of section 13(4) of the Law Reform (Miscellaneous Provisions) (Scotland) Act 1968.

---

[1] Substituted by S.I. 1970 No. 456.

**4.** Subject to the provisions of section 15(8) of the Law Reform (Miscellaneous Provisions) (Scotland) Act 1968, a party upon whom a counter-notice has been served in terms of paragraph 3 hereof shall not be entitled to rely upon the statement in the document to which the notice under paragraph 1 hereof related, unless the counter-notice shall have been withdrawn by the party who gave it or unless the court shall be satisfied that the counter-notice was complied with so far as was reasonably possible.

**5.** Any party to whom information is furnished under a counter-notice by virtue of paragraph 3 hereof may, not later than twenty-eight days before the date of the proof or trial, by notice in writing require that the party wishing to rely on the statement in the document produced by a computer should call as a witness any person of whom particulars were furnished under sub-paragraph (b) or (c) of paragraph 3 hereof.

**6.**

(i) Subject to the provisions of section 15(8) of the Law Reform (Miscellaneous Provisions) (Scotland) Act 1968 a party who has been required to call any person as a witness in terms of paragraph 5 hereof shall not be entitled to rely upon the statement in the document to which the notice under paragraph 1 hereof related unless the notice requiring that person to be called as a witness shall have been withdrawn by the party who gave it, or unless that person shall be adduced as a witness, or unless the court shall be satisfied that such person is dead, or beyond the seas, or unfit by reason of his bodily or mental condition to attend as a witness, or cannot with reasonable diligence be identified or found, or cannot reasonably be expected (having regard to the passage of time and to all the circumstances) to have any recollection of matters relevant to the accuracy or otherwise of the statement in the document.

(ii) In the event that such person is not to be adduced as a witness for any reason aforesaid, the party wishing to rely on the statement in the document produced by a computer shall give notice in writing to every other party to the proceedings that such witness is not to be adduced and the reason therefor.

(iii) The notice referred to in sub-paragraph (ii) hereof shall be given not later than fourteen days after the date of the notice under paragraph 5 hereof or, if such reason could not reasonably have become known to him within that period, immediately such reason shall become known.

**7.** This Act of Sederunt shall apply to all civil proceedings in the Sheriff Court.

**8.** This Act of Sederunt may be cited as the Act of Sederunt (Computer Evidence in the Sheriff Court) 1969, and shall come into operation on 1st December 1969.

*[Edinburgh] 7 November 1973.*

The Lords of Council and Session, under and by virtue of the powers conferred on them by section 32 of the Sheriff Courts (Scotland) Act 1971 and of all other powers enabling them in that behalf, and after consultation with the Sheriff Court Rules Council, do hereby enact and declare as follows:—

**1.** This Act of Sederunt may be cited as the Act of Sederunt (Appeals against Poinding) 1973 and shall come into operation on 1st January 1974.

**2.**—(1) In this Act of Sederunt, unless the context otherwise requires—

"the Act" means the Law Reform (Diligence) (Scotland) Act 1973[1];
"appeal" means an appeal under section 1 (4) of the Act; "sheriff clerk" includes sheriff clerk depute.

(2) The Interpretation Act 1889 shall apply to the interpretation of this Act of Sederunt as it applies to the interpretation of an Act of Parliament.

**3.** On the execution of a poinding in a dwellinghouse the poinding sheriff officer or messenger-at-arms shall deliver to the possessor of the poinded effects a notice in the Form A in the Schedule hereto.

**4.** Appeals shall be made by lodging with the sheriff clerk a form in, or as nearly as is practicable in, the Form B in the Schedule hereto.

**5.** On the lodging of an appeal the sheriff shall grant warrant for intimation and shall fix a date for hearing the appeal not sooner than the seventh day after such intimation, which warrant may be in the Form C in the Schedule hereto.

**6.** On the granting of a warrant for intimation the sheriff clerk shall forthwith intimate the appeal to the respondent and to the poinding sheriff officer or messenger-at-arms by transmitting a copy of the appeal and warrant, duly certified by him, by registered post or by recorded delivery first class service to each of the said respondent and sheriff officer or messenger-at arms at the address or addresses stated in the appeal. A certificate of execution of intimation may be in the Form D in the Schedule hereto.

**7.** All appeals shall be entered in a book to be kept for the purpose and such entries shall set forth the names and designations of the appellant, respondent, and poinding officer, the date of the poinding, the articles in respect of which the appeal is taken and the several deliverances and the dates thereof, which book shall be signed by the sheriff. The determinations and deliverances of the sheriff may be written on the principal appeal or separately, shall be signed by the sheriff clerk and shall have the force and effect of extract.

SCHEDULE

*Form A.*
Notice to the possessor of poinded effects.
The Law Reform (Diligence) (Scotland) Act 1973 provides that an article shall not be liable to be poinded at the instance of a creditor in respect of a debt due to him by a debtor if it is an article to which

---

[1] See Division B.

the Act applies and, being at the time of the poinding in a dwellinghouse in which the debtor is residing, it is reasonably necessary to enable him and any other person living in family with him in that dwellinghouse to continue to reside there without undue hardship. The Act at present applies to beds or bedding material, chairs, tables, furniture or plenishings providing facilities for cooking, eating or storing food, and furniture or plenishings providing facilities for heating.

Where any article is poinded in respect of a debt, then, without prejudice to any other remedy available to him, a debtor may within seven days from the date of the poinding appeal to the Sheriff on the ground that, by virtue of the provisions of the Act, the said article is not liable to be poinded.

Any enquiry relating to the making of such an appeal may be directed to the Sheriff Clerk's Office at ...............

*Form B.*

In the Sheriff Court at .......... Appeal under section 1(4) of the Law Reform (Diligence) (Scotland) Act 1973

Appeal by ..............

*Applicant*

in the poinding at the ...............

instance of ...............

*Respondent*

1. The Appellant is the defender in an action at the instance of .......... the respondent in .......... (court) .......... in which decree was granted on .......... (date) .......... against the Appellant for payment of (or as the case may be)..........

2. .......... (name), .......... Sheriff Officer, .......... (address), .......... on the instructions of the respondent executed a poinding of the appellant's effects on .......... (date) .......... at the dwellinghouse at .......... (address) ...............

Included amongst the effects poinded were the following articles:—

   (a)   ...............

   (b)   ...............

3. These articles are reasonably necessary to enable the appellant and the persons living in family with him in that dwellinghouse to continue to reside there without undue hardship.

4. This appeal is made under section 1(4) of the Law Reform (Diligence) (Scotland) Act 1973.

THEREFORE the Appellant craves the Court—

   (a)   To find that the articles referred to are articles to which section 1 of the Law Reform (Diligence) (Scotland) Act 1973 applies and are not liable to be poinded.

   (b)   To order that said articles be released from the poinding.

   (c)   To deal with the expenses of this Appeal as the Court may think fit.

   (d)   To sist meantime all further execution in respect of said articles.

*Appellant*

*or*

Appellant's Solicitors.

*Form C.*

Grants Warrant to intimate the foregoing Appeal and this warrant to the respondent and the therein designed Sheriff Officer/Messenger-at-Arms and Appoints them, if they intend to oppose the Appeal, to answer within the Sheriff Court a t.......... on the .......... day of .......... at .......... o'clock .......... noon. Further Appoints the said Sheriff Officer/Messenger-at-Arms to lodge a copy of the schedule of poinded effects in the hands of the clerk of court. Meantime, Grants interim sist of execution as craved.

*Form D.*

I, .........., Sheriff Clerk (Depute), did lawfully intimate the foregoing Appeal to the respondent and to the poinding Sheriff Officer/Messenger-at-Arms by posting a certified copy of the Appeal and warrant in a registered letter (or through the recorded delivery service) to each of them. The Post Office receipts for the said registered (or recorded delivery) letters are attached hereto.

Signed Sheriff Clerk or Sheriff Clerk Depute.

# INTEREST IN SHERIFF COURT DECREES OR EXTRACTS 1975

(SI 1975/948)

*4 June 1975.*

The Lords of Council and Session, under and by virtue of the powers conferred upon them by section 4 of the Administration of Justice (Scotland) Act 1972 and of all other powers competent to them in that behalf, do hereby enact and declare as follows:—

**1.**[1]   In the case of any decree or extract in an action commenced on or after 1st July 1975 the provisions of section 9 of the Sheriff Courts (Scotland) Extracts Act 1892 as amended by the Act of Sederunt (Interest in Sheriff Court Decrees or Extracts) 1972 shall not apply. Instead there shall be substituted a new section 9 as follows:—

> "where interest is included in a decree or extract, it shall be deemed to be at the rate of eight per *centum* per annum, unless otherwise stated".

**2.**   This Act of Sederunt may be cited as the Act of Sederunt (Interest in Sheriff Court Decrees or Extracts) 1975, and shall come into operation on 2nd July 1975.

---

[1] Twelve per cent substituted for eleven per cent, with effect from 5th April 1983, by SI 1983/409.
Fifteen per cent substituted for twelve per cent, with effect from 16th August 1985, by SI 1985/1179.
Eight per cent substituted for fifteen per cent, with effect from 1st April 1993, by SI 1993/769.

431

## FATAL ACCIDENTS AND SUDDEN DEATHS INQUIRY PROCEDURE (SCOTLAND) RULES 1977

(SI 1977/191)

**D2.18**

*7 February 1977.*

In exercise of the powers conferred on me by section 7(1) of the Fatal Accidents and Sudden Deaths Inquiry (Scotland) Act 1976 and of all other powers enabling me in that behalf I hereby make the following rules:—

### Citation and commencement

**1.** These rules may be cited as the Fatal Accidents and Sudden Deaths Inquiry Procedure (Scotland) Rules 1977 and shall come into operation on 1st March 1977.

### Interpretation

**2.**—(1) In these rules, unless the context otherwise requires,—

"the Act" means the Fatal Accidents and Sudden Deaths Inquiry (Scotland) Act 1976;

"inquiry" means an inquiry under the Act;

"officer of law" has the meaning assigned to it by section 462 of the Criminal Procedure (Scotland) Act 1975;

"the Ordinary Cause Rules" means Schedule 1 to the Sheriff Courts (Scotland) Act 1907;[1]

"procurator fiscal" has the meaning assigned to it by section 462 of the Criminal Procedure (Scotland) Act 1975;

"sheriff clerk" includes sheriff clerk depute and any person duly authorised to execute the duties of sheriff clerk.

(2) In these rules, unless the context otherwise requires, a reference to any enactment shall be construed as a reference to that enactment as amended or re-enacted by any subsequent enactment.

(3) The Interpretation Act 1889 shall apply for the interpretation of these rules as it applies for the interpretation of an Act of Parliament.

### Application for holding of inquiry

**3.** The application for the holding of an inquiry in accordance with section 1(1) of the Act and the sheriffs first warrant thereon shall be in the case of such a death as is referred to in section 1(1)(a) of the Act in the form as nearly as may be of Form 1 of the Schedule to these rules, and in the case of such a death as is referred to in section 1(1)(b) of the Act in the form as nearly as may be of Form 2 of the said Schedule.

### Notice of holding of inquiry

**4.**—(1) Intimation of the holding of an inquiry in accordance with section 3(2)(a) of the Act shall be made by notice in writing in the form as nearly as may be of Form 3 of the Schedule to these rules, given not less than 21 days before the date of the inquiry.

---

[1] As inserted by the Fatal Accidents and Sudden Deaths Inquiry Procedure (Scotland) Amendment Rules (SSI 2007/478), r.2(2)(c) (effective November 1, 2007).

(2)   Such notice shall be given to the following persons, besides those specified in the said section 3(2)(a),—

> (za)[1]   any civil partner of the person who has died;
>
> (a)   in the case of such a death as is referred to in section 1(1)(a)(i) of the Act, to the Health and Safety Commission;
>
> (b)   in the case of such a death as is referred to in section 1(1)(a)(ii) of the Act, to any minister, government department or other authority in whose legal custody the person who has died was at the time of his death;
>
> (c)[2]   in the case of a death occurring in the circumstances specified in section 9 of the Act, or a death resulting from an accident occurring in those circumstances, to the Secretary of State for Employment;
>
> (d)   in any case where it is competent for a minister or government department under any statute other than the Act to cause public inquiry to be made into the circumstances of the death, to such minister or government department.

(3)   Public notice of the holding of an inquiry in accordance with section 3(2)(b) of the Act shall be given by publishing in at least two newspapers circulating in the sheriff court district where the inquiry is to be held, not less than 21 days before the date of the inquiry, an advertisement in the form as nearly as may be of Form 4 of the Schedule to these rules.

**Custody of productions**

**5.**   The sheriff may at the time of making an order for the holding of an inquiry or at any time thereafter, upon the application of the procurator fiscal, or of any other person entitled to appear at the inquiry or at his own instance, grant warrant to officers of law to take possession of anything connected with the death which is the subject of inquiry and which it may be considered necessary to produce at the inquiry and to hold any such thing in safe custody, subject to inspection by any persons interested.

**Inspection of land, premises, etc.**

**6.**   The sheriff may at the time of making an order for the holding of an inquiry or at any time thereafter, upon the application of the procurator fiscal or of any other person entitled to appear at the inquiry or at his own instance, inspect or grant warrant for any person to inspect any land, premises, article or other thing the inspection of which the sheriff considers desirable for the purposes of the inquiry.

**Representation**

**7.**—(1)   The procurator fiscal may appear on his own behalf at an inquiry or be represented by an assistant or depute procurator fiscal or by Crown counsel.

(2)   Any person entitled to appear at an inquiry in terms of section 4(2) of the Act may appear on his own behalf or be represented by an advocate or a solicitor or, with the leave of the sheriff, by any other person.

---

[1] As inserted by the Fatal Accidents and Sudden Deaths Inquiry Procedure (Scotland) Amendment Rules (SSI 2007/478), r.2(3) (effective November 1, 2007).
[2] As amended by SI 1992/1568 (effective July 3, 1992).

## Citation of witnesses or havers

**8.** The citation of a witness or haver to appear at an inquiry shall be in the form as nearly as may be of Form 5 of the Schedule to these rules, and an execution of citation in the form as nearly as may be of Form 6 of the said Schedule shall be sufficient evidence of such citation.

## Vulnerable witness procedure—forms

**8A.**—[1](1) This rule applies where a vulnerable witness (within the meaning of section 11(1) of the 2004 Act) is to give evidence at an inquiry and the application of the Ordinary Cause Rules in relation to the vulnerable witness would otherwise require any of the forms in column 1 of the Table below to be used.

(2) The form used instead shall be as nearly as may be the corresponding form of the Schedule to these Rules that is specified in column 2 of the Table.

**Table 1**

| Column 1—Ordinary Cause Rules form | Column 2—Inquiry form |
| --- | --- |
| child witness notice (Form G19) | Form 7 |
| vulnerable witness application (Form G20) | Form 8 |
| certificate of intimation (Form G21) | Form 9 |
| review application (Form G22) | Form 10 |
| certificate of intimation (Form G23) | Form 11 |

## Vulnerable witness procedure—preliminary hearing

**8B.**[2] If any preliminary hearing is held before the inquiry, the sheriff shall ascertain whether there is or is likely to be a vulnerable witness (within the meaning of section 11(1) of the 2004 Act) who is to give evidence at the inquiry, consider any child witness notice or vulnerable witness application that has been lodged where no order has been made under section 12 of the 2004 Act and consider whether any order under section 12 of that Act requires to be made.

## Adjournment of inquiry

**9.** The sheriff may at any time adjourn the inquiry to a time and place specified by him at the time of adjournment.

## Written statements

**10.**—(1) The sheriff may admit in place of oral evidence by any person in an inquiry, to the like extent as such oral evidence, a written statement by that person signed by that person and sworn or affirmed to be true by that person before a notary public, commissioner for oaths or justice of the peace, or before a commissioner appointed by the sheriff for that purpose:

---

[1] As inserted by the Fatal Accidents and Sudden Deaths Inquiry Procedure (Scotland) Amendment Rules (SSI 2007/478), r.2(4) (effective November 1, 2007).
[2] As inserted by the Fatal Accidents and Sudden Deaths Inquiry Procedure (Scotland) Amendment Rules (SSI 2007/478), r.2(4) (effective November 1, 2007).

Provided that such a statement may only be admitted if—

    (a)   all persons who appear or are represented at the inquiry agree to its admission; or

    (b)   the sheriff considers that its admission will not result in unfairness in the conduct of the inquiry to any person who appears or is represented at the inquiry.

(2)   A certificate that the statement has been so sworn and affirmed, annexed to the statement and signed by the person making the statement and by the person before whom it is sworn or affirmed, shall be sufficient evidence that it has been so sworn or affirmed.

(3)   Any statement which is admitted in evidence by virtue of this rule shall, unless the sheriff otherwise directs, be read aloud at the inquiry; and where the sheriff directs that a statement or any part of it shall not be read aloud he shall state his reason for so directing and, where appropriate, an account shall be given orally of what the sheriff has directed not to be read aloud.

(4)   Any document or object referred to as a production and identified in a written statement tendered in evidence under this rule shall be treated as if it had been produced and had been identified in court by the maker of the statement.

## Sheriff's determination

11.—(1)   The sheriffs determination shall be in writing and shall be signed by him.

(2)   The sheriffs determination shall, except in the circumstances specified in paragraph (3) of this rule, be read out by him in public.

(3)   Where the sheriff requires time to prepare his determination and considers that in the circumstances it is not reasonable to fix an adjourned sitting of the inquiry for the sole purpose of reading out the determination, the sheriff shall not be required to read out the determination, but the sheriff clerk shall send free of charge a copy of the determination, to the procurator fiscal and to any person who appeared or was represented at the inquiry and shall allow any person to inspect a copy of the determination at the sheriff clerk's office free of charge during the period of three months after the date when the determination was made.

## Assessors

12.—(1)   A request to the sheriff to summon a person to act as an assessor in terms of section 4(6) of the Act shall be made by written motion lodged with the sheriff clerk not less than seven days before the date of the inquiry.

(2)   The appointment of an assessor shall not affect the admissibility of expert evidence in the inquiry.

## Recording of evidence

13.   Evidence given in an inquiry shall be recorded in the same manner as evidence given in an ordinary civil cause in the sheriff court:

Provided that where the evidence shall have been taken down in shorthand it shall not be necessary to extend such evidence unless the sheriff shall so direct or unless a copy of the transcript of evidence shall be duly requested by any person entitled thereto in terms of the Act and these rules.

**Time-limit for obtaining copy of transcript of evidence**

**14.** A person shall be entitled to obtain a copy of the transcript of the evidence in accordance with section 6(5)(b) of the Act only if he makes application therefor to the sheriff clerk within a period of three months after the date when the sheriffs determination was made.

**Fee on obtaining copy of determination, or of transcript of evidence**

**15.**—(1) The fee payable upon obtaining a copy of the sheriffs determination in accordance with section 6(5)(a) of the Act shall be such fee as is payable to sheriff clerks for copying documents relating to civil proceedings in the sheriff court.

(2) The fee payable upon obtaining a copy of the transcript of the evidence in accordance with section 6(5)(b) of the Act shall be—

(a) where the copy is made by a shorthand writer, such copying fee as is payable by the sheriff clerk to the shorthand writer;

(b) where the copy is made by the sheriff clerk, such fee as is payable to sheriff clerks for copying documents relating to civil proceedings in the sheriff court.

**Service of documents**

**16.**—(1) The notice intimating the holding of an inquiry in accordance with section 3(2)(a) of the Act, the citation of a witness for precognition by the procurator fiscal, the citation of a witness or haver to attend at an inquiry, and any interlocutor, warrant or other order of the sheriff or writ following thereon issued in connection with an inquiry may be served on a person in any of the following manners:—

(a) the procurator fiscal or the solicitor for any person entitled to appear at the inquiry, as appropriate, may post the document in a registered or recorded delivery letter addressed to the person on whom the document requires to be served at his residence or place of business or at any address specified by him for the purpose of receiving documents;

(b) a police officer (where the document is issued by the procurator fiscal) or a sheriff officer may—

(i) serve the document personally on the person on whom it requires to be served; or

(ii) leave the document in the hands of an inmate or employee at that person's residence or place of business or any address specified by him for the purpose of receiving documents;

(iii) introduce the document into that person's residence or place of business or any address so specified by means of a letterbox or other lawful means; or

(iv) affix the document to the door of that person's residence or place of business or any place so specified;

Provided that when it proves difficult for any reason to serve any document on any person the sheriff, on being satisfied that all reasonable steps have been taken to serve it, may dispense with service of such document or order such other steps as he may think fit.

**Dispensing power of sheriff**

**17.** The sheriff may in his discretion relieve any person from the consequences of any failure to comply with the provisions of these rules if the failure resulted from mistake, oversight or any cause other than wilful non-observance of these rules and in granting such relief may impose such terms and conditions as appear to him to be just; and in any such case the sheriff may make such order as appears to him to be just regarding extension of time, lodging or amendment of papers or otherwise, so as to enable the inquiry to proceed as if such failure had not happened.

SCHEDULE

**Rule 3**

Form 1

Under the Fatal Accidents and Sudden Deaths Inquiry (Scotland) Act 1976

To the Sheriff of..........at (*place of court*)

The APPLICATION of the Procurator Fiscal for the District of

From information received by the applicant it appears that (*narrate briefly the apparent facts of the death*);

In terms of the said Act an inquiry requires to be held into the circumstances of said death.

May it therefore please your Lordship to fix a time and place for the holding by your Lordship of such in inquiry; to grant warrant to cite witnesses and havers to attend at such inquiry, at the instance of the applicant, and of any other person who may be entitled by virtue of said Act to appear thereat; to grant warrant to officers of law to take possession of, and hold in safe custody, subject to inspection by any person interested, anything which it may be considered necessary to produce at the inquiry.

According to Justice, &c.

(*Signature*)

Procurator Fiscal

(*Place and date*). The Sheriff having considered the foregoing application orders that inquiry into the circumstances of the death of..........within designed, be held on the..........day of..........19.........., at (*time*), within the Sheriff Court House at..........; grants warrant to cite witnesses and havers as craved; also grants warrant to officers of law to take possession of, and to hold in safe custody, subject to the inspection by any person interested, anything which it may be considered necessary to produce at the inquiry.

(*Signature*)

Rule 3

Form 2

Under the Fatal Accidents and Sudden Deaths Inquiry (Scotland) Act 1976

To the Sheriff of..........at (*place of court*)

The APPLICATION of the Procurator Fiscal for the District of

From information received by the applicant is appears that (*narrate briefly the apparent facts of the death*);

and it appears to the Lord Advocate to be expedient in the public interest that an inquiry under the said Act should be held into the circumstances of said death.

May it therefore please your Lordship to fix a time and place for the holding by your Lordship of such an inquiry; to grant warrant to cite witnesses and havers to attend at such inquiry, at the instance of the applicant and of any other person who may be entitled by virtue of said Act to appear thereat; to grant warrant to officers of law to take possession of, and hold in safe custody, subject to inspection by any person interested, anything which it may be considered necessary to produce at the inquiry.

According to Justice, &c.

(*Signature*)

Procurator Fiscal

(*Place and date*). The Sheriff having considered the foregoing application orders that inquiry into the circumstances of the death of..........within designed, be held on the..........day of..........19.........., at (*time*) within the Sheriff Court House at..........; grants warrant to cite witnesses and havers as craved; also grants warrant to officers of law to take possession of, and to hold in safe custody, subject to the inspection by any person interested, anything which it may be considered necessary to produce at the inquiry.

(*Signature*)

Rule 4(1)

Form 3

(*Address of procurator fiscal*)

(*Date*)

(*Name and address of person to whom notice is given*)

Dear Sir

DEATH OF (*insert name of deceased*)

I have to intimate that an inquiry under the Fatal Accidents and Sudden Deaths Inquiry (Scotland) Act 1976 into the circumstances of the death of (*insert name and address of deceased*) will be held on..........the..........day of..........at (*time*) within the Sheriff Court House at (*address*).

\* [You have the right to appear, call witnesses and lead evidence at the inquiry. You may attend in person or be represented by an advocate or a solicitor instructed by you or, with the leave of the sheriff, by some other person.]

Yours faithfully,

(*Signature*)

Procurator Fiscal

\* To be inserted only when the person to whom notice is given is the wife, husband or nearest known relative, or the employer, of the deceased.

Rule 4(3)

FORM 4

ADVERTISEMENT

Under the Fatal Accidents and Sudden Deaths Inquiry (Scotland) Act 1976

The Sheriff of.............. ....................will hold an inquiry on the..............day of (*month*) 19..........at (*time*) within the Sheriff Court House at (*address*) into the circumstances of the death of (*name, occupation, address*).

The Sheriff of..............will hold an inquiry on the..............day of (*month*) 19..........at (*time*) within the Sheriff Court House at (*address*) into the circumstances of the death of (*name, occupation, address*).

(*Signature*)

Procurator Fiscal for the District of

Rule 8

FORM 5

To (*name and designation*).

YOU are cited to attend at the Sheriff Court House at (*address*) on (*date*) at (*time*) as a witness at the instance of (*insert* "the Procurator Fiscal for the District of.........." *or name and address of person calling witness*) at the INQUIRY then to be held into the circumstances of the DEATH of (*name and address of deceased*) [and are required to bring with you..........] and if you fail to attend you may be ordered to pay a penalty not exceeding\*

(*Signature and designation of procurator fiscal, police officer, sheriff officer or solicitor*)

\* (Insert penalty specified in rule [74(2)] of the First Schedule to the Sheriff Courts (Scotland) Act 1907 [as amended]).

Rule 8

FORM 6

I certify that on (*date*) I lawfully cited (*name and designation*) to attend at the Sheriff Court House at (*address*) on (*date*) at (*time*) as a witness at the instance of (*insert* "the Procurator Fiscal for the District of.........." *or name and address of person calling witness*) at the INQUIRY then to be held into the circumstances of the DEATH of (*name and address of deceased*) [and I required him to bring with him..........].

This I did by (*specify exactly how served*).

(*Signature and designation of procurator fiscal, police officer, sheriff officer or solicitor*)

# APPLICATIONS UNDER THE MATRIMONIAL HOMES (FAMILY PROTECTION) (SCOTLAND) ACT 1981, 1982[1]

(SI 1982/1432)

D2.21

*7 October 1982.*

The Lords of Council and Session, under and by virtue of the powers conferred on them by section 32 of the Sheriff Courts (Scotland) Act 1971 and of all other powers competent to them in that behalf do hereby enact and declare:—

### Citation and commencement

**1.** This Act of Sederunt may be cited as the Act of Sederunt (Applications under the Matrimonial Homes (Family Protection) Act 1981) 1982 and shall come into operation on 29th October 1982.

### Interpretation

**2.**—(1) In this Act of Sederunt, unless the context otherwise requires:—

"the 1981 Act" means the Matrimonial Homes (Family Protection) (Scotland) Act 1981.

(2) Unless the context otherwise requires, words and expressions used in these rules and in the 1981 Act shall have the same meaning in these rules as they have in the Act.

### Intimation to third parties

**3.**—(1) The applicant shall intimate a copy of the application or the terms of the motion by which the application is made—

    (a) in an application under sections 2(1)(e) and 2(4)(a)(authorisation of non-essential repairs etc.), 4 (exclusion orders), 7 (dispensation with consent to dealing), 13 (transfer of tenancy) and 18 (occupancy rights of cohabiting couples) of the 1981 Act, to the landlord if the entitled spouse is a tenant of the matrimonial home;

    (b) in an application under sections 2(1) (rights consequential to occupancy), 2(4)(a), 3(1) and (2) (rights of occupancy), 4, 7 and 18 of the 1981 Act, to the third party if the entitled spouse is permitted by a third party to occupy the matrimonial home;

    (c) to any person as the sheriff may order in any application.

(2) A person to whom intimation of an application has been made in terms of this paragraph may lodge answers within such period as the sheriff may allow or if the application is made by motion may appear or be represented and may oppose the motion.

**4.** An order for intimation to be made under the last foregoing paragraph may be contained in the original warrant for citation or intimation may be appointed to be made at a later date.

---

[1] Revoked except for para. 7 (other than the proviso) and para. 8 by S.I. 1993 No. 1956, in relation to causes commenced on or after 1st January 1994.

### Form of applications

**5.**—(1)  Except as otherwise provided in this Act of Sederunt an application under the 1981 Act shall be brought as an ordinary cause except where the application falls within the definition of a summary cause in section 35 of the Sheriff Courts (Scotland) Act 1971 in which case it shall be brought as a summary cause.

(2)  Where civil proceedings to which this paragraph refers (hereinafter referred to as "the principal proceedings") have been raised it shall be competent for a defender in the principal proceedings or other person who is entitled to make an application under the 1981 Act to lodge such an application in the process of the principal proceedings.

(3)  An application lodged in terms of this paragraph shall be by minute signed by the applicant or his solicitor, shall be served upon the pursuer in the principal proceedings and shall contain:

    (a)  a crave or craves in a form which, if the application had been made by way of a separate action would have been appropriate in such separate action;

    (b)  a statement of facts setting out in numbered paragraphs the facts on which the application is founded; and

    (c)  a note of the pleas-in-law which are necessary to support the application.

(4)  In any application lodged in terms of this paragraph the sheriff may make such order for any warrant for intimation, service or arrestment and may regulate the procedure as he thinks fit and may dispose of the application as if it had been stated in a substantive action.

(5)  The principal proceedings are:

    (i)  an action of separation and aliment;

    (ii)  an action of adherence and aliment;

    (iii)  an action of interim aliment;

    (iv)  an action of affiliation and aliment;

    (v)  any application under the 1981 Act.

**6.**—(1)  Applications for the variation or recall of orders which have been made under sections 3 or 4 of the 1981 Act shall be made by minute lodged in the original process in which the order was made.

(2)  The sheriff shall order that any minute lodged in terms of this paragraph be served on the opposite party or parties and be intimated to—

    (a)  the landlord if the entitled spouse is a tenant of the matrimonial home,

    (b)  the third party if the entitled spouse is permitted to occupy the matrimonial home by a third party,

    (c)  any other person as the sheriff may order.

(3)  The sheriff shall appoint answers to be lodged to any minute lodged in terms of this paragraph within a specified time and shall thereafter, without closing the record, and after such proof or other procedure as he may deem necessary, dispose of the application.

**7.**  An application for an order under section 7 of the 1981 Act shall be made by initial writ under the Sheriff Courts (Scotland) Acts 1907 and 1913 and such application shall be dealt with as a summary application as defined in those Acts:

Provided that in any civil proceedings which involve proceedings in relation to a matrimonial home an application for an order under section 7 of the 1981 Act, by any party to such proceedings entitled to make such an application, shall be made by motion.

**8.** An application under section 11 (poinding) for a declarator or order of the 1981 Act shall be made by initial writ under the Sheriff Courts (Scotland) Acts 1907 and 1913 and such application shall be dealt with as a summary application as defined in those Acts.

**9.**[1] Where a matrimonial interdict, to which there is attached a power of arrest, is varied or recalled or the power of arrest ceases to have effect by reason of decree of divorce being granted, the spouse who applied for variation or recall, or in whose favour decree of divorce has been granted, shall ensure that there is delivered as soon as possible—

(a) to the chief constable of the police area in which the matrimonial home is situated; and

(b) if the spouse who applied for the interdict resides in another police area, to the chief constable of that other police area,

a copy of the application for variation or recall and of the interlocutor granting variation or recall or, as the case may be, a copy of the interlocutor granting decree of divorce and shall immediately thereafter lodge with the sheriff clerk a certificate of delivery.

---

[1] Added by S.I. 1984 No. 255.

# VARIATION AND RECALL OF ORDERS IN CONSISTORIAL CAUSES 1984[1]

(SI 1984/667)

*9 May 1984.*

The Lords of Council and Session, by virtue of the powers conferred upon them by section 32 of the Sheriff Courts (Scotland) Act 1971, section 8(4) of the Law Reform (Miscellaneous Provisions) (Scotland) Act 1966 and of all other powers competent to them in that behalf, after consultation with the Sheriff Court Rules Council, do hereby enact and declare:—

### Citation and commencement

**1.**—(1)  This Act of Sederunt may be cited as the Act of Sederunt (Variation and Recall of Orders in Consistorial Causes) 1984 and shall come into operation on 1st June 1984.

(2)  This Act of Sederunt shall be inserted in the Books of Sederunt.

### Procedure for variation and recall of orders under 1966 Act

**2.**—(1)  This Act of Sederunt shall apply to applications to the sheriff for variation or recall of any order to which section 8 of the said Act of 1966 applies.

(2)  All such applications shall be commenced by initial writ and, subject to the provisions of this Act of Sederunt, shall proceed as an ordinary cause and shall be subject to the same rights of appeal as any ordinary cause.

**3.**—(1)  In all such applications there shall be lodged in the sheriff court along with the initial writ a copy of the interlocutor which it is sought to vary certified by the appropriate officer of the Court of Session.

(2)  Before lodging the initial writ in terms of paragraph (1), a copy of the initial writ certified by the pursuer or his solicitor shall be lodged in or sent by first class recorded delivery post to the Court of Session to be lodged in the process of the Court of Session action in which the original order was made and the pursuer or his solicitor shall attach a certificate of execution of intimation to the principal initial writ lodged in the sheriff court.

(3)  The sheriff may, on cause shown, prorogate the time for lodging such certified copy interlocutor.

**4.**  Where no notice of intention to defend has been lodged, the cause shall be called on the next convenient court day when the sheriff shall hear the pursuer or his solicitor and thereafter may grant decree or make such other order as he thinks appropriate.

**5.**  Where a notice of intention to defend has been lodged and no request is made under paragraph 8, the pursuer shall, within 14 days after tabling or within such period as the sheriff may order, lodge in process in the sheriff court the following documents (or copies) from the process in the Court of Session action in which the original order was made—

    (a)  the pleadings;

    (b)  the interlocutor sheets;

---

[1] Revoked by SI 1993/1956, in relation to causes commenced on or after 1st January 1994.

(c)   any opinions of the court; and

(d)   the inventory of productions together with any productions upon which he seeks to found.

**6.**   Where a notice of intention to defend has been lodged and no request is made under paragraph 8, the sheriff may, on the joint motion of the parties made at any time after the lodging of the documents mentioned in paragraph 5, dispense with proof, and whether defences have been lodged or not hear the parties and thereafter may grant decree or otherwise dispose of the cause as he thinks appropriate.

**7.**—(1)   Where decree has been granted or the cause otherwise disposed of and the days of appeal have elapsed, the sheriff clerk shall transmit to the Court of Session the sheriff court process together with those Court of Session documents which have been lodged in the sheriff court.

(2)   A sheriff court process so transmitted shall form part of the process of the Court of Session action in which the original order was made.

**8.**—(1)   A request for a remit to the Court of Session under section 8(3) of the said Act of 1966 shall be made by way of minute signed by the applicant or his solicitor and lodged at or before tabling.

(2)   The sheriff shall in respect of any such minute at tabling order that the cause be remitted to the Court of Session and within four days after the date of such order the sheriff clerk shall transmit the whole sheriff court process to the Court of Session.

**9.**—(1)   A cause remitted to the Court of Session in terms of paragraph 8 shall form part of the process of the Court of Session action in which the original order was made.

## Revocation

**10.**   The Act of Sederunt (Variation and Recall of Orders in Consistorial Causes) 1970 is revoked.

*2 May 1985.*

The Lords of Council and Session, under and by virtue of the powers conferred on them by sections 70(3), 73(8), 75(5) and 141(5) of the Consumer Credit Act 1974, section 32 of the Sheriff Courts (Scotland) Act 1971 and of all other powers competent to them in that behalf, do hereby enact and declare:—

## Citation and commencement

**1.**—(1)   This Act of Sederunt may be cited as the Act of Sederunt (Consumer Credit Act 1974) 1985 and shall come into operation on 19th May 1985.

(2)   This Act of Sederunt shall be inserted in the Books of Sederunt.

## Interpretation

**2.**—(1)[1, 2]   In this Act of Sederunt, "the 1974 Act" means the Consumer Credit Act 1974 and "Sheriff Court Summary Application Rules" means the Sheriff Court Summary Application Rules 1999.

(2)   Expressions used in this Act of Sederunt which are used in the 1974 Act have the same meaning as in that Act.

## Revocation

**3.**   The Act of Sederunt (Sheriff Court Procedure, Consumer Credit) 1977 is revoked.

PART I

ORDINARY AND SUMMARY CAUSES

**4.**   In a cause relating to a regulated agreement, the sheriff may, on cause shown on the motion of any party to the cause before or at proof, in relation to any party to that agreement or any surety, dispense with the requirement in section 141(5) of the 1974 Act to make that party or surety a party to the cause.

**5.**   In any cause relating to a regulated agreement brought by a person who has acquired rights or liabilities of a former creditor under the agreement by assignation or by operation of law, the requirement in section 141(5) of the 1974 Act that all parties to the regulated agreement shall be made parties to the cause shall not apply to the former creditor unless the sheriff so directs.

## Application for a time order

**5A.**[3]   Where there are no proceedings in respect of the regulated agreement before the court, an application for a time order under section 129 or an ancillary

---

[1] As amended by S.I. 1995 No. 1877 (effective 7th August 1995).

[2] As substituted by the Act of Sederunt (Sheriff Court Rules) (Miscellaneous Amendments) 2008 (SSI 2008/223) r.15(2) (effective July 1, 2008).

[3] Inserted by S.I. 1995 No. 1877 (effective 7th August 1995) and substituted by the Act of Sederunt (Sheriff Court Rules) (Miscellaneous Amendments) 2008 (SSI 2008/223) r.15 (effective July 1, 2008: substitution has effect subject to savings provision specified in SSI 2008/223 r.15(4)).

order under sections 132, 133, 135, 136, 139 or 140B of the 1974 Act shall be by summary application and made as nearly as may be in accordance with Form 1 of the Schedule to this Act of Sederunt and rule 2.4(1) and Form 1 of the Sheriff Court Summary Application rules shall not apply to such an application.

### Application for variation or revocation of a time order

**5B.**[1] An application for variation or revocation of a time order under section 130(6) of the 1974 Act shall be by minute or incidental application, as appropriate, in the proceedings in which the time order was granted.

### PART II

### SUMMARY CAUSES

**6.**—(1)[2] Where, in a summary cause to which this sub-paragraph applies, a defender has a claim against a third party who is jointly and severally liable with the defender to the pursuer in respect of the subject-matter of the cause and who is not already a party to the cause or whom the pursuer is not bound to call as a defender, the defender may apply to the sheriff under rule 11 of the Act of Sederunt (Summary Cause Rules) 2002 (third party procedure) (incidental applications) for an order making the third party a party to the cause.

(2) Sub-paragraph (1) applies to a cause in which an application is made by virtue of—

    (a)   section 70(3) of the 1974 Act (supplier may be made a party to proceedings against the creditor for recovery of money on cancellation of a regulated agreement);

    (b)   section 73(8) of the 1974 Act (negotiator may be made a party to proceedings against the creditor for recovery of money on cancellation of a regulated agreement where goods were taken in part-exchange); or

    (c)   section 75(5) of the 1974 Act (supplier may be made a party to proceedings against the creditor for misrepresentation or breach of contract by the supplier).

**7.** If an application under paragraph 6(1) is granted, the sheriff shall appoint a date on which he will regulate further procedure and shall grant warrant to the defender to serve on the third party—

    (a)   a copy of the summons;

    (b)   a copy of the statement of defence, which shall contain the grounds upon which it is claimed that the third party is liable; and

    (c)[3]   a notice as nearly as may be in accordance with the form 2 set out in the Schedule to this Act of Sederunt.

**8.** On, or after, the date appointed for the regulation of further procedure under paragraph 7, the sheriff may—

    (a)   regulate procedure; or

    (b)   grant such decree, interlocutor or order as he considers appropriate.

---

[1] Inserted by S.I. 1995 No. 1877 (effective 7th August 1995).

[2] As substituted by the Act of Sederunt (Sheriff Court Rules) (Miscellaneous Amendments) 2008 (SSI 2008/223) r.15(5) (effective July 1, 2008).

[3] As amended by S.I. 1995 No. 1877 (effective 7th August 1995).

**9.** A decree or other interlocutor granted against a third party under this Part shall take effect and be extractable in the same way as a decree or other interlocutor against a pursuer or defender.

SCHEDULE

Paragraph 5A

Form 1[1]

**The Consumer Credit Act 1974, Section 129**
Sheriff Court..............

APPLICATION
FOR TIME OR-
DER

*(1) insert your name and address*

(1)..............

..............19.........

..............

(court reference no.)

.............. APPLICANT

*(2) insert full name and address of the person against whom the order is sought*

(2)..............

..............

..............RESPONDENT

*\* delete as appropriate*

*(3) insert the section number of the Consumer Credit Act 1974 under which any ancillary order is craved*

| Part I | Order Sought |
| --- | --- |

The applicant asks the court to make

*(a) a time order under section 129 of the Consumer Credit Act 1974;

*(b) an order in terms of section (3)..........of the Consumer Credit Act 1974

| *Part II | Proposals for Payment |
| --- | --- |

My proposal for payment of the arrears and future instalments is £..........per week/month.

No time to pay direction or time to pay order has been made in relation to this debt.

*\* delete whichever box not appropriate*

| *Part III | Proposals to Remedy Breach of Agreement |
| --- | --- |

I have breached the terms of the agreement, as follows—

..............
..............
..............

My proposals for remedying the breach(es) are as follows*mdash;

..............
..............

---

[1] Inserted by S.I. 1995 No. 1877 (effective August 7, 1995).

*delete box if not appropriate*

**\*Part IV**            **Ancillary orders sought**

The ancillary order(s) sought in addition to the time order are sought for the following reasons (4).........

*(4) insert here the reasons why you have sought any ancillary order in addition to a time order*

...............
...............
...............

---

**Part V**         **Details of Regulated Agreement**

*(5) Attach a copy of the agreement to the application form if you have retained it or delete*

i. Date of agreement.........and reference number
.........(5)
* A copy of the agreement is attached.

*insert details of the agreement where known–refer to your copy of the agreement if you have retained it*

ii. Names and addresses of other parties to the agreement
...............
...............

iii. Name and address of person (if any) who acted as surety
...............
...............

iv. Reason why respondent is now creditor (applies where agreement transferred to another company)
...............
...............

v. Place where agreement signed (eg the shop where agreement signed, include name and address)
...............

*\* delete as appropriate*

vi. Details of payment arrangements

a. The agreement is to pay by instalments of £.......... per week/month*

b. The unpaid balance is £........./I do not know the unpaid balance*

c. I am £.......... in arrears/I do not know the amount of arrears*

vii. The respondent served on me a—
default notice/section 76(1) notice/section 98(1) notice*

A copy of the notice is/is not* attached to this application.

---

Signed...............APPLICANT/SOLICITOR FOR APPLICANT
    Date...............

TO HELP THE COURT PLEASE PROVIDE DETAILS OF YOUR FINANCIAL POSITION IN THE BOXES BELOW

    (If necessary attach a separate sheet)

| Income | |
|---|---|
| My income is: | |
| *(give average weekly figures, after deductions)* | |
| Pay | £ |
| *(include overtime, bonuses etc)* | |
| Pensions | £ |
| State Benefits | £ |
| Other income | £ |
| Total | £ |

| Expenditure | |
|---|---|
| My expenditure is: | |
| *(give average weekly figures)* | |
| Rent/Mortgage | £ |
| Council Tax | £ |
| Heating/Light | £ |
| Food | £ |
| Payments for credit cards | £ |
| hire purchase etc | £ |
| Other payments (specify) | |
| | £ |
| Total | £ |

**Dependants**

List the names and ages of members of the household who are financially dependent on you.

Paragraph 7(c)

FORM 2

Notice to Third Party

Third Party Notice in the case of

A.B., Pursuer v. CD.,
Defender

and

E.F., Third Party

To E.F. (*name and address*)

This Notice is served upon you by C.D. by virtue of an order granted by the Sheriff of..........at..........on..........in the action raised against C.D., defender, by A.B., pursuer. The pursuer claims against the defender for (*describe pursuer's claim*) in respect of (*describe contract*) as more fully appears in the summons.

The defender admits *[or denies]* liability to the pursuer but [or and] claims that [if he is found liable to the pursuer] you are liable to relieve him wholly [or in part] of his liability for the reasons set out in the statement of defence enclosed herewith.

Take notice that if you wish to resist either the claim of the pursuer against the defender or the claim of the defender against you or to make an offer in settlement you are required to appear at the Sheriff Court House at (*address*) on (*day and date*) at (*time*).

If you do not appear decree may be granted against you in your absence.

Dated this..........day of..........19.

(*Signed*)
Solicitor for Defender

NOTES:

1. You may attend court in person or be represented by an advocate or a solicitor.

451

2. If you are ordered to pay a sum of money by instalments any failure to pay such instalments at the proper time may result in your forfeiting the right to pay by instalments and the whole amount outstanding will then become due.

3. If decree is granted against you this may, among other possible steps, lead to the arrestment of your wages and/or seizure of your possessions.

**D2.24**

*13 November 1986.*

The Lords of Council and Session, under and by virtue of the powers conferred on them by section 32 of the Sheriff Courts (Scotland) Act 1971, section 48 of the Civil Jurisdiction and Judgments Act 1982 and of all other powers enabling them in that behalf, do hereby enact and declare:—

### Citation and commencement

**1.**—(1)   This Act of Sederunt may be cited as the Act of Sederunt (Enforcement of Judgments under the Civil Jurisdiction and Judgments Act 1982) 1986 and shall come into operation on 1st January 1987.

(2)   This Act of Sederunt shall be inserted in the Books of Sederunt.

### Interpretation

**2.**—(1)[1]   In this Act of Sederunt—

"the 1982 Act" means the Civil Jurisdiction and Judgments Act 1982;
"the 1968 Convention" and "the Lugano Convention" have the meanings respectively assigned in section 1 of the 1982 Act;
"authentic instrument" means an instrument referred to in Articles 50 or 51 of the 1968 Convention and the Lugano Convention;
"court settlement" means a settlement referred to in Article 51 of the 1968 Convention and the Lugano Convention; and
"Ordinary Cause Rules" means the First Schedule to the Sheriff Courts (Scotland) Act 1907.

(2)   A form referred to by number means the form so numbered in the Schedule to this Act of Sederunt or a form substantially to the same effect, with such variation as circumstances may require.

### Enforcement of sheriff court judgments in other parts of the United Kingdom (Money provisions)

**3.**—(1)   An application for a certificate under paragraph 2 of Schedule 6 to the 1982 Act shall be made in writing to the sheriff clerk and shall be accompanied by an affidavit—

(a)   stating the sum or aggregate of the sums, including expenses, payable and unsatisfied;

(b)   verifying that the time for bringing an appeal against the judgment has expired and no appeal has been brought within that time, or that any appeal has been finally disposed of; and that enforcement of the judgment has not been suspended and the time available for the enforcement has not expired; and

(c)   stating the address of the party entitled to enforce, and the usual or last known address of the party liable to execution on, the judgment.

---

[1] As amended by SI 1993/2346 (effective October 25, 1993).

(2) A certificate under paragraph 4 of Schedule 6 to the 1982 Act shall be in Form 1 and be signed by the sheriff clerk.

## Enforcement of sheriff court judgments in other parts of the United Kingdom (Non-money provisions)

**4.**—(1) An application for a certified copy of an interlocutor or extract decree and, where appropriate, a copy of the note or opinion of the sheriff under paragraph 2 of Schedule 7 to the 1982 Act shall be made in writing to the sheriff clerk and shall be accompanied by an affidavit—

> (a) verifying that the time for bringing an appeal against the judgment has expired and no appeal has been brought within that time, or any appeal has been finally disposed of; and that enforcement of the judgment has not been suspended and the time available for the enforcement has not expired; and
>
> (b) stating the address of the party entitled to enforce, and the usual or last known address of the party liable to execution on, the judgment.

(2) A copy of an interlocutor, decree, note or opinion issued under paragraph 4 of Schedule 7 to the 1982 Act shall have appended to it a certificate in Form 2 signed by the sheriff clerk.

## Enforcement of sheriff court interlocutors and decrees in another Contracting State

**5.**—(1)[1] Before an application is made under section 12 of the 1982 Act for a copy of a judgment or a certificate giving particulars relating to the judgment and the proceedings in which it was given, the party wishing to enforce the judgment shall serve the judgment on all parties against whom the judgment has been given in accordance with rule 5.4 or 5.5 of the Ordinary Cause Rules, as the case may be, accompanied by a notice in Form 4; and the execution of such service shall be in Form 5 unless a form of execution of service is provided by the person effecting service in the other Contracting State where service was effected.

(2) An application under section 12 of the 1982 Act shall be made in writing to the sheriff clerk for—

> (a) a certificate in Form 3;
>
> (b) a certified copy interlocutor; and
>
> (c) if required, a certified copy of the opinion of the sheriff.

(3) A certificate shall not be issued under sub-paragraph (2)(a) unless there is produced and lodged in the process of the cause an execution of service required under sub-paragraph (1).

## Recognition and enforcement in Scotland of foreign maintenance orders

**6.** *[Repealed by SI 1997/291, r.1.4, Sch.2 (effective April 1, 1997).]*

**6A.**—[2](1) Paragraphs 5 and 6 shall apply to the recognition and enforcement of an authentic instrument or court settlement as they apply to the recognition and enforcement of a judgment under the 1982 Act, but with such modifications as circumstances may require.

---

[1] As amended by SI 1993/2346 (effective October 25, 1993).
[2] Inserted by SI 1993/2346 (effective October 25, 1993).

(2)   Where paragraph 5 applies in relation to an authentic instrument, an application under section 12 of the 1982 Act shall be made, in writing, to the sheriff clerk for—

(a)   a certificate in Form 3A; and

(b)   a certified copy of the authentic instrument.

## Consequential amendments

**7.**—(1)   In paragraph 2 of the Act of Sederunt (Enforcement Abroad of Sheriff Court Judgments) 1962, for the word "abroad" wherever it occurs, substitute the words "in a country other than a country to which Parts I and II of the Civil Jurisdiction and Judgments Act 1982 applies".

(2)   In rule 13(1) of the Act of Sederunt (Maintenance Orders (Reciprocal Enforcement) Act 1972 Rules) 1974, after the word "Act", where it second and third appears in that rule, insert the words "or any other enactment".

SCHEDULE

Paragraph 3(2)

FORM 1

Certificate by sheriff clerk under section 18 of, and paragraph 4(1) of Schedule 6 to, the Civil Jurisdiction and Judgments Act 1982

Sheriff Court (*address*)

...............(Pursuer)v...........(Defender)

I,.........Sheriff Clerk at.........Sheriff Court,.............hereby certify:—

1.   That [AB] obtained judgment against [CD] in the above sheriff court on (*date*) for payment of.........with.........of expenses of which.........is unsatisfied.

2.   That the money provision in the judgment carries interest at the rate.........of *per centum per annum* from the.........day of.........19.........until payment.

3.   That the time for appealing against the judgment has expired [and no appeal has been brought within that time] *[or* and an appeal having been brought within that time has been finally disposed of].

4.   That enforcement of the judgment has not for the time being been suspended and that the time available for its enforcement has not expired.

5.   That this certificate is issued under section 18 of, and paragraph 4(1) of Schedule 6 to, the Civil Jurisdiction and Judgments Act 1982 and paragraph 3(2) of the Act of Sederunt (Enforcement of Judgments under the Civil Jurisdiction and Judgments Act 1982) 1986.

Dated at (*place*) this day of.........19.........

(*Signed*)

Sheriff Clerk

Paragraph 4(2)

FORM 2

Certificate by sheriff clerk under section 18 of, and paragraph 4(1)(*b*) of Schedule 7 to, the Civil Jurisdiction and Judgments Act 1982

Sheriff Court (*address*)

I,.........Sheriff Clerk at.........Sheriff Court,.............hereby certify:—

1.   That [AB] obtained judgment against [CD] in the above sheriff court on (*date*).

2.   That the copy of the interlocutor attached is a true copy of the decree *[or other order]* [and that the copy of the note or opinion of the sheriff attached is a true copy thereof].

3.   That the time for appealing against the interlocutor has expired [and no appeal has been brought within that time] *[or* and an appeal having been brought within that time has been finally disposed of].

4.   That enforcement of the decree *[or other order]* has not for the time being been suspended and that the time available for its enforcement has not expired.

5.   That this certificate is issued under section 18 of, and paragraph 4(1)(*b*) of Schedule 7 to, the Civil Jurisdiction and Judgments Act 1982 and paragraph 4(2) of the Act of Sederunt (Enforcement of Judgments under the Civil Jurisdiction and Judgments Act 1982) 1986.

Dated at (*place*) this.........day of 19............

(*Signed*)

Sheriff Clerk

Paragraph 5(2)

## FORM 3

Certificate by sheriff clerk under section 12 of the Civil Jurisdiction and Judgments Act 1982

Sheriff Court (*address*)

...............(Pursuer) v...........(Defender)

I,..........Sheriff Clerk at..........Sheriff Court,..............hereby certify:—

1.  That the initial writ raised by the pursuer, [AB] (*address*), was executed by citation of the defender, [CD] (*address*), served on him on the..........day of..........19..........by (*state mode of service*).

2.  That in the initial writ the pursuer sought [payment of the sum of £..........in respect of (*state briefly the nature of the claim*) [and (*state other craves of the writ*)].

3.  That [no] notice of intention to defend the action was lodged by the defender [on the-day of..........19..........] [and lodged defences on the..........day of..........19..........].

4.  That decree *[or other order]* was granted against the defender by the Sheriff of..........at.......... for payment of the sum of £.......... *[or state briefly the terms of the interlocutor or opinion of the sheriff]* [and (*state briefly any other craves of the initial writ*)] together with expenses of the action in the sum of £.........., all in terms of the certified copy interlocutor attached hereto.

5.  That [no] objection to the jurisdiction of the court has been made [on the grounds that..............].

6.  That the decree includes interest at the rate of..........*per centum per annum* on the total of the sum of £..........and expenses of £..........from the..........day of..........19..........until payment.

7.  That the interlocutor containing the decree has been served on the defender.

8.  That the time within which an appeal may be brought against the interlocutor [expires on..........*[or* has expired]].

9.  That an *[or* no] appeal against the interlocutor has been brought [and has been finally disposed of].

10.  That enforcement of the decree has not for the time being been suspended and the time available for its enforcement has not expired.

11.  That the whole pleadings of the parties are contained in the closed record *[or* initial writ] a copy of which is attached.

12.  That the pursuer *[or* defender] benefited from legal aid.

13.  That this certificate is issued under section 12 of the Civil Jurisdiction and Judgments Act 1982 and paragraph 5(2) of the Act of Sederunt (Enforcement of Judgments under the Civil Jurisdiction and Judgments Act 1982) 1986.

Dated at (*place*) this..........day of..........19..........

(*Signed*)

Sheriff Clerk

Paragraph 6A(2)

## [1]FORM 3A

Certificate by Sheriff Clerk under Section 12 of the Civil Jurisdiction and Judgments Act 1982
(Authentic Instruments)

Sheriff Court (*address*)

Authentic Instrument between (*names of parties*)

I, (*name*) sheriff clerk at (*name of court*) Sheriff Court, (*address*) hereby certify:—

1.  That the attached copy instrument is a true copy of an authentic instrument registered in the Sheriff Court Books on (*date*).

2.  That a copy of the authentic instrument so registered was served on the said (*name of debtor*) on (*date*).

3.  That (*state briefly the obligation contained in the authentic instrument*).

4.  That enforcement of the authentic instrument has not for the time being been suspended and the time available for enforcement has not expired.

5.  That this certificate is issued under section 12 of the Civil Jurisdiction and Judgments Act 1982 as modified by the Civil Jurisdiction and Judgments (Authentic Instruments and Court Settlements) Order 1993.

Dated at (*insert place*) this..........day of..........19..........

(*Signed*)

Sheriff Clerk

Paragraph 5(1)

---

[1] Inserted by SI 1993/2346 (effective 25th October 1993).

FORM 4

Notice to accompany service copy of judgment

To [AB] (*address*)

You are hereby served with a copy of the interlocutor of the Sheriff of..........at..........given on the..........day of..........19...........[In terms of this interlocutor you are required to (*state requirements of interlocutor*). Your failure to do so may result in further steps being taken to enforce the interlocutor.]

(*Signed*)

(*Address*)

Solicitor [*or* Sheriff Officer]

(*Place and date*)

Paragraph 5(1)

FORM 5

Execution of service of judgment and notice where service effected by officer of court or solicitor in Scotland

(*place and date*)

I, [AB] (*address*), hereby certify that upon the..........day of..........19.........., I duly served a copy of this judgment together with notice in terms of paragraph 5(1) of the Act of Sederunt (Enforcement of Judgments under the Civil Jurisdiction and Judgments Act 1982) 1986 upon [CD], defender. This I did by posting (*set forth mode of service; if by officer and not by post, add* in presence of EF (*address*) witness, hereto with me subscribing).

(*Signed*)

(*Address*)

Solicitor for Pursuer

[*or* Defender]

[or

(*Signed*)

Sheriff Officer

(*Signed*)

Witness]

Paragraph 6(8)

FORM 6

*[Revoked by SI 1997/291, r.1.4, Sched. 2 (effective April 1, 1997).]*

# SMALL CLAIMS (SCOTLAND) ORDER 1988

(SI 1988/1999)

*15 November 1988.*

The Lord Advocate, in exercise of the powers conferred on him by sections 35(2) and 36B(1) and (2) of the Sheriff Courts (Scotland) Act 1971, and of all other powers enabling him in that behalf, hereby makes the following Order, a draft of which has been laid before and approved by resolution of each House of Parliament:

## Citation and commencement

**1.** This Order may be cited as the Small Claims (Scotland) Order 1988 and shall come into force on 30th November 1988.

## Proceeding to be small claims

**2.**[1] The form of summary cause process, to be known as a "small claim", shall be used for the purposes of summary cause proceedings of one or other of the following descriptions, namely—

 (a) actions for payment of money not exceeding £3000 in amount (exclusive of interest and expenses), other than actions in respect of aliment and interim aliment, actions of defamation and actions for personal injury;

 (b) actions *ad factum praestandum* and actions for the recovery of possession of moveable property where in any such action *ad factum praestandum* or for recovery there is included, as an alternative to the claim, a claim for payment of a sum not exceeding £3,000 (exclusive of interest and expenses).

**2A.**[2] In article 2(a), "actions for personal injury" mean actions to which section 17 or 18 of the Prescription and Limitation (Scotland) Act 1973 applies.

**3.** For the purpose of article 2, actions *ad factum praestandum* include actions for delivery and actions for implement but do not include actions for count, reckoning and payment.

## Limit on award of expenses in small claims

**4.**—(1) The provisions of this article are without prejudice to the provisions of section 36B(3) of the Sheriff Courts (Scotland) Act 1971.

(2) No award of expenses shall be made in a small claim as specified in article 2 of this Order in which the value of the claim does not exceed £200.

(3)[3] In the case of any small claim other than a small claim to which paragraph (2) applies, the sheriff may award expenses—

 (a) not exceeding £150, where the value of the claim is £1500 or less; or

---

[1] As amended by the Small Claims (Scotland) Amendment Order (SSI 2007/496), art.2(2) (effective January 14, 2008).

[2] As inserted by the Small Claims (Scotland) Amendment Order (SSI 2007/496), art.2(3) (effective January 14, 2008).

[3] As substituted by the Small Claims (Scotland) Amendment Order (SSI 2007/496), art.2(4) (effective January 14, 2008).

(b)   not exceeding 10% of the value of the claim, where the value of the claim is greater than £1500.

# PROCEEDINGS IN THE SHERIFF COURT UNDER THE DEBTORS (SCOTLAND) ACT 1987, 1988

(SI 1988/2013)                                                        **D2.27**

*16 November 1988.*

ARRANGEMENT OF RULES

PART I INTRODUCTORY

The Lords of Council and Session, under and by virtue of the powers conferred on them by section 97 of the Debtors (Scotland) Act 1987 and of all other powers enabling them in that behalf, do hereby enact and declare:—

## PART I

## INTRODUCTORY

### Citation and commencement

**1.**—(1) This Act of Sederunt may be cited as the Act of Sederunt (Proceedings in the Sheriff Court under the Debtors (Scotland) Act 1987) 1988 and shall come into force on 30th November 1988.

(2) This Act of Sederunt shall be inserted in the Books of Sederunt.

### Interpretation

**2.** In this Act of Sederunt—
   (a) "the Act" means the Debtors (Scotland) Act 1987; and
   (b) a reference to a "form" means the form so numbered in the Schedule to this Act of Sederunt or a form substantially to the same effect with such variation as circumstances may require.

## PART II

## EXTENSION OF TIME TO PAY DEBTS AND RELATED MATTERS

### Notice of interest claimed

**3.**—(1) A creditor wishing to recover interest under a decree of the sheriff court shall serve on the defender the notice referred to in sections 1(7) and 5(7) of the Act (notice claiming and specifying amount of interest), either by posting it by recorded delivery post or by having it served personally by an officer of court—

(a) in the case of a decree requiring payment by instalments, no later than 14 days before the date on which the last instalment is due to be paid; or

(b) in the case of a decree requiring payment by lump sum within a certain period, no later than 14 days before the last day of such period.

## Applications for variation or recall of time to pay directions or for recall or restriction of arrestments

**4.**—(1) An application under section 3(1) of the Act for an order for variation or recall of a time to pay direction, or where appropriate, for recall or restriction of an arrestment, shall be in form 1.

(2) An application to which paragraph (1) of this rule applies shall be lodged with the sheriff clerk who shall—

(a) fix a date for the hearing of the application (which date shall be not less than seven days from the date of intimation made under subparagraph (c) of this paragraph);

(b) obtain from the sheriff a warrant to intimate the application to the debtor and the creditor;

(c) intimate the application and warrant to the debtor and the creditor; and

(d) complete a certificate of intimation.

## Applications for time to pay orders

**5.**—(1) A party who intends to apply for a time to pay order under section 5 of the Act shall complete and lodge with the sheriff clerk an application in form 2.

(2) An order by the sheriff under section 6(4) of the Act (creditor to furnish particulars of decree or other document) shall require a creditor to furnish the following information—

(a) the date of the decree or other document;

(b) the parties named in it;

(c) where appropriate, the court which granted it;

(d) details of the debt and any interest due; and

(e) any further information, relating to the decree or other document, as the sheriff shall consider necessary to enable him to determine the application.

(3) Service by the sheriff clerk of an application under paragraph (1) of this rule, or of any *interim* order of the sheriff under section 6(3) of the Act, shall be by recorded delivery post and the sheriff clerk shall serve, in like manner and at the same time, a copy of any *interim* order upon the applicant.

(4) Where a creditor fails to comply with an order referred to in subparagraph (2) of this rule, any order giving him an opportunity to make representations under section 6(5) of the Act shall be intimated to him by the sheriff clerk.

(5) A creditor may, within 14 days after the date of service of an application under paragraph (1) of this rule, object to the granting of the application by lodging with the sheriff clerk the appropriate portion of form 2 or a letter specifying his objections, including any counter-proposals on it.

(6) If no written objections are received from the creditor within the time specified in paragraph (5) of this rule, the sheriff shall make a time to pay order in accordance with the application.

(7) If written objections are received from the creditor within the time specified in paragraph (5) of this rule, the sheriff clerk shall—

    (a)   appoint a date for the hearing of the application;

    (b)   intimate that date to the parties and a copy of the written objections to the applicant; and

    (c)   advise the applicant that he may accept any counter-proposal prior to the date fixed for the hearing.

(8)   Where the debtor accepts counter-proposals made by the creditor in accordance with paragraph (5) of this rule, he shall intimate his acceptance to the sheriff clerk who shall intimate the acceptance to the creditor and advise parties that the hearing of the application will not proceed; and the sheriff shall make a time to pay order in terms of the counter-proposals.

(9)   The sheriff clerk shall intimate the decision of the sheriff on the application and any order relating to it to the parties by first class post and at the same time shall advise the creditor of the date when intimation was made to the debtor.

## Applications for variation or recall of time to pay orders, attachments or arrestments

6.—[1](1)   An application under section 10(1) of the Act for an order for variation or recall of a time to pay order or, where appropriate, for recall of an attachment or for recall or restriction of an arrestment shall be in form 3.

(2)   An application to which paragraph (1) of this rule applies shall be lodged with the sheriff clerk who shall—

    (a)   fix a date for the hearing of the application (which date shall be not less than seven days from the date of intimation made under subparagraph (c) of this paragraph);

    (b)   obtain from the sheriff a warrant to intimate the application to the debtor and the creditor;

    (c)   intimate the application and warrant to the debtor and the creditor; and

    (d)   complete a certificate of intimation.

(3)   The sheriff may, where he considers it appropriate, make an order requiring any person in possession of a summons or other writ or who holds an execution of diligence in respect of the debt to deliver it to the court.

## Consumer Credit Act 1974

7.—(1)   In any proceedings by a creditor or owner to enforce a regulated agreement or any related security within the meaning of the Consumer Credit Act 1974, the pursuer shall lodge a copy of any existing or previous time order relating to the debt.

(2)   Where a time to pay order is applied for, the applicant shall specify in his application whether a time order, within the meaning of the Consumer Credit Act 1974, relating to the debt has been made.

(3)   Where a time order is applied for under the Consumer Credit Act 1974, the applicant shall specify whether a time to pay direction or order relating to the debt has been made.

PART III[2]

---

[1] As amended by the Act of Sederunt (Debt Arrangement and Attachment (Scotland) Act 2002) 2002 (SSI 2002/560), art.4, Sch.3 (effective December 30, 2002).

[2] Revoked by the Act of Sederunt (Debt Arrangement and Attachment (Scotland) Act 2002) 2002 (SSI 2002/560), art.5, Sch.4 (effective December 30, 2002), subject to savings outlined in art.5.

PART IV

DILIGENCE AGAINST EARNINGS

### Earnings arrestment schedules

**38.**—(1)   An earnings arrestment schedule under section 47(2)(a) of the Act shall be in form 30.

(2)   An earnings arrestment schedule shall state—

(a)   the name, designation and address of the creditor, the debtor, the employer and any person residing in the United Kingdom to whom payment under the arrestment is to be made;

(b)   the decree or other document constituting the debt and when, where and by whom it was granted or issued;

(c)   the date on which any charge for payment was served; and

(d)   the debt outstanding and the manner of its calculation.

(3)[1]   There shall be attached to or reproduced upon the earnings arrestment schedule, and any copy intimated to the debtor, the terms of section 49(1) to (6) and section 49A of, and Schedule 2 to, the Act.

### Intimation of regulations made under section 49(7) of the Act

**39.**—(1)   The form of intimation to an employer under section 49(8) of the Act of regulations under section 49(7) of the Act varying Tables A, B or C of Schedule 2 to the Act or the percentages specified in section 49(5) or (6)(a)(ii) of the Act shall be in form 31.

(2)   The form of intimation required under paragraph (1) of this rule shall specify—

(a)   the date of service of the earnings arrestment schedule;

(b)   the name and address of the creditor, the debtor and the employer;

(c)[2]   that changes in the tables or percentages, as the case may be, have been made by regulations made by the Lord Advocate or the Scottish Ministers, the date when they were made and the date of their coming into force.

(3)   There shall be attached to or reproduced upon such a form of intimation the full text of the statutory deduction tables as varied by the regulations.

### Applications for orders that earnings arrestments invalid etc.

**40.**—(1)   An application under section 50(1) of the Act for declarator that an earnings arrestment is invalid or has ceased to have effect shall be in form 32.

(2)   An application to which paragraph (1) of this rule applies shall state—

(a)   the name and address of the creditor, the debtor, the officer of court who served the earnings arrestment schedule and the person on whom the schedule was served;

---

[1] As amended by the Act of Sederunt (Sheriff Court Rules Amendment) (Diligence) (SSI 2008/121) r.10(2) (effective April 1, 2008).

[2] As amended by SI 1999/1820, art.4, Sch.2, para.145 (effective July 1, 1999).

(b)   the court which granted the original decree and the date of that decree, or details of the summary warrant or other document, upon which the earnings arrestment proceeded;

(c)   the date of service of the earnings arrestment schedule;

(d)   the form of order sought;

(e)   the reasons for the application; and

(f)   any competent crave for expenses.

(3)   A copy of the earnings arrestment schedule shall, where practicable, be attached to such an application.

(4)   On the lodging of such an application the sheriff clerk shall—

(a)   fix a date for a hearing;

(b)   obtain from the sheriff a warrant for intimation;

(c)   intimate the application and warrant to the applicant, the creditor and, as appropriate, the debtor or the person on whom the earnings arrestment schedule was served; and

(d)   complete a certificate of intimation.

### Determination of disputes as to operation of earnings arrestment

**41.**—(1)   An application under section 50(3) of the Act for determination of any dispute as to the operation of an earnings arrestment shall be in form 33.

(2)   An application to which paragraph (1) of this rule applies shall specify—

(a)   the name and address of the creditor, the debtor, the officer of court who served the earnings arrestment schedule and the employer;

(b)   the court which granted the original decree and the date of that decree, or details of the summary warrant or other document, upon which the earnings arrestment proceeded;

(c)   the date of service of the earnings arrestment schedule;

(d)   the subject matter of the dispute;

(e)   the form of order sought, including any sum sought to be reimbursed or paid;

(f)   any claim for interest and the date from which such interest should run; and

(g)   any competent crave for expenses.

(3)   A copy of the earnings arrestment schedule shall, where practicable, be attached to such an application.

(4)   On the lodging of such an application the sheriff clerk shall—

(a)   fix a date for a hearing;

(b)   obtain from the sheriff a warrant for intimation;

(c)   intimate the application and warrant to the applicant and, as appropriate, the creditor, the debtor and the employer; and

(d)   complete a certificate of intimation.

(5)   The sheriff clerk shall intimate the sheriff's decision on such an application to any person to whom intimation of the application was made but who was not present when the application was determined.

### Current maintenance arrestment schedules

**42.**—(1)   A current maintenance arrestment schedule under section 51(2)(a) of the Act shall be in form 34.

(2)   A current maintenance schedule shall state—

(a)   the name, designation and address of the creditor, the debtor, the employee and any person residing in the United Kingdom to whom payment under the arrestment is to be made;

(b) the maintenance order constituting the current maintenance, when and by whom it was granted or issued, and, where appropriate, details of its registration or confirmation;

(c) the maintenance payable under the maintenance order by the debtor expressed as a daily rate;

(d) where appropriate, the date of intimation made to the debtor under section 54(1) of the Act and particulars of default; and

(e) whether or not income tax falls to be deducted from the maintenance payable by the debtor.

(3) There shall be attached to or reproduced upon the current maintenance schedule, and any copy intimated to the debtor, the terms of section 53(1) and (2) of the Act.

## Intimation of regulations made under section 53(3) of the Act

**43.**—(1) The form of intimation to an employer under section 53(4) of the Act of regulations under section 53(3) of the Act varying the sum specified in section 53 (2)(b) of the Act shall be in form 35.

(2) The form of intimation required under paragraph (1) of these rules shall state—

(a) the date of service of the current maintenance arrestment schedule;

(b) the name and address of the creditor, the debtor and the employer; and

(c)[1] the new sum which is applicable in accordance with regulations made by the Lord Advocate or the Scottish Ministers, the date when they were made and the date of their coming into force.

## Intimation of changes in small maintenance payments limits

**44.**—(1) The form of intimation to an employer under section 53(5) of the Act of a change in the small maintenance payments limits shall be in form 36.

(2) The form of intimation required under paragraph (1) of this rule shall specify—

(a) the date of service of the current maintenance arrestment schedule;

(b) the name and address of the creditor, the debtor and the employer; and

(c) that changes have been made to section 351(2) of the Income and Corporation Taxes Act 1988, what these changes are and the date of their coming into force.

(3) There shall be attached to or reproduced upon such a form of intimation the full text of section 351(2) of the Income and Corporation Taxes Act 1988.

## Notice to debtor prior to service of current maintenance arrestment

**45.**—[2](1) Intimation to a debtor under a maintenance order required by section 54(1)(a) of the Act prior to service of a current maintenance arrestment shall be given by intimating to him a notice in form 37 together with a copy of the relevant maintenance order.

(2) The notice referred to in paragraph (1) of this rule shall contain—

(a) the name and address of the creditor and of the debtor;

---

[1] As amended by S.I. 1999 No. 1820, Art. 4, Sched. 2, para. 145 (effective July 1, 1999).
[2] Substituted by S.I. 1991 No. 1920.

    (b)   details of the making, registration or confirmation of the maintenance order;

    (c)   guidance as to the manner in which payment may be made; and

    (d)   a statement of the consequences of failure to comply with the maintenance order.

(3)   Intimation in accordance with this rule shall—

    (a)   where the debtor resides in the United Kingdom, be by recorded delivery post; and

    (b)   where the debtor resides outside the United Kingdom, be by any competent method of service appropriate to that place.

(4)   The creditor shall prepare a certificate that intimation has been made in accordance with this rule and shall retain the certificate while the current maintenance arrestment is in force.

(5)   Where, in the exercise of his powers under section 24B of the Social Security Act 1986, the Secretary of State seeks to enforce a maintenance order on behalf of a claimant, the following notice shall be appended to form 37:—

    "The Secretary of State for Social Security ('the creditor') intends to enforce this maintenance order under the powers conferred on him by section 24B of the Social Security Act 1986.".

## Applications for orders that current maintenance arrestments are invalid etc.

**46.**—(1)   An application under section 55(1) of the Act for declarator that a current maintenance arrestment is invalid or has ceased to have effect shall be in form 38.

(2)   An application to which paragraph (1) of this rule applies shall specify—

    (a)   the name and address of the creditor, the debtor, the officer of court who served the current maintenance arrestment schedule and the person on whom the schedule was served;

    (b)   the maintenance order and when, where and by whom it was granted or issued and, where appropriate, details of its registration or confirmation;

    (c)   the date of service of the current maintenance arrestment schedule;

    (d)   the reasons for seeking the order;

    (e)   the form of order sought; and

    (f)   any competent crave for expenses.

(3)   A copy of the current maintenance arrestment schedule shall, where practicable, be attached to such an application.

(4)   On the lodging of such an application the sheriff clerk shall—

    (a)   fix a date for a hearing;

    (b)   obtain from the sheriff a warrant for intimation;

    (c)   intimate the application and warrant to the applicant, the creditor and, as appropriate, the debtor or the person on whom the current maintenance arrestment schedule was served; and

    (d)   complete a certificate of intimation.

## Recall of current maintenance arrestments

**47.**—(1)   An application under section 55(2) of the Act for a recall of a current maintenance arrestment shall be in form 39.

(2)   An application to which paragraph (1) of this rule applies shall specify—

    (a)   the name and address of the creditor, the debtor, the officer of court who served the current maintenance arrestment schedule and the employer;

    (b)   the maintenance order and when, where and by whom it was granted or issued and, where appropriate, details of its registration or confirmation;

    (c)   the date of service of the current maintenance arrestment schedule;

    (d)   such information as the applicant considers appropriate to satisfy the sheriff that he will not default again in paying maintenance;

    (e)   the order sought; and

    (f)   any competent crave for expenses.

(3)   A copy of the current maintenance arrestment schedule shall, where practicable, be attached to such an application.

(4)   On the lodging of such an application the sheriff clerk shall—

    (a)   fix a date for a hearing;

    (b)   obtain from the sheriff a warrant for intimation;

    (c)   intimate the application and warrant to the applicant and the creditor; and

    (d)   complete a certificate of intimation.

## Determination of disputes as to operation of current maintenance arrestments

**48.**—(1)   An application under section 55(5) of the Act for determination of any dispute as to the operation of a current maintenance arrestment shall be in form 40.

(2)   An application to which paragraph (1) of this rule applies shall specify—

    (a)   the name and address of the creditor, the debtor, the officer of court who served the current maintenance arrestment schedule and the employer;

    (b)   the maintenance order and when, where and by whom it was granted or issued and, where appropriate, details of its registration or confirmation;

    (c)   the date of service of the current maintenance arrestment schedule;

    (d)   the subject matter of the dispute;

    (e)   the form of order sought, including any sum sought to be reimbursed or paid;

    (f)   any claim for interest and the date from which such interest should run; and

    (g)   any competent crave for expenses.

(3)   A copy of the current maintenance arrestment schedule shall, where practicable, be attached to such an application.

(4)   On the lodging of such an application the sheriff clerk shall—

    (a)   fix a date for hearing;

    (b)   obtain from the sheriff a warrant for intimation;

    (c)   intimate the application and warrant to the applicant and, as appropriate, the creditor, the debtor and the employer; and

    (d)   complete a certificate of intimation.

## Intimation by sheriff clerk where non-Scottish maintenance order ceases to have effect

**49.**   Where a maintenance order pronounced outwith Scotland and registered in a sheriff court for enforcement in Scotland ceases to have effect because the debtor no longer resides in Scotland, the sheriff clerk of that court shall, so far as reasonably practicable, intimate those facts—

    (a)   where a current maintenance arrestment is in force, to the person upon whom the current maintenance arrestment schedule was served; and

(b) where a conjoined arrestment order is in force, to the sheriff clerk to whom payments require to be made by the employer in terms of such order.

## Intimation by creditor under section 57(4) of the Act

**50.** Intimation by the creditor to an employer required by section 57(4) of the Act shall be in writing.

## Applications by debtors for payment by creditors

**51.**—(1) An application under section 57(6) of the Act by a debtor for an order requiring a creditor to pay an amount not exceeding twice the amount recoverable by the debtor under section 57(5) of the Act shall be in form 41.

(2) An application to which paragraph (1) of this rule applies shall specify—

(a) the name and address of the debtor, the creditor, the officer of court who served the arrestment and the employer;

(b) the court which granted the original decree and the date of that decree, or details of the summary warrant or other document, upon which arrestment proceeded;

(c) the amount of the debt or the sum to be deducted from the debtor's earnings;

(d) where appropriate, the expenses of diligence;

(e) where appropriate, whether the debt recoverable under the earnings arrestment is paid or otherwise extinguished and, if so, from what date and in what circumstances;

(f) where appropriate, whether the current maintenance arrestment has ceased to have effect and, if so, from what date and in what circumstances;

(g) where appropriate, whether the debt being enforced by the earnings arrestment has ceased to be enforceable by diligence and, if so, from what date and in what circumstances;

(h) the calculation showing the sum alleged to have been received by the creditor in excess of entitlement;

(i) the sum sought from the creditor and the grounds for seeking such sum; and

(j) any competent crave for expenses.

(3) A copy of the relevant arrestment schedule shall, where practicable, be attached to such an application.

(4) On the lodging of such an application the sheriff clerk shall—

(a) fix a date for a hearing;

(b) obtain from the sheriff a warrant for intimation;

(c) intimate the application and warrant to the applicant and to the creditor; and

(d) complete a certificate of intimation.

(5) The sheriff clerk shall intimate the sheriff's decision in such an application to the creditor if the creditor was not present when the application was determined.

## Applications by second creditors for information

**52.**—(1) An application by a second creditor under section 59(5) of the Act for an order to ordain an employer to give information relating to any other earnings arrestment or current maintenance arrestment to the second creditor shall be in form 42.

(2) An application to which paragraph (1) of this rule applies shall specify—

    (a) the name and address of the applicant, the debtor, the employer and the officer of court who served the arrestment schedule in respect of the debt due to the applicant;

    (b) the date of service of the applicant's earnings arrestment or current maintenance arrestment schedule;

    (c) that the arrestment did not come into effect by virtue of section 59 of the Act;

    (d) the information required by the applicant and which he alleges has not been provided by the employer;

    (e) the order sought; and

    (f) any competent crave for expenses.

(3) On the lodging of such an application the sheriff clerk shall—

    (a) fix a date for a hearing;

    (b) obtain from the sheriff a warrant for intimation;

    (c) intimate the application and warrant to the applicant and the employer; and

    (d) complete a certificate of intimation.

(4) The sheriff clerk shall intimate the sheriff's decision in such an application to the employer if the employer was not present when the application was determined.

## Applications for conjoined arrestment orders

**53.**—(1) An application under section 60(2) of the Act by a qualified creditor for a conjoined arrestment order shall be in form 43.

(2) An application to which paragraph (1) of this rule applies shall specify—

    (a) the name and address of the applicant, the debtor, the employer and any person residing in the United Kingdom to whom payment is to be made in respect of the applicant's debt;

    (b) such information relating to the debt due to the applicant as would require to be specified in an earnings arrestment schedule or, as the case may be, a current maintenance arrestment schedule;

    (c) in respect of each earnings arrestment or current maintenance arrestment already in effect against the debtor in the hands of the same employer—

        (i) the name and address of the creditor;

        (ii) the date and the place of the execution of such arrestments; and

        (iii) the debt recoverable specified in the earnings arrestment schedule or, as the case may be, the daily rate of maintenance specified in the current maintenance Schedule; and

    (d) the expenses of the application.

(3) On the lodging of such an application the sheriff clerk shall—

    (a) intimate the application, together with a form of notice and response in form 44, to the debtor and any other creditor of the debtor already enforcing a debt by an earnings arrestment or current maintenance arrestment in the hands of the same employer; and

(b)  complete a certificate of intimation.

(4)  Where a creditor or the debtor intends to object to such an application, he shall complete and lodge with the sheriff clerk the form of notice and response in form 44 within 14 days after the date of intimation.

(5)  On receipt of such a form of notice and response the sheriff clerk shall fix a date for a hearing and intimate the date to the applicant and any person who received intimation of the application.

(6)  Where such a form of notice and response is not timeously lodged with the sheriff clerk, the sheriff may grant the application or may make such other order as he considers appropriate.

## Conjoined arrestment orders

**54.**—(1)  A conjoined arrestment order shall be in form 45.

(2)  A conjoined arrestment order shall—

(a)  specify any earnings arrestment or current maintenance arrestment in effect against the earnings of the debtor in the hands of the same employer;

(b)  notify the employer that he must deduct a sum calculated in accordance with section 63 of the Act from the debtor's net earnings on any pay day and to pay the sum deducted to the sheriff clerk as soon as is reasonably practicable for so long as the order is in effect;

(c)  specify, as appropriate, the amount recoverable in respect of the debt or debts and maintenance, expressed as a daily rate or aggregate of the daily rates;

(d)  state the address of the sheriff clerk to whom payments are to be sent and, where appropriate, a court reference number; and

(e)  if appropriate, include an award of expenses.

(3)  The sheriff clerk shall serve a copy of the conjoined arrestment order (or such final order of the sheriff in an application under rule 53 above) on the applicant, the employer, the debtor and the creditors in any earnings arrestment or current maintenance arrestment recalled by the order.

(4)  There shall be attached to or reproduced upon every copy conjoined arrestment order as served on any person the full text of section 63(1) to (6) of the Act.

(5)  There shall be enclosed with a conjoined arrestment order served on any person a notice in form 46 which shall require all creditors whose arrestments have been recalled to inform the sheriff clerk, within 14 days of the date of service of the notice, of the name and address of the person within the United Kingdom to whom payments should be made in respect of his debt.

(6)  Subject to paragraphs (7) and (8) of this rule, service under this rule shall be by recorded delivery post.

(7)  Where such service has been unsuccessful, reservice—

(a)  in the case of service on the employer, shall be effected by an officer of court on payment of his fee by the applicant; and

(b)  in any other case of service on a person within the United Kingdom, shall be by ordinary first class post.

(8)  Service under this rule on a person outside the United Kingdom which cannot be effected by recorded delivery post shall be by any other competent method of service.

## Applications by sheriff clerks for warrants for diligence

**55.**—(1) An application by a sheriff clerk under section 60(9)(c) of the Act for a warrant for diligence against an employer for recovery of sums which are claimed to be due shall be in form 47.

(2) An application to which paragraph (1) of this rule applies shall specify—

    (a) the name and address of the sheriff clerk, the employer, the debtor and the creditors under the conjoined arrestment order;

    (b) the date of the conjoined arrestment order and details of its service on the employer;

    (c) the sum claimed to be due by the employer and details of its calculation; and

    (d) the circumstances in which the sum is said to be due and, if appropriate, any reasons given to the sheriff clerk for its not having been paid.

(3) On preparing such an application the sheriff clerk shall—

    (a) fix a date for a hearing;

    (b) obtain from the sheriff a warrant for intimation;

    (c) intimate the application and warrant to the employer, the debtor and the creditors under the conjoined arrestment order; and

    (d) complete a certificate of intimation.

## Applications by creditors for information under section 62 of the Act

**56.**—(1) An application by a creditor under section 62(4) of the Act for an order for information which an employer requires to provide in accordance with section 62(2) or (3) of the Act shall be in form 48.

(2) An application to which paragraph (1) of this rule applies shall specify—

    (a) the name and address of the applicant, the debtor, the employer and the officer of court who served the arrestment schedule in respect of the debt due to the applicant;

    (b) the date of service of the applicant's earnings arrestment or current maintenance arrestment schedule;

    (c) the reason for that arrestment not coming into effect or ceasing to have effect;

    (d) the information required by the applicant and which he alleges has not been provided by the employer; and

    (e) any competent crave for expenses.

(3) On the lodging of such an application the sheriff clerk shall—

    (a) fix a date for a hearing;

    (b) obtain from the sheriff a warrant for intimation;

    (c) intimate the application and warrant to the applicant and the employer; and

    (d) complete a certificate of intimation.

(4) The sheriff clerk shall intimate the sheriff's decision on such an application to the employer if the employer was not present when the application was determined.

## Application for variation of conjoined arrestment orders

**57.**—(1) An application under section 62(5) of the Act for variation of a conjoined arrestment order by a creditor whose debt is not being enforced under a conjoined arrestment order but would, but for the order, be entitled to enforce the debt by an earnings arrestment or current maintenance order shall be in form 49.

(2)　An application to which paragraph (1) of this rule applies shall specify—

    (a)　the name and address of the applicant, the debtor, the employer and any person residing in the United Kingdom to whom payment is to be made in respect of the applicant's debt;

    (b)　the date of the conjoined arrestment order;

    (c)　such information relating to the debt due to the applicant as would require to be specified in an earnings arrestment schedule or, as the case may be, a current maintenance arrestment schedule; and

    (d)　the expenses of the application.

(3)　On the lodging of such an application the sheriff clerk shall—

    (a)　intimate the application together with a form of notice and response in form 50 to the debtor and any creditor whose debt is being enforced under the conjoined arrestment order; and

    (b)　complete a certificate of intimation.

(4)　Where a creditor or the debtor wishes to object to such an application, he shall complete and lodge with the sheriff clerk the form of notice and response in form 50 within 14 days after the date of intimation.

(5)　On receipt of such a form of notice and response, the sheriff clerk shall fix a date for a hearing and intimate the date to the applicant and to those who received intimation of the application.

(6)　Where such a form of notice and response is not timeously lodged with the sheriff clerk, the sheriff may grant the application or may make such other order as he considers appropriate.

(7)　Where an application to which paragraph (1) of this rule applies has been granted, there shall be served by the sheriff clerk with the sheriffs decision—

    (a)　a copy of the conjoined arrestment order as varied; and

    (b)　a notice in form 51.

(8)　Subject to paragraphs (9) and (10) of this rule, service under this rule and section 62(6) of the Act shall be by recorded delivery post.

(9)　Where such service has been unsuccessful, reservice—

    (a)　in the case of service on the employer, shall be effected by an officer of court on payment of his fee by the applicant; and

    (b)　in any other case of service on a person within the United Kingdom, shall be by ordinary first class post.

(10)　Service under this rule and section 62(6) of the Act on a person outside the United Kingdom which cannot be effected by recorded delivery post shall be by any other competent method of service.

### Intimation of changes to calculation of sum payable by employer

**58.**—(1)　Intimation by the sheriff clerk to an employer operating a conjoined arrestment order—

    (a)　under section 63(7) of the Act, shall be in form 52; or

    (b)　under section 63(8) of the Act, shall be in form 53.

(2)　A form of intimation required under paragraph (1) of this rule shall state—

    (a)　the date of the conjoined arrestment order and any variation of it and the date of service of it on the employer;

    (b)　the name and address of the debtor, the employer and the sheriff clerk; and

    (c)　that changes to—

        (i)　Tables A, B and C of Schedule 2 to the Act;

    (ii)   the percentages specified in section 49(5) and (6)(a)(ii) of the Act;

    (iii)  the sums specified in section 63(4)(b) of the Act; or

    (iv)  the small maintenance payments limits mentioned in section [351(2)] of the Income and Corporation Taxes Act [1988] have been made and the date when they were made and of their coming into force.

(3)   There shall be attached to or reproduced upon form 52 the full text of the appropriate provisions of the Act.

(4)   There shall be attached to or reproduced upon form 53 the full text of section 351(2) of the Income and Corporation Taxes Act 1988.

### Determination of disputes as to operation of conjoined arrestment orders

**59.**—(1)   An application under section 65(1) of the Act for determination of any dispute as to the operation of a conjoined arrestment order shall be in form 54.

(2)   An application to which paragraph (1) of this rule applies shall specify—

    (a)   the name and address of the applicant, the debtor, the creditors whose debts are being enforced by the conjoined arrestment order, the employer and the sheriff clerk;

    (b)   the date of the conjoined arrestment order and the court which made the order;

    (c)   the subject matter of the dispute;

    (d)   the order sought, including details of any sum for which reimbursement or repayment is sought;

    (e)   any claim for interest and the date from which such interest shall run; and

    (f)   any competent crave for expenses.

(3)   On the lodging of such an application the sheriff clerk shall—

    (a)   fix a date for a hearing;

    (b)   obtain from the sheriff a warrant for intimation;

    (c)   intimate the application and warrant to the applicant and, as appropriate, the debtor, the creditors whose debts are being enforced by the conjoined arrestment order and the employer; and

    (d)   complete the certificate of intimation.

(4)   The sheriff clerk shall intimate the sheriff's decision on such an application to any person to whom intimation of the application was made but who was not present when the application was determined.

### Applications for payment by creditors to debtors

**60.**—(1)   An application under section 65(7) of the Act for an order requiring the creditor to pay to the debtor a sum not exceeding twice the sum recoverable by the sheriff clerk in accordance with section 65(6) of the Act shall be in form 55.

(2)   An application in which paragraph (1) of this rule applies shall specify—

    (a)   the name and address of the debtor and creditor;

    (b)   the date of the conjoined arrestment order and the court which made the order;

    (c)   whether, in the case of an ordinary debt, the debt has been paid, otherwise extinguished or has ceased to be enforceable by diligence and also why and from what date;

    (d)   whether, in the case of current maintenance, the obligation to pay maintenance has ceased or has ceased to be enforceable by diligence and if so why and from what date;

    (e)   the calculation showing the sum alleged to have been received by the creditor in excess of entitlement;

    (f)   the sum sought from the creditor;

    (g)   the applicant's grounds for seeking such sum;

    (h)   any competent crave for expenses.

(3)   On the lodging of such an application the sheriff clerk shall—

    (a)   fix a date for a hearing;

    (b)   obtain from the sheriff a warrant for intimation;

    (c)   intimate the application and warrant to the applicant and the creditor; and

    (d)   complete a certificate of intimation.

(4)   The sheriff clerk shall intimate the sheriff's decision on such an application to the creditor if the creditor was not present when the application was determined.

### Recall of conjoined arrestment orders under section 66(1)(a) of the Act

**61.**—(1)   An application under section 66(1)(a) of the Act by a debtor, creditor, employer, sheriff clerk or interim, or permanent, trustee in the debtor's sequestration for recall of a conjoined arrestment order shall be in form 56.

(2)   An application to which paragraph (1) of this rule applies shall specify—

    (a)   the name and address of the debtor, the creditors whose debts are being enforced under the conjoined arrestment order, the person on whom a copy of the order or an order varying the order was served under section 60(7) or 62(6) of the Act, any trustee in the debtor's sequestration and the sheriff clerk to whom payment is made under the order;

    (b)   the date of the conjoined arrestment order and the court which made the order;

    (c)   if appropriate, that the conjoined arrestment order is invalid and why it is claimed to be invalid;

    (d)   if appropriate, that all ordinary debts enforced by the order have been paid or otherwise extinguished or have ceased to be enforceable and in each case when and how this occurred;

    (e)   if appropriate, that all obligations to pay current maintenance enforced by the order have ceased or have ceased to be enforceable by diligence and in either case when and how this occurred;

    (f)   if appropriate, that the debtor's estate has been sequestrated and when this occurred;

    (g)   the order sought and any consequential order; and

    (h)   any competent crave for expenses.

(3)   Subject to paragraph (4) of this rule, on the lodging of such an application the sheriff clerk shall—

    (a)   fix a date for a hearing;

    (b)   obtain from the sheriff a warrant for intimation;

    (c)   intimate the application and warrant to the applicant and, as appropriate, the debtor, the creditors whose debts are being enforced under the order, the person on whom a copy of the order or an order varying the order was served under section 60(7) or 62(6) of the Act and the interim, or permanent, trustee in the debtor's sequestration; and

    (d)   complete a certificate of intimation.

(4)   Where such an application has been made by all of the creditors whose debts are being enforced by the conjoined arrestment order or where the sheriff clerk has previously received intimation from all of those creditors as to the matters referred to in section 66(1)(a)(ii) of the Act, the sheriff may grant the application without requiring intimation or any hearing of the application.

### Recall of conjoined arrestment orders under section 66(1)(b) of the Act

**62.**—(1)   An application under section 66(1)(b) of the Act by all creditors whose debts are being enforced for recall of a conjoined arrestment order shall be in form 57.

(2)   An application to which paragraph (1) of this rule applies shall specify—
   (a)   the names and addresses of the applicants and the debtors; and
   (b)   the date of the conjoined arrestment order and the court which made the order;
   (c)   the reasons for the application; and
   (d)   any consequential order sought.

(3)   On the lodging of such an application the sheriff may grant it immediately or may make such other order as he considers appropriate.

### Applications for variation of conjoined arrestment orders

**63.**—(1)   An application under section 66(4) of the Act for variation of a conjoined arrestment order shall be in form 58.

(2)   An application to which paragraph (1) of this rule applies shall specify—
   (a)   the name and address of the debtor, the employer, the creditors whose debts are being enforced by the conjoined arrestment order and the sheriff clerk;
   (b)   the date of the conjoined arrestment order and the court which made the order;
   (c)   if appropriate, that any ordinary debt being enforced by the order has been paid, otherwise extinguished or has ceased to be enforceable by diligence and in each case when and how this occurred;
   (d)   if appropriate, that an order or decree varying, superseding or recalling any maintenance order has come into effect and when and by whom the order or decree was granted;
   (e)   if appropriate, that an obligation to pay maintenance has ceased or has ceased to be enforceable in Scotland and in either case when or how this occurred;
   (f)   the order sought; and
   (g)   any competent crave for expenses.

(3)   On the lodging of such an application the sheriff clerk shall—
   (a)   fix a date for a hearing;
   (b)   obtain from the sheriff a warrant for intimation;
   (c)   intimate the application and warrant to the applicant and, as appropriate, to the debtor, the creditors whose debts are being enforced by the conjoined arrestment order and the employer; and
   (d)   complete a certificate of intimation.

### Requests by creditors to cease enforcement of debts by conjoined arrestment orders

**64.**—(1)   A request by a creditor to the sheriff under section 66(6) of the Act to vary a conjoined arrestment order, by ordering that a debt being enforced by him under it shall cease to be so enforced, shall be in writing.

(2)   The sheriff may grant or refuse such a request or may make such order as he considers appropriate.

### Service of sheriff's decision in applications for recall or variation of conjoined arrestment orders

**65.**—(1)   Subject to the following paragraphs of this rule, the final order of the sheriff in an application to which rule 61, 62, 63 or 64 applies shall be served upon the applicant, the employer, the debtor and the creditors whose debts are being enforced under the conjoined arrestment order by recorded delivery post.

(2)   Where such service has been unsuccessful, reservice—

    (a)   in the case of service on the employer, shall be effected by an officer of court on payment of his fee by the applicant; and

    (b)   in any other case of service on a person within the United Kingdom, shall be by ordinary first class post.

(3)   Where an application for variation of a conjoined arrestment order to which rule 63 above applies has been granted, there shall be served by the sheriff clerk with the final order—

    (a)   a copy of the conjoined arrestment order as varied; and

    (b)   a notice in form 59.

(4)   Service under this rule on a person outwith the United Kingdom which cannot be effected by recorded delivery post shall be by any other competent method of service.

### Application where employer fails to give notice under section 70A (5) of the Act

**65A.**—[1](1)   An application by a creditor under section 70B of the Act shall be in Form 59a.

(2)   An application to which paragraph (1) of this rule applies shall specify—

    (a)   the name and address of the applicant, the debtor, the employer and the officer of court who served the arrestment schedule in respect of the debt due to the applicant; and

    (b)   the date of service of the applicant's earnings arrestment schedule, current maintenance arrestment schedule or conjoined arrestment order.

(3)   On the lodging of such an application the sheriff clerk shall—

    (a)   fix a date for a hearing;

    (b)   obtain from the sheriff a warrant for intimation;

    (c)   intimate the application and warrant to the applicant and the employer; and

    (d)   complete a certificate of intimation.

---

[1] As inserted by the Act of Sederunt (Sheriff Court Rules Amendment) (Diligence) (SSI 2008/121) r.10(3) (effective April 1, 2008).

(4) The sheriff clerk shall intimate the sheriff's decision on such an application to the employer if the employer was not present when the application was determined.

### Service by post of arrests against earnings

**66.** On the face of the envelope used for service of an earnings arrestment schedule, a current maintenance arrestment schedule or a conjoined arrestment order there shall be written or printed the following notice—

"ARRESTMENT OF EARNINGS OF AN EMPLOYEE
This letter contains an earnings arrestment schedule/current maintenance arrestment schedule/ conjoined arrestment order. If delivery of the letter cannot be made at the address shown it is to be returned immediately to (*name and address*).".

### Certificates of execution

**67.** The certificate of execution of an earnings arrestment or a current maintenance arrestment shall be in form 60.

PART V

WARRANTS FOR DILIGENCE

### Summary warrants

**68.**—[1] A summary warrant for recovery of any sum shall be in form 61 or 62, as the case may be.

### Applications by creditors for warrants to enforce acquired rights

**69.**—(1) An application to the sheriff clerk under section 88(2) of the Act by a person, who has acquired a right by assignation, confirmation as executor or otherwise to a decree, obligation, order or determination referred to in section 88(1) of the Act for a warrant authorising diligence, shall be made by minute endorsed on the extract decree or other document.

(2) The sheriff clerk shall, where he is satisfied that the applicant's right is established, endorse the warrant sought in such an application on the extract decree or other document.

PART VA[2]

ARRESTMENT IN EXECUTION

### Certificate of execution

**69A.** A certificate of execution of an arrestment in execution shall be in Form 63B.

---

[1] As amended by S.I. 1996 No. 2709 (effective November 11, 1996).
[2] As inserted by the Act of Sederunt (Sheriff Court Rules Amendment) (Diligence) 2009 (SSI 2009/ 107) (effective April 22, 2009).

### Service of final decree

**69B.** The copy final decree served under section 73C(2) of the Act (arrestment on the dependence followed by decree) shall be in Form 63C.

### Failure to disclose information

**69C.**—(1) An application under section 73H(1) of the Act (failure to disclose information)—

    (a)   shall be in Form 63D; and

    (b)   must be intimated by the creditor to the debtor and to the arrestee.

  (2)  On the lodging of an application under paragraph (1) the sheriff may—

    (a)   fix a date for a hearing; and

    (b)   order the sheriff clerk to intimate the date of the hearing in Form 63E to such persons as the sheriff considers appropriate.

### Notice of objection

**69D.**—(1) A notice of objection under section 73M of the Act (notice of objection) shall be in Form 63F.

  (2)  On the lodging of a notice of objection under paragraph (1) the sheriff must—

    (a)   fix a date for the hearing; and

    (b)   order the sheriff clerk to intimate the date of the hearing in Form 63E to such persons as the sheriff considers appropriate.

### Application for release of property where arrestment unduly harsh

**69E.**—(1) An application under section 73Q(2) of the Act (application for release of property where arrestment unduly harsh) shall be in Form 63G.

  (2)  On the lodging of an application under paragraph (1) the sheriff must—

    (a)[1]  fix a date for the hearing; and

    (b)   order the sheriff clerk to intimate the date of the hearing in Form 63E to such persons as the sheriff considers appropriate.

### Power of sheriff to make orders

**69F.** The sheriff may make such other order for the progress of an application under this Part as he considers appropriate in the circumstances of the case.

---

[1] As amended by the Act of Sederunt (Sheriff Court Rules) (Miscellaneous Amendments) 2009 (SSI 2009/294) r.13 (effective October 1, 2009).

## Service of documents

**69G.** Rules 5.3 to 5.6 of the Ordinary Cause Rules in the First Schedule to the Sheriff Courts (Scotland) Act 1907 are to apply to the service or intimation of any document under this Part as they apply to the service or intimation of any document under those Rules.

Part VI

Miscellaneous

## Representation

**70.** A party to any proceedings under the Act shall be entitled to be represented by a person other than an advocate or a solicitor if the sheriff is satisfied that such person is a suitable representative and is duly authorised to represent the party.

## Powers of sheriff

**71.**—[1](1) Without prejudice to any other powers competent to him, the sheriff, in the exercise of the powers conferred on him by these rules, shall have the same powers as regards the summoning and examination of witnesses, the production of documents, the administration of oaths and the correcting of interlocutors as those which he has in an ordinary cause to which the Ordinary Cause Rules in the First Schedule to the Sheriff Courts (Scotland) Act 1907(1) apply and in particular shall have the same powers as regards the identification and treatment of vulnerable witnesses within the meaning of section 11(1) of the Vulnerable Witnesses (Scotland) Act 2004 as those which he has under Chapter 45 of the Ordinary Cause Rules.

## Appeals

**72.**—(1) An application for leave to appeal from a decision of the sheriff under the Act shall be made in writing to the sheriff clerk within seven days of the making of the decision and shall specify the question of law upon which the appeal is to proceed.

(2) The sheriff may consider such an application without hearing parties unless it appears to him to be necessary to hold a hearing on the application in which case the sheriff clerk shall intimate the date, place and time of the hearing to the parties.

(3) Subject to section 103(2) of the Act, an appeal shall—

    (a) be made by note of appeal written by the appellant on the written record containing the order appealed against or on a separate sheet lodged with the sheriff clerk;

    (b) be as nearly as may be in the following terms—

> "The applicant *[or* respondent or *other]* appeals to the sheriff principal/Court of Session";

    (c) be signed by the appellant or his representative and bear the date on which it is signed; and

    (d) where appeal is made to the Court of Session, bear the name and address of the solicitors in Edinburgh who will be acting for the appellant.

---

[1] As substituted by the Act of Sederunt (Proceedings in the Sheriff Court under the Debtors (Scotland) Act 1987) Amendment (Vulnerable Witnesses (Scotland) Act 2004) (SSI 2007/465) art.2(2) (effective November 1, 2007).

(4)   The appellant shall, at the same time as marking his appeal under paragraph (3) of this rule, intimate that he is doing so to the other parties.

(5)   The sheriff shall, on an appeal being marked under paragraph (3) of this rule, state in writing the reasons for his original decision.

(6)   Where an appeal is marked, the sheriff clerk shall transmit the process within four days to the sheriff principal or to the Deputy Principal Clerk of Session, as the case may be.

## Intimation

**73.**—(1)   A warrant for intimation referred to in these rules shall be in form 64.

(2)   The sheriff may order intimation to persons other than those to whom intimation is required under these rules as he considers appropriate.

## Hearings

**74.**   At any hearing (other than the hearing of an appeal) fixed under these rules the cause to be dealt with may be—

(a)   determined;

(b)   continued for such further procedure as the sheriff considers appropriate; or

(c)   if no party appears, dismissed.

## Dispensing power of sheriff

**75.**   The sheriff may relieve any party from the consequences of any failure to comply with the provisions of these rules which is shown to be due to mistake, oversight or other cause, not being wilful non-observance of the same, on such terms and conditions as seem just; and in any such case the sheriff may make such order as seems just by way of extension of time, lodging or amendment of papers or otherwise so as to enable the cause to proceed as if such failure had not happened.

### SCHEDULE

#### FORMS

*Arrangement of Forms*

**Extension of Time to Pay and Related Matters**

| Form No. | Title | Rule |
|---|---|---|
| 1 | Application for variation or recall of a time to pay direction and arrestment | 4(1) |
| 2 | Application for time to pay order | 5(1) |
| 3 | Application tor variation or recall or a time to pay order, arrestment and attachment | 6(1) |
| | *Poindings and warrant sales* | |
| 4–29 | *Revoked* | |
| | *Diligence against earnings* | |
| 30 | Earnings arrestment schedule | 38(1) |
| 31 | Intimation to employer under section 49(8) of the Debtors (Scotland) Act 1987 | 39(1) |
| 32 | Application for declarator that earnings arrestment invalid or ceased to have effect | 40(1) |

| Form No. | Title | Rule |
|---|---|---|
| 33 | Application for determination of dispute in operation of earnings arrestment | 41(1) |
| 34 | Current maintenance arrestment schedule | 42(1) |
| 35 | Intimation to employer under section 53(4) of the Debtors (Scotland) Act 1987 | 43(1) |
| 36 | Intimation to employer under section 53(5) of the Debtors (Scotland) Act 1987 | 44(1) |
| 37 | Intimation to debtor under section 54(1)(a) of the Debtors (Scotland) Act 1987 | 45(1) |
| 38 | Application for declarator that current maintenance arrestment invalid or ceased to have effect | 46(1) |
| 39 | Application for recall of a current maintenance arrestment | 47(1) |
| 40 | Application for determination of dispute in operation of current maintenance arrestment | 48(1) |
| 41 | Application for payment by creditor to debtor of penalty sum | 51(1) |
| 42 | Application for order on employer to provide information | 52(1) |
| 43 | Application for conjoined arrestment order | 53(1) |
| 44 | Form of notice of application for a conjoined arrestment order | 53(4) |
| 45 | Conjoined arrestment order | 54(1) |
| 46 | Notice of service of conjoined arrestment order | 54(5) |
| 47 | Application for warrant for diligence against employer | 55(1) |
| 48 | Application for order on employer to provide information | 56(1) |
| 49 | Application for variation of a conjoined arrestment order | 57(1) |
| 50 | Form of notice of application for variation of a conjoined arrestment order | 57(3)(a) |
| 51 | Notice of service of an order varying a conjoined arrestment order in terms of section 62(5) of the Debtors (Scotland) Act 1987 | 57(7)(b) |
| 52 | Intimation to employer in terms of section 63(7) of the Debtors (Scotland) Act 1987 | 58(1)(a) |
| 53 | Intimation to employer in terms of section 63(8) of the Debtors (Scotland) Act 1987 | 58(1)(b) |
| 54 | Application for determination of dispute in operation of conjoined arrestment order | 59(1) |
| 55 | Application for payment by creditor to debtor of penalty sum (conjoined arrestment order) | 60(1) |
| 56 | Application for recall of conjoined arrestment order | 61(1) |
| 57 | Application for recall of conjoined arrestment order by all creditors whose debts are being enforced by it | 62(1) |
| 58 | Application for variation of conjoined arrestment order | 63(1) |
| 59 | Notice of service of an order varying a conjoined arrestment order in terms of section 66 of the Debtors (Scotland) Act 1987 | 65(3)(b) |
| 59a | The Debtors (Scotland) Act 1987, section 70B | 65A |
| 60 | Certificate of execution of earnings arrestment schedule/current maintenance arrestment schedule | 67 |
| *Warrants for diligence* | | |
| 61 | Summary warrant for recovery of rates or community charge | 68(1) |
| 62 | Summary warrant for recovery of rates | 68(2) |
| 63 | Summary warrant for recovery of taxes etc. | 68(3) |
| 63A | *Revoked* | |
| 63B | Form of certificate of execution of arrestment in execution CERTIFICATE OF EXECUTION | 69A |
| 63C | The Debtors (Scotland) Act 1987 Form of Service of copy final decree under section 73C | 69B |
| 63D | The Debtors (Scotland) Act 1987 Application under section 73H(1) | |
| 63E | The Debtors (Scotland) Act 1987 Form of intimation of hearing | Rule |

| Form No. | Title | Rule |
|----------|-------|------|
| | | 69C(2), 69D(2) and 69E(2) |
| 63F | The Debtors (Scotland) Act 1987 Notice of objection under section 73M(1) | 69D |
| 63G | The Debtors (Scotland) Act 1987 Application under section 73Q(2) | 69E |
| | *Miscellaneous* | |
| 64 | Warrant for intimation | 73(1) |

Rule 4(1)

## Form 1
*The Debtors (Scotland) Act 1987, section 3*

Sheriff Court ............... .......... 19..........

(Court Ref. No.)

APPLICATION FOR BY VARIATION OR RE-   BY ...............
CALL OF A TIME TO PAY DIRECTION AND   ...............
ARRESTMENT   ...............

...............Applicant

* delete as appropriate                              against

...............

...............

...............

............... Respondent

The sheriff on ............... 19.......... granted an order for payment by the defender to the pursuer of the sum of £.......... along with expenses amounting to £.......... and interest ............... and made a time to pay direction directing that the total sum ordered be paid by ...............

*(a)   Instalments of £.......... each .......... which started on ............... 19..........

*(b)   A deferred lump sum which became payable by ............... 19..........

To the best of the applicant's knowledge and belief the amount which remains outstanding under the said direction at the date of this application is £...........

The applicant who is the defender/pursuer wishes the time to pay direction recalled or varied as follows (*please give details including reasons for application*):— ..........

....................

....................

**or**

seeks to have recalled or restricted an arrestment made on .......... (*give details*) .......... 19.......... at ............... in respect of ...............

Therefore the applicant asks the court:

*(a)   To recall or vary the time to pay direction as sought.

*(b)   To recall/restrict the arrestment referred to.

Date .......... 19..........                              (*signed*)

Applicant

Rule 5(1)

## Form 2[1, 2]
*The Debtors (Scotland) Act 1987*

Sheriff Court ...............                              .......... 19..........

(Court Ref. No.)

**Part A**

APPLICATION FOR TIME TO PAY ORDER      BY ...............

---

[1] As amended by the Act of Sederunt (Debt Arrangement and Attachment (Scotland) Act 2002) 2002 (SSI 2002/560), art.4, Sch.3 (effective December 30, 2002).

[2] As substituted by the Act of Sederunt (Sheriff Court Rules) (Miscellaneous Amendments) 2009 (SSI 2009/294) r.8 (effective October 1, 2009).

...............
...............Applicant
PERSON TO WHOM DEBT DUE

...............
...............
...............Creditor

**PART B**                *(a)                     The applicant is the defender
                                                   in an action raised in this
                                                   Sheriff Court/ Court of Ses-
                                                   sion by the creditor in which
                                                   decree was granted on ..........
                                                   19.......... for £..........;

*delete as appropriate                                       **or**

                          *(b)                     The debt due by the applicant
                                                   is payable under a document
                                                   bearing a warrant for dili-
                                                   gence (*give details of this
                                                   document*):—

The applicant states that to the best of his knowledge and belief that no time to pay direction or order relating to the debt has been made and that at the date of this application the amount outstanding is £.......... (*this figure should take account of interest, court expenses and any paymenu made to account*).

The applicant states that the following steps have been taken in respect of the debt, namely

*(a)   A charge for payment has been served on the applicant;

*(b)   An arrestment has been carried out;

*(c)   An action for adjudication of debt has been commenced.

**PART C**   The applicant offers to pay the outstanding amount

             *(a)                     By instalments of £.......... each

**or**

                                      (*Tick one box only*) Week ☐ Fortnight ☐ Month ☐

             *(b)                     In one payment within.......... weeks/months

Applicant's financial position

I am employed / self-employed / unemployed

| **My net income is:** | weekly, fortnightly or monthly | **My** **outgoings** **are:** | weekly, fort-nightly or monthly |
|---|---|---|---|
| Wages | £ | Mortgage/rent | £ |
| State benefits | £ | Council tax | £ |
| Tax credits | £ | Gas/electricity etc | £ |
| Other | £ | Food | £ |
| | | Credit and loans | £ |
| | | Phone | £ |
| | | Other | £ |
| Total | £ | Total | £ |

People who rely on your income (e.g. spouse/civil partner/partner/child)— how many

Here list all capital (if any) e.g. value of house; amount in bank/building society account; shares or other investments:—

Here list any outstanding debts:—

Here specify any action taken by creditor to enforce the debt (e.g. *arrestment; attachment; etc*):—

The applicant asks the court—

             1.                       To make a "time to pay order"

             *2.                      To make an order recalling the following attachment (*give details*):—

             *3.                      To recall or restrict the following arrestment(s) (*give *details*):—

or

*delete
as appro-
priate

\*4.     To order that no further steps shall be taken by the creditor or the sheriff officer in the diligence concerned, other than in the case of an attachment making a report of the attachment under section 17 of the Debt Arrangement and Attachment (Scotland) Act 2002, or applying for an order under sections 17(1), 20(1), and 21(10) of that Act.

(*signed*)

Date     19.............Applicant

## EXTRACT FROM SECTION 5(4) AND (5) OF THE DEBTORS (SCOTLAND) ACT 1987

"(4)   It shall not be competent for the sheriff to make a time to pay order:—

(a)   where the amount of the debt outstanding at the date of the making of the application under subsection (2) above (exclusive of any interest) exceeds £10,000 or such amount as may be prescribed in regulations made by the Lord Advocate;

(b)   where, in relation to the debt, a time to pay direction or a time to pay order has previously been made (whether such direction or order is in effect or not);

(c)[1]   where, in relation to the debt, a summary warrant has been granted;

(d)   in relation to a debt including any sum recoverable by or on behalf of the Inland Revenue in respect of tax or as if it were tax;

(e)[2]   in relation to a debt including any sum due to—

(i)   a rating authority for payment of rates;

(ii)   a regional or islands council for the payment of any community charge, community water charge, council tax, or council water charge;

(iii)   a collecting authority (within the meaning of section 79 of the Local Government etc. (Scotland) Act 1994) in respect of any charges payable to them by virtue of that section; or

(iv)   a regional or islands council for payment of any amount payable as a civil penalty within the meaning of subsection (9) below.

(f)   in relation to a debt including—

(i)   any duty due under the Betting and Gaming Duties Act 1981;

(ii)   car tax due under the Car Tax Act 1983; or

(iii)   value added tax due under the Value Added Tax Act 1983 or any sum recoverable as if it were value added tax.

(5)   Where in respect of a debt to which this section applies:—

(a)[3]   articles belonging to the debtor have been attached and notice of an auction given under section 27(4) of the Debt Arrangement and Attachment (Scotland) Act 2002 (asp 17) but no auction has yet taken place;

(aa)[4]   money owed by the debtor has been attached and removed;

(b)   moveable property of the debtor has been arrested and in respect of the arrested property—

(i)   a decree in an action of forthcoming has been granted but has not been enforced; or

(ii)   a warrant of sale has been granted but the warrant has not been executed; or

---

[1] Repealed by the Act of Sederunt (Sheriff Court Rules Amendment) (Diligence) (SSI 2008/ 121) r.3(2)(a) (effective April 1, 2008). These subsections will continue to have effect for the purpose of any application for a time to pay order made before April 1, 2008.

[2] Repealed by the Act of Sederunt (Sheriff Court Rules Amendment) (Diligence) (SSI 2008/ 121) r.3(2)(a) (effective April 1, 2008). These subsections will continue to have effect for the purpose of any application for a time to pay order made before April 1, 2008.

[3] As substituted by the Act of Sederunt (Sheriff Court Rules Amendment) (Diligence) (SSI 2008/121) r.3(2)(b) (effective April 1, 2008).

[4] As inserted by the Act of Sederunt (Sheriff Court Rules Amendment) (Diligence) (SSI 2008/ 121) r.3(2)(b) (effective April 1, 2008).

(c) a decree in an action of adjudication for debt has been granted and the creditor has, with the debtor's consent or acquiescence, entered into possession of any property adjudged by the decree or has obtained a decree of maills and duties, or a decree of removing or ejection, in relation to any such property,

it shall not be competent for the sheriff to make a time to pay order in respect of that debt until the diligence has been completed or has otherwise ceased to have effect."

The sheriff having considered the foregoing application and being satisfied that it is properly made, meantime sists all diligence in terms of section 8(1) of the Debtors (Scotland) Act 1987 pending the disposal of the application.

Appoints the creditor to furnish the sheriff with particulars of the decree or other document under which the debt is payable within .......... days of intimation hereof.

Appoints the sheriff clerk to intimate a copy of the application and this interlocutor to the creditor; appoints him if he objects to the granting of this application to make written representations to the court within 14 days of the date of intimation hereof.

Sheriff

(Court Ref. No.)<br>..........19..........

To: The Sheriff Clerk

Sheriff Court ..........

I have read the application for a "Time to Pay Order" by ...............

*1. I do not object to the proposal made and agree to the making of a "Time to Pay Order".

*2. I object to the granting of the application for the following reasons:—

*delete as
appropri-
ate

*3. I object to the making of a "Time to Pay Order" as proposed, and wish to make the following alternative proposals:—

*4. I intend*/do not intend to appear at the hearing.

*(Signed)*<br>............... Creditor

Date

..........

19..........

Please Note:—This form (or if you wish, a letter with the same information) should be returned by ............... 19..........

Form 3 [1]

Rule 6(1)

*The Debtors (Scotland) Act 1987, section 10*

Sheriff Court ...............

...............<br>(Court Ref. No.)

APPLICATION FOR VARIATION OR RECALL  BY ...............
OF A TIME TO PAY ORDER, ARRESTMENT   ...............
AND ATTACHMENT                       ...............
                                     ...............Applicant

Against

---

[1] As amended by the Act of Sederunt (Debt Arrangement and Attachment (Scotland) Act 2002) 2002 (SSI 2002/560), art.4, Sch.3 (effective December 30, 2002).

..............
..............
..............
.......... Respondent
*delete as appropriate

1. *(a) On (*date*).......... decree was granted in this Sheriff Court/Court of Session for payment by the defender to the pursuer of the sum of £.......... along with expenses of £.......... and interest.

*(b) The debt due by the applicant/respondent is payable under a document bearing a warrant for diligence (*give details of this document*):—

2. The sheriff on (*date*).......... made a time to pay order, that the debt outstanding amounting to £.......... be paid:—

*(a) By instalments of £.......... each .............. which started on

*(b) As a lump sum which became payable by

To the best of the applicant's knowledge and belief the amount which remains outstanding under the said order at the time of this application is £..........

3. The applicant who is the debtor/creditor:—

*(a) Wishes the time to pay order recalled or varied as follows (*specify order sought*):— ..............
....................

*(b) Seeks the recall or restriction of an arrestment (*give details of arrestment served, person on whom served, and date, and specify order sought*):— ..........
..............

*(c) Seeks the recall of the attachment carried out on the instructions of the creditor at (*place of attachment*) on (*date of attachment*).

Give reasons for this application— ..............
....................

4. The applicant asks the court:—

*1.    To recall or vary the time to pay order as requested.
*2.    To recall or restrict the arrestment referred to.
*3.    To recall the attachment referred to
*4.    (*Specify any other order sought and the diligence to which it relates*).
....................

Date .......... Signed ..............

Applicant

Forms 4–29 [1]
Form 30 [2]

Rule 38(1)

*The Debtors (Scotland) Act 1987, section 47*
*Earnings Arrestment Schedule*

On the date of service of this schedule there comes into effect an earnings arrestment. Particulars of the arrestment and of the requirement on the employer on a pay-day to pay sums deducted from the debtor's earnings to the creditor are given in the schedule.

*Particulars of earnings arrestment*

|  |  |  |
|---|---|---|
| Employer : | (*name, designation and address*) | |
| Debtor (employee) : | (em- | (*name, designation and address*) |
| Creditor : | (*name, designation and address*) | |

| Where there is more than one debt state details relating to each | The debt recoverable: | debt | ordinary debt | — |
|  |  |  | expenses | — |
|  |  |  | interest | — |

---

[1] Revoked by the Act of Sederunt (Debt Arrangement and Attachment (Scotland) Act 2002) 2002 (SSI 2002/560), art.5, Sch.4 (effective December 30, 2002), subject to savings outlined in art.5.
[2] As amended by the Act of Sederunt (Sheriff Court Rules Amendment) (Diligence) (SSI 2008/121) r.10(4) (effective April 1, 2008).

separately     less paid to account   — ..........

           expenses of serving charge  — ..........

           expenses of executing this

           earnings arrestment   — ..........

                  TOTAL ..........

Particulars of decree: (*specify*)

or other documents or summary

warrant upon which this arrestment

proceeds

Date of any charge:

(*Place and date*)

To (*name of employer*)

You are served with this earnings arrestment schedule along with a copy of sections 49(1) to (6), section 49A and Schedule 2 to the Debtors (Scotland) Act 1987.

         (*Signed*) ..............

           Officer of Court

          (*name, designation and address*)

### NOTE TO OFFICER OF COURT:

A copy of this earnings arrestment schedule and a copy of section 49(1) to (6), section 49A and Schedule 2 to the Debtors (Scotland) Act 1987 is to be intimated to the debtor by you, if reasonably practicable.

### EFFECT OF EARNINGS ARRESTMENT

An earnings arrestment has the general effect of requiring the employer of a debtor:—

(1) to deduct a sum calculated in accordance with the Debtors (Scotland) Act 1987 from the debtor's net earnings on every pay-day; and

(2) to pay any sum so deducted to the creditor as soon as is reasonably practicable.

The arrestment remains in effect until the debt has been paid or otherwise extinguished, the debtor has ceased to be employed by the employer or the arrestment has been recalled or abandoned by the creditor or has ceased to have effect.

*Instructions to Employer*

Please read these instructions carefully.

1. When this earnings arrestment schedule is served on you, you are required to make a deduction from your employee's net earnings on every pay-day unless you are already making deductions from his earnings under a previous earnings arrestment or a conjoined arrestment order in which case read sections 59 and 62 of the Debtors (Scotland) Act 1987.

2.

(1) You must begin deducting on the first pay-day occurring after a period of seven days after the date of service of this schedule on you.

(2) Where any pay-day occurs within this seven day period you are entitled but not required to begin deducting.

3. The sum to be deducted is calculated in accordance with section 49 of the Debtors (Scotland) Act 1987. (A copy of section 49(1) to (6), section 49A and Schedule 2 to the Act is attached) [*officer of court to attach*].

4. As soon as is reasonably practicable you must pay the sum deducted to [*officer of court to insert name and address of a person in the United Kingdom to whom payment is to be made*].

5. You must continue to make deductions and payments until:—

(1) the debt recoverable has been paid or otherwise extinguished;

(2) the debtor has ceased to be employed by you or;

(3) the arrestment has been recalled or abandoned by the creditor or has for any other reason ceased to have effect.

6. You are entitled to charge your employee a fee (at present ..........) on each occasion you make a payment to the creditor.

7. For further information read the following notes.

### NOTES

(1) The debt recoverable by the arrestment consists of the sums as set out in section 48 of the Act.

(2) "Earnings" and "net earnings" from which deductions are to be made, are defined in section 73 of the Act.

(3) You are also referred to the following sections of the Act:—

| | |
|---|---|
| 50(1): | Sheriff's power on an application by the debtor or the person on whom the earnings arrestment schedule was served to make an order declaring that the earnings arrestment is invalid or has ceased to have effect. |
| 50(3): | Sheriff's power on an application by the debtor, the creditor or the employer to determine any dispute as to the operation of an earnings arrestment. |
| 57(1): | Employer's liability where he fails to comply with an earnings arrestment. |
| 58(1): | Provisions regarding the simultaneous operation of one earnings arrestment and one current maintenance arrestment. |
| 59(1): | While an earnings arrestment is in effect, no other earnings arrestment against the earnings of the same debtor payable by the same employer is competent. |
| 59(4): | Employer's duty, on receipt of a second earnings arrestment schedule to give certain information to the "second creditor". |
| 62(2) and (3): | Employer's duty, when a conjoined arrestment order is in effect, to give certain information to a creditor who is not included in the conjoined arrestment order and who has served or has in effect an earnings arrestment. |
| 69(3): | If deductions are not made on the first pay-day after the service of the earnings arrestment schedule in accordance with section 69(2) of the Act, deductions made on a subsequent pay-day are not to include any deductions in respect of the first pay-day. |
| 69(5)(a): | Intimations the employer may expect to receive from the creditor or the sheriff clerk. |
| 70(4A) | Employer's duty to intimate a copy of an earnings arrestment schedule to the debtor and to give certain information to the debtor. |
| 70A | Employer's duty to give certain information to the creditor or, as the case may be, the sheriff clerk and to send a copy of certain information to the debtor. |

Further information and advice about the Act is available from solicitors' offices, Citizens' Advice Bureaux and other local advice centres and sheriff clerks' offices.

Form 31 [1]

Rule 39(1)

*The Debtors (Scotland) Act 1987*
*Intimation to employer in terms of* section 49(8)

The employer ...............:(*name and address*)

The debtor (employee) ...............:(*name and address*)

The creditor ...............:(*name and address*)

Date earnings arrestment schedule served on employer:(*specify*)

*To the em-* —Take note that on (*date*) the Lord Advocate/Scottish
*ployer*

Ministers made regulations which varied

*delete as
appropriate.

*(a) Tables A, B and C of Schedule 2 to the Debtors (Scotland) Act 1987 (the statutory deduction tables)

*(b) the percentage specified in subsection (5) and (6)(a)(ii) of section 49 of the Debtors (Scotland) Act 1987 to (*specify change*)

The regulations come into force on (*date*)

Date ..........(*Signed*) ...............

Creditor/Debtor

(i) This intimation should be considered carefully by the employer as the variation referred to may affect the sum to be deducted by him under the earnings arrestment (see further section 69(1), (2) and (3) of the Debtors (Scotland) Act 1987).

(ii) The person intimating this form to the employer must attach the statutory deduction tables as revised where these have been varied by the regulations.

---

[1] As amended by S.I. 1999 No. 1820, Art.4, Sched. 2, para.145 (effective July 1, 1999).

Form 32

Rule 40(1)

*The Debtors (Scotland) Act 1987, section 50(1)*

Sheriff Court ..........

APPLICATION FOR DECLARA-
TION THAT EARNINGS ARREST-
MENT INVALID OR CEASED TO
HAVE EFFECT

(1)

........19..(Court
Ref. No.) AP-
PLICANT

\* delete as appropriate

A. The applicant is
   \*(a)  The debtor
   \*(b)  The person on whom the earnings arrestment schedule was served

(1) Insert name and address

B. Other persons having an interest are
   (c)   The creditor (1)
   \*(d)  The debtor (1)
   \*(e)  The person on whom the earnings arrestment schedule was served (1)

(2) Insert name

C. Decree was granted in an action by the pursuer(s) (2).............. in the Court of Session/Sheriff Court at............... on.......... 19.......... against the defender(s) (2).............. (*or give details of other document or summary warrant upon which the earnings arrestment proceeded*):—

D. An earnings arrestment schedule against the earnings of the debtor (2)............... was served on (2).............. by (1).............. sheriff officer/messenger-at-arms on the instructions of the creditor (2)............... on.............. 19..........
A copy of the said schedule is attached.

E. The earnings arrestment is invalid/has ceased to have effect because (*Give reasons for application*):—

This application is made under section 50(1) of the Debtors (Scotland) Act 1987.

491

F.  The applicant asks the court:—
1.  To fix a hearing.
2.  To order the sheriff clerk to intimate this application and the date of the hearing to the applicant and to those persons stated above as having an interest.
3.  To make an order declaring that the earnings arrestment is invalid or has ceased to have effect.
4.  To make the following consequential order (*give details*).
5.  To award expenses (if competent).

Date ..........19..........(*Signed*)...............

Applicant

IF YOU WISH FURTHER ADVICE CONTACT ANY CITIZENS ADVICE BUREAU/ LOCAL ADVICE CENTRE/SHERIFF CLERK OR SOLICITOR

**Form 33**

Rule 41(1)

*The* Debtors (Scotland) Act 1987, section 50(3)

Sheriff Court ...............

APPLICATION FOR DETERMINA-   (1)
TION OF DISPUTE IN OPERATION
OF EARNINGS ARRESTMENT

........19..(Court Ref. No.) AP-PLICANT

*delete as appropriate

A.  The applicant is
    *(a)    The debtor
    *(b)    The creditor
    *(c)    The employer

(1)    Insert name and address

B.  Other persons having an interest are
    *(d)    The debtor (1)
    *(e)    The creditor (1)
    *(f)    The employer (1)

(2)    Insert name

C.  Decree was granted in an action by the pursuer(s) (2)............... in the Court of Session/Sheriff Court at............... on............... 19......... against the defender(s) (2)............... (*or give details of other document or summary warrant upon which the poinding proceeded*):—

D.  An earnings arrestment schedule against the earnings of the debtor (2)............... was served on the employer

> (2).............. by (1).............. sheriff off ker/messenger-at-arms on the instructions of the creditor (2)..............
> on.......... 19..........
> A copy of the said schedule is attached.

E.

> The following dispute as to the operation of the earnings arrestment requires to be determined (*specify nature of the dispute*):—

This application is made under section 50(3) of the Debtors (Scotland) Act 1987.

F.

The applicant asks the court:—

1. To fix a hearing.
2. To order the sheriff clerk to intimate this application and the date of the hearing to the applicant and to those persons stated above as having an interest.
3. To make an order determining the dispute (*specify order sought*):—
*4. To order the reimbursement by (*name person*) to (*name person*) of £.......... with interest thereon at the rate of (*specify rate*) from (*specify date*) or such other date as the court may consider appropriate.
*5. To order the payment by (*name person*) to (*name person*) of £.......... with interest thereon at the rate of (*specify rate*) from (*specify date*) or such other date as the court may consider appropriate.
6. To award expenses (if competent).

Date ..........19.......... (*Signed*)..............

Applicant

**IF YOU WISH FURTHER ADVICE CONTACT ANY CITIZENS ADVICE BUREAU/LOCAL ADVICE CENTRE/SHERIFF CLERK OR SOLICITOR**

Form 34 [1]

Rule 42(1)

*The Debtors (Scotland) Act 1987, section 51*
*Current Maintenance Arrestment Schedule*

On the date of service of this schedule there comes into effect a current maintenance arrestment. Particulars of the arrestment and of the requirement on the employer on a pay-day to pay sums deducted from the debtor's earnings to the creditor are given in the schedule.

*Particulars of current maintenance arrestment*

Employer ..............:      (*name, designation and address*)

Debtor (employee) ..............:      (*name, designation and address*)

Creditor ..............:      (*name, designation and ad-*

---

[1] As amended by the Act of Sederunt (Child Support Rules) (SI 1993/920) r.7(3) (effective April 5, 1993) and the Act of Sederunt (Sheriff Court Rules Amendment) (Diligence) (SSI 2008/121) r.10(5) (effective April 1, 2008).

*dress*)

Particulars of maintenance order(s) (*specify*) upon: which this arrestment proceeds

Maintenance payable by the debtor: (*state*) expressed as a daily rate (see section 51(5))

Date of any intimation made under sec-:tion 54(1)

The debtor has defaulted in his (*give particulars of default* payments: under the maintenance or- *with reference to either* sub-der(s) section (1) or (2) of section 54 of the Act)

*delete as appropriate    The debtor *is/*is not entitled to deduct: income tax from the maintenance payable to the creditor

(*Place and date*)

To (*name of employer*)

You are served with this earnings arrestment schedule along with a copy of sections 53(1) to (2) of the Debtors (Scotland) Act 1987.

(*Signed*) ..............

Officer of Court

(*name, designation and address*)

NOTE TO OFFICER OF COURT:

A copy of this current maintenance arrestment schedule and a copy of section 53(1) to (2) of the Debtors (Scotland) Act 1987 is to be intimated to the debtor by you. if reasonably practicable.

EFFECT OF CURRENT MAINTENANCE ARRESTMENT

A current maintenance arrestment has the general effect of requiring the employer of a debtor:—

(1)    to deduct a sum calculated in accordance with the Debtors (Scotland) Act 1987 from the debtor's net earnings on every pay-day; and

(2)    to pay any sum so deducted to the creditor as soon as is reasonably practicable.

The arrestment remains in effect until the debtor has ceased to be employed by the employer or the arrestmment has been recalled or abandoned by the creditor or has ceased to have effect.

*Instructions to employer*

Please read these instructions carefully.

1.    When this current maintenance arrestment schedule is served on you, you are required to make a deduction from your employee's net earnings on every pay-day unless you are already making deductions from his earnings under a previous current maintenance arrestment or a conjoined arrestment order in which case read sections 59 and 62 of the Debtors (Scotland) Act 1987.

2.

(1)    You must begin deducting on the first pay-day occurring after a period of seven days after the date of service of this schedule on you.

(2)    Where any pay-day occurs within this seven day period you are entitled but not required to begin deducting.

3.

(1)    The sum to be deducted is calculated in accordance with section 53 of the Debtors (Scotland) Act 1987. (A copy of sections 53(1) and (2) is attached) [*officer of court to attach.*]

(2)    You may be required to make deductions under both an earnings arrestment and a current maintenance arrestment. If this is the case and on any pay-day the net earnings of your employee are less than the total sums to be deducted by you, you must first deduct under the earnings arrestment and then under the current maintenance arrestment on the balance of the net earnings in accordance with section 53(1) of the Act.

4.    As soon as is reasonably practicable you must pay the sum deducted to [*officer of court to insert name and address of a person in the United Kingdom to whom payment is to be made*].

5.    You must continue to make deductions and payments until:—

(1)    the debtor has ceased to be employed by you;

(2)    the arrestment has been recalled or abandoned by the creditor;

(3) the arrestment has ceased to have effect under section 55(8) of the Act or for any other reason.

6. You are entitled to charge your employee a fee (at present ..........) on each occasion you make a payment to the creditor.

7. For further information read the following notes.

### NOTES FOR EMPLOYER

(1) "Earnings" and "net earnings" from which deductions are to be made, are defined in section 73 of the Act as amended by the Child Support Act 1991.

(2) You are also referred to the following sections of the Act:—

| | |
|---|---|
| 55(1): | Sheriffs power on an application by the debtor or the person on whom the current maintenance arrestment schedule was served to make an order declaring that a current maintenance arrestment is invalid or has ceased to have effect. |
| 55(2): | Sheriffs power on an application by the debtor to recall a current maintenance arrestment if satisfied that the debtor is unlikely to default again in paying maintenance. |
| 55(5): | Sheriffs power on an application by the debtor, the creditor or the employer to determine any dispute as to the operation of a current maintenance arrestment. |
| 57(1): | Employer's liability where he fails to comply with a current maintenance arrestment. |
| 58: | Provisions regarding the simultaneous operation of one earnings arrestment and one current maintenance arrestment. |
| 59(2): | While a current maintenance arrestment is in effect, no other current maintenance arrestment against the earnings of the same debtor payable by the same employer is competent. |
| 59(4): | Employer's duty, on receipt of a second current maintenance arrestment schedule to give certain information to the "second creditor". |
| 62(2) and (3): | Employer's duty, when a conjoined arrestment order is in effect, to give certain information to a creditor who is not included in the conjoined arrestment order and who has served or has in effect a current maintenance arrestment. |
| 68: | Creditor's power to authorise the Secretary of State to receive any sums payable under the current maintenance arrestment direct from the employer. |
| 69(3): | If deductions not made on the first pay-day after service of the schedule in accordance with section 69(2) of the Act, deductions made on subsequent pay-day not to include any deductions in respect of first pay-day. |
| 69(5)(6): | Intimations the employer may expect to receive from the creditor or the sheriff clerk. |
| 70(4A) | Employer's duty to intimate a copy of a current maintenance arrestment schedule to the debtor and to give certain information to the debtor. |
| 70A | Employer's duty to give certain information to the creditor or, as the case may be, the sheriff clerk and to send a copy of certain information to the debtor. |

Further information and advice about the Act is available from solicitors' offices, Citizens' Advice Bureaux and other local advice centres and sheriff clerks' offices.

Form 35 [1]

Rule 431(1)

*The Debtors (Scotland) Act 1987*

*Intimation to employer in terms of* section 53(4)

The employer ...............:(*name and address*)

The debtor (employee) ...............:(*name and address*)

The creditor ...............:(*name and address*)

Date current maintenance arrestment schedule served on employer ...............:(*specify*)

*To the employer:* Take note that on (*date*) the Lord Advocate/Scottish Ministers made regulations which varied the sum specified in subsection 2(b) of section 53 of the Debtors (Scotland) Act 1987 to £..........

---

[1] As amended by SI 1999/1820, art.4, Sch.2, para.145 (effective July 1, 1999).

The regulations come into operation on (*date*)

Date...............                                   (*Signed*)...............

Creditor/Debtor

This intimation should be considered carefully by the employer as the variation referred to may affect the sum to be deducted by him under the current maintenance arrestment (see further section 69(1), (2) and (3) of the Debtors (Scotland) Act 1987.

Form 36

Rule 44(1)

*The Debtors (Scotland) Act 1987*
*Intimation to employer in terms of* section 53(4)

The employer (*name and address*)
...............:

The debtor (em- (*name and address*)
ployee) ...............:

The creditor (*name and address*)
...............:

Date current main- (*specify*)
tenance arrestment
schedule served on
employer ...............:

*To the employer:* Take note that on (*date*) the small maintenance payment limits mentioned in section 65(1A) of the Income and Corporation Taxes Act 1970 were changed to (*specify changes*)

The changes come into operation on (*date*)

Date.......... (*Signed*)..........

Creditor/Debtor

(i) This intimation should be considered carefully by the employer as the changes made may affect the sum to be deducted by him under the current maintenance arrestment.

(ii) The person intimating this form to the employer must attach a copy of section 65(1A) of the Income and Corporation Taxes Act 1970 as amended or varied.

Form 37 [1]

Rules 45(1) and 45(5)

*The Debtors (Scotland) Act 1987*
*Intimation to debtor in terms of* section 54(1) (a)

To (*name and address of debtor*)

Take note that a maintenance order, in which you are ordered to make payments to (*name and address*) was [granted/made/registered/confirmed] on (*date*) by/in (*name of court*). A copy of the order is attached. [Here insert reference to enforcement by Secretary of State for Social Security if appropriate]

Date .......... (*Signed*) ...............

[Creditor/Solicitor/Sheriff Officer/Authorised lay representative]

GUIDANCE ABOUT THE PAYMENT OF MAINTENANCE
(You should read this section carefully)
**WHAT CAN HAPPEN IF YOU DO NOT MAKE REGULAR PAYMENTS?**

If you do not make regular payments and get into arrears amounting in value one instalment of maintenance, a document called a Current Maintenance Arrestment Schedule (referred to here as an arrestment) may be sent to your employer.

The arrestment will instruct your employer to make deductions from your net earnings on every pay day, and pay these sums over to the creditor (i.e. the person to whom the payment of maintenance is due).

The arrestment of your earnings will remain in force for so long as you are employed by your current employer or until the arrestment is recalled or abandoned by the creditor or ceases to have effect.

If an arrestment is sent to your employer you have the right to apply to the sheriff for the order to be recalled. If the sheriff is satisfied that you are unlikely to default in paying maintenance again he may recall the order.

---

[1] Substituted by SI 1991/1920. As amended by SI 1993/920 (effective April 5, 1993).

## HOW CAN YOU PAY MAINTENANCE?

To avoid the risk of an arrestment it is best to make arrangements to pay the maintenance regularly. This can be done in various ways, including

—   by cash payment
—   by standing order through a bank or building society
—   by personal cheque
—   by bank giro credit

Probably the simplest way to make payments is by standing order. This will also provide you with a clear record of payments made. Any bank or building society will give you further advice on this.

## WHERE CAN YOU GET ADVICE?

FURTHER ADVICE MAY BE OBTAINED BY CONTACTING ANY CITIZENS ADVICE BUREAU, OTHER LOCAL ADVICE CENTRE, SHERIFF CLERK OR SOLICITOR

## PAYMENT ARRANGEMENTS

The debtor ...............:                                       *(name and address)*

The creditor ...............:                                    *(name and address)*

*Creditor's agent ...............:                            *(name and address)*

**To the debtor: Take note that payment of sums due under this maintenance order should be sent to** * **the creditor at the above address/the account number referred to below/the creditor's agent at the above address.**

## * PAYMENT TO BANK, BUILDING SOCIETY OR OTHER ACCOUNT

**To the debtor:** Payment should be made direct to the following account—

ACCOUNT NUMBER:

SORT CODE:

NAME OF BANK, BUILDING SOCIETY, ETC:

ADDRESS:

*(Details to be inserted by or on behalf of the creditor)*

**To debtor:** If it is not possible for payment by standing order to start on the due date you must ensure that payment is made direct to the creditor until such time as the standing order comes into operation.

**Do not delay** in making payments while you are making arrangements with your own bank or building society. Otherwise you may inadvertently breach the terms of the court order. This could result in a current maintenance arrestment order being served on your employer.

    * Delete as appropriate.

Form 38

Rule 46(1)

*The Debtors (Scotland) Act 1987, section 55(1)*
Sheriff Court ..........

APPLICATION FOR DEC-  (1)                          .......... 19..........
LARATION THAT CUR-                                (Court Ref. No.)
RENT MAINTENANCE
INVALID OR CEASED TO                                     APPLICANT
HAVE EFFECT

* delete as ap-  A.
propriate

    The applicant is
      *(a)    The debtor
      *(b)    The person on whom the current maintenance arrestment schedule was served

(1)    Insert  B.
name and ad-
dress

    Other persons having an interest are
      (c)    The creditor (1)
      *(d)    The debtor (1)
      *(e)    The person on whom the current maintenance arrestment schedule was served (1)

C.

> Specify details of maintenance order and when and by whom granted or issued and where appropriate details of its registration or confirmation:—

(2)   Insert
name

D.

> A current maintenance arrestment schedule against the earnings of the debtor (2) ......... was served on (2) ......... by (1) ......... sheriff officer/messenger-at-arms on the instructions of the creditor (2) ............... on ......... 19 ........... A copy of the said schedule is attached

E.

> The current maintenance arrestment is invalid/has ceased to have effect because (*give reasons for application*):—

This application is made under section 55(1) of the Debtors (Scotland) Act 1987.

F.

The applicant asks the court:—

1. To fix a hearing.

2. To order the sheriff clerk to intimate this application and the date of the hearing to the applicant, and to those persons stated above as having an interest.

3. To make an order declaring that the current maintenance arrestment is invalid or has ceased to have effect.

4. To make the following consequential order (*give details*):

5. To award expenses (if competent).

Date ............... 19..........                    (*Signed*)...............

Applicant

IF YOU WISH FURTHER ADVICE CONTACT ANY CITIZENS ADVICE BUREAU/LOCAL ADVICE CENTRE/SHERIFF CLERK OR SOLICITOR

Form 39

Rule 47(1)

*The Debtors (Scotland) Act 1987, section 55(2)*

Sheriff Court ..........

APPLICATION FOR RE-   (1)
CALL OF A CURRENT
MAINTENANCE   AR-
RESTMENT

.......... 19..........
(Court Ref. No.)

APPLICANT

A.

> The applicant is
> The debtor

(1)   Insert
name and ad-
dress

B.

> Other persons having an interest are
> The creditor (1)

C.  Specify details of maintenance order and when and by whom granted or issued and where appropriate details of its registration or confirmation:—

(2) Insert name

D.  A current maintenance arrestment schedule against the earnings of the debtor (2) .......... was served on the employer (1) .......... by (1) .......... sheriff officer/messenger-at-arms on the instructions of the creditor (2) ...............on .......... 19 ........... A copy of the said schedule is attached

E.  The current maintenance arrestment should be recalled (*state why you say that you are unlikely to default again in payment maintenance*):—

This application is made under section 55(2) of the Debtors (Scotland) Act 1987.

F.  The applicant asks the court:—

1. To fix a hearing.

2. To order the sheriff clerk to intimate this application and the date of the hearing to the applicant and to the creditor.

3. To recall the current maintenance arrestment.

4. To award expenses (if competent).

Date ............... 19..........          (*Signed*)...............
                                                    Applicant

IF YOU WISH FURTHER ADVICE CONTACT ANY CITIZENS ADVICE BUREAU/LOCAL ADVICE CENTRE/SHERIFF CLERK OR SOLICITOR

Form 40

**Rule 48(1)**

*The* Debtors (Scotland) Act 1987, section 55(5)

Sheriff Court ..........

APPLICATION FOR DE-TERMINATION OF DISPUTE IN OPERATION OF CURRENT MAINTENANCE ARRESTMENT

(1)

.......... 19..........
(Court Ref. No.)
APPLICANT

*delete as appropriate

A.  The applicant is
* a)  The debtor
* b)  The creditor
* (c)  The employer

(1) Insert name and address

B.  Other persons having an interest are
* (d)  The debtor (1)
* (e)  The creditor (1)
* (f)  The employer (1)

C. | Specify details of maintenance order and when and by whom granted or issued and where appropriate details of its registration or confirmation:—

(2) Insert name

D. | A current maintenance arrestment schedule against the earnings of the debtor (2).......... was served on the employer (2).......... by (1).......... sheriff officer/messenger-at-arms on the instructions of the creditor (2).......... on.......... 19.......... A copy of the said schedule is attached

E. | The following dispute as to the operation of the current maintenance arrestment requires to be determined (*specify nature of the dispute*):—

This application is made under section 55(5) of the Debtors (Scotland) Act 1987.

F. The applicant asks the court:—

1. To fix a hearing.

2. To order the sheriff clerk to intimate this application and the date of the hearing to the applicant, and to those persons stated above as having an interest.

3. To make an order determining the dispute (*specify order sought*):—

*4. To order the reimbursement by (*name person*) to (*name person*) of £.......... with interest thereon at the rate of (*specify rate*) from (*specify date*) or such other date as the court may consider appropriate.

*5. To order the payment by (*name person*) to (*name person*) of £.......... with interest thereon at the rate of (*specify rate*) from (*specify date*) or such other date as the court may consider appropriate.

6. To award expenses (if competent).

Date ...............19..........          (*Signed*) ..........

Applicant

IF YOU WISH FURTHER ADVICE CONTACT ANY CITIZENS ADVICE BUREAU/ LOCAL ADVICE CENTRE/SHERIFF CLERK OR SOLICITOR

Form 41

**Rule 51(1)**

*The* Debtors (Scotland) Act 1987, section 57(6)

Sheriff Court ..........

APPLICATION FOR PAY-   (1)
MENT BY CREDITOR TO
DEBTOR OF PENALTY
SUM

.......... 19..........
(Court Ref. No.)

APPLICANT

A. | The applicant is
The debtor

| | | |
|---|---|---|
| (1) Insert name and address | B. | Other persons having an interest are<br>The creditor (1) |

| | | |
|---|---|---|
| (2) Insert name | C. | Decree was granted in an action by the pursuer(s) (2)..........<br>in the Court of Session/Sheriff Court at ...............on<br>............... 19.......... against the Defender(s) (2) ...............(*or give details of other document or summary warrant or maintenance order upon which earnings arrestment or current maintenance arrestment proceeded*):— |

| | | |
|---|---|---|
| | D. | An earnings arrestment schedule/a current maintenance arrestment schedule against the earnings of the debtor (2).......... was served on the employer (2).......... by (1)............... sheriff officer/messenger-at-arms on the instructions of the creditor (2) on............... 19..........<br>A copy of the said schedule is attached |

| | | |
|---|---|---|
| *delete as appropriate | E. | The amount of the debt or the sum to be deducted from the earnings of the debtor was (*specify*):—<br>The expenses of diligence were (*specify*):—<br>The creditor failed to intimate to the debtor's employer that<br>  *(a)  the debt recoverable under the earnings arrestment had been paid or otherwise extinguished (*specify from what date and in what circumstances*):—<br>  *(b)  the current maintenance arrestment has ceased to have effect under section 55(8) of the Debtors (Scotland) Act 1987 (*specify from what date and in what circumstances*):—<br>  *(c)  the debt being enforced by the earnings arrestment had ceased to be enforceable by diligence (*specify from what date and in what circumstances*):—<br>The employer overpaid £.......... as a result of this failure. (*Give details of the calculation of this sum and grounds for seeking the sum sought from the creditor*):— |

This application is made under section 57(6) of the Debtors (Scotland) Act 1987.

F.     The applicant asks the court:—

1. To fix a hearing.

2. To order the sheriff clerk to intimate this application and the date of the hearing to the applicant and to the creditor.

3. To order the creditor to pay to the debtor £.......... (*specify amount requested*).

4. To award expenses (if competent).

Date ...............19..........              (*Signed*)...............

                                                    Applicant

IF YOU WISH FURTHER ADVICE CONTACT ANY CITIZENS ADVICE BUREAU/ LOCAL ADVICE CENTRE/SHERIFF CLERK OR SOLICITOR

Form 42

**Rule 52(1)**

*The* Debtors (Scotland) Act 1987, section 59(5)

Sheriff Court ..........

APPLICATION FOR OR- (1)
DER ON EMPLOYER TO
PROVIDE INFORMATION

.......... 19..........

(Court Ref. No.)

APPLICANT

A.

> The applicant is
> A second creditor in terms of section 59(4) of the Debtors
> (Scotland) Act 1987

(1) Insert B.
name and ad-
dress

> Other persons having an interest are
> The employer (1)

C.

> An earnings arrestment schedule/a current maintenance
> arrestment schedule against the earnings of the debtor
> (1).......... was served on the said employer by (1)..........
> sheriff officer/messenger-at-arms on the instructions of the
> applicant.............. on.......... 19..........

D.

> The arrestment did not come into effect because of the
> terms of section 59 of the Debtors (Scotland) Act 1987
> The employer has failed without reasonable cause to give
> the following information to the applicant (*specify infor-
> mation not given*):—
> The applicant is entitled to this information

This application is made under section 59(5) of the Debtors
(Scotland) Act 1987.

E.      The applicant asks the court:—

1. To fix a hearing.

2. To order the sheriff clerk to intimate this application and
the date of the hearing to the applicant and to the employer.

3. To order the employer to give the information requested
to the applicant within such period as the court may order.

4. To award expenses (if competent).

Date ..............19..........        (*Signed*) ..............

Applicant

IF YOU WISH FURTHER ADVICE CONTACT ANY CITIZENS ADVICE BUREAU/ LOCAL
ADVICE CENTRE/SHERIFF CLERK OR SOLICITOR

Form 43 [1]

**Rule 53(1)**

*The* Debtors (Scotland) Act 1987, section 60(2)

---

[1] As amended by the Act of Sederunt (Debt Arrangement and Attachment (Scotland) Act 2002) 2002
(SSI 2002/560) art.4 Sch.3 (effective December 30, 2002) and by the Act of Sederunt (Sheriff Court
Rules) (Miscellaneous Amendments) 2009 (SSI 2009/294) r.9 (effective October 1, 2009).

Sheriff Court ..........

*Application for a conjoined arrestment order*

1. The applicant ..........: (*name and address*)

   The debtor (employee) ..........: (*name and address*)

   The employer ..........: (*name and address*)

   Debtor's place of employment ..........: (*address*)

2. The applicant is a creditor of the debtor and wishes to enforce his debt by executing an earnings arrestment and/or a current maintenance arrestment against earnings payable to the debtor by the employer.

3. The applicant cannot execute this arrestment as there is already an earnings arrestment and/ or a current maintenance arrestment in effect against these earnings.

4. No conjoined arrestment order has been made against these earnings.

5. The applicant's debt consists of

| **ORDINARY DEBT** | **CURRENT MAINTENANCE** |
|---|---|
| (Where there is more than one ordinary debt state details relating to each separately.) | Maintenance payable by the debtor : expressed as a daily rate |
| Sum due under decree or other: document or summary warrant | Is the debtor entitled to deduct income tax from maintenance payable? : Yes/No |
| expenses : | Particulars of maintenance order(s) : |
| interest : | which constituted the obligation to pay |
| less paid to account : .......... | maintenance |
| expenses of executing current maintenance arrestment : | Date of any intimation made under section 54(1) of the Act : |
| expenses of serving charge : | Specify particulars of debtors default : |
| expenses of executing : | in his payments under the maintenance |
| earnings arrestment expenses of this : | order(s) with reference to either sub- |
| application | section (1) or (2) of section 54 of the Act |

TOTAL AMOUNT RECOVERABLE ..........

..........

Particulars of decree or other document or summary warrant upon which the attachment proceeded: (*specify*)

Date of any charge :

6. The person within the United Kingdom to whom payments are to be made is:.......... (*name and address*).

7. Specify the following information for each of the earnings and/or current maintenance arrestments already in effect against the earnings payable to the debtor by the employer.

   The creditor:.......... (*name and address*)

   Date and place of execution of the arrestment:..........

   Debt recoverable or daily rate of maintenance as specified in the arrestment:..........

8. A debt advice and information package was provided to the debtor on (*insert date*). The applicant asks the court to make a conjoined arrestment order which

   a. Recalls the earnings and/or current maintenance arrestment(s) presently in effect against earnings payable to the debtor by the employer.

   b. Orders the employer, while the conjoined arrestment order is in effect to deduct a sum calculated in accordance with section 63 of the Debtors (Scotland) Act 1987 from the debtors net earnings on any pay-day and to pay this sum as soon as is reasonably practicable to the sheriff clerk at (*place*).

Date.............. Signed ..............

Applicant

Form 44

**Rule 53(4)**

*The* Debtors (Scotland) Act 1987

Sheriff Court: .......... Court Ref. No. ..........

*Form of notice of application for a conjoined arrestment order*

1. (*Place and date*)

To (*name and address of person to whom intimation given*).

This application for a conjoined arrestment order by (*name and address of applicant*) is intimated to you this date.

..........

Sheriff Clerk

2. IF YOU WISH TO OBJECT to the granting of the application you must fill in the box below

I intend to object to the granting of the application
Date .......... Signature ...............

3.     If you have filled in the box above you must return this form to the court within 14 days from the date of this intimation

The address of the court is: THE SHERIFF CLERK, ...............

4.     You will then be advised by the sheriff clerk of the date fixed for the hearing of the application when you should attend or be represented at court.

5.     PLEASE NOTE if you fail to return this form to the court as directed or if having returned it you fail to attend or be represented at the hearing the application may be dealt with in your absence.

IF YOU WISH FURTHER ADVICE CONTACT ANY CITIZENS ADVICE BUREAU/ LOCAL ADVICE CENTRE, SHERIFF CLERK OR SOLICITOR

Form 45 [1]

**Rule 54(1)**

SHERIFF COURT, (*Place*)

UNDER THE DEBTORS (SCOTLAND) ACT 1987, SECTION 60

CONJOINED ARRESTMENT ORDER IN THE APPLICATION BY

(*name and address*)

(*Place and date*). The Sheriff RECALLS the following arrestment(s) which have been served on (*name and address of employer*), the employer of the debtor (*name and address of debtor*) on the following dates:—

1.     On (*date*), for (*amount*), on behalf of (*name*)

2.     Etc.

SPECIFIES the amount(s) recoverable under this order as:—

(a)     Ordinary debt(s)

        Name of creditor                  Amount recoverable

(b)     Current maintenance debt

        Name of each maintenance creditor      Daily rate recoverable £

Aggregrate daily rate £

REQUIRES the said employer of the debtor, while this order is in effect to deduct a sum calculated in accordance with section 63 of the Debtors (Scotland) Act 1987 from the said debtor's net earnings on any pay-day and to pay it as soon as is reasonably practical to the sheriff clerk, (*address of sheriff clerk's office*);

Sheriff

**INSTRUCTIONS TO EMPLOYER**

*Please read these instructions carefully*

1.     As soon as this conjoined arrestment order comes into effect, any earnings arrestment and/or current maintenance arrestment against earnings payable by you to your employee is recalled and you must stop making deductions under the(se) arrestments.

2.     While this conjoined arrestment order is in effect you are required to deduct a sum from your employee's net earnings on any pay-day and to pay it as soon as is reasonably practicable to the sheriff clerk at (*address of sheriff clerk's office*).

3.     When making payment to the sheriff clerk you are required to supply him with the following information:—

     (1)    Name and address of your employee

---

[1] As amended by the Act of Sederunt (Child Support Rules) (SI 1993/920) r.7(3) (effective April 5, 1993), the Act of Sederunt (Sheriff Court Rules Amendment) (Diligence) (SSI 2008/ 121) r.10(6) (effective April 1, 2008) and by the Act of Sederunt (Sheriff Court Rules) (Miscellaneous Amendments) 2009 (SSI 2009/294) r.9 (effective October 1, 2009).

    (2)    Date of the conjoined arrestment order

    (3)    Sum deducted from his earnings for ordinary debt(s)

    (4)    Sum deducted from his earnings for current maintenance

    (5)    Total sum being paid to the sheriff clerk

    (6)    Whether income tax was deducted from the sum due for current maintenance

4.    The sum to be deducted is calculated in accordance with section 63 of the Debtors (Scotland) Act 1987 (a copy of sections 63(1) to (6) is attached) (*sheriff clerk to attach*).

5.    You must continue to make these deductions and payments until either—

    (1)    a copy of an order recalling the conjoined arrestment order has been served on you under section 66(7) of the Debtors (Scotland) Act 1987; or

    (2)    the debtor ceases to be employed by you.

    If the debtor ceases to be employed by the employer, the employer must, as soon as is reasonably practicable, notify the sheriff clerk of that fact and, so far as is known to him, of the name and address of any new employer of the debtor.

6.    You are entitled to charge your employee a fee (at present ..........) on each occasion you make a payment to the sheriff clerk under the conjoined arrestment order.

7.    For further information read the following notes.

(1) "Earnings" and "net earnings" from which deductions are to be made are defined in section 73 of the Act as amended by the Child Support Act 1991.

    (2) You are also referred to the following sections of the Act:—

| | |
|---|---|
| 60(9): | employer's liability where he fails to comply with a conjoined arrestment order |
| 62(2) and (3): | employer's duty, when a conjoined arrestment order is in effect, to give certain information to a creditor who is not included in the conjoined arrestment order and who has served or has in effect an earnings arrestment or a current maintenance arrestment. |
| 65(1): | Sheriff's power on an application by the debtor, a creditor whose debt is being enforced by a conjoined arrestment order, the employer or the sheriff clerk to determine any dispute as to the operation of a conjoined arrestment order. |
| 66(1): | Sheriff's power to recall a conjoined arrestment order where, in particular, all ordinary debts have been paid and all obligations to pay current maintenance have ceased. |
| 66(4): | Sheriff's power to vary a conjoined arrestment order where, for example an ordinary debt is paid or a maintenance order being enforced is varied or recalled. |
| 69(3): | If deductions are not made on the first pay-day after service of the conjoined arrestment order in accordance with section 69(2) of the Act, deductions made on a subsequent pay-day are not to include any deductions in respect of the first pay-day. |
| 70(4A) | Employer's duty to intimate a copy of a conjoined arrestment order to the debtor and to give certain information to the debtor. |
| 70A | Employer's duty to give certain information to the creditor or, as the case may be, the sheriff clerk and to send a copy of certain information to the debtor. |

Further information and advice about the Act is available from solicitors' offices, Citizens' Advice Bureaux and other local advice centres and sheriff clerks' offices.

Form 46 [1]

**Rule 54(5)**

### SHERIFF COURT:
### NOTICE OF SERVICE OF CONJOINED ARRESTMENT ORDER

To .............., the debtor's employer.

To .............., debtor.

To .............., creditor.

You are served with a copy of the foregoing conjoined arrestment order along with a copy of sections 63(1) to (6) of the Debtors (Scotland) Act 1987. It comes into effect seven days after service of the copy order on the employer and remains in effect until a copy of an order recalling it is served on the employer under section 66(7) of the Debtors (Scotland) Act 1987 or the debtor ceases to be employed by him. If the

---

[1] As amended by the Act of Sederunt (Sheriff Court Rules) (Miscellaneous Amendments) 2009 (SSI 2009/294) r.9 (effective October 1, 2009).

debtor ceases to be employed by the employer, the employer must, as soon as is reasonably practicable, notify the sheriff clerk of that fact and, so far as is known to him, of the name and address of any new employer of the debtor.

Sheriff Clerk

Sheriff Clerk's Office

(*Address and date*)

Officer of Court

(*name and address, designation*)

All creditors whose arrestments have been recalled by the foregoing conjoined arrestment order and are included in it must inform the sheriff clerk in writing within 14 days of receiving this notice of the name and address of a person within the United Kingdom to whom payments are to be made by him under the order.

**Form 47**

**Rule 55(1)**

*The* Debtors (Scotland) Act 1987, section 60(9)(c)

Sheriff Court ..........

| APPLICATION FOR WARRANT FOR DILIGENCE AGAINST EMPLOYER | (1) | | .......... 19.......... (Court Ref. No.) APPLICANT |

A.

The applicant is
(a)    The sheriff clerk

(1)    Insert name and address

B.

Other persons having an interest are
(b)    The employer (1)
(c)    The debtor (1)
(d)    The creditors whose debts are being enforced by the conjoined arrestment order (1)

(2)    Insert name

C.

A conjoined arrestment order against the earnings of the debtor (2)..........was made on (*date*)..........by the sheriff at (*place*)..........and was served on the employer (2)..........by or on the instructions of the sheriff clerk (*place*) on (*date*)..........

D.

The employer has failed to comply with the conjoined arrestment order (*specify manner and circumstances of this failure*):—
The employer is accordingly liable to pay to the sheriff clerk £ which he would have paid if he had complied with the order.

This application is made under section 60(9)(c) of the Debtors (Scotland) Act 1987.

E.

The applicant asks the court:—

1. To fix a hearing.

2. To order the sheriff clerk to intimate this application and the date of the hearing to the employer, the debtor and the

creditors whose debts are being enforced by the conjoined arrestment order.

3. To order the employer to pay to the sheriff clerk (*place*).......... £..........

4. To grant warrant for diligence against the employer for recovery of this sum or such other sum as appears to the court to be due.

5. To award expenses (if competent).

Date ...............19..........         (*Signed*) ...............

Applicant

IF YOU WISH FURTHER ADVICE CONTACT ANY CITIZENS ADVICE BUREAU/ LOCAL ADVICE CENTRE/SHERIFF CLERK OR SOLICITOR

**Form 48**

**Rule 56(1)**

*The* Debtors (Scotland) Act 1987, section 62(4)

Rule 54(5)                  Sheriff Court ..........

APPLICATION FOR OR- (1)         .......... 19..........
DER ON EMPLOYER TO            (Court Ref. No.)
PROVIDE INFORMATION        APPLICANT

A.      The applicant is
The creditor who requires information under section 62(2) or (3)

(1) Insert B.    Other persons having an interest are
name and ad-     The employer (1)
dress

* delete as ap- C.    *An earnings arrestment schedule/*a current maintenance
propriate         arrestment schedule against the earnings of the debtor
                 (1).......... was served on the said employer by (1)..............
                 sheriff officer/messenger-at-arms on the instructions of the
                 applicant on..............

D.      The arrestment *did not come into effect/*has ceased to
have effect as a conjoined arrestment order is in effect.
The employer has failed without reasonable excuse to inform the applicant which court made the conjoined ar-restment order.
The applicant is entitled to this information.

This application is made under section 62(4) of the Debtors (Scotland) Act 1987.

E.      The applicant asks the court:—

1. To fix a hearing.

2. To order the sheriff clerk to intimate this application and the date of the hearing to the applicant and to the employer.

3. To order the employer to inform the applicant which court made the conjoined arrestment order within such period as the court may order.

4. To award expenses (if competent).

Date ...............19.........  (*Signed*) ...............

Applicant

IF YOU WISH FURTHER ADVICE CONTACT ANY CITIZENS ADVICE BUREAU/ LOCAL ADVICE CENTRE/SHERIFF CLERK OR SOLICITOR

## Form 49

**Rule 57(1)**

*The* Debtors (Scotland) Act 1987, section 62(5)

Sheriff Court .........

*Application for variation of a conjoined arrestment order*

1. The applicant..........: (*name and address*)

The debtor (employee)..........: (*name and address*)

The employer..........: (*name and address*)

2. The applicant is a creditor of the debtor and wishes to enforce his debt by executing an earnings arrestment and/or a current maintenance arrestment against earnings payable to the debtor by the employer.

3. The debt cannot be enforced by executing an earnings arrestment or a current maintenance arrestment as a conjoined arrestment order is in effect against these earnings.

4. The conjoined arrestment order was made on (*date*) by the court at (*address of court*).

5. The applicant's debt consists of

| ORDINARY DEBT | CURRENT MAINTENANCE |
|---|---|
| (Where there is more than one ordinary debt state details relating to each separately.) | Maintenance payable by the debtor : expressed as a daily rate |
| Sum due under decree or other document or summary warrant : | Is the debtor entitled to deduct income : Yes/No tax from maintenance payable? |
| expenses : | Particulars of maintenance order(s) |
| interest : | which constituted the obligation to |
| less paid to account : ......... | pay maintenance : |
| expenses of executing current maintenance arrestment : | Date of any intimation made under section 54(1) of the Act : |
| expenses of serving charge : | Particulars of debtors default in his payments under the maintenance |
| expenses of executing earnings arrestment : | order(s) with reference to either subsection (1) or (2) of section 54 of : the Act |
| expenses of this application : | |
| TOTAL AMOUNT RECOVERABLE ......... | |
| ......... | |
| Particulars of decree or other document : or summary warrant which constituted the debt (*specify*) | |
| Date of any charge : | |

6. The person within the United Kingdom to whom payments are to be made is: (*name and address*).

The applicant asks the court:—

To vary the conjoined arrestment order granted on (*date*) to include the applicant's debt among the debts being enforced by the conjoined arrestment order.

Date ............... Signed ...............

Applicant

**Form 50**

**Rule 57(3)(a)**

*The* Debtors (Scotland) Act 1987

Sheriff Court: ..........                    Court Ref. No. ..........

*Form of notice of application for variation of a conjoined arrestment order*

1. (*Place and date*)

To (*name and address of person to whom intimation given*).

This application for a variation of a conjoined arrestment order by (*name and address of applicant*) is intimated to you this date.

..............

Sheriff Clerk

2. IF YOU WISH TO OBJECT to the granting of the application you must fill in this box below

> I intend to object to the granting of the application
>
> Date .......... Signature ..........

3. If you have filled in the box above you must return this form to the court within 14 days from the date of this intimation

The address of the court is: THE SHERIFF CLERK, ..............

4.    You will then be advised by the sheriff clerk of the date fixed for the hearing of the application when you should attend or be represented at court.

5.    PLEASE NOTE if you fail to return this form to the court as directed or if having returned it, you fail to attend or be represented at the hearing, the application may be dealt with in your absence.

IF YOU WISH FURTHER ADVICE CONTACT ANY CITIZENS ADVICE BUREAU/ LOCAL ADVICE CENTRE, SHERIFF CLERK OR SOLICITOR

Form 51 [1]

**Rule 57(7)(b)**

*SHERIFF COURT*

*Notice of Service of an Order Varying a Conjoined Arrestment Order under* Section 62(5) of the Debtors (Scotland) Act 1987

To .............., the debtor's employer.

To .............., debtor.

To .............., creditor.

You are served with (1) copy of an order dated.......... varying a conjoined arrestment order made on (2) a copy of the conjoined arrestment order as varied

(3) a copy of subsections (1) to (6) of section 63 of the Debtors (Scotland) Act 1987

The employer is required to operate the conjoined arrestment order as varied seven days after service of the copy order on him, although he may operate it on any pay-day occurring within this seven day period. The conjoined arrestment order as varied remains in effect untila copy of an order recalling it is served on the employer under section 66(7) of the Debtors (Scotland) Act 1987 or the debtor ceases to be employed by him. If the debtor ceases to be employed by the employer, the employer must, as soon as is reasonably practicable, notify the sheriff clerk of that fact and, so far as is known to him, of the name and address of any new employer of the debtor.

Sheriff Clerk

Sheriff Clerk's Office

(*Address and date*)

Officer of Court

(*name and address, designation*)

**Rule 58(1)(a)**                        **Form 52**

*The* Debtors (Scotland) Act 1987

*Intimation to employer under* section 63(7)

The employer ..............: (*name and address*)

The debtor (employee) ..............: (*name and address*)

The sheriff clerk ..............: (*name and address*)

Date of conjoined arrestment order ..............: (*specify*)

Date order served on employer ..............: (*specify*)

---

[1] As amended by the Act of Sederunt (Sheriff Court Rules) (Miscellaneous Amendments) 2009 (SSI 2009/294) r.9 (effective October 1, 2009).

Date of order varying the conjoined arrestment order ..........: (*specify*)

Date varied order served on employer ...............: (*specify*)

*To the employer*—Take note that on (*date*) the Lord Advocate made regulations which varied

*(a) Tables A, B and C of Schedule 2 to the Debtors (Scotland) Act 1987 (the statutory deduction tables)

*(b) The percentage specified in subsection (5) and (6)(a)(ii) of section 49 of the Debtors (Scotland) Act 1987 to (*specify change*)

*(c) The sum specified in subsection 4(b) of section 63 of the Debtors (Scotland) Act 1987 to £

The regulations come into operation on (*date*)

*delete as appropriate

Date ............... (*Signed*) ...............

Sheriff Clerk

(i) This intimation should be considered carefully by the employer as the variation(s) made by regulations referred to may affect the sum to be deducted by him under the conjoined arrestment order (see further section 69(1), (2) and (3) of the Debtors (Scotland) Act 1987).

(ii) The sheriff clerk must attach to this intimation the statutory deduction tables as revised where these have been varied by the regulations.

**Rule 58(1)(b)**        Form 53

*The* Debtors (Scotland) Act 1987

*Intimation to employer under* section 63(8)

The employer ...............: (*name and address*)

The debtor (employee) ...............: (*name and address*)

The sheriff clerk ...............: (*name and address*)

Date of conjoined arrestment order ...............: (*specify*)

Date order served on employer ...............: (*specify*)

Date of order varying the conjoined arrestment order ..........: (*specify*)

Date varied order served on employer ...............: (*specify*)

*To the employer*—Take note that on (*date*) the small maintenance limits mentioned in section 351(2) of the Income and Corporation Taxes Act 1988 were changed to (*specify change*):—

The changes come into operation on (*date*)

Date ............... (*Signed*) ...............

Sheriff Clerk

(i) This intimation should be considered carefully by the employer as the change made may affect the sum to be deducted by him under the conjoined arrestment order.

(ii) The sheriff clerk must attach to this intimation a copy of section 351(2) of the Income and Corporation Taxes Act 1988.

Form 54

**Rule 59(1)**

*The* Debtors (Scotland) Act 1987, section 65(1)

Sheriff Court ...............

| APPLICATION FOR DE-TERMINATION OF DISPUTE IN OPERATION OF CONJOINED ARREST-MENT ORDER | (1) | | .......... 19......... (Court Ref. No.) |
|---|---|---|---|
| | | | APPLICANT |

*delete as appropriate

(1) Insert B.

A. The applicant is
*(a) The debtor
*(b) A creditor whose debt is being enforced by the conjoined arrestment order
*(c) The employer
*(d) The sheriff clerk (1)

Other persons having an interest are

510

name and ad-
dress

*(e)    The debtor (1)
*(f)    (Other) creditors whose debts are being enforced by the conjoined arrestment order (1)
*(g)    The employer (1)
*(h)    The sheriff clerk (1)

C.

A conjoined arrestment order against the earnings of the debtor (1)............... was made on (*date*)............... by the sheriff at (*place*)...............

D.

The following dispute as to the operation of the conjoined arrestment order requires to be determined (*specify nature of the dispute*)

This application is made under section 65(1) of the Debtors (Scotland) Act 1987.

E.

The applicant asks the court:—

1. To fix a hearing.

2. To order the sheriff clerk to intimate this application and the date of the hearing to the applicant and to those persons stated above as having an interest other than himself.

3. To make an order determining the dispute (*specify order sought*).

*4. To order the reimbursement by (*name person*) to (*name person*) of £.......... with interest thereon at the rate of (*specify rate*) from (*specify date*) or such other date as the court may consider appropriate.

*5. To order the payment by (*name person*) to (*name person*) of £.......... with interest thereon at the rate of (*specify rate*) from (*specify date*) or such other date as the court may consider appropriate.

6. To award expenses (if competent).

Date ............... 19..........        (*Signed*) ...............

Applicant

IF YOU WISH FURTHER ADVICE CONTACT ANY CITIZENS ADVICE BUREAU/LOCAL ADVICE CENTRE/SHERIFF CLERK OR SOLICITOR

**Rule 60(1)**                    Form 55

*The* Debtors (Scotland) Act 1987, section 65(7)

Sheriff Court ...............

APPLICATION FOR PAY-  (1)
MENT BY CREDITOR TO
DEBTOR OF PENALTY
SUM (CONJOINED AR-
RESTMENT ORDER)

.......... 19..........
(Court Ref. No.)
APPLICANT

A.

The applicant is
The debtor

(1)    Insert  B.

Other persons having an interest are

511

| name and address | | The creditor (1) |
|---|---|---|

| | C. | A conjoined arrestment order against the earnings of the debtor was made on (*date*).......... by the sheriff at (*place*).......... |
|---|---|---|

| (2) Insert name *delete as appropriate | D. | *An ordinary debt/*current maintenance due to the said creditor (2).......... was included in the conjoined arrestment order.<br>The creditor failed to intimate to the sheriff clerk (*place*) that:—<br>*(a) The debt recoverable had been paid or otherwise extinguished.<br>*(b) The debt had ceased to be enforceable by diligence.<br>*(c) The obligation to pay the current maintenance had ceased.<br>*(d) The obligation to pay the current maintenance had ceased to be enforceable by diligence.<br>(*Specify when and how (a), (b), (c) or (d) occurred*):—<br>The debtor overpaid £.......... as a result of this failure. (*Give details of the calculation of this sum and grounds for seeking the sum sought from the creditor*):— |
|---|---|---|

|  |  | This application is made under section 65(7) of the Debtors (Scotland) Act 1987. |
|---|---|---|
|  | E. | The applicant asks the court:— |
|  |  | 1. To fix a hearing. |
|  |  | 2. To order the sheriff clerk to intimate this application and the date of the hearing to the applicant and to the creditor. |
|  |  | 3. To order the creditor to pay to the debtor £.......... (*specify amount requested*). |
|  |  | 4. To award expenses (if competent). |

Date ............... 19..........                    (*Signed*) ...............

Applicant

IF YOU WISH FURTHER ADVICE CONTACT ANY CITIZENS ADVICE BUREAU/LOCAL ADVICE CENTRE/SHERIFF CLERK OR SOLICITOR

**Rule 61(1)**                    Form 56

*The* Debtors (Scotland) Act 1987, section 66(1)(a)

Sheriff Court ...............

| APPLICATION FOR RE-<br>CALL OF CONJOINED<br>ARRESTMENT ORDER | (1) |  |
|---|---|---|

.......... 19..........

(Court Ref. No.)

APPLICANT

| *delete as appropriate | A. | The applicant is<br>*(a) The debtor<br>*(b) A creditor whose debt is being enforced by the conjoined arrestment order<br>*(c) The person on whom a copy of the conjoined arrestment order or an order varying the order was |
|---|---|---|

served under section 60(7) or 62(6) of the Act
*(d)   The sheriff clerk
*(e)   An interim/permanent trustee of the debtor

(1)   Insert B.
name and ad-
dress

Other persons having an interest are
*(f)   The debtor (1)
*(g)   (Other) creditors whose debts are being enforced under the conjoined arrestment order (1)
*(h)   (Other) persons on whom a copy of the conjoined arrestment order or an order varying the order was served under section 60(7) or 62(6) of the Act (including the employer) (1)
*(i)   The sheriff clerk (1)
*(j)   An interim/permanent trustee of the debtor (1)

(2)   Insert C.
name

A conjoined arrestment order against the earnings of the debtor (2).............. was made on (date).............. by the sheriff at (place)..............

D.

*(a)   The conjoined arrestment order is invalid. (Specify why it is claimed to be invalid):—
*(b)   All the ordinary debts being enforced by the conjoined arrestment order have been paid or otherwise extinguished or have ceased to be enforceable by diligence and all the obligations to pay current maintenance being so enforced have ceased or have ceased to be enforceable by diligence. (Specify when and how these matters occurred):—
*(c)   The debtor's estate has been sequestrated (specify date of sequestration)

This application is made under section 66(1)(a) of the Debtors (Scotland) Act 1987.

E.   The applicant asks the court:—

1. To fix a hearing.

2. To order the sheriff clerk to intimate this application and the date of the hearing to the applicant and to those persons stated above as having an interest other than himself.

*3. To dispense with a hearing and intimation.

4. To recall the conjoined arrestment order.

*5. To make the following consequential order (specify order sought).

6. To award expenses (if competent).

Date .............. 19.........        (Signed) ..............

Applicant

IF YOU WISH FURTHER ADVICE CONTACT ANY CITIZENS ADVICE BUREAU/LOCAL ADVICE CENTRE/SHERIFF CLERK OR SOLICITOR

Rule 62(1)                    Form 57

The Debtors (Scotland) Act 1987, section 66(1)(b)

Sheriff Court ..........

APPLICATION FOR RE-
CALL OF CONJOINED
ARRESTMENT ORDER
(BY ALL CREDITORS
WHOSE DEBTS ARE BE-
ING ENFORCED BY IT)

(1)

.......... 19..........
(Court Ref. No.)

APPLICANT

A. The applicants are
The creditors whose debts are being enforced by a conjoined arrestment order(1)

(1) Insert
name
and ad-
dress

B. Other persons having an interest are
The debtor (1)

(2) Insert
name

C. A conjoined arrestment order against the earnings of the debtor (2)..........was
made on (date)..........by the sheriff at (place)...............

D. The conjoined arrestment order should be recalled (specify reasons for application and any consequential order sought)

This application is made under section 66(1)(b) of the Debtors (Scotland) Act
1987.

E. The applicants ask the court:—
1. To order such intimation (if any) and
further procedure that the court considers
appropriate.
2. To recall the conjoined arrestment order.
3. To make the following consequential
order (specify order sought).
4. To award expenses (if competent).

Date .......... (Signed) ...............
19..........

Applicant

IF YOU WISH FURTHER ADVICE CONTACT ANY CITIZENS ADVICE BUREAU/LOCAL
ADVICE CENTRE/SHERIFF CLERK OR SOLICITOR

Rule 63(1)                                         Form 58
The Debtors (Scotland) Act 1987, section 66(4)
Sheriff Court ..........

APPLICATION FOR VARI-
ATION OF CONJOINED
ARRESTMENT ORDER

(1)

.......... 19..........
(Court Ref. No.)

APPLICANT

*delete
as appro-
priate

A. The applicant is
*(a)    The debtor
*(b)    A creditor whose debt is being enforced by the conjoined arrestment
order
*(c)    The employer
*(d)    The sheriff clerk

| (1) Insert name and ad- dress | B. | Other persons having an interest are <br> *(e)  The debtor (1) <br> *(f)  (Other) creditors whose debts are being enforced by the conjoined arrestment order (1) <br> *(g)  The employer (1) <br> *(h)  The sheriff clerk (1) |

| (2) Insert name | C. | A conjoined arrestment order against the earnings of the debtor (2).........was made on (*date*)..........by the sheriff at (*place*)............... |

| | D. | *(a)  An ordinary debt being enforced by the conjoined arrestment order has been paid or otherwise extinguished or has ceased to be enforceable by diligence (*give details of when and how this occurred*):— <br> *(b)  An order or decree has come into effect which varies/supersedes/recalls a maintenance order being enforced by the conjoined arrestment order (*give details of the order or decree which varied, superseded or recalled the maintenance order*):—. <br> *(c)  An obligation to pay maintenance being enforced by the conjoined arrestment order has ceased to be enforceable in Scotland (*give details of when and how this occurred*):— <br> The conjoined arrestment order should accordingly be varied (*specify variation required*):— |

This application is made under section 66(4) of the Debtors (Scotland) Act 1987.

E.  The applicant asks the court:—

1. To fix a hearing.
2. To order the sheriff clerk to intimate this application and the date of the hearing to the applicant and to those persons stated above as having an interest other than himself.
3. To vary the conjoined arrestment order as requested.
4. To award expenses (if competent).

Date      .......... (*Signed*) ...............
19..........

Applicant

IF YOU WISH FURTHER ADVICE CONTACT ANY CITIZENS ADVICE BUREAU/LOCAL ADVICE CENTRE/SHERIFF CLERK OR SOLICITOR

Rule 65(3)(b)                 Form 59

*SHERIFF COURT:*

*Notice of Service of an Order Varying a Conjoined Arrestment Order under* Section 66 of the Debtors (Scotland) Act 1987

To (*Name and address of persons upon whom service is made*)

You are served with    (1) a copy of an order dated .......... varying a conjoined arrestment order made on

(2) a copy of the conjoined arrestment order as varied

(3) a copy of subsections (1) to (6) of section 63 of the Debtors (Scotland) Act 1987.

The variation comes into effect seven days after service of the copy order on the employer and the conjoined arrestment order as varied remains in effect until a copy of an order recalling it is served on the employer under section 66(7) of the Debtors (Scotland) Act 1987 or the debtor ceases to be employed by the employer. The employer should notify the sheriff clerk in writing immediately if the debtor ceases to be employed by him.

Sheriff Clerk
Sheriff Clerk's Office
(*Address and date*)

Officer of Court
(*Name, designation and address*)

Rule 65A                              Form 59a [1]

*The* Debtors (Scotland) Act 1987, section 70B

Sheriff Court..........

(Court Ref No. )

APPLICATION UNDER SECTION 70B OF THE ACT

APPLICANT:

A. The applicant is:

B. The employer is:

C. The debtor is:

D. The *earnings arrestment/current maintenance assessment schedule/conjoined arrestment order*\** was served on the employer by [*insert name*] *sheriff officer / messenger-at-arms*\* on the instructions of the applicant on [*insert date*].

E. The employer has ceased to be the employer of the debtor but has failed to give notice under section 70.4(5) of the Debtors (Scotland) Act 1987 of that fact and of the name and address of any new employer of the debtor.

This application is made under section 70B(1) of the Debtors (Scotland) Act 1987.

F. The applicant asks the court—

1. to fix a hearing;
2. to order the sheriff clerk to intimate this application and the date of the hearing to the applicant and the employer;
3. to make an order under section 70B(1) in respect of the employer; and
4. to award expenses (if competent).

*Date*                           (*Signed*)

*Applicant*

• *delete as applicable*

Rule 67                                Form 60

*Certificate of execution of earnings arrestment schedule/current maintenance arrestment* schedule

(*Place and date*)

I .............. certify that on (*date*) I served the foregoing earnings arrestment schedule/current maintenance arrestment schedule on (*name and address of employer*) employer of the debtor (*name and address of debtor*). This I did by (*state method of service*).

Officer of Court
(*Name, designation and address*)

Rule 68                                Form 61 [2]

SUMMARY WARRANT FOR THE RECOVERY OF

(*insert type of sum due e.g. Rates, Community Charge, Council Tax, etc.*)

under (*insert section and statute under which sum due*)

(*Place and date*)

The sheriff having considered the application dated (*date*) by (*name and address of applicant*) along with certificate produced and it being stated in the application that an action has not been commenced for the recovery of any amount due, grants a summary warrant authorising recovery of the amount remaining due and unpaid by each person specified in the application along with a surcharge of 10 per cent of that amount by:

(a)    a poinding and sale in accordance with Schedule 5 to the Debtors (Scotland) Act 1987;

(b)    an earnings arrestment;

(c)    an arrestment and action of furthcoming or sale;

and grants warrant to enter premises in the occupancy of any person specified in the application in order to execute a poinding or sale or the removal and sale of poinded articles and, for any of those purposes, to open shut and lockfast places.

Rule 68                                Form 62 [3]

---

[1] As inserted by the Act of Sederunt (Sheriff Court Rules Amendment) (Diligence) (SSI 2008/121) r.10(7) (effective April 1, 2008).

[2] As substituted by SI 1996/2709 (effective November 11, 1996).

[3] As substituted by SI 1996/2709 (effective November 11, 1996).

*SUMMARY WARRANT FOR THE RECOVERY OF*
*(insert type of sum due e.g. Car Tax, Value Added Tax, etc.)*
under *(insert section and statute under which sum due)*
*(Place and date)*

The sheriff having considered the application dated *(date)* by *(name and address of applicant)* along with certificate produced, grants a summary warrant authorising recovery of the amount remaining due and unpaid by each person specified in the application by:

(a) a poinding and sale in accordance with Schedule 5 to the Debtors (Scotland) Act 1987;

(b) an earnings arrestment;

(c) an arrestment and action of furthcoming or sale;

and grants warrant to enter premises in the occupancy of any person specified in the application in order to execute a poinding or sale or the removal and sale of poinded articles and, for any of those purposes, to open shut and lockfast places.

| Rule 68(3) | Form 63 [1] |
|---|---|

| Rule 68(4) | Form 63A [2] |
|---|---|

| Rule 69A | Form 63B [3] |
|---|---|

Form of certificate of execution of arrestment in execution
CERTIFICATE OF EXECUTION

I, *(name)*, Sheriff Officer, certify that I executed an arrestment, by virtue of:—

* a decree by the sheriff at *(place)* on *(date)*

* a document of debt as defined by section 73A(4) of the Debtors (Scotland) Act 1987 [and registered for execution in *(insert place of execution)* on *(insert date)*, if appropriate],

obtained at the instance of *(name and address of party arresting)* against *(name and address of defender)* on *(name of arrestee)*—

* by delivering the schedule of arrestment to *(name of arrestee or other person)* at *(place)* personally on *(date)*.

* by leaving the schedule of arrestment with *(name and occupation of person with whom left)* at *(place)* on *(date)*, [and by posting a copy of the schedule to the arrestee by registered post or first class recorded delivery to the address specified on the receipt annexed to this certificate].

* by depositing the schedule of arrestment in *(place)* on *(date)*. *(Specify that enquiry made and reasonable grounds exist for believing that the person on whom service is to be made resides at the place but is not available)* [and by posting a copy of the schedule to the arrestee by registered post or first class recorded delivery to the address specified on the receipt annexed to this certificate].

* by affixing the schedule of arrestment to the door at *(place)* on *(date)*. *(Specify that enquiry made and that reasonable grounds exist for believing that the person on whom service is to be made resides at the place but is not available)* [and by posting a copy of the schedule to the arrestee by registered post or first class recorded delivery to the address specified on the receipt annexed to this certificate].

* by leaving the schedule of arrestment with *(name and occupation of person with whom left)* at *(place of business)* on *(date)* [and by posting a copy of the schedule to the arrestee by registered post or first class recorded delivery to the address specified on the receipt annexed to this certificate].

* by depositing the schedule of arrestment at *(place of business)* on *(date)*. *(Specify that enquiry made and that reasonable grounds exist for believing that the person on whom service is to be made carries on business at that place)* [and by posting a copy of the schedule to the arrestee by registered post or first class recorded delivery to the address specified on the receipt annexed to this certificate].

* by affixing the schedule of arrestment to the door at *(place of business)* on *(date)*. *(Specify that enquiry made and that reasonable grounds exist for believing that the person on whom service is to be made carries on business at that place.)* [and by posting a copy of the schedule to the arrestee by registered post or first class recorded delivery to the address specified on the receipt annexed to this certificate].

---

[1] Substituted by SI 1991/1920, and as amended by SI 1994/3086 (effective December 22, 1994) and 1995 No.1876 (effective August 7, 1995). Revoked by SI 1996/2709 (effective November 11, 1996).

[2] As inserted by SI 1994/3086. Revoked by SI 1995/1876 (effective August 7, 1995).

[3] As inserted by the Act of Sederunt (Sheriff Court Rules Amendment) (Diligence) 2009 (SSI 2009/107) r.2 (effective April 22, 2009).

* by leaving the schedule of arrestment at (*registered office*) on (*date*), in the hands of (*name of person*) [and by posting a copy of the schedule to the arrestee by registered post or first class recorded delivery to the address specified on the receipt annexed to this certificate].

* by depositing the schedule of arrestment at (*registered office*) on (*date*) [and by posting a copy of the schedule to the arrestee by registered post or first class recorded delivery to the address specified on the receipt annexed to this certificate].

* by affixing the schedule of arrestment to the door at (*registered office*) on (*date*) [and by posting a copy of the schedule to the arrestee by registered post or first class recorded delivery to the address specified on the receipt annexed to this certificate].

I did this in the presence of (*name, occupation and address of witness*).

(*Signed*)

Sheriff Officer

(Address)

(*Signed*)

(Witness)

*Delete where not applicable

Form 63C [1]

Rule 69B

*The* Debtors (Scotland) Act 1987

**Form of Service of copy final decree under section 73C**

Sheriff Court ..............          Court Ref No ..............

1.     (*Place and date*)

       To (*name and address of arrestee*)

2.     On (*date*) the court granted decree against (*name of debtor*) for payment of £ (*insert sum*) to (*insert name of creditor*). A copy of the final decree is attached.

3.     An arrestment on the dependence of this action attaching funds in your hands was executed on (*insert date*).

4.     You are now required to release to the creditor, on the expiry of the period of 14 weeks beginning with this date (or earlier where a mandate authorises you to do so) the lowest of—
       (a)    the sum attached by the arrestment;
       (b)    the sum due by you to the debtor; or
       (c)    the sum of £(*insert sum*), which is the sum calculated in accordance with section 73K(c) of the Debtors (Scotland) Act 1987.

5.     This must be done unless:
       (a)    an application is made under section 73M(1) of the Debtors (Scotland) Act 1987;
       (b)    the debtor applies to the sheriff under section 73Q(2) of that Act;
       (c)    an action of multiplepoinding is raised in relation to the funds attached by the arrestment;
       (d)    the arrestment is recalled, restricted or otherwise ceases to have effect.

(*Signed*)                                                    Date ..........

Creditor [*or* Solicitor for Creditor]

IF YOU WISH FURTHER ADVICE CONTACT ANY CITIZENS ADVICE BUREAU/ LOCAL ADVICE CENTRE/SHERIFF CLERK OR SOLICITOR

Form 63D [2]

Rule 69C(1)

*The* Debtors (Scotland) Act 1987

**Application under** section 73H(1)

Sheriff Court ..............

---

[1] As inserted by the Act of Sederunt (Sheriff Court Rules Amendment) (Diligence) 2009 (SSI 2009/107) r.2 (effective April 22, 2009).

[2] As inserted by the Act of Sederunt (Sheriff Court Rules Amendment) (Diligence) 2009 (SSI 2009/107) r.2 (effective April 22, 2009).

APPLICATION (1)
FOR ORDER
REQUIRING
ARRESTEE TO
MAKE
PAYMENT TO
CREDITOR

.............. 20 .........

(Court Ref. No.)

APPLICANT

* delete as appropriate

**A.** The applicant is
*(a) the creditor who has arrested in pursuance of a warrant granted for diligence on the dependence of an action
*(b) the creditor who has arrested in execution of a decree (or document of debt)

(1) Insert name and address

**B** Other persons having an interest are
*(c) the arrestee (1)
*(d) the debtor (1)

**C** The Creditor obtained decree against the debtor at (*insert name of court*) on (*insert date*) (*or give details of other document upon which the arrestment proceeded*).

>

**D** The sum of £ (*insert sum*) was arrested on the hands of the arrestee on (*insert date*).

**E** (*Where applicable*) The Creditor served a copy of the final decree on the arrestee on (*insert date*)

**F** The arrestee has failed without reasonable excuse to send to the creditor the information referred to in section 73G(2) of the Debtors (Scotland) Act 1987.

**G** The applicant asks the court:-
1. To fix a hearing;
2. To order the sheriff clerk to intimate this application and the date of the hearing to the applicant, the arrestee and the debtor;
3. To make an order requiring the arrestee to pay to the creditor—
*(a) the sum of £ (*insert sum*) which is the sum due to the creditor by the debtor
*(b) the sum of £ (*insert sum*) which is the

| | |
|---|---|
| | sum first mentioned in column 1 of Table B in Schedule 2 to the Debtors (Scotland) Act 1987 (being the sum representing the net monthly earnings from which no reduction would be made under an earnings arrestment were such an arrestment in effect). |
| | *4. To make a finding of contempt of court. |

IF YOU WISH FURTHER ADVICE CONTACT ANY CITIZENS ADVICE BUREAU/LOCAL ADVICE CENTRE/SHERIFF CLERK OR SOLICITOR

Form 63E [1]

Rules 69C(2), 69D(2) and 69E(2)

*The* Debtors (Scotland) Act 1987

**Form of intimation of hearing**

Sheriff Court ...............          Court Ref No ..........

1.          (*Place and date*)

          To (*name and address of person to whom intimation is given*)

2.          An application under [*section 73H(1) or 73M(1) or 73Q(1)] of the Debtors (Scotland) Act 1987 was made by (*name of applicant*) on (*date*).

3.          The hearing of the application will take place on (*insert date*) at (*insert time*) in (*insert court*).

4.          If you fail to attend or be represented at the hearing the application may be dealt with in your absence.

*delete as appropriate

(*Signed*)          Date ..........

Sheriff Clerk

IF YOU WISH FURTHER ADVICE CONTACT ANY CITIZENS ADVICE BUREAU/ LOCAL ADVICE CENTRE/SHERIFF CLERK OR SOLICITOR

Form 63F [2]

Rule 69D

*The* Debtors (Scotland) Act 1987

**Notice of objection under** section 73M(1)

Sheriff Court ...................

APPLICATION     (1)

FOR ORDER                    ............... 20 ..........

RECALLING                                        (Court Ref. No.)

OR

RESTRICTING          APPLICANT

ARRESTMENT

| | |
|---|---|
| (1) Insert name and address | A. |
| | The applicant is |
| | *(a)    the debtor (1) |
| | *(b)    the arrestee (1) |
| | *(c)    a third party (1) |

---

[1] As inserted by the Act of Sederunt (Sheriff Court Rules Amendment) (Diligence) 2009 (SSI 2009/107) r.2 (effective April 22, 2009).

[2] As inserted by the Act of Sederunt (Sheriff Court Rules Amendment) (Diligence) 2009 (SSI 2009/107) r.2 (effective April 22, 2009).

|   |   |
|---|---|

| *delete as appropriate* | B | Other persons entitled to receive notice of this application are<br>*(d)  the debtor (1)<br>*(e)  the arrestee (1)<br>*(f)  the creditor (1)<br>*(g)  a third party (1)<br>(h)  the sheriff clerk (1) |

| | C | The Creditor has arrested the sum of £ (*insert sum*) on (*insert date*) in relation to the decree granted at (*insert name of court*) *[and served upon the arrestee on (*insert date*)] (*or give details of the document upon which the arrestment proceeded*). |

| | D | The applicant objects to the arrestment on the following grounds—<br>*(i)  the warrant in execution of which the arrestment was executed is invalid (*give details*)<br>*(j)  the arrestment has been executed incompetently or irregularly (*give details*)<br>*(k)  the funds attached are due to the third party solely or in common with the debtor (*give details*) |

| | E | The applicant asks the court—<br>1.  To fix a hearing;<br>2.  To order the sheriff clerk to intimate the date of the hearing to the applicant and those persons mentioned in Part B;<br>3.  To make an order *recalling *or* restricting the arrestment. |

**Note:**  You must give this notice of objection to the creditor, the sheriff clerk, the debtor or, as the case may be, the arrestee and, in so far as known to you, any third party, before the expiry of the period of 4 weeks beginning with the date of service of a copy of the final decree under section 73C(2) of the Debtors (Scotland) Act 1987 or, as the case may be, the date of service of the schedule of arrestment.

IF YOU WISH FURTHER ADVICE CONTACT ANY CITIZENS ADVICE BUREAU/ LOCAL ADVICE CENTRE/SHERIFF CLERK OR SOLICITOR

Form 63G [1]

Rule 69E

*The* Debtors (Scotland) Act 1987

**Application under** *section 73Q(2)*

Sheriff Court ..............

---

[1] As inserted by the Act of Sederunt (Sheriff Court Rules Amendment) (Diligence) 2009 (SSI 2009/ 107) r.2 (effective April 22, 2009).

| | |
|---|---|
| APPLICATION (1)<br>FOR RELEASE<br>OF PROPERTY<br>WHERE<br>ARRESTMENT<br>UNDULY<br>HARSH | ............... 20 .........<br>(Court Ref. No.)<br><br>APPLICANT |

| A. | The applicant is<br>The debtor |
|---|---|

| (1) *Insert name and address* | B | Other persons having an interest are<br>(a) The creditor (1)<br>(b) The arrestee (1)<br>(c) Other (1) |
|---|---|---|

| C | The creditor has arrested the sum of £ (*insert sum*) in the hands of the arrestee on (*insert date*) in relation to the decree granted at (*insert name of court*) (*or give details of other document upon which the arrestment proceeded*) and that arrestment attaches funds due to or other moveable property of the debtor. |
|---|---|

| D | The applicant considers that the arrestment is unduly harsh for the following reasons:— (*give details*) |
|---|---|

| E | The applicant asks the court—<br>1. To fix a hearing<br>2. To order the sheriff clerk to intimate this application and the date of the hearing to the creditor, the arrestee and any other person appearing to the court to have an interest<br>3. To make an order—<br>   (a) providing that the arrestment ceases to have effect in relation to—(*specify funds or property*); and<br>   (b) requiring the creditor to release the funds (*or* property) detailed above to the debtor. |
|---|---|

Date ............... 20 .........        (*Signed*) ...............

IF YOU WISH FURTHER ADVICE CONTACT ANY CITIZENS ADVICE BUREAU/LOCAL ADVICE CENTRE/SHERIFF CLERK OR SOLICITOR

Form 64 [1]

Rule 73(1)

---

[1] As amended by the Act of Sederunt (Debt Arrangement and Attachment (Scotland) Act 2002) 2002 (SSI 2002/560), art.4, Sch.3 (effective December 30, 2002).

WARRANT FOR INTIMATION

(*Place and date*)

*delete as appropriate/ state other person(s) as the Sheriff may direct — The sheriff grants warrant to intimate the foregoing application and this warrant to the applicant, to the other person(s) stated in the application as having an interest [or to the therein designed] and *to the sheriff officer/ appropriate messenger-at-arms named in the application.

Fixes as a hearing (*date*) at (*time*) within the Sheriff Court House (*address of court*).

1. *Requires the applicant* to appear or be represented at the hearing to show why the application should be granted.

2. *Requires the other persons to whom intimation is given* to appear or be represented at the hearing if they intend to oppose the application.

*3. *Directs the sheriff officer/messenger-at-arms* to send a copy of the attachment schedule to the sheriff clerk before the date of the hearing.

Sheriff

To (*name of person receiving intimation*)

The application and warrant is hereby intimated to you.

Sheriff Clerk Depute
Date

TAKE NOTE

*To the applicant*

If you fail to appear or be represented at the hearing fixed your application may be dismissed.

*To the other persons to whom intimation is given*

If you fail to appear or be represented at the hearing fixed the application may be dealt with in your absence.

# FORM OF CHARGE FOR PAYMENT[1]

(SI 1988/2059)

*24 November 1988.*

The Lords of Council and Session, under and by virtue of the powers conferred on them by section 5 of the Court of Session Act 1988, section 32 of the Sheriff Courts (Scotland) Act 1971 and of all other powers enabling them in that behalf, do hereby enact and declare:—

## Citation and commencement

**1.**—(1)   This Act of Sederunt may be cited as the Act of Sederunt (Form of charge for payment) 1988 and shall come into force on 30th November 1988.

(2)   This Act of Sederunt shall be inserted in the Books of Sederunt.

## Form of charge for payment

**2.**   The form of charge for payment of money to be used by a messenger-at-arms or a sheriff officer under section 90 of the Debtors (Scotland) Act 1987 shall be in the form in the Schedule to this Act of Sederunt or a form substantially to the same effect with such variation as circumstances may require.

SCHEDULE

FORM OF CHARGE FOR PAYMENT OF MONEY[2]

**Paragraph 2**

CHARGE FOR PAYMENT OF MONEY
in
[AB] (*address*)
PURSUER
against
[CD] (*address*)
DEFENDER

To (*name and address of debtor*)

On (*date*) a decree against you was granted in the Court of Session [*or* the sheriff court at (*place*)] for payment of a sum of money in the above action [*or give details of other document upon which charge proceeds*].

The decree was extracted on (*date*).

I, (*name and address*), messenger-at-arms [or sheriff officer], by virtue of the extract decree, in Her Majesty's name and authority and in the name and authority of the Lords of Council and Session [*or* the sheriff], charge you to pay the total sum due as set out below [together with any further interest] within [14] days after the date of this charge to (*name and address of person to whom payment to be made*).

If you do not pay this sum within [14] days you are liable to have further action taken against you including arrestment of your earnings and the attachment and auction of articles belonging to you. You are also liable to be sequestrated (declared bankrupt).

This charge is served on you today by me by (*state method of service*) and is witnessed by (*name and address of witness*).

Dated the .......... day of .......... 19..........

---

[1] In relation to its application to the Court of Session, SI 1988/2059 is repealed by the Act of Sederunt (Rules of the Court of Session 1994) (SI 1994/1443), Sch.5, para.1 (effective September 5, 1994).

[2] As amended by the Act of Sederunt (Debt Arrangement and Attachment (Scotland) Act 2002) 2002 (SSI 2002/560), art.4, Sch.3 (effective December 30, 2002).

|  |  |  |  |
|---|---|---|---|
| (*Signed*) |  | (*Signed*) |  |
| Witness |  | Messenger-at-arms [or sheriff officer] |  |

| The sum now due by you is:— | |
|---|---|
| Principal sum | £ |
| Interest to date | £ |
| Expenses | £ |
| TOTAL | £ ......... |
| Less paid to account | £ |
| Agent's fee | £ ......... |
| Expenses of messenger-at-arms [*or* sheriff officer] | £ |
|     Charge fee | £ |
|     Travelling | £ |
|     Witness fee | £ |
|     Other outlays in connection with service of charge (*specify*) | £ ......... |
| TOTAL SUM DUE | £ |
| [Interest on the principal sum will continue to run until the date of payment.] | |

IF YOU ARE NOT SURE WHAT TO DO YOU SHOULD CONSULT A SOLICITOR, CITIZENS ADVICE BUREAU OR OTHER LOCAL ADVICE CENTRE IMMEDIATELY.

# APPLICATIONS UNDER SECTION 57C OF THE SOCIAL SECURITY PENSIONS ACT 1975, 1990

(SI 1990/2116)

D2.30

*12 November 1990.*

The Lords of Council and Session, under and by virtue of the powers conferred on them by section 32 of the Sheriff Courts (Scotland) Act 1971 and of all other powers enabling them in that behalf, having approved, with modifications, draft rules submitted to them by the Sheriff Court Rules Council under section 34 of that Act, do hereby enact and declare:

## Citation and commencement

**1.**—(1) This Act of Sederunt may be cited as the Act of Sederunt (Applications under section 57C of the Social Security Pensions Act 1975) 1990 and shall come into force on 12th November 1990.

(2) This Act of Sederunt shall be inserted in the Books of Sederunt.

(3) In this Act of Sederunt, the expression "acting as an insolvency practitioner" has the meaning assigned to it by section 57C(8) of the Social Security Pensions Act 1975.

## Application

**2.** This Act of Sederunt applies to applications under section 57C(6) of the Social Security Pensions Act 1975 for an order requiring a person acting as an insolvency practitioner to discharge his duties under section 57C(2) of that Act.

## Procedure

**3.** An application to which this Act of Sederunt applies shall be made—

(a) by note in the process of the proceedings by virtue of which or in relation to which the person acting as insolvency practitioner was appointed; or

(b) where there have been no such proceedings, by summary application.

# APPLICATIONS IN THE SHERIFF COURT IN RESPECT OF DEFECTIVE COMPANY ACCOUNTS

(SI 1991/24)

*4 February 1991.*

The Lords of Council and Session, under and by virtue of the powers conferred on them by section 32 of the Sheriff Courts (Scotland) Act 1971 and of all other powers enabling them in that behalf, having approved draft rules submitted to them by the Sheriff Court Rules Council under section 34 of that Act, do hereby enact and declare:

## Citation and commencement

**1.**—(1)   This Act of Sederunt may be cited as the Act of Sederunt (Applications in the Sheriff Court in respect of Defective Company Accounts) 1991 and shall come into force on 4th February 1991.

(2)   This Act of Sederunt shall be inserted in the Books of Sederunt.

## Applications under section 245B of the Companies Act 1985

**2.**—(1)   An application to the sheriff under section 245B of the Companies Act 1985 (application for declarator that annual accounts of a company do not comply with the requirements of that Act) shall be made by summary application.

(2)   A copy of such an application shall be intimated to every director of the company at the time the accounts are approved.

*25 February 1991.*

The Lords of Council and Session, under and by virtue of the powers conferred on them by section 32 of the Sheriff Courts (Scotland) Act 1971 and of all other powers enabling them in that behalf, having approved draft rules submitted to them by the Sheriff Court Rules Council in accordance with section 34 of that Act, do hereby enact and declare:

### Citation and commencement

**1.**—(1)   This Act of Sederunt may be cited as the Act of Sederunt (Applications under Part VII of the Companies Act 1989) 1991 and shall come into force on 25th February 1991.

(2)   This Act of Sederunt shall be inserted in the Books of Sederunt.

(3)   In this Act of Sederunt, "insolvency proceedings" means proceedings commenced by a petition in accordance with rules 10 (administration orders), 15 (appointment of receiver) or 18 (winding up of a company) of the Act of Sederunt (Sheriff Court Company Insolvency Rules) 1986, a petition for sequestration under sections 5 or 6 of the Bankruptcy (Scotland) Act 1985 or a summary petition under section 11A of the Judicial Factors (Scotland) Act 1889.

### Applications under Part VII of the Companies Act 1989

**2.**—(1)   An application for an order or direction under the provisions of the Companies Act 1989 ("the Act") specified in sub-paragraph (2) below shall be made:
- (a)   where there are before the sheriff insolvency proceedings to which the application relates, by note in the process of those proceedings; or
- (b)   where there are no such proceedings before the sheriff, by summary application.

(2)   The provisions of the Act referred to in sub-paragraph (1) above are—
- (a)   section 161(1) (interim order in relation to party to market contract dissipating or applying assets to prevent recovery by relevant officeholder);
- (b)   section 161(3) (order altering or dispensing from compliance with duties of relevant office-holder);
- (c)   section 163(4) (direction that profit arising from a sum is not recoverable by relevant office-holder);
- (d)   section 164(4) (direction that profit from a market contract or the amount or value of a margin is not recoverable by relevant officeholder);
- (e)   section 175(2) (order to ensure that charge under a prior or pari passu ranked charge is not prejudiced by enforcement of market charge);
- (f)   section 175(5) (direction that profit from a property disposition is not recoverable by relevant office-holder); and
- (g)   section 182(4) (order to achieve same result as if provisions of Schedule 22 to the Act had been in force).

### Intimation

**3.**   Without prejudice to any other order in respect of intimation which the sheriff may make, he shall not make an order under section 175(2) of the Act unless intimation has been made to such persons having an interest as he considers necessary and any such person has had an opportunity to be heard.

# SUMMARY SUSPENSION 1993

(SI 1993/3128)

*10 December 1993.*

The Lords of Council and Session, under and by virtue of the powers conferred on them by section 32 of the Sheriff Courts (Scotland) Act 1971 and of all other powers enabling them in that behalf, having approved, with modifications, draft rules submitted to them by the Sheriff Court Rules Council in accordance with section 34 of that Act, do hereby enact and declare:

## Citation and commencement

**1.**—(1)   This Act of Sederunt may be cited as the Act of Sederunt (Summary Suspension) 1993 and shall come into force on 1st January 1994.

(2)   This Act of Sederunt shall be inserted in the Books of Sederunt.

## Summary application for suspension of charge

**2.**   Where a charge for payment has been executed on any decree to which section 5(5) of the Sheriff Courts (Scotland) Act 1907 applies the person so charged may apply to the sheriff in the sheriff court having jurisdiction over him for suspension of such charge and diligence.

## Sist of diligence

**3.**—(1)   On sufficient caution being found or other security given for—

(a)   the sum charged for with interest and expenses, and

(b)   a further sum to be fixed by the sheriff in respect of expenses to be incurred in the suspension process.

the sheriff may sist diligence, order intimation and answers, and proceed to dispose of the cause in a summary manner.

(2)   The following rules of the Ordinary Cause Rules 1993 shall, with the necessary modifications, apply to an applicant under paragraph 2—

rule 27.4 (methods of finding caution or giving security)

rule 27.5 (cautioners and guarantors)

rule 27.6 (forms of bonds of caution and other securities)

rule 27.7 (sufficiency of caution or security and objections)

rule 27.8 (insolvency or death of cautioner or guarantor).

## Objections

**4.**   Where objections are taken to the competency or regularity of suspension proceedings, the decision of the sheriff on such objections may be appealed to the sheriff principal whose decision shall be final and not subject to appeal.

## Savings for proceedings arising out of causes already commenced

**5.**   Nothing in this Act of Sederunt shall affect suspension proceedings arising out of causes commenced before the date of coming into force of this Act of Sederunt, which shall proceed according to the law and practice in force immediately before that date.

# ACT OF SEDERUNT (REQUIREMENTS OF WRITING) 1996

## (SI 1996/1534)

*7 January 1996.*

The Lords of Council and Session, under and by virtue of the powers conferred on them by section 32 of the Sheriff Courts (Scotland) Act 1971 and of all other powers enabling them in that behalf, having approved, with modifications, draft rules submitted to them by the Sheriff Court Rules Council in accordance with section 34 of that Act, do hereby enact and declare:

## Citation and commencement

**1.**—(1)   This Act of Sederunt may be cited as the Act of Sederunt (Requirements of Writing) 1996 and shall come into force on 1st July 1996.

(2)   This Act of Sederunt shall be inserted in the Books of Sederunt.

## Interpretation

**2.**—(1)   In this Act of Sederunt, "the Act of 1995" means the Requirements of Writing (Scotland) Act 1995.

(2)   Unless the context otherwise requires, words and expressions used in this Act of Sederunt which are also used in the Act of 1995 have the same meaning as in that Act.

(3)   Unless the context otherwise requires, a reference to a specified paragraph or form is a reference to the paragraph so specified, or the form so specified in the Schedule, in this Act of Sederunt.

## Application

**3.**—(1)   Subject to sub-paragraph (2) below, this Act of Sederunt shall apply to an application under the following provisions of the Act of 1995:—

section 4(1) or (2),

section 5(6),

paragraph 2(1) or (2) of Schedule 1,

paragraph 7 of Schedule 3.

paragraph 14 of Schedule 3.

(2)   This Act of Sederunt shall not apply to an application under a provision mentioned in sub-paragraph (1) above which is a summary application within the meaning of section 3 of the Sheriff Courts (Scotland) Act 1907.

## Application in commissary proceedings

**4.**   An application to which this Act of Sederunt applies for a certificate or decree in connection with a document, made incidental to and in the course of an application for confirmation of an executor, shall be made as nearly as may be in accordance with Form 1.

## Application in other proceedings

**5.**   An application to which this Act of Sederunt applies for a certificate or decree in connection with a document, made incidental to and in the course of any proceedings other than an application for confirmation of an executor, shall be made by minute, incidental application or note, as appropriate, in those proceedings.

## Intimation

**6.**—(1)   Except where it appears to the sheriff that an application under paragraph 4 should be intimated to a person having an interest, the application shall be considered and determined by the sheriff without intimation or any period of notice.

(2)   Where it appears to the sheriff that an application under paragraph 4 should be intimated, the application shall be intimated to such persons and in such manner as the sheriff shall direct.

## Affidavit evidence

**7.**   Evidence given by affidavit in an application under paragraph 4 or 5 shall be made as nearly as may be in accordance with Form 2.

## Decree, interlocutor and certificate

**8.**   Where the sheriff grants an application under paragraph 4 or 5 he shall—

    (a)   where the document has been registered in the Books of Council and Session or the sheriff court books, grant decree in those terms; or

    (b)   in any other case—

        (i)   issue an interlocutor; and

        (ii)   direct the sheriff clerk to endorse a certificate on the document as nearly as may be in accordance with Form 3.

SCHEDULE

**Paragraph 4**

FORM 1

Form of Application

SHERIFFDOM OF (*insert name of sheriffdom*)

AT (*insert place of sheriff court*)

APPLICATION UNDER THE REQUIREMENTS OF WRITING (SCOTLAND) ACT 1995

by

[A.B.] (*name and address*)

APPLICANT

1. The applicant is (*insert name and address of applicant and his interest in the document, e.g. executor-nominate/dative*).

2. This application is made (*insert details of the circumstances under which the application is made, e.g. incidental to the application by the above named executor(s) for confirmation to the estate of the deceased*).

3. (*Insert details of document and the reasons for seeking certification by the court or decree, as appropriate; e.g.* "The document is a will dated (*insert date of will*) which bears to be signed by the deceased. No person has subscribed as a witness to the will as required by section 3(1) of the Requirements of Writing (Scotland) Act 1995. The document cannot therefore be presumed to have been subscribed by the granter").

4. The applicant seeks a certificate [*or* decree] under (*insert appropriate statutory reference*) of the Requirements of Writing (Scotland) Act 1995 with respect to the aforementioned document.

    (Signed)................

Applicant

[*or* [X. Y.] (*insert name and
business address*)

Solicitor for applicant]

    (Date)..........

**Paragraph 7**

FORM 2

Form of Affidavit

AT (*place and date*) in the presence of [C.D.] (*address*) Justice of the Peace for (*place*) [*or* Notary Public] [*or* Commissioner for Oaths *or other such person entitled to administer oaths (specify capacity)*].

Compeared [E.F.] (*name and address*) who, being solemnly sworn and examined depones [*or* solemnly and sincerely affirms] that (*insert evidence of the deponent in relation to the document and order sought, e.g.* "I am well acquainted with the signature of [A.B.] (*full name and address*) and have seen and examined the signature on the will dated (*date*) and confirm that it is the signature of the said [A.B.]" [*or* "I was present at (*place of execution*) on (*date of execution*) and confirm that the alterations to the will were made by [A.B.] (*full name and address*) before execution" [*or* as the case may be]).

All of which is the truth as the deponent shall answer to God [*or* All of which is affirmed to be the truth].

Date.........                                        Signed..............

                                                 [E.F.]

                          Signed..............

                                               [C.D.]

The document referred to is produced herewith and signed by the deponent and the said [C.D.] as relative hereto.

**Paragraph 8**                                        FORM 3

Form of Certificate of Sheriff Clerk

AT (*insert name of sheriff court*)

DATE (*insert date of certificate*)

By interlocutor of the sheriff dated (*insert date*) it is hereby certified in terms of (*insert appropriate statutory reference*) of the Requirements of Writing (Scotland) Act 1995 that (*insert details of document and extent of certification, e.g.* this will was subscribed by the granter [A.B.], or this will was subscribed on (*date*) and at (*place*)).

Signed....................

                                    Sheriff clerk

# REPORTERS (CONDUCT OF PROCEEDINGS BEFORE THE SHERIFF) (SCOTLAND) REGULATIONS 1997

(SI 1997/714)

*1 April 1997.*

The Secretary of State and the Lord Advocate, in exercise of the powers conferred on them by section 40(4) of the Children (Scotland) Act 1995[1] and of all powers enabling them in that behalf, hereby make the following regulations:

## Citation and commencement

**1.** These Regulations may be cited as the Reporters (Conduct of Proceedings before the Sheriff) (Scotland) Regulations 1997 and shall come into operation on 1st April 1997.

## Interpretation

**2.**[2] In these regulations, unless the content otherwise requires—

"the Act" means the Children (Scotland) Act 1995; and
"reporter" means for any period prior to 1st April 1996 a person holding an appointment under section 36 of the Social Work (Scotland) Act 1968.

## Power to conduct proceedings before the sheriff

**3.** Any reporter having the experience prescribed in regulation 4 of these Regulations shall be entitled, whether or not he is an advocate or a solicitor, to conduct before a sheriff any proceedings which under Chapters 2 or 3 of Part II of the Act are heard by the sheriff.

## Prescription of experience required

**4.** For the purposes of regulation 3 of these regulations the experience prescribed shall be the experience of having been a reporter for any period or periods amounting to not less than one year.

---

[1] As amended by SI 1997/1084 (effective April 1, 1997).
[2] As amended by SI 1997/1084 (effective April 1, 1997).

# CHILD CARE AND MAINTENANCE RULES 1997

(SI 1997/291)

*1 April 1997.*

ARRANGEMENT OF RULES

### Chapter 1: Preliminary

### Chapter 2: Adoption of Children

#### PART I GENERAL

#### PART II APPLICATION FOR AN ORDER DECLARING A CHILD FREE FOR ADOPTION

#### PART III REVOCATION ORDERS, ETC.

#### PART IV ADOPTION ORDERS

#### PART IVA CONVENTION ADOPTION ORDERS

#### PART V PARENTAL RESPONSIBILITIES ORDERS

#### PART VI HUMAN FERTILISATION AND EMBRYOLOGY

Chapter 5: Maintenance Orders

PART I GENERAL

PART II OUTGOING ORDERS UNDER THE 1950 ACT

PART III OUTGOING ORDERS UNDER THE 1972 ACT

PART IV INCOMING ORDERS UNDER THE 1950 ACT

PART V INCOMING ORDERS UNDER THE 1972 ACT

The Lords of Council and Session, under and by virtue of the powers conferred on them by sections 17, 20, 22, 23, 24 and 28(1) of the Maintenance Orders Act 1950, sections 2(4)(c), 2A(1) and 21(1) of the Maintenance Orders Act 1958, section 32 of the Sheriff Courts (Scotland) Act 1971, section 59 of the Adoption (Scotland) Act 1978 (as modified and applied in relation to parental orders under section 30 of the Human Fertilisation and Embryology Act 1990 and applications for such orders by paragraph 15 of Schedule 1 to the Parental Orders (Human Fertilisation and Embryology) (Scotland) Regulations 1994, section 48 of the Civil Jurisdiction and Judgments Act 1982, sections 27(2), 28(1) and 42(1) of the Family Law Act 1986 and section 91 of the Children (Scotland) Act 1995 and of all other powers enabling them in that behalf, having approved, with modifications, draft rules submitted to them by the Sheriff Court Rules Council in accordance with section 34 of the Sheriff Courts (Scotland) Act 1971, do hereby enact and declare:

CHAPTER 1

PRELIMINARY

**Citation and commencement**

**1.1**—(1)   This Act of Sederunt may be cited as the Act of Sederunt (Child Care and Maintenance Rules) 1997 and shall come into force on 1st April 1997.

(2)   This Act of Sederunt shall be inserted in the Books of Sederunt.

**Interpretation**

**1.2**—(1)   In this Act of Sederunt, unless the context otherwise requires—

"Ordinary Cause Rules" means the First Schedule to the Sheriff Courts (Scotland) Act 1907;

"Principal Reporter" is the person referred to in section 14 of the Children's Hearings (Scotland) Act 2011 or any person carrying out the functions of the Principal Reporter by virtue of paragraph 10(1) of schedule 3 to that Act;[1]

"sheriff clerk" includes sheriff clerk depute.

(2)   Unless the context otherwise requires, any reference in this Act of Sederunt to a specified Chapter, Part or rule shall be construed as a reference to the Chapter, Part or rule bearing that number in this Act of Sederunt, and a reference to a specified paragraph, sub-paragraph or head shall be construed as a reference to the paragraph, sub-paragraph or head so numbered or lettered in the provision in which that reference occurs.

(3)   Any reference in this Act of Sederunt to a numbered Form shall be construed as a reference to the Form so numbered in Schedule 1 to this Act of Sederunt and includes a form substantially to the same effect with such variation as circumstances may require.

**Affidavits**

**1.3**   An affidavit required in terms of any provision of this Act of Sederunt may be emitted—

(a)   in the United Kingdom, before an notary public or any other competent authority;

(b)   outwith the United Kingdom, before a British diplomatic or consular officer, or any person authorised to administer an oath or affirmation under the law of the place where the oath or affirmation is made.

**Revocations and transitional provisions**

**1.4**—(1)   Subject to paragraphs (2) and (3), the Acts of Sederunt mentioned in column (1) of Schedule 2 to this Act of Sederunt are revoked to the extent specified in column (3) of that Schedule.

---

[1] As substituted by the Act of Sederunt (Children's Hearings (Scotland) Act 2011) (Miscellaneous Amendments) 2013 (SSI 2013/172) para.3 (effective June 24, 2013).

(2)    Nothing in paragraph (1) or in Chapter 2 shall affect any cause which has been commenced before 1st April 1997 and to which that Chapter would otherwise apply, and such a cause shall proceed according to the law and practice in force immediately before that date.

(3)    Nothing in paragraph (1) shall affect any cause to which paragraph 8(1) of Schedule 3 to the Children (Scotland) Act applies, and such a cause shall proceed according to the law and practice in force immediately before 1st April 1997.

### Vulnerable witnesses

**1.5.**—[1](1)    This rule shall apply to proceedings under these rules, except those proceedings to which the rules in Part XI of Chapter 3 apply.

(2)    At any hearing on an application under these rules, the sheriff shall ascertain whether there is or is likely to be a vulnerable witness who is to give evidence at or for the purposes of any proof or hearing, consider any child witness notice or vulnerable witness application that has been lodged where no order has been made under section 12(1) or (6) of the Vulnerable Witnesses (Scotland) Act 2004 and consider whether any order under section 12(1) of that Act requires to be made.

(3)    Except where the sheriff otherwise directs, where a vulnerable witness is to give evidence at or for the purposes of any proof or hearing in an application under these rules, any application in relation to the vulnerable witness or special measure that may be ordered shall be dealt with in accordance with the rules within Chapter 45 of the Ordinary Cause Rules.

(4)    In this rule, "vulnerable witness" means a witness within the meaning of section 11(1) of the Vulnerable Witnesses (Scotland) Act 2004.

### Lodging audio or audio-visual recordings of children

**1.6.**—[2](1)    In this rule "child" is a person under the age of 16 on the date of commencement of the proceedings and "children" shall be construed accordingly.

(2)    Except where the sheriff otherwise directs, where a party seeks to lodge an audio or audio-visual recording of a child as a production in an application under this Act of Sederunt, this shall be done in accordance with and regulated by Chapter 50 of the Ordinary Cause Rules.

(3)    A party who has lodged a recording of a child shall—
- (a)    within 28 days after the final determination of the application, where no subsequent appeal has been marked, or
- (b)    within 28 days after the disposal of any appeal marked on the final determination of the application,

uplift the recording from process.

(4)    Where a recording has not been uplifted as required by paragraph (3), the sheriff clerk shall intimate to—
- (a)    the solicitor who lodged the recording, or
- (b)    where no solicitor is acting, the party or such other party as seems appropriate,

---

[1] As inserted by the Act of Sederunt (Child Care and Maintenance Rules 1997) Amendment (Vulnerable Witnesses (Scotland) Act 2004) 2007, r.2 (effective November 1, 2007).

[2] As inserted by the Act of Sederunt (Sheriff Court Rules) (Miscellaneous Amendments) (No.3) 2012 (SSI 2012/271) para.4 (effective November 1, 2012).

that if he or she fails to uplift the recording within 28 days after the date of such intimation, it will be disposed of in such a manner as the sheriff directs.

## CHAPTER 2

## ADOPTION OF CHILDREN

## Part I

## General

### Interpretation

**2.1**[1]  In this Chapter, unless the context otherwise requires—

"the Act" means the Adoption (Scotland) Act 1978;

"the 1995 Act" means the Children (Scotland) Act 1995;

"Her Majesty's Forces" means the regular forces as defined in section 374 of the Armed Forces Act 2006;[2]

"Registrar General" means the Registrar General of Births, Deaths and Marriages for Scotland.

### Expenses

**2.2**  The sheriff may make such an order with regard to the expenses, including the expenses of a reporting officer and a curator ad litem or any other person who attended a hearing, of an application under this Chapter as he thinks fit and may modify such expenses or direct them to be taxed on such scale as he may determine.

### Intimation to Principal Reporter

**2.3**  *[Repealed by the Act of Sederunt (Sheriff Court Rules Amendment) (Adoption and Children (Scotland) Act 2007) 2009 (SSI 2009/284) r.4(1)(a)(ii) (effective September 28, 2009: subject to savings and transitional provisions specified in SSI 2009/284 r.4(2) to (7)).]*

---

[1] As amended by the Act of Sederunt (Child Care and Maintenance Rules 1997) (Amendment) (Adoption and Children Act 2002) 2006 (SI 2006/411) (effective August 18, 2006) and by the Act of Sederunt (Sheriff Court Rules Amendment) (Adoption and Children (Scotland) Act 2007) 2009 (SSI 2009/284) (effective September 28, 2009).

[2] As substituted by the Act of Sederunt (Sheriff Court Rules) (Miscellaneous Amendments) 2009 (SSI 2009/294) r.17 (effective October 1, 2009).

**Timetables under section 25A of the Act**

**2.4** *[Repealed by the Act of Sederunt (Sheriff Court Rules Amendment) (Adoption and Children (Scotland) Act 2007) 2009 (SSI 2009/284) r.4(1)(a)(ii) (effective September 28, 2009: subject to savings and transitional provisions specified in SSI 2009/284 r.4(2) to (7)).]*

Part II

**Application for an Order Declaring a Child Free for Adoption**

K2.23

*[Repealed by the Act of Sederunt (Sheriff Court Rules Amendment) (Adoption and Children (Scotland) Act 2007) 2009 (SSI 2009/284) r.4(1) (effective September 28, 2009: repeal has effect subject to savings and transitional provisions specified in SSI 2009/284 r.4(2)–(7)).]*

Part III

**Revocation Orders, etc**

*[Repealed by the Act of Sederunt (Sheriff Court Rules Amendment) (Adoption and Children (Scotland) Act 2007) 2009 (SSI 2009/284) r.4(1) (effective September 28, 2009: repeal has effect subject to savings and transitional provisions specified in SSI 2009/284 r.4(2)–(7)).]*

Part IV

**Adoption Orders**

*[Repealed by the Act of Sederunt (Sheriff Court Rules Amendment) (Adoption and Children (Scotland) Act 2007) 2009 (SSI 2009/284) r.4(1) (effective September 28, 2009: repeal has effect subject to savings and transitional provisions specified in SSI 2009/284 r.4(2)–(7)).]*

Part IVA

**Convention Adoption Orders**

*[Repealed by the Act of Sederunt (Sheriff Court Rules Amendment) (Adoption and Children (Scotland) Act 2007) 2009 (SSI 2009/284) r.4(1) (effective September 28, 2009: repeal has effect subject to savings and transitional provisions specified in SSI 2009/284 r.4(2)–(7)).]*

Part V

**Parental Responsibilities Orders**

*[Repealed by the Act of Sederunt (Sheriff Court Rules Amendment) (Adoption and Children (Scotland) Act 2007) 2009 (SSI 2009/284) r.4(1) (effective September 28, 2009: repeal has effect subject to savings and transitional provisions specified in SSI 2009/284 r.4(2)–(7)).]*

Part VI[1]

**Human Fertilisation and Embryology**

K2.24

## Interpretation

**2.45.** In this Part—

"2007 Act" means the Adoption and Children (Scotland) Act 2007;

"2008 Act" means the Human Fertilisation and Embryology Act 2008;

"parental order" means an order under section 54 of the 2008 Act; and

"the Regulations" means the Human Fertilisation and Embryology (Parental Orders) Regulations 2010.

## Form of application and productions

**2.46.**—(1) An application for a parental order is to be made by petition in Form 22.

(2) The following documents must be lodged in process along with the petition—

(a) an extract or a certified copy of the entry in the Register of Births relating to the child who is the subject of the application;

(b) extracts or certified copies of any entries in the Register of Births relating to the birth of each of the petitioners;

(c) in the case of an application under section 54(2)(a) of the 2008 Act, an extract or a certified copy of the entry in the Register of Marriages relating to the marriage of the petitioners;

(d) in the case of an application under section 54(2)(b) of the 2008 Act, an extract or a certified copy of the entry in the Register of Civil Partnerships relating to the civil partnership of the petitioners; and

(e) any other document founded on by the petitioners in support of the terms of the petition.

## Confidentiality

**2.47.**—(1) Unless the sheriff otherwise directs, all documents lodged in process (including the reports by the curator ad litem and reporting officer) are to be available only to the sheriff, the curator ad litem, the reporting officer and the parties; and such documents must be treated as confidential by all persons involved in, or party to, the proceedings and by the sheriff clerk.

(2) The reporting officer and the curator ad litem—

(a) must treat all information obtained in the exercise of their duties as confidential; and

(b) must not disclose any such information to any person unless disclosure of such information is necessary for the purpose of their duties.

(3) This rule is subject to rule 2.53.

## Orders for evidence

**2.48.**—(1) The sheriff may, before determining the cause, order—

(a) production of further documents (including affidavits); or

(b) parole evidence.

(2) A party may apply by motion for the evidence of a person to be received in evidence by affidavit; and the sheriff may make such order as the sheriff thinks fit.

---

[1] As substituted by the Act of Sederunt (Child Care and Maintenance Rules) Amendment (Human Fertilisation and Embryology Act 2008) 2010 (SSI 2010/137) r.2(2) (effective April 6, 2010: substitution has effect subject to transitional provisions and savings as specified in SSI 2010/137 r.3).

## Protection of identity of petitioners

**2.49.**—(1)   Where persons who propose to apply for a parental order wish to prevent their identities being disclosed to any person whose agreement to the parental order is required, they may, before presenting the petition, apply by letter to the sheriff clerk for a serial number to be assigned to them for all purposes connected with the petition.

(2)   On receipt of an application under paragraph (1), the sheriff clerk must—

    (a)   assign a serial number to the applicants; and

    (b)   enter a note of the number opposite the name of the applicants in a register of serial numbers kept by the sheriff clerk.

(3)   The contents of the register of serial numbers and the names of the persons to whom each number relates must be treated as confidential by the sheriff clerk and must not be disclosed to any person other than the sheriff.

(4)   Where a serial number has been assigned under paragraph (2)(a), any form of agreement to a parental order under section 54(6) of the 2008 Act—

    (a)   must refer to the petitioners by means of the serial number assigned to them;

    (b)   must not contain the names and designation of the petitioners; and

    (c)   must specify the year in which and the court by which the serial number was assigned.

## Appointment of a curator ad litem and reporting officer

**2.50.**—(1)   The sheriff must on the lodging of a petition under rule 2.46, appoint a curator ad litem and reporting officer.

(2)   The same person may be appointed as curator ad litem and reporting officer in the same petition, if the sheriff considers that doing so is appropriate in the circumstances.

(3)   The sheriff may appoint a person who is not a member of a panel established under regulations made by virtue of section 101(1) of the 1995 Act to be curator ad litem or a reporting officer.

(4)   The sheriff may, on cause shown, appoint a reporting officer prior to the lodging of such a petition.

(5)   An application for an appointment under paragraph (4) is to be made by letter addressed to the sheriff clerk specifying the reasons for the appointment, and shall not require to be intimated to any other person.

(6)   The sheriff clerk must intimate the appointment of a curator ad litem and reporting officer under paragraph (1) or (4) to the petitioner and to the person or persons appointed.

(7)   Where the curator ad litem is not also the reporting officer, the sheriff may order the reporting officer to make available to the curator ad litem any report or information in relation to the child.

## Duties of reporting officer and curator ad litem

**2.51.**—(1)   The other duties of a reporting officer appointed under rule 2.50(1) prescribed for the purposes of section 108(1)(b) of the 2007 Act as modified and applied in relation to applications for parental orders by regulation 4 of, and Schedule 3, to the Regulations (rules: appointment of curators ad litem and reporting officers) are—

    (a)   to ascertain the whereabouts of all persons whose agreement to the making of a parental order in respect of the child is required;

(b)    to ascertain whether there is any person other than those mentioned in the petition upon whom notice of the petition should be served;

(c)    in the case of each person who is not a petitioner and whose agreement to the making of a parental order is required under section 54(6) of the 2008 Act—

    (i)    to ascertain whether that person understands the effect of the parental order;

    (ii)    to ascertain whether alternatives to a parental order have been discussed with that person;

    (iii)    to confirm that that person understands that he or she may withdraw his or her agreement at any time before an order is made;

    (iv)    to ascertain whether that person suffers or appears to suffer from a mental disorder within the meaning of section 328 of the Mental Health (Care and Treatment) (Scotland) Act 2003; and

(d)    to ascertain whether the conditions in subsections (2) to (8) of section 54 of the 2008 Act have been satisfied;

(e)    to draw to the attention of the court any matter which may be of assistance; and

(f)    to report in writing on the matters mentioned in subparagraphs (a) to (e) to the sheriff within 4 weeks from the date of the interlocutor appointing the reporting officer, or within such other period as the sheriff in his or her discretion may allow.

(2)[1]    A curator ad litem appointed under rule 2.50 must—

(a)    have regard to safeguarding the interests of the child as his or her paramount duty;

(b)    enquire, so far as he or she considers necessary, into the facts and circumstances stated in the petition;

(c)    establish that the petitioners understand the nature and effect of a parental order and in particular that the making of the order will render them responsible for the maintenance and upbringing of the child;

(d)    ascertain whether any money or other benefit which is prohibited by section 54(8) of the 2008 Act (prohibition on gift or receipt of money or other benefit) has been received or agreed upon;

(e)    ascertain whether it may be in the interests of the welfare of the child that the sheriff should make the parental order subject to particular terms and conditions or require the petitioners to make special provision for the child and, if so, what provision;

(f)    ascertain whether it would be better for the child that the court should make the order than it should not make the order;

(g)    establish whether the proposed parental order is likely to safeguard and promote the welfare of the child throughout the child's life; and

(h)    ascertain from the child whether he or she wishes to express a view and, where a child indicates his or her wish to express a view, ascertain that view.

---

[1] As substituted by the Act of Sederunt (Sheriff Court Rules) (Miscellaneous Amendments) 2010 (SSI 2010/279) r.7(4) (effective July 29, 2010).

(3)    Subject to paragraph (4), the curator ad litem must report in writing on the matters mentioned in paragraph (2) to the sheriff within 4 weeks from the date of the interlocutor appointing the curator, or within such other period as the sheriff in his or her discretion may allow.

(4)    Subject to any order made by the sheriff under rule 2.53(1), the views of the child ascertained in terms of paragraph (2)(h) may, if the curator ad litem considers appropriate, be conveyed to the sheriff orally.

(5)    The reporting officer must, on completion of his or her report in terms of paragraph (1), in addition send to the sheriff clerk—

(a)    a copy of his or her report for each party; and

(b)    any agreement for the purposes of section 54(6) of the 2008 Act.

(6)    The curator ad litem must, on completion of his or her report in terms of paragraph (3), in addition send a copy of it for each party to the sheriff clerk.

### Agreement

**2.52.**—(1)    The agreement of a person required by section 54(6) of the 2008 Act is to be in Form 23.

(2)[1]    The form of agreement mentioned in paragraph (1) must be witnessed—

(a)    where it is executed in Scotland, by the reporting officer appointed under rule 2.50;

(b)    where it is executed outwith Scotland but within the United Kingdom, by a justice of the peace or commissioner for oaths;

(c)    where it is executed outwith the United Kingdom—

(i)    if the person who executes the agreement is serving in Her Majesty's Forces, by an officer holding a commission in any of those forces; or

(ii)    in any other case, by a British diplomatic or consular official or any person authorised to administer an oath or affirmation under the law of the place where the agreement is executed.

### Procedure where child wishes to express a view

**2.53**—(1)    Where a child to whom section 54(11) of the 2008 Act applies indicates his or her wish to express a view, the sheriff, without prejudice to rule 2.51(2)(h)—

(a)    may order such procedural steps to be taken as the sheriff considers appropriate to ascertain the views of that child; and

(b)    must not make an order under this Part unless an opportunity has been given for the views of that child to be obtained or heard.

(2)    Where the views of a child, whether obtained under this rule or under rule 2.51(2)(h) have been recorded in writing, the sheriff may direct that such a written record is to—

(a)    be sealed in an envelope marked "Views of the child — confidential";

(b)    be available to a sheriff only;

(c)    not be opened by any person other than a sheriff; and

(d)    not form a borrowable part of the process.

---

[1] As substituted by the Act of Sederunt (Sheriff Court Rules) (Miscellaneous Amendments) 2010 (SSI 2010/279) r.7(4) (effective July 29, 2010).

**Hearing**

**2.54**—(1)   On receipt of the reports referred to in rule 2.51, the sheriff must fix a hearing.

(2)   The sheriff may—

    (a)   order any person whose agreement is required to attend the hearing;

    (b)   order intimation of the date of the hearing to any person not mentioned in paragraph (3)(a), (b) or (c); and

    (c)   order the reporting officer or curator ad litem to perform additional duties to assist him or her in determining the petition.

(3)   The petitioners or, where a serial number has been assigned under rule 2.49, the sheriff clerk, must intimate the date of the hearing in Form 24 by registered post or recorded delivery letter to—

    (a)   every person whose whereabouts are known to them and whose agreement is required;

    (b)[1]   the reporting officer appointed under rule 2.50;

    (c)[2]   the curator ad litem appointed under rule 2.50; and

    (d)   any person on whom intimation has been ordered under paragraph (2)(b).

(4)   At the hearing—

    (a)   the petitioners, the reporting officer and the curator ad litem must, if required by the sheriff, appear and may be represented;

    (b)   any other person required by the sheriff to attend the hearing must appear and may be represented; and

    (c)   any other person to whom intimation was made under paragraph (3) (a) or (d) may appear or be represented.

**Applications under sections 22 and 24 of the 2007 Act**

**2.55**—(1)   An application under section 22(3) (restrictions on removal: application for parental order pending), section 24(1) (return of child removed in breach of certain provisions) or section 24(2) (order directing person not to remove child) of the 2007 Act all as modified and applied in relation to applications for parental orders by regulation 4 of, and Schedule 3 to, the Regulations, is to be made by minute in the process of the petition for a parental order to which it relates.

(2)   A minute under paragraph (1) must include an appropriate crave and statement of facts.

(3)   On receipt of a minute under paragraph (1), the sheriff must—

    (a)   order a diet of hearing to be fixed; and

    (b)   ordain the minuter, or where a serial number has been assigned under rule 2.49, the sheriff clerk, to send a notice of such hearing in Form 25 together with a copy of the minute, by recorded delivery letter to the curator ad litem in the original petition, to any person who may have care and possession of the child and to such other persons as the sheriff considers appropriate.

---

[1] As substituted by the Act of Sederunt (Sheriff Court Rules) (Miscellaneous Amendments) 2010 (SSI 2010/279) r.7(4) (effective July 29, 2010).

[2] As substituted by the Act of Sederunt (Sheriff Court Rules) (Miscellaneous Amendments) 2010 (SSI 2010/279) r.7(4) (effective July 29, 2010).

### Amendment of parental order

**2.56**—(1)   An application under paragraph 7 of Schedule 1 to the 2007 Act, as modified and applied in relation to parental orders by regulation 4 of, and Schedule 3 to, the Regulations (amendment of orders and rectification of registers) is to be made by petition to the court which made the parental order.

(2)   The sheriff may order the petitioners to intimate the petition to such persons as the sheriff considers appropriate.

### Communication to the Registrar General

**2.57**   The communication to the Registrar General of a parental order required to be made by the sheriff clerk under paragraph 4(1) of Schedule 1 to the 2007 Act, as modified and applied in relation to parental orders by regulation 4 of, and Schedule 3 to, the Regulations (registration of parental orders), is to be made by sending a certified copy of the order to the Registrar General either by recorded delivery post in an envelope marked "Confidential", or by personal delivery by the sheriff clerk in a sealed enveloped marked "Confidential".

### Extract of order

**2.58**   An extract of a parental order must not be issued except by order of the court on an application to it—
  (a)   where there is a petition for the parental order depending before the court, by motion in that process; or
  (b)   where there is no such petition depending before the court, by petition.

### Final procedure

**2.59**—(1)   After the granting of a parental order the court process must, immediately upon the communication under rule 2.57 being made or, in the event of an extract of the order being issued under rule 2.58, immediately upon such issue, be sealed by the sheriff clerk in an envelope marked "Confidential".

(2)   The envelope referred to in paragraph (1) is not to be unsealed by the sheriff clerk or by any other person having control of the records of that or any court, and the process is not to be made accessible to any person for one hundred years after the date of the granting of the order except—
  (a)   to the person who is the subject of the parental order after he or she has reached the age of 16 years; and
  (b)   to a person on the granting of an application made by him or her to the sheriff setting forth the reason for which access to the process is required.

### Appeals

**2.60.**—(1)   Chapter 31 of the Ordinary Cause Rules is to apply, with any necessary modifications, to an appeal against an order of the sheriff under this Part as it applies to an appeal against an order of the sheriff under the Ordinary Cause Rules.

CHAPTER 3[1]

K2.25

---

[1] Chapter 3 heading and r.3.1 as amended by the Act of Sederunt (Children's Hearings (Scotland) Act 2011) (Miscellaneous Amendments) 2013 (SSI 2013/172) para.3 (effective June 24, 2013).

CHILDREN'S HEARINGS: APPLICATION TO THE SHERIFF

## Part I

## Interpretation

**Interpretation**

**3.1**—[1](1)   In this Chapter, unless the context otherwise requires—

"1995 Act" means the Children (Scotland) Act 1995 and (except where the context otherwise requires) references to terms defined in that Act have the same meaning here as given there;

"2011 Act" means the Children's Hearings (Scotland) Act 2011 and (except where the context otherwise requires) references to terms defined in that Act have the same meaning here as given there;

"relevant person" means—

   (aa)   a person referred to in section 200(1) of the 2011 Act or

   (bb)   a person deemed a relevant person by virtue of section 81(3) or 160(4)(b) of the 2011 Act;

"service" includes citation, intimation or the giving of notice as required in terms of this Chapter.

(2)   In this Chapter any reference, however expressed, to disputed grounds shall be construed as a reference to a statement of grounds which forms the subject of an application under section 93(2)(a) or 94(2)(a) of the 2011 Act.

(3)   Except as otherwise provided, this Chapter applies to applications to the sheriff (including reviews and appeals) under the 1995 Act or the 2011 Act.

(4)   All hearings in respect of applications to the sheriff must be held in private.

## Part II

## General Rules

*Procedure in Respect of Children*

**Application of rules 3.3 to 3.5A**

**3.2**—[1](1)   Rules 3.3 to 3.5 apply where a sheriff is coming to a decision about a matter relating to a child within the meaning of section 27 of the 2011 Act.

(2)   Rule 3.5A applies in the circumstances referred to in paragraph (1) and in respect of applications under Part V of this Chapter.

**Power to dispense with service on child**

**3.3**[2]   Where the sheriff is satisfied, so far as practicable and taking account of the age and maturity of the child, that it would be inappropriate to order service on the child, the sheriff may dispense with service on the child.

---

[1] Chapter 3 heading and r.3.1 as amended by the Act of Sederunt (Children's Hearings (Scotland) Act 2011) (Miscellaneous Amendments) 2013 (SSI 2013/172) para.3 (effective June 24, 2013).

[2] As substituted by the Act of Sederunt (Children's Hearings (Scotland) Act 2011) (Miscellaneous Amendments) 2013 (SSI 2013/172) para.3 (effective June 24, 2013).

### Child to attend hearing

**3.3A**—[1](1)   This rule applies where an application is made to the sheriff under the 2011 Act, other than where section 103 or 112 of the 2011 Act applies.

(2)   A child must attend all hearings, unless the sheriff otherwise directs.

(3)   A child may attend a hearing even if the child is excused from doing so.

(4)   If the child is not excused from attending the hearing but does not attend the sheriff may grant a warrant to secure attendance in relation to the child.

(5)   Paragraph (6) applies if—

    (a)   the hearing of the application is to be continued to another day; and

    (b)   the sheriff is satisfied that there is reason to believe that the child will not attend on that day.

(6)   The sheriff may grant a warrant to secure attendance in relation to the child.

### Service on child

**3.4**—(1)   Subject to rule 3.3 and to paragraph (2), after the issue of the first order or warrant to cite, as the case may be, the applicant shall forthwith serve a copy of the application and first order or warrant to cite on the child, together with a notice or citation in—

    (a)   Form 26 in respect of an application for a child assessment order under Part III of this Chapter;

    (b)[2]   Form 27 in respect of an application to vary or terminate a child protection order in terms of rule 3.33;

    (c)   Form 28 in respect of an application for an exclusion order in terms of rules 3.34 to 3.39;

    (d)   Form 29 in respect of an application to vary or recall an exclusion order in terms of rule 3.40;

    (e)   *[Repealed by the Act of Sederunt (Children's Hearings (Scotland) Act 2011) (Miscellaneous Amendments) 2013 (SSI 2013/172) para.3 (effective June 24, 2013).]*

    (f)[3]   subject to subparagraph (g), in Form 31 in respect of an application under section 93(2)(a) or 94(2)(a) of the 2011 Act;

    (g)[4]   Form 31A in respect of an application under section 94(2)(a) of the 2011 Act where a procedural hearing has been fixed; and

    (h)[5]   Form 31B in respect of an application under section 110(2) of the 2011 Act.

(2)   The sheriff may, on application by the applicant or of his own motion, order that a specified part of the application is not served on the child.

---

[1] As substituted by the Act of Sederunt (Children's Hearings (Scotland) Act 2011) (Miscellaneous Amendments) 2013 (SSI 2013/172) para.3 (effective June 24, 2013).

[2] As amended by the Act of Sederunt (Children's Hearings (Scotland) Act 2011) (Miscellaneous Amendments) 2013 (SSI 2013/172) para.3 (effective June 24, 2013).

[3] As substituted by the Act of Sederunt (Children's Hearings (Scotland) Act 2011) (Miscellaneous Amendments) 2013 (SSI 2013/172) para.3 (effective June 24, 2013).

[4] As substituted by the Act of Sederunt (Children's Hearings (Scotland) Act 2011) (Miscellaneous Amendments) 2013 (SSI 2013/172) para.3 (effective June 24, 2013).

[5] As substituted by the Act of Sederunt (Children's Hearings (Scotland) Act 2011) (Miscellaneous Amendments) 2013 (SSI 2013/172) para.3 (effective June 24, 2013).

## Procedure for obtaining a child's view

**3.5**—(1)[1]  Subject to section 27(3) of the 2011 Act, the sheriff—

    (a)  may order such steps to be taken as he considers appropriate to ascertain the views of that child; and

    (b)[2]  shall not come to a decision about a matter relating to a child within the meaning of section 27 of the 2011 Act unless an opportunity has been given for the views of that child to be obtained or heard.

(2)  Subject to any order made by the sheriff under paragraph (1)(a) and to any other method as the sheriff in his discretion may permit, the views of the child may be conveyed—

    (a)  by the child orally or in writing;

    (b)  by an advocate or solicitor acting on behalf of the child;

    (c)  by any safeguarder; or

    (ca)[3]  by any curator ad litem

    (d)  by any other person (either orally or in writing), provided that the sheriff is satisfied that that person is a suitable representative and is duly authorised to represent the child.

(3)  Where the views of the child are conveyed orally to the sheriff, the sheriff shall record those views in writing.

(4)  The sheriff may direct that any written views given by a child, or any written record of those views, shall—

    (a)  be sealed in an envelope marked "Views of the child—confidential";

    (b)  be kept in the court process without being recorded in the inventory of process;

    (c)  be available to a sheriff only;

    (d)  not be opened by any person other than a sheriff, and

    (e)  not form a borrowable part of the process.

## Confidentiality

**3.5A.**—[4](1)  Unless the sheriff otherwise directs, all documents lodged in process are to be available only to the sheriff, the reporter, the safeguarder, the curator ad litem and the parties; and such documents must be treated as confidential by all persons involved in, or party to, the proceedings and by the sheriff clerk.

(2)  The safeguarder and the curator ad litem must—

    (a)  treat all information obtained in the exercise of their duties as confidential; and

    (b)  not disclose any such information to any person unless disclosure of such information is necessary for the purpose of their duties.

(3)  This rule is subject to rule 3.5.

---

[1] As amended by the Act of Sederunt (Children's Hearings (Scotland) Act 2011) (Miscellaneous Amendments) 2013 (SSI 2013/172) para.3 (effective June 24, 2013).

[2] As substituted by the Act of Sederunt (Children's Hearings (Scotland) Act 2011) (Miscellaneous Amendments) 2013 (SSI 2013/172) para.3 (effective June 24, 2013).

[3] As inserted by the Act of Sederunt (Children's Hearings (Scotland) Act 2011) (Miscellaneous Amendments) 2013 (SSI 2013/172) para.3 (effective June 24, 2013).

[4] As inserted by the Act of Sederunt (Children's Hearings (Scotland) Act 2011) (Miscellaneous Amendments) 2013 (SSI 2013/172) para.3 (effective June 24, 2013).

*Safeguarders*

## Application

**3.6**[1]   Rules 3.7 to 3.9 apply, as regards a safeguarder, to all applications and proceedings to which this Chapter applies except for an application under section 37 of the Act for a child protection order.

## Appointment of safeguarder

**3.7**—(1)[2]   Where a safeguarder has not been appointed for the child, the sheriff—
  (a)   shall, as soon as reasonably practicable after the lodging of an application or the commencing of any proceedings, consider whether it is necessary to appoint a safeguarder in the application or proceedings; and
  (b)   may at that stage, or at any later stage of the application or proceedings, appoint a safeguarder.

  (2)   [2] Where a sheriff appoints a safeguarder, the appointment and the reasons for it must be recorded in an interlocutor.

## Rights, powers and duties of safeguarder on appointment

**3.8**   A safeguarder appointed in an application shall—
  (a)   have the powers and duties at common law of a curator ad litem in respect of the child;
  (b)   be entitled to receive from the Principal Reporter copies of the application, all of the productions in the proceedings and any papers which were before the children's hearing;
  (c)   subject to rule 3.5(1)(a), determine whether the child wishes to express his views in relation to the application and, if so, where the child so wishes to transmit his views to the sheriff;
  (d)   make such enquiries so far as relevant to the application as he considers appropriate; and
  (e)   without delay, and in any event before the hearing on the application, intimate in writing to the sheriff clerk whether or not he intends to become a party to the proceedings.
  (f)[3]   whether or not a party, be entitled to receive from the sheriff clerk all interlocutors subsequent to his or her appointment.

## Representation of safeguarder[4]

**3.9**[3]   A safeguarder may appear personally in the proceedings or instruct an advocate or solicitor to appear on his behalf.

  (2)   Where an advocate or a solicitor is appointed to act as a safeguarder, he shall not act also as advocate or solicitor for the child in the proceedings.

---

[1] As amended by the Act of Sederunt (Children's Hearings (Scotland) Act 2011) (Miscellaneous Amendments) 2013 (SSI 2013/172) para.3 (effective June 24, 2013).
[2] As amended by the Act of Sederunt (Children's Hearings (Scotland) Act 2011) (Miscellaneous Amendments) 2013 (SSI 2013/172) para.3 (effective June 24, 2013).
[3] As inserted by the Act of Sederunt (Children's Hearings (Scotland) Act 2011) (Miscellaneous Amendments) 2013 (SSI 2013/172) para.3 (effective June 24, 2013).
[4] As amended by the Act of Sederunt (Childrensquo;s Hearings (Scotland) Act 2011) (Miscellaneous Amendments) 2013 (SSI 2013/172) para.3 (effective June 24, 2013).

## Provision where safeguarder intimates his intention not to become a party to the proceedings

**3.10** *[Repealed by the Act of Sederunt (Children's Hearings (Scotland) Act 2011) (Miscellaneous Amendments) 2013 (SSI 2013/172) para.3 (effective June 24, 2013).]*

### Fixing of First Hearing

## Assigning of diet for hearing

**3.11**[1] Except where otherwise provided in these Rules, after the lodging of any application the sheriff clerk shall forthwith assign a diet for the hearing of the application and shall issue a first order or a warrant to cite in Form 32, Form 32A or Form 33, as the case may be.

### Service, Citation and Notice

## Service and notice to persons named in application

**3.12**—(1) Subject to the provisions of rule 3.4 (service on child), after the issue of the first order or warrant to cite, as the case may be, the applicant shall forthwith give notice of the application by serving a copy of the application and the first order or warrant to cite together with a notice or citation, as the case may be, on the persons named in the application or, as the case may be, a person who should receive notice of the application (subject to paragraph (2)) in—

    (a) Form 34 in respect of an application for a child assessment order under Part III of this Chapter;

    (b)[2] Form 35 in respect of an application to vary or terminate a child protection order in terms of rule 3.33;

    (c) Form 36 in respect of an application for an exclusion order in terms of rules 3.34 to 3.39;

    (d) Form 37 in respect of an application to vary or recall an exclusion order in terms of rule 3.40;

    (e) *[Repealed by the Act of Sederunt (Children's Hearings (Scotland) Act 2011) (Miscellaneous Amendments) 2013 (SSI 2013/172) para.3 (effective June 24, 2013).]*

    (f)[3] subject to subparagraph (g), in Form 39 in respect of an application under section 93(2)(a) or 94(2)(a) of the 2011 Act made under Part VII of this Chapter; or

    (g)[4] in Form 39A where a procedural hearing has been fixed in respect of an application under section 94(2)(a) of the 2011 Act made under Part VII of this Chapter.

---

[1] As amended by the Act of Sederunt (Children's Hearings (Scotland) Act 2011) (Miscellaneous Amendments) 2013 (SSI 2013/172) para.3 (effective June 24, 2013).

[2] As amended by the Act of Sederunt (Children's Hearings (Scotland) Act 2011) (Miscellaneous Amendments) 2013 (SSI 2013/172) para.3 (effective June 24, 2013).

[3] As substituted by the Act of Sederunt (Children's Hearings (Scotland) Act 2011) (Miscellaneous Amendments) 2013 (SSI 2013/172) para.3 (effective June 24, 2013).

[4] As substituted by the Act of Sederunt (Children's Hearings (Scotland) Act 2011) (Miscellaneous Amendments) 2013 (SSI 2013/172) para.3 (effective June 24, 2013).

(2)[1]  Notice of the application shall be given in the case of a safeguarder or curator ad litem by serving a copy of the application and the first order or warrant to cite together with notice in Form 40.

## Period of notice

**3.13**—(1)  Subject to paragraph (2), citation or notice authorised or required by this Chapter shall be made not later than forty-eight hours, or in the case or postal citation seventy-two hours, before the date of the diet to which the citation or notice relates.

(2)  Paragraph (1) shall not apply in relation to citation or notice of the following applications or proceedings—

    (a)[2]  an appeal referred to in section 157(1), 160(1), 161(1) or 162(3) of the 2011 Act;

    (b)  a hearing in respect of an exclusion order where an interim order has been granted in terms of rule 3.36;

    (c)[3]  a hearing on an application to vary or terminate a child protection order;

    (d)  an application for a child assessment order,

in which cases the period of notice and the method of giving notice shall be as directed by the sheriff.

## Citation of witnesses, parties and persons having an interest

**3.14**—(1)  The following shall be warrants for citation of witnesses, parties and havers—

    (a)[4]  the warrant for the hearing on evidence in an application;

    (b)  an interlocutor fixing a diet for the continued hearing of an application; and

    (c)  an interlocutor assigning a diet for a hearing of an appeal or application.

(2)  In an application or an appeal, witnesses or havers may be cited in Form 41.

(3)  The certificate of execution of citation of witnesses and havers shall be in Form 42.

## Modes of service

**3.15**—(1)  Service authorised or required by this Chapter shall be made by any mode specified in paragraphs (2) and (3).

(2)  It shall be deemed legal service to or on any person if such service is—

    (a)  delivered to him personally;

    (b)  left for him at his dwelling-house or place of business with some person resident or employed therein;

    (c)  where it cannot be delivered to him personally and he has no known dwelling-house or place of business, left for him at any other place at which he may at the time be resident;

---

[1] As amended by the Act of Sederunt (Children's Hearings (Scotland) Act 2011) (Miscellaneous Amendments) 2013 (SSI 2013/172) para.3 (effective June 24, 2013).

[2] As substituted by the Act of Sederunt (Children's Hearings (Scotland) Act 2011) (Miscellaneous Amendments) 2013 (SSI 2013/172) para.3 (effective June 24, 2013).

[3] As substituted by the Act of Sederunt (Children's Hearings (Scotland) Act 2011) (Miscellaneous Amendments) 2013 (SSI 2013/172) para.3 (effective June 24, 2013).

[4] As amended by the Act of Sederunt (Children's Hearings (Scotland) Act 2011) (Miscellaneous Amendments) 2013 (SSI 2013/172) para.3 (effective June 24, 2013).

    (d)   where he is the master of, or a seaman or other person employed in, a vessel, left with a person on board or connected with the vessel;

    (e)   sent by first class recorded delivery post, or the nearest equivalent which the available postal service permits, to his dwelling-house or place of business, or if he has no known dwelling-house or place of business to any other place in which he may at the time be resident;

    (f)   where the person has the facility to receive facsimile or other electronic transmission, by such facsimile or other electronic transmission; or

    (g)   where the person has a numbered box at a document exchange, given by leaving at the document exchange.

(3)   Where service requires to be made and there is not sufficient time to employ any of the methods specified in paragraph (2), service shall be effected orally or in such other manner as the sheriff directs.

### Persons who may effect service

**3.16.**—(1)   Subject to paragraphs (2) and (3), service shall be effected—

    (a)   in the case of any of the modes specified in rule 3.15(2), by a sheriff officer;

    (b)[1]   in the case of any of the modes specified in rule 3.15(2)(e) to (g), by a solicitor, the sheriff clerk, the Principal Reporter or an officer of the local authority; or

    (c)   in the case of any mode specified by the sheriff in terms of rule 3.15(3), by such person as the sheriff directs.

(2)   In relation to the citation of witnesses, parties and havers in terms of rule 3.14 or service of any application, "officer of the local authority" in paragraph (1)(b) includes any officer of a local authority authorised to conduct proceedings under these Rules in terms of rule 3.21 (representation).

(3)[2]   Where required by the sheriff, the sheriff clerk shall cite the Principal Reporter, the authors or compilers of any reports or statements and any other person whom the sheriff may wish to examine under section 155(5) of the 2011 Act (procedure in appeal to sheriff against decision of children's hearing).

### Production of certificates of execution of service

**3.17.**—(1)   The production before the sheriff of—

    (a)   a certificate of execution of service in Form 43; and

    (b)[3]   additionally in the case of postal service, a post office receipt of the registered or recorded delivery letter,

shall be sufficient evidence that service was duly made.

(2)   It shall be sufficient to lodge the execution of service at the hearing, unless the sheriff otherwise directs or on cause shown.

---

[1] As amended by the Act of Sederunt (Children's Hearings (Scotland) Act 2011) (Miscellaneous Amendments) 2013 (SSI 2013/172) para.3 (effective June 24, 2013).

[2] As substituted by the Act of Sederunt (Children's Hearings (Scotland) Act 2011) (Miscellaneous Amendments) 2013 (SSI 2013/172) para.3 (effective June 24, 2013).

[3] As amended by the Act of Sederunt (Children's Hearings (Scotland) Act 2011) (Miscellaneous Amendments) 2013 (SSI 2013/172) para.3 (effective June 24, 2013).

## Power to dispense with service

**3.18.** Subject to rule 3.3, the sheriff may, on cause shown, dispense with service on any person named.

*Miscellaneous*

## Expenses

**3.19.** No expenses shall be awarded in any proceedings in which this Chapter applies.

## Record of proceedings

**3.20.** Proceedings under this Chapter shall be conducted summarily.

## Representation

**3.21.**—(1) In any proceedings any party may be represented by an advocate or a solicitor or, subject to paragraphs (2) and (3), other representative authorised by the party.

(2) Such other representative must throughout the proceedings satisfy the sheriff that he is a suitable person to represent the party and that he is authorised to do so.

(3) Such other representative may in representing a party do all such things for the preparation and conduct of the proceedings as may be done by an individual on his own behalf.

## Applications for evidence by live link

**3.22.**—[1](1) On cause shown, a party may apply in the form prescribed in paragraph (3) for authority for the whole or part of—

    (a) the evidence of a witness or party; or

    (b) a submission,

to be made through a live link.

(2) In paragraph (1)—

> "witness" means a person who has been or may be cited to appear before the sheriff as a witness (including a witness who is outwith Scotland), except in circumstances where such witness is a vulnerable witness within the meaning of section 11(1) of the Vulnerable Witnesses (Scotland) Act 2004;
>
> "submission" means any oral submission which would otherwise be made to the court by the party or such party's representative in person including an oral submission in support of an application;
>
> "live link" means a live television link or such other arrangement as may be specified in the application by which the witness, party or representative, as the case may be, is able to be seen and heard in the proceedings or heard in the proceedings and is able to see and hear or hear the proceedings while at a place which is outside the courtroom.

(3) An application under paragraph (1) shall be made—

    (a) in Form 44A in the case of a witness or party;

---

[1] As substituted by the Act of Sederunt (Children's Hearings (Scotland) Act 2011) (Miscellaneous Amendments) 2013 (SSI 2013/172) para.3 (effective June 24, 2013).

(b)  in Form 44B in the case of a submission.

(4)  The application shall be lodged with the sheriff clerk prior to the hearing at which the witness is to give evidence or the submission is to be made (except on special cause shown).

(5)  The sheriff shall—

(a)  order intimation of the application to be made to the other party or parties to the proceedings in such form as he or she prescribes; and

(b)  hear the application as soon as reasonably practicable.

### Orders and transfer of cases

**3.23.**—(1)  The sheriff who hears an application under rule 3.22 shall, after hearing the parties and allowing such further procedure as the sheriff thinks fit, make an order granting or refusing the application.

(2)  Where the sheriff grants the application, he may—

(a)  transfer the case to be heard in whole; or

(b)  hear the case himself or such part of it as he shall determine, in another sheriff court in the same sheriffdom.

### Exclusion of certain enactments

**3.24.**  The enactments specified in column (1) of Schedule 3 to this Act of Sederunt (being enactments relating to matters with respect to which this Chapter is made) shall not, to the extent specified in column (3) of that Schedule, apply to an application or appeal.

## Part III

## Child Assessment Orders

### Interpretation

**3.25.**[1]  In this Part, "application" means an application for a child assessment order in terms of section 35(1) of the 2011 Act.

### Form of application

**3.26.**  An application shall be made in Form 45.

### Orders

**3.27.**—(1)  After hearing parties and allowing such further procedure as he thinks fit, the sheriff shall make an order granting or refusing the application.

(2)  Where an order is made granting the application, that order shall be made in Form 46 and shall contain the information specified therein.

(3)[2]  Where the sheriff, in terms of section 36(3) of the 2011 Act, has decided to make a child protection order pursuant to an application, rules 3.31 to 3.33 shall apply.

---

[1] As amended by the Act of Sederunt (Children's Hearings (Scotland) Act 2011) (Miscellaneous Amendments) 2013 (SSI 2013/172) para.3 (effective June 24, 2013).

[2] As amended by the Act of Sederunt (Children's Hearings (Scotland) Act 2011) (Miscellaneous Amendments) 2013 (SSI 2013/172) para.3 (effective June 24, 2013).

**Intimation**

**3.28.** The local authority shall intimate the grant or refusal of an application to such persons, if any, as the sheriff directs.

## Part IV

## Child Protection Orders

**Interpretation**

**3.29**[1] In this Part, "application" means, except in rule 3.33, an application for a child protection order in terms of section 37 of the 2011 Act.

**Form of application**

**3.30** An application made by a local authority shall be in Form 47 and an application made by any other person shall be in Form 48.

**Determination of application**

**3.31**—(1) On receipt of an application, the sheriff, having considered the grounds of the application and the supporting evidence, shall forthwith grant or refuse it.

(2)[2] Where an order is granted, it shall be in Form 49 and it shall contain any directions made under section 40, 41 or 42 of the 2011 Act.

**Intimation of making of order**

**3.32** Where an order is granted, the applicant shall forthwith serve a copy of the order on—

    (a)   the child, along with a notice in Form 50;

    (b)[3]  the persons referred to in section 43(1)(a), (c), (d) and (e) of the 2011 Act, along with a notice in Form 51; and

    (c)   such other persons as the sheriff may direct and in such manner as he or she may direct.

**Application to vary or terminate a child protection order**

**3.33**—[4](1) An application under section 48 of the 2011 Act for the variation or termination of a child protection order or a direction given under section 58 of the Act or such an order shall be made in Form 52.

(2) A person applying under section 48 of the 2011 Act for the variation or termination of a child protection order shall require the lodge with his application a copy of that order.

---

[1] As amended by the Act of Sederunt (Children's Hearings (Scotland) Act 2011) (Miscellaneous Amendments) 2013 (SSI 2013/172) para.3 (effective June 24, 2013).

[2] As amended by the Act of Sederunt (Children's Hearings (Scotland) Act 2011) (Miscellaneous Amendments) 2013 (SSI 2013/172) para.3 (effective June 24, 2013).

[3] As substituted by the Act of Sederunt (Children's Hearings (Scotland) Act 2011) (Miscellaneous Amendments) 2013 (SSI 2013/172) para.3 (effective June 24, 2013).

[4] As amended by the Act of Sederunt (Children's Hearings (Scotland) Act 2011) (Miscellaneous Amendments) 2013 (SSI 2013/172) para.3 (effective June 24, 2013).

(3)    Without prejudice to rule 3.5, any person on whom service is made under section 49 of the 2011 Act may appear or be represented at the hearing of the application.

(4)    The sheriff, after hearing parties and allowing such further procedure as he thinks fit, shall grant or refuse the application.

(5)    Where an order is made granting the application for variation, the order shall be in Form 53.

(6)    Where the sheriff so directs, intimation of the granting or refusing of an application shall be given by the applicant to such persons as the sheriff shall direct.

## Part V

## Exclusion Orders

### Interpretation

**3.34**[1]    In this Part, "application" means, except in rule 3.40, an application by a local authority for an exclusion order in terms of sections 76 to 80 of the 1995 Act; and "ancillary order" and "interim order" shall be construed accordingly.

### Form of application

**3.35**    An application shall be made in Form 54.

### Hearing following interim order

**3.36**[2]    Where an interim order is granted under subsection (4) of section 76 of the 1995 Act, the hearing under subsection (5) of that section shall take place not later than 3 working days after the granting of the interim order.

### Orders

**3.37**—(1)    After hearing parties and allowing such further procedure as he thinks fit, the sheriff shall make an order granting or refusing the application.

(2)    Where the sheriff grants an order in terms of paragraph (1), it shall be in Form 55 and shall be served forthwith by the local authority on—

    (a)    the named person;
    (b)    the appropriate person;
    (c)    the relevant child; and
    (d)    the Principal Reporter.

### Certificates of delivery of documents to chief constable

**3.38**—[3](1)    After the local authority have complied with section 78(4) of the 1955 Act, they shall forthwith lodge in process a certificate of delivery in Form 56.

(2)    After a person has complied with section 78(5) of the 1995 Act, he shall lodge in process a certificate of delivery in Form 56.

---

[1] As amended by the Act of Sederunt (Children's Hearings (Scotland) Act 2011) (Miscellaneous Amendments) 2013 (SSI 2013/172) para.3 (effective June 24, 2013).
[2] As amended by the Act of Sederunt (Children's Hearings (Scotland) Act 2011) (Miscellaneous Amendments) 2013 (SSI 2013/172) para.3 (effective June 24, 2013).
[3] As amended by the Act of Sederunt (Children's Hearings (Scotland) Act 2011) (Miscellaneous Amendments) 2013 (SSI 2013/172) para.3 (effective June 24, 2013).

## Power to make child protection order in an application for an exclusion order

**3.39**[1]   Where the sheriff, in terms of section 76(8) of the 1995 Act, has decided to make a child protection order under Part 5 of the 2011 Act pursuant to an application, rules 3.31 to 3.33 shall apply.

## Variation or recall of an exclusion order

**3.40**—[2](1)   Any application for the variation or recall of an exclusion order and any warrant, interdict, order or direction granted or made under section 77 of the 1995 Act shall be in Form 57.

(2)   After hearing parties and allowing such further procedure as he thinks fit, the sheriff shall make an order granting or refusing the application.

(3)   Where an order is made granting the application for variation, that order shall be in Form 58.

(4)   Intimation of the granting or refusing of an application shall be given by the applicant to such persons as the sheriff shall direct.

## Part VI

## Warrant for Further Detention of a Child

**3.41–3.44**   *[Repealed by the Act of Sederunt (Children's Hearings (Scotland) Act 2011) (Miscellaneous Amendments) 2013 (SSI 2013/172) para.3 (effective June 24, 2013).]*

## Form of application

**3.42**   An application shall be made in Form 59.

## Orders

**3.43**   After hearing parties and allowing such further procedure as he thinks fit, the sheriff shall make an order granting or refusing the application.

## Part VII

## Procedure in Applications under Section 93(2)(a) or 94(2)(a) of the 2011 Act[3]

## Interpretation

**3.44**[4]   In this Part, "application" means an application under section 93(2)(a) or 94(2)(a) of the 2011 Act.

---

[2] As amended by the Act of Sederunt (Children's Hearings (Scotland) Act 2011) (Miscellaneous Amendments) 2013 (SSI 2013/172) para.3 (effective June 24, 2013).
[3] As amended by the Act of Sederunt (Children's Hearings (Scotland) Act 2011) (Miscellaneous Amendments) 2013 (SSI 2013/172) para.3 (effective June 24, 2013).
[4] As amended by the Act of Sederunt (Children's Hearings (Scotland) Act 2011) (Miscellaneous Amendments) 2013 (SSI 2013/172) para.3 (effective June 24, 2013).

## Lodging of application, etc.

**3.45**—[1](1)  Within a period of 7 days beginning with the date on which the Principal Reporter was directed in terms of section 93(2)(a) or 94(2)(a) of the 2011 Act to make an application to the sheriff, the Principal Reporter shall lodge an application in Form 60 with the sheriff clerk of the sheriff court district in which the child is habitually resident.

(1A)  Paragraph (1) is subject to the terms of section 102(2) of the 2011 Act.

(1B)  The sheriff may, on cause shown, remit any application to another sheriff court.

(1C)  Not later than 28 days after the day on which the application is lodged the sheriff clerk shall fix a hearing on evidence as required under section 101(2) of the 2011 Act.

(2)  Where a safeguarder has been appointed by the chairman at the children's hearing, the Principal Reporter shall intimate such appointment to the sheriff clerk and shall lodge along with the application any report made by the safeguarder.

(3)  Paragraphs (4) to (7) apply where an application under paragraph (1) is made by virtue of section 94(2)(a) of the 2011 Act.

(4)  The sheriff may fix a procedural hearing to determine whether or not the section 67 grounds in the statement of grounds are accepted by each relevant person.

(5)  Such procedural hearing must take place before the expiry of the period of 7 days beginning with the day on which the application is lodged.

(6)  The sheriff shall appoint service and intimation of the procedural hearing as the sheriff thinks fit.

(7)  Subject to paragraph (9)(a) and (b), subsequent to the procedural hearing the sheriff may discharge the hearing on evidence and determine the application.

(8)  Where paragraph (7) applies the sheriff shall make such orders for intimation as the sheriff thinks fit.

(9)  Where—

    (a)  a relevant person does not accept the section 67 grounds in the statement of grounds at the procedural hearing;

    (b)  section 106(2)(a) or (b) of the 2011 Act applies; or

    (c)  the sheriff has not fixed a procedural hearing;

a hearing on evidence must take place in accordance with rule 3.47.

## Withdrawal of application

**3.46**—[2](1)  At any stage of the proceedings before the application is determined the Principal Reporter may withdraw the application, either in whole or in part, by lodging a minute to that effect or by motion at the hearing.

(2)  The Principal Reporter shall intimate such withdrawal to—

    (a)  the child, except where service on the child had been dispensed with in terms of rule 3.3;

    (b)  any relevant person whose whereabouts are known to the Principal Reporter; and

    (c)  any safeguarder appointed by the sheriff and curator ad litem.

---

[1] As amended by the Act of Sederunt (Children's Hearings (Scotland) Act 2011) (Miscellaneous Amendments) 2013 (SSI 2013/172) para.3 (effective June 24, 2013).

[2] As amended by the Act of Sederunt (Children's Hearings (Scotland) Act 2011) (Miscellaneous Amendments) 2013 (SSI 2013/172) para.3 (effective June 24, 2013).

(3)   In the event of withdrawal in whole in terms of paragraph (1), the sheriff shall dismiss the application and discharge the referral.

### Expeditious determination of application

**3.46A**[1]   Prior to or at a hearing on evidence under rule 3.47 (or any adjournment or continuation thereof under rule 3.49), the sheriff may order parties to take such steps as the sheriff deems necessary to secure the expeditious determination of the application, including but not limited to—
- (a)   instructing a single expert;
- (b)   using affidavits;
- (c)   restricting the issues for proof;
- (d)   restricting witnesses;
- (e)   applying for evidence to be taken by live link in accordance with rule 3.22.

### Hearing on evidence

(A1)   If, at a hearing on evidence (or any adjournment or continuation thereof under rule 3.49), the section 67 grounds (or as they may be amended) are no longer in dispute, the sheriff may determine the application without hearing evidence.

(1)   In the case of every section 67 ground, the sheriff shall, in relation to any ground of referral which is in dispute, hear evidence tendered by or on behalf of the Principal Reporter, including evidence given pursuant to an application granted under rule 3.23.

(2)   At the close of the evidence led by the Principal Reporter in a case where it is disputed that the ground set out in section 67(2)(j) of the 2011 Act applies, the sheriff shall consider whether sufficient evidence has been led to establish that ground and shall give all the parties an opportunity to be heard on the question of sufficiency of evidence.

(3)   Where the sheriff is not satisfied that sufficient evidence has been led as mentioned in paragraph (2), he shall make a determination to that effect.

(4)   Paragraph (4A) applies where—
- (a)   paragraph (2) applies and the sheriff is satisfied that sufficient evidence has been led;
- (b)   any other section 67 ground is in dispute.

(4A)   The child, the relevant person and any safeguarder may give evidence and may, with the approval of the sheriff, call witnesses with regard to the ground in question.

(5)   Where the sheriff excuses the child from attending all or part of the hearing in accordance with section 103(3) of the 2011 Act, the following persons shall be permitted to remain during the absence of the child—
- (a)   any safeguarder appointed in relation to the child;
- (b)   any curator ad litem appointed in relation to the child;
- (c)   any relevant person;
- (d)   the child's representative.

---

[1] As amended by the Act of Sederunt (Children's Hearings (Scotland) Act 2011) (Miscellaneous Amendments) 2013 (SSI 2013/172) para.3 (effective June 24, 2013).

(6)    Subject to paragraph (7), the sheriff may exclude any person, including the relevant person, while any child is giving evidence if the sheriff is satisfied that this is necessary in the interests of the child and that—

(a)    he must do so in order to obtain the evidence of the child; or

(b)    the presence of the person or persons in question is causing, or is likely to cause, significant distress to the child.

(7)    Where the relevant person is not legally represented at the hearing and has been excluded under paragraph (6), the sheriff shall inform that relevant person of the substance of any evidence given by the child and shall give that relevant person an opportunity to respond by leading evidence or otherwise.

(8)    Where evidence has been heard in part and a safeguarder thereafter becomes a party to proceedings, the sheriff may order the evidence to be reheard in whole or in part.

### Amendment of the statement of grounds

**3.48**[1]    The sheriff may at any time, on the application of any party or on his own motion, allow amendment of any statement of grounds.

### Adjournment for inquiry, etc.

**3.49**[2]    The sheriff on the motion of any party or on his own motion may continue the hearing fixed under rule 3.45(1B) in order to allow time for further inquiry into any application, in consequence of the amendment of any statement under rule 3.48, or for any other necessary cause, for such reasonable time as he may in the circumstances consider necessary.

### Power of sheriff in making findings as to offences

**3.50**[3]    Where in a statement of grounds it is alleged that an offence has been committed by or against any child, the sheriff may determine that any other offence established by the facts has been committed.

### Decision of sheriff

**3.51**—[4](1)    Subject to rule 3.47(3), the sheriff shall give his decision orally at the conclusion of the hearing.

(2)    The sheriff clerk shall forthwith send a copy of the interlocutor containing that decision to—

(a)    the child, except where service on the child has been dispensed with in terms of rule 3.3;

(b)    any relevant person whose whereabouts are known;

(c)    any safeguarder and curator ad litem;

(d)    the Principal Reporter; and

---

[1] As amended by the Act of Sederunt (Children's Hearings (Scotland) Act 2011) (Miscellaneous Amendments) 2013 (SSI 2013/172) para.3 (effective June 24, 2013).

[2] As amended by the Act of Sederunt (Children's Hearings (Scotland) Act 2011) (Miscellaneous Amendments) 2013 (SSI 2013/172) para.3 (effective June 24, 2013).

[3] As amended by the Act of Sederunt (Children's Hearings (Scotland) Act 2011) (Miscellaneous Amendments) 2013 (SSI 2013/172) para.3 (effective June 24, 2013).

[4] As amended by the Act of Sederunt (Children's Hearings (Scotland) Act 2011) (Miscellaneous Amendments) 2013 (SSI 2013/172) para.3 (effective June 24, 2013).

(e)   such other persons as the sheriff may direct.

(3)   The sheriff may, when giving his decision in terms of paragraph (1) or within 7 days thereafter, issue a note of the reasons for his decision and the sheriff clerk shall forthwith send a copy of such a note to the persons referred to in paragraph (2).

### Signature of warrants

**3.52**—[1](1)   Subject to paragraph (3) a warrant granted under the 2011 Act may be signed by the sheriff or the sheriff clerk.

(2)   A warrant signed by the sheriff clerk shall be treated for all purposes as if it had been signed by the sheriff.

(3)   A warrant to secure attendance must be signed by the sheriff.

## Part VIII[2]

## Procedure in Appeals to the Sheriff against Decisions of Children's Hearings

### Form of appeal

**3.53**—[3](1)   This Part applies to appeals to the sheriff under sections 154(1), 160(1), 161(1) and 162(3) of the 2011 Act.

(1A)   An appeal to the sheriff under the sections of the 2011 Act prescribed in paragraph (1B) must be—
  (a)   made in the form prescribed in paragraph (1B);
  (b)   accompanied by a copy of the decision complained of and any document relevant to it that was before the children's hearing; and
  (c)   lodged with the sheriff clerk of the sheriff court district in which the child is habitually resident or, on cause shown, such other court as the sheriff may direct.

(1B)   The prescribed sections and form of appeal are—
  (a)   in the case of an appeal under section 154(1) (appeal to sheriff against decision of children's hearing), in Form 61;
  (b)   in the case of an appeal under section 160(1) (appeal to sheriff against relevant person determination), in Form 62;
  (c)   in the case of an appeal under section 161(1) (appeal to sheriff against decision affecting contact or permanence order), in Form 63;
  (d)   in the case of an appeal under section 162(3) (appeal to sheriff against decision to implement secure accommodation authorisation), in Form 63A.

(2)   Subject to paragraph (3), the appeal shall be signed by the appellant or his representative.

(3)   An appeal by a child may be signed on his behalf by any safeguarder.

(4)   Where leave to appeal is required by virtue of section 159(2) of the 2011 Act, such application for leave shall be—
  (a)   made by letter addressed to the sheriff clerk setting out the grounds on which the application is made;

---

[1] As substituted by the Act of Sederunt (Children's Hearings (Scotland) Act 2011) (Miscellaneous Amendments) 2013 (SSI 2013/172) para.3 (effective June 24, 2013).
[2] As amended by the Act of Sederunt (Children's Hearings (Scotland) Act 2011) (Miscellaneous Amendments) 2013 (SSI 2013/172) para.3 (effective June 24, 2013).
[3] As amended by the Act of Sederunt (Children's Hearings (Scotland) Act 2011) (Miscellaneous Amendments) 2013 (SSI 2013/172) para.3 (effective June 24, 2013).

(b) accompanied by a copy of the decision referred to in section 159(2) of the 2011 Act;

(c) lodged with the sheriff clerk with the relevant form of appeal.

(5) On receipt of such application the sheriff clerk shall forthwith fix a hearing and intimate the application and the date of the hearing to the other parties to the proceedings.

(6) Where leave to appeal is granted, the appeal will proceed in accordance with rule 3.54.

## Appointment and intimation of first diet

**3.54**—[1](1) On the lodging of the appeal, the sheriff clerk shall forthwith assign a date for the hearing and shall at the same time intimate to the appellant or his representative and, together with a copy of the appeal, to—

(a) the Principal Reporter;

(b) subject to the provisions of paragraph (4), the child (if not the appellant);

(c) any relevant person (if not the appellant);

(d) any safeguarder; and

(e) any other person the sheriff considers necessary, including those referred to in section 155(5)(c) and (e) of the 2011 Act.

(f) in the case of appeals under section 162(3), the chief social work officer of the relevant local authority for the child.

(2) The sheriff clerk shall endorse on the appeal a certificate of execution of intimation under paragraph (1).

(3) Intimation to a child in terms of paragraph (1)(b) shall be in Form 64.

(4) The sheriff may dispense with intimation to a child in terms of paragraph (1)(b) where he considers that such dispensation is appropriate.

(5) The date assigned for the hearing under paragraph (1) shall be within the time limits prescribed in, or by virtue of, the 2011 Act and in any event, no later than 28 days after the lodging of the appeal.

## Answers

**3.55**—(1)[2] Subject to paragraph (1A), if any person on whom service of the appeal has been made wishes to lodge answers to the appeal, he or she must do so not later than 7 days before the diet fixed for the hearing of the appeal.

(1A)[3] Paragraph (1) does not apply to those appeals referred to in section 157(1), 160(1), 161(1) or 162(3) of the 2011 Act.

(2) Any person who has lodged answers shall forthwith intimate a copy thereof to any other person on whom service has been made under rule 3.54(1).

---

[1] As amended by the Act of Sederunt (Children's Hearings (Scotland) Act 2011) (Miscellaneous Amendments) 2013 (SSI 2013/172) para.3 (effective June 24, 2013).

[2] As substituted by the Act of Sederunt (Children's Hearings (Scotland) Act 2011) (Miscellaneous Amendments) 2013 (SSI 2013/172) para.3 (effective June 24, 2013).

[3] As substituted by the Act of Sederunt (Children's Hearings (Scotland) Act 2011) (Miscellaneous Amendments) 2013 (SSI 2013/172) para.3 (effective June 24, 2013).

## Procedure at hearing of appeal

**3.56**—[1](1)  Before proceeding to examine the Principal Reporter and the authors or compilers of any reports or statements, the sheriff shall hear the appellant or his representative and any party to the appeal.

(2)  On receipt of any further report required by the sheriff under or by virtue of the 2011 Act, the sheriff shall direct the Principal Reporter to send a copy of the report to every party to the appeal.

(3)  At any appeal the sheriff may hear evidence—

    (a)  where a ground of the appeal is an alleged irregularity in the conduct of a hearing, as to that irregularity;

    (b)  in any other circumstances where he considers it appropriate to do so.

(4)  Where the nature of the appeal or of any evidence is such that the sheriff is satisfied that it is in the interests of the child that he should not be present at any stage of the appeal, the sheriff may exclude the child from the hearing during that stage and, in that event, any safeguarder appointed and any relevant person or representative of the child shall be permitted to remain during the absence of the child.

(5)  Subject to paragraph (6), the sheriff may exclude any relevant person, or that person and any representative of his, or any such representative from any part or parts of the hearing for so long as he considers it is necessary in the interests of any child, where he is satisfied that—

    (a)  he must do so in order to obtain the views of the child in relation to the hearing; or

    (b)  the presence of the person or persons in question is causing, or is likely to cause, significant distress to the child.

(6)  Where any relevant person has been excluded under paragraph (5) the sheriff shall, after that exclusion has ended, explain to him the substance of what has taken place in his absence and shall give him an opportunity to respond to any evidence given by the child by leading evidence or otherwise.

(7)  Where an appeal has been heard in part and a safeguarder thereafter becomes a party to the appeal, the sheriff may order the hearing of the appeal to commence of new.

## Adjournment or continuaton of appeals

**3.57**—[2](1)  The sheriff may, on the motion of any party or on his own motion, adjourn or continue the hearing of the appeal for such reasonable time and for such purpose as may in the circumstances be appropriate.

(2)  In the event of such adjournment or continuation the sheriff may make such order as the sheriff deems necessary to secure the expeditious determination of the appeal.

---

[1] As amended by the Act of Sederunt (Children's Hearings (Scotland) Act 2011) (Miscellaneous Amendments) 2013 (SSI 2013/172) para.3 (effective June 24, 2013).

[2] As amended by the Act of Sederunt (Children's Hearings (Scotland) Act 2011) (Miscellaneous Amendments) 2013 (SSI 2013/172) para.3 (effective June 24, 2013).

### Decision of sheriff in appeals

**3.58**—[1](1)   The sheriff shall give his decision orally either at the conclusion of the appeal or on such day as he shall appoint, subject to the provisions of, or by virtue of, the 2011 Act.

(2)   The sheriff may issue a note of the reasons for his decision, and shall require to do so where he takes any of the steps referred to in section 156(2) or (3) of the 2011 Act.

(3)   Any note in terms of paragraph (2) shall be issued at the time the sheriff gives his decision or within 7 days thereafter.

(4)   The sheriff clerk shall forthwith send a copy of the interlocutor containing the decision of the sheriff, and where appropriate of the note referred to in paragraph (2), to the Principal Reporter, to the appellant (and to any child or the relevant person, if not the appellant), any safeguarder and such other persons as the sheriff may direct, and shall also return to the Principal Reporter any documents lodged with the sheriff clerk.

(5)   Where section 159 of the 2011 Act applies the sheriff clerk shall send a copy of the interlocutor containing the decision of the sheriff to the Scottish Legal Aid Board.

## Part VIIIA[2]

### Applications for Review by Local Authority

### Review applications by local authority

**3.58A**—[3](1)   This Part of Chapter 3 applies to applications to the sheriff for a review under section 166(2) of the 2011 Act.

(2)   An application shall be made in Form 64A and must contain—

    (a)   the name and address of the local authority;

    (b)   the name of the child in respect of whom the duty was imposed and the child's representative (if any);

    (c)   the name and address of any relevant person in relation to the child and such person's representative (if any);

    (d)   the name and address of any safeguarder;

    (e)   the name and address of any curator ad litem ;

    (f)   the name and address of any other party to the application;

    (g)   the name and address of any other local authority with an interest;

    (h)   the date and determination made and the place of the sheriff court which made the determination, or alternatively the date and decision made by the children's hearing;

        (i)   the grounds for the making of the application;

    (j)   any reports, affidavits and productions upon which the applicant intends to rely.

---

[1] As amended by the Act of Sederunt (Children's Hearings (Scotland) Act 2011) (Miscellaneous Amendments) 2013 (SSI 2013/172) para.3 (effective June 24, 2013).

[2] As inserted by the Act of Sederunt (Children's Hearings (Scotland) Act 2011) (Miscellaneous Amendments) 2013 (SSI 2013/172) para.3 (effective June 24, 2013).

[3] As inserted by the Act of Sederunt (Children's Hearings (Scotland) Act 2011) (Miscellaneous Amendments) 2013 (SSI 2013/172) para.3 (effective June 24, 2013).

**Hearing on application**

**3.58B**—[1](1)   After lodging the application in terms of rule 3.58A, the sheriff clerk shall assign a date for hearing the application and shall issue a warrant to cite in Form 64B, which shall require any party to lodge answers if so advised within such time as the sheriff shall appoint.

(2)   Subject to the provisions of rule 3.3 (power to dispense with service on child), after the issue of the warrant to cite, the applicant shall forthwith give notice of the application by serving a copy and the warrant on the persons referred to in rule 3.58A.

(3)   At the hearing the sheriff may determine the application or allow such further procedure as the sheriff thinks fit.

(4)   The provisions of rule 3.51 shall apply to any order made under this Part.

## Part IX

### Procedure in Appeals by Stated Case under Part 15 of the 2011 Act[2]

**Appeals**

(A1)   This Part applies to appeals by stated case under section 163(1), 164(1), 165(1) and 167(1) of the 2011 Act.

(1)[3]   An application to the sheriff to state a case for the purposes of an appeal to the sheriff principal to which this Part applies shall specify the point of law upon which the appeal is to proceed or the procedural irregularity, as the case may be.

(2)[4]   The appellant shall, at the same time as lodging the application for a stated case, intimate the lodging of an appeal from the decision of the sheriff to—

    (a)   the Principal Reporter;

    (b)   the child (if not the appellant), except where service on the child has been dispensed with in terms of rule 3.3;

    (c)   any relevant person (if not the appellant);

    (d)   any safeguarder;

    (e)   any other party to proceedings.

(3)[5]   The sheriff shall, within 21 days of the lodging of the application for a stated case, issue a draft stated case—

    (a)   containing findings in fact and law or, where appropriate, a narrative of the proceedings before him;

    (b)   containing appropriate questions of law or setting out the procedural irregularity concerned; and

    (c)   containing a note stating the reasons for his decisions in law,

and the sheriff clerk shall send a copy of the draft stated case to the appellant and to parties referred to in paragraph (2).

(4)   Within 7 days of the issue of the draft stated case—

    (a)   the appellant or a party referred to in paragraph (2) may lodge with the sheriff clerk a note of any adjustments which he seeks to make;

---

[1] As inserted by the Act of Sederunt (Children's Hearings (Scotland) Act 2011) (Miscellaneous Amendments) 2013 (SSI 2013/172) para.3 (effective June 24, 2013).

[2] As amended by the Act of Sederunt (Children's Hearings (Scotland) Act 2011) (Miscellaneous Amendments) 2013 (SSI 2013/172) para.3 (effective June 24, 2013).

[3] As amended by SI 1998/2130, effective September 1, 1998.

[4] As amended by SI 1998/2130, effective September 1, 1998.

[5] As amended by SI 1998/2130, effective September 1, 1998.

(b)    the appellant or such a party may state any point of law or procedural irregularity which he wishes to raise in the appeal; and

(c)    the note of adjustment and, where appropriate, point of law or procedural irregularity shall be intimated to the appellant and the other such parties.

(5)    The sheriff may, on the motion of the appellant or a party referred to in paragraph (2) or of his own accord, and shall where he proposes to reject any proposed adjustment, allow a hearing on adjustments and may provide for such further procedure under this rule prior to the hearing of the appeal as he thinks fit.

(6)    The sheriff shall, within 14 days after—

(a)    the latest date on which a note of adjustments has been or may be lodged; or

(b)    where there has been a hearing on adjustments, that hearing,

and after considering such note and any representations made to him at the hearing, state and sign the case.

(7)    The stated case signed by the sheriff shall include—

(a)    questions of law, framed by him, arising from the points of law stated by the parties and such other questions of law as he may consider appropriate;

(b)    any adjustments, proposed under paragraph (4), which are rejected by him;

(c)    a note of the procedural irregularity averred by the parties and any questions of law or other issue which he considers arise therefrom,

as the case may be.

(8)    After the sheriff has signed the stated case, the sheriff clerk shall—

(a)    place before the sheriff principal all documents and productions in the appeal together with the stated case; and

(b)    send to the appellant and the parties referred to in paragraph (2) a copy of the stated case together with a written note of the date, time and place of the hearing of the appeal.

(9)    In the hearing of an appeal, a party referred to in paragraph (2) shall not be allowed to raise questions of law or procedural irregularities of which notice has not been given except on cause shown and subject to such conditions as the sheriff principal may consider appropriate.

(10)    The sheriff may, on an application by any party or on his own motion, reduce any of the periods mentioned in paragraph (3), (4) or (6) to such period or periods as he considers reasonable.

(11)    Where the sheriff is temporarily absent from duty for any reason, the sheriff principal may extend any period specified in paragraph (3) or (6) for such period or periods as he considers reasonable.

## Lodging of reports and information in appeals

3.60.[1]    Where, in an appeal—

(a)    it appears to the sheriff that any report or information lodged under section 155(2) of the 2011 Act is relevant to any issue which is likely to arise in the stated case; and

(b)    the report or information has been returned to the Principal Reporter,

---

[1] As amended by the Act of Sederunt (Children's Hearings (Scotland) Act 2011) (Miscellaneous Amendments) 2013 (SSI 2013/172) para.3 (effective June 24, 2013).

the sheriff may require the Principal Reporter to lodge the report or information with the sheriff clerk.

## Hearing

**3.61.**—(1)   The sheriff principal, on hearing the appeal, may either pronounce his decision or reserve judgment.

(2)   Where judgment is so reserved, the sheriff principal shall within 28 days give his decision in writing which shall be intimated by the sheriff clerk to the parties.

## Leave of the sheriff principal to appeal to the Court of Session

**3.61A**—(1)   This rule applies to applications for leave to appeal under section 163(2), 164(2) or 165(2) of the 2011 Act.

(2)   An application shall be made by letter addressed to the sheriff clerk, which must—

  (a)   state the point of law or procedural irregularity upon which the appeal is to proceed;

  (b)   be lodged with the sheriff clerk before the expiry of the period of 7 days beginning with the day on which the determination or decision appealed against was made.

(3)   On receipt of such application the sheriff clerk shall—

  (a)   forthwith fix a hearing which should take place no later than 14 days from the date of receipt of the application;

  (b)   intimate the application and the date of the hearing to the other parties to the proceedings.

(4)   Where leave to appeal is granted, the appeal shall be lodged in accordance with the timescales prescribed in the relevant section of the 2011 Act.

### Part X[1]

### Applications for Review of Grounds Determination

## Application

**3.62**—[2](1)   An application under section 110 of the 2011 Act for a review of a grounds determination made in terms of section 108 of the 2011 Act (determination that grounds for referral established) shall contain—

  (a)   the name and address of the applicant and his or her representative (if any);

  (b)   the name and address (if known) of the person who is the subject of the grounds determination (even if that person is no longer a child), if not the applicant;

  (c)   the name and address of the safeguarder (if any);

  (d)   the name and address of the curator ad litem (if any);

---

[1] As amended by the Act of Sederunt (Children's Hearings (Scotland) Act 2011) (Miscellaneous Amendments) 2013 (SSI 2013/172) para.3 (effective June 24, 2013).
[2] As substituted by the Act of Sederunt (Children's Hearings (Scotland) Act 2011) (Miscellaneous Amendments) 2013 (SSI 2013/172) para.3 (effective June 24, 2013).

(e)   the name and address of any person who is, or was at the time the grounds determination was made, a relevant person in relation to the child, if not the applicant;

(f)   the date and grounds determination made and the place of the sheriff court which made the grounds determination;

(g)   the grounds for the making of the application;

(h)   specification of the nature of evidence in terms of section 111(3) of the 2011 Act not considered by the sheriff who made the grounds determination;

      (i)   the explanation for the failure to lead such evidence on the original application; and

(j)   any reports, affidavits and productions upon which the applicant intends to rely.

(2)   Where the applicant does not wish to disclose the address or whereabouts of the child or any other person to persons receiving notice of the application, the applicant shall set out his or her reasons for this.

### Hearing on application

**3.63**—[1](1)   Where an application has been lodged in terms of rule 3.62, the sheriff clerk shall—

(a)   assign a diet for hearing the application;

(b)   issue a warrant to cite in Form 65 requiring the Principal Reporter to lodge answers if so advised within such time as the sheriff shall appoint.

(2)   Subject to the provisions of rule 3.4 (service on child), after the issue of the warrant to cite, the applicant shall forthwith give notice of the application by serving a copy and the warrant on the persons named in rule 3.62 and such other person as the sheriff directs.

(3)   After hearing parties and having considered the terms of section 111(3) of the 2011 Act and allowing such further procedure as the sheriff thinks fit to secure the expeditious determination of the application, the sheriff shall make an order as appropriate.

(4)   The provisions of rule 3.51 shall apply to any order made under paragraph (3).

### Hearing to consider the evidence

**3.64.**   *[Repealed by the Act of Sederunt (Children's Hearings (Scotland) Act 2011) (Miscellaneous Amendments) 2013 (SSI 2013/172) para.3 (effective June 24, 2013).]*

### Part XA[2]

---

[1] As amended by the Act of Sederunt (Children's Hearings (Scotland) Act 2011) (Miscellaneous Amendments) 2013 (SSI 2013/172) para.3 (effective June 24, 2013).

[2] As inserted by the Act of Sederunt (Children's Hearings (Scotland) Act 2011) (Miscellaneous Amendments) 2013 (SSI 2013/172) para.3 (effective June 24, 2013).

## Orders under the Children's Hearings (Scotland) Act 2011

### Interim compulsory supervision order

**3.64A**—[1](1)   Where a sheriff makes an interim compulsory supervision order under section 100, 109 or 156(3)(d) of the 2011 Act, such order shall be in Form 65A and, subject to rule 3.3, shall be intimated forthwith to the child by the Principal Reporter in Form 65B.

(2)   An application for the extension or extension and variation of an interim compulsory supervision order shall be made to the sheriff in Form 65C.

(3)   An application for the further extension or further extension and variation of an interim compulsory supervision order shall be made to the sheriff in Form 65D.

(4)   Subject to rule 3.3, an application under paragraph (2) or (3) must be intimated forthwith by the applicant to the child and each relevant person and such other persons as the sheriff determines and in such manner as the sheriff determines.

(5)   Where the sheriff grants an application under paragraph (2) or (3), the interlocutor shall state the terms of such extension or extension and variation and subject to rule 3.3, shall be intimated forthwith to the child by the Principal Reporter in Form 65B.

(6)   Subject to paragraphs (1) and (5), where the sheriff—

    (a)   makes an interim compulsory supervision order under paragraph (1); or

    (b)   grants an application under paragraph (2) or (3),

the Principal Reporter shall intimate the order forthwith to the implementation authority and to such other persons as the sheriff determines in Form 65E.

### Compulsory supervision order

**3.64B.**[2]   Where a sheriff varies or continues a compulsory supervision order, the interlocutor shall state the terms of such variation or continuation and shall be intimated forthwith by the sheriff clerk to the parties and the relevant implementation authority.

### Medical examination order

**3.64C.**[3]   Where a sheriff varies or continues a medical examination order, the interlocutor shall state the terms of such variation or continuation and shall be intimated forthwith by the sheriff clerk to the parties and the relevant local authority or establishment.

## Part XI[4]

---

[1] As inserted by the Act of Sederunt (Children's Hearings (Scotland) Act 2011) (Miscellaneous Amendments) 2013 (SSI 2013/172) para.3 (effective June 24, 2013).

[2] As inserted by the Act of Sederunt (Children's Hearings (Scotland) Act 2011) (Miscellaneous Amendments) 2013 (SSI 2013/172) para.3 (effective June 24, 2013).

[3] As inserted by the Act of Sederunt (Children's Hearings (Scotland) Act 2011) (Miscellaneous Amendments) 2013 (SSI 2013/172) para.3 (effective June 24, 2013).

[4] As inserted by the Act of Sederunt (Child Care and Maintenance Rules) Amendment (Vulnerable Witnesses (Scotland) Act 2004) 2005 (SSI 2005/190) r.2(3) (effective April 1, 2005).

## Vulnerable Witnesses (Scotland) Act 2004

### Interpretation

**3.65.**[1]   In this Part—

"the Act of 2004" means the Vulnerable Witnesses (Scotland) Act 2004;
"child witness notice" has the meaning given in section 12(2) of the Act of 2004;
"review application" means an application for review of arrangements for vulnerable witnesses pursuant to section 13 of the Act of 2004;
"vulnerable witness application" has the meaning given in section 12(6)(a) of the Act of 2004.[2]

### Extent of application of this Part

**3.66.**[3]   This Part of Chapter 3 shall apply to proceedings where an application is made to the sheriff under section 93(2)(a), 94(2)(a) or 110 of the 2011 Act or an appeal is made under Part 15 of the 2011 Act.

### Child Witness Notice

**3.67.**   A child witness notice lodged in accordance with section 12(2) of the Act of 2004 shall be in Form 75.

**3.68.**—[4](1)   The party lodging a child witness notice shall intimate a copy of the child witness notice to all other parties to the proceedings and to any safeguarder and complete a certificate of intimation.

(2)   A certificate of intimation referred to in this rule shall be in Form 76 and shall be lodged together with the child witness notice.

**3.69.**—(1)   On receipt of a child witness notice, a sheriff may—

(a)   make an order under section 12(1) of the Act of 2004 without holding a hearing;

(b)   require of any of the parties further information before making any further order;

(c)   fix a date for a hearing of the child witness notice and grant warrant to cite witnesses and havers.

(2)   The sheriff may, subject to any statutory time limits, make an order altering the date of the proof or other hearing at which the child is to give evidence and make such provision for intimation of such alteration to all parties concerned as he deems appropriate.

(3)   An order fixing a hearing for a child witness notice shall be intimated by the sheriff clerk—

(a)   on the day the order is made; and

(b)   in such manner as may be prescribed by the sheriff,

---

[1] As amended by the Act of Sederunt (Children's Hearings (Scotland) Act 2011) (Miscellaneous Amendments) 2013 (SSI 2013/172) para.3 (effective June 24, 2013).
[2] As inserted by the Act of Sederunt (Child Care and Maintenance Rules) Amendment (Vulnerable Witnesses (Scotland) Act 2004) 2006 (SSI 2006/75) r.2(2) (effective April 1, 2006).
[3] As amended by the Act of Sederunt (Children's Hearings (Scotland) Act 2011) (Miscellaneous Amendments) 2013 (SSI 2013/172) para.3 (effective June 24, 2013).
[4] As amended by the Act of Sederunt (Children's Hearings (Scotland) Act 2011) (Miscellaneous Amendments) 2013 (SSI 2013/172) para.3 (effective June 24, 2013).

to all parties to the proceedings and such other persons as are named in the order where such parties or persons are not present at the time the order is made.

**3.69A.**[1]   A vulnerable witness application made in accordance with section 12(6)(a) of the Act of 2004 shall be in Form 76A.

**3.69B.**—[2,3](1)   The party making a vulnerable witness application shall intimate a copy of the vulnerable witness application to all other parties to the proceedings and to any safeguarder and complete a certificate of intimation.

(2)   A certificate of intimation referred to in this rule shall be in Form 76B and shall be lodged together with the vulnerable witness application.

**3.69C.**—[4](1)   On receipt of a vulnerable witness application a sheriff may—

- (a)   make an order under section 12(6) of the Act of 2004 without holding a hearing;
- (b)   require of any of the parties further information before making any further order; or
- (c)   fix a date for a hearing of the vulnerable witness application and grant warrant to cite witnesses and havers.

(2)   The sheriff may, subject to any statutory time limits, make an order altering the date of the proof or other hearing at which the vulnerable witness is to give evidence and make such provision for intimation of such alteration to all parties concerned as he deems appropriate.

(3)   An order fixing a hearing for a vulnerable witness application shall be intimated by the sheriff clerk—

- (a)   on the day the order is made; and
- (b)   in such manner as may be prescribed by the sheriff,

to all parties to the proceedings and such other persons as are named in the order where such parties or persons are not present at the time the order is made.

### Review of arrangements for vulnerable witnesses

**3.70.**—(1)   A review application shall be in Form 77.

(2)   Where the review application is made during the sheriff's hearing of the case, the sheriff may dispense with the requirements of paragraph (1).

**3.71.**—[5](1)   Where a review application is in Form 77, the applicant shall intimate a copy of the review application to all other parties to the proceedings and to any safeguarder and complete a certificate of intimation.

(2)   A certificate of intimation referred to in this rule shall be in Form 78 and shall be lodged together with the review application.

**3.72.**—(1)   On receipt of a review application, a sheriff may—

- (a)   if he is satisfied that he may properly do so, make an order under sec-

---

[1] As inserted by the Act of Sederunt (Child Care and Maintenance Rules) Amendment (Vulnerable Witnesses (Scotland) Act 2004) 2006 (SSI 2006/75) r.2(3) (effective April 1, 2006).

[2] As inserted by the Act of Sederunt (Child Care and Maintenance Rules) Amendment (Vulnerable Witnesses (Scotland) Act 2004) 2006 (SSI 2006/75) r.2(3) (effective April 1, 2006).

[3] As amended by the Act of Sederunt (Children's Hearings (Scotland) Act 2011) (Miscellaneous Amendments) 2013 (SSI 2013/172) para.3 (effective June 24, 2013).

[4] As inserted by the Act of Sederunt (Child Care and Maintenance Rules) Amendment (Vulnerable Witnesses (Scotland) Act 2004) 2006 (SSI 2006/75) r.2(3) (effective April 1, 2006).

[5] As amended by the Act of Sederunt (Children's Hearings (Scotland) Act 2011) (Miscellaneous Amendments) 2013 (SSI 2013/172) para.3 (effective June 24, 2013).

tion 13(2) of the Act of 2004 without holding a hearing or, if he is not so satisfied, make such an order after giving the parties an opportunity to be heard;

    (b)   require of any of the parties further information before making any further order;

    (c)   fix a date for a hearing of the review application and grant warrant to cite witnesses and havers.

(2)[1]   The sheriff may, subject to any statutory time limits, make an order altering the date of the proof or other hearing at which the witness is to give evidence and make such provision for intimation of such alteration to all parties concerned as he deems appropriate.

(3)   An order fixing a hearing for a review application shall be intimated by the sheriff clerk—

    (a)   on the day the order is made; and

    (b)   in such manner as may be prescribed by the sheriff,

to all parties to the proceedings and such other persons as are named in the order where such parties or persons are not present at the time the order is made.

### Determination of special measures

**3.73.**[2]   When making an order under section 12(1), 12(6) or 13(2) of the Act of 2004 a sheriff may, in light thereof, make such further orders as he deems appropriate in all the circumstances.

### Intimation of an order under section 12(1), 12(6) or 13(2)

**3.74.**[3]   An order under section 12(1), 12(6) or 13(2) of the Act of 2004 shall be intimated by the sheriff clerk—

    (a)   on the day the order is made; and

    (b)   in such manner as may be prescribed by the sheriff,

to all parties to the proceedings and such other persons as are named in the order where such parties or persons are not present at the time the order is made.

### Lodging audio and audio-visual recordings and documents[4]

**3.75.**—[5](1)[6]   Where evidence is taken on commission pursuant to an order made under section 12(1), 12(6) or 13(2) of the Act of 2004 the commissioner shall lodge any audio or audio-visual recording of the commission and relevant documents with the sheriff clerk.

(2)   On any audio or audio-visual recording and any documents being lodged the sheriff clerk shall—

---

[1] As substituted by the Act of Sederunt (Child Care and Maintenance Rules) Amendment (Vulnerable Witnesses (Scotland) Act 2004) 2006 (SSI 2006/75) r.2(4) (effective April 1, 2006).

[2] As amended by the Act of Sederunt (Child Care and Maintenance Rules) Amendment (Vulnerable Witnesses (Scotland) Act 2004) 2006 (SSI 2006/75) r.2(5) (effective April 1, 2006).

[3] As amended by the Act of Sederunt (Child Care and Maintenance Rules) Amendment (Vulnerable Witnesses (Scotland) Act 2004) 2006 (SSI 2006/75) r.2(5) (effective April 1, 2006).

[4] As amended by the Act of Sederunt (Children's Hearings (Scotland) Act 2011) (Miscellaneous Amendments) 2013 (SSI 2013/172) para.3 (effective June 24, 2013).

[5] As amended by the Act of Sederunt (Children's Hearings (Scotland) Act 2011) (Miscellaneous Amendments) 2013 (SSI 2013/172) para.3 (effective June 24, 2013).

[6] As amended by the Act of Sederunt (Child Care and Maintenance Rules) Amendment (Vulnerable Witnesses (Scotland) Act 2004) 2006 (SSI 2006/75) r.2(5) (effective April 1, 2006).

    (a)  note—
        (i)  the documents lodged;
        (ii)  by whom they were lodged; and
        (iii)  the date on which they were lodged, and
    (b)  intimate what he has noted to all parties concerned.

### Custody of audio or audio-visual recordings and documents[1]

**3.76.**—[2](1)  The audio or audio-visual recording and documents referred to in rule 3.75 shall, subject to paragraph (2), be kept in the custody of the sheriff clerk.

(2)  Where the audio or audio-visual recording of the evidence of a witness is in the custody of the sheriff clerk under this rule and where intimation has been given to that effect under rule 3.75(2), the name and address of that witness and the record of his evidence shall be treated as being in the knowledge of the parties; and no party shall be required, notwithstanding any enactment to the contrary—

    (a)  to include the name of that witness in any list of witnesses; or
    (b)  to include the record of his evidence in any list of productions.

### Part XIA[3]

### Cases Involving Sexual Behaviour

### Interpretation and application of this Part

**3.76A**—[4](1)  This Part of Chapter 3 applies to proceedings where—

    (a)  an application is made to the sheriff under section 93(2)(a), 94(2)(a) or 110 of the 2011 Act or an appeal is made under Part 15 of the 2011 Act; and
    (b)  the section 67 ground involves sexual behaviour engaged in by any person.

(2)  In the case of relevant appeals the provisions of sections 173 to 175 of the 2011 Act shall be deemed to apply as they apply to applications.

(3)  The evidence referred to in section 173(2) of the 2011 Act may be in writing or take the form of an audio or audio-visual recording.

(4)  In this Part an "admission application" means an application to the sheriff for an order as to evidence pursuant to section 175(1) of the 2011 Act.

### Application for admission of restricted evidence

**3.77.**—(1)  An admission application shall be in Form 79.

(2)  Where an admission application is made during the sheriff's hearing of the case, the sheriff may dispense with the requirements of paragraph (1).

---

[1] As amended by the Act of Sederunt (Children's Hearings (Scotland) Act 2011) (Miscellaneous Amendments) 2013 (SSI 2013/172) para.3 (effective June 24, 2013).
[2] As amended by the Act of Sederunt (Children's Hearings (Scotland) Act 2011) (Miscellaneous Amendments) 2013 (SSI 2013/172) para.3 (effective June 24, 2013).
[3] As inserted by the Act of Sederunt (Children's Hearings (Scotland) Act 2011) (Miscellaneous Amendments) 2013 (SSI 2013/172) para.3 (effective June 24, 2013).
[4] As inserted by the Act of Sederunt (Children's Hearings (Scotland) Act 2011) (Miscellaneous Amendments) 2013 (SSI 2013/172) para.3 (effective June 24, 2013).

**3.78.**—[1](1)   Where an admission application is made under rule 3.77, the applicant shall intimate a copy of the admission application to all other parties to the proceedings and to any safeguarder and complete a certificate of intimation.

(2)   A certificate of intimation referred to in this rule shall be in Form 80 and shall be lodged together with the admission application.

**3.79.**—[2](1)   On receipt of an admission application, a sheriff may—

    (a)   grant the admission application in whole or in part;

    (b)   require of any of the parties further information before making any further order;

    (c)   fix a date for a hearing of the admission application and grant warrant to cite witnesses and havers.

(2)   The sheriff may, subject to any statutory time limits, make an order altering the date of the proof or other hearing to which the admission application relates and make such provision for intimation of such alteration to all parties concerned as he deems appropriate.

(3)   An order fixing a hearing for an admission application shall be intimated by the sheriff clerk—

    (a)   on the day the order is made; and

    (b)   in such manner as may be prescribed by the sheriff,

to all parties to the proceedings and such other persons as are named in the order where such parties or persons are not present at the time the order is made.

**3.80.**—(1)   When making an order pursuant to rule 3.79(1)(a) a sheriff may, in light thereof, make such further orders as he deems appropriate in all the circumstances.

**3.81.**—(1)   An order made pursuant to rule 3.79(1)(a) shall be intimated by the sheriff clerk—

    (a)   on the day the order is made; and

    (b)   in such manner as may be prescribed by the sheriff,

to all parties to the proceedings and such other persons as are named in the order where such parties or persons are not present at the time the order is made.

## Lodging restricted evidence

**3.81A.**—[3](1)   Where the sheriff makes an order under section 175(1) or (c) of the 2011 Act, the applicant shall lodge any relevant recording and documents with the sheriff clerk.

(2)   On the recording and documents being lodged the sheriff clerk shall—

    (a)   note—

        (i)   the evidence lodged;

        (ii)   by whom they were lodged;

        (iii)   the date on which they were lodged; and

    (b)   intimate what he or she has noted to all parties concerned.

(3)   The recording and documents referred to in paragraph (1) shall, subject to paragraph (4), be kept in the custody of the sheriff clerk.

---

[1] As amended by the Act of Sederunt (Children's Hearings (Scotland) Act 2011) (Miscellaneous Amendments) 2013 (SSI 2013/172) para.3 (effective June 24, 2013).

[2] As inserted by the Act of Sederunt (Children's Hearings (Scotland) Act 2011) (Miscellaneous Amendments) 2013 (SSI 2013/172) para.3 (effective June 24, 2013).

[3] As inserted by the Act of Sederunt (Children's Hearings (Scotland) Act 2011) (Miscellaneous Amendments) 2013 (SSI 2013/172) para.3 (effective June 24, 2013).

(4)    Where the recording of the evidence of a witness is in the custody of the sheriff clerk under this rule and where intimation has been given to that effect under paragraph (2), the name and address of that witness and the record of his or her evidence shall be treated as being in the knowledge of the parties; and no party shall be required, notwithstanding any enactment to the contrary—

    (a)    to include the name of that witness in any list of witnesses; or

    (b)    to include the record of his or her evidence in any list of productions.

## CHAPTER 4

K2.26

### REGISTRATION OF CHILD CUSTODY ORDERS

**Interpretation**

**4.1.**    In this Chapter, unless the context otherwise requires—

"the Act" means the Family Law Act 1986;

"appropriate court" means the High Court in England and Wales or the High Court in Northern Ireland or, in relation to a specified dependent territory, the corresponding court of that territory, as the case may be;

"appropriate register" means the sheriff court book in which there is registered the action in which the Part I order was made;

"corresponding court", in relation to a specified dependent territory, means the corresponding court specified in relation to that territory in Schedule 3 to the Family Law Act 1986 (Dependent Territories) Order 1991;

"Part I order" has the meaning assigned to it by sections 1, 32 42(5) and 42(6) of the Act;

"proper officer" means the Secretary of the Principal Registry of the Family Division of the High Court in England and Wales or the Master (Care and Protection) of the High Court in Northern Ireland or, in relation to a specified dependent territory, the corresponding officer of the appropriate court in that territory, as the case may be; and

"specified dependent territory" means a territory specified in column 1 of Schedule 1 to the Family Law Act 1986 (Dependent Territories) Order 1991.

**Applications for registration of Part I order in another court**

**4.2**—(1)    An application under section 27 of the Act (registration) to register a Part I order made by a sheriff court in an appropriate court shall be made by letter to the sheriff clerk of the court in which the order was made.

(2)    An application under paragraph (1) of this rule shall be accompanied by—

    (a)    a copy of the letter of application;

    (b)    an affidavit by the applicant;

    (c)    a copy of that affidavit;

    (d)    a certified copy of the interlocutor making the Part I order and any variation thereto which is still in force; and

    (e)    any other document relevant to the application together with a copy of it.

(3)    The affidavit required under this rule shall set out—

    (a)    the name and address of the applicant and his right under the Part I order;

    (b)    the name and date of birth of the child in respect of whom the Part I order was made, the present whereabouts or suspected whereabouts of the child and the name of any person with whom he is alleged to be;

(c) the name and address of any other person who has an interest in the Part I order;

(d) the appropriate court in which it is sought to register the Part I order;

(e) whether the Part I order is in force;

(f) whether the Part I order is already registered and, if so, where it is registered; and

(g) details of any order known to the applicant which affects the child and is in force in the jurisdiction in which the Part I order is to be registered.

### Transmission of application for registration

**4.3**—(1) Unless it appears to the court that the Part I order is no longer in force, the sheriff clerk shall send the documents mentioned in section 27(3) of the Act to the proper officer of the court in which the Part I order is to be registered.

(2) For the purposes of section 27(3) of the Act the prescribed particulars of any variation of a Part I order which is in force shall be a certified copy of the interlocutor making any such variation.

(3) On sending an application under paragraph (1) of this rule, the sheriff clerk shall record the date and particulars of the application and the Part I order in the appropriate register.

(4) On receiving notification from the appropriate court that the Part I order has been registered in that court under section 27(4) of the Act, the sheriff clerk shall record the date of registration in the appropriate register.

### Notification of refusal of application

**4.4** Where the court refuses to send an application under rule 4.2 to the appropriate court on the ground that the Part I order is no longer in force, the sheriff clerk shall notify the applicant in writing of the court's decision.

### Retention of application and related documents

**4.5** The sheriff clerk shall retain the letter of application under rule 4.2 together with any documents which accompanied it and which are not transmitted to the appropriate court under section 27(3) of the Act.

### Cancellation or variation of registered Part I order

**4.6**—(1) Where the court revokes, recalls or varies a Part I order which it has made and which has been registered under section 27(4) of the Act, the sheriff clerk shall—

(a) send a certified copy of the appropriate interlocutor to the proper officer of the court in which the Part I order is registered;

(b) record the transmission of the certified copy in the appropriate register; and

(c) record the revocation, recall or variation in the appropriate register.

(2)   On receiving notification from the court in which the Part I order is registered that the revocation, recall or variation has been recorded, the sheriff clerk shall record that fact in the appropriate register.

CHAPTER 5

MAINTENANCE ORDERS

Part I

General

**K2.27**

### Interpretation

**5.1.**[1, 2]   In this Chapter, unless the context otherwise requires—

"the 1950 Act" means the Maintenance Orders Act 1950;

"the 1958 Act" means the Maintenance Orders Act 1958;

"the 1972 Act" means the Maintenance Orders (Reciprocal Enforcement) Act 1972;

"the 1982 Act" means the Civil Jurisdiction and Judgments Act 1982;

"2011 Regulations" means the Civil Jurisdiction and Judgments (Maintenance) Regulations 2011;

"clerk of court" means the clerk to the magistrates' court in England or Northern Ireland and, in relation to a county court in England or Northern Ireland, means the registrar of that court;

"clerk of the magistrates' court" means the clerk to the magistrates' court in England or Northern Ireland as the case may be;

"Court in a Hague Convention Country" includes any judicial or administrative authority in a Hague Convention Country;

"Maintenance Decision" has the meaning given to "decision" by Article 2(1) of the Maintenance Regulation;

"Maintenance Regulation" means Council Regulation (EC) No 4/2009of 18th December 2008 including as applied in relation to Denmark by virtue of the Agreement made on 19th October 2005 between the European Community and the Kingdom of Denmark;

"Maintenance Regulation State" in the application of any provision in relation to the Maintenance Regulation, refers to any of the Member States;

"order" includes decree;

"reciprocating country" has the meaning assigned to it by section 1 of the 1972 Act;

"the Registrar", in relation to the High Court in England, means the Senior Registrar of the principal Registry of the Family Division of the High Court in England; and

### Application

**5.2**—(1)   Part II of this Chapter shall have effect in relation to the registration in other parts of the United Kingdom of orders granted by the sheriff to which the 1950

---

[1] As amended by the Act of Sederunt (Child Care and Maintenance Rules) Amendment 2009 (SSI 2009/29) r.2(2) (effective March 2, 2009).

[2] As amended by the Act of Sederunt (Sheriff Court Rules) (Miscellaneous Amendments) (No.3) 2011 (SSI 2011/386) para.9 (effective November 28, 2011).

and 1958 Acts apply and such orders are referred to in this Chapter as "outgoing orders under the 1950 Act".

(2)    Part III of this Chapter shall have effect in relation to the registration outwith the United Kingdom of orders to which the 1972 Act, or the 1972 Act as amended by any Order in Council made under Part III of the 1972 Act, applies and such orders are referred to as "outgoing orders under the 1972 Act".

(3)    Part IV of this Chapter shall have effect in relation to the registration in the sheriff court of orders made by courts in other parts of the United Kingdom to which the 1950 Act applies and such orders are referred to in this Chapter as "incoming orders under the 1950 Act".

(4)    Part V of this Chapter shall have effect in relation to the registration in the sheriff court of orders made by courts outwith the United Kingdom to which the 1972 Act, or the 1972 Act as amended by any Order in Council made under Part III of the 1972 Act, applies and such orders are referred to in this Chapter as "incoming orders under the 1972 Act".

(5)    Part VI of this Chapter shall have effect in relation to the registration in the sheriff court of orders made by courts outwith the United Kingdom to which the 1982 Act applies and such orders are referred to in this Chapter as "incoming orders under the 1982 Act".

(6)[1]    Part VII of this Chapter shall have effect in relation to a Maintenance Decision.

(7)[2]    Part VIII of this Chapter shall have effect only in relation to—

    (a)    a Maintenance Decision made by a court in Denmark; and

    (b)    a Maintenance Decision to which sections 2 and 3 of Chapter IV of the Maintenance Regulation apply by virtue of Article 75(2)(a) or (b) of that Regulation.

**Prescribed officer**

    **5.3**—(1)    The sheriff clerk shall be—

    (a)[3]    the prescribed officer for the purposes of the 1950, 1958 and 1972 Acts, the 1972 Act as amended by any Order in Council, the 1982 Act and the 2011 Regulations; and

    (b)    the proper officer for the purposes of Schedules 6 and 7 to the 1982 Act (enforcement of UK judgments).

(2)    Unless otherwise provided, all communications which the prescribed officer is required to send to—

    (a)    an addressee in the United Kingdom shall be sent by first class recorded delivery post; and

    (b)    an addressee outwith the United Kingdom shall be sent by registered letter or the nearest equivalent which the available postal service permits.

---

[1] As inserted by the Act of Sederunt (Sheriff Court Rules) (Miscellaneous Amendments) (No.3) 2011 (SSI 2011/386) para.9 (effective November 28, 2011).

[2] As inserted by the Act of Sederunt (Sheriff Court Rules) (Miscellaneous Amendments) (No.3) 2011 (SSI 2011/386) para.9 (effective November 28, 2011).

[3] As amended by the Act of Sederunt (Sheriff Court Rules) (Miscellaneous Amendments) (No.3) 2011 (SSI 2011/386) para.9 (effective November 28, 2011).

## Maintenance Orders Register

**5.4**—[1](1)   The sheriff clerk shall maintain a Register called "the Maintenance Orders Register" for the purpose of the 1950, 1958 and 1972 Acts, the 1972 Act as amended by any Order in Council, the 1982 Act and the Maintenance Regulation, Part I of which shall relate to outgoing orders and Part II to incoming orders.

(2)   The sheriff clerk shall make appropriate entries in the Maintenance Orders Register in respect of any action taken by him or notified to him in accordance with the relevant provisions, and shall keep in such manner as he considers appropriate any documents sent to him in connection with any such action.

(3)   Every entry registering a maintenance order shall specify the relevant provision including where appropriate any Order in Council under which the maintenance order in question is registered.

(4)   When a registered maintenance order is varied, revoked or cancelled, the sheriff clerk shall make an appropriate entry against the entry for the original order.

## Inspection

**5.5**—(1)   The sheriff clerk shall, on an application by—

(a)   any person entitled to, or liable to make, payments under an order in respect of which any entry has been made in the Maintenance Orders Register; or

(b)   a solicitor acting on behalf of any such person,

permit that person or his solicitor, as the case may be, to inspect any such entry and any document in his possession relating to that entry and to take copies of any such entry or document.

(2)   On an application by or on behalf of any other person, the sheriff clerk may, on being satisfied of that person's interest, grant that person or his solicitor permission to inspect or take copies of any such entry or document.

## Part II

## Outgoing Orders under the 1950 Act

## Commencement of proceedings

**5.6**—(1)   Every writ by which proceedings are begun in a sheriff court having jurisdiction under or by virtue of Part I of the 1950 Act against a person residing in another part of the United Kingdom, and all parts of process (other than productions) lodged in any proceedings taken in a sheriff court under or by virtue of the 1950 Act or the 1958 Act, shall be headed "Maintenance Orders Act 1950" or as the case may be "Maintenance Orders Act 1958".

(2)   The warrant of citation upon any writ which by virtue of those Acts is to be served upon a person residing in another part of the United Kingdom shall proceed upon a period of notice of 21 days, and such warrant of citation may be signed by the sheriff clerk.

(3)   In connection with the service under section 15 of the 1950 Act (service of process) of a writ from a sheriff court the expressions "initial writ", "writ" and "summons" in the said section and in the forms contained in the Second Schedule to that Act shall include the warrant of citation relative thereto.

---

[1] As amended by the Act of Sederunt (Sheriff Court Rules) (Miscellaneous Amendments) (No.3) 2011 (SSI 2011/386) para.9 (effective November 28, 2011).

## Application for registration

**5.7**—(1)   An application for registration in a magistrates' court in England or Northern Ireland of an order granted by a sheriff court to which the 1950 Act applies shall be made by lodging with the sheriff clerk—

    (a)   a letter of application;

    (b)   an affidavit by the applicant;

    (c)   a copy of that affidavit; and

    (d)   a certified copy of the order.

  (2)   An affidavit under this rule shall include—

    (a)   the name and address of the person liable to make payments under the order;

    (b)   details of any arrears due under the order and the date to which they are calculated;

    (c)   the reason for the application; and

    (d)   a statement that the order is not already registered under the 1950 Act.

## Transmission

**5.8**   On the grant of an application under rule 5.7, the sheriff clerk shall send to the clerk of the magistrates' court—

    (a)   the affidavit of the applicant;

    (b)   the certified copy of the order; and

    (c)   a letter requesting registration of the order.

## Application to adduce evidence

**5.9**—(1)   An application to a sheriff court under section 22(5) of the 1950 Act to adduce evidence in connection with an order granted by that court and registered in a court in England or Northern Ireland shall be made by initial writ.

  (2)   Any evidence adduced in pursuance of such an application shall be recorded in such manner as the sheriff shall direct and the record of evidence certified by the sheriff shall be the transcript or summary of the evidence adduced, and shall be signed by the deponent, together with any documentary productions referred to therein.

  (3)   Where the sheriff clerk of a court in which an order was granted receives a transcript or summary of evidence connected with that order adduced, under section 22(5) of the 1950 Act, in the court where the order was registered, he shall lodge such transcript or summary in the process containing that order.

## Re-registration in the High Court

**5.10**—(1)   When an order has been registered in the magistrates' court, an application to the sheriff court for the re-registration of that order in the High Court in England under the 1958 Act shall be made by lodging with the sheriff clerk—

    (a)   a letter of application;

    (b)   an affidavit by the applicant;

    (c)   a certified copy of that affidavit; and

    (d)   a certified copy of the order.

  (2)   An affidavit under this rule shall include—

    (a)   the name and address of the person liable to make payments under the order;

(b) details of any arrears due under the order and the date to which they are calculated;

(c) the reason for the application;

(d) the date and place of the original registration;

(e) where the order has been re-registered, the date and place of the last re-registration and whether or not that has been cancelled, or where any of these facts is not known a statement to that effect; and

(f) a declaration that no process remains in force for the enforcement of the registered order

### Transmission for re-registration

**5.11**  If an application under rule 5.10 is granted, the sheriff clerk shall send to the Registrar—

(a) the affidavit of the applicant; and

(b) a letter stating that the application has been granted and requesting him to take steps to have the order registered in the High Court.

### Discharge and variation

**5.12**  Where an interlocutor is pronounced in the sheriff court varying or discharging an order registered under the 1950 Act or the 1958 Act, the sheriff clerk shall send to the clerk of the magistrates' court and, as the case may be, to the Registrar—

(a) a certified copy of the interlocutor; and

(b) a letter requesting the clerk of the magistrates' court and, as the case may be, the Registrar to take the appropriate action under those Acts, in accordance with the interlocutor, and to notify him of the result.

### Cancellation of registration

**5.13**—(1)  An application under section 24(2) of the 1950 Act (cancellation of registration) in connection with an order granted by a sheriff court and registered in a court in England or Northern Ireland shall be made by lodging with the sheriff clerk an affidavit by the person liable to make payments under the order stating the facts on which the application is founded.

(2)  Where it appears to the sheriff clerk that the applicant has ceased to reside in England or Northern Ireland, as the case may be, the sheriff clerk shall send notice to that effect to the clerk of the magistrates' court and the Registrar, as the case may be, of any court in which the order is registered.

### Part III

### Outgoing Orders under the 1972 Act

### Application for transmission of order for enforcement in a reciprocating country

**5.14**—(1)  An application for the transmission of a maintenance order for enforcement in a reciprocating country shall be made by letter addressed to the sheriff clerk.

(2)  There shall be lodged with any such application—

(a) a certified copy of the relevant order;

   (b)   a statement signed by the applicant or his solicitor of any arrears outstanding in respect of the order;

   (c)   a statement signed by the applicant or his solicitor giving such information as to the whereabouts of the payer as he possesses;

   (d)   a statement signed by the applicant or his solicitor giving such information as the applicant possesses for facilitating the identification of the payer;

   (e)   where available, a photograph of the payer.

### Application for transmission of order for enforcement in the Republic of Ireland

**5.15—** *[Repealed by the Act of Sederunt (Sheriff Court Rules) (Miscellaneous Amendments) (No.3) 2011 (SSI 2011/386) para.9 (effective November 28, 2011).]*

### Application for transmission of order to Hague Convention Country

**5.16—**(1)   An application for the transmission of a maintenance order to a Court in a Hague Convention Country for registration and enforcement shall be made by letter addressed to the sheriff clerk.

   (2)   There shall be lodged with any such application—

   (a)   a certified copy of the relevant order;

   (b)   a statement signed by the applicant or his solicitor of any arrears outstanding in respect of that order;

   (c)   a statement signed by the applicant or his solicitor giving such information as to the whereabouts of the payer as he possesses;

   (d)   a statement signed by the applicant or his solicitor giving such information as the applicant possesses for facilitating the identification of the payer;

   (e)   where available, a photograph of the payer;

   (f)   a statement signed by the applicant or his solicitor which establishes that notice of the order was sent to the payer;

   (g)   if the payee received legal aid in the proceedings, a statement to that effect; and

   (h)   if the payer did not appear in the proceedings in which the maintenance order was made, the original or a certified true copy of a document which establishes that notice of the institution of the proceedings was served on the payer.

### Application for transmission of order for enforcement in the USA[1]

**5.16A.—**(1)   An application for the transmission of a maintenance order to the United States of America for enforcement shall be made by letter addressed to the sheriff clerk.

   (2)   There shall be lodged with any such application—

   (a)   three certified copies of the maintenance order;

   (b)   a certificate of arrears signed by the applicant or his solicitor;

   (c)   a sworn statement signed by the payee—

       (i)   giving the address of the payee;

---

[1] As inserted by the Act of Sederunt (Child Care and Maintenance Rules) Amendment 2000 (SSI 2000/388) (effective November 20, 2000) and amended by the Act of Sederunt (Child Care and Maintenance Rules) Amendment 2009 (SSI 2009/29) r.2(3) and (4) (effective March 2, 2009).

(ii) giving such information as is known as to the whereabouts of the payer; and

(iii) giving a description, so far as is known, of the nature and location of any assets of the payer available for execution; and

(d) a statement signed by the applicant giving such information as the applicant possesses for facilitating the identification of the payer including a photograph if available.

### Service on defender in Hague Convention Country

**5.17** For the purposes of section 4(4) of the 1972 Act as applied in respect of a defender in a Hague Convention Country, service on such a defender shall be effected in accordance with the Ordinary Cause Rules.

### Service of notice of proceedings on payer residing in USA

**5.17A.**[1] Where service of a document is executed in accordance with section 5(4)(a) of the 1972 Act as applied to the United States of America, the Scottish Ministers shall obtain and lodge with the sheriff clerk a certificate by a person who is conversant with the law of the United States of America and who practises or who has practised law in that country or is a duly accredited representative of the Government of the United States of America, stating that the method of service employed is in accordance with the law of the place where service was executed.

### Provisional order made with a view to transmission to a reciprocating country

**5.18** A certificate signed by the sheriff clerk in terms of section 3(5)(c) of the 1972 Act (certificate of grounds), as read with section 4(6) thereof, shall also be signed by the sheriff.

### Evidence adduced prior to confirmation of provisional order

**5.19**—(1) Where under section 5(9) of the 1972 Act it appears to the sheriff that a provisional order ought not to have been made, the sheriff clerk shall send by first class recorded delivery a notice in Form 66 to the person on whose application the order was made.

(2) Where such a person wishes to make representations, he shall lodge with the sheriff clerk within 21 days of the date of posting of the notice a minute narrating the representations and the further evidence which he intends to adduce.

(3) On the expiry of the period of 21 days, the cause shall be enrolled before the sheriff who shall appoint a diet for the hearing of further evidence or make such other order as may be appropriate.

### Provisions in relation to intimation and entering appearance

**5.20**—(1) Where the 1972 Act provides that on intimation to a payee of the receipt by the court of a provisional order the payee is to enter appearance within a prescribed period, intimation shall be given in Form 67 and the period shall be—

(a) 21 days from the date of posting where the payee is resident in Europe; and

---

[1] As inserted by the Act of Sederunt (Child Care and Maintenance Rules) Amendment 2009 (SSI 2009/29) r.2(5) (effective March 2, 2009).

(b)   42 days from the date of posting where the payee is resident outside Europe.

(2)   To enter appearance in terms of section 5(6) of the 1972 Act, the payee shall lodge an application—

    (a)   stating that he opposes confirmation of the order; and

    (b)   setting forth averments in answer to the case upon which the provisional order was made, supported by the appropriate pleas-in-law.

(3)   Where the payee enters appearance in terms of section 5(6) of the 1972 Act, the sheriff shall appoint a diet for the hearing of evidence or make such other order as may be appropriate to enable the court to proceed in accordance with the procedure and practice in ordinary civil proceedings in the sheriff court as if the application for the variation or revocation of the maintenance order had been made to it.

**Authentication of documents**

**5.21**   Where the 1972 Act provides that a document is to be authenticated in a prescribed manner, it shall be authenticated by a certificate signed by the sheriff clerk declaring that the document is authentic.

**Application under section 4 or 5 of the 1972 Act**

**5.22**[1]   An application for a provisional order under section 4 of the 1972 Act or an application under section 5 of that Act for variation or revocation of a maintenance order shall proceed as an ordinary cause in accordance with the terms of Chapter 33 (family actions) or 33A (civil partnership actions), as the case may be, of the Ordinary Cause Rules.

**Representations or evidence by payer residing in the USA**

**5.22A.**—[2](1)   Where notices are provided in accordance with section 5(4) of the 1972 Act as applied to the United States of America, the sheriff clerk shall notify the recipients of the notices that if the payer wishes the court in Scotland to take into account any representations made by him or any evidence adduced by him or on his behalf, then such representations or evidence must be lodged with the sheriff clerk not later than 21 days before the date fixed for the hearing.

(2)   Where such representations are lodged, or such evidence is lodged, the sheriff clerk shall serve a copy of the representations or evidence—

    (a)   where the payee is represented by a solicitor, on that solicitor, by—

        (i)   personal delivery;

        (ii)   facsimile transmission;

        (iii)   first class ordinary post; or

        (iv)   delivery to a document exchange; and

    (b)   where the payee is not represented by a solicitor, on the payee, by any of the methods of service provided for in Chapter 5 of the Ordinary Cause Rules (citation, service and intimation).

---

[1] As amended by the Act of Sederunt (Child Care and Maintenance Rules) Amendment 2009 (SSI 2009/29) r.2(6) (effective March 2, 2009).

[2] As inserted by the Act of Sederunt (Child Care and Maintenance Rules) Amendment 2009 (SSI 2009/29) r.2(7) (effective March 2, 2009).

### Application by payer residing in the USA for variation or revocation of order

**5.22B.**—[1](1)   Where an application is made in accordance with section 5(6) of the 1972 Act as applied to the United States of America, the sheriff clerk shall give notice of institution of the proceedings, including notice of the substance of the application, in accordance with subparagraph (2) or (3).

(2)   Where the payee is represented by a solicitor, the document referred to in subparagraph (1) shall be served on that solicitor by—

    (a)   personal delivery;

    (b)   facsimile transmission;

    (c)   first class ordinary post; or

    (d)   delivery to a document exchange.

(3)   Where the payee is not represented by a solicitor, the document referred to in subparagraph (1) shall be served on the payee by any of the methods of service provided for in Chapter 5 of the Ordinary Cause Rules (citation, service and intimation).

### Evidence

**5.23**—(1)[2]   Where any request to take evidence is made by or on behalf of a court in terms of section 14 of the 1972 Act, or section 14 of the 1972 Act as amended by any Order in Council made under Part III of that Act, or by the Secretary of State in terms of section 38 thereof, such evidence shall be taken before a sheriff of the sheriffdom in which the witness resides and shall be—

    (a)   recorded by tape recording or other mechanical means approved by the court; or

    (b)   taken down by a shorthand writer, or where the sheriff so directs, by the sheriff,

and the extended notes of evidence certified by the sheriff shall be the notes of the evidence taken.

(2)   Where a provisional order is made under section 4 or 5 of the 1972 Act and evidence has been taken by a shorthand writer, the applicant or his solicitor shall provide the sheriff clerk with a copy of the extended notes of evidence.

### Taking of evidence at request of a court in the USA

**5.23A.**[3]   Where evidence is taken by a sheriff under section 14(1) of the 1972 Act as applied to the United States of America, rules 29.7 (citation of witnesses), 29.9 (second diligence against a witness) and 29.10 (failure of witness to attend) of the Ordinary Cause Rules shall apply in respect of the matters set out in those rules.

### Requests for the taking of evidence by a court in the USA

**5.23B.**[4]   An application made to a sheriff for the purposes of section 14(5) of the 1972 Act as applied to the United States of America shall follow as nearly as may

---

[1] As inserted by the Act of Sederunt (Child Care and Maintenance Rules) Amendment 2009 (SSI 2009/29) r.2(7) (effective March 2, 2009).

[2] As substituted by the Act of Sederunt (Child Care and Maintenance Rules) Amendment 2009 (SSI 2009/29) r.2(8) (effective March 2, 2009).

[3] As inserted by the Act of Sederunt (Child Care and Maintenance Rules) Amendment 2009 (SSI 2009/29) r.2(9) (effective March 2, 2009).

[4] As inserted by the Act of Sederunt (Child Care and Maintenance Rules) Amendment 2009 (SSI 2009/29) r.2(9) (effective March 2, 2009).

be the procedure set out in rule 28.14 of the Ordinary Cause Rules (letters of request), subject to any modifications necessitated by that provision of the 1972 Act as so applied.

## Communication with courts in the USA

**5.23C.**[1]   In so far as applicable to outgoing orders under the 1972 Act to the United States of America, for the purposes of the provisions in Part I of the 1972 Act, the sheriff may communicate with a court or courts in the United States of America in such circumstances and in such manner as he thinks fit.

## Disapplication of provisions where payer resides or has assets in the USA

**5.23D.**[2]   In any case in which the payer under a maintenance order made by a court in Scotland is residing or has assets in the United States of America, none of the provisions in this Part shall apply except this rule and rules 5.16A, 5.17A, 5.21, 5.22, 5.22A, 5.22B, 5.23, 5.23A, 5.23B and 5.23C.

## Part IV

## Incoming Orders under the 1950 Act

### Registration

**5.24**—(1)   On receiving a certified copy of a maintenance order made by a court in England or Northern Ireland, the sheriff clerk shall—

  (a)  retain any certificate or affidavit sent with the certified copy of the order as to the amount of any arrears due under the order;

  (b)  endorse on the certified copy order a declaration in Form 68 and retain such certified copy order and declaration; and

  (c)  notify the clerk of the court which made the order that it has been registered.

(2)   The sheriff clerk may issue an extract of the order with the declaration thereon, and such extract shall have the same force and effect as, and may be enforced in all respects as if it was, an extract decree of the sheriff court in which the certified copy is registered.

### Variation of rate of payment

**5.25**   An application to a sheriff court under section 22(1) of the 1950 Act for variation of the rate of payment under a maintenance order made by a court in England or Northern Ireland and registered in that sheriff court shall be made by initial writ.

---

[1] As inserted by the Act of Sederunt (Child Care and Maintenance Rules) Amendment 2009 (SSI 2009/29) r.2(9) (effective March 2, 2009).

[2] As inserted by the Act of Sederunt (Child Care and Maintenance Rules) Amendment 2009 (SSI 2009/29) r.2(9) (effective March 2, 2009).

## Application to adduce evidence

**5.26**—(1)   An application to a sheriff court under section 22(5) of the 1950 Act to adduce evidence in connection with a maintenance order made by a court in England or Northern Ireland and registered in that sheriff court shall be made by initial writ.

(2)   Any evidence adduced in pursuance of such an application shall be recorded in such manner as the sheriff shall direct and the record of evidence certified by the sheriff shall be the transcript or summary of the evidence adduced.

(3)   Where the sheriff clerk of a court in which an order is registered receives a transcript or summary of evidence connected with that order adduced under section 22(5) of the 1950 Act in the court where that order was made, he shall lodge such transcript or summary in the process of any proceedings for variation of the order before the sheriff court.

## Discharge and variation

**5.27**—(1)   Where a maintenance order made by a court in England or Northern Ireland and registered under the 1950 Act in a sheriff court is varied by that sheriff court, the sheriff clerk shall give notice of the variation to the clerk of the court by which the order was made by sending him a certified copy of the interlocutor varying the order.

(2)   Where a maintenance order made by a court in England or Northern Ireland and registered in a sheriff court is discharged or varied by any court other than that sheriff court, the sheriff clerk shall on receipt of a certified copy of the order discharging or varying the registered order notify the clerk of the appropriate court that the discharge or variation has been entered in the Maintenance Orders Register.

(3)   Paragraphs (1)(a) and (b) and (2) of rule 5.24 shall apply to an order varying a registered order as they apply to the registered order.

## Cancellation of registration

**5.28**—(1)   An application under section 24(1) of the 1950 Act for the cancellation of the registration of a maintenance order made by a court in England or Northern Ireland and registered in a sheriff court shall be made by lodging with the sheriff clerk—

    (a)   an application for that purpose which shall state the date of the registration of the order; and

    (b)   a copy of the order the registration of which is sought to be cancelled.

(2)   Where under section 24(1) or (2) of the 1950 Act the sheriff clerk cancels the registration of a maintenance order, he shall—

    (a)   notify the clerk of the court by which the order was made; and

    (b)   notify the person liable to make payments under the order.

## Part V

## Incoming Orders under the 1972 Act

### Provisions in relation to intimation and entering appearance

**5.29**—(1)   Where the 1972 Act provides that on intimation to a payer of the receipt by the court of a provisional order the payer is to enter appearance within a prescribed period, intimation shall be given in Form 67 and the period shall be—

    (a)   21 days from the date of posting where the payer is resident in Europe; and

    (b)   42 days from the date of posting where the payer is resident outside Europe.

(2)   To enter appearance in terms of section 7(4) or 9(7) of the 1972 Act, the payer shall lodge an application—

    (a)   stating that he opposes confirmation of the order; and

    (b)   setting forth averments in answer to the case upon which the provisional order was made, supported by appropriate pleas-in-law.

(3)   Where the payer enters appearance in terms of section 7(4) of the 1972 Act, the sheriff shall appoint a diet for the hearing of evidence or make such other order as may be appropriate to enable the court to proceed in accordance with the procedure and practice in ordinary civil proceedings in the sheriff court as if an application for a maintenance order against the payer had been made to it.

(4)   Where the payer enters appearance in terms of section 9(7) of the 1972 Act, the sheriff shall appoint a diet for the hearing of evidence or make such other order as may be appropriate to enable the court to proceed in accordance with the procedure and practice in ordinary civil proceedings in the sheriff court as it an application for the variation of the maintenance order had been made to it.

### Authentication of documents

**5.30**   Where the 1972 Act provides that a document is to be authenticated in a prescribed manner, it shall be authenticated by a certificate signed by the sheriff clerk declaring that the document is authentic.

### Application under sections 9 and 20 of the 1972 Act

**5.31**—(1)   An application under section 9 of the 1972 Act (variation and revocation of maintenance orders) for variation or revocation of a maintenance order shall be brought as an ordinary cause.

(2)   An application under section 20 of the 1972 Act (restriction on enforcement of arrears) for leave to enforce the payment of any arrears due under a maintenance order registered in Scotland shall be made by lodging a minute in the process.

### Information to be provided where payer has ceased to reside in Scotland

**5.32**—(1)   Where the registration of an order is cancelled in the circumstances set out in section 10(2) of the 1972 Act, the payee or his solicitor shall provide the sheriff clerk so far as is possible with information to enable the sheriff clerk to prepare the certificate and statement referred to in section 10(7) of the 1972 Act.

(2)   Where the sheriff clerk is required in terms of section 32(1) of the 1972 Act (transfer of orders) to send to the Secretary of State the related documents specified in section 32(8) of that Act, the payee or his solicitor shall provide the sheriff clerk so far as possible with information to enable the sheriff clerk to prepare the certificate and statement to be included among those documents.

### Evidence

**5.33**   Where a provisional order is made under section 9 of the 1972 Act and evidence has been taken by a shorthand writer, the applicant or his solicitor shall provide the sheriff clerk with a copy of the extended notes of evidence.

### Intimation of registration of, or of decision not to register, an order made in the Republic of Ireland

**5.34** *[Repealed by the Act of Sederunt (Sheriff Court Rules) (Miscellaneous Amendments) (No.3) 2011 (SSI 2011/386) para.9 (effective November 28, 2011).]*

### Application to set aside registration of, or to set aside decision not to register, an order made in the Republic of Ireland

**5.35** *[Repealed by the Act of Sederunt (Sheriff Court Rules) (Miscellaneous Amendments) (No.3) 2011 (SSI 2011/386) para.9 (effective November 28, 2011).]*

### Intimation of registration of, or refusal to register, an order made in a Hague Convention Country

**5.36**—(1)    Intimation of the registration of a maintenance order in terms of section 6 of the 1972 Act as applied to an order made in a Hague Convention Country shall be given by the sheriff clerk—

    (a)    to the payer, by sending an intimation in Form 72; and

    (b)    to the payee, by sending a notice in Form 70.

(2)    Notice of a refusal to register a maintenance order on any of the grounds set out in section 6(5), (6) or (7) of the 1972 Act as applied to an order made in a Hague Convention Country shall be given by the sheriff clerk to the payee, by sending a notice in Form 71.

### Application to set aside registration of, or to set aside decision not to register, an order made in a Hague Convention Country

**5.37**    Application to the court under section 6(9) or (12) of the 1972 Act as applied to an order made in a Hague Convention Country shall be made by summary application setting out the grounds of the application.

### Taking of evidence at the request of a court in the USA

**5.37A.**[1]    Where evidence is taken under section 38(2) of the 1972 Act in consequence of a request made by a court in the United States of America under section 38(1) of that Act, rules 29.7 (citation of witnesses), 29.9 (second diligence against a witness) and 29.10 (failure of witness to attend) of the Ordinary Cause Rules shall apply in respect of the matters set out in those rules.

### Communication with courts in the USA

**5.37B.**[2]    In so far as applicable to incoming orders under the 1972 Act from the United States of America, for the purposes of the provisions in Part I of the 1972 Act, the sheriff may communicate with a court or courts in the United States of America in such circumstances and in such manner as he thinks fit.

---

[1] As inserted by the Act of Sederunt (Child Care and Maintenance Rules) Amendment 2009 (SSI 2009/29) r.2(10) (effective March 2, 2009).

[2] As inserted by the Act of Sederunt (Child Care and Maintenance Rules) Amendment 2009 (SSI 2009/29) r.2(10) (effective March 2, 2009).

## Disapplication of provisions in respect of orders made by courts in the USA

**5.37C.**[1]   In any case in which a maintenance order is made by a court in the United States of America which falls to be dealt with under sections 6 to 11 of the 1972 Act as those provisions are applied to the United States of America, none of the provisions in this Part shall apply except this rule and rules 5.30, 5.32, 5.37A and 5.37B.

## Part VI

## Incoming Orders under the 1982 Act

### Applications under section 5A of the 1982 Act

**5.38**—[2](1)   Applications under section 5A of the 1982 Act shall be in writing addressed to the Scottish Ministers, signed by the applicant, or a solicitor or professional person qualified to act in such matters in the Contracting State of origin on his behalf, and shall specify—

(a)   an address within Scotland for service on the applicant;

(b)   the usual and last known address of the person against whom judgment was granted;

(c)   the place where the applicant seeks to enforce the judgment;

(d)   whether at the date of the application the judgment has been satisfied in whole or in part;

(e)   whether interest is recoverable under the judgment in accordance with the law of the country in which it was granted and, if so, the rate of interest and the date from which interest became due; and

(f)   whether the time for bringing an appeal against the judgment has expired without an appeal having been brought or whether an appeal has been brought against the judgment and is pending or has been finally disposed of.

(2)   An application under paragraph (1) shall be accompanied by—

(a)   a copy of the judgment authenticated by the court which made the order;

(b)   documents which establish that, according to the law of the country in which the judgment has been given, the judgment is enforceable and has been served;

(c)   in the case of a judgment given in default, documents which establish that the party in default was served with the documents instituting the proceedings;

(d)   where appropriate, a document showing that the applicant is in receipt of legal aid in the country in which the judgment was given; and

(e)   where the judgment or any of the documents specified in sub-paragraphs (b) to (d) are in a language other than English, a translation into English certified by a person qualified to do so in one of the Contracting States.

(3)   Where the applicant does not produce a document required under paragraph (2)(c) or (d), the sheriff clerk may—

---

[1] As inserted by the Act of Sederunt (Child Care and Maintenance Rules) Amendment 2009 (SSI 2009/29) r.2(10) (effective March 2, 2009).

[2] Heading and section as amended by the Act of Sederunt (Child Care and Maintenance Rules) Amendment (No.2) 2009 (SSI 2009/449) r.2 (effective January 1, 2010) and the Act of Sederunt (Sheriff Court Rules) (Miscellaneous Amendments) (No.3) 2011 (SSI 2011/386) para.9 (effective November 28, 2011).

   (a)   fix a time within which the document is to be produced;

   (b)   accept an equivalent document; or

   (c)   dispense with production of the document.

### Address of applicant's solicitor for service

**5.39**   Where the sheriff clerk is informed by a solicitor practising in Scotland that he is acting on behalf of the applicant, the business address of the solicitor shall thereafter be treated as the address for service on the applicant.

### Notice of determination of application

**5.40**   Immediately after determination of an application for the recognition or enforcement of an order, the sheriff clerk shall serve, in accordance with the Ordinary Cause Rules so far as not inconsistent with the terms of this Chapter, a notice in Form 73 on the applicant and on the person against whom enforcement is sought.

### Appeal by party against whom enforcement is authorised

**5.41**—(1)   Where enforcement of a maintenance order is authorised to any extent, the party against whom enforcement is authorised may appeal by way of summary application to the sheriff against the decision of the sheriff clerk—

   (a)   within one month from the date of service of the notice under rule 5.40; or

   (b)   if the person against whom enforcement is sought is domiciled in a Contracting State other than the United Kingdom, within two months from the date of service of such notice.

(2)   The determination of the sheriff of such a summary application shall be subject to a final appeal on a point of law to the Inner House of the Court of Session in accordance with the Ordinary Cause Rules.

### Appeal by applicant

**5.42**—(1)   Where the application for enforcement of a maintenance order is refused, the applicant may appeal by way of summary application to the sheriff within one month from the date of service of the notice under rule 5.40.

(2)   The determination of the sheriff of such a summary application shall be subject to a final appeal on a point of law to the Inner House of the Court of Session in accordance with the Ordinary Cause Rules.

### Enforcement of registered order

**5.43**[1]   The applicant may obtain an extract of a registered order and proceed to arrest in execution, to intimate the order (for the purposes of section 54(1) of the Debtors (Scotland) Act 1987), to inhibit and to charge and attach thereon, but may not proceed to an action of furthcoming in respect of an arrestment, serve a current maintenance arrestment schedule, make application for a conjoined arrestment order, proceed to adjudication in respect of inhibition or auction in respect of an attachment until the time for appeal against the determination of the sheriff under rules 5.41 or 5.42 has elapsed and any appeal has been disposed of.

---

[1] As amended by SSI 2002/560, Sch.3, para.7.

## Part VII[1]

## Maintenance Decisions under the Maintenance Regulation

### Application for transmission of a Maintenance Decision to another Maintenance Regulation State

**5.44.**—(1)  This rule applies to applications under Article 40 of the Maintenance Regulation to enforce a Maintenance Decision of a sheriff in another Maintenance Regulation State.

(2)  On receipt of an application in the form of a letter, the sheriff clerk will provide the applicant with a certified copy of the Maintenance Decision and a completed extract from the decision in the form of Annex I or II to the Maintenance Regulation as the case may be.

(3)  The letter must be addressed to the sheriff clerk and must include—

(a)  the name and National Insurance number (if known) of the parties to the proceedings;

(b)  the date, or approximate date, of the proceedings in which the Maintenance Decision was made and the nature of those proceedings;

(c)  the Maintenance Regulation State in which the application for recognition or enforcement has been made or is to be made; and

(d)  the postal address of the applicant.

### Enforcement of a Maintenance Decision made by a court in a Maintenance Regulation State other than Denmark

**5.45.**  The "enforcing court" under paragraph 4(2) of Schedule 1 to the 2011 Regulations, means the sheriff court having jurisdiction in the matter in accordance with Schedule 8 to the 1982 Act.

## Part VIII[2]

### Recognition and Enforcement of Maintenance Decisions made by Courts in Denmark etc.

### Recognition and enforcement of a Maintenance Decision made in Denmark etc.

**5.46.**  The "registering court" under paragraph 6(2) of Schedule 1 to the 2011 Regulations, means the sheriff court having jurisdiction in the matter in accordance with Schedule 8 to the 1982 Act.

### Intimation of registration of, or refusal to register, a Maintenance Decision made in Denmark etc.

**5.47.**—(1)  Intimation of the registration of a Maintenance Decision in accordance with Article 31 of the Maintenance Regulation shall be given by the sheriff clerk—

---

[1] As inserted by the Act of Sederunt (Sheriff Court Rules) (Miscellaneous Amendments) (No.3) 2011 (SSI 2011/386) para.9 (effective November 28, 2011).

[2] As inserted by the Act of Sederunt (Sheriff Court Rules) (Miscellaneous Amendments) (No.3) 2011 (SSI 2011/386) para.9 (effective November 28, 2011).

(a) to the payer, by sending an intimation in Form 73A; and

(b) to the payee, by sending a notice in Form 73B.

(2) Notice of a refusal to register a Maintenance Decision shall be given by the sheriff clerk to the payee, by sending a notice in Form 73C.

## Application to set aside registration of, or to set aside decision not to register, a Maintenance Decision made in Denmark etc.

**5.48.** An application under Article 32 of the Maintenance Regulation shall be by summary application setting out the grounds of the application.

## Sist of proceedings

**5.49.** An application under Article 35 of the Maintenance Regulation shall be made by motion.

CHAPTER 6

**K2.28**

APPLICATIONS UNDER THE SOCIAL SECURITY ADMINISTRATION ACT 1992

## Interpretation

**6.1** In this Chapter "the Act" means the Social Security Administration Act 1992 and, unless the context otherwise requires, expressions used in this Chapter which are also used in that Act shall have the meaning assigned to them by the Act.

## Applications under section 106 of the Act

**6.2**—(1) An application to the sheriff under section 106(1) of the Act (recovery of expenditure on benefit from person liable for maintenance) shall be by summary application.

(2) Where, in such an application, a sum is craved which represents or includes a personal allowance element, that element shall be identified in the application.

## Transfer of rights under section 107 of the Act

**6.3**—(1) The sheriff clerk, on receiving notice from the Secretary of State of a transfer of rights to an order by virtue of section 107(3) or (8) of the Act, shall endorse on the interlocutor sheet a certificate in Form 74.

(2) Where, following a transfer by virtue of section 107(3) or (8) of the Act, the dependent parent or the Secretary of State requests an extract of the order originally granted, the sheriff clerk shall issue an extract with a certified copy of the latest certificate referred to in paragraph (1) endorsed on it.

## Notice to Secretary of State under section 108(5) of the Act

**6.4** The notice required to be given to the Secretary of State by the sheriff clerk under section 108(5) of the Act (notice of application to vary etc. a maintenance order), as read with regulation 3 of the Income Support (Liable Relatives) Regulations 1990, shall—

(a) be in writing;

(b) specify any date assigned for the hearing of the application;

(c) be accompanied by a copy of the application; and

(d) be sent by recorded delivery post.

## Notice to Secretary of State of making of maintenance order

**6.5** Where an order granted by the sheriff in favour of the Secretary of State under section 106(2) of the Act has been transferred to the dependent parent in accordance with section 107(3) of the Act and a maintenance order is subsequently granted by the sheriff in favour of the dependent relative, the sheriff clerk shall forthwith notify the Secretary of State in writing and by recorded delivery post of the granting of the maintenance order.

SCHEDULE 1

**Rule 1.2(3)**

FORM 1

Rule 2.5(1)

APPLICATION FOR AN ORDER DECLARING A CHILD FREE FOR ADOPTION UNDER SECTION 18 OF THE ADOPTION (SCOTLAND) ACT 1978<br>[A.B. (address)], Petitioner<br>[or serial number where allocated]<br>For an order in relation to the child, CD.

([Full Name])..............
([Date of Birth])..............
[(Address or serial number where allocated])..............

The Petitioner craves the court [(1)] to make an order declaring the child, CD., free for adoption; and (2) to dispense with the agreement [or consent] of.......... on the ground that..............

The following documents are produced herewith:

    a.    An extract of the entry in the Register of Births, relating to the child;
    b.    *Consent of ([name and address]) to the making of this application;
    c.    *Consent by the child dated
    d.    *Adoption agency report dated

Signed ..........<br>[designation]..........<br>Date ..........

*Delete as appropriate

FORM 2

Rule 2.6(1)

FORM OF PARENTAL AGREEMENT UNDER SECTION 18(1)(a) OF THE ADOPTION (SCOTLAND) ACT 1978

In the petition by (adoption agency, name and address).............. for an order declaring the child—..............(full name of child)..........free for adoption,

I, (name, address).............. confirm that I am the mother/father/guardian of the child. I fully understand that on the making of an order under section 18 of the Adoption (Scotland) Act 1978 any parental responsibility or right which I have at present relating to the child vests in the petitioners and that the effect of an adoption order will be to deprive me of these parental responsibilities or rights permanently. I freely agree generally and unconditionally to the making of an adoption order in relation to the child.

I have signed this agreement at (place of signing).............. on the.......... day of.......... Nineteen hundred and ninety.......... years.

(Signature) ..............
This agreement was signed in the presence of:—..............
(Signature of reporting officer or other person authorised)..............
Full name..............
Address..............

FORM 3

Rule 2.6(1)

FORM OF PARENTAL CONSENT UNDER SECTION 18(2) OF THE ADOPTION (SCOTLAND) ACT 1978

604

In the petition by (adoption agency, name and address).............. for an order declaring the child—..............(full name of child).........free for adoption,..............

I, (name, address)............... confirm that I am the mother/father/guardian of the child. I fully understand that on the making of an order under section 18 of the Adoption (Scotland) Act 1978 any parental responsibility or right which I have at present relating to the child vests in the petitioners and that the effect of an adoption order will be to extinguish these parental responsibilities or rights. I freely consent, generally and unconditionally to the making of an application to the court for an order declaring the child free for adoption.

I have signed this consent at [place].......... on the.......... day of.......... Nineteen hundred and ninety.......... years.

(Signature) ...............

This consent was signed in the presence of:—...............

(Signature of reporting officer or other person authorised) ...............

Full name...............

Address...............

*delete as appropriate.

FORM 4

Rules 2.6(1) and 2.23(1)

FORM OF CONSENT UNDER SECTION 12(8) OR 18(8) OF THE ADOPTION (SCOTLAND) ACT 1978

in the

petition by

(Name and address).......... Petitioner...............

I, (full name of child) confirm that I understand the nature and effect of any order declaring me free for adoption/adoption order for which application is made. I hereby consent to the making of such an order in the petitioner's favour in respect of myself.

I have signed this consent at (place of signing)................... on the.......... day of.......... Nineteen hundred and.......... years.

(Signature)...............

This consent was signed in the presence of:—...............

(Signature of reporting officer or other person authorised) ...............

Full name...............

Address...............

FORM 5

Rules 2.10(1) and 2.13(3)

DECLARATION UNDER SECTION 18(6) OR SECTION 19(4) OF THE ADOPTION (SCOTLAND) ACT 1978

In the petition by (adoption agency, name and address).............. for an order declaring the child [full name]............... free for adoption,..........

I/We,.............. being the............... of the child hereby declare that I/we prefer not to be involved in future questions concerning the adoption of the child.

In witness whereof I/we have signed this declaration on the.......... day of.......... Nineteen hundred and ninety..........

Signature...............

Signature...............

Signed in the presence of..............

(Signature)...............

Full name...............

Designation.......... and Reporting Officer

Address...............

FOR OFFICIAL USE ONLY

The foregoing declaration was received at the Sheriff Clerk's Office,.......... on.......... 19.........., and has been duly entered in the Adoption Register of that court.

Signature ..........

Sheriff Clerk Depute

FORM 6

Rule 2.10(5)

WITHDRAWAL OF DECLARATION UNDER SECTION 18(6) OR SECTION 19(4) OF THE ADOPTION (SCOTLAND) ACT 1978

In the petition by (adoption agency, name and address).......... for an order declaring the child [full name]............... free for adoption,...............

I/We,............... being the (*insert relationship to the child*)............... of the child hereby withdraw the declaration dated (*insert date of declaration*) that I/we prefer not to be involved in future questions concerning the adoption of the child.

I/we have signed this withdrawal of declaration on the.......... day of.......... Nineteen hundred and ninety..........

Signature ...............

Signature ...............

....................

### FOR OFFICIAL USE ONLY

The foregoing withdrawal of declaration was received at the Sheriff Clerk's Office, on 19.........., and has been duly entered in the Adoption Register of that court and intimation of the withdrawal made to the Local Authority.

Signature ..........

Sheriff Clerk Depute

### FORM 7

Rules 2.11(2) and 2.28(3) and (4)

### FORM OF INTIMATION OF DIET OF HEARING UNDER SECTION 12 OR SECTION 18 OF THE ADOPTION (SCOTLAND) ACT 1978

To:...............

(Full name and address of person to whom this intimation is to be sent)..........

Notice is given that a hearing will take place at (Name of sheriff court) Sheriff Court (Full address of court) on.......... (date) at.......... (time) in relation to the child (full name of child as given in the birth certificate)

when the court will consider an application for an order declaring the child free for adoption [or an application for adoption of the child].

You do not need to attend this hearing if you do not wish to be heard by the court.

If you do not attend this hearing the court may make an order as noted above.

Signature ...............

Designation...............

Date...............

### FORM 8

Rule 2.15(1)

### APPLICATION TO REVOKE AN ORDER FREEING A CHILD FOR ADOPTION UNDER SECTION 20(1) OF THE ADOPTION (SCOTLAND) ACT 1978

### MINUTE

by

....................

[full name, address]

in relation to the child

....................

[full name and date of birth]

The minuter craves the court to revoke the order declaring the child free for adoption on the ground that he/she wishes to resume parental responsibilities and rights and condescends as follows:

1. An order freeing the child for adoption was made on...........
2. More than 12 months have elapsed since the child was freed for adoption.
3. No adoption order has been made in respect of the child.
4. The child at present resides at.......... and does not have his home with a person with whom he had been placed for adoption.
5. The minuter makes the following proposals for the future well-being of the child:—

Signed ..........

[designation]

Date ..........

### FORM 9

Rule 2.19(1)

### APPLICATION (FOR LEAVE OF COURT) TO PLACE CHILD FOR ADOPTION UNDER SECTION 20(2) OF THE ADOPTION (SCOTLAND) ACT 1978

### MINUTE

by

....................
[full name, address]
in relation to the child

....................
[full name and date of birth]
residing at present at...............
The minuters crave leave of the court to place the child for adoption and condescend as follows:

a. An order in terms of section 18 of the Adoption (Scotland) Act 1978 declaring the child free for adoption was made by the court on.......... 19.........., in a petition by the minuters.

b. An application to revoke the aforesaid order was lodged on.......... 19..........,by and that application for revocation has not yet been determined by the court.

c. [Set out here the circumstances justifying the placing of the child]

Date ..........
Signature ..........

[designation]

FORM 10

Rule 2.20

FURTHER APPLICATION BY FORMER PARENT TO REVOKE AN ORDER FREEING A CHILD FOR ADOPTION UNDER SECTION 20(5) OF THE ADOPTION (SCOTLAND) ACT 1978

MINUTE

by

....................
[full name, address]
in relation to the child

....................
[full name and address] born on [date of birth]
The minuter craves leave of the court to make this further application on the ground that:—
[narrate the change in circumstances or other proper reason for application]..........
The minuter craves the court to revoke the order declaring the child free for adoption on the ground that he wishes to resume parental responsibilities and rights and condescends as follows:

a. An order freeing the child for adoption was made on..........

b. An application to the court to revoke the order was made on.........., but was refused on..........

c. More than 12 months have elapsed since the child was freed for adoption.

d. No adoption order has been made in respect of the child.

e. The child at present resides at .......... and does not have his home with a person with whom he has been placed for adoption.

f. The minuter makes the following proposals for the future well-being of the child:—

Date..........
Signature..........

[designation]

FORM 11

Rule 2.21(1)

PETITION FOR ADOPTION ORDER UNDER SECTION 12 OF THE ADOPTION (SCOTLAND) ACT 1978

PETITION OF

[A.B., full name]...............
[and (full name of spouse)...............
Maiden surname...............
Any previous married surname]...............
[Address]...............

For authority to adopt the child
[Full name of child as shown on birth certificate], born on...............
[Child's date of birth]...............
[Child's present address]...............

The petitioner(s) crave(s) the court [(1)] to make an adoption order in his/her/their favour under section 12 of the Adoption (Scotland) Act 1978, in relation to the child [; and to dispense with the agreement [or consent] of.......... on the ground that.......... ] and condescends as follows:

1.[1]>

    a. The petitioner(s) is/are domiciled in.......... and reside(s) at.......... [or the male/female petitioner is domiciled in.......... and both petitioners reside at.......... ].

    b. The occupation(s) of the petitioner(s) is/are.......... .

    c. The petitioner(s) is/are married [or unmarried or widow or widower]. (If married, state whether spouse resides with, or apart from, the petitioner.)

    d. The petitioner(s) is/are [respectively].......... [and].......... years of age.

    e. The petitioner(s) has/have resident with him/her/them the following persons, namely..........

    f. The child was received into the home of the petitioners on (date).

    g. The child has continuously had his home with the petitioner(s) since the date shown above.

    h. *Arrangements for placing the child in the care of the petitioner(s) were made by (give full name and address of the agency or authority or person making such arrangement) [*and therefore notification in terms of section 22(1) of the Adoption (Scotland) Act 1978 is not required].

    i. The petitioner(s) notified (give name of local authority notified) of his/their intention to apply for an adoption order in relation to the child on (date).

    j. An order freeing the child for adoption was made at.......... Sheriff Court on (date).......... [or an order declaring the child free for adoption has not been made].

    k. No reward or payment has been given or received by the petitioner(s) for or of in consideration of the adoption of the child or the giving of consent to the making of an adoption order.

    l. *Each parent or guardian of the child has consented under section 20(1) (advance consent to adoption: England and Wales) of the Adoption and Children Act 2002 and has not withdrawn that consent.

    m. *By notice under section 20(4)(a) (notice that information about application for adoption order not required: England and Wales) of the Adoption and Children Act 2002 (*name of parent or guardian*) [and (*name of parent or guardian*] stated that he [or she or they] did not wish to be informed of any application for an adoption order and that statement has not been withdrawn.

    n. *The child has been placed for adoption by an adoption agency within the meaning of section 2(1) (adoption agencies in England and Wales) of the Adoption and Children Act 2002 with the petitioner(s) and the child was placed for adoption [*under section 19(1) (placing children with parental consent: England and Wales) of that Act with the consent of each parent or guardian and the consent of the mother was given when the child was at least six weeks old] [*under an order made under section 21(1) (placement orders: England and Wales) of that Act and the child was at least six weeks old when that order was made].

(*Delete as appropriate)

2.

    a. The child is.......... years of age, having been born on the.......... day of.......... 19.......... , at.......... in the County of..............

    b. The child is not and never has been married and is male/female.

    c. The child's natural mother is (full name and address).

    d. *The child's natural father is (full name and address).

    e. *Paternity of the child has not been admitted or established by decree of any court.

(*Delete either (d) or (e) as appropriate)

    f. The child is of British/or.......... nationality.

    g. The child is entitled to the following property, namely..........

    h. The child has the following tutors, curators or guardians. (Either give full names and addresses or delete the paragraph if it does not apply.)..........

3. .......... is/are liable to contribute to the support of the child.

4. The child has not been the subject of an adoption order or of a petition for an adoption order save that..............

5. The petitioner(s) is/are prepared to undertake, if any order is made on this petition, to make the said child the following provisions, namely—..............

6. There is lodged along with this application the following documents

  (i) extract birth certificate relating to the child

  (ii) extract marriage certificate relating to the petitioner(s)

(Note: this need be lodged only in the case of a joint application by spouses)

---

[1] As amended by the Act of Sederunt (Child Care and Maintenance Rules 1997) (Amendment) (Adoption and Children Act 2002) 2006 (SSI 2006/411) (effective August 18, 2006).

(iii)    medical certificate relating to the health of the male petitioner

(iv)    medical certificate relating to the health of the female petitioner

(Note: medical certificate need not be produced where either the petitioner or one of the joint petitioners is a parent of the child)

(v)    *agreement to the adoption by the child's natural mother

(vi)    *agreement to the adoption by the child's natural father

(vii)    *consent to the adoption by the child

(viii)    *consent to the adoption by the tutor or curator

(ix)    *extract of the order freeing the child for adoption

(x)    *acknowledgement by local authority of letter by petitioner(s) intimating intention to apply for adoption order

(xi)    *report by local authority in terms of section 22(2) of the Adoption (Scotland) Act 1978

(xii)    *report by the adoption agency in terms of section 23 of the Adoption (Scotland) Act 1978

(xiii)    *any other document not referred to above.

(*Delete as appropriate)

7.......... have taken part in the arrangements for placing the child in the care of the petitioner(s)—

The petitioner(s) crave(s) the court to dispense with intimation and to order notice of this petition to be served on such persons, if any, as the court may think proper, and thereafter, on resuming consideration hereon, to make an adoption order in favour of the petitioner(s) under section 12 of the Adoption (Scotland) Act 1978 on such terms and conditions (if any) as the court may think fit, and to direct the Registrar General for Scotland to make an entry regarding the adoption in the Adopted Children Register in the form prescribed by him, giving.......... as the forename(s), and the surname of the adopter(s) as the surname of.......... in the form; and further, upon proof to the satisfaction of the court in the course of the proceedings to follow hereon, that (name of child).......... was born on the.......... day of.......... in the year Nineteen hundred and.......... and is identical with the.......... to whom any entry numbered.......... and made on the.......... day of.......... in the year 19.........., in the Register of Births for the Registration District of.......... in the.......... relates, to direct the said Registrar General to cause such birth entry to be marked with the word "adopted" and to include the abovementioned date of birth in the entry recording the adoption in the manner indicated in the Schedule to the said Act.......... and to pronounce such other or further orders or directions upon such matters, including the expenses of this petition, as the court may think fit.

..............

Signature of male petitioner

..............

Signature of female petitioner

or

..............

Signature of solicitor with designation and address

..............

..............

FORM 12

Rule 2.21(1)

PETITION FOR AN ORDER UNDER SECTION 49 OF THE ADOPTION (SCOTLAND) ACT 1978

PETITION OF..............

[A.B. full name]..............

[and (full name of spouse)..............

Maiden surname..............

Previous married surname]..............

For an order vesting in him/her/them the parental rights and responsibilities relating to the child..........

[Full name of child as shown on birth certificate], born on..............

[Child's date of birth]..............

[Child's present address]..............

1. The petitioner(s) crave(s) the court [(1)] to make an order under section 49 of the Adoption (Scotland) Act 1978 vesting in him/her/them the parental rights and responsibilities relating to the child [; and to dispense with the agreement [or consent] of.......... on the ground that..........] and condescends as follows:

a.    The petitioner(s) is/are domiciled in..........and reside(s) at..........

b.    The occupation(s) of the petitioner(s) is/are..............

c.    The petitioner(s) is/are married [or unmarried or widow or widower]. (If married, state whether spouse resides with, or apart from, the petitioner)..........

    d.    The petitioner(s) is/are [respectively].......... [and].......... years of age

    e.    The petitioner(s) has/have resident with him/her/them the following persons, namely.........

    f.    The child was received into the home of the petitioners on (date).........

    g.    The child has continuously had his home with the petitioner(s) since the date shown above

    h.    *Arrangements for placing the child in the care of the petitioner(s) were made by (give full name and address of agency or authority or person making such arrangements) and therefore notification in terms of section 22(1) of the Adoption (Scotland) Act 1978 is not required

    i.    *The petitioner(s) notified (give name of local authority notified) of his/her/their intention to apply for an adoption order in relation to the child on (date).........

(*Delete as appropriate)

    j.    An order freeing the child for adoption was made at.......... Sheriff Court on (date) [or an order declaring the child free for adoption has not been made]..........

    k.    No reward or payment has been given or received by the petitioner(s) for or in consideration of the adoption fo the child or the giving of consent to the making of an adoption order

2.

    a.    The child is.......... years of age, having been born on the.......... day of 19.........., at.......... in the County of...............

    b.    The child is not and never has been married and is male/female

    c.    The child's natural mother is............... (full name and address)

    d.    *The child's natural father is............... (full name and address)

OR

    e.    *Paternity of the child has not been admitted or established by decree of any court

(*Delete either (d) or (e) as appropriate)

    f.    The child is of British/or.......... nationality

    g.    The child is entitled to the following property, namely...............

    h.    The child has the following tutors, curators or guardians. (Either give full names and addresses or delete the paragraph if it does not apply)

3. .......... is/are liable to contribute to the support of the child.

4. The child has not been the subject of an adoption order or of a petition for an adoption order save that...............

5. The petitioner(s) is/are prepared to undertake, if any order is made on this petition, to make for the said child the following provisions, namely:—...............

6. There is lodged along with this application the following documents—

    (i)    extract birth certificate relating to the child

    (ii)    extract marriage certificate relating to the petitioner(s)

(Note: this need be lodged only in the case of a joint application by spouses)

    (iii)    medical certificate relating to the health of the male petitioner

    (iv)    medical certificate relating to the health of the female petitioner

(Note: medical certificate need not be produced where either the petitioner or one of the joint petitioners is a parent of the child)

    (v)    *agreement to the adoption by the child's natural mother

    (vi)    *agreement to the adoption by the child's natural father

    (vii)    *consent to the adoption by the child

    (viii)    *consent to the adoption by the tutor or curator

    (ix)    *extract of the order freeing the child for adoption

    (x)    *acknowledgement by local authority of letter by petitioner(s) intimating intention to apply for adoption order

    (xi)    *report by local authority in terms of section 22(2) of the Adoption (Scotland) Act 1978

    (xii)    *report by the adoption agency in terms of section 23 of the Adoption (Scotland) Act 1978

    (xiii)    *an affidavit by.......... who is conversant with the law of adoption of.......... and has practised law as a.......... [or represents that country as (state capacity).......... in the United Kingdom]

(*Delete where appropriate)

7. .......... have taken part in the arrangements for placing the child in the care of the petitioner(s)—

The petitioner(s) crave(s) the court to dispense with intimation and to order notice of this petition to be served on such persons, if any, as the court may think proper, and thereafter, on resuming consideration hereon, to make an adoption order in favour of the petitioner(s) under the Adoption (Scotland) Act 1978 section 49, vesting in the petitioners the parental responsibilities and rights relating to (name of child) on such terms and conditions (if any) as the court may think fit, to authorise removal of the child for the purpose of adoption under the laws of..........; to find the petitioners entitled to the custody of the child pending such adoption and to direct the Registrar General for Scotland to make an entry regarding the order in the Adopted Children Register in the form prescribed by him, giving.......... as the forename(s), and the surname of the adopters as the surname of.......... in the form; and further, upon proof to the satisfaction of the court in the course of the proceedings to follow hereon, that the child.......... was born on the.......... day of.......... in the year Nineteen hundred and.......... and is identical with the.......... to whom any entry numbered.......... and made on the.......... day of.......... in the year 19.........., in the Register of Births for the Registration District of.......... in the.......... relates, to direct the said Registrar General to cause such birth entry to be marked with the words "proposed foreign adoption" and to include the abovementioned date of birth in the entry recording the order in the manner indicated in the Schedule to the said Act; and to pronounce such other or further orders or directions upon such matters, including the expenses of this petition, as the court may think fit.

..............
Signature of male petitioner or agent

..............
Signature of female petitioner or agent

or

..............
Signature of solicitor with designation and address

..............

## FORM 13

Rule 2.23(1)

FORM OF PARENTAL AGREEMENT UNDER SECTION 16(1)(b)(i) OF THE ADOPTION (SCOTLAND) ACT 1978[1]

In the petition relating to the adoption of..............
(Insert the full name of the child as it is given in the birth certificate)
to which petition the court has assigned the serial number..........
I, (name and addess)..............
confirm that I am the mother/father/guardian of the child. I fully understand that the effect of the adoption order for which application has been made will be to deprive me permanently of all parental rights or responsibilities which I have at present over the child. I freely agree generally and unconditionally to the making of an adoption order in relation to the child.

I have signed this agreement at (place of signing)....................on the.......... day of.......... Nineteen hundred and..............

This agreement was signed in the presence of:—....................(Signature of reporting officer)

..............
Full name of Reporting Officer

..............
Address

## FORM 14[1]

Rule 2.23(1)

FORM OF PARENTAL AGREEMENT UNDER SECTION 15(1)(aa) AND 16(1)(b)(i) OF THE ADOPTION (SCOTLAND) ACT 1978

In the petition relating to the adoption of..............(Insert the full name of the child as it is given in the birth certificate)

I, (name and address)..............confirm that I am the mother/father/guardian of the child. I fully understand that the effect of the adoption order for which application has been made will be to share with the petitioner all parental responsibilities and rights which I have at present over the child. I freely agree generally and unconditionally to the making of an adoption order in relation to the child.

I have signed this agreement at (place of signing)..............on the.......... day of..............

This agreement was signed in the presence of:—..............(Signature of reporting officer)

..............
Full name of Reporting Officer

..............
Address

## FORM 15

Rule 2.36(3)

FORM OF INTIMATION OF DIET OF HEARING UNDER SECTION 27, 28, 29 OR 30 OF THE ADOPTION (SCOTLAND) ACT 1978

Notice of hearing of minute in petition for authority to adopt..........(Full name of child as given in the birth certificate)

To:—...................(Full name and address of person to whom this intimation is to be sent)

Notice is hereby given that a hearing in the petition for authority to adopt the child, which hearing will be restricted to matters bearing upon the crave of the minute, a copy of which is attached hereto, will take place at (name of sheriff court).......... Sheriff Court (address) on.......... (date) at.......... (time) when you may appear and be heard personally or be represented by solicitor or counsel.

Signature ...............

Designation...............

Date...............

FORM 16

Rule 2.38(1)

APPLICATION FOR A PARENTAL RESPONSIBILITIES ORDER UNDER SECTION 86 OF THE CHILDREN (SCOTLAND) ACT 1995

Case No..........

Date lodged..........

Application to Sheriff Court at...............for a Parental Responsibilities Order under section 86 of the Children (Scotland) Act 1995

1

| | |
|---|---|
| APPLICANT | *[insert name, address, telephone and fax numbers, and details of the capacity of the person making the application on behalf of the local authority, e.g. solicitor for local authority, social worker]* |
| CHILD | *[insert name, address, gender and date of birth exactly as given in birth certificate]* |
| RELEVANT PERSON(S) | *[insert name, address and the basis for the person being a relevant person within the meaning of* section 86(4) of the Act] |
| REPORTING OFFICER | *[insert name and address and details of appointment of Reporting Officer appointed prior to the application in terms of* rules 2.7 or 2.25] |
| ANY OTHER PERSON WHO SHOULD RECEIVE NOTICE OF THE APPLICATION | *[insert name, address of person and provide details of their interest in the appication and/or child]* |

2. GROUNDS I OR MAKING APPLICATION

The Applicant asks the Court to make a Parental Responsibilities Order for the following reasons:— *[applicant to provide details of grounds for making the application]*

OTHER APPLICATIONS AND ORDERS WHICH AFFECT THE CHILD

*[insert details of any other applications or orders made which affect or are relevant to the child who is the subject of this application including any details of a supervision requirement of a Children's Hearing]*

3. REQUEST FOR ORDER

1. The applicants request the court to make a Parental Responsibilities Order transferring the appropriate parental rights and responsibilities to them.

2. The petitioners request the court to dispense with the agreement of

...................

...................

on the ground that ...............[in terms of section 86(2)(b)]

4. REPORTS/DOCUMENTARY EVIDENCE ETC.

*delete as appropriate

The following documents are produced with this petition:—

a) An extract of the entry in the Register of Births relating to the child

b) Agreement of relevant persons within the meaning of Section 86(4) of the Act

c) * Any other document founded upon by the petitioner in support of the terms of the petition

5. OTHER ORDERS

*In terms of section 88(3) of the Act the sheriff is requested to make the following is directions as to contact with the child by *[insert name and address of persons and his or her relationship with the child]* *[insert details of any directions sought as to contact with the child]*

*delete as appropriate

*[insert details of any other orders craved e.g. Crave for warrant for delivery of the child and warrant to open shut and lockfast places]*

## 6. DETAILS OF FIRST ORDER SOUGHT FROM SHERIFF

The applicant requests the sheriff to appoint a curator ad litem and a Reporting Officer to the child for the purpose of investigating and reporting to the court within 4 weeks and on receipt of the reports by the curator ad litem and reporting officer to fix a hearing

SIGNED ..............

DATE ..............

*[insert Name, Address, telephone, DX and Fax number]*..............

FORM 17

Rule 2.38(2)

## FORM OF AGREEMENT OF RELEVANT PERSON UNDER SECTION 86(2) OF THE CHILDREN (SCOTLAND) ACT 1995

In the application for a Parental Responsibilities Order in respect of...................*(Insert the full name of the child as it is given in the birth certificate)*

I, *(insert name and address)*...............confirm that I am the *mother/*father/*person with parental rights. I fully understand that the effect of the Parental Responsibilities Order for which application has been made will be to transfer my parental rights and responsibilities to *(insert name and address of Local Authority)*.......... during such period as the Order remains in force. I freely, and with full understanding of what is involved, agree unconditionally to the making of a Parental Responsibilities Order in relation to the child.

.....................
*(Signature of relevant person)*

.....................
*(Signature of Reporting Officer)*

I have signed this agreement at *(place of signing)*...............on the.......... day of.......... 199...............

This agreement was signed in the presence of *(Full name and address of Reporting Officer)*..........

*delete as appropriate

YOU SHOULD GET ADVICE FROM A SOLICITOR OR LOCAL ADVICE AGENCY OR LAW CENTRE about the application and bout Legal Aid.

FORM 18

Rule 2.42(2)

## FORM OF INTIMATION OF DIET OF HEARING UNDER SECTION 86 OF THE CHILDREN (SCOTLAND) ACT 1995

To:...............*(Full name and address of person to whom this intimation is to be sent)*

Notice is given that a hearing will take place at *(Name of Sheriff Court)* Sheriff Court *(Full address of Sheriff Court)* on.......... *(date)* at.......... *(time)* in relation to the child *(full name of child as given in the birth certificate)*...............when the court will consider an application for a Parental Responsibilities Order in relation to the child.

Signature..............

Designation..............

Date..............

WHAT YOU SHOULD DO

You need not attend this hearing if you do not wish to be heard by the court.

If you do not attend or are not represented at the hearing, the application may be determined in your absence.

YOU SHOULD GET ADVICE FROM A SOLICITOR OR LOCAL ADVICE AGENCY OR LAW CENTRE about the application and about Legal Aid.

FORM 19

Rule 2.43(2)

## PARENTAL RESPONSIBILITIES ORDER UNDER SECTION 86 OF THE CHILDREN (SCOTLAND) ACT 1995

IN THE SHERIFF COURT

at ..............

on ..............

Case No

The sheriff orders tht all parental rights and responsibilities relating to the child *[insert name, address, gender and date of birth]* except any right to agree, or decline to agree—

(a) to the making of an application in relation to the child under section 18 (freeing for adoption) or 55 (adoption abroad) of the Adoption Act 1976, under section 18 or 49 of the Adoption (Scotland) Act 1978 or under Article 17, 18 or 57 of the Adoption (Northern Ireland) Order 1987 (corresponding provision for Scotland and Northern Ireland); or

(b) to the making of an Adoption Order are transferred to *[insert name and address of Local Authority]* during the period that the Parental Responsibilities Order remains in force.

*In terms of section 88 of the Act the sheriff makes the following directions as to contact with the child by *[insert name and address of person and his or her relationships with child]*—

*[insert details of any other orders granted e.g. Warrant for delivery of the child etc.]*

*delete as appropriate

........................

*For the purpose of enforcing this order warrant is granted for all lawful execution, including warrant to open shut and lockfast places.

........................

Signed ..........
Sheriff of .......... at ..........
Date ..........

FORM 20

Rule 2.44(6)

FORM OF INTIMATION OF DIET OF HEARING UNDER SECTION 86(5) OF THE CHILDREN (SCOTLAND) ACT 1995

To: ..............

*(Full name and address of person to whom this intimation is to be sent)*

Notice is given that a hearing will take place at *(Name of Sheriff Court)* Sheriff Court *(Full address of Sheriff Court)* on ..........*(date)* at ..........*(time)* in relation to the child *(full name and date of birth of child as given in the birth certificate)*....................when the court will consider an application for *variation/ discharge of the Parental Responsibilities Order in relation to the child dated *(insert date of Order)*. A copy of the minute for *variation/discharge is attached.

Signature ..............
Designation ..............
Date ..............

*delete as appropriate

WHAT YOU SHOULD DO

You need not attend this hearing if you do not wish to be heard by the court.

If you do not attend or are not represented at the hearing, the application may be determined in your absence.

YOU SHOULD GET ADVICE FROM A SOLICITOR OR LOCAL ADVICE AGENCY OR LAW CENTRE about the application and about Legal Aid

FORM 21

Rule 2.44(7)

FORM OF DISCHARGE OR VARIATION OF PARENTAL RESPONSIBILITIES ORDER UNDER SECTION 86(5) OF THE CHILDREN (SCOTLAND) ACT 1995

To: ..............

*(Full name and address of person to whom intimation of the order is to be sent)*

[N.B. See Rule 2.44(7)]

In the application for *variation/discharge of Parental Responsibilities Order in relation to the child...................*(full name and date of birth of child as given in the birth certificate)*

At *(Name of Sheriff Court)* on *(date of Order)*, the Sheriff

(1) Discharged the Parental Responsibilities Order dated *(insert date of original Order)*

*or*

(2) Varied the Parental Responsibilities Order dated *(insert date of original Order)* by *(insert details of variation)*

Signature ..............
Designation ..............
Date ..............
*delete as appropriate

FORM 22[1]

**Rule 2.46(1)**

FORM OF PETITION FOR PARENTAL ORDER UNDER SECTION 54 OF THE HUMAN
FERTILISATION AND EMBRYOLOGY ACT 2008
SHERIFFDOM OF (*insert name of sheriffdom*)
AT (*insert place of sheriff court*)
PETITION
of
[A.B.] (*designation and address*)*
and
[C.D.] (*designation and address*)*
[*or serial number where one has been assigned*]

Petitioners

for
a parental order under section 54 of the Human Fertilisation and Embryology Act 2008
in respect of
[E.F.] (*name as in birth certificate*)

The petitioners condescend as follows—

1. The petitioners are [married to each other] *or* [civil partners of each other] *or* [two persons who are living as partners in an enduring family relationship and are not within prohibited degrees of relationship in relation to each other], are domiciled in the [United Kingdom][Channel Islands]*or* [Isle of Man] and reside at (*state full address*).

2. The petitioners are respectively .......... and .......... years of age.

3. (*State name of child, the subject of the petition*) is [male] *or* [female] and is .......... [months] *or* [years] old having been born on .......... at ...........

4. [A court has not previously refused the petitioners' application for a parental order in respect of the child] *or* [A court has previously refused the petitioners' application for a parental order in respect of the child but the court directed that section 33(1) of the Adoption and Children (Scotland) Act 2007 as modified, should not apply] *or* [A court has previously refused the petitioners' application for a parental order in respect of the child but the petitioners aver that it is proper for the court to hear the application because .......... (*give full details*)].

5. The child is not and never has been married or a civil partner.

6. The child's home is with the petitioners.

7. The child was carried by a woman who is not one of the petitioners as the result of [the placing in her of an embryo] *or* [the placing in her of sperm and eggs] *or* [her artificial insemination].

8. The gametes of (*state which petitioner or if both state both petitioners*) were used to bring about the creation of the embryo of the child.

9. The child is not the subject of any other pending or completed court proceedings (*if the child is so subject give full details*).

[10. (*State full name and address of the other parent of the child*), who is [the father of the child by virtue of sections 35 or 36 of the Human Fertilisation and Embryology Act 2008] *or* [the other parent of the child by virtue of sections 42 or 43 of the Human Fertilisation and Embryology Act 2008] or [the other parent of the child by virtue of (*specify*)], where he or she is not one of the petitioners has freely and with full understanding of what is involved, agreed unconditionally to the making of the order sought.]

[[11.] (*State full name and address of the woman who carried the child*), is the woman who carried the child and has freely and with full understanding of what is involved, agreed unconditionally to the making of the order sought.]

[12.] No money or benefit, other than for expenses reasonably incurred, has been given or received by the petitioners for or in consideration of
  (a) the making of the order sought;
  (b) any agreement required for the making of the order sought;
  (c) the handing over of the child to the petitioners, or
  (d) the making of any arrangements with a view to the making of the order,
  [other than (*state any money or other benefit given or received by authority of the court and specify such authority*)].

[[13.] [The father of the child by virtue of sections 35 or 36 of the Human Fertilisation and Embryology Act 2008] *or* [The other parent of the child by virtue of sections 42 or 43 of the Human Fertilisation and Embryology Act 2008] *or* [The other parent of the child by virtue of (*specify*)] [and] [or] [The woman who carried the child] [cannot be found (*state the efforts which have been made to find the person(s) concerned)] or* [is [*or are*] incapable of giving agreement by reason of (*state reasons*)].]

The petitioners crave the court—

1. To order notice of the petition to be intimated to such person or persons as the court thinks fit.

2. To appoint a reporting officer and a curator ad litem to the child and direct them to report.

[3. To dispense with the agreement of the other parent of the child [*and*] [*or*] [the woman who carried the child] [who cannot be found] *or* [who is [*or are*] incapable of giving agreement].]

[4.] On resuming consideration of this petition and the reports by the reporting officer and the curator ad litem, to make a parental order in their favour under section 54 of the Human Fertilisation and Embryology Act 2008 in respect of the child.

[5.] To direct the Registrar General for Scotland to make an entry regarding the parental order in the Parental Order Register in the form prescribed by him or her giving [*insert forename(s)*] as the forename(s) and [*insert surname*] as the surname of the child; and upon proof to the satisfaction of the court in the course of the proceedings to follow hereon, to find that the child was born on the [*insert date*] day of [*insert month*] in the year [*insert year*] and is identical with the child to whom an entry numbered [*insert entry number*] and made on the [*insert date*] day of [*insert month*] in the year [*insert year*], in the Register of Births for the registration district of [*insert district*] relates; and to direct the Registrar General for Scotland to cause such birth entry to be marked with the words "Parental Order" and to include the above mentioned date of birth in the entry recording the parental order in the manner indicated in that form.

[6.] To pronounce such other or further orders or directions upon such matters, including the expenses of this petition, as the court thinks fit.

[(*Signed*)

First Petitioner

(*Signed*)

Second petitioner]

or [(*Signed*)

Solicitor for petitioners]

(*Address*)

FORM 23¹>>

**Rule 2.48(1)**

FORM OF AGREEMENT TO A PARENTAL ORDER UNDER SECTION 54(6) OF THE HUMAN FERTILISATION AND EMBRYOLOGY ACT 2008

In the petition applying for a parental order in relation to (*insert the full name of the child as it is given in the birth certificate*).

[\*to which petition the court has assigned the serial number (*insert serial number*).] (\**delete as appropriate*)

I, (*insert name and address*), confirm that I am [the woman who carried the child] *or* [the father of the child by virtue of sections 35 or 36 of the Human Fertilisation and Embryology Act 2008] *or* [the other parent of the child by virtue of sections 42 or 43 of the Human Fertilisation and Embryology Act 2008] *or* [the other parent of the child by virtue of (*specify*)]. I confirm that:—

(1) I fully understand that the effect of the making of a parental order in respect of the child will be to extinguish all the parental responsibilities and parental rights which I have at present in respect of the child.

(2) I understand that the court cannot make a parental order in relation to the child without my agreement [and the agreement of [the woman who carried the child] *or* [the father of the child by virtue of sections 35 or 36 of the Human Fertilisation and Embryology Act 2008] *or* [the other parent of the child by virtue of sections 42 or 43 of the Human Fertilisation and Embryology Act 2008] *or* [the other parent of the child by virtue of (*specify*)], where he or she is not one of the petitioners] unless the court dispenses with agreement on the ground that the person concerned cannot be found or is incapable of giving agreement.

(3) I understand that when the hearing of the petition to determine the application for a parental order in relation to the child is heard, this document may be used as evidence of my agreement to the making of the order unless I inform the court that I no longer agree.

(4) I freely, and with full understanding of what is involved, agree unconditionally to the making of a parental order in relation to the child.

(5) I have not received or given any money or benefit, other than for expenses reasonably incurred, for or in consideration of—

(a)    the making of the parental order,

(b)    the execution of this agreement,

(c)    the handing over of the child to the petitioners, or

(d)    the making of any arrangements with a view to the making of a parental order,

[other than (*state any money or other benefit given or received by authority of the court and specify such authority*)].

I have signed this agreement at (*place of signing*) on the .......... day of .......... Two thousand and ...........

(*Signed by the [woman who carried the child] [father] or [other parent of the child]*)

This agreement was signed in the presence of:—

...............

(*Signature of witness*)

...............

[*Insert full name and address of witness*]

FORM 24[1]

**Rule 2.54(3)**

FORM OF INTIMATION OF DIET OF THE HEARING OF APPLICATION FOR A PARENTAL ORDER UNDER SECTION 54 OF THE HUMAN FERTILISATION AND EMBRYOLOGY ACT 2008

To: (*insert full name and address of person to whom this intimation is to be sent*)

You are given NOTICE that a hearing will take place at (*insert name and address of sheriff court*) on (*insert date*) at (*insert time*) in relation to the child (*insert full name of child as given in the birth certificate*)

when the court will consider an application for a parental order under section 54 of the Human Fertilisation and Embryology Act 2008 in respect of the child.

You are [not] obliged to attend the hearing [unless you wish to do so].

If you do not attend this hearing the court may make an order as noted above.

[While the petition is pending you must not, except with the leave of the court, remove the child from the care of the petitioners.]

[The court has been requested to dispense with your agreement to the making of an order on the ground[s] that (*specify ground(s)*)].

Date (*insert date*)

[*(Signed)*
First petitioner
*(Signed)*
Second petitioner]
or [*(Signed)*
[*Solicitor for petitioners*] or [*sheriff clerk*\*]
(*Address*)]
\*where serial number assigned

FORM 25[1]

Rule 2.55(3)(b)

FORM OF INTIMATION OF DIET OF THE HEARING OF APPLICATION UNDER SECTIONS 22(1) OR 24 OF THE HUMAN FERTILISATION AND EMBRYOLOGY ACT 2008

To: (*insert full name and address of person to whom this intimation is to be sent*)

You are given NOTICE that a hearing will take place at (*insert name and address of sheriff court*) on (*insert date*) at (*insert time*) in relation to the child (*insert full name of child as given in the birth certificate*)

when the court will consider a minute of application under rule 2.55 of the Act of Sederunt (Child Care and Maintenance Rules) 1997 in respect of the child. A copy of the application is attached.

You do not need to attend this hearing if you do not wish to be heard by the court.

Date (*insert date*)

*(Signed)*
Minuter
or [*(Signed)*
[*Solicitor for minuter*] or [*sheriff clerk*\*]
(*Address*)]
\*where serial number has been assigned

FORM 26[1]

**Rule 3.4(1)(a)**

NOTICE TO CHILD OF APPLICATION FOR A CHILD ASSESSMENT ORDER UNDER SECTION 35 OF THE CHILDREN'S HEARINGS (SCOTLAND) ACT 2011

Court ref. no.:

Dear *[insert name by which child is known]*

I am writing to tell you that because there are worries about the way you are being treated the sheriff [the person who has to decide] is being asked to make a "Child Assessment Order" to make sure that you are being treated properly.

The application to the sheriff has been made by *[insert in simple language the person making the application, the reason for making it and the order(s) sought]*. The sheriff would like to hear your views about what you would like to happen before making a decision.

You can tell the sheriff what you think by:

**Going to see the Sheriff**

The sheriff will consider what to do next on *[insert date, time and place of hearing]*.

You can take someone like a friend, parent, teacher or a social worker with you to see the sheriff to support you; or

You can ask a lawyer to come with you and tell the sheriff your views.

If you think you would like to go to see the sheriff it is usually best to talk it over with a lawyer.

**Not going to see the Sheriff**

You can fill in the attached form or write down your views on a separate sheet of paper and send them back in the enclosed stamped addressed envelope **before** the date on which the sheriff is to hear the application, which is at the end of this letter.

**REMEMBER**

That someone like a friend or teacher can help you to fill in the form or write down your views.

— If you return the form it will be given to the sheriff and, if he needs more information, he will ask the Sheriff Clerk who works with him to contact you about this.

**IMPORTANT NOTE**—You do not have to do any of these things if you would prefer not to; however, it is very important for you to understand that, if you do not do anything, the sheriff might make an order without knowing what your views are.

---

**If you are unsure about what to do you can get free legal advice from a Lawyer or Local Advice Agency or Law Centre about the application and about legal aid.**
**The Scottish Child Law Centre can refer you to specially trained lawyers who can help you.**
**They give advice on their free phone no (0800 328 8970) any time between 9.30 am and 4.00 pm Monday to Friday.**

---

**The hearing to consider the application will be held on [insert date] at [insert time], in [insert name of court] SHERIFF COURT, [insert address of court].**

You will see that, along with this letter, there is a copy of the application to the sheriff and the sheriff's order fixing the hearing. If you decide to get advice, or to be represented, make sure that you give your advisor a copy of the application, and the sheriff's order.

Signed Date ............... Date ..........

To the Sheriff Clerk

I would like the Sheriff to know what I have to say before he or she makes a decision.

**Write what you want to say here, or you can use a separate sheet of paper.**

...............

Name ...............

Address ...............

...............

...............

Court Reference Number ..........

(if you know it)

FORM 27

Rule 3.4(1)(b)

NOTICE TO CHILD OF APPLICATION TO VARY OR SET ASIDE CHILD PROTECTION ORDER UNDER SECTION 60 OF THE CHILDREN (SCOTLAND) ACT 1995

---

CASE NUMBER

---

**KEEPING YOU SAFE**

Dear *[insert name by which child is known]*

A Child Protection Order was made on .......... to keep you safe from harm.

The sheriff [the person who has to decide] made the order, which says that you are to continue to live at *[insert address]* at present.

Now the sheriff has been asked to have another look at your situation, *[insert in simple language the person making the application, the reason for making it and the order(s) sought]*. The sheriff would like to hear your views about what you would like to happen before making a decision.

You can tell the sheriff what you think by:—

**Going to see the Sheriff**

You can take someone like a friend, parent, a teacher or a social worker with you to see the sheriff to support you; or you can ask a lawyer to come with you and tell the sheriff your views.

**Not going to see the Sheriff**

You can fill in the attached form and send it back in the enclosed stamped addressed envelope before the hearing date which is at the end of this letter.

**REMEMBER**

That someone can help you to fill in the form.

If you return the form it will be given to the sheriff and, if he needs more information, he will ask the Sheriff Clerk who works with him to contact you about this.

**IMPORTANT NOTE**—You do not have to do any of these things if you would prefer not to; however, it is very important for you to understand that, if you do not do anything, the sheriff might make an order without knowing what your views are.

---

**If you are unsure about what to do you can get free legal advice from a Lawyer or Local Advice Agency or Law Centre about the application and about legal aid.**
**The Scottish Child Law Centre can refer you to specially trained lawyers who can help you. They give advice on their free phone no (0800 317 500) any time between 9.00 am and 5.00 pm Monday to Friday.**

---

The hearing to consider the application will be held on [insert date] at [insert time], in [insert name of court] SHERIFF COURT, [insert address of court].

You will see that, along with this letter, there is a copy of the application to the sheriff, and the sheriff's order fixing the hearing. If you decide to get advice, or to ask someone to go to see the sheriff for you, make sure that you give your advisor a copy of the application, and the sheriff's order.

SIGNED ...............

DATE: ...............

To the Sheriff Clerk

I would like the Sheriff to know what I have to say before he or she makes a decision.

**Write what you want to say here, or you can use a separate sheet of paper.**

...................

Name ...............

Address ...............

...............

...............

Court Reference Number ..........

(if you know it)

FORM 28[1]

Rule 3.4(1)(c)

NOTICE TO CHILD OF APPLICATION FOR AN EXCLUSION ORDER UNDER SECTION 76 OF THE CHILDREN (SCOTLAND) ACT 1995

---

Court ref. no.:

---

**KEEPING YOU SAFE**

Dear *[insert name by which child is known]*

I am writing to tell you that because there are worries about your safety the sheriff [the person who has to decide] has been asked to sort out some practical arrangements to make sure you can be kept safe. The sheriff is being asked to make an "Exclusion Order" to make sure that *[insert name of person]* does not come into the family home at *[insert address]*. You are to stay [at home/where you are]* at present.

---

[1] As amended by the Act of Sederunt (Children's Hearings (Scotland) Act 2011) (Miscellaneous Amendments) 2013 (SSI 2013/172) para.4 (effective June 24, 2013).

*delete as appropriate

The application to the sheriff has been made by *[insert in simple language the person making the application, the reason for making it and the order(s) sought]*. The sheriff would like to hear your views about what you would like to happen before making a decision.

You can tell the sheriff what you think by:—

**Going to see the Sheriff**

You can take someone like a friend, parent, a teacher or a social worker with you to see the sheriff to support you; or you can ask a lawyer to come with you and tell the sheriff your views.

If you think you would like to go to see the sheriff it is usually best to talk it over with a lawyer.

**Not going to see the Sheriff**

You can fill in the attached form or write down your views on a separate sheet of paper and send them back in the enclosed stamped addressed envelope **before** the date on which the court is to hear the application, which is at the end of this letter.

**REMEMBER**

That someone like a friend or teacher can help you to fill in the form or write down your views.

If you return the form it will be given to the sheriff, and, if he needs more information, he will ask the Sheriff Clerk who works with him to contact you about this.

**IMPORTANT NOTE**—You do not have to do any of these things if you would prefer not to; however, it is very important for you to understand that, if you do not do anything, the sheriff might make an order without knowing what your views are.

---

**If you are unsure about what to do you can get free legal advice from a Lawyer or Local Advice Agency or Law Centre about the application and about legal aid.**
**The Scottish Child Law Centre can refer you to specially trained lawyers who can help you.**
**They give advice on their free phone no (0800 328 8970) any time between 9.30 am and 4.00 pm Monday to Friday.**

---

The hearing to consider the application will be held on [insert date] at [insert time], in [insert name of court] SHERIFF COURT, [insert address of court].

You will see that, along with this letter, there is a copy of the application to the sheriff and the sheriff's order fixing the hearing. If you decide to get advice, or to ask someone to go to see the sheriff for you, make sure that you give your advisor a copy of the application, and the sheriff's order.

SIGNED ............... DATE: .........

To the Sheriff Clerk

I would like the Sheriff to know what I have to say before he or she makes a decision.

**Write what you want to say here, or you can use a separate sheet of paper.**

.....................

Name ...............

Address ...............

...............

...............

Court Reference Number .........
(if you know it)

FORM 29[1]

Rule 3.4(1)(d)

NOTICE TO CHILD OF APPLICATION TO VARY AN EXCLUSION ORDER UNDER SECTION 79(3) OF THE CHILDREN (SCOTLAND) ACT 1995

---

Court ref. no.:

---

**CHANGING THE ARRANGEMENTS FOR KEEPING YOU SAFE**

Dear *[insert name by which child is known]*

---

[1] As amended by the Act of Sederunt (Children's Hearings (Scotland) Act 2011) (Miscellaneous Amendments) 2013 (SSI 2013/172) para.4 (effective June 24, 2013).

I am writing to tell you that the sheriff has been asked to look again at the arrangements that were made to make sure you can be kept safe. The sheriff is being asked to *[change or cancel]** the "Exclusion Order" he made on *[insert date]*. You are to stay *[at home/where you are]** at present.

*delete as appropriate

The application to the sheriff has been made by *[insert in simple language the person making the application, the reason for making it and the order(s) sought]*. The sheriff would like to hear your views about what you would like to happen before making a decision.

You can tell the sheriff what you think in the same way that you did when the original order was made. If you told the sheriff your views last time you might want to do so again using the same method again. You can if you prefer use a different method to tell the sheriff this time.

Even if you did not tell anything to the sheriff last time he would like to hear your views.

You can tell the sheriff what you think by:—

**Going to see the Sheriff**

You can take someone like a friend, parent, a teacher or a social worker with you to see the sheriff to support you; or you can ask a lawyer to come with you and tell the sheriff your views.

If you think you would like to see the sheriff it is usually best to talk it over with a lawyer.

**Not going to see the Sheriff**

You can fill in the attached form or write down your views on a separate sheet of paper and send them back in the enclosed stamped addressed envelope **before** the date on which the sheriff is to hear the application, which is at the end of this letter.

**REMEMBER**

That someone like a friend or teacher can help you to fill in the form or write down your views.

If you return the form it will be given to the sheriff and, if he needs more information, he will ask the Sheriff Clerk who works with him to contact you about this.

**IMPORTANT NOTE**—You do not have to do any of these things if you would prefer not to; however, it is very important for you to understand that, if you do not do anything, the sheriff might make an order without knowing what your views are.

---

**If you are unsure about what to do you can get free legal advice from a Lawyer or Local Advice Agency or Law Centre The Scottish Child Law Centre can refer you to specially trained lawyers who can help you.**
**They give advice on their free phone no (0800 328 8970) any time between 9.30 am and 4.00 pm Monday to Friday.**

---

The hearing to consider the application will be held on [insert place] at [insert time], in [insert name] SHERIFF COURT, [insert address of sheriff].

You will see that, along with this letter, there is a copy of the application to the sheriff, and the sheriff's order fixing the hearing. If you decide to get advice, or to ask someone to go to sheriff for you, make sure that you give your advisor a copy of the application, and the sheriff's order.

SIGNED........................ DATE:..........

To the Sheriff Clerk

I would like the Sheriff to know what I have to say before he or she makes a decision.

**Write what you want to say here, or you can use a separate sheet of paper.**

....................

Name ...............

Address ...............

...............

...............

Court Reference Number ..........

(if you know it)

FORM 30

Rule 3.4(1)(e)

NOTICE TO CHILD OF APPLICATION FOR A FURTHER DETENTION WARRANT UNDER SECTION 67 OF THE CHILDREN (SCOTLAND) ACT 1995

*[Repealed by the Act of Sederunt (Children's Hearings (Scotland) Act 2011) (Miscellaneous Amendments) 2013 (SSI 2013/172) para.4 (effective June 24, 2013).]*

FORM 31[1]

Rule 3.4(1)(f)

CITATION OF CHILD IN APPLICATION UNDER SECTION 93(2)(A) OR 94(2)(A) OF THECHILDREN'S HEARINGS (SCOTLAND) ACT 2011 (NO PROCEDURAL HEARING FIXED)

Court ref. no.:

Dear [insert name by which child is known],

As you know at the Children's Hearing held on [insert date] not everyone agreed that the information given to you in the statement of grounds was correct. *[The information on the statement of grounds was not accepted by [insert name of person who did not accept the grounds]] or [The hearing was satisfied that *you/[insert name of relevant person] *could not/did not understand the reasons why you were there]. This means that your case has been sent to a sheriff,who will decide whether the information given to you in the statement of grounds is correct.

**WHAT THE SHERIFF DOES:** A sheriff assists for lots of different reasons, but this time the purpose is to help the Children's Hearing. If the sheriff decides that the worries about you are justified the case will go back to the Children's Hearing who will decide what is to happen in your case.

**HEARING ON EVIDENCE:** The sheriff has set a date for a hearing on evidence. The hearing on evidence will take place on [insert time and date of hearing] at [insert address of sheriff court].

[*You are required to attend court on that date or You are not required to attend court on that date, but you may wish to do so.]

At the hearing on evidence the sheriff will listen to the evidence in your case, and will make a decision. This decision is very important for you [*and it is necessary for you to attend the hearings to tell the sheriff about your circumstances and how you feel. You might be asked some questions. You can be represented by a solicitor or another person].

*[IMPORTANT NOTE: IT IS VERY IMPORTANT THAT YOU ATTEND on the date and time given. If an emergency arises and you cannot attend you must contact the sheriff clerk on (insert telephone number) or the Principal Reporter because it is possible, if you do not attend, you may be detained and kept in a safe place until a later date.]

*[The sheriff has said that you do not have to attend the hearing on [insert date] at [insert time] at [insert name and address of sheriff court], but if you want to go along to hear what is said at the hearing then you can. If you do not want to go to court then you can still let the sheriff know what you think by filling in the attached form or you can write down what you want to say on a separate sheet of paper and send them back in the enclosed stamped addressed envelope before the date on which the sheriff is to hear the application, which is at the end of this letter. Alternatively, you can ask a lawyer to go to the hearing to tell the sheriff your views.]

**If you are unsure about what to do you can get free legal advice from a Lawyer or Local Advice Agency or Law Centre about the application and about legal aid. The Scottish Child Law Centre can refer you to specially trained lawyers who can help you. They give advice on their free phone number (0800 328 8970) any time between 9.30am and 4.00pm Monday to Friday.**

You will see that, along with this letter, there is a copy of the application to the sheriff, and the sheriff's order fixing the hearing. If you decide to get advice, or to ask someone to go with you to see the sheriff, make sure that you give them a copy of the application and the sheriff's order.

....................

(Signed)             (Date)

(*delete as appropriate)

To the Sheriff Clerk:

**I would like the Sheriff to know what I have to say before he or she makes a decision** (write what you want to say here, or you can use a separate sheet of paper):

Your Name:

Your Address:

Court Reference Number (if you know it):

FORM 31A[2]

---

[1] As substituted by the Act of Sederunt (Children's Hearings (Scotland) Act 2011) (Miscellaneous Amendments) 2013 (SSI 2013/172) para.4 (effective June 24, 2013).
[2] As inserted by the Act of Sederunt (Children's Hearings (Scotland) Act 2011) (Miscellaneous Amendments) 2013 (SSI 2013/172) para.4 (effective June 24, 2013).

Rule 3.4(1)(g)

CITATION OF CHILD IN APPLICATION UNDER SECTION 94(2)(A) OF THE CHILDREN'S HEARINGS (SCOTLAND) ACT 2011 (PROCEDURAL HEARING FIXED)

Court ref. no.:

Dear [*insert name by which child is known*],

As you know at the Children's Hearing held on [*insert date*] not everyone agreed that the information given to you in the statement of grounds was correct. The hearing was satisfied that you *could not/did not understand the reasons why you were there. This means that your case has been sent to a sheriff, who will decide whether the information given to you in the statement of grounds is correct.

**WHAT THE SHERIFF DOES:** A sheriff assists for lots of different reasons, but this time the purpose is to help the Children's Hearing. If the sheriff decides that the worries about you are justified the case will go back to the Children's Hearing who will decide what is to happen in your case.

**PROCEDURAL HEARING:** The sheriff has arranged a procedural hearing to determine whether or not each relevant person (whose names are [*insert names of relevant persons*]) accepts that the information given to you in the statement of grounds is correct. The procedural hearing will take place on [*insert time and date of hearing*] at [*insert address of sheriff court*]. [*You are required to attend court on that date or You are not required to attend court on that date, but you may wish to do so.*] If, at the procedural hearing, all the relevant persons accept that that the information that has been given is correct then the sheriff may make a decision without hearing evidence. You have the right though to ask the sheriff to hear evidence, even if all relevant persons accept that the information in the statement of grounds is correct.

**HEARING ON EVIDENCE:** The sheriff has also set a date for a hearing on evidence. Unless you receive notice that the sheriff has discharged the hearing on evidence, it will take place on [*insert time and date of hearing*] at [*insert address of sheriff court*]. [*You are required to attend court on that date or You are not required to attend court on that date, but you may wish to do so.*]

At the hearing on evidence the sheriff will listen to the evidence in your case, and will make a decision. This decision is very important for you [*and it is necessary for you to attend the hearing to tell the sheriff about your circumstances and how you feel. You might be asked some questions. You can be represented by a solicitor or another person*].

*[**IMPORTANT NOTE: IT IS VERY IMPORTANT THAT YOU ATTEND** on the dates and times given. If an emergency arises and you cannot attend you must contact the sheriff clerk on (*insert telephone number*) or the Principal Reporter because it is possible, if you do not attend, you may be detained and kept in a safe place until a later date.]

*[The sheriff has said that you do not have to attend the hearing on [*insert date*] at [*insert time*] at [*insert name and address of sheriff court*], but if you want to go along to hear what is said at the hearing then you can. If you do not want to go to court then you can still let the sheriff know what you think by filling in the attached form or you can write down what you want to say on a separate sheet of paper and send them back in the enclosed stamped addressed envelope before the date on which the sheriff is to hear the application, which is at the end of this letter. Alternatively, you can ask a lawyer to go to the hearing to tell the sheriff your views.]

**If you are unsure about what to do you can get free legal advice from a Lawyer or Local Advice Agency or Law Centre about the application and about legal aid. The Scottish Child Law Centre can refer you to specially trained lawyers who can help you. They give advice on their free phone number (0800 328 8970) any time between 9.30am and 4.00pm Monday to Friday.**

You will see that, along with this letter, there is a copy of the application to the sheriff, and the sheriff's order fixing the hearings. If you decide to get advice, or to ask someone to go with you to see the sheriff, make sure that you give them a copy of the application and the sheriff's order.

...................

(Signed)                    (Date)

(*\*delete as appropriate*)

To the Sheriff Clerk:

**I would like the Sheriff to know what I have to say before he or she makes a decision** (write what you want to say here, or you can use a separate sheet of paper):

Your Name:

Your Address:

Court Reference Number (if you know it):

FORM 31B[1]

Rule 3.4(1)(h)

NOTICE TO CHILD OF APPLICATION FOR REVIEW OF GROUNDS DETERMINATION
UNDER THE CHILDREN'S HEARINGS (SCOTLAND) ACT 2011

Court ref. no.:

Dear [insert name by which child is known],

I am writing to tell you that the sheriff has been asked to look again at the decision that [he or she]* made on [insert date], which found that [insert details in simple terms of the grounds determination]. You are to stay [at home/where you are]* at present.

The application to the sheriff has been made by [insert in simple language the person making the application]. That person thinks that before making the grounds determination the sheriff should have considered [insert in simple language the evidence that was not considered by the sheriff and why]. The sheriff would like to hear your views about what you would like to happen before making a decision.

*[So that you can tell the sheriff what you think, you need to go and see the sheriff on [insert date] at [insert time] at [insert name and address of sheriff court]. It is very important that you turn up on this date. You can take someone like a friend, parent, a teacher or a social worker with you to see the sheriff and to support you. Alternatively, you can ask a lawyer to come with you and tell the sheriff your views. If you think you would like to go to see the sheriff it is usually best to talk it over with a lawyer.] OR

*[The sheriff has said that you do not have to attend the hearing on [insert date] at [insert time] at [insert name and address of sheriff court], but if you want to go along to hear what is said at the hearing then you can. If you do not want to go to court then you can still let the sheriff know what you think by filling in the attached form or you can write down what you want to say on a separate sheet of paper and send them back in the enclosed stamped addressed envelope before the date on which the sheriff is to hear the application, which is at the end of this letter. Alternatively, you can ask a lawyer to go to the hearing to tell the sheriff your views.

**REMEMBER** that someone like a friend or teacher can help you to fill in the form or write down your views. If you return the form it will be given to the sheriff and, if the sheriff needs more information, he or she will ask the sheriff clerk who works with the sheriff to contact you about this.]

**If you are unsure about what to do you can get free legal advice from a Lawyer or Local Advice Agency or Law Centre. The Scottish Child Law Centre can refer you to specially trained lawyers who can help you. They give advice on their free phone number (0800 328 8970) any time between 9.30am and 4.00pm Monday to Friday.**

You will see that, along with this letter, there is a copy of the application to the sheriff, and the sheriff's order fixing the hearing. If you decide to get advice, or to ask someone to go with you to see the sheriff, make sure that you give them a copy of the application and the sheriff's order.

....................

(Signed)                    (Date)

*(*delete as appropriate)*

To the Sheriff Clerk:

**I would like the Sheriff to know what I have to say before he or she makes a decision** (write what you want to say here, or you can use a separate sheet of paper):

Your Name:

Your Address:

Court Reference Number (if you know it):

FORM 32[2]

Rule 3.11

FORM OF FIRST ORDER UNDER THE CHILDREN (SCOTLAND) ACT 1995

Court ref. no.:

SECTION 76 (Application for Exclusion Order),

SECTION 79 (Application to vary or recall Exclusion Order) and

---

[1] As inserted by the Act of Sederunt (Children's Hearings (Scotland) Act 2011) (Miscellaneous Amendments) 2013 (SSI 2013/172) para.4 (effective June 24, 2013).

[2] As amended by the Act of Sederunt (Children's Hearings (Scotland) Act 2011) (Miscellaneous Amendments) 2013 (SSI 2013/172) para.4 (effective June 24, 2013).

*[Place and date]*

The court assigns *[date]* at *[hour]* within the *[name court]* in chambers at *[place]* for the hearing of the application;

appoints the applicant forthwith to give notice of the application and hearing to the persons listed in PART I of the application by serving a copy of the application and this order together with notices in Forms *[insert form Nos.]*;

*dispenses with notice and service on *[insert name]* for the following reason(s) *[insert reason(s)]*.

[Note: *Insert details of any other order granted and in an application under* section 76 of the Children (Scotland) Act 1995 *for an exclusion order insert as appropriate*

Meantime grants an interim exclusion order; *or* interim interdict; *or otherwise as the case may be.]* ..............

.............................
*Sheriff or sheriff clerk

*delete as appropriate

FORM 32A[1]

Rule 3.11

FORM OF FIRST ORDER UNDER THE CHILDREN'S HEARINGS (SCOTLAND) ACT 2011

Court ref. no.:

Section 35 (Application for Child Assessment Order),

Section 48 (Application to vary or terminate a Child Protection Order)

*[Place and date]*

The court assigns *[date]* at *[hour]* within chambers at *[insert name and address of sheriff court]* for the hearing of the application;

appoints the applicant forthwith to give notice of the application and hearing to the persons listed in PART I of the application by serving a copy of the application and this order together with notices in Forms *[insert Form Numbers]*;

*dispenses with notice and service on *[insert name]* for the following reason(s) *[insert reason(s)]*.

[Note: *In the case of* section 48 *applications only, insert details of the* Child Protection Order.] ..............

.............................
(Sheriff or sheriff clerk)

(**delete as appropriate*)

FORM 33[2]

Rule 3.11

FORM OF WARRANT TO CITE CHILD AND TO GIVE NOTICE/INTIMATE TO RELEVANT PERSON(S) AND SAFEGUARDER IN APPLICATIONS UNDER SECTION 93(2)(a) or 94(2)(a) OF THE CHILDREN'S HEARINGS (SCOTLAND) ACT 2011

Court ref. no.:

*[Place and date]*

The court

1. Assigns *[date]* at *[hour]* within the *[name court]* in chambers at *[place]* for the hearing of the application;

*[and fixes a procedural hearing to take place on *[insert date]* at *[insert time]* within *[name court]* in chambers at *[place]*]

2. Appoints the Principal Reporter forthwith

to cite AB *[name of child]*,

to give notice/intimate to BB *[insert name of relevant person or persons (within the meaning of* Rule 3.1(1) *)]* whose whereabouts are known and to [CD] (name and design) the safeguarder *[and [EF] (name and design) the curator *ad litem*],

by serving a copy of the application and relative statement of grounds of referral;

---

[1] As inserted by the Act of Sederunt (Children's Hearings (Scotland) Act 2011) (Miscellaneous Amendments) 2013 (SSI 2013/172) para.4 (effective June 24, 2013).

[2] As amended by the Act of Sederunt (Children's Hearings (Scotland) Act 2011) (Miscellaneous Amendments) 2013 (SSI 2013/172) para.4 (effective June 24, 2013).

3. Grants warrant to cite witnesses and havers.

4. *Dispenses with notice and service on *[insert name]* for the following reason(s) *[insert reason(s)]*.

5. *Dispenses with the obligation to attend of *[insert name of child]* for the following reason(s) *[insert reason(s)]*.

................

*Sheriff or Sheriff Clerk

*delete as appropriate

FORM 34[1]

Rule 3.12(1)(a)

NOTICE OF APPLICATION FOR A CHILD ASSESSMENT ORDER TO A PERSON NAMED IN APPLICATION UNDER SECTION 35(1) OF THE CHILDREN'S HEARINGS (SCOTLAND) ACT 2011

Court ref. no.:

**Application to Sheriff Court at** *[insert name]*

for a Child Assessment Order under section 35 of the Children's hearings (Scotland) Act 2011

To *[insert name and address of person to whom notice is given]*.

...................

You are given notice that the court will hear this application—

*[applicant to insert details of the date, time and place for hearing the application]*

on...............

at...............

in...............

Along with this notice there is attached a copy of the application and the court's order fixing this hearing.

Signed .............. Date .........

WHAT YOU SHOULD DO

YOU SHOULD ATTEND OR BE REPRESENTED AT THE HEARING.

If you do not attend in person you may instruct someone else to represent you.

**If you do not attend or are not represented at the hearing, the court may decide the case in your absence.**

YOU SHOULD OBTAIN ADVICE FROM A SOLICITOR OR LOCAL ADVICE AGENCY OR LAW CENTRE. You may be entitled to legal aid. Advice about legal aid is available from any solicitor, advice agency or law centre.

FORM 35[2]

Rule 3.12(1)(b)

NOTICE OF APLICATION TO VARY OR TERMINATE CHILD PROTECTION ORDER TO PERSON NAMED IN APPLICATION UNDER SECTION 48 OF THE CHILDREN'S HEARINGS (SCOTLAND) ACT 2011

Court ref. no.:

**Application to Sheriff Court at** *[insert name]*...............

to vary or terminate a Child Protection Order under section 48 of the Children's Hearings (Scotland) Act 2011

To *(insert name and address)*...............

You are given notice that the court will hear this application—

*[applicant to insert details of the date, time and place for hearing the application]*

The application is to *(insert details of purpose application)*

on...............

at...............

in...............

Along with this notice there is attached a copy of the application and the court's order fixing this hearing.

Signed .............. Date .........

WHAT YOU SHOULD DO

---

[1] As amended by the Act of Sederunt (Children's Hearings (Scotland) Act 2011) (Miscellaneous Amendments) 2013 (SSI 2013/172) para.4 (effective June 24, 2013).

[2] As amended by the Act of Sederunt (Children's Hearings (Scotland) Act 2011) (Miscellaneous Amendments) 2013 (SSI 2013/172) para.4 (effective June 24, 2013).

YOU SHOULD ATTEND OR BE REPRESENTED AT THE HEARING.

If you do not attend in person you may instruct someone else to represent you.

**If you do not attend or are not represented at the hearing, the court may decide the case in your absence.**

YOU SHOULD OBTAIN ADVICE FROM A SOLICITOR OR LOCAL ADVICE AGENCY OR LAW CENTRE. You may be entitled to legal aid. Advice about legal aid is available from any solicitor, advice agency or law centre.

FORM 36[1]

Rule 3.12(1)(c)

NOTICE OF APPLICATION FOR AN EXCLUSION ORDER TO PERSON NAMED IN APPLICA-TION OR ANY OTHER PERSON UNDER SECTION 76 OF THE CHILDREN (SCOTLAND) ACT 1995

Court ref. no.:

**Application to Sheriff Court at** *(insert name)*

for an exclusion order under section 76 of the Children (Scotland) Act 1995 in respect of

\*you/*[insert name and address of named person]*

\*delete as appropriate

To *[insert name and address of person to whom notice is given]*.

You are given notice that the court will hear this application—

*[applicant to insert details of the date, time and place for hearing the application]*

on..............

at..............

in..............

Along with this notice there is attached a copy of the application and the court's order fixing this hearing \*which includes details of any interim orders granted.

Signed .......... Date ..........

WHAT YOU SHOULD DO

YOU SHOULD ATTEND OR BE REPRESENTED AT THE HEARING.

**If you do not attend or are not represented at the hearing, the court may decide the case in your absence**. If the order sought is to exclude you then the granting of the order will have an effect on a number of your rights including the suspending of any rights of occupancy you have.

Details of the orders sought are contained in the application form.

YOU SHOULD OBTAIN ADVICE FROM A SOLICITOR OR LOCAL ADVICE AGENCY OR LAW CENTRE. You may be entitled to legal aid. Advice about legal aid is available from any solicitor, advice agency or law centre.

\*delete as appropriate

FORM 37[2]

Rule 3.12(1)(d)

NOTICE OF APPLICATION TO VARY OR RECALL AN EXCLUSION ORDER TO PERSON NAMED IN APPLICATION OR ANY OTHER PERSON UNDER SECTION 79 OF THE CHILDREN (SCOTLAND) ACT 1995

Court ref. no.:

Application to Sheriff Court at **(insert name)**

to vary or recall\* an exclusion order under section 79 of the Children (Scotland) Act 1995 in respect of \*you/*[insert name and address of named person]*

\*delete as appropriate

To *[insert name and address of person to whom notice is given]*

You are given notice that the court will hear this application—

*[applicant to insert details of the date, time and place for hearing the application]*

on..............

at..............

in..............

---

[1] As amended by the Act of Sederunt (Children's Hearings (Scotland) Act 2011) (Miscellaneous Amendments) 2013 (SSI 2013/172) para.4 (effective June 24, 2013).

[2] As amended by the Act of Sederunt (Children's Hearings (Scotland) Act 2011) (Miscellaneous Amendments) 2013 (SSI 2013/172) para.4 (effective June 24, 2013).

Along with this notice there is attached a copy of the application and the court's order fixing the hearing

Signed .......... Date ..........

WHAT YOU SHOULD DO

YOU SHOULD ATTEND OR BE REPRESENTED AT THE HEARING.

**If you do not attend or are not represented at the hearing, the court may decide the case in your absence.** Details of the orders sought are contained in the application form.

YOU SHOULD OBTAIN ADVICE FROM A SOLICITOR OR LOCAL ADVICE AGENCY OR LAW CENTRE. You may be entitled to legal aid. Advice about legal aid is available from any solicitor, advice agency or law centre. If you instructed any person to represent you at the original hearing which granted the application you should consider bringing this application to their attention without delay.

FORM 38

Form 3.12(1)(e)

NOTICE OF APPLICATION FOR FURTHER DETENTION OF CHILD TO PERSON NAMED IN APPLICATION OR ANY OTHER PERSON UNDER SECTION 67 OF THE CHILDREN (SCOTLAND) ACT 1995

*[Repealed by the Act of Sederunt (Children's Hearings (Scotland) Act 2011) (Miscellaneous Amendments) 2013 (SSI 2013/172) para.4 (effective June 24, 2013).]*

FORM 39[1]

Rule 3.12(1)(f)

NOTICE TO RELEVANT PERSON IN APPLICATION UNDER SECTION 93(2)(a) or 94(2)(a) OF THE CHILDREN'S HEARINGS (SCOTLAND) ACT 2011 (NO PROCEDURAL HEARING)

Court ref. no.:

1. *[Place and Date]*

To *[name and address of relevant person (within the meaning of* Rule 3.1(1) *)]*

TAKE NOTICE that the court has received the application which accompanies this intimation.

2. **YOU MAY ATTEND COURT** for the hearing of the application as shown below.

3.      Place of Hearing:               Sheriff Court ..............

                                     Address ..............

                                          ..............

                                          ..............

                                          ..............

             Date of hearing:                    ..............

             Time of hearing:                   ..............

                                          ..............

(Signed)

Principal Reporter

WHAT YOU SHOULD DO

YOU SHOULD ATTEND OR BE REPRESENTED AT THE HEARING.

**If you do not attend or are not represented at the hearing, the court may decide the case in your absence.** Details of the orders sought are contained in the application form.

YOU SHOULD OBTAIN ADVICE FROM A SOLICITOR OR LOCAL ADVICE AGENCY OR LAW CENTRE. You may be entitled to legal aid. Advice about legal aid is available from any solicitor, advice agency or law centre.

FORM 39A[2]

Rule 3.12(1)(g)

NOTICE TO RELEVANT PERSON IN APPLICATION UNDER SECTION 94(2)(A) OF THE CHILDREN'S HEARINGS (SCOTLAND) ACT 2011 (PROCEDURAL HEARING FIXED)

Court ref. no.:

1. *[Insert place and date]*

---

[1] As amended by the Act of Sederunt (Children's Hearings (Scotland) Act 2011) (Miscellaneous Amendments) 2013 (SSI 2013/172) para.4 (effective June 24, 2013).

[2] As inserted by the Act of Sederunt (Children's Hearings (Scotland) Act 2011) (Miscellaneous Amendments) 2013 (SSI 2013/172) para.4 (effective June 24, 2013).

To [*insert name and address of relevant person (within the meaning of* Rule 3.1(1) *)*]

TAKE NOTICE that the court has received the application which accompanies this intimation.

2. **PROCEDURAL HEARING:** The sheriff has fixed a procedural hearing to determine whether or not the section 67 grounds in the statement of grounds are accepted by each relevant person. The procedural hearing will take place on [*insert time and date of hearing*] at [*insert address of sheriff court*]. If you accept the grounds YOU SHOULD ATTEND OR BE REPRESENTED AT COURT ON THAT DATE so that you can tell the sheriff that you accept the section 67 grounds. If you do not attend the procedural hearing, then you should attend the hearing on evidence referred to in paragraph 3 below.

If, at the procedural hearing, all the relevant persons accept that that the information that has been given is correct then the sheriff may make a decision without hearing evidence. You have the right though to ask the sheriff to hear evidence, even if all other relevant persons accept that the information in the statement of grounds is correct.

3. A hearing on evidence has also been fixed. Unless you receive notice in accordance with rule 3.45(8) of the Act of Sederunt (Child Care and Maintenance Rules) 1997 that the sheriff has discharged that hearing, the hearing on evidence will take place on [*insert time and date of hearing*] at [*insert address of sheriff court*]. YOU SHOULD ATTEND COURT on that date for the hearing of the application.

(*signed*)

Principal Reporter

**WHAT YOU SHOULD DO:**

**YOU SHOULD ATTEND OR BE REPRESENTED AT THE HEARINGS.**

If you do not attend or are not represented at the hearings, the court may decide the case in your absence. Details of the orders sought are contained in the application form.

**YOU SHOULD OBTAIN ADVICE FROM A SOLICITOR OR LOCAL ADVICE AGENCY OR LAW CENTRE.** You may be entitled to legal aid. Advice about legal aid is available from any solicitor, advice agency or law centre.

FORM 40[1]

Rule 3.12(2)

NOTICE TO SAFEGUARDER/CURATOR *AD LITEM IN* APPLICATION UNDER SECTION 93(2)(A) OR 94(2)(A) OF THE CHILDREN'S HEARINGS (SCOTLAND) ACT 2011

Court ref. no.:

1. *[Place and Date]*

To *[name and address of safeguarder and/or curator ad litem]*

TAKE NOTICE that the court has received the application which accompanies this intimation.

2. A hearing of evidence in respect of the application has been fixed as follows:

Place of Hearing:                  Sheriff Court ...............

                                       Address ...............

                                         ...............

                                         ...............

Date of hearing:                    ...............

Time of hearing:                   ...............

*(In addition, a procedural hearing has been fixed to take place on [*insert date*] at [*insert time*] within [*name court*] in chambers at [*place*])

(Signed)

Principal Reporter

**PLEASE NOTE:**

Your attention is drawn to the provisions of rules 3.6 to 3.9 of the Act of Sederunt (Child Care and Maintenance Rules) 1997 which regulate the appointment and duties of safeguarders.

(*\*delete as appropriate*)

---

[1] As amended by the Act of Sederunt (Children's Hearings (Scotland) Act 2011) (Miscellaneous Amendments) 2013 (SSI 2013/172) para.4 (effective June 24, 2013).

FORM 41[1]

Rule 3.14(2)

CITATION OF WITNESS OR HAVER UNDER THE CHILDREN'S HEARINGS (SCOTLAND)
ACT 2011 OR THE CHILDREN (SCOTLAND) ACT 1995

Court ref. no.:

KL [address], you are required to attend at .......... Sheriff Court on .......... at .......... to give evidence in
the hearing of [an application by the Principal Reporter] to the sheriff for a determination of whether the
section 67 grounds in the case of *[insert name of child]* are established]

OR

[an appeal to the sheriff against a decision of a children's hearing in the case of [name of child]]

OR

[an application by *[insert name and address]* for [insert details of purpose of hearing]]

[You are required to bring with you [specify documents]].

**If you fail to attend without reasonable excuse having demanded and been paid your travelling
expenses, warrant may be granted for your arrest.**

Signed PQ, Sheriff Officer;

or

XY Solicitor/Sheriff Clerk/ Principal Reporter/Officer of the Local Authority
[address]

Note:

Within certain specified limits claims for necessary outlays and loss of earnings will be met.

Claims should be made to the person who has cited you to attend and proof of any loss of earnings
should be given to that person. If you wish your travelling expenses to be paid prior to your attendance
you should apply to the person who has cited you.

FORM 42[2]

Rule 3.14(3)

CERTIFICATE OF EXECUTION OF CITATION UNDER THE CHILDREN'S HEARINGS
(SCOTLAND) ACT 2011 OR THE CHILDREN (SCOTLAND) ACT 1995

Court ref. no.:

1. [Place and Date]

I [Name and designation] hereby certify that on the above date, I duly.............. cited [full name of
witness]

by

*posting, on [date] between the hours of (..........) and (..........) at the [place], a copy of [the foregoing
application, warrant and] *citation/*intimation to *him/*her, in a *registered/*recorded delivery letter
addressed as follows—[full name and address]

and the receipt for that letter accompanies this certificate.

*or by [set forth the mode of citation or intimation]

(signed, A B Principal Reporter)
C D Sheriff Officer
E F (Witness)
G H Solicitor

*delete as appropriate

FORM 43[3]

Rule 3.17(3)

*CERTIFICATE OF EXECUTION OF CITATION OF SERVICE UNDER THE CHILDREN'S
HEARINGS (SCOTLAND) ACT 2011 OR THE CHILDREN (SCOTLAND) ACT 1995

Court ref. no.

---

[1] As amended by the Act of Sederunt (Children's Hearings (Scotland) Act 2011) (Miscellaneous
Amendments) 2013 (SSI 2013/172) para.4 (effective June 24, 2013).

[2] As amended by the Act of Sederunt (Children's Hearings (Scotland) Act 2011) (Miscellaneous
Amendments) 2013 (SSI 2013/172) para.4 (effective June 24, 2013).

[3] As amended by the Act of Sederunt (Children's Hearings (Scotland) Act 2011) (Miscellaneous
Amendments) 2013 (SSI 2013/172) para.4 (effective June 24, 2013).

1. *[Place, date]*

I *[Name and designation]* hereby certify that on the date shown above, I duly

*cited *[full name of child]*

*gave notice to *[full name of person]*

by

*posting, on *[date]* between the hours of [..........] and [..........] at the *[place]*, a copy of the foregoing application, warrant and *citation/*intimation to *him/*her, in a *registered/*recorded delivery letter addressed as follows—*[full name and address]*

and the receipt for that letter accompanies this certificate.

*or by *[set forth the mode of citation or intimation]*

[signed]

*Principal Reporter

or solicitor for applicant

[Officer of Local Authority/Sheriff clerk]

or Sheriff Officer

*[name and business address]*

and *[name and address of any witness]*

*Delete as appropriate

FORM 44A[1]

Rule 3.22(3)(a)

APPLICATION FOR AUTHORISATION OF THE GIVING OF EVIDENCE BY A WITNESS OR PARTY BY MEANS OF A LIVE LINK

Court ref. no.:

*[Insert name, address and designation of applicant*

*e.g. Principal Reporter/Parent/Safeguarder]*

in the case of

*[insert name of child]*

1. On *[insert date of application]* the Principal Reporter made an application to the sheriff to find whether the section 67 grounds [[*not accepted by the said *[insert name of child]* or *[insert name of relevant person(s) within the meaning of Rule 3.1(1)]]* or [*not understood by the said *[insert name of child]* are established] or [*as the case may be].

2. The court assigned *[insert date]* at *[insert time]* in chambers at *[insert name and address of sheriff court]* for the hearing of the application.

*3. That *[insert name and address of witness]* is a witness in the application.

4. That *[here state reasons for application]*.

5. *[Insert name of applicant]* therefore applies to the sheriff under Rule 3.22(1) of the Act of Sederunt (Child Care and Maintenance Rules) 1997 for an order that the evidence of the said *[insert name of witness]* shall be given by means of live link.

*[Signed]*

[*Principal Reporter /Parent/

Safeguarder etc. as appropriate]

[state designation, address and contact

numbers]

(*delete as appropriate)

FORM 44B[2]

---

[1] As inserted by the Act of Sederunt (Children's Hearings (Scotland) Act 2011) (Miscellaneous Amendments) 2013 (SSI 2013/172) para.4 (effective June 24, 2013).

[2] As inserted by the Act of Sederunt (Children's Hearings (Scotland) Act 2011) (Miscellaneous Amendments) 2013 (SSI 2013/172) para.4 (effective June 24, 2013).

Rule 3.22(3)(b)

APPLICATION FOR AUTHORISATION OF THE MAKING OF A SUBMISSION BY MEANS OF A LIVE LINK

Court ref. no.:

*[Insert name, address and designation of applicant]*
*e.g. Principal Reporter/Parent/Safeguarder*
in the case of
*[insert name of child]*

1. On *[insert date of application]* the Principal Reporter made an application to the sheriff to find whether the section 67 grounds [[*not accepted by the said *[insert name of child]* or *[insert name of relevant person(s) within the meaning of* Rule 3.1(1)]] or [*not understood by the said *[insert name of child]* are established] or [*as the case may be].

2. The court assigned *[insert date]* at *[insert time]* in chambers at *[insert name and address of sheriff court]* for the hearing of the application.

3. That *[insert name and address of person]* wishes to make a submission in respect of the application.

4. That *[here state reasons for application]*.

5. The *[insert name of applicant]* therefore applies to the sheriff under Rule 3.22(1) of the Act of Sederunt (Child Care and Maintenance Rules) 1997 for an order that the submission of the said *[insert name]* shall be given by means of live link.

*[Signed]*
[*Principal
Reporter/Parent/Safeguarder
etc. as appropriate]
[state designation, address and
contact numbers]

*(*delete as appropriate)*

FORM 45[1]

Rule 3.26

APPLICATION FOR A CHILD ASSESSMENT ORDER UNDER SECTION 35 OF THE CHILDREN'S HEARINGS (SCOTLAND) ACT 2011

Court ref. no.:
Date lodged..........

**Application to Sheriff Court at**

for a Child Assessment Order under section 35 of the Children's Hearings (Scotland) Act 2011

**PART 1. DETAILS OF APPLICANT AND OTHER PERSONS WHO THE APPLICANT BELIEVES SHOULD RECEIVE NOTICE OF THE APPLICATION**

| | |
|---|---|
| APPLICANT | *[insert name, address, telephone, DX and fax numbers of local authority]* |
| CHILD | **[insert name, address, gender and date of birth]*** |
| RELEVANT PERSON(S) | *[insert name, address and the basis for the person being a relevant person within the meaning of* Rule 3.1(1) of the Act] |
| SAFEGUARDER | *[insert name, address, telephone, DX and fax numbers (if known) of any safeguarder]* |
| THE PRINCIPAL REPORTER | *[insert address, telephone, DX and fax numbers]* |
| ANY OTHER PERSON WHO SHOULD RECEIVE NOTICE OF THE APPLICATION | [For example, any person who is caring for the child at the time of the application being made: *insert name, address and telephone number of person and provide details of their interest in the application and/or child]* |
| | [The court may seek views from applicants in relation to other persons on whom service should be made.] |

---

[1] As amended by the Act of Sederunt (Children's Hearings (Scotland) Act 2011) (Miscellaneous Amendments) 2013 (SSI 2013/172) para.4 (effective June 24, 2013).

*Note: Information to be provided in Part 3 where applicant does not wish to disclose the address or whereabouts of the child or any other person to persons receiving notice of the application.

**PART 2. INFORMATION ABOUT THE APPLICATION AND ORDERS SOUGHT**

GROUNDS FOR MAKING APPLICATION

*[applicant to provide details of grounds for making the application: including reasons why a Child Protection Order is not being sought]*

*OTHER APPLICATIONS AND ORDERS WHICH AFFECT THE CHILD

*[insert details of any other applications or orders made which affect or are relevant to the child who is the subject of this application]*

REPORTS/DOCUMENTARY EVIDENCE ETC.

The following reports/documentary evidence is attached/will be produced*—*[list any reports, statements or affidavits which are or will be produced at any subsequent hearing of the application]*

*delete as appropriate

**PART 3. DETAILS OF THE ASSESSMENT AND ORDERS SOUGHT**

ASSESSMENT

*[in terms of* section 35(2) *insert the following details of the assessment sought]*

- a. The type of assessment is [provide details of the type of assessment that is sought including information on the child's health or development or the way in which the child has been or is being treated or neglected].
- b. The assessment would begin on *[insert date] (which must be no later than 24 hours after the order is granted).*
- c. The assessment will have effect for *[insert number of days]* from that date (*which must not exceed the maximum period of 3 days* ).
- d. The person(s) to be authorised to carry out any assessment is/are *[insert name(s), designation and address]*
- e. *[insert name and address]* would be required to produce the child to the authorised person and permit that person or any other authorised person to carry out an assessment in accordance with the order.

OTHER ORDERS

*[in terms of* section 35(3) *provide the following information about any other order sought]*

- *a. In terms of section 35(3)(b) an order is sought to permit the child to be taken to *[insert details of the place]* for the purpose of the assessment, and to authorise the child to be kept at that place or any other place for [specify period].
- *b. In terms of section 35(3)(c) the sheriff is requested to make the following directions as to contact with the child by *[insert name and address of person and his or her relationship with child]* while the child is in the aforementioned place

*[insert details of any directions sought as to contact with the child]*

*[insert details and grounds for any order sought in relation*

- a) *to non-disclosure of address or whereabouts of child; or*
- b) *service of restricted documents on child.]*

*delete as appropriate

**PART 4. DETAILS OF FIRST ORDER SOUGHT FROM THE SHERIFF**

The applicant requests the sheriff to:

- a. Fix a hearing.
- *b. Order service on the child, together with a notice in form 26* or order service of the following documents only *[insert details of documents to be served on child, e.g. notice in form 26 only]*
- *c. Order service of a copy of the application and the first order on the persons listed in Part 1 of this application, together with a notice in form 34.
- *d. Order that the address of *[insert name]* should not be disclosed in the application.
- *e. Dispense with service on the child or any other person for the following reasons *[insert details]*.

*delete as appropriate

Signed .......... Date ..........

[name, designation and address
telephone, DX and fax numbers]

FORM 46[1]

Rule 3.27(2)

CHILD ASSESSMENT ORDER UNDER SECTION 35 OF THE CHILDREN'S HEARINGS (SCOTLAND) ACT 2011

Court ref. no.:

**IN THE SHERIFF COURT**

**at**...............

**on**...............

The sheriff orders that there shall be a *[insert details of assessment]* assessment of the child *[insert name, address, gender and date of birth]*

This order has effect from [ *insert time and date (to be no later than 24 hours after the order is granted)* ] until [ *insert time and date (not exceeding 3 days from time the order took effect)* ]

The person authorised to carry out the assessment is *[insert name, designation and address]*

* The sheriff orders that *[insert name and address]* is required to produce the child to the authorised person and permit that person or any other authorised person to carry out the assessment in accordance with this order.

In terms of section 35(3)(b) the sheriff permits the child to be taken to [ *insert details of the place* ] for the purpose of the assessment, and authorises the child to be kept at that place or any other place for [ *specify period* ].

* In terms of section 35(3)(c) the sheriff makes the following directions as to contact with the child by *[insert name and address of person and his or her relationship with child]* while the child is in the aforementioned place—

*[insert details of any directions sought as to contact with the child]*

*delete as appropriate

For the purpose of enforcing this order, warrant is granted to officers of law for all lawful execution, including-

(a)     searching for and apprehending the child;

(b)     taking the child to the authorised place;

(c)     where (i) it is not reasonably practicable to take the child immediately to the authorised place; and (ii) the authorised place is not a place of safety, taking the child to and detaining the child in a place of safety for as short a period of time as is practicable;

(d)     so far as necessary, by breaking open shut and lockfast places.

Signed ..........

Sheriff ..........

Time ..........

FORM 47[2]

Rule 3.30

APPLICATION FOR A CHILD PROTECTION ORDER BY LOCAL AUTHORITY UNDER SECTION 37 OF THE CHILDREN'S HEARINGS (SCOTLAND) ACT 2011

Court ref. no.:

Date lodged ..........

**Application to Sheriff at**

for a Child Protection Order under section 37(1) of the Children's Hearings (Scotland) Act 2011

**PART 1. DETAILS OF APPLICANT AND OTHER PERSONS WHO THE APPLICANT BELIEVES SHOULD RECEIVE NOTICE OF THE APPLICATION**

| APPLICANT | *[insert name, address, telephone, DX and fax numbers of the local authority]* |
|---|---|
| CHILD | *[insert name, address, gender and date of birth]* |
| RELEVANT PERSON(S) | *[insert name, address and the basis for the person being a relevant person within the meaning of section Rule 3.1(1) of the Act]* |
| SAFEGUARDER | *[insert name, address, telephone, DX and fax numbers (if* |

---

[1] As amended by the Act of Sederunt (Children's Hearings (Scotland) Act 2011) (Miscellaneous Amendments) 2013 (SSI 2013/172) para.4 (effective June 24, 2013).

[2] As amended by the Act of Sederunt (Children's Hearings (Scotland) Act 2011) (Miscellaneous Amendments) 2013 (SSI 2013/172) para.4 (effective June 24, 2013).

*known) of any safeguarder]*

| | |
|---|---|
| THE PRINCIPAL REPORTER | *[insert address, telephone, DX and fax numbers]* |
| ANY OTHER PERSON WHO SHOULD RECEIVE NOTICE OF THE APPLICATION | *[For example, any person who is caring for the child at the time of the application being made: insert name, address and telephone number of person and provide details of their interest in the application and/or child]* |

**\*Note: Information to be provided in Part 3 where applicant does not wish to disclose the address or whereabouts of the child or any other person to persons receiving notice of the application.**

### PART 2. INFORMATION ABOUT THE APPLICATION AND ORDERS SOUGHT

GROUNDS FOR MAKING APPLICATION

*[applicant to provide details of grounds for making the application: see section 38(2) and 39(2) of the Act]*

OTHER APPLICATIONS AND ORDERS WHICH AFFECT THE CHILD

*[insert details of any other applications or orders made which affect or are relevant to the child who is the subject of this application]*

SUPPORTING EVIDENCE

The following supporting evidence is produced—

*[list reports, statements, affidavits or other evidence produced]*

### PART 3. DETAILS OF ORDER AND DIRECTION(S) SOUGHT

ORDER SOUGHT: The applicant requests the sheriff to make a Child Protection Order in respect of the child *[insert name]*

In terms of section 37 the applicant seeks an order to *[insert details of the order sought including details of the specified person (if appropriate)]*.

\*DIRECTIONS IN RELATION TO THE EXERCISE OR FULFILMENT OF PARENTAL RESPONSIBILITIES OR PARENTAL RIGHTS

In terms of section 42(1) the applicant seeks the following direction(s)—

*insert details of the direction(s) sought]*.

*ANY OTHER AUTHORISATION, REQUIREMENT OR DIRECTION(S) SOUGHT*

*[insert here details and grounds for any other authorisation, requirement or direction sought including—*

(a) *an information non-disclosure direction under* section 40;

(b) *a contact direction under* section 41.]

### PART 4. DETAILS OF ORDER SOUGHT

The applicant requests the sheriff to:

a.    Make a child protection order in respect of the said child *[insert name of the child]* including any authorisation, requirement or direction set out in Part 3 of the application.

\*b.    Order the applicant to forthwith serve a copy of the Child Protection Order *[and a copy of the application]* on,

    i.    the child, together with a notice in form 50\* or orders service of the following documents only *[insert details of documents to be served on child, e.g. notice in form 50 only]*; and

    ii.    the other persons listed in Part 1 of this application, together with a notice in form 51.

\*c.    Order that the address of *[insert name]* should not be disclosed in the application.

\*d.    Dispense with service on the child or any other person for the following reasons *[insert details]*.

\*delete as appropriate

Signed .............. Date ..........

[name, designation and address

telephone, DX and fax numbers]

FORM 48[1]

Rule 3.30

---

[1] As amended by the Act of Sederunt (Children's Hearings (Scotland) Act 2011) (Miscellaneous Amendments) 2013 (SSI 2013/172) para.4 (effective June 24, 2013).

APPLICATION FOR A CHILD PROTECTION ORDER BY ANY PERSON (OTHER THAN A LO-CAL AUTHORITY) UNDER SECTION 37 OF THE CHILDREN'S HEARINGS (SCOTLAND) ACT 2011

Court ref. no.:

Date lodged..........

**Application to Sheriff at**

for a Child Protection Order under section 37(1) of the Children's Hearings (Scotland) Act 2011

**PART 1. DETAILS OF APPLICANT OR OTHER PERSONS WHO THE APPLICANT BELIEVES SHOULD RECEIVE NOTICE OF THE APPLICATION**

| | |
|---|---|
| APPLICANT | *[insert name and address, telephone, DX and fax numbers and capacity in which application is made]* |
| CHILD | *[insert name, address, gender and date of birth]** |
| RELEVANT PERSON(S) | *[insert name, address and the basis for the person being a relevant person within the meaning of Rule 3.1(1) of the Act]* |
| SAFEGUARDER | *[insert name, address, telephone, DX and fax numbers (if known) of any safeguarder]* |
| LOCAL AUTHORITY | *[insert and address, DX and telephone and fax numbers]* |
| THE PRINCIPAL REPORTER | *[insert address, telephone, DX and fax numbers]* |
| ANY OTHER PERSON WHO SHOULD RECEIVE NOTICE OF THE APPLICATION | *[For example, any person who is caring for the child at the time of the application being made: insert name and address of person and provide details of their interest in the application and/or child]* |

**\*Note: Information to be provided in Part 3 where applicant does not wish to disclose the address or whereabouts of the child or any other person to persons receiving notice of the application.**

**PART 2. INFORMATION ABOUT THE APPLICATION AND ORDERS SOUGHT**

GROUNDS FOR MAKING APPLICATION

*[applicant to provide details of grounds for making the application: see section 39(2) of the Act ]*

OTHER APPLICATIONS AND ORDERS WHICH AFFECT THE CHILD

*[insert details of any other applications or orders made which affect or are relevant to the child who is the subject of this application]*

SUPPORTING EVIDENCE

The following supporting evidence is produced—

*[list reports, statements, affidavits or other evidence produced]*

**PART 3. DETAILS OF ORDER AND DIRECTION SOUGHT ETC.**

ORDER SOUGHT: The applicant requests the sheriff to make a Child Protection Order in respect of the child *[insert name]*

In terms of section 37 the applicant seeks an order to

*[insert details of the order sought including details of the specified person (if appropriate)].*

\*DIRECTIONS IN RELATION TO THE EXERCISE OR FULFILMENT OF PARENTAL RE-SPONSIBILITIES OR PARENTAL RIGHTS

In terms of section 42(1) the applicant seeks the following direction(s)—

*[insert details of the direction(s) sought].*

*ANY OTHER AUTHORISATION, REQUIREMENT OR DIRECTION(S) SOUGHT*

*[insert here details and grounds for any other authorisation, requirement or direction sought includ-ing—*

(a)  *an information non-disclosure direction under section 40;*

(b)  *a contact direction under section 41.]*

\*delete as appropriate

**PART 4. DETAILS OF FIRST ORDER SOUGHT FROM THE SHERIFF**

The applicant requests the sheriff to:

a.  Make a child protection order in respect of the said child *[insert name of the child]* including any authorisation, requirement or direction set out in Part 3 of the application.

\*b.  Order the applicant to forthwith serve a copy of the Child Protection Order [and a copy of the application] on,

    i.  the child, together with a notice in form 50\* or orders service of the following documents only *[insert details of documents to be served on child, e.g. notice in form 50 only]*; and

    ii.  the other persons listed in Part 1 of this application, together with a notice in form 51.

*c.   Order that the address of *[insert name]* should not be disclosed in the application.

*d.   Dispense with service on the child or any other person for the following reasons *[insert details].*

*delete as appropriate

Signed .......... Date ..........

[name, designation and address

telephone, DX and fax numbers]

FORM 49[1]

Rule 3.31(2)

CHILD PROTECTION ORDER UNDER SECTION 37 OF THE CHILDREN'S HEARINGS (SCOTLAND) ACT 2011

Court ref. no.:

**IN THE SHERIFF COURT**

**at**..........

**on**..........

In the application by *[insert name and address]* for a Child Protection Order/Child Assessment Order *the sheriff makes a Child Protection Order in respect of the child *[insert name, address (unless an information non disclosure order made), gender and date of birth of the child]*

*The sheriff orders that *[insert name and address of person]* is required to produce the child to a specified person *[insert name and address of the specified person].*

*The sheriff authorises the removal of the child by the specified person to **[insert details of the place]* a place of safety and for the keeping of the child at that place.

*The sheriff authorises the prevention of the removal of the child from *[insert details of the place].*

*The sheriff authorises the carrying out (subject to section 186) of an assessment of—

(a)   the child's health or development, or

(b)   the way in which the child has been or is being treated or neglected.

DIRECTIONS

The Sheriff directs that—

(a)   *the location of any place of safety; and

(b)   *any other information *[specify information]*

must not be disclosed (directly or indirectly) to the following persons *(specify person or class of persons)*

*(*delete as applicable)*

*In terms of section 41 the sheriff gives the following directions to the applicant as to contact with the child—

*[insert details of any directions]*

*In terms of section 42 the sheriff gives the following directions as to the exercise or fulfilment of parental responsibilities or parental rights in repect of the child—

*[insert details of any directions]*

*delete as appropriate

For the purpose of enforcing this order, warrant is granted to officers of law for all lawful execution, including—

(a)   searching for and apprehending the child;

(b)   taking the child to the authorised place;

(c)   where (i) it is not reasonably practicable to take the child immediately to the authorised place; and (ii) the authorised place is not a place of safety, taking the child to and detaining the child in a place of safety for as short a period of time as is practicable;

(d)   so far as necessary, by breaking open shut and lockfast places.

Signed..........

Sheriff..........

Time..........

FORM 50[2]

Rule 3.32(a)

NOTICE OF CHILD PROTECTION ORDER TO CHILD IN TERMS OF SECTION 37 OF THE CHILDREN'S HEARINGS (SCOTLAND) ACT 2011

---

[1] As amended by the Act of Sederunt (Children's Hearings (Scotland) Act 2011) (Miscellaneous Amendments) 2013 (SSI 2013/172) para.4 (effective June 24, 2013).

[2] As amended by the Act of Sederunt (Children's Hearings (Scotland) Act 2011) (Miscellaneous Amendments) 2013 (SSI 2013/172) para.4 (effective June 24, 2013).

## ARRANGEMENTS TO KEEP YOU SAFE

Court ref. no.:

Dear *[insert name by which child is known]*

I am writing to tell you that because there were worries about your safety the court was asked to sort out some practical arrangements to make sure you are kept safe.

After hearing about your situation the court made an order, called a "Child Protection Order". That means that the court gave permission to *[insert in simple language the order(s) and any directions granted and their effect on the child]*

If you are unhappy with this order or any authorisation, requirement or direction you can ask the court to change it. For example, you might want to ask the court to allow you *[insert an example e.g. to allow more contact with certain members of the family etc.]*

**Any change must be requested without delay**

If you want to do this you can ask the court which made the order to listen to you. You will need a lawyer to help you.

**Remember** that if you do not agree with the order or any directions you must get advice **IMMEDIATELY.**

*In the meantime you must do what the order says.*

---

**If you are unsure about what to do you can get free legal advice from a Lawyer or Local Advice Agency or Law Centre about the application and about legal aid.
The Scottish Child Law Centre can refer you to specially trained lawyers who can help you.
They give advice on their free phone no (0800 328 8970) any time between 9.30 am and 4.00 pm Monday to Friday.**

---

You will see that, along with this letter, there is [a copy of the application which was made to the court, and the order the court (delete if appropriate)] has made which affects you. If you decide to get advice, or to ask someone to go to court for you, make sure that you give your advisor a copy of the application, and the court's order.

Signed:.............. Date: ..............

Time.........

FORM 51[1]

Rule 3.32(b)

NOTICE OF CHILD PROTECTION ORDER TO A NAMED PERSON UNDER **SECTION 37 OF THE CHILDREN'S HEARINGS (SCOTLAND) ACT 2011**

Court ref. no.:

**Notice of Child Protection Order made under section 37 of the Children's Hearings (Scotland) Act 2011 in the Sheriff Court at**

To *[insert name and address of person to whom notice is given].*

You are given notice of the making of a Child Protection Order in respect of the child *[insert name, address, gender and date of birth of child]* by the sheriff at *[name of sheriff court]* on *[date of order].*

Along with this notice there is attached a copy of the application and the order.

Signed .......... Date ..........

WHAT YOU SHOULD DO

**YOU MUST COMPLY WITH THE ORDER AND ANY AUTHORISATION, REQUIRE-MENT OR DIRECTION CONTAINED WITHIN IT. FAILURE TO COMPLY IS AN OFFENCE UNDER SECTION 59 OF THE CHILDREN'S HEARINGS (SCOTLAND) ACT 2011 AND COULD LEAD TO YOU BEING FINED.**

\*YOU MAY WISH TO OBTAIN ADVICE FROM A SOLICITOR OR LOCAL ADVICE AGENCY OR LAW CENTRE. You may be entitled to legal aid. Advice about legal aid is available from any solicitor, advice agency or law centre.

**\*You may be able to contest or vary the order, and in such circumstances you should obtain legal advice without delay.**

\*delete as appropriate

FORM 52[2]

---

[1] As amended by the Act of Sederunt (Children's Hearings (Scotland) Act 2011) (Miscellaneous Amendments) 2013 (SSI 2013/172) para.4 (effective June 24, 2013).

[2] As amended by the Act of Sederunt (Children's Hearings (Scotland) Act 2011) (Miscellaneous Amendments) 2013 (SSI 2013/172) para.4 (effective June 24, 2013).

APPLICATION TO VARY OR TERMINATE A CHILD PROTECTION ORDER UNDER SECTION 48 OF THE CHILDREN'S HEARINGS (SCOTLAND) ACT 2011

Court ref. no.:

Date lodged..........

**Application to Sheriff at**

to vary or terminate a Child Protection Order under section 48 of the Children's Hearings (Scotland) Act 2011

## PART 1. DETAILS OF APPLICANT AND OTHER PERSONS WHO THE APPLICANT BELIEVES SHOULD RECEIVE NOTICE OF THE APPLICATION

| | |
|---|---|
| APPLICANT | *[insert name, address, telephone, DX and fax numbers, and details of the capacity of the person making the application]* |
| CHILD | *[insert name, address, gender and date of birth]** |
| SAFEGUARDER | **If not applicant** *[insert name, address, telephone, DX and fax numbers (if known) of any safeguarder]* |
| RELEVANT PERSON(S) | **If not applicant** *[insert name, address and telephone number (if known) and the basis for the person being a relevant person within the meaning of section Rule 3.1(1) of the Act ]* |
| LOCAL AUTHORITY | *[insert name, address, telephone, DX and fax numbers]* |
| THE PRINCIPAL REPORTER | *[insert address, telephone, DX and fax numbers]* |
| ANY OTHER PERSON WHO SHOULD RECEIVE NOTICE OF THE APPLICATION | *[For example, any person who is caring for the child at the time of the application being made any person who applied for the child protection order or any person specified in the order under section 37(2)(a) , unless the person is the applicant: insert name, address and telephone number of person and provide details of their interest in the application and/or child]* |

**\*Note: Information to be provided in Part 3 where applicant does not wish to disclose the address or whereabouts of the child or any other person to persons receiving notice of the application.**

### PART 2. INFORMATION ABOUT THE APPLICATION AND ORDERS SOUGHT

On *[date of order]* the Sheriff made a Child Protection Order in the following terms *[insert full details of order, including any authorisation, requirement or direction attaching to it]* *[Copy original order must be attached in terms of* Rule 3.33 *]*.

OTHER APPLICATIONS AND ORDERS WHICH AFFECT THE CHILD

*[insert details of any other applications or orders made which affect or are relevant to the child who is the subject of this application]*

ORDER(S), INCLUDING ANY AUTHORISATION, REQUIREMENT OR DIRECTION THE VARIATION OR TERMINATION OF WHICH ARE SOUGHT

*[applicant to insert details of order now sought]*

GROUNDS FOR MAKING APPLICATION

*[applicant to provide details of grounds for seeking the variation or termination]*

SUPPORTING EVIDENCE

The following supporting evidence is produced—

*[list reports, statements, affidavits or other evidence produced]*

### PART 3. DETAILS OF ORDER SOUGHT AND ANY TERMS, CONDITIONS OR DIRECTIONS

FIRST ORDER

The applicant requests the sheriff to:

a. Assign a hearing on the application.

\*b. Order the applicant to forthwith serve a copy of the application together with the date of hearing on,

    i. The Principal Reporter

    ii. The Local Authority

    iii. The child, together with a notice in form 27; and

    iv. The other persons listed in part 1 of this application, together with a notice in form 35.

\*c. Dispense with service on the child or any other person for the following reasons *[insert details]*.

And thereafter to *[enter details of what you want the sheriff to vary or terminate]*.
   *delete as appropriate
   Signed ...............

Date .........

   [name, designation and address
   telephone, DX and fax numbers}

FORM 53[1]

Rule 3.33(5)

VARIATION OR TERMINATION OF CHILD PROTECTION ORDER UNDER SECTION 48 OF
THE CHILDREN'S HEARINGS (SCOTLAND) ACT 2011

Court ref. no.:

**IN THE SHERIFF COURT**
   **at..........**
   **on..........**
   The sheriff makes the following order in the application by *[insert name and address]* to vary or terminate a Child Protection Order in respect of the child *[insert name, address (unless order made re non disclosure), gender and date of birth of the child]*
   *[insert order granted in this application]*
AUTHORISATIONS, REQUIREMENTS AND DIRECTIONS IN FORCE UNDER CHILD PROTEC-
TION ORDER AFTER VARIATION
   **[insert name and address of person]* is ordered to produce the child to the specified person *[insert name and address of the specified person]*.
   *the removal of the child by the specified person to * *[insert details of the place]* a place of safety and for the keeping of the child at that place is authorised.
   *the prevention of the removal of the child from *[insert details of the place]* is authorised.
   *the carrying out (subject to section 186 of the Act) of an assessment of—
   (a)   the child's health or development, or
   (b)   the way in which the child has been or is being treated or neglected
is authorised.
   DIRECTIONS
   The Sheriff directs that—
   (a)   *the location of any place of safety; and
   (b)   *any other information *[specify information]*
must not be disclosed (directly or indirectly) to the following person or class of person *(specify person or class of person)*
   (*delete as applicable)
   *In terms of section 41 the sheriff gives the following directions to the applicant as to contact with the child—
   *[insert details of any directions]*
   *In terms of section 42 the sheriff gives the following directions as to the exercise or fulfilment of parental responsibilities or parental rights in respect of the child—
   *[insert details of any directions]*
   *delete as appropriate
   For the purpose of enforcing this order, warrant is granted to officers of law for all lawful execution, including—
   (a)   searching for and apprehending the child;
   (b)   taking the child to the authorised place;
   (c)   where (i) it is not reasonably practicable to take the child immediately to the authorised place; and (ii) the authorised place is not a place of safety, taking the child to and detaining the child in a place of safety for as short a period of time as is practicable;
   (d)   so far as necessary, by breaking open shut and lockfast places.
Signed .........
   Sheriff .........
   Time.........

---

[1] As amended by the Act of Sederunt (Children's Hearings (Scotland) Act 2011) (Miscellaneous Amendments) 2013 (SSI 2013/172) para.4 (effective June 24, 2013).

FORM 54[1]

Rule 3.35

APPLICATION FOR EXCLUSION ORDER BY LOCAL AUTHORITY UNDER SECTION 76 OF THE CHILDREN (SCOTLAND) ACT 1995

Court ref. no.:

**Application to Sheriff at**                                        Date lodged..........

for an Exclusion Order under section 76(1) of the Children (Scotland) Act 1995

### PART 1. DETAILS OF APPLICANT AND OTHER PERSONS WHO THE APPLICANT BELIEVES SHOULD RECEIVE NOTICE OF THE APPLICATION

| | |
|---|---|
| APPLICANT | *[insert name and address, telephone, DX and fax numbers]* |
| CHILD | *[insert name, address, gender and date of birth]** |
| THE NAMED PERSON | *[insert name and address of person to be excluded]* |
| SAFEGUARDER | *[insert name, address, telephone, DX and fax numbers (if known) of any safeguarder appointed by a children's hearing or court in respect of the child]* |
| RELEVANT PERSON(S) | *[insert name, address and the basis for the person being a relevant person within the meaning of Rule 3.1(1) of the Act]* |
| THE APPROPRIATE PERSON | *[insert name and address of person who is to have care of the child if the order is made]* |
| THE PRINCIPAL REPORTER | *[insert address, telephone, DX and fax numbers]* |
| ANY OTHER PERSON WHO SHOULD RECEIVE NOTICE OF THE APPLICATION | *[insert name, address and telephone number of person and provide details of their interest in the aplication and/or child]* |

*Note: Information to be provided in Part 3 where applicant does not wish to disclose the address or whereabouts of the child or any other person to persons receiving notice of the application.

### PART 2. INFORMATION ABOUT THE APPLICATION AND ORDERS SOUGHT

CONDITIONS FOR MAKING APPLICATION

*[applicant to provide details of grounds for making the application including the address of the family home and details of all persons resident there.]*

ANY OTHER RELEVANT APPLICATION OR ORDER WHICH AFFECTS THE CHILD

*[insert details of any other aplications or orders made which affect or are relevant to the child who is the subject of this application]*

SUPPORTING EVIDENCE

The following supporting evidence is produced—

*[list reports, statements, affidavits or other evidence produced]*

PROPOSALS BY THE LOCAL AUTHORITY FOR FINANCIAL OR OTHER SUPPORT FOR THE NAMED PERSON

*[insert details; Section 76(9) and (10) of the Act refer]*

### PART 3. DETAILS OF ORDER SOUGHT AND ANY TERMS, CONDITIONS OR DIRECTIONS

ORDER SOUGHT: The applicant requests the sheriff to *[insert details of the order sought and any terms and conditions to be attached to the ordeer]* in respect of the child *[insert name]*

ANCILLARY OR INTERIM ORDERS SOUGHT

In terms of section 77(3) the following orders or interim orders are sought:

*[specify orders sought and provide information about the reasons for seeking order]*

TERMS AND CONDITIONS TO BE ATTACHED TO ORDER

In terms of section 77(7) the applicant seeks an order to:

*[insert details of the order sought].*

DIRECTIONS AS TO PRESERVATION OF NAMED PERSON'S PROPERTY

---

[1] As amended by the Act of Sederunt (Children's Hearings (Scotland) Act 2011) (Miscellaneous Amendments) 2013 (SSI 2013/172) para.4 (effective June 24, 2013).

In terms of section 77(5) the applicant seeks the following direction:

*[insert details of the direction sought].*

In terms of section 78(1) a power of arrest is sought in relation to:

*[insert details of interdict and provide information about the reasons for seeking power of arrest]*

### PART 4. DETAILS OF FIRST ORDER SOUGHT FROM THE SHERIFF

The applicant requests the sheriff to:

a. Fix a hearing.

b. Order the applicant to forthwith serve a copy of the application on

  i. the child, together with a notice in form 28;

  ii. the named person, together with a notice in Form 36 and

  iii. the persons listed in paragraph 1 of this application, together with a notice in form 36.

*c. Dispense with service on the child or any other person for the following reasons *[insert details]*

*d. Make an interim exclusion order excluding the named person from the child's family home in terms of part 2 *on the terms and conditions set out in part 3 above, and subject to the directions sought.

*e. Grant the following ancillary order. *[specify order sought]*

*f. Grant a power of arrest.

*delete as appropriate

Signed.................... Date..............

[name, designation and address

telephone, DX and fax numbers]

FORM 55[1]

Rule 3.37(2)

EXCLUSION ORDER UNDER SECTION 76 OF THE CHILDREN (SCOTLAND) ACT 1995

Court ref. no.:

### IN THE SHERIFF COURT

**at..........**

**on..........**

In the application by the Local Authority for an exclusion order in terms of section 76 of the Act the sheriff orders that *[insert name and address of named person]* shall be excluded from *[insert address of child's family home]* *forthwith/from *[insert date]* until *[insert date when order shall cease to have effect]*.

*From the effective date the rights of occupancy of *[insert name]* from the said address are suspended.

*delete as appropriate

ANCILLARY ORDERS

In terms of section 77 the sheriff makes the following ancillary orders:

*[insert details of the orders granted and any terms and conditions or directions made by the sheriff or power of arrest attached to any interdict]*

For the purpose of enforcing this order warrant is granted for all lawful execution, including warrant to open shut and lockfast places.

Signed..............

Sheriff at..........

Time..........

FORM 56[2, 3]

Rule 3.38(1) and (2)

---

[1] As amended by the Act of Sederunt (Children's Hearings (Scotland) Act 2011) (Miscellaneous Amendments) 2013 (SSI 2013/172) para.4 (effective June 24, 2013).

[2] As amended by the Act of Sederunt (Sheriff Court Rules) (Miscellaneous Amendments) 2013 (SI 2013/135) para.5 (effective May 27, 2013).

[3] As amended by the Act of Sederunt (Children's Hearings (Scotland) Act 2011) (Miscellaneous Amendments) 2013 (SSI 2013/172) para.4 (effective June 24, 2013).

CERTIFICATE OF DELIVERY TO THE CHIEF CONSTABLE UNDER SECTION 78 OF THE CHILDREN (SCOTLAND) ACT 1995

Court ref. no.:

*[Insert place and date]*I,.......... hereby certify that upon the..........day of I duly delivered to the chief constable of the Police Service of Scotland (*insert details of the documents delivered*). This I did by (*state method of service*).

Signed..........

(name, designation and address)

(*add designation and business address*)

FORM 57[1]

Rule 3.40(1)

APPLICATION TO VARY OR RECALL AN EXCLUSION ORDER UNDER SECTION 79(3) OF THE CHILDREN (SCOTLAND) ACT 1995

Court ref. no.:

Date lodged..........

**Application to Sheriff at**

to vary or recall an Exclusion Order under section 79(3) of the Children (Scotland) Act 1995

**PART 1. DETAILS OF A APPLICANT AND OTHER PERSONS WHO THE APPLICANT BELIEVES SHOULD RECEIVE NOTICE OF THE APPLICATION**

| | |
|---|---|
| APPLICANT | *[insert name, address, telephone, DX and fax numbers, and details of the capacity of the person making the application]* |
| CHILD | *[insert name, address, gender and date of birth]** |
| THE NAMED PERSON | **If not applicant** *[insert name and address of person excluded]* |
| SAFEGUARDER | *[insert name, address, telephone, DX and fax numbers (if known) of any safeguarder appointed by a children's hearing or court in respect of the child]* |
| APPROPRIATE PERSON(S) | **If not applicant** *[insert name, address and the basis for the person being an appropriate person within the meaning of section 76(2)(c) of the Act ]* |
| RELEVANT PERSON | *[insert name, address, and the basis for the person being a relevant person within the meaning of Rule 3.1(1) ]* |
| THE PRINCIPAL REPORTER | *[insert address, telephone, DX and fax numbers]* |
| ANY OTHER PERSON WHO SHOULD RECEIVE NOTICE OF THE APPLICATION | *[insert name, address and telephone numbers of person and provide details of their interest in the application and/or child]* |

***Note: Information to be provided in Part 3 where applicant does not wish to disclose the address or whereabouts of the child or any other person to persons receiving notice of the application**

PART2. INFORMATION ABOUT THE APPLICATION AND ORDERS SOUGHT

On *[date of order]* the sheriff made an exclusion order in the following terms *[insert full details of order and conditions attaching to it]* *[Copy original order to be attached]*.

OTHER APPLICATIONS AND ORDERS WHICH AFFECT THE CHILD

*[insert details of any other applications or orders made which affect or are relevant to the child who is the subject of this application]*

SUPPORTING EVIDENCE

The following supporting evidence is produced—

*[list reports, statements, affidavits or other evidence including financial information produced]*

**PART 3. DETAILS OF ORDER SOUGHT AND ANY TERMS, CONDITIONS OR DIRECTIONS**

---

[1] As amended by the Act of Sederunt (Children's Hearings (Scotland) Act 2011) (Miscellaneous Amendments) 2013 (SSI 2013/172) para.4 (effective June 24, 2013).

ORDER SOUGHT: The applicant requests the sheriff to *[insert details of the variation or recall sought and any terms and conditions to be attached to the order]* in respect of the child [insert name] *[insert here details and grounds for any order sought in relation*

a) *to non-disclosure of address or whereabouts of child; or*

b) *service of restricted documents on child.]*

## PART 4. DETAILS OF FIRST ORDER SOUGHT FROM THE SHERIFF

The applicant requests the sheriff to:

a. Fix a hearing.

\*b. Order the applicant to forthwith serve a copy of the application on

    i. the Principal Reporter

    ii. the Local Authority

    iii. the named person, together with a notice in Form 37; and

    iv. the child, together with a notice in form 29;

    v. the persons listed in part 1 of this application, together with a notice in Form 37.

\*c. Dispense with service on the child or any other person for the following reasons *[insert details]*

\*d. Grant the following ancillary order, *[specify order sought]*

\*e. Grant a power of arrest.

\*delete as appropriate

Signed.................... Date...............

[name, designation and address

telephone, DX and fax numbers]

FORM 58[1]

Rule 3.40(3)

VARIATION OF EXCLUSION ORDER UNDER SECTION 79 OF THE CHILDREN (SCOTLAND) ACT 1995

Court ref. no.:

### IN THE SHERIFF COURT

**at..........**

**on..........**

The sheriff makes the following order in the application by *[insert name and address]* to vary or recall an exclusion order in respect of *[insert name and address of named person]* in relation to

*[insert address of child's family home]*

*[insert order granted in this application]*

TERMS AND CONDITIONS IN FORCE UNDER EXCLUSION ORDER AFTER VARIATION

\* *[insert name and address of named person]* is excluded from *[insert address of child's family home]* from *[insert date]* until *[insert date when order shall cease to have effect]*.

\*from *[insert date]* the rights of occupancy of *[insert name]* from the said address are suspended.

\*the following ancillary orders are in force in terms of section 77:

*[insert details of any orders in force and any terms and conditions or directions made by the sheriff or power of arrest attached to any interdict]*

\*delete as appropriate

For the purpose of enforcing any of these orders warrant is granted for all lawful execution, including warrant to open shut and lockfast places.

Signed..............

Sheriff..............

Time..............

FORM 59

Rule 3.42

APPLICATION BY PRINCIPAL REPORTER FOR FURTHER DETENTION OF CHILD UNDER SECTION 67 OF THE CHILDREN (SCOTLAND) ACT 1995

*[Repealed by the Act of Sederunt (Children's Hearings (Scotland) Act 2011) (Miscellaneous Amendments) 2013 (SSI 2013/172) para.4 (effective June 24, 2013).]*

---

[1] As amended by the Act of Sederunt (Children's Hearings (Scotland) Act 2011) (Miscellaneous Amendments) 2013 (SSI 2013/172) para.4 (effective June 24, 2013).

FORM 60[1]

Rule 3.45(1)

FORM OF APPLICATION TO SHERIFF UNDER SECTION 93(2)(A) OR 94(2)(A) OF THE
CHILDREN'S HEARINGS (SCOTLAND) ACT 2011

Court ref. no.:

SHERIFF COURT AT (*insert place of sheriff court*)

Application to sheriff under section *93(2)(a) and/or 94(2)(a) of the Children's Hearings (Scotland) Act
2011

by

**The Principal Reporter**

in the case of

[*insert name of child*]

1. At [*insert location of children's hearing*] on [*insert date*] a children's hearing gave a direction to
the Principal Reporter under section *93(2)(a) and/or 94(2)(a) of the Children's Hearings (Scotland) Act
2011 in respect of [*insert name of child*]

2. *The hearing appointed [*insert name and designation*] as a safeguarder/no safeguarder was
appointed.

3. *[An interim compulsory supervision order is in force in relation to the said [*insert name of child*],
which [*insert details of what that order specifies*]] OR [No interim compulsory supervision order is in
force in relation to the said [*insert name of child*]].

4. A copy of the statement of grounds by the Principal Reporter setting out the section 67 grounds of
referral of the case of the said [*insert name of child*] to the children's hearing is attached [*together with
the report(s) of the safeguarder].

5. (a) The said *[*insert name of child*] and/or *[*insert name and address and status of the relevant
person or persons (within the meaning of* Rule 3.1(1) *)]* did not accept [*specify ground(s) not accepted*]
of the statement of grounds.

(b) The *[children's hearing][grounds hearing] was satisfied that the said *[*insert name of child*]
and/or *[*insert name and address and status of the relevant person or persons (within the meaning of*
Rule 3.1(1) *)]* would not be capable of understanding or has not understood the explanation given in
compliance with section 90(1) of the 2011 Act in relation to a section 67 ground.

6. The Principal Reporter applies to the sheriff to determine whether the section 67 ground(s) not accepted by the said *[*insert name of child*] or [*insert name of relevant person or persons (within the meaning of* Rule 3.1(1) *)]* are established.

7. The Principal Reporter intends to call the following witnesses (*specify names and roles of witnesses*):

*8. The Principal Reporter requests the sheriff to remove the obligation on the child to attend the hear-
ing in view of [*insert reason*]. The Principal Reporter requests the sheriff to dispense with service on
[*insert name of child*] on the basis that [*insert reason*].

(*Signed*)
(*name, designation and address,
telephone number, [DX and fax
numbers]*)
(*Date*)

[*Insert place and date*]

The sheriff—

1. Assigns [*insert date*] at [*insert time*] within chambers at [*insert name and place of court*] for the
hearing of evidence in respect of the application.

*2. Appoints the Principal Reporter forthwith to serve a copy of the application and relative statement
of grounds and this warrant on—

a. the child, *[together with a notice in [*Form 31 or Form 31A]] *or* [orders service of the following
documents only [*insert details of documents to be served on child e.g. notice in Form 31/Form 31A
only*]]; and

b. [*insert name of relevant person or persons (within the meaning of* Rule 3.1(1) *)]* together with a
notice in Form 39 or Form 39A as the case may be.

c. any safeguarder [*insert name and designation*].

*3. Orders that the address of [*insert name*] should not be disclosed in the application.

*4. Dispenses with service on the child or any other person for the following reasons [*insert details*].

---

[1] As substituted by the Act of Sederunt (Children's Hearings (Scotland) Act 2011) (Miscellaneous
Amendments) 2013 (SSI 2013/172) para.4 (effective June 24, 2013).

*5 Dispenses with the obligation on the child to attend the hearing in view of [*insert details*].

6. Grants warrant to cite witnesses and havers.

(*Signed*)

(Sheriff or Sheriff clerk)

*7-day hearing (where child unable to understand grounds)

[*Insert place and date*]

The sheriff assigns [*insert date*] at [*insert time*] within chambers at [*insert name and place of court*] for a procedural hearing in terms of section 106(4) of the 2011 Act and ordains parties to attend if so advised.

(*Signed*)

(Sheriff or Sheriff clerk)

(*\*delete as appropriate*)

FORM 61[1]

Rule 3.53(1B)(a)

APPEAL TO SHERIFF UNDER SECTION 154(1) OF THE CHILDREN'S HEARINGS (SCOTLAND) ACT 2011

Court ref. no.:

SHERIFF COURT AT (*insert place of sheriff court*)

Appeal under section 154(1) of the Children's Hearings (Scotland) Act 2011

by

[*insert names of child; and names and address of relevant person(s) and/or safeguarder (as appropriate)*]

Appellant

against

a decision of the children' hearing at [*state location of children's hearing*]

1. On [*insert date*] a children's hearing at [*insert location of children's hearing*] decided that [*insert details of relevant decision as referred to in section 154(3) of the Children's Hearings (Scotland) Act 2011*].

2. *[The children's hearing appointed [*insert name and address*] to act as safeguarder] *or* [No safeguarder has been appointed].

3. The following person(s) is/are* relevant persons [*insert name(s) and address(es) of relevant person(s) (within the meaning of Rule 3.1(1) )*].

4. The decision is not justified because [*state briefly the reasons why the decision is being appealed against*].

5. The said [*insert names of child, relevant person(s) (within the meaning of* Rule 3.1(1) ) *or safeguarder (as appropriate)*] appeals to the sheriff against the decision.

(*Signed*)

*[Appellant(s)] *or* [Solicitor for Appellant(s) [*insert name and address*]]

[*Insert place and date*]

The sheriff assigns [*insert date*] at [*insert time*] within chambers at [*insert name and address of sheriff court*] for the hearing of the application;

The sheriff—

1. Appoints the sheriff clerk forthwith to intimate a copy of the application and this warrant to—

(a) the Principal Reporter;

*(b) the child together with a notice in Form 64;

*(c) [insert name of relevant person(s) (*within the meaning of* Rule 3.1(1) )];

*(d) [insert name of any safeguarder];

*(e) [insert names of any other person the sheriff thinks necessary].

*2. Dispenses with service on the child for the following reasons [*insert details*].

---

[1] As substituted by the Act of Sederunt (Children's Hearings (Scotland) Act 2011) (Miscellaneous Amendments) 2013 (SSI 2013/172) para.4 (effective June 24, 2013).

*3. Appoints answers to be lodged, if so advised, not later than [*insert number of days*] before the said diet.

4. Grants warrant to cite witnesses and havers.

(*Signed*)
(Sheriff or Sheriff clerk)

(*Insert Place/Date*)
Intimated this day by me in terms of Rule 3.54(1).

(*Signed*)
(Sheriff Clerk/Depute)
[Date]

(*\*delete as appropriate*)


FORM 62[1]

Rule 3.53(1B)(b)
APPEAL TO SHERIFF UNDER SECTION 160(1) OF THE CHILDREN'S HEARINGS
(SCOTLAND) ACT 2011

Court ref. no.:

SHERIFF COURT AT (*insert place of sheriff court*)
Appeal under section 160(1) of the Children's Hearings (Scotland) Act 2011
by
[*insert name of child; and names and addresses of relevant person(s) and/or individual deemed not to be a relevant person (as appropriate)*]

Appellant
against
a determination of a pre-hearing panel or children's hearing at [*state location of pre-hearing panel/ children's hearing*]

1. On [*insert date*] the *[[pre-hearing panel] *or* [children's hearing]] at [*insert location of children's hearing or pre-hearing panel*] determined that [*insert details of relevant person determination*]. A copy of the relevant person determination is attached.

2. *[The [pre-hearing panel] *or* [children's hearing] appointed [*insert name and address*] to act as safeguarder] *or* [No safeguarder has been appointed].

3. The following person(s) is/are* relevant persons [*insert name(s) and address(es) of relevant person(s) (within the meaning of Rule 3.1(1))*].

4. The determination is not justified because [*state briefly the reasons why the determination is being appealed against*].

5. The said [*insert names of child, relevant person(s) (within the meaning of Rule 3.1(1)) or individual deemed not to be a relevant person (as appropriate)*] appeals to the sheriff against the determination.

(*Signed*)

*[Appellant(s)] *or* [Solicitor for
Appellant(s) [*insert name and address*]]
[*Insert place and date*]

The sheriff assigns [*insert date*] at [*insert time*] within chambers at [*insert name and address of sheriff court*] for the hearing of the application;

The sheriff—

1. Appoints the sheriff clerk forthwith to intimate a copy of the application and this warrant to—
(a) the Principal Reporter;
*(b) the child together with a notice in Form 64;
*(c) [insert name of relevant person(s) (*within the meaning of* Rule 3.1(1) )];
*(d) [insert name of any safeguarder];
*(e) [insert names of any other person the sheriff thinks necessary].

*2. Dispenses with service on the child for the following reasons [*insert details*].

3. Grants warrant to cite witnesses and havers.

---

[1] As substituted by the Act of Sederunt (Children's Hearings (Scotland) Act 2011) (Miscellaneous Amendments) 2013 (SSI 2013/172) para.4 (effective June 24, 2013).

*(Signed)*
(Sheriff or Sheriff clerk)

Intimated this day by me in terms of Rule 3.54(1).

*(Signed)*
(Sheriff Clerk/Depute)
[Date]

*(\*delete as appropriate)*

FORM 63[1]

Rule 3.53(1B)(c)

APPEAL TO SHERIFF UNDER SECTION 161(1) OF THE CHILDREN'S HEARINGS (SCOTLAND) ACT 2011

Court ref. no.:

SHERIFF COURT AT *(insert place of sheriff court)*
Appeal under section 161(1) of the Children's Hearings (Scotland) Act 2011
by
*[insert names and addresses of appellant within the meaning of* section 161(2) of the Children's Hearings (Scotland) Act 2011 *)]*

Appellant

against
a decision of the children's hearing at *[state location of children's hearing]*

1. On *[insert date]* the children's hearing at *[insert location of children's hearing]* decided that *[insert details of relevant decision as referred to in* section 161(3) of the Children's Hearings (Scotland) Act 2011]. A copy of the relevant decision is attached.

2. \*[The children's hearing appointed *[insert name and address]* to act as safeguarder] *or* [No safeguarder has been appointed].

3. The following person(s) is/are\* relevant persons *[insert name(s) and address(es) of relevant person(s) (within the meaning of* Rule 3.1(1) *)]*.

4. The decision is not justified because *[state briefly the reasons why the decision is being appealed against]*.

5. The said *[insert name of appellant]* appeals to the sheriff against the decision.

*(Signed)*
\*[Appellant(s)] *or* [Solicitor
for Appellant(s) *[insert name
and address]]*

*[Insert place and date]*

The sheriff assigns *[insert date]* at *[insert time]* within chambers at *[insert name and address of sheriff court]* for the hearing of the application;

The sheriff—

1. Appoints the sheriff clerk forthwith to intimate a copy of the application and this warrant to—

(a) the Principal Reporter;

\*(b) the child together with a notice in Form 64;

\*(c) [insert name of relevant person(s) *(within the meaning of* Rule 3.1(1) *)]*;

\*(d) [insert name of any safeguarder];

\*(e) [insert names of any other person the sheriff thinks necessary].

\*2. Dispenses with service on the child for the following reasons *[insert details]*.

3. Grants warrant to cite witnesses and havers.

*(Signed)*
(Sheriff or Sheriff clerk)

Intimated this day by me in terms of Rule 3.54(1).

*(Signed)*
(Sheriff Clerk/Depute)
[Date]

*(\*delete as appropriate)*

---

[1] As substituted by the Act of Sederunt (Children's Hearings (Scotland) Act 2011) (Miscellaneous Amendments) 2013 (SSI 2013/172) para.4 (effective June 24, 2013).

FORM 63A[1]

Rule 3.53(1B)(d)

APPEAL TO SHERIFF UNDER SECTION 162(3) OF THE CHILDREN'S HEARINGS (SCOTLAND) ACT 2011

Court ref. no.:

SHERIFF COURT AT (*insert place of sheriff court*)

Appeal under section 162(3) of the Children's Hearings (Scotland) Act 2011

by

[*insert name of child and/or name and address of relevant person(s)*]

Appellant

against

a decision of the chief social work officer at [*insert location of local authority*]

1. On [*insert date*], the chief social work officer at [*insert location of local authority*] decided that [*insert details of relevant decision as referred to in* section 162(4) of the Children's Hearings (Scotland) Act 2011]. A copy of the relevant decision is attached.

2. *[The children's hearing that made a relevant order or warrant in relation to the child appointed [*insert name and address*] to act as safeguarder] *or* [No safeguarder has been appointed].

3. The following person(s) is/are* relevant persons [*insert name(s) and address(es) of relevant person(s) (within the meaning of* Rule 3.1(1) )].

4. The decision is not justified because [*state briefly the reasons why the decision is being appealed against*].

5. The said [*insert name of child and/or relevant person(s)*] appeals to the sheriff against the decision.

[*Signed*]

*[Appellant(s)] *or* [Solicitor for Appellant(s) [*insert name and address*]]

[*Insert place and date*]

The sheriff assigns [*insert date*] at [*insert time*] within chambers at [*insert name and address of sheriff court*] for the hearing of the application;

The sheriff—

1. Appoints the sheriff clerk forthwith to intimate a copy of the application and this warrant to—

(a) the Principal Reporter;

*(b) the child together with a notice in Form 64;

*(c) [insert name of relevant person(s) (*within the meaning of Rule 3.1(1) )*];

*(d) [insert name of any safeguarder];

*(e) [insert names of any other person the sheriff thinks necessary];

(f) [insert name of the chief social work officer].

*2. Dispenses with service on the child for the following reason [*insert details*].

3. Grants warrant to cite witnesses and havers.

[*Signed*]

[Sheriff or Sheriff clerk]

Intimated this day by me in terms of Rule 3.54(1).

[*Signed*]

[Sheriff Clerk/Depute]

[Date]

(*delete as appropriate)

FORM 64[2]

Rule 3.54(3)

INTIMATION TO CHILD IN RESPECT OF APPEALS TO THE SHERIFF UNDER THE CHILDREN'S HEARINGS (SCOTLAND) ACT 2011

---

[1] As inserted by the Act of Sederunt (Children's Hearings (Scotland) Act 2011) (Miscellaneous Amendments) 2013 (SSI 2013/172) para.4 (effective June 24, 2013).

[2] As substituted by the Act of Sederunt (Children's Hearings (Scotland) Act 2011) (Miscellaneous Amendments) 2013 (SSI 2013/172) para.4 (effective June 24, 2013).

Court ref. no.:

Dear [*insert name by which child is known*],

As you know at the *Children's Hearing/pre-hearing panel held on [*insert date*] not everyone agreed with the decision that was made. Since the decision of the hearing to [*insert details of decision being appealed*] was not accepted by [*insert name of person(s) who did not accept the decision*] your case has been sent to a sheriff who will decide whether the decision made by the *Children's Hearing/pre-hearing panel is correct.

**WHAT THE SHERIFF DOES:** A sheriff assists for lots of different reasons, but this time the purpose is to help the *Children's Hearing/pre-hearing panel. If the sheriff decides that the decision should be reconsidered the case may go back to the *Children's Hearing/pre-hearing panel to think again what is to happen in your case.

**HEARING:** The sheriff has set a date for hearing your case. The hearing will take place on [*insert time and date of hearing*] at [*insert address of sheriff court*]. [*You are required to attend court on that date *or* You are not required to attend court on that date, but you may wish to do so.*]

At the hearing the sheriff will listen to the evidence in your case, and will make a decision. This decision is very important for you [*and it is necessary for you to attend the hearing to tell the sheriff about your circumstances and how you feel. You might be asked some questions. You can be represented by a solicitor or another person].

*[**IMPORTANT NOTE: IT IS VERY IMPORTANT THAT YOU ATTEND** on the date and time given. If an emergency arises and you cannot attend you must contact the sheriff clerk on (*insert telephone number*) or the Principal Reporter because it is possible, if you do not attend, you may be detained and kept in a safe place until a later date.]

*[The sheriff has said that you do not have to attend the hearing on [*insert date*] at [*insert time*] at [*insert name and address of sheriff court*], but if you want to go along to hear what is said at the hearing then you can. If you do not want to go to court then you can still let the sheriff know what you think by filling in the attached form or you can write down what you want to say on a separate sheet of paper and send them back in the enclosed stamped addressed envelope before the date on which the sheriff is to hear the application, which is at the end of this letter. Alternatively, you can ask a lawyer to go to the hearing to tell the sheriff your views.]

**If you are unsure about what to do you can get free legal advice from a Lawyer or Local Advice Agency or Law Centre about the application and about legal aid. The Scottish Child Law Centre can refer you to specially trained lawyers who can help you. They give advice on their free phone number (0800 328 8970) any time between 9.30am and 4.00pm Monday to Friday.**

You will see that, along with this letter, there is a copy of the application to the sheriff, and the sheriff's order fixing the hearing. If you decide to get advice, or to ask someone to go with you to see the sheriff, make sure that you give them a copy of the application and the sheriff's order.

......................                                    ......................

(Signed)                                    (Date)

*(*delete as appropriate)*

To the Sheriff Clerk:

**I would like the Sheriff to know what I have to say before he or she makes a decision** (write what you want to say here, or you can use a separate sheet of paper):

Your Name:

Your Address:

Court Reference Number (if you know it):

FORM 64A[1]

Rule 3.58A(2)

FORM OF APPLICATION UNDER SECTION 166(2) OF THE CHILDREN'S HEARINGS (SCOTLAND) ACT 2011

Court ref. no.:

SHERIFF COURT AT (*insert place of sheriff court*)

Application to sheriff under section 166(2) of the Children's Hearings (Scotland) Act 2011 to review requirement imposed on local authority

---

[1] As substituted by the Act of Sederunt (Children's Hearings (Scotland) Act 2011) (Miscellaneous Amendments) 2013 (SSI 2013/172) para.4 (effective June 24, 2013).

by

*[insert name and address of local authority]*

Applicant

in the case of

*[insert name of child]*

PART 1: DETAILS OF PERSONS WHOM THE APPLICANT BELIEVES SHOULD RECEIVE NOTICE OF THE APPLICATION

THE NATIONAL
CONVENER
THE PRINCIPAL
REPORTER

CHILD *[insert name of child in respect of whom the duty was imposed and the child's representative (if any)]*

RELEVANT PERSON *[insert name and address of relevant person(s) (within the meaning of* Rule 3.1(1)*) and such person's representative(s) (if any)]*

SAFEGUARDER *[insert name and address of any safeguarder]*

CURATOR *AD LITEM [insert name and address of any curator ad litem]*

ANY OTHER PARTY *[insert name and address of any other party to the application]*

ANY OTHER
LOCAL AUTHORITY *[insert name and address of any other local authority with an interest]*

*\*Note: Information to be provided in Part 2 where applicant does not wish to disclose the address or whereabouts of the child or any other person to persons receiving notice of the application*

PART 2: INFORMATION ABOUT THE APPLICATION AND THE ORDERS SOUGHT

On *[insert date]*, \*[the sheriff at *[insert place]* made a determination in the following terms *[insert full details of order and conditions attaching to it]* OR [the children's hearing at *[insert place]* imposed a duty on the applicant local authority in respect of *[insert name of child]* in the following terms *[insert full details of order and conditions attaching to it]*. A copy of the relevant order is attached.

The applicant local authority is satisfied for the following reasons that it is not the relevant local authority for the child in respect of whom the duty has been imposed and requests the sheriff to review the decision or determination that imposed the duty on it: *[insert details of the basis on which such application is made]*.

The following supporting evidence is produced *(insert details of the evidence produced in support of the application)*—

\**[Insert here details and grounds where applicant does not wish to disclose the address or whereabouts of any person to persons receiving notice of the application.]*

*[Signed]*
\*[Solicitor for the local authority
*[insert name and address]]*

*(\*delete as appropriate)*

FORM 64B[1]

Rule 3.58B(1)

APPLICATION UNDER SECTION 166(2) OF THE CHILDREN'S HEARINGS (SCOTLAND) ACT 2011:
FORM OF WARRANT TO CITE

Court ref. no.:

*[Insert place and date]*

The sheriff—

1. Assigns *[insert date]* at *[insert time]* within chambers at *[insert name and address of sheriff court]* for the hearing of the application;

2. Appoints the Applicant forthwith to serve a copy of the application and this warrant to—

(a) the National Convener;

\*(b) the Principal Reporter;

\*(c) the child together with a notice in Form 64;

---

[1] As substituted by the Act of Sederunt (Children's Hearings (Scotland) Act 2011) (Miscellaneous Amendments) 2013 (SSI 2013/172) para.4 (effective June 24, 2013).

*(d) [insert name of relevant person(s) (*within the meaning of Rule 3.1(1)* )];

*(e) [insert name of any safeguarder];

*(f) [insert name of any curator *ad litem*];

*(g) [insert name of local authority(ies)];

*(h) [insert names of any other person the sheriff thinks necessary].

*3. Dispenses with service on the child for the following reason [*insert details*].

4. Grants warrant to cite witnesses and havers.

5. Orders that answers must be lodged (if so advised) by (*insert date*).

[*Signed*]

[Sheriff or Sheriff clerk]

(*\*delete as appropriate*)

FORM 65[1]

Rule 3.63(1)

APPLICATION UNDER SECTION 110 OF THE CHILDREN'S HEARINGS (SCOTLAND) ACT 2011: FORM OF WARRANT TO CITE PRINCIPAL REPORTER

Court ref. no.:

[*Place and date*]

The court

1.  Assigns [*date*] at [*hour*] within the [*name court*] in chambers at [*place*] for the hearing of the application.

2.  Appoints the Applicant to forthwith cite the Principal Reporter to lodge answers, if so advised, within [*enter period set by sheriff*]

3.  Appoints the Applicant to forthwith intimate the application to

    i    BB* [*insert name of relevant person or persons (within the meaning of Rule 3.1(1) (if not the Applicant))*] whose whereabouts are known and

    ii    [AB]* (name and design) the safeguarded

    (iia)    [YZ] ( name and design ) any curator *ad litem*

    iii    [BC]* (name and design) a party to the application,

    by serving a copy of the application and this warrant upon [*each of*] *them;

    (iv)    [CD]* (*insert name of child (if not the Applicant)*)

4.  Grants warrant to cite witnesses and havers.

5.  *Dispenses with notice and service on [*insert name*] for the following reason(s) [*insert reason(s)*].

..............

Sheriff Clerk

*delete as appropriate

FORM 65A[2]

Rule 3.64A(1)

INTERIM COMPULSORY SUPERVISION ORDER UNDER THE CHILDREN'S HEARINGS (SCOTLAND) ACT 2011

Court ref. no.:

[*Insert place and date*]

In the application under [*specify relevant section of the Children's Hearings (Scotland) Act 2011*\*] the sheriff—

1. Made an interim compulsory supervision order in relation to [*insert name of child*] because the sheriff was satisfied that [*insert details why the child's circumstances are such that it was necessary as a matter of urgency for the sheriff to make the order*].

*2. Ordered that the interim compulsory supervision order includes the following measures—

---

[1] As amended by the Act of Sederunt (Children's Hearings (Scotland) Act 2011) (Miscellaneous Amendments) 2013 (SSI 2013/172) para.4 (effective June 24, 2013).

[2] As substituted by the Act of Sederunt (Children's Hearings (Scotland) Act 2011) (Miscellaneous Amendments) 2013 (SSI 2013/172) para.4 (effective June 24, 2013).

*(a) a requirement that the child reside at (*insert address of specified place OR a place of safety away from the place where the child predominantly resides at (insert address of predominant residence))*;

*(b) a direction authorising the person who is in charge of the place specified in paragraph (a) to restrict the child's liberty to the extent that the person considers appropriate having regard to the measures included in this order;

*(c) a prohibition on the disclosure (whether directly or indirectly) of a place specified under paragraph (a);

*(d) a movement restriction condition in the following terms: [*insert relevant details*];

*(e) a secure accommodation authorisation in the following terms: [*insert relevant details*];

*(f) a requirement that the implementation authority arrange (*insert details of the specified medical or other examination of the child OR the specified medical or other treatment for the child*];

*(g) a direction regulating contact between the child and [*insert name and address of specified person OR specify class of person*];

*(h) a requirement that the child comply with [*specify any other condition*];

*(i) a requirement that the implementation authority carry out the following duties in relation to the child: (*insert specified duties*).

3. Specified that [*insert name and address of local authority*] (the implementation authority) is to be responsible for giving effect to the measures included in the order.

4. Specified that this order has effect until [*specify the relevant period*].

5. [Ordered the *[Principal Reporter to intimate this order to the child in Form 65B]] *or* [dispensed with intimation to the child].

6. Ordered the Principal Reporter to intimate this order to the implementation authority.

*7. Ordered the Principal Reporter to intimate this order to [*insert name of other persons*] in Form 65E.

[*Signed*]

[Sheriff clerk]

*(\*delete as appropriate)*

For the purpose of enforcing this order warrant is granted to officers of law for all lawful execution, including—

(a) searching for and apprehending the child;

(b) taking the child to the authorised place;

(c) where (i) it is not reasonably practicable to take the child immediately to the authorised place; and (ii) the authorised place is not a place of safety, taking the child to and detaining the child in a place of safety for as short a period of time as is practicable;

(d) so far as necessary, by breaking open shut and lockfast places.

[*Signed*]

[Sheriff or Sheriff clerk]

Date & time ..............

FORM 65B[1]

Rule 3.64A

NOTICE TO CHILD OF AN INTERIM COMPULSORY SUPERVISION ORDER UNDER THE CHILDREN'S HEARINGS (SCOTLAND) ACT 2011

Court ref. no.:

Dear [*insert name by which child is known*],

I am writing to let you know that because there are worries about your safety, the sheriff has made an order to keep you safe. This order is called an interim compulsory supervision order. It means that [*insert details in simple terms of what the order means for the child and refer to any previous order if appropriate*]. This is because the sheriff is concerned that [*insert the reason why the sheriff made the order*]. The interim compulsory supervision order will be in force until [*insert date — see section 86(3) of the Children's Hearings (Scotland) Act 2011*]. A copy of the order is attached.

---

[1] As substituted by the Act of Sederunt (Children's Hearings (Scotland) Act 2011) (Miscellaneous Amendments) 2013 (SSI 2013/172) para.4 (effective June 24, 2013).

**If you are unsure about what to do you can get free legal advice from a Lawyer or Local Advice Agency or Law Centre. The Scottish Child Law Centre can refer you to specially trained lawyers who can help you. They give advice on their free phone number (0800 328 8970) any time between 9.30am and 4.00pm Monday to Friday.**

*(Principal Reporter)*                 *(Date)*

FORM 65C[1]

Rule 3.64A(2)

APPLICATION TO EXTEND OR EXTEND AND VARY AN INTERIM COMPULSORY SUPERVISION ORDER UNDER THE CHILDREN'S HEARINGS (SCOTLAND) ACT 2011

Court ref. no.:

SHERIFF COURT AT *(insert place of sheriff court)*

Application to sheriff under *[insert relevant section]* of the Children's Hearings (Scotland) Act 2011 to [*extend *OR* extend and vary] an interim compulsory supervision order

by

**The Principal Reporter**

in the case of

*[insert name of child]*

PART 1: DETAILS OF PERSONS WHOM THE APPLICANT BELIEVES SHOULD RECEIVE NOTICE OF THE APPLICATION

CHILD                *[insert name, gender and date of birth*]*

RELEVANT

PERSON           *[insert name(s) and address(es) of relevant person(s) (within the meaning of Rule 3.1(1) )]*

SAFEGUARDER     *[insert name, address and telephone numbers (if known) of any safeguarder]*

IMPLEMENTATION

AUTHORITY       *[insert name of local authority, if appropriate]*

ANY OTHER

PERSON          *[insert name, address and telephone numbers (if known) of any other persons and provide details of their interest in the application]*

*\*Note: Information to be provided in Part 2 where applicant does not wish to disclose the address or whereabouts of the child or any other person to persons receiving notice of the application*

PART 2: INFORMATION ABOUT THE APPLICATION AND THE ORDERS SOUGHT

On *[insert date]*, the children's hearing at *[insert place]* made an interim compulsory supervision order in respect of *[insert name and address of child]* in the following terms *[insert full details of order and conditions attaching to it]*. A copy of the relevant order is attached.

The applicant requests the sheriff to [*extend *OR* extend and vary] the order in the following terms: *[insert details of the extension or extension and variation sought]*.

The following supporting evidence is produced *(insert details of the evidence produced in support of the application)*—

*\*[Insert here details and grounds where applicant does not wish to disclose the address of any person to persons receiving notice of the application.]*

[*Signed*]

*\*[Principal Reporter] or*

[Solicitor for Principal Reporter

*[insert name and address]*]]

PART 3: FORM OF INTERLOCUTOR

*[Insert place and date]*

The sheriff—

1. Assigns *[insert date]* at *[insert time]* within chambers at *[insert name and address of sheriff court]* for the hearing of the application;

2. Appoints the Applicant forthwith to serve a copy of the application and this warrant to—

---

[1] As substituted by the Act of Sederunt (Children's Hearings (Scotland) Act 2011) (Miscellaneous Amendments) 2013 (SSI 2013/172) para.4 (effective June 24, 2013).

(a) the child;

(b) the other persons listed in Part 1 of this application.

*3. Dispenses with service on the child or any other person for the following reason [*insert details*].

4. Grants warrant to cite witnesses and havers.

5. Appoints answers to be lodged, if so advised, not later than [*insert number of days*] before the said diet.

[*Signed*]

[Sheriff clerk]

(**delete as appropriate*)

FORM 65D[1]

Rule 3.64A(3)

APPLICATION TO FURTHER EXTEND OR FURTHER EXTEND AND VARY AN INTERIM COMPULSORY SUPERVISION ORDER UNDER THE CHILDREN'S HEARINGS (SCOTLAND) ACT 2011

Court ref. no.:

SHERIFF COURT AT (*insert place of sheriff court*)

Application to sheriff under section 99 of the Children's Hearings (Scotland) Act 2011 to [*further extend OR further extend and vary] an interim compulsory supervision order

by

**The Principal Reporter**

in the case of

[*insert name of child*]

PART 1: DETAILS OF PERSONS WHOM THE APPLICANT BELIEVES SHOULD RECEIVE NOTICE OF THE APPLICATION

| | |
|---|---|
| CHILD | [*insert name, gender and date of birth**] |
| RELEVANT PERSON | [*insert name(s) and address(es) of relevant person(s) (within the meaning of Rule 3.1(1) )*] |
| SAFEGUARDER | [*insert name, address and telephone numbers (if known) of any safeguarder*] |
| IMPLEMENTATION AUTHORITY | [*insert name of local authority, if appropriate*] |
| ANY OTHER PERSON | [*insert name, address and telephone numbers (if known) of any other persons and provide details of their interest in the application*] |

**Note: Information to be provided in Part 2 where applicant does not wish to disclose the address or whereabouts of the child or any other person to persons receiving notice of the application*

PART 2: INFORMATION ABOUT THE APPLICATION AND THE ORDERS SOUGHT

On [*insert date*], the children's hearing at [*insert place*] [*extended OR extended and varied OR further extended OR further extended and varied] an interim compulsory supervision order in respect of [*insert name and address of child*] in the following terms [*insert full details of order and conditions attaching to it*]. A copy of the relevant order [as extended OR extended and varied OR further extended OR further extended and varied] is attached.

The applicant requests the sheriff to [*further extend OR further extend and vary] the order in the following terms: [*insert details of the further extension or further extension and variation sought*].

The following supporting evidence is produced (*insert details of the evidence produced in support of the application)—*

*[*Insert here details and grounds where applicant does not wish to disclose the address of any person to persons receiving notice of the application.*]

[*Signed*]

*[Principal Reporter] or

[Solicitor for Principal Reporter

[*insert name and address*]]

PART 3: FORM OF INTERLOCUTOR

---

[1] As substituted by the Act of Sederunt (Children's Hearings (Scotland) Act 2011) (Miscellaneous Amendments) 2013 (SSI 2013/172) para.4 (effective June 24, 2013).

[*Insert place and date*]

The sheriff—

1. Assigns [*insert date*] at [*insert time*] within chambers at [*insert name and address of sheriff court*] for the hearing of the application;

2. Appoints the Applicant forthwith to serve a copy of the application and this warrant to—

(a) the child;

(b) the other persons listed in Part 1 of this application.

*3. Dispenses with service on the child or any other person for the following reason [*insert details*].

4. Grants warrant to cite witnesses and havers.

5. Appoints answers to be lodged, if so advised, not later than [*insert number of days*] before the said diet.

[*Signed*]

[Sheriff clerk]

(**delete as appropriate*)

FORM 65E[1]

Rule 3.64A(6)

NOTICE OF INTIMATION OF AN INTERIM COMPULSORY SUPERVISION ORDER UNDER THE CHILDREN'S HEARINGS (SCOTLAND) ACT 2011

Court ref. no.:

To [*insert name and address of person receiving intimation as required by the sheriff under* Rule 3.64A(6)]

I am writing to let you know that the sheriff has made an interim compulsory supervision order in respect of [*insert name of child*]. It means that [*insert details of what the order means for the child and the specified person (if appropriate, and refer to any previous order if appropriate*]. This is because the sheriff is concerned that [*insert the reason why the sheriff made the order*]. The interim compulsory supervision order will be in force until [*insert date — see section 86(3) of the Children's Hearings (Scotland) Act 2011*]. A copy of the order is attached.

*[YOU SHOULD OBTAIN ADVICE FROM A SOLICITOR OR LOCAL ADVICE AGENCY OR LAW CENTRE. You may be entitled to legal aid. Advice about legal aid is available from any solicitor, advice agency or law centre.]

(*Date*)                                             (*signed*)

Principal Reporter

(**delete as appropriate*)

FORM 66                                             Rule 5.19(1)

(Place).......... (Date)...............

AB (design)

Intimation is hereby given that there has been received at (..........) Sheriff Court evidence relative to the provisional maintenance order made on your application on .........., as a result of which it appears that the provisional order ought not to have been made.

*A copy of the document summarising that evidence taken by the [name of Court] in proceedings relating to the confirmation of the provisional order accompanies this intimation.

or

*A copy of the note of that evidence taken at [name of Court] Sheriff Court accompanies this intimation.

IF YOU WISH TO MAKE REPRESENTATIONS AND ADDUCE FURTHER EVIDENCE with respect to the evidence received you must lodge a minute narrating the representations and the further evidence you intend to adduce with the Sheriff Clerk at [name and address of Sheriff Court] within 21 days afer the date of this intimation.

IF YOU DO NOTHING IN ANSWER TO THIS INTIMATION the Court may revoke the provisional maintenance order.

[Signed]

---

[1] As substituted by the Act of Sederunt (Children's Hearings (Scotland) Act 2011) (Miscellaneous Amendments) 2013 (SSI 2013/172) para.4 (effective June 24, 2013).

Sheriff Clerk

*Delete as appropriate

FORM 67 Rules 5.20(1) and 5.29(1)

MAINTENANCE ORDERS (RECIPROCAL ENFORCEMENT) ACT 1972

(Place).......... (Date)..............

AB (Design)

Intimation is hereby given of the receipt at [name and address of Sheriff Court] of a provisional order made by [name of Court] at .......... on ...............

A copy of the provisional order together with a summary of the evidence upon which the order was made [*and a statement of the grounds upon which the order might have been opposed] accompanies this intimation.

IF YOU WISH TO OPPOSE THE ORDER, you must lodge an application with the Sheriff Clerk at [name and address of Sheriff Court] within 21/42* days after the date of this intimation and at the same time present this copy intimation.

IF YOU DO NOTHING IN ANSWER TO THIS INTIMATION the order will be confirmed.

[Signed]
Sheriff Clerk

*Delete as appropriate

FORM 68 Rule 5.24(1)(b)

FORM OF DECLARATION

I hereby declare that the foregoing certified copy of a maintenance order has been duly registered by me in Part II of the Maintenance Orders Register kept in this Court in terms of the Maintenance Orders Act 1950, and of Chapter 5 of the Act of Sederunt (Child Care and Maintenance Rules) 1997.

[Signed]
Sheriff Clerk Depute

FORM 69 Rule 5.34(1)(a)

NOTICE OF REGISTRATION FOR ENFORCEMENT IN SCOTLAND OF A MAINTENANCE ORDER MADE IN THE REPUBLIC OF IRELAND

*[Repealed by the Act of Sederunt (Sheriff Court Rules) (Miscellaneous Amendments) (No.3) 2011 (SSI 2011/386) para.9 (effective November 28, 2011).]*

FORM 70[1] Rules 5.34(1)(b) and 5.36(1)(b)

NOTICE OF REGISTRATION FOR THE PURPOSES OF ENFORCEMENT IN SCOTLAND OF A MAINTENANCE ORDER MADE IN A HAGUE CONVENTION COUNTRY

(Place).......... (Date)..............

AB (Design)

Notice is hereby given of the registration in the Maintenance Order Register kept at [name and address of Sheriff Court] of a maintenance order made by [name and address of Court in Hague Convention Country] on [date of making order].

In terms of said maintenance order CD [design payer] is required to pay to you [narrate terms of order].

[Signed]
Sheriff Clerk

FORM 71[2] Rules 5.34(2) and 5.36(2)

NOTICE OF A DECISION NOT TO REGISTER, FOR THE PURPOSES OF THE ENFORCEMENT IN SCOTLAND, A MAINTENANCE ORDER MADE IN A HAGUE CONVENTION COUNTRY

(Place).......... (Date)..............

---

[1] As amended by the Act of Sederunt (Sheriff Court Rules) (Miscellaneous Amendments) (No.3) 2011 (SSI 2011/386) para.9 (effective November 28, 2011).
[2] As amended by the Act of Sederunt (Sheriff Court Rules) (Miscellaneous Amendments) (No.3) 2011 (SSI 2011/386) para.9 (effective November 28, 2011).

AB (Design)

Notice is hereby given that the maintenance order made by [name and address of Court in Hague Convention Country] on [date of making order] requiring CD (design) to pay to you [narrate terms of order] has NOT been registered in the Maintenance Orders Register kept at this Sheriff Court.

The Order has not been registered on the grounds that [narrate grounds].

You may within one calendar month from the date of this notice make application to this Sheriff Court to set aside the decision not to register the order by lodging at this Sheriff Court a summary application setting out the grounds of your application.

[Signed]
Sheriff Clerk

FORM 72[1]                                                   Rule 5.36(1)(a)

INTIMATION OF REGISTRATION FOR ENFORCEMENT IN SCOTLAND OF A MAINTENANCE ORDER MADE IN A HAGUE CONVENTION COUNTRY

(Place).......... (Date)...............

AB (Design)

Intimation is hereby given of the registration in the Maintenance Orders Register kept at [name and address of Sheriff Court] of a maintenance order made by [name and address of Court in Hague Convention Country] on [date of making order].

In terms of the said maintenance order you are required [narrate terms of order and payee].

You may within one calendar month from the date of this intimation make application to [name and address of Sheriff Court] to set aside the registration of the order by lodging with the Sheriff Clerk at [name and address of Sheriff Court] a summary application setting out the grounds of the application.

The grounds upon which application to set aside the registration may be made are

(a)   [name of Court in Hague Convention Country] did not have jurisdiction to make the order;

(b)   registration is manifestly contrary to public policy;

(c)   the order was obtained by fraud in connection with a matter of procedure;

(d)   proceedings between you and the payee under the mainenance order and having the same purpose are pending before a court in Scotland and those proceedings were the first to be instituted;

(e)   the order is incompatible with an order made in proceedings between you and the payee and having the same purpose either in the United Kingdom or in another country, provided that the latter order fulfils the conditions necessary for registration and enforcement;

(f)   you did not appear in the proceedings in the Hague Convention Country and you were not served in accordance with the institution of proceedings including notice of the substance of the claim in sufficient time, having regard to the circumstances, to enable you to defend the proceedings.

[Signed]
Sheriff Clerk

FORM 73[2]                                                   Rule 5.40

NOTICE OF DETERMINATION BY SHERIFF CLERK OF APPLICATION UNDER SECTION 5A OF THE CIVIL JURISDICTION AND JUDGMENTS ACT 1982

Sheriff Court (Address)

.............. (Applicant) v. .............. (Respondent)

TAKE NOTICE that the application by [name and address], for the recognition and/or enforcement of a maintenance order granted by [state Court of Tribunal] on the .......... day of ..........; has been *GRANTED/REFUSED (state reasons in brief for refusal); and has been registered in the Books of Court to the extent that (state the extent).

(Signed)
Sheriff Clerk
Date

NOTE:

---

[1] As amended by the Act of Sederunt (Sheriff Court Rules) (Miscellaneous Amendments) (No.3) 2011 (SSI 2011/386) para.9 (effective November 28, 2011).

[2] As amended by the Act of Sederunt (Sheriff Court Rules) (Miscellaneous Amendments) (No.3) 2011 (SSI 2011/386) para.9 (effective November 28, 2011).

1. If the application has been granted to any extent, the person against whom enforcement is sought may appeal against this decision within one month from the date of service of this Notice, unless he is domiciled in another Contracting State in which case he may appeal within two months from the date of service.

2. If the application has been refused or not granted in full the Applicant may appeal against the decision within one month from the date of service of this Notice.

3. A solicitor qualified in Scots law should be consulted for the purposes of any appeal.

*Delete as appropriate

Rule 5.47(1)(a)                  FORM 73A[1]

INTIMATION OF REGISTRATION FOR ENFORCEMENT IN SCOTLAND OF A MAINTENANCE DECISION MADE BY A COURT IN DENMARK ETC.

(*Insert place*) ...............

(*Insert date*) ...............

[A.B.], (*Design*)

Intimation is hereby given of the registration in the Maintenance Orders Register kept at [*insert name and address of sheriff court*] of a Maintenance Decision made by [*name and address of Court*] on [*insert date of making order*].

In terms of the said Maintenance Decision you are required [*narrate terms of order and payee*].

You may within [30 days] *or* [*where the party against whom enforcement is sought has his/her habitual residence outwith the United Kingdom*, 45 days] from the date of this intimation make an application to [*insert name and address of sheriff court*] to set aside the registration of the order by lodging with the sheriff clerk at [*insert name and address of sheriff court*] a summary application setting out the grounds of the application.

The grounds upon which an application to set aside the registration may be made are:

(a)    the court does not have jurisdiction;

(b)    such registration is manifestly contrary to public policy in any part of the United Kingdom. The test of public policy may not be applied to the rules relating to jurisdiction;

(c)    where the decision was given in default of appearance, if you were not served with the document which instituted the proceedings or with an equivalent document in sufficient time and in such a way as to enable you to arrange for your defence, unless you failed to commence proceedings to challenge the decision when it was possible for you to do so;

(d)    if the decision is irreconcilable with a Maintenance Decision given in a dispute between the same parties in Scotland or another part of the United Kingdom;

(e)    if the decision is irreconcilable with an earlier decision given in another Member Regulation State or in a third State in a dispute involving the same cause of action and between the same parties, provided that the earlier decision fulfils the conditions necessary for its recognition in Scotland or another part of the United Kingdom.

**Note: A Maintenance Decision which has the effect of modifying an earlier Maintenance Decision on the basis of changed circumstances shall not be considered an irreconcilable decision within the meaning of points (d) and (e).**

                                                     [*Signed*]

                                              (Sheriff Clerk)

Rule 5.47(1)(b)                  FORM 73B[2]

NOTICE OF REGISTRATION FOR THE PURPOSES OF ENFORCEMENT IN SCOTLAND OF A MAINTENANCE DECISION MADE BY A COURT IN DENMARK ETC.

(*Insert place*)

(*Insert date*)

[A.B.], (*Design*)

Notice is hereby given of the registration in the Maintenance Orders Register kept at [*insert name and address of sheriff court*] of a Maintenance Decision made by [*insert name and address of Court*] on [*insert date of making order*].

---

[1] As inserted by the Act of Sederunt (Sheriff Court Rules) (Miscellaneous Amendments) (No.3) 2011 (SSI 2011/386) para.9 (effective November 28, 2011).

[2] As inserted by the Act of Sederunt (Sheriff Court Rules) (Miscellaneous Amendments) (No.3) 2011 (SSI 2011/386) para.9 (effective November 28, 2011).

In terms of the said Maintenance Decision CD [*design payer*] is required to pay to you [*narrate terms of order*].

[*Signed*]
(Sheriff Clerk)

Rule 5.47(2)                                   FORM 73C[1]

NOTICE OF A DECISION NOT TO REGISTER, FOR THE PURPOSES OF THE ENFORCEMENT IN SCOTLAND, A MAINTENANCE DECISION MADE BY A COURT IN DENMARK ETC.
(*Insert place*)
(*Insert date*)
[A.B.], (*Design*)

Notice is hereby given that the Maintenance Decision made by [*insert name and address of Court*] on [*insert date of making order*] requiring CD [*design payer*] to pay to you [*narrate terms of order*] has NOT been registered in the Maintenance Orders Register kept at this Sheriff Court.

The Maintenance Decision has not been registered on the grounds that [*narrate grounds*].

You may within 30 days from the date of this intimation make an application to [*insert name and address of sheriff court*] to set aside the decision not to register the order by lodging with the sheriff clerk at [*insert name and address of sheriff court*] a summary application setting out the grounds of the application.

[*Signed*]
(Sheriff Clerk)

FORM 74                                   Rule 6.3(1)

FORM OF CERTIFICATE OF A TRANSFER OF RIGHTS TO AN ORDER BY VIRTUE OF SECTION 107 OF THE SOCIAL SECURITY ADMINISTRATION ACT 1992
(Place).......... (Date)..............

I certify that notice has today been received from the Secretary of State under section 107 of the Social Security Administration Act 1992 of a transfer of rights under an order granted on (date) from (name and design) to (name and design) with effect from (date).

(Signed)
Sheriff Clerk [Depute]

FORM 75[2]                                   Rule 3.67

CHILD WITNESS NOTICE
VULNERABLE WITNESSES (SCOTLAND) ACT 2004 Section 12

Received the ............... day of ............... 20.....
(Date of receipt of this notice)
.......... [signed]
Sheriff Clerk

**CHILD WITNESS NOTICE**

Sheriff Court ............... ............... 20.....

(Court Ref. No.)

1. [A.B.] (the Applicant) is a party to an [application under section [93(2)(a), 94(2)(a) *or* 110] of the Children's Hearings (Scotland) Act 2011] *or* [an appeal under Part 15 of the 2011 Act]. [*State the nature of the interest of the party*].".

2. The applicant [has cited [or intends to cite]] [C.D.] (*date of birth*) as a witness.

3. [C.D.] is a child witness under section 11 of the Vulnerable Witnesses (Scotland) Act 2004 [and was under the age of sixteen on the date of the commencement of proceedings].

4. The applicant considers [that the following special measure[s] is [are] the most appropriate for the purpose of taking the evidence of [C.D.]] *or* [that [C.D.] should give evidence without the benefit of any special measure]:–

(*delete as appropriate and specify any special measure(s) sought*).

---

[1] As inserted by the Act of Sederunt (Sheriff Court Rules) (Miscellaneous Amendments) (No.3) 2011 (SSI 2011/386) para.9 (effective November 28, 2011).

[2] As amended by the Act of Sederunt (Children's Hearings (Scotland) Act 2011) (Miscellaneous Amendments) 2013 (SSI 2013/172) para.4 (effective June 24, 2013).

5. [(a) The reason[s] this [these] special measure[s] is [are] considered the most appropriate is [are] as follows:–

(*here specify reason(s) for the special measure(s) sought*).]

OR

[(b) The reason[s] it is considered that [C.D.] should give evidence without the benefit of any special measure is [are]–

(*here explain why it is felt that no special measures are required*).

6. [C.D.] [and the parent[s] of] *or* [person[s] with parental responsibility for] [C.D.]] have expressed the following view[s] on [the special measure[s] that is [are] considered most appropriate] *or* [the appropriateness of [C.D.] giving evidence without the benefit of any special measure]:–

(*delete as appropriate and set out the view(s) expressed and how they were obtained*).

7. Other information considered relevant to this application is as follows:–

(*here set out any other information relevant to the child witness notice*).

8. The applicant asks the court to–

(a)  consider this child witness notice;

(b)  make an order authorising the special measure[s] sought; *or*

(c)  make an order authorising the giving of evidence by [C.D.] without the benefit of special measures.

(*delete as appropriate*)

.......... (Signed)

[A.B.]

*or* [Legal representative of A.B.] (*include full designation*)

*NOTE: This form should be suitably adapted where* section 16 of the Act of 2004 *applies.*

FORM 76          Rule 3.68

CERTIFICATE OF INTIMATION

VULNERABLE WITNESSES (SCOTLAND) ACT 2004 Section 12

Sheriff Court .................... .......... 20.....

(Court Ref. No.)

I certify that intimation of the child witness notice relating to [name of child] was made to (*insert names of parties or solicitors for parties, as appropriate*) by (*insert method of intimation; where intimation is by facsimile transmission, insert fax number to which intimation sent*) on (*insert date of intimation*).

Date: ..............

.............. Signed

Solicitor [or Sheriff Officer]

(*include full business designation*)

FORM 76A[1, 2]         Rule 3.67

VULNERABLE WITNESS APPLICATION

VULNERABLE WITNESSES (SCOTLAND) ACT 2004 Section 12

Received the .............. day of .............. 20.....

(Date of receipt of this notice)

........................ [signed]

Sheriff Clerk

**VULNERABLE WITNESS APPLICATION**

Sheriff Court .................... .............. 20.....

(Court Ref. No.)

1. [A.B.] (the Applicant) is a party to an [application under section [93(2)(a), 94(2)(a) *or* 110] of the Children's Hearings (Scotland) Act 2011] *or* [an appeal under Part 15 of the 2011 Act]. [*State the nature of the interest of the party*].

2. The applicant [has cited [or intends to cite]] [C.D.] (*date of birth*) as a witness.

---

[1] As inserted by the Act of Sederunt (Child Care and Maintenance Rules) Amendment (Vulnerable Witnesses (Scotland) Act 2004) 2006 (SSI 2006/75) Sch.1 para.1 (effective April 1, 2006).

[2] As amended by the Act of Sederunt (Children's Hearings (Scotland) Act 2011) (Miscellaneous Amendments) 2013 (SSI 2013/172) para.4 (effective June 24, 2013).

3. The applicant considers that [C.D.] is a vulnerable witness under section 11(1)(b) of the Vulnerable Witnesses (Scotland) Act 2004 for the following reasons:– (*here specify reasons witness is considered to be a vulnerable witness*).

4. The applicant considers that the following special measure[s] is [are] the most appropriate for the purpose of taking the evidence of [C.D.]. (*specify any special measure(s) sought*)

5. The reason[s] this [these] special measure[s] is [are] considered the most appropriate is [are] as follows:– (*here specify reason(s) for the special measure(s) sought*).]

6. [C.D.] has expressed the following view[s] on [the special measure[s] that is [are] considered most appropriate]:– (*set out the views expressed and how they were obtained*).

7. Other information considered relevant to this application is as follows:–
(*here set out any other information relevant to the vulnerable witness application*).

8. The applicant asks the court to–
(a)     consider this vulnerable witness application;
(b)     make an order authorising the special measure[s] sought.
.......... (Signed)
[A.B.]
*or* [Legal representative of A.B.] (*include full designation*)
*NOTE: This form should be suitably adapted where* section 16 of the Act of 2004 *applies.*

FORM 76B[1]                    Rule 3.71(2)

CERTIFICATE OF INTIMATION
VULNERABLE WITNESSES (SCOTLAND) ACT 2004
Sheriff Court ............... ......... 20.....

(Court Ref. No.)

CERTIFICATE OF INTIMATION
I certify that intimation of the vulnerable witness application relating to [name of witness] was made to (*insert names of parties or solicitors for parties, as appropriate*) by (*insert method of intimation; where intimation is by facsimile transmission, insert fax number to which intimation sent*) on (*insert date of intimation*).
Date: ...............
.......... Signed
Solicitor [or Sheriff Officer]
(*include full business designation*)

FORM 77[2, 3]                    Rule 3.70

APPLICATION FOR REVIEW OF ARRANGEMENTS FOR VULNERABLE WITNESS
VULNERABLE WITNESSES (SCOTLAND) ACT 2004 SECTION 13
Received the ............... day of ............... 20.....
(Date of receipt of this notice)
............... [signed]
Sheriff Clerk
**APPLICATION FOR REVIEW OF ARRANGEMENTS FOR VULNERABLE WITNESS**
Sheriff Court ............... ............... 20.....

(Court Ref. No.)

1. [A.B.] (the Applicant) is a party to an [application under section [93(2)(a), 94(2)(a) *or* 110] of the Children's Hearings (Scotland) Act 2011] *or* [an appeal under Part 15 of the 2011 Act]. [ *State the nature of the interest of the party* ].

2. A hearing is fixed for [(*date*)] at [(*time*)].

3. [C.D.] is a witness who is to give evidence at, or for the purposes of, the hearing. [C.D.] is a vulnerable witness under section 11 of the Vulnerable Witnesses (Scotland) Act 2004.

---

[1] As inserted by the Act of Sederunt (Child Care and Maintenance Rules) Amendment (Vulnerable Witnesses (Scotland) Act 2004) 2006 (SSI 2006/75) Sch.1 para.1 (effective April 1, 2006).
[2] As amended by the Act of Sederunt (Child Care and Maintenance Rules) Amendment (Vulnerable Witnesses (Scotland) Act 2004) 2006 (SSI 2006/75) Sch.1 para.2 (effective April 1, 2006).
[3] As amended by the Act of Sederunt (Children's Hearings (Scotland) Act 2011) (Miscellaneous Amendments) 2013 (SSI 2013/172) para.4 (effective June 24, 2013).

4. The current arrangements for taking the evidence of [C.D.] are (*here specify current arrangements*).

5. The current arrangements should be reviewed as (*here specify reasons for review*).

6. [C.D.] and [the parent[s] of] *or* [person[s] with parental responsibility for] [C.D.]] has [or have] expressed the following view[s] on [the special measure[s] that is [or are] considered most appropriate] *or* [the appropriateness of [C.D.] giving evidence without the benefit of any special measure]:–

(*delete as appropriate and set out the view(s) expressed and how they were obtained*).

7. The applicant seeks (*here specify the order sought*).

.............. (Signed)

[A.B.]

[*or* Legal representative of A.B.] (*include full designation*)

*NOTE: This form should be suitably adapted where* section 16 of the Act of 2004 *applies.*

FORM 78                                           Rule 3.71(2)

CERTIFICATE OF INTIMATION
VULNERABLE WITNESSES (SCOTLAND) ACT 2004 SECTION 13

Sheriff Court .............. .............. 20.....

(Court Ref. No.)

CERTIFICATE OF INTIMATION

I certify that intimation of the review application relating to [name of witness] was made to (insert names of parties or solicitors for parties, as appropriate) by (insert method of intimation; where intimation is by facsimile transmission, insert fax number to which intimation sent) on (insert date of intimation).

Date ..............

.............. Signed

Solicitor [or Sheriff Officer]

(*include full business designation*)

FORM 79[1]                         Rule 3.77

APPLICATION TO SHERIFF FOR ORDER AS TO EVIDENCE UNDER SECTION 175 OF THE
CHILDREN'S HEARINGS (SCOTLAND) ACT 2011

Received the .............. day of .............. 20.....

(Date of receipt of this notice)

.......... [signed]

Sheriff Clerk

**Application for admission of evidence or allowance of questioning**

Sheriff Court .............. .............. 20.....

(Court Ref. No.)

1. [A.B.] (the Applicant) is a party to an [application under section [93(2)(a), 94(2)(a) *or* 110] of the Children's Hearings (Scotland) Act 2011] *or* [an appeal under Part 15 of the 2011 Act] in relation to the child [C.D.]. [ *State the nature of the interest of the party* ].

2. A hearing is fixed for [(*date*)] at [(*time*)].

3. The applicant asks the court to admit, or allow questioning designed to elicit or enable to be taken by commissioner, evidence which shows or tends to show that [C.D.] or [other person]:

* is not of good character (whether in relation to sexual matters or otherwise);

* has, at any time, engaged in sexual behaviour not forming part of the subject matter of the statement of grounds;

* has, at any time (other than shortly before, at the same time as or shortly after the acts which form part of the subject-matter of the ground), engaged in behaviour (not being sexual behaviour), that might found an inference that the person is not credible or the person's evidence is not reliable;

* has, at any time, been subject to any condition or predisposition that might found the inference that the person is not credible or the person's evidence is not reliable.

4. The circumstances justifying this application are:

(*here set out these circumstances with particular reference to* section 175 of the 2011 Act).

---

[1] As amended by the Act of Sederunt (Children's Hearings (Scotland) Act 2011) (Miscellaneous Amendments) 2013 (SSI 2013/172) para.4 (effective June 24, 2013).

.......... (Signed)

[A.B.]

*or* [Legal representative of A.B.] (*include full designation*)

(*\*delete as appropriate*)

FORM 80[1]        Rule 3.78

CERTIFICATE OF INTIMATION UNDER SECTION 175 OF THE CHILDREN'S HEARINGS (SCOTLAND) ACT 2011

Sheriff Court ............... .......... 20.....

(Court Ref. No.)

I certify that intimation of the application for [admission of evidence]/[allowance of questioning] was made to (*insert names of parties or solicitors for parties, as appropriate*) by (*insert method of intimation; where intimation is by facsimile transmission, insert fax number to which intimation sent* on (*insert date of intimation*).

Date ...............

............... Signed

Solicitor [or Sheriff Officer]

(*include full business designation*)

SCHEDULE 2

REVOCATIONS

**Rule 1.4(1)**

| (1) Act of Sederunt revoked | (2) Reference | (3) Extension of revocation |
|---|---|---|
| Act of Sederunt (Social Work) (Sheriff Court Procedure Rules) 1971 | SI 1971/92 | The whole Act of Sederunt |
| Act of Sederunt (Social Work) (Sheriff Court Procedure Rules Amendment) 1972 | SI 1972/1671 | The whole Act of Sederunt |
| Act of Sederunt (Maintenance Orders (Reciprocal Enforcement) Act 1972 Rules) 1974 | SI 1974/939 | In rule 1(2) the words ""Sheriff Clerk" includes Sheriff Clerk depute"; in rule 2 the words from "and the provisions" to the end; in rule 3(1) the words "and the Sheriff Clerk shall be the "prescribed officer" for the Sheriff Court"; rule 3(1A) and Part III |
| Act of Sederunt (Maintenance Orders (Reciprocal Enforcement) Act 1972 Amendment Rules) 1975 | SI 1975/474 | The whole Act of Sederunt |
| Act of Sederunt (Reciprocal Enforcement of Maintenance Orders (Republic of Ireland) Order 1974 Rules) 1975 | SI 1975/475 | In rule 1(2) the words ""Sheriff Clerk" includes Sheriff Clerk Depute"; in rule 2 the words "and the provisions of Part III of this Act of Sederunt shall apply for the purposes of the Act to orders made by or registered in the Sheriff Court"; in rule 3(1) the words "and the Sheriff Clerk shall be the "prescribed officer" for the Sheriff Court"; and Part III |
| Act of Sederunt (Reciprocal Enforce- | SI 1980/291 | In rule 2(1) the words " "Sheriff Clerk" |

---

[1] As amended by the Act of Sederunt (Children's Hearings (Scotland) Act 2011) (Miscellaneous Amendments) 2013 (SSI 2013/172) para.4 (effective June 24, 2013).

| (1)<br>Act of Sederunt | (2)<br>Reference | (3)<br>Extension of revocation |
|---|---|---|
| revoked | | |
| ment of Maintenance Orders) (Hague Convention Countries) 1980 | | includes the Sheriff Clerk Depute"; rule 3(2); rule 4(1)(b); in rule 4(2) the words "and the Sheriff Clerk"; and Part III |
| Act of Sederunt (Reciprocal Mainte-nance Orders (America)) Rules 1980 | SI 1980/423 | The whole Act of Sederunt |
| Act of Sederunt (Social Work) (Sheriff Court Procedure Rules Amendment) 1980 | SI 1980/1443 | The whole Act of Sederunt |
| Act of Sederunt (Maintenance Orders Acts, Rules) 1980 | SI 1980/1732 | The whole Act of Sederunt |
| Act of Sederunt (Adoption of Children) 1984 | SI 1984/1013 | The whole Act of Sederunt |
| Act of Sederunt (Social Work (Scot-land) Act 1968) (Safeguarders) 1985 | SI 1985/780 | The whole Act of Sederunt |
| Act of Sederunt (Social Work) (Sheriff Court Procedure Rules 1971) (Amend-ment) 1985 | SI 1985/781 | The whole Act of Sederunt |
| Act of Sederunt (Social Work) (Sheriff Court Procedure Rules 1971) (Amend-ment No. 2) 1985 | SI 1985/1976 | The whole Act of Sederunt |
| Act of Sederunt (Enforcement of Judg-ments under the Civil Jurisdiction and Judgments Act 1982) 1986 | SI 1986/1947 | Paragraph 6 and Form 6 |
| Act of Sederunt (Rules for the Registra-tion of Custody Orders of the Sheriff Court) 1988 | SI 1988/613 | The whole Act of Sederunt |
| Act of Sederunt (Applications under the Social Security Act 1986) 1990 | SI 1990/2238 | The whole Act of Sederunt |
| Act of Sederunt (Rules for the Registra-tion of Custody Orders of the Sheriff Court) (Amendment) 1991 | SI 1991/2205 | The whole Act of Sederunt |
| Act of Sederunt (Adoption of Children) (Amendment) 1992 | SI 1992/1076 | The whole Act of Sederunt |
| Act of Sederunt (Sheriff Court Parental Orders (Human Fertilisation and Em-bryology) Rules) 1994 | SI 1994/2805 | The whole Act of Sederunt |

SCHEDULE 3[1]

EXCLUSION OF ENACTMENTS

**Rule 3.24**

| Column (1)<br>Enactment excluded | Column (2)<br>Reference | Column (3)<br>Extent of exclusion |
|---|---|---|
| The Citation Act 1592 | 1592 c.59 (S. ) | The whole Act |
| The Citation Act 1686 | 1686 c.5 (S. ) | The whole Act |

[1] As amended by the Act of Sederunt (Child Care and Maintenance Rules 1997) Amendment (Vulner-able Witnesses (Scotland) Act 2004) 2007, r.2(3) (effective November 1, 2007) and by the Act of Sederunt (Sheriff Court Rules) (Miscellaneous Amendments) (No.3) 2012 (SSI 2012/271) para.4 (ef-fective November 1, 2012).

| Column (1) Enactment excluded | Column (2) Reference | Column (3) Extent of exclusion |
|---|---|---|
| The Debtors (Scotland) Act 1838, section 32 (as applied by the Citation (Scotland) Act 1846) | 1838 c.114 | The words "and more than one witness shall not be required for service or execution thereof" |
| The Citation Amendment (Scotland) Act 1882 | 1882 c.77 | The whole Act |
| The Sheriff Courts (Scotland) Act 1907, section 39 and the First Schedule | 1907 c.51 | The whole section; the whole Schedule except rule 29.10 (failure of witness to attend) and Chapter 45 (Vulnerable Witnesses (Scotland) Act 2004) and Chapter 50 (lodging recordings of children) |

# ACT OF SEDERUNT (SUMMARY APPLICATIONS, STATUTORY APPLICATIONS AND APPEALS ETC. RULES) 1999

(SI 1999/929)

*19 March 1999.*

ARRANGEMENT OF RULES

CHAPTER 1: GENERAL

Schedule 1

Forms

Schedule 2

Revocations

The Lords of Council and Session, under and by virtue of the powers conferred on them by Schedule 1, paragraphs 24(1), 28D and 28(2), Schedule 2, paragraph 7 and Schedule 3, paragraph 13(3) to the Betting Gaming and Lotteries Act 1963, Schedule 2, paragraphs 33(1), 34(1), 45 and 47, and Schedule 9, paragraph 15 to the Gaming Act 1968, section 32 of the Sheriff Courts (Scotland) Act 1971, sections 66(5A) and 75 of the Sex Discrimination Act 1975, section 39(9) of the Licensing (Scotland) Act 1976, Schedule 3, paragraph 12 to the Lotteries and Amusements Act 1976, sections 136, 139, 146, 147, 152, 153, 182(3) and 185 of the Representation of the People Act 1983, sections 114(3), 204(3) and 231(3) of the Copyright, Designs and Patents Act 1988, section 19(3) of the Trade Marks Act 1994, section 46 of the Drug Trafficking Act 1994, Regulation 5(3) of the Olympics Association Right (Infringement Proceedings) Regulations 1995, and sections 31(5) and 48 of, and Schedule 1, paragraph 11 to, the Proceeds of Crime (Scotland) Act 1995 and of all other powers enabling them in that behalf, having approved draft rules submitted to them by the Sheriff Court Rules Council in accordance with section 34 of the Sheriff Courts (Scotland) Act 1971, do hereby enact and declare:

## CHAPTER 1

### GENERAL

**Citation and commencement**

1.1—(1)   This Act of Sederunt may be cited as the Act of Sederunt (Summary Applications, Statutory Applications and Appeals etc. Rules) 1999 and shall come into force on 1st July 1999.

(2)   This Act of Sederunt shall be inserted in the Books of Sederunt.

**Interpretation**

1.2—(1)[1]   In this Act of Sederunt, unless the context otherwise requires—

"the 2004 Act" means the Vulnerable Witnesses (Scotland) Act 2004;[2]

"enactment" includes an enactment comprised in, or in an instrument made under, an Act of the Scottish Parliament;

"Ordinary Cause Rules" means the First Schedule to the Sheriff Courts (Scotland) Act 1907;

"sheriff clerk" includes sheriff clerk depute; and

"summary application" has the meaning given by section 3(p) of the Sheriff Courts (Scotland) Act 1907.

---

[1] As amended by the Act of Sederunt (Ordinary Cause, Summary Application, Summary Cause and Small Claim Rules) Amendment (Miscellaneous) 2007 (SSI 2007/6), para.3(2) (effective January 29, 2007).

[2] As inserted by the Act of Sederunt (Ordinary Cause, Summary Application, Summary Cause and Small Claim Rules) Amendment (Vulnerable Witnesses (Scotland) Act 2004) (SSI 2007/463), r.3(2) (effective November 1, 2007).

(2)    Unless the context otherwise requires, any reference in this Act of Sederunt to a specified Chapter, Part or rule shall be construed as a reference to the Chapter, Part or rule bearing that number in this Act of Sederunt, and a reference to a specified paragraph, sub-paragraph or head shall be construed as a reference to the paragraph, sub-paragraph or head so numbered or lettered in the provision in which that reference occurs.

(3)    Any reference in this Act of Sederunt to a numbered Form shall, unless the context otherwise requires, be construed as a reference to the Form so numbered in Schedule 1 to this Act of Sederunt and includes a form substantially to the same effect with such variation as circumstances may require.

(4)[1]    In this Act of Sederunt, references to a solicitor include a reference to a member of a body which has made a successful application under section 25 of the Law Reform (Miscellaneous Provisions) (Scotland) Act 1990 but only to the extent that the member is exercising rights acquired by virtue of section 27 of that Act.

## Revocation

**1.3**    The Acts of Sederunt mentioned in column (1) of Schedule 2 to this Act of Sederunt are revoked to the extent specified in column (3) of that Schedule.

## Application

**1.4**    Unless otherwise provided in this Act of Sederunt or in any other enactment, any application or appeal to the sheriff shall be by way of summary application and the provisions of Chapter 2 of this Act of Sederunt shall apply accordingly.

CHAPTER 1A[2]

LAY REPRESENTATION

## Application and interpretation

**1A.1.**—(1)    This Chapter is without prejudice to any enactment (including any other provision in these Rules) under which provision is, or may be, made for a party to a particular type of case before the sheriff to be represented by a lay representative.

(2)    In this Chapter, a "lay representative" means a person who is not—
   (a)    a solicitor;
   (b)    an advocate, or
   (c)    someone having a right to conduct litigation, or a right of audience, by virtue of section 27 of the Law Reform (Miscellaneous Provisions) (Scotland) Act 1990.

## Lay representation for party litigants

**1A.2.**—(1)    In any proceedings in respect of which no provision as mentioned in rule 1A.1(1) is in force, the sheriff may, on the request of a party litigant, permit a

---

[1] As inserted by the Act of Sederunt (Sheriff Court Rules Amendment) (Sections 25 to 29 of the Law Reform (Miscellaneous Provisions) (Scotland) Act 1990) 2009 (SSI 2009/164) r.3 (effective May 20, 2009).

[2] As inserted by the Act of Sederunt (Sheriff Court Rules) (Lay Representation) 2013 (SSI 2013/91) r.3 (effective April 4, 2013).

named individual (a "lay representative") to appear, along with the litigant, at a specified hearing for the purpose of making oral submissions on behalf of the litigant at that hearing.

(2)   An application under paragraph (1)—

    (a)   is to be made orally on the date of the first hearing at which the litigant wishes a named individual to make oral submissions; and

    (b)   is to be accompanied by a document, signed by the named individual, in Form A1.

(3)   The sheriff may grant an application under paragraph (1) only if the sheriff is of the opinion that it would assist his or her consideration of the case to grant it.

(4)   It is a condition of permission granted by the sheriff that the lay representative does not receive directly or indirectly from the litigant any remuneration or other reward for his or her assistance.

(5)   The sheriff may grant permission under paragraph (1) in respect of one or more specified hearings in the case; but such permission is not effective during any period when the litigant is legally represented.

(6)   The sheriff may, of his or her own accord or on the motion of a party to the proceedings, withdraw permission granted under paragraph (1).

(7)   Where permission has been granted under paragraph (1), the litigant may—

    (a)   show the lay representative any document (including a court document); or

    (b)   impart to the lay representative any information,

which is in his or her possession in connection with the proceedings without being taken to contravene any prohibition or restriction on the disclosure of the document or the information; but the lay representative is then to be taken to be subject to any such prohibition or restriction as if he or she were the litigant.

(8)   Any expenses incurred by the litigant in connection with lay representation under this rule are not recoverable expenses in the proceedings.

CHAPTER 2

SUMMARY APPLICATION RULES

Part I

**Interpretation**

**Interpretation**

    **2.1**   In this Chapter, unless the context otherwise requires—

        "decree" includes any judgment, deliverance, interlocutor, act, order, finding or authority which may be extracted;

        "defender" means any person other than the pursuer who is a party to a summary application; and "pursuer" means any person making a summary application.

## Part II

## General Rules

### Application

**2.2**   This Part applies to summary applications.

### Lay support

**2.2A**—[1](1)   At any time during proceedings the sheriff may, on the request of a party litigant, permit a named individual to assist the litigant in the conduct of the proceedings by sitting beside or behind (as the litigant chooses) the litigant at hearings in court or in chambers and doing such of the following for the litigant as he or she requires—

    (a)   providing moral support;
    (b)   helping to manage the court documents and other papers;
    (c)   taking notes of the proceedings;
    (d)   quietly advising on—
        (i)   points of law and procedure;
        (ii)   issues which the litigant might wish to raise with the sheriff;
        (iii)   questions which the litigant might wish to ask witnesses.

(2)   It is a condition of such permission that the named individual does not receive from the litigant, whether directly or indirectly, any remuneration for his or her assistance.

(3)   The sheriff may refuse a request under paragraph (1) only if—

    (a)   the sheriff is of the opinion that the named individual is an unsuitable person to act in that capacity (whether generally or in the proceedings concerned); or
    (b)   the sheriff is of the opinion that it would be contrary to the efficient administration of justice to grant it.

(4)   Permission granted under paragraph (1) endures until the proceedings finish or it is withdrawn under paragraph (5); but it is not effective during any period when the litigant is represented.

(5)   The sheriff may, of his or her own accord or on the motion of a party to the proceedings, withdraw permission granted under paragraph (1); but the sheriff must first be of the opinion that it would be contrary to the efficient administration of justice for the permission to continue.

(6)   Where permission has been granted under paragraph (1), the litigant may—

    (a)   show the named individual any document (including a court document); or
    (b)   impart to the named individual any information,

which is in his or her possession in connection with the proceedings without being taken to contravene any prohibition or restriction on the disclosure of the document or the information; but the named individual is then to be taken to be subject to any such prohibition or restriction as if he or she were the litigant.

---

[1] As inserted by the Act of Sederunt (Sheriff Court Rules) (Miscellaneous Amendments) (No.2) 2010 (SSI 2010/416) r.3 (effective January 1, 2011).

(7)  Any expenses incurred by the litigant as a result of the support of an individual under paragraph (1) are not recoverable expenses in the proceedings.

## Relief from failure to comply with rules

**2.3**—(1)  The sheriff may relieve a party from the consequences of failure to comply with a provision in this Part which is shown to be due to mistake, oversight or other excusable cause, on such conditions as he thinks fit.

(2)  Where the sheriff relieves a party from the consequences of a failure to comply with a provision in this Part of these Rules under paragraph (1), he may make such order as he thinks fit to enable the summary application to proceed as if the failure to comply with the provision had not occurred.

## The initial writ

**2.4**—(1)  Unless otherwise prescribed by any other enactment, a summary application shall be commenced by initial writ in Form 1.

(2)  The initial writ shall be written, typed or printed on A4 size paper of durable quality and shall not be backed or folded.

(3)  Where the pursuer has reason to believe that an agreement exists prorogating jurisdiction over the subject-matter of the summary application to another court, the initial writ shall contain details of that agreement.

(4)  Where the pursuer has reason to believe that proceedings are pending before another court involving the same cause of action and between the same parties as those named in the instance of the initial writ, the initial writ shall contain details of those proceedings.

(4A)[1]  In an action which relates to a regulated agreement within the meaning given by section 189(1) of the Consumer Credit Act 1974 the initial writ shall include an averment that such an agreement exists and details of the agreement.

(5)  An article of condescendence shall be included in the initial writ averring—

    (a)  the ground of jurisdiction; and

    (b)  the facts upon which the ground of jurisdiction is based.

(6)  Where the residence, registered office or place of business, as the case may be, of the defender is not known and cannot reasonably be ascertained, the pursuer shall set out in the instance of the initial writ that the whereabouts of the defender are not known and aver in the condescendence what steps have been taken to ascertain his present whereabouts.

(7)  The initial writ shall be signed by the pursuer or his solicitor (if any) and the name and address of that solicitor shall be stated on the back of every service copy of that writ.

(8)  The initial writ shall include averments about those persons who appear to the pursuer to have an interest in the application and in respect of whom a warrant for citation is sought.

(9)[2]  Where warrant to arrest on the dependence is sought, the initial writ shall include averments to justify the grant of such a warrant.

---

[1] As inserted by the Act of Sederunt (Sheriff Court Rules) (Miscellaneous Amendments) 2009 (SSI 2009/294) r.3 (effective December 1, 2009) as substituted by the Act of Sederunt (Amendment of the Act of Sederunt (Sheriff Court Rules) (Miscellaneous Amendments) 2009) 2009 (SSI 2009/402) (effective November 30, 2009).

[2] As inserted by the Act of Sederunt (Ordinary Cause, Summary Application and Small Claim Rules) Amendment (Miscellaneous) 2004 (SSI 2004/197) para.3(2) (effective May 21, 2004).

### Order for intimation to interested persons by sheriff

**2.5** The sheriff may make an order for intimation to any person who appears to him to have an interest in the summary application.

### Time limits

**2.6**—(1)[1] This rule applies to a summary application where the time within which the application being an appeal under statute or an application in the nature of an appeal may be made is not otherwise prescribed.

(2) An application to which this rule applies shall be lodged with the sheriff clerk within 21 days after the date on which the decision, order, scheme, determination, refusal or other act complained of was intimated to the pursuer.

(3) On special cause shown, the sheriff may hear an application to which this rule applies notwithstanding that it was not lodged within the period prescribed in paragraph (2).

### Warrants, forms and certificate of citation

**2.7**—[2](1) Subject to paragraph (2), a warrant for citation or intimation may be signed by the sheriff or sheriff clerk.

(1A)[3] A warrant for arrestment on the dependence may be signed by the sheriff, if the sheriff considers it appropriate.

(2) A warrant containing a period of notice shorter than the period of notice to be given to a defender under rule 3.6(1)(a) or (b), as the case may be, of the Ordinary Cause Rules or any other warrant which the sheriff clerk may not sign, shall be signed by the sheriff.

(3) Where the sheriff clerk refuses to sign a warrant which he may sign, the party presenting the summary application may apply to the sheriff for the warrant.

(4) Where citation is necessary—

    (a)[4, 5] the warrant of citation shall, subject to paragraphs (5) and (7ZA)(a) and rule 3.18.3(1) (appeals under section 103J of the Local Government (Scotland) Act 1973), be in Form 2; and

    (b)[6 7] citation shall, subject to paragraphs (7) and (7ZA)(b) and rules 2.13 (service where address of person is not known) and 3.18.3(2) (appeals under section 103J of the Local Government (Scotland) Act 1973), be in Form 3.

---

[1] As amended by the Act of Sederunt (Ordinary Cause, Summary Application and Small Claim Rules) Amendment (Miscellaneous) 2004 (SSI 2004/197) para.3(3) (effective May 21, 2004).

[2] As amended by the Act of Sederunt (Ordinary Cause, Summary Application, Summary Cause and Small Claim Rules) Amendment (Miscellaneous) 2007 (SSI 2007/6), para.3(3) (effective January 29, 2007).

[3] As inserted by the Act of Sederunt (Ordinary Cause, Summary Application and Small Claim Rules) Amendment (Miscellaneous) 2004 (SSI 2004/197) para.3(4) (effective May 21, 2004).

[4] As amended by the Act of Sederunt (Summary Applications, Statutory Applications and Appeals etc. Rules) Amendment (No.2) (Local Government (Scotland) Act 1973) 2002 (SSI 2002/130) para.2(2) (effective March 8, 2002).

[5] As amended by the Act of Sederunt (Sheriff Court Rules)(Miscellaneous Amendments) 2013 (SSI 2013/135) para.2 (effective May 27, 2013).

[6] As amended by the Act of Sederunt (Summary Applications, Statutory Applications and Appeals etc. Rules) Amendment (No.2) (Local Government (Scotland) Act 1973) 2002 (SSI 2002/130) para.2(2) (effective March 8, 2002).

[7] As amended by the Act of Sederunt (Sheriff Court Rules)(Miscellaneous Amendments) 2013 (SSI 2013/135) para.2 (effective May 27, 2013).

(5) Where a time to pay direction under the Debtors (Scotland) Act 1987 or a time order under the Consumer Credit Act 1974 may be applied for by the defender, the warrant of citation shall be in Form 4.

(6) Where a warrant of citation in accordance with Form 4 is appropriate, there shall be served on the defender (with the initial writ and warrant) a notice in Form 5.

(7) Where a time to pay direction under the Debtors (Scotland) Act 1987 or a time order under the Consumer Credit Act 1974 may be applied for by the defender, citation shall be in Form 6 which shall be attached to a copy of the initial writ and warrant of citation.

(7ZA) In an application for enforcement of security over residential property within the meaning of Part IV of Chapter 3—

    (a) the warrant of citation will be in Form 6ZA;

    (b) citation will be in Form 6ZB which is to be attached to a copy of the initial writ,

Form 11C and warrant of citation.

(7A) *[Repealed by the Act of Sederunt (Sheriff Court Rules) (Enforcement of Securities over Heritable Property) 2010 (SSI 2010/324) para.2 (effective September 30, 2010).]*

(8) Where citation is necessary, the certificate of citation shall be in Form 7 which shall be attached to the initial writ.

(9) Where citation is by a sheriff officer, one witness shall be sufficient for the execution of citation.

(10) Where citation is by a sheriff officer, the certificate of citation shall be signed by the sheriff officer and the witness and shall state—

    (a) the method of citation; and

    (b) where the method of citation was other than personal or postal citation, the full name and designation of any person to whom the citation was delivered.

(11) Where citation is executed under paragraph (3) of rule 2.11 (depositing or affixing by sheriff officer), the certificate shall include a statement—

    (a) of the method of service previously attempted;

    (b) of the circumstances which prevented such service being executed; and

    (c) that a copy of the document was sent in accordance with the provisions of paragraph (4) of that rule.

**Orders against which caveats may be lodged**

**2.8** *[Omitted by Act of Sederunt (Sheriff Court Caveat Rules) 2006 (SI 2006/ 198), effective April 28, 2006]*

**Form, lodging and renewal of caveats**

**2.9** *[Omitted by Act of Sederunt (Sheriff Court Caveat Rules) 2006 (SI 2006/ 198), effective April 28, 2006]*

**Postal service or intimation**

**2.10**—(1) In any summary application in which service or intimation of any document or citation of any person may be by recorded delivery, such service, intimation or citation shall be by the first class recorded delivery service.

(2) Notwithstanding the terms of section 4(2) of the Citation Amendment (Scotland) Act 1882 (time from which period of notice reckoned), where service or

intimation is by post, any period of notice contained in the warrant of citation shall run from the beginning of the day after the date of posting.

(3) On the face of the envelope used for postal service or intimation under this rule there shall be written or printed the following notice:—

"This envelope contains a citation to or intimation from (*specify the court*). If delivery cannot be made at the address shown it is to be returned immediately to:— The Sheriff Clerk (*insert address of sheriff clerk's office*).".

(4) The certificate of citation or intimation in the case of postal service shall have attached to it any relevant postal receipts.

### Service within Scotland by sheriff officer

**2.11**—(1) An initial writ, decree, charge, warrant or any other order or writ following upon such initial writ or decree served by a sheriff officer on any person shall be served—

    (a) personally; or

    (b) by being left in the hands of a resident at the person's dwelling place or an employee at his place of business.

(2) Where service is executed under paragraph (1)(b), the certificate of citation or service shall contain the full name and designation of any person in whose hands the initial writ, decree, charge, warrant or other order or writ, as the case may be, was left.

(3) Where a sheriff officer has been unsuccessful in executing service in accordance with paragraph (1), he may, after making diligent enquiries, serve the document question by—

    (a) depositing it in that person's dwelling place or place of business; or

    (b)[1] by leaving it at that person's dwelling place or place of business in such a way that it is likely to come to the attention of that person.

(4) Subject to rule 2.18 (service of schedule of arrestment), where service is executed under paragraph (3), the sheriff officer shall, as soon as possible after such service, send a letter containing a copy of the document by ordinary first class post to the address at which he thinks it most likely that the person on whom service has been executed may be found.

(5)[2] Where the firm which employs the sheriff officer has in its possession—

    (a) the document or a copy of it certified as correct by the pursuer's solicitor, the sheriff officer may serve the writ upon the defender without having the document or certified copy in his possession, in which case he shall if required to do so by the person on whom service is executed and within a reasonable time of being so required, show the document or certified copy to the person; or

    (b) a certified copy of the interlocutor pronounced allowing service of the document, the sheriff officer may serve the document without having in his possession the certified copy interlocutor if he has in his possession a facsimile copy of the certified copy interlocutor (which he shall show, if required, to the person on whom service is executed).

---

[1] As substituted by the Act of Sederunt (Sheriff Court Rules) (Miscellaneous Amendments) 2011 (SSI 2011/193) r.3 (effective April 4, 2011).

[2] As inserted by the Act of Sederunt (Ordinary Cause, Summary Application, Summary Cause and Small Claim Rules) Amendment (Miscellaneous) 2003 (SSI 2003/26), para.3(3) (effective January 24, 2003).

(6)[1]   Where service is executed under paragraphs (1)(b) or (3), the document and the citation or notice of intimation, as the case may be, must be placed in an envelope bearing the notice "This envelope contains a citation to or intimation from (*insert name of sheriff court*) " and sealed by the sheriff officer.

## Service on persons furth of Scotland

**2.12—**[2, 3](1)   Subject to the following provisions of this rule, an initial writ, decree, charge, warrant or any other order or writ following upon such initial writ or decree served on a person furth of Scotland shall be served—

(a)   at a known residence or place of business in England, Wales, Northern Ireland, the Isle of Man, the Channel Islands or any country with which the United Kingdom does not have a convention providing for service of writs in that country—

(i)   in accordance with the rules for personal service under the domestic law of the place in which service is to be executed; or

(ii)   by posting in Scotland a copy of the document in question in a registered letter addressed to the person at his residence or place of business;

(b)   in a country which is a party to the Hague Convention on the Service Abroad of Judicial and Extra-Judicial Documents in Civil or Commercial Matters dated 15th November 1965 or the Convention in Schedule 1 or 3C to the Civil Jurisdiction and Judgments Act 1982—

(i)   by a method prescribed by the internal law of the country where service is to be executed for the service of documents in domestic actions upon persons who are within its territory;

(ii)[4]   by or through the central, or other appropriate, authority in the country where service is to be executed at the request of the Scottish Ministers;

(iii)   by or through a British Consular Office in the country where service is to be executed at the request of the Secretary of State for Foreign and Commonwealth Affairs;

(iv)   where the law of the country in which the person resides permits, by posting in Scotland a copy of the document in a registered letter addressed to the person at his residence; or

(v)   where the law of the country in which service is to be executed permits, service by an *huissier*, other judicial officer or competent official of the country where service is to be executed; or

(c)   in a country with which the United Kingdom has a convention on the

---

[1] As inserted by the Act of Sederunt (Sheriff Court Rules) (Miscellaneous Amendments) 2011 (SSI 2011/193) r.3 (effective April 4, 2011).

[2] As amended by the Act of Sederunt (Ordinary Cause, Summary Application, Summary Cause and Small Claim Rules) Amendment (Miscellaneous) 2003 (SSI 2003/26), para.3(4) (effective January 24, 2003).

[3] As amended and inserted by the Act of Sederunt (Ordinary Cause, Summary Application and Small Claim Rules) Amendment (Miscellaneous) 2004 (SSI 2004/197) (effective May 21, 2004), para.3(5) and substituted by the Act of Sederunt (Sheriff Court Ordinary Cause, Summary Application, Summary Cause and Small Claims Rules) Amendment (Council Regulation (EC) No. 1348 of 2000 Extension to Denmark) 2007 (SSI 2007/440) r.3(2) (effective October 9, 2007).

[4] As substituted by the Act of Sederunt (Sheriff Court Rules) (Miscellaneous Amendments) 2011 (SSI 2011/193) r.6 (effective April 4, 2011).

service of writs in that country other than the conventions mentioned in sub-paragraph (b), by one of the methods approved in the relevant convention.

(1A)[1, 2]  In a country to which the EC Service Regulation applies, service—

(a)  may be effected by the methods prescribed in paragraph (1)(b)(ii) or (iii) only in exceptional circumstances; and

(b)  is effected only if the receiving agency has informed the person that acceptance of service may be refused on the ground that the document has not been translated in accordance with paragraph (6).

(2)  Any document which requires to be posted in Scotland for the purposes of this rule shall be posted by a solicitor or a sheriff officer, and on the face of the envelope there shall be written or printed the notice set out in rule 2.10(3).

(3)  In the case of service by a method referred to in paragraph (1)(b)(ii) and (iii), the pursuer shall—

(a)[3]  send a copy of the writ and warrant of service with citation attached, or other document, as the case may be, with a request for service by the method indicated in the request to the Scottish Ministers or, as the case may be, the Secretary of State for Foreign and Commonwealth Affairs; and

(b)  lodge in process a certificate signed by the authority which executed service stating that it has been, and the manner in which it was, served.

(4)  In the case of service by a method referred to in paragraph (1)(b)(v), the pursuer or the sheriff officer shall—

(a)  send a copy of the writ and warrant for service with citation attached, or other document, as the case may be, with a request for service by the method indicated in the request to the official in the country in which service is to be executed; and

(b)  lodge in process a certificate of the official who executed service stating that it has been, and the manner in which it was, served.

(5)  Where service is executed, in accordance with paragraph (1)(a)(i) or (1)(b)(i) other than on another party in the United Kingdom, the Isle of Man or the Channel Islands, the party executing service shall lodge a certificate by a person who is conversant with the law of the country concerned and who practises or has practised law in that country or is a duly accredited representative of the Government of that country, stating that the method of service employed is in accordance with the law of the place where service was executed.

(6)  Every writ, document, citation or notice on the face of the envelope mentioned in rule 2.10(3) shall be accompanied by a translation in—

(a)[4]  an official language of the country in which service is to be executed; or

---

[1] As amended and inserted by the Act of Sederunt (Ordinary Cause, Summary Application and Small Claim Rules) Amendment (Miscellaneous) 2004 (SSI 2004/197) (effective May 21, 2004), para.3(5) and substituted by the Act of Sederunt (Sheriff Court Ordinary Cause, Summary Application, Summary Cause and Small Claims Rules) Amendment (Council Regulation (EC) No. 1348 of 2000 Extension to Denmark) 2007 (SSI 2007/440) r.3(2) (effective October 9, 2007).

[2] As amended by the Act of Sederunt (Sheriff Court Rules) (Miscellaneous Amendments) (No.2) 2008 (SSI 2008/365) r.8(a) (effective November 13, 2008).

[3] As amended by the Act of Sederunt (Sheriff Court Rules) (Miscellaneous Amendments) 2011 (SSI 2011/193) r.7 (effective April 4, 2011).

[4] As amended and inserted by the Act of Sederunt (Ordinary Cause, Summary Application and Small Claim Rules) Amendment (Miscellaneous) 2004 (SSI 2004/197) (effective May 21, 2004), para.3(5) and substituted by the Act of Sederunt (Sheriff Court Ordinary Cause, Summary Application, Sum-

(b) in a country to which the EC Service Regulation applies, a language of the member state of transmission that is understood by the person on whom service is being executed.

(7) A translation referred to in paragraph (6) shall be certified as correct by the person making it and the certificate shall—

    (a) include his full name, address and qualifications; and

    (b) be lodged with the execution of citation or service.

(8)[1] In this rule "the EC Service Regulation" means Regulation (EC) No. 1393/2007 of the European Parliament and of the Council of 13th November 2007 on the service in the Member States of judicial and extrajudicial documents in civil or commercial matters (service of documents), and repealing Council Regulation (EC) No. 1348/2000, as amended from time to time.

### Service where address of person is not known

**2.13**—(1) Where the address of a person to be cited or served with a document is not known and cannot reasonably be ascertained, the sheriff shall grant warrant for citation or service upon that person by—

    (a) the publication of an advertisement in Form 9 in a specified newspaper circulating in the area of the last known address of that person; or

    (b) displaying on the walls of court a copy of the instance and crave of the initial writ, the warrant of citation and a notice in Form 10;

and any period of notice contained in the warrant of citation shall run from the date of publication of the advertisement or display on the walls of court, as the case may be.

(2) Where service requires to be executed under paragraph (1), the pursuer shall lodge a service copy of the initial writ and a copy of any warrant of citation with the sheriff clerk from whom they may be uplifted by the person for whom they are intended.

(3) Where a person has been cited or served in accordance with paragraph (1) and, after the summary application has commenced, his address becomes known, the sheriff may allow the initial writ to be amended subject to such conditions as to re-service, intimation, expenses or transfer of the summary application as he thinks fit.

(4) Where advertisement in a newspaper is required for the purpose of citation or service under this rule, a copy of the newspaper containing the advertisement shall be lodged with the sheriff clerk by the pursuer.

(5) Where display on the walls of court is required under paragraph (1)(b), the pursuer shall supply to the sheriff clerk for that purpose a certified copy of the instance and crave of the initial writ and any warrant of citation.

### Persons carrying on business under trading or descriptive name

**2.14**—(1) A person carrying on a business under a trading or descriptive name may be designed in the instance of the initial writ by such trading or descriptive name alone, and an extract of a—

    (a) decree pronounced in the sheriff court; or

---

mary Cause and Small Claims Rules) Amendment (Council Regulation (EC) No. 1348 of 2000 Extension to Denmark) 2007 (SSI 2007/440) r.3(2) (effective October 9, 2007).

[1] As substituted by the Act of Sederunt (Sheriff Court Rules) (Miscellaneous Amendments) (No.2) 2008 (SSI 2008/365) r.8(b) (effective November 13, 2008).

(b) decree proceeding upon any deed, decree arbitral, bond, protest of a bill, promissory note or banker's note or upon any other obligation or document on which execution may proceed, recorded in the sheriff court books,

against such person under such trading or descriptive name, shall be a valid warrant for diligence against such person.

(2) An initial writ, decree, charge, warrant or any other order or writ following upon such initial writ or decree in a summary application in which a person carrying on business under a trading or descriptive name is designed in the instance of the initial writ by that name shall be served—

(a) at any place of business or office at which such business is carried on within the sheriffdom of the sheriff court in which the cause is brought; or

(b) where there is no place of business within that sheriffdom, at any place where such business is carried on (including the place of business or office of the clerk or secretary of any company, corporation or association or firm).

### Endorsation unnecessary

**2.15** An initial writ, decree, charge, warrant or any other order or writ following upon such initial writ or decree may be served, enforced or otherwise lawfully executed anywhere in Scotland without endorsation by a sheriff clerk and, if executed by a sheriff officer, may be so executed by a sheriff officer of the court which granted it or by a sheriff officer of the sheriff court district in which it is to be executed.

Re-service

**2.16** Where it appears to the sheriff that there has been any failure or irregularity in citation or service on a person, he may order the pursuer to re-serve the initial writ on such conditions as the sheriff thinks fit.

### No objection to regularity of citation, service or intimation

**2.17**—(1) A person who appears in a summary application shall not be entitled to state any objection to the regularity of the execution of citation, service or intimation on him, and his appearance shall remedy any defect in such citation, service or intimation.

(2) Nothing in paragraph (1) shall preclude a party from pleading that the court has no jurisdiction.

### Service of schedule of arrestment

**2.18** If a schedule of arrestment has not been personally served on an arrestee, the arrestment shall have effect only if a copy of the schedule is also sent by registered post or the first class recorded delivery service to—

(a) the last known place of residence of the arrestee; or

(b) if such a place of residence is not known, or if the arrestee is a firm or corporation, to the arrestee's principal place of business if known, or, if not known, to any known place of business of the arrestee,

and the sheriff officer shall, on the certificate of execution, certify that this has been done and specify the address to which the copy of the schedule was sent.

## Form of schedule of arrestment on the dependence

**2.18A.**—[1](1)   An arrestment on the dependence shall be served by serving the schedule of arrestment on the arrestee in Form 10A.

(2)   A certificate of execution shall be lodged with the sheriff clerk in Form 10B.

## Arrestment on dependence before service

**2.19**—(1)   An arrestment on the dependence of a summary application used before service shall cease to have effect if the initial writ is not served within 20 days from the date of arrestment and either—

    (a)   in the case where the pursuer is entitled to minute for decree in absence on the expiry of a period of notice contained in the warrant of citation, decree in absence has not been pronounced within 20 days after the expiry of the period of notice; or

    (b)   in the case where the pursuer is not entitled to minute for decree in absence prior to the first hearing of the summary application, there is no appearance by the pursuer at the first hearing and the summary application drops from the roll.

(2)   After such an arrestment has been executed, the party who executed it shall forthwith report the execution to the sheriff clerk.

## Movement of arrested property

**2.20**—(1)   Any person having an interest may apply by motion for a warrant authorising the movement of a vessel or cargo which is the subject of an arrestment to found jurisdiction or on the dependence of a summary application.

(2)   Where the court grants a warrant sought under paragraph (1), it may make such further order as it thinks fit to give effect to that warrant.

## Transfer to another sheriff court

**2.21**—(1)   The sheriff may, on cause shown, remit a summary application to another sheriff court.

(2)   Subject to paragraph (4), where a summary application in which there are two or more defenders has been brought in the sheriff court of the residence or place of business of one of them, the sheriff may transfer the summary application to any other sheriff court which has jurisdiction over any of the defenders.

(3)   Subject to paragraph (4), where a plea of no jurisdiction is sustained, the sheriff may transfer the summary application to the sheriff court before which it appears to him the summary application ought to have been brought.

(4)   The sheriff shall not transfer a summary application to another sheriff court under paragraph (2) or (3) except—

    (a)   on the motion of a party; and

    (b)   where he considers it expedient to do so having regard to the convenience of the parties and their witnesses.

(5)   On making an order under paragraph (1), (2) or (3), the sheriff—

    (a)   shall state his reasons for doing so in the interlocutor; and

    (b)   may make the order on such conditions as to expenses or otherwise as he thinks fit.

---

[1] As inserted by the Act of Sederunt (Sheriff Court Rules Amendment) (Diligence) 2009 (SSI 2009/107) r.4(effective April 22, 2009).

(6)   The court to which a summary application is transferred under paragraph (1), (2) or (3) shall accept the summary application.

(7)   A transferred summary application shall proceed in all respects as if it had been originally brought in the court to which it is transferred.

(8)   An interlocutor transferring a summary application may, with leave of the sheriff, be appealed to the sheriff principal but shall not be subject to appeal to the Court of Session.

**Applications for time to pay directions or time orders**

2.22—[1](1)   This rule applies to a summary application in which—

    (a)   a time to pay direction may be applied for under the Debtors (Scotland) Act 1987; or

    (b)   a time order may be applied for under the Consumer Credit Act 1987.

(2)   A defender may apply for a time to pay direction or time order and, where appropriate, for recall or restriction of an arrestment—

    (a)   by appearing and making the appropriate motion at a diet fixed for hearing of the summary application;

    (b)[2]   except where the warrant of citation contains a shorter period of notice than the period of notice to be given to a defender under rule 3.6(1)(a) or (b), as the case may be, of the Ordinary Cause Rules, by completing and returning the appropriate portion of Form 5 to the sheriff clerk at least 14 days before the first diet fixed for hearing of the summary application or the expiry of the period of notice or otherwise, as the case may be in the warrant of citation; or

    (c)   by application to the court at any stage before final decree.

(3)[3]   On lodging an application under paragraph (2)(b), the defender shall send a copy of it to the pursuer by first class ordinary post.

(4)[4]   Where the pursuer objects to the application of the defender lodged under paragraph (2)(b) he shall—

    (a)   complete and lodge with the sheriff clerk Form 5A prior to the date fixed for the hearing of the summary application; and

    (b)   send a copy of that form to the defender.

(5)[5]   The sheriff clerk shall then fix a hearing in relation to the application under paragraph (2)(b) and intimate the hearing to the pursuer and the defender.

(6)[6]   The sheriff may determine an application under paragraph (2)(c) without the defender having to appear.

---

[1] As amended by the Act of Sederunt (Ordinary Cause, Summary Application, Summary Cause and Small Claim Rules) Amendment (Miscellaneous) 2007 (SSI 2007/6), para.3(4) (effective January 29, 2007).

[2] As amended by the Act of Sederunt (Sheriff Court Rules) (Miscellaneous Amendments) 2009 (SSI 2009/294) r.3 (effective December 1, 2009).

[3] Para.(3) substituted for paras (3)–(6) by the Act of Sederunt (Sheriff Court Rules) (Miscellaneous Amendments) 2009 (SSI 2009/294) r.3 (effective December 1, 2009).

[4] Para.(3) substituted for paras (3)–(6) by the Act of Sederunt (Sheriff Court Rules) (Miscellaneous Amendments) 2009 (SSI 2009/294) r.3 (effective December 1, 2009).

[5] Para.(3) substituted for paras (3)–(6) by the Act of Sederunt (Sheriff Court Rules) (Miscellaneous Amendments) 2009 (SSI 2009/294) r.3 (effective December 1, 2009).

[6] Para.(3) substituted for paras (3)–(6) by the Act of Sederunt (Sheriff Court Rules) (Miscellaneous Amendments) 2009 (SSI 2009/294) r.3 (effective December 1, 2009).

## Applications under the Mortgage Rights (Scotland) Act 2001

**2.22A** *[Repealed by the Act of Sederunt (Sheriff Court Rules) (Enforcement of Securities over Heritable Property) 2010 (SSI 2010/324) para.2 (effective September 30, 2010).]*

## Remuneration of assessors

**2.23** Where an assessor is appointed by the sheriff to assist him in determining the summary application, the remuneration to be paid to such assessor shall be part of the expenses of the application.

## Deposits for expenses

**2.24** Where, under any enactment, the sheriff requires the pursuer to deposit a sum of money to cover the expenses of an appeal under the enactment, such sum shall, subject to the provisions of that enactment, not exceed an amount which is twenty-five times the amount of the fee payable at that time in respect of lodging the initial writ.

## When decrees extractable

**2.25**—(1)   Subject to the following paragraphs—
  (a)   subject to sub-paragraph (c), a decree in absence may be extracted after the expiry of 14 days from the date of decree;
  (b)   subject to sub-paragraph (c), any decree pronounced in a defended summary application may be extracted at any time after whichever is the later of the following—
    (i)   the expiry of the period within which an application for leave to appeal may be made and no such application has been made;
    (ii)   the date on which leave to appeal has been refused and there is no right of appeal from such refusal;
    (iii)   the expiry of the period within which an appeal may be marked and no appeal has been marked; or
    (iv)   the date on which an appeal has been finally disposed of; and
  (c)   where the sheriff has, in pronouncing decree, reserved any question of expenses, extract of that decree may be issued only after the expiry of 14 days from the date of the interlocutor disposing of the question of expenses unless the sheriff otherwise directs.

(2)   The sheriff may, on cause shown, grant a motion to allow extract to be applied for and issued earlier than a date referred to in paragraph (1).

(3)   In relation to a decree referred to in paragraph (1)(b) or (c), paragraph (2) shall not apply unless—
  (a)   the motion under that paragraph is made in the presence of the parties; or
  (b)   the sheriff is satisfied of proper intimation of the motion has been made in writing to every party not present at the hearing of the motion.

(4)   Nothing in this rule shall affect the power of the sheriff to supersede extract.

## Form of extract decree

**2.26**   The extract of a decree shall be in Form 11.

### Form of warrant for execution

**2.27** An extract of a decree on which execution may proceed shall include a warrant for execution in the following terms:— "This extract is warrant for all lawful execution hereon.".

### Date of decree in extract

**2.28**—(1) Where the sheriff principal has adhered to the decision of the sheriff following an appeal, the date to be inserted in the extract decree as the date of decree shall be the date of the decision of the sheriff principal.

(2) Where a decree has more than one date it shall not be necessary to specify in an extract what was done on each date.

### Decrees in absence where defender furth of Scotland

**2.29**—(1) Where a defender is domiciled in another part of the United Kingdom or in another Contracting State, the sheriff shall not grant decree in absence until it has been shown that the defender has been able to receive the initial writ in sufficient time to arrange for his defence or that all necessary steps have been taken to that end, and for the purposes of this paragraph—

(a) the question whether a person is domiciled in another part of the United Kingdom shall be determined in accordance with sections 41 and 42 of the Civil Jurisdiction and Judgments Act 1982;

(b) the question whether a person is domiciled in another Contracting State shall be determined in accordance with Article 52 of the Convention in Schedule 1 or 3C to that Act, as the case may be; and

(c) the term "Contracting State" has the meaning assigned in section 1 of that Act.

(2) Where an initial writ has been served in a country to which the Hague Convention on the Service Abroad of Judicial and Extra-Judicial Documents in Civil or Commercial Matters dated 15th November 1965 applies, decree shall not be granted until it is established to the satisfaction of the sheriff that the requirements of Article 15 of the Convention have been complied with.

### Motion procedure

**2.30** Except where the sheriff otherwise directs, any motion relating to a summary application shall be made in accordance with, and regulated by, Chapter 15 of the Ordinary Cause Rules.

### Power of sheriff to make orders

**2.31** The sheriff may make such order as he thinks fit for the progress of a summary application in so far as it is not inconsistent with section 50 of the Sheriff Courts (Scotland) Act 1907.

### Live links

**2.32**—[1](1)   On cause shown, a party may apply by motion for authority for the whole or part of—

    (a)   the evidence of a witness or the party to be given; or

    (b)   a submission to be made,

through a live link.

    (2)   In paragraph (1)—

    "witness" means a person who has been or may be cited to appear before the court as a witness, except a vulnerable witness within the meaning of section 11(1) of the 2004 Act;[2]

    "submission" means any oral submission which would otherwise be made to the court by the party or his representative in person including an oral submission in support of a motion; and

    "live link" means a live television link or such other arrangement as may be specified in the motion by which the witness, party or representative, as the case may be, is able to be seen and heard in the proceedings or heard in the proceedings and is able to see and hear or hear the proceedings while at a place which is outside the courtroom.

### Enquiry when fixing hearing

**2.33.**[3]   Where the sheriff fixes a hearing he shall make enquiry whether there is or is likely to be a vulnerable witness within the meaning of section 11(1) of the 2004 Act who is to give evidence at any proof or hearing, consider any child witness notice or vulnerable witness application that has been lodged where no order has been made and consider whether any order under section 12(1) of the 2004 Act requires to be made.

### Vulnerable witness procedure

**2.34.**[4]   Except where the sheriff otherwise directs, where a vulnerable witness is to give evidence in a hearing of a summary application any child witness notice or vulnerable application relating to the vulnerable witness shall be made in accordance with and regulated by Chapter 45 of the Ordinary Cause Rules.

---

[1] As inserted by the Act of Sederunt (Ordinary Cause, Summary Application, Summary Cause and Small Claim Rules) Amendment (Miscellaneous) 2007 (SSI 2007/6), para.3(5) (effective January 29, 2007).

[2] As amended by the Act of Sederunt (Ordinary Cause, Summary Application, Summary Cause and Small Claim Rules) Amendment (Vulnerable Witnesses (Scotland) Act 2004) 2007 (SSI 2007/463), r.3(3) (effective November 1, 2007).

[3] As inserted by the Act of Sederunt (Ordinary Cause, Summary Application, Summary Cause and Small Claim Rules) Amendment (Vulnerable Witnesses (Scotland) Act 2004) 2007 (SSI 2007/463) r.3(4) (effective November 1, 2007).

[4] As inserted by the Act of Sederunt (Ordinary Cause, Summary Application, Summary Cause and Small Claim Rules) Amendment (Vulnerable Witnesses (Scotland) Act 2004) 2007 (SSI 2007/463), r.3(4) (effective November 1, 2007).

**Representation**

**2.35.**—[1](1)   A party may be represented by any person authorised under any enactment to conduct proceedings in the sheriff court in accordance with the terms of that enactment.

(2)   The person referred to in paragraph (1) may do everything for the preparation and conduct of an action as may have been done by an individual conducting his own action.

**Expenses**

**2.36.**—[2](1)   A party who—

    (a)   is or has been represented by a person authorised under any enactment to conduct proceedings in the sheriff court; and

    (b)   would have been found entitled to expenses if he had been represented by a solicitor or an advocate,

May be awarded expenses or outlays to which a party litigant may be found entitled under the Litigants in Person (Costs and Expenses) Act 1975 or any enactment under that Act.

**Interventions by the CEHR**

**2.37.**—[3](1)   In this rule and in rule 2.38, "the CEHR" means the Commission for Equality and Human Rights.

(2)   The CEHR may apply to the sheriff for leave to intervene in any summary application in accordance with this Rule.

(3)   An application for leave to intervene shall be by way of minute of intervention in Form 11AA and the CEHR shall—

    (a)   send a copy of it to all the parties; and

    (b)   lodge it in process, certifying that sub-paragraph (a) has been complied with.

(4)   A minute of intervention shall set out briefly—

    (a)   the CEHR's reasons for believing that the proceedings are relevant to a matter in connection with which the CEHR has a function;

    (b)   the issue in the proceedings which the CEHR wishes to address; and

    (c)   the propositions to be advanced by the CEHR and the CEHR's reasons for believing that they are relevant to the proceedings and that they will assist the sheriff.

(5)   The sheriff may—

    (a)   refuse leave without a hearing;

    (b)   grant leave without a hearing unless a hearing is requested under paragraph (6);

    (c)   refuse or grant leave after such a hearing.

---

[1] As inserted by the Act of Sederunt (Ordinary Cause, Summary Application, Summary Cause and Small Claim Rules) Amendment (Miscellaneous) 2007 (SSI 2007/6), para.3(5) (effective January 29, 2007).

[2] As renumbered by the Act of Sederunt (Sheriff Court Rules) (Miscellaneous Amendments) 2008 (SSI 2008/223) r.14(2) (effective July 1, 2008).

[3] As inserted by the Act of Sederunt (Sheriff Court Rules) (Miscellaneous Amendments) 2008 (SSI 2008/223) r.5(2) (effective July 1, 2008).

(6)   A hearing, at which the applicant and the parties may address the court on the matters referred to in paragraph (8)(c) may be held if, within 14 days of the minute of intervention being lodged, any of the parties lodges a request for a hearing.

(7)   Any diet in pursuance of paragraph (6) shall be fixed by the sheriff clerk who shall give written intimation of the diet to the CEHR and all the parties.

(8)   The sheriff may grant leave only if satisfied that—

    (a)   the proceedings are relevant to a matter in connection with which the CEHR has a function;

    (b)   the propositions to be advanced by the CEHR are relevant to the proceedings and are likely to assist him; and

    (c)   the intervention will not unduly delay or otherwise prejudice the rights of the parties, including their potential liability for expenses.

(9)   In granting leave the sheriff may impose such terms and conditions as he considers desirable in the interests of justice, including making provision in respect of any additional expenses incurred by the parties as a result of the intervention.

(10)   The sheriff clerk shall give written intimation of a grant or refusal of leave to the CEHR and all the parties.

(11)   This rule is without prejudice to any other entitlement of the CEHR by virtue of having title and interest in relation to the subject matter of any proceedings by virtue of section 30(2) of the Equality Act 2006 or any other enactment to seek to be sisted as a party in those proceedings.

(12)   Nothing in this rule shall affect the power of the sheriff to make such other direction as he considers appropriate in the interests of justice.

(13)   Any decision of the sheriff in proceedings under this rule and rule 2.38 shall be final and not subject to appeal.

### Form of intervention

**2.38.**—[1](1)   An intervention by the CEHR shall be by way of a written submission which (including any appendices) shall not exceed 5000 words.

(2)   The CEHR shall lodge the submission and send a copy of it to all the parties by such time as the sheriff may direct.

(3)   The sheriff may in exceptional circumstances—

    (a)   allow a longer written submission to be made;

    (b)   direct that an oral submission is to be made.

(4)   Any diet in pursuance of paragraph (3)(b) shall be fixed by the sheriff clerk who shall give written intimation of the diet to the CEHR and all the parties.

### Interventions by the SCHR

**2.39.**—[2](1)   In this rule and in rules 2.40 and 2.41—

"the Act of 2006" means the Scottish Commission for Human Rights Act 2006; "the SCHR" means the Scottish Commission for Human Rights.

(2)   An application for leave to intervene shall be by way of minute of intervention in Form 11AB and the SCHR shall—

    (a)   send a copy of it to all the parties; and

---

[1] As inserted by the Act of Sederunt (Sheriff Court Rules) (Miscellaneous Amendments) 2008 (SSI 2008/223) r.5(2) (effective July 1, 2008).

[2] As inserted by the Act of Sederunt (Sheriff Court Rules) (Miscellaneous Amendments) 2008 (SSI 2008/223) r.5(2) (effective July 1, 2008).

(b) lodge it in process, certifying that subparagraph (a) has been complied with.

(3) In granting leave the sheriff may impose such terms and conditions as he considers desirable in the interests of justice, including making provision in respect of any additional expenses incurred by the parties as a result of the intervention.

(4) The sheriff clerk shall give written intimation of a grant or refusal of leave to the SCHR and all the parties.

(5) Any decision of the sheriff in proceedings under this rule and rules 2.40 and 2.41 shall be final and not subject to appeal.

### Invitations to intervene

**2.40.**—[1](1) An invitation to intervene under section 14(2)(b) of the Act of 2006 shall be in Form 11AC and the sheriff clerk shall send a copy of it to the SCHR and all the parties.

(2) An invitation under paragraph (1) shall be accompanied by—
    (a) a copy of the pleadings in the proceedings; and
    (b) such other documents relating to those proceedings as the sheriff thinks relevant.

(3) In issuing an invitation under section 14(2)(b) of the Act of 2006, the sheriff may impose such terms and conditions as he considers desirable in the interests of justice, including making provision in respect of any additional expenses incurred by the parties as a result of the intervention.

### Form of intervention

**2.41.**—[2](1) An intervention by the SCHR shall be by way of a written submission which (including any appendices) shall not exceed 5000 words.

(2) The SCHR shall lodge the submission and send a copy of it to all the parties by such time as the sheriff may direct.

(3) The sheriff may in exceptional circumstances—
    (a) allow a longer written submission to be made;
    (b) direct that an oral submission is to be made.

(4) Any diet in pursuance of paragraph (3)(b) shall be fixed by the sheriff clerk who shall give written intimation of the diet to the SCHR and all the parties.

### Lodging audio or audio-visual recordings of children

**2.42.**—[3](1) In this rule "child" is a person under the age of 16 on the date of commencement of the proceedings and "children" shall be construed accordingly.

(2) Except where the sheriff otherwise directs, where a party seeks to lodge an audio or audio-visual recording of a child as a production in a summary application, this shall be done in accordance with and regulated by Chapter 50 of the Ordinary Cause Rules.

(3) A party who has lodged a recording of a child shall—

---

[1] As inserted by the Act of Sederunt (Sheriff Court Rules) (Miscellaneous Amendments) 2008 (SSI 2008/223) r.5(2) (effective July 1, 2008).
[2] As inserted by the Act of Sederunt (Sheriff Court Rules) (Miscellaneous Amendments) 2008 (SSI 2008/223) r.5(2) (effective July 1, 2008).
[3] As inserted by the Act of Sederunt (Sheriff Court Rules) (Miscellaneous Amendments) (No.3) 2012 (SSI 2012/271) para.3 (effective November 1, 2012).

(a) within 14 days after the final determination of the application, where no subsequent appeal has been marked, or

(b) within 14 days after the disposal of any appeal marked on the final determination of the application,

uplift the recording from process.

(4) Where a recording has not been uplifted as required by paragraph (3), the sheriff clerk shall intimate to—

(a) the solicitor who lodged the recording, or

(b) where no solicitor is acting, the party or such other party as seems appropriate,

that if he or she fails to uplift the recording within 28 days after the date of such intimation, it will be disposed of in such a manner as the sheriff directs.

## Chapter 3

### Rules on Applications under Specific Statutes

### Part I

### Administration of Justice (Scotland) Act 1972

### Interpretation and application

3.1.1—[1](1) In this Part,

(a) "the Act" means the Administration of Justice (Scotland) Act 1972; and

(b) "listed items" means a list of the documents and other property which the applicant in terms of rule 3.1.2 wishes to be made the subject of the order.

(2) This Part applies to applications under section 1(1) of the Act.

### Applications under section 1(1) of the Act

3.1.2—(1) An application for an order under section 1(1) of the Act (orders for inspection of documents and other property, etc.) shall be made by summary application where the proceedings in respect of which the application is made have not been commenced.

(2)[2] The summary application shall contain—

(a) the listed items;

(b) the address of the premises within which the applicant believes the listed items are to be found; and

(c) the facts which give rise to the applicant's belief that, were the order not to be granted, the listed items, or any of them, would cease to be available for the purposes of section 1 of the Act.

---

[1] As amended by the Act of Sederunt (Summary Applications, Statutory Applications and Appeals etc. Rules) Amendment (No.2) (Administration of Justice (Scotland) Act 1972) 2000 (SSI 2000/387) (effective November 20, 2000).

[2] As inserted by the Act of Sederunt (Summary Applications, Statutory Applications and Appeals etc. Rules) Amendment (No.2) (Administration of Justice (Scotland) Act 1972) 2000 (SSI 2000/387) r.2(4) (effective November 20, 2000).

**Accompanying documents**

**3.1.3**[1]  The applicant shall lodge with the summary application—
- (a)  an affidavit supporting the averments in the summary application; and
- (b)  an undertaking by the applicant that he—
  - (i)  will comply with any order of the sheriff as to payment of compensation if it is subsequently discovered that the order, or the implementation of the order, has caused loss to the respondent or, where the haver is not the respondent, to the haver;
  - (ii)  will bring within a reasonable time of the execution of the order any proceedings which he decides to bring; and
  - (iii)  will not, without leave of the sheriff, use any information, documents or other property obtained as a result of the order, except for the purpose of any proceedings which he decides to bring and to which the order relates.

**Modification of undertakings**

**3.1.4**[2]  The sheriff may, on cause shown, modify, by addition, deletion or substitution, the undertaking mentioned in rule 3.1.3.

**Intimation and service of application**

**3.1.5**—[3](1)  Before granting the summary application, the sheriff may order such intimation or service of the summary application to be given or executed, as the case may be, as he thinks fit.

(2)  Any person receiving intimation or service of the summary application by virtue of an order under paragraph (1) may appear and oppose the summary application.

**Form of order**

**3.1.6**[4]  An order made under this Part shall—
- (a)  be in Form 11A; and
- (b)  include in addition a warrant of citation in Form 2.

---

[1] As inserted by the Act of Sederunt (Summary Applications, Statutory Applications and Appeals etc. Rules) Amendment (No.2) (Administration of Justice (Scotland) Act 1972) 2000 (SSI 2000/387) r.2(4) (effective November 20, 2000).

[2] As inserted by the Act of Sederunt (Summary Applications, Statutory Applications and Appeals etc. Rules) Amendment (No.2) (Administration of Justice (Scotland) Act 1972) 2000 (SSI 2000/387) r.2(4) (effective November 20, 2000).

[3] As inserted by the Act of Sederunt (Summary Applications, Statutory Applications and Appeals etc. Rules) Amendment (No.2) (Administration of Justice (Scotland) Act 1972) 2000 (SSI 2000/387) r.2(4) (effective November 20, 2000).

[4] As inserted by the Act of Sederunt (Summary Applications, Statutory Applications and Appeals etc. Rules) Amendment (No.2) (Administration of Justice (Scotland) Act 1972) 2000 (SSI 2000/387) r.2(4) (effective November 20, 2000).

**Caution and other security**

**3.1.7**[1]  On granting, in whole or in part, the summary application the sheriff may order the applicant to find such caution or other security as he thinks fit.

**Execution of an order**

**3.1.8**[2]  The order made in terms of rule 3.1.6 shall be served by the Commissioner in person and it shall be accompanied by a copy of the affidavit referred to in rule 3.1.3(a).

**Duties of a Commissioner**

**3.1.9**[3]  The Commissioner appointed by the sheriff shall, on executing the order—

    (a)   give to the haver a copy of the notice in Form 11B;

    (b)   explain to the haver—

        (i)   the meaning and effect of the order; and

        (ii)   that he may be entitled to claim that some or all of the listed items are confidential or privileged;

    (c)[4]  inform the haver of his right to seek legal advice and to ask the sheriff to vary or recall the order;

    (d)   enter the premises and take all reasonable steps to fulfil the terms of the order;

    (e)   where the order has authorised the recovery of any of the listed items, prepare an inventory of all the listed items to be recovered before recovering them; and

    (f)   send any recovered listed items to the sheriff clerk to await the further order of the sheriff.

**Confidentiality**

**3.1.10**—[5](1)  Where confidentiality is claimed for any listed item, that listed item shall, where practicable, be enclosed in a sealed envelope.

(2)  A motion to have such a sealed envelope opened may be made by the party who obtained the order and he shall intimate the terms of the motion, by registered post or first class recorded delivery, to the person claiming confidentiality.

(3)  A person claiming confidentiality may oppose a motion made under paragraph (2).

---

[1] As inserted by the Act of Sederunt (Summary Applications, Statutory Applications and Appeals etc. Rules) Amendment (No.2) (Administration of Justice (Scotland) Act 1972) 2000 (SSI 2000/387) r.2(4) (effective November 20, 2000).

[2] As inserted by the Act of Sederunt (Summary Applications, Statutory Applications and Appeals etc. Rules) Amendment (No.2) (Administration of Justice (Scotland) Act 1972) 2000 (SSI 2000/387) r.2(4) (effective November 20, 2000).

[3] As inserted by the Act of Sederunt (Summary Applications, Statutory Applications and Appeals etc. Rules) Amendment (No.2) (Administration of Justice (Scotland) Act 1972) 2000 (SSI 2000/387) r.2(4) (effective November 20, 2000).

[4] As amended by the Act of Sederunt (Sheriff Court Rules) (Miscellaneous Amendments) (No.3) 2011 (SSI 2011/386) para.6 (effective November 28, 2011).

[5] As inserted by the Act of Sederunt (Summary Applications, Statutory Applications and Appeals etc. Rules) Amendment (No.2) (Administration of Justice (Scotland) Act 1972) 2000 (SSI 2000/387) r.2(4) (effective November 20, 2000).

## Restrictions on service

**3.1.11—**[1](1)   Except on cause shown, the order may be served on Monday to Friday only, between the hours of 9am and 5pm only.

(2)   The order shall not be served at the same time as a search warrant granted in the course of a criminal investigation.

(3)   The Commissioner may be accompanied only by—

    (a)   any person whom he considers necessary to assist him to execute the order;

    (b)   such representatives of the applicant as are named in the order, and if it is likely that the premises will be occupied by an unaccompanied female and the Commissioner is not female, one of the people accompanying the Commissioner shall be female.

(4)   If it appears to the Commissioner when he comes to serve the order that the premises are occupied by an unaccompanied female and the Commissioner is neither female nor accompanied by a female, the Commissioner shall not enter the premises.

## Right of haver to consult

**3.1.12—**[2](1)   The haver may seek legal or other professional advice of his or her choice.

(2)   Where the purpose of seeking this advice is to help the haver to decide whether to ask the sheriff to vary or recall the order, the haver may ask the Commissioner to delay starting the search for up to 2 hours or such other longer period as the Commissioner may permit.

(3)   Where the haver is seeking advice under this rule, he or she must—

    (a)   inform the Commissioner and the applicant's agent of that fact;

    (b)   not disturb or remove any listed items;

    (c)   permit the Commissioner to enter the premises, but not to start the search.

## Part II

### Betting and Gaming Appeals

*[Revoked by the Act of Sederunt (Sheriff Court Rules) (Miscellaneous Amendments) 2008 (SSI 2008/223) para.14(3)(effective July 1, 2008).]*

## Part III

### Coal Mining Subsidence Act 1991

## Interpretation and application

**3.3.1—**(1)   In this Part—

"the Act" means the Coal Mining Subsidence Act 1991;

---

[1] As inserted by the Act of Sederunt (Summary Applications, Statutory Applications and Appeals etc. Rules) Amendment (No.2) (Administration of Justice (Scotland) Act 1972) 2000 (SSI 2000/387) r.2(4) (effective November 20, 2000).

[2] As inserted by the Act of Sederunt (Summary Applications, Statutory Applications and Appeals etc. Rules) Amendment (No. 2) (Administration of Justice (Scotland) Act 1972) 2000 (SSI 2000/387) (effective November 20, 2000) and substituted by the Act of Sederunt (Sheriff Court Rules) (Miscellaneous Amendments) (No.3) 2011 (SSI 2011/386) para.6 (effective November 28, 2011).

"agreement or consent" means the agreement or consent referred to in section 41 of the Act);

"person" means a person referred to in section 41 of the Act;

"any person with responsibility for subsidence affecting any land" has the meaning given in section 43 of the Coal Industry Act 1994.

(2)   This Part applies to proceedings under section 41 of the Act.

### Applications under section 41 of the Act

**3.3.2**—(1)   An application under section 41 of the Act (disputes about withholding of agreement or consent) shall specify—

  (a)   the person with whom any person with responsibility for subsidence affecting any land has reached agreement and from whom any person with responsibility for subsidence affecting any land obtained consent; and

  (b)   the steps which have been taken to obtain the agreement or consent of the person who is withholding such agreement or consent.

(2)   An application under section 41 of the Act made in relation to the exercise of a power under section 5(3) or (5) of the Act, shall, when lodged with the sheriff clerk, be accompanied by the notice of proposed remedial action under section 4(2) of the Act.

**Part IV[1]**

**Enforcement of Securities over Heritable Property**

*Section 1*

### Interpretation

**3.4.1.**   In this Part—

"the 1894 Act" means the Heritable Securities (Scotland) Act 1894;

"the 1970 Act" means the Conveyancing and Feudal Reform (Scotland) Act 1970;

"application for enforcement of security over residential property" means any of the following—

  (a)   an application under section 24(1B) of the 1970 Act alone ("a 1970 Act only application");

  (b)   an application under section 5(1) of the 1894 Act, in a case falling within section 5(2) of that Act, alone ("an 1894 Act only application");

  (c)   an application under paragraphs (a) and (b) together ("a combined 1970 Act and 1894 Act application");

"entitled resident" means—

  (a)   in a 1970 Act only application, a person falling within the definition of that expression provided by section 24C of the 1970 Act;

  (b)   in an 1894 Act only application, a person falling within the definition of that expression provided by section 5D of the 1894 Act;

---

[1] As substituted by the Act of Sederunt (Sheriff Court Rules) (Enforcement of Securities over Heritable Property) 2010 (SSI 2010/324) para.2 (effective September 30, 2010).

    (c)   in a combined 1970 Act and 1894 Act application, a person falling
within either of those definitions;

"entitled resident application" means any of the following—

    (a)   an application under section 24B of the 1970 Act alone;

    (b)   an application under section 5C of the 1894 Act alone;

    (c)   an application under paragraphs (a) and (b) together.

"pre-action requirements" means—

    (a)   in a 1970 Act only application, the requirements specified in sec-
tions 24A(2) to (6) of the 1970 Act, together with any provision
made under section 24A(8) of that Act;

    (b)   in an 1894 Act only application, the requirements specified in sec-
tions 5B(2) to (6) of the 1894 Act, together with any provision
made under section 5B(8) of that Act;

    (c)   in a combined 1970 Act and 1894 Act application, both of those
sets of requirements;

"a recall of decree application" means any of the following—

    (a)   an application under section 24D of the 1970 Act alone;

    (b)   an application under section 5E of the 1894 Act alone;

    (c)   an application under paragraphs (a) and (b) together.

*Section 2*

## Disposal of applications under Part II of the 1970 Act for non-residential purposes

**3.4.2.**—(1)   This rule applies to an application or counter-application made by
virtue of paragraph (3)(2)(b) of the Act of Sederunt (Sheriff Court Rules) (Enforcement of Securities over Heritable Property) 2010.

(2)   An interlocutor of the sheriff disposing of an application or counter-
application is final and not subject to appeal except as to a question of title or as to
any other remedy granted.

*Section 3*

## Initial writ

**3.4.3.**—(1)   An application for enforcement of security over residential property
must include averments that the pre-action requirements have been complied with.

(2)   The pursuer must lodge Form 11C with the initial writ.

(3)   The initial writ must specify the name and particulars of all persons known
by the pursuer to be entitled residents; and crave warrant for intimation to such
persons.

*Section 4*

## Appointment of Hearing

**3.4.4.**   On an application being submitted under rule 3.4.3, the sheriff must—

    (a)   fix a hearing;

(b)   appoint service and intimation of the initial writ and Form 11C.

*Section 5*

### Answers

**3.4.5.**—(1)   Where a defender opposes an application, the sheriff may order answers to be lodged within such period that the sheriff specifies.

(2)   The answers must—

(a)   specify the name and particulars of all persons known by the defender to be entitled residents who have not already been named in the initial writ; and crave warrant for intimation to such persons; or

(b)   state that to the best of the defender's knowledge there are no other entitled residents.

*Section 6*

### Intimation to known entitled residents

**3.4.6.**   The sheriff must order that a copy of the initial writ together with a notice in Form 11D and Form 11E be intimated to all entitled residents referred to in rules 3.4.3(3) and 3.4.5(2)(a).

*Section 7*

### Application to court by entitled residents

**3.4.7.**—(1)   This rule applies to an entitled resident application.

(2)   Such application is to be made by lodging a minute in Form 11E in the principal application to which the application relates.

(3)   On a Form 11E being lodged, the sheriff must—

(a)   fix a hearing of the entitled resident application;

(b)   order parties to lodge answers (where the sheriff considers it appropriate to do so) within such period that the sheriff specifies;

(c)   order the applicant to serve upon every party and intimate to every entitled resident—

(i)   a copy of the entitled resident application;

(ii)   a note of the date, time and place of the hearing.

*Section 8*

### Recall of decree

**3.4.8.**—(1)   This rule applies to a recall of decree application.

(2)   Such application is to be made by lodging a minute in Form 11F.

(3)   On a Form 11F being lodged, the sheriff clerk must fix a hearing of the recall of decree application.

(4)   Where a hearing has been fixed under paragraph (3) the person seeking recall must, not less than seven days before the date fixed for the hearing, serve upon every party and intimate to every entitled resident—

(a)   a copy of the recall of decree application;

(b)   a note of the date, time and place of the hearing.

(4A)[1]  Where service or intimation under this rule is to be made to a party represented in the cause by a solicitor, a notice sent to such party's solicitor shall be held to be notice to the party.

(5)  At a hearing fixed under paragraph (3), the sheriff must recall the decree so far as not implemented and the hearing will then proceed as a hearing held under rule 3.4.4(a).

(6)  A minute for recall of a decree, when lodged and served or intimated in terms of this rule, will have the effect of preventing any further action being taken to enforce the decree.

(7)  If it appears to the sheriff that there has been any failure or irregularity in service or intimation of the minute for recall of a decree, the sheriff may order re-service or re-intimation of the minute (as the case may be) on such conditions as he or she thinks fit.

(8)  Where the person seeking recall does not appear or is not represented at the hearing for recall, the sheriff will pronounce an interlocutor ordaining that person to appear or be represented at a peremptory diet fixed by the sheriff to state whether or not that person intends to proceed with the person's defence or application, under certification that if that person fails to do so the sheriff may grant decree or make such other order or finding as the sheriff thinks fit.

(9)  The diet fixed in the interlocutor under paragraph (8) must not be less than 14 days after the date of the interlocutor unless the sheriff otherwise orders.

(10)  The sheriff must appoint a party to intimate to the person seeking recall a copy of the interlocutor and a notice in Form 11G.

(11)  Where a person on whom a notice and interlocutor has been intimated under paragraph (10) fails to appear or be represented at a diet fixed under paragraph (8) and to state his or her intention as required by that paragraph, the sheriff may grant decree of new or make such other order or finding as the sheriff thinks fit.

## Part V

## Copyright, Designs and Trade Marks

### Interpretation

**3.5.1**  In this Part

"the 1988 Act" means the Copyright, Designs and Patents Act 1988;
"the 1994 Act" means the Trade Marks Act 1994; and
"the 1995 Regulations" means the Olympics Association Right (Infringement Proceedings) Regulations 1995.

### Orders for delivery up, forfeiture, destruction or other disposal

**3.5.2**  An application to the sheriff made under sections 99, 114, 195, 204, 230, 231 or 298 of the 1988 Act, under sections 16 or 19 of the 1994 Act or under Regulation 3 or 5 of the 1995 Regulations, shall be made—

(a)  by motion or incidental application, as the case may be, where proceedings have been commenced; or

(b)  by summary application where no proceedings have been commenced.

---

[1] As inserted by the Act of Sederunt (Sheriff Court Rules)(Miscellaneous Amendments) 2013 (SSI 2013/135) para.2 (effective May 27, 2013).

**Service of notice on interested persons**

**3.5.3.** Where an application has been made under section 114, 204, 231 or 298 of the 1988 Act, section 19 of the 1994 Act or Regulation 5 of the 1995 Regulations—

    (a)  the application shall—

        (i)  specify the name and address of any person known or believed by the applicant to have an interest in the subject matter of the application; or

       (ii)  state that to the best of the applicant's knowledge and belief no other person has such an interest; and

    (b)  the sheriff shall order that there be intimated to any person who has such an interest, a copy of the pleadings and any motion, incidental application or summary application, as the case maybe.

**Procedure where leave of court required**

**3.5.4**—(1)  Where leave of the court is required under the 1988 Act before the action may proceed, the pursuer shall lodge along with the initial writ or summons a motion or incidental application, as the case may be, stating the grounds upon which leave is sought.

(2)  The sheriff may hear the pursuer on the motion or incidental application and may grant or refuse it or make such other order in relation to it as he considers appropriate prior to determination.

(3)  Where such motion or incidental application is granted, a copy of the sheriff's interlocutor shall be served upon the defender along with the warrant of citation.

## Part VI

### Drug Trafficking Act 1994

*[Revoked by the Act of Sederunt (Summary Applications, Statutory Applications and Appeals etc. Rules) Amendment (No.5) (Proceeds of Crime Act 2002) 2002 (SSI 2002/563), para.2(3) (effective December 30, 2002), subject to savings outlined in para.2(3).]*

## Part VII

### Licensing (Scotland) Act 1976

**Interpretation and application**

**3.7.1**—(1)  In this Part, "the Act" means the Licensing (Scotland) Act 1976.

(2)  This Part applies to appeals under section 39 of the Act.

**Service**

**3.7.2**  The appellant shall serve a copy of the initial writ on—

    (a)  the clerk to the licensing board and the chief constable;

    (b)  if he was the applicant at the hearing before the licensing board, upon all parties who appeared at the hearing; and

    (c)  if he was an objector at the hearing, upon the applicant.

### Statement of reasons of licensing board

**3.7.3**—(1)   Where the appellant has received from the licensing board a statement of reasons for its decision, he shall lodge a copy thereof with the sheriff clerk along with the initial writ.

(2)   The sheriff may, at any time prior to pronouncing a final interlocutor, require the licensing board to state the ground of refusal of an application and to give their reasons for finding such ground to be established.

## Part VIII

## Mental Health (Scotland) Act 1984

### Interpretation and application

**3.8.1**—(1)   In this Part, "the Act" means the Mental Health (Scotland) Act 1984.

(2)   This Part applies to—
- (a) applications for admission submitted to a sheriff under section 21 of the Act;
- (b) guardianship applications submitted to a sheriff under section 40 of the Act; and
- (c) community care applications submitted under section 35A of the Act.

### Appointment of hearing

**3.8.2**—(1)   On an application being submitted, the sheriff shall appoint a hearing subject, in the case of an application for admission, to section 21(3A) of the Act.

(2)   The sheriff may, where he considers it appropriate in all the circumstances, appoint that the hearing of an application shall take place in a hospital or other place.

### Service of application

**3.8.3**—(1)   The sheriff clerk shall serve or cause to be served on the patient a copy of the application, with the exception of any medical recommendation, together with a notice in Form 12.

(2)   Where the patient is not a resident patient in a hospital, the notice and copy application shall be served on him personally by sheriff officer.

(3)   Where the patient is a resident patient in a hospital, the notice and copy application shall be served together with a notice in Form 13 on his responsible medical officer—
- (a) by first class recorded delivery service; or
- (b) personally by sheriff officer.

(4)   Where the patient is already the subject of a guardianship order, the notice and copy application (including any medical recommendations) shall, in addition to any other service required by this rule, be served on the guardian—
- (a) by first class recorded delivery service; or
- (b) personally a sheriff officer.

### Duties of responsible medical officer

**3.8.4**—(1)   On receipt of a notice in Form 13 the responsible medical officer shall, subject to rule 3.8.5(1)—
- (a) deliver the notice in Form 12 to the patient; and

    (b)   as soon as practicable thereafter, complete and return to the court a certificate of such delivery in Form 14.

(2)[1]   Where, in the opinion of the responsible medical officer, it would be prejudicial to the patient's health or treatment if the patient were to be present during the proceedings—

    (a)   in an application to which rule 3.8.3(3) applies, the responsible medical officer shall set forth his reasons for his opinion in the certificate in Form 14; and

    (b)   in any other case, the responsible medical officer or the special medical officer, as the case may be, shall set forth his reasons for his opinion in writing and send them to the sheriff clerk.

### Appointment of curator ad litem

**3.8.5**—(1)   Where two medical certificates are produced stating that it would be prejudicial to the health or treatment of the patient if personal service were effected in terms of rule 3.8.3(2) or 3.8.4(1) the sheriff—

    (a)   may dispense with such service; and

    (b)   if he does so, shall appoint a curator ad litem to receive the application and represent the interest of that patient.

(2)   The sheriff may appoint a curator ad litem to represent the interests of the patient where he is satisfied that—

    (a)   the patient should be excluded from the whole or any part of the proceedings under section 113(2) of the Act; or

    (b)   in any other case, it is in all the circumstances appropriate to do so.

(3)   The sheriff clerk shall serve the application on the curator ad litem by handing, or sending by first class recorded delivery service, to him a copy of the application and of the order appointing him as the curator.

### Appointment of solicitor by court

**3.8.6**   Where the patient has indicated that he wishes to be represented at the hearing but has not nominated a representative, the sheriff may appoint a solicitor to take instructions from the patient.

### Intimation to representatives

**3.8.7**   Where in any proceedings under the Act, the sheriff clerk is aware that the patient is represented by any person and that representative would not otherwise receive intimation of any diet, a copy of the notice served on the patient shall be intimated to the representative by the sheriff clerk by first class recorded delivery service.

### Service by sheriff officer

**3.8.8**—(1)   Where a copy of an application and any notice has been served personally by sheriff officer, he shall prepare and return to the court an execution of such service setting forth in detail the manner and circumstances of such service.

(2)   Where a sheriff officer has been unable to effect personal service under this Part, he shall report to the court the reason why service was not effected.

---

[1] As amended by SSI 2003/26, para.3(5) (clerical error).

## Variation of conditions of community care order

**3.8.9**—(1)   Where, after consulting the persons referred to in subsections (1) and (2) of section 35D of the Act (variation of conditions of community care order), an application is made by the special medical officer for the variation of a community care order under that section, the special medical officer shall—

    (a)    complete Form 22 in Schedule 2 to the Mental Health (Prescribed Forms) (Scotland) Regulations 1996; and

    (b)    lodge that form with the sheriff clerk, together with a certified copy of the community care order to which the application for variation relates.

## Hearing

**3.8.10**—(1)   Any hearing to determine an application under rule 3.8.9 shall take place within 28 days after receipt by the sheriff clerk of Form 22 and the community care order referred to in that rule.

(2)   Intimation of the date of the hearing referred to in paragraph (1) shall be given by the Stationery sheriff clerk by first class recorded delivery service to such persons as the sheriff may direct; and any intimation of such date to the patient shall be made personally by sheriff officer.

## Appeal against community care order

**3.8.11**   An application by way of appeal for the revocation of a community care order under section 35F of the Act shall be in Form 15.

## Part IX

## Proceeds of Crime (Scotland) Act 1995

## Interpretation and application

**3.9.1**—(1)   In this Part—

"the Act" means the Proceeds of Crime (Scotland) Act 1995; and
"administrator" means the person appointed under paragraph 1(1) of Schedule 1 to Act.

(2)   This Part applies to proceedings under sections 28, 29, 30, 31 and 33 of, and paragraphs 1, 2, 4, 6 and 12 of Schedule 1 to, the Act.

## Service of restraint orders

**3.9.2**   Where the sheriff pronounces an interlocutor making a restraint order under section 28(1) of the Act (application for restraint order), the prosecutor shall serve a copy of that interlocutor on every person named in the interlocutor as restrained by the order.

## Recall or variation of restraint orders

**3.9.3**—(1)   An application to the sheriff under any of the following provisions of the Act shall be made by note in the process containing the interlocutor malting the restraint order to which the application relates—

    (a)    section 29(4) or (5) (recall of restraint orders in relation to realisable property);

(b)   section 30(3) or (4) (recall of restraint orders in relation to forfeitable property);

(c)   section 31(1) (variation or recall of restraint order).

(2)   In respect of an application by note under paragraph (1)(c) by a person having an interest for an order for variation or recall under section 31(1)(b) of the Act—

(a)   *[Revoked by the Act of Sederunt (Ordinary Cause, Summary Application, Summary Cause and Small Claim Rules) Amendment (Miscellaneous) 2005 (SSI 2005/648) r.3(2) (effective January 2, 2006).]*

(b)   the period of notice for lodging answers to the note shall be 14 days or such other period as the sheriff thinks fit.

### Applications for interdict

**3.9.4**—(1)   An application to the sheriff under section 28(8) of the Act (interdict) may be made—

(a)   in the application made under section 28(1) of the Act; or

(b)   if made after a restraint order has been made, by note in the process of the application for that order.

(2)   An application under section 28(8) of the Act by note under paragraph (1)(b) shall not be intimated, served or advertised before that application is granted.

### Applications in relation to arrestment

**3.9.5**—(1)   An application to the sheriff under section 33(1) of the Act (arrestment of property affected by restraint order by the prosecutor for warrant for arrestment may be made—

(a)   in the application made under section 28(1) of the Act; or

(b)   if made after a restraint order has been applied for, by note in the process of the application for that order.

(2)   An application to the sheriff under section 33(2) of the Act, to loose, restrict or recall an arrestment shall be made by note in the process of the application for the restraint order.

(3)   An application to the sheriff under section 33(4) of the Act (recall or restriction of arrestment) shall be made by note in the process containing the interlocutor making the restraint order to which the application relates.

### Appeals to the Court of Session

**3.9.6**—(1)   This rule applies to appeals against an interlocutor of the sheriff refusing, varying or recalling or refusing to vary or recall a restraint order.

(2)   An appeal to which this rule applies shall be marked within 14 days after the date of the interlocutor concerned.

(3)   An appeal to which this rule applies shall be marked by writing a note of appeal on the interlocutor sheet, or other written record containing the interlocutor appealed against, or on a separate sheet lodged with the sheriff clerk, in the following terms:— "The applicant appeals to the Court of Session.".

(4)   A note of appeal to which this rule applies shall—

(a)   be signed by the appellant;

(b)   bear the date on which it is signed; and

(c)   where the appellant is represented, specify the name and address of the solicitor or other agent who will be acting for him in the appeal.

(5)   The sheriff clerk shall transmit the process within 4 days after the appeal is marked to the Deputy Principal Clerk of Session.

(6) Within the period specified in paragraph (5), the sheriff clerk shall—

    (a) send written notice of the appeal to every other party; and

    (b) certify on the interlocutor sheet that he has done so.

(7) Failure of the sheriff clerk to comply with paragraph (6) shall not invalidate the appeal.

### Applications for appointment of administrators

**3.9.7**—(1) An application to the sheriff under paragraph 1 of Schedule 1 to the Act (appointment of administrators) shall be made—

    (a) where made after a restraint order has been made, by note in the process of the application for that order; or

    (b) in any other case, by summary application.

(2) The notification to be made by the sheriff clerk under paragraph 1(3)(a) of Schedule 1 to the Act shall be made by intimation of a copy of the interlocutor to the person required to give possession of property to an administrator.

### Incidental applications in an administration

**3.9.8**—(1) An application to the sheriff under any of the following provisions of Schedule to the Act shall be made by note in the process of the application for appointment of the administrator—

    (a) paragraph 1(1) with respect to an application after appointment of an administrator to require a person to give property to him;

    (b) paragraph 1(4) (making or altering a requirement or removal of administrator);

    (c) paragraph 1(5) (appointment of new administrator on death, resignation or removal of administrator);

    (d) paragraph 2(1)(n) (directions as to functions of administrator);

    (e) paragraph 4 (directions for application of proceeds).

(2) An application to the sheriff under any of the following provisions of Schedule 1 to the Act shall be made in the application for appointment of an administrator under paragraph 1(1) of that Schedule or, if made after the application has been made, by note in the process—

    (a) paragraph 2(1)(o) (special powers of administrator);

    (b) paragraph 2(3) (vesting of property in administrator);

    (c) paragraph 12 (order to facilitate the realisation of property).

### Requirements where order to facilitate realisation of property considered

**3.9.9** Where the sheriff considers making an order under paragraph 12 of Schedule 1 to the Act (order to facilitate the realisation of property)—

    (a) the sheriff shall fix a date for a hearing in the first instance; and

    (b) the applicant or noter, as the case may be, shall serve a notice in Form 16 on any person who has an interest in the property.

### Documents for Accountant of Court

**3.9.10**—(1) A person who has lodged any document in the process of an application for the appointment of an administrator shall forthwith send a copy of that document to the Accountant of Court.

(2)   The sheriff clerk shall transmit to the Accountant of Court any part of the process as the Accountant of Court may request in relation to an administration which is in dependence before the sheriff unless such part of the process is, at the time of request, required by the sheriff.

### Procedure for fixing and finding caution

**3.9.11**   Rules 9 to 12 of the Act of Sederunt (Judicial Factors Rules) 1992 (fixing and finding caution in judicial factories) shall, with the necessary modifications, apply to the fixing and finding of caution by an administrator under this Part as they apply to the fixing and finding of caution by a judicial factor.

### Administrator's title to act

**3.9.12**   An administrator appointed under this Part shall not be entitled to act until he has obtained a copy of the interlocutor appointing him.

### Duties of administrator

**3.9.13**—(1)   The administrator shall, as soon as possible, but within three months after the date of his appointment, lodge with the Accountant of Court—
>   (a)   an inventory of the property in respect of which he has been appointed;
>   (b)   all vouchers, securities, and other documents which are in his possession; and
>   (c)   a statement of that property which he has in his possession or intends to realise.

(2)   An administrator shall maintain accounts of his intromissions with the property in his charge and shall, subject to paragraph (3)—
>   (a)   within six months after the date of his appointment; and
>   (b)   at six monthly intervals after the first account during the subsistence of his appointment,

lodge with the Accountant of Court an account of his intromissions in such form, with such supporting vouchers and other documents, as the Accountant of Court may require.

(3)   The Accountant of Court may waive the lodging of an account where the administrator certifies that there have been no intromissions during a particular accounting period.

### State of funds and scheme of division

**3.9.14**—(1)   The administrator shall—
>   (a)   where there are funds available for division, prepare a state of funds after application of sums in accordance with paragraph 4(2) of Schedule 1 to the Act, and a scheme of division amongst those who held property which has been realised under the Act and lodge them and all relevant documents with the Accountant of Court; or
>   (b)   where there are no funds available for division, prepare a state of funds only and lodge it with the Accountant of Court, and give to the Accountant of Court such explanations as he shall require.

(2)   The Accountant of Court shall—
>   (a)   make a written report on the state of funds and any scheme of division including such observations as he considers appropriate for consideration by the sheriff; and

(b) return the state of funds and any scheme of division to the administrator with his report.

(3) The administrator shall, on receiving the report of the Accountant of Court—

(a) lodge in process the report, the state of funds and any scheme of division;

(b) intimate a copy of it to the prosecutor; and

(c) intimate to each person who held property which has been realised under the Act a notice stating—

(i) that the state of funds and scheme of division or the state of funds only, as the case may be, and the report of the Accountant of Court, have been lodged in process; and

(ii) the amount for which that person has been ranked, and whether he is to be paid in full, or by a dividend, and the amount of it, or that no funds are available for payment.

## Objections to scheme of division

**3.9.15**—(1) A person wishing to be heard by the sheriff in relation to the distribution of property under paragraph 4(3) of Schedule 1 to the Act shall lodge a note of objection in the process to which the scheme of division relates within 21 days of the date of the notice intimated under rule 3.9.14(3)(c).

(2) After the period for lodging a note of objection has expired and no note of objection has been lodged, the administrator may apply by motion for approval of the scheme of division and state of funds, or the state of funds only, as the case may be.

(3) After the period for lodging a note of objection has expired and a note of objection has been lodged, the sheriff shall dispose of such objection after hearing any objector and the administrator and making such inquiry as he thinks fit.

(4) If any objection is sustained to any extent, the necessary alterations shall be made to the state of funds and any scheme of division and shall be approved by the sheriff.

## Application for discharge of administrator

**3.9.16**—(1) Where the scheme of division is approved by the sheriff and the administrator delivered or conveyed to the persons entitled the sums or receipts allocated to them in the scheme, the administrator may apply for his discharge.

(2) An application to the sheriff for discharge of the administrator shall be made by note in the process of the application under paragraph 1(1) of Schedule 1 to the Act.

**Appeals against determination of outlays and remuneration**

**3.9.17**    An appeal to the sheriff under paragraph 6(2) of Schedule 1 to the Act (appeal against a determination by the Accountant of Court) shall be made by note in the process of the application in which the administrator was appointed.

## Part X

## Rating (Disabled Persons) Act 1978

### Interpretation and application

**3.10.1**—(1)    In this Part, "the Act" means the Rating (Disabled Persons) Act 1978.

(2)    This Part applies to appeals under section 6(5) or 6(5A) of the Act.

### Appeals under section 6(5) or 6(5A) of the Act

**3.10.2**    Any appeal under this Part shall be lodged within 42 days of the date on which the application to the rating authority is refused by the authority.

## Part XI

## Representation of the People Act 1983

### Interpretation and application

**3.11.1**—[1](1)    In this Part—

"sheriff clerk" means, except in rules 3.11.2, 3.11.22 and 3.11.23 the sheriff clerk of the sheriff court district where the trial of the election petition is to take place;
"the Act" means the Representation of the People Act 1983.

(2)    In this Part—

(a)    rules 3.11.2 to 3.11.21 apply to election petitions under the Act; and
(b)    rules 3.11.22 to 3.11.24 apply to registration appeals under section 56 of the Act where the appellant is a person—
    (i)    whose entry in the register is an anonymous entry; or
    (ii)    who has applied for such an entry.

### Initiation of proceedings

**3.11.2**—(1)    The election petition shall be lodged with the sheriff clerk of a sheriff court district within which the election questioned has taken place.

(2)    The sheriff clerk shall without delay transmit it to the sheriff principal who shall forthwith appoint—

(a)    the time and place for trial of the petition;
(b)    the amount of the security to be given by the petitioner; and
(c)    if he thinks fit, answers to be lodged within a specified time after service.

---

[1] As substituted by the Act of Sederunt (Summary Applications, Statutory Applications and Appeals etc. Rules) Amendment (Registration Appeals) 2008 (SSI 2008/41), r.2(2) (effective March 17, 2008).

(3)    Service in terms of section 136(3) of the Act (security for costs) shall be effected—

    (a)    personally within—

        (i)    5 days; or

        (ii)    such other period as the sheriff principal may appoint, of the giving of security; or

    (b)    by first class recorded delivery post within—

        (i)    5 days; or

        (ii)    such other period as the sheriff principal may appoint, of the giving of security.

### Security for expenses by bond of caution

**3.11.3**—(1)    If the security proposed is in whole or in part by bond of caution, it shall be given by lodging with the sheriff clerk a bond for the amount specified by the sheriff principal.

(2)    Such bond shall—

    (a)    recite the nature of the petition; and

    (b)    bind and oblige the cautioner and the petitioner jointly and severally, and their respective heirs, executors and successors whomsoever, that the petitioner shall make payment of all costs, charges and expenses that may be payable by him to any person by virtue of any order or decree pronounced in the petition.

(3)    The sufficiency of the cautioner must be attested to the satisfaction of the sheriff clerk, as in the case of judicial bonds of caution.

### Objections to bond of caution

**3.11.4**—(1)    Objections to a bond of caution shall be lodged with the sheriff clerk within 14 days of service in terms of section 136(3) of the Act.

(2)    Objections shall be heard and disposed of by the sheriff clerk.

(3)    If any objection is allowed, it may be removed by a deposit of such sum of money as the sheriff clerk shall determine, made in the manner provided in rule 3.11.5 and within 5 days after the date of the sheriff clerk's determination.

### Security by deposit

**3.11.5**—(1)    Security tendered in whole or in part by deposit of money shall be made in such bank the sheriff clerk may select.

(2)    The deposit receipt shall be—

    (a)    taken in joint name of the petitioner and the sheriff clerk;

    (b)    handed to the sheriff clerk; and

    (c)    held by the sheriff clerk subject to the orders of the court in the petition.

### Amendment of pleadings

**3.11.6**—(1)    Subject to paragraph (2), the sheriff principal shall have power at any stage to allow petition and any answers to be amended upon such condition as to expenses or otherwise as he shall think fit.

(2)    No amendment altering the ground upon which the election was questioned in the petition as presented shall be competent, except to the extent sanctioned by section 129(6) of the Act (time for presentation or amendment of petition questioning local election).

### Notice of date and place of trial

**3.11.7**—(1)   The sheriff clerk shall, as soon as he receives intimation of the time and place fixed for trial—

(a)   display a notice thereof on the walls of his principal office; and

(b)   send by first class post one copy of such notice to—

    (i)   the petitioner;

    (ii)   the respondent;

    (iii)   the Lord Advocate; and

    (iv)   the returning officer.

(2)   The returning officer on receipt of notice from the sheriff clerk shall forthwith publish the time and place fixed for trial in the area for which the election questioned was held.

(3)   Subject to paragraph (4), display of a notice in accordance with paragraph (1)(a) shall be deemed to be notice in the prescribed manner within the meaning of section 139(1) of the Act (trial of petition) and such notice shall not be vitiated by any miscarriage of or relating to all or any copies sent by post.

(4)   At any time before the trial it shall be competent for any party interested to bring any miscarriage of notice sent by post before the sheriff principal, who shall deal therewith as he may consider fit.

### Clerk of court

**3.11.8**   The sheriff clerk shall attend and act as clerk of court at the trial of the petition.

### Shorthand writer's charges

**3.11.9**   The shorthand writer's charges, as approved by the sheriff principal, shall be paid in the first instance by the petitioner.

### Appeals

**3.11.10**   The application to state a special case referred to in section 146(1) of the (special case for determination of the Court of Session) shall be made by minute in the petition proceedings.

### List of votes objected to and of objections

**3.11.11**—(1)   When a petitioner claims the seat for an unsuccessful candidate, alleging that such candidate had a majority of lawful votes, he and the respondent shall, 5 days before the day fixed for the trial, respectively deliver to the sheriff clerk, and send by first class post to the other party and the Lord Advocate, a list of the votes intended to be objected to, and of the objections to each such vote.

(2)   The sheriff clerk shall allow inspection of such list to all parties concerned.

(3)   No evidence shall be allowed to be given against any vote or in support of any objection not specified in such list, except by leave of the sheriff principal granted upon such terms as to the amendment of the list, postponement of the trial, and payment of expenses as to him may seem fit.

### Petition against undue return

**3.11.12**—(1)   When on the trial of a petition complaining of an undue return and claiming the office for some person, the respondent intends to give evidence to prove that that person was not duly elected, such respondent shall, 5 days before the day appointed for the trial, deliver to the sheriff clerk, and send by first class post to the petitioner and the Lord Advocate, a list of the objections to the election upon which he intends to rely.

(2) No evidence shall be allowed to be given by a respondent in support of any objection to the election not specified in such list except by leave of the sheriff principal granted upon such terms as to the amendment of the list, postponement of the trial, and payment of expenses as to him may seem fit.

## Prescribed officer

**3.11.13** The sheriff clerk shall be the prescribed officer for the purposes of sections 143(1) (expense of witnesses) and 155(2) (neglect or refusal to pay costs) of the Act.

## Leave to abandon

**3.11.14**—(1) Application for leave to withdraw a petition in terms of section 147(1) of the Act (withdrawal of petition), shall be made by minute in Form 17 and shall be preceded by written notice of the intention to make it, sent by first class post to—

(a) the respondent;

(b) the Lord Advocate; and

(c) the returning officer.

(2) The returning officer shall forthwith publish the fact of his having received such notice in the area for which the election questioned was held.

(3) The sheriff principal, upon the application being laid before him, shall by interlocutor, fix the time, not being earlier than 8 days after the date of the interlocutor, and place for hearing it.

(4) The petitioner shall, at least 6 days before the day fixed for the hearing, publish in a newspaper circulating in the district named in the interlocutor a notice in Form 18.

## Death of petitioner

**3.11.15**—(1) In the event of the death of the sole petitioner, or of the last survivor of several petitioners, the sheriff clerk shall forthwith, upon the fact being brought to his knowledge, insert in a newspaper circulating in the district a notice in Form 19.

(2) The time within which any person who might have been a petitioner in respect of the election may apply to the court by minute in the petition proceedings to be substituted as a petitioner shall be 21 days from the date of publication of such notice.

## Notice by respondent that he does not oppose petition

**3.11.16**—(1) Notice that a respondent does not intend to oppose a petition shall be given by leaving a written notice to that effect at the office of the sheriff clerk at least 6 days (exclusive of the day of leaving such notice) before the day fixed for the trial.

(2)   On such notice being left with the sheriff clerk, or on its being brought to his knowledge that a respondent other than a returning officer has died, resigned, or otherwise ceased to hold the office to which the petition relates, the sheriff clerk shall forthwith—

   (a)   advertise the fact once in a newspaper circulating in the district; and
   (b)   send intimation thereof by first class post to—
      (i)   the petitioner;
      (ii)   the Lord Advocate; and
      (iii)   the returning officer, who shall publish the fact in the district.

(3)   The advertisement to be made by the sheriff clerk shall state the last day on which, under this Part, application to be admitted as a respondent to oppose the petition can be made.

### Application to be admitted as respondent

**3.11.17**   Application to be admitted as a respondent to oppose a petition on the occurrence of any of the events mentioned in section 153(1) of the Act (withdrawal and substitution of respondents before trial) must be made by minute in the petition proceedings within 10 days after the date of publication of the advertisement mentioned in rule 3.11.16, unless the sheriff principal on cause shown sees fit to extend the time.

### Public notice of trial not proceeding

**3.11.18**—(1)   This rule applies where after the notice of trial has been published the sheriff clerk receives notice

   (a)   the petitioner's intention to apply for leave to withdraw;
   (b)   the respondent's intention not to oppose;
   (c)   the abatement of the petition by death; or
   (d)   the occurrence of any of the events mentioned in section 153(1) of the
         Act.

(2)   Where this rule applies the sheriff clerk shall forthwith give notice by advertisement inserted once in a newspaper circulating in the district, that the trial will not proceed on the day fixed.

### Notice to a party's agent sufficient

**3.11.19**   Where a party to proceedings under this Part is represented by a solicitor any reference to such party shall, where appropriate, be construed as a reference to the solicitor representing that party and a notice sent to his solicitor shall be held to be notice to the party.

### Cost of publication

**3.11.20**   Where under this Part the returning officer or the sheriff clerk requires to have published a notice or advertisement, the cost shall be paid in the first instance by the petitioner or in the case of a notice under rule 3.11.15 from the estate of the sole or last surviving petitioner and shall form part of the general expenses of the petition.

## Expenses

**3.11.21**    The expenses of petitions and other proceedings under the Act shall be taxed by the auditor of the sheriff court.

## Application for serial number

**3.11.22**—[1](1)    Where a person desiring to appeal wishes to prevent his identity being disclosed he may, before lodging the appeal, apply to the sheriff clerk for a serial number to be assigned to him for all purposes connected with the appeal.

(2)    On receipt of an application for a serial number, the sheriff clerk shall assign such a number to the applicant and shall enter a note of it opposite the name of the applicant in the register of such serial numbers.

(3)    The contents of the register of serial numbers and the names of the persons to whom each number relates shall be treated as confidential by the sheriff clerk and shall not be disclosed to any person other than—

    (a)    the sheriff;

    (b)    the registration officer whose decision or determination is the subject of the appeal.

(4)    In this rule and in rule 3.11.23 "sheriff clerk" means the sheriff clerk of the sheriff court district in which the appeal is or is to be raised.

## Confidentiality

**3.11.23**[2]    Unless the sheriff otherwise directs, all documents lodged in process of an appeal to which this rule applies are to be available only to the sheriff and the parties; and such documents are to be treated as confidential by all persons involved in, or party to, the proceedings and by the sheriff clerk.

## Hearing

**3.11.24**[3]    The hearing of an appeal to which this rule applies is to be in private.

## Part XII

## Requests or Applications under the Model Law on International Commercial Arbitration

## Interpretation

**3.12.1**    In this Part, "the Model Law" means the United Nations Commission on International Trade Law Model Law on International Commercial Arbitration as set out in Schedule 7 to the Law Reform (Miscellaneous Provisions) (Scotland) Act 1990.

---

[1] As inserted by the Act of Sederunt (Summary Applications, Statutory Applications and Appeals etc. Rules) Amendment (Registration Appeals) (SSI 2008/41), r.2(3) (effective March 17, 2008).

[2] As inserted by the Act of Sederunt (Summary Applications, Statutory Applications and Appeals etc. Rules) Amendment (Registration Appeals) (SSI 2008/41), r.2(3) (effective March 17, 2008).

[3] As inserted by the Act of Sederunt (Summary Applications, Statutory Applications and Appeals etc. Rules) Amendment (Registration Appeals) (SSI 2008/41), r.2(3) (effective March 17, 2008).

**Application**

**3.12.2**—(1)  Subject to sub-paragraph (2), any request or application which may be made to the sheriff under the Model Law shall be made by summary application.

(2)  Where proceedings involving the same arbitration and the same parties are already pending before the sheriff under this Part, a further application or request may be made by note in the same process.

(3)  The sheriff shall order service of such summary application or note to be made on such persons as he considers appropriate.

**Recognition and enforcement of awards**

**3.12.3**—(1)  There shall be lodged along with an application under Article 35 of the Model Law—

    (a)  the original arbitration agreement or certified copy thereof;

    (b)  the duly authenticated original award or certified copy thereof and

    (c)  where appropriate, a duly certified translation in English of the agreement and award.

(2)  An application under this paragraph shall specify whether to the knowledge of the applicant—

    (a)  the arbitral award has been recognised, or is being enforced, in any other jurisdiction; and

    (b)  an application for setting aside or suspension of the arbitral award has been made to a court of the country in which or under whose law the award was made.

(3)  Where the sheriff is satisfied that an arbitral award should be recognised and enforced, he shall so order and shall instruct the sheriff clerk to register the award in the Books of the Sheriff Court for execution.

## Part XIII

### Sex Discrimination Act 1975

*[Omitted by the Act of Sederunt (Ordinary Cause, Summary Application, Summary Cause and Small Claim Rules) Amendment (Equality Act 2006 etc.) 2006 (SSI 2006/ 509) (effective November 3, 2006).]*

## Part XIV[1]

### Access to Health Records Act 1990

**Interpretation and application**

**3.14.1**—(1)  In this Part—

"the Act" means the Access to Health Records Act 1990; and

"the Reg" means the Access to Health Records (Steps to Secure Compliance and Complaints Procedures) (Scotland) Regulations 1991.

(2)  This Part applies to applications under section 8(1) of the Act (applications to the court for order to comply with requirement of the Act).

---

[1] As inserted by the Act of Sederunt (Summary Applications, Statutory Applications and Appeals etc. Rules) Amendment 2000 (SSI 2000/148), para.2(2) (effective July 3, 2000).

## Accompanying documents

**3.14.2**　An application shall specify those steps prescribed in the Regulations which have been taken by the person concerned to secure compliance with any requirement of the Act, and when lodged in process shall be accompanied by—

    (a)　a copy of the application under section 3 of the Act (applications for access to a health record);

    (b)　a copy of the complaint under regulation 3 or 4 of the Regulations (complaint about non-compliance with the Act); and

    (c)　if applicable, a copy of the report under regulation 6 of the Regulations (report in response to complaint).

## Time of making application

**3.14.3**　The application shall be made where the applicant—

    (a)　has received a report in accordance with regulation 6 of the Regulations, within one year of the date of the report;

    (b)　has not received such a report, within 18 months of the date of the complaint.

## Part XV

## Race Relations Act 1976

*[Omitted by the Act of Sederunt (Ordinary Cause, Summary Application, Summary Cause and Small Claim Rules) Amendment (Equality Act 2006 etc.) 2006 (SSI 2006/509) (effective November 3 2006).]*

## Part XVI[1]

## Adults with Incapacity (Scotland) Act 2000

## Interpretation

**3.16.1**[2]　In this Part—

"the 2000 Act" means the Adults with Incapacity (Scotland) Act 2000;

"the 2003 Act" means the Mental Health (Care and Treatment) (Scotland) Act 2003;[3]

"adult" means a person who is the subject of an application under the 2000 Act and—

    (a)　has attained the age of 16 years; or

    (b)　in relation to an application for a guardianship order, will attain the age of 16 years within 3 months of the date of the application;[4]

---

[1] As inserted by the Act of Sederunt (Summary Applications, Statutory Applications and Appeals etc. Rules) Amendment (Adults with Incapacity) 2001 (SSI 2001/142), r.3(2).

[2] As amended by the the Mental Health (Care and Treatment) (Scotland) Act 2003 (Modification of Subordinate Legislation) Order 2005 (SSI 2005/445) (effective October 5, 2005).

[3] Inserted by the the Mental Health (Care and Treatment) (Scotland) Act 2003 (Modification of Subordinate Legislation) Order 2005 (SSI 2005/445) (effective October 5, 2005).

[4] As substituted by the Act of Sederunt (Summary Applications, Statutory Applications and Appeals etc. Rules) Amendment (Adult Support and Protection (Scotland) Act 2007) 2008 (SSI 2008/111) r.3(1) (effective April 1, 2008).

"authorised establishment" has the meaning ascribed to it in section 35(2) of the 2000 Act;

"continuing attorney" means a person on whom there has been conferred a power of attorney granted under section 15(1) of the 2000 Act;

"guardianship order" means an order made under section 58(4) of the 2000 Act;[1]

"incapable" has the meaning ascribed to it at section 1(6) of the 2000 Act, and "incapacity" shall be construed accordingly;

"intervention order" means an order made under section 53(1) of the 2000 Act;[2]

"local authority" has the meaning ascribed to it by section 87(1) of the 2000 Act;[3]

"managers" has the meaning ascribed to it in paragraph 1 of Schedule 1 to the 2000 Act;

"Mental Welfare Commission" has the meaning ascribed to it by section 87(1) of the 2000 Act;[4]

"named person" has the meaning ascribed to it by section 329 of the Mental Health (Care and Treatment) (Scotland) Act 2003;[5]

"nearest relative" means, subject to section 87(2) of the 2000 Act, the person who would be, or would be exercising the functions of, the adult's nearest relative under sections 53 to 57 of the 1984 Act if the adult were a patient within the meaning of that Act and notwithstanding that the person neither is or was caring for the adult for the purposes of section 53(3) of that Act;

"power of attorney" includes a factory and commission;

"primary carer" means the person or organisation primarily engaged in caring for an adult;

"Public Guardian" shall be construed in accordance with section 6 of the 2000 Act; and

"welfare attorney" means a person on whom there has been conferred a power of attorney granted under section 16(1) of the 2000 Act.

## Appointment of hearing

**3.16.2** On an application or other proceedings being submitted under or in pursuance of the 2000 Act the sheriff shall—

(a) fix a hearing;

(b) order answers to be lodged (where he considers it appropriate to do so) within a period that he shall specify; and

(c) appoint service and intimation of the application or other proceedings.

---

[1] As amended by the Act of Sederunt (Summary Applications, Statutory Applications and Appeals etc. Rules) Amendment (No.3) (Adults with Incapacity) 2002 (SSI 2002/146), r.2(2).

[2] As amended by the Act of Sederunt (Summary Applications, Statutory Applications and Appeals etc. Rules) Amendment (No.3) (Adults with Incapacity) 2002 (SSI 2002/146), r.2(2).

[3] As amended by the Act of Sederunt (Summary Applications, Statutory Applications and Appeals etc. Rules) Amendment (No.3) (Adults with Incapacity) 2002 (SSI 2002/146), r.2(2).

[4] As amended by the Act of Sederunt (Summary Applications, Statutory Applications and Appeals etc. Rules) Amendment (No.3) (Adults with Incapacity) 2002 (SSI 2002/146), r.2(2).

[5] As inserted by the Act of Sederunt (Summary Applications, Statutory Applications and Appeals etc. Rules) Amendment (Adult Support and Protection (Scotland) Act 2007) 2008 (SSI 2008/111) r.2(1) (effective April 1, 2008).

**Place, and privacy, of any hearing**

**3.16.3**[1]   The sheriff may, where he considers it appropriate in all the circumstances, appoint that the hearing of an application or other proceedings shall take place—

    (a)   in a hospital, or any other place than the court building;

    (b)   in private.

**Service of application and renewal proceedings**[2]

**3.16.4**—(2)   Where the applicant is an individual person without legal representation service shall be effected by the sheriff clerk.

(3)   Where the adult is in an authorised establishment the person effecting service shall not serve Form 20 on the adult under paragraph (1)(a) but shall instead serve Forms 20 and 21, together with Form 22, on the managers of that authorised establishment by—

    (a)   first class recorded delivery post; or

    (b)   personal service by a sheriff officer.

(4)   On receipt of Forms 20 and 21 in terms of paragraph (3) the managers of the authorised establishment shall, subject to rule 3.16.5—

    (a)   deliver the notice in Form 20 to the adult; and

    (b)   as soon as practicable thereafter complete and return to the sheriff clerk a certificate of such delivery in Form 22.

(5)   Where the application or other proceeding follows on a remit under rule 3.16.9 the order for service of the application shall include an order for service on the Public Guardian or other party concerned.

(6)[3]   Where the application is for an intervention order or a guardianship order, copies of the reports lodged in accordance with section 57(3) of the 2000 Act (reports to be lodged in court along with application) shall be served along with Forms 20, 21 and 22 as the case may be.

[3] As substituted by the Act of Sederunt (Sheriff Court Rules)(Miscellaneous Amendments) (No.3) 2013 (SSI 2013/171) para.2 (effective June 25, 2013)

**Dispensing with service on adult**

**3.16.5**—(1)   Where, in relation to any application or proceeding under or in pursuance of the 2000 Act, two medical certificates are produced stating that intimation of the application or other proceeding, or notification of any interlocutor relating to such application or other proceeding, would be likely to pose a serious risk to the health of the adult the sheriff may dispense with such intimation or notification.

(2)   Any medical certificates produced under paragraph (1) shall be prepared by medical practitioners independent of each other.

---

[1] As substituted by the Act of Sederunt (Ordinary Cause, Summary Application and Small Claim Rules) Amendment (Miscellaneous) 2004 (SSI 2004/197) para.3(7) (effective May 21, 2004).

[2] As amended by the Act of Sederunt (Sheriff Court Rules)(Miscellaneous Amendments) (No.3) 2013 (SSI 2013/171) para.2 (effective June 25, 2013).

[3] As amended by the Act of Sederunt (Summary Applications, Statutory Applications and Appeals etc. Rules) Amendment (No.3) (Adults with Incapacity) 2002 (SSI 2002/146), r.2(2).

(3)[1]  In any case where the incapacity of the adult is by reason of mental disorder, one of the two medical practitioners must be a medical practitioner approved for the purposes of section 22(4) of the 2003 Act as having special experience in the diagnosis or treatment of mental disorder.

## Hearing

**3.16.6**—(1)[2]  A hearing to determine any application or other proceeding shall take place within 28 days of the interlocutor fixing the hearing under rule 3.16.2 unless any person upon whom the application is to be served is outside Europe.

(2)  At the hearing referred to in paragraph (1) the sheriff may determine the application or other proceeding or may order such further procedure as he thinks fit.

## Prescribed forms of application

**3.16.7**—(1)  An application submitted to the sheriff under or in pursuance of the 2000 Act, other than an appeal or remitted matter, shall be in Form 23.

(2)  An appeal to the sheriff under or in pursuance of the 2000 Act shall be in Form 24.

## Subsequent applications

**3.16.8**—(1)[3]  Unless otherwise prescribed in the Part or under the 2000 Act, any application or proceedings subsequent to an initial application or proceeding considered by the sheriff including an application to renew an existing order, shall take the form of a minute lodged in the process.

(1A)[4]  Except where the sheriff otherwise directs, any such minute shall be lodged in accordance with, and regulated by, Chapter 14 of the Ordinary Cause Rules.

(2)  Where any subsequent application or proceedings under paragraph (1) above are made to a court in another sheriffdom the sheriff clerk shall transmit the court process to the court dealing with the current application or proceeding.

(3)  Transmission of the process in terms of paragraph (2) shall be made within 4 days of it being requested by the sheriff clerk of the court in which the current application or proceedings have been raised.

(4)[5]  Where the application is for renewal of a guardianship order, a copy of any report lodged under section 60 of the 2000 Act shall be served along with the minute.

---

[1] As amended by the the the Mental Health (Care and Treatment) (Scotland) Act 2003 (Modification of Subordinate Legislation) Order (SSI 2005/445) (effective October 5, 2005).

[2] As amended by the Act of Sederunt (Summary Applications, Statutory Applications and Appeals etc. Rules) Amendment (No.3) (Adults with Incapacity) 2002 (SSI 2002/146), r.2(2) (effective April 1, 2002).

[3] As amended the Act of Sederunt (Summary Applications, Statutory Applications and Appeals etc. Rules) Amendment (No.3) (Adults with Incapacity) 2002 (SSI 2002/146) r.2(2) and the Act of Sederunt (Summary Applications, Statutory Applications and Appeals etc. Rules) Amendment (Adult Support and Protection (Scotland) Act 2007) 2008 (SSI 2008/111) r.3(2)(a) (effective April 1, 2008).

[4] As amended the Act of Sederunt (Summary Applications, Statutory Applications and Appeals etc. Rules) Amendment (No.3) (Adults with Incapacity) 2002 (SSI 2002/146) r.2(2) and the Act of Sederunt (Summary Applications, Statutory Applications and Appeals etc. Rules) Amendment (Adult Support and Protection (Scotland) Act 2007) 2008 (SSI 2008/111) r.3(2)(a) (effective April 1, 2008).

[5] As amended the Act of Sederunt (Summary Applications, Statutory Applications and Appeals etc. Rules) Amendment (No.3) (Adults with Incapacity) 2002 (SSI 2002/146) r.2(2) and the Act of Sederunt (Summary Applications, Statutory Applications and Appeals etc. Rules) Amendment (Adult Support and Protection (Scotland) Act 2007) 2008 (SSI 2008/111) r.3(2)(a) (effective April 1, 2008).

(5)  *[Repealed by the Act of Sederunt (Sheriff Court Rules)(Miscellaneous Amendments) (No.3) 2013 (SSI 2013/171) para.2 (effective June 25, 2013).]*

## Remit of applications by the Public Guardian etc.

**3.16.9**  Where an application is remitted to the sheriff by the Public Guardian or by any other party authorised to do so under the 2000 Act the party remitting the application shall, within 4 days of the decision to remit, transmit the papers relating to the application to the sheriff clerk of the court where the application is to be considered.

## Caution and other security[1]

**3.16.10**—[2](1)  Where the sheriff requires a person authorised under an intervention order or any variation of an intervention order, or appointed as a guardian, to find caution he shall specify the amount and period within which caution is to be found in the interlocutor authorising or appointing the person or varying the order (as the case may be).

(1A)[3]  The amount of caution specified by the sheriff in paragraph (1) may be calculated and expressed as a percentage of the value of the adult's estate.

(2)  The sheriff may, on application made by motion before the expiry of the period for finding caution and on cause shown, allow further time for finding caution in accordance with paragraph (1).

(3)  Caution shall be lodged with the Public Guardian.

(4)  Where caution has been lodged to the satisfaction of the Public Guardian he shall notify the sheriff clerk.

(5)  The sheriff may at any time while a requirement to find caution is in force—

    (a)  increase the amount of, or require the person to find new, caution; or

    (b)  authorise the amount of caution to be decreased.

(6)[4]  Where the sheriff requires the person referred to in paragraph (1) to give security other than caution, the rules of Chapter 27 of the Ordinary Cause Rules shall apply with the necessary modifications.

## Appointment of interim guardian

**3.16.11**[5]  An application under section 57(5) of the 2000 Act (appointment of interim guardian) may be made in the crave of the application for a guardianship order to which it relates or, if made after the submission of the application for a guardianship order, by motion in the process of that application.

---

[1] As amended by the Act of Sederunt (Summary Applications, Statutory Applications and Appeals etc. Rules) Amendment (Adult Support and Protection (Scotland) Act 2007) 2008 (SSI 2008/111) r.4 (effective April 1, 2008).

[2] As inserted by the Act of Sederunt (Summary Applications, Statutory Applications and Appeals etc. Rules) Amendment (No.3) (Adults with Incapacity) 2002 (SSI 2002/146), r.2(2).

[3] As inserted by the Act of Sederunt (Summary Applications, Statutory Applications and Appeals etc. Rules) Amendment (Adult Support and Protection (Scotland) Act 2007) 2008 (SSI 2008/111) r.4 (effective April 1, 2008).

[4] As inserted by the Act of Sederunt (Summary Applications, Statutory Applications and Appeals etc. Rules) Amendment (Adult Support and Protection (Scotland) Act 2007) 2008 (SSI 2008/111) r.4 (effective April 1, 2008).

[5] As inserted by the Act of Sederunt (Summary Applications, Statutory Applications and Appeals etc. Rules) Amendment (No.3) (Adults with Incapacity) 2000 (SSI 2002/146), r.2(2) (effective April 1, 2002).

### Registration of intervention order or guardianship order relating to heritable property

**3.16.12**[1]   Where an application for an intervention order or a guardianship order seeks to vest in the person authorised under the order, or the guardian, as the case may be, any right to deal with, convey or manage any interest in heritable property which is recorded or capable of being recorded in the General Register of Sasines or is registered or capable of being registered in the Land Register of Scotland, the applicant must specify the necessary details of the property in the application to enable it to be identified in the Register of Sasines or the Land Register of Scotland, as the case may be.

### Non-compliance with decisions of guardians with welfare powers

**3.16.13**—[2](1)   Where the court is required under section 70(3) of the 2000 Act to intimate an application for an order or warrant in relation to noncompliance with the decision of a guardian with welfare powers, the sheriff clerk shall effect intimation in Form 20 in accordance with paragraphs (2) and (3).

(2)   Intimation shall be effected—

   (a)   where the person is within Scotland, by first class recorded delivery post, or, in the event that intimation by first class recorded delivery post is unsuccessful, by personal service by a sheriff officer; or

   (b)   where the person is furth of Scotland, in accordance with rule 2.12 (service on persons furth of Scotland).

(3)   Such intimation shall include notice of the period within which any objection to the application shall be lodged.

Part XVII[3]

Anti-Terrorism, Crime and Security Act 2001

### Interpretation

**3.17.1**   In this Part, any reference to a specified paragraph shall be construed as a reference to the paragraph bearing that number in Schedule 1 to the Anti-terrorism, Crime and Security Act 2001.

### Applications for extended detention of cash

**3.17.2**—(1)   An application to the sheriff for an order under paragraph 3(2) (extended detention of seized cash) shall be made by summary application.

(2)   An application for any further order for the detention of cash under paragraph 3(2) shall be made by minute in the original process and shall be proceeded with in accordance with sub-paragraph (3) below.

---

[1] As inserted by the Act of Sederunt (Summary Applications, Statutory Applications and Appeals etc. Rules) Amendment (No.3) (Adults with Incapacity) 2002 (SSI 2002/146), r.2(2) (effective April 1, 2002).

[2] As inserted by the Act of Sederunt (Summary Applications, Statutory Applications and Appeals etc. Rules) Amendment (No.3) (Adults with Incapacity) 2002 (SSI 2002/146), r.2(2) (effective April 1, 2002).

[3] As inserted by the Act of Sederunt (Summary Applications, Statutory Applications and Appeals etc. Rules) Amendment (Detention and Forfeiture of Terrorist Cash) 2002 (SSI 2002/ 129), para.2(2) (effective March 8, 2002).

(3) On the lodging of an application for any further order the sheriff shall—

    (a) fix a date for determination of the application; and

    (b) order service of the application together with notice of such date for determination on any persons whom he considers may be affected.

### Applications for release of detained cash

**3.17.3**—(1) An application to the sheriff under paragraph 5(2) (application for release of detained cash) or under paragraph 9(1) (application by person who claims that cash belongs to him) shall, where the court has made an order under paragraph 3(2), be made by minute in the original process of the application for that order, and in any other case shall be made by summary application.

(2) On the lodging of such an application the sheriff shall—

    (a) fix a date for a hearing; and

    (b) order service of the application together with notice of such hearing on the procurator fiscal and any other person whom he considers may be affected by the granting of such an application.

### Applications for forfeiture of detained cash

**3.17.4**—(1) An application to the sheriff under paragraph 6(1) (application for forfeiture of detained cash) shall, where the court has made an order under paragraph 3(2), be made by minute in the original process of the application for that order, and in any other case shall be made by summary application.

(2) On the lodging of such an application the sheriff shall—

    (a) fix a date for a hearing; and

    (b) order service of the application together with notice of such hearing on any person whom he considers may be affected by the granting of such an application.

### Applications for compensation

**3.17.5**—(1) An application to the sheriff under paragraph 10(1) (application for compensation) shall, where the court has made an order under paragraph 3(2), be made by minute in the original process of the application for that order, and in any other case shall be made by summary application.

(2) On the lodging of such an application the sheriff shall—

    (a) fix a date for a hearing; and

    (b) order service of the application together with notice of such hearing on any person whom he considers may be affected by the granting of such an application.

Part XVIII[1]

---

[1] As inserted by the Act of Sederunt (Summary Applications, Statutory Applications and Appeals etc. Rules) Amendment (No.2) (Local Government (Scotland) Act 1973) 2002 (SSI 2002/130), r.2(3) (effective March 8, 2002).

## Local Government (Scotland) Act 1973

### Application

**3.18.1—** This Part applies to appeals to the sheriff principal under section 103J of the Local Government (Scotland) Act 1973 (appeals from the Accounts Commission for Scotland).

### Appeals

**3.18.2—**(1) An appeal under this Part shall be made by summary application.

(2) A summary application made under paragraph (1) shall include grounds of appeal stating—

(a) the finding or sanction or suspension being appealed;

(b) reasons why the appeal should be allowed; and

(c) the date of sending of the finding or imposition of the sanction or suspension concerned,

and shall be accompanied by a copy of such finding, sanction or suspension.

### Warrant and form of citation

**3.18.3—**(1) A warrant for citation in an appeal under this Part shall be in Form 2A and shall state—

(a) the date by which answers should be lodged; and

(b) the date and time when the appeal will call.

(2) Citation in respect of a warrant granted under paragraph (1) shall be in Form 3A.

(3) Where a party on whom service has been made lodges answers under paragraph (1)(a) that party shall, at the same time, send a copy to the applicant.

(4) In Schedule 1 (forms)—

(a) after Form 2 insert Form 2A; and

(b) after Form 3 insert Form 3A,

as set out in the Schedule to this Act of Sederunt.

## Part XIX[1]

### Proceeds of Crime Act 2002

*General*

### Interpretation and application

**3.19.1.—**[2](1) In this Part—

"the Act" means the Proceeds of Crime Act 2002;

references to an administrator are to an administrator appointed under section 125(1) or 128(3);

a reference to a specified section is a reference to the section bearing that number

---

[1] As inserted by the Act of Sederunt (Summary Applications, Statutory Applications and Appeals etc. Rules) Amendment (No.5) (Proceeds of Crime Act 2002) 2002 (SSI 2002/563), r.2(2) (effective December 30, 2002).

[2] As substituted by the Act of Sederunt (Summary Applications, Statutory Applications and Appeals etc. Rules) Amendment (No.6) (Proceeds of Crime Act 2002) 2003 (SSI 2003/98), r.2(2)(a) (effective February 24, 2003 for provisions specified in SSI 2003/98 para.1(1)(b)(ii); March 24, 2003 otherwise).

in the Act; and any reference to a specified paragraph in a specified Schedule is a reference to the paragraph bearing that number in the Schedule of that number in the Act.

(2) This Part applies to applications to the sheriff under Parts 3, 5 and 8 of the Act; but it only applies to applications under Part 8 in relation to property that is the subject of a civil recovery investigation.

*Recovery of cash in summary proceedings*

### Applications for extended detention of cash

**3.19.2.**—(1) An application to the sheriff for an order under sections 295(2) and (7) (extended detention of seized cash) shall be made by summary application.

(2) An application for any further order for the detention of cash under section 295(2) shall be made by minute in the process of the original application for extended detention of seized cash and shall be proceeded with in accordance with sub-paragraph (3) below.

(3) On the lodging of an application for any further order the sheriff shall—
    (a) fix a date for determination of the application; and
    (b) order service of the application together with notice of such date for determination on any persons whom he considers may be affected.

### Applications for release of detained cash

**3.19.3.**—(1) An application to the sheriff under section 297(3) (application for release of detained cash) or under section 301(1) (application by person who claims that cash belongs to him) shall, where the court has made an order under section 295(2), be made by minute in the process of the application for that order, and in any other case shall be made by summary application in the course of the proceedings or at any other time.

(2) On the lodging of such an application the sheriff shall—
    (a) fix a date for a hearing; and
    (b) order service of the application together with notice of such hearing on the procurator fiscal and any other person whom he considers may be affected by the granting of such an application.

### Applications for forfeiture of detained cash

**3.19.4.**—(1) An application to the sheriff under section 298(1)(b) (application by the Scottish Ministers for forfeiture of detained cash) shall, where the court has made an order under section 295(2), be made by minute in the process of the application for that order, and in any other case shall be made by summary application.

(2) On the lodging of such an application the sheriff shall—
    (a) fix a date for a hearing; and
    (b) order service of the application together with notice of such hearing on any person whom he considers may be affected by the granting of such an application.

### Applications for compensation

**3.19.5.**—(1) An application to the sheriff under section 302(1) (application for compensation) shall, where the court has made an order under section 295(2), be made by minute in the process of the application for that order, and in any other case shall be made by summary application.

(2)   On the lodging of such an application the sheriff shall—

    (a)   fix a date for a hearing; and

    (b)   order service of the application together with notice of such hearing on any person whom he considers may be affected by the granting of such an application.

*Restraint and administration orders[1]*

### Service of restraint orders

**3.19.6.**   The intimation to be made by the prosecutor under section 121(3) shall be made by serving a copy of the interlocutor granting a restraint order on every person named in the interlocutor as restrained by the order.

### Recall or variation of restraint orders

**3.19.7.**   An application to the sheriff under section 121(5) (variation or recall of restraint order) shall be made by minute in the process of the application for the restraint order.

### Appeals to the Court of Session

**3.19.8.**—(1)   An appeal against an interlocutor of the sheriff refusing, varying or recalling or refusing to vary or recall a restraint order shall be marked within 14 days after the date of the interlocutor concerned.

(2)   Such an appeal shall be marked by writing a note of appeal on the interlocutor sheet, or other written record containing the interlocutor appealed against, or on a separate sheet lodged with the sheriff clerk, in the following terms—

    "The applicant appeals to the Court of Session.".

(3)   The note of appeal shall—

    (a)   be signed by the appellant;

    (b)   bear the date on which it is signed; and

    (c)   where the appellant is represented, specify the name and address of the solicitor or other agent who will be acting for him in the appeal.

(4)   The sheriff clerk will transmit the process within 4 days after the appeal is marked to the Deputy Principal Clerk of Session.

(5)   Within the period specified in paragraph (4), the sheriff clerk shall—

    (a)   send written notice of the appeal to every other party; and

    (b)   certify on the interlocutor sheet that he has done so.

(6)   Failure of the sheriff clerk to comply with paragraph (5) shall not invalidate the appeal.

### Applications in relation to arrestment

**3.19.9.**—(1)   An application to the sheriff under section 124(1) (arrestment of property affected by restraint order) by the prosecutor for warrant for arrestment may be made—

---

[1] Inserted by the Act of Sederunt (Summary Applications, Statutory Applications and Appeals etc. Rules) Amendment (No.6) (Proceeds of Crime Act 2002) 2003 (SSI 2003/98), r.2(2)(b) (effective February 24, 2003 for provisions specified in SSI 2003/98 para.1(1)(b)(ii); March 24, 2003 otherwise).

(a) in the application made under section 121(2) (application for restraint order); or

(b) if made after a restraint order has been applied for, by minute in the process of the application for that order.

(2) An application to the sheriff under section 124(3) (recalling, loosing or restricting arrestment) or under section 124(6) (recall or restriction of arrestment) shall be made by minute in the process of the application for the restraint order.

### Applications for appointment of administrators

**3.19.10.**—(1) An application to the sheriff under section 125(1) (appointment of management administrator) shall be made by minute in the process of the application for the restraint order.

(2) An application to the sheriff under section 128(2) (appointment of enforcement administrator) shall be made—

(a) where made after a restraint order has been made, by minute in the process of the application for that order; or

(b) in any other case, by summary application.

(3) The notification to be made by the sheriff clerk under section 125(3) or 128(8) (as the case may be) shall be made by intimation of a copy of the interlocutor to the accused and the persons subject to the order.

### Incidental applications in relation to an administration

**3.19.11.** An application to the sheriff subsequent to the appointment of an administrator relating to any matter incidental to that appointment shall be made by minute in the process of the application in which the administrator was appointed.

### Documents for Accountant of Court

**3.19.12.**—(1) A person who has lodged any document in the process of an application for the appointment of an administrator shall forthwith send a copy of that document to the Accountant of Court.

(2) The sheriff clerk shall transmit to the Accountant of Court any part of the process as the Accountant of Court may request in relation to an administration which is in dependence before the sheriff unless such part of the process is, at the time of request, required by the sheriff.

### Procedure for fixing and finding caution

**3.19.13.**—(1) The Accountant of Court shall forthwith, on receiving intimation of an application for the appointment of an administrator, fix the caution to be found in the event of appointment being made and shall notify the amount to the sheriff clerk and the applicant.

(2) During the subsistence of the appointment of the administrator, the Accountant of Court may, at any time—

(a) require the administrator to increase the amount of or find new or additional caution; or

(b) authorise the administrator to decrease the amount of existing caution.

**Time for finding caution**

**3.19.14.**—(1)   Where the time within which caution is to be found is not stipulated in the interlocutor appointing the administrator, the time allowed for finding caution shall be, subject to paragraph (2) of this rule, limited to one calendar month from the date of the interlocutor.

(2)   The sheriff may, on application made before the expiry of the period for finding caution, and, on cause shown, allow further time for finding caution.

**Procedure on finding caution**

**3.19.15.**—(1)   Caution shall be lodged with the Accountant of Court.

(2)   Where caution has been found to the satisfaction of the Accountant of Court, he shall notify the sheriff clerk.

**Issue of certified copy interlocutor**

**3.19.16.**—(1)   A certified copy interlocutor of appointment of an administrator shall not be issued by the sheriff clerk until he receives notification from the Accountant of Court in accordance with rule 3.19.15(2).

**Administrator's title to act**

**3.19.17.**   An administrator shall not be entitled to act until he has obtained a certified copy of the interlocutor appointing him.

**Accounts**

**3.19.18.**—(1)   An administrator shall maintain accounts of his intromissions with the property in his charge and shall, subject to paragraph (2)—

    (a)   within six months after the date of his appointment; and

    (b)   at six monthly intervals after the first account during the subsistence of his appointment,

lodge with the Accountant of Court an account of his intromissions in such form, with such supporting vouchers and other documents, as the Accountant of Court may require.

(2)   The Accountant of Court may waive the lodging of an account where the administrator certifies that there have been no intromissions during a particular accounting period.

**Application for discharge of administrator**

**3.19.19.**   An application to the sheriff for discharge of an administrator shall be made by minute in the process of the application in which the administrator was appointed.

**Appeals against determination of outlays and remuneration**

**3.19.20.**   An appeal to the sheriff under paragraph 9(1) of Schedule 3 (appeal against a determination by the Accountant of Court) shall be made by minute in the process of the application in which the administrator was appointed.

## Production orders

**3.19.21.**—(1)   An application to the sheriff under section 382(2) (order to grant entry to premises) may be made—

(a)   in the application for the production order; or

(b)   if made after the production order has been made, by minute in the process of the application for that order.

(2)   A report to the sheriff under section 385(4) (report of failure to bring production order made in relation to an authorised government department to the attention of the officer concerned) shall take the form of a letter to the sheriff clerk.

(3)   An application to the sheriff under section 386(4) (discharge or variation of a production order or an order to grant entry) shall be made by minute in the process of the application for the production order.

## Search warrants

**3.19.22.**   An application to the sheriff under section 387(1) (search warrant) shall be in the form of a summary application.

## Customer information orders

**3.19.23.**   An application under section 403(4) (discharge or variation of a customer information order) shall be made by minute in the process of the application for the customer information order.

## Account monitoring orders

**3.19.24.**   An application under section 408(4) (discharge or variation of an account monitoring order) shall be made by minute in the process of the application for the account monitoring order.

Part XX[2]

## International Criminal Court (Scotland) Act 2001

*General*

## Interpretation and application

**3.20.1.**—(1)   In this Part—

"the Act" means the International Criminal Court (Scotland) Act 2001;

"ICC crime" has the same meaning as in section 28(1) of the Act; and a reference to a specified section is a reference to the section bearing that number

---

[1] As inserted by the Act of Sederunt (Summary Applications, Statutory Applications and Appeals etc. Rules) Amendment (No.6) (Proceeds of Crime Act 2002) 2003 (SSI 2003/98), r.2(2)(b) (effective February 24, 2003 for provisions specified in SSI 2003/98 para.1(1)(b)(ii); March 24, 2003 otherwise).
[2] As inserted by the Act of Sederunt (Summary Applications, Statutory Applications and Appeals etc. Rules) Amendment (International Criminal Court) 2003 (SSI 2003/27), r.2(2) (effective January 24, 2003).

in the Act, and any reference to a specified paragraph in a specified schedule is a reference to the paragraph bearing that number in the schedule of that number to the Act.

(2)    This Part applies to applications to the sheriff under Parts 1 and 2 of schedule 5 to the Act.

## Investigations of proceeds of ICC crime

### Production or access orders

**3.20.2.**—(1)    An order under Part 1 of schedule 5 to the Act may be made by the sheriff on a summary application by a person authorised for the purpose under section 19 of the Act.

(2)    Any such application may be made on an ex parte application to a sheriff in chambers.

(3)    Any such application must set out reasonable grounds for suspecting—

(a)    that a specified person has benefited from an ICC crime; and

(b)    that the material to which the application relates is likely to be of substantial value (whether by itself or together with other material) to the investigation for the purposes of which the application is made.

(4)    Any application for variation or discharge of an order under Part 1 of schedule 5 to the Act shall be made by minute.

### Search warrants

**3.20.3.**—(1)    On a summary application by a person authorised under section 19 of the Act to the sheriff sitting as a court of civil jurisdiction, the sheriff may issue a warrant under Part 2 of the Act.

(2)    Any such application must set out grounds sufficient to satisfy the sheriff—

(a)    that a production or access order made in relation to material on the premises has not been complied with;

(b)    that—

(i)    there are reasonable grounds for suspecting that a specified person has benefited from an ICC crime;

(ii)    there are grounds for making a production and access order in relation to material on the premises; and

(iii)    it would not be appropriate to make a production and access order in relation to the material for any of the reasons specified in paragraph 10(4) of schedule 5 to the Act; or

(c)    that—

(i)    there are reasonable grounds for suspecting that a specified person has benefited from an ICC crime;

(ii)    there are reasonable grounds for suspecting that there is material on the premises which cannot be particularised at the time of the application, but which—

(aa)    relates to the specified person, or to the question of whether that person has benefited from an ICC crime, or to any question as to the extent or whereabouts of the proceeds of an ICC crime; and

(bb)    is likely to be of substantial value (whether by itself or together with other material) to the investigation for the purposes of which the application is made; and

(iii)    any of the circumstances specified in paragraph 10(6) of schedule 5 to the Act applies.

Part XXI[1]

## Immigration And Asylum Act 1999

### Interpretation

**3.21.1.**    In this Part—

"the Act" means the Immigration and Asylum Act 1999; and
"an appeal" means an appeal to the sheriff under section 35A(1) or section 40B(1) of the Act.

### Appeals

**3.21.2.**—(1)    A person making an appeal against a decision by the Secretary of State to impose a penalty under section 32 or a charge under section 40 of the Act must, subject to paragraph (2), bring an appeal within 21 days after receiving the penalty notice or charge notice.

(2)    Where the appellant has given notice of objection to the Secretary of State under section 35(4) or section 40A(3) of the Act within the time prescribed for doing so, he must bring an appeal within 21 days after receiving notice of the Secretary of State's decision under section 35(7) or section 40A(6) respectively of the Act in response to the notice of objection.

Part XXII[2]

## Crime and Disorder Act 1998

*[Revoked by the Act of Sederunt (Summary Applications, Statutory Applications and Appeals etc. Rules) Amendment (Antisocial Behaviour etc. (Scotland) Act 2004) 2004 (SSI 2004/455) r.2(2) (effective October 28, 2004: repeal has effect subject to transitional provisions specified in SSI 2004/455 r.2(3)).]*

Part XXIII[3]

## Ethical Standards in Public Life etc. (Scotland) Act 2000

### Application

**3.23.1.**    This Part applies to appeals to the sheriff principal under sections 22 (appeals from commission) or 26 (appeals by water industry commissioner) of the Ethical Standards in Public Life etc. (Scotland) Act 2000.

---

[1] As inserted by the Act of Sederunt (Summary Applications, Statutory Applications and Appeals etc. Rules) Amendment (Immigration and Asylum) 2003 (SSI 2003/261), r.2(2) (effective May 24, 2003).
[2] As inserted by the Act of Sederunt (Summary Applications, Statutory Applications and Appeals etc. Rules) Amendment (Standards Commission for Scotland) 2003 (SSI 2003/346), r.2(2) (effective July 4, 2003).
[3] As inserted by the Act of Sederunt (Summary Applications, Statutory Applications and Appeals etc. Rules) Amendment (Standards Commission for Scotland) 2003 (SSI 2003/346), r.2(2) (effective July 4, 2003).

## Appeals

**3.23.2.**—(1)  An appeal under this Part shall be made by summary application.

(2)  A summary application made under paragraph (1) shall include grounds of appeal stating—

    (a)  which of the findings of, or sanction or suspension imposed by, the Standards Commission for Scotland is being appealed;

    (b)  reasons why the appeal should be allowed; and

    (c)  the date of the sending of that finding, or imposition of that sanction or suspension,

and shall be accompanied by a copy of that finding, sanction or suspension.

## Warrant and form of citation

**3.23.3.**—(1)  A warrant for citation in an appeal under this Part shall be in Form 2A, or a form as near thereto as circumstances permit, and shall state—

    (a)  the date by which answers should be lodged; and

    (b)  the date and time when the appeal will call.

(2)  Citation in respect of a warrant granted under paragraph (1) shall be in Form 3A, or a form as near thereto as circumstances permit.

(3)  Where a party on whom service has been made lodges answers under paragraph (1)(a) that party shall, at the same time, send a copy to the appellant.

Part XXIV[1]

**International Protection of Adults**

## Interpretation

**3.24.1.**  In this Part—

"the Act" means the Adults with Incapacity (Scotland) Act 2000;

"the Convention" means the Hague Convention of 13th January 2000 on the International Protection of Adults;

"international measure" means any measure taken under the law of a country other than Scotland for the personal welfare, or the protection of property, of an adult with incapacity, where—

    (a)  jurisdiction in the other country was based on the adult's habitual residence there; or

    (b)  the other country and the United Kingdom were when that measure was taken parties to the Convention, and jurisdiction in that other country was based on a ground of jurisdiction in the Convention; and

"Public Guardian" shall be construed in accordance with section 6 (the public guardian and his functions) of the Act.

## Application

**3.24.2.**—(1)  An application to register an international measure under paragraph 8(1) of schedule 3 to the Act shall be by summary application made under this Part.

---

[1] As inserted by the Act of Sederunt (Summary Applications, Statutory Applications and Appeals etc. Rules) Amendment (International Protection of Adults) 2003 (SSI 2003/556), r.2(2) (effective November 14, 2003).

(2) The original document making the international measure, or a copy of that document duly certified as such by an officer of the issuing or a requesting body, shall be lodged with an application under paragraph (1), together with (as necessary) an English translation of that document and that certificate.

(3) Any translation under paragraph (2) must be certified as a correct translation by the person making it, and the certificate must contain the full name, address and qualifications of the translator.

## Intimation of application

**3.24.3.**—(1) The sheriff shall order intimation of an application to register an international measure—

    (a) except where the sheriff is satisfied that the person to whom the international measure relates had an opportunity to be heard in the country where that measure was taken, to that person;

    (b) which if registered would have the effect of placing the adult to whom the international measure relates in an establishment in Scotland, to the—

        (i) Scottish Central Authority; and

        (ii) Mental Welfare Commission;

    (c) to the Public Guardian; and

    (d) to any other person whom the sheriff considers appropriate.

  (2) In this rule—

    (a) "Scottish Central Authority" means an authority—

        (i) designated under Article 28 of the Convention for the purposes of acting as such; or

        (ii) appointed by the Scottish Ministers for the purposes of carrying out the functions to be carried out under schedule 3 of the Act by the Scottish Central Authority, where no authority is designated for the purposes of sub paragraph (i); and

    (b)[1] "Mental Welfare Commission" means the Mental Welfare Commission for Scotland continued in being by section 4 of the Mental Health (Care and Treatment) (Scotland) Act 2003.

## Notice to the Public Guardian

**3.24.4.** The sheriff clerk shall within 7 days after the date of an order registering an international measure, provide the Public Guardian with—

    (a) a copy of that order; and

    (b) a copy of the international measure, and of any translation.

## Register of recognised foreign measures

**3.24.5.**—(1) There shall be a register of international measures ("the register") registered by order under this Part.

  (2) The register shall include—

    (a) the nature of the international measure;

    (b) the date of the international measure;

---

[1] As amended by the Mental Health (Care and Treatment) (Scotland) Act 2003 (Modification of Subordinate Legislation) Order 2005 (SSI 2005/445) Sch.1 para.29(1)(b) (effective October 5, 2005).

(c) the date of the order under this Part granting recognition of the international measure;

(d) the name and address of—

    (i) the person who applied for recognition of the international measure under this Part;

    (ii) the person in respect of whom the international measure was taken; and

    (iii) if applicable, the person on whom any power is conferred by the international measure; and

(e) a copy of the international measure, and of any translation.

(3) The Public Guardian shall maintain the register, and make it available during normal office hours for inspection by members of the public.

(4) The Public Guardian shall if requested by any person certify that an international measure registered under this Part has been entered in the register.

## Part XXV[1]

### Sexual Offences Act 2003

**Interpretation**

**3.25.1.** In this Part—

"the Act" means the Sexual Offences Act 2003;

"main application" has the same meaning as in section 109(1) of the Act,[2]

and words and expressions used in this Part and in the Act shall have the meanings given in the Act.

**Time limit for service of a notice under section 99(3)**

**3.25.2.** If the person in respect of whom a notification order is sought wishes to serve on the applicant a notice under section 99(3) of the Act, that person must do so no later than 3 working days before the hearing date for the application for the relevant notification order.

**Time limit for service of a notice under section 106(11)**

**3.25.3.** If the person in respect of whom a sexual offences prevention order is sought wishes to serve on the applicant a notice under section 106(11) of the Act, that person must do so no later than 3 working days before the hearing date for the application for the relevant sexual offences prevention order.

---

[1] As inserted by the Act of Sederunt (Summary Applications, Statutory Applications and Appeals etc. Rules) Amendment (Sexual Offences Act 2003) 2004 (SSI 2004/222) r.2(2) (effective May 21, 2004).

[2] As inserted by the Act of Sederunt (Summary Applications, Statutory Applications and Appeals etc. Rules) Amendment (Protection of Children and Prevention of Sexual Offences (Scotland) Act 2005) 2005 (SSI 2005/473) r.2(2)(a) (effective October 7, 2005).

### Time limit for service of a notice under section 116(6)

**3.25.4.** If the person in respect of whom a foreign travel order is sought wishes to serve on the applicant a notice under section 116(6) of the Act, that person must do so no later than 3 working days before the hearing date for the application for the relevant foreign travel order.

### Variation, renewal or discharge of SOPOs

**3.25.5.**—[1](1) Where an application under section 108(1) of the Act for an order varying, renewing or discharging a sexual offences prevention order is made in a sheriff court other than the sheriff court in which the process relating to the sexual offences prevention order is held—

(a) the initial writ containing the application shall contain averments as to the sheriff court in which the process relating to the sexual offences prevention order is held;

(b) the sheriff clerk with whom the application is lodged shall notify the sheriff clerk of the sheriff court in which the process relating to the sexual offences prevention order is held; and

(c) the sheriff clerk of the sheriff court in which the process relating to the sexual offences prevention order is held shall, not later than 4 days after receipt of such notification, transfer the process relating to the sexual offences prevention order to the sheriff clerk of the sheriff court in which the application is made.

(2) For the purposes of paragraph (1), the sheriff court in which the process relating to the order is held is the sheriff court in which the sexual offences prevention order was granted or, where the process has been transferred under that paragraph, the last sheriff court to which the process has been transferred.

(3) A failure of the sheriff clerk to comply with paragraph (1) shall not invalidate the application.

### Variation, renewal or discharge of FTOs

**3.25.6.**—[2](1) Subject to paragraph (2), an application under section 118 of the Act for an order varying, renewing or discharging a foreign travel order shall be made by minute in the process relating to the foreign travel order.

(2) Where an application under section 118(1) of the Act for an order varying, renewing or discharging a foreign travel order is made in a sheriff court other than the sheriff court in which the process relating to the foreign travel order is held—

(a) the application shall be made by summary application;

(b) the initial writ containing the application shall contain averments as to the sheriff court in which the process relating to the foreign travel order is held;

(c) the sheriff clerk with whom the application is lodged shall notify the sheriff clerk of the sheriff court in which the process relating to the foreign travel order is held; and

---

[1] As substituted by the Act of Sederunt (Summary Applications, Statutory Applications and Appeals etc. Rules) Amendment (Protection of Children and Prevention of Sexual Offences (Scotland) Act 2005) 2005 (SSI 2005/473) r.2(2)(b) (effective October 7, 2005).

[2] As substituted by the Act of Sederunt (Summary Applications, Statutory Applications and Appeals etc. Rules) Amendment (Protection of Children and Prevention of Sexual Offences (Scotland) Act 2005) 2005 (SSI 2005/473) r.2(2)(b) (effective October 7, 2005).

(d) the sheriff clerk of the sheriff court in which the process relating to the foreign travel order is held shall, not later than 4 days after receipt of such notification, transfer the process relating to the foreign travel order to the sheriff clerk of the sheriff court in which the application is made.

(3) For the purposes of paragraph (2), the sheriff court in which the process relating to the foreign travel order is held is the sheriff court in which the foreign travel order was granted or, where the process has been transferred under that paragraph, the last sheriff court to which the process has been transferred.

(4) A minute under paragraph (1) shall be made in accordance with and regulated by Chapter 14 of the Ordinary Cause Rules.

(5) A failure of the sheriff clerk to comply with paragraph (2) shall not invalidate the application.

## Interim SOPOs

**3.25.7.**—[1](1) Subject to paragraph (2), an application under section 109(2) of the Act for an interim sexual offences prevention order shall—

(a) be made by crave in the initial writ containing the main application; and

(b) once craved, be moved by motion to that effect.

(2) Where an application under section 109(2) of the Act for an interim sexual offences prevention order is made in a sheriff court other than the sheriff court in which the main application was lodged, the application for an interim sexual offences prevention order shall be made by summary application.

(3) The initial writ in a summary application under paragraph (2) shall contain averments as to the sheriff court in which the main application was lodged.

(4) On receipt of a summary application under paragraph (2), the sheriff clerk shall notify the sheriff clerk of the sheriff court in which the main application was lodged.

(5) There shall be produced with a summary application under paragraph (2) copies of the following documents, certified as correct by the applicant's solicitor or the sheriff clerk—

(a) the initial writ containing the main application;

(b) any answers to the main application; and

(c) any interlocutors pronounced in the main application.

(6) The sheriff clerk shall send a certified copy of any interlocutor disposing of a summary application under paragraph (2) to the sheriff clerk of the sheriff court in which the main application was lodged.

(7) A failure of the sheriff clerk to comply with paragraph (4) or (6) shall not invalidate the main application or the summary application under paragraph (2).

(8) Paragraphs (3) to (7) shall apply to an application for the variation, renewal or discharge of an interim sexual offences prevention order subject to the following modifications—

(a) for references to a summary application under paragraph (2) there shall be substituted references to a summary application for the variation, renewal or discharge of an interim sexual offences prevention order;

(b) references to the main application shall include references to any ap-

---

[1] As inserted by the Act of Sederunt (Summary Applications, Statutory Applications and Appeals etc. Rules) Amendment (Protection of Children and Prevention of Sexual Offences (Scotland) Act 2005) 2005 (SSI 2005/473) r.2(2)(b) (effective October 7, 2005).

plication for an interim sexual offences prevention order and any previous application for the variation, renewal or discharge of such an order; and

(c) references to any interlocutors pronounced in the main application shall include any interlocutors pronounced in an application for an interim sexual offences prevention order or previous application for the variation, renewal or discharge of an interim sexual offences prevention order.".

Part XXVI[1]

## Protection of Children (Scotland) Act 2003

### Interpretation

**3.26.1.** In this Part—

"the Act" means the Protection of Children (Scotland) Act 2003; and
"the list" means the list of individuals considered unsuitable to work with children kept by the Scottish Ministers under section 1(1) of the Act, and cognate expressions shall be construed accordingly.

### Application

**3.26.2.** An application under section 7(6) or 14(1) or an appeal under section 15(1) of the Act shall be made by summary application.

### Provisional inclusion in the list

**3.26.3.** The sheriff may consider and dispose of an application by the Scottish Ministers under section 7(6) of the Act without intimation to, or representation by, any other person.

### Applications for removal from the list

**3.26.4.**—(1) A listed individual shall combine in a single application—

(a) a request for leave to make an application under section 14(1) of the Act;
(b) the grounds on which that individual considers that the sheriff should grant leave; and
(c) the grounds on which that individual considers that the sheriff should grant such an application.

(2) An application under paragraph (1) shall be intimated to the Scottish Ministers.

(3) The sheriff shall consider and dispose of at a preliminary hearing that part of an application relating to the request for leave under paragraph (1)(a).

---

[1] As inserted by the Act of Sederunt (Summary Applications, Statutory Applications and Appeals etc. Rules) Amendment (Protection of Children (Scotland) Act 2003) 2004 (SSI 2004/334), r.2(2) (effective July 30, 2004) and renumbered by the Act of Sederunt (Ordinary Cause, Summary Application, Summary Cause and Small Claim Rules) Amendment (Miscellaneous) 2005 (SSI 2005/648), r.3(3) (effective January 2, 2006).

### Appeal: inclusion in lists under section 5 or 6 of the Act

**3.26.5.** An appeal under section 15(1) of the Act against inclusion in the list in terms of section 5 or 6 of the Act shall be intimated to the Scottish Ministers.

### Appeals: to the sheriff principal or to the Inner House of the Court of Session

**3.26.6.** An appeal under section 15(4) of the Act to the sheriff principal or an appeal under section 15(6)(a) of the Act to the Inner House of the Court of Session shall be intimated to the Scottish Ministers.

Part XXVII[1]

**Antisocial Behaviour etc. (Scotland) Act 2004**

### Interpretation

**3.27.1.**—(1)   In this Part—

"the Act" means the Antisocial Behaviour etc. (Scotland) Act 2004;
"ASBO" means an antisocial behaviour order under section 4(1) of the Act;
"interim ASBO" means an interim ASBO under section 7(2) of the Act;
"parenting order" means a parenting order under section 13 or 102 of the Act; and
"the Principal Reporter" means the Principal Reporter appointed under section 127 of the Local Government etc. (Scotland) Act 1994.

(2)   Any reference to a section shall, unless the context otherwise requires, be a reference to a section of the Act.

### Applications for variation or revocation of ASBO s to be made by minute in the original process

**3.27.2.**—(1)   An application under section 5 (variation and revocation of antisocial behaviour orders) shall be made by minute in the original process of the application for the ASBO in relation to which the variation or revocation is sought.

(2)   Where the person subject to the ASBO is a child, a written statement containing the views of the Principal Reporter on the application referred to in rule 3.27.2(1) shall, where practicable, be lodged with that application.

### Application for an interim ASBO

**3.27.3.**—(1)   An application for an interim ASBO shall be made by crave in the initial writ in which an ASBO is sought.

(2)   An application for an interim ASBO once craved shall be moved by motion to that effect.

(3)   The sheriff shall not consider an application for an interim ASBO until after the initial writ has been intimated to the person in respect of whom that application is made and, where that person is a child, a written statement containing the views of the Principal Reporter on that application has been lodged.

---

[1] As inserted by the Act of Sederunt (Summary Applications, Statutory Applications and Appeals etc. Rules) Amendment (Antisocial Behaviour etc. (Scotland) Act 2004) 2004 (SSI 2004/455) r.2(4) (effective January 31, 2005 in relation to the provisions specified in SSI 2004/455 r.l(2)(a); April 4, 2005 in relation to the provisions specified in SSI 2004/455 r.l(2)(b); November 15, 2005 in relation to the provisions specified in SSI 2004/455 r.l(2)(c); October 28, 2004 otherwise).

**Notification of making etc. of ASBOs and interim ASBOs**

**3.27.4.** *[Repealed by the Act of Sederunt (Ordinary Cause and Summary Application Rules) Amendment (Miscellaneous) 2006 (SSI 2006/410) r.3(2) (effective August 18, 2006).]*

**Parenting orders**

**3.27.5.**—(1)   Where a sheriff is considering making a parenting order under section 13 (sheriffs power to make parenting order), the sheriff shall order the applicant for the ASBO to—

(a)   intimate to any parent in respect of whom the parenting order is being considered—

(i)   that the court is considering making a parenting order in respect of that parent;

(ii)   that if that parent wishes to oppose the making of such a parenting order, he or she may attend or be represented at the hearing at which the sheriff considers the making of the parenting order;

(iii)   the place, date and time of the hearing set out in sub-paragraph (a)(ii) above; and

(iv)   that if that parent fails to appear and is not represented at the hearing, a parenting order may be made in respect of the parent; and

(b)   serve on any parent in respect of whom the parenting order is being considered a copy of the initial writ in which the ASBO is sought.

(2)   Any parent in respect of whom a parenting order under section 13 is being considered may be sisted as a party to the action on their own motion, on the motion of either party or by the sheriff of his own motion.

**Closure notice**

**3.27.6.**—(1)   A closure notice served under section 27 (service etc.) shall be in the form of Form 25 and shall (in addition to the requirements set out in section 27(5))—

(a)   state that it has been authorised by a senior police officer;

(b)   specify the date, time and place of the hearing of the application for a closure order under section 28; and

(c)   state that any person living on or having control of, responsibility for or an interest in the premises to which the closure notice relates who wishes to oppose the application should attend or be represented.

(2)   Certification of service of a copy of the closure notice to all persons identified in accordance with section 27(2)(b) shall be in the form of Form 26.

**Application for closure orders**

**3.27.7.**   An application to the sheriff for a closure order under section 28 shall be in the form of Form 27.

**Application for extension of closure orders**

**3.27.8.**   An application to the sheriff for an extension of a closure order under section 32 shall be by minute in the form of Form 28 lodged in the original process of the application for the closure order in relation to which the extension is sought and shall be lodged not less than 21 days before the closure order to which it relates is due to expire.

### Application for revocation of closure order

**3.27.9.** An application to the sheriff for revocation of a closure order under section 33 shall be by minute in the form of Form 29 lodged in the original process of the application for the closure order in relation to which the revocation is sought.

### Application for access to premises

**3.27.10.** An application to the sheriff for an order for access to premises under section 34 shall be by minute in the form of Form 30 lodged in the original process of the application for the closure order in relation to which the access order is sought.

### Applications by summary application

**3.27.11.** An application under section 35 (Reimbursement of expenditure), 63 (Appeal against graffiti removal notice) or 64 (Appeal against notice under section 61(4)) shall be by summary application.

**3.27.12.** An application under section 71 (Failure to comply with notice: order as to rental income), 74 (Failure to comply with notice: management control order) or 97 (Appeals against notice under section 94) shall be by summary application.

### Revocation and suspension of order as to rental income

**3.27.13.** An application under section 73(2) for the revocation or suspension of an order relating to rental income shall be by minute lodged in the original process of the application for the order relating to rental income in relation to which the order for revocation or suspension is sought.

### Revocation of management control order

**3.27.14.** An application under section 76(1) for the revocation of a management control order shall be by minute lodged in the original process of the application for the management control order in relation to which the order for revocation is sought.

### Review of parenting order

**3.27.15.**—(1) An application under section 105(1) for revocation or variation of a parenting order shall be by minute lodged in the original process of the application for the parenting order in relation to which the order for revocation or variation is sought.

(2) Where the court that made a parenting order makes an order under section 105(5) that court shall within 4 days transmit the original process relating to the parenting order to the court specified in that order.

### Procedural requirements relating to parenting orders

**3.27.16.** Where the sheriff is considering making a parenting order, or a revocation or variation of a parenting order, and it is practicable, having regard to the age and maturity of the child to—

(a) give the child an opportunity to indicate whether the child wishes to express views; and

(b) if the child so wishes, give the child an opportunity to express those views,

the sheriff shall order intimation in the form of Form 31 to the child in respect of whom the order was or is proposed to be made.

**3.27.17.** Where the sheriff is considering making a parenting order or revoking or varying a parenting order and does not already have sufficient information about the child, the sheriff shall order intimation in the form of Form 32 to the local authority for the area in which the child resides.

## Enforcement of local authorities' duties under section 71 of the Children (Scotland) Act 1995

**3.27.18.** An application under section 71A(2) of the Children (Scotland) Act 1995 by the Principal Reporter shall be by summary application to the sheriff principal of the Sheriffdom in which the principal office of the local authority is situated.

Part XXVIII[1]

### Land Reform (Scotland) Act 2003

## Interpretation

**3.28.1.** In this Part—

"the Act" means the Land Reform (Scotland) Act 2003.

## Public notice of appeal against section 14(2) remedial notice

**3.28.2.** Where an owner of land appeals by summary application undersection 14(4) of the Act against a notice served on him under section 14(2) of the Act, the owner must at the same time as, or as closely in time as practicable to, the lodging of the application, advertise by publication of an advertisement in a newspaper circulating in the area of the land details of the application including details of the notice appealed against.

## Restriction on number of persons being party to section 14(4) application

**3.28.3.** Persons interested in the exercise of access rights over the land to which a summary application under section 14(2) of the Act relates, and persons or bodies representative of such persons, may be parties to the summary application proceedings, but the court may order that any one or more of the persons or bodies who have the same interests and no others, may take an active part in the proceedings.

---

[1] As inserted by the Act of Sederunt (Summary Applications, Statutory Applications and Appeals, etc. Rules) Amendment (Land Reform) (Scotland) Act 2005 (SSI 2005/61), r.2(2)(effective February 9, 2005).

**Public notice and restriction on number of parties to section 15 application**

**3.28.4.**　The provisions in rules 3.28.2 and 3.28.3 above apply with necessary modifications to a summary application appealing against a notice served under section 15(2) of the Act.

**Public notice and restriction on number of parties to section 28 application**

**3.28.5.**—(1)　The provisions in rules 3.28.2 and 3.28.3 above apply with necessary modifications to a summary application for a declaration under section 28(1) or (2) of the Act.

(2)　A summary application under section 28(1) or (2) of the Act may be made at any time.

Part XXIX[1]

### Risk of Sexual Harm Orders

**Interpretation**

**3.29.1.**　In this Part

"the Act" means the Protection of Children and Prevention of Sexual Offences (Scotland) Act 2005[5];

"main application" has the same meaning as in section 5 of the Act,

and words and expressions used in this Part and in the Act shall have the meanings given in the Act.

**Variation, renewal or discharge of RSHOs**

**3.29.2.**—(1)　Subject to paragraph (2), an application under section 4(1) of the Act for an order varying, renewing or discharging a risk of sexual harm order shall be made by minute in the process relating to the risk of sexual harm order.

(2)　Where an application under section 4(1) of the Act for an order varying, renewing or discharging a risk of sexual harm order is made in a sheriff court other than the sheriff court in which the process relating to the risk of sexual harm order is held—

　(a)　the application shall be made by summary application;

　(b)　the initial writ containing the application shall contain averments as to the sheriff court in which the process relating to the risk of sexual harm order is held;

　(c)　the sheriff clerk with whom the application is lodged shall notify the sheriff clerk of the sheriff court in which the process relating to the risk of sexual harm order is held; and

　(d)　the sheriff clerk of the sheriff court in which the process relating to the risk of sexual harm order is held shall, not later than 4 days after receipt of such notification, transfer the process relating to the risk of sexual harm order to the sheriff clerk of the sheriff court in which the application is made.

---

[1] As inserted by Act of Sederunt (Summary Applications, Statutory Applications and Appeals etc. Rules) Amendment (Protection of Children and Prevention of Sexual Offences (Scotland) Act 2005) 2005 (SSI 2005/473) r.2(3) (effective October 7, 2005).

(3)   For the purposes of paragraph (2), the sheriff court in which the process relating to the risk of sexual harm order is held is the sheriff court in which the risk of sexual harm order was granted or, where the process has been transferred under that paragraph, the last sheriff court to which the process has been transferred.

(4)   A minute under paragraph (1) shall be made in accordance with and regulated by Chapter 14 of the Ordinary Cause Rules.

(5)   A failure of the sheriff clerk to comply with paragraph (2) shall not invalidate the application.

## Interim RSHOs

**3.29.3.**—(1)   Subject to paragraph (2), an application under section 5(2) of the Act for an interim risk of sexual harm order shall—

(a)   be made by crave in the initial writ containing the main application; and

(b)   once craved, be moved by motion to that effect.

(2)   Where an application under section 5(2) of the Act for an interim risk of sexual harm order is made in a sheriff court other than the sheriff court in which the main application was lodged, the application for an interim risk of sexual harm order shall be made by summary application.

(3)   The initial writ in a summary application under paragraph (2) shall contain averments as to the sheriff court in which the main application was lodged.

(4)   On receipt of a summary application under paragraph (2), the sheriff clerk shall notify the sheriff clerk of the sheriff court in which the main application was lodged.

(5)   There shall be produced with a summary application under paragraph (2) copies of the following documents, certified as correct by the applicant's solicitor or the sheriff clerk:—

(a)   the initial writ containing the main application;

(b)   any answers to the main application; and

(c)   any interlocutors pronounced in the main application.

(6)   The sheriff clerk shall send a certified copy of any interlocutor disposing of a summary application under paragraph (2) to the sheriff clerk of the sheriff court in which the main application was lodged.

(7)   Rule 3.29.2 (variation, renewal or discharge of RSHOs) shall apply to an application for an order under section 5(6) of the Act for variation, renewal or discharge of an interim risk of sexual harm order subject to the following modifications:—

(a)   for references to section 4(1) of the Act there shall be substituted references to section 5(6) of the Act; and

(b)   for references to a risk of sexual harm order there shall be substituted references to an interim risk of sexual harm order.

(8)   A failure of the sheriff clerk to comply with paragraph (4) or (6) shall not invalidate the main application or the summary application under paragraph (2).

## Service of RSHOs

**3.29.4.**—(1)   This rule applies to—

(a)   a risk of sexual harm order;

(b)   an interim risk of sexual harm order; and

(c)   an order varying or renewing an order mentioned in sub-paragraph (a) or (b).

(2)[1] The sheriff clerk shall serve a copy of the order on the person against whom it has effect.

(3)[2] For the purposes of paragraph (2), the copy of the order is served—

   (a) where the person against whom the order has effect is present in court when the order is made—

      (i) by giving it to the person and obtaining a receipt therefor;

      (ii) by sending it to the person by recorded delivery or registered post; or

      (iii) by causing it to be served by sheriff officer; or

   (b) where the person against whom the order has effect is not present in court when the order is made—

      (i) by sending it to the person by recorded delivery or registered post; or

      (ii) by causing it to be served by sheriff officer.

(4) A failure by the sheriff clerk to comply with this rule shall not invalidate the order.

## Part XXX[3]

## Mental Health (Care and Treatment) (Scotland) Act 2003

### Interpretation

**3.30.1.** In this Part "the Act" means the Mental Health (Care and Treatment) (Scotland) Act 2003.

### Applications for removal orders

**3.30.2.**—(1) An application under section 293 of the Act (removal order to place of safety) shall be lodged with the sheriff clerk who shall fix a date for hearing the application.

(2) An order fixing a hearing shall be intimated in such manner and within such timescales as may be prescribed by the sheriff.

### Applications for recall or variation of removal orders

**3.30.3.**—(1) An application under section 295 of the Act (recall or variation of removal order) shall be lodged with the sheriff clerk who shall fix a date for hearing the application.

(2) An order fixing a hearing shall be intimated by the sheriff clerk in such manner and within such timescales as may be prescribed by the sheriff.

### Remit to Court of Session

**3.30.4.**—(1) Where the sheriff principal to whom an appeal is made remits the appeal to the Court of Session under section 320 of the Act (appeals), the sheriff

---

[1] As substituted by the Act of Sederunt (Ordinary Cause and Summary Application Rules) Amendment (Miscellaneous) 2006 (SSI 2006/410) r.3(3) (effective August 18, 2006).

[2] As substituted by the Act of Sederunt (Ordinary Cause and Summary Application Rules) Amendment (Miscellaneous) 2006 (SSI 2006/410) r.3(3) (effective August 18, 2006).

[3] As inserted by Act of Sederunt (Summary Applications, Statutory Applications and Appeals etc. Rules) Amendment (Mental Health (Care and Treatment) (Scotland) Act 2003) 2005 (SSI 2005/504) r.2(2) (effective October 6, 2005).

clerk shall, within four days after the sheriff principal has pronounced the interlocutor remitting the appeal to the Court of Session, transmit the process to the Deputy Principal Clerk of Session.

(2)  On transmitting the process under paragraph (1), the sheriff clerk shall—

(a)  send written notice of the remit and transmission of the process to each party; and

(b)  certify on the interlocutor sheet that he has done so.

## Part XXXI[1]

### Football Banning Orders

#### Interpretation

**3.31.1.**  In this Part—

"the Act" means the Police, Public Order and Criminal Justice (Scotland) Act 2006;

"football banning order" means an order made under section 52(4) of the Act.

#### Applications for variation or termination of a football banning order

**3.31.2.**—(1)  An application under—

(a)  section 57(1) of the Act for variation of a football banning order; or

(b)  section 58(1) of the Act for termination of a football banning order, shall be made by minute in the process relating to the football banning order.

(2)  A minute under paragraph (1) shall be made in accordance with and regulated by Chapter 14 of the Ordinary Cause Rules.

## Part XXXII[2]

### Animal Health and Welfare

#### Interpretation

**3.32.1.**  In this Part—

"the 1981 Act" means the Animal Health Act 1981; and

"the 2006 Act" means the Animal Health and Welfare (Scotland) Act 2006.

#### Interim orders

**3.32.2.**—(1)  An application for an interim order under—

(a)  section 28G(10) of the 1981 Act; or

(b)  section 41(9) of the 2006 Act, or

(c)[3]  section 48(9) of the Animal Welfare Act 2006,

---

[1] As inserted by the Act of Sederunt (Summary Applications, Statutory Applications and Appeals etc. (Rules) Amendment (Miscellaneous) 2006 (SSI 2006/437) r.2(2) (effective September 1, 2006).

[2] As inserted by the Act of Sederunt (Summary Applications, Statutory Applications and Appeals etc. Rules) Amendment (Miscellaneous) 2006 (SSI 2006/437) r.2(2) (effective September 1, 2006).

[3] As inserted by the Act of Sederunt (Summary Applications, Statutory Applications and Appeals etc. Rules) Amendment (Animal Welfare Act 2006) 2007 (SSI 2007/233) r.2(2) (effective March 26, 2007).

shall be made by crave in the initial writ in which a seizure order is sought.

(2)   An application for an interim order once craved shall be moved by motion to that effect.

### Interim orders pending appeal

**3.32.3.**   An application for an interim order under—
(a)   section 28H(2) of the 1981 Act; or
(b)   section 43(5) of the 2006 Act, or
(c)[1]   section 49(5) of the Animal Welfare Act 2006,
where a seizure order is suspended or inexecutable shall be made by motion.

Part XXXIII[2]

## The Equality Act 2010

### Interpretation and application

**3.33.1.**—[3](1)   In this Part—

"the Commission" means the Commission for Equality and Human Rights; and "the 2010 Act" means the Equality Act 2010.

(2)   This Part applies to claims made by virtue of section 114(1) of the 2010 Act not including a claim for damages.

### Intimation to Commission

**3.33.2.**[4]   The applicant shall, except where the applicant is the Commission, send a copy of the initial writ to the Commission by registered or recorded delivery post.

### Assessor

**3.33.3.**—(1)   The sheriff may, of his own motion or on the motion of any party, appoint an assessor.

(2)   The assessor shall be a person who the sheriff considers has special qualifications to be of assistance in determining the cause.

### Taxation of Commission expenses

**3.33.4.**   *[Omitted by the Act of Sederunt (Sheriff Court Rules) (Miscellaneous Amendments) 2008 (SSI 2008/223) r.5(3)(c) (effective July 1, 2008).]*

---

[1] As inserted by the Act of Sederunt (Summary Applications, Statutory Applications and Appeals etc. Rules) Amendment (Animal Welfare Act 2006) 2007 (SSI 2007/233) r.2(3) (effective March 26, 2007).

[2] As inserted by the Act of Sederunt (Ordinary Cause, Summary Application, Summary Cause and Small Claim Rules) Amendment (Equality Act 2006 etc.) 2006 (SSI 2006/509), (effective November 3, 2006). Chapter title amended by the Act of Sederunt (Sheriff Court Rules) (Equality Act 2010) 2010 (SSI 2010/340) para.3 (effective October 1, 2010).

[3] As substituted by the Act of Sederunt (Sheriff Court Rules) (Equality Act 2010) 2010 (SSI 2010/340) para.3 (effective October 1, 2010).

[4] As inserted by the Act of Sederunt (Sheriff Court Rules) (Miscellaneous Amendments) 2008 (SSI 2008/223) r.5(3)(b) (effective July 1, 2008).

**National security**

**3.33.5.**—[1](1)   Where, on a motion under paragraph (3) or of the sheriffs own motion, the sheriff considers it expedient in the interests of national security, the sheriff may—

    (a)   exclude from all or part of the proceedings—

        (i)   the pursuer;

        (ii)   the pursuer's representatives;

        (iii)   any assessors;

    (b)   permit a pursuer or representative who has been excluded to make a statement to the court before the commencement of the proceedings or the part of the proceedings, from which he or she is excluded;

    (c)   take steps to keep secret all or part of the reasons for his or her decision in the proceedings.

    (2)   The sheriff clerk shall, on the making of an order under paragraph (1) excluding the pursuer or the pursuer's representatives, notify the Advocate General for Scotland of that order.

    (3)   A party may apply by motion for an order under paragraph (1).

    (4)   The steps referred to in paragraph (1)(c) may include the following—

    (a)   directions to the sheriff clerk; and

    (b)   orders requiring any person appointed to represent the interests of the pursuer in proceedings from which the pursuer or the pursuer's representatives are excluded not to communicate (directly or indirectly) with any persons (including the excluded pursuer)—

        (i)   on any matter discussed or referred to;

        (ii)   with regard to any material disclosed,

during or with reference to any part of the proceedings from which the pursuer or the pursuer's representatives are excluded.

    (5)   Where the sheriff has made an order under paragraph (4)(b), the person appointed to represent the interests of the pursuer may apply by motion for authority to seek instructions from or otherwise communicate with an excluded person.

**Transfer to Employment Tribunal**

**3.33.6.**—[2](1)   On transferring proceedings to an employment tribunal under section 140(2) of the 2010 Act, the sheriff—

    (a)   shall state his or her reasons for doing so in the interlocutor; and

    (b)   may make the order on such conditions as to expenses or otherwise as he or she thinks fit.

    (2)   The sheriff clerk must, within 7 days from the date of such order—

    (a)   transmit the relevant process to the Secretary of the Employment Tribunals (Scotland);

    (b)   notify each party to the proceedings in writing of the transmission under subparagraph (a); and

    (c)   certify, by making an appropriate entry on the interlocutor sheet, that he or she has made all notifications required under subparagraph (b).

---

[1] As substituted by the Act of Sederunt (Sheriff Court Rules) (Equality Act 2010) 2010 (SSI 2010/340) para.3 (effective October 1, 2010).

[2] As inserted by the Act of Sederunt (Sheriff Court Rules) (Equality Act 2010) 2010 (SSI 2010/340) para.3 (effective October 1, 2010).

(3)   Transmission of the process under paragraph (2)(a) will be valid notwithstanding any failure by the sheriff clerk to comply with paragraph (2)(b) and (c).

**Transfer from Employment Tribunal**

**3.33.7.**—[1](1)   On receipt of the documentation in proceedings which have been remitted from an employment tribunal under section 140(3) of the 2010 Act, the sheriff clerk must—

    (a)   record the date of receipt on the first page of the documentation;

    (b)   fix a hearing to determine further procedure not less than 14 days after the date of receipt of the process; and

    (c)   forthwith send written notice of the date of the hearing fixed under subparagraph (b) to each party.

(2)   At the hearing fixed under paragraph (1)(b) the sheriff may make such order as he or she thinks fit to secure so far as practicable that the cause thereafter proceeds in accordance with these Rules.

## Part XXXIV[2]

### Licensing (Scotland) Act 2005

**Appeals**

**3.34.**—(1)   An appeal under section 131 of the Licensing (Scotland) Act 2005 is to be made by summary application.

(2)   An application under paragraph (1) must be lodged with the sheriff clerk of the sheriff court district in which the principal office of the Licensing Board is situated not later than 21 days after the relevant date.

(3)   In paragraph (2) "relevant date" means—

    (a)   the date of the decision of the Licensing Board; or

    (b)   where a statement of reasons has been required under section 51(2) of the 2005 Act, the date of issue of the statement of reasons.

## Part XXXV[3]

### Adult Support and Protection (Scotland) Act 2007

**Interpretation**

**3.35.1.**   In this Part—

"the Act" means the Adult Support and Protection (Scotland) Act 2007;
"the adult at risk" has the same meaning as in section 3 of the Act.

---

[1] As inserted by the Act of Sederunt (Sheriff Court Rules) (Equality Act 2010) 2010 (SSI 2010/340) para.3 (effective October 1, 2010).

[2] As inserted by the Act of Sederunt (Summary Applications, Statutory Applications and Appeals etc. Rules) Amendment (Licensing (Scotland) Act 2005) 2008 (SSI 2008/9) r.2(2) (effective February 1, 2008) and substituted by the Act of Sederunt (Sheriff Court Rules) (Miscellaneous Amendments) (No.2) 2010 (SSI 2010/416) r.9 (effective December 13, 2010).

[3] As inserted by the Act of Sederunt (Summary Applications, Statutory Applications and Appeals etc. Rules) Amendment (Adult Support and Protection (Scotland) Act 2007) (No.2) 2008 (SSI 2008/335) r.2(2) (effective October 29, 2008).

## Variation or recall of removal order

**3.35.2.**—(1)   An application under section 17 of the Act (variation or recall of removal order) for variation or recall of a removal order shall be made by minute in the process relating to the removal order.

(2)   A minute under paragraph (1) shall be made in accordance with and regulated by Chapter 14 of the Ordinary Cause Rules.

## Applications—banning orders and temporary banning orders

**3.35.3.**—(1)   Where in an application under subsection (1) of section 19 of the Act (banning orders) an order is sought under subsection (2)(a) or (b) of that section there shall, where appropriate and unless the sheriff otherwise directs, be lodged a plan which clearly identifies the area specified in the application.

(2)   An application under section 21 of the Act (temporary banning orders) shall—

    (a)   be made by crave in the application for the banning order concerned; and

    (b)   once craved, be moved by motion to that effect.

(3)   Where a temporary banning order is granted, the related application for a banning order shall be determined within 6 months of the date of the lodging of that application.

(4)   An application under section 24(1)(a) of the Act (variation or recall of banning order) shall be made by minute in the process relating to the banning order.

(5)   An application under section 24(1)(b) of the Act (variation or recall of temporary banning order) shall be moved by motion to that effect in the process relating to the application for the banning order concerned.

(6)   A minute under paragraph (4) shall be made in accordance with and regulated by Chapter 14 of the Ordinary Cause Rules.

## Attachment of power of arrest

**3.35.4.**—(1)   The following documents shall be served under section 25(2) of the Act (powers of arrest) along with a power of arrest—

    (a)   a copy of the application for the order;

    (b)   a copy of the interlocutor granting the order and the power of arrest; and

    (c)   where the application to attach the power of arrest was made after the order was granted, a copy of the certificate of service of the order.

(2)   The following documents shall be delivered to the chief constable in accordance with section 27(1) of the Act (notification to police)—

    (a)   a copy of the application for the order;

    (b)   a copy of the interlocutor granting the order;

    (c)   a copy of the certificate of service of the order; and

    (d)   where the application to attach the power of arrest was made after the order was granted—

        (i)   where applicable, a copy of the application for the power of arrest;

        (ii)   a copy of the interlocutor granting it; and

        (iii)   a copy of the certificate of service of the power of arrest and the documents that required to be served along with it in accordance with section 25(2).

(3) *[Revoked by the Act of Sederunt (Summary Applications, Statutory Applications and Appeals etc. Rules) Amendment (Adult Support and Protection (Scotland) Act 2007) (No.3) 2008 (SSI 2008/375) r.2(2) (effective November 20, 2008).]*

### Notification to adult at risk etc.

**3.35.5.**[1]   Where section 26(1)(b) of the Act (notification to the adult at risk etc. on the variation or recall of a banning order or temporary banning order) applies, the person prescribed for the purposes of section 26(2) is the sheriff clerk.

### Certificate of delivery of documents

**3.35.6.**[2]   Where a person is in any circumstances required to comply with section 26(2), 27(1) or 27(2) of the Act he shall, after such compliance, lodge in process a certificate of delivery in Form 34.

### Warrants for entry

**3.35.7.**—(1)   An application for a warrant for entry under section 38(2) of the Act (criteria for granting warrants of entry under section 7) shall be in Form 35.

(2)   The application may be granted without a hearing.

### Form of appeal to the sheriff principal

**3.35.8.**—(1)   An appeal under section 51(2) of the Act (appeals) against an interlocutor of the sheriff granting, or refusing to grant, a banning order shall be lodged within 14 days after the date of the interlocutor concerned.

(2)   An application for leave to appeal against an interlocutor of the sheriff granting, or refusing to grant, a temporary banning order under section 51(2) of the Act shall be made within 7 days after the date of the interlocutor concerned.

(3)   An appeal against an interlocutor referred to in paragraph (2) shall be lodged within 7 days after the date of the interlocutor granting leave to appeal.

### Privacy of any hearing

**3.35.9.**   The sheriff may, where he considers it appropriate in all the circumstances, appoint that the hearing of an application or other proceedings under this Part shall take place in private.

### Part XXXVI[3]

---

[1] As substituted by the Act of Sederunt (Summary Applications, Statutory Applications and Appeals etc. Rules) Amendment (Adult Support and Protection (Scotland) Act 2007) (No.3) 2008 (SSI 2008/375) r.2(3) (effective November 20, 2008).

[2] As substituted by the Act of Sederunt (Summary Applications, Statutory Applications and Appeals etc. Rules) Amendment (Adult Support and Protection (Scotland) Act 2007) (No.3) 2008 (SSI 2008/375) r.2(4) (effective November 20, 2008).

[3] As inserted by the Act of Sederunt (Sheriff Court Rules) (Miscellaneous Amendments) (No.2) 2008 (SSI 2008/365) r.6 (effective November 25, 2006).

## Interpretation

**3.36.1.** In this Part—

"the Act" means the UK Borders Act 2007; and
"an appeal" means an appeal to the sheriff under section 11(1) of the Act.

## Appeals

**3.36.2.**—(1) Subject to paragraph (2), an appeal must be lodged with the sheriff clerk not later than 21 days after the date the penalty notice was received by the appellant.

(2) Where the appellant has given notice of objection under section 10(1) of the Act, an appeal must be lodged with the sheriff clerk not later than 21 days after the date that notice of the Secretary of State's decision under section 10(4) of the Act was received by the appellant.

Part XXXVII[1]

### Employment Tribunals Act 1996

### Conciliation: recovery of sums payable under compromises

**3.37.1.**—(1) An application to the sheriff for a declaration under section 19A(4) of the Employment Tribunals Act 1996 shall be made not later than 42 days from the date of issue of the certificate stating that a compromise has been reached.

(2) An application to the sheriff for a declaration under section 19A(4) of that Act is pending for the purposes of subsection (7) of that section from the date on which it is lodged with the sheriff clerk until the date upon which final judgment on the application has been extracted.

Part XXXVIII[2]

### Counter-Terrorism Act 2008

### Variation, renewal or discharge of foreign travel restriction order

**3.38.**—(1) Where an application under paragraph 9 of Schedule 5 to the Counter-Terrorism Act 2008 for an order varying, renewing or discharging a foreign travel restriction order is made in a sheriff court other than the sheriff court in which the process relating to the foreign travel restriction order is held—

    (a) the initial writ containing the application shall contain averments as to the sheriff court in which the process relating to the foreign travel restriction order is held;

    (b) the sheriff clerk with whom the application is lodged shall notify the sheriff clerk of the sheriff court in which the process relating to the foreign travel restriction order is held; and

---

[1] As inserted by the Act of Sederunt (Summary Applications, Statutory Applications and Appeals etc. Rules) Amendment (Employment Tribunals Act 1996) 2009 (SSI 2009/109) r.2 (effective April 1, 2009).

[2] As inserted by the Act of Sederunt (Sheriff Court Rules) (Miscellaneous Amendments) 2009 (SSI 2009/294) r.18 (effective October 1, 2009).

(c)   the sheriff clerk of the sheriff court in which the process relating to the foreign travel restriction order is held shall, not later than 4 days after receipt of such notification, transfer the process relating to the foreign travel restriction order to the sheriff clerk of the sheriff court in which the application is made.

(2)   For the purposes of paragraph (1), the sheriff court in which the process relating to the order is held is the sheriff court in which the foreign travel restriction order was granted or, where the process has been transferred under that paragraph, the last sheriff court to which the process has been transferred.

(3)   A failure of the sheriff clerk to comply with paragraph (1) shall not invalidate the application.

## Part XXXIX[1]

## Public Health etc. (Scotland) Act 2008

### Interpretation

**3.39.1.**   In this Part—

"the Act" means the Public Health etc. (Scotland) Act 2008;

"an investigator" means a person appointed under section 21 of the Act;

"health board competent person" has the same meaning as in section 124 of the Act, and words and expressions used in this Part and in the Act shall have the same meaning given in the Act.

### Application for a public health investigation warrant

**3.39.2.**—(1)   An application made by an investigator for a warrant under section 27(2) of the Act (public health investigation warrants) shall be in Form 36.

(2)   Where such a warrant is granted by the sheriff it shall be in Form 37.

### Application for an order for medical examination

**3.39.3.**—(1)   An application made by a health board for an order under section 34(1) of the Act (order for medical examination) shall be in Form 38.

(2)   On receipt of an application mentioned in paragraph (1), the sheriff may order intimation of the application to such persons, within such a timescale and by such method as he sees fit.

(3)   Where an order for a medical examination is granted by the sheriff it shall be in Form 39.

(4)   Subject to the requirements of section 34(6)(b)(i) and (ii) of the Act, where an order for a medical examination is granted, the sheriff may direct that the order be notified to such persons, within such a timescale and by such method as he sees fit.

(5)   For the avoidance of doubt, the method of intimation or notification referred to in paragraphs (2) and (4) may include intimation or notification by telephone, email or facsimile transmission.

---

[1] As inserted by the Act of Sederunt (Summary Applications, Statutory Applications and Appeals etc. Rules) Amendment (Public Health etc. (Scotland) Act 2008) 2009 (SSI 2009/320) r.2 (effective October 1, 2009).

## Application for a quarantine order

**3.39.4.**—(1)   An application made by a health board for a quarantine order under section 40(1) of the Act (quarantine orders) shall be in Form 40.

(2)   On receipt of an application mentioned in paragraph (1), the sheriff may order intimation of the application to such persons, within such a timescale and by such method as he sees fit.

(3)   Where a quarantine order is granted by the sheriff it shall be in Form 41.

(4)   Subject to the requirements of section 40(6)(b)(i) and (ii) of the Act, where a quarantine order is granted, the sheriff may direct that the order be notified to such persons, within such a timescale and by such method as he sees fit.

(5)   For the avoidance of doubt, the method of intimation or notification referred to in paragraphs (2) and (4) may include intimation or notification by telephone, email or facsimile transmission.

## Application for a short term detention order

**3.39.5.**—(1)   An application made by a health board for a short term detention order under section 42(1) of the Act (order for removal to and detention in hospital) shall be in Form 42.

(2)   An application made by a health board for a short term detention order under section 43(1) of the Act (order for detention in hospital) shall be in Form 44.

(3)   On receipt of an application mentioned in paragraph (1) or (2), the sheriff may order intimation of the application to such persons, within such a timescale and by such method as he sees fit.

(4)   Where a short term detention order is granted by the sheriff under section 42(1) of the Act it shall be in Form 43.

(5)   Where a short term detention order is granted by the sheriff under section 43(1) of the Act it shall be in Form 45.

(6)   Subject to the requirements of sections 42(4)(b)(i) and (ii) and 43(4)(b)(i) and (ii) of the Act, where a short term detention order is granted under section 42(1) or 43(1) of the Act, the sheriff may direct that the order be notified to such persons, within such a timescale and by such method as he sees fit.

(7)   For the avoidance of doubt, the method of intimation or notification referred to in paragraphs (3) and (6) may include intimation or notification by telephone, email or facsimile transmission.

## Application for an exceptional detention order

**3.39.6.**—(1)   An application made by a health board for an exceptional detention order under section 45(1) of the Act (exceptional detention order) shall be in Form 46.

(2)   On receipt of an application mentioned in paragraph (1), the sheriff may order intimation of the application to such persons, within such a timescale and by such method as he sees fit.

(3)   Where an exceptional detention order is granted by the sheriff it shall be in Form 47.

(4)   Subject to the requirements of section 45(4)(b)(i) and (ii) of the Act, where an exceptional detention order is granted, the sheriff may direct that the order be notified to such persons, within such a timescale and by such method as he sees fit.

(5)   For the avoidance of doubt, the method of intimation or notification referred to in paragraphs (2) and (4) may include intimation or notification by telephone, email or facsimile transmission.

### Application for extension of a quarantine order, short term detention order or exceptional detention order

**3.39.7.**—(1)   An application made by a health board for an extension to a quarantine order, a short term detention order or an exceptional detention order under section 49(5) of the Act (extension of quarantine and hospital detention orders) shall be in Form 48.

(2)   On receipt of an application mentioned in paragraph (1), the sheriff may order intimation of the application to such persons, within such a timescale and by such method as he sees fit.

(3)   Where an order extending a quarantine order, a short term detention order or an exceptional detention order is granted by the sheriff it shall be in Form 49.

(4)   Subject to the requirements of section 49(10)(b)(i) and (ii) of the Act, where an order mentioned in paragraph (3) is granted, the sheriff may direct that the order be notified to such persons, within such a timescale and by such method as he sees fit.

(5)   For the avoidance of doubt, the method of intimation or notification referred to in paragraphs (2) and (4) may include intimation or notification by telephone, email or facsimile transmission.

### Application for modification of a quarantine order, short term detention order or exceptional detention order

**3.39.8.**—(1)   An application made by a health board for an order modifying a quarantine order, a short term detention order or an exceptional detention order under section 51(1) of the Act (variation of quarantine and hospital detention orders) shall be in Form 50.

(2)   On receipt of an application mentioned in paragraph (1), the sheriff may order intimation of the application to such persons, within such a timescale and by such method as he sees fit.

(3)   Where an order modifying a quarantine order, a short term detention order or an exceptional detention order is granted by the sheriff it shall be in Form 51.

(4)   Subject to the requirements of section 51(5)(b)(i) and (ii) of the Act, where an order mentioned in paragraph (3) is granted, the sheriff may direct that the order be notified to such persons, within such a timescale and by such method as he sees fit.

(5)   For the avoidance of doubt, the method of intimation or notification referred to in paragraphs (2) and (4) may include intimation or notification by telephone, email or facsimile transmission.

### Application for recall of an order granted in the absence of the person to whom it relates

**3.39.9.**—(1)   An application for recall of a quarantine order, a short term detention order or an exceptional detention order under section 59 of the Act (recall of orders granted in absence of persons to whom application relates) shall be in Form 52.

(2)    Subject to section 59(6) of the Act, on receipt of an application mentioned in paragraph (1), the sheriff may order intimation of the application to such persons, within such a timescale and by such method as he sees fit.

(3)    Where an order recalling a quarantine order, a short term detention order or an exceptional detention order is granted by the sheriff it shall be in Form 53.

(4)    Where an order mentioned in paragraph (3) is granted, the sheriff may direct that the order be notified to such persons, within such a timescale and by such method as he sees fit.

(5)    For the avoidance of doubt, the method of intimation or notification referred to in paragraphs (2) and (4) may include intimation or notification by telephone, email or facsimile transmission.

### Intimation of applications in relation to a child

**3.39.10.**—(1)    This rule applies where an application is made under this Part and the person who it is proposed will be subject to the order is under 16.

(2)    On receipt of an application mentioned in paragraph (1), the sheriff may, in particular, order intimation of the application to a person who has day-to-day care or control of the person mentioned in paragraph (1).

### Intimation of orders on the person to whom they apply

**3.39.11.**    Where a sheriff, in the absence of the person to whom it applies, grants—

(a)    a quarantine order under section 40(1) of the Act;

(b)    a short term detention order under section 42(1) of the Act;

(c)    an exceptional detention order under section 45 of the Act,

and the order is intimated to the person to whom it applies, a copy of Form 52 shall be delivered to that person along with the order.

### Appeal to the sheriff against an exclusion order or a restriction order

**3.39.12.**—(1)    An appeal to the sheriff under section 61 of the Act (appeal against exclusion orders and restriction orders) in respect of an exclusion order or a restriction order shall be marked by lodging a note of appeal in Form 54.

(2)    On the lodging of a note of appeal, the sheriff clerk shall send a copy of the note of appeal to—

(a)    the health board competent person who made the exclusion order or restriction order; and

(b)    the person in relation to whom the order applies, where that person is not the appellant.

(3)    The sheriff shall make such order as he thinks fit in order to dispose of the appeal.

### Application for a warrant to enter premises and take steps under Part 5 of the Act

**3.39.13.**—(1)    An application made by a local authority for a warrant under section 78(2) of the Act (warrant to enter and take steps) shall be in Form 55.

(2)    Where such a warrant is granted by the sheriff it shall be in Form 56.

**Application for an order for disposal of a body**

**3.39.14.**—(1)    An application made by a local authority for an order for the disposal of a body under section 93 of the Act (power of sheriff to order removal to mortuary and disposal) shall be in Form 57.

(2)    Where such an order is granted by the sheriff it shall be in Form 58.

**Application for appointment of a single arbiter to determine a dispute in relation to compensation**

**3.39.15.**    An application under sections 30(6), 56(5), 57(3), 58(4) or 82(3) of the Act for the appointment of a single arbiter to determine a dispute in relation to compensation may be made by written application in the form of a letter addressed to the sheriff clerk.

Part XL[1]

**Forced Marriage etc. (Protection and Jurisdiction) (Scotland) Act 2011**

**Interpretation**

**3.40.1.**    In this Part (except where the context otherwise requires) references to terms defined in Part 1 of the Forced Marriage etc. (Protection and Jurisdiction) (Scotland) Act 2011 have the same meaning here as given there.

**Applications for leave for a forced marriage protection order**

**3.40.2.**—(1)    This rule applies where leave of the court is required to make an application for a forced marriage protection order.

(2)    Leave shall be sought at the time of presenting the initial writ by letter addressed to the sheriff clerk.

(3)    The letter shall include a statement of—

    (a)    the grounds on which leave is sought;

    (b)    whether or not the applicant has applied for legal aid.

(4)    Where the applicant has applied for legal aid he or she must also present along with the initial writ written confirmation from the Scottish Legal Aid Board that it has determined, under regulation 7(2)(b) of the Civil Legal Aid (Scotland) Regulations 2002, that notification of the application should be dispensed with or postponed.

(5)    An application under paragraph (2) shall not be served or intimated unless the sheriff otherwise directs.

(6)    The sheriff may hear the pursuer on the application and may grant or refuse it or make such other order in relation to it as the sheriff considers appropriate.

(7)    Where leave is granted, a copy of the interlocutor allowing leave must be served upon the defender along with the warrant of citation.

---

[1] As inserted by the Act of Sederunt (Sheriff Court Rules) (Miscellaneous Amendments) (No.3) 2011 (SSI 2011/386) para.7 (effective November 28, 2011).

## Applications for variation, recall or extension of a forced marriage protection order

**3.40.3.**—(1)   An application for variation, recall or extension of a forced marriage protection order must be made by minute in the process relating to the forced marriage protection order.

(2)   Except where the sheriff otherwise directs, any such minute must be lodged in accordance with, and regulated by, Chapter 14 of the Ordinary Cause Rules.

(3)   Paragraph (4) applies where leave of the court is required under section 7(1)(d) or 8(3)(d) of the 2011 Act before an application for variation, or recall or extension of a forced marriage protection order may be made.

(4)   Leave shall be sought at the time of presenting the minute by letter addressed to the sheriff clerk.

(5)   The letter shall include a statement of—
  (a)   the grounds on which leave is sought;
  (b)   whether or not the applicant has applied for legal aid.

(6)   Where the applicant has applied for legal aid he or she must also present along with the minute confirmation from the Scottish Legal Aid Board that it has determined, under regulation 7(2)(b) of the Civil Legal Aid (Scotland) Regulations 2002, that notification of the application should be dispensed with or postponed.

(7)   An application under paragraph (4) shall not be served or intimated unless the sheriff otherwise directs.

(8)   The sheriff may hear the applicant on the application and may grant or refuse it or make such other order in relation to it as the sheriff considers appropriate.

(9)   Where leave is granted, a copy of the interlocutor allowing leave must be intimated along with the minute.

## Part XLI[1, 2]

### Reporting Restrictions under the Contempt of Court Act 1981

## Interpretation and application of this Part

**3.41.1.**   In this Part "the 1981 Act" means the Contempt of Court Act 1981.

## Notification of reporting restrictions etc.

**3.41.2.**—(1)   Paragraph (2) applies where the sheriff makes an order under section 4(2) of the 1981 Act (order postponing publication of report of legal proceedings).

(2)   The sheriff clerk shall immediately arrange—
  (a)   for a copy of the order to be sent to those persons who have asked to see any such order made by the sheriff and whose names are on the list kept by the Lord President for that purpose;
  (b)   for the publication of the making of the order on the website used to provide official information about the Scottish courts.

---

[1] As inserted by the Act of Sederunt (Sheriff Court Rules) (Miscellaneous Amendments) (No.3) 2011 (SSI 2011/386) para.8 (effective November 28, 2011).

[2] As amended by the Act of Sederunt (Sheriff Court Rules) (Miscellaneous Amendments) 2012 (SSI 2012/188) para.12 (effective August 1, 2012).

## Applications for variation or revocation

**3.41.3.**—(1)  A person aggrieved by the terms of an order made under section 4(2) of the 1981 Act may apply to the sheriff for its variation or revocation.

(2)  An application shall be made by letter addressed to the sheriff clerk.

(3)  On an application being made the sheriff shall—

(a)  appoint the application for a hearing;

(b)  order written intimation of the date and time of the hearing, together with a copy of the application, to the parties to the proceedings.

(4)  The hearing shall—

(a)  unless there are exceptional circumstances or a later date is requested by the applicant, take place within 48 hours of receipt of the application by the sheriff clerk;

(b)  so far as reasonably practicable, be before the sheriff who made the order.

(5)  The decision of the sheriff is final.

## Part XLII[1]

### Regulation of Investigatory Powers Act 2000

## Interpretation

**3.42.1.**  In this Part—

"the 2000 Act" means the Regulation of Investigatory Powers Act 2000; and words and expressions used in this Part and in the 2000 Act shall have the same meaning given in the 2000 Act.

## Authorisations requiring judicial approval

**3.42.2.**—(1)  An application under section 23B(1) of the 2000 Act (procedure for judicial approval) for an order under section 23A(2) (authorisations requiring judicial approval)—

(a)  approving the grant or renewal of an authorisation; or

(b)  the giving or renewal of a notice,

shall be in Form 59, which must be signed by a solicitor on behalf of the local authority.

(2)  The application (and any order made in relation to it) must not be intimated to—

(a)  the person to whom the authorisation or notice which is the subject of the application or order relates; or

(b)  such person's representatives.

(3)  The application must be heard and determined by the sheriff in private.

(4)  Where an application is granted by the sheriff the order shall be in Form 60.

---

[1] As inserted by the Act of Sederunt (Sheriff Court Rules) (Miscellaneous Amendments) (No.3) 2012 (SSI 2012/271) para.10 (effective November 1, 2012).

SCHEDULE 1

FORMS

**Rule 1.2(3)**


Form A1[1]

Rule 1A.2(2)(b)

Statement by prospective lay representative for Pursuer/Defender*

Case Ref. No.:

in the cause

SHERIFFDOM OF (*insert name of sheriffdom*)

AT (*insert place of sheriff court*)

[A.B.], (*insert designation and address*), Pursuer

against

[C.D.], (*insert designation and address*), Defender

Court ref. no:

| Name and address of prospective lay representative who requests to make oral submissions on behalf of party litigant: | |
|---|---|
| Identify hearing(s) in respect of which permission for lay representation is sought: | |
| The prospective lay representative declares that: | |
| (a) | I have no financial interest in the outcome of the case *or* I have the following financial interest in it:* |
| (b) | I am not receiving remuneration or other reward directly or indirectly from the litigant for my assistance and will not receive directly or indirectly such remuneration or other reward from the litigant. |
| (c) | I accept that documents and information are provided to me by the litigant on a confidential basis and I undertake to keep them confidential. |
| (d) | I have no previous convictions *or* I have the following convictions: (list convictions)* |
| (e) | I have not been declared a vexatious litigant under the Vexatious Actions (Scotland) Act 1898 *or* I was declared a vexatious litigant under the Vexatious Actions (Scotland) Act 1898 on [insert date].* |

(*Signed*)

[Name of prospective lay representative]

[Date]

(*Insert Place/Date*)

The Sheriff grants/refuses* the application.

[*Signed*]

Sheriff Clerk

[Date]

(*\*delete as appropriate*)

Form 1

Rule 2.4(1)

Form of initial writ

SUMMARY APPLICATION UNDER (*title & section of statute or statutory instrument*)

INITIAL WRIT

SHERIFFDOM OF (*insert name of sheriffdom*)

AT (*insert place of sheriff court*)

[A.B.] (*design and state any special capacity in which the pursuer is suing*) Pursuer

---

[1] As inserted by the Act of Sederunt (Sheriff Court Rules) (Lay Representation) 2013 (SSI 2013/91) r.3 (effective April 4, 2013).

against

[C.D.] (*design and state any special capacity in which the defender is being sued*) Defender

The Pursuer craves the court (*here state the specific decree, warrant or order sought*)

CONDESCENDENCE

(*State in numbered paragraphs the facts which form the ground of action*)

PLEAS-IN-LAW

(*State in numbered sentences*)

Signed

[A.B.], Pursuer

or [X.Y.], solicitor for the Pursuer

(*state designation and business address*)

FORM 2

Rule 2.7(4)(a)

[Form of warrant of citation]

(*Insert place and date*). Grants warrant to cite the defender (*insert name and address*) by serving upon him [*or* her] a copy of the writ and warrant [on a period of notice of (*insert period of notice*) days], [and ordains him [*or* her] to answer within the Sheriff Court House (*insert place of sheriff court*) [in Room No. .........., or in Chambers, *or otherwise, as the case may be*], on the .......... day of .......... at .......... o'clock .......... noon] [*or otherwise, as the case may be*] [and grants warrant to arrest on the dependence].

Signed

Sheriff [*or* sheriff clerk]

Rule 3.18.3(1)                              FORM 2A[1]

Form of warrant of citation

(*Insert place and date*). Grants warrant to cite (*insert name and address of parties specified by sheriff principal*) by serving upon them a copy of the writ and warrant on a period of notice of 21 days and ordains them if they wish to oppose the application—

(a) to lodge answers within the period of notice; and

(b) to be represented within the Sheriff Court House (*insert place and address of sheriff court*) [in Room No..........., *or otherwise, as the case may be*], on the..........day of at..........o'clock.......... noon [*or otherwise, as the case may be*].

Signed

Sheriff [*or* sheriff clerk]

Rule 2.7(4)(b)                              FORM 3

Form of citation for summary application

CITATION FOR SUMMARY APPLICATION

SHERIFFDOM OF (*insert name of sheriffdom*)

AT (*insert place of sheriff court*)

[A.B.], (*insert designation and address*) Pursuer

against

[C.D.], (*insert designation and address*) Defender

Court ref. no.

(*Insert place and date*). You [.CD.] are hereby served with this copy writ and warrant, and are required to answer it.

**IF YOU ARE UNCERTAIN AS TO WHAT ACTION TO TAKE** you should consult a solicitor. You may be eligible for legal aid depending on your income, and you can get information about legal aid from a solicitor. You may also obtain advice from any Citizens' Advice Bureau or other advice agency.

**PLEASE NOTE THAT IF YOU DO NOTHING IN ANSWER TO THIS DOCUMENT** the court may regard you as admitting the claim made against you and the pursuer may obtain decree against you in your absence.

---

[1] Inserted by the Act of Sederunt (Summary Applications, Statutory Applications and Appeals etc. Rules) Amendment (No.2) (Local Government (Scotland) Act 1973) 2002 (S.S.I. 2002 No. 130), para.2(4) and Sched.

Signed
[PQ.], Sheriff Officer,
or [X.Y] (*add designation and business address*)
Solicitor for the Pursuer

Rule 3.18.3(2)                                   FORM 3A[1]

Form of citation for summary application
CITATION FOR SUMMARY APPLICATION
SHERIFFDOM OF (*insert name of sheriffdom*)
AT (*insert place of sheriff court*)
[A.B.], (*insert designation and address*), Applicant
against
[C.D.], (*insert designation and address*), Respondent
Court ref. no.

(*Insert place and date*). You [C.D.] are hereby served with this copy writ and warrant, and are required to answer it.

If you wish to oppose the application, you—

(a) must lodge answers with the sheriff clerk at (*insert place and address of sheriff court*) sheriff court, (*insert address*) not later than (*insert date*), and at the same time, send a copy of the answers to the Applicant; and

(b) should be represented within the Sheriff Court House (*insert place and address of sheriff court*) [in Room No..........., or otherwise, as the case may be] on the day of at..........o'clock.......... noon [*or otherwise as the case maybe*].

**PLEASE NOTE THAT IF YOU DO NOTHING IN ANSWER TO THIS DOCUMENT** the court may regard you as admitting the appeal and the Applicant may obtain decree against you in your absence.

Signed
[P.Q.], Sheriff Officer, or [X.Y.]
(*add designation and business address*)
Solicitor for the Applicant

Rule 2.7(5)                                   FORM 4[2]

Form of warrant of citation where time to pay direction or time order may be applied for

(*Insert place and date*). *Grants warrant to cite the defender (insert name and address*) by serving a copy of the writ and warrant, together with Form 5, [on a period of notice of (*insert period of notice*) days*] and ordains him [*or* her] if he [*or* she]—

(a) intends to defend the action or make any claim [to answer within the Sheriff Court House (*insert place and address of sheriff court*) [in Room No..........., or in Chambers, *or otherwise, as the case may be*], on the..........day of..........at..........o'clock..........noon] [*or otherwise as the case may be*] or

(b) admits the claim and intends to apply for a time to pay direction or time order (and where appropriate apply for recall or restriction of an arrestment) [either to appear at that diet and make such application or] to lodge the appropriate part of Form 5 duly completed with the sheriff clerk at (*insert place of sheriff court*) at least fourteen days before [the diet or the expiry of the period of notice *or otherwise, as the case may be*] [and grants warrant to arrest on the dependence].

Signed
Sheriff [*or* sheriff clerk]

Rule 2.7(6) and 2.22(2)(b)                       FORM 5[3, 4]

---

[1] Inserted by the Act of Sederunt (Summary Applications, Statutory Applications and Appeals etc. Rules) Amendment (No.2) (Local Government (Scotland) Act 1973) 2002 (S.S.I. 2002 No. 130), para.2(4) and Sched.

[2] As amended by SSI 2007/6 (effective January 29, 2007) and SSI 2009/294 (effective December 1, 2009).

[3] As amended by SSI 2007/6 (effective January 29, 2007) and substituted by Act of Sederunt (Sheriff Court Rules)(Miscellaneous Amendments) 2009 (SSI 2009/294) r.2 (effective December 1, 2009).

[4] As amended by the Act of Sederunt (Sheriff Court Rules)(Miscellaneous Amendments) 2011 (SSI 2011/193) r.10 (effective April 3, 2011).

Form of notice to be served on defender where time to pay direction or time order may be applied for

Rule 2.7(6) and 2.22(2)(b)                    ACTION RAISED BY

                             PURSUER                    DEFENDER

AT...............SHERIFF COURT
(Including address)
COURT REF. NO.

**THIS SECTION MUST BE COMPLETED BY THE PURSUER BEFORE SERVICE**

(1) Time to pay directions

The Debtors (Scotland) Act 1987 gives you the right to apply to the court for a "time to pay direction" which is an order permitting you to pay any sum of money you are ordered to pay to the pursuer (which may include interest and court expenses) either by way of instalments or deferred lump sum. A deferred lump sum means that you must pay all the amount at one time within a period specified by the court.

When making a time to pay direction the court may recall or restrict an arrestment made on your property by the pursuer in connection with the action or debt (for example, your bank account may have been frozen).

(2) Time Orders

The Consumer Credit Act 1974 allows you to apply to the court for a "time order" during a court action, to ask the court to give you more time to pay a loan agreement. **A time order is similar to a time to pay direction, but can only be applied for where the court action is about a credit agreement regulated by the Consumer Credit Act**. The court has power to grant a time order in respect of a regulated agreement to reschedule payment of the sum owed. This means that a time order can change:

- the amount you have to pay each month
- how long the loan will last
- in some cases, the interest rate payable

A time order can also stop the creditor taking away any item bought by you on hire purchase or conditional sale under the regulated agreement, so long as you continue to pay the instalments agreed.

**HOW TO APPLY FOR A TIME TO PAY DIRECTION OR TIME ORDER WHERE YOU ADMIT THE CLAIM AND YOU DO NOT WANT TO DEFEND THE ACTION**

1. The appropriate application forms are attached to this notice. After completing the appropriate form it should be returned to the Sheriff Court at least fourteen days before the date of the first hearing or expiry of the period of notice or otherwise, as the case may be, in the warrant of citation. The address of the court is shown on page 1 of the application. No court fee is payable when lodging the application.

2. Before completing the application please read carefully the notes on how to complete the application. In the event of difficulty you may contact the court's civil department at the address above or any sheriff clerk's office, solicitor, Citizens Advice Bureau or other advice agency. Written guidance can also be obtained from the Scottish Court Service website (www.scotcourts.gov.uk).

**WHAT WILL HAPPEN NEXT**

If the pursuer objects to your application, a hearing will be fixed and the court will advise you in writing of the date and time.

If the pursuer does not object to your application, a copy of the court order for payment (called an extract decree) will be served on you by the pursuer's solicitor advising when instalment payments should commence or deferred payment be made.

Court ref. no.

**APPLICATION FOR A TIME TO PAY DIRECTION UNDER THE DEBTORS (SCOTLAND) ACT 1987**

**\*PART A**                              BY

**\*(This section must be
completed by pursuer
before service)**

                                        DEFENDER

                                        **In an action raised by**
                                        PURSUER

**HOW TO COMPLETE THE APPLICATION**
PLEASE WRITE IN INK USING BLOCK CAPITALS

**PART A** of the application will have been completed in advance by the pursuer and gives details of the pursuer and you as the defender.

**PART B** If you wish to apply to pay by instalments enter the amount and tick the appropriate box at B3(1). If you wish to apply to pay the full sum due in one deferred payment enter the period of deferment you propose at B3(2).

**PART C** Give full details of your financial position in the space provided.

**PART D** If you wish the court, when making the time to pay direction to recall or restrict an arrestment made in connection with the action, enter the appropriate details about what has been arrested and the place and date of the arrestment at D5, and attach the schedule of arrestment or copy.

Sign the application where indicated. Retain the copy initial writ and the form of notice which accompanied this application form as you may need them at a later stage. The application should be returned to the Sheriff Court at least fourteen days before the date of the first hearing or expiry of the period of notice or otherwise, as the case may be, in the warrant of citation. The address of the court is shown on page 1 of the application.

| | |
|---|---|
| **PART B** | 1. The applicant is a defender in the action brought by the above named pursuer. |
| | 2. The defender admits the claim and applies to the court for a time to pay direction. |
| | 3. The defender applies |
| | (1) To pay by instalments of £ |
| | (Tick one box only) |
| | EACH WEEK    FORTNIGHT    MONTH |
| | OR |
| | (2) To pay the sum ordered in one payment within WEEKS/MONTHS |
| | Please state in this box why you say a time to pay direction should be made. In doing so, please consider the Note below. |
| | **NOTE** |
| | **Under the 1987 Act, the court is required to make a time to pay direction if satisfied that it is reasonable in the circumstances to do so, and having regard in particular to the following matters—** |
| | **The nature of and reasons for the debt in relation to which decree is granted or the order is sought Any action taken by the creditor to assist the debtor in paying the debt** |
| | **The debtor's financial position The reasonableness of any proposal by the debtor to pay that debt** |
| | **The reasonableness of any refusal or objection by the creditor to any proposal or offer by the debtor to pay the debt.** |

| | |
|---|---|
| **PART C** | **4. Defender's financial position** |
| | I am employed /self employed / unemployed |

| **My net income is:** | weekly, fortnightly or monthly | **My outgoings are:** | weekly, fortnightly or monthly |
|---|---|---|---|
| Wages | £ | Mortgage/rent | £ |
| State benefits | £ | Council tax | £ |
| Tax credits | £ | Gas/electricity etc | £ |
| Other | £ | Food | £ |
| | | Credit and loans | £ |
| | | Phone | £ |
| | | Other | £ |
| Total | £ | Total | £ |

People who rely on your income (e.g.

spouse/civil partner/partner/ children)

—how many

Here list all assets (if any) e.g. value of house; amounts in bank or building society accounts; shares or other investments:

Here list any outstanding debts:

**PART D**    5. The defender seeks to recall or restrict an arrestment of which the details are as follows (*please state, and attach the schedule of arrestment or copy*).

6. This application is made under sections 1(1) and 2(3) of the Debtors (Scotland) Act 1987.

Therefore the defender asks the court

*to make a time to pay direction

*to recall the above arrestment

*to restrict the above arrestment (*in which case state restriction wanted*)

Date (*insert date*)

Signed

Defender

**Court ref. no**.

## APPLICATION FOR A TIME ORDER UNDER THE CONSUMER CREDIT ACT 1974

**\*PART A**    By

**\*(This section must be completed by pursuer before service)**

DEFENDER

**In an action raised by**

PURSUER

### HOW TO COMPLETE THE APPLICATION
PLEASE WRITE IN INK USING BLOCK CAPITALS

**PART A** of the application will have been completed in advance by the pursuer and gives details of the pursuer and you as the defender.

**PART B** If you wish to apply to pay by instalments enter the amount and tick the appropriate box at B3. If you wish the court to make any additional orders, please give details at B4. Please give details of the regulated agreement at B5.

**PART C** Give full details of your financial position in the space provided.

Sign the application where indicated. Retain the copy initial writ and the form of notice which accompanied this application form as you may need them at a later stage. The application should be returned to the Sheriff Court at least fourteen days before the date of the first hearing or expiry of the period of notice or otherwise, as the case may be, in the warrant of citation. The address of the court is shown on page 1 of the application.

**PART B**    1. The Applicant is a defender in the action brought by the above named pursuer.

**I/WE WISH TO APPLY FOR A TIME ORDER under the Consumer Credit Act 1974**

**2. Details of order(s) sought**

The defender wishes to apply for a time order under section 129 of the Consumer Credit Act 1974

The defender wishes to apply for an order in terms of section..........of the Consumer Credit Act 1974

**3. Proposals for payment**

I admit the claim and apply to pay the arrears and future instalments as follows:

By instalments of £..........per *week/fortnight/month

No time to pay direction or time to pay order has been made in relation to this debt.

**4. Additional orders sought**

The following additional order(s) is (are) sought: (*specify*)

The order(s) sought in addition to the time order is (are) sought for the following reasons:

5. **Details of regulated agreement**

*(Please attach a copy of the agreement if you have retained it and insert details of the
agreement where known)*

(a) Date of agreement

(b) Reference number of agreement

(c) Names and addresses of other parties to agreement

(d) Name and address of person (if any) who acted as surety (guarantor) to the agreement

(e) Place where agreement signed (e.g. the shop where agreement signed, including name and address)

(f) Details of payment arrangements

　　i. The agreement is to pay instalments of £..........per week/month

　　ii. The unpaid balance is £..........I do not know the amount of arrears

　　iii. I am £..........in arrears / I do not know the amount of arrears

**PART C**　　　　　　　　**Defender's financial position**

I am employed /self employed / unemployed

| | My net income is: | weekly, fortnightly or monthly | My outgoings are: | weekly, fortnightly or monthly |
|---|---|---|---|---|
| | Wages | £ | Mortgage/rent | £ |
| | State benefits | £ | Council tax | £ |
| | Tax credits | £ | Gas/electricity etc | £ |
| | Other | £ | Food | £ |
| | | | Credit and loans | £ |
| | | | Phone | £ |
| | | | Other | £ |
| | Total | £ | Total | £ |

People who rely on your income (e.g. spouse/civil partner/partner/children)—how many

Here list all assets (if any) e.g. value of house; amounts in bank or building society accounts; shares or other investments:

Here list any outstanding debts:

Therefore the defender asks the court to make a time order

Date　　　　　　　　　　　　　　　　　Signed

　　　　　　　　　　　　　　　　　　　Defender

Rule 2.22(4)　　　　　　　　　　FORM 5A[1]

**Form of pursuer's response objecting to application for time to pay direction or time order**

**Court ref no:..........**

SHERIFFDOM OF *(insert name of sheriffdom)*

AT *(insert place of sheriff court)*

PURSUER'S RESPONSE OBJECTING TO APPLICATION FOR TIME TO PAY DIRECTION OR TIME ORDER

in the cause

[A.B.], *(insert designation and address)*, Pursuer

---

[1] As inserted by the Act of Sederunt (Sheriff Court Rules) (Miscellaneous Amendments) 2009 (SSI 2009/294) r.2 (effective December 1, 2009).

against

[C.D.], (*insert designation and address*), Defender

1. The pursuer received a copy application for a time to pay direction or time order lodged by the defender on (*date*).
2. The pursuer does not accept the offer.
3. The debt is (*please specify the nature of the debt*).
4. The debt was incurred on (*specify date*) and the pursuer has contacted the defender in relation to the debt on (*specify date(s)*).
*5. The contractual payments were (*specify amount*).
*6. (*Specify any action taken by the pursuer to assist the defender to pay the debt*).
*7. The defender has made payment(s) towards the debt of (*specify amount(s)*) on (*specify date(s)*).
*8. The debtor has made offers to pay (*specify amount(s)*) on (*specify date(s)*) which offer(s) was [were] accepted [*or* rejected] and (*specify amount*) was paid on (*specify date(s)*).
9. (*Here set out any information you consider relevant to the court's determination of the application*).

*delete as appropriate

(*Signed*)

Pursuer *or* Solicitor for pursuer

(*Date*)

Rule 2.7(7)                                    FORM 6[1]

Form of citation where time to pay direction or time order may be applied for in summary application

SHERIFFDOM OF (*insert name of sheriffdom*)

AT (*insert place of sheriff court*)

[A.B.], (*insert designation and address*) Pursuer

against

[C.D.], (*insert designation and address*) Defender

Court ref. no.

(*Insert place and date*). You [CD.], are hereby served with this copy writ and warrant, together with Form 5 (application for time to pay direction in summary application).

**Form 5** is served on you because it is considered that you may be entitled to apply for a time to pay direction or time order [and for the recall or restriction of an arrestment used on the dependence of the action or in security of the debt referred to in the copy writ]. See Form 5 for further details.

**IF YOU ADMIT THE CLAIM AND WISH TO APPLY FOR A TIME TO PAY DIRECTION OR TIME ORDER,** you must complete Form 5 and return it to the sheriff clerk at the above address at least 7 days before the hearing or the expiry of the period of notice or otherwise, as the case may be, in the warrant of citation.

**IF YOU ADMIT THE CLAIM AND WISH TO AVOID A COURT ORDER BEING MADE AGAINST YOU,** the whole sum claimed including interest and any expenses due should be paid to the pursuer or his solicitor by the court date.

**IF YOU ARE UNCERTAIN AS TO WHAT ACTION TO TAKE** you should consult a solicitor. You may be eligible for legal aid depending on your income, and you can get information about legal aid from a solicitor. You may also obtain advice from any Citizens' Advice Bureau, or other advice agency.

**PLEASE NOTE THAT IF YOU DO NOTHING IN ANSWER TO THIS DOCUMENT** the court may regard you as admitting the claim made against you and the pursuer may obtain decree against you in your absence.

Signed

[P.Q.], Sheriff Officer,

or [X.Y.] (*add designation and business address*)

Solicitor for the Pursuer

FORM 6ZA[2]

Rule 2.7(7ZA)(a)

---

[1] As amended by the Act of Sederunt (Ordinary Cause, Summary Application, Summary Cause and Small Claim Rules) Amendment (Miscellaneous) 2007 (SSI 2007/6), para.3(6) (effective January 29, 2007).

[2] As inserted by the Act of Sederunt (Sheriff Court Rules) (Miscellaneous Amendments) 2013 (SSI 2013/135) para.2 (effective May 27, 2013).

Form of warrant of citation in an application to which rule 2.7(7ZA)(a) applies

(*Insert place and date*). Grants warrant to cite the defender (*insert name and address*) by serving a copy of the writ and warrant together with Form 6ZB and Form 11C [*on a period of notice of (*insert period of notice*) days] and ordains him [*or* her] if he [*or* she] intends to oppose the application—

To be present or represented at the diet on (*insert date and time*) within (*insert name and address of sheriff court*) [*or otherwise as the case may be*].

Signed

Sheriff [*or* sheriff clerk]

(*\*delete as appropriate*)

## FORM 6ZB[1]

Rule 2.7(7ZA)(b)

Form of citation in an application to which rule 2.7(7ZA)(b) applies

SHERIFFDOM OF (*insert name of sheriffdom*)

AT (*insert place of sheriff court*)

[A.B.], (*insert designation and address*), Pursuer

Against

[C.D.], (*insert designation and address*), Defender

Court ref. no:

To: (*insert name and address of defender*)

Attached to this notice is a copy of an application by (*insert name of pursuer*) under [*insert reference to provision or provisions under which application is made*]. **IF THE APPLICATION IS GRANTED, THE PROPERTY AT (*INSERT ADDRESS OF SECURITY SUBJECTS*) MAY BE REPOSSESSED AND YOU WOULD NO LONGER HAVE THE RIGHT TO RESIDE THERE.**

**The hearing will be held at (*insert name and address of sheriff court*) on (*insert date*) at (*insert time*).**

**IF YOU WISH TO OPPOSE THE APPLICATION** you should be present or represented at the hearing.

**IF YOU ARE UNCERTAIN AS TO WHAT ACTION TO TAKE** you should consult a solicitor. You may be eligible for legal aid depending on your income, and you can get information about legal aid from a solicitor. You may also obtain advice from an approved lay representative, or any Citizens' Advice Bureau or other advice agency.

**PLEASE NOTE THAT IF YOU DO NOTHING IN ANSWER TO THIS DOCUMENT** the court may consider the application in the absence of you or your representative.

Signed

[P.Q.], Sheriff Officer,

or [X.Y.], (*add designation and business address*)

Solicitor for the Pursuer

## FORM 6A

*[Repealed by the Act of Sederunt (Sheriff Court Rules) (Enforcement of Securities over Heritable Property) 2010 (SSI 2010/324) para.2 (effective September 30, 2010).]*

## FORM 6B

*[Repealed by the Act of Sederunt (Sheriff Court Rules) (Enforcement of Securities over Heritable Property) 2010 (SSI2010/324) para.2 (effective September 30, 2010).]*

Rule 2.7(8)                                   FORM 7[2, 3, 4, 5]

---

[1] As inserted by the Act of Sederunt (Sheriff Court Rules) (Miscellaneous Amendments) 2013 (SSI 2013/135) para.2 (effective May 27, 2013).

[2] Inserted by the Act of Sederunt (Amendment of Ordinary Cause Rules and Summary Applications, Statutory Applications and Appeals etc. Rules) Applications under the Mortgage Rights (Scotland) Act 2001) 2002 (SSI 2002/7), para.3(4) and Sch.2.

[3] As amended by the Act of Sederunt (Ordinary Cause, Summary Application, Summary Cause and Small Claim Rules) Amendment (Miscellaneous) 2007 (SSI 2007/6), para.3(6) (effective January 29, 2007).

[4] As amended by the Act of Sederunt (Sheriff Court Rules) (Enforcement of Securities over Heritable Property) 2010 (SSI 2010/324) para.2 (effective September 30, 2010).

Form of certificate of citation

## CERTIFICATE OF CITATION

(Insert place and date) I, hereby certify that upon the day of I duly cited [CD.], Defender, to answer the foregoing writ. I did this by (*state method of service; [if by officer and not by post, add*: in the presence of [L.M.], (*insert designation*), witness hereto with me subscribing;] *and where service executed by post state whether by registered post or the first class recorded delivery service*).

(*In actions in which a time to pay direction or time order may be applied for, state whether Form 4 and Form 5 were sent in accordance with rule 2.7(5)* and (6).)

(*In applications for enforcement of security over residential property within the meaning of Part IV of Chapter 3 , state whether Forms 6ZA, 6ZB and 11C were provided in accordance with rule 2.7(7ZA)*).

Signed

[P.Q.], Sheriff Officer

[L.M.], witness

or [X.Y.] (*add designation and business address*)

Solicitor for the Pursuer

Rule 2.9(1)                                    FORM 8

Form of caveat

*[Repealed by the Act of Sederunt (Sheriff Court Caveat Rules) 2006 (SI 2006/198), effective April 28, 2006.]*

Rule 2.13(1)(a)                                FORM 9

Form of advertisement

NOTICE TO [C.D.]

Court ref. no.

An action has been raised in Sheriff Court by [A.B.], Pursuer calling as a Defender [CD.], whose last known address was (*insert last known address of defender*).

If [CD.] wishes to defend the action he [*or* she] should immediately contact the sheriff clerk (*insert address*) from whom the service copy initial writ may be obtained. If he [*or* she] fails to do so decree may pass against him [*or* her] [when the case calls in court on (*date*) or on the expiry of the period of notice *or otherwise, as the case may be in the warrant of citation*].

Signed

[X.Y.], (*add designation and business address*)

Solicitor for the Pursuer

or [P.Q.] (*add business address*)

Rule 2.13(1)(b)                                FORM 10

Form of notice for walls of court

NOTICE TO [CD.]

Court ref. no.

An action has been raised in..........Sheriff Court by [A.B.], Pursuer calling as a Defender [CD.], whose last known address was (*insert last known address of defender*).

If [C.D.] wishes to defend the action he [*or* she] should immediately contact the sheriff clerk at (*insert address*) from whom the service copy initial writ may be obtained. If he [*or* she] fails to do so decree may pass against him [*or* her] [when the case calls in court on (*date*) or on the expiry of the period of notice *or otherwise, as the case may he in the warrant of citation*].

Date (*insert date*)

Signed

Sheriff clerk (*depute*)

Telephone no. (*insert telephone number of sheriff clerk's office*)

Rule 2.18A                                     FORM 10A[1]

---

[5] As amended by the Act of Sederunt (Sheriff Court Rules) (Miscellaneous Amendments) 2013 (SSI 2013/135) para.2 (effective May 27, 2013).

[1] As inserted by the Act of Sederunt (Sheriff Court Rules Amendment) (Diligence) 2009 (SSI 2009/107) (effective April 22, 2009).

Form of schedule of arrestment on the dependence

### SCHEDULE OF ARRESTMENT ON THE DEPENDENCE

Date: (*date of execution*)

Time: (*time arrestment executed*)

To: (*name and address of arrested*)

IN HER MAJESTY'S NAME AND AUTHORITY AND IN NAME AND AUTHORITY OF THE SHERIFF.1, (*name*). Sheriff Officer, by virtue of:

- an initial writ containing warrant which has been granted for arrestment on the dependence of the action at the instance of (*name and address of pursuer*) against (*name and address of defender*) and dated (*date*);

- a counterclaim containing a warrant which has been granted for arrestment on the dependence of the claim by (*name and address of creditor*) againts (*name and address of debtor*) and dated (*date of warrant*);

- an order of the Sheriff at (*place*) dated (*dated of order*) granting warrant [for arrestment on the dependence of the action mised at the instance of (*name and address of pursuer*) against (*name and address of defender*).] [or for arrestment on the dependence of the claim in the counterclaim [or third party notice] by (*name and address of creditor*) against (*name and address of debtor*)].

arrest in your hands (i) the sum of (*amount*), in excess of the Protected Minimum Balance; where applicable (*see Note 1*), more or less, due by you to (*defender's name*)[*or name and address of common debtor i common debtor is not the defender*] or to any other person on his [*or her*] [*or its*] [*or their*] behalf, and (ii) all moveable things in your hands belonging or pertaining to the said (*name of common debtor*), to remain in your hands under arrestment until they are made forthcoming to (*name of pursuer*) [*or name and address of creditor if he is not the pursuer*] or until further order of the court.

This I do in the presence of (*name, occupation and address of witness*).

(*Signed*)

Sheriff Officer

(*Address*)

### NOTE

1.    This Schedule arrests in your hands (i) funds due by you to (*name of common debtor*) and (ii) goods or other moveables held by you for him. **You should not pay any funds to him or hand over any goods or other moveables to him without taking legal advice.**

2.    This Schedule may be used to arrest a ship or cargo. If it is, you should consult your legal adviser about the effect of it.

3.    The Protected Minimum Balance is the sum referred to in section 73F(4) of the Debtors (Scotland) Act 1987. This sum is currently set at [*insert current sum*]. The Protected Minimum Balance applies where the arrestment attaches funds standing to the credit of a debtor in an account held by a bank or other financial institution and the debtor is an individual. The Protected Minimum Balance does not apply where the account is held in the name of a company, a limited liability partnership, a partnership or an unincorporated association or where the account is operated by the debtor as a trading account.

4.    Under section 73G of the Debtors (Scotland) Act 1987 you must also, within the period of 3 weeks beginning with the day on which the arrestment is executed, disclose to the creditor the nature and value of the funds and/or moveable property which have been attached. This disclosure must be in the form set out in Schedule 8 to the Diligence (Scotland) Regulations 2009. Failure to comply may lead to a financial penalty under section 73G of the Debtors (Scotland) Act 1987 and may also be dealt with as a contempt of court. You must, at the same time, send a copy of the disclosure to the debtor and to any person known to you who owns (or claims to own) attached property and to any person to whom attached funds are (or are claimed to be due), solely or in common with the debtor.

**IF YOU WISH FURTHER ADVICE CONTACT ANY CITIZENS ADVICE BUREAU/LOCAL ADVICE CENTRE/SHERIFF CLERK OR SOLICITOR**

Rule 2.18A                    FORM 10B[1]

Form of certificate of execution of arrestment on the dependence

### CERTIFICATE OF EXECUTION

---

[1] As inserted by the Act of Sederunt (Sheriff Court Rules Amendment) (Diligence) 2009 (SSI 2009/107) (effective April 22, 2009).

I, (*name*), Sheriff Officer, certify that I executed an arrestment on the dependence, by virtue of an interlocutor of the Sheriff at (*place*) on (*date*) obtained at the instance of (*name and address of party arresting*) against (*name and address of defender*) on (*name of arrestee*)—

* by delivering the schedule of arrestment to (*name of arrestee or other person*) at (*place*) personally on (*date*).

* by leaving the schedule of arrestment with (*name and occupation of person with whom left*) at (*place*) on (*date*) [and by posting a copy of the schedule to the arrestee by registered post or first class recorded delivery to the address specified on the receipt annexed to this certificate].

* by depositing the schedule of arresment in (*place*) on (*date*). (*Specify that enquiry made and reasonable grounds exist for believing that the person on whom service is to be made resides at the place but is not available*) [and by posting a copy of the schedule to the arrestee by registered post or first class recorded delivery to the address specified on the receipt annexed to this certificate].

* by affixing the schedule of arrestment to the door at (*place*) on (*date*). (*Specify that enquiry made and that reasonable grounds exist for believing that the person on whom service is to be made resides at the place but is not available*) [and by posting a copy of schedule to the arrestee by registered post or first class recorded delivery to the address specified on the receipt annexed to this certificate].

* by leaving the schedule of arrestment with (*name and occupation of person with whom left*) at (*place of business*) on (*date*) [and by posting a copy of schedule to the arrestee by registered post or first class recorded delivery to the address specified on the receipt annexed to this certificate].

* by depositing the schedule of arresment at (*place of business*) on (*date*). (*Specify that enquiry made and that reasonable grounds exist for believing that the person on whom service is to be made carries on business at that place.*) [and by posting a copy of the schedule to the arrestee by registered post or first class recorded delivery to the address specified on the receipt annexed to this certificate].

* by affixing the schedule of arrestment to the door at (*place of business*) on (*date*). (*Specify that enquiry made and that reasonable grounds exist for believing that the person on whom service is to be made carries on business at that place.*) [and by posting a copy of schedule to the arrestee by registered post or first class recorded delivery to the address specified on the receipt annexed to this certificate].

* by leaving the schedule of arrestment at (*registered office*) on (*date*), in the hands of (*name of person*) [and by posting a copy of the schedule to the arrestee by registered post or first class recorded delivery to the address specified on the receipt annexed to this certificate].

* by depositing the schedule of arrestment at (*registered office*) on (*date*) [and by posting a copy of the schedule to the arrestee by registered post or first class recorded delivery to the address specified on the receipt annexed to this certificate].

* by affixing the schedule of arrestment to the door at (*registered office*) on (*date*) [and by posting a copy of the schedule to the arrestee by registered post or first class recorded delivery to the address specified on the receipt annexed to this certificate].

I did this in the presence of (*name, occupation and address of witness*).

(*Signed*)
Sheriff Officer
(*Address*)
(*Signed*)
(Witness)

*Delele where not applicable

NOTE

A copy of the Schedule of arrestment on the dependence is to be attached to this certificate.

Rule 2.26                              FORM 11

Form of extract decree
EXTRACT DECREE

Sheriff Court                    Court Ref. No.
Date of decree                   *In absence
Pursuer(s)                       Defender(s)
The Sheriff
and granted decree against the              for payment of expenses of £
This extract is warrant for all lawful execution hereon.
Date (*insert date*)                   Sheriff clerk (*depute*)
*Delete as appropriate

Rule 2.37(3)                                  FORM 11AA[1]

Form of minute of intervention by the Commission for Equality and Human Rights

SHERIFFDOM OF (*insert name of sheriffdom*)      Court ref. no.
AT (insert place of sheriff court)

APPLICATION FOR LEAVE TO INTERVENE BY THE COMMISSION FOR EQUALITY AND
HUMAN RIGHTS
in the cause
[A.B.] (*designation and address*), Pursuer
against
[CD.] (*designation and address*), Defender

[*Here set out briefly:*
(a)   the Commission's reasons for believing that the proceedings are relevant to a matter in connec-
      tion with which the Commission has a function;
(b)   the issue in the proceedings which the Commission wishes to address; and
(c)   the propositions to be advanced by the Commission and the Commission's reasons for believ-
      ing that they are relevant to the proceedings and that they will assist the court]

Rule 2.39(2)                                  FORM 11AB[2]

Form of minute of intervention by the Scottish Commission for Human Rights

SHERIFFDOM OF (*insert name of sheriffdom*)      Court ref. no.
AT (*insert place of sheriff court*)

APPLICATION FOR LEAVE TO INTERVENE BY THE SCOTTISH COMMISSION FOR HUMAN
RIGHTS
in the cause
[A.B.] (*designation and address*), Pursuer
against
[C.D.] (*designation and address*), Defender

[*Here set out briefly:*
(a)   *the issue in the proceedings which the Commission intends to address;*
(b)   *a summary of the submission the Commission intends to make.*]

Rule 2.40(1)                                  FORM 11AC[3]

Invitation to the Scottish Commission for Human Rights to intervene

SHERIFFDOM OF *(insert name of sheriffdom)*      Court ref. no.
AT *(insert place of sheriff court)*

INVITATION TO THE SCOTTISH COMMISSION FOR HUMAN RIGHTS TO INTERVENE
in the cause
[A.B.] (*designation and address*), Pursuer
against
[C.D.] (*designation and address*), Defender

[*Here set out briefly:*
(a)   *the facts, procedural history and issues in the proceedings;*
(b)   *the issue in the proceedings on which the court seeks a submission*]

---

[1] As inserted by the Act of Sederunt (Sheriff Court Rules) (Miscellaneous Amendments) 2008 (SSI
2008/223) para.5(4) (effective July 1, 2008).
[2] As inserted by the Act of Sederunt (Sheriff Court Rules) (Miscellaneous Amendments) 2008 (SSI
2008/223) para.5(4) (effective July 1, 2008).
[3] As inserted by the Act of Sederunt (Sheriff Court Rules) (Miscellaneous Amendments) 2008 (SSI
2008/223) para.5(4) (effective July 1, 2008).

Rule 3.1.6                                                  FORM 11A[1]

Form of order for recovery of documents etc. under the Administration of Justice (Scotland) Act 1972

SHERIFFDOM OF (*insert name of sheriffdom*)

AT (*insert place of sheriff court*)

in the Summary Application

of

[A.B.] (*designation and address*)

Applicant

against

[C.D.] (*designation and address*)

Respondent

Date: (*date of interlocutor*)

To: (*name and address of party or parties or named third party haver, from whom the documents and other property are sought to be recovered*)

**THE SHERIFF** having heard the applicant and being satisfied that it is appropriate to make an order under section 1 of the Administration of Justice (Scotland) Act 1972:

**ORDERS** the Summary Application to be served upon the person(s) named and designed in the application;

APPOINTS (*name and designation of Commissioner*) to be Commissioner of the court;

**GRANTS** commission and diligence;

**ORDERS** the Commissioner to explain to the haver on executing the order—

(1)    the meaning and effect of the order;

(2)    that the haver may be entitled to claim that certain of the documents and other property are confidential or privileged;

(3)    that the haver has a right to seek legal or other professional advice of his or her choice and to apply to vary or recall the order;

and to give the haver a copy of the Notice in Form 11B of Schedule 1 to the Act of Sederunt (Summary Applications, Statutory Applications and Appeals etc. Rules) 1999.

*GRANTS* warrant to and authorises the said Commissioner, whether the haver has allowed entry or not—

(1)    to enter, between the hours of 9am and 5pm on Monday to Friday, (*or, where the sheriff has found cause shown under* rule 3.1.11(1), *otherwise specify the time [and day]*) the premises at (*address of premises*) and any other place in Scotland owned or occupied by the haver at which it appears to the Commissioner that any of the items set out in the statement of facts in the application to the court (the "listed items") may be located;

(2)    to search for and take all other steps which the Commissioner considers necessary to take possession of or preserve (*specify the listed items*);

(3)    to take possession of and to preserve all or any of the listed items and to consign them with the Sheriff Clerk at (*enter name and address of sheriff court*) to be held by him or her pending the further orders of the sheriff;

and for that purpose,

**ORDERS** the haver or his/her servants or agents to allow the Commissioner, any person whom the Commissioner considers necessary to assist him/her, and the Applicant's representatives to enter the premises named in the order and to allow them—

(1)    to search for the listed items and take such other steps as the Commissioner considers it reasonable to take to execute the order;

(2)    to remain in the premises until such time as the search is complete, including allowing them to continue the search on subsequent days if necessary.

**FURTHER ORDERS** the haver or his/her servants or agents—

(1)    (*if appropriate*) to provide access to information stored on any computer owned or used by him/her by supplying or providing the means to overcome any and all security mechanisms inhibiting access thereto;

(2)    to inform the Commissioner immediately of the whereabouts of the listed items;

(3)    to provide the Commissioner with a list of the names and addresses of everyone to whom he or she has given any of the listed items;

---

[1] As substituted by the Act of Sederunt (Sheriff Court Rules) (Miscellaneous Amendments) (No.3) 2011 (SSI 2011/386) para.6 (effective November 28, 2011).

and not to destroy, conceal or tamper with any of the listed items except in accordance with the terms of this order;

**FURTHER AUTHORISES** (*specify the representatives*) to be the sole representatives of the Applicant to accompany the Commissioner for the purpose of identification of the said documents and other property.

*(Signed)*

Sheriff

## SCHEDULE TO THE ORDER
### Undertakings given by the Applicant

The Applicant has given the following undertakings—

1. That he/she will comply with any order of the sheriff as to payment of compensation if it is subsequently discovered that the order, or the implementation of the order, has caused loss to the respondent or, where the respondent is not the haver, to the haver.
2. That he/she will bring within a reasonable time of the execution of the order any proceedings which he/she decides to bring.
3. That he/she will not, without leave of the sheriff, use any information, documents or other property obtained as a result of the order, except for the purpose of any proceedings which he/she decides to bring and to which the order relates.

(*or as modified under* rule 3.1.4)

Rule 3.1.9(a)                                    FORM 11B[1]

Notice to accompany order in Form 11A when served by Commissioner

**IMPORTANT**
**NOTICE TO PERSON ON WHOM THIS ORDER IS SERVED**

1. This order orders you to allow the person appointed and named in the order as Commissioner to enter your premises to search for, examine and remove or copy the items mentioned in the order.
2. It also allows entry to the premises to any person appointed and named in the order as a representative of the person who has been granted the order and to any person accompanying the Commissioner to assist him/her.
3. No-one else is given authority to enter the premises.
4. You should read the order immediately.
5. You have the right to seek legal or other professional advice of your choice and you are advised to do so as soon as possible.
6. Consultation under paragraph 5 will not prevent the Commissioner from entering your premises for the purposes mentioned in paragraph 1 but if the purpose of your seeking advice is to help you to decide if you should ask the sheriff to vary or recall the order you are entitled to ask the Commissioner to delay searching the premises for up to 2 hours or such other longer period as the Commissioner may permit.
7. The Commissioner is obliged to explain the meaning and effect of the order to you.
8. The Commissioner is also obliged to explain to you that you are entitled to claim that the items, or some of them, are protected as confidential or privileged.
9. You are entitled to ask the sheriff to vary or recall the order provided that—
   (a) you take steps to do so at once; and
   (b) you allow the Commissioner, any person appointed as a representative of the person who has been granted the order and any person accompanying the Commissioner to assist him/her, to enter the premises meantime.
10. The Commissioner and the persons mentioned as representatives or assistants have a right to enter the premises even if you refuse to allow them to do so, unless—
    (a) you are female and alone in the premises and there is no female with the Commissioner (where the Commissioner is not herself female), in which case they have no right to enter the premises;
    (b) the Commissioner serves the order before 9am or after 5pm on a weekday or at any time on a Saturday or Sunday (except where the sheriff has specifically allowed this, which will be stated in the order);
    in which cases you should refuse to allow entry.

---

[1] As substituted by the Act of Sederunt (Sheriff Court Rules) (Miscellaneous Amendments) (No.3) 2011 (SSI 2011/386) para.6 (effective November 28, 2011).

11.　You are entitled to insist that there is no-one (*or* no-one other than X) present who could gain commercially from anything which might be read or seen on your premises.

12.　You are required to hand over to the Commissioner any of the items mentioned in the order which are in your possession.

13.　You may be found liable for contempt of court if you refuse to comply with the order.

Rule 3.4.3(2)　　　　　　　　　　　FORM 11C[1, 2]

Form of certificate of completion of pre-action requirements

Certificate of completion of pre-action requirements in an application under [insert reference to provision or provisions under which application is made] of the property at (*insert address of security subjects*).

in the cause

SHERIFFDOM OF (*insert name of sheriffdom*)

AT (*insert place of sheriff court*)

[A.B.], (*insert designation and address*), Pursuer

against

[C.D.], (*insert designation and address*), Defender

Court ref. no:

(Insert name of pursuer), pursuer and creditor in the security with (*insert name of defender*), the defender, in respect of the premises at (*insert address of security subjects*) aver(s) that the pre-action requirements, have been complied with (*tick boxes to confirm*)—

1.　As soon as reasonably practicable upon the defender entering into default, the pursuer provided the defender with clear information about—[3]

    (a)　the terms of the security;

    (b)　the amount due to the pursuer under the security, including any arrears and any charges in respect of late payment, broken down so as to show—

        (i)　the total amount of the arrears;

        (ii)　the total outstanding amount due including any charges already incurred;

    (c)　the nature and the level of any charges that may be incurred by virtue of the contract to which the security relates if the default is not remedied; and

    (d)　any other obligation under the security in respect of which the defender is in default.

Please provide details of (a) the date on which the information mentioned in 1(a) was provided; and (b) how the requirements of 1(b), (c) and (d) were complied with including a copy of the information provided under those paragraphs:

---

[1] As inserted by the Act of Sederunt (Sheriff Court Rules) (Enforcement of Securities over Heritable Property) 2010 (SSI 2010/324) (effective September 30, 2010).

[2] As amended by the Act of Sederunt (Sheriff Court Rules) (Miscellaneous Amendments) 2013 (SSI 2013/135) para.2 (effective May 27, 2013).

[3] As amended by the Act of Sederunt (Sheriff Court Rules) (Miscellaneous Amendments) 2013 (SSI 2013/135) para.2 (effective May 27, 2013).

2.  The pursuer has made reasonable efforts to agree with the defender proposals in respect of future payments to the pursuer under the security and the fulfilment of any other obligation under the security in respect of which the defender is in default, including—[1]

    (a)  making reasonable attempts to contact the defender to discuss the default;

    (b)  providing the defender with details of any proposals made by the pursuer, set out in such a way as to allow the defender to consider the proposal;

    (c)  allowing the defender reasonable time to consider any proposals made by the pursuer;

    (d)  notifying the defender within a reasonable time of any decision taken by the pursuer to accept or reject a proposal made by the defender and, where the pursuer rejects such proposal, the pursuer has provided reasons for rejecting the proposal in writing within 10 working days of notifying the defender it is rejecting the proposal;

    (e)  considering the affordability of any proposal for the defender taking into account, where known to the pursuer, the defender's personal and financial circumstances.

Provide details:

> 

*3.  Where the defender has failed to comply with a condition of an agreement reached with the pursuer in respect of any proposal and the defender has not previously failed to comply with a condition of the agreement—

    (a)  the pursuer has given the defender notice in writing of its decision to make an application under [*insert reference to provision or provisions under which application is made*] and the ground of the proposed application before making the application;

    (b)  the pursuer has not made an application before the expiry of 15 working days**, beginning with the date on which the defender is deemed to have received the notice referred to at paragraph (a);

    (c)  the default by the defender in respect of which the application is intended to be made has not been remedied during that notice period.

Provide details of the defender's failure to comply with a condition of the agreement:

> 

*Indicate here if not applicable

**In this paragraph, "working day" means a day that is not a Saturday or Sunday, or any day that is a bank holiday under the Banking and Financial Dealings Act 1971 in any part of the United Kingdom.

4.  The defender has not taken steps that are likely to result in—

    (a)  the payment to the pursuer within a reasonable time of any arrears, or the whole amount, due to the pursuer under the security; and

    (b)  fulfilment by the defender within a reasonable time of any other obligation under the security in respect of which the defender is in default.

Indicate what (if any) steps have been taken by the defender and why those steps are not considered to be effective:

> 

---

[1] As amended by the Act of Sederunt (Sheriff Court Rules) (Miscellaneous Amendments) 2013 (SSI 2013/135) para.2 (effective May 27, 2013).

5.   The pursuer has provided the defender with information about sources of advice and assistance in relation to management of debt, including—

(a)   where the security is regulated, any relevant information sheet published by the appropriate regulatory body;

(b)   a local citizens advice bureau or other advice organisation; and

(c)   the housing department of the local authority in whose area the property which is subject to the security is situated.

6.   The pursuer has encouraged the defender to contact the local authority in whose area the security subjects are situated.

7.   The pursuer has had regard to any guidance issued by the Scottish Ministers.

(Signed)

[X. Y,], (*add designation and business address*)

Pursuer's solicitor

Rule 3.4.6                                    FORM 11D[1]

Form of notice to entitled residents in an application for enforcement of security over residential property

Notice to an entitled resident in an application for repossession of the property at (*insert address of security subjects*).

**SHERIFFDOM OF** (*insert name of sheriffdom*)

**AT** (*insert place of sheriff court*)

[A.B.], (*insert designation and address*), Pursuer

against

[C.D.], (*insert designation and address*), Defender

Court ref. no:

To: (*insert name and address of entitled resident*)

Attached to this notice is a copy of an application by (*insert name of pursuer*) under [insert reference to provision or provisions under which application is made]. **IF THE APPLICATION IS GRANTED, THE PROPERTY AT** *(INSERT ADDRESS OF SECURITY SUBJECTS)* **MAY BE REPOSSESSED AND YOU WOULD NO LONGER HAVE THE RIGHT TO RESIDE THERE**. A Form 11E application form is also attached.

This Notice—

(a)   gives you warning that an application has been made to the sheriff court for an order which may affect your interest as an entitled resident under [*insert reference to relevant provision or provisions*] in the property at (*insert address of security subjects*); and

(b)   informs you that an entitled resident may apply to the court to continue the proceedings or make any other order [*insert reference to relevant provision or provisions*] of that Act.

**IF YOU WISH TO MAKE AN APPLICATION FOR AN ORDER UNDER [INSERT REFERENCE TO RELEVANT PROVISION OR PROVISIONS]** you should complete and lodge Form 11E with the sheriff clerk at (*insert name and address of sheriff court*).

**IF YOU ARE UNCERTAIN AS TO WHAT ACTION TO TAKE** you should consult a solicitor. You may be eligible for legal aid depending on your income, and you can get information about legal aid from a solicitor. You may also obtain advice from an approved lay representative, or any Citizens Advice Bureau or other advice agency.

**PLEASE NOTE THAT IF YOU DO NOTHING IN ANSWER TO THIS DOCUMENT** the court will consider the application in the absence of you or your representative.

(Signed)

[P.Q.], Sheriff Officer, or

[X.Y.] (*add designation and business address*) Solicitor

---

[1] As inserted by the Act of Sederunt (Sheriff Court Rules) (Enforcement of Securities over Heritable Property) 2010 (SSI 2010/324) (effective September 30, 2010).

Rules 3.4.6 and 3.4.7          FORM 11E[1]

Form of application to court by entitled resident

Application to court by an entitled resident in proceedings for repossession of the property at (*insert address of security subjects*).

Sheriff Court:..........

Date:

Court ref. no.

1.     This application is made [by/on behalf of] (*delete as appropriate*) (*insert name and address of entitled resident*).

2.     The applicant is an entitled resident within the meaning of section 24C(1) of the Conveyancing and Feudal Reform (Scotland) Act 1970 and/or, as the case may be, section 5D of the Heritable Securities (Scotland) Act 1894 because his or her sole or main residence is the security subjects (in whole or in part) at (*insert address of security subjects) and (*tick one box as appropriate*)—

     (a)    *he or she is the proprietor of the security subjects (where the proprietor is* ☐ *not the debtor in the security);*

     (b)    *her or she is the non-entitled spouse of the debtor or the proprietor of* ☐ *security subjects which are (in whole or in part) a matrimonial home;*

     (c)    *he or she is the non-entitled civil partner of the debtor or the proprietor of* ☐ *security subjects which are (in whole or in part) a family home;*

     (d)    *he or she is a person living together with the debtor or the proprietor as* ☐ *husband and wife;*

     (e)    *he or she is a person living together with the debtor or the proprietor in a* ☐ *relationship which has the characteristics of the relationship between civil partners;*

     (f)    *he or she lived together with the debtor or the proprietor in a relationship* ☐ *described in (d) or (e) and—*

         (i)    *the security subjects (in whole or in part) are not the sole or main residence of the debtor or the proprietor;*

         (ii)    *he or she lived together with the debtor or the proprietor throughout the period of 6 months ending with the date on which the security subjects ceased to be the sole or main residence of the debtor or the proprietor; and*

         (iii)    *the security subjects (in whole or in part) are the sole or main residence of a child aged under 16 who is a child of both parties in that relationship.*

3.     The applicant believes that the court should consider this application because (*insert relevant details*)—

4.     The applicant asks the court to make an order under section 24B(1) of the Conveyancing and Feudal Reform (Scotland) Act 1970 and/or section 5C(1) of the Heritable Securities (Scotland) Act 1894 for (*insert details of what you wish the court to do and why*—)

*WHAT HAPPENS NEXT:* When you lodge this form at the sheriff clerk's office, the sheriff will fix a hearing for all those with an interest to appear and be heard. You are required to serve upon every party and intimate to every entitled resident a copy of this form, together with details of the date, time and place of the hearing.

---

[1] As inserted by the Act of Sederunt (Sheriff Court Rules) (Enforcement of Securities over Heritable Property) 2010 (SSI 2010/324) (effective September 30, 2010).

*IF YOU ARE UNCERTAIN AS TO WHAT ACTION TO TAKE* you should consult a solicitor. You may be eligible for legal aid depending on your income, and you can get information about legal aid from a solicitor. You may also obtain advice from an approved lay representative or any Citizens Advice Bureau or other advice agency,

Date (*insert date*)

> (Signed)
>
> [P.Q.], (Applicant),
>
> or [X.Y.], (*add designation and address of Applicant's representative*)

## DIET ASSIGNED

At (*insert place*) on (*insert date*), the court assigns the (*insert date of hearing*) at (*insert time*) at (*insert name of sheriff court*) as a diet for hearing parties on the Form 11E application.

Date (*insert date*)

> (*Signed*)
>
> Sheriff Clerk

## EXECUTION OF CITATION

At (*insert place*) on (*insert date*), I hereby certify that upon the (*insert date*), I duly served upon every party and intimated to every entitled resident a copy of this Form HE application, together with details of the hearing. This I did by (*insert method of service/intimation*).

Date (*insert date*)

> (*Signed*)
>
> [P.Q.], Sheriff Officer, or
>
> [X.Y.] (*add designation and business address*) Applicant's Solicitor

Rule 3.4.8(2)                                    FORM 11F[1]

Form of minute for recall of decree

Minute for recall of decree in an application for repossession of the property at (*insert address of security subjects*).

Sheriff Court:..........

Date:

Court ref. no.

A.B. (*pursuer*) against C.D. (*defender(s)*)

(*insert name*), being (*tick one box as appropriate*)—

| | |
|---|---|
| The Pursuer*; | ☐ |
| The Defender*; or | ☐ |

An entitled resident within the meaning of section 24C(1) of the Conveyancing and Feudal Reform (Scotland) Act 1970 and/or, as the case may be, section 5D of the Heritable Securities (Scotland) Act 1894 because my sole or main residence is the security subjects (in whole or in part) at (*insert address of security subjects*) and—*

(a)     *I am the proprietor of the security subjects (where the proprietor is not the* ☐ *debtor in the security);*

(b)     *I am the non-entitled spouse of the debtor or the proprietor of security subjects* ☐ *which are (in whole or in part) a matrimonial home;*

(c)     *I am the non-entitled civil partner of the debtor or the proprietor of security* ☐ *subjects which are (in whole or in part) a family home;*

(d)     *I am a person living together with the debtor or the. proprietor as husband and* ☐ *wife;*

(e)     *I am a person living together with the debtor or the proprietor in a relationship* ☐ *which has the characteristics of the relationship between civil partners;*

(f)     *I am a person who lived together with the debtor or the proprietor in a relation-* ☐

---

[1] As inserted by the Act of Sederunt (Sheriff Court Rules) (Enforcement of Securities over Heritable Property) 2010 (SSI 2010/324) (effective September 30, 2010).

ship described in (d) or (e) and—

(i) the security subjects (in whole or in part) are not the sole or main residence of the debtor or the proprietor;

(ii) I lived together with the debtor or the proprietor throughout the period of 6 months ending with the date on which the security subjects ceased to be the sole or main residence of the debtor or the proprietor; and

(iii) the security subjects (in whole or in part) are the sole or main residence of a child aged under 16 who is a child of both parties in that relationship.

moves the court to recall the decree pronounced on (insert date) in this case.

**WHAT HAPPENS NEXT:** When you lodge this form at the sheriff clerk's office, the sheriff clerk will fix a hearing for all those with an interest to appear and be heard. You are required to serve upon every party and intimate to every entitled resident a copy of this form, together with details of the date, time and place of the hearing.

If you wish to proceed with this application for recall of decree **YOU MUST ATTEND OR BE REPRESENTED AT THAT HEARING.**

**YOU ARE STRONGLY ADVISED TO SEEK IMMEDIATE LEGAL ADVICE FROM A SOLICITOR.** You may be eligible for legal aid depending on your income, and you can get information about legal aid from a solicitor. You may also obtain advice from an approved lay representative or any Citizens Advice Bureau or other advice agency.

Date (insert date)

(Signed)

[P.Q.], (Applicant),

or [X.Y.], (add designation and address of Applicant's representative)

**DIET ASSIGNED**

At (insert place) on (insert date), the court assigns the (insert date of hearing) at (insert time) at (insert name of sheriff court) as a diet for hearing parties on the Form 11F application.

Date (insert date)

(Signed)

Sheriff Clerk

**EXECUTION OF CITATION**

At (insert place) on (insert date), I hereby certify that upon the (insert date), I duly served upon every party and intimated to every entitled resident a copy of this Form 11F application, together with details of the hearing. This I did by (insert method of service/intimation).

Date (insert date)

(Signed)

[P.Q.], Sheriff Officer, or

[X.Y.] (add designation and business address) Applicant's Solicitor

Rule 3.4.8(10)                    FORM 11G[1]

Form of intimation where peremptory diet fixed in a recall of decree application

Intimation of peremptory diet fixed in an application for repossession of the property at (insert address of security subjects).

**SHERIFFDOM OF** (insert name of sheriffdom)

**AT** (insert place of sheriff court)

[A.B.], (insert designation and address), Pursuer

against

(C.D.] (insert designation and address), Defender

Court ref. no:

---

[1] As inserted by the Act of Sederunt (Sheriff Court Rules) (Enforcement of Securities over Heritable Property) 2010 (SSI 2010/324) (effective September 30, 2010).

The court noted that you did not appear at the Hearing to consider your application for recall of decree on (*insert date*). In your absence the decree for repossession of the property at (*insert address of security subjects*) has been recalled. As a result of your non-appearance the sheriff has ordered that you appear or be represented on (*insert date*) at (*insert time*) within (*insert name and address of sheriff court*) in order to ascertain whether you intend to proceed with your defence or your application.

A copy of the order is attached.

When you appear you will be asked by the sheriff to state whether you intend to proceed with your defence or your application.

**IF YOU ARE UNCERTAIN AS TO WHAT ACTION TO TAKE** you should consult a solicitor. You may be eligible for legal aid depending on your income, and you can get information about legal aid from a solicitor. You may also obtain advice from an approved lay representative or any Citizens Advice Bureau or other advice agency.

**PLEASE NOTE THAT IF YOU DO NOT APPEAR OR ARE NOT REPRESENTED AT THAT HEARING** the sheriff may regard you as no longer wishing to proceed with your defence or your application arid the sheriff may award decree of new against you in your absence and you will not be allowed to make a further application for recall.

Date (*insert date*)

(*Signed*)

(*add designation and address*)

Rule 3.8.3(1)            FORM 12

FORM OF NOTICE TO BE SERVED ON PERSON WHO IS SUBJECT OF HOSPITAL ORDER, GUARDIANSHIP ORDER OR COMMUNITY CARE ORDER PROCEEDINGS.

To [*name and address of patient*]

Attached to this notice is a copy of—

*an application to the managers of [*name of hospital*] for your admission to that hospital in accordance with section 21 of the Mental Health (Scotland) Act 1984.

*an application to the sheriff at [*name of Sheriff Court*] for a Community Care Order in accordance with section 35A of the Mental Health (Scotland) Act 1984.

*an application to the [*name of local authority*] for your reception into guardianship in accordance with Section 40 of the Mental Health (Scotland) Act 1984.

**The hearing will be held at** [*place*] .......... **on** [*date*] .......... **at** [*time*].

You may appear personally at the hearing of this application unless the court decides otherwise on medical recommendations.

In any event, if you are unable or do not wish to appear personally you may request any person to appear on your behalf.

If you do not appear personally or by representative, the sheriff will consider the application in the absence of you or your representative.

[*Signed*]
Sheriff Clerk

[*Place and date*]
*delete as appropriate

Rule 3.8.3(3)          | FORM 13

FORM OF NOTICE TO RESPONSIBLE MEDICAL OFFICER

To [*name and address of responsible medical officer*]

In accordance with the Mental Health (Scotland) Act 1984, a copy of the application and notice of hearing is sent with this notice.

1. You are requested to deliver it personally to [*name of patient*] and to explain the contents of it to him.
2. You are also required to arrange if the patient so wishes, for the attendance of [*name of patient*] at the hearing at [*place of hearing*] on [*date*] so that he may appear and be heard in person.
3. You are further requested to complete and return to me in the enclosed envelope the certificate appended hereto before the date of the hearing.
4. If in your opinion it would be prejudicial to the patient's health or treatment for him to appear and be heard personally you may so recommend in writing, with reasons on the certificate.

[*Signed*]
Sheriff Clerk

[*Place and date*]

Rule 3.8.4(1)(b) and                                    FORM 14
3.8.4(2)(a)

FORM OF CERTIFICATE OF DELIVERY BY RESPONSIBLE MEDICAL OFFICER

I, [*name and designation*], certify that—

1. I have on the..........day of..........personally delivered to [*name of patient*] a copy of the application and the intimation cf the hearing; and have explained the contents or purport to him [*or* her].

2. The patient does [not] wish to attend the hearing.

3. The patient does [not] wish to be represented at the hearing [and has nominated [*name and address of representative*] to represent him].

4. I shall arrange for the attendance of the patient at the hearing [*or* in my view it would be prejudicial to the patient's health or treatment for him [*or* her] to appear and be heard in person for the following reasons [*give reasons*]].

                                                    [*Signature and designation*]

[*Address and date*]

Rule 3.8.11                                          FORM 15

FORM OF APPEAL FOR REVOCATION OF A COMMUNITY CARE ORDER UNDER SECTION 35F OF THE MENTAL HEALTH (SCOTLAND) ACT 1984

SHERIFFDOM OF (*insert name of sheriffdom*)

AT (*insert name of Sheriff Court*)

I, [*insert name and address of applicant*],

appeal to the sheriff for revocation of a community care order made on [*insert date of order* on the following grounds:—

[*State grounds on which appeal is to proceed*]

The community care order was renewed under section 35C(5) of the Mental Health (Scotland) Act 1984 on [*insert date of renewal*] and is still in force.

The special medical officer specified in the community care order is [*insert name and address of special medical officer*].

                                        [*Signed*]..........
                                        Applicant..........
                                        [*or* Solicitor for Applicant]..........
                                        [*Insert designation and address*]..........

**Rule 3.9.9(b)**                                   FORM 16

FORM OF NOTICE TO PERSON WITH INTEREST IN PROPERTY SUBJECT TO AN APPLICATION FOR AN ORDER UNDER PARAGRAPH 12 OF SCHEDULE 1 TO THE PROCEEDS OF CRIME (SCOTLAND) ACT 1995

IN THE SHERIFF COURT

in the

PETITION [*or* NOTE]

of

[A.B.] (*name and address*)

for an order under paragraph 12 of Schedule 1 to the Proceeds of Crime (Scotland) Act 1995

in respect of the estates of [CD.] (*name and address*)

Court Ref No.

Date: (*date of posting or other method of service*)

To: (name and address of person on whom notice is to be served)

This Notice—

(a) gives you warning that an application has been made to the sheriff court for an order which may affect your interest in property; and

(b) informs you that you have an opportunity to appear and make representations to the court before the application is determined.

TAKE NOTICE

1. That on (*date*) in the sheriff court at (*place*) a confiscation order was made under section 1 of the Proceeds of Crime (Scotland) Act 1995 in respect of [CD.] (name and address).

2. That on (*date*) the administrator appointed under paragraph 1(1)(a) of Schedule 1 to the Proceeds of Crime (Scotland) Act 1995 on (*date*) was empowered to realise property belonging to [CD.].

or

2. That on (*date*) the administrator was appointed under paragraph 1 (1)(b) of Schedule 1 to the Proceeds of Crime (Scotland) Act 1995 on (*date*) to realise property belonging to [CD.].

3. That application has been made by petition [*or* note] for an order under paragraph 12 of Schedule 1 to the Proceeds of Crime (Scotland) Act 1995 (*here set out briefly the nature of the order sought*). A copy of the petition [*or* note] is attached.

4. That you have the right to appear before the court in person or by counsel or other person having a right of audience and make such representations as you may have in respect of the order applied for. The court has fixed (*insert day and date fixed for hearing the application*), at (*insert time and place fixed for hearing*) as the time when you should appear to do this.

5. That if you do not appear or are not represented on the above date, the order applied for may be made in your absence.

IF YOU ARE UNCERTAIN ABOUT THE EFFECT OF THIS NOTICE, you should consult a Solicitor, Citizen's Advice Bureau or other local advice agency or adviser immediately.

> (*Signed*) ..........
>
> Sheriff Officer ..........
>
> [*or* Solicitor [*or* Agent] for petitioner [*or* noter]] ..........
>
> (*Address*)..........

**Rule 3.11.14(1)** FORM 17

### Representation of the People Act 1983

In the petition questioning the election for the .......... of .........., in which .......... is petitioner and .......... is respondent.

The petitioner desires to withdraw his petition on the following grounds [*state grounds*], and craves that a diet may be appointed for hearing his application. He has, in compliance, with rule 3.11.14 of the Act of Sederunt (Summary Applications, Statutory Applications and Appeals etc. Rules) 1999, given the written notice of his intention to present this application to the respondent, to the Lord Advocate, and to the returning officer.

[*To be signed by the petitioner or his solicitor.*]

**Rule 3.11.14(4)** FORM 18

### Representation of the People Act 1983

In the petition questioning the election for the .......... of .........., in which .......... is the petitioner and .......... is respondent.

Notice is hereby given that the above petitioner has applied for leave to withdraw his petition, and that the sheriff principal has, by interlocutor dated the .......... day of .........., assigned the .......... day of .......... at .......... o'clock .......... noon within the .......... as a diet for hearing the application.

Notice is further given that under the Act any person who might have been a petitioner in respect of the said election may at the above diet apply to the sheriff principal to be substituted as a petitioner.

[*To be signed by the petitioner or his solicitor.*]

**Rule 3.11.15(1)** FORM 19

### Representation of the People Act 1983

In the petition questioning the election for the .......... of .........., in which .......... was the petitioner [*or* last surviving petitioner] and .......... is the respondent.

Notice is hereby given that the above petition stands abated by the death of the petitioner [*or* last surviving petitioner], and that any person who might have been a petitioner in respect of the said election and who desires to be substituted as a petitioner must, within 21 days from this date, lodge with the undersigned sheriff clerk of [*name sheriff court district*], a minute craving to be so substituted.

Date (*insert date*)

[*To be signed by the sheriff clerk*]

**Rule 3.16.4(1)**                    FORM 20[1]

### FORM OF NOTICE OF AN APPLICATION UNDER THE ADULTS WITH INCAPACITY (SCOTLAND) ACT 2000

To *(insert name and address)*

Attached to this notice is a copy of an application for *(insert type of application)* under the Adults with Incapacity (Scotland) Act 2000.

**The hearing will be held at (insert place) on (insert date) at (insert time)**

You may appear personally at the hearing of this application.

In any event, if you are unable or do not wish to appear personally you may appoint a legal representative to appear on your behalf.

If you are uncertain as to what action to take you should consult a solicitor. You may be eligible for legal aid, and you can obtain information about legal aid from any solicitor. You may also obtain information from any Citizens Advice Bureau or other advice agency.

If you do not appear personally or by legal representative, the sheriff may consider the application in the absence of you or your legal representative.

*(insert place and date)*..........

*(signed)*..........
Sheriff Clerk ..........
or
[P.Q.] Sheriff Officer ..........
or
[X.Y.],Solicitor ..........

**Rule 3.16.4(3)**                    FORM 21[2]

### FORM OF NOTICE TO MANAGERS

To *(insert name and address of manager)*

A copy of an application made under the Adults with Incapacity (Scotland) Act 2000 and notice of hearing is sent with this notice.

1. You are requested to deliver it personally to (name of adult) and to explain the contents of it to him or her.

2. You are further requested to complete and return to the sheriff clerk in the enclosed envelope the certificate (Form 22) appended hereto before the date of the hearing.

*(insert place and date)*..........

*(signed)*..........
Sheriff Clerk ..........
or
[P.Q.] Sheriff Officer ..........
or
[X.Y.],Solicitor ..........

**Rule 3.16.4(4)**                    FORM 22[3]

### FORM OF CERTIFICATE OF DELIVERY BY MANAGER

I, *(insert name and designation)*, certify that—

I have on *(insert date)* personally delivered to (name of adult) a copy of the application and the intimation of the hearing and have explained the contents to him/her.

Date *(insert date)*..........

*(signed)*..........
Manager ..........
*(add designation and address)*..........

---

[1] As inserted by the Act of Sederunt (Summary Applications, Statutory Applications and Appeals etc. Rules) Amendment (Adults with Incapacity) 2001 (SSI 2001/142), (effective April 2, 2001).

[2] As inserted by the Act of Sederunt (Summary Applications, Statutory Applications and Appeals etc. Rules) Amendment (Adults with Incapacity) 2001 (SSI 2001/142), (effective April 2, 2001).

[3] As inserted by the Act of Sederunt (Summary Applications, Statutory Applications and Appeals etc. Rules) Amendment (Adults with Incapacity) 2001 (SSI 2001/142), (effective April 2, 2001).

**Rule 3.16.7(1)** FORM 23[1]

SUMMARY APPLICATION UNDER THE ADULTS WITH INCAPACITY (SCOTLAND) ACT 2000

SHERIFFDOM OF *(insert name of sheriffdom)*

AT *(insert place of Sheriff Court)*

[A.B.] *(design and state capacity in which the application is made)*, Pursuer

The applicant craves the court *(state here the specific order(s) sought by reference to the provisions in the Adults with Incapacity (Scotland) Act 2000 .)*

**STATEMENTS OF FACT**

*(State in numbered paragraphs the facts on which the application is made, including:*

1. *The designation of the adult concerned (if other than the applicant).*

(a) *the adult's nearest relative;*

(b) *the adult's primary carer;*

(ba) *the adult's named person;*

(c) *any guardian, continuing attorney or welfare attorney of the adult; and*

(d) *any other person who may have an interest in the application.*

3. *The adult's place of habitual residence and/or the location of the property which is the subject of the application.)*

*(insert place and date)* ..........        *(signed)* ..........

[A.B.], Pursuer or

[X.Y.], *(state designation and business address)*..........

Solicitor for the Pursuer ..........

**Rule 3.16.7(2)** FORM 24[2]

APPEAL TO THE SHERIFF UNDER THE ADULTS WITH INCAPACITY (SCOTLAND) ACT 2000

SHERIFFDOM OF *(insert name of sheriffdom)*

AT *(insert place of Sheriff Court)*

[A.B.] *(design and state capacity in which the appeal is being made)*, Pursuer

This appeal is made in respect of *(state here the decision concerned, the date on which it was intimated to the pursuer, and refer to the relevant provisions in the Adults with Incapacity (Scotland) Act 2000 )*.

*(State here, in numbered paragraphs*:

1. *The designation of the adult concerned (if other than the applicant).*

2. *The designation of:*

(a) *the adult's nearest relative;*

(b) *the adult's primary carer;*

(ba) *the adult's named person;*

(c) *any guardian, continuing attorney or welfare attorney of the adult; and*

(d) *any other person who may have an interest in the application.*

3. *The adult's place of habitual residence and/or the location of the property which is the subject of the application.)*

The pursuer appeals against the decision on the following grounds *(state here in separate paragraphs the grounds on which the appeal is made).*

The pursuer craves the court *(state here orders sought in respect of appeal).*

---

[1] As inserted by the Act of Sederunt (Summary Applications, Statutory Applications and Appeals etc. Rules) Amendment (Adults with Incapacity) 2001 (SSI 2001/142), (effective April 2, 2001) and amended by the Act of Sederunt (Summary Applications, Statutory Applications and Appeals etc. Rules) Amendment (Adult Support and Protection (Scotland) Act 2007) (SSI 2008/111) r.2(3) (effective April 1, 2008).

[2] As inserted by the Act of Sederunt (Summary Applications, Statutory Applications and Appeals etc. Rules) Amendment (Adults with Incapacity) 2001 (SSI 2001/142), r.3(3), (effective April 2, 2001) and amended by the Act of Sederunt (Summary Applications, Statutory Applications and Appeals etc. Rules) Amendment (Adult Support and Protection (Scotland) Act 2007) (SSI 2008/111) r.2(3) (effective April 1, 2008).

*(insert place and date)* .........

*(signed)*..........

[A.B.], Pursuer or

[X.Y.], *(state designation and business address)*..........

Solicitor for the Pursuer .........

**Rule 3.27.6(1)**                    FORM 25[1]

ANTISOCIAL BEHAVIOUR ETC. (SCOTLAND) ACT 2004
CLOSURE NOTICE

Section 27

1. The service of this closure notice is authorised by a senior police officer under section 26(1) of the Antisocial Behaviour etc. (Scotland) Act 2004 ("the Act").

2. The premises to which this closure notice relates are: *(specify premises)*.

3. Access to those premises by any person other than—

(a) a person who habitually resides in the premises; or

(b) the owner of the premises,

is prohibited.

4. Failure to comply with this notice is an offence which may result in a fine of up to £2,500 or imprisonment for a term of up to 3 months (or both). The penalties may be higher for repeated failure to comply with this (or any other) closure notice.

5. An application for the closure of these premises will be made under section 28 of the Act and will be considered at *(insert place including Room No. if appropriate)* on the ......... day of ......... at ......... am/pm.

6. On such an application as set out in paragraph 5 being made, the sheriff may make a closure order under section 29 of the Act in respect of these premises.

7. The effect of the Closure Order in respect of these premises would be to close the premises to all persons (other than any person expressly authorised access by the sheriff in terms of section 29(3) of the Act) for such period not exceeding 3 months as is specified in the order. Measures may be taken to ensure that the premises are securely closed against entry by any person.

8. If you live on or have control of, responsibility for or an interest in the premises to which this closure notice relates and wish to oppose the application for a closure order, you should attend or be represented at the hearing mentioned in paragraph 5 of this notice.

9. If you would like further information or advice about housing or legal matters you can contact—

*(specify at least two persons or organisations (including name and means of contacting) based in the locality of the promises who or which will be able to provide advice about housing and legal matters)*. You also have a legal right to advice from your local authority should you be threatened with possible homelessness.

**Rule 3.27.6(2)**                    FORM 26[2]

ANTISOCIAL BEHAVIOUR ETC. (SCOTLAND) ACT 2004
**CERTIFICATION OF SERVICE**

Section 27

I *(insert designation, including address and rank, of police officer)* certify that a copy of the closure notice which was authorised by *(insert designation of senior police officer)* on *(insert date on which closure notice was authorised)* in respect of *(insert details of the premises to which closure notice relates)* was served on: *(insert name and address of each person to whom a copy of the notice was given, including date)*

.....................

.....................

.....................

.....................

.....................

---

[1] Inserted by SSI 2004/455, para 5 and Sch. (effective October 28, 2004).
[2] Inserted by SSI 2004/455, para 5 and Sch. (effective October 28, 2004).

by *(insert designation, including address and rank, of police officer who served the copy or copies of the closure notice and, if more than one, indicate which police officer served a copy of the notice on which of the persons listed above).*

.....................

Signed

*(insert designation, including rank, of police officer)*

**Rule 3.27.7**                                        FORM 27[1]

ANTISOCIAL BEHAVIOUR ETC. (SCOTLAND) ACT 2004

Section 28

Sheriff Court.................... 20..........

(Court Ref No.)

**PART A**

APPLICATION FOR CLOSURE ORDER IN RESPECT OF PREMISES AT:

.....................

.....................

.....................

("the Premises")

**PART B**

1. This application is made [by/on behalf of] *(delete as appropriate) (insert name and rank of senior police officer)* of *(insert details of police force).*

2. Service of a closure notice on the Premises was authorised by *(insert details of senior police officer)* on the .......... day of .......... A copy of [the authorisation/written confirmation of such authorisation] *(delete as appropriate)* is attached.

3. A copy of the closure notice was, on the .......... day of ..........,—

(a) fixed to:

*(insert details of all locations in, or used as part of the Premises, to which a copy of the notice was fixed)*

.....................

.....................

.....................

.....................

.....................

(b) given to:

*(insert name and address of each person to whom a copy of the notice was given)*

.....................

.....................

.....................

.....................

.....................

4. Certification in the prescribed form of service of the closure notice to the persons described at paragraph 3(b) above is attached.

5. This application is made on the following grounds:

*(insert reasons for making application)*

.....................

.....................

.....................

.....................

.....................

6. The following evidence is [attached/supplied] *(delete as appropriate)* in respect of this application *(insert short details of supporting evidence).*

---

[1] Inserted by SSI 2004/455, para 5 and Sch. (effective October 28, 2004) and amended by SSI 2010/416 (effective December 13, 2010).

**PART C**

7. The applicant asks the court to—

(a) assign the hearing for the .......... day of .......... at .......... am/pm; and

(b) make a closure order in respect of the Premises.

..........Signed

Senior Police Officer for [Police Force] (Applicant)

or [X.Y.] Solicitor for Senior Police Officer

*(add designation and business address)*

FORM OF INTERLOCUTOR

Sheriff Court .......... .......... 20..........

(Court Ref No.)

The sheriff having considered this application assigns .......... at .......... within .......... as a hearing, this date having been previously intimated to known interested persons and published in the closure notice.

..........Signed

Sheriff

FORM OF INTERLOCUTOR

Sheriff Court .................... 20..........

(Court Ref No.)

The sheriff having heard *(insert details of parties who attended the hearing)* and having considered the application [, being satisfied that the conditions mentioned in [section 30(2)] [section 30(2A)] of the Antisocial Behaviour etc. (Scotland) Act 2004 are met] *(delete as appropriate)* and having regard to the matters mentioned in section 30(3) of the Antisocial Behaviour etc. (Scotland) Act 2004 ("the Act"),

*1. makes an order under section 29(1) of the Act that the premises at *(insert details of premises)* are closed to all persons for a period of *(insert period)*.

*2. directs intimation of this interlocutor to *(insert details of all known interested persons)* and by posting a copy thereof at prominent places on the premises at *(indicate where copies have been posted)*.

*3. refuses to make a closure order in respect of the premises at *(insert details of premises)*.

*4. postpones the determination of the application until *(insert date)* at *(insert time)* within *(insert location)*.

*delete as appropriate

..........Signed

Sheriff

**Rule 3.27.8**                                        FORM 28[1]

ANTISOCIAL BEHAVIOUR ETC. (SCOTLAND) ACT 2004
Minute

Section 32

Application for extension of closure order

Sheriff Court ..........: .............. 20..........

(Court Ref No.)

**PART A**

PREMISES IN RESPECT OF WHICH CLOSURE ORDER HAS BEEN MADE:

....................

....................

....................

("the Premises")

**PART B**

1. This application is made [by/on behalf of] *(delete as appropriate) (insert name and rank of senior police officer) of (insert details of police force)*.

2. A copy of the closure order made in respect of the Premises is attached. The closure order has effect until *(enter date)*.

3. The applicant believes that it is necessary to extend the period for which the closure order has effect for the purpose of preventing [relevant harm] [the commission of an exploitation offence] *(delete as appropriate)*, on the following grounds: *(specify reasons for extension)*.

---

[1] Inserted by SSI 2004/455, para 5 and Sch. (effective October 28, 2004) and amended by SSI 2010/416 (effective December 13, 2010).

4. *(Insert details of local authority)* has been consulted about the applicant's intention to make this application.

PART C

5. The applicant asks the court to—

(c) fix a hearing;

(d) order the applicant to intimate this application and the date of the hearing to such persons as the sheriff considers appropriate; and

(e) extend the closure order in respect of the Premises for a period of .......... [months/days] *(delete as appropriate)* or for such period not exceeding 6 months as the court may consider appropriate.

..........Signed

Senior Police Officer for [Police Force] (Applicant)

or [X.Y.] Solicitor for Senior Police Officer

*(add designation and business address)*

FORM OF INTERLOCUTOR

Sheriff Court.................... 2..........

(Court Ref No.)

The sheriff having considered this minute orders the applicant to intimate this application and interlocutor to .........., assigns .......... at .......... within .......... as a hearing and directs any person wishing to oppose the granting of the application to appear or be represented at the hearing to show cause why the application should not be granted.

..........Signed

Sheriff

FORM OF INTERLOCUTOR

Sheriff Court ....................20..........

(Court Ref No.)

The sheriff having heard *(insert details of parties who attended the hearing)* [and] having considered this minute [and being satisfied that the condition mentioned in [section 32(1)] [section 32(1 A)] of the Antisocial Behaviour etc. (Scotland) Act 2004 is met] *(delete as appropriate)*,

*1. makes an order extending the closure order made under section 29(1) of the Antisocial Behaviour etc. (Scotland) Act 2004 in respect of the premises at *(insert details of premises)* for a period of *(insert period)*.

*2. directs intimation of this interlocutor to *(insert details of persons to whom sheriff considers it to he appropriate to intimate)* and by posting a copy thereof at prominent places on the premises at *(indicate where copies have been posted)*.

*3. refuses to make an order extending the closure order in respect of the premises at *(insert details of premises)*.

*4. postpones the determination of the application until *(insert date)* at *(insert time)* within *(insert location)*.

*delete as appropriate

..........Signed

Sheriff

**Rule 3.27.9**                                        FORM 29[1]

ANTISOCIAL BEHAVIOUR ETC. (SCOTLAND) ACT 2004

Minute

Section 33

Application for revocation of closure order

Sheriff Court .................... 20..........

(Court Ref No.)

**PART A**

PREMISES IN RESPECT OF WHICH CLOSURE ORDER HAS BEEN MADE:

....................

....................

....................

("the Premises")

---

[1] Inserted by SSI 2004/455, para 5 and Sch. (effective October 28, 2004) and amended by SSI 2010/416 (effective December 13, 2010).

The applicant is *(insert name and address of applicant)* who is:

*1. a senior police officer of the police force for the area within which the Premises (or part thereof) are situated.

*2. the local authority for the area within which the Premises or part thereof are situated.

*3. a person on whom a copy of the closure notice relating to the Premises in respect of which the closure order has effect was served under section 27(2)(b) or (3) of the Antisocial Behaviour etc. (Scotland) Act 2004.

*4. a person who has an interest in these premises but on whom the closure notice was not served.

*delete as appropriate

**PART B**

1. A copy of the closure order made in respect of the Premises is attached.

2. The applicant believes that a closure order in respect of the Premises is no longer necessary to prevent [the occurrence of relevant harm][the commission of an exploitation offence] *(delete as appropriate)* for the following reasons *(specify grounds for application for revocation)*.

**PART C**

3. The applicant asks the court to:
   (a) fix a hearing;
   (b) order the applicant to intimate this application and the date of the hearing to such persons as the sheriff considers appropriate and, where the applicant is not a senior police officer, to such senior police officer as the sheriff considers appropriate; and
   (c) order the revocation of the closure order.

..........Signed

Applicant *(include full designation)*

or [X.Y.] Solicitor for Applicant *(include full designation and business address)*

FORM OF INTERLOCUTOR

Sheriff Court.......... ..........20..............

(Court Ref No.)

The sheriff having considered this minute orders the applicant to intimate this application and interlocutor to.........., assigns...........within...........as a hearing and directs any person wishing to oppose the granting of the application to appear or be represented at the hearing to show cause why the application should not be granted.

..........Signed

Sheriff

FORM OF INTERLOCUTOR

Sheriff Court..............20...........

(Court Ref No.)

The sheriff having heard *(insert details of parties who attended the hearing)* [and] having considered this minute [and being satisfied that a closure order is no longer necessary to prevent [the occurrence of relevant harm][the commission of an exploitation offence] *(delete as appropriate)*,

*1. makes an order revoking the closure order made under section 29(1) of the Antisocial Behaviour etc. (Scotland) Act 2004 in respect of the premises at (insert details of the premises).

*2. directs intimation of this interlocutor to (insert details of persons to whom sheriff considers it to be appropriate to intimate).

*3. refuses to make an order revoking the closure order in respect of the premises at (insert details of the premises).

*4. postpones the determination of the application until *(insert date)* at *(insert time)* within *(insert location)*.

*delete as appropriate

..........Signed

Sheriff

**Rule 3.27.10**                    FORM 30[1]

ANTISOCIAL BEHAVIOUR ETC. (SCOTLAND) ACT 2004
Minute

Section 34

Application for access to premises in respect of which a closure order is in force

---

[1] Inserted by SSI 2004/455, para 5 and Sch. (effective October 28, 2004).

Sheriff Court.......... ...........20...........

(Court Ref No.)

**PART A**

PREMISES IN RESPECT OF WHICH CLOSURE ORDER HAS BEEN MADE:

...................

...................

...................

("the Premises")

PREMISES IN RESPECT OF WHICH APPLICATION FOR ACCESS IS BEING MADE:

...................

...................

...................

**PART B**

1. A copy of the closure order made in respect of the Premises is attached. The closure order has effect until (*insert date*).

2. The applicant (*insert details of applicant*) [owns/occupies] (*delete as appropriate*) the following [part of] (delete as appropriate) building or structure in which the Premises are situated and in respect of which the closure order does not have effect.

**PART C**

3. The applicant asks the court to:

(a) fix a hearing;

(b) order the applicant to intimate this application and the date of the hearing to such persons as the sheriff considers appropriate and, where the applicant is not a senior police officer, to such senior police officer as the sheriff considers appropriate; and

(c) make an order allowing access (detail access provisions requested).

..........Signed

Applicant (*include full designation*)

or [X.Y.] Solicitor for Applicant (*include full designation and business address*)

FORM OF INTERLOCUTOR

Sheriff Court...............20...........

(Court Ref No.)

The sheriff having considered this minute orders the applicant to intimate this application and interlocutor to.........., assigns..........at..........within.......... as a hearing and directs any person wishing to oppose the granting of the application to appear or be represented at the hearing to show cause why the application should not be granted.

..........Signed

Sheriff

FORM OF INTERLOCUTOR

Sheriff Court...............20..........

(Court Ref No.)

The sheriff having heard (*insert details of parties who attended the hearing*) and having considered this minute,

*1. makes an order an order allowing (*insert name and address*)

...................

...................

...................

access to the following part or parts of the premises at (*insert details of premises*) in relation to which a closure order has been made under section 29(1) of the Antisocial Behaviour etc. (Scotland) Act 2004: (*insert details of parts of premises to which access order is to apply*)

*2. directs intimation of this interlocutor to (*insert details of all known interested persons to whom the sheriff considers it to be appropriate to intimate*).

*3. refuses to make an access order in respect of the premises at (*insert details of premises*).

*4. postpones the determination of the application until (insert date) at (insert time) within (*insert location*).

*delete as appropriate

.......... Signed

Sheriff

FORM 31

ANTISOCIAL BEHAVIOUR ETC. (SCOTLAND) ACT 2004 Section 13, 102 or 105

Intimation that court may make or revoke or vary a parenting order

Sheriff Court .......... .......... 20 ..........

(Court Ref No.)

**PART A**

**This part must be completed by the applicant's solicitor in language a child is capable of understanding**

To **(1)**

The Sheriff (the person who has to decide about the parenting order) has been asked by **(2)** to decide:—

(a)   **(3)** and **(4)**;

(b)   **(5)**;

(c)   **(6)**.

If you want to tell the Sheriff what you think about the things **(2)** has asked the Sheriff to decide about your future you should complete Part B of this form and send it to the Sheriff Clerk at **(7)** by **(8)**. An envelope which does not need a postage stamp is enclosed for you to use to return the form.

**IF YOU DO NOT UNDERSTAND THIS FORM OR IF YOU WANT HELP TO COMPLETE IT you may get free help from a SOLICITOR or contact the SCOTTISH CHILD LAW CENTRE ON the FREE ADVICE TELEPHONE LINE ON 0800 317 500.**

If you return the form it will be given to the Sheriff. The Sheriff may wish to speak with you and may ask you to come and see him or her.

NOTES FOR COMPLETION

| | |
|---|---|
| (1) Insert name and address of child. | (2) Insert description of party making the application to the court. |
| (3) Insert appropriate wording for parenting order sought. | (4) Insert appropriate wording, if relevant, for Antisocial Behaviour Order. |
| (5) Insert appropriate wording for contact. | (6) Insert appropriate wording for any other order sought or determinations to be made by sheriff. |
| (7) Insert address of sheriff clerk. | (8) Insert the date occurring 21 days after the date on which intimation is given. |
| (9) Insert court reference number. | (10) Insert name and address of parties to the action. |

**PART B**

**IF YOU WISH THE SHERIFF TO KNOW YOUR VIEWS ABOUT THE PARENTING ORDER YOU SHOULD COMPLETE THIS PART OF THE FORM**

To the Sheriff Clerk, (7)

Court Ref. No. (9)

(10)..........

**QUESTION (1): DO YOU WISH THE SHERIFF TO KNOW WHAT YOUR VIEWS ARE ABOUT THE PARENTING ORDER?**

(PLEASE TICK BOX)

| | |
|---|---|
| YES | |
| NO | |

If you have ticked YES please also answer Question (2) or (3)

**QUESTION (2): WOULD YOU LIKE A FRIEND, RELATIVE OR OTHER PERSON TO TELL THE SHERIFF YOUR VIEWS ABOUT THE PARENTING ORDER?**

(PLEASE TICK BOX)

| | |
|---|---|
| YES | |
| NO | |

If you have ticked YES please write the name and address of the person you wish to tell the Sheriff your views in Box (A) below. You should also tell that person what your views are about the parenting order.

| BOX A: | (NAME) | | | | |
|---|---|---|---|---|---|
| | .................... | | | | |
| | (ADDRESS) | | | | |
| | .................... | | | | |
| | .................... | | | | |
| | .................... | | | | |
| | Is this person— | A friend? | | A relative? | |
| | | A teacher? | | Other? | |

OR

**QUESTION (3): WOULD YOU LIKE TO WRITE TO THE SHERIFF AND TELL HIM
WHAT YOUR VIEWS ARE ABOUT THE PARENTING ORDER?**
(PLEASE TICK BOX)

| YES | |
|---|---|
| NO | |

If you decide that you wish to write to the Sheriff you can write what your views are about the parenting
order in Box (B) below or on a separate piece of paper. If you decide to write your views on a separate
piece of paper you should send it along with this form to the Sheriff Clerk in the envelope provided.

| BOX B: | WHAT I HAVE TO SAY ABOUT THE PARENTING ORDER:— |
|---|---|
| | |

NAME: ..........
    ADDRESS: ..........
    DATE: ..........

**Rule 3.27.17**                           FORM 32[1]

ANTISOCIAL BEHAVIOUR ETC. (SCOTLAND) ACT 2004
Section 13, 102 or 105
Form of notice to local authority requesting a report in respect of a child
Sheriff Court.......... .......... 20..........
(Court Ref No.)
To (*insert name and address*)

**1. YOU ARE GIVEN NOTICE** that in an action in the Sheriff Court at (*insert address*) an application for [the variation/revocation of] (*delete as appropriate*) a parenting order is being considered in
respect of a parent of the child (*insert name of child*). A copy of the application is enclosed.

2. You are required to submit to the court a report on all the circumstances of the child, including but
not limited to:—

    (a)    the current or proposed arrangements for the case and upbringing of the child;

    (b)    information about the family circumstances of the parent; and

    (c)    the likely effect of a parenting order on the family circumstances of the parent and the child.

3. This report should be sent to the Sheriff Court at .......... on or before .......... (*insert date*).

Date (*insert date*)
..........Signed:
Applicant (*include full designation*)
or [X.Y.] Solicitor for Applicant (*include full designation and business address*)
or Sheriff Clerk

**Rule 3.34.2**                           FORM 33

NOTE OF APPEAL UNDER LICENSING (SCOTLAND) ACT 2005
*[Repealed by the Act of Sederunt (Sheriff Court Rules) (Miscellaneous Amend-
ments) (No.2) 2010 (SSI 2010/416) r.8 (effective December 13, 2010).]*

---

[1] Inserted by SSI 2004/455, para 5 and Sch. (effective October 28, 2004).

**Rule 3.35.6**                                               FORM 34[1]

Form of certificate of delivery of document under section 26(2), 27(1) or 27(2) of the Adult Support and Protection (Scotland) Act 2007

Court ref no:

(Insert place and date) I, (insert name and designation), hereby certify that on (date) I duly delivered to (insert name and address) (insert details of the document delivered). This I did by (state method of delivery).

*Signed*

*(add designation and address or business address)*

FORM 35[2]

FORM OF APPLICATION FOR WARRANT FOR ENTRY UNDER SECTION 38(2) OF THE ADULT SUPPORT AND PROTECTION (SCOTLAND) ACT 2007

SHERIFFDOM OF *(insert name of sheriffdom)*

AT *(insert place of sheriff court)*

[A.B.] *(design and state capacity in which the application is made)*, Applicant

The applicant craves the court to grant a warrant for entry in terms of sections 37 and 38(2) of the Adult Support and Protection (Scotland) Act 2007 to *(state address of specified place to which entry is sought)*.

**Rule 3.39.2(1)**                                               FORM 36[3]

FORM OF APPLICATION FOR WARRANT UNDER SECTION 27 OF THE PUBLIC HEALTH ETC. (SCOTLAND) ACT 2008

SHERIFFDOM OF *(insert name of sheriffdom)*

AT *(insert place of sheriff court)*

[A.B.] (design and state address), Applicant

**Order sought from the court**

The applicant applies to the court to grant warrant to him:

1.   to enter the premises at *(insert address of premises to which entry is sought)*.
2.   to take with him any other person he may authorise and, if he has reasonable cause to expect any serious obstruction in obtaining access, a constable.
3.   to take with him any equipment or materials required for any purpose for which the power of entry is being exercised.
4.   to direct that those premises (or any part of them) are, or any thing in or on them is, to be left undisturbed (whether generally or in particular respects) for so long as he considers appropriate.
5.   to exercise any of the powers conferred by sections 23, 24 and 25 of the Public Health etc. (Scotland) Act 2008 ("the Act").

**Statement**

*Delete as appropriate

1.   This application is made pursuant to section 27 of the Act.
2.   The applicant is an investigator duly appointed in terms of section 21(2) of the Act to carry out a public health investigation.
3.   The said premises are*/are not* a dwellinghouse.
4.   The said premises are within the jurisdiction of this court.
5.   The applicant considers it necessary for the purpose of, or in connection with, a public health investigation to exercise the powers of entry available to him under section 22 of the Act, the other investigatory powers mentioned in section 23 of the Act, the power to ask questions

---

[1] As inserted by the Act of Sederunt (Summary Applications, Statutory Applications and Appeals etc. Rules) Amendment (Adult Support and Protection (Scotland) Act 2007) (No.2) 2008 (SSI 2008/335) r.2(3) (effective October 29, 2008) and substituted by the Act of Sederunt (Summary Applications, Statutory Applications and Appeals etc. Rules) Amendment (Adult Support and Protection (Scotland) Act 2007) (No.3) 2008 (SSI 2008/375) para.2(5) (effective November 20, 2008).

[2] As inserted by the Act of Sederunt (Summary Applications, Statutory Applications and Appeals etc. Rules) Amendment (Adult Support and Protection (Scotland) Act 2007) (No.2) 2008 (SSI 2008/335) r.2(3) (effective October 29, 2008).

[3] As inserted by the Act of Sederunt (Summary Applications, Statutory Applications and Appeals etc. Rules) Amendment (Public Health etc. (Scotland) Act 2008) 2009 (SSI 2009/320) r.2 (effective October 1, 2009).

mentioned in section 24 of the Act and any supplementary power mentioned in section 25 of the Act (*insert here a brief statement of reasons*).

*6. [*If the said premises are a dwellinghouse*] The applicant has in terms of section 26(2) of the Act given 48 hours notice of the proposed entry to a person who appears to be the occupier of the dwellinghouse and the period of notice has expired.

*7. The applicant is an investigator entitled to enter premises under section 22 of the Act and *the applicant has been refused entry to the said premises, or *the applicant reasonably anticipates that entry will be refused

OR

*7. The said premises are premises which the applicant is entitled to enter and they are unoccupied.

**OR**

*7. The said premises are premises which the applicant is entitled to enter and the occupier thereof is temporarily absent and there is urgency because (*here state briefly why there is urgency*).

**OR**

*7. The applicant is an investigator entitled to exercise a power under section 23 or 24 of the Act and
* has been prevented from exercising that power, or
* reasonably anticipates being prevented from exercising that power.

**OR**

*7 An application for admission to the said premises would defeat the object of the public health investigation.

8. In the circumstances narrated the applicant is entitled to the warrant sought and it should be granted accordingly.

> (*signed*)
> [A.B.] Applicant
> or [X.Y.] (*add designation and business address*)
> Solicitor for applicant
> (*insert date*)

**Rule 3.39.2(2)**                                                          FORM 37[1]

FORM OF WARRANT FOR A PUBLIC HEALTH INVESTIGATION

Sheriff Court...............20...............

(Court Ref. No.)

* *Delete as appropriate*

The sheriff, having considered an application made under section 27 of the Public Health etc. (Scotland) Act 2008 ("the Act") *[and productions lodged therewith] *[and (*where the premises referred to below are a dwellinghouse*) being satisfied that due notice has been given under section 26(2) of the Act and has expired],

Grants warrant to the applicant (*insert name*) as sought and authorises him:

(a)  to enter the premises at (*insert address*),

(b)  on entering the premises referred to at paragraph (a), to take—

(i)  any other person authorised by him and, if he has reasonable cause to expect any serious obstruction in obtaining access, a constable; and

(ii)  any equipment or materials required for any purpose for which the power of entry is being exercised,

(c)  to direct that—

(i)  those premises (or any part of them) are; or

(ii)  any thing in or on those premises is, to be left undisturbed (whether generally or in particular respects) for so long as he considers appropriate.

(d)  to exercise any power mentioned in sections 23 to 25 of the Act.

(*signed*)

Sheriff

---

[1] As inserted by the Act of Sederunt (Summary Applications, Statutory Applications and Appeals etc. Rules) Amendment (Public Health etc. (Scotland) Act 2008) 2009 (SSI 2009/320) r.2 (effective October 1, 2009).

FORM 38[1]

FORM OF APPLICATION FOR MEDICAL EXAMINATION OF A PERSON UNDER SECTION 34
OF THE PUBLIC HEALTH ETC. (SCOTLAND) ACT 2008

SHERIFFDOM OF (*insert name of sheriffdom*)

AT (*insert place of sheriff court*)

[A.B.] (*design health board*), Applicant

### Order sought from the court

*\* Delete as appropriate*

The applicant applies to the court to grant an order under section 34(1) of the Public Health etc.
(Scotland) Act 2008 ("the Act") authorising the medical examination of (*insert name, address and date
of birth of person to be medically examined*) ("the person").

*\*And (if necessary, request any specialities in connection with the examination, about which the
court's additional authority is sought pursuant to section 34(3) of the Act).*

### Statement

*\*Delete as appropriate*

1.   This application is made pursuant to sections 33 and 34 of the Act.
2.   The person is present within the applicant's area. The applicant is a health board operating
     within the jurisdiction of this court. This court accordingly has jurisdiction.
3.   The person is aged 16 years or over.

**OR**

The person is under 16. The parent or other person who has day-to-day care or control of the person is
(*insert name, address and relationship to the person*).

4.
   (a)   The applicant *knows/*suspects that the person—
        *(i)    has an infectious disease, namely [*insert name of disease*];
        *(ii)   has been exposed to an organism which causes an infectious disease [*insert
                name of disease*];
        *(iii)  is contaminated; or
        *(iv)   has been exposed to a contaminant,

(*insert here a brief statement indicating the basis upon which these matters are known or suspected by
the applicant*)

**AND**

   (b)   It appears to the applicant that as a result—
        (i)    there is or may be a significant risk to public health; and
        (ii)   it is necessary, to avoid or minimise that risk, for the person to be medically examined.

(*Insert here a brief statement indicating the reason why the applicant considers that there is or may be a
significant risk to public health and that it is necessary, to avoid or minimise that risk, for the person to
be medically examined*).

5. The applicant proposes that the examination be carried out by (*insert proposed class or classes of
health care professional*).

6. The applicant proposes that the examination be (*insert nature of the proposed examination*).

*7. The applicant has explained to the person—
   (a)   that there is a significant risk to public health;
   (b)   the nature of that risk; and
   (c)   why the applicant considers it necessary for the proposed action to be taken in relation to that
         person.

**OR**

*7. The applicant states that the person is incapable of understanding any explanation of the matters
referred to at section 31(3) of the Act (*state reason*) and has explained to (*insert name and address of a
person mentioned in section 31(5)(a) or (b) of the Act and their relationship to the person*)—
   (a)   that there is a significant risk to public health;
   (b)   the nature of that risk; and

---

[1] As inserted by the Act of Sederunt (Summary Applications, Statutory Applications and Appeals etc.
Rules) Amendment (Public Health etc. (Scotland) Act 2008) 2009 (SSI 2009/320) r.2 (effective
October 1, 2009).

(c) why the applicant considers it necessary for the proposed action to be taken in relation to that person.

**OR**

*7. The applicant states that no explanation has been given in relation to this application under section 31(3) or (5) of the Act because (*state why it was not reasonably practicable to do so*).

*8. The applicant states that *a response was made/*representations were made on behalf of the person in the following terms (*insert response or representations made*).

9. The applicant attaches to this application a certificate signed by a health board competent person which indicates that the competent person is satisfied as to the matters mentioned in statement 4 [*and (*in a case where medical examination of a group is sought*) that it is necessary, to avoid or minimise an actual or anticipated significant risk to public health, for all the persons in the group to be medically examined].

10. In the circumstances narrated the applicant is entitled to the order sought and it should be granted accordingly.

(*signed*)

[X.Y.] (*add designation and business address*)

Solicitor for applicant

(*insert date*)

FORM 39[1]

**Rule 3.39.3(3)**

FORM OF ORDER FOR A MEDICAL EXAMINATION

Sheriff Court................

............... 20.......... at [*insert time*]

(Court Ref. No.)

The sheriff, having considered an application made under section 33(2) of the Public Health etc. (Scotland) Act 2008 ("the Act") *[and productions lodged therewith], and being satisfied as necessary as to the matters mentioned in section 34(2) of the Act,

1. Makes an order in terms of section 34(1) of the Act authorising the medical examination of (insert details of the person as given in the application) and authorises (insert the class or classes of health care professional by whom the medical examination is to be carried out) to carry out the examination,

*And (*add any additional matters to be dealt with in the order in terms of* section 34(3) of the Act).

2. Directs notification of this order (*insert details of method and timing of notice*) to (*the person to whom the order applies*)

*and (*the name and designation of any person to whom an explanation was given under* section 31(5) of the Act)

*and (*insert the name and designation of any other person whom the sheriff considers appropriate*).

* Delete *as appropriate*

(*signed*)

Sheriff

FORM 40[2]

**Rule 3.39.4(1)**

FORM OF APPLICATION FOR QUARANTINE ORDER UNDER SECTION 40 OF THE PUBLIC HEALTH ETC. (SCOTLAND) ACT 2008

SHERIFFDOM OF (*insert name of sheriffdom*)

AT (*insert place of sheriff court*)

[A.B.] (*design health board*), Applicant

**Order sought from the court**

* Delete *as appropriate*

---

[1] As inserted by the Act of Sederunt (Summary Applications, Statutory Applications and Appeals etc. Rules) Amendment (Public Health etc. (Scotland) Act 2008) 2009 (SSI 2009/320) r.2 (effective October 1, 2009).

[2] As inserted by the Act of Sederunt (Summary Applications, Statutory Applications and Appeals etc. Rules) Amendment (Public Health etc. (Scotland) Act 2008) 2009 (SSI 2009/320) r.2 (effective October 1, 2009).

The applicant applies to the court for a quarantine order under section 40(1) of the Public Health etc. (Scotland) Act 2008 ("the Act") authorising the quarantining of (*insert name, address and date of birth of person to be quarantined*) (*"the person"*) for a period of (*insert period*).

*and the person's removal to (*insert place of quarantine*) [by (*insert, if sought, the name and designation of a person mentioned in* section 4()(4)(d) of the Act)].

*authorising the taking in relation to the person of the following steps, namely *disinfection/
*disinfestation/*decontamination (*specify which steps are sought*)

*and imposing the following conditions in relation to the quarantine (insert conditions sought).

**Statement**

*Delete as appropriate*

1. This application is made pursuant to sections 39 and 40 of the Act.

2. The person is present within the applicant's area. The applicant is a health board operating within the jurisdiction of this court. This court accordingly has jurisdiction.

3. The person is aged 16 years or over.

**OR**

The person is under 16. The parent or other person who has day-to-day care or control of the person is (*insert name, address and relationship to the person*).

4. (a) The applicant *knows/*has reasonable grounds to suspect that the person—

*(i)    has an infectious disease, namely [*insert name of disease*];

*(ii)   has been exposed to an organism which causes an infectious disease [*insert name of disease*];

*(iii)  is contaminated; or

*(iv)   has been exposed to a contaminant,

(*insert here a brief statement indicating the basis upon which these matters are known or suspected by the applicant*)

**AND**

(b) that as a result—

(i)    there is or may be a significant risk to public health; and

(ii)   it is necessary, to avoid or minimise that risk, for the person to be quarantined.

(*Insert here a brief statement indicating the reason why the applicant considers that there is or may be a significant risk to public health and that it is necessary, to avoid or minimise that risk, for the person to be quarantined*).

5. The applicant proposes that the person be quarantined at (*insert place and address*) *[and that he should be removed there by (*insert name and designation of person under* section 40(4) (d) of the Act)]. (*Indicate briefly why this is proposed*).

6. The applicant proposes that the person be quarantined for (*insert period of time*).

7. The applicant considers it necessary to *disinfect/*disinfest/*decontaminate the person (*insert details and reasons*).

*8. The applicant considers the conditions sought to be included in the order to be necessary because (*insert reasons*).

*9. The applicant has explained to the person—

(a)    that there is a significant risk to public health;

(b)    the nature of that risk; and

(c)    why the applicant considers it necessary for the proposed action to be taken in relation to that person.

**OR**

*9. The applicant states that the person is incapable of understanding any explanation of the matters referred to at section 31(3) of the Act (*state reason*) and has explained to (*insert name and address of a person mentioned in* section 31(5) (a) or (b) of the Act *and their relationship to the person*)—

(a)    that there is a significant risk to public health;

(b)    the nature of that risk; and

(c)    why the applicant considers it necessary for the proposed action to be taken in relation to that person.

**OR**

*9 The applicant states that no explanation has been given in relation to this application under section 31(3) or (5) of the Act because (*state why it was not reasonably practicable to do so*).

*10. The applicant states that *a response was made/*representations were made on behalf of the person in the following terms (*insert response or representations made*).

11. The applicant attaches to this application a certificate signed by a health board competent person which indicates that the competent person is satisfied as to the matters mentioned in statement 4.

12. In the circumstances narrated the applicant is entitled to the order sought and it should be granted accordingly.

*(signed)*

[X.Y.] *(add designation and business address)*

Solicitor for applicant

*(insert date)*

FORM 41[1]

**Rule 3.39.4(3)**

FORM OF QUARANTINE ORDER

Sheriff Court................

................ 20..........at *(insert time)*

(Court Ref. No.)

The sheriff, having considered an application made under section 39(2) of the Public Health etc. (Scotland) Act 2008 ("the Act") *[and productions lodged therewith], and being satisfied as necessary as to the matters mentioned in section 40(2) of the Act,

1. Makes an order in terms of section 40(1) of the Act authorising the quarantining of *(insert details of the person as given in the application)* in *(insert the place in which the person is to be quarantined)* for a period of (insert the period for which the person is to be quarantined) and

Authorising the removal of *(insert name of the person)* to *(insert address at which the person is to be quarantined)*

Further *(insert any authorisation for disinfection/disinfestation/decontamination)*,

*(Insert any conditions imposed by the order including the name and designation of any person authorised under* section 40(4) (d) of the Act *to effect a removal)*, and

2. Directs notification of this order *(insert details of method and timing of notice)* to (the person to whom the order applies)

*and *(the name and designation of any person to whom an explanation was given under* section 31(5) of the Act)

*and *(insert the name and designation of any other person whom the sheriff considers appropriate)*.

**Delete as appropriate*

*(signed)*

Sheriff

FORM 42[2]

**Rule 3.39.5(1)**

FORM OF APPLICATION TO HAVE A PERSON REMOVED TO AND DETAINED IN HOSPITAL
UNDER SECTION 42 OF THE PUBLIC HEALTH ETC. (SCOTLAND) ACT 2008

SHERIFFDOM OF *(insert name of sheriffdom)*

AT *(insert place of sheriff court)*

[A.B.] *(design health board)*, Applicant

**Order sought from the court**

**Delete as appropriate*

The applicant applies to the court for a short term detention order under section 42(1) of the Public Health etc. (Scotland) Act 2008 ("the Act") in respect of *(insert name, address and date of birth of person to be subject to the order)* ("the person").

1. authorising the person's removal to hospital *[by *(insert name and designation of a person mentioned in* section 42(1)(a) of the Act)] and the person's detention in hospital for the period of *(insert period)*, and

2. authorising the taking in relation to the person of the following steps, namely *disinfection/ *disinfestation/*decontamination *(specify which steps are sought)*.

**Statement**

**Delete as appropriate*

---

[1] As inserted by the Act of Sederunt (Summary Applications, Statutory Applications and Appeals etc. Rules) Amendment (Public Health etc. (Scotland) Act 2008) 2009 (SSI 2009/320) r.2 (effective October 1, 2009).

[2] As inserted by the Act of Sederunt (Summary Applications, Statutory Applications and Appeals etc. Rules) Amendment (Public Health etc. (Scotland) Act 2008) 2009 (SSI 2009/320) r.2 (effective October 1, 2009).

1. This application is made pursuant to sections 41 and 42 of the Act.

2. The person is present within the applicant's area. The applicant is a health board operating within the jurisdiction of this court. This court accordingly has jurisdiction.

3. The person is aged 16 years or over.

**OR**

The person is under 16. The parent or other person who has day-to-day care or control of the person is (*insert name, address and relationship to the person*).

4. (a) The applicant knows that the person—

*(i)   has an infectious disease, namely [*insert name of disease*]; or

*(ii)   is contaminated,

(*insert here a brief statement indicating the basis upon which these matters are known to the applicant*)

**AND**

(b) it appears to the applicant that as a result—

(i)   there is a significant risk to public health; and

(ii)   it is necessary, to avoid or minimise that risk, for the person to be detained in hospital

(*Insert here a brief statement indicating the reason why the applicant considers that there is a significant risk to public health and that it is necessary, to avoid or minimise that risk, for the person to be detained in hospital*).

5. The applicant proposes that the person be detained at (*insert name and address of hospital*) *[and that he should be removed there by (*insert name and designation of person under* section 42(1)(a) of the Act *and indicate briefly why this is proposed*)].

6. The applicant proposes that the person be detained for (*insert period of time*).

7. The applicant considers it necessary to *disinfect,/*disinfest/*decontaminate the person (*insert details and reasons*).

*8. The applicant has explained to the person—

(a)   that there is a significant risk to public health;

(b)   the nature of that risk; and

(c)   why the applicant considers it necessary for the proposed action to be taken in relation to that person.

**OR**

*8. The applicant states that the person is incapable of understanding any explanation of the matters referred to at section 31(3) of the Act (*state reason*) and has explained to (*insert name and address of a person mentioned in* section 31(5)(a) or (b) of the Act *and their relationship to the person*)—

(a)   that there is a significant risk to public health;

(b)   the nature of that risk; and

(c)   why the applicant considers it necessary for the proposed action to be taken in relation to that person.

*OR*

*8. The applicant states that no explanation has been given in relation to this application under section 31(3) or (5) of the Act because (*state why it was not reasonably practicable to do so*).

*9. The applicant states that *a response was made/*representations were made on behalf of the person in the following terms (*insert response or representations made*).

10. The applicant attaches to this application a certificate signed by a health board competent person which indicates that the competent person is satisfied as to the matters mentioned in statement 4.

11. In the circumstances narrated the applicant is entitled to the order sought and it should be granted accordingly.

(*signed*)

Solicitor for applicant

[X. Y.] (add designation and business address)

(insert date)

FORM 43[1]

**Rule 3.39.5(4)**

FORM OF SHORT TERM DETENTION ORDER—REMOVAL TO AND DETENTION IN HOSPITAL

---

[1] As inserted by the Act of Sederunt (Summary Applications, Statutory Applications and Appeals etc. Rules) Amendment (Public Health etc. (Scotland) Act 2008) 2009 (SSI 2009/320) r.2 (effective October 1, 2009).

Sheriff Court...............

............... 20............... at (*insert time*)

(Court Ref. No.)

The sheriff, having considered an application made under section 41(2) of the Public Health etc. (Scotland) Act 2008 ("the Act") *[and productions lodged therewith], and being satisfied as necessary as to the matters mentioned in section 42(2) of the Act,

1. Makes an order in terms of section 42(1) of the Act authorising the short term detention in hospital of (*insert details of the person as given in the application*),

Authorising the removal of that person by (*specify person authorised to carry out removal in terms of* section 42(1)(a) of the Act) to (*specify hospital at which the person is to he detained, including the address*), there to be detained for (*insert period of detention*)

Further (*insert any authorisation for disinfectionjdisinfestationjdecontamination*), and

2. Directs notification of this order (*insert details of method and timing of notice) to (the person to whom the order applies*)

*and (*the name and designation of any person to whom an explanation was given under section* 31(5) of the Act)

*and (*insert the name and designation of any other person whom the sheriff considers appropriate*).

* *Delete as appropriate*

(signed)

Sheriff

FORM 44[1]

**Rule 3.39.5(2)**

FORM OF APPLICATION FOR A SHORT TERM DETENTION ORDER UNDER SECTION 43 OF
THE PUBLIC HEALTH ETC. (SCOTLAND) ACT 2008

SHERIFFDOM OF (*insert name of sheriffdom*)

AT (*insert place of sheriff court*)

[A.B.] (*design health hoard*), Applicant

**Order sought from the court**

* *Delete as appropriate*

The applicant applies to the court for a short term detention order under section 43(1) of the Public Health etc. (Scotland) Act 2008 ("the Act") in respect of (*insert name, address and date of birth of person to be subject to the order*) ("the person").

1. authorising the person's detention in hospital for a period of (*insert period*), and

2. authorising the taking in relation to the person of the following steps, namely *disinfection/ *disinfestation/*decontamination (*specify which steps are sought*).

**Statement**

* *Delete as appropriate*

1. This application is made pursuant to sections 41 and 43 of the Act.

2. The person is present within the applicant's area. The applicant is a health board operating within the jurisdiction of this court. This court accordingly has jurisdiction.

3. The person is aged 16 years or over.

**OR**

The person is under 16. The parent or other person who has day-to-day care or control of the person is (*insert name, address and relationship to the person*).

4. (a) The applicant knows that the person—

*(i)   has an infectious disease, namely [*insert name of disease*]; or

*(ii)   is contaminated,

(*insert here a brief statement indicating the basis upon which these matters are known to the applicant*)

**AND**

(b) it appears to the applicant that as a result—

(i)   there is a significant risk to public health; and

(ii)   it is necessary, to avoid or minimise that risk, for the person to be detained in hospital.

---

[1] As inserted by the Act of Sederunt (Summary Applications, Statutory Applications and Appeals etc. Rules) Amendment (Public Health etc. (Scotland) Act 2008) 2009 (SSI 2009/320) r.2 (effective October 1, 2009).

(*Insert here a brief statement indicating the reason why the applicant considers that there is a significant risk to public health and that it is necessary, to avoid or minimise that risk, for the person to be detained in hospital*).

5. The person is currently in (*insert name and address of hospital*). The applicant proposes that the person be detained at (*insert name and address of hospital*).

6. The applicant proposes that the person be detained for (*insert period of time*).

7. The applicant considers it necessary to \*disinfect/\*disinfest/\*decontaminate the person (*insert details and reasons*).

\*8. The applicant has explained to the person—
(a)    that there is a significant risk to public health;
(b)    the nature of that risk; and
(c)    why the applicant considers it necessary for the proposed action to be taken in relation to that person.

**OR**

\*8. The applicant states that the person is incapable of understanding any explanation of the matters referred to at section 31(3) of the Act (*state reason*) and has explained to (*insert name and address of a person mentioned in* section 31(5)(a) or (b) of the Act *and their relationship to the person*)—
(a)    that there is a significant risk to public health; Release 104: September 2009
(b)    the nature of that risk; and
(c)    why the applicant considers it necessary for the proposed action to be taken in relation to that person.

**OR**

\*8. The applicant states that no explanation has been given in relation to this application under section 31(3) or (5) of the Act because {*state why it was not reasonably practicable to do so*).

\*9. The applicant states that \*a response was made/\*representations were made on behalf of the person in the following terms (*insert response or representations made*).

10. The applicant attaches to this application a certificate signed by a health board competent person which indicates that the competent person is satisfied as to the matters mentioned in statement 4.

11. In the circumstances narrated the applicant is entitled to the order sought and it should be granted accordingly.

(*signed*)
[X.Y.] (*add designation and business address*)
Solicitor for applicant
(*insert date*)

FORM 45[1]

**Rule 3.39.5(5)**
FORM OF SHORT TERM DETENTION ORDER—DETENTION IN HOSPITAL
Sheriff Court...............
............... 20.......... at (*insert time*)
(Court Ref. No.)

The sheriff, having considered an application made under section 41(2) of the Public Health etc. (Scotland) Act 2008 ("the Act") \*[and productions lodged therewith], and being satisfied as necessary as to the matters mentioned in section 43(2) of the Act,

1. Makes an order in terms of section 43(1) of the Act authorising the short term detention in hospital of (*insert details of the person as given in the application*) at (*insert name and address of hospital*) for (*insert period of detention*)

Further (*insert any authorisation for disinfection/disinfestationi/decontamination*), and

2. Directs notification of this order (*insert details of method and timing of notice*) to (*the person to whom the order applies*)

\*and (*the name and designation of any person to whom an explanation was given under* section 31(5) of the Act)

\*and (*insert the name and designation of any other person whom the sheriff considers appropriate*).

\**Delete as appropriate*
(*signed*)

---

[1] As inserted by the Act of Sederunt (Summary Applications, Statutory Applications and Appeals etc. Rules) Amendment (Public Health etc. (Scotland) Act 2008) 2009 (SSI 2009/320) r.2 (effective October 1, 2009).

Sheriff

**Rule 3.39.6(1)**

FORM OF APPLICATION FOR EXCEPTIONAL DETENTION ORDER UNDER SECTION 45 OF THE PUBLIC HEALTH ETC. (SCOTLAND) ACT 2008

SHERIFFDOM OF (*insert name of sheriffdom*)

AT (*insert place of sheriff court*)

[A.B.] (*design health board*), Applicant

**Order sought from the court**

*\*Delete as appropriate*

The applicant applies to the court for an exceptional detention order under section 45(1) of the Public Health etc. (Scotland) Act 2008 ("the Act") in respect of (*insert name, address and date of birth of person to be subject to the order*) ("the person").

1. authorising the person's continued detention in hospital for a period of (*insert period*), and

2. authorising the taking in relation to the person of the following steps, namely ""disinfection/ *disinfestation/*decontamination (*specify which steps are sought*).

**Statement**

*\* Delete as appropriate*

1. This application is made pursuant to sections 44 and 45 of the Act.

2. The person is presently detained in a hospital within the applicant's area by virtue of a short term detention order. The applicant is a health board operating within the jurisdiction of this court and applied for the short term detention order. This court accordingly has jurisdiction.

3. The person is aged 16 years or over.

**OR**

*The person is under 16. The parent or other person who has day-to-day care or control of the person is (*insert name, address and relationship to the person*).

4. The applicant is satisfied—

(a) that the person—

*(i)    has an infectious disease, namely [*insert name of disease*]; or

*(ii)    is contaminated,

**AND**

(b) that as a result there is a significant risk to public health,

(*insert here a brief statement indicating the basis upon which the applicant is satisfied of these matters*)

**AND**

(c) that it continues to be necessary, to avoid or minimise that risk, for the person to be detained in hospital (*insert here a brief statement indicating the reason why the applicant considers it necessary for the person to be detained in hospital*),

**AND**

(d) that it is necessary, to avoid or minimise that risk, for the person to be detained for a period exceeding the maximum period for which the person could be detained by virtue of the short term detention order were that order to be extended under section 49(5)(a) of the Act(*insert here a brief statement indicating the reason why the applicant considers it necessary for the person to be detained beyond that maximum period*).

5. The person is currently detained in (*insert name and address of hospital*) by virtue of a short term detention order granted on (*insert date*). The said order is extant until [*insert date*]. The applicant proposes that the person be detained at (*insert name and address of hospital*).

6. The applicant applies to the court to order that the person continue to be detained in (*insert name and address of hospital*) for (*insert period of time*) from (*insert date from which the order is to commence*).

7. The applicant considers it necessary to *disinfect/*disinfest/*decontaminate the person (*insert details and reasons*).

*8. The applicant has explained to the person—

(a)    that there is a significant risk to public health;

(b)    the nature of that risk; and

---

[1] As inserted by the Act of Sederunt (Summary Applications, Statutory Applications and Appeals etc. Rules) Amendment (Public Health etc. (Scotland) Act 2008) 2009 (SSI 2009/320) r.2 (effective October 1, 2009).

(c)   why the applicant considers it necessary for the proposed action to be taken in relation to that person.

**OR**

*8. The applicant states that the person is incapable of understanding any explanation of the matters referred to at section 31(3) of the Act (*state reason*) and has explained to (*insert name and address of a person mentioned in* section 31(5) (a) or (b) of the Act *and their relationship to the person*)—
(a)   that there is a significant risk to public health;
(b)   the nature of that risk; and
(c)   why the applicant considers it necessary for the proposed action to be taken in relation to that person.

**OR**

*8. The applicant states that no explanation has been given in relation to this application under section 31(3) or (5) of the Act because (*state why it was not reasonably practicable to do so*).

*9. The applicant states that *a response was made/*representations were made on behalf of the person in the following terms (*insert response or representations made*).

10. The applicant attaches to this application a certificate signed by a health board competent person which indicates that the competent person is satisfied as to the matters mentioned in statement 4.

11. In the circumstances narrated the applicant is entitled to the order sought and it should be granted accordingly.

(*signed*)
[X.Y.] (*add designation and business address*)
Solicitor for applicant
(*insert date*)
**FORM 47**[1]

**Rule 3.39.6(3)**

FORM OF EXCEPTIONAL DETENTION ORDER

Sheriff Court..........
..........20..........at (insert time)
(Court Ref. No.)
The sheriff, having considered an application made under section 44(3) of the Public Health etc. (Scotland) Act 2008 ("the Act") *[and productions lodged therewith], and being satisfied as to the matters mentioned in section 45(2) of the Act,

1. Makes an exceptional detention order in terms of section 45(1) of the Act authorising the continued detention of (*insert details of the person as given in the application*) at (*insert name and address of hospital*) for (*insert period of detention*).

Further (*insert any authorisation for disinfection/disinfestation/decontamination*), and

2. Directs notification of this order (*insert details of method and timing of notice*) to (*the person to whom the order applies*)

*and (*the name and designation of any person to whom an explanation was given under* section 31(5) of the Act)

*and (*insert the name and designation of any other person whom the sheriff considers appropriate*).

* Delete as appropriate

(*signed*)
Sheriff

**FORM 48**[2]

**Rule 3.39.7(1)**

FORM OF APPLICATION FOR EXTENSION OF A QUARANTINE ORDER, SHORT TERM DETENTION ORDER OR EXCEPTIONAL DETENTION ORDER UNDER SECTION 49 OF THE PUBLIC HEALTH ETC. (SCOTLAND) ACT 2008
SHERIFFDOM OF (*insert name of sheriffdom*)
**AT** (*insert place of sheriff court*)

---

[1] As inserted by the Act of Sederunt (Summary Applications, Statutory Applications and Appeals etc. Rules) Amendment (Public Health etc. (Scotland) Act 2008) 2009 (SSI 2009/320) r.2 (effective October 1, 2009).
[2] As inserted by the Act of Sederunt (Summary Applications, Statutory Applications and Appeals etc. Rules) Amendment (Public Health etc. (Scotland) Act 2008) 2009 (SSI 2009/320) r.2 (effective October 1, 2009).

[**A.B.**] (*design health hoard*), Applicant

### Order sought from the court

*\*Delete as appropriate*

The applicant applies to the court to extend for a period of (insert period):

\*the quarantine order granted on (*insert date*) in respect of (*insert name, address and date of birth of the person in respect of whom the order was granted*) ("the person") **OR**

\*the short term detention order granted on (insert date) in respect of (*insert name, address and date of birth of the person*) ("the person") **OR**

\*the exceptional detention order granted on (*insert date*) in respect of (*insert name, address and date of birth of the person*) ("the person").

### Statement

*\*Delete as appropriate*

1. This application is made pursuant to section 49 of the Public Health etc. (Scotland) Act 2008.

2. The person is presently \*quarantined/\*detained in hospital within the applicant's area by virtue of \*a quarantine order/\*a short term detention order/\*an exceptional detention order granted on (*insert date*) which expires on (*insert date*). This court accordingly has jurisdiction.

3. The person is aged 16 years or over.

**OR**

The person is under 16. The parent or other person who has day-to-day care or control of the person is (*insert name, address and relationship to the person*).

4. The applicant attaches to this application a certificate signed by a health board competent person which indicates that the competent person is satisfied as to the following matters:

\*[*in relation to a proposed extension of a quarantine order*] That it is known, or there are reasonable grounds to suspect, that the person—

\*(i)    has an infectious disease;

\*(ii)   has been exposed to an organism which causes an infectious disease;

\*(iii)  is contaminated; or

\*(iv)   has been exposed to a contaminant,

**AND** that as a result there is or may be significant risk to public health,

  **AND** that it is necessary, to avoid or minimise that risk, for the person to continue to be quarantined.
  **OR**

\*[in relation to a proposed extension of a short term detention order or an exceptional detention order] That the person—

\*(i)    has an infectious disease; or

\*(ii)   is contaminated,

**AND** that as a result there is significant risk to public health,

  **AND** that it is necessary, to avoid or minimise that risk, for the person to continue to be detained in hospital.

5. The court is asked to extend the order for a period of (*insert period*) from (*insert date from which the order is to commence*).

\*6. An extension of the quarantine order, as sought, will not result in the person being quarantined for a continuous period exceeding 12 weeks.

**OR**

\*6 An extension of the short term detention order, as sought, will not result in the person being detained in hospital for a continuous period exceeding 12 weeks.

**OR**

\*6 An extension of the exceptional detention order, as sought, will not result in the person being detained in hospital for a continuous period exceeding 12 months.

7. In the circumstances narrated the applicant is entitled to the order sought and it should be granted accordingly.

(signed)

[X.Y.] (*add designation and business address*)

Solicitor for applicant

(*insert date*)

FORM 49[1]

**Rule 3.39.7(3)**

FORM OF ORDER EXTENDING A QUARANTINE ORDER, SHORT TERM DETENTION ORDER
OR EXCEPTIONAL DETENTION ORDER

Sheriff Court..........

..........20..........at (*insert time*)

(Court Ref. No.)

The sheriff, having considered an application made under section 49(2) of the Public Health etc.
(Scotland) Act 2008 ("the Act") and productions lodged therewith, and being satisfied as to the matters
mentioned in section 49(6) of the Act,

1. Makes an order in terms of section 49(5) of the Act extending *the quarantine order/*the short term
detention order/*the exceptional detention order which was granted in respect of (*insert details of the
person as given in the application*) on (*insert date*) for a period of (*insert period*) and

2. Directs notification of this order (*insert details of method and timing of notice*) to (*the person to
whom the order applies*)

*and (*the name and designation of any person to whom an explanation was given under* section 31(5)
of the Act)

*and (*insert the name and designation of any other person whom the sheriff considers appropriate*).

* *Delete as appropriate*

(*signed*)

Sheriff

FORM 50[2]

**Rule 3.39.8(1)**

FORM OF APPLICATION FOR MODIFICATION OF A QUARANTINE ORDER, SHORT TERM
DETENTION ORDER OR EXCEPTIONAL DETENTION ORDER UNDER SECTION 51 OF THE
PUBLIC HEALTH ETC. (SCOTLAND) ACT 2008

**SHERIFFDOM OF** (*insert name of sheriffdom*)

**AT** (*insert place of sheriff court*)

[**A.B.**] (*design health hoard*), Applicant

**Order sought from the court**

*\*Delete as appropriate*

The applicant applies to the court to modify:

*the quarantine order granted on (insert date) in respect of (insert name, address and date of birth of
the person in respect of whom the order was granted) ("the person") **OR**

*the short term detention order granted on (insert date) in respect of (insert name, address and date of
birth of the person) ("the person") **OR**

*the exceptional detention order granted on (*insert date*) in respect of (*insert name, address and date
of birth of the person*) ("the person")

by (*specify details of the modification sought*).

**Statement**

*\*Delete as appropriate*

1. This application is made pursuant to sections 50 and 51 of the Public Health etc. (Scotland) Act
2008.

2. The person is presently *quarantined/*detained in hospital within the applicant's area by virtue of
*a quarantine order/*a short term detention order/*an exceptional detention order granted on (*insert
date*) which expires on (*insert date*). This court accordingly has jurisdiction.

3. The person is aged 16 years or over.

**OR**

The person is under 16. The parent or other person who has day-to-day care or control of the person is
(*insert name, address and relationship to the person*).

---

[1] As inserted by the Act of Sederunt (Summary Applications, Statutory Applications and Appeals etc.
Rules) Amendment (Public Health etc. (Scotland) Act 2008) 2009 (SSI 2009/320) r.2 (effective
October 1, 2009).

[2] As inserted by the Act of Sederunt (Summary Applications, Statutory Applications and Appeals etc.
Rules) Amendment (Public Health etc. (Scotland) Act 2008) 2009 (SSI 2009/320) r.2 (effective
October 1, 2009).

4. The applicant attaches to this application a certificate signed by a health board competent person which indicates that the competent person is satisfied as to the following matters:

*[*in relation to a proposed modification of a quarantine order*] That it is known, or there are reasonable grounds to suspect, that the person—

*(i)   has an infectious disease;

*(ii)  has been exposed to an organism which causes an infectious disease;

*(iii) is contaminated; or

*(iv)  has been exposed to a contaminant,

AND that as a result there is or may be significant risk to public health,

AND that it is necessary, to avoid or minimise that risk, for the person to continue to be quarantined.

OR

*[*in relation to a proposed modification of a short term detention order or an exceptional detention order*] That the person—

*(i)   has an infectious disease; or

*(ii)  is contaminated,

AND that as a result there is significant risk to public health

AND that it is necessary, to avoid or minimise that risk, for the person to continue to be detained in hospital.

5. The modification is sought for the following reasons (*here insert a brief statement of reasons*).

6. In the circumstances narrated the applicant is entitled to the order sought and it should be granted accordingly.

(*signed*)

[X.Y.] (*add designation and business address*)

Solicitor for applicant

(*insert date*)

## FORM 51[1]

**Rule 3.39.8(3)**

FORM OF MODIFICATION OF A QUARANTINE ORDER, SHORT TERM DETENTION ORDER OR EXCEPTIONAL DETENTION ORDER

Sheriff Court..........

..........20..........at [insert time]

(Court Ref. No.)

The sheriff, having considered an application made under section 50(2) of the Public Health etc. (Scotland) Act 2008 ("the Act") *[and productions lodged therewith], and being satisfied as to the matters mentioned in section 51(2) of the Act,

1. Makes an order in terms of section 51(1) of the Act modifying *the quarantine order/*the short term detention order/*the exceptional detention order which was granted in respect of (*insert details of the person as given in the application*) on (*insert date*), by

(*insert details of modification and, if applicable, name and designation of person considered appropriate under* section 51(4)(a)(iv) of the Act).

2. Directs notification of this order (*insert details of method and timing of notice*) to (*the person to whom the order applies*)

*and (*the name and designation of any person to whom an explanation was given under* section 31(5) of the Act)

*and (*insert the name and designation of any other person whom the sheriff considers appropriate*).

*Delete as appropriate

(*signed*)

Sheriff

## FORM 52 [2]

Rule 3.39.9(1)

---

[1] As inserted by the Act of Sederunt (Summary Applications, Statutory Applications and Appeals etc. Rules) Amendment (Public Health etc. (Scotland) Act 2008) 2009 (SSI 2009/320) r.2 (effective October 1, 2009).

[2] As inserted by the Act of Sederunt (Summary Applications, Statutory Applications and Appeals etc. Rules) Amendment (Public Health etc. (Scotland) Act 2008) 2009 (SSI 2009/320) r.2 (effective October 1, 2009).

| Official use only |
|---|
| Court ref: |
| Date and time of receipt: |

## FORM OF APPLICATION FOR RECALL OF AN ORDER GRANTED IN THE ABSENCE OF THE PERSON TO WHOM IT APPLIES UNDER SECTION 59 OF THE PUBLIC HEALTH ETC. (SCOTLAND) ACT 2008

**NOTES**

This form should be used if you wish to apply to the sheriff for an order recalling a quarantine order OR a short term detention order OR an exceptional detention order which was made in the absence of the person to whom the order applies.

If you are the person to whom the order applies, you or your solicitor should complete and sign **PART A** and deliver it to the sheriff clerk of the sheriff court at which you wish to make your application.

If you are not the person to whom the order applies but instead are a person who has an interest in the welfare of the person to whom the order applies, you or your solicitor should complete and sign **PART B** and deliver it to the sheriff clerk of the sheriff court at which you wish to make your application.

Your application MUST be received by the sheriff clerk before the expiry of the period of 72 hours beginning with the time at which the order which you wish to be recalled was notified to you (or, as the case may be, the person to whom the order applies).

You should note that, despite the making of your application, the order which you wish recalled will REMAIN IN FORCE unless and until it is revoked by the sheriff.

Before determining your application the sheriff must give you and various other parties (who are specified in section 59(7) of the Act) the opportunity of making representations (whether orally or in writing) and of leading, or producing, evidence.

IF YOU ARE UNCERTAIN WHAT ACTION TO TAKE you should consult a solicitor. You may be entitled to legal aid depending on your financial circumstances, and you can get information about legal aid from a solicitor. You may also obtain advice from any Citizens Advice Bureau or other advice agency.

**PART A**

Sheriff Court (*Insert name of court*)  |  1.

Details of applicant (*Insert full name, address and telephone number and, if available, e-mail address and fax number*)  |  2.

Type of order you wish the sheriff to recall (*Tick as appropriate*)  |  3. Quarantine Order ☐ / Short Term Detention Order ☐ / Exceptional Detention Order ☐

Date of order (*Insert date of order you wish the sheriff to recall*)  |  4.

Sheriff Court at which the order was made, if it was not the court specified in box 1 (*Insert name of court*)  |  5.

If available, a copy of the order which you wish the sheriff to recall should be attached to this application.

Date and time at which the order was notified to you (*Insert date and exact time of day*) | 6.

I ask the sheriff to recall the order specified in boxes 3 and 4 on the following grounds:

(*State why you wish the order to be recalled. If necessary, continue on a separate sheet of paper*):

Signed:
   Date:
   (A solicitor should add his or her name and contact details)
**PART B**

Sheriff Court (*Insert name of court*) | 1.

Details of applicant (*Insert full name, address and telephone number and, if available, email address and fax number*) | 2.

Type of order you wish the sheriff to recall (*Tick as appropriate*) | 3. Quarantine Order ☐
Short Term Detention Order ☐
Exceptional Detention Order ☐

Date of order (*Insert date of order you wish the sheriff to recall*) | 4.

Sheriff Court at which the order was made, if it was not the court specified in box 1 (*Insert name of court*) | 5.

Details of person to whom the order applies (*Insert name, address and telephone number and, if available, e-mail address and fax number*) | 6.

If available, a copy of the order which you wish the sheriff to recall should be attached to this application.

Date and time at which the order was notified to the person named in box 6 (*Insert date and exact time of day*) | 7.

I have an interest in the welfare of the person named in box 6 for the following reasons:

(*State why you have an interest in the welfare of this person. If necessary, continue on a separate sheet of paper*):

I ask the sheriff to recall the order specified in boxes 3 and 4 on the following grounds:

*(State why you wish the order to he recalled. If necessary, continue on a separate sheet of paper)*:

Signed:

    Date:

    (A solicitor should add his or her name and contact details)

**Rule 3.39.9(3)**                 FORM 53[1]

FORM OF ORDER RECALLING A QUARANTINE ORDER, SHORT TERM DETENTION ORDER
OR EXCEPTIONAL DETENTION ORDER

    Sheriff Court..............

    ...............20..........

    (Court Ref. No.)

    The sheriff, having considered an application made under section 59(2) of the Public Health etc. (Scotland) Act 2008 for recall of *the quarantine order/*the short term detention order/*the exceptional detention order which was granted in respect of *(insert details of the person as given in the application)* on *(insert date)*,

    Refuses the application and Confirms the said order

    OR

    *Grants the application and Revokes the said order,

    And Directs notification of this order *(insert details of method and timing of notice)* to *(enter details of any other person whom the sheriff considers appropriate).*

    **Delete as appropriate*

    (signed)

    Sheriff

**Rule 3.39.12(1)**                 FORM 54[2]

Official use only

Court ref:

Date and time of receipt:

FORM OF NOTE OF APPEAL UNDER SECTION 61 OF THE PUBLIC HEALTH ETC. (SCOTLAND) ACT 2008

    *NOTES*

---

[1] As inserted by the Act of Sederunt (Summary Applications, Statutory Applications and Appeals etc. Rules) Amendment (Public Health etc. (Scotland) Act 2008) 2009 (SSI 2009/320) r.2 (effective October 1, 2009).

[2] As inserted by the Act of Sederunt (Summary Applications, Statutory Applications and Appeals etc. Rules) Amendment (Public Health etc. (Scotland) Act 2008) 2009 (SSI 2009/320) r.2 (effective October 1, 2009).

This form should be used if you wish to appeal to the sheriff under section 61 of the Public Health etc. (Scotland) Act 2008 in relation to an exclusion order OR a restriction order. A copy of the section is set out below.

If you are the person to whom the order applies, you or your solicitor should complete and sign PART A and deliver it to the sheriff clerk of the sheriff court at which you wish to appeal.

If you are not the person to whom the order applies but instead are a person who has an interest in the welfare of the person to whom the order applies, you or your solicitor should complete and sign PART B and deliver it to the sheriff clerk of the sheriff court at which you wish to appeal.

The form MUST be received by the sheriff clerk before the expiry of 14 days beginning with the day on which the order, modification or, as the case may be, decision against which you wish to appeal was made.

IF YOU ARE UNCERTAIN WHAT ACTION TO TAKE you should consult a solicitor. You may be entitled to legal aid depending on your financial circumstances, and you can get information about legal aid from a solicitor. You may also obtain advice from any Citizens Advice Bureau or other advice agency.

**61 Appeal against exclusion orders and restriction orders**

(1)     This section applies where a person is subject to—
    (a)     an exclusion order; or
    (b)     a restriction order.

(2)     A person mentioned in subsection (3) may appeal to the sheriff against—
    (a)     the making of the order;
    (b)     any conditions imposed by the order;
    (c)     any modification of the order under section 48(2); or
    (d)     a decision of a health board competent person under section 52(4) or 53(3) not to revoke the order.

(3)     The person referred to in subsection (2) is—
    (a)     the person in relation to whom the order applies; or
    (b)     any person who has an interest in the welfare or such a person.

(4)     An appeal under this section must be made before the expiry of the period of 14 days beginning with the day on which the order, modification or, as the case may be, decision appealed against is made.

(5)     On an appeal under this section, the sheriff may—
    (a)     confirm the order appealed against;
    (b)     modify the order;
    (c)     revoke the order;
    (d)     confirm the decision appealed against;
    (e)     quash that decision;
    (f)     make such other order as the sheriff considers appropriate.

(6)     In subsection (5)(b), "modify" is to be construed in accordance with section 48.

*PART A*

Sheriff Court (*Insert name of court*)     | 1.

Details of appellant (*Insert full name, address and telephone number and, if available, email address and fax number*)     | 2.

Type of order (*Tick as appropriate to indicate what type of order the appeal is about*)     | 3. Exclusion Order ☐
Restriction Order ☐

Date of order (*Insert date of order indicated in box 3*)     | 4.

Name and address of person who made the order
(*Insert name and address. You should find this on the order*)

> 5.

If available, a copy of the order specified in boxes 3 and 4 should be attached to this application.

I appeal to the sheriff on the following grounds:

> *(State here with reasons*
> *(i) what it is about the order that you wish to appeal. You should specify at least one of the options given in* section 61(2).
> *(ii) what it is that you want the sheriff to do. You should specify one of the options given in* section 61(5). *If you choose the option given in* section 61(5)(f) *you should specify what order you wish the sheriff to make.*
> *If necessary, continue on a separate sheet of paper)*

Signed:
> Date:
> (A solicitor should add his or her name and contact details)

**PART B**

Sheriff Court (*Insert name of court*)

> 1.

Details of appellant (*Insert full name, address and telephone number and, if available, email address and fax number*)

> 2.

Type of order (*Tick as appropriate to indicate what type of order the appeal is about*)

> 3. Exclusion Order Restriction Order ☐

Date of order (*Insert date of order indicated in box 3*)

> 4.

Name and address of person who made the order
(*Insert name and address. You should find this on the order*)

> 5.

Details of person to whom the order applies (*Insert full name, address and telephone number and, if available, email address and fax number*)

> 6.

If available, a copy of the order specified in boxes 3 and 4 should be attached to this application.

I have an interest in the welfare of the person named in box 6 for the following reasons:

*(State why you have an interest in the welfare of this person. If necessary, continue on a separate sheet of paper)*:

I appeal to the sheriff on the following grounds:

*(State here with reasons
(i) what it is about the order that you wish to appeal. You should specify at least one of the options given in section 61(2).
(ii) what it is that you want the sheriff to do. You should specify one of the options given in section 61(5). If you choose the option given in section 61(5)(f) you should specify what order you wish the sheriff to make.
If necessary, continue on a separate sheet of paper)*

Signed:
    Date:
    (A solicitor should add his or her name and contact details)

*Rule 3.39.13(1)*                                  FORM 55[1]

FORM OF APPLICATION FOR WARRANT TO ENTER PREMISES AND TAKE STEPS UNDER SECTION 78 OF THE PUBLIC HEALTH ETC. (SCOTLAND) ACT 2008

SHERIFFDOM OF *(insert name of sheriffdom)*

AT *(insert place of sheriff court)*

[A.B.] (design and state address), Applicant

*Order sought from the court*

The applicant applies to the court to grant warrant to *(insert name)*, an officer of the local authority

1. to enter the premises at *(insert address of premises to which entry is sought)*.
2. to take with him any other person he may authorise and, if he has reasonable cause to expect any serious obstruction in obtaining access, a constable.
3. to direct that those premises (or any part of them) are, or any thing in or on them is to be left undisturbed (whether generally or in particular respects) for so long as the officer considers appropriate.
4. to take any step mentioned in section 73(2) of the Public Health etc. (Scotland) Act 2008 ("the Act") or to remove any thing from the premises for the purpose of taking any such step at any other place.

*Statement*

    *\*Delete as appropriate*

1. This application is made pursuant to section 78 of the Act.
2. The applicant is a local authority and the said officer is an authorised officer within the meaning give in section 73(8) of the Act.
3. The said premises \*are/\*are not a dwellinghouse within the meaning given in section 26 of the Act.
4. The said premises are within the jurisdiction of this court.
5. The applicant considers it necessary that the authorised officer should exercise the powers of entry and take the other steps mentioned in section 73(2) of the Act *(insert here a brief statement of reasons)*.

\*6. The authorised officer Release 104: September 2009

\*has been refused entry to the said premises, or

    \*reasonably anticipates that entry will be refused.

*OR*

    \*6    The said premises are premises which the authorised officer is entitled to enter and they are unoccupied.

*OR*

    \*6    The said premises are premises which the authorised officer is entitled to enter and the occupier

---

[1] As inserted by the Act of Sederunt (Summary Applications, Statutory Applications and Appeals etc. Rules) Amendment (Public Health etc. (Scotland) Act 2008) 2009 (SSI 2009/320) r.2 (effective October 1, 2009).

thereof is temporarily absent and there is urgency because (here state briefly why there is urgency).

OR

*6    The authorised officer

*has been prevented from taking any steps which he is entitled to take under Part 5 of the Act, or

*reasonably anticipates being prevented from taking any steps that he is entitled to take under Part 5 of the Act.

*7    [*If the said premises are a dwellinghouse*] The authorised officer has in terms of section 77(2) of the Act given 48 hours notice of the proposed entry to a person who appears to be the occupier of the dwellinghouse and the period of notice has expired.

8.    In the circumstances narrated the applicant is entitled to the warrant sought and it should be granted accordingly.

(*signed*)

[X.Y.[(*add designation and business address*)

Solicitor for applicant

(*insert date*)

*Rule 3.39.13(2)*                                         FORM 56[1]

FORM OF WARRANT TO ENTER PREMISES AND TAKE STEPS UNDER PART 5 OF THE PUBLIC HEALTH ETC. (SCOTLAND) ACT 2008

Sheriff Court...............

...............20 ..........

(Court Ref. No.)

*Delete as appropriate

The sheriff, having considered an application made under section 78 of the Public Health etc. (Scotland) Act 2008 ("the Act") *[and any productions lodged therewith], [*and (where the premises referred to below are a dwellinghouse) being satisfied that due notice has been given under section 77(2) of the Act and has expired],

Grants warrant authorising the authorised person, (insert name):

(a)    to enter the premises at (insert address)

(b)    on entering the premises referred to at paragraph (a), to take any other person authorised by him and, if he has reasonable cause to expect any serious obstruction in obtaining access, a constable; and

(c)    to direct that:

(i)    those premises (or any part of them) are; or

(ii)    any thing in or on those premises is,

to be left undisturbed (whether generally or in particular respects) for so long as he considers appropriate;

(d)    to take any steps mentioned in section 73(2) of the Act; and

(e)    to remove any thing from the premises for the purpose of taking any such step at any other place.

(signed)

Sheriff

*Rule 3.39.14(1)*                                         FORM 57[2]

FORM OF APPLICATION FOR AN ORDER FOR DISPOSAL OF A BODY UNDER SECTION 93 OF THE PUBLIC HEALTH ETC. (SCOTLAND) ACT 2008

SHERIFFDOM OF (*insert name of sheriffdom*)

AT (*insert place of sheriff court*)

[A.B.] (*design local authority*), Applicant

*Order sought from the court*

---

[1] As inserted by the Act of Sederunt (Summary Applications, Statutory Applications and Appeals etc. Rules) Amendment (Public Health etc. (Scotland) Act 2008) 2009 (SSI 2009/320) r.2 (effective October 1, 2009).

[2] As inserted by the Act of Sederunt (Summary Applications, Statutory Applications and Appeals etc. Rules) Amendment (Public Health etc. (Scotland) Act 2008) 2009 (SSI 2009/320) r.2 (effective October 1, 2009).

*Delete as appropriate*

*The applicant applies to the court to make an order authorising the applicant to remove the body of (*insert name and date of birth of deceased person and address of premises in which the body is being retained*) to a mortuary or other similar premises and to dispose of that body before the expiry of (*insert period sought*).

OR

The applicant applies to the court to make an order authorising the applicant to dispose of the body of (*insert name and date of birth of deceased person and address of premises in which the body is being retained*) as soon as reasonably practicable.

Statement

*Delete as appropriate*

1. This application is made pursuant to section 93 of the Public Health etc. (Scotland) Act 2008.
2. The applicant's area falls within the jurisdiction of the court. The court accordingly has jurisdiction.
3. The body of the said (*insert details of deceased person) is being retained in (*insert name and address of premises*).
4. The applicant is a local authority in whose area the said premises are situated.
5. The applicant considers that the appropriate arrangements have not been made for the disposal of the said body.
6. The applicant is satisfied that as a result there is a significant risk to public health and it is necessary, to avoid or minimise that risk, for the body to be appropriately disposed of.
*7. The applicant considers that the risk to public health is such that it is necessary for the body to be disposed of immediately because (*insert here brief reasons why immediate disposal of the body is sought*).
8. The applicant attaches to this application a certificate signed by a local authority competent person which indicates that the competent person is satisfied as to the matters mentioned in statements 3, 4, 5 and 6.
9. In the circumstances narrated the applicant is entitled to the order sought and it should be granted accordingly.

(*signed*)

[X.Y.] (*add designation and business address*)

Solicitor for applicant

(*insert date*)

Rule 3.39.14(2)                                                FORM 58[1]

FORM OF ORDER FOR DISPOSAL OF A BODY

Sheriff Court..............

..............20..........

(Court Ref. No.)

*Delete as appropriate*

The sheriff, having considered an application made under section 93 of the Public Health etc. (Scotland) Act 2008 and any productions lodged,

*Being satisfied that there is a significant risk to public health, makes an order authorising the applicant to remove the body of (*insert details of deceased person*) to a mortuary or other similar premises and to dispose of that body before the expiry of (*insert period sought*).

OR

* Being satisfied that the risk to public health is such that it is necessary for the body of (*insert details of deceased person*) to be disposed of immediately, makes an order authorising the applicant to dispose of the body as soon as reasonably practicable.

(*signed*)

Sheriff

FORM 59

Rule 3.42.2(1)

---

[1] As inserted by the Act of Sederunt (Summary Applications, Statutory Applications and Appeals etc. Rules) Amendment (Public Health etc. (Scotland) Act 2008) 2009 (SSI 2009/320) r.2 (effective October 1, 2009).

FORM OF APPLICATION FOR JUDICIAL APPROVAL UNDER SECTION 23B(1) OF THE REGULATION OF INVESTIGATORY POWERS ACT 2000

Court ref. no.

SHERIFFDOM OF *(insert name of sheriffdom)*

AT *(insert place of sheriff court)*

*[A.B.], (insert designation and address of local authority)*, Applicant

### Order sought from the court

*\*Delete as appropriate*

The Applicant applies to the court under section 23B(1) of the Regulation of Investigatory Powers Act 2000 ("the Act") to grant an order under section 23A(2) of the Act approving [\*[the grant or renewal of an authorisation] *or* [the giving or renewal of a notice]] to obtain communications data [\*about *(insert name and address of person (if known) or other identifying details]* [\*from *(insert name and address of postal or telecommunications operator from whom the communications data is to be obtained)*].

### Statement

*\*Delete as appropriate*

**1.** This application is made pursuant to section 23B(1) of the Act.

**2.** The Applicant is a local authority the area of which is situated within the jurisdiction of this court. This court accordingly has jurisdiction.

**3.**[1] *[Insert name and office, rank or position of relevant person]*, a relevant person within the meaning of section 23A(6) of the Act, has—

* \*(a)   granted or renewed an authorisation under section 22(3), (3B) or (3F) of the Act;
* \*(b)   given or renewed a notice under section 22(4) of the Act

*(insert here a brief statement indicating when the authorisation or notice was given, granted or renewed and the terms of such authorisation or notice)*

**4.** At the time the relevant person [\*[\*granted or renewed] the authorisation under section [\*22(3), (3B) or (3F)]] *or* [\*[\*gave or renewed] a notice under section 22(4)] of the Act there were reasonable grounds for believing that it was necessary to obtain communications data—

* \*(a)   in the interests of national security;
* \*(b)   for the purpose of preventing or detecting crime or of preventing disorder;
* \*(c)   in the interests of the economic well-being of the United Kingdom;
* \*(d)   in the interests of public safety;
* \*(e)   for the purpose of protecting public health;
* \*(f)   for the purpose of assessing or collecting any tax, duty, levy or other imposition, contribution or charge payable to a government department;
* \*(g)   for the purpose, in an emergency, of preventing death or injury or any damage to a person's physical or mental health, or of mitigating any injury or damage to a person's physical or mental health; or
* \*(h)   for any purpose (not falling within paragraphs (a) to (g)) which is specified for the purposes of section 22(2)(h) by an order made by the Secretary of State *(specify relevant details)*.

*(insert here a brief statement indicating the basis upon which such grounds were believed to exist)*

**5.** At the time the relevant person [\*[\*granted or renewed] the authorisation under section [\*22(3), (3B) or (3F)]] or [\*[\*gave or renewed] a notice under section 22(4)] of the Act there were reasonable grounds for believing that obtaining the data in question by the conduct authorised or required by the authorisation or notice was proportionate to what was sought to be achieved by so obtaining the data.

*(insert here a brief statement indicating the basis upon which so obtaining the data was believed to be proportionate)*

**6.** At the time that the authorisation or notice was given, granted or renewed the relevant conditions set out in section 23A(5)(a) or (c) of the Act were satisfied.

*(insert here a brief statement indicating the basis upon which the relevant conditions were satisfied)*

**7.** There remain reasonable grounds for believing that the matters referred to in paragraphs 4, 5 and 6 are satisfied in relation to the authorisation or notice.

*(insert here a brief statement indicating the basis for this averment)*

**8.** In the circumstances narrated the Applicant is entitled to the order sought and it should be granted accordingly.

---

[1] As amended by the Act of Sederunt (Sheriff Court Rules)(Miscellaneous Amendments) 2013 (SSI 2013/135) para.6 (effective May 27, 2013).

*(signed)*
[X.Y.] *(add designation and business address)*
Solicitor for Applicant
*(insert date)*

FORM 60[1]

Rule 3.42.2(4)

FORM OF ORDER UNDER SECTION 23A(2) OF THE REGULATION OF INVESTIGATORY POWERS ACT 2000

Sheriff Court .........
......... 20 .........
(Court Ref. No.)

*\*Delete as appropriate*

The sheriff, having considered an application made under section 23B(1) of the Regulation of Investigatory Powers Act 2000 ("the Act") for an order under section 23A(2) of the Act,

*Being satisfied as necessary as to the matters mentioned in section [\*23A(3) or 23A(4)] of the Act:

**1.** Makes an order in terms of section 23A(2) of the Act [\*approving the grant or renewal of the authorisation OR the giving or renewal of the notice].

[**\*2.** Directs notification of this order by (insert details of method and timing of notice) to (insert name and address of postal or telecommunications operator from whom the communications data is to be obtained).]

OR

*Refuses to approve the [\*grant or renewal of the authorisation concerned OR the giving or renewal of the notice concerned] [\*and makes an order under section 23B(3) of the Act quashing the authorisation OR notice.]

*Delete as appropriate
*(signed)*
Sheriff

SCHEDULE 2

REVOCATIONS

Rule 1.3

| (1) Act of Sederunt | (2) Reference | (3) Extent of Revocation |
|---|---|---|
| Codifying Act of Sederunt 1913 | SR & O 1913/638 | Book L, Chapter X (proceedings under the Representation of the People Act 1983) |
| Codifying Act of Sederunt 1913 | SR & O 1913/638 | Book L, Chapter XI (appeals to the Court under the Pilotage Act 1913) |
| Act of Sederunt Regulating Appeals under the Pharmacy and Poisons Act 1933 | SR & O 1935/1313 | The whole Act of Sederunt |
| Act of Sederunt (Betting, Gaming and Lotteries Act Appeals) 1965 | 1965/1168 | The whole Act of Sederunt |
| Act of Sederunt (Housing Appeals) 1966 | 1966/845 | The whole Act of Sederunt |
| Act of Sederunt (Sheriff Court Procedure under Part IV of the Housing (Scotland) Act 1969) 1970 | 1970/1508 | The whole Act of Sederunt |
| Act of Sederunt (Proceedings under Sex Discrimination Act 1975) 1976 | 1976/374 | The whole Act of Sederunt |
| Act of Sederunt (Proceedings under Sex Discrimi- | 1976/1851 | The whole Act of Sederunt |

---

[1] As amended by the Act of Sederunt (Sheriff Court Rules) (Miscellaneous Amendments) 2013 (SSI 2013/135) para.6 (effective May 27, 2013).

| (1) | (2) | (3) |
| --- | --- | --- |
| **Act of Sederunt** | **Reference** | **Extent of Revocation** |
| nation Act 1975) No 2 1976 | | |
| Act of Sederunt (Proceedings under Sex Discrimination Act 1975) 1977 | 1977/973 | The whole Act of Sederunt |
| Act of Sederunt (Appeals under the Licensing (Scotland) Act 1976) 1977 | 1977/1622 | The whole Act of Sederunt |
| Act of Sederunt (Betting and Gaming Appeals) 1978 | 1978/229 | The whole Act of Sederunt |
| Act of Sederunt (Appeals under the Rating (Disabled Persons) Act 1978) 1979 | 1979/446 | The whole Act of Sederunt |
| Act of Sederunt (Copyright, Deisgns and Patents) 1990 | 1990/380 | The whole Act of Sederunt |
| Act of Sederunt (Proceedings in the Sheriff Court under the Model Law on International Commercial Arbitration) 1991 | 1991/2214 | The whole Act of Sederunt |
| Act of Sederunt (Coal Mining Subsidence Act 1991) 1992 | 1992/798 | The whole Act of Sederunt |
| Act of Sederunt (Applications under Part III of the Criminal Justice (International Co-operation) Act 1990) 1992 | 1992/1077 | The whole Act of Sederunt |
| Act of Sederunt (Sheriff Court Summary Application Rules) 1993 | 1993/3240 | The whole Act of Sederunt |
| Act of Sederunt (Mental Health Rules) 1996 | 1996/2149 | The whole Act of Sederunt |
| Act of Sederunt (Proceeds of Crime Rules) 1996 | 1996/2446 | The whole Act of Sederunt |

# ACT OF SEDERUNT (PROCEEDINGS FOR DETERMINATION OF DEVOLUTION ISSUES RULES) 1999

## (SI 1999/1347)

The Lords of Council and Session, under and by virtue of the powers conferred on them by section 32 of the Sheriff Courts (Scotland) Act 1971, paragraph 37 of Schedule 6 to the Scotland Act 1998, paragraph 38 of Schedule 10 to the Northern Ireland Act 1998 and paragraph 36 of Schedule 8 to the Government of Wales Act 1998 and of all other powers enabling them in that behalf, having approved, draft rules submitted to them by the Sheriff Court Rules Council in accordance with section 34 of the Sheriff Courts (Scotland) Act 1971, do hereby enact and declare:

### Citation

**1.**—(1)   This Act of Sederunt may be cited as the Act of Sederunt (Proceedings for Determination of Devolution Issues Rules) 1999 and shall come into force on 6th May 1999.

(2)   This Act of Sederunt shall be inserted in the Books of Sederunt.

### Interpretation

**2.**—[1](1)   In this Act of Sederunt—

"Advocate General" means the Advocate General for Scotland;
"devolution issue" means a devolution issue within the meaning of—
    (a)   Schedule 6 to the Scotland Act 1998;
    (b)   Schedule 10 to the Northern Ireland Act 1998; or
    (c)   Schedule 9 to the Government of Wales Act 2006;
"initiating document" means the initial writ, summons, petition or other document by which the proceedings are initiated;
"relevant authority" means the Advocate General and—
    (a)   in the case of a devolution issue within the meaning of Schedule 6, the Lord Advocate;
    (b)   in the case of a devolution issue within the meaning of Schedule 10, the Attorney General for Northern Ireland, the First Minister and the deputy First Minister;
    (c)   in the case of a devolution issue within the meaning of Schedule 9, the Counsel General to the Welsh Assembly Government.

(2)   Any reference in this Act of Sederunt to a numbered Form shall be construed as a reference to the Form so numbered in Schedule 1 to this Act of Sederunt, and any reference to a rule shall be a reference to the rule so numbered in this Act of Sederunt.

### Proceedings for determination of a devolution issue

**3.**   Where the initiating document contains an averment or crave which raises a devolution issue, the initiating document shall include a crave for warrant to intimate it to the relevant authority, unless he is a party to the action.

---

[1] As amended by the Act of Sederunt (Proceedings for Determination of Devolution Issues Rules) Amendment 2007 (SSI 2007/362) r.2(2) (effective August 15, 2007) and by the Act of Sederunt (Devolution Issues) (Appeals and References to the Supreme Court) 2009 (SSI 2009/323) (effective October 1, 2009).

## Time for raising devolution issue

**4.** It shall not be competent for a party to any proceedings to raise a devolution issue after proof is commenced, unless the sheriff, on cause shown, otherwise determines.

## Specification of devolution issue

**5.**—(1) Any party raising a devolution issue shall specify—

    (a) where he initiates the action, in the initiating document;

    (b) in the written defences or answers; or

    (c) in any other case, in Form 1,

the facts and circumstances and contentions of law on the basis of which it is alleged that the devolution issue arises in sufficient detail to enable the sheriff to determine whether such an issue arises in the proceedings.

(2) Where a pay wishes to raise a devolution issue after lodging any writ mentioned in paragraph (1) above he shall do so—

    (a) by way of adjustment or minute of amendment; or

    (b) in proceedings in which there is no procedure for adjustment or amendment, in Form 1,

so as to provide specification of the matters mentioned in that paragraph.

## Intimation of devolution issue

**6.**—(1) Intimation of a devolution issue shall be given to the relevant authority (unless he is a party to the proceedings) in accordance with this rule.

(2) Where the devolution issue is raised in the initiating document, the sheriff shall order intimation of the devolution issue as craved in the warrant for service.

(3) In any case other than that described in paragraph (2) above, the party raising the devolution issue shall lodge a motion or incidental application, as the case may be, craving a warrant for intimation of the devolution issue on the relevant authority, and on considering the motion or incidental application, where it appears to the sheriff that a devolution issue arises, he shall order such intimation of the devolution issue.

(4) Where intimation is ordered in accordance with paragraphs (2) or (3) above, such intimation shall be in Form 2 and be made in such manner as the sheriff considers appropriate in the circumstances.

(5) The intimation of a devolution issue shall specify 14 days, or such other period as the sheriff thinks fit, as the period within which the relevant authority may enter appearance as a party in the proceedings.

(6)[1] Where, after determination at first instance of any proceedings in which a devolution issue has been raised under this Act of Sederunt, a party to those proceedings marks an appeal under rule 31.3 or 31.4 of the Ordinary Cause Rules 1993 in Schedule 1 to the Sheriff Courts (Scotland) Act 1907, that party shall, unless the relevant authority is already a party to the proceedings, intimate the note of appeal to the relevant authority together with a notice in Form 2A.

---

[1] As inserted by the Act of Sederunt (Proceedings for Determination of Devolution Issues Rules) Amendment 2007 (SSI 2007/362) r.2(3) (effective August 15, 2007).

**Response to intimation of devolution issue**

**7.**—(1)   This rule applies where the relevant authority receives intimation of a devolution issue.

(2)   Where the relevant authority intends to enter an appearance as a party in the proceedings, he shall lodge a minute stating that he intends to do so.

(3)   Upon receipt of the minute lodged in accordance with paragraph (2) above, the sheriff shall sist the relevant authority as a party to the action.

(4)   Upon the relevant authority being sisted as a party in accordance with paragraph (3) above, the sheriff shall order the relevant authority to lodge a note of his written submissions in respect of the devolution issue specifying those matters mentioned in rule 5(1) within 7 days, or such other period as the sheriff thinks fit.

(5)   A copy of the minute lodged in accordance with paragraph (2) above and a copy of any note lodged in accordance with paragraph (4) above shall, at the same time as lodging the minute or any note, be intimated by the party lodging such to all other parties in the proceedings.

(6)   At any time after the note mentioned in paragraph (4) above has been lodged, the sheriff may regulate such further procedure in the proceedings as he thinks fit.

(7)[1]   Where a relevant authority does not take part as a party in the proceedings at first instance the court may allow him to take part as a party in any subsequent appeal to the sheriff principal.

**Intimation under section 102 of the Scotland Act 1998, section 81 of the Northern Ireland Act 1998 or section 153 of the Government of Wales Act 2006**

**8.**—[2](1)   This rule applies to orders made under—
  (a)   section 102 of the Scotland Act 1998 (powers of courts or tribunals to vary retrospective decisions);
  (b)   section 81 of the Northern Ireland Act 1998 (powers of courts or tribunals to vary retrospective decisions); or
  (c)   section 153 of the Government of Wales Act 2006 (power to vary retrospective decisions).

(2)   Where the sheriff is considering whether to make an order under any of the provisions mentioned in paragraph (1) above, he shall order intimation of that fact to be given to every person to whom intimation is required to be given by that provision.

(3)   The intimation mentioned in paragraph (2) above shall—
  (a)   be made forthwith by the sheriff clerk in Form 3 by first class recorded delivery post; and
  (b)   specify 14 days, or such other period as the sheriff thinks fit, as the period within which a person may enter an appearance as a party in the proceedings so far as they relate to the making of the order.

**Response to intimation of order under rule 8**

**9.**—(1)   This rule applies where a person receives intimation in accordance with rule 8.

---

[1] As inserted by the Act of Sederunt (Proceedings for Determination of Devolution Issues Rules) Amendment 2007 (SSI 2007/362) r.2(4) (effective August 15, 2007).
[2] As amended by the Act of Sederunt (Proceedings for Determination of Devolution Issues Rules) Amendment 2007 (SSI 2007/362) r.2(5)–(6) (effective August 15, 2007).

(2)   Where a person intends to enter an appearance as a party in the proceedings, he shall lodge a minute stating that he intends to do so.

(3)   Upon receipt of the minute lodged in accordance with paragraph (2) above, the sheriff shall sist the person as a party to the action.

(4)   Upon a person being sisted as a party in accordance with paragraph (3) above, the sheriff shall order the person to lodge a note of his written submissions in respect of the making of the order within 7 days, or such other period as the sheriff thinks fit.

(5)   A copy of the minute lodged in accordance with paragraph (2) above and a copy of any note lodged in accordance with paragraph (4) above shall, at the same time as lodging the minute or any note, be intimated by the party lodging such to all other parties in the proceedings.

(6)   At any time after the note mentioned in paragraph (4) above has been lodged, the sheriff may regulate such further procedure in the proceedings as he thinks fit.

### Reference of devolution issue to Inner House of the Court of Session or Supreme Court

**10.**—[1](1)   This rule applies where—
- (a)   any reference of a devolution issue is made to the Inner House of the Court of Session; or
- (b)   the sheriff is required by the relevant authority to refer a devolution issue to the Supreme Court.

(2)   Where a reference is made in accordance with paragraph (1) above, the sheriff shall pronounce an interlocutor giving directions about the manner and time in which the reference is to be drafted and adjusted.

(3)   When the reference has been drafted and adjusted in accordance with paragraph (2) above, the sheriff shall sign the reference.

(4)   The reference shall include such matters as are prescribed in Schedule 2 to this Act of Sederunt, and shall have annexed to it the interlocutor making the reference and any other order of the court in the cause.

(5)   The sheriff clerk shall send a copy of the reference by first class recorded delivery post to—
- (a)   the parties to the proceedings; and
- (b)   the relevant authority (if he is not already a party) who may have a potential interest in the proceedings,

and shall certify on the back of the principal reference that a copy has been sent and to whom.

### Sist of cause on reference to Inner House of the Court of Session or Supreme Court

**11.**[2]   On a reference being made in accordance with rule 10, the cause shall, unless the sheriff when making the reference otherwise orders, be sisted until the devolution issue has been determined.

---

[1] As amended by the Act of Sederunt (Devolution Issues) (Appeals and References to the Supreme Court) 2009 (SSI 2009/323) (effective October 1, 2009).

[2] As amended by the Act of Sederunt (Devolution Issues) (Appeals and References to the Supreme Court) 2009 (SSI 2009/323) (effective October 1, 2009).

## Interim Orders

**12.**—[1](1) Notwithstanding the reference of a devolution issue to the Inner House of the Court of Session or to the Supreme Court in accordance with rule 10, the sheriff shall have power to make any interim order which a due regard to the interests of the parties may require.

(2) The sheriff may recall a sist made under rule 11 for the purpose of making the interim order mentioned in paragraph (1) above.

## Transmission of reference

**13.**—(1) The sheriff clerk shall forthwith transmit the principal copy of the reference—

    (a) to the Deputy Principal Clerk of the Court of Session; or

    (b)[2] together with seven copies, to the Registrar of the Supreme Court, as the case may be.

(2) Unless the sheriff otherwise directs, the principal copy of the reference shall not be transmitted in accordance with paragraph (1) above, where an appeal against the making of the reference is pending.

(3) For the purpose of paragraph (2) above, an appeal shall be treated as pending—

    (a) until the expiry of the time for making that appeal; or

    (b) where an appeal has been made, until that appeal has been determined.

## Procedure following determination on reference or appeal

**14.**—[3](1) This rule applies where either the Inner House of the Court of Session or the Supreme Court have determined—

    (a) a devolution issue referred to them in accordance with rule 10; or

    (b) an appeal ma to them.

(2) Upon receipt of the determination of the Inner House of the Court of Session or the Supreme Court, as the case may be, the sheriff clerk shall forthwith place before the sheriff a copy of the determination and the court process.

(3) The sheriff may *ex proprio motu* or shall upon the lodging of a motion or incidental application by any of the parties to the proceedings, pronounce an interlocutor ordering such further procedure as may be required.

(4) Where the sheriff *ex proprio motu* pronounces an interlocutor in accordance with paragraph (3) above, the sheriff clerk shall forthwith intimate a copy of the interlocutor to all parties in the proceedings.

SCHEDULE 1

**Rule 2(2)**

Rules 5(1)(c) and 5(2)(b)

---

[1] As amended by the Act of Sederunt (Devolution Issues) (Appeals and References to the Supreme Court) 2009 (SSI 2009/323) (effective October 1, 2009).

[2] As amended by the Act of Sederunt (Devolution Issues) (Appeals and References to the Supreme Court) 2009 (SSI 2009/323) (effective October 1, 2009).

[3] As amended by the Act of Sederunt (Devolution Issues) (Appeals and References to the Supreme Court) 2009 (SSI 2009/323) (effective October 1, 2009).

FORM 1[1]

FORM OF SPECIFICATION OF DEVOLUTION ISSUE

SHERIFFDOM OF (*insert name of sheriffdom*)

AT (*insert place of sheriff court*).........Court Ref No...........

In the action of

[A.B.] (*designation and address*)

Pursuer

against

[C.D.] (*designation and address*)

Defender

1. The *Pursuer/Defender (*if other please specify*) wishes to raise a devolution issue in the above action.

[*The Pursuer or Defender or other party, as the case may be, should then insert the following information—*

- *the facts and circumstances and contentions of law on the basis of which it is alleged that the devolution issue arises in sufficient detail to enable the sheriff to determine whether such an issue arises in the proceedings;*
- *details of the relevant law including the relevant provisions of the* Scotland Act 1998, the Government of Wales Act 2006 or the Northern Ireland Act 1998, *as the case may be; and*
- *the reason why the resolution of the devolution issue is considered necessary for the purpose of disposing of the proceedings*].

Date (*insert date*)

(*Signed*)

Solicitor for the *Pursuer/Defender (*if other please specify*)

*Delete as appropriate

Rule 6(4)

FORM 2

FORM OF INTIMATION TO RELEVANT AUTHORITY OF A DEVOLUTION ISSUE RAISED IN CIVIL PROCEEDINGS IN THE SHERIFF COURT

To (*insert name and address*).........Court Ref No.........

1. You are given notice that in the Sheriff Court at (*insert address*),

*an action has been raised which includes a crave in respect of a devolution issue;

*a devolution issue has been raised in an action;

A copy of the * initial writ/pleadings in the case (*as adjusted*) is enclosed. A copy of the interlocutor appointing intimation is also enclosed.

2. If you wish to enter appearance as a party to the proceedings, you must lodge with the Sheriff Clerk (*insert name and address*) a notice in writing stating that you intend to appear as a party in the proceedings. The notice must be lodged within 14 days of (*insert date on which intimation was given*).

Date (*insert date*).........

(*Signed*).........

Solicitor for *Pursuer/Defender.........

*Delete as appropriate.

Rule 6(6)

FORM 2A[2]

FORM OF INTIMATION TO RELEVANT AUTHORITY OF APPEAL IN PROCEEDINGS IN WHICH A DEVOLUTION ISSUE HAS BEEN RAISED

To: (*name and address of relevant authority*).......... Court Ref No:..........

You are given notice that an appeal has been marked in proceedings in which a devolution issue has been raised. A copy of the note of appeal is enclosed.

Date (*insert date*).......... (*Signed*)..........

Solicitor for the Appellant

(*add designation and business address*)

---

[1] As amended by the Act of Sederunt (Proceedings for Determination of Devolution Issues Rules) Amendment 2007 (SSI 2007/362) r.2(7)(a) (effective August 15, 2007).

[2] As inserted by the Act of Sederunt (Proceedings for Determination of Devolution Issues Rules) Amendment 2007 (SSI 2007/362) r.2(7)(b) (effective August 15, 2007).

# Act of Sederunt (Proceedings for Determination of Devolution Issues Rules) 1999

## FORM 3[1]

FORM OF INTIMATION UNDER *SECTION 102 OF THE SCOTLAND ACT 1998/SECTION 81 OF THE NORTHERN IRELAND ACT 1998/SECTION 153 OF THE GOVERNMENT OF WALES ACT 2006

To (*insert name and address*).......... Court Ref No:..........

1. You are given notice that in an action raised in the Sheriff Court at (*insert address*), the sheriff has decided

*that an Act/provision of an Act of the Scottish Parliament is not within the legislative competence of the Parliament;

*a member of the Scottish Executive does not have the power to make, confirm or approve a provision of subordinate legislation he has purported to make, confirm or approve;

A copy of the *initial writ/pleadings in the case (*as adjusted*) is enclosed. A copy of the interlocutor appointing intimation is also enclosed.

2. The sheriff is considering whether to make an order under *section 102 of the Scotland Act 1998/ section 81 of the Northern Ireland Act 1998/section 153 of the Government of Wales Act 2006 either removing or limiting the retrospective effect of the decision, or suspending the effect of the decision to allow the defect to be corrected.

3. If you wish to enter appearance as a party to the proceedings so far as they relate to the making of the order, you must lodge with the sheriff clerk (insert name and address) a notice in writing stating that you intend to appear as a party in the proceedings. The notice must be lodged within 14 days of (*insert date on which intimation was given*).

Date (*insert date*).......... (*Signed*)

Sheriff Clerk

*Delete as appropriate

## SCHEDULE 2[2]

DETAILS TO BE INCLUDED WHERE REFERENCE MADE TO *THE INNER HOUSE OF THE COURT OF SESSION/SUPREME COURT

**Rule 10(4)**

1. The question(s) referred.

2. The addresses of the parties.

3. A concise statement of the background to the matter, including—

    (i)   the facts of the case, including any relevant findings of fact by the referring court; and

    (ii)  the main issues in the case and contentions of the parties with regard to them.

4. The relevant law including the relevant provisions of the *Scotland Act 1998/Government of Wales Act 2006/Northern Ireland Act 1998.

5. The reasons why an answer to the question(s) *is/are considered necessary for the purpose of disposing of the proceedings.

*Note*: A copy of the interlocutor making the reference and a copy of any judgment in the proceedings must be annexed to the reference.

*Delete as appropriate.

---

[1] As amended by the Act of Sederunt (Proceedings for Determination of Devolution Issues Rules) Amendment 2007 (SSI 2007/352) r.2(7)(c) (effective August 15, 2007).

[2] As amended by the Act of Sederunt (Proceedings for Determination of Devolution Issues Rules) Amendment 2007 (SSI 2007/362) r.2(8) (effective August 15, 2007) and by the Act of Sederunt (Devolution Issues) (Appeals and References to the Supreme Court) 2009 (SSI 2009/323) (effective October 1, 2009).

# ACT OF SEDERUNT (EVIDENCE OF JUDGMENTS ETC.) (HUMAN RIGHTS ACT 1998) 2000

## (SSI 2000/314)

The Lords of Council and Session, under and by virtue of the powers conferred on them by section 32 of the Sheriff Courts (Scotland) Act 1971, and of all other powers enabling them in that behalf, having approved draft rules submitted to them by the Sheriff Court Rules Council in accordance with section 34 of that Act, do hereby enact and declare:

### Citation and commencement

**1.**—(1)   This Act of Sederunt may be cited as the Act of Sederunt (Evidence of Judgments etc.) (Human Rights Act 1998) 2000 and shall come into force on 2nd October 2000.

(2)   This Act of Sederunt shall be inserted in the Books of Sederunt.

### Evidence of judgments etc

**2.**—(1)   Evidence of any judgment, decision, declaration or opinion of which account has to be taken by the court under section 2 of the Human Rights Act 1998 shall be given by reference to any authoritative and complete report of the said judgment, decision, declaration or opinion and may be given in any manner.

(2)   Evidence given in accordance with paragraph (1) shall be sufficient evidence of that judgment, decision, declaration or opinion.

# PART-TIME SHERIFFS (REMOVAL TRIBUNAL) REGULATIONS 2001

(SI 2001/205)

## Citation and commencement

**1.** These Regulations may be cited as the Part-Time Sheriffs (Removal Tribunal) Regulations 2001 and shall come into force on the day after the day on which they are made.

## Interpretation

**2.** In these Regulations—

"the Act" means the Sheriff Courts (Scotland) Act 1971;
"investigation" means an investigation carried out under section 11C(2) of the Act;
"sheriff" means the part-time sheriff who is the subject of the investigation;
"tribunal" means the tribunal constituted by and under section 11C(3) of the Act.

## Commencement of investigation

**3.** Prior to an investigation by the tribunal commencing, the Scottish Ministers shall give the sheriff written notice of the investigation and of their reasons for requesting the investigation.

## Payments to members

**4.** The Scottish Ministers may pay to a member of the tribunal such sums as they consider appropriate in respect of the performance of that person's duties as a member.

## Change in membership of tribunal

**5.**—(1) This regulation shall apply where, after commencement of an investigation, any member of the tribunal—

(a) dies;
(b) resigns; or
(c) is, in the opinion of the Lord President, unable to act.

(2) Subject to paragraph (3), the Lord President shall appoint a new member to replace the member referred to in paragraph (1).

(3) Where the member referred to in paragraph (1) is not the person presiding over the tribunal, a new member need not be appointed under paragraph (2) unless the sheriff so wishes.

(4) On a new member being appointed under paragraph (2), the tribunal may (but need not) commence the investigation again.

## Procedure—general

**6.** Other than as specified in these Regulations, the procedure to be followed by and before the tribunal shall be that determined by the tribunal.

## Procedure—further provisions

**7.**—(1) The tribunal may receive oral or written evidence from such persons as it thinks fit.

(2) The tribunal shall give the sheriff the opportunity to make written and, if the sheriff wishes, oral representations regarding the matters which are the subject of the investigation.

(3) Representations under paragraph (2) may be made by the sheriff personally or by anyone acting on his or her behalf.

(4) The tribunal shall sit in private and no member shall disclose information received in the course of an investigation other than for the purposes of carrying out the functions conferred on the tribunal by the Act and these Regulations.

### Suspension

**8.**—(1) At any time during an investigation, the tribunal may suspend the sheriff from office.

(2) A suspension imposed under paragraph (1) shall terminate—

    (a) on the tribunal deciding not to order removal of the sheriff from office; or

    (b) before then, on the tribunal deciding to bring the suspension to an end.

(3) If the tribunal so directs, a sheriff suspended under this regulation may remain in office as a part-time sheriff but only for the purpose of continuing to deal with proceedings commenced prior to the suspension taking effect.

### Draft findings to be sent to sheriff

**9.**—(1) The tribunal shall send to the sheriff a draft of its findings on the investigation and shall give the sheriff an opportunity to make comments on the draft by such date as the tribunal may specify.

(2) The tribunal shall have regard to any comments made under paragraph (1), but need not give the sheriff an opportunity to comment on any alterations made to the draft prior to submission of the final report under regulation 10.

### Report and decisions

**10.**—(1) On completion of its investigation, the tribunal shall submit a written report to the Scottish Ministers specifying—

    (a) its findings on the investigation;

    (b) its decision on whether to order removal of the sheriff from office; and

    (c) where appropriate, the date of removal from office.

(2) At the same time as submitting its report under paragraph (1), the tribunal shall send a copy of it to the sheriff.

# ACT OF SEDERUNT (SUMMARY CAUSE RULES) 2002

## (SSI 2002/132)

The Lords of Council and Session, under and by virtue of the powers conferred by section 32 of the Sheriff Courts (Scotland) Act 1971 (a) and of all other powers enabling them in that behalf, having approved draft rules submitted to them by the Sheriff Court Rules Council in accordance with section 34 of the said Act of 1971, do hereby enact and declare:

## Citation and commencement

**1.**—(1)   This Act of Sederunt may be cited as the Act of Sederunt (Summary Cause Rules) 2002 and shall come into force on 10th June 2002.

(2)   This Act of Sederunt shall be inserted in the Books of Sederunt.

## Summary Cause Rules

**2.**   The provisions of Schedule 1 to this Act of Sederunt shall have effect for the purpose of providing rules for a summary cause other than a small claim.

## Transitional provision

**3.**   Nothing in Schedule 1 to this Act of Sederunt shall apply to a summary cause commenced before 10th June 2002 and any such action shall proceed according to the law and practice in force immediately before that date.

## Revocation

**4.**   The Acts of Sederunt mentioned in column (1) of Schedule 2 to this Act of Sederunt are revoked to the extent specified in column (3) of that Schedule except—

(a)   in relation to any summary cause commenced before 10th June 2002; and

(b)   for the purposes of the Act of Sederunt (Small Claim Rules) 1988.

SCHEDULE 1

SUMMARY CAUSE RULES 2002

**Paragraph 2**

### Arrangement of Rules

## Chapter 9
### *Incidental applications and sists*

## Chapter 10
### *Counterclaim*

## Chapter 11
### *Third party procedure*

## Chapter 12
### *Summary decree*

## Chapter 13
### *Alteration of summons etc.*

## Chapter 14
### *Additional defender*

## Chapter 14A
### *Interventions by the Commission for Equality and Human Rights*

## Chapter 14B
### *Interventions by the Scottish Commission for Human Rights*

## Chapter 15
### *Application for sist of party and transference*

## Chapter 16
### *Transfer and remit of actions*

Appendix 1A

**Schedule of timetable under personal injuries procedure**

Appendix 2

**Glossary**

CHAPTER 1

CITATION, INTERPRETATION AND APPLICATION

**Citation, interpretation and application**

**1.1**—[1](1)   These Rules may be cited as the Summary Cause Rules 2002.

(2)   In these Rules—

"the 1907 Act" means the Sheriff Courts (Scotland) Act 1907;
"the 1971 Act" means the Sheriff Courts (Scotland) Act 1971;
"the 1975 Act" means the Litigants in Person (Costs and Expenses) Act 1975;
"the 2004 Act" means the Vulnerable Witnesses (Scotland) Act 2004;[2]
"authorised lay representative" means a person to whom section 32(1) of the Solicitors (Scotland) Act 1980 (offence to prepare writs) does not apply by virtue of section 32(2)(a) of that Act;
"enactment" includes an enactment comprised in, or in an instrument made under, an Act of the Scottish Parliament;
"small claim" has the meaning assigned to it by section 35(2) of the 1971 Act;
"summary cause" has the meaning assigned to it by section 35(1) of the 1971 Act.

(3)   Any reference to a specified Chapter or rule shall be construed as a reference to the Chapter or rule bearing that number in these Rules, and a reference to a specified paragraph, subparagraph or head shall be construed as a reference to the paragraph, sub-paragraph or head so numbered or lettered in the provision in which that reference occurs.

(4)   A form referred to by number means the form so numbered in Appendix 1 to these Rules or a form substantially of the same effect with such variation as circumstances may require.

(4A)[3]   In these Rules, references to a solicitor include a reference to a member of a body which has made a successful application under section 25 of the Law Reform (Miscellaneous Provisions) (Scotland) Act 1990 but only to the extent that the member is exercising rights acquired by virtue of section 27 of that Act.

(5)   The glossary in Appendix 2 to these Rules is a guide to the meaning of certain legal expressions used in these Rules, but is not to be taken as giving those expressions any meaning which they do not have in law generally.

---

[1] As amended by the Act of Sederunt (Ordinary Cause, Summary Application, Summary Cause and Small Claim Rules) Amendment (Miscellaneous) 2007 (SSI 2007/6) r.4(2) (effective January 29, 2007).

[2] As inserted by the Act of Sederunt (Ordinary Cause, Summary Application, Summary Cause and Small Claim Rules) Amendment (Vulnerable Witnesses (Scotland) Act 2004) 2007 (SSI 2007/463) r.4(2) (effective November 1, 2007).

[3] As inserted by the Act of Sederunt (Sheriff Court Rules Amendment) (Sections 25 to 29 of the Law Reform (Miscellaneous Provisions) (Scotland) Act 1990) 2009 (SSI 2009/164) r.4(2) (effective May 20, 2009).

(6)   These Rules shall apply to a summary cause other than a small claim.

Chapter 2

Representation

**Representation**

**2.1.**—[1](1)   A party may be represented by—

    (a)   an advocate;

    (b)   a solicitor;

    (c)   a person authorised under any enactment to conduct proceedings in the sheriff court, in accordance with the terms of that enactment; and

    (d)   subject to paragraphs (2) and (4), an authorised lay representative.

(2)   An authorised lay representative shall not appear in court on behalf of a party except at the hearing held in terms of rule 8.2(1) and, unless the sheriff otherwise directs, any subsequent or other calling where the action is not defended on the merits or on the amount of the sum due.

(3)   Subject to the provisions of this rule, the persons referred to in paragraph (1)(c) and (d) above may, in representing a party, do everything for the preparation and conduct of an action as may be done by an individual conducting his own action.

(4)   If the sheriff finds that the authorised lay representative is—

    (a)   not a suitable person to represent the party; or

    (b)   not in fact authorised to do so,

that person must cease to represent the party.

(5)   A party may be represented by a person other than an advocate or solicitor at any stage of any proceedings under the Debtors (Scotland) Act 1987, other than appeals to the sheriff principal, if the sheriff is satisfied that that person is a suitable person to represent the party at that stage and is authorised to do so.

**Lay support**

**2.2.**—[2](1)   At any time during proceedings the sheriff may, on the request of a party litigant, permit a named individual to assist the litigant in the conduct of the proceedings by sitting beside or behind (as the litigant chooses) the litigant at hearings in court or in chambers and doing such of the following for the litigant as he or she requires—

    (a)   providing moral support;

    (b)   helping to manage the court documents and other papers;

    (c)   taking notes of the proceedings;

    (d)   quietly advising on—

        (i)    points of law and procedure;

        (ii)   issues which the litigant might wish to raise with the sheriff;

        (iii)  questions which the litigant might wish to ask witnesses.

(2)   It is a condition of such permission that the named individual does not receive from the litigant, whether directly or indirectly, any remuneration for his or her assistance.

(3)   The sheriff may refuse a request under paragraph (1) only if—

    (a)   the sheriff is of the opinion that the named individual is an unsuitable person to act in that capacity (whether generally or in the proceedings concerned); or

    (b)   the sheriff is of the opinion that it would be contrary to the efficient administration of justice to grant it.

(4)   Permission granted under paragraph (1) endures until the proceedings finish or it is withdrawn under paragraph (5); but it is not effective during any period when the litigant is represented.

(5)   The sheriff may, of his or her own accord or on the incidental application of a party to the proceedings, withdraw permission granted under paragraph (1); but the sheriff must first be of the opinion that it would be contrary to the efficient administration of justice for the permission to continue.

(6)   Where permission has been granted under paragraph (1), the litigant may—

    (a)   show the named individual any document (including a court document); or

    (b)   impart to the named individual any information,

---

[1] As amended by the Act of Sederunt (Ordinary Cause, Summary Application, Summary Cause and Small Claim Rules) Amendment (Miscellaneous) 2007 (SSI 2007/6) r.4(3) (effective January 29, 2007).

[2] As inserted by the Act of Sederunt (Sheriff Court Rules) (Miscellaneous Amendments) (No.2) 2010 (SSI 2010/416) r.4 (effective January 1, 2011).

which is in his or her possession in connection with the proceedings without being taken to contravene any prohibition or restriction on the disclosure of the document or the information; but the named individual is then to be taken to be subject to any such prohibition or restriction as if he or she were the litigant.

(7) Any expenses incurred by the litigant as a result of the support of an individual under paragraph (1) are not recoverable expenses in the proceedings.

Chapter 2A[1]

Lay Representation

**Application and interpretation**

**2A.1.**—(1) This Chapter is without prejudice to any enactment (including any other provision in these Rules) under which provision is, or may be, made for a party to a particular type of case before the sheriff to be represented by a lay representative.

(2) In this Chapter, a "lay representative" means a person who is not—

    (a)    a solicitor;

    (b)    an advocate, or

    (c)    someone having a right to conduct litigation, or a right of audience, by virtue of section 27 of the Law Reform (Miscellaneous Provisions) (Scotland) Act 1990.

**Lay representation for party litigants**

**2A.2.**—(1) In any proceedings in respect of which no provision as mentioned in rule 2A.1(1) is in force, the sheriff may, on the request of a party litigant, permit a named individual (a "lay representative") to appear, along with the litigant, at a specified hearing for the purpose of making oral submissions on behalf of the litigant at that hearing.

(2) An application under paragraph (1)—

    (a)    is to be made orally on the date of the first hearing at which the litigant wishes a named individual to make oral submissions; and

    (b)    is to be accompanied by a document, signed by the named individual, in Form A1.

(3) The sheriff may grant an application under paragraph (1) only if the sheriff is of the opinion that it would assist his or her consideration of the case to grant it.

(4) It is a condition of permission granted by the sheriff that the lay representative does not receive directly or indirectly from the litigant any remuneration or other reward for his or her assistance.

(5) The sheriff may grant permission under paragraph (1) in respect of one or more specified hearings in the case; but such permission is not effective during any period when the litigant is legally represented.

(6) The sheriff may, of his or her own accord or on the motion of a party to the proceedings, withdraw permission granted under paragraph (1).

(7) Where permission has been granted under paragraph (1), the litigant may—

    (a)    show the lay representative any document (including a court document); or

    (b)    impart to the lay representative any information,

which is in his or her possession in connection with the proceedings without being taken to contravene any prohibition or restriction on the disclosure of the document or the information; but the lay representative is then to be taken to be subject to any such prohibition or restriction as if he or she were the litigant.

(8) Any expenses incurred by the litigant in connection with lay representation under this rule are not recoverable expenses in the proceedings.

Chapter 3

Relief from failure to comply with rules

**Dispensing power of sheriff**

**3.1.**—(1) The sheriff may relieve any party from the consequences of any failure to comply with the provisions of these Rules which is shown to be due to mistake, oversight or other excusable cause, on such conditions as he thinks fit.

---

[1] As inserted by the Act of Sederunt (Sheriff Court Rules) (Lay Representation) 2013 (SSI 2013/91) r.4 (effective April 4, 2013).

(2) Where the sheriff relieves a party from the consequences of the failure to comply with a provision in these Rules under paragraph (1), he may make such order as he thinks fit to enable the action to proceed as if the failure to comply with the provision had not occurred.

### Chapter 4

#### Commencement of action

### Form of summons

**4.1.**—(1) A summary cause action shall be commenced by summons, which shall be in Form 1.

(2) The form of claim in a summons may be in one of Forms 2, 3, 4, 5, 6, 7, 8 or 9.

### Statement of claim

**4.2.** The pursuer must insert a statement of his claim in the summons to give the defender fair notice of the claim; and the statement must include—

    (a) details of the basis of the claim including relevant dates; and

    (b) if the claim arises from the supply of goods or services, a description of the goods or services and the date or dates on or between which they were supplied and, where relevant, ordered.

### Actions relating to regulated agreements

**4.2A.**[1] In an action which relates to a regulated agreement within the meaning given by section 189(1) of the Consumer Credit Act 1974 the statement of claim shall include an averment that such an agreement exists and details of the agreement.

### Defender's copy summons

**4.3.** A copy summons shall be served on the defender—

    (a) where the action is for, or includes a claim for, payment of money—

        (i) in Form 1a where an application for a time to pay direction under the Debtors (Scotland) Act 1987 or time order under the Consumer Credit Act 1974 may be applied for; or

        (ii) in Form 1b in every other case;

    (b) where the action is not for, and does not include a claim for, payment of money, in Form 1c; or

    (c) in an action of multiplepoinding, in Form 1d.

### Authentication and effect of summons

**4.4.**—(1) A summons shall be authenticated by the sheriff clerk in some appropriate manner except where—

    (a) he refuses to do so for any reason;

    (b) the defender's address is unknown; or

    (c) a party seeks to alter the normal period of notice specified in rule 4.5(2); or

    (d)[2] a warrant for arrestment on the dependence, or to found jurisdiction, is sought.[2]

(2) If any of paragraphs (1)(a) to (d) applies, the summons shall be authenticated by the sheriff, if he thinks it appropriate.

(3) The authenticated summons shall be warrant for—

    (a) service on the defender; and

    (b) where the appropriate warrant has been sought in the summons—

        (i) arrestment on the dependence; or

        (ii) arrestment to found jurisdiction,

    as the case may be.

(4)[3, 4] Where a warrant for arrestment to found jurisdiction, is sought, averments to justify that warrant must be included in the statement of claim.

---

[1] As inserted by the Act of Sederunt (Sheriff Court Rules) (Miscellaneous Amendments) 2009 (SSI 2009/294) r.4 (effective December 1, 2009) as substituted by the Act of Sederunt (Amendment of the Act of Sederunt (Sheriff Court Rules) (Miscellaneous Amendments) 2009) 2009 (SSI 2009/402) (effective November 30, 2009).

[2] As inserted by the Act of Sederunt (Ordinary Cause, Summary Application and Small Claim Rules) Amendment (Miscellaneous) (SSI 2004/197) r.4(2) (effective May 21, 2004).

[3] As inserted by the Act of Sederunt (Ordinary Cause, Summary Application and Small Claim Rules) Amendment (Miscellaneous) (SSI 2004/197) r.4(2) (effective May 21, 2004).

**Period of notice**

**4.5.**—(1)  An action shall proceed after the appropriate period of notice of the summons has been given to the defender prior to the return day.

(2)  The appropriate period of notice shall be—

(a)  21 days where the defender is resident or has a place of business within Europe; or

(b)  42 days where the defender is resident or has a place of business outwith Europe.

(3)  The sheriff may, on cause shown, shorten or extend the period of notice on such conditions as to the form of service as he may direct, but in any case where the period of notice is reduced at least two days' notice must be given.

(4)  If a period of notice expires on a Saturday, Sunday, public or court holiday, the period of notice shall be deemed to expire on the next day on which the sheriff clerk's office is open for civil court business.

(5)  Notwithstanding the terms of section 4(2) of the Citation Amendment (Scotland) Act 1882, where service is by post the period of notice shall run from the beginning of the day next following the date of posting.

(6)  The sheriff clerk shall insert in the summons—

(a)  the return day, which is the last day on which the defender may return a form of response to the sheriff clerk; and

(b)  the calling date, which is the date set for the action to call in court.

(7)[1]  The calling date shall be 14 days after the return day.

**Intimation**

**4.6.**  Any provision in these Rules requiring papers to be sent to or any intimation to be made to any party, applicant or claimant shall be construed as if the reference to the party, applicant or claimant included a reference to the solicitor representing that party, applicant or claimant.

Chapter 5

Register of Summary Causes, service and return of the summons

**Register of Summary Causes**

**5.1.**—(1)  The sheriff clerk shall keep a register of summary cause actions and incidental applications made in such actions, which shall be known as the Register of Summary Causes.

(2)  There shall be entered in the Register of Summary Causes a note of all actions, together with a note of all minutes under rule 24.1(1) (recall of decree) and the entry for each action or minute must contain the following particulars where appropriate:—

(a)  the names, designations and addresses of the parties;

(b)  whether the parties were present or absent at any hearing, including an inspection, and the names of their representatives;

(c)  the nature of the action;

(d)  the amount of any claim;

(e)  the date of issue of the summons;

(f)  the method of service;

(g)  the return day;

(h)  the calling date;

(i)  whether a form of response was lodged and details of it;

(j)  the period of notice if shortened or extended in accordance with rule 4.5(3);

(k)  details of any minute by the pursuer regarding an application for a time to pay direction or time order, or minute by the pursuer requesting decree or other order;

(l)  details of any interlocutors issued;

(m)  details of the final decree and the date of it; and

(n)  details of any variation or recall of a decree.

(3)  There shall be entered in the Register of Summary Causes in the entry for the action to which they relate details of incidental applications including, where appropriate—

(a)  whether parties are present or absent at the hearing of the application, and the names of their representatives;

(b)  the nature of the application; and

---

[4] As substituted by the Act of Sederunt (Sheriff Court Rules) (Miscellaneous Amendments) 2009 (SSI 2009/294) r.7 (effective October 1, 2009).

[1] As amended by the Act of Sederunt (Sheriff Court Rules) (Miscellaneous Amendments) 2009 (SSI 2009/294) r.7 (effective December 1, 2009).

    (c)    the interlocutor issued or order made.

(4)    The Register of Summary Causes must be—

    (a)    authenticated in some appropriate manner by the sheriff in respect of each day any order is made or application determined in an action; and

    (b)    open for inspection during normal business hours to all concerned without fee.

(5)    The Register of Summary Causes may be kept in electronic or documentary form.

**Persons carrying on business under trading or descriptive name**

**5.2.**—(1)    A person carrying on a business under a trading or descriptive name may sue or be sued in such trading or descriptive name alone.

(2)    An extract of—

    (a)    a decree pronounced in an action; or

    (b)    a decree proceeding upon any deed, decree arbitral, bond, protest of a bill, promissory note or banker's note or upon any other obligation or document on which execution may proceed, recorded in the sheriff court books, against such person under such trading or descriptive name shall be a valid warrant for diligence against such person.

(3)    A summons, decree, charge or other document following upon such summons or decree in an action in which a person carrying on business under a trading or descriptive name sues or is sued in that name may be served—

    (a)    at any place of business or office at which such business is carried on within the sheriffdom of the sheriff court in which the action is brought; or

    (b)    if there is no place of business within that sheriffdom, at any place where such business is carried on (including the place of business or office of the clerk or secretary of any company, corporation or association or firm).

**Form of service and certificate thereof**

**5.3.**—(1)    Subject to rule 5.5 (service where address of defender is unknown), a form of service in Form 11 must be enclosed with the defender's copy summons.

(2)    After service has been effected a certificate of execution of service in Form 12 must be prepared and signed by the person effecting service.

(3)    When service is by a sheriff officer, the certificate of execution of service must—

    (a)    be signed by him; and

    (b)    specify whether the service was personal or, if otherwise, the mode of service and the name of any person to whom the defender's copy summons was delivered.

(4)    If service is effected in accordance with rule 5.4(2), the certificate must also contain a statement of—

    (a)    the mode of service previously attempted; and

    (b)    the circumstances which prevented such service from being effected.

**Service within Scotland by sheriff officer**

**5.4.**—(1)    A sheriff officer may validly serve any summons, decree, charge or other document following upon such summons or decree issued in an action by—

    (a)    personal service; or

    (b)    leaving it in the hands of—

        (i)    a resident at the person's dwelling place; or

        (ii)    an employee at the person's place of business.

(2)    If a sheriff officer has been unsuccessful in effecting service in accordance with paragraph (1), he may, after making diligent inquiries, serve the document—

    (a)    by depositing it in the person's dwelling place or place of business by means of a letter box or by other lawful means; or

    (b)[1]    by leaving it at that person's dwelling place or place of business in such a way that it is likely to come to the attention of that person.

(3)    Subject to the requirements of rule 6.1 (service of schedule of arrestment), if service is effected in accordance with paragraph (2), the sheriff officer must thereafter send by ordinary post to the address at which he thinks it most likely that the person may be found a letter containing a copy of the document.

(4)    In proceedings in or following on an action, it shall be necessary for any sheriff officer to be accompanied by a witness except where service, citation or intimation is to be made by post.

---

[1] As substituted by the Act of Sederunt (Sheriff Court Rules) (Miscellaneous Amendments) 2011 (SSI 2011/193) r.4 (effective April 4, 2011).

(5) Where the firm which employs the sheriff officer has in its possession—

    (a) the document or a copy of it certified as correct by the pursuer's solicitor, the sheriff officer may serve the document upon the defender without having the document or certified copy in his possession (in which case he shall if required to do so by the person on whom service is executed and within a reasonable time of being so required, show the document or certified copy to the person); or

    (b) a certified copy of the interlocutor pronounced allowing service of the document, the sheriff officer may serve the document without having in his possession the certified copy interlocutor if he has in his possession a facsimile copy of the certified copy interlocutor (which he shall show, if required, to the person on whom service is executed).

(6)[1] Where service is executed under paragraphs (1)(b) or (2), the document and the citation or notice of intimation, as the case may be, must be placed in an envelope bearing the notice "This envelope contains a citation to or intimation from (*insert name of sheriff court*)" and sealed by the sheriff officer.

### Service on persons whose address is unknown

**5.5.**—(A1)[2] Subject to rule 6.A7, this rule applies to service where the address of a person is not known.

(1) If the defender's address is unknown to the pursuer and cannot reasonably be ascertained by him, the sheriff may grant warrant to serve the summons—

    (a) by the publication of an advertisement in Form 13 in a newspaper circulating in the area of the defender's last known address; or

    (b) by displaying on the walls of court a notice in Form 14.

(2) Where a summons is served in accordance with paragraph (1), the period of notice, which must be fixed by the sheriff, shall run from the date of publication of the advertisement or display on the walls of court, as the case may be.

(3) If service is to be effected under paragraph (1), the pursuer must lodge a service copy of the summons with the sheriff clerk.

(4) The defender may uplift from the sheriff clerk the service copy of the summons lodged in accordance with paragraph (3).

(5) If display on the walls of court is required under paragraph (1)(b), the pursuer must supply to the sheriff clerk for that purpose a completed copy of Form 14.

(6) In every case where advertisement in a newspaper is required for the purpose of service, a copy of the newspaper containing said advertisement must be lodged with the sheriff clerk.

(7) If service has been made under this rule and thereafter the defender's address becomes known, the sheriff may allow the summons to be amended and, if appropriate, grant warrant for reservice subject to such conditions as he thinks fit.

### Service by post

**5.6.**—(A1) [Repealed by the Act of Sederunt (Sheriff Court Rules) (Miscellaneous Amendments) 2009 (SSI 2009/294) r.11 (effective October 1, 2009).]

(1) If it is competent to serve or intimate any document or to cite any person by recorded delivery, such service, intimation or citation, must be made by the first class recorded delivery service.

(2) On the face of the envelope used for postal service under this rule, there must be written or printed a notice in Form 15.

(3) The certificate of execution of postal service must have annexed to it any relevant postal receipt.

### Service on persons outwith Scotland

**5.7.**—(1) If any summons, decree, charge or other document following upon such summons or decree, or any charge or warrant, requires to be served outwith Scotland on any person, it must be served in accordance with this rule.

(2) If the person has a known home or place of business in—

    (a) England and Wales, Northern Ireland, the Isle of Man or the Channel Islands; or

    (b) any country with which the United Kingdom does not have a convention providing for service of writs in that country,

the document must be served either—

---

[1] As inserted by the Act of Sederunt (Sheriff Court Rules) (Miscellaneous Amendments) 2011 (SSI 2011/193) r.4 (effective April 4, 2011).

[2] As inserted by the Act of Sederunt (Sheriff Court Rules) (Miscellaneous Amendments) 2009 (SSI 2009/294) r.11 (effective October 1, 2009).

  (i) by posting in Scotland a copy of the document in question in a registered letter addressed to the person at his residence or place of business; or

  (ii) in accordance with the rules for personal service under the domestic law of the place in which the document is to be served.

(3) Subject to paragraph (4), if the document requires to be served in a country which is a party to the Hague Convention on the Service Abroad of Judicial and Extra-Judicial Documents in Civil or Commercial Matters dated 15th November 1965 or the European Convention on Jurisdiction and Enforcement of Judgments in Civil and Commercial Matters as set out in Schedule 1 or 3C to the Civil Jurisdiction and Judgments Act 1982, it must be served—

 (a) by a method prescribed by the internal law of the country where service is to be effected for the service of documents in domestic actions upon persons who are within its territory;

 (b) by or through a British consular authority at the request of the Secretary of State for Foreign and Commonwealth Affairs;

 (c)[1] by or through a central authority in the country where service is to be effected at the request of the Scottish Ministers;

 (d) where the law of the country in which the person resides permits, by posting in Scotland a copy of the document in a registered letter addressed to the person at his residence; or

 (e) where the law of the country in which service is to be effected permits, service by an *huissier*, other judicial officer or competent official of the country where service is to be made.

(4)[2] If the document requires to be served in a country to which the EC Service Regulation applies, service—

 (a) may be effected by the methods prescribed in paragraph (3)(b) or (c) only in exceptional circumstances; and

 (b) is effected only if the receiving agency has informed the person that acceptance of service may be refused on the ground that the document has not been translated in accordance with paragraph (12).

(5) If the document requires to be served in a country with which the United Kingdom has a convention on the service of writs in that country other than the conventions specified in paragraph (3) or the regulation specified in paragraph (4), it must be served by one of the methods approved in the relevant convention.

(6) Subject to paragraph (9), a document which requires to be posted in Scotland for the purposes of this rule must be posted by a solicitor or a sheriff officer, and the form of service and certificate of execution of service must be in Forms 11 and 12 respectively.

(7) On the face of the envelope used for postal service under this rule there must be written or printed a notice in Form 15.

(8) Where service is effected by a method specified in paragraph (3)(b) or (c), the pursuer must—

 (a)[3] send a copy of the summons and warrant for service with form of service attached, or other document, with a request for service to be effected by the method indicated in the request to the Scottish Ministers or, as the case may be, the Secretary of State for Foreign and Commonwealth Affairs; and

 (b) lodge in process a certificate of execution of service signed by the authority which has effected service.

(9) If service is effected by the method specified in paragraph (3)(e), the pursuer must—

 (a) send to the official in the country in which service is to be effected a copy of the summons and warrant for service, with citation attached, or other document, with a request for service to be effected by delivery to the defender or his residence; and

 (b) lodge in process a certificate of execution of service by the official who has effected service.

(10) Where service is executed in accordance with paragraph (2)(b)(ii) or (3)(a) other than on another party in—

 (a) the United Kingdom;

 (b) the Isle of Man; or

---

[1] As substituted by the Act of Sederunt (Sheriff Court Rules) (Miscellaneous Amendments) 2011 (SSI 2011/193) r.6 (effective April 4, 2011).

[2] As substituted by Act of Sederunt (Ordinary Cause, Summary Application, Summary Cause and Small Claim Rules) Amendment (Miscellaneous) 2004 (SSI 2004/197) r.4(3)(a) (effective May 21, 2004) and amended by the Act of Sederunt (Sheriff Court Rules) (Miscellaneous Amendments) (No.2) 2008 (SSI 2008/365) r.9(a) (effective November 13, 2008).

[3] As amended by the Act of Sederunt (Sheriff Court Rules) (Miscellaneous Amendments) 2011 (SSI 2011/193) r.7 (effective April 4, 2011).

(c) the Channel Islands, the party executing service must lodge a certificate stating that the form of service employed is in accordance with the law of the place where the service was executed.

(11)    A certificate lodged in accordance with paragraph (10) shall be given by a person who is conversant with the law of the country concerned and who—

(a) practises or has practised law in that country; or
(b) is a duly accredited representative of the government of that country.

(12)[1]    Every summons or document and every citation and notice on the face of the envelope referred to in paragraph (7) must be accompanied by a translation in an official language of the country in which service is to be executed, unless English is—

(a) an official language of the country in which service is to be executed; or
(b) in a country to which the EC Service Regulation applies, a language of the member state of transmission that is understood by the person on whom service is being executed.

(13)    A translation referred to in paragraph (12) must be certified as a correct translation by the person making it and the certificate must contain the full name, address and qualifications of the translator and be lodged along with the execution of such service.

(14)[2]    In this rule "the EC Service Regulation" means Regulation (EC) No. 1393/2007 of the European Parliament and of the Council of 13th November 2007 on the service in the Member States of judicial and extrajudicial documents in civil or commercial matters (service of documents), and repealing Council Regulation (EC) No. 1348/2000, as amended from time to time.

### Endorsation by sheriff clerk of defender's residence not necessary

**5.8.**    Any summons, decree, charge or other document following upon a summons or decree may be served, enforced or otherwise lawfully executed in Scotland without endorsation by a sheriff clerk and, if executed by a sheriff officer, may be so executed by a sheriff officer of the court which granted the summons, or by a sheriff officer of the sheriff court district in which it is to be executed.

### Contents of envelope containing defender's copy summons

**5.9.**    Nothing must be included in the envelope containing a defender's copy summons except—

(a) the copy summons
(b) a response or other notice in accordance with these Rules; and
(c) any other document approved by the sheriff principal.

### Re-service

**5.10.**—(1)    If it appears to the sheriff that there has been any failure or irregularity in service upon a defender, the sheriff may order the pursuer to re-serve the summons on such conditions as he thinks fit.

(2)    If re-service has been ordered in accordance with paragraph (1) or rule 5.5(7) the action shall proceed thereafter as if it were a new action.

### Defender appearing barred from objecting to service

**5.11.**—(1)    A person who appears in an action shall not be entitled to state any objection to the regularity of the execution of service or intimation on him and his appearance shall remedy any defect in such service or intimation.

(2)    Nothing in paragraph (1) shall preclude a party pleading that the court has no jurisdiction.

### Return of summons

**5.12.**—(1)    If any appearance in court is required on the calling date in respect of any party—

(a) the summons; and
(b) the relevant certificate of execution of service, shall be returned to the sheriff clerk not later than two days before the calling date.

(2)    If no appearance by any party is required on the calling date, only the certificate of execution of service need be returned to the sheriff clerk, not later than two days before the calling date.

---

[1] As substituted for existing text by the Act of Sederunt (Ordinary Cause, Summary Application, Summary Cause and Small Claim Rules) Amendment (Miscellaneous) 2004 (SSI 2004/197) r.4(3)(b) (effective May 21, 2004) and by the Act of Sederunt (Sheriff Court Rules) (Miscellaneous Amendments) (No.2) 2008 (SSI 2008/365) r.9(a) (effective November 13, 2008).

[2] As substituted by the Act of Sederunt (Sheriff Court Rules) (Miscellaneous Amendments) (No.2) 2008 (SSI 2008/365) r.9(b) (effective November 13, 2008).

(3) If the pursuer fails to proceed in accordance with paragraph (1) or (2) as appropriate, the sheriff may dismiss the action.

Chapter 6[1]

Interim Diligence

### Interpretation

**6.A1.** In this Chapter—

"the 1987 Act" means the Debtors (Scotland) Act 1987; and

"the 2002 Act" means the Debt Arrangement and Attachment (Scotland) Act 2002.

### Application for interim diligence

**6.A2.**—(1) The following shall be made by incidental application—

(a) an application under section 15D(1) of the 1987 Act for warrant for diligence by arrestment or inhibition on the dependence of an action or warrant for arrestment on the dependence of an admiralty action;

(b) an application under section 9C of the 2002 Act for warrant for interim attachment.

(2) Such an application must be accompanied by a statement in Form 15a.

(3) A certified copy of an interlocutor granting an application under paragraph (1) shall be sufficient authority for execution of the diligence concerned.

### Effect of authority for inhibition on the dependence

**6.A3.**—(1) Where a person has been granted authority for inhibition on the dependence of an action, a certified copy of the interlocutor granting the application may be registered with a certificate of execution in the Register of Inhibitions and Adjudications.

[2](2) A notice of a certified copy of an interlocutor granting authority for inhibition under rule 6.A2 may be registered in the Register of Inhibitions and Adjudications; and such registration is to have the same effect as registration of a notice of inhibition under section 155(2) of the Titles to Land Consolidation (Scotland) Act 1868.

### Recall etc of arrestment or inhibition

**6.A4.**—(1) An application by any person having an interest—

(a) to loose, restrict, vary or recall an arrestment or an interim attachment; or

(b) to recall, in whole or in part, or vary, an inhibition,

shall be made by incidental application.

(2) Paragraph (1) does not apply to an application made orally at a hearing under section 15K that has been fixed under section 15E(4) of the Act of 1987.

### Incidental applications in relation to interim diligence, etc.

**6.A5.** An application under Part 1A of the 1987 Act or Part 1A of the 2002 Act other than mentioned above shall be made by incidental application.

### Form of schedule of inhibition on the dependence

**6.A6.** *[Revoked by the Act of Sederunt (Sheriff Court Rules Amendment) (Diligence) 2009 (SSI 2009/107) r.5 (effective April 22, 2009).]*

### Service of inhibition on the dependence where address of defender not known

**6.A7.**—(1) Where the address of a defender is not known to the pursuer, an inhibition shall be deemed to have been served on the defender if the schedule of inhibition is left with or deposited at the office of the sheriff clerk of the sheriff court district where the defender's last known address is located.

(2) Where service of an inhibition on the dependence is executed under paragraph (1), a copy of the schedule of inhibition shall be sent by the sheriff officer by first class post to the defender's last known address.

---

[1] Chapter renamed and rr.6.A1–6.A7 inserted by the Act of Sederunt (Sheriff Court Rules Amendment) (Diligence) 2008 (SSI 2008/121) r.6 (effective April 1, 2008).

[2] As substituted by the Act of Sederunt (Sheriff Court Rules Amendment) (Diligence) 2009 (SSI 2009/107) r.5 (effective April 22, 2009).

### Form of schedule of arrestment on the dependence

**6.A8.**—(1)[1]    An arrestment on the dependence shall be served by serving the schedule of arrestment on the arrestee in Form 15b.

(2)    A certificate of execution shall be lodged with the sheriff clerk in Form 15c.

### Service of schedule of arrestment

**6.1.**    If a schedule of arrestment has not been personally served on an arrestee, the arrestment shall have effect only if a copy of the schedule is also sent by registered post or the first class recorded delivery service to—

(a)    the last known place of residence of the arrestee; or

(b)    if such place of residence is not known, or if the arrestee is a firm or corporation, to the arrestee's principal place of business if known, or, if not known, to any known place of business of the arrestee,

and the sheriff officer must, on the certificate of execution, certify that this has been done and specify the address to which the copy of the schedule was sent.

### Arrestment before service

**6.2.**—(1)[2]    An arrestment to found jurisdiction used prior to service shall cease to have effect, unless the summons is served within 21 days from the date of execution of the arrestment.

(2)    When such an arrestment as is referred to in paragraph (1) has been executed, the party using it must forthwith report the execution to the sheriff clerk.

### Recall and restriction of arrestment

**6.3**—(1)    The sheriff may order that an arrestment on the dependence of an action or counterclaim shall cease to have effect if the party whose funds or property are arrested—

(a)    pays into court; or

(b)    finds caution to the satisfaction of the sheriff clerk in respect of, the sum claimed together with the sum of £50 in respect of expenses.

(2)    Without prejudice to paragraph (1), a party whose funds or property are arrested may at any time apply to the sheriff to exercise his powers to recall or restrict an arrestment on the dependence of an action or counterclaim, with or without consignation or caution.

(3)    An application made under paragraph (2) must be intimated by the applicant to the party who instructed the arrestment.

(4)    On payment into court in accordance with paragraph (1), or if the sheriff recalls or restricts an arrestment on the dependence of an action in accordance with paragraph (2) and any condition imposed by the sheriff has been complied with, the sheriff clerk must—

(a)    issue to the party whose funds or property are arrested a certificate in Form 16 authorising the release of any sum or property arrested to the extent ordered by the sheriff; and

(b)    send a copy of the certificate to—

(i)    the party who instructed the arrestment; and

(ii)    the party who has possession of the funds or property that are arrested.

Chapter 7

Undefended action

### Undefended action

**7.1.**—(1)    Subject to paragraphs (4), (5) and (6), where the defender has not lodged a form of response on or before the return day—

(a)    the action shall not require to call in court on the calling date; and

(b)    the pursuer must lodge a minute in Form 17 before the sheriff clerk's office closes for business on the second day before the calling date.

(2)    If the pursuer does not lodge a minute in terms of paragraph (1), the sheriff must dismiss the action.

(3)    If the sheriff is not prepared to grant the order requested in Form 17, the sheriff clerk must—

(a)    fix a date, time and place for the pursuer to be heard; and

(b)    inform the pursuer of—

---

[1] As inserted by the Act of Sederunt (Sheriff Court Rules Amendment) (Diligence) 2009 (SSI 2009/107) r.5 (effective April 22, 2009).

[2] As amended by the Act of Sederunt (Sheriff Court Rules Amendment) (Diligence) 2008 (SSI 2008/121) r.6(5) (effective April 1 2008).

      (i)    that date, time and place; and

      (ii)   the reasons for the sheriff wishing to hear him.

(4)   Where no form of response has been lodged in an action—

    (a)   for recovery of possession of heritable property; or

    (b)   of sequestration for rent, the action shall call in court on the calling date and the sheriff shall determine the action as he thinks fit.

(5)   Where no form of response has been lodged in an action of multiplepoinding the action shall proceed in accordance with rule 27.9(1)(a).

(6)   Where no form of response has been lodged in an action of count, reckoning and payment the action shall proceed in accordance with rule 29.2.

(7)   If the defender does not lodge a form of response in time or if the sheriff is satisfied that he does not intend to defend the action on the merits or on the amount of the sum due, the sheriff may grant decree with expenses against him.

**Application for time to pay direction or time order**

7.2.—(1)   If the defender admits the claim, he may, where competent—

    (a)   make an application for a time to pay direction (including, where appropriate, an application for recall or restriction of an arrestment) or a time order by completing the appropriate part of the form of response contained in the defender's copy summons and lodging it with the sheriff clerk on or before the return day; or

    (b)   lodge a form of response indicating that he admits the claim and intends to apply orally for a time to pay direction (including, where appropriate, an application for recall or restriction of an arrestment) or time order.

(1A)[1]   The sheriff clerk must on receipt forthwith intimate to the pursuer a copy of any response lodged under paragraph (1).

(2)[2]   Where the defender has lodged an application in terms of paragraph (1)(a), the pursuer may intimate that he does not object to the application by lodging a minute in Form 18 before the time the sheriff clerk's office closes for business on the day occurring 9 days before the calling date stating that he does not object to the defender's application and seeking decree.

(3)   If the pursuer intimates in accordance with paragraph (2) that he does not object to the application—

    (a)   the sheriff may grant decree on the calling date;

    (b)   the parties need not attend; and

    (c)   the action will not call in court.

(4)[3]   If the pursuer wishes to oppose the application for a time to pay direction or time order made in accordance with paragraph (1)(a) he must before the time the sheriff clerk's office closes for business on the day occurring 9 days before the calling date—

    (a)   lodge a minute in Form 19; and

    (b)   send a copy of that minute to the defender.

(5)   Where the pursuer objects to an application in terms of paragraph (1)(a) or the defender has lodged a form of response in accordance with paragraph (1)(b), the action shall call on the calling date when the parties may appear and the sheriff must decide the application and grant decree accordingly.

(6)   The sheriff shall decide an application in accordance with paragraph (5) whether or not any of the parties appear.

(7)   Where the defender has lodged an application in terms of paragraph (1)(a) and the pursuer fails to proceed in accordance with either of paragraphs (2) or (4) the sheriff may dismiss the claim.

**Decree in actions to which the Hague Convention or Civil Jurisdiction and Judgements Act 1982 apply**

7.3.—(1)   If the summons has been served in a country to which the Hague Convention on the Service Abroad of Judicial and Extra-Judicial Documents in Civil or Commercial Matters dated 15th November 1965 applies, decree must not be granted until it is established to the satisfaction of the sheriff that the requirements of Article 15 of that Convention have been complied with.

---

[1] As inserted by the Act of Sederunt (Sheriff Court Rules) (Miscellaneous Amendments) 2009 (SSI 2009/294) r.4 (effective December 1, 2009).

[2] As substituted by the Act of Sederunt (Sheriff Court Rules) (Miscellaneous Amendments) 2009 (SSI 2009/294) r.4 (effective December 1, 2009).

[3] As substituted by the Act of Sederunt (Sheriff Court Rules) (Miscellaneous Amendments) 2009 (SSI 2009/294) r.4 (effective December 1, 2009).

(2)   Where a defender is domiciled in another part of the United Kingdom or in another Contracting State, the sheriff shall not grant decree until it has been shown that the defender has been able to receive the summons in sufficient time to arrange his defence or that all necessary steps have been taken to that end.

(3)   For the purposes of paragraph (2)—

(a)   the question whether a person is domiciled in another part of the United Kingdom shall be determined in accordance with sections 41 and 42 of the Civil Jurisdiction and Judgments Act 1982;

(b)   the question whether a person is domiciled in another Contracting State shall be determined in accordance with Article 52 of the Convention in Schedule 1 or 3C to that Act; and

(c)   the term "Contracting State" has the meaning assigned in section 1 of that Act.

Chapter 8

Defended action

## Response to summons

**8.1.**—(1)   If the defender intends—

(a)   to challenge the jurisdiction of the court or the competency of the action;

(b)   to defend the action (whether as regards the amount claimed or otherwise); or

(c)   state a counterclaim,

he must complete and lodge with the sheriff clerk on or before the return day the form of response contained in the defender's copy summons including a statement of his response which gives fair notice to the pursuer.

(2)   The sheriff clerk must upon receipt intimate to the pursuer a copy of any response lodged under paragraph (1).

## Procedure in defended action

**8.2.**—(1)   Where the defender has lodged a form of response in accordance with rule 8.1(1) the action will call in court for a hearing.

(2)   The hearing shall be held on the calling date.

(3)   The sheriff may continue the hearing to such other date as he considers appropriate.

(4)   The defender must either be present or be represented at the hearing.

(5)   Where the defender—

(a)   does not appear or is not represented; and

(b)   the pursuer is present or is represented,

decree may be granted against the defender in terms of the summons.

(6)   Where at the hearing—

(a)   the pursuer does not appear or is not represented; and

(b)   the defender is present or represented, the sheriff shall dismiss the action and may grant decree in terms of any counterclaim.

(7)   If all parties fail to appear at the hearing, the sheriff shall, unless sufficient reason appears to the contrary, dismiss the action and any counterclaim.

## Purpose of hearing

**8.3.**—(1)   If, at the hearing, the sheriff is satisfied that the action is incompetent or that there is a patent defect of jurisdiction, he must grant decree of dismissal in favour of the defender or, if appropriate, transfer the action in terms of rule 16.1(2).

(2)   At the hearing, the sheriff shall—

(a)   ascertain the factual basis of the action and any defence, and the legal basis on which the action and defence are proceeding; and

(b)   seek to negotiate and secure settlement of the action between the parties.

(3)   If the sheriff cannot secure settlement of the action between the parties, he shall—

(a)   identify and note on the summons the issues of fact and law which are in dispute;

(b)   note on the summons any facts which are agreed;

(c)   where it appears that the claim as stated or any defence stated in response to it is not soundly based in law in whole or in part, hear parties forthwith on that matter and may grant decree in favour of any party; and

(d)   if satisfied that the claim and any defence have or may have a sound basis in law and that the dispute between the parties depends upon resolution of disputed issues of fact, fix a diet of proof or, alternatively, if satisfied that the claim and any defence have a sound basis in law and that the facts of the case are sufficiently agreed, hear parties forthwith on the merits of the action and may grant decree in whole or in part in favour of any party.

(e)[1] enquire whether there is or is likely to be a vulnerable witness within the meaning of section 11(1) of the 2004 Act who is to give evidence at any proof or hearing, consider any child witness notice or vulnerable witness application that has been lodged where no order has been made and consider whether any order under section 12(1) of the 2004 Act requires to be made.

(4) Where the sheriff fixes a proof, the sheriff clerk shall make up a folder for the case papers.

## Remit to person of skill

**8.4.**—(1) The sheriff may, on an incidental application by any party or on a joint application, remit to any person of skill, or other person, to report on any matter of fact.

(2) If a remit under paragraph (1) is made by joint application or of consent of all parties, the report of such person shall be final and conclusive with respect to the matter of fact which is the subject of the remit.

(3) If a remit under paragraph (1) is made—

(a) on the application of one of the parties, the expenses of its execution must, in the first instance, be met by that party; or

(b) on a joint application or of consent of all parties, the expenses must, in the first instance, be met by the parties equally, unless the sheriff otherwise orders.

## Inspection and recovery of documents

**8.5.**—(1) Each party shall, within 28 days after the date of the fixing of a proof, intimate to every other party, and lodge with the sheriff clerk, a list of documents, which are or have been in his possession or control which he intends to use or put in evidence at the proof, including the whereabouts of those documents.

(2) A party who has received a list of documents from another party under paragraph (1) may inspect those documents which are in the possession or control of the party intimating the list at a time and place fixed by that party which is reasonable to both parties.

(3) Nothing in this rule shall affect—

(a) the law relating, or the right of a party to object, to the inspection of a document on the ground of privilege or confidentiality; or

(b) the right of a party to apply under rule 18.1 for a commission and diligence for recovery of documents or under rule 18.3 for an order under section 1 of the Administration of Justice (Scotland) Act 1972.

## Exchange of lists of witnesses

**8.6.**—(1) Within 28 days after the date of the fixing of a proof, each party shall intimate to every other party, and lodge with the sheriff clerk, a list of witnesses, including any skilled witnesses, whom he intends to call to give evidence.

(2) A party who seeks to call as a witness a person not on his list intimated and lodged under paragraph (1) shall, if any other party objects to such a witness being called, seek leave of the sheriff to call that person as a witness; and such leave may be granted on such conditions, if any, as the sheriff thinks fit.

(3)[2] The list of witnesses intimated under paragraph (1) shall include the name, occupation (where known) and address of each intended witness and indicate whether the witness is considered to be a vulnerable witness within the meaning of section 11(1) of the 2004 Act and whether any child witness notice or vulnerable witness application has been lodged in respect of that witness.

## Exchange of reports of skilled witnesses

**8.7.**—(1) Not less than 28 days before the diet of proof, a party shall—

(a) disclose to every other party in the form of a written report the substance of the evidence of any skilled person whom he intends to call as a witness; and

(b) lodge a copy of that report in process.

---

[1] As inserted by the Act of Sederunt (Ordinary Cause, Summary Application, Summary Cause and Small Claim Rules) Amendment (Vulnerable Witnesses (Scotland) Act 2004) 2007 (SSI 2007/463) r.4(3) (effective November 1, 2007).

[2] As amended by the Act of Sederunt (Ordinary Cause, Summary Application, Summary Cause and Small Claim Rules) Amendment (Vulnerable Witnesses (Scotland) Act 2004) 2007 (SSI 2007/463) r.4(4) (effective November 1, 2007).

(2)   Except on special cause shown, a party may only call as a skilled witness any person the substance of whose evidence has been disclosed in accordance with paragraph (1).

### Evidence generally

**8.8.**   Where possible, the parties shall agree photographs, sketch plans, and any statement or document not in dispute.

### Notices to admit and notices of non-admission

**8.8A.**—[1](1)   At any time after a form of response has been lodged, a party may intimate to any other party a notice or notices calling on him or her to admit for the purposes of that cause only—

    (a)   such facts relating to an issue averred in the statement of claim or form of response as may be specified in the notice;

    (b)   that a particular document lodged with the sheriff clerk and specified in the notice is—

        (i)   an original and properly authenticated document; or

        (ii)   a true copy of an original and properly authenticated document.

(2)   Where a party on whom a notice is intimated under paragraph (1)—

    (a)   does not admit a fact specified in the notice, or

    (b)   does not admit, or seeks to challenge, the authenticity of a document specified in the notice,

he or she must, within 21 days after the date of intimation of the notice under paragraph (1), intimate a notice of non-admission to the party intimating the notice to him or her under paragraph (1) stating that he or she does not admit the fact or document specified.

(3)   A party who fails to intimate a notice of non-admission under paragraph (2) will be deemed to have admitted the fact or document specified in the notice intimated to him or her under paragraph (1); and such fact or document may be used in evidence at a proof if otherwise admissible in evidence, unless the sheriff, on special cause shown, otherwise directs.

(4)   The party serving a notice under paragraph (1) or (2) must lodge a copy of it with the sheriff clerk.

(5)   A deemed admission under paragraph (3) must not be used—

    (a)   against the party by whom it was deemed to be made other than in the cause for the purpose for which it was deemed to be made; or

    (b)   in favour of any person other than the party by whom the notice was given under paragraph (1).

(6)   The sheriff may, at any time, allow a party to amend or withdraw an admission made by him or her on such conditions, if any, as the sheriff thinks fit.

(7)   A party may, at any time, withdraw in whole or in part a notice of non-admission by intimating a notice of withdrawal.

### Hearing parts of action separately

**8.9.**—(1)   In any action which includes a claim for payment of money, the sheriff may—

    (a)   of his own accord; or

    (b)   on the incidental application of any party,

order that proof on liability or any specified issue be heard separately from proof on any other issue and determine the order in which the proofs shall be heard.

(2)   The sheriff shall pronounce such interlocutor as he thinks fit at the conclusion of the first proof of any action ordered to be heard in separate parts under paragraph (1).

---

[1] As inserted by the Act of Sederunt (Sheriff Court Rules) (Miscellaneous Amendments) 2010 (SSI 2010/279) r.6 (effective July 29, 2010).

**Returning borrowed parts of process before proof**

**8.10.** All parts of process which have been borrowed must be returned to process not later than noon on the day preceding the proof.

**Conduct of proof**

**8.11** The pursuer must lead in the proof unless the sheriff, on the incidental application of any of the parties which has been intimated to the other parties not less than seven days before the diet of proof, directs otherwise.

**Administration of oath or affirmation to witness**

**8.12.** The sheriff must administer the oath to a witness in Form 20 or, where the witness elects to affirm, the affirmation in Form 21.

**Noting of evidence, etc.**

**8.13.**—(1) The sheriff who presides at the proof may make a note of any facts agreed by the parties since the hearing held in terms of rule 8.2(1).

(2) The parties may, and must if required by the sheriff, lodge a joint minute of admissions of the facts upon which they have reached agreement.

(3) The sheriff must—

    (a) make for his own use notes of the evidence led at the proof, including any evidence the admissibility of which is objected to, and of the nature of any such objection; and

    (b) retain these notes until after any appeal has been disposed of.

**Parties to be heard at close of proof**

**8.14.**—(1) After all the evidence has been led relevant to the particular proof, the sheriff must hear parties on the evidence.

(2) At the conclusion of that hearing, the sheriff may—

    (a) pronounce his decision; or

    (b) reserve judgment.

**Objections to admissibility of evidence**

**8.15.** If in the course of a proof an objection is made to the admissibility of any evidence and that line of evidence is not abandoned by the party pursuing it, the sheriff must except where—

    (a) he is of the opinion that the evidence is clearly irrelevant or scandalous; or

    (b) it is an objection falling within rule 8.16(1),

note the terms of the objection and allow the evidence to be led reserving the question of its admissibility to be decided by him at the close of the proof.

**Incidental appeal against rulings on confidentiality of evidence and production of documents**

**8.16.**—(1) Where a party or any other person objects to the admissibility of oral or documentary evidence on the ground of confidentiality or to the production of a document on any ground, he may, if dissatisfied with the ruling of the sheriff on the objection, express immediately his formal dissatisfaction with the ruling and, with leave of the sheriff, appeal to the sheriff principal.

(2) The sheriff principal shall dispose of an appeal under paragraph (1) with the least possible delay.

(3) Except as provided in paragraph (1), no appeal may be made during a proof against any decision of the sheriff as to the admissibility of evidence or the production of documents.

(4) The appeal referred to in paragraph (1) shall not remove the action from the sheriff who may proceed with the action in relation to any issue which is not dependent on the ruling appealed against.

**Application for time to pay direction or a time order in defended action**

**8.17.** A defender in an action which proceeds as defended may, where it is competent to do so, make a incidental application or apply orally at any hearing, at any time before decree is granted, for a time to pay direction (including where appropriate, an order recalling or restricting an arrestment on the dependence) or time order.

**Pronouncement of decision**

**8.18.**—(1) If the sheriff pronounces his decision at the end of the hearing held in terms of rule 8.2(1) or any proof, he must state briefly the grounds of his decision, including the reasons for his decision on any question of law or of admissibility of evidence.

(2) If the sheriff pronounces his decision after reserving judgement, he must give to the sheriff clerk within 28 days—

    (a) a statement of his decision; and

    (b) a brief note of the matters mentioned in paragraph (1).

(3)   The sheriff clerk must send copies of the documents mentioned in paragraphs (2)(a) and (b) to each of the parties.

Chapter 9

Incidental applications and sists

**General**

**9.1.**—(1)   Except where otherwise provided, any incidental application in an action may be made—
   (a)   orally with the leave of the sheriff during any hearing of the action; or
   (b)   by lodging the application in written form with the sheriff clerk.

(2)   An application lodged in accordance with paragraph (1)(b) may only be heard after not less than two days' notice has been given to the other party.

(3)   Where the party receiving notice of an incidental application lodged in accordance with paragraph (1)(b) intimates to the sheriff clerk and the party making the application that the application is not opposed, the application shall not require to call in court unless the sheriff so directs.

(4)   Any intimation made under paragraph (3) shall be made not later than noon on the day before the application is due to be heard.

**Application to sist action**

**9.2.**—(1)   Where an incidental application to sist an action is made, the reason for the sist—
   (a)   shall be stated by the party seeking the sist; and
   (b)   shall be recorded in the Register of Summary Causes and on the summons.

(2)   Where an action has been sisted, the sheriff may, after giving parties an opportunity to be heard, recall the sist.

Chapter 10

Counterclaim

**Counterclaim**

**10.1.**—(1)   If a pursuer intends to oppose a counterclaim, he must lodge answers within seven days of the lodging of the form of response.

(2)   The pursuer must at the same time as lodging answers intimate a copy of any answers to every other party.

(3)[1]   The defender may apply for warrant for interim diligence in respect of a counterclaim.

(4)–(5)   *[Repealed by the Act of Sederunt (Sheriff Court Rules) (Miscellaneous Amendments) 2009 (SSI 2009/294) r. 11 (effective October 1, 2009).]*

Chapter 11

Third party procedure

**Application for third party notice**

**11.1.**—(1)   Where in an action a defender claims that—
   (a)   he has in respect of the subject matter of the action a right of contribution, relief or indemnity against any person who is not a party to the action; or
   (b)   a person whom the pursuer is not bound to call as a defender should be made a party to the action along with the defender in respect that such person is—
      (i)   solely liable, or jointly or jointly and severally liable with the defender to the pursuer in respect of the subject matter of the action; or
      (ii)   liable to the defender in respect of the claim arising from or in connection with the liability, if any, of the defender to the pursuer,
   he may apply by incidental application for an order for service of a third party notice upon that other person.

(2)   An application for service of a third party notice shall be made at the time when the defender lodges a form of response, unless the sheriff on cause shown shall permit a later application.

(3)   Where—
   (a)   a pursuer against whom a counterclaim is made; or
   (b)   a third party convened in the action,

---

[1]  As amended by the Act of Sederunt (Sheriff Court Rules) (Miscellaneous Amendments) 2009 (SSI 2009/294) r.11 (effective October 1, 2009).

seeks, in relation to the claim against him, to make against a person who is not a party, a claim mentioned in paragraph (1) as a claim which could be made by a defender against a third party, he shall apply by incidental application for an order for service of a third party notice; and rules 11.2 and 11.3 shall, with the necessary modifications, apply to such a claim as they apply in relation to a counterclaim by a defender.

**Procedure**

**11.2.**—(1)  If an application in terms of rule 11.1 is granted, the sheriff shall—

    (a)  fix a date on which he will regulate further procedure; and

    (b)  grant warrant to serve on the third party—

        (i)  a copy of the summons;

        (ii)  a copy of the grounds upon which it is claimed that the third party is liable; and

        (iii)  a notice in Form 22 and a copy of Form 23.

(2)  A copy of the third party notice, and any certificate of execution of service, shall be lodged by the defender before the hearing fixed under paragraph (1)(a).

(3)  A third party seeking to answer the claim against him shall complete and lodge the form of response no later than seven days before the hearing fixed under paragraph (1)(a).

(4)  The sheriff clerk must upon receipt intimate to the other parties a copy of any response lodged under paragraph (3).

**Warrants for diligence on third party notice**

**11.3.**—(1)[1]  A defender who applies for an order for service of a third party notice may apply for—

    (a)  a warrant for arrestment to found jurisdiction;

    (b)  a warrant for interim diligence,

which would have been permitted had the warrant been sought in an initial writ in a separate action.

(1A)[2]  On an application under paragraph (1)(a) being made—

    (a)  the sheriff may grant the application if he thinks it appropriate; and

    (b)  the sheriff shall not grant the application unless averments to justify the warrant sought have been made.

(2)  A certified copy of the interlocutor granting warrant for diligence shall be sufficient authority for execution of the diligence.

Chapter 12

Summary decree

**Application of chapter**

**12.1.**  This chapter applies to any action other than an action of multiplepoinding.

**Application for summary decree**

**12.2.**—(1)  A pursuer may at any time after a defender has lodged a form of response apply by incidental application for summary decree against any defender on the ground that there is no defence to the action or any part of it.

(2)  In applying for summary decree the pursuer may ask the sheriff to dispose of the whole or part of the subject matter of the action.

(3)  The pursuer shall intimate an application under paragraph (1) by registered or recorded delivery post to every other party not less than seven days before the date fixed for the hearing of the application.

(4)  On an application under paragraph (1), the sheriff may ordain any party, or a partner, director, officer or office-bearer of any party—

    (a)  to produce any relevant document or article; or

    (b)  to lodge an affidavit in support of any assertion of fact made in the action or at the hearing of the incidental application.

(5)  Notwithstanding the refusal of an application for summary decree, a subsequent application may be made on a change of circumstances.

---

[1] As substituted by the Act of Sederunt (Sheriff Court Rules) (Miscellaneous Amendments) 2009 (SSI 2009/294) r.11 (effective October 1, 2009).

[2] As inserted by the Act of Sederunt (Ordinary Cause, Summary Application, Summary Cause and Small Claim Rules) Amendment (Miscellaneous) 2004 (SSI 2004/197) r.4(5) (effective May 21, 2004) and amended by the Act of Sederunt (Sheriff Court Rules) (Miscellaneous Amendments) 2009 (SSI 2009/294) r.11 (effective October 1, 2009).

**Summary decree in a counterclaim etc.**

**12.3.** Rule 12.2 shall apply with the necessary modifications to an application by any other party for summary decree.

Chapter 13

Alteration of summons etc.

**Alteration of summons etc.**

**13.1.**—(1) The sheriff may, on the incidental application of a party, allow amendment of the summons, form of response, counterclaim or answers to a counterclaim and adjust the note of disputed issues at any time before final judgment is pronounced on the merits.

(2) In an undefended action, the sheriff may order the amended summons to be re-served on the defender on such period of notice as he thinks fit.

(3) Paragraph (1) includes amendment for the following purposes:-

    (a)    increasing or reducing the sum claimed;

    (b)    seeking a different remedy from that originally sought;

    (c)    correcting or supplementing the designation of a party;

    (d)    enabling a party to sue or be sued in a representative capacity; and

    (e)    sisting a party in substitution for, or in addition to, the original party.

(4) Where an amendment sists an additional or substitute defender to the action the sheriff shall order such service and regulate further procedure as he thinks fit.

Chapter 14

Additional defender

**Additional defender**

**14.1**—(1) Any person who has not been called as a defender may apply by incidental application to the sheriff for leave to enter an action as a defender, and to state a defence.

(2) An application under this rule must specify—

    (a)    the applicant's title and interest to enter the action; and

    (b)    the grounds of the defence which he proposes to state.

(3) On the lodging of an application under this rule—

    (a)    the sheriff must appoint a date for hearing the application; and

    (b)    the applicant must forthwith serve a copy of the application and of the order for a hearing on the parties to the action.

(4) After hearing the applicant and any party to the action the sheriff may, if he is satisfied that the applicant has shown title and interest to enter the action, grant the application.

(5) Where an application is granted under paragraph (4)—

    (a)    the applicant shall be treated as a defender; and

    (b)    the sheriff must forthwith consider whether any decision already taken in the action on the issues in dispute between the parties requires to be reconsidered in light of the terms of the application.

(6)[1] Paragraph (5)(b) does not apply to a personal injuries action raised under Chapter 34.

---

[1] As inserted by the Act of Sederunt (Summary Cause Rules Amendment) (Personal Injuries Actions) 2012 (SSI 2012/144) para.2 (effective September 1, 2012).

(7)[1]   Where an application is granted under paragraph (4) in a personal injuries action raised under Chapter 34, the sheriff may make such further order as the sheriff thinks fit.

Chapter 14A[2]

Interventions by the Commission for Equality and Human Rights

**Interpretation**

**14A.1.**   In this Chapter "the CEHR" means the Commission for Equality and Human Rights.

**Interventions by the CEHR**

**14A.2.**—(1)   The CEHR may apply to the sheriff for leave to intervene in any summary cause action in accordance with this Chapter.

(2)   This Chapter is without prejudice to any other entitlement of the CEHR by virtue of having title and interest in relation to the subject matter of any proceedings by virtue of section 30(2) of the Equality Act 2006 or any other enactment to seek to be sisted as a party in those proceedings.

(3)   Nothing in this Chapter shall affect the power of the sheriff to make such other direction as he considers appropriate in the interests of justice.

(4)   Any decision of the sheriff in proceedings under this Chapter shall be final and not subject to appeal.

**Applications to intervene**

**14A.3.**—(1)   An application for leave to intervene shall be by way of minute of intervention in Form 23A and the CEHR shall-

    (a)   send a copy of it to all the parties; and

    (b)   lodge it in process, certifying that subparagraph (a) has been complied with.

(2)   A minute of intervention shall set out briefly—

    (a)   the CEHR's reasons for believing that the proceedings are relevant to a matter in connection with which the CEHR has a function;

    (b)   the issue in the proceedings which the CEHR wishes to address; and

    (c)   the propositions to be advanced by the CEHR and the CEHR's reasons for believing that they are relevant to the proceedings and that they will assist the sheriff.

(3)   The sheriff may—

    (a)   refuse leave without a hearing;

    (b)   grant leave without a hearing unless a hearing is requested under paragraph (4);

    (c)   refuse or grant leave after such a hearing.

(4)   A hearing, at which the applicant and the parties may address the court on the matters referred to in paragraph (6)(c) may be held if, within 14 days of the minute of intervention being lodged, any of the parties lodges a request for a hearing.

(5)   Any diet in pursuance of paragraph (4) shall be fixed by the sheriff clerk who shall give written intimation of the diet to the CEHR and all the parties.

(6)   The sheriff may grant leave only if satisfied that—

    (a)   the proceedings are relevant to a matter in connection with which the CEHR has a function;

    (b)   the propositions to be advanced by the CEHR are relevant to the proceedings and are likely to assist him; and

    (c)   the intervention will not unduly delay or otherwise prejudice the rights of the parties, including their potential liability for expenses.

(7)   In granting leave the sheriff may impose such terms and conditions as he considers desirable in the interests of justice, including making provision in respect of any additional expenses incurred by the parties as a result of the intervention.

(8)   The sheriff clerk shall give written intimation of a grant or refusal of leave to the CEHR and all the parties.

---

[1] As inserted by the Act of Sederunt (Summary Cause Rules Amendment) (Personal Injuries Actions) 2012 (SSI 2012/144) para.2 (effective September 1, 2012).

[2] As inserted by the Act of Sederunt (Sheriff Court Rules) (Miscellaneous Amendments) 2008 (SSI 2008/223) r.6(2) (effective July 1, 2008). Originally named Chapter 13B Interventions by the Scottish Commission for Human Rights in a possible drafting error.

**Form of intervention**

**14A.4.**—(1)   An intervention shall be by way of a written submission which (including any appendices) shall not exceed 5000 words.

(2)   The CEHR shall lodge the submission and send a copy of it to all the parties by such time as the sheriff may direct.

(3)   The sheriff may in exceptional circumstances-

    (a)   allow a longer written submission to be made;

    (b)   direct that an oral submission is to be made.

(4)   Any diet in pursuance of paragraph (3)(b) shall be fixed by the sheriff clerk who shall give written intimation of the diet to the CEHR and all the parties.

Chapter 14B[1]

Interventions by the Scottish Commission for Human Rights

**Interpretation**

**14B.1.**   In this Chapter—

"the Act of 2006" means the Scottish Commission for Human Rights Act 2006; and

"the SCHR" means the Scottish Commission for Human Rights.

**Applications to intervene**

**14B.2.**—(1)   An application for leave to intervene shall be by way of minute of intervention in Form 23B and the SCHR shall—

    (a)   send a copy of it to all the parties; and

    (b)   lodge it in process, certifying that subparagraph (a) has been complied with.

(2)   In granting leave the sheriff may impose such terms and conditions as he considers desirable in the interests of justice, including making provision in respect of any additional expenses incurred by the parties as a result of the intervention.

(3)   The sheriff clerk shall give written intimation of a grant or refusal of leave to the SCHR and all the parties.

(4)   Any decision of the sheriff in proceedings under this Chapter shall be final and not subject to appeal.

**Invitations to intervene**

**14B.3.**—(1)   An invitation to intervene under section 14(2)(b) of the Act of 2006 shall be in Form 23C and the sheriff clerk shall send a copy of it to the SCHR and all the parties.

(2)   An invitation under paragraph (1) shall be accompanied by—

    (a)   a copy of the pleadings in the proceedings; and

    (b)   such other documents relating to those proceedings as the sheriff thinks relevant.

(3)   In issuing an invitation under section 14(2)(b) of the Act of 2006, the sheriff may impose such terms and conditions as he considers desirable in the interests of justice, including making provision in respect of any additional expenses incurred by the parties as a result of the intervention.

**Form of intervention**

**14B.4.**—(1)   An intervention shall be by way of a written submission which (including any appendices) shall not exceed 5000 words.

(2)   The SCHR shall lodge the submission and send a copy of it to all the parties by such time as the sheriff may direct.

(3)   The sheriff may in exceptional circumstances—

    (a)   allow a longer written submission to be made;

    (b)   direct that an oral submission is to be made.

---

[1] As inserted by the Act of Sederunt (Sheriff Court Rules) (Miscellaneous Amendments) 2008 (SSI 2008/223) r.6(2) (effective July 1, 2008).

(4)   Any diet in pursuance of paragraph (3)(b) shall be fixed by the sheriff clerk who shall give written intimation of the diet to the SCHR and all the parties.

## Chapter 15

### Application for sist of party and transference

**Application for sist of party and transference**

**15.1.**—(1)   If a party dies or becomes legally incapacitated while an action is depending, any person claiming to represent that party or his estate may apply by incidental application to be sisted as a party to the action.

(2)   If a party dies or becomes legally incapacitated while an action is depending and the provisions of paragraph (1) are not invoked, any other party may apply by incidental application to have the action transferred in favour of or against, as the case may be, any person who represents that party or his estate.

## Chapter 16

### Transfer and remit of actions

**Transfer to another court**

**16.1.**—(1)   The sheriff may transfer an action to any other sheriff court, whether in the same sheriffdom or not, if the sheriff considers it expedient to do so.

(2)   If the sheriff is satisfied that the court has no jurisdiction, he may transfer the action to any sheriff court in which it appears to the sheriff that it ought to have been brought.

(3)   An action so transferred shall proceed in all respects as if it had been brought originally in the court to which it is transferred.

**Remit between procedures**

**16.2.**—(1)   If the sheriff makes a drection that an action is to be treated as an ordinary cause, he must, at the time of making that direction—

    (a)   direct the pursuer to lodge an initial writ, and intimate it to every other party, within 14 days of the date of the direction;

    (b)   direct the defender to lodge defences within 28 days of the date of the direction; and

    (c)   fix a date and time for an Options Hearing and that date shall be the first suitable court day occurring not sooner than ten weeks, or such lesser period as he considers appropriate, after the last date for lodging the initial writ.

(2)   If the sheriff directs that an ordinary cause or small claim is to be treated as an action under these rules—

    (a)   he must specify the next step of procedure to be followed in the action; and

    (b)   in the case of an ordinary cause, the initial writ shall be deemed to be a summary cause summons.

**Remit from Court of Session**

**16.3.**   On receipt of the process in an action which has been remitted from the Court of Session under section 14 of the Law Reform (Miscellaneous Provisions) (Scotland) Act 1985, the sheriff clerk must—

    (a)   record the date of receipt in the Register of Summary Causes;

    (b)   fix a hearing to determine further procedure on the first court day occurring not earlier than 14 days after the date of receipt of the process; and

    (c)   forthwith send written notice of the date of the hearing fixed under paragraph (b) to each party.

## Chapter 17

### Productions and documents

**Lodging of productions**

**17.1.**—(1)   A party who intends to rely at a proof upon any documents or articles in his possession, which are reasonably capable of being lodged with the court, must—

    (a)   lodge them with the sheriff clerk together with a list detailing the items no later than 14 days before the proof; and

    (b)   at the same time send a copy of the list to the other party.

(2)   The documents referred to in paragraph (1) include any affidavit or other written statement admissible under section 2 (1) of the Civil Evidence (Scotland) Act 1988.

(3)   A party lodging a document under this rule must send a copy of it to every other party, unless it is not practicable to do so.

(4)   Subject to paragraph (5), only documents or articles produced—

(a)   in accordance with paragraph (1) (and, if it was a document to which rule 8.5 (1) applies, was on the list lodged in accordance with that rule);

(b)   at a hearing under rule 8.2; or

(c)   under rule 18.2 (2) or (3), may be used or put in evidence.

(5)   Documents other than those mentioned in paragraph (4) may be used or put in evidence only with the—

(a)   consent of the parties; or

(b)   permission of the sheriff on cause shown, and on such terms as to expenses or otherwise as to him seem proper.

## Copy productions

**17.2.**—(1)   A copy of every production, marked with the appropriate number of process of the principal production, must be lodged for the use of the sheriff at a proof not later than 48 hours before the diet of proof.

(2)   Each copy production consisting of more than one sheet must be securely fastened together by the party lodging it.

## Borrowing of productions

**17.3.**—(1)   Any productions borrowed must be returned not later than noon on the day preceding the date of the proof.

(2)   A receipt for any production borrowed must be entered in the list of productions and that list must be retained by the sheriff clerk.

(3)   Subject to paragraph (4), productions may be borrowed only by—

(a)   a solicitor; or

(b)   his authorised clerk for whom he shall be responsible.

(4)   A party litigant or an authorised lay representative may borrow a production only with permission of the sheriff and subject to such conditions as the sheriff may impose.

(5)   Productions may be inspected within the office of the sheriff clerk during normal business hours, and copies may be obtained by a party litigant, where practicable, from the sheriff clerk.

## Penalty for failure to return productions

**17.4.**—(1)   If a solicitor has borrowed a production and fails to return it for any diet at which it is required, the sheriff may impose upon such solicitor a fine not exceeding £50.

(2)   A fine imposed under paragraph (1) shall—

(a)   be payable to the sheriff clerk; and

(b)   be recoverable by civil diligence.

(3)   An order imposing a fine under this rule shall not be subject to review except that the sheriff who granted it may, on cause shown, recall it.

## Documents lost or destroyed

**17.5.**—(1)   This rule applies to any—

(a)   summons;

(b)   form of response;

(c)   answers to a counterclaim;

(d)   third party notice or answers to a third party notice;

(d)   Register of Summary Causes; or

(e)   other document lodged with the sheriff clerk in connection with an action.

(2)   Where any document mentioned in paragraph (1) is—

(a)   lost; or

(b)   destroyed,

a copy of it, authenticated in such manner as the sheriff may require, may be substituted and shall, for the purposes of the action including the use of diligence, be equivalent to the original.

## Documents and productions to be retained in custody of sheriff clerk

**17.6.**—(1)   This rule applies to all documents or other productions which have at any time been lodged or referred to during a hearing or proof.

(2)   The sheriff clerk must retain in his custody any document or other production mentioned in paragraph (1) until—

(a)   after the expiry of the period during which an appeal is competent; and

(b)   any appeal lodged has been disposed of.

(3)   Each party who has lodged productions in an action shall—

(a) after the final determination of the claim, where no appeal has been lodged, within 14 days after the appeal period has expired; or

(b) within 14 days after the disposal of any appeal lodged on the final determination of the action, uplift the productions from the sheriff clerk.

(4) Where any production has not been uplifted as required by paragraph (3), the sheriff clerk shall intimate to—

(a) the solicitor who lodged the production; or

(b) where no solicitor is acting, the party himself or such other party as seems appropriate, that if he fails to uplift the production within 28 days after the date of such intimation, it will be disposed of in such manner as the sheriff directs.

## Chapter 18

### Recovery of evidence and attendance of witnesses

**Diligence for recovery of documents**

**18.1.**—(1) At any time after a summons has been served, a party may make an incidental application in writing to the sheriff to grant commission and diligence to recover documents.

(2) A party who makes an application in accordance with paragraph (1) must list in the application the documents which he wishes to recover.

(3) A copy of the incidental application made under paragraph (1) must be intimated by the applicant to—

(a) every other party; and

(b) where necessary, the Advocate General for Scotland or the Lord Advocate (and if there is any doubt, both).

(4) The Advocate General for Scotland and the Lord Advocate may appear at the hearing of any incidental application under paragraph (1).

(5) The sheriff may grant commission and diligence to recover those documents in the list mentioned in paragraph (2) which he considers relevant to the action.

**Optional procedure before executing commission and diligence**

**18.2.**—(1) Any party who has obtained a commission and diligence for the recovery of documents may, at any time before executing it, serve by first class recorded delivery post on the person from whom the documents are sought to be recovered (or on his known solicitor or solicitors) an order with certificate attached in Form 24.

(2) Documents recovered in response to an order under paragraph (1) must be sent to, and retained by, the sheriff clerk who shall, on receiving them, advise the parties that the documents are in his possession and may be examined within his office during normal business hours.

(3) If the party who served the order is not satisfied that full production has been made under the specification, or that adequate reasons for non-production have been given, he may execute the commission and diligence in normal form, notwithstanding his adoption in the first instance of the foregoing procedure by order.

(4) At the commission, the commissioner shall—

(a) administer the appropriate oath or affirmation to any clerk and any shorthand writer appointed for the commission; and

(b) administer to the haver the oath in Form 20, or where the haver elects to affirm, the affirmation in Form 21.

(5) Documents recovered under this rule may be tendered as evidence at any hearing or proof without further formality, and rules 18.4(2), (3) and (4) shall apply to such documents.

**Applications for orders under section 1 of the Administration of Justice (Scotland) Act 1972**

**18.3**—(1) An application by a party for an order under section 1 of the Administration of Justice (Scotland) Act 1972, must be made by incidental application in writing.

(2) At the time of lodging an incidental application under paragraph (1), a specification of—

(a) the document or other property sought to be inspected, photographed, preserved, taken into custody, detained, produced, recovered, sampled or experimented with or upon, as the case may be; or

(b) the matter in respect of which information is sought as to the identity of a person who might be a witness or a defender, must be lodged in process.

(3) A copy of the specification lodged under paragraph (2) and the incidental application made under paragraph (1) must be intimated by the applicant to—

(a) every other party;

(b) any third party haver; and

(c) where necessary, the Advocate General for Scotland or the Lord Advocate (and if there is any doubt, both).

(4) If the sheriff grants an incidental application under paragraph (1) in whole or in part, he may order the applicant to find such caution or give such other security as he thinks fit.

(5) The Advocate General for Scotland and the Lord Advocate may appear at the hearing of any incidental application under paragraph (1).

**Confidentiality**

**18.4**—(1) Confidentiality may be claimed for any evidence sought to be recovered under rule 18.2 or 18.3.

(2) Where confidentiality is claimed under paragraph (1), the documents or property in respect of which confidentiality is claimed shall be enclosed in a separate, sealed packet.

(3) A sealed packet referred to in paragraph (2) shall not be opened except by authority of the sheriff obtained on the incidental application of the party who sought the commission and diligence or order.

(4) The incidental application made under paragraph (3) must be intimated by the applicant to the party or parties from whose possession the documents specified in the commission and diligence or order were obtained.

(5) Any party received intimation under paragraph (4) may appear at the hearing of the application.

**Preservation and obtaining of evidence**

**18.5**—(1) Evidence in danger of being lost may be taken to be retained until required and, if satisfied that it is desirable so to do, the sheriff may, upon the application of any party at any time, either take it himself or grant authority to a commissioner to take it.

(2) The interlocutor granting such a commission shall be sufficient authority for citing the witness to appear before the commission.

(3) The evidence of any witness who—

    (a) is resident beyond the sheriffdom;

    (b) although resident within the sheriffdom, resides at some place remote from the court in which the proof is to be held; or

    (c) is by reason of illness, age, infirmity or other sufficient cause unable to attend the proof, may be taken in the same manner as is provided in paragraph (1).

(4) On special cause shown, evidence may be taken from any witness or haver on a ground other than one mentioned in paragraph (1) or (3).

(5) Evidence taken under paragraph (1), (3) or (4) may be taken down by—

    (a) the sheriff;

    (b) the commissioner; or

    (c) a clerk or shorthand writer nominated by the sheriff or commissioner, and such evidence may be recorded in narrative form or by question and answer as the sheriff or commissioner shall direct and the extended notes of such evidence certified by such clerk or shorthand writer shall be the notes of such oral evidence.

(6) At the commission, the commissioner shall or where the sheriff takes evidence himself, the sheriff shall—

    (a) administer the appropriate oath or affirmation to any clerk and any shorthand writer appointed for the commission; and

    (b) administer to the witness the oath in Form 20, or where the witness elects to affirm, the affirmation in Form 21.

**Warrants for production of original documents from public records**

**18.6**—(1) If a party seeks to obtain from the keeper of any public record production of the original of any register or deed in his custody for the purposes of an action, he must apply to the sheriff by incidental application.

(2) Intimation of an incidental application under paragraph (1) must be given to the keeper of the public record concerned at least seven days before the incidental application is lodged.

(3) In relation to a public record kept by the Keeper of the Registers of Scotland or the Keeper of the Records of Scotland—

    (a) where it appears to the sheriff that it is necessary for the ends of justice that an incidental application under this rule should be granted, he must pronounce an interlocutor containing a certificate to that effect; and

    (b) the party applying for production may apply by letter (enclosing a copy of the interlocutor duly certified by the sheriff clerk), addressed to the Deputy Principal Clerk of Session, for an order from the Court of Session authorising the Keeper of the Registers or the Keeper of the Records, as the case may be, to exhibit the original of any register or deed to the sheriff.

(4)   The Deputy Principal Clerk of Session must submit the application sent to him under paragraph (3) to the Lord Ordinary in chambers who, if satisfied, shall grant a warrant for production or exhibition of the original register or deed sought.

(5)   A certified copy of the warrant granted under paragraph (4) must be served on the keeper of the public record concerned.

(6)   The expense of the production or exhibition of such an original register or deed must be met, in the first instance, by the party who applied by incidental application under paragraph (1).

### Letter of request

**18.7**—(1)[1]   Subject to paragraph (7), this rule applies to an application for a letter of request to a court or tribunal outside Scotland to obtain evidence of the kind specified in paragraph (2), being evidence obtainable within the jurisdiction of that court or tribunal, for the purpose of an action depending before the sheriff.

(2)   An application to which paragraph (1) applies may be made in relation to a request—
- (a)   for the examination of a witness;
- (b)   for the inspection, photographing, preservation, custody, detention, production or recovery of, or the taking of samples of, or the carrying out of any experiment on or with, a document or other property, as the case may be;
- (c)   for the medical examination of any person;
- (d)   for the taking and testing of samples of blood from any person; or
- (e)   for any other order for obtaining evidence, for which an order could be obtained from the sheriff.

(3)   Such an application must be made by minute in Form 25 together with a proposed letter of request in Form 25a.

(4)   It shall be a condition of granting a letter of request that any solicitor for the applicant, or a party litigant, as the case may be, is to be personally liable, in the first instance, for the whole expenses which may become due and payable in respect of the letter of request to the court or tribunal obtaining the evidence and to any witness who may be examined for the purpose; and he must consign into court such sum in respect of such expenses as the sheriff thinks fit.

(5)   Unless the court or tribunal to which a letter of request is addressed is a court or tribunal in a country or territory—
- (a)   where English is an official language; or
- (b)   in relation to which the sheriff clerk certifies that no translation is required, then the applicant must, before the issue of the letter of request, lodge in process a translation of that letter and any interrogatories and cross-interrogatories into the official language of that court or tribunal.

(6)[2]   The letter of request when issued, any interrogatories and cross-interrogatories and the translations (if any) must be forwarded by the sheriff clerk to the Scottish Ministers or to such person and in such manner as the sheriff may direct.

(7)[3]   This rule does not apply to any request for the taking of evidence under Council Regulation (EC) No. 1206/2001 of 28th May 2001 on cooperation between the courts of the Member States in the taking of evidence in civil or commercial matters.

### Taking of evidence in the European Community

**18.7A.**—[4](1)   This rule applies to any request—
- (a)   for the competent court of another Member State to take evidence under Article 1.1(a) of the Council Regulation; or
- (b)   that the court shall take evidence directly in another Member State under Article 1.1(b) of the Council Regulation.

---

[1] As amended by the Act of Sederunt (Taking of Evidence in the European Community) 2003 (SSI 2003/601) r.5(2) (effective January 1, 2004).
[2] As substituted by the Act of Sederunt (Sheriff Court Rules) (Miscellaneous Amendments) 2011 (SSI 2011/193) r.8 (effective April 4, 2011).
[3] As inserted by the Act of Sederunt (Taking of Evidence in the European Community) 2003 (SSI 2003/601) r.5(2) (effective January 1, 2004).
[4] As inserted by the Act of Sederunt (Taking of Evidence in the European Community) 2003 (SSI 2003/601) r.5(3) (effective January 1, 2004).

(2)   An application for a request under paragraph (1) shall be made by minute in Form 25B, together with the proposed request in form A or I (as the case may be) in the Annex to the Council Regulation.

(3)   In this rule, "the Council Regulation" means Council Regulation (EC) No. 1206/2001 of 28th May 2001 on cooperation between the courts of the Member States in the taking of evidence in civil or commercial matters.

### Citation of witnesses

**18.8.**—(1)   The citation of a witness or haver must be in Form 26 and the certificate of it must be in Form 26a.

(2)   A party shall be responsible for securing the attendance of his witnesses or havers at a hearing and shall be personally liable for their expenses.

(3)   The summons or the copy served on the defender shall be sufficient warrant for the citation of witnesses and havers.

(4)   The period of notice given to witnesses or havers cited in terms of paragraph (3) must be not less than seven days.

(5)   A witness or haver shall be cited—

    (a)   by registered post or the first class recorded delivery service by the solicitor for the party on whose behalf he is cited; or

    (b)   by a sheriff officer—

        (i)   personally;

        (ii)   by a citation being left with a resident at the person's dwelling place or an employee at his place of business;

        (iii)   by depositing it in that person's dwelling place or place of business;

        (iv)   by affixing it to the door of that person's dwelling place or place of business; or

        (v)   by registered post or the first class recorded delivery service.

(6)   Where service is effected under paragraph (5) (b) (iii) or (iv), the sheriff officer shall, as soon as possible after such service, send by ordinary post to the address at which he thinks it most likely that the person may be found, a letter containing a copy of the citation.

### Citation of witnesses by party litigants

**18.9.**—(1)   Where a party to an action is a party litigant he shall—

    (a)   not later than 28 days before the diet of proof apply to the sheriff by incidental application to fix caution for expenses in such sum as the sheriff considers reasonable having regard to the number of witnesses he proposes to cite and the period for which they may be required to attend court; and

    (b)   before instructing a solicitor or a sheriff officer to cite a witness, find caution in the sum fixed in accordance with paragraph (1).

(2)   A party litigant who does not intend to cite all the witnesses referred to in his application under paragraph 1(a), may apply by incidental application for variation of the amount of caution.

### Witnesses failing to attend

**18.10.**—(1)   A hearing must not be adjourned solely on account of the failure of a witness to appear unless the sheriff, on cause shown, so directs.

(2)   A witness or haver who fails without reasonable excuse to answer a citation after having been properly cited and offered his travelling expenses if he has asked for them may be ordered by the sheriff to pay a penalty not exceeding £250.

(3)   The sheriff may grant decree for payment of a penalty imposed under paragraph (2) above in favour of the party on whose behalf the witness or haver was cited.

(4)   The sheriff may grant warrant for the apprehension of the witness or haver and for bringing him to court.

(5)   A warrant mentioned in paragraph (4) shall be effective in any sheriffdom without endorsation and the expenses of it may be awarded against the witness or haver.

Chapter 18A[1]

Vulnerable Witnesses (Scotland) Act 2004

### Interpretation

**18A.1.**   In this Chapter—

"child witness notice" has the meaning given in section 12(2) of the 2004 Act;
"review application" means an application for review of arrangements for vulnerable witnesses pursuant to section 13 of the 2004 Act;
"vulnerable witness application" has the meaning given in section 12(6) of the 2004 Act.

### Child Witness Notice

**18A.2.**   A child witness notice lodged in accordance with section 12(2) of the 2004 Act shall be in Form 26B.

### Vulnerable Witness Application

**18A.3.**   A vulnerable witness application lodged in accordance with section 12(6) of the 2004 Act shall be in Form 26C.

### Intimation

**18A.4.**—(1)   The party lodging a child witness notice or vulnerable witness application shall intimate a copy of the child witness notice or vulnerable witness application to all the other parties to the proceedings and complete a certificate of intimation.

(2)   A certificate of intimation referred to in paragraph (1) shall be in Form 26D and shall be lodged with the child witness notice or vulnerable witness application.

### Procedure on lodging child witness notice or vulnerable witness application

**18A.5.**—(1)   On receipt of a child witness notice or vulnerable witness application, the sheriff may—

    (a)   make an order under section 12(1) or (6) of the 2004 Act without holding a hearing;
    (b)   require further information from any of the parties before making any further order;
    (c)   fix a date for a hearing of the child witness notice or vulnerable witness application.

(2)   The sheriff may, subject to any statutory time limits, make an order altering the date of the proof or other hearing at which the child or vulnerable witness is to give evidence and make such provision for intimation of such alteration to all parties concerned as he deems appropriate.

(3)   An order fixing a hearing for a child witness notice or vulnerable witness application shall be intimated by the sheriff clerk—

    (a)   on the day the order is made; and
    (b)   in such manner as may be prescribed by the sheriff,

to all parties to the proceedings and such other persons as are named in the order where such parties or persons are not present at the time the order is made.

### Review of arrangements for vulnerable witnesses

**18A.6.**—(1)   A review application shall be in Form 26E.

(2)   Where the review application is made orally, the sheriff may dispense with the requirements of paragraph (1).

### Intimation of review application

**18A.7.**—(1)   Where a review application is lodged, the applicant shall intimate a copy of the review application to all other parties to the proceedings and complete a certificate of intimation.

(2)   A certificate of intimation referred to in paragraph (1) shall be in Form 26F and shall be lodged together with the review application.

### Procedure on lodging a review application

**18A.8.**—(1)   On receipt of a review application, the sheriff may—

    (a)   if he is satisfied that he may properly do so, make an order under section 13(2) of the

---

[1] As inserted by the Act of Sederunt (Ordinary Cause, Summary Application, Summary Cause and Small Claim Rules) Amendment (Vulnerable Witnesses (Scotland) Act 2004) 2007 (SSI 2007/463) r.4(5) (effective November 1, 2007).

2004 Act without holding a hearing or, if he is not so satisfied, make such an order after giving the parties an opportunity to be heard;

(b)    require of any of the parties further information before making any further order;

(c)    fix a date for a hearing of the review application.

(2)    The sheriff may, subject to any statutory time limits, make an order altering the date of the proof or other hearing at which the child or vulnerable witness is to give evidence and such provision for intimation of such alteration to all parties concerned as he deems appropriate.

(3)    An order fixing a hearing for a review application shall be intimated by the sheriff clerk—

(a)    on the day the order is made; and

(b)    in such manner as may be prescribed by the sheriff,

to all parties to the proceedings and such other persons as are named in the order where such parties or persons are not present at the time the order is made.

### Determination of special measures

**18A.9.**    When making an order under section 12(1) or (6) or 13(2) of the 2004 Act the sheriff may, in light thereof, make such further orders as he deems appropriate in all the circumstances.

### Intimation of an order under section 12(1) or (6) or 13(2)

**18A.10.**    An order under section 12(1) or (6) or 13(2) of the 2004 Act shall be intimated by the sheriff clerk—

(a)    on the day the order is made; and

(b)    in such manner as may be prescribed by the sheriff,

to all parties to the proceedings and such other persons as are named in the order where such parties or persons are not present at the time the order is made.

### Taking of evidence by commissioner

**18A.11.**—(1)    An interlocutor authorising the special measure of taking evidence by a commissioner shall be sufficient authority for the citing the witness to appear before the commissioner.

(2)    At the commission the commissioner shall—

(a)    administer the oath de fideli administratione to any clerk appointed for the commission; and

(b)    administer to the witness the oath in Form 20, or where the witness elects to affirm, the affirmation in Form 21.

(3)    The commission shall proceed without interrogatories unless, on cause shown, the sheriff otherwise directs.

### Commission on interrogatories

**18A.12.**—(1)    Where interrogatories have not been dispensed with, the party citing or intending to cite the vulnerable witness shall lodge draft interrogatories in process.

(2)    Any other party may lodge cross-interrogatories.

(3)    The interrogatories and cross-interrogatories, when adjusted, shall be extended and returned to the sheriff clerk for approval and the settlement of any dispute as to their contents by the sheriff.

(4)    The party who cited the vulnerable witness shall—

(a)    provide the commissioner with a copy of the pleadings (including any adjustments and amendments), the approved interrogatories and any cross-interrogatories and a certified copy of the interlocutor of his appointment;

(b)    instruct the clerk; and

(c)    be responsible in the first instance for the fee of the commissioner and his clerk.

(5)    The commissioner shall, in consultation with the parties, fix a diet for the execution of the commission to examine the witness.

### Commission without interrogatories

**18A.13.**    Where interrogatories have been dispensed with, the party citing or intending to cite the vulnerable witness shall—

(a)    provide the commissioner with a copy of the pleadings (including any adjustments and amendments) and a certified copy of the interlocutor of his appointment;

(b)    fix a diet for the execution of the commission in consultation with the commissioner and every other party;

(c)    instruct the clerk; and

(d)    be responsible in the first instance for the fees of the commissioner and his clerk.

**Lodging of video record and documents**

**18A.14.**—(1)   Where evidence is taken on commission pursuant to an order made under section 12(1) or (6) or 13(2) of the 2004 Act the commissioner shall lodge the video record of the commission and relevant documents with the sheriff clerk.

(2)   On the video record and any documents being lodged the sheriff clerk shall—

    (a)   note—

        (i)   the documents lodged;

        (ii)   by whom they were lodged; and

        (iii)   the date on which they were lodged, and

    (b)   intimate what he has noted to all parties concerned.

**Custody of video record and documents**

**18A.15.**—(1)   The video record and documents referred to in rule 18A.14 shall, subject to paragraph (2), be kept in the custody of the sheriff clerk.

(2)   Where the video record of the evidence of a witness is in the custody of the sheriff clerk under this rule and where intimation has been given to that effect under rule 18A.14(2), the name and address of that witness and the record of his evidence shall be treated as being in the knowledge of the parties; and no party shall be required, notwithstanding any enactment to the contrary—

    (a)   to include the name of that witness in any list of witnesses; or

    (b)   to include the record of his evidence in any list of productions.

**Application for leave for party to be present at the commission**

**18A.16.**   An application for leave for a party to be present in the room where the commission proceedings are taking place shall be by incidental application..

(2)   In rule 37.1(2) (live links) at the end of the definition of "witness" there shall be inserted the following—

", except a vulnerable witness within the meaning of section 11(1) of the 2004 Act.".

(3)   In Appendix 1—

    (a)   for Form 26 there shall be substituted the form in Part 1 of Schedule 2 to this Act of Sederunt; and

    (b)   after Form 26A there shall be inserted the forms set out in Part 2 of Schedule 2 to this Act of Sederunt.

Chapter 19

Challenge of documents

**Challenge of documents**

**19.1.**—(1)   If a party relies on a deed or other document to support his case, any other party may object to the deed or document without having to bring an action of reduction.

(2)   If an objection is made, the sheriff may order the objector, if an action of reduction would otherwise have been competent, to find caution or to consign with the sheriff clerk a sum of money as security.

Chapter 20

European Court

**Interpretation of rules 20.2 to 20.5**

**20.1.**—(1)   In rules 20.2 to 20.5—

"the European Court" means the Court of Justice of the European Communities;

"reference" means a reference to the European Court for—

    (a)   a preliminary ruling under Article 234 of the E.E.C. Treaty, Article 150 of the Euratom Treaty or Article 41 of the E.C.S.C. Treaty; or

    (b)   a ruling on the interpretation of the Conventions, as defined in section 1(1) of the Civil Jurisdiction and Judgments Act 1982, under Article 3 of Schedule 2 to that Act.

(2)   The expressions "E.E.C. Treaty", "Euratom Treaty" and "E.C.S.C. Treaty" have the meanings assigned respectively in Schedule 1 to the European Communities Act 1972.

**Application for reference**

**20.2.**—(1)   The sheriff may, on the application of a party or of his own accord make a reference.

870

(2)    A reference must be made in the form of a request for a preliminary ruling of the European Court in Form 27.

**Preparation of case for reference**

**20.3.**—(1)    If the sheriff decides that a reference shall be made, he must within four weeks draft a reference.

(2)    On the reference being drafted, the sheriff clerk must send a copy to each party.

(3)    Within four weeks after the date on which copies of the draft have been sent to parties, each party may—

    (a)    lodge with the sheriff clerk; and

    (b)    send to every other party, a note of any adjustments he seeks to have made in the draft reference.

(4)    Within 14 days after the date on which any such note of adjustments may be lodged, the sheriff, after considering any such adjustments, must make and sign the reference.

(5)    The sheriff clerk must forthwith intimate the making of the reference to each party.

**Sist of action**

**20.4.**—(1)    Subject to paragraph (2), on a reference being made, the action must, unless the sheriff when making the reference otherwise orders, be sisted until the European Court has given a preliminary ruling on the question referred to it.

(2)    The sheriff may recall a sist made under paragraph (1) for the purpose of making an interim order which a due regard to the interests of the parties may require.

**Transmission of reference**

**20.5.**    A copy of the reference, certified by the sheriff clerk, must be transmitted by the sheriff clerk to the Registrar of the European Court.

Chapter 21

Abandonment

**Abandonment of action**

**21.1.**—(1)    A pursuer may before an order granting absolvitor or dismissing the action has been pronounced, offer to abandon the action.

(2)    Where the pursuer offers to abandon the action in accordance with paragraph (1), the sheriff clerk shall, subject to the approval of the sheriff, fix the amount of the defender's expenses to be paid by the pursuer in accordance with rule 23.3 and the action must be continued to the first appropriate court occurring not sooner than 14 days after the amount has been fixed.

(3)    If before the continued diet the pursuer makes payment to the defender of the amount fixed under paragraph (2), the sheriff must dismiss the action unless the pursuer consents to absolvitor.

(4)    If before the continued diet the pursuer fails to pay the amount fixed under paragraph (2), the defender shall be entitled to decree of absolvitor with expenses.

Chapter 22

Decree by default

**Decree by default**

**22.1.**—(1)    If, after a proof has been fixed under rule 8.3(3)(d), a party fails to appear at a hearing where required to do so, the sheriff may grant decree by default.

(2)    If all parties fail to appear at a hearing or proof where required to do so, the sheriff must, unless sufficient reason appears to the contrary, dismiss the action and any counterclaim.

(3)    If, after a proof has been fixed under rule 8.3(3)(d), a party fails to implement an order of the court, the sheriff may, after giving him an opportunity to be heard, grant decree by default.

(4)   The sheriff shall not grant decree by default solely on the ground that a party has failed to appear at the hearing of an incidental application.

Chapter 22A[1]

Dismissal of Action due to Delay

### Dismissal of action due to delay

**22A.1.**—(1)   Any party to an action may, while that action is depending before the court, apply by written incidental application to the court to dismiss the action due to inordinate and inexcusable delay by another party or another party's agent in progressing the action, resulting in unfairness.

(2)[2]   An application under paragraph (1) shall include a statement of the grounds on which it is proposed that the application should be allowed.

(3)   In determining an application made under this rule, the court may dismiss the action if it appears to the court that—

    (a)   there has been an inordinate and inexcusable delay on the part of any party or any party's agent in progressing the action; and

    (b)   such delay results in unfairness specific to the factual circumstances, including the procedural circumstances, of that action.

(4)   In determining whether or not to dismiss an action under paragraph (3), the court shall take account of the procedural consequences, both for the parties and for the work of the court, of allowing the action to proceed.

(5)   Rule 9.1 shall, with the necessary modifications, apply to an application under paragraph (1).

Chapter 23

Decrees, extracts, execution and variation

### Decree

**23.1.**   The sheriff must not grant decree against—

    (a)   a defender or a third party in respect of a claim; or

    (b)   a pursuer in respect of a counterclaim, under any provision of these Rules unless satisfied that a ground of jurisdiction exists.

### Final decree

**23.2.**[3]   The final decree of the sheriff principal or the sheriff shall be granted, where expenses are awarded, only after expenses have been dealt with in accordance with rules 23.3, 23.3A and 23.3B.

### Expenses

**23.3.**—[4, 5](1)[6]   Subject to rule 23.3A and paragraphs (2) to (4), the sheriff clerk must, with the approval of the sheriff, assess the amount of expenses including the fees and outlays of witnesses awarded in any cause, in accordance with the applicable statutory table of fees.

(2)   A party litigant, who is not represented by a solicitor or advocate and who would have been entitled to expenses if he had been so represented, may be awarded any outlays or expenses to which he might be found entitled by virtue of the 1975 Act or any enactment under that Act.

(3)   A party who is or has been represented by an authorised lay representative or a person authorised under any enactment to conduct proceedings in the sheriff court and who would have been found entitled to expenses if he had been represented by a solicitor or an advocate may be awarded any outlays or expenses to which a party litigant might be found entitled in accordance with paragraph (2).

---

[1] As inserted by the Act of Sederunt (Sheriff Court Rules) (Miscellaneous Amendments) 2009 (SSI 2009/294) r.15 (effective October 1, 2009).

[2] As amended by the Act of Sederunt (Sheriff Court Rules) (Miscellaneous Amendments) 2010 (SSI 2010/279) r.7 (effective July 29, 2010).

[3] As substituted by the Act of Sederunt (Summary Cause Rules) (Amendment) 2002 (SSI 2002/516) r.2(2) (effective January 1, 2003).

[4] As amended by the Act of Sederunt (Summary Cause Rules) (Amendment) 2002 (SSI 2002/516) r.2(3) (effective January 1, 2003).

[5] As amended by the Act of Sederunt (Ordinary Cause, Summary Application, Summary Cause and Small Claim Rules) Amendment (Miscellaneous) 2007 (SSI 2007/6) r.4(4) (effective January 29, 2007).

[6] As amended by the Act of Sederunt (Sheriff Court Rules Amendment) (Sections 25 to 29 of the Law Reform (Miscellaneous Provisions) (Scotland) Act 1990) 2009 (SSI 2009/164) r.4(3) (effective May 20, 2009).

(4) A party who is not an individual, and—

    (i) is or has been represented by an authorised lay representative or a person authorised under any enactment to conduct proceedings in the sheriff court;

    (ii) if unrepresented, could not represent itself; and

    (iii) would have been found entitled to expenses if it had been represented by a solicitor or an advocate,

may be awarded any outlays to which a party litigant might be found entitled under the 1975 Act or any enactment made under that Act.

(5) Except where an account of expenses is allowed to be taxed under rule 23.3A, in every case including an appeal where expenses are awarded, the sheriff clerk shall hear the parties or their solicitors on the claims for expenses including fees, if any, and outlays.

(6) Except where the sheriff principal or the sheriff has reserved judgment or where he orders otherwise, the hearing on the claim for expenses must take place immediately upon the decision being pronounced.

(7) When that hearing is not held immediately, the sheriff clerk must—

    (a) fix the date, time and place when he shall hear the parties or their solicitors; and

    (b) give all parties at least 14 days' notice in writing of the hearing so fixed.

(8) The party awarded expenses must—

    (a) lodge his account of expenses in court at least seven days prior to the date of any hearing fixed under paragraph (7); and

    (b) at the same time forward a copy of that account to every other party.

(9) The sheriff clerk must—

    (a) fix the amount of the expenses; and

    (b) report his decision to the sheriff principal or the sheriff in open court for his approval at a diet which the sheriff clerk has intimated to the parties.

(10) The sheriff principal or the sheriff, after hearing parties or their solicitors if objections are stated, must pronounce final decree including decree for payment of expenses as approved by him.

(11) In an appeal, the sheriff may pronounce decree under paragraph (10) on behalf of the sheriff principal.

(12) Failure by—

    (a) any party to comply with any of the foregoing provisions of this rule; or

    (b) the successful party or parties to appear at the hearing on expenses, must be reported by the sheriff clerk to the sheriff principal or the sheriff at a diet which the sheriff clerk has intimated to the parties.

(13) In either of the circumstances mentioned in paragraphs (12)(a) or (b), the sheriff principal or sheriff must, unless sufficient cause be shown, pronounce decree on the merits of the action and find no expenses due to or by any party.

(14) A decree pronounced under paragraph (13) shall be held to be the final decree for the purposes of these Rules.

(15) The sheriff principal or sheriff may, if he thinks fit, on the application of the solicitor of any party to whom expenses may be awarded, made at or before the time of the final decree being pronounced, grant decree in favour of that solicitor for the expenses of the action.

**Taxation**

**23.3A.**—(1)[1] Either—

    (a) the sheriff, on his own motion or on the motion of any party; or

    (b) the sheriff clerk on cause shown,

may allow an account of expenses to be taxed by the auditor of court instead of being assessed by the sheriff clerk under rule 23.3.

(2) Where an account of expenses is lodged for taxation, the account and process shall be transmitted by the sheriff clerk to the auditor of court.

(3) The auditor of court shall—

    (a) assign a diet of taxation not earlier than 7 days from the date he receives the account from the sheriff clerk; and

    (b) intimate that diet forthwith from to the party who lodged the account.

(4) The party who lodged the account of expenses shall, on receiving intimation from the auditor of court under paragraph (3)—

---

[1] As inserted by the Act of Sederunt (Summary Cause Rules) (Amendment) 2002 (SSI 2002/516) r.2(4) (effective January 1, 2003).

(a)　send a copy of the account; and

(b)　intimate the date, time and place of the diet of taxation, to every other party.

(5)　After the account has been taxed, the auditor of court shall transmit the process with the account and his report to the sheriff clerk.

(6)　Where the auditor of court has reserved consideration of the account at the date of the taxation, he shall intimate his decision to the parties who attended the taxation.

(7)　Where no objections are lodged under rule 23.3B (objections to auditor's report), the sheriff may grant decree for the expenses as taxed.

**23.3B.—**　Objections to auditor's report

(1)[1]　A party may lodge a note of objections to an account as taxed only where he attended the diet of taxation.

(2)　Such a note shall be lodged within 7 days after—

(a)　the diet of taxation; or

(b)　where the auditor of court reserved consideration of the account under paragraph (6) of rule 23.3A, the date on which the auditor of court intimates his decision under that paragraph.

(3)　The sheriff shall dispose of the objection in a summary manner, with or without answers.

**Correction of interlocutor or note**

**23.4.**　At any time before extract, the sheriff may correct any clerical or incidental error in an interlocutor or note attached to it.

**Taxes on funds under control of the court**

**23.5.—**(1)　Subject to paragraph (2), in an action in which money has been consigned into court under the Sheriff Court Consignations (Scotland) Act 1893, no decree, warrant or order for payment to any person shall be granted until there has been lodged with the sheriff clerk a certificate by an authorised officer of the Inland Revenue stating that all taxes or duties payable to the Commissioners of Inland Revenue have been paid or satisfied.

(2)　In an action of multiplepoinding, it shall not be necessary for the grant of a decree, warrant or order for payment under paragraph (1) that all of the taxes or duties payable on the estate of a deceased claimant have been paid or satisfied.

**Extract of decree**

**23.6.—**(1)　Extract of a decree signed by the sheriff clerk may be issued only after the lapse of 14 days from the granting of the decree unless the sheriff on application orders earlier extract.

(2)　In an action (other than an action to which rule 30.2 applies) where an appeal has been lodged, the extract may not be issued until the appeal has been disposed of.

(3)　The extract decree—

(a)　may be written on the summons or on a separate paper;

(b)　may be in one of Forms 28 to 28k; and

(c)　shall be warrant for all lawful execution.

**Charge**

**23.7.—**(1)　The period for payment specified in any charge following on a decree for payment granted in an action shall be—

(a)　14 days if the person on whom it is served is within the United Kingdom; and

(b)　28 days if he is outside the United Kingdom or his whereabouts are unknown.

(2)　The period in respect of any other form of charge on a decree in an action shall be 14 days.

**Service of charge where address of defender is unknown**

**23.8.—**(1)　If the address of a defender is not known to the pursuer, a charge shall be deemed to have been served on the defender if it is—

(a)　served on the sheriff clerk of the sheriff court district where the defender's last known address is located; and

(b)　displayed by the sheriff clerk on the walls of court for the period of the charge.

(2)　On receipt of such a charge, the sheriff clerk must display it on the walls of court and it must remain displayed for the period of the charge.

---

[1] As inserted by the Act of Sederunt (Summary Cause Rules) (Amendment) 2002 (SSI 2002/516) r.2(4) (effective January 1, 2003).

(3)   The period specified in the charge shall run from the first date on which it was displayed on the walls of court.

(4)   On the expiry of the period of charge, the sheriff clerk must endorse a certificate in Form 29 on the charge certifying that it has been displayed in accordance with this rule and must then return it to the sheriff officer by whom service was executed.

**Diligence on decree in actions for delivery**

**23.9.**—(1)   In an action for delivery, the court may, when granting decree, grant warrant to search for and take possession of goods and to open shut and lockfast places.

(2)   A warrant granted under paragraph (1) shall only apply to premises occupied by the defender.

**Applications in same action for variation, etc. of decree**

**23.10.**—(1)   If by virtue of any enactment the sheriff, without a new action being initiated, may order that—

(a)   a decree granted be varied, discharged or rescinded; or

(b)   the execution of that decree in so far as it has not already been executed be sisted or suspended,

the party requesting the sheriff to make such an order must do so by lodging a minute to that effect, setting out briefly the reasons for the application.

(2)   On the lodging of such a minute by the pursuer, the sheriff clerk must grant warrant for service upon the defender (provided that the pursuer has returned the extract decree).

(3)   On the lodging of such a minute by the defender, the sheriff clerk must grant warrant for service upon the pursuer ordaining him to return the extract decree and may, where appropriate, grant interim sist of execution of the decree.

(4)   Subject to paragraph (5), the minute shall not be heard in court unless seven days' notice of the minute and warrant has been given to the other parties by the party lodging the minute.

(5)   The sheriff may, on cause shown, alter the period of seven days referred to in paragraph (4) but may not reduce it to less than two days.

(6)   This rule shall not apply to any proceedings under the Debtors (Scotland) Act 1987 or to proceedings which may be subject to the provisions of that Act.

Chapter 24

Recall of decree

**Recall of decree**

**24.1.**—[1](1)   A party may apply for recall of a decree granted under any of the following provisions—

(a)   rule 7.1; or

(b)   paragraph (5), (6) or (7) of rule 8.2.

(2)   The application is to be by minute in Form 30, which must be lodged with the sheriff clerk.

(3)   The application must include where appropriate (and if not already lodged with the sheriff clerk), the proposed defence or the proposed answer to the counterclaim.

(4)   A party may apply for recall of a decree in the same action on one occasion only.

(5)   A minute for recall of a decree of dismissal must be lodged within 14 days of the date of decree.

(6)   Subject to paragraphs (7) to (9), a minute for recall of any other kind of decree may be lodged at any time before the decree is fully implemented.

(7)   Subject to paragraphs (8) and (9), where a charge or arrestment has been executed following the decree, the minute must be lodged within 14 days of that execution (or the first such execution where there has been more than one).

(8)   Subject to paragraph (9), in the case of a party seeking recall who was served with the action under rule 5.7, the minute must be lodged—

(a)   within a reasonable time of such party having knowledge of the decree against him or her; but

(b)   in any event, within one year of the date of decree.

(9)   Where the decree includes a decree for removing from heritable property to which section 216(1) of the Bankruptcy and Diligence etc. (Scotland) Act 2007 applies, the minute may be lodged at any time before the defender has been removed from the subjects or premises.

---

[1] As substituted by the Act of Sederunt (Sheriff Court Rules) (Miscellaneous Amendments) 2011 (SSI 2011/193) r.16 (effective April 4, 2011).

(10)   On the lodging of a minute for recall of a decree, the sheriff clerk must fix a date, time and place for a hearing of the minute.

(11)   Where a hearing has been fixed under paragraph (10), the party seeking recall must, not less than 7 days before the date fixed for the hearing, serve upon the other party—

    (a)   a copy of the minute in Form 30a; and

    (b)   a note of the date, time and place of the hearing.

(12)   At a hearing fixed under paragraph (10), the sheriff must recall the decree so far as not implemented and the hearing must then proceed as a hearing held under rules 8.2(3) to (7) and 8.3.

(13)   A minute for recall of a decree, when lodged and served in terms of this rule, will have the effect of preventing any further action being taken by the other party to enforce the decree.

(14)   On receipt of the copy minute for recall of a decree, any party in possession of an extract decree must return it forthwith to the sheriff clerk.

(15)   If it appears to the sheriff that there has been any failure or irregularity in service of the minute for recall of a decree, the sheriff may order re-service of the minute on such conditions as the sheriff thinks fit.

## Chapter 25

## Appeals

### Appeals

**25.1.**—(1)   An appeal to the sheriff principal, other than an appeal to which rule 25.4 applies, must be by note of appeal in Form 31 lodged with the sheriff clerk not later than 14 days after the date of final decree—

    (a)   requesting a stated case; and

    (b)   specifying the point of law upon which the appeal is to proceed.

(2)   The appellant must, at the same time as lodging a note of appeal, intimate a copy of it to every other party.

(3)   The sheriff must, within 28 days of the lodging of a note of appeal, issue a draft stated case containing—

    (a)   findings in fact and law or, where appropriate, a narrative of the proceedings before him;

    (b)   appropriate questions of law; and

    (c)   a note stating the reasons for his decisions in law,

and the sheriff clerk must send a copy of the draft stated case to the parties.

(4)   In an appeal where questions of admissibility or sufficiency of evidence have arisen, the draft stated case must contain a description of the evidence led at the proof to which these questions relate.

(5)   Within 14 days of the issue of the draft stated case—

    (a)   a party may lodge with the sheriff clerk a note of any adjustments which he seeks to make;

    (b)   a respondent may state any point of law which he wishes to raise in the appeal; and

    (c)   the note of adjustment and, where appropriate, point of law must be intimated to every other party.

(6)   The sheriff may, on the motion of a party or of his own accord, and must where he proposes to reject any proposed adjustment, allow a hearing on adjustments and may provide for such further procedure under this rule prior to the hearing of the appeal as he thinks fit.

(7)   The sheriff must, within 14 days after—

    (a)   the latest date on which a note of adjustments has been or may be lodged; or

    (b)   where there has been a hearing on adjustments, that hearing, and after considering such note and any representations made to him at the hearing, state and sign the case.

(8)   If the sheriff is temporarily absent from duty for any reason, the sheriff principal may extend any period specified in paragraphs (3) or (7) for such period or periods as he considers reasonable.

(9)   The stated case signed by the sheriff must include questions of law, framed by him, arising from the points of law stated by the parties and such other questions of law as he may consider appropriate.

(10)   After the sheriff has signed the stated case, the sheriff clerk must—

    (a)   place before the sheriff principal all documents and productions in the case together with the stated case; and

    (b)   send to the parties a copy of the stated case together with a written note of the date, time and place of the hearing of the appeal.

### Effect of and abandonment of appeal

**25.2.**—(1)   When a note of appeal has been lodged, it may be insisted on by all other parties in the action although they may not have lodged separate appeals.

(2) After a note of appeal has been lodged, the appellant shall not be at liberty to withdraw it, except—

- (a) with the consent of the other parties which may be incorporated in a joint minute; or
- (b) by leave of the sheriff principal and on such terms as to expenses or otherwise as to him seem proper.

### Hearing of appeal

**25.3.**—(1) The sheriff principal shall hear the parties or their solicitors orally on all matters connected with the appeal including liability for expenses, but if any party moves that the question of liability for expenses be heard after the sheriff principal has given his decision the sheriff principal may grant that motion.

(2) In the hearing of an appeal, a party shall not be allowed to raise questions of law of which notice has not been given except on cause shown and subject to such conditions as to expenses or otherwise as the sheriff principal may consider appropriate.

(3) The sheriff principal may permit a party to amend any question of law or to add any new question in accordance with paragraph (2).

(4) The sheriff principal may—

- (a) adhere to or vary the decree appealed against;
- (b) recall the decree appealed against and substitute another therefor; or
- (c) remit, if he considers it desirable, to the sheriff, for any reason other than to have further evidence led.

(5) At the conclusion of the hearing, the sheriff principal may either pronounce his decision or reserve judgment in which latter case he must within 28 days thereof give his decision in writing and the sheriff clerk must forthwith intimate it to the parties.

### Appeal in relation to a time to pay direction

**25.4.**—(1) This rule applies to appeals to the sheriff principal or to the Court of Session which relate solely to any application in connection with a time to pay direction.

(2) Rules 25.1, 25.2, 25.3(2) and (3) and 25.7 shall not apply to appeals under this rule.

(3) An application for leave to appeal against a decision in an application for a time to pay direction or any order connected therewith must—

- (a) be made in Form 32 within seven days of that decision, to the sheriff who made the decision; and
- (b) must specify the question of law upon which the appeal is to proceed.

(4) If leave to appeal is granted, the appeal must be lodged in Form 33 and intimated by the appellant to every other party within 14 days of the order granting leave and the sheriff must state in writing his reasons for his original decision.

(5) An appeal under this rule to the sheriff principal shall proceed in accordance with paragraphs (1), (4) and (5) of rule 25.3.

### Sheriff to regulate interim possession

**25.5**—(1) Notwithstanding an appeal, the sheriff shall have power—

- (a) to regulate all matters relating to interim possession;
- (b) to make any order for the preservation of any property to which the action relates or for its sale, if perishable;
- (c) to make any order for the preservation of evidence; or
- (d) to make in his discretion any interim order which a due regard for the interests of the parties may require.

(2) An order under paragraph (1) shall not be subject to review except by the appellate court at the hearing of the appeal.

### Provisions for appeal in actions for recovery of heritable property to which rule 30.2 applies

**25.6.** In an action to which rule 30.2 applies—

- (a) it shall not be competent to shorten or dispense with the period for appeal specified in rule 25.1;
- (b) it shall be competent to appeal within that period for appeal irrespective of the early issue of an extract decree; and
- (c) the lodging of a note of appeal shall not operate so as to suspend diligence unless the sheriff directs otherwise.

**Appeal to the Court of Session**

**25.7.**—(1)   A certificate that an action is suitable for appeal to the Court of Session may be applied for by completing and lodging an application in Form 34 with the sheriff clerk.

(2)   An application made in accordance with paragraph (1) must be lodged within 14 days of the date of the final decree.

(3)   The sheriff clerk must put the application before the sheriff principal who, after hearing the parties or their solicitors, shall grant or refuse the certificate.

Chapter 26

Management of damages payable to persons under legal disability

**Orders for payment and management of money**

**26.1.**—(1)   In an action of damages in which a sum of money becomes payable, by virtue of a decree or an extra-judicial settlement, to or for the benefit of a person under legal disability (other than a person under the age of 18 years), the sheriff shall make such order regarding the payment and management of that sum for the benefit of that person as he thinks fit.

(2)   Any order required under paragraph (1) shall be made on the granting of decree for payment or of absolvitor.

**Methods of management**

**26.2.**   In making an order under rule 26.1(1), the sheriff may—

    (a)   order the money to be paid to—

        (i)   the Accountant of Court; or

        (ii)   the guardian of the person under legal disability, as trustee, to be applied, invested or otherwise dealt with and administered under the directions of the sheriff for the benefit of the person under legal disability;

    (b)   order the money to be paid to the sheriff clerk of the sheriff court district in which the person under legal disability resides, to be applied, invested or otherwise dealt with and administered, under the directions of the sheriff of that district, for the benefit of the person under legal disability; or

    (c)   order the money to be paid directly to the person under legal disability.

**Subsequent orders**

**26.3.**—(1)   If the sheriff has made an order under rule 26.1(1), any person having an interest may apply for an order under rule 26.2, or any other order for the payment or management of the money, by incidental application.

(2)   An application for directions under rule 26.2(a) or (b) may be made by any person having an interest by incidental application.

**Management of money paid to sheriff clerk**

**26.4.**—(1)   A receipt in Form 35 by the sheriff clerk shall be a sufficient discharge in respect of the amount paid to him under rules 26.1 to 26.3.

(2)   The sheriff clerk shall, at the request of any competent court, accept custody of any sum of money in an action of damages ordered to be paid to, applied, invested or otherwise dealt with by him, for the benefit of a person under legal disability.

(3)   Any money paid to the sheriff clerk under rules 26.1 to 26.3 must be paid out, applied, invested or otherwise dealt with by the sheriff clerk only after such intimation, service and enquiry as the sheriff may order.

(4)   Any sum of money invested by the sheriff clerk under rules 26.1 to 26.3 must be invested in a manner in which trustees are authorised to invest by virtue of the Trustee Investments Act 1961.

**Management of money payable to children**

**26.5.** If the sheriff has made an order under section 13 of the Children (Scotland) Act 1995, an application by a person for an order by virtue of section 11(1)(d) of that Act must be made in writing.

Chapter 27

Action of multiplepoinding

**Application of Chapter**

**27.1.** This Chapter applies to an action of multiplepoinding.

**Application of other rules**

**27.2.**—(1) Rule 8.1 shall not apply to an action of multiplepoinding.

(2) Rules 8.2 to 8.17 shall only apply to an action of multiplepoinding in accordance with rule 27.7.

**Pursuer in multiplepoinding**

**27.3.** An action of multiplepoinding may be raised by any party holding or having an interest in or claim on the fund or subject *in medio*.

**Parties**

**27.4.** The pursuer must call as defenders—

    (a) all persons so far as known to him as having an interest in the fund or subject *in medio*; and

    (b) where he is not the holder of the fund or subject, the holder of that fund or subject.

**Statement of fund or subject in medio**

**27.5.**—(1) Where the pursuer is the holder of the fund or subject *in medio* he shall include a statement of the fund or subject in his statement of claim.

(2) Where the pursuer is not the holder of the fund or subject *in medio*, the holder shall, before the return day—

    (a) lodge with the sheriff clerk a statement in Form 5a providing—

        (i) a statement of the fund or subject;

        (ii) a statement of any claim or lien which he may profess to have on the fund or subject; and

        (iii)[1] a list of all persons known to him as having an interest in the fund or subject; and

    (b) intimate the statement in Form 5a to the pursuer, the defenders and all persons listed in the statement as having an interest in the fund or subject.

**Response to summons**

**27.6.**—(1) If a defender intends to—

    (a) challenge the jurisdiction of the court or the competency of the action;

    (b) object to the extent of the fund or subject *in medio*; or

    (c) make a claim on the fund, he must complete and lodge with the sheriff clerk on or before the return day the form of response contained in the defender's copy summons as appropriate, including a statement of his response which gives fair notice to the pursuer.

(2) The sheriff clerk must upon receipt intimate to the pursuer a copy of any response lodged under paragraph (1).

**Procedure where response lodged**

**27.7.** Where in a form of response a defender states a defence in accordance with rule 27.6(1)(a)—

    (a) the provisions of rules 8.2 to 8.17 shall, with the necessary modifications, apply to the resolution of the issues raised under that sub-paragraph; and

    (b) rules 27.8 to 27.10 shall apply only once those issues have been so dealt with.

**Objections to fund or subject in medio**

**27.8.**—(1) If objections to the fund or subject *in medio* have been lodged, the sheriff must, after disposal of any defence—

    (a) fix a hearing; and

    (b) state the order in which the claimants shall be heard at the hearing.

---

[1] As substituted by SSI 2003/26, r.4(3) (clerical error).

(2)　If no objections to the fund or subject in medio have been lodged, or if objections have been lodged and disposed of, the sheriff may approve the fund or subject and if appropriate find the holder liable only in one single payment.

## Claims hearing

**27.9.**—(1)　This rule applies where—

    (a)　no defence or objection to the extent of the fund or subject in medio has been stated;

    (b)　any defence stated has been repelled; or

    (c)　any such objection stated has been dealt with.

(2)　The sheriff must—

    (a)　order claims in Form 5b to be lodged within 14 days; and

    (b)　must fix a claims hearing at which all parties may appear or be represented.

(3)　The sheriff clerk must intimate to the parties, the order for claims and the date and time of any claims hearing fixed in terms of paragraph (2).

## Procedure at claims hearing

**27.10.**—(1)　If there is no competition between the claimants who appear at the claims hearing, the sheriff may order the holder of the fund or subject *in medio*, or the sheriff clerk if it is consigned with him in terms of rule 27.12, to make it over to the claimants in terms of their claims or otherwise and subject to such provisions as to expenses as he directs.

(2)　If the sheriff is unable at the claims hearing to resolve competing claims, he shall pronounce an order—

    (a)　fixing a date, time and place for a further hearing; and

    (b)　regulating the nature and scope of the hearing and the procedure to be followed.

(3)　The sheriff may require that evidence be led at the further claims hearing fixed under paragraph (2).

(4)　The sheriff clerk must intimate to all claimants the date, time and place of any hearing fixed under paragraph (2).

(5)　At the conclusion of the claims hearing or the further claims hearing fixed under paragraph (2), the sheriff may either pronounce his decision or reserve judgement in which case he must give his decision in writing within 28 days and the sheriff clerk must forthwith intimate it to the parties.

(6)　In giving his decision under paragraph (5) the sheriff—

    (a)　must dispose of the action;

    (b)　may order the holder of the fund or subject *in medio*, or the sheriff clerk if it is consigned with him in terms of rule 27.12, to make it over to such claimants and in such quantity or amount as he may determine; and

    (c)　must deal with all questions of expenses.

## Advertisement

**27.11.**　If it appears to the sheriff at any stage in the multiplepoinding that there may be other potential claimants who are not parties to the action, he may order such advertisement or intimation of the order for claims as he thinks proper.

## Consignation and discharge of holder

**27.12.**—(1)　At any stage in an action of multiplepoinding the sheriff may order that—

    (a)　the fund or subject *in medio* be consigned in the hands of the sheriff clerk; or

    (b)　any subject *in medio* be sold and the proceeds of sale consigned in the hands of the sheriff clerk.

(2)　After such consignation the holder of the fund or subject may apply for his exoneration and discharge.

(3)   The sheriff may allow the holder of the fund or subject, on his exoneration and discharge, his expenses out of the fund as a first charge on the fund.

Chapter 28

Action of furthcoming

**Expenses included in claim**

**28.1.**   The expenses of bringing an action for furthcoming, including the expenses of the arrestment, shall be deemed to be part of the arrestor's claim which may be paid out of the arrested fund or subject.

Chapter 29

Action of count, reckoning and payment

**Response to summons**

**29.1.**   If a defender wishes to admit liability to account in an action for count, reckoning and payment, this must be stated on the form of response.

**Accounting hearing**

**29.2.**—(1)   This rule applies where in an action of count, reckoning and payment—
(a)   no form of response has been lodged;
(b)   the defender has indicated on the form of response that he admits liability to account; or
(c)   any defence stated has been repelled.

(2)   Where paragraph 1(a) or (b) applies, the pursuer must lodge with the sheriff clerk a minute in Form 17 before close of business on the second day before the calling date.

(3)   If the pursuer does not lodge a minute in accordance with paragraph (2), the sheriff must dismiss the action.

(4)   Where the pursuer has lodged a minute in accordance with paragraph (2), or any defence stated has been repelled, the sheriff shall pronounce an order—
(a)   for the lodging of accounts within 14 days and objections within such further period as the sheriff may direct;
(b)   fixing a date, time and place for an accounting hearing; and
(c)   regulating the nature and scope of the accounting hearing and the procedure to be followed.

(5)   The sheriff may require that evidence be led at an accounting hearing fixed under paragraph (4) to prove the accounts and in support of any objection taken.

(6)   The sheriff clerk must intimate to all claimants the date, time and place of any hearing fixed under paragraph (4).

Chapter 30

Recovery of possession of heritable property

**Action raised under section 38 of the 1907 Act**

**30.1.**   An action for the recovery of possession of heritable property made in terms of section 38 of the 1907 Act may be raised by—
(a)   a proprietor;
(b)   his factor; or
(c)   any other person authorised by law to pursue a process of removing.

**Action against persons in possession of heritable property without right or title**

**30.2.**—(1)   Subject to paragraph (2), this rule applies only to an action for recovery of possession of heritable property against a person or persons in possession of heritable property without right or title to possess the property.

(2)   This rule shall not apply with respect to a person who has or had a title or other right to occupy the heritable property and who has been in continuous occupation since that title or right is alleged to have come to an end.

(3)   Where the name of a person in occupation of a heritable property is not known and cannot reasonably be ascertained, the pursuer shall call that person as a defender by naming him as an "occupier".

(4)   Where the name of a person in occupation of the heritable property is not known and cannot reasonably be ascertained, the summons shall be served (whether or not it is also served on a named person), unless the sheriff otherwise directs, by an officer of the court—
(a)   affixing a copy of the summons and a citation in Form 11 addressed to "the occupiers" to

the main door or other conspicuous part of the premises, and if practicable, depositing a copy of each of those documents in the premises; or

(b) in the case of land only, inserting stakes in the ground at conspicuous parts of the occupied land to each of which is attached a sealed transparent envelope containing a copy of the summons and a citation in Form 11 addressed to "the occupiers".

(5) In an action to which this rule applies, the sheriff may in his discretion, and subject to rule 25.6, shorten or dispense with any period of time provided anywhere in these rules.

(6) An application by a party under this rule to shorten or dispense with any period may be made orally and the provisions in rule 9.1 shall not apply, but the sheriff clerk must enter details of any such application in the Register of Summary Causes.

### Effect of decree

**30.3.** When decree for the recovery of possession is granted, it shall have the same force and effect as—

    (a) a decree of removing;

    (b) a decree of ejection;

    (c) a summary warrant of ejection;

    (d) a warrant for summary ejection in common form; or

    (e) a decree pronounced in a summary application for removing, in terms of sections 36, 37 and 38 respectively of the 1907 Act.

### Preservation of defender's goods and effects

**30.4.**[1] When decree is pronounced, the sheriff may give such directions as he deems proper for the preservation of the defender's goods and effects.

### Action of removing where fixed term of removal

**30.5.**—(1) Subject to section 21 of the Agricultural Holdings (Scotland) Act 1991—

    (a) if the tenant has bound himself to remove by writing, dated and signed—

        (i) within 12 months after the term of removal; or

        (ii) where there is more than one ish, after the ish first in date to remove, an action of removing may be raised at any time; and

    (b) if the tenant has not bound himself, an action of removing may be raised at any time, but—

        (i) in the case of a lease of lands exceeding two acres in extent for three years and upwards, an interval of not less than one year nor more than two years must elapse between the date of notice of removal and the term of removal first in date;

        (ii) in the case of a lease of lands exceeding two acres in extent, whether written or oral, held from year to year or under tacit relocation, or for any other period less than three years, an interval of not less than six months must elapse between the date of notice of removal and the term of removal first in date; and

        (iii) in the case of a house let with or without land attached not exceeding two acres in extent, as also of land not exceeding two acres in extent without houses, as also of mills, fishings, shootings, and all other heritable subjects excepting land exceeding two acres in extent and let for a year or more, 40 days at least must elapse between the date of notice of removal and the term of removal first in date.

(2) In any defended action of removing, the sheriff may order the defender to find caution for violent profits.

### Form of notices and letter

**30.6.**—(1) A notice under section 34, 35 or 36 of the 1907 Act must be in Form 3a.

(2) A notice under section 37 of the 1907 Act must be in Form 3b.

(3) A letter of removal must be in Form 3c.

### Giving notice of removal

**30.7.**—(1) A notice under section 34, 35, 36, 37 or 38 of the 1907 Act may be given by—

    (a) a sheriff officer;

---

[1] As amended by the Act of Sederunt (Ordinary Cause, Summary Application, Summary Cause and Small Claim Rules) Amendment (Miscellaneous) 2007 (SSI 2007/6) r.4(6) (effective January 29, 2007).

(b)    the person entitled to give such notice; or

(c)    the solicitor or factor of such person,

posting the notice by registered post or the first class recorded delivery service at any post office within the United Kingdom in time for it to be delivered at the address on the notice before the last date on which by law such notice must be given, addressed to the person entitled to receive such notice, and bearing the address of that person at the time, if known, or, if not known, to the last known address of that person.

(2)    A sheriff officer may also give notice under any section of the 1907 Act mentioned in paragraph (1) in any manner in which he may serve an initial writ; and, accordingly, rule 5.4 shall, with the necessary modifications, apply to the giving of notice under this paragraph as it applies to service of a summons.

### Evidence of notice to remove

**30.8.**—(1)    It shall be sufficient evidence that notice has been given if—

(a)    a certificate of the sending of notice under rule 30.7 dated and endorsed on the lease or an extract of it, or on the letter of removal, is signed by the sheriff officer or the person sending the notice, his solicitor or factor; or

(b)    an acknowledgement of the notice is endorsed on the lease or an extract of it, or on the letter of removal, by the party in possession or his agent.

(2)    If there is no lease, a certificate of the sending of such notice must be endorsed on a copy of the notice or letter of removal.

**30.9**[1]    Where, in response to a summons for the recovery of heritable property which includes a claim for payment of money, a defender makes a written application about payment, he shall not thereby be taken to be admitting the claim for recovery of possession of the heritable property.

Chapter 31

Action of sequestration for rent

*[Repealed by the Act of Sederunt (Sheriff Court Rules Amendment) (Diligence) 2008 (SSI 2008/121) r.2(1)(b) (effective April 1, 2008).]*

Chapter 32

Action for aliment

### Recall or variation of decree for aliment

**32.1.**—(1)    Applications for the recall or variation of any decree for payment of aliment pronounced in the small debt court under the Small Debt Acts or in a summary cause under the 1971 Act must be made by summons.

(2)    The sheriff may make such interim orders in relation to such applications or in relation to actions brought under section 3 of the Sheriff Courts (Civil Jurisdiction and Procedure) (Scotland) Act 1963 as he thinks fit.

(3)    In paragraph (1) "the Small Debt Acts" means and includes the Small Debt (Scotland) Acts 1837 to 1889 and Acts explaining or amending the same.

### Warrant and forms for intimation

**32.2.**    In the summons in an action brought under section 3 of the Sheriff Courts (Civil Jurisdiction and Procedure) (Scotland) Act 1963, the pursuer must include an application for a warrant for intimation—

(a)    in an action where the address of the defender is not known to the pursuer and cannot reasonably be ascertained, to—

    (i)    every child of the marriage between the parties who has reached the age of 16 years; and

    (ii)    one of the next-of-kin of the defender who has reached that age,

    unless the address of such a person is not known to the pursuer and cannot reasonably be ascertained, and a notice of intimation in Form 36 must be attached to the copy of the summons intimated to any such person; or

(b)    in an action where the defender is a person who is suffering from a mental disorder, to—

    (i)    those persons mentioned in paragraphs (a)(i) and (ii), unless the address of such person is not known to the pursuer and cannot reasonably be ascertained; and

---

[1] As inserted by the Act of Sederunt (Sheriff Court Rules) (Miscellaneous Amendments) 2008 (SSI 2008/223) r.8 (effective July 1, 2008).

(ii)    the guardian of, the defender, if one has been appointed, and a notice in Form 37 must be attached to the copy of the summons intimated to any such person.

### Chapter 33

### Child Support Act 1991

**Interpretation of rules 33.2 to 33.4**

**33.1.**    In rules 33.2 to 33.4 below—

"the 1991 Act" means the Child Support Act 1991;

"child" has the meaning assigned in section 55 of the 1991 Act;

"claim relating to aliment" means a crave for decree of aliment in relation to a child or for recall or variation of such a decree; and

"maintenance calculation" has the meaning assigned in section 54 of the 1991 Act.

**Statement of claim**

**33.2.**—(1)    Any summons or counterclaim which contains a claim relating to aliment and to which section 8(6), (7), (8) or (10) of the 1991 Act applies must—

    (a)    state, where appropriate—

        (i)    that a maintenance calculation under section 11 of the 1991 Act (maintenance calculations) is in force;

        (ii)    the date of the maintenance calculation;

        (iii)    the amount and frequency of periodical payments of child support maintenance fixed by the maintenance calculation; and

        (iv)    the grounds on which the sheriff retains jurisdiction under section 8(6), (7), (8) or (10) of the 1991 Act; and

    (b)    unless the sheriff on cause shown otherwise directs, be accompanied by any document issued by the Secretary of State to the party intimating the making of the maintenance calculation referred to in sub-paragraph (a).

(2)    Any summons or counterclaim which contains a claim relating to aliment and to which section 8(6), (7), (8) or (10) of the 1991 Act does not apply must include a statement—

    (a)    that the habitual residence of the absent parent, person with care or qualifying child, within the meaning of section 3 of the 1991 Act, is outwith the United Kingdom; or

    (b)    that the child is not a child within the meaning of section 55 of the 1991 Act.

(3)    A summons or counterclaim which involves parties in respect of whom a decision has been made in any application, review or appeal under the 1991 Act must—

    (a)    include in the statement of claim statements to the effect that such a decision has been made and give details of that decision; and

    (b)    unless the sheriff on cause shown otherwise directs, be accompanied by any document issued by the Secretary of State to the parties intimating that decision.

**Effect of maintenance calculations**

**33.3.**—(1)    On receiving notification that a maintenance calculation has been made, cancelled or has ceased to have effect so as to affect an order of a kind prescribed for the purposes of section 10 of the 1991 Act, the sheriff clerk must enter in the Register of Summary Causes in respect of that order a note to that effect.

(2)    The note mentioned in paragraph (1) must state that—

    (a)    the order ceases or ceased to have effect from the date two days after the making of the maintenance calculation; or

    (b)    the maintenance calculation has been cancelled or has ceased to have effect.

**Effect of maintenance calculations on extacts of decrees relating to aliment**

**33.4**—(1)    Where a decree relating to aliment is affected by a maintenance calculation, any extract of that decree issued by the sheriff clerk must be endorsed with the following certificate:—

"A maintenance calculation having been made under the Child Support Act 1991 on (*insert date*), this order, in so far as it relates to the making or securing of periodical payments to or for the benefit of (*insert name(s) of child/children*), ceases to have effect from (*insert date two days after the date on which the maintenance calculation was made*).".

(2)    Where a decree relating to aliment has ceased to have effect on the making of a maintenance calculation and that maintenance calculation is later cancelled or ceases to have effect, any extract of that order issued by the sheriff clerk must be endorsed also with the following certificate:—

"The jurisdiction of the child support officer under the Child Support Act 1991 having terminated on (*insert date*), this order, in so far as it relates to (*insert name(s) of child/children*), again shall have effect as of (*insert date of termination of child support officer's jurisdiction*).".

Chapter 34[1]

Action of Damages for, or Arising from, Personal Injuries

*Application and interpretation*

### Application and interpretation of this Chapter

**34.1.**—(1)   This Chapter applies to a personal injuries action.

(2)   In this Chapter—

"personal injuries action" means an action of damages for, or arising from, personal injuries or death of a person from personal injuries;

"personal injuries procedure" means the procedure that applies to a personal injuries action as established by rules 34.7 to 34.11;

"1982 Act" means the Administration of Justice Act 1982.

(3)   In the definition of "personal injuries action", "personal injuries" includes any disease or impairment, whether physical or mental.

*Raising a personal injuries action*

### Form of summons

**34.2.**—(1)   In a personal injuries action the form of claim to be inserted in box 4 of Form 1 (summary cause summons) shall be in Form 2 (form of claim in a summons for payment of money).

(2)   The pursuer must, instead of stating the details of claim in box 7 of Form 1, attach to Form 1 a statement of claim in Form 10 (form of statement of claim in a personal injuries action), which must give the defender fair notice of the claim and include—

(a)   a concise statement of the grounds of the claim in numbered paragraphs relating only to those facts necessary to establish the claim;

(b)   the names of every medical practitioner from whom, and every hospital or other institution in which, the pursuer or, in an action in respect of the death of a person, the deceased, received treatment for the personal injuries.

(3)   A summons may include—

(a)   an application for warrants for intimation so far as permitted under these Rules; and

(b)   a specification of documents containing such of the calls in Form 10b (form of order of court for recovery of documents etc.) as the pursuer considers appropriate.

### Defender's copy summons

**34.3.**—(1)   A copy summons shall be served on the defender—

(a)   in Form 1e where an application for a time to pay direction under the Debtors (Scotland) Act 1987 may be applied for; or

(b)   in Form 1f in every other case,

in each case, including a copy statement of claim in Form 10.

(2)   A form of response in Form 10a shall accompany the defender's copy summons when it is served on the defender.

### Response to summons

**34.4.**—(1)   If a defender intends to—

(a)   challenge the jurisdiction of the court or the competency of the action;

(b)   defend the action (whether as regards the amount claimed or otherwise); or

(c)   state a counterclaim,

the defender must complete and lodge with the sheriff clerk on or before the return day the form of response contained in the defender's copy summons and Form 10a stating, in a manner which gives the pursuer fair notice, the grounds of fact and law on which the defender intends to resist the claim.

(2)   A counterclaim may include—

---

[1] As substituted by the Act of Sederunt (Summary Cause Rules Amendment) (Personal Injuries Actions) 2012 (SSI 2012/144) para.2 (effective September 1, 2012; not applicable to an action raised before September 1, 2012).

> (a) an application for warrants for intimation so far as permitted under these Rules; and
>
> (b) a specification of documents containing such of the calls in Form 10b as the defender considers appropriate.

(3) The sheriff clerk must, upon receipt, intimate to the pursuer a copy of any response lodged under paragraph (1).

(4) Within 7 days of receipt of intimation under paragraph (3), the pursuer shall return to the sheriff clerk the summons and the relevant certificate of execution of service.

### Inspection and recovery of documents

**34.5.**—(1) This rule applies where the summons or counterclaim in a personal injuries action contains a specification of documents by virtue of rule 34.2(3)(b) or rule 34.4(2)(b).

(2) On the summons being authenticated or counterclaim received, an order granting commission and diligence for the production and recovery of the documents mentioned in the specification shall be deemed to have been granted and the sheriff clerk shall certify Form 10b to that effect by attaching thereto a docquet in Form 10c (form of docquet etc.).

(3) An order which is deemed to have been granted under paragraph (2) shall be treated for all purposes as an interlocutor granting commission and diligence signed by the sheriff.

(4) The pursuer or defender in the case of a counterclaim may serve an order under paragraph (2) and the provisions of Chapter 18 (recovery of evidence and attendance of witnesses) shall thereafter apply, subject to any necessary modifications, as if the order were an order obtained on an incidental application made under rule 18.1 (diligence for recovery of documents).

(5) Nothing in this rule shall affect the right of a party to apply under rule 18.1 for a commission and diligence for recovery of documents or under rule 18.3 for an order under section 1 of the Administration of Justice (Scotland) Act 1972 in respect of any document or other property whether or not mentioned in the specification annexed to the summons.

*Personal injuries action: application of other rules*

### Application of other rules

**34.6.**—(1) The following rules do not apply to a personal injuries action—

rule 4.1(2) (form of claim in a summons);

rule 4.2 (statement of claim);

rule 4.3 (defender's copy summons);

rule 8.1 (response to summons);

rule 8.2 (procedure in defended action);

rule 8.3 (purpose of hearing);

rule 8.5 (inspection and recovery of documents);

rule 8.6 (exchange of lists of witnesses);

rule 8.13(1) (noting of evidence, etc.).

(2) In the application of Chapter 11 (third party procedure)—

> (a) rule 11.1(2) (application for third party notice) shall not apply;
>
> (b) in the application of rule 11.2(1) (procedure) a copy of Form 10 and any timetable already issued in terms of rule 34.7(1)(c) shall also be served on the third party; and
>
> (c) where a third party lodges a form of response under rule 11.2(3), any timetable already issued under rule 34.7(1)(c) shall apply to the third party.

(3) In respect of adjustments to the parties' respective statements made in accordance with the timetable issued under rule 34.7(1)(c), the requirement under rule 13.1 (alteration of summons etc.) to make an incidental application in respect of such adjustments shall not apply.

(4) In relation to an action proceeding in accordance with personal injuries procedure references elsewhere in these Rules to the statement of claim in the summons shall be construed as references to the statement required under rule 34.2(2) and the numbered paragraphs of that statement.

*Personal injuries procedure*

### Allocation of diets and timetables

**34.7.**—(1) The sheriff clerk shall, on the lodging of the form of response in pursuance of rule 34.4(1) or, where there is more than one defender, the first lodging of a form of response—

> (a) discharge the hearing assigned to take place on the calling date specified in the summons;
>
> (b) allocate a diet for proof of the action, which shall be no earlier than 4 months (unless the sheriff on cause shown directs an earlier diet to be fixed) and no later than 9 months from the date of the first lodging of the form of response; and
>
> (c) issue a timetable stating—

(i)    the date of the diet mentioned in subparagraph (b); and

(ii)   the dates no later than which the procedural steps mentioned in paragraph (2) are to take place.

(2)   Those procedural steps are—

(a)    application for a third party notice under rule 11.1;

(b)    the pursuer serving a commission for recovery of documents under rule 34.5;

(c)    the parties adjusting their respective statements;

(d)    the pursuer lodging with the sheriff clerk a statement of valuation of claim;

(e)    the pursuer lodging with the sheriff clerk a certified adjusted statement of claim;

(f)    the defender (and any third party to the action) lodging with the sheriff clerk a certified adjusted response to statement of claim;

(g)    the defender (and any third party to the action) lodging with the sheriff clerk a statement of valuation of claim;

(h)    the parties lodging with the sheriff clerk a list of witnesses together with any productions upon which they wish to rely; and

(i)    the pursuer lodging with the sheriff clerk the minute of the pre-proof conference.

(3)   The dates mentioned in paragraph (1)(c)(ii) are to be calculated by reference to periods specified in Appendix 1A, which, with the exception of the period specified in rule 34.10(2), the sheriff principal may vary for his or her sheriffdom or for any court within his or her sheriffdom.

(4)   A timetable issued under paragraph (1)(c) shall be in Form 10d and shall be treated for all purposes as an interlocutor signed by the sheriff; and so far as the timetable is inconsistent with any provision in these Rules which relates to a matter to which the timetable relates, the timetable shall prevail.

(5)   Where a party fails to comply with any requirement of a timetable other than that referred to in paragraph (10) or rule 34.10(3), the sheriff clerk may fix a date and time for the parties to be heard by the sheriff.

(6)   The relevant parties must lodge with the sheriff clerk the following documents by the date specified in the timetable and intimate that fact to the other parties at the same time—

(a)    in the case of the pursuer, a certified adjusted statement of claim; and

(b)    in the case of the defender (and any third party to the action), a certified adjusted response to statement of claim.

(7)   The pursuer shall, on lodging the certified adjusted statement of claim required by paragraph (6)(a), apply by incidental application to the sheriff, craving the court—

(a)    to allow parties a preliminary proof on specified matters;

(b)    to allow a proof; or

(c)    to make some other specified order.

(8)   The application lodged under paragraph (7) shall specify the anticipated length of the preliminary proof, or proof, as the case may be.

(9)   In the event that any party proposes to crave the court to make any order other than an order allowing a proof under paragraph (7)(b), that party shall, on making or opposing (as the case may be) the pursuer's application, specify the order to be sought and give full notice of the grounds of their application or their grounds of opposition to such application.

(10)   Where a party fails to lodge the documents required under paragraph (6) by the date specified in the timetable issued under paragraph (1)(c), the sheriff clerk must fix a date and time for the parties to be heard by the sheriff.

(11)   A party who seeks to rely on the evidence of a person not on his or her list lodged in accordance with paragraph (2)(h) must, if any other party objects to such evidence being admitted, seek leave of the sheriff to admit that evidence whether it is to be given orally or not; and such leave may be granted on such conditions, if any, as the sheriff thinks fit.

(12)   The list of witnesses intimated in accordance with paragraph (2)(h) must include the name, occupation (where known) and address of each intended witness and indicate whether the witness is considered to be a vulnerable witness within the meaning of section 11(1) of the 2004 Act and whether any child witness notice or vulnerable witness application has been lodged in respect of that witness.

(13)   A production which is not lodged in accordance with paragraph (2)(h) shall not be used or put in evidence at proof unless—

(a)    by consent of the parties; or

(b)    with the leave of the sheriff on cause shown and on such conditions, if any, as to expenses or otherwise as the sheriff thinks fit.

(14)   In a cause which is one of a number of causes arising out of the same cause of action, the sheriff may—

(a)    on the application of a party to that cause; and

(b)    after hearing parties to all those causes,

appoint that cause or any part of those causes to be the leading cause and to sist the other causes pending the determination of the leading cause.

(15)    In this rule, "pursuer" includes additional pursuer or applicant as the case may be.

### Applications for sist or for variation of timetable

**34.8.**—(1)    The action may be sisted or the timetable varied by the sheriff on the incidental application of any party to the action.

(2)    An application under paragraph (1)—

    (a)    shall be placed before the sheriff; and

    (b)    shall be granted only on special cause shown.

(3)    Any sist of an action in terms of this rule shall be for a specific period.

(4)    Where the timetable issued under rule 34.7(1)(c) is varied under this rule, the sheriff clerk shall issue a revised timetable in Form 10d.

(5)    A revised timetable issued under paragraph (4) shall have effect as if it were a timetable issued under rule 34.7(1)(c) and any reference in this Chapter to any action being taken in accordance with the timetable shall be construed as a reference to its being taken in accordance with the timetable as varied under this rule.

### Statements of valuation of claim

**34.9.**—(1)    Each party to the action shall make a statement of valuation of claim in Form 10e.

(2)    A statement of valuation of claim (which shall include a list of supporting documents) shall be lodged with the sheriff clerk.

(3)    Each party shall, on lodging a statement of valuation of claim—

    (a)    intimate the list of documents included in the statement of valuation of claim to every other party; and

    (b)    lodge each of those documents with the sheriff clerk.

(4)    Nothing in paragraph (3) shall affect—

    (a)    the law relating to, or the right of a party to object to, the recovery of a document on the ground of privilege or confidentiality; or

    (b)    the right of a party to apply under rule 18.1 for a commission and diligence for recovery of documents or under rule 18.3 for an order under section 1 of the Administration of Justice (Scotland) Act 1972.

(5)    Without prejudice to rule 34.11(2), where a party has failed to lodge a statement of valuation of claim in accordance with a timetable issued under rule 34.7(1)(c), the sheriff may, at any hearing under paragraph (5) of that rule—

    (a)    where the party in default is the pursuer, dismiss the action; or

    (b)    where the party in default is the defender, grant decree against the defender for an amount not exceeding the pursuer's valuation.

### Pre-proof conferences

**34.10.**—(1)    For the purposes of this rule, a pre-proof conference is a conference of the parties, which shall be held not later than four weeks before the date assigned for the proof—

    (a)    to discuss settlement of the action; and

    (b)    to agree, so far as is possible, the matters which are not in dispute between them.

(2)    Subject to any variation of the timetable in terms of rule 34.8, a joint minute of a pre-proof conference, made in Form 10f, shall be lodged with the sheriff clerk by the pursuer not later than three weeks before the date assigned for proof.

(3)    Where a joint minute in Form 10f has not been lodged in accordance with paragraph (2) and by the date specified in the timetable the sheriff clerk must fix a date and time for the parties to be heard by the sheriff.

(4)    If a party is not present during the pre-proof conference, the representative of such party shall have access to the party or another person who has authority to commit the party in settlement of the action.

### Incidental hearings

**34.11.**—(1)    Where the sheriff clerk fixes a date and time for a hearing under rules 34.7(5) or (10) or rule 34.10(3), the sheriff clerk must—

    (a)    fix a date not less than seven days after the date of the notice referred to in subparagraph (b);

    (b)    give notice to the parties to the action—

(i)    of the date and time of the hearing; and

(ii)   requiring the party in default to lodge with the sheriff clerk a written explanation as to why the timetable has not been complied with and to intimate a copy to all other parties not less than two clear working days before the date of the hearing.

(2)   At the hearing, the sheriff—

(a)   must consider any explanation provided by the party in default;

(b)   may award expenses against that party; and

(c)   may make any other appropriate order, including decree of dismissal.

*Personal injuries action: additional provisions*

### Intimation to connected persons in certain actions of damages

**34.12.**—(1)   This rule applies to an action of damages in which, following the death of any person from personal injuries, damages are claimed—

(a)   in respect of the injuries from which the deceased died; or

(b)   in respect of the death of the deceased.

(2)   In this rule "connected person" means a person, not being a party to the action, who has title to sue the defender in respect of the personal injuries from which the deceased died or in respect of his or her death.

(3)   The pursuer shall state in the summons, as the case may be—

(a)   that there are no connected persons;

(b)   that there are connected persons, being the persons specified in the application for warrant for intimation; or

(c)   that there are connected persons in respect of whom intimation should be dispensed with on the ground that—

    (i)   the names or whereabouts of such persons are not known to, and cannot reasonably be ascertained by, the pursuer; or

    (ii)  such persons are unlikely to be awarded more than £200 each.

(4)   Where the pursuer makes a statement in accordance with paragraph (3)(b), the summons shall include an application for warrant for intimation to any such persons.

(5)   A notice of intimation in Form 10g shall be attached to the copy of the summons, where intimation is given on a warrant under paragraph (4).

(6)   Where the pursuer makes a statement in accordance with paragraph (3)(c), the summons shall include an application for an order to dispense with intimation.

(7)   In determining an application under paragraph (6), the sheriff shall have regard to—

(a)   the desirability of avoiding a multiplicity of actions; and

(b)   the expense, inconvenience or difficulty likely to be involved in taking steps to ascertain the name or whereabouts of the connected person.

(8)   Where the sheriff is not satisfied that intimation to a connected person should be dispensed with, the sheriff may—

(a)   order intimation to a connected person whose name and whereabouts are known;

(b)   order the pursuer to take such further steps as the sheriff may specify in the interlocutor to ascertain the name or whereabouts of any connected person; and

(c)   order advertisement in such manner, place and at such times as the sheriff may specify in the interlocutor.

(9)   Where the name or whereabouts of a person, in respect of whom the sheriff has dispensed with intimation on a ground specified in paragraph (3)(c), subsequently becomes known to the pursuer, the pursuer shall apply to the sheriff by incidental application for a warrant for intimation to such a person; and such intimation shall be made in accordance with paragraph (5).

(10)   A connected person may apply by incidental application to be sisted as an additional pursuer to the action.

(11)   An application under paragraph (10) shall also seek leave of the sheriff to adopt the existing grounds of action and to amend the summons and statement of claim.

(12)   Where an application under paragraph (10) is granted, any timetable already issued under rule 34.7(1)(c)—

(a)   shall apply to such connected person; and

(b)   must be intimated to such person by the sheriff clerk.

(13)   Where a connected person to whom intimation is made—

(a)   does not apply to be sisted as an additional pursuer to the action;

(b)   subsequently raises a separate action against the same defender in respect of the same personal injuries or death; and

    (c)    would, apart from this rule, be awarded the expenses or part of the expenses of that action,

such person shall not be awarded those expenses except on cause shown.

### Provisional damages for personal injuries

**34.13.**—(1)   In this rule—

    "further damages" means the damages referred to in section 12(4)(b) of the 1982 Act; and
    "provisional damages" means the damages referred to in section 12(4)(a) of the 1982 Act.

(2)   An application for an order under section 12(2)(a) of the 1982 Act (application for provisional damages) shall be made by including in the summons a claim for provisional damages in Form 10h, and where such application is made, a concise statement as to the matters referred to in paragraphs (a) and (b) of section 12(1) of that Act must be included in the statement of claim.

(3)   An application for further damages by a pursuer in respect of whom an order has been made under section 12(2)(b) of the 1982 Act (application for further damages) shall be made by lodging an incidental application with the sheriff clerk in Form 10i, which shall include—

    (a)    a claim for further damages;
    (b)    a concise statement of the facts supporting that claim;
    (c)    an application for warrant to serve the incidental application on—
        (i)    every other party; and
        (ii)   where such other parties are insured or otherwise indemnified, their insurer or indemnifier, if known to the pursuer; and
    (d)    a request for the sheriff to fix a hearing on the application.

(4)   A notice of intimation in Form 10j shall be attached to every copy of the incidental application served on a warrant granted under paragraph (3)(c).

(5)   At the hearing fixed under paragraph (3)(d), the sheriff may determine the application or order such further procedure as the sheriff thinks fit.

### Mesothelioma actions: special provisions

**34.14.**—[1](1)   This rule applies where liability to a relative of the pursuer may arise under section 5 of the Damages (Scotland) Act 2011 (discharge of liability to pay damages: exception for mesothelioma).

(2)   On settlement of the pursuer's claim, the pursuer may apply by incidental application for all or any of the following—

    (a)    a sist for a specified period;
    (b)    discharge of any diet;
    (c)    where the action is one to which the personal injuries procedure applies, variation of the timetable issued under rule 34.7(1)(c).

(3)   Paragraphs (4) to (7) apply where an application under paragraph (2) has been granted.

(4)   As soon as reasonably practicable after the death of the pursuer, any agent who immediately prior to the death was instructed in a cause by the deceased pursuer shall notify the court of the death.

(5)   The notification under paragraph (4) shall be by letter to the sheriff clerk and shall be accompanied by a certified copy of the death certificate relative to the deceased pursuer.

(6)   A relative of the deceased may apply by incidental application for the recall of the sist and for an order for further procedure.

(7)   On expiration of the period of any sist pronounced on an application under paragraph (2), the sheriff clerk may fix a date and time for the parties to be heard by the sheriff.

### Chapter 35

### Electronic transmission of documents

### Extent of provision

**35.1.**—(1)   Any document referred to in these rules which requires to be—

    (a)    lodged with the sheriff clerk;
    (b)    intimated to a party; or
    (c)    sent by the sheriff clerk,

may be in electronic or documentary form, and if in electronic form may be lodged, intimated or sent by e-mail or similar means.

---

[1] In relation to any action raised in respect of any death occurring before July 7, 2011, rule 34.14 of the Summary Cause Rules shall be construed in accordance with art.4 of the Damages (Scotland) Act 2011 (Commencement, Transitional Provisions and Savings) Order 2011.

(2)    Paragraph (1) does not apply to any certificate of execution of service, citation or arrestment, or to a decree or extract decree of the court.

(3)    Where any document is lodged by e-mail or similar means the sheriff may require any principal document to be lodged.

**Time of lodgement**

**35.2.**    The time of lodgement, intimation or sending shall be the time when the document was sent or transmitted.

Chapter 36[1]

The Equality Act 2010

**Interpretation and application**

**36.1.**—[2](1)    In this Chapter—

"the Commission" means the Commission for Equality and Human Rights; and
"the 2010 Act" means the Equality Act 2010.

(2)    This Chapter applies to claims made by virtue of section 114(1) of the 2010 Act including a claim for damages.

**Intimation to Commission[3]**

**36.2.**    The pursuer shall send a copy of the summons to the Commission by registered or recorded delivery post.

**Assessor**

**36.3.**—(1)    The sheriff may, of his own motion or on the incidental application of any party, appoint an assessor.

(2)    The assessor shall be a person who the sheriff considers has special qualifications to be of assistance in determining the cause.

**Taxation of Commission expenses**

**36.4.**    *[Repealed by the Act of Sederunt (Sheriff Court Rules) (Miscellaneous Amendments) 2008 (SSI 2008/223) r.6(3)(c) (effective July 1, 2008).]*

**National security**

**36.5.**—[4](1)    Where, on an incidental application under paragraph (3) or of the sheriff's own motion, the sheriff considers it expedient in the interests of national security, the sheriff may—

    (a)    exclude from all or part of the proceedings—

        (i)    the pursuer;

        (ii)    the pursuer's representatives;

        (iii)    any assessors;

    (b)    permit a pursuer or representative who has been excluded to make a statement to the court before the commencement of the proceedings or the part of the proceedings, from which he or she is excluded;

    (c)    take steps to keep secret all or part of the reasons for his or her decision in the proceedings.

(2)    The sheriff clerk shall, on the making of an order under paragraph (1) excluding the pursuer or the pursuer's representatives, notify the Advocate General for Scotland of that order.

(3)    A party may make an incidental application for an order under paragraph (1).

(4)    The steps referred to in paragraph (1)(c) may include the following—

    (a)    directions to the sheriff clerk; and

    (b)    orders requiring any person appointed to represent the interests of the pursuer in proceed-

---

[1]  As inserted by the Act of Sederunt (Ordinary Cause, Summary Application, Summary Cause and Small Claim Rules) Amendment (Equality Act 2006 etc.) 2006 (SSI 2006/509) r.4(2) (effective November 3, 2006). Chapter title amended by the Act of Sederunt (Sheriff Court Rules) (Equality Act 2010) 2010 (SSI 2010/340) para.4 (effective October 1, 2010).

[2]  As substituted by the Act of Sederunt (Sheriff Court Rules) (Equality Act 2010) 2010 (SSI 2010/340) para.4 (effective October 1, 2010).

[3]  As substituted by the Act of Sederunt (Sheriff Court Rules) (Miscellaneous Amendments) 2008 (SSI 2008/223) r.6(3)(b) (effective July 1, 2008).

[4]  As substituted by the Act of Sederunt (Sheriff Court Rules) (Equality Act 2010) 2010 (SSI 2010/340) para.4 (effective October 1, 2010).

ings from which the pursuer or the pursuer's representatives are excluded not to communicate (directly or indirectly) with any persons (including the excluded pursuer)—

    (i)    on any matter discussed or referred to;

    (ii)   with regard to any material disclosed,

during or with reference to any part of the proceedings from which the pursuer or the pursuer's representatives are excluded.

(5)   Where the sheriff has made an order under paragraph (4)(b), the person appointed to represent the interests of the pursuer may make an incidental application for authority to seek instructions from or otherwise communicate with an excluded person.

(6)   The sheriff may, on the application of a party intending to lodge an incidental application in written form, reduce the period of notice of two days specified in rule 9.1(2) or dispense with notice.

(7)   An application under paragraph (6) shall be made in the written incidental application, giving reasons for such reduction or dispensation.

### Transfer to Employment Tribunal

**36.6.**—[1](1)   On transferring proceedings to an employment tribunal under section 140(2) of the 2010 Act, the sheriff —

    (a)   shall state his or her reasons for doing so in the interlocutor; and

    (b)   may make the order on such conditions as to expenses or otherwise as he or she thinks fit.

(2)   The sheriff clerk must, within 7 days from the date of such order—

    (a)   transmit the relevant process to the Secretary of the Employment Tribunals (Scotland);

    (b)   notify each party to the proceedings in writing of the transmission under subparagraph (a); and

    (c)   certify, by making an appropriate entry in the Register of Summary Causes, that he or she has made all notifications required under subparagraph (b).

(3)   Transmission of the process under paragraph (2)(a) will be valid notwithstanding any failure by the sheriff clerk to comply with paragraph (2)(b) and (c).

### Transfer from Employment Tribunal

**36.7.**—[2](1)   On receipt of the documentation in proceedings which have been remitted from an employment tribunal under section 140(3) of the 2010 Act, the sheriff clerk must—

    (a)   record the date of receipt on the first page of the documentation;

    (b)   fix a hearing to determine further procedure not less than 14 days after the date of receipt of the process; and

    (c)   forthwith send written notice of the date of the hearing fixed under subparagraph (b) to each party.

(2)   At the hearing fixed under paragraph (1)(b) the sheriff may make such order as he or she thinks fit to secure so far as practicable that the cause thereafter proceeds in accordance with these Rules.

Chapter 37[3]

Live Links

**37.1.**—(1)   On cause shown, a party may apply by incidental application for authority for the whole or part of—

    (a)   the evidence of a witness or the party to be given; or

    (b)   a submission to be made,

through a live link.

(2)   in paragraph (1)—

    "witness" means a person who has been or may be cited to appear before the court as a witness except a vulnerable witness within the meaning of section 11(1) of the Act of 2004;[4]

---

[1] As inserted by the Act of Sederunt (Sheriff Court Rules) (Equality Act 2010) 2010 (SSI 2010/340) para.4 (effective October 1, 2010).

[2] As inserted by the Act of Sederunt (Sheriff Court Rules) (Equality Act 2010) 2010 (SSI 2010/340) para.4 (effective October 1, 2010).

[3] As inserted by the Act of Sederunt (Ordinary Cause, Summary Application, Summary Cause and Small Claim Rules) Amendment (Miscellaneous) 2007 (SSI 2007/6) r.4(7) (effective January 29, 2007).

[4] As amended by the Act of Sederunt (Ordinary Cause, Summary Application, Summary Cause and Small Claim Rules) Amendment (Vulnerable Witnesses (Scotland) Act 2004) 2007 (SSI 2007/463) r.4(6) (effective November 1, 2007).

"submission" means any oral submission which would otherwise be made to the court by the party or his representative in person including an oral submission in support of an incidental application; and

"live link" means a live television link or such other arrangement as may be specified in the incidental application by which the witness, party or representative, as the case may be, is able to be seen and heard in the proceedings or heard in the proceedings and is able to see and hear or hear the proceedings while at a place which is outside the court room.

**Appendix 1**

**FORMS**

**Rule 1.1(4)**

Rule 4.1(1)

[1]FORM A1

Rule 2A.2(2)(b)

Statement by prospective lay representative for Pursuer/Defender*

Case Ref. No.:

in the cause

SHERIFFDOM OF (*insert name of sheriffdom*)

AT (*insert place of sheriff court*)

[A.B.], (*insert designation and address*), Pursuer

against

[C.D.], (*insert designation and address*), Defender

Court ref. no:

| | |
|---|---|
| Name and address of prospective lay representative who requests to make oral submissions on behalf of party litigant: | |
| Identify hearing(s) in respect of which permission for lay representation is sought: | |
| The prospective lay representative declares that: | |
| (a) | I have no financial interest in the outcome of the case *or* I have the following financial interest in it:* |
| (b) | I am not receiving remuneration or other reward directly or indirectly from the litigant for my assistance and will not receive directly or indirectly such remuneration or other reward from the litigant. |
| (c) | I accept that documents and information are provided to me by the litigant on a confidential basis and I undertake to keep them confidential. |
| (d) | I have no previous convictions *or* I have the following convictions: (list convictions)* |
| (e) | I have not been declared a vexatious litigant under the Vexatious Actions (Scotland) Act 1898 *or* I was declared a vexatious litigant under the Vexatious Actions (Scotland) Act 1898 on [insert date].* |

*(Signed)*

[Name of prospective lay representative]

[Date]

*(Insert Place/Date)*

The Sheriff grants/refuses* the application.

[*Signed*]

Sheriff Clerk

[Date]

*(*delete as appropriate)*

---

[1] As inserted by the Act of Sederunt (Sheriff Court Rules) (Lay Representation) 2013 (SSI 2013/91) r.4 (effective April 4, 2013).

<sup></sup>¹FORM 1
*Summons*

FORM 1

# Summary Cause Summons

**Action for/of**

(state type, e.g. payment of money)

OFFICIAL USE ONLY
SUMMONS No.

| | | |
|---|---|---|
| Sheriff Court (name, address, e-mail and telephone no.) | 1 | |
| Name and address of person raising the action (**pursuer**) | 2 | |
| Name and address of person against whom action raised (**defender, arrestee, etc.**) | 3 | |
| Name(s) and address(s) of any interested party (eg. connected person) | 3a | |
| Claim (form of decree or other order sought) | 4 | |
| Name, full address, telephone no, and e-mail address of pursuer's solicitor or representative (if any) acting in the case | 5 | |
| Fee Details (Enter these only if forms sent electronically to court) | 5a | |

| | 6 | | |
|---|---|---|---|
| | | **RETURN DAY** | 20 |
| | | **CALLING DATE** | 20   at   am. |

*Sheriff Clerk to delete as appropriate

The pursuer is authorised to serve a copy summons in form *1a/1b/1c/1d/1e/1f, on the defender, and give intimation to any interested party, not less than * 21/42 days before the **RETURN DAY** shown in the box above. The summons is warrant for service, and for citation of witnesses to attend court on any future date at which evidence may be led.

*Court Authentication*

Sheriff clerk depute (name)      Date:.......... 20

---

¹ As amended by the Act of Sederunt (Sheriff Court Rules Amendment) (Diligence) 2008 (SSI 2008/121) r.6(6) (effective April 1, 2008) and by the Act of Sederunt (Summary Cause Rules Amendment) (Personal Injuries Actions) 2012 (SSI 2012/144) para.2 (effective September 1, 2012).

**NOTE: The pursuer should complete boxes 1 to 5a above and box 7 on page 2. The sheriff clerk will complete box 6.**

| | |
|---|---|
| 7. | **STATE DETAILS OF CLAIM HERE (all cases) and PARTICULARS OF ARREST-MENT (furthcoming actions only)** |

**(To be completed by the pursuer. If space is insufficient, a separate sheet may be attached)**

The details of the claim are:..............

**FOR OFFICIAL USE ONLY**

Sheriff's notes as to:

1. Issues of fact and law in dispute

2. Facts agreed

3. Reasons for any final disposal at the hearing held on the calling date.

[1, 2]**FORM 1a**

Rule 4.3(a)

*Defender's copy summons—claim for or including payment of money where time to pay direction or time order may be applied for*

| |
|---|
| **OFFICIAL USE ONLY** |
| **SUMMONS No.** |

---

[1] As amended by the Act of Sederunt (Sheriff Court Rules Amendment) (Diligence) 2008 (SSI 2008/121) r.6(8) (effective April 1, 2008) and substituted by the Act of Sederunt (Sheriff Court Rules) (Miscellaneous Amendments) 2009 (SSI 2009/294) r.4 (effective December 1, 2009).

[2] As amended by the Act of Sederunt (Sheriff Court Rules) (Miscellaneous Amendments) 2011 (SSI 2011/193) r.11 (effective April 4, 2011) and by the Act of Sederunt (Summary Cause Rules Amendment) (Personal Injuries Actions) 2012 (SSI 2012/144) para.2 (effective September 1, 2012).

**Summary Cause Summons**
    Action for/of
    (state type, e.g. payment of money)
    **DEFENDER'S COPY: Claim for or including payment of money (where time to pay direction or time order may be applied for)**

| | | |
|---|---|---|
| Sheriff Court (name, address, e-mail and telephone no.) | **1** | |
| Name and address of person raising the action (**pursuer**) | **2** | |
| Name and address of person against whom action raised (**defender, arrestee, etc.**) | **3** | |
| Name(s) and address(s) of any interested party (e.g. connected person) | **3a** | |
| Claim (form of decree or other order sought) | **4** | |
| Name, full address, telephone no., and e-mail address of pursuer's solicitor or representative (if any) acting in the case | **5** | |

| **6** | | | | |
|---|---|---|---|---|
| | **RETURN DAY** | 20 | | |
| | **CALLING DATE** | 20 | at | am. |

**NOTE: You will find details of claim on page 2.**

| 7. | STATEMENT OF CLAIM |
|---|---|

    **PARTICULARS OF ARRESTMENT (furthcoming actions only)**

    **(To be completed by the pursuer. If space is insufficient, a separate sheet may be attached)**

    The details of the claim are:

| | |
|---|---|
| **8.** | **SERVICE ON DEFENDER** |

**(PLACE)**..............

**(DATE)**.........

**To:**..............

**(Defender)**.........

You are hereby served with a copy of the above summons.

Solicitor/sheriff officer
*delete as appropriate*

NOTE: The pursuer should complete boxes 1 to 6 on page 1, the statement of claim in box 7 on page 2 and section A on page 6 before service on the defender. The person serving the Summons will complete box 8, above.

PAGE 2

## WHAT MUST I DO ABOUT THIS SUMMONS?

The RETURN DAY (on page 1 of this summons) is the deadline by which you need to reply to the court. You must send the correct forms back (see below for details) by this date if you want the court to hear your case. If you do not do this, in most cases there will not be a hearing about your case and the court will make a decision in your absence.

The CALLING DAY (on page 1 of this summons) is the date for the court hearing.

Note: If your case is about **recovery of possession of heritable property** (eviction) there will be a hearing even if you do not send back the forms, so you should attend court on the calling date. If you make an application for time to pay in such a case and the court accepts your application, it may still make an order for eviction, so you should attend court if you wish to defend the action for eviction.

**You should decide whether you wish to dispute the claim and/or whether you owe any money or not, and how you wish to proceed.** Then, look at the 5 options listed below. Find the one that covers your decision and follow the instructions given there.

If you are not sure what you need to do, contact the sheriff clerk's office before the return day. Written guidance can also be obtained from the Scottish Court Service website (www.scotcourts.gov.uk).

### OPTIONS

1.  **ADMIT LIABILITY FOR THE CLAIM and settle it with the pursuer now.**
    If you wish to avoid the possibility of a court order passing against you, you should settle the claim (including any question of expenses) with the pursuer or his representative **in good time before the return day.** Please do not send any payment direct to the court. Any payment should be made to the pursuer or his representative.

2.  **ADMIT LIABILITY FOR THE CLAIM and make <u>written</u> application to pay by instalments or by <u>deferred</u> lump sum.**

Complete Box 1 of section B on page 6 of this form and return pages 6, 8 and 9 to the court to arrive on or before the return day. You should then contact the court to find out whether or not the pursuer has accepted your offer. If he has not accepted it, the case will then call in court on the calling date, when the court will decide how the amount claimed is to be paid.

NOTE: If you fail to return pages 6, 8 and 9 as directed, or if, having returned them, you fail to attend or are not represented at the calling date if the case is to call, the court may decide the claim in your absence.

3. ADMIT LIABILITY FOR THE CLAIM and attend at court to make application to pay by instalments or deferred lump sum.

Complete Box 2 on page 6. Return page 6 to the court so that it arrives on or before the return day.

**PAGE 3**

You must attend personally, or be represented, at court on the calling date. Your representative may be a Solicitor, or someone else having your authority. It may be helpful if you or your representative bring pages 1 and 2 of this form to the court.

NOTE: If you fail to return page 6 as directed, or if, having returned it, you fail to attend or are not represented at the calling date, the court may decide the claim in your absence.

4. DISPUTE THE CLAIM and attend at court to do any of the following:
- Challenge the jurisdiction of the court or the competency of the action
- Defend the action (whether as regards the sum claimed or otherwise)
- State a counterclaim

Complete Box 3 on page 6. Return page 6 to the court so that it arrives **on or before the return day. You must attend personally, or be represented, at court on the calling date.** Your representative may be a solicitor, or someone else having your authority. It may be helpful if you or your representative bring pages 1 and 2 of this form to the court.

NOTE: If you fail to return page 6 as directed, or if, having returned it, you fail to attend or are not represented at the calling date, the court may decide the claim in your absence.

**WRITTEN NOTE OF PROPOSED DEFENCE**

You must send to the court by the return day a written note of any proposed defence, or intimate that you intend to dispute the sum claimed or wish to dispute the court's jurisdiction. You must also attend or be represented at court on the calling date.

5. ADMIT LIABILITY FOR THE CLAIM and make written application for a time order under the Consumer Credit Act 1974.

Complete Box 4 on page 6 and return pages 6 and 10 to 12 to the court to arrive on or before the return day. You should then contact the court to find out whether or not the pursuer has accepted your offer. Where you have been advised that the pursuer has not accepted your offer then the case will call in court on the calling date. You should appear in court on the calling date as the court will decide how the amount claimed is to be paid.

NOTE: If you fail to return pages 6 and 10 to 12 as directed, or if, having returned them, you fail to attend or are not represented at the calling date if the case is to call, the court may decide the claim in your absence.

<u>PLEASE NOTE</u>

If you do nothing about this summons, the court will almost certainly, where appropriate, grant decree against you and order you to pay the pursuer the sum claimed, including any interest and expenses found due.

YOU ARE ADVISED TO KEEP PAGES 1 AND 2, AS THEY MAY BE USEFUL AT A LATER STAGE OF THE CASE.

**PAGE 4**

Notes:

(1) **Time to pay directions**

The Debtors (Scotland) Act 1987 gives you the right to apply to the court for a "time to pay direction". This is an order which allows you to pay any sum which the court orders you to pay either in instalments or by deferred lump sum. A "deferred lump sum" means that you will be ordered by the court to pay the whole amount at one time within a period which the court will specify.

If the court makes a time to pay direction it may also recall or restrict any arrestment made on your property by the pursuer in connection with the action or debt (for example, your bank account may have been frozen).

No court fee is payable when making an application for a time to pay direction.

If a time to pay direction is made, a copy of the court order (called an extract decree) will be sent to you by the pursuer telling you when payment should start or when it is you have to pay the lump sum.

If a time to pay direction is not made, and an order for immediate payment is made against you, an order to pay (called a charge) may be served on you if you do not pay.

### (2) Determination of application

Under the 1987 Act, the court is required to make a time to pay direction if satisfied that it is reasonable in the circumstances to do so, and having regard in particular to the following matters—

- The nature of and reasons for the debt in relation to which decree is granted
- Any action taken by the creditor to assist the debtor in paying the debt
- The debtor's financial position
- The reasonableness of any proposal by the debtor to pay that debt
- The reasonableness of any refusal or objection by the creditor to any proposal or offer by the debtor to pay the debt.

### (3) Time Orders

The Consumer Credit Act 1974 allows you to apply to the court for a "time order" during a court action, to ask the court to give you more time to pay a loan agreement. **A time order is similar to a time to pay direction, but can only be applied for where the court action is about a credit agreement regulated by the Consumer Credit Act.** The court has power to grant a time order in respect of a regulated agreement to reschedule payment of the sum owed. This means that a time order can change:

- the amount you have to pay each month
- how long the loan will last
- in some cases, the interest rate payable

A time order can also stop the creditor taking away any item bought by you on hire purchase or conditional sale under the regulated agreement, so long as you continue to pay the instalments agreed.

No court fee is payable when making an application for a time order.

**PAGE 5**

---

**SECTION A**

This section must be
completed before service

| Summons No |
| --- |
| Return Day |
| Calling Date |

SHERIFF COURT (Includ-
ing address)

PURSUER'S FULL NAME
AND ADDRESS

DEFENDER'S FULL
NAME AND ADDRESS

**SECTION B**      **DEFENDER'S RESPONSE TO THE SUMMONS**

        ** **Delete those boxes which do not apply**

**\*\*Box 1**

**ADMIT LIABILITY FOR THE CLAIM and make** written **application to pay by instalments or by** deferred **lump sum**.

I do not intend to defend the case but admit liability for the claim.

I wish to make a written application about payment.

I have completed the application form on pages 8 and 9.

**\*\*Box 2**

**ADMIT LIABILITY FOR THE CLAIM and** attend at court **to make application to pay by instalments or deferred lump sum**.

I admit liability for the claim.

|  |  |
|---|---|
|  | I intend to appear or be represented at court on the calling date. |
| **Box 3 | **DISPUTE THE CLAIM (or the amount due) and attend at court** |
|  | *I intend to challenge the jurisdiction of the court. |
|  | *I intend to challenge the competency of the action. |
|  | *I intend to defend the action. |
|  | *I wish to dispute the amount due only. |
|  | *I apply for warrant to serve a third party notice (see page 14). |
|  | I intend to appear or be represented in court on the calling date. |
|  | ............... |
|  | *I attach a note of my proposed defence/counterclaim. |
|  | *delete as necessary |
| **Box 4 | **ADMIT LIABILITY FOR THE CLAIM and apply for a time order under the** Consumer Credit Act 1974. |
|  | I do not intend to defend the case but admit liability for the claim. |
|  | I wish to apply for a time order under the Consumer Credit Act 1974. |
|  | I have completed the application form on pages 10 to 12. |

**PAGE 6**

**WRITTEN NOTE OF PROPOSE DEFENCE / COUNTERCLAIM**

State which facts in the statement of claim are admitted:

State briefly any facts regarding the circumstances of the claim on which you intent to rely:

State details of counterclaim, if any:

<table>
<tr><td> <br><br><br><br><br><br><br><br><br></td></tr>
</table>

**PLEASE REMEMBER:** You must send your response to the court to **arrive on or before the return day** if you have completed a response in Section B. If you have admitted the claim, please do not send any payment direct to the court. **Any payments you wish to make should be made to the pursuer or his solicitor**.

APPLICATION IN WRITING FOR A TIME TO PAY DIRECTION UNDER THE DEBTORS (SCOTLAND) ACT 1987

**I WISH TO APPLY FOR A TIME TO PAY DIRECTION**

*I admit the claim* and make application to pay as follows:

(1) By instalments of £ .......... per *week / fortnight / month

**OR**

(2) In one payment within .......... *weeks / months from the date of the court order.

The debt is for (*specify the nature of the debt*) and has arisen (*here set out the reasons the debt has arisen*)

Please also state why you say a time to pay direction should be made. In doing so, please consider the Notes (1) and (2) on page 5.

To help the court please provide details of your financial position in the boxes below.

I am employed / self-employed / unemployed

**\*Please also indicate whether payment/receipts are weekly, fortnightly or monthly**

| My outgoings are: | *Weekly / fortnightly/ monthly | | My net income is | *Weekly / fortnightly/ monthly |
|---|---|---|---|---|
| Rent/mortgage | £ | | Wages/pensions | £ |
| Council tax | £ | | State benefits | £ |
| Gas/electricity etc | £ | | Tax credits | £ |
| Food | £ | | Other | £ |
| Loans and credit agreements | £ | | | |
| Phone | £ | | | |
| Other | £ | | | |
| Total | £ | | Total | £ |

| People who rely on your | |
|---|---|

| income (e.g. spouse/ civil partner/ partner/chil- dren)— how many | |
|---|---|

**Please list details of all capital held, e.g. value of house; amount in savings account, shares or other investments:**

I am of the opinion that the payment offer is reasonable for the following reason(s):

*Here set out any information you consider relevant to the court's determination of the application. In doing so, please consider Note (2) on page 5.*

---

**\*APPLICATION FOR RECALL OR RESTRICTION OF AN ARRESTMENT**

I seek the recall or restriction of the arrestment of which the details are as follows:

---

Date:

   *\*Delete if inapplicable*

| | | **APPLICATION FOR A TIME ORDER UNDER THE CONSUMER CREDIT ACT 1974** |
|---|---|---|
| | | By |
| | | DEFENDER |
| | | **In an action raised by** |
| | | |

| | |
|---|---|
| | PURSUER |
| | PLEASE WRITE IN INK USING BLOCK CAPITALS |
| | If you wish to apply to pay by instalments enter the amount at box 3.<br><br>If you wish the court to make any additional orders, please give details at box 4. Please give details of the regulated agreement at box 5 and details of your financial position in the spaces provided below box 5.<br><br>Sign and date the application where indicated. You should ensure that your application arrives at the court along with the completed page 6 on or before the return day. |
| | 1. The Applicant is a defender in the action brought by the above named pursuer.<br><br>**I/WE WISH TO APPLY FOR A TIME ORDER under the Consumer Credit Act 1974** |
| | **2. Details of order(s) sought**<br><br>The defender wishes to apply for a time order under section 129 of the Consumer Credit Act 1974<br><br>The defender wishes to apply for an order in terms of section .......... of the Consumer Credit Act 1974 |
| | **3. Proposals for payment**<br><br>I admit the claim and apply to pay the arrears and future instalments as follows:<br><br>By instalments of £ .......... per *week/fortnight/month<br><br>No time to pay direction or time to pay order has been made in relation to this debt. |
| | **4. Additional orders sought**<br><br>The following additional order(s) is (are) sought: (*specify*)<br><br>The order(s) sought in addition to the time order is (are) sought for the following reasons: |
| | **5. Details of regulated agreement**<br><br>*(Please attach a copy of the agreement if you have retained it and insert details of the agreement where known)*<br><br>(a) Date of agreement<br><br>(b) Reference number of agreement |

|  | (c) Names and addresses of other parties to agreement |
|---|---|
|  | (d) Name and address of person (if any) who acted as surety (guarantor) to the agreement |
|  | (e) Place where agreement signed (e.g. the shop where agreement signed, including name and address) |
|  | (f) Details of payment arrangements<br>i. The agreement is to pay instalments of £ .......... per week/month<br>ii. The unpaid balance is £ .......... / I do not know the amount of arrears<br>iii. I am £ .......... in arrears / I do not know the amount of arrears |

**PAGE 11**

| | Defender's financial position | | | |
|---|---|---|---|---|
| | I am employed /self employed / unemployed | | | |
| | **My net income is:** | weekly, fort-nightly or monthly | **My outgoings are:** | weekly, fort-nightly or monthly |
| | Wages | £ | Mortgage/rent | £ |
| | State benefits | £ | Council tax | £ |
| | Tax credits | £ | Gas/electricity etc | £ |
| | Other | £ | Food | £ |
| | | | Credit and loans | £ |
| | | | Phone | £ |
| | | | Other | £ |
| | Total | £ | Total | £ |
| | People who rely on your income (e.g. spouse/civil partner/partner/children)— how many | | | |
| | Here list all assets (if any) e.g. value of house; amounts in bank or building society accounts; shares or other investments:.................... | | | |
| | Here list any outstanding debts:................... | | | |
| | Therefore the defender asks the court to make a time order | | | |
| | Date:.............. | | Signed:.............. | |
| | | | Defender:.............. | |

**PAGE 12**

APPLICATION FOR SERVICE OF A THIRD PARTY NOTICE
NOTE:
You can apply to have another party added to the action if:

**(A)**　　　　　　　　**You think that, as regards the matter which the action is about, that other party has a duty to:**

1. Indemnify you; or
2. Make a contribution in respect of the matter; or
3. Relieve you from any responsibility as regards it.

**or**

**(B)**　　　　　　　　**You think that other party is:**
1. Solely liable to the pursuer; or

2. Liable to the pursuer along with you; or

3. Has a liability to you as a result of the pursuer's claim against you.

You may apply for warrant to found jurisdiction if you wish to do so.

**PAGE 13**

---

FORM OF APPLICATION

### (TO BE RETURNED TO THE COURT ALONG WITH YOUR RESPONSE)

I request the court to grant warrant for service of a third party notice on the following party:

**Name:** ...............

**Address:** ...............

The reason I wish a third party notice to be served on the party mentioned above is as follows:

**(Give details below of the reasons why you wish the party to be made a defender in the action.)**

---

*I apply for warrant to found jurisdiction

**delete as appropriate**

**Date:** ...............

---

[1] FORM 1b

Rule 4.3(a)

---

[1] As amended by the Act of Sederunt (Sheriff Court Rules Amendment) (Diligence) 2008 (SSI 2008/121) r.6(8) (effective April 1, 2008) and by the Act of Sederunt (Summary Cause Rules Amendment) (Personal Injuries Actions) 2012 (SSI 2012/144) para.2 (effective September 1, 2012).

*Defender's copy summons - claim for or including payment of money (where time to pay direction or time order may not be applied for)*

**FORM 1b**

OFFICIAL USE ONLY
SUMMONS No.

# Summary Cause Summons
## Action for/of
(state type, e.g. payment of money)

**DEFENDER'S COPY: Claim for or including payment of money (where time to pay direction or time order may not be applied for)**

| | | |
|---|---|---|
| Sheriff Court (name, address, e-mail and telephone no.) | **1** | |
| Name and address of person raising the action (**pursuer**) | **2** | |
| Name and address of person against whom action raised (**defender, arrestee, etc.**) | **3** | |
| Name(s) and address(s) of any interested party (e.g. connected person) | **3a** | |
| Claim (Form of decree or other order sought) | **4** | |
| Name, full address, telephone no., and e-mail address of pursuer's solicitor or representative (if any) | **5** | |

| | | | | |
|---|---|---|---|---|
| **6** | **RETURN DAY** | 20 | | |
| | **CALLING DATE** | 20 | at | am. |

**NOTE: You will find details of claim on page 2.**

PAGE 1

7. **STATEMENT OF CLAIM**
   **PARTICULARS OF ARRESTMENT (furthcoming actions only.)**
   (To be completed by the pursuer. If space is insufficient, a separate sheet may be attached)
   The details of the claim are:

8. **SERVICE ON DEFENDER**
   (Place)...............                    (Date)..........

To:...............           (defender)..........

You are hereby served with a copy of the above summons.

Solicitor / sheriff officer

*delete as appropriate*

**NOTE: The pursuer should complete boxes 1 to 6 on page 1, the statement of claim in box 7 on page 2 and section A on page 5 before service on the defender. The person serving the Summons will complete box 8.**

WHAT MUST I DO ABOUT THIS SUMMONS?

Decide whether you wish to dispute the claim, or admit any liability for the claim and whether you owe any money or not, and how you wish to proceed. Thereafter, look at the 2 options listed below. Find the one which covers your decision and follow the instructions given there. You will find the RETURN DAY and the CALLING DATE on page one of the summons.

Written guidance on summary cause procedure can be obtained from the sheriff clerk at any sheriff clerk's office. Further advice can also be obtained by contacting any of the following:

Citizen's Advice Bureau, Consumer Advice Centre, Trading Standards or Consumer Protection Department or a Solicitor. (Addresses can be found in the guidance booklets)

**Options**

**1. ADMIT LIABILITY FOR THE CLAIM and settle it with the pursuer now.**

If you wish to avoid the possibility of a court order passing against you, you should settle the claim (including any question of expenses) with pursuer or his representative **in good time before the return day**. Please do not send any payment direct to the court. Any payment should be made to the pursuer or his representative.

**2. DISPUTE THE CLAIM and attend at court to do any of the following:**

- Challenge the jurisdiction of the court or the competency of the action
- Defend the action
- Dispute the sum claimed
- State a counterclaim

Complete Section B on page 4. Return your response to the court so that it arrives **on or before the return day. You must attend personally, or be represented, at court on the calling date.**

Your representative may be a solicitor, or someone else having your authority. It may be helpful if you or your representative bring pages 1 and 2 of this form to the court.

**NOTE: If you fail to return your response as directed, or if, having returned it, you fail to attend or are not represented at the calling date, the court will almost certainly decide the claim in your absence.**

**Written Note of Proposed Defence**

You must send to the court by the return day a written note of any proposed defence, or intimate that you intend to dispute the sum claimed or wish to challenge the court's jurisdiction. You must also attend or be represented at court on the calling date.

**Please Note:**

If you do nothing about this summons, the court will almost certainly, where appropriate, grant decree against you and order you to pay the pursuer the sum claimed, including any interest and expenses found due.

**You Are Advised to Keep Pages 1 And 2, as They May Be Useful at a Later Stage of the Case.**

| **SECTION A** This section must be completed before service | | Summons No |
| --- | --- | --- |
| | | Return Day |
| | | Calling Date |
| | SHERIFF COURT (Including address) | |

| PURSUER'S FULL NAME AND ADDRESS | DEFENDER'S FULL NAME AND ADDRESS |
|---|---|

**SECTION B**  **DEFENDER'S RESPONSE TO THE SUMMONS**

---

**DISPUTE THE CLAIM (or the amount due) and attend at court**

\* I intend to challenge the jurisdiction of the court.

\* I intend to challenge the competency of the action.

\* I intend to defend the claim.

\* I wish to dispute the amount due only.

\* I apply for warrant to serve a third party notice (see page 6).

\* I intend to appear or be represented in court on the calling date.

........................

\* I attach a note of my proposed defence/counterclaim (see page 5).

\* *delete as necessary*

---

**WRITTEN NOTE OF PROPOSED DEFENCE / COUNTERCLAIM**

State which facts in the statement of claim are admitted:


State briefly any facts regarding the circumstances of the claim on which you intend to rely:


State details of counterclaim, if any:


---

**PLEASE REMEMBER:** You must send your response to the court to **arrive on or before the return day** if you have completed a response in Section B. If you have admitted the claim, please do not send any payment direct to the court. **Any payments you wish to make should be made to the pursuer or his solicitor.**

**APPLICATION FOR SERVICE OF A THIRD PARTY NOTICE**

**NOTE:**

You can apply to have another party added to the action if:

**(A) You think that, as regards the matter which the action is about, that other party has a duty to:**

1.   Indemnify you; or

2.   Make a contribution in respect of the matter; or

3.   Relieve you from any responsibility as regards it.

or

(B) You think that other party is:

4.   Solely liable to the pursuer; or

908

5. Liable to the pursuer along with you; or

6. Has a liability to you as a result of the pursuer's claim against you.

You may apply for warrant to found jurisdiction if you wish to doso.

---

FORM OF APPLICATION

### (TO BE RETURNED TO THE COURT ALONG WITH YOUR RESPONSE)

**I request the court to grant warrant for service of a third party notice on the following party:**

Name:...............

Address:...............

**The reason I wish a third party notice to be served on the party mentioned above is as follows:** (Give details below of the reasons why you wish the party to be made a defender in the action.)

**\* I apply for warrant to found jurisdiction**

\* delete as appropriate

---

Form 1c[1]

*Defender's copy summons — non monetary claim*

Rule 4.3(b)

### FORM 1c

| | OFFICIAL USE ONLY |
| --- | --- |
| | SUMMONS No. |

# Summary Cause Summons
# Action for/of
(state type, e.g. delivery)

**DEFENDER'S COPY: Non Monetary Claim**

| | | |
| --- | --- | --- |
| Sheriff Court (name, address, e-mail and telephone no.) | **1** | |
| Name and address of person raising the action (**pursuer**) | **2** | |
| Name and address of Person against whom Action raised (**defender**) | **3** | |

---

[1] As amended by the Act of Sederunt (Sheriff Court Rules Amendment) (Diligence) 2008 (SSI 2008/121) r.6(8) (effective April 1, 2008).

| Claim (Form of decree or other order sought) 4 | |
|---|---|

| Name, full address, telephone no, and e-mail address of pursuer's solicitor or representative (if any) 5 | |
|---|---|

| 6 | **RETURN DAY** | 20 | | |
|---|---|---|---|---|
| | **CALLING DATE** | 20 | at | am. |

**NOTE: You will find details of claim on page 2.**

---

7.  **STATE DETAILS OF CLAIM HERE OR ATTACH A STATEMENT OF CLAIM**
    **(to be completed by the pursuer. If space is insufficient, a separate sheet may be attached)**

    The details of the claim are:

8.  **SERVICE ON DEFENDER**

    (Place)...............                                           (Date).........

    To:...............                                                      (defender)

    You are hereby served with a copy of the above summons.

                                                    * Solicitor / sheriff officer
                                                    (delete as appropriate)

---

**NOTE: The pursuer should complete boxes 1 to 6 on page 1, the statement of claim in box 7 on page 2 and section A on page 5 before service on the defender. The person serving the Summons will complete box 8.**

### WHAT MUST I DO ABOUT THIS SUMMONS?

**Decide whether you wish to dispute the action and how you wish to proceed.** Thereafter, look at the 2 options listed below. Find the one which covers your decision and follow the instructions given there. You will find the RETURN DAY and the CALLING DATE on page one of the summons.

**Written guidance on summary cause procedure can be obtained from the sheriff clerk at any sheriff clerk's office. Further advice can also be obtained by contacting any of the following:**

**Citizen's Advice Bureau, Consumer Advice Centre, Trading Standards or Consumer Protection Department or a Solicitor. (Addresses can be found in the guidance booklets)**

**Options**

**1. ADMIT LIABILITY FOR THE CLAIM and settle it with the pursuer now.**

If you wish to avoid the possibility of a court order passing against you, you should settle the claim (including any liability for expenses) with the pursuer or his representative in good time before the return day.

**2. DISPUTE THE CLAIM and attend at court to do any of the following:**
- Challenge the jurisdiction of the court or the competency of the action
- Defend the action
- State a counterclaim

Complete Section B on page 4. Return page 4 to the court so that it arrives **on or before the return day. You must attend personally, or be represented, at court on the calling date.**

Your representative may be a solicitor, or someone else having your authority. It may be helpful if you or your representative bring pages 1 and 2 of this form to the court.

**NOTE: If you fail to return page 4 as directed, or if, having returned it, you fail to attend or are not represented at the calling date, the court will almost certainly decide the claim in your absence.**

**Written Note of Proposed Defence**

You must send to the court by the return day a written note of any proposed defence, or intimate that you wish to challenge the jurisdiction of the court. You must also attend or be represented at court on the calling date.

**Please Note**

If you do nothing about this summons, the court will almost certainly, where appropriate, grant decree against you, including any interest and expenses found due.

**You Are Advised to Keep Pages 1 And 2, as They May Be Useful at a Later Stage of the Case.**

**SECTION A**
This section must
Be completed
Before service

Summons No

Return Day

Calling Date

SHERIFF COURT (Including address)

PURSUER'S FULL NAME AND ADDRESS

DEFENDER'S FULL NAME AND ADDRESS

**SECTION B**

**DEFENDER'S RESPONSE TO THE SUMMONS**

**DISPUTE THE CLAIM and attend at court**

* I intend to challenge the jurisdiction of the court.
* I intend to challenge the competency of the court.
* I wish to defend the action.
* I apply for warrant to serve a third party notice (see page 6).

I intend to appear or be represented in court on the calling date.
*I attach a note of my proposed defence/counterclaim (see page 5).

* *delete as necessary*

**WRITTEN NOTE OF PROPOSED DEFENCE / COUNTERCLAIM**
State which facts in the statement of claim are admitted:

State briefly any facts regarding the circumstances of the claim on which you intend to rely:

State details of counterclaim, if any:

**PLEASE REMEMBER:** You must send your response to the court to **arrive** on or **before the return day** if you have completed a response in Section B.

### APPLICATION FOR SERVICE OF A THIRD PARTY NOTICE
**NOTE:**

You can apply to have another party added to the action if:

**(A) You think that, as regards the matter which the action is about, that other party has a duty to:**

1. Indemnify you; or
2. Make a contribution in respect of the matter; or
3. Relieve you from any responsibility as regards it.

or

(B) You think that other party is:

4. Solely liable to the pursuer; or
5. Liable to the pursuer along with you; or
6. Has a liability to you as a result of the pursuer's claim against you.

You may apply for warrant to found jurisdiction if you wish to do so.

---

**Form of Application**

(TO BE RETURNED TO THE COURT ALONG WITH YOUR RESPONSE)

**I request the court to grant warrant for service of a third party notice on the following party:**

Name:...............

Address:...............

**The reason I wish a third party notice to be served on the party mentioned above is as follows:**

(Give details below of the reasons why you wish the party to be made a defender in the action.)

**\* I apply for warrant to found jurisdiction**

delete as appropriate

---

Form 1d

Defender's copy summons - multiplepoinding

Rule 4.3(c)

**FORM 1d**

# Summary Cause Summons

Action of Multiplepoinding

| OFFICIAL USE ONLY |
| SUMMONS No. |

**DEFENDER'S COPY**

| Sheriff Court (name, address, e-mail and telephone no.) | 1 | |
|---|---|---|
| Name and address of person raising the action (**pursuer**) | 2 | |
| Name and address of person against whom action raised (**defenders**) | 3 | |
| Claim (Form of decree or other order sought - see Form 5) | 4 | |
| Name, full address, telephone no., and e-mail address of pursuer's solicitor (if any) | 5 | |

| 6 | **RETURN DAY** | 20 | | |
|---|---|---|---|---|
| | **CALLING DATE** | 20 | at | am. |

**NOTE: You will find details of claim on page 2.**

| 7. | **STATE DETAILS OF CLAIM HERE OR ATTACH A STATEMENT OF CLAIM** |
|---|---|
| | (to be completed by the pursuer. If space is insufficient, a separate sheet may be attached) |
| | The details of the claim are: |

8.  **SERVICE ON DEFENDER**

(Place)............... (Date).........

To:............... (Defender.)

You are hereby served with the above summons. The pursuer has been authorised by the court to serve it on you.

Solicitor / sheriff officer
(delete as appropriate)

**NOTE: The Pursuer should complete boxes 1 to 6 on page 1, the statement of claim in box 7 on page 2 and section A on page 5 before service on the defender. The person serving the Summons will complete box 8.**

### WHAT MUST I DO ABOUT THIS SUMMONS?

**Decide whether you wish to dispute the action and how you wish to proceed.** Thereafter, look at the 2 options listed below. Find the one which covers your decision and follow the instructions given there. You will find the RETURN DAY and the CALLING DATE on page one of the summons.

**Written guidance on summary cause procedure can be obtained from the sheriff clerk at any sheriff clerk's office. Further advice can also be obtained by contacting any of the following:**

**Citizen's Advice Bureau, Consumer Advice Centre, Trading Standards or Consumer Protection Department or a solicitor. (Addresses can be found in the guidance booklets)**

### OPTIONS

1. ADMIT LIABILITY FOR THE CLAIM and settle it with the pursuer now.

If you wish to avoid the possibility of a court order passing against you, you should attempt to settle the claim (including any liability for expenses) with the pursuer or his Solicitor **in good time before the return day.**

**2. DISPUTE THE CLAIM and attend at court to do any of the following:**

- Challenge the jurisdiction of the court or the competency of the action.
- Object to the extent of the fund or subject detailed in the statement of claim on page 2.
- Make a claim on the fund or subject.

Complete Section B on page 4. Return page 4 to the court so that it arrives **on or before the return day. You must attend personally, or be represented, at court on the calling date.**

Your representative may be a Solicitor, or someone else having your authority. It may be helpful if you or your representative bring pages 1 and 2 of this form to the court.

**NOTE: If you fail to return page 4 as directed, or if, having returned it, you fail to attend or are not represented at the calling date, the court will almost certainly deal with the action in your absence.**

**NOTES:**

1. If you do nothing about this summons, the court will almost certainly deal with the action in your absence.

2. **IF YOU ARE THE HOLDER OF THE FUND,** you must complete the enclosed form 5a and send it to the sheriff clerk before the return day. You must also, before the return day, send a copy of form 5a to the pursuer, the other defenders in the action and to all the persons you have listed in form 5a as having an interest in the fund or subject.

**YOU ARE ADVISED TO KEEP PAGES 1 AND 2, AS THEY MAY BE USEFUL AT A LATER STAGE OF THE CASE.**

| **SECTION A** This section must be completed Before service | | | Summons No |
|---|---|---|---|
| | | | Return Day |
| | | | Calling Date |
| | SHERIFF COURT (Including address) | | |

|  |  |
|---|---|
| PURSUER'S FULL NAME AND AD- DRESS | DEFENDER'S FULL NAME AND AD- DRESS |

**SECTION B**  **DEFENDER'S RESPONSE TO THE SUMMONS**

---

**DISPUTE THE CLAIM and attend at court**

**I intend to:**

* (1) Challenge the jurisdiction of the court or the competency of the action.

* (2) Object to the extent of the fund or subject detailed in the statement of claim.

* (3) Make a claim on the fund or subject.

I intend to appear or be represented in court on the calling date.

* *delete as necessary*

**Please give below brief details of your reason(s) for disputing the claim in accordance with your response to 1, 2 or 3 above:**

---

¹ FORM 1e

Form 1e

| OFFICIAL USE ONLY |
|---|
| SUMMONS No. |

Rule 34.3(1)(a)

*Summary Cause Summons—Personal Injuries Action*

**DEFENDER'S COPY: Claim for payment of money in a personal injuries action (where time to pay direction may be applied for)**

| Sheriff Court (name, address, e-mail and telephone no.) | 1 | |
|---|---|---|
| Name and address of person raising the action (**pursuer**) | 2 | |
| Name and address of person against whom | 3 | |

---

¹ As inserted by the Act of Sederunt (Summary Cause Rules Amendment) (Personal Injuries Actions) 2012 (SSI 2012/144) para.2 (effective September 1, 2012; not applicable to an action raised before September 1, 2012).

| action raised (de-fender, arrestee, etc.) | | |
|---|---|---|
| Name(s) and ad-dress(es) of any inter-ested party (e.g. con-nected person) | **3a** | |
| Claim (form of decree of other order sought) | **4** | |
| Name, full address, telephone no., and e-mail address of pur-suer's solicitor or rep-resentative (if any) act-ing in the case | **5** | |

| **6** | **RETURN DAY** | **20** | | |
|---|---|---|---|---|
| | **CALLING DATE** | **20** | **at** | **am.** |

**NOTE: You will find details of the claim in the attached Form 10 (statement of claim in a personal injuries action).**

---

**7.**      **STATEMENT OF CLAIM**

        **(Pursuer to attach copy Form 10 (statement of claim in a personal injuries action))**

        The details of the claim are as stated in the attached copy Form 10.

---

**8.**      **SERVICE ON DEFENDER**

        **(Place)**...............                            **(Date)**.........

        **To:**...............                              **(Defender)**.........

        **You are hereby served with a copy of the above summons.**

<table>
<tr><td>Solicitor / sheriff officer<br>*delete as appropriate*</td></tr>
</table>

NOTE: The pursuer should complete boxes 1 to 6 on page 1, attach a copy of the Form 10, (statement of claim) and complete section A on page 6 before service on the defender. The pursuer should also enclose a form of response in Form 10a. The person serving the Summons will complete box 8, above.

**PAGE 2**

### WHAT MUST I DO ABOUT THIS SUMMONS?

The RETURN DAY (on page 1 of this summons) is the deadline by which you need to reply to the court. You must send the correct forms back (see below for details) by this date if you want the court to hear your case. If you do not do this, in most cases there will not be a hearing about your case and the court will make a decision in your absence.

The CALLING DAY (on page 1 of this summons) is the date when the court will deal with your case should you not respond to this summons, or the date of the court hearing should you admit the claim and the court is required to consider your application to pay the sum claimed by instalments or by deferred lump sum.

**You should decide whether you wish to dispute the claim and/or whether you owe any money or not, and how you wish to proceed.** Then, look at the 4 options listed below. Find the one that covers your decision and follow the instructions given there.

You may have a policy of insurance that could indemnify you against this claim. This could be motor, home contents, buildings, travel or some other form of liability insurance that may offer cover to meet legal costs to defend this claim or to meet any claim against you that is admitted or proved. If you believe you have any such insurance cover, you should **immediately** contact your insurer and take steps to forward to them details of this claim.

**IF YOU ARE UNCERTAIN WHAT ACTION TO TAKE** you should consult a solicitor. You may also obtain advice from a Citizens Advice Bureau or other advice agency. Alternatively, if you are not sure what you need to do, contact the sheriff clerk's office before the return day. Written guidance is available from the Scottish Court Service website (www.scotcourts.gov.uk).

### OPTIONS

**1. ADMIT LIABILITY FOR THE CLAIM and settle it with the pursuer now.**

If you wish to avoid the possibility of a court order passing against you, you should settle the claim (including any question of expenses) with the pursuer or their representative **in good time before the return day.** Please do not send any payment direct to the court. Any payment should be made to the pursuer or their representative.

**2. ADMIT LIABILITY FOR THE CLAIM and make written application to pay by instalments or by deferred lump sum.**

Complete Box 1 of section B on page 6 of this form and return pages 6, 7 and 8 to the court **to arrive on or before the return day.** You should then contact the court to find out whether or not the pursuer has accepted your offer. If the pursuer has not accepted it, the case will then call in court on the calling date, when the court will decide how the amount claimed is to be paid.

**NOTE: If you fail to return pages 6, 7 and 8 as directed, or if, having returned them, you fail to attend or are not represented at the calling date if the case is to call, the court may decide the claim in your absence.**

**3. ADMIT LIABILITY FOR THE CLAIM and attend at court to make application to pay by instalments or deferred lump sum.**

Complete Box 2 of section B on page 6 of this form. Return page 6 to the court so that it arrives **on or before the return day.**

**PAGE 3**

**You must attend personally, or be represented, at court on the calling date.** Your representative may be a solicitor, or someone else having your authority. It may be helpful if you or your representative bring pages 1 and 2 of this Form and Form 10 to the court.

**NOTE: If you fail to return page 6 as directed, or if, having returned it, you fail to attend or are not represented at the calling date, the court may decide the claim in your absence.**

**4. DISPUTE THE CLAIM for any of the following reasons:**
- Challenge the jurisdiction of the court or the competency of the action;
- Defend the action;
- Dispute the sum claimed; or
- State a counterclaim.

You must complete Box 3 of Section B on page 6 and the attached form of response in Form 10a, stating in a manner which gives the pursuer fair notice, the grounds of fact and law on which you intend to resist the claim, or counterclaim, and return these to the court so that they arrive **on or before the return day.** Thereafter, the case **will not** call in court on the calling date and you do not require to attend or be represented at court on that date. The sheriff clerk will send to you or your representative a timetable confirming the anticipated date for the hearing of evidence and the dates by which various procedural matters must be undertaken. Your representative may be a solicitor or someone else having your authority.

**NOTE: If you fail to return page 6 and the completed Form 10a as directed, the case may call on the calling date, and the court may decide the claim in your absence.**

**PLEASE NOTE**

If you do nothing about this summons, the court will almost certainly, where appropriate, grant decree against you and order you to pay the pursuer the sum claimed, including any interest and expenses found due.

**YOU ARE ADVISED TO KEEP PAGES 1 AND 2 AND FORM 10, AS THEY MAY BE USE-FUL AT A LATER STAGE OF THE CASE.**

PAGE 4

**Notes:**

**(1) Time to pay directions**

The Debtors (Scotland) Act 1987 gives you the right to apply to the court for a "time to pay direction". This is an order which allows you to pay any sum which the court orders you to pay either in instalments or by deferred lump sum. A "deferred lump sum" means that you will be ordered by the court to pay the whole amount at one time within a period which the court will specify.

If the court makes a time to pay direction it may also recall or restrict any arrestment made on your property by the pursuer in connection with the action or debt (for example, your bank account may have been frozen).

No court fee is payable when making an application for a time to pay direction.

If a time to pay direction is made, a copy of the court order (called an extract decree) will be sent to you by the pursuer telling you when payment should start or when it is you have to pay the lump sum.

If a time to pay direction is not made, and an order for immediate payment is made against you, an order to pay (called a charge) may be served on you if you do not pay.

**(2) Determination of application**

Under the 1987 Act, the court is required to make a time to pay direction if satisfied that it is reasonable in the circumstances to do so, and having regard in particular to the following matters—
- The nature of and reasons for the debt in relation to which decree is granted
- Any action taken by the creditor to assist the debtor in paying the debt
- The debtor's financial position
- The reasonableness of any proposal by the debtor to pay that debt
- The reasonableness of any refusal or objection by the creditor to any proposal or offer by the debtor to pay the debt.

PAGE 5

| **SECTION A** | | **Summons No** |
|---|---|---|
| This section must be | | |
| completed before service | | **Return Day** |
| | | |
| | | **Calling Date** |
| SHERIFF COURT (Including address) | | |

918

```
┌─────────────┐        ┌─────────────┐
│             │        │             │
│             │        │             │
│             │        │             │
└─────────────┘        └─────────────┘
```

PURSUER'S FULL NAME          DEFENDER'S   FULL
AND ADDRESS                  NAME AND ADDRESS

**SECTION B**       **DEFENDER'S RESPONSE TO THE SUMMONS**

** Delete those boxes which do not apply

**\*\*Box 1**

> **ADMIT LIABILITY FOR THE CLAIM and make written application to pay by instalments or by deferred lump sum.**
>
> I do not intend to defend the case but admit liability for the claim.
>
> I wish to make a written application about payment.
>
> I have completed the application form on pages 7 and 8.

**\*\*Box 2**

> **ADMIT LIABILITY FOR THE CLAIM and attend at court to make application to pay by instalments or deferred lump sum.**
>
> I admit liability for the claim.
>
> I intend to appear or be represented at court on the calling date.

**\*\*Box 3**

> **DISPUTE THE CLAIM (or the amount due)**
>
> *I intend to challenge the jurisdiction of the court.
>
> *I intend to challenge the competency of the action.
>
> *I intend to defend the action/state a counterclaim.
>
> *I wish to dispute the amount due only.
>
> *I apply for warrant to serve a third party notice (see page 10).
>
> *delete as necessary
>
> ...............
>
> I attach completed Form 10a stating my proposed defence/counterclaim.

**PLEASE REMEMBER:** You must send your response to the court to **arrive on or before the return day** if you have completed a response in Section B. If you have admitted the claim, please do not send any payment direct to the court. **Any payments you wish to make should be made to the pursuer or their solicitor.**

**PAGE 6**

APPLICATION IN WRITING FOR A TIME TO PAY DIRECTION UNDER THE DEBTORS
(SCOTLAND) ACT 1987

> **I WISH TO APPLY FOR A TIME TO PAY DIRECTION**
>
> **I admit the claim** and make application to pay as follows:
>
> (1) By instalments of £ .......... per *week / fortnight / month
>
> **OR**
>
> (2) In one payment within .......... *weeks / months from the date of the court order.
>
> The debt is for (*specify the nature of the debt*) and has arisen (*here set out the reasons the debt has arisen*)

Please also state why you say a time to pay direction should be made. In doing so, please consider the Notes (1) and (2) on page 5.

To help the court please provide details of your financial position in the boxes below.

I am employed / self-employed / unemployed
**\*Please also indicate whether payment/receipts are weekly, fortnightly or monthly**

| My outgoings are: | *Weekly / fortnightly/ monthly | | My net income is | *Weekly / fortnightly/ monthly |
|---|---|---|---|---|
| Rent/mortgage | £ | | Wages/pensions | £ |
| Council tax | £ | | State benefits | £ |
| Gas/electricity etc | £ | | Tax credits | £ |
| Food | £ | | Other | £ |
| Loans and credit agreements | £ | | | |
| Phone | £ | | | |
| Other | £ | | | |
| Total | £ | | Total | £ |

People who rely on your income (e.g. spouse/ civil partner/ partner/children)— how many

**Please list details of all capital held, e.g. value of house; amount in savings account, shares or other investments:**

I am of the opinion that the payment offer is reasonable for the following reason(s):

*Here set out any information you consider relevant to the court's determination of the application. In doing so, please consider Note (2) on page 5.*

**\*APPLICATION FOR RECALL OR RESTRICTION OF AN ARRESTMENT**

I seek the recall or restriction of the arrestment of which the details are as follows:

---

*Delete if inapplicable

Date:

APPLICATION FOR SERVICE OF A THIRD PARTY NOTICE

NOTE:

You can apply to have another party added to the action if:

**(A)**           **You think that, as regards the matter which the action is about, that other party has a duty to:**

          1. Indemnify you; or

          2. Make a contribution in respect of the matter; or

          3. Relieve you from any responsibility as regards it.

          **or**

**(B)**           **You think that other party is:**

          1. Solely liable to the pursuer; or

          2. Liable to the pursuer along with you; or

          3. Has a liability to you as a result of the pursuer's claim against you.

You may apply for warrant to found jurisdiction if you wish to do so.

---

FORM OF APPLICATION

**(TO BE RETURNED TO THE COURT ALONG WITH YOUR RESPONSE)**

I request the court to grant warrant for service of a third party notice on the following party:

**Name:**...............

**Address:**...............

The reason I wish a third party notice to be served on the party mentioned above is as follows:

**(Give details below of the reasons why you wish the party to be made a defender in the action.)**

*I apply for warrant to found jurisdiction

---

*delete as appropriate

Date:...............

[1] FORM 1f

Form 1f

OFFICIAL USE ONLY
SUMMONS No.

Rule 34.3(1)(b)

*Summary Cause Summons—Personal Injuries Action*

**DEFENDER'S COPY: Claim for payment of money in a personal injuries action (where time to pay direction may be applied for)**

| | | |
|---|---|---|
| Sheriff Court (name, address, e-mail and telephone no.) | **1** | |
| Name and address of person raising the action (**pursuer**) | **2** | |
| Name and address of person against whom action raised (**defender, arrestee, etc.**) | **3** | |
| Name(s) and address(es) of any interested party (e.g. connected person) | **3a** | |
| Claim (form of decree of other order sought) | **4** | |
| Name, full address, telephone no., and e-mail address of pursuer's solicitor or representative (if any) act- | **5** | |

---

[1] As inserted by the Act of Sederunt (Summary Cause Rules Amendment) (Personal Injuries Actions) 2012 (SSI 2012/144) para.2 (effective September 1, 2012; not applicable to an action raised before September 1, 2012).

ing in the case

|   |   |   |   |   |
|---|---|---|---|---|
| 6 | RETURN DAY | 20 |   |   |
|   | CALLING DATE | 20 | at | am. |

NOTE: You will find details of the claim in the attached Form 10 (statement of claim in a personal injuries action).

**PAGE 1**

---

7.        **STATEMENT OF CLAIM**

       **(Pursuer to attach copy Form 10 (statement of claim in a personal injuries action))**

       The details of the claim are as stated in the attached copy Form 10.

---

8.        **SERVICE ON DEFENDER**

       **(Place)..............**                          **(Date)..........**

       **To:...............**                              **(Defender)..........**

       **You are hereby served with a copy of the above summons.**

                                      **Solicitor / sheriff officer**

                                      *delete as appropriate*

---

NOTE: The pursuer should complete boxes 1 to 6 on page 1, attach a copy of the Form 10, (statement of claim) and complete section A on page 6 before service on the defender. The pursuer should also enclose a form of response in Form 10a. The person serving the Summons will complete box 8, above.

**PAGE 2**

## WHAT MUST I DO ABOUT THIS SUMMONS?

The RETURN DAY (on page 1 of this summons) is the deadline by which you need to reply to the court. You must send the correct forms back (see below for details) by this date if you want the court to hear your case. If you do not do this, in most cases there will not be a hearing about your case and the court will make a decision in your absence.

The CALLING DAY (on page 1 of this summons) is the date when the court will deal with your case should you not respond to this summons.

**You should decide whether you wish to dispute the claim and/or whether you owe any money or not, and how you wish to proceed.** Then, look at the 2 options listed on the next page. Find the one that covers your decision and follow the instructions given there.

You may have a policy of insurance that could indemnify you against this claim. This could be motor, buildings, travel or some other form of liability insurance that may offer cover to meet legal costs to defend this claim or to meet any claim against you that is admitted or proved. If you believe you have any such insurance cover, you should **immediately** contact your insurer and take steps to forward to them details of this claim.

**IF YOU ARE UNCERTAIN WHAT ACTION TO TAKE** you should consult a solicitor. You may also obtain advice from a Citizens Advice Bureau or other advice agency. Alternatively, if you are not sure what you need to do, contact the sheriff clerk's office before the return day. Written guidance is available from the Scottish Court Service website (www.scotcourts.gov.uk).

PAGE 3

## OPTIONS

**1. ADMIT LIABILITY FOR THE CLAIM and settle it with the pursuer now.**

If you wish to avoid the possibility of a court order passing against you, you should settle the claim (including any question of expenses) with the pursuer or their representative **in good time before the return day.** Please do not send any payment direct to the court. Any payment should be made to the pursuer or their representative.

**2. DISPUTE THE CLAIM for any of the following reasons:**
- Challenge the jurisdiction of the court or the competency of the action;
- Defend the action;
- Dispute the sum claimed; or
- State a counterclaim.

You must complete Section B on page 5 and the attached form of response in Form 10a, stating in a manner which gives the pursuer fair notice, the grounds of fact and law on which you intend to resist the claim, or counterclaim, and return these to the court so that they arrive **on or before the return day.** Thereafter, the case **will not** call in court on the calling date and you do not require to attend or be represented at court on that date. The sheriff clerk will send to you or your representative a timetable confirming the anticipated date for the hearing of evidence and the dates by which various procedural matters must be undertaken. Your representative may be a solicitor or someone else having your authority.

**NOTE: If you fail to return page 5 and the completed Form 10a as directed, the case may call on the calling date, and the court may decide the claim in your absence.**

## PLEASE NOTE

If you do nothing about this summons, the court will almost certainly, where appropriate, grant decree against you and order you to pay the pursuer the sum claimed, including any interest and expenses found due.

**YOU ARE ADVISED TO KEEP PAGES 1 AND 2 AND FORM 10, AS THEY MAY BE USEFUL AT A LATER STAGE OF THE CASE.**

Page 4

| SECTION A | | Summons No |
|---|---|---|
| This section must be completed before service | | Return Day |
| | | Calling Date |

SHERIFF COURT (Including address)

|  |  |
|---|---|
| PURSUER'S FULL NAME AND ADDRESS | DEFENDER'S FULL NAME AND ADDRESS |

**SECTION B**      **DEFENDER'S RESPONSE TO THE SUMMONS**

**\*\* Delete those boxes which do not apply**

| **DISPUTE THE CLAIM (or the amount due)** |
|---|
| *I intend to challenge the jurisdiction of the court. |
| *I intend to challenge the competency of the action. |
| *I intend to defend the action/state a counterclaim. |
| *I wish to dispute the amount due only. |
| *I apply for warrant to serve a third party notice (see page 6). |
| *delete as necessary |
| ............... |
| I attach completed Form 10a stating my proposed defence/counterclaim. |

**PLEASE REMEMBER:** You must send your response to the court to **arrive on or before the return day** if you have completed a response in Section B. If you have admitted the claim, please do not send any payment direct to the court. **Any payments you wish to make should be made to the pursuer or their solicitor.**

**PAGE 5**

APPLICATION FOR SERVICE OF A THIRD PARTY NOTICE

NOTE:

You can apply to have another party added to the action if:

**(A)**      **You think that, as regards the matter which the action is about, that other party has a duty to:**

    1.                                       Indemnify you; or

    2.                                         Make a contribution in respect of the matter; or

    3.                                       Relieve you from any responsibility as regards it.

                                                **or**

**(B)**      **You think that other party is:**

    1.                                       Solely liable to the pursuer; or

    2.                                       Liable to the pursuer along with you; or

    3.                                       Has a liability to you as a result of the pursuer's claim against you.

You may apply for warrant to found jurisdiction if you wish to do so.

**PAGE 6**

FORM OF APPLICATION

925

---

**(TO BE RETURNED TO THE COURT ALONG WITH YOUR RESPONSE)**

I request the court to grant warrant for service of a third party notice on the following party:

Name:...............

Address:...............

The reason I wish a third party notice to be served on the party mentioned above is as follows:
**(Give details below of the reasons why you wish the party to be made a defender in the action.)**

---

*I apply for warrant to found jurisdiction

*delete as appropriate

Date:...............

---

**PAGE 7**

**Rule 4.1(2)**                                        FORM 2

Form of claim in a summons for payment of money..........The pursuer claims from the defender(s) the sum of £..........with..........interest on that sum at the rate of..........annually from the date of service, together with the expenses of bringing the action.

**Rule 4.1(2)**                                        FORM 3

Form of claim in a summons for recovery of possession of heritable property The pursuer claims that, in the circumstances described in the statement contained on page 2 of this copy summons, he is entitled to recover possession of the property at (*address*), and that you refuse or delay to remove from said property.

The pursuer therefore asks the court to grant a decree against you, removing you, and your family, sub-tenants and dependants (if any) with your goods and possessions from the said property.

The pursuer also claims from you the expenses of bringing the action.

**Rule 30.6(1)**                                       FORM 3A

Form of notice of removal under sections 34, 35 or 36 of the Sheriff Courts (Scotland) Act 1907

To: (*name, designation and address of party in possession*)

You are hereby required to remove from (*describe subjects*) at the term of (*or, if different terms, state them and the subjects to which they apply*), in terms of (*describe lease, terms of letter of removal or otherwise*).

*(date)*                                                    *(signature, designation and address)*

**Rule 30.6(2)**                             FORM 3B

Form of notice of removal under section 37 of the Sheriff Courts (Scotland) Act 1907

NOTICE OF REMOVAL UNDER SECTION 37 OF THE SHERIFF COURTS (SCOTLAND) ACT 1907

To:...............

*(name, designation and address)*

You are hereby required to remove from (*describe subjects*) at the term of *(Whitsunday or Martinmas)*, *(date)*.

*(date)*                                                    *signature, designation and address*

**Rule 30.6(3)**                             FORM 3C

Form of letter of removal

To: (*name, designation and address*)...............(*place and date*). I am to remove from (describe subjects by usual name or give a short description sufficient for identification) at the term of (*insert term and date*).

*(date)*                                                    *(signature, designation and address)*

**Rule 4.1(2)**                             FORM 4

Form of claim in a summons of sequestration for rent

*[Repealed by the Act of Sederunt (Sheriff Court Rules Amendment) (Diligence) 2008 (SSI 2008/121) r.2(1)(b) (effective April 1, 2008).]*

**Rule 31.2(2)**                             FORM 4A

Notice informing defender of right to apply for certain orders under the Debtors (Scotland) Act 1987

*[Repealed by the Act of Sederunt (Sheriff Court Rules Amendment) (Diligence) 2008 (SSI 2008/121) r.2(1)(b) (effective April 1, 2008).]*

**Rule 31.2(2)**                             FORM 4B

Certificate of Sequestration

*[Repealed by the Act of Sederunt (Sheriff Court Rules Amendment) (Diligence) 2008 (SSI 2008/121) r.2(1)(b) (effective April 1, 2008).]*

**Rule 4.1(2)**                             FORM 5

Form of claim in a summons of multiplepoinding

The pursuer claims that, in the circumstances described in the statement contained on page 2 of this copy summons, the (*state party*) is the holder of a fund (*or subject*) valued at £.......... on which competing claims are being made by the defenders.

The pursuer therefore asks the court to grant a decree finding the holder of the said fund or subject liable to make payment of, or to deliver, same to the party found by the court to be entitled thereto.

The pursuer also asks that the expenses of bringing the action be deducted from the value of the said fund or subject before payment is made.

**Rule 27.5(2)(a)**                             FORM 5A

Form of statement by holder of fund or subject when not the pursuer

(1) I, (*name, address*), hereby state that the fund or subject in the summary cause summons raised at the instance of AB (*design*) against CD, *(EF and GH) (design)* is as follows: (*description and details of fund or subject*).

(2) I have the following claim or lien on said fund or subject (give details, including a reference to any document founded upon in support of the claim).

(3) I am aware that the persons listed below have an interest in the said fund/subject:

(*list names and addresses*)

(4) I certify that I have today intimated a copy of this statement to each of the persons contained in the list at (3) above.

(*date*)

**Rule 27.9(2)(a)**                                             FORM 5B

Form of claim on the fund or subject in action of multiplepoinding

I, EF, claim to be preferred on the fund in the multiplepoinding raised in the name of AB against CD, EF etc. for the sum of £.......... by reason of (*state ground of claim, including a reference to any document founded upon in support thereof*) with interest thereon from (*date*).

I also claim any appropriate court expenses which I may incur by appearing in this action.

(*signature*)

**Rule 4.1(2)**                                             FORM 6

Form of claim in a summons of furthcoming

The pursuer claims that, in the circumstances described in the statement contained on page 2 of this copy summons, the said (*name of common debtor*) is due to him the sum of £...........

He further claims that he has lawfully arrested in the hands of the said (*name of arrestee*) the goods or money valued at £.......... and described in the said statement of claim, which ought to be made furthcoming to him.

He therefore asks the court to order that you make furthcoming and deliver to him the said arrested goods or money or so much thereof as will satisfy (*or part satisfy*) the said sum of £.......... owing to him.

The pursuer also claims from you the expenses of bringing this action. If the value of the arrested funds are insufficient to meet the sum owing to the pursuer plus the expenses of the action, the pursuer claims those expenses from the said (*name of common debtor*).

**Rule 4.1(2)**                                             FORM 7

Form of claim in a summons for delivery

The pursuer claims that, in the circumstances described in the statement contained on page 2 of this copy summons, he has right to the possession of the article(s) described therein.

He therefore asks the court to grant a decree ordering you to deliver the said articles to the pursuer.

Alternatively, if you do not deliver said articles, the pursuer asks the court to grant a decree ordering you to pay to him the sum of £.......... with interest on that sum at the rate of.......... % annually from (*date*) until payment.

The pursuer also claims from you the expenses of bringing the action.

**Rule 4.1(2)**                                             FORM 8

Form of claim in a summons for implement of an obligation

The pursuer claims that, in the circumstances described in the statement contained on page 2 of this copy summons, you are obliged to

He therefore asks the court to grant a decree ordering you to implement the said obligation.

Alternatively, if you do not fulfil the obligation, the pursuer asks the court to grant a decree ordering you to pay to him the sum of £.......... with interest on that sum at the rate of.......... % annually from (*date*) until payment.

The pursuer also claims from you the expenses of bringing the action.

**Rule 4.1(2)**                                             FORM 9

Form of claim in a summons for count, reckoning and payment

The pursuer claims that, in the circumstances described in the statement contained on page 2 of this copy summons, you have intromitted with (*describe briefly the fund or estate*), in which he has an interest.

He therefore asks the court to grant a decree ordering you to produce a full account of your intromissions therewith, and for payment to him of the sum of £.......... , or such other sum as appears to the court to be the true balance due by you, with interest thereon at the rate of.......... % annually from (*date*) until payment.

Alternatively, if you do not produce such an account, the pursuer asks the court to grant a decree ordering you to pay to him the said sum of £.......... with interest thereon at the rate of.......... % annually from (*date*) until payment.

The pursuer also claims from you the expenses of bringing the action.

**Rule 34.2(2)** FORM 10 [1]

Form of statement of claim in a personal injuries action

1. The pursuer is (*state designation, address, occupation, date of birth and National Insurance number (where applicable) of the pursuer*). (*In an action arising out of the death of a relative state designation of the deceased and relation to the pursuer*).
2. The defender is (*state designation, address and occupation of the defender*).
3. The court has jurisdiction to hear this claim against the defender because (*state briefly ground of jurisdiction*).
4. (*State briefly the facts necessary to establish the claim*).
5. (*State briefly the personal injuries suffered and the heads of claim. Give names and addresses of medical practitioners and hospitals or other institutions in which the person injured received treatment*).
6. (*State whether claim based on fault at common law or breach of statutory duty; if breach of statutory duty, state provision of enactment*).

**Rules 34.3(2) and 34.4(1)** FORM 10A [2]

Form of response (action for damages: personal injuries)

Court ref. no:

SHERIFFDOM OF (*insert name of sheriffdom*)
AT (*insert place of sheriff court*)
*in the cause*
[A.B.], (*insert name and address*), Pursuer
against
[C.D.], (*insert name and address*), Defender
RESPONSE TO STATEMENT OF CLAIM

| Question | Response |
|---|---|
| 1. Is it intended to dispute the description and designation of the pursuer? If so, why? | |
| 2. Is the description and designation of the defender disputed? If so, why? | |
| 3. Is there any dispute that the court has jurisdiction to hear the claim? If so, why? | |
| 4. (a) State which facts in paragraph 4 of the statement of claim are admitted. | |
| (b) State any facts regarding the circumstances of the claim upon which the defender intends to rely. | |
| 5. (a) State whether the nature and extent of the pursuer's injuries is disputed and whether medical reports can be agreed. | |
| (b) If the defender has a medical report upon which he or she intends to rely to contradict the pursuer's report in any way, state the details. | |
| (c) State whether the claims for other losses are disputed in whole or in part. | |

---

[1] As inserted by the Act of Sederunt (Summary Cause Rules Amendment) (Personal Injuries Actions) 2012 (SSI 2012/144) para.2 (effective September 1, 2012; not applicable to an action raised before September 1, 2012).

[2] As inserted by the Act of Sederunt (Summary Cause Rules Amendment) (Personal Injuries Actions) 2012 (SSI 2012/144) para.2 (effective September 1, 2012; not applicable to an action raised before September 1, 2012).

| Question | Response |
|---|---|
| 6. (a) Does the defender accept that the common law duty or duties in the statement of claim were incumbent upon them in the circumstances? If not, state why. | |
| (b) Does the defender accept that the statutory duty or duties alleged in the statement of claim were incumbent upon them in the circumstances? If not, state why. | |
| (c) State any other provisions or propositions upon which the defender proposes to rely in relation to the question of their liability for the accident including, if appropriate, details of any allegation of contributory negligence. | |
| (d) Does the defender allege that the accident was caused by any other wrongdoer? If so, give details. | |
| (e) Does the defender allege that they are entitled to be indemnified or relieved from any liability they might have to the pursuer? If so, give details. | |
| 7. Does the defender intend to pursue a counter-claim against the pursuer? If so, give details. | |

*(Insert date)*                              *(signature, designation and address)*

**Rules 34.2(3)(b)** and **34.4(2)(b)**                    FORM 10B [1]

Form of order of court for recovery of documents in personal injuries action

Court ref. no:

SHERIFFDOM OF *(insert name of sheriffdom)*

AT *(insert place of sheriff court)*

SPECIFICATION OF DOCUMENTS

*in the cause*

[A.B.], *(insert name and address)*, Pursuer

against

[C.D.], *(insert name and address)*, Defender

To: *(insert name and address of party or parties from whom the following documents are sought to be recovered)*.

You are hereby required to produce to the sheriff clerk at *(insert address)* within seven days of the service on you of this Order:

*[Insert such of the following calls as are required]*

1. All books, medical records, reports, charts, X-rays, notes and other documents of *(specify the name of each medical practitioner or general practitioner practice named in summons in accordance with* rule 34.2(2)(b))*, and relating to the pursuer *[or, as the case may be, the deceased]* from *(insert date)*, in order that excerpts may be taken therefrom at the sight of the Commissioner of all entries showing or tending to show the nature, extent and cause of the pursuer's *[or, as the case may be, the deceased's]* injuries when he or she attended his or her doctor on or after *(specify date)* and the treatment received by him or her since that date.

2. All books, medical records, reports, charts, X-rays, notes and other documents of *(specify, in separate calls, the name of each hospital or other institution named in summons in accordance with* rule 34.2(2)(b))*, and relating to the pursuer *[or, as the case may be, the deceased]* from *(insert date)*, in order that excerpts may be taken therefrom at the sight of the Commissioner of all entries showing or tending to show the nature, extent and cause of the pursuer's *[or, as the case may be, the deceased's]* injuries when he or she was admitted to that institution on or about *(specify date)*, the treatment received by him or her since that date and his or her certificate of discharge, if any.

3. The medical records and capability assessments held by the defender's occupational health department relating to the pursuer *[or, as the case may be, the deceased]*, except insofar as prepared for or in

---

[1] As inserted by the Act of Sederunt (Summary Cause Rules Amendment) (Personal Injuries Actions) 2012 (SSI 2012/144) para.2 (effective September 1, 2012; not applicable to an action raised before September 1, 2012).

contemplation of litigation, in order that excerpts may be taken therefrom at the sight of the Commissioner of all entries showing or tending to show the nature and extent of any injuries, symptoms and conditions from which the pursuer [or, as the case may be, the deceased] was suffering and the nature of any assessment and diagnosis made thereof on or subsequent to (specify date).

4. All wage books, cash books, wage sheets, computer records and other earnings information relating to the pursuer [or, as the case may be, the deceased] (N.I. number (specify number)) held by or on behalf of (specify employer), for the period (specify dates commencing not earlier than 26 weeks prior to the date of the accident or the first date of relevant absence, as the case may be) in order that excerpts may be taken therefrom at the sight of the Commissioner of all entries showing or tending to show—

(a)    the pursuer's [or, as the case may be, the deceased's] earnings, both gross and net of income tax and employee National Insurance Contributions, over the said period;

(b)    the period or periods of the pursuer's [or, as the case may be, the deceased's] absence from employment over the said period and the reason for absence;

(c)    details of any increases in the rate paid over the period (specify dates) and the dates on which any such increases took effect;

(d)    the effective date of, the reasons for and the terms (including any terms relative to any pension entitlement) of the termination of the pursuer's [or, as the case may be, the deceased's] employment;

(e)    the nature and extent of contributions (if any) to any occupational pension scheme made by the pursuer [or, as the case may be, the deceased] and his or her employer;

(f)    the pursuer's present entitlement (if any) to any occupational pension and the manner in which said entitlement is calculated.

5. All accident reports, memoranda or other written communications made to the defender or anyone on his or her behalf by an employee of the defender who was present at or about the time at which the pursuer [or, as the case may be, the deceased] sustained the injuries in respect of which the summons in this cause was issued and relevant to the matters contained in the statement of claim.

6. Any assessment current at the time of the accident referred to in the summons or at the time of the circumstances referred to in the summons giving rise to the cause of action (as the case may be) undertaken by or on behalf of the defender for the purpose of regulation 3 of the Management of Health and Safety at Work Regulations 1992 and subsequently regulation 3 of the Management of Health and Safety at Work Regulations 1999 [or (specify the regulations or other legislative provision under which the risk assessment is required)] in order that excerpts may be taken therefrom at the sight of the Commissioner of all entries relating to the risks posed to workers [or (specify the matters set out in the statement of claim to which the risk assessment relates)].

7. Failing principals, drafts, copies or duplicates of the above or any of them.

Date (insert date of posting or other method of    (Insert signature, name and business address of
service)    the agent for the pursuer)

**NOTES:**

1. The documents recovered will be considered by the parties to the action and they may or may not be lodged with the sheriff clerk. A written receipt will be given or sent to you by the sheriff clerk, who may thereafter allow them to be inspected by the parties. The party in whose possession the documents are will be responsible for their safekeeping.

2. Payment may be made, within certain limits, in respect of claims for outlays incurred in relation to the production of documents. Claims should be made in writing to the person who has obtained an order that you produce the documents.

3. If you claim that any of the documents produced by you is **confidential** you must still produce such documents but may place them in a separate sealed packet by themselves, marked "CONFIDENTIAL". Any party who wishes to open the sealed packet must apply to the sheriff by incidental application. A party who makes such an application must intimate the application to you.

4. Subject to paragraph 3 above, you may produce these documents by sending them by registered post or by recorded delivery service, or by hand delivery to the sheriff clerk at (insert address).

**CERTIFICATE**

I hereby certify with reference to the above order of the sheriff at (insert name of sheriff court) in the case (insert court reference number) and the enclosed specification of documents, served on me and marked respectively X and Y—

1. That the documents which are produced and which are listed in the enclosed inventory signed by me and marked Z, are all the documents in my possession falling within the specification.

*or*

That I have no documents in my possession falling within the specification.

2. That, to the best of my knowledge and belief, there are in existence other documents falling within the specification, but not in my possession. These documents are as follows—(*describe them by reference to the descriptions of documents in the specification*). They were last seen by me on or about (*date*), at (*place*), in the hands of (*insert name and address of the person*).

*or*

That I know of the existence of no documents in the possession of any person, other than me, which fall within the specification.

(*Insert date*)          (*Signed*)

                                        (*Name and address*)

**Rule 34.5(2)**                 FORM 10C [1]

Form of docquet for deemed grant of recovery of documents in a personal injuries action

Court ref. no:

Court (*insert court*)

Commission and diligence for the production and recovery of the documents called for in this specification of documents is deemed to have been granted.

Date (*insert date*)           (*Signed*)

                                 Sheriff Clerk (depute)

**Rule 34.7(1)(c) and (4)**            FORM 10D [2]

Form of timetable

Court ref. no:

TIMETABLE

*in the cause*

[A.B.], (*insert name and address*), Pursuer

against

[C.D.], (*insert name and address*), Defender

This timetable has effect as if it were an interlocutor of the sheriff.

1. The diet allocated for the proof in this action will begin on (*date*). Subject to any variation under rule 34.8, this order requires the parties to undertake the conduct of this action within the periods specified in paragraphs 2 to 10 below.

2. An application under rule 11.1 (third party procedure) shall be made by (*date*).

3. Where the pursuer has obtained a commission and diligence for the recovery of documents by virtue of rule 34.5, the pursuer shall serve the order not later than (*date*).

4. For the purposes of rule 34.7(2)(c), the adjustment period shall end on (*date*).

5. The pursuer shall lodge with the sheriff clerk a statement of valuation of claim under rule 34.9 not later than (*date*).

6. The pursuer shall lodge with the sheriff clerk a certified adjusted statement of claim not later than (*date*).

7. The defender (and any third party to the action) shall lodge with the sheriff clerk a certified adjusted response to statement of claim not later than (*date*).

8. The defender (and any third party to the action) shall lodge with the sheriff clerk a statement of valuation of claim under rule 34.9 not later than (*date*).

9. Not later than (*date*) the parties shall lodge with the sheriff clerk lists of witnesses and productions.

10. Not later than (*date*) the pursuer shall lodge with the sheriff clerk a pre-proof minute under rule 34.10.

(*Insert date*)          (*Signed*)

                                 Sheriff Clerk (depute)

---

[1] As inserted by the Act of Sederunt (Summary Cause Rules Amendment) (Personal Injuries Actions) 2012 (SSI 2012/144) para.2 (effective September 1, 2012; not applicable to an action raised before September 1, 2012).

[2] As inserted by the Act of Sederunt (Summary Cause Rules Amendment) (Personal Injuries Actions) 2012 (SSI 2012/144) para.2 (effective September 1, 2012; not applicable to an action raised before September 1, 2012).

**Rule 34.9**                                                                    FORM 10E[1]

Form of statement of valuation of claim

Court ref. no:

SHERIFFDOM OF (*insert name of sheriffdom*)

AT (*insert place of sheriff court*)
STATEMENT OF VALUATION OF CLAIM
*in the cause*
[A.B.], (*insert name and address*), Pursuer
against
[C.D.], (*insert name and address*), Defender

| Head of Claim | Components | Valuation |
|---|---|---|
| Solatium | Past | £x |
| | Future | £x |
| Interest on past solatium | Percentage applied to past solatium (*state percentage rate*) | £x |
| Past wage loss | Date from which wage loss claimed: (*date*) | £x |
| | Date to which wage loss claimed: (*date*) | |
| | Rate of net wage loss (*per week, per month or per annum*) | |
| Interest on past wage loss | Percentage applied to past wage loss: (*state percentage rate*) | £x |
| Future wage loss | Multiplier: (*state multiplier*) | £x |
| | Multiplicand: (*state multiplicand and show how calculated*) | |
| | Discount factor applied (if appropriate): (*state factor*) | |
| | Or specify any other method of calculation | |
| Past services | Date from which services claimed: (*date*) | £x |
| | Date to which services claimed: (*date*) | |
| | Nature of services: (............) | |
| | Person by whom services provided: (............) | |
| | Hours per week services provided: (............) | |
| | Net hourly rate claimed: (..........) | |
| | Total amount claimed: (..........) | |
| | Interest | |
| Future loss of capacity to provide personal services | Multiplier: (*insert multiplier*) | £x |
| | Multiplicand: (*insert multiplicand, showing how calculated*) | |
| Needs and other expenses | One off | £x |
| | Multiplier: (*insert multiplier*) | |
| | Multiplicand: (*insert multiplicand*) | |
| | Interest | |

---

[1] As inserted by the Act of Sederunt (Summary Cause Rules Amendment) (Personal Injuries Actions) 2012 (SSI 2012/144) para.2 (effective September 1, 2012; not applicable to an action raised before September 1, 2012).

| Head of Claim | Components | Valuation |
|---|---|---|
| Any other heads as appropriate (*specify*) | | £x |
| Total | | £x (*insert total valuation of claim*) |
| List of Supporting Documents:— | | |

(*Insert date*)                                        (*Signed*)

(*Name and address*)

**Rule 34.10(2)**                                  FORM 10F [1]

Minute of pre-proof conference

Court ref. no.:

SHERIFFDOM OF (*insert sheriffdom*)

AT (*insert place of sheriff court*)

JOINT MINUTE OF PRE-PROOF CONFERENCE

in the cause

[*A.B.*], Pursuer

against

[*C.D.*], Defender

[E.F.] for the pursuer and

[G.H.] for the defender hereby state to the court:

1. That the pre-proof conference was held in this case [*at (place) or by (telephone conference or video conference or other remote means)*] on [*date*].

2. That the following persons were present—

(*State names and designations of persons attending conference*)

3. That the following persons were available to provide instructions by telephone or video conference—

(*State names and designations or persons available to provide instructions by telephone or video conference*)

4. That the persons participating in the conference discussed settlement of the action.

5. That the following questions were addressed—

**Section 1**

|  |  | Yes | No |
|---|---|---|---|
| 1. | Is the diet of proof still required? | | |
| 2. | If the answer to question 1 is "yes", does the defender admit liability? (If "no", complete section 2) | | |
|  | If yes, does the defender plead contributory negligence? | | |
|  | If yes, is the degree of contributory negligence agreed? | | |
|  | If yes, state % degree of fault attributed to the pursuer. | | |
| 3. | If the answer to question 1 is "yes", is the quantum of damages agreed? (If "no", complete section 3) | | |

**Section 2**

[*To be inserted only if the proof is still required*]

It is estimated that the hearing will last [*insert number*] [*days/hours*].

*NB. If the estimate is more than one day then this should be brought to the attention of the sheriff clerk. This may affect prioritisation of the case.*

---

[1] As inserted by the Act of Sederunt (Summary Cause Rules Amendment) (Personal Injuries Actions) 2012 (SSI 2012/144) para.2 (effective September 1, 2012; not applicable to an action raised before September 1, 2012).

During the course of the pre-proof conference, the pursuer called on the defender to agree certain facts, questions of law and matters of evidence.

Those calls, and the defender's responses, are as follows—

| Call | Response | |
|------|----------|--|
| | *Admitted* | *Denied* |
| 1. | | |
| 2. | | |
| 3. | | |
| 4. | | |

During the course of the pre-proof conference, the defender called on the pursuer to agree certain facts, questions of law and matters of evidence.

Those calls, and the pursuer's responses, are as follows—

| Call | Response | |
|------|----------|--|
| | *Admitted* | *Denied* |
| 1. | | |
| 2. | | |
| 3. | | |
| 4. | | |

**Section 3**

Quantum of damages

Please indicate where agreement has been reached on an element of damages

| Head of claim | Components | Not agreed | Agreed at |
|---------------|-----------|------------|-----------|
| Solatium | Past Future | | |
| Interest on past solatium | Percentage applied to past solatium (*state percentage*) | | |
| Past wage loss | Date from which wage loss claimed | | |
| | Date to which wage loss claimed | | |
| | Rate of net wage loss (*per week, per month or per annum*) | | |
| Interest on past wage loss | | | |
| Future wage loss | Multiplier | | |
| | Multiplicand (*showing how calculated*) | | |
| Past necessary services | Date from which services claimed | | |
| | Date to which services claimed | | |
| | Hours per week services provided | | |
| | Net hourly rate claimed | | |
| Past personal services | Date from which services claimed | | |
| | Date to which services claimed | | |
| | Hours per week services provided | | |
| | Net hourly rate claimed | | |
| Interest on past services | | | |

| Head of claim | Components | Not agreed | Agreed at |
|---|---|---|---|
| Future necessary services | Multiplier | | |
| | Multiplicand (*showing how calculated*) | | |
| Future personal services | Multiplier | | |
| | Multiplicand (*showing how calculated*) | | |
| Needs and other expenses | One off | | |
| | Multiplier | | |
| | Multiplicand (*showing how calculated*) | | |
| Any other heads as appropriate (specify) | | | |

(*Insert date of signature*)                    (*Signed by each party/his or her solicitor*)

**Rule 34.12(5)**                              FORM 10G[1]

Form of intimation to connected persons

Court ref. no:

SHERIFFDOM OF (*insert sheriffdom*)
AT (*insert place of sheriff court*)
in the cause
[*A.B.*], Pursuer
against
[*C.D.*], Defender

To: (*insert name and address as in warrant*)

You are hereby given notice that an action has been raised in the above sheriff court against (*insert name of defender*), by your (*insert relationship, e.g. father, brother or other relative as the case may be*). A copy of the summons is attached.

It is believed that you may have a title or interest to sue (*name of defender*) in this action, which is based upon (*the injuries from which the late (insert name and designation) died) (or the death of the late (insert name and designation)*). You may therefore be entitled to enter this action as an additional pursuer. This may be done by lodging an incidental application with the sheriff clerk at (*insert address of sheriff court*).

If you wish to appear as a party in the action, or are uncertain about what action to take, you should contact a solicitor. You may, depending on your financial circumstances, be entitled to legal aid, and you can get information about legal aid from a solicitor.

You may also obtain advice from any Citizen's Advice Bureau, other advice agency or any sheriff clerk's office.

(*Insert date of signature*)                    (*Signed*)

(*Solicitor for the pursuer*)

**Rule 34.13(2)**                              FORM 10H[2]

Form of claim for provisional damages

Court ref. no:

SHERIFFDOM OF (*insert sheriffdom*)
AT (*insert place of sheriff court*)
in the cause
[*A.B.*], Pursuer

---

[1] As inserted by the Act of Sederunt (Summary Cause Rules Amendment) (Personal Injuries Actions) 2012 (SSI 2012/144) para.2 (effective September 1, 2012; not applicable to an action raised before September 1, 2012).

[2] As inserted by the Act of Sederunt (Summary Cause Rules Amendment) (Personal Injuries Actions) 2012 (SSI 2012/144) para.2 (effective September 1, 2012; not applicable to an action raised before September 1, 2012).

against

[*C.D.*], Defender

For payment to the pursuer by the defender of the sum of (*amount in words and figures*) as provisional damages under section 12(2)(a) of the Administration of Justice Act 1982.

(*Statements to include that there is a risk that the pursuer will as result of the act or omission which gave rise to the cause of action develop serious disease or serious deterioration of condition in the future; and that the defender was, at the time of the act or omission which gave rise to the cause of action, a public authority, public corporation or insured or otherwise indemnified in respect of the claim*).

(*Insert date of signature*)　　　　　　　　　　(*Signed*)

　　　　　　　　　　　　　　　　　　　　　　(*Solicitor for the pursuer*)

**Rule 34.13(3)**　　　　　　　　　　　FORM 10I[1]

Form of application for further damages

Court ref. no:

SHERIFFDOM OF (*insert sheriffdom*)
AT (*insert place of sheriff court*)
APPLICATION FOR FURTHER DAMAGES
in the cause
[*A.B.*], Pursuer
against
[*C.D.*], Defender

The pursuer claims payment from the defender of the sum (*insert amount* in words and figures) as further damages under section 12(2)(b) of the Administration of Justice Act 1982.

(*Insert concise statement of facts supporting claim for further damages*).

The pursuer requests the sheriff to fix a hearing on this incidental application and applies for warrant to serve the application on—

(*Here state names and addresses of other parties to the action; and, where such other parties are insured or otherwise indemnified, their insurers or indemnifiers, if known to the pursuer*).

(*Insert date of signature*)　　　　　　　　　　(*Signed*)

　　　　　　　　　　　　　　　　　　　　　　(*Solicitor for the pursuer*)

**Rule 34.13(4)**　　　　　　　　　　　FORM 10J[2]

Form of application for further damages

Court ref. no:

SHERIFFDOM OF (*insert sheriffdom*)
AT (*insert place of sheriff court*)
APPLICATION FOR FURTHER DAMAGES
in the cause
[*A.B.*], Pursuer
against
[*C.D.*], Defender

To:

TAKE NOTICE

(*Pursuer's name and address*), pursuer, raised an action against (*defender's name and address*), defender, in the sheriff court at (*insert name of sheriff court*).

In the action, the sheriff on (*date*) made an award of provisional damages in accordance with section 12(2)(a) of the Administration of Justice Act 1982 in favour of the pursuer against (*you or name of party*). [The sheriff specified that the pursuer may apply for an award of further damages under section

---

[1] As inserted by the Act of Sederunt (Summary Cause Rules Amendment) (Personal Injuries Actions) 2012 (SSI 2012/144) para.2 (effective September 1, 2012; not applicable to an action raised before September 1, 2012).

[2] As inserted by the Act of Sederunt (Summary Cause Rules Amendment) (Personal Injuries Actions) 2012 (SSI 2012/144) para.2 (effective September 1, 2012; not applicable to an action raised before September 1, 2012).

12(2)(b) of that Act at any time before (*date*)]. The pursuer has applied by incidental application for an award of further damages against you [or name of party]. A copy of the incidental application is attached.

A hearing on the incidental application has been fixed for (*date and time*) at (*place of sheriff court*). If you wish to be heard on the incidental application, you should attend or be represented at court on that date.

| | |
|---|---|
| (*Insert date of signature*) | (*Signed*) |
| | (*Solicitor for the pursuer*) |

**Rule 5.3(1)** FORM 11

Form of service

XY, you are hereby served with a copy of the above (or attached) summons.

(*signature of solicitor or sheriff officer*)

**Rule 5.3(2)** FORM 12

Form of certificate of execution of service

Case name:

Court ref: no:

(*Place and date*)...............

I,..........,hereby certify that on the..........day of.........., 20..........,I duly cited XY to answer the foregoing summons. This I did by (*set forth the mode of service*).

(*Signature of solicitor or sheriff officer*)

**Rule 5.5(1)(a)** FORM 13

Service on person whose address is unknown Form of advertisement

A summary cause action has been raised in the sheriff court at..........by AB, pursuer against CD, defender, whose last known address was..........

If the said CD wishes to defend the action he should immediately contact the sheriff clerk's office at the above court.

Address of court:
Telephone no:
Fax no:
E-mail address:

**Rule 5.5(1)(b)** FORM 14

Service on person whose address is unknown

Form of notice to be displayed on the walls of court

A summary cause action has been raised in this court by AB, pursuer against CD, defender, whose last known address was...............

If the said CD wishes to defend the action he should immediately contact the sheriff clerk's office.

| | |
|---|---|
| (*Date*) | Displayed on the walls of court of this date. |

Sheriff clerk depute

**Rule 5.6(2)** FORM 15

Service by post—form of notice

This letter contains a citation to or intimation from the sheriff court at..........

If delivery cannot be made the letter must be returned immediately to the sheriff clerk at (*insert full address*).

**Rule 6.A2(2)** FORM 15A [1]

Statement to accompany application for interim diligence

---

[1] As inserted by the Act of Sederunt (Sheriff Court Rules Amendment) (Diligence) 2008 (SSI 2008/ 121) r.6(9) (effective April 1, 2008).

DEBTORS (SCOTLAND) ACT 1987 Section 15D [or DEBT ARRANGEMENT AND ATTACH-
MENT (SCOTLAND) ACT 2002 Section 9C]

Sheriff Court:...............

In the Cause (Cause Reference No. )

[A.B.] (*designation and address*)

Pursuer

against

[C.D.] (*designation and address*)

Defender

STATEMENT

1. The applicant is the pursuer [*or* defender] in the action by [A.B] (*design*) against [C.D.] (*design*).

2. [The following persons have an interest [*specify names and addresses*].]

3. The application is [*or* is not] seeking the grant under section 15E(1) of the 1987 Act of warrant for diligence [or section 9D(1) of the 2002 Act of interim attachment] in advance of a hearing on the application.

4. [*Here provide such other information as may be prescribed by regulations made by the Scottish Ministers under* section 15D(2)(d) of the 1987 Act *or* 9C(2)(d,) of the 2002 Act]

(*Signed*)

Solicitor [*or* Agent] for A.B. [*or* C.D.]

(*include full designation*)

**Rule 6.A8**                                    FORM 15B [1]

Form of schedule of arrestment on the dependence

SCHEDULE OF ARRESTMENT ON THE DEPENDENCE

**Rule 6.A8**                                    FORM 15C [2]

Form of certificate of execution of arrestment on the dependence

CERTIFICATE OF EXECUTION

* by affixing the schedule of arrestment to the door at (*place*) on (*date*). (*Specify that enquiry made and that reasonable grounds exist for believing that the person on whom service is to be made resides at the place but is not available*) [and by posting a copy of the schedule to the arrestee by registered post or first class recorded delivery to the address specified on the receipt annexed to this certificate].

* by leaving the schedule of arrestment with (*name and occupation of person with whom left*) at (*place of business*) on (*date*).[and by posting a copy of the schedule to the arrestee by registered post or first class recorded delivery to the address specified on the receipt annexed to this certificate].

* by depositing the schedule of arrestment at (*place of business*) on (*date*). (*Specify that enquiry made and that reasonable grounds exist for believing that the person on whom service is to be made carries on business at that place.*) [and by posting a copy of the schedule to the arrestee by registered post or first class recorded delivery to the address specified on the receipt annexed to this certificate].

* by affixing the schedule of arrestment to the door at (*place of business*) on (*date*). (*Specify that enquiry made and that reasonable grounds exist for believing that the person on whom service is to be made carries on business at that place.*) [and by posting a copy of the schedule to the arrestee by registered post or first class recorded delivery to the address specified on the receipt annexed to this certificate].

* by leaving the schedule of arrestment at (*registered office*) on (*date*), in the hands of (*name of person*) [and by posting a copy of the schedule to the arrestee by registered post or first class recorded delivery to the address specified on the receipt annexed to this certificate].

* by depositing the schedule of arrestment at (*registered office*) on (*date*) [and by posting a copy of the schedule to the arrestee by registered post or first class recorded delivery to the address specified on the receipt annexed to this certificate].

---

[1] As inserted by the Act of Sederunt (Sheriff Court Rules Amendment) (Diligence) 2008 (SSI 2008/121) r.6(9) (effective April 1, 2008) and substituted by the Act of Sederunt (Sheriff Court Rules Amendment) (Diligence) 2009 (SSI 2009/107) (effective April 22, 2009).

[2] As inserted by the Act of Sederunt (Sheriff Court Rules Amendment) (Diligence) 2008 (SSI 2008/121) r.6(9) (effective April 1, 2008) and substituted by the Act of Sederunt (Sheriff Court Rules Amendment) (Diligence) 2009 (SSI 2009/107) (effective April 22, 2009).

* by affixing the schedule of arrestment to the door at (*registered office*) on (*date*). [and by posting a copy of the schedule to the arrestee by registered post or first class recorded delivery to the address specified on the receipt annexed to this certificate].

I did this in the presence of (*name, occupation and address of witness*).

(*Signed*)
Sheriff Officer
(*Address*)
(*Signed*)
(Witness)

*Delete where not applicable

**NOTE**

**A copy of the Schedule of arrestment on the dependence is to be attached to this certificate.**

**Rule 6.3(4)(a)**                                                              FORM 16

Recall or restriction of arrestment
Certificate authorising the release of arrested funds or property

Sheriff court, (*place*)..............

Court ref. no.:...........AB (pursuer) against CD (defender)

I, (*name*), hereby certify that the sheriff on (*date*) authorised the release of the funds or property arrested on the *dependence of the action/counterclaim/third party notice to the following extent:

(*details of sheriff's order*)

(*Date*)                                                    Sheriff clerk depute

*delete as appropriate

Copy to:
Party instructing arrestment
Party possessing arrested funds/property

**Rule 7.1(1)**                                                                FORM 17

Form of minute—no form of response lodged by defender

Sheriff court, (*place*)..............

Calling date:..............

In respect that the defender(s) has/have failed to lodge a form of response to the summons, the pursuer respectfully craves the court to make the orders specified in the following case(s):

Court ref. No                 Name(s) of defender(s)                          Minute(s)

**Rule 7.1(2)**                                                                FORM 18 [1]

Form of minute—pursuer not objecting to application for a time to pay direction or time order

Sheriff court, (*place*)..............

Court ref. no.:..............

Name(s) of defender(s)..............

Calling date:..............

I do not object to the defender's application for
*a time to pay direction
*recall or restriction of an arrestment
*a time order

The pursuer requests the court to grant decree or other order in terms of the following minute(s)

*delete as appropriate

FORM 19 [2]

Rule 7.2(4)

---

[1] As amended by the Act of Sederunt (Ordinary Cause, Summary Application, Summary Cause and Small Claim Rules) Amendment (Miscellaneous) 2003 (SSI 2003/26) r.4(4)(b) (effective January 24, 2003).

[2] As substituted by the Act of Sederunt (Sheriff Court Rules) (Miscellaneous Amendments) 2009 (SSI 2009/294) r.4 (effective December 1, 2009).

Form of minute—pursuer opposing an application for a time to pay direction or time order

**Sheriff court (place):...............**

**Court ref no:...............**

Name(s) of defender(s):...............

Calling date:...............

I oppose the defender's application for

*a time to pay direction

*recall or restriction of arrestment

*a time order

* *delete as appropriate*

1. The debt is (*please specify the nature of the debt*).

2. The debt was incurred on (*specify date*) and the pursuer has contacted the defender in relation to the debt on (*specify date(s)*).

*3. The contractual payments were (*specify amount*).

*4. (*Specify any action taken by the pursuer to assist the defender to pay the debt*).

*5. The defender has made payment(s) towards the debt of (*specify amount(s)*) on (*specify date(s)*).

*6. The debtor has made offers to pay (*specify amount(s)*) on (*specify date(s)*) which offer(s) was [were] accepted] [or rejected] and (*specify amount*) was paid on (*specify date(s)*).

7. (*Here set out any information you consider relevant to the court's determination of the application*).

8. The pursuer requests the court to grant decree.

* *delete as appropriate*

(*Signed*)

Pursuer [*or* Solicitor for Pursuer]

(*Date*)

Rule 8.12

FORM 20

Form of oath for witnesses

I swear by Almighty God that I will tell the truth, the whole truth and nothing but the truth.

Rule 8.12

FORM 21

Form of affirmation for witnesses

I solemnly, sincerely and truly declare and affirm that I will tell the truth, the whole truth and nothing but the truth.

Rule 11.2(1)(b)(iii)

FORM 22

Form of third party notice

Court ref. no.

SHERIFF COURT, (*place*)

THIRD PARTY NOTICE

in the cause

(AB) (*insert designation and address*), pursuer

against

(CD) (*insert designation and address*), defender

To (EF)

You are given notice by (CD) of an order granted by the sheriff at (*insert place of court*) in which (AB) is the pursuer and (CD) is the defender. A copy of the order is enclosed herewith.

In the action, the pursuer claims from the defender (*insert a brief account of the circumstances of the claim*) as more fully appears in the copy summons enclosed.

The defender claims that,...............(* *delete as appropriate*).

*if he is liable to the pursuer, you are liable to relieve him wholly/partially of his liability, as more fully appears in the copy grounds upon which the defender relies for this, which are also enclosed.

*he is not liable to the pursuer for the claim made against him. He maintains that any liability to the pursuer in respect of this claim rests solely on you, as more fully appears in the copy grounds upon which the defender relies for this, which are also enclosed.

*if he is liable to the pursuer in respect of this claim, he shares that liability with you, as more fully appears in the copy grounds upon which the defender relies for this, which are also enclosed.

*You are liable to him in respect of the claim, as more fully appears in the copy grounds upon which the defender relies for this, which are also enclosed.

If you wish to resist the claim(s) made by the defender as detailed above, you must—

(a) return the form of response enclosed to the sheriff clerk at (*address*) by (*date seven days before the date of hearing*); and

(b) attend or be represented at a hearing on (*date and time*).

(*Date*)...............(*Signature of person serving notice*)

Rule 11.2(1)(b)(iii)

FORM 23

Form of response to third party notice
in the cause

(AB) (*insert designation and address*), pursuer

against

(CD) (*insert designation and address*), defender

I wish to answer the claim made against me by (CD), defender. (*here state briefly the grounds of opposition to the defender's claim.*)

(*date*)

Rule 14A.3(1)

FORM 23A [1]

Form of minute of intervention by the Commission for Equality and Human Rights

SHERIFF COURT, (place)..........Court ref. no...........

**APPLICATION FOR LEAVE TO INTERVENE BY THE COMMISSION FOR EQUALITY AND HUMAN RIGHTS**

in the cause

[A.B.] (designation and address), Pursuer

against

[C.D.] (designation and address), Defender

[Here set out briefly:

(a) the Commission's reasons for believing that the proceedings are relevant to a matter in connection with which the Commission has a function;

(b) the issue in the proceedings which the Commission wishes to address; and

(c) the propositions to be advanced by the Commission and the Commission's reasons for believing that they are relevant to the proceedings and that they will assist the court.]

Rule 14B.2(1)

FORM 23B [2]

Form of minute of intervention by the Scottish Commission for Human Rights

SHERIFF COURT, (place)..........Court ref. no...........

**APPLICATION FOR LEAVE TO INTERVENE BY THE SCOTTISH COMMISSION FOR HUMAN RIGHTS**

in the cause

[A.B.] (designation and address), Pursuer

against

[C.D.] (designation and address), Defender

[Here set out briefly:

(a) the issue in the proceedings which the Commission intends to address; and

(b) a summary of the submission the Commission intends to make.]

Rule 14B.3(1)

FORM 23C[3]

Invitation to the Scottish Commission for Human Rights to intervene

SHERIFF COURT, (place)..........Court ref. no...........

**INVITATION TO THE SCOTTISH COMMISSION FOR HUMAN RIGHTS TO INTERVENE**

in the cause

[A.B.] (designation and address), Pursuer

---

[1] As inserted by the Act of Sederunt (Sheriff Court Rules) (Miscellaneous Amendments) 2008 (SSI 2008/223) Sch.3 (effective July 1, 2008).

[2] As inserted by the Act of Sederunt (Sheriff Court Rules) (Miscellaneous Amendments) 2008 (SSI 2008/223) Sch.3 (effective July 1, 2008).

[3] As inserted by the Act of Sederunt (Sheriff Court Rules) (Miscellaneous Amendments) 2008 (SSI 2008/223) Sch.3 (effective July 1, 2008).

against

[C.D.] (designation and address), Defender

[Here set out briefly:

   (a)   the facts, procedural history and issues in the proceedings;

   (b)   the issue in the proceedings on which the court seeks a submission.]

Rule 18.2(1)

### FORM 24 [1]

Order by the court and certificate in optional procedure for recovery of documents

Sheriff Court, (*place and address*)

In the cause (*court ref. no.*)

in which

AB (*design*) is the pursuer

and

CD (*design*) is the defender

To: (*name and designation of party or haver from whom the documents are sought to be recovered.*)

You are required to produce to the sheriff clerk at (*address*) within..........days of the service upon you of this order:

(1) This order itself (which must be produced intact);

(2) The certificate marked 'B' attached;

(3) All documents within your possession covered by the specification which is enclosed; and

(4) A list of those documents. You can produce the items listed above either:

(a) by delivering them to the sheriff clerk at the address shown above; or

(b) sending them to the sheriff clerk by registered or recorded delivery post.

(*date*)..........(*Signature, name, address and designation of person serving order*)

PLEASE NOTE:

If you claim confidentiality for any of the documents produced by you, you must still produce them. However, they may be placed in a separate envelope by themselves, marked "confidential". The court will, if necessary, decide whether the envelope should be opened or not.

Claims for necessary outlays within certain specified limits may be paid. Claims should be made in writing to the person who has obtained an order that you produce the documents.

CERTIFICATE

B

Sheriff Court, (*place and address*)

In the cause (*court ref. no.*)

in which

AB (*design*) is the pursuer

and

CD (*design*) is the defender.

Order for recovery of documents dated..........

With reference to the above order and relative specification of documents, I certify:

*\* delete as appropriate*

\*that the documents produced herewith and the list signed by me which accompanies them are all the documents in my possession which fall under the specification.

\* I have no documents in my possession falling under the specification.

\* I believe that there are other documents falling within the specification which are not in my possession. These documents are (*list the documents as described in the specification*) These documents were last seen by me on (*date*) in the possession of (*name and address of person/company, if known*).

\* I know of no documents falling within the specification which are in the possession of any other person.

(*name*) (*date*)

Rule 18.7(3)

### FORM 25

Form of minute in an application for letter of request

Sheriff Court, (*place and address*)

---

[1] As substituted by Act of Sederunt (Ordinary Cause, Summary Application, Summary Cause and Small Claim Rules) Amendment (Miscellaneous) 2005 (SSI 2005/648) (effective January 2, 2006).

MINUTE
for (*designation*)
In the cause (court ref. no.)
in which
AB (*design*) is the pursuer
and
CD (*design*) is the defender.

The minuter states to the court that the evidence specified in the proposed letter of request lodged with this minute is required for the purpose of this cause. The minuter respectfully asks the court to issue a letter of request in terms of the proposed letter of request to (*central authority of the country or territory in which the evidence is to be obtained*) in order to obtain the evidence so specified.

(*designation of minuter*)

Rule 18.7(3)

FORM 25A
Form of letter of request
PART A—items to be included in every letter of request

1.    Sender                                                (*Identity and address*)..........
      ...............

2.    Central authority of the requested state             (*Identity and address*)..........
      ...............

3.    Persons to whom the executed request is to be        (*Identity and address*)..........
      returned
      ...............

4.    The undersigned applicant has the honour to
      submit the following request:

5.    a. Requesting Judicial authority                     (*Identity and address*)..........
      ...............

      b. To the competent authority                        (*the requested state*)..........
      ...............

6.    Names and addresses of the parties and their
      representatives
      a. pursuer                                           ...............
      b. defender                                          ...............
      c. other parties                                     ...............

7.    Nature and purpose of the proceedings and sum-       ...............
      mary of the facts
      ...............

8.    Evidence to be obtained or other judicial act to be  ...............
      performed
      ...............

PART B—items to be completed where applicable

9.    Identity and address of any person to be examined    ...............
      ...............

10.   Questions to be put to the person to be examined,    (*or, see attached list*)..........
      or statement of the subject matter about which
      they are to be examined
      ...............
      ...............
      ...............

11.   Documents or other property to be inspected          (*specify whether to be produced, copied,
                                                            valued etc.*)...............

944

12. Any requirement that the evidence be given on oath or affirmation and any special form to be used *(in the event that the evidence cannot be taken in the manner requested, specify whether it is to be taken in such manner as provided by local law for the formal taking of evidence)*

13. Special methods or procedure to be followed   ...............
   ...............

14. Request for notification of the time and place for   ............... the execution of the request and identity and address of any person to be notified

   ...............
   ...............
   ...............

15. Request for attendance or participation of judicial   ............... personnel of the requesting authority at the execution of the letter of request

   ...............
   ...............
   ...............

16. Specification of privilege or duty to refuse to give   ............... evidence under the law of the state of origin

   ...............
   ...............

17. The fees and expenses incurred will be borne by   *(identity and address)*..........

   ...............

PART C—to be included in every letter of request

18. Date of request, signature and seal of the request-   ............... ing authority

   ...............

**Rule 18.7A(2)**

FORM 25B [1]

Form of minute in application for taking of evidence in the European Community
Sheriff Court, *(place and address)*

MINUTE
for *(designation)*
In the cause (court ref. no.)
in which
AB *(design)* is the pursuer
and
CD *(design)* is the defender.

The minuter states to the court that the evidence specified in the proposed Form A [or Form I] lodged with this minute is required for the purpose of this cause. The minuter respectfully asks the court to issue that Form to *(specify the applicable court, tribunal, central body or competent authority)* in order to obtain the evidence specified.

Signed *(designation of minuter)*

**Rule 18.8(1)**

FORM 26 [2]

Form of citation of witness or haver

---

[1] As inserted by the Act of Sederunt (Taking of Evidence in the European Community) 2003 (SI 2003/601).

[2] As substituted by the Act of Sederunt (Ordinary Cause, Summary Application, Summary Cause and Small Claim Rules) Amendment (Vulnerable Witnesses (Scotland) Act 2004) 2007 (SSI 2007/463) (effective November 1, 2007).

(*date*)

CITATION

SHERIFFDOM OF (*insert name of sheriffdom*)

AT (*insert place of sheriff court*)

TO [*A.B.*] (design)

(*Name*) who is pursuing/defending a case against (*name*) [*or is a (specify) in the case of (name) against (name)*] has asked you to be a witness. You must attend the above sheriff court on (*insert date*) at (*insert time*) for that purpose, [*and bring with you (specify documents)*].

If you

• would like to know more about being a witness

• are a child under the age of 16

• think you may be a vulnerable witness within the meaning of section 11(1) of the Vulnerable Witnesses (Scotland) Act 2004 (that is someone the court considers may be less able to give their evidence due to mental disorder or fear or distress connected to giving your evidence at the court hearing).

you should contact (*specify the solicitor acting for the party or the party litigant citing the witness*) for further information.

If you are a vulnerable witness (including a child under the age of 16) then you should be able to use a special measure (such measures include use of a screen, a live TV link or a supporter, or a commissioner) to help you give evidence.

**Expenses**

You may claim back money which you have had to spend and any earnings you have lost within certain specified limits, because you have to come to court on the above date. These may be paid to you if you claim within specified time limits. Claims should be made to the person who has asked you to attend court. Proof of any loss of earnings should be given to that person.

If you wish your travelling expenses to be paid before you go to court, you should apply for payment to the person who has asked you to attend court.

**Failure to attend**

**It is very important that you attend court and you should note that failure to do so may result in a warrant being granted for your arrest. In addition, if you fail to attend without any good reason, having requested and been paid your travelling expenses, you may be ordered to pay a penalty not exceeding £250.**

If you have any questions about anything in this citation, please contact (*specify the solicitor acting for the party or the party litigant citing the witness*) for further information.

Signed

[P.Q.] Sheriff Officer

or [X.Y.], (*add designation and business address*)

Solicitor for the pursuer [*or defender*] [*or (specify)*]

Rule 18.8(1)

FORM 26A

Form of certificate of witness citation

I certify that on (*date*) I duly cited AB (*design*) to attend at (*name of court*) on (*date*) at (*time*) as a witness for the (*design party*) in the action at the instance of CD (*design*) against EF (*design*) (and I required him to bring with him ....). This I did by ....

(*Signature of solicitor or sheriff officer*)

**Rule 18A.2**

FORM 26B [1]

Form of child witness notice

VULNERABLE WITNESSES (SCOTLAND) ACT 2004 SECTION 12

Received the..........day of..........20

(*Date of receipt of this notice*)

...............(*signed*)

Sheriff Clerk

CHILD WITNESS NOTICE

Sheriff Court...............20

---

[1] As inserted by the Act of Sederunt (Ordinary Cause, Summary Application, Summary Cause and Small Claim Rules) Amendment (Vulnerable Witnesses (Scotland) Act 2004) 2007 (SSI 2007/463) (effective November 1, 2007).

Court Ref. No.

1. The applicant is the pursuer [or defender] in the action by [A.B.] (*design*) against [C.D.] (*design*).

2. The applicant has cited [or intends to cite] [E.F.] (*date of birth*) as a witness.

3. [E.F.] is a child witnesses under section 11 of the Vulnerable Witnesses (Scotland) Act 2004 [and was under the age of sixteen on the date of the commencement of proceedings].

4. The applicant considers that the following special measure[s] is [are] the most appropriate for the purpose of taking the evidence of [E.F.]*[or that [E.F.] should give evidence without the benefit of any special measure]*:—

(*delete as appropriate and specify any special measure(s) sought*).

5. [(a) The reason][s] this [these] special measure[s] is [are] considered the most appropriate is [are] as follows:—

(*here specify the reason(s) for the special measure(s) sought*).

OR

[(b) The reason][s] it is considered that [E.F.] should give evidence without the benefit of any special measure is [are]:—

(*here explain why it is felt that no special measures are required*).

6. [E.F.] and the parent[s] of *[or person[s] with parental responsibility for]* [E.F.] has [have] expressed the following view[s] on the special measure[s] that is [are] considered most appropriate *[or the appropriateness of [E.F.] giving evidence without the benefit of any special measure]*:—

(*delete as appropriate and set out the views(s) expressed and how they were obtained*)

7. Other information considered relevant to this application is as follows:—

(*here set out any other information relevant to the child witness notice*).

8. The applicant asks the court to —

(a) consider this child witness notice;

(b) make an order authorising the special measure[s] sought;

or

(c) make an order authorising the giving of evidence by [E.F.] without the benefit of special measures.

(*delete as appropriate*)

(*Signed*)

[A.B. *or* C.D.]

[or Representative of A.B. *[or C.D.]]* (*include full designation*)

NOTE: *This form should he suitably adapted where* section 16 of the Act of 2004 *applies.*

FORM 26C[1]

Form of vulnerable witness application

Rule 18A.3

VULNERABLE WITNESSES (SCOTLAND) ACT 2004 Section 12

Received the..........day of..........20..........

(*Date of receipt of this notice*)

..........(*signed*)

Sheriff Clerk

VULNERABLE WITNESS APPLICATION

Sheriff Court................ ..........20..........

Court Ref. No.

1. The applicant is the pursuer *[or defender]* in the action by [A.B] (*design*) against [C.D.] (*design*).

2. The applicant has cited *[or intends to cite]* [E.F.] (*date of birth*) as a witness.

3. The applicant considers that [E.F.] is a vulnerable witness under section 11(1)(b) of the Vulnerable Witnesses (Scotland) Act 2004 for the following reasons:—

(*here specify reasons witness is considered to be a vulnerable witness*).

4. The applicant considers that the following special measure[s] is [are] the most appropriate for the purpose of taking the evidence of [E.F.]:—

(*specify any special measure(s) sought*).

5. The reason[s] this [these] special measure[s] is [are] considered the most appropriate is [are] as follows:—

[1] As inserted by the Act of Sederunt (Ordinary Cause, Summary Application, Summary Cause and Small Claim Rules) Amendment (Vulnerable Witnesses (Scotland) Act 2004) 2007 (SSI 2007/463) (effective November 1, 2007).

*(here specify the reason(s) for the special measures(s) sought).*

6. [E.F.] has expressed the following view[s] on the special mcasure[s] that is [are] considered most appropriate:—

*(set out the views expressed and how they were obtained).*

7. Other information considered relevant to this application is as follows:—

*(here set out any other information relevant to the vulnerable witness application).*

8. The applicant asks the court to—

(a)    consider this vulnerable witness application;

(b)    make an order authorising the special measure[s] sought.

*(Signed)*

[A.B. or CD]

*[or Representative of A.B. [or C.D.]] (include full designation)*

*NOTE: This form should be suitably adapted where section 16 of the Act of 2004 applies.*

FORM 26D[1]

Form of certificate of intimation

Rule 18A.4(2)

VULNERABLE WITNESSES (SCOTLAND) ACT 2004 Section 12

CERTIFICATE OF INTIMATION

Sheriff Court.................... 20

Court Ref. No.

I certify that intimation of the child witness notice *[or vulnerable witness application]* relating to *(insert name of witness)* was made to *(insert names of parties or solicitors for parties, as appropriate)* by *(insert method of intimation; where intimation is by facsimile transmission, insert fax number to which intimation sent)* on *(insert dale of intimation).*

Date:..........

*(Signed)*

Solicitor/or Sheriff Officer

*(include full business designation)*

FORM 26E[2]

Form of application for review

Rule 18A.6(1)

VULNERABLE WITNESSES (SCOTLAND) ACT 2004 Section 13

Received the...........day of.........20.........

*(date of receipt of this notice)*

...............(signed)

Sheriff Clerk

APPLICATION FOR REVIEW OF ARRANGEMENTS FOR VULNERABLE WITNESS

Sheriff Court....................20.....

Court Ref. No.

1.    The applicant is the pursuer *[or* defender] in the action by [A.B.] *(design)* against [C.D.] *(design).*

2.    A proof *[or* hearing] is fixed for *(date)* at *(time).*

3.    [E.F.] is a witness who is to give evidence at, or for the purposes of, the proof *[or* hearing]. [E.F.] is a child witness *[or* vulnerable witness] under section 11 of the Vulnerable Witnesses (Scotland) Act 2004.

4.    The current arrangements for taking the evidence of [E.F.] are *(here specify current arrangements).*

5.    The current arrangements should be reviewed as *(here specify reasons for review).*

6.    [E.F.] [and the parent[s] of *[or* person[s] with parental responsibility for] [E.F.]] has [have] expressed the following view[s] on [the special measure[s] that is [are] considered most ap-

---

[1] As inserted by the Act of Sederunt (Ordinary Cause, Summary Application, Summary Cause and Small Claim Rules) Amendment (Vulnerable Witnesses (Scotland) Act 2004) 2007 (SSI 2007/463) (effective November 1, 2007).

[2] As inserted by the Act of Sederunt (Ordinary Cause, Summary Application, Summary Cause and Small Claim Rules) Amendment (Vulnerable Witnesses (Scotland) Act 2004) 2007 (SSI 2007/463) (effective November 1, 2007).

propriate] *[or* the appropriateness of [E.F.] giving evidence without the benefit of any special measure]:–

*(delete as appropriate and set out the view(s) expressed and how they were obtained).*

7.  The applicant seeks (here specify the order sought).

*(Signed)*

[A.B. or C.D.]

*[or* Representative of A.B. *[or* C.D.]] (*include full designation)*

*NOTE: This form should be suitably adapted where* section 16 of the Act of 2004 *applies.*

FORM 26F[1]

Form of certificate of intimation

Rule 18A.7(2)

VULNERABLE WITNESSES (SCOTLAND) ACT 2004 Section 13

CERTIFICATE OF INTIMATION

Sheriff Court..........................20... ......

Court Ref. No.

I certify that intimation of the review application relating to *(insert name of witness)* was made to *(insert names of parties or solicitors for parties, as appropriate)* by *(insert method of intimation; where intimation is by facsimile transmission, insert fax number to which intimation sent)* on *(insert date of intimation).*

Date:..........

*(Signed)*

Solicitor *[or* Sheriff Officer]

*(include full business designation)*

FORM 27

Form of reference to the European Court

Rule 20.2(2)

REQUEST

for

PRELIMINARY RULING

of

THE COURT OF JUSTICE OF THE EUROPEAN COMMUNITIES

from

THE SHERIFFDOM OF *(insert name of sheriffdom)* at *(insert place of court)*

In the cause

AB *(insert designation and address),*

Pursuer

Against

CD *(insert designation and address)*

Defender

*(Here set out a clear and succinct statement of the case giving rise to the request for a ruling of the European Court in order to enable the European Court to consider and understand the issues of Community law raised and to enable governments of Member states and other interested parties to submit observations. The statement of the case should include:*

(a)  *particulars of the parties;*

(b)  *the history of the dispute between the parties;*

(c)  *the history of the proceedings;*

(d)  *the relevant facts as agreed by the parties or found by the court or, falling such agreement or finding, the contentions of the parties on such facts;*

(e)  *the nature of the issues of law and fact between the parties;*

(f)  *the Scots law, so far as relevant;*

(g)  *the Treaty provisions or other acts, instruments or rules of Community law concerned;*

(h)  *an explanation of why the reference is being made).*

The preliminary ruling of the Court of Justice of the European Communities is accordingly requested on the following questions:

---

[1] As inserted by the Act of Sederunt (Ordinary Cause, Summary Application, Summary Cause and Small Claim Rules) Amendment (Vulnerable Witnesses (Scotland) Act 2004) 2007 (SSI 2007/463) (effective November 1, 2007).

1,2,etc. (*Here set out the question(s) on which the ruling is sought, identifying the Treaty provisions or other acts, instruments or rules of Community law concerned.*)

Dated .........the..........day of..........20

## FORM 28
### Form of extract decree–basic
Rule 23.6(3)

| | |
|---|---|
| Sheriff Court | Court ref. no. |
| Date of decree | *in absence |
| Pursuer(s) | Defender(s) |
| The sheriff | |

and granted decree against..........the for payment of expenses of £..........against the (name of party).
This extract is warrant for all lawful execution thereon.

Date                                                                    Sheriff clerk depute

*delete as appropriate*

## FORM 28A
### Form of extract decree–payment
Rule 23.6(3)

| | |
|---|---|
| Sheriff Court | Court ref. no. |
| Date of decree | *in absence |
| Pursuer(s) | Defender(s) |

The sheriff granted decree against the..........for payment to the..........the undernoted sums:
 (1)   Sum(s) decerned for: £
 (2)   Interest at per cent per year from (*date*) until payment.
 (3)   Expenses of £..........against the (*name of party*).
*A time to pay direction was made under section 1(1) of the Debtors (Scotland) Act 1987.
 *A time order was made under section 129(1) of the Consumer Credit Act 1974.
 *The amount is payable by instalments of £percommencing within
 *days/weeks/months of intimation of this extract decree.
 *The amount is payable by lump sum within*days/weeks/months of intimation of this extract decree.
This extract is warrant for all lawful execution thereon.

Date                                                                    Sheriff clerk depute

*delete as appropriate*

## FORM 28B [1]
### Form of extract decree—recovery of possession of heritable property (no rent arrears)
Rule 23.6(3)

| | |
|---|---|
| Sheriff Court | Court ref. no. |
| Date of decree | *in absence |
| Pursuer(s) | Defender(s) |
| The sheriff | |

 (1)   granted warrant for ejecting the defender (and others mentioned in the summons) from the premises at.........., such ejection being not sooner than (*date*) at 12 noon.
 (2)   granted decree against the defender for payment to the pursuer of the sum of £.......... of expenses.
This extract is warrant for all lawful execution thereon.

Date                                                                    Sheriff clerk depute

Rule 23.6(3)

---

[1] As amended by the Act of Sederunt (Sheriff Court Rules) (Miscellaneous Amendments) 2012 (SSI 2012/188) para.11 (effective August 1, 2012).

FORM 28BA [1]

Form of extract decree—recovery of possession of heritable property in accordance with section 16(5A) of the Housing (Scotland) Act 2001 (non-payment of rent)

| | |
|---|---|
| Sheriff Court | Court ref no. |
| Date of decree | * in absence |
| Pursuer(s) | Defender(s) |

The sheriff—

(1)  granted warrant for ejecting the defender (and others mentioned in the summons) from the premises at (*insert address of premises*) on (*insert date*) and specified a period of (*number*) (*days/weeks/months\**) from that date as the period for which the pursuer's right to eject shall have effect.

(2)  granted decree against the defender for payment to the pursuer of the undernoted sums:
  (a)  Sum(s) decerned for: £(*insert sum*).
  (b)  Interest at (*insert rate of interest*) per cent per year from (*insert date*) until payment.
  (c)  Expenses of £(*insert amount*) against the (*insert name of party*).

*A time to pay direction was made under section 1(1) of the Debtors (Scotland) Act 1987.

*The amount is payable by instalments of £(*insert sum*) per (*insert period*) commencing within (*insert timescale*) *days/weeks/months of intimation of this extract decree.

The amount is payable by lump sum within (*insert timescale*) *days/weeks/months of intimation of this extract decree.

This extract is warrant for all lawful execution thereon.

| | |
|---|---|
| Date | (Sheriff clerk depute) |

*delete as appropriate

FORM 28BB [2, 3]

Rule 23.6(3)

Form of extract decree—recovery of possession of heritable property in other cases (non-payment of rent)

| | |
|---|---|
| Sheriff Court | Court ref no. |
| Date of decree | *in absence |
| Pursuer(s) | Defender(s) |

The sheriff—
(1)  granted warrant for ejecting the defender (and others mentioned in the summons) from the premises at (*insert address of premises*), such ejection being not sooner than (*insert date*) at 12 noon.

(2)  granted decree against the defender for payment to the pursuer of the undernoted sums:
  (a)  Sum(s) decerned for: £(*insert sum*).
  (b)  Interest at (*insert rate of interest*) per cent per year from (*insert date*) until payment.
  (c)  Expenses of £(*insert amount*) against the (*insert name of party*).

*A time to pay direction was made under section 1(1) of the Debtors (Scotland) Act 1987.

*The amount is payable by instalments of £(*insert sum*) per (*insert period*) commencing within (*insert timescale*) *days/weeks/months of intimation of this extract decree.

* The amount is payable by lump sum within (*insert timescale*) *days/weeks/months of intimation of this extract decree.

This extract is warrant for all lawful execution thereon.

| | |
|---|---|
| Date | (*Sheriff clerk depute*) |

*delete as appropriate

---

[1] As inserted by the Act of Sederunt (Sheriff Court Rules) (Miscellaneous Amendments) 2012 (SSI 2012/188) para.11 (effective August 1, 2012).

[2] As inserted by the Act of Sederunt (Sheriff Court Rules) (Miscellaneous Amendments) 2013 (SSI 2013/135) para.3 (effective May 27, 2013).

[3] As amended by the Act of Sederunt (Sheriff Court Rules) (Miscellaneous Amendments) (No.3) 2013 (SSI 2013/171) para.5 (effective June 25, 2013).

## FORM 28C
### Form of extract decree and warrant to sell in sequestration for rent and sale
Rule 23.6(3)

*[Repealed by the Act of Sederunt (Sheriff Court Rules Amendment) (Diligence) 2008 (SSI 2008/121) r.2(1)(b) (effective April 1, 2008).]*

## FORM 28D
### Form of extract—warrant for ejection and to re-let in sequestration for rent and sale
Rule 23.6(3)

*[Repealed by the Act of Sederunt (Sheriff Court Rules Amendment) (Diligence) 2008 (SSI 2008/121) r.2(1)(b) (effective April 1, 2008).]*

## FORM 28E
### Form of extract decree—furthcoming
Rule 23.6(3)

| | |
|---|---|
| Sheriff Court | Court ref. no. |
| Date of decree | *in absence |
| Date of original decree | |
| Pursuer(s) | |
| Defender(s)/Arrestee(s) | |
| Common debtor | |

The sheriff granted decree
(1)  against the arrestee(s) for payment of £, or such other sum(s) as may be owing by the arrestee(s) to the common debtor(s) by virtue of the original decree mentioned above in favour of the pursuer(s) against the common debtor(s).
(2)  for expenses of £

*payable out of the arrested fund.
*payable by the common debtor.

*delete as appropriate*
This extract is warrant for all lawful execution thereon.

Date                                    Sheriff clerk depute

## FORM 28F
### Form of extract decree—delivery
Rule 23.6(3)

| | |
|---|---|
| Sheriff Court | Court ref. no. |
| Date of decree | *in absence |
| Pursuer(s) | |
| Defender(s) | |

The sheriff granted decree against the defender
(1)  for delivery to the pursuer of (*specify articles*)
(2)  for expenses of £

*Further, the sheriff granted warrant to officers of court to (1) open shut and lockfast places occupied by the defender and (2) search for and take possession of said goods in the possession of the defender.

*delete as appropriate*
This extract is warrant for all lawful execution thereon.

Date                                    Sheriff clerk depute

## FORM 28G
### Form of extract decree—delivery—payment failing delivery
Rule 23.6(3)

| | |
|---|---|
| Sheriff Court | Court ref. no. |
| Date of decree | *in absence |
| Pursuer(s) | |
| Defender(s) | |

The sheriff, in respect that the defender has failed to make delivery in accordance with the decree granted in this court on (*date*), granted decree for payment against the defender of the undernoted sums:

(1)    Sum(s) decerned for: £.........., being the alternative crave claimed.

(2)    Interest at..........per cent per year from (*date*) until payment.

(3)    Expenses of £..........against the (*name of party*).

*A time to pay direction was made under section 1(1) of the Debtors (Scotland) Act 1987.

*A time order was made under section 129(1) of the Consumer Credit Act 1974.

*The amount is payable by instalments of £..........per...........commencing within..........*days/weeks/months..........of intimation of this extract decree.

*The amount is payable by lump sum within..........*days/weeks/months of intimation of this extract decree.

*delete as appropriate

This extract is warrant for all lawful execution thereon.

Date                                  Sheriff clerk depute

## FORM 28H
### Form of extract decree—aliment

Rule 23.6(3)

Sheriff Court                              Court ref. no.

Date of decree                            *in absence

Pursuer(s)

Defender(s)

The sheriff

Granted decree against the defender for payment to the pursuer of aliment at the rate of £.......... per *week/month.

*delete as appropriate

This extract is warrant for all lawful execution thereon.

Date                                  Sheriff clerk depute

## FORM 28I
### Form of extract decree—ad factum praestandum

Rule 23.6(3)

Sheriff Court                              Court ref. no.

Date of decree                              *in absence

Pursuer(s)

Defender(s)

The sheriff

(1)    ordained the defender(s)

(2)    granted decree for payment of expenses of £against the defender(s).

*delete as appropriate

This extract is warrant for all lawful execution thereon.

Date                                  Sheriff clerk depute

## FORM 28J
### Form of extract decree—absolvitor

Rule 23.6(3)

Sheriff Court                              Court ref. no.

Date of decree                              *in absence

Pursuer(s)

Defender(s)

The sheriff

(1)    absolved the defender(s)

(2)     granted decree for payment of expenses of £.......... against the
*delete as appropriate
This extract is warrant for all lawful execution thereon.

Date                                                                    Sheriff clerk depute

FORM 28K
Form of extract decree—dismissal
Rule 23.6(3)

Sheriff Court                                                          Court ref. no.
Date of decree                                                      *in absence
Pursuer(s)
Defender(s)

The sheriff
(1)     dismissed the action against the defender(s)
*(2)     granted decree for payment of expenses of £.......... against the
*(3)     found no expenses due to or by either party
*delete as appropriate
This extract is warrant for all lawful execution thereon.

Date                                                                    Sheriff clerk depute

FORM 29
Form of certificate by sheriff clerk
Service of charge where address of defender is unknown
Rule 23.8(4)

I certify that the foregoing charge was displayed on the walls of court on (date) and that it remained so displayed for a period of (period of charge) from that date.

(date)                                                                  Sheriff clerk depute

FORM 30 [1]
Minute for recall of decree
Rule 24.1(1)

Sheriff Court:                              (place)
Court ref. no.:

AB (pursuer) against CD (defender(s))
The *(pursuer/defender/third party) moves the court to recall the decree pronounced on (date) in this case * and in which execution of a charge/arrestment was effected on (date)
*Proposed defence/answer:
*delete as appropriate
Rule 24.1(6)(a)

FORM 30A[2]
Minute for recall of decree—service copy

Sheriff Court:..........(place)
Court ref. no.:..........

AB (pursuer) against CD (defender(s))
The *(pursuer/defender/third party) moves the court to recall the decree pronounced on (date) in this case * and in which execution of a charge/arrestment was effected on (date)
*Proposed defence/answer:
*delete as appropriate

---

[1] As amended by the Act of Sederunt (Sheriff Court Rules) (Miscellaneous Amendments) 2011 (SSI 2011/193) r.16 (effective April 4, 2011).
[2] As amended by the Act of Sederunt (Sheriff Court Rules) (Miscellaneous Amendments) 2011 (SSI 2011/193) r.16 (effective April 4, 2011).

NOTE: You must return the summons to the sheriff clerk at the court mentioned at the top of this form by (*insert date 2 days before the date of the hearing.*)

Rule 25.1(1)

## FORM 31
### Form of note of appeal to the sheriff principal

SHERIFF COURT (*place*)

Court ref. no...........AB (pursuer) against CD (defender)

The pursuer/defender appeals the sheriff's interlocutor of (*date*) to the sheriff principal and requests the sheriff to state a case.

The point(s) of law upon which the appeal is to proceed is/are: (*give brief statement*)

(*date*)

Rule 25.4(3)(a)

## FORM 32
### Application for leave to appeal against time to pay direction

SHERIFF COURT (*place*)

Court ref. no........... AB (pursuer) against CD (defender)

The pursuer/defender requests the sheriff to grant leave to appeal the decision made on (*date*) in respect of the defender's application for a time to pay direction to the sheriff principal/Court of Session.

The point(s) of law upon which the appeal is to proceed is/are: (*give brief statement*)

(*date*)

Rule 25.4(4)

## FORM 33
### Appeal against time to pay direction

SHERIFF COURT (*place*)

Court ref. no........... AB (pursuer) against CD (defender)

The pursuer/defender appeals the decision made on (*date*) in respect of the defender's application for a time to pay direction to the sheriff principal/Court of Session.

(*date*)

Rule 25.7(1)

## FORM 34
### Application for certificate of suitability for appeal to the Court of Session

The pursuer/defender in the summary cause at the instance of AB against CD hereby moves the sheriff principal to certify that the cause is suitable for appeal to the Court of Session.

Rule 26.4(1)

## FORM 35
### Form of receipt for money paid to the sheriff clerk

In the sheriff court of (*name of sheriffdom*) at (*place of sheriff court*).

In the cause (*state names of parties or other appropriate description*)

AB (*designation*) has this day paid into court the sum of £.........., being a payment made in terms of rule 26(4)(1) of the Summary Cause Rules 2002.

*Custody of this money has been accepted at the request of (*insert name of court making the request*)

*delete as appropriate

(Date)                                                                         Sheriff clerk depute

Rule 32.2(a)

## FORM 36
### Action for aliment
### Form of notice of intimation to children and next of kin where address of defender is unknown

Court ref. no.

To: (*insert name and address as in warrant*)

You are hereby given notice that an action for aliment has been raised against (*name*), your (*insert relationship, e.g, father, brother or other relative as the case may be*). A copy of the summons is enclosed.

If you know of his/her present address, you are requested to inform the sheriff clerk at (*insert full address*) in writing immediately.

If you wish to appear as a party in the action, or are uncertain about what action to take, you should contact a solicitor. You may, depending on your financial circumstances, be entitled to legal aid, and you can get information about legal aid from a solicitor.

You may also obtain advice from any Citizen's Advice Bureau, other advice agency or any sheriff clerk's office.

Rule 32.2(b)

FORM 37

Action for aliment

Form of notice of intimation to children, next of kin and guardian where defender suffers from mental disorder

Court ref. no.

To: (*insert name and address as in warrant*)

You are hereby given notice that an action for aliment has been raised against (*name*), your (*insert relationship, e.g, father or other relative, or ward, as the case may be*). A copy of the summons is enclosed.

If you wish to appear as a party in the action, or are uncertain about what action to take, you should contact a solicitor immediately. You may, depending on your financial circumstances, be entitled to legal aid, and you can get information about legal aid from a solicitor.

You may also obtain advice from any Citizen's Advice Bureau, other advice agency or any sheriff clerk's office.

Appendix IA[1]

SCHEDULE OF TIMETABLE UNDER PERSONAL INJURIES PROCEDURE

| Steps referred to under rule 34.7(1)(c) | Period of time within which action must be carried out* |
|---|---|
| Application for a third party notice under rule 11.1 (rule 34.7(2)(a)) | Not later than 28 days after the form of response has been lodged |
| Pursuer serving a commission for recovery of documents under rule 34.5 (rule 34.7(2)(b)) | Not later than 28 days after the form of response has been lodged |
| Parties adjusting their respective statements (rule 34.7(2)(c)) | Not later than 8 weeks after the form of response has been lodged |
| Pursuer lodging a statement of valuation of claim (rule 34.7(2)(d)) | Not later than 8 weeks after the form of response has been lodged |
| Pursuer lodging a certified adjusted statement of claim (rule 34.7(2)(e)) | Not later than 10 weeks after the form of response has been lodged |
| Defender (and any third party to the action) lodging a certified adjusted response to statement of claim (rule 34.7(2)(f)) | Not later than 10 weeks after the form of response has been lodged |
| Defender (and any third party to the action) lodging a statement of valuation of claim (rule 34.7(2)(g)) | Not later than 12 weeks after the form of response has been lodged |
| Parties lodging a list of witnesses together with any productions on which they wish to rely (rule 34.7(2)(h)) | Not later than 8 weeks before the date assigned for the proof |
| Pursuer lodging the minute of the pre-proof conference (rule 34.7(2)(i)) | Not later than 21 days before the date assigned for the proof |
| *NOTE: Where there is more than one defender in an action, references in the above table to the form of response having been lodged should be read as references to the first lodging of a form of response. | |

[1] As inserted by the Act of Sederunt (Summary Cause Rules Amendment) (Personal Injuries Actions) 2012 (SSI 2012/144) para.2 (effective September 1, 2012; not applicable to an action raised before September 1, 2012).

## Appendix 2

## GLOSSARY

*Absolve*

To find in favour of and exonerate the defender.

*Absolvitor*

An order of the court granted in favour of and exonerating the defender which means that the pursuer is not allowed to bring the same matter to court again.

*Action of count, reckoning and payment*

A legal procedure for requiring someone to account for their dealings with assets under their stewardship. For example, a trustee might be subject to such an action.

*Action of furthcoming*

A final stage of diligence or enforcement. It results in whatever has been subject to arrestment being made over to the person who is suing. For example, where a bank account has been arrested this results in the appropriate amount being transferred to the pursuer.

*Appellant*

A person making an appeal against the sheriff's decision. This might be the pursuer or the defender.

*Arrestee*

A person subject to an arrestment.

*Arrestment on the dependence*

A court order to freeze the goods or bank account of the defender until the court has heard the case.

*Arrestment to found jurisdiction*

A court order to used against a person who has goods or other assets in Scotland to give the court jurisdiction to hear a case. This is achieved by preventing anything being done with the goods or assets until the case has been disposed of.

*Authorised lay representative*

A person other than a lawyer who represents a party to a summary cause.

*Calling date*

The date on which the case will first be heard in court.

*Cause*

Another word for case or claim.

*Caution (pronounced kay-shun)*

A security, usually a sum of money, given to ensure that some obligation will be carried out.

*Certificate of execution of service*

The document recording that an application to, or order or decree of, the court for service of documents has been effected.

*Charge*

An order to obey a decree of a court. A common type is one served on the defender by a sheriff officer on behalf of the pursuer who has won a case demanding payment of a sum of money.

*Claim*

The part of the summons which sets out the legal remedy which the pursuer is seeking.

*Commission and diligence*

Authorisation by the court for someone to take the evidence of a witness who cannot attend court or to obtain the production of documentary evidence. It is combined with a diligence authorising the person appointed to require the attendance of the witness and the disclosure of documents.

*Consignation*

The deposit in court, or with a third party, of money or an article in dispute.

*Continuation*

An order made by the sheriff postponing the completion of a hearing until a later date or dates.

*Contribution, Right of*

The right of one person who is legally liable to pay money to someone to claim a proportionate share from others who are also liable.

*Counterclaim*

A claim made by a defender in response to the pursuer's case and which is not necessarily a defence to that case. It is a separate but related case against the pursuer which is dealt with at the same time as the pursuer's case.

*Damages*

Money compensation payable for a breach of contract or some other legal duty.

*Declarator of irritancy of a lease*

957

A decision of a court finding that a tenant has failed to observe a term of a lease which may lead to the termination of the lease.

*Decree*

An order of the court containing the decision of the case in favour of one of the parties and granting the remedy sought or disposing of the case.

*Decree of ejection*

A decree ordering someone to leave land or property which they are occupying. For example, it is used to remove tenants in arrears with their rent.

*Decree of removing*

A court order entitling someone to recover possession of heritable property and ordering a person to leave land which he is occupying. For example, it is used to remove tenants in arrears with their rent.

*Defender*

Person against whom a summary cause is started.

*Deliverance*

A decision or order of a court.

*Diet*

Date for a court hearing.

*Diligence*

The collective term for the procedures used to enforce a decree of a court. These include arrestment of wages, goods or a bank account.

*Dismissal*

An order bringing to an end the proceedings in a summary cause. It is usually possible for a new summary cause to be brought if not time barred.

*Domicile*

The place where a person is normally resident or where, in the case of a company, it has its place of business or registered office.

*Execution of service*

See *Certificate of execution of service*.

*Execution of a charge*

The intimation of the requirement to obey a decree or order of a court.

*Execution of an arrestment*

The carrying out of an order of arrestment.

*Expenses*

The costs of a court case.

*Extract decree*

The document containing the order of the court made at the end of the summary cause. For example, it can be used to enforce payment of a sum awarded.

*Fund in medio*

See *Multiplepoinding*.

*Haver*

A person who holds documents which are required as evidence in a case.

*Heritable property*

Land and buildings as opposed to moveable property.

*Huissier*

An official in France and some other European countries who serves court documents.

*Incidental application*

An application that can be made during the course of a summary cause for certain orders. Examples are applications for the recovery of documents or to amend the statement of claim.

*Interlocutor*

The official record of the order or judgment of a court.

*Interrogatories*

Written questions put to someone in the course of a court case and which must be answered on oath.

*Intimation*

Giving notice to another party of some step in a summary cause.

*Jurisdiction*

The authority of a court to hear particular cases.

*Ish*

The date on which a lease terminates.

*Letter of request*

A document issued by the sheriff court requesting a foreign court to take evidence from a specified person within its jurisdiction or to serve Scottish court documents on that person.

*Messenger at arms*

Officers of court who serve documents issued by the Court of Session.

*Minute*

A document produced in the course of a case in which a party makes an application or sets out his position on some matter.

*Minute for recall*

A form lodged with the court by one party asking the court to recall a decree.

*Multiplepoinding* (pronounced "multiple pinding")

A special type of summary cause in which the holder of property, etc. (referred to as the fund*in medio*) requires claimants upon it to appear and settle claims in court. For example, where the police come into possession of a stolen car of which two or more people claim to be owner this procedure could be used.

*Options Hearing*

A preliminary stage in an ordinary cause action.

*Ordinary cause*

Another legal procedure for higher value cases available in the sheriff court.

*Party litigant*

A person who conducts his own case.

*Process*

The court file containing the collection of documents relating to a case.

*Productions*

Documents or articles which are used in evidence.

*Pursuer*

The person who starts a summary cause.

*Recall of an arrestment*

A court order withdrawing an arrestment.

*Restriction of an arrestment*

An order releasing part of the money or property arrested.

*Recall of a decree*

An order revoking a decree which has been granted.

*Recovery of documents*

The process of obtaining documentary evidence which is not in the possession of the person seeking it (e.g. hospital records necessary to establish the extent of injuries received in a road accident).

*Remit between procedures*

A decision of the sheriff to transfer the summary cause to another court procedure e.g. small claim or ordinary cause procedure.

*Respondent*

When a decision of the sheriff is appealed against, the person making the appeal is called the appellant. The other side in the appeal is called the respondent.

*Return day*

The date by which the defender must send a written reply to the court and, where appropriate, the pursuer must return the summons to court.

*Schedule of arrestment*

The list of items which may be arrested.

*Serve / service*

Sending a copy of the summons or other court document to the defender or another party.

*Sheriff clerk*

The court official responsible for the administration of the sheriff court.

*Sheriff officer*

A person who serves court documents and enforces court orders.

*Sist of action*

The temporary suspension of a court case by court order.

*Sist as a party*

To add another person as a litigant in a case.

*Small claim*

Another legal procedure in the sheriff court for claims having a lower value than summary cause.

*Specification of documents*

A list lodged in court of documents for the recovery of which a party seeks a court order.

*Stated case*

An appeal procedure where the sheriff sets out his findings and the reasons for his decision and states the issues on which the decision of the sheriff principal is requested.

*Statement of claim*

The part of the summons in which pursuers set out details of their cases against defenders.

*Summons*

The form which must be filled in to begin a summary cause.

*Time to pay direction*

A court order for which a defender who is an individual may apply permitting a sum owed to be paid by instalments or by a single payment at a later date.

*Time order*

A court order which assists debtors who have defaulted on an agreement regulated by the Consumer Credit Act 1974 (c.39) and which may be applied for during a court action.

*Warrant for diligence*

Authority to carry out one of the diligence procedures.

*Writ*

A legally significant writing.

SCHEDULE 2

REVOCATIONS

**Paragraph 4**

| (1) Act of Sederunt | (2) Reference | (3) Extent of revocation |
|---|---|---|
| Act of Sederunt (Summary Cause Rules, Sheriff Court) 1976 | S.I. 1976/476 | The whole Act of Sederunt |
| Act of Sederunt (Summary Cause Rules, Sheriff Court) (Amendment) 1978 | S.I. 1978/112 | The whole Act of Sederunt |
| Act of Sederunt (Summary Cause Rules, Sheriff court) (Amendment no. 2) 1978 | S.I. 1978/1805 | The whole Act of Sederunt |
| Act of Sederunt (Summary Cause Rules, Sheriff Court) (Amendment) 1980 | S.I. 1980/455 | The whole Act of Sederunt |
| Act of Sederunt (Ordinary Cause Rules, Sheriff Court) 1983 | S.I. 983/747 | Paragraph 4 |
| Act of Sederunt (Civil Jurisdiction of the Sheriff Court) 1986 | S.I. 1986/1946 | Paragraph 3 |
| Act of Sederunt (Miscellaneous Amendments) 1986 | S.I. 1986/1966 | Paragraph 3 |
| Act of Sederunt (Small Claim Rules) 1988 | S.I. 1988/1976 | Paragraph 3 |
| Act of Sederunt (Amendment of Sheriff Court Ordinary Cause, and Summary Cause, Rules) 1988 | S.I. 1988/1978 | Paragraphs 19 to 35 and Schedule 2 |
| Act of Sederunt (Amendment of Ordinary Cause and Summary Cause Rules) (Written Statements) 1989 | S.I. 1989/436 | Paragraph 3 |
| Act of Sederunt (Amendment of Sheriff Court Ordinary Cause, Summary Cause and Small Claim, Rules) 1990 | S.I. 1990/661 | Paragraph 3 |
| Act of Sederunt (Amendment of Sheriff Court Ordinary Cause, Summary Cause and Small Claim, Rules) (No. 2) 1990 | S.I. 1990/2105 | Paragraph 3 |
| Act of Sederunt (Amendment of Summary Cause and Small Claim Rules) 1991 | S.I. 1991/821 | The whole Act of Sederunt |

| (1) Act of Sederunt | (2) Reference | (3) Extent of revocation |
|---|---|---|
| Act of Sederunt (Amendment of Ordinary Cause, Summary Cause and Small Claim Rules) 1992 | S.I. 1992/ 249 | Paragraph 3 |
| Act of Sederunt (Child Support Act 1991) (Amendment of Ordinary Cause and Summary Cause Rules) 1993 | S.I. 1993/ 919 | Paragraph 4 |
| Act of Sederunt (Sheriff Court Ordinary Cause Rules) 1993 | S.I. 1993/ 1956 | Paragraph 3 |

# ACT OF SEDERUNT (SMALL CLAIM RULES) 2002

## (SSI 2002/133)

### *10 June 2002.*

The Lords of Council and Session, under and by virtue of the powers conferred by section 32 of the Sheriff Courts (Scotland) Act 1971 and of all other powers enabling them in that behalf, having approved draft rules submitted to them by the Sheriff Court Rules Council in accordance with section 34 of the said Act of 1971, do hereby enact and declare:

## Citation and commencement

**1.**—(1)  This Act of Sederunt may be cited as the Act of Sederunt (Small Claim Rules) 2002 and shall come into force on 10th June 2002.

(2)  This Act of Sederunt shall be inserted in the Books of Sederunt.

## Small Claim Rules

**2.**  The provisions of Schedule 1 to this Act of Sederunt shall have effect for the purpose of providing rules for the form of summary cause process known as a small claim.

## Transitional provision

**3.**  Nothing in Schedule 1 to this Act of Sederunt shall apply to a small claim commenced before 10th June 2002 and any such claim shall proceed according to the law and practice in force immediately before that date.

## Revocation

**4.**  The Acts of Sederunt mentioned in column (1) of Schedule 2 to this Act of Sederunt are revoked to the extent specified in column (3) of that Schedule except in relation to any small claim commenced before 10th June 2002.

SCHEDULE 1

SMALL CLAIM RULES 2002

Arrangement of Rules

*Chapter 1*

*Citation, interpretation and application*

*Chapter 2*

*Representation*

*Chapter 2A*

*Lay Representation*

*Chapter 3*

964

966

**Appendix 1**

**FORMS**

**Appendix 2**

**GLOSSARY**

Chapter 1

Citation, interpretation and application

### Citation, interpretation and application

**1.1.**—[1](1)  These Rules may be cited as the Small Claim Rules 2002.

(2)  In these rules—

"the 1971 Act" means the Sheriff Courts (Scotland) Act 1971;

"the 1975 Act" means the Litigants in Person (Costs and Expenses) Act 1975;

"the 2004 Act" means the Vulnerable Witnesses (Scotland) Act 2004;[2]

"authorised lay representative" means a person to whom section 32(1) of the Solicitors (Scotland) Act 1980 (offence to prepare writs) does not apply by virtue of section 32(2)(a) of that Act;

"enactment" includes an enactment comprised in, or in an instrument made under, an Act of the Scottish Parliament;

"small claim" has the meaning assigned to it by section 35(2) of the 1971 Act;

"summary cause" has the meaning assigned to it by section 35(1) of the 1971 Act.

(3)  Any reference in these Rules to a specified rule shall be construed as a reference to the rule bearing that number in these Rules, and a reference to a specified paragraph, sub-paragraph or head shall be construed as a reference to the paragraph, sub-paragraph or head so numbered or lettered in the provision in which that reference occurs.

(4)  A form referred to by number in these Rules means the form so numbered in Appendix 1 to these rules or a form substantially of the same effect with such variation as circumstances may require.

(4A)[3]  In these Rules, references to a solicitor include a reference to a member of a body which has made a successful application under section 25 of the Law Reform (Miscellaneous Provisions) (Scotland) Act 1990 but only to the extent that the member is exercising rights acquired by virtue of section 27 of that Act.

(5)  The glossary in Appendix 2 to these Rules is a guide to the meaning of certain legal expressions used in these Rules, but is not to be taken as giving those expressions any meaning which they do not have in law generally.

---

[1] As amended by the Act of Sederunt (Ordinary Cause, Summary Application, Summary Cause and Small Claim Rules) Amendment (Miscellaneous) 2007 (SSI 2007/6) r.5(a) (effective January 29, 2007).

[2] As inserted by the Act of Sederunt (Ordinary Cause, Summary Application, Summary Cause and Small Claim Rules) Amendment (Vulnerable Witnesses (Scotland) Act 2004) 2007 (SSI 2007/463) r.5(2) (effective November 1, 2007).

[3] As inserted by the Act of Sederunt (Sheriff Court Rules Amendment) (Sections 25 to 29 of the Law Reform (Miscellaneous Provisions) (Scotland) Act 1990) 2009 (SSI 2009/164) r.5(2) (effective May 20, 2009).

(6)　These Rules shall apply to a small claim.

CHAPTER 2

REPRESENTATION

**Representation**

**2.1.**—[1](1)　A party may be represented by—

    (a)　an advocate;

    (b)　a solicitor;

    (c)　a person authorised under any enactment to conduct proceedings in the sheriff court, in accordance with the terms of that enactment; and

    (d)　subject to paragraph (3), an authorised lay representative.

(2)　The persons referred to in paragraph (1)(c) and (d) above may in representing a party do everything for the preparation and conduct of a small claim as may be done by an individual conducting his own claim.

(3)　If the sheriff finds that the authorised lay representative is—

    (a)　not a suitable person to represent the party; or

    (b)　not in fact authorised to do so,

that person must cease to represent the party.

**Lay support**

**2.2**—[2](1)　At any time during proceedings the sheriff may, on the request of a party litigant, permit a named individual to assist the litigant in the conduct of the proceedings by sitting beside or behind (as the litigant chooses) the litigant at hearings in court or in chambers and doing such of the following for the litigant as he or she requires—

    (a)　providing moral support;

    (b)　helping to manage the court documents and other papers;

    (c)　taking notes of the proceedings;

    (d)　quietly advising on—

        (i)　points of law and procedure;

        (ii)　issues which the litigant might wish to raise with the sheriff;

        (iii)　questions which the litigant might wish to ask witnesses.

(2)　It is a condition of such permission that the named individual does not receive from the litigant, whether directly or indirectly, any remuneration for his or her assistance.

(3)　The sheriff may refuse a request under paragraph (1) only if—

    (a)　the sheriff is of the opinion that the named individual is an unsuitable person to act in that capacity (whether generally or in the proceedings concerned); or

    (b)　the sheriff is of the opinion that it would be contrary to the efficient administration of justice to grant it.

(4)　Permission granted under paragraph (1) endures until the proceedings finish or it is withdrawn under paragraph (5); but it is not effective during any period when the litigant is represented.

(5)　The sheriff may, of his or her own accord or on the incidental application of a party to the proceedings, withdraw permission granted under paragraph (1); but the sheriff must first be of the opinion that it would be contrary to the efficient administration of justice for the permission to continue.

(6)　Where permission has been granted under paragraph (1), the litigant may—

    (a)　show the named individual any document (including a court document); or

    (b)　impart to the named individual any information,

which is in his or her possession in connection with the proceedings without being taken to contravene any prohibition or restriction on the disclosure of the document or the information; but the named individual is then to be taken to be subject to any such prohibition or restriction as if he or she were the litigant.

(7)　Any expenses incurred by the litigant as a result of the support of an individual under paragraph (1) are not recoverable expenses in the proceedings.

---

[1] As amended by the Act of Sederunt (Ordinary Cause, Summary Application, Summary Cause and Small Claim Rules) Amendment (Miscellaneous) 2007 (SSI 2007/6) r.5(b) (effective January 29, 2007).

[2] As inserted by the Act of Sederunt (Sheriff Court Rules) (Miscellaneous Amendments) (No.2) 2010 (SSI 2010/416) r.5 (effective January 1, 2011).

## Chapter 2A[1]

### Lay Representation

**Application and interpretation**

**2A.1.**—(1)  This Chapter is without prejudice to any enactment (including any other provision in these Rules) under which provision is, or may be, made for a party to a particular type of case before the sheriff to be represented by a lay representative.

(2)  In this Chapter, a "lay representative" means a person who is not—

    (a)    a solicitor;

    (b)    an advocate, or

    (c)    someone having a right to conduct litigation, or a right of audience, by virtue of section 27 of the Law Reform (Miscellaneous Provisions) (Scotland) Act 1990.

**Lay representation for party litigants**

**2A.2.**—(1)  In any proceedings in respect of which no provision as mentioned in rule 2A.1(1) is in force, the sheriff may, on the request of a party litigant, permit a named individual (a "lay representative") to appear, along with the litigant, at a specified hearing for the purpose of making oral submissions on behalf of the litigant at that hearing.

(2)  An application under paragraph (1)—

    (a)    is to be made orally on the date of the first hearing at which the litigant wishes a named individual to make oral submissions; and

    (b)    is to be accompanied by a document, signed by the named individual, in Form A1.

(3)  The sheriff may grant an application under paragraph (1) only if the sheriff is of the opinion that it would assist his or her consideration of the case to grant it.

(4)  It is a condition of permission granted by the sheriff that the lay representative does not receive directly or indirectly from the litigant any remuneration or other reward for his or her assistance.

(5)  The sheriff may grant permission under paragraph (1) in respect of one or more specified hearings in the case; but such permission is not effective during any period when the litigant is legally represented.

(6)  The sheriff may, of his or her own accord or on the motion of a party to the proceedings, withdraw permission granted under paragraph (1).

(7)  Where permission has been granted under paragraph (1), the litigant may—

    (a)    show the lay representative any document (including a court document); or

    (b)    impart to the lay representative any information, which is in his or her possession in connection with the proceedings without being taken to contravene any prohibition or restriction on the disclosure of the document or the information; but the lay representative is then to be taken to be subject to any such prohibition or restriction as if he or she were the litigant.

(8)  Any expenses incurred by the litigant in connection with lay representation under this rule are not recoverable expenses in the proceedings.

## Chapter 3

### Relief from Failure to Comply with Rules

**Dispensing power of sheriff**

**3.1.**—(1)  The sheriff may relieve any party from the consequences of any failure to comply with the provisions of these Rules which is shown to be due to mistake, oversight or other excusable cause, on such conditions as he thinks fit.

(2)  Where the sheriff relieves a party from the consequences of the failure to comply with a provision in these Rules under paragraph (1), he may make such order as he thinks fit to enable the claim to proceed as if the failure to comply with the provision had not occurred.

## Chapter 4

### Commencement of Claim

**Form of summons**

**4.1.**—(1)  A small claim shall be commenced by summons, which shall be in Form 1.

(2)  The claim in a small claim summons may be in one of Forms 2 to 4.

---

[1] As inserted by the Act of Sederunt (Sheriff Court Rules) (Lay Representation) 2013 (SSI 2013/91) r.5 (effective April 4, 2013).

**Statement of claim**

**4.2.** The pursuer must insert a statement of his claim in the summons to give the defender fair notice of the claim; and the statement must include—

    (a)    details of the basis of the claim including relevant dates; and

    (b)    if the claim arises from the supply of goods or services, a description of the goods or services and the date or dates on or between which they were supplied and, where relevant, ordered.

**Actions relating to regulated agreements**

**4.2A.**[1] In an action which relates to a regulated agreement within the meaning given by section 189(1) of the Consumer Credit Act 1974 the statement of claim shall include an averment that such an agreement exists and details of the agreement.

**Defender's copy summons**

**4.3.** A copy summons shall be served on the defender—

    (a)    in Form 1 a where—

        (i)    the small claim is for, or includes a claim for, payment of money; and

        (ii)    an application for a time to pay direction under the Debtors (Scotland) Act 1987 or time order under the Consumer Credit Act 1974 may be applied for;

        or

    (b)    in Form 1b in every other case.

**Authentication and effect of summons**

**4.4.**—(1) A summons shall be authenticated by the sheriff clerk in some appropriate manner except where—

    (a)    he refuses to do so for any reason;

    (b)    the defender's address is unknown; or

    (c)    a party seeks to alter the normal period of notice specified in rule 4.5(2); or

    (d)[2]    a warrant for arrestment on the dependence, or to found jurisdiction, is sought

(2)[3] If any of paragraphs (1)(a) to (d) applies, the summons shall be authenticated by the sheriff, if he thinks it appropriate.

(3) The authenticated summons shall be warrant for—

    (a)    service on the defender; and

    (b)    where the appropriate warrant has been sought in the summons—

        (i)    arrestment on the dependence; or

        (ii)    arrestment to found jurisdiction, as the case may be.

(4)[4] Where a warrant for arrestment to found jurisdiction, is sought, averments to justify that warrant must be included in the statement of claim.

**Period of notice**

**4.5.**—(1) A claim shall proceed after the appropriate period of notice of the summons has been given to the defender prior to the return day.

(2) The appropriate period of notice shall be—

    (a)    21 days where the defender is resident or has a place of business within Europe; or

    (b)    42 days where the defender is resident or has a place of business outwith Europe.

---

[1] As inserted by the Act of Sederunt (Sheriff Court Rules) (Miscellaneous Amendments) 2009 (SSI 2009/294) r.5 (effective December 1, 2009) as substituted by the Act of Sederunt (Amendment of the Act of Sederunt (Sheriff Court Rules) (Miscellaneous Amendments) 2009) 2009 (SSI 2009/402) (effective November 30, 2009).

[2] As inserted by the Act of Sederunt (Ordinary Cause, Summary Application and Small Claim Rules) Amendment (Miscellaneous) 2004 (SSI 2004/197) r.5(2) (effective May 21, 2004) and amended by the Act of Sederunt (Sheriff Court Rules) (Miscellaneous Amendments) 2009 (SSI 2009/294) r.12 (effective October 1, 2009).

[3] As substituted by the Act of Sederunt (Ordinary Cause, Summary Application, Summary Cause and Small Claim Rules) Amendment (Miscellaneous) 2004 (SSI 2004/197) r.5(2)(b) (effective May 21, 2004).

[4] As inserted by the Act of Sederunt (Ordinary Cause, Summary Application and Small Claim Rules) Amendment (Miscellaneous) 2004 (SSI 2004/197) r.5(2) (effective May 21, 2004) and amended by the Act of Sederunt (Sheriff Court Rules) (Miscellaneous Amendments) 2009 (SSI 2009/294) r.12 (effective October 1, 2009).

(3)   The sheriff may, on cause shown, shorten or extend the period of notice on such conditions as to the form of service as he may direct, but in any case where the period of notice is reduced at least two days' notice must be given.

(4)   If a period of notice expires on a Saturday, Sunday, public or court holiday, the period of notice shall be deemed to expire on the next day on which the sheriff clerk's office is open for civil court business.

(5)   Notwithstanding the terms of section 4(2) of the Citation Amendment (Scotland) Act 1882, where service is by post the period of notice shall run from the beginning of the day next following the date of posting.

(6)   The sheriff clerk shall insert in the summons—
>   (a)   the return day, which is the last day on which the defender may return a form of response to the sheriff clerk; and
>   (b)   the hearing date, which is the date set for the hearing of the claim.

### Intimation

**4.6.**   Any provision in these Rules requiring papers to be sent to or any intimation to be made to any party or applicant shall be construed as if the reference to the party or applicant included a reference to the solicitor representing that party or applicant.

CHAPTER 5

REGISTER OF SMALL CLAIMS

### Register of Small Claims

**5.1.**—(1)   The sheriff clerk shall keep a register of claims and incidental applications made in claims, which shall be known as the Register of Small Claims.

(2)   There shall be entered in the Register of Small Claims a note of all claims, together with a note of all minutes under rule 22.1(1) (recall of decree) and the entry for each claim or minute must contain the following particulars where appropriate:—
>   (a)   the names, designations and addresses of the parties;
>   (b)   whether the parties were present or absent at any hearing, including an inspection, and the names of their representatives;
>   (c)   the nature of the claim;
>   (d)   the amount of any claim;
>   (e)   the date of issue of the summons;
>   (f)   the method of service;
>   (g)   the return day;
>   (h)   the hearing date;
>   (i)   whether a form of response was lodged and details of it;
>   (j)   the period of notice if shortened or extended in accordance with rule 4.5(3);
>   (k)   details of any minute by the pursuer regarding a time to pay direction or time order, or minute by the pursuer requesting decree or other order;
>   (l)   details of any interlocutors issued;
>   (m)   details of the final decree and the date of it; and
>   (n)   details of any variation or recall of a decree by virtue of the Debtors (Scotland) Act 1987.

(3)   There shall be entered in the Register of Small Claims, in the entry for the claim to which they relate, details of incidental applications including, where appropriate—
>   (a)   whether parties are present or absent at the hearing of the application, and the names of their representatives;
>   (b)   the nature of the application; and
>   (c)   the interlocutor issued or order made.

(4)   The Register of Small Claims must be—
>   (a)   authenticated in some appropriate manner by the sheriff in respect of each day any order is made or application determined in a claim; and
>   (b)   open for inspection during normal business hours to all concerned without fee.

(5)   The Register of Small Claims may be kept in electronic or documentary form.

CHAPTER 6

SERVICE AND RETURN OF THE SUMMONS

### Persons carrying on business under trading or descriptive name

**6.1.**—(1)   A person carrying on a business under a trading or descriptive name may sue or be sued in such trading or descriptive name alone.

972

(2)   An extract of a decree pronounced in a claim against such person under such trading or descriptive name shall be a valid warrant for diligence against that person.

(3)   A summons, decree, charge or other document following upon such summons or decree in a claim in which a person carrying on business under a trading or descriptive name sues or is sued in that name may be served—

> (a)   at any place of business or office at which such business is carried on within the sheriffdom of the sheriff court in which the claim is brought; or
>
> (b)   if there is no place of business within that sheriffdom, at any place where such business is carried on (including the place of business or office of the clerk or secretary of any company, corporation or association or firm).

### Form of service

**6.2.**—(1)   Subject to rule 6.6 (service where address of defender is unknown), a form of service in Form 5 must be enclosed with the defender's copy summons.

(2)   After service has been effected a certificate of execution of service in Form 6 must be prepared and signed by the person effecting service.

(3)   When service is effected by a sheriff officer the certificate of execution of service must specify whether the service was personal or, if otherwise, the mode of service and the name of any person to whom the defender's copy summons was delivered.

(4)   If service is effected in accordance with rule 6.4(2) (service within Scotland by sheriff officer where personal service etc. unsuccessful) the certificate must also contain a statement of—

> (a)   the mode of service previously attempted; and
>
> (b)   the circumstances which prevented the service from being effected.

### Service of the summons

**6.3.**—(1)   Subject to rule 6.5 (service on persons outwith Scotland), a copy summons may be served on the defender—

> (a)   by the pursuer's solicitor, a sheriff officer or the sheriff clerk sending it by first class recorded delivery post; or
>
> (b)   in accordance with rule 6.4 (service within Scotland by sheriff officer).

(2)   On the face of the envelope used for postal service in terms of this rule, there must be printed or written a notice in Form 7.

(3)   The certificate of execution of service in the case of postal service must have annexed to it any relevant postal receipt.

(4)   If the pursuer requires the sheriff clerk to effect service on his behalf by virtue of section 36A of the 1971 Act (pursuer not being a partnership, body corporate or acting in a representative capacity) under paragraph (1), he may require the sheriff clerk to supply him with a copy of the summons.

### Service within Scotland by sheriff officer

**6.4.**—(1)   A sheriff officer may validly serve any summons, decree, charge or other document following upon such summons or decree issued in a claim by—

> (a)   personal service; or
>
> (b)   leaving it in the hands of—
>
>> (i)[1]   a resident at the person's dwelling place; or
>>
>> (ii)   an employee at the person's place of business.

(2)   If a sheriff officer has been unsuccessful in effecting service in accordance with paragraph (1), he may, after making diligent inquiries, serve the document—

> (a)   by depositing it in the person's dwelling place or place of business by means of a letter box or by other lawful means; or
>
> (b)[2]   by leaving it at that person's dwelling place or place of business in such a way that it is likely to come to the attention of that person.

(3)   If service is effected in accordance with paragraph (2), the sheriff officer must thereafter send by ordinary post to the address at which he thinks it most likely that the person may be found a letter containing a copy of the document.

---

[1] As substituted by the Act of Sederunt (Sheriff Court Rules) (Miscellaneous Amendments) 2011 (SSI 2011/193) r.5 (effective April 4, 2011).

[2] As substituted by the Act of Sederunt (Sheriff Court Rules) (Miscellaneous Amendments) 2011 (SSI 2011/193) r.5 (effective April 4, 2011).

(4)   In proceedings in or following on a claim, it shall be necessary for any sheriff officer to be accompanied by a witness except where service, citation or intimation is to be made by post.

(5)   Where the firm which employs the sheriff officer has in its possession—

(a)   the document or a copy of it certified as correct by the pursuer's solicitor or the sheriff clerk, the sheriff officer may serve the document upon the defender without having the document or certified copy in his possession (in which case he shall if required to do so by the person on whom service is executed and within a reasonable time of being so required, show the document or certified copy to the person); or

(b)   a certified copy of the interlocutor pronounced allowing service of the document, the sheriff officer may serve the document without having in his possession the certified copy interlocutor if he has in his possession a facsimile copy of the certified copy interlocutor (which he shall show, if required, to the person on whom service is executed).

(6)   If the pursuer requires the sheriff clerk to effect service of the summons on his behalf by virtue of section 36A of the 1971 Act, the sheriff clerk may instruct a sheriff officer to effect service in accordance with this rule on payment to the sheriff clerk by the pursuer of the fee prescribed by order of the Scottish Ministers.

(7)[1]   Where service is executed under paragraphs (1)(b) or (2), the document and the citation or notice of intimation, as the case may be, must be placed in an envelope bearing the notice "This envelope contains a citation to or intimation from (*insert name of sheriff court*)" and sealed by the sheriff officer.

### Service on persons outwith Scotland

6.5.—(1)   If any summons, decree, charge or other document following upon such summons or decree, or any charge or warrant, requires to be served outwith Scotland on any person, it must be served in accordance with this rule.

(2)   If the person has a known home or place of business in—

(a)   England and Wales, Northern Ireland, the Isle of Man or the Channel Islands; or

(b)   any country with which the United Kingdom does not have a convention providing for service of writs in that country,

the document must be served either—

(i)   by posting in Scotland a copy of the document in question in a registered letter addressed to the person at his residence or place of business; or

(ii)   in accordance with the rules for personal service under the domestic law of the place in which the document is to be served.

(3)   Subject to paragraph (4), if the document requires to be served in a country which is a party to the Hague Convention on the Service Abroad of Judicial and Extra-Judicial Documents in Civil or Commercial Matters dated 15th November 1965 or the European Convention on Jurisdiction and Enforcement of Judgments in Civil and Commercial Matters as set out in Schedule 1 or 3C to the Civil Jurisdiction and Judgments Act 1982, it must be served—

(a)   by a method prescribed by the internal law of the country where service is to be effected for the service of documents in domestic actions upon persons who are within its territory;

(b)   by or through a British consular authority at the request of the Secretary of State for Foreign and Commonwealth Affairs;

(c)[2]   by or through a central authority in the country where service is to be effected at the request of the Scottish Ministers;

(d)   where the law of the country in which the person resides permits, by posting in Scotland a copy of the document in a registered letter addressed to the person at his residence; or

(e)   where the law of the country in which service is to be effected permits, service by an *huissier*, other judicial officer or competent official of the country where service is to be made.

(4)[3, 4]   If the document requires to be served in a country to which the EC Service Regulation applies, service—

---

[1]   As inserted by the Act of Sederunt (Sheriff Court Rules) (Miscellaneous Amendments) 2011 (SSI 2011/193) r.5 (effective April 4, 2011).

[2]   As substituted by the Act of Sederunt (Sheriff Court Rules) (Miscellaneous Amendments) 2011 (SSI 2011/193) r.6 (effective April 4, 2011).

[3]   As substituted by the Act of Sederunt (Ordinary Cause, Summary Application, Summary Cause and Small Claim Rules) Amendment (Miscellaneous) 2004 (SSI 2004/197) r.5(3) (effective May 21, 2004).

[4]   As substituted by Act of Sederunt (Sheriff Court Rules) (Miscellaneous Amendments) (No.2) 2008 (SSI 2008/365) r.10(a) (effective November 13, 2008).

   (a)    may be effected by the methods prescribed in paragraph (3)(b) or (c) only in exceptional circumstances; and

   (b)    is effected only if the receiving agency has informed the person that acceptance of service may be refused on the ground that the document has not been translated in accordance with paragraph (12).

(5)   If the document requires to be served in a country with which the United Kingdom has a convention on the service of writs in that country other than the conventions specified in paragraph (3) or the regulation specified in paragraph (4), it must be served by one of the methods approved in the relevant convention.

(6)   Subject to paragraph (9), a document which requires to be posted in Scotland for the purposes of this rule must be posted by a solicitor, the sheriff clerk or a sheriff officer, and the form for service and the certificate of execution of service must be in Forms 5 and 6 respectively.

(7)   On the face of the envelope used for postal service under this rule there must be written or printed a notice in Form 7.

(8)   Where service is effected by a method specified in paragraph (3)(b) or (c), the pursuer must—

   (a)[1]   send a copy of the summons and warrant for service with form of service attached, or other document, with a request for service to be effected by the method indicated in the request to the Scottish Ministers or, as the case may be, the Secretary of State for Foreign and Commonwealth Affairs; and

   (b)    lodge in process a certificate of execution of service signed by the authority which has effected service.

(9)   If service is effected by the method specified in paragraph (3)(e), the pursuer must—

   (a)    send to the official in the country in which service is to be effected a copy of the summons and warrant for service, with citation attached, or other document, with a request for service to be effected by delivery to the defender or his residence; and

   (b)    lodge in process a certificate of execution of service by the official who has effected service.

(10)   Where service is executed in accordance with paragraph (2)(b)(ii) or (3)(a) other than on another party in—

   (a)    the United Kingdom;

   (b)    the Isle of Man; or

   (c)    the Channel Islands,

the party executing service must lodge a certificate stating that the form of service employed is in accordance with the law of the place where the service was executed.

(11)   A certificate lodged in accordance with paragraph (10) shall be given by a person who is conversant with the law of the country concerned and who—

   (a)    practises or has practised law in that country; or

   (b)    is a duly accredited representative of the government of that country.

(12)[2]   Every summons or document and every citation and notice on the face of the envelope referred to in paragraph (7) must be accompanied by a translation in—

   (a)    an official language of the country in which service is to be executed; or

   (b)[3]   in a country to which the EC Service Regulation applies, a language of the member state of transmission that is understood by the person on whom service is being executed.

(13)   A translation referred to in paragraph (12) must be certified as a correct translation by the person making it and the certificate must contain the full name, address and qualifications of the translator and be lodged along with the execution of such service.

(14)   If the pursuer requires the sheriff clerk to effect service on his behalf under this rule by virtue of section 36A of the 1971 Act (pursuer not a partnership, body corporate or acting in a representative capacity)—

   (a)    the cost must be borne by the pursuer;

   (b)    no service shall be instructed by the sheriff clerk until such cost has been paid to him by the pursuer; and

---

[1] As amended by the Act of Sederunt (Sheriff Court Rules) (Miscellaneous Amendments) 2011 (SSI 2011/193) r.7 (effective April 4, 2011).

[2] As substituted by the Act of Sederunt (Ordinary Cause, Summary Application, Summary Cause and Small Claim Rules) Amendment (Miscellaneous) 2004 (SSI 2004/197) r.5(3) (effective May 21, 2004).

[3] As substituted by Act of Sederunt (Sheriff Court Rules) (Miscellaneous Amendments) (No.2) 2008 (SSI 2008/365) r.10(a) (effective November 13, 2008).

(c) the pursuer may require the sheriff clerk to supply him with a copy of the summons.

(15)[1] In this rule "the EC Service Regulation" means Regulation (EC) No. 1393/2007 of the European Parliament and of the Council of 13th November 2007 on the service in the Member States of judicial and extrajudicial documents in civil or commercial matters (service of documents), and repealing Council Regulation (EC) No. 1348/2000, as amended from time to time.

### Service where address of defender is unknown

**6.6.**—(A1)[2] Subject to rule 7.A7 this rule applies to service where the address of a person is not known.

(1) If the defender's address is unknown to the pursuer and cannot reasonably be ascertained by him, the sheriff may grant warrant to serve the summons—

   (a) by the publication of an advertisement in Form 8 in a newspaper circulating in the area of the defender's last known address; or
   (b) by displaying on the walls of court a copy of a notice in Form 9.

(2) Where a summons is served in accordance with paragraph (1), the period of notice, which must be fixed by the sheriff, shall run from the date of publication of the advertisement or display on the walls of court, as the case may be.

(3) If service is to be effected under paragraph (1), the pursuer must lodge a defender's copy summons with the sheriff clerk.

(4) The defender may uplift from the sheriff clerk the copy summons lodged in accordance with paragraph (3).

(5) If the pursuer requires the sheriff clerk to effect service on his behalf under paragraph (1) by virtue of section 36A of the 1971 Act (pursuer not a partnership, body corporate or acting in a representative capacity)—

   (a) the cost of any advertisement required under sub-paragraph (a) of that paragraph must be borne by the pursuer;
   (b) no advertisement required under sub-paragraph (a) of that paragraph shall be instructed by the sheriff clerk until such cost has been paid to him by the pursuer; and
   (c) the pursuer may require the sheriff clerk to supply him with a copy of the summons.

(6) A copy of the newspaper containing the advertisement referred to in paragraph (1)(a) must be lodged with the sheriff clerk unless the sheriff clerk instructed such advertisement.

(7) If display on the walls of court is required under paragraph (1)(b), the pursuer must supply to the sheriff clerk for that purpose a completed copy of Form 9.

(8) If service has been made under this rule and thereafter the defender's address becomes known, the sheriff may allow the summons to be amended and, if appropriate, grant warrant for resservice subject to such conditions as he thinks fit.

### Endorsation by sheriff clerk of defender's residence not necessary

**6.7.** Any summons, decree, charge or other document following upon a summons or decree may be served, enforced or otherwise lawfully executed in Scotland without endorsation by a sheriff clerk and, if executed by a sheriff officer, may be so executed by a sheriff officer of the court which granted the summons, or by a sheriff officer of the sheriff court district in which it is to be executed.

### Contents of envelope containing defender's copy summons

**6.8.** Nothing must be included in the envelope containing a defender's copy summons except—

   (a) the copy summons;
   (b) a response or other notice in accordance with these Rules; and
   (c) any other document approved by the sheriff principal.

### Re-service

**6.9.**—(1) If it appears to the sheriff that there has been any failure or irregularity in service upon a defender, the sheriff may order the pursuer to re-serve the summons on such conditions as he thinks fit.

---

[1] As inserted by the Act of Sederunt (Ordinary Cause, Summary Application, Summary Cause and Small Claim Rules) Amendment (Miscellaneous) 2004 (SSI 2004/197) r.5(3) (effective May 21, 2004) and substituted by the Act of Sederunt (Sheriff Court Ordinary Cause, Summary Application, Summary Cause and Small Claim Rules) Amendment (Council Regulation (EC) No.1348 of 2000 Extension to Denmark) 2007 (SSI 2007/440) (effective October 9, 2007) and the Act of Sederunt (Sheriff Court Rules) (Miscellaneous Amendments) (No.2) 2008 (SSI 2008/365) r.10(b) (effective November 13, 2008).

[2] As inserted by the Act of Sederunt (Sheriff Court Rules Amendment) (Diligence) 2008 (SSI 2008/121) r 7(2) (effective April 1, 2008).

(2)   If re-service has been ordered in accordance with paragraph (1) or rule 6.6(8), the claim shall proceed thereafter as if it were a new claim.

**Defender appearing barred from objecting to service**

**6.10.**—(1)   A person who appears in any claim shall not be entitled to state any objection to the regularity of the execution of service or intimation on him and his appearance shall remedy any defect in such service or intimation.

(2)   Nothing in paragraph (1) shall preclude a party pleading that the court has no jurisdiction.

**Return of summons and execution**

**6.11.**—(1)   If—

(a)   someone other than the sheriff clerk has served the summons; and
(b)   the case requires to call in court for any reason on the hearing date, the pursuer must return the summons and the certificate of execution of service to the sheriff clerk at least two days before the hearing date.

(2)   If the case does not require to call in court on the hearing date, the pursuer must return the certificate of execution of service to the sheriff clerk by the date mentioned in paragraph (1) above.

(3)   If the pursuer fails to return the summons or certificate of execution of service in accordance with paragraph (1) or (2) as appropriate, the sheriff may dismiss the claim.

CHAPTER 7

INTERIM DILIGENCE[1]

**Interpretation**

**7.A1.**[2]   In this Chapter—

"the 1987 Act" means the Debtors (Scotland) Act 1987; and
"the 2002 Act" means the Debt Arrangement and Attachment (Scotland) Act 2002.

**Application for interim diligence**

**7.A2.**—[3](1)   The following shall be made by incidental application—

(a)   an application under section 15D(1) of the 1987 Act for warrant for diligence by arrestment or inhibition on the dependence of an action or warrant for arrestment on the dependence of an admiralty action;
(b)   an application under section 9C of the 2002 Act for interim attachment.

(2)   Such an application must be accompanied by a statement in Form 9a.

(3)   A certified copy of an interlocutor granting an application under paragraph (1) shall be sufficient authority for execution of the diligence concerned.

**Effect of authority for inhibition on the dependence**

**7.A3.**—[4](1)   Where a person has been granted authority for inhibition on the dependence of an action, a certified copy of the interlocutor granting the application may be registered with a certificate of execution in the Register of Inhibitions and Adjudications.

(2)[5]   A notice of a certified copy of an interlocutor granting authority for inhibition under rule 7.A2 may be registered in the Register of Inhibitions and Adjudications; and such registration is to have the same effect as registration of a notice of inhibition under section 155(2) of the Titles to Land Consolidation (Scotland) Act 1868.

---

[1] Chapter renamed by the Act of Sederunt (Sheriff Court Rules Amendment) (Diligence) 2008 (SSI 2008/121) r.7(3) (effective April 1, 2008).
[2] As inserted by the Act of Sederunt (Sheriff Court Rules Amendment) (Diligence) 2008 (SSI 2008/121) r.7(4) (effective April 1, 2008).
[3] As inserted by the Act of Sederunt (Sheriff Court Rules Amendment) (Diligence) 2008 (SSI 2008/121) r.7(4) (effective April 1, 2008).
[4] As inserted by the Act of Sederunt (Sheriff Court Rules Amendment) (Diligence) 2008 (SSI 2008/121) r.7(4) (effective April 1, 2008).
[5] As substituted by the Act of Sederunt (Sheriff Court Rules Amendment) (Diligence) 2009 (SSI 2009/107) r.6 (effective April 22, 2009).

**Recall etc of arrestment or inhibition**

**7.A4.**—[1](1)    An application by any person having an interest—

    (a)    to loose, restrict, vary or recall an arrestment or an interim attachment; or

    (b)    to recall, in whole or in part, or vary, an inhibition,

shall be made by incidental application.

(2)    Paragraph (1) does not apply to an application made orally at a hearing under section 15K that has been fixed under section 15E(4) of the Act of 1987.

**Incidental applications in relation to interim diligence, etc**

**7.A5.**[2]    An application under Part 1A of the 1987 Act or Part 1A of the 2002 Act other than mentioned above shall be made by incidental application.

**Form of schedule of inhibition on the dependence**

**7.A6.**    *[Revoked by the Act of Sederunt (Sheriff Court Rules Amendment) (Diligence) 2009 (SSI 2009/107) r.6 (effective April 22, 2009).]*

**Service of inhibition on the dependence where address of defender not known**

**7.A7.**—[3](1)    Where the address of a defender is not known to the pursuer, an inhibition shall be deemed to have been served on the defender if the schedule of inhibition is left with or deposited at the office of the sheriff clerk of the sheriff court district where the defender's last known address is located.

(2)    Where service of an inhibition on the dependence is executed under paragraph (1), a copy of the schedule of inhibition shall be sent by the sheriff officer by first class post to the defender's last known address.

**Form of schedule of arrestment on the dependence**

**7.A8.**—[4](1)    An arrestment on the dependence shall be served by serving the schedule of arrestment on the arrestee in Form 9b.

(2)    A certificate of execution shall be lodged with the sheriff clerk in Form 9c.

**Service of schedule of arrestment**

**7.1.**    If a schedule of arrestment has not been personally served on an arrestee, the arrestment shall have effect only if a copy of the schedule is also sent by registered post or the first class recorded delivery service to—

    (a)    the last known place of residence of the arrestee; or

    (b)    if such place of residence is not known, or if the arrestee is a firm or corporation, to the arrestee's principal place of business if known, or, if not known, to any known place of business of the arrestee,

and the sheriff officer must, on the certificate of execution, certify that this has been done and specify the address to which the copy of the schedule was sent.

**Arrestment on dependence before service**

**7.2.**—[5](1)    An arrestment to found jurisdiction used prior to service shall cease to have effect, unless the summons is served within 21 days from the date of execution of the arrestment.

(2)    When such an arrestment as is referred to in paragraph (1) has been executed, the party using it must forthwith report the execution to the sheriff clerk.

**Recall and restriction of arrestment**

**7.3.**—(1)    The sheriff may order that an arrestment on the dependence of a claim or counterclaim shall cease to have effect if the party whose funds or property are arrested—

    (a)    pays into court; or

---

[1]  As inserted by the Act of Sederunt (Sheriff Court Rules Amendment) (Diligence) 2008 (SSI 2008/121) r.7(4) (effective April 1, 2008).

[2]  As inserted by the Act of Sederunt (Sheriff Court Rules Amendment) (Diligence) 2008 (SSI 2008/121) r.7(4) (effective April 1, 2008).

[3]  As inserted by the Act of Sederunt (Sheriff Court Rules Amendment) (Diligence) 2008 (SSI 2008/121) r.7(4) (effective April 1, 2008).

[4]  As inserted by the Act of Sederunt (Sheriff Court Rules Amendment) (Diligence) 2009 (SSI 2009/107) r.6 (effective April 22, 2009).

[5]  As amended by the Act of Sederunt (Sheriff Court Rules Amendment) (Diligence) (SSI 2008/121) r.7(5) (effective April 1, 2008). This rule as it applied immediately before April 1, 2008 continues to have effect for the purpose of any application for arrestment on the dependence made before that date.

(b)   finds caution to the satisfaction of the sheriff clerk in respect of, the sum claimed together with the sum of £50 in respect of expenses.

(2)   Without prejudice to paragraph (1), a party whose funds or property are arrested may at any time apply to the sheriff to exercise his powers to recall or restrict an arrestment on the dependence of a claim or counterclaim, with or without consignation or caution.

(3)   An application made under paragraph (3) must be intimated by the applicant to the party who instructed the arrestment.

(4)   On payment into court or the finding of caution to the satisfaction of the sheriff clerk in accordance with paragraph (1), or if the sheriff recalls or restricts an arrestment on the dependence of a claim in accordance with paragraph (2) and any condition imposed by the sheriff has been complied with, the sheriff clerk must—

(a)   issue to the party whose funds or property are arrested a certificate in Form 10 authorising the release of any sum or property arrested to the extent ordered by the sheriff; and

(b)   send a copy of the certificate to—

(i)   the party who instructed the arrestment; and

(ii)   the party who has possession of the funds or property that are arrested.

CHAPTER 8

UNDEFENDED CLAIM

## Undefended claim

**8.1.**—(1)   Where the defender has not lodged a form of response on or before the return day, the claim shall not require to call in court.

(2)   Where paragraph (1) applies, the pursuer must lodge a minute in Form 11 before the sheriff clerk's office closes for business on the second day before the date set for the hearing.

(3)   Where the pursuer has lodged a minute in accordance with paragraph (2), the sheriff may grant decree or other competent order sought in terms of that minute.

(4)   Where the pursuer has not lodged a minute in accordance with paragraph (2), the sheriff must dismiss the claim.

## Application for time to pay direction or time order

**8.2.**—(1)   If the defender admits the claim, he may, where competent—

(a)   make an application for a time to pay direction (including, where appropriate, an application for recall or restriction of an arrestment) or a time order by completing the appropriate parts of the Form 1a and lodging it with the sheriff clerk on or before the return day; or

(b)   lodge a form of response indicating that he admits the claim and intends to apply orally for a time to pay direction (including, where appropriate, an application for recall or restriction of an arrestment) or time order.

(1A)[1]   The sheriff clerk must on receipt forthwith intimate to the pursuer a copy of any response lodged under paragraph (1).

(2)[2]   Where the defender has lodged an application in terms of paragraph (1)(a), the pursuer may intimate that he does not object to the application by lodging a minute in Form 12 before the time the sheriff clerk's office closes for business on the day occurring 9 days before the hearing date stating that he does not object to the defender's application and seeking decree.

(3)   If the pursuer intimates in accordance with paragraph (2) that he does not object to the application—

(a)   the sheriff may grant decree on the hearing date;

(b)   the parties need not attend; and

(c)   the action will not call in court.

(4)[3]   If the pursuer wishes to oppose the application for a time to pay direction or time order made in accordance with paragraph (1)(a) he must before the time the sheriff clerk's office closes for business on the day occurring 9 days before the hearing date—

(a)   lodge a minute in Form 13; and

(b)   send a copy of that minute to the defender.

---

[1] As inserted by the Act of Sederunt (Sheriff Court Rules) (Miscellaneous Amendments) 2009 (SSI 2009/294) r.5 (effective December 1, 2009).

[2] As substituted by the Act of Sederunt (Sheriff Court Rules) (Miscellaneous Amendments) 2009 (SSI 2009/294) r.5 (effective December 1, 2009).

[3] As substituted by the Act of Sederunt (Sheriff Court Rules) (Miscellaneous Amendments) 2009 (SSI 2009/294) r.5 (effective December 1, 2009).

(5) Where the pursuer objects to an application in terms of paragraph (1)(a) or the defender has lodged a form of response in accordance with paragraph (1)(b), the action shall call in court on the hearing date when the parties may appear and the sheriff must decide the application and grant decree accordingly.

(6) The sheriff shall decide an application in accordance with paragraph (5) whether or not any of the parties appear.

(7) Where the defender has lodged an application in terms of paragraph (1)(a) and the pursuer fails to proceed in accordance with either of paragraphs (2) or (4) the sheriff may dismiss the claim.

### Decree in claims to which the Hague Convention or the Civil Jurisdiction and Judgments Act 1982 apply

**8.3.**—(1) If the summons has been served in a country to which the Hague Convention on the Service Abroad of Judicial and Extra-Judicial Documents in Civil or Commercial Matters dated 15th November 1965 applies, decree must not be granted until it is established to the satisfaction of the sheriff that the requirements of Article 15 of that Convention have been complied with.

(2) Where a defender is domiciled in another part of the United Kingdom or in another Contracting State, the sheriff shall not grant decree until it has been shown that the defender has been able to receive the summons in sufficient time to arrange his defence or that all necessary steps have been taken to that end.

(3) For the purposes of paragraph (2)—

    (a) the question whether a person is domiciled in another part of the United Kingdom shall be determined in accordance with sections 41 and 42 of the Civil Jurisdiction and Judgments Act 1982;

    (b) the question whether a person is domiciled in another Contracting State shall be determined in accordance with Article 52 of the Convention in Schedule 1 or 3C to that Act; and

    (c) the term "Contracting State" has the meaning assigned in section 1 of that Act.

CHAPTER 9

DEFENDED CLAIM

### The Hearing

**9.1.**—(1) Where a defender intends to—

    (a) challenge the jurisdiction of the court;

    (b) state a defence (including, where appropriate, a counterclaim); or

    (c) dispute the amount of the claim, he must complete the form of response part of Form 1a or 1b as appropriate indicating that intention and lodge it with the sheriff clerk on or before the return day.

(2) Where the defender has lodged a form of response in accordance with paragraph (1) the claim will call in court for a hearing ("the Hearing").

(3)[1] The Hearing shall be held on the hearing date which shall be 14 days after the return day.

(4) If the claim is not resolved at the Hearing, the sheriff may continue the Hearing to such other date as he considers to be appropriate.

(5) The defender must attend or be represented at the Hearing and the sheriff shall note any challenge, defence or dispute, as the case may be, on the summons.

(6) Where at the Hearing the defender—

    (a) does not appear or is not represented; and

    (b) the pursuer is present or is represented, decree may be granted against the defender in terms of the summons.

(7) Where at the Hearing—

    (a) the pursuer does not appear or is not represented; and

    (b) the defender is present or represented, the sheriff may grant decree of dismissal.

(8) If all parties fail to appear at the Hearing, the sheriff shall, unless sufficient reason appears to the contrary, dismiss the claim.

---

[1] As substituted by the Act of Sederunt (Sheriff Court Rules) (Miscellaneous Amendments) 2009 (SSI 2009/294) r.7 (effective December 1, 2009).

**Purpose of the Hearing**

**9.2.**—(1) If, at the Hearing, the sheriff is satisfied that the claim is incompetent or that there is a patent defect of jurisdiction, he must grant decree of dismissal in favour of the defender or, if appropriate, transfer the claim in terms of rule 15.1(2).

(2) At the Hearing, the sheriff shall—

    (a) ascertain the factual basis of the claim and any defence, and the legal basis on which the claim and defence are proceeding; and

    (b) seek to negotiate and secure settlement of the claim between the parties.

(3) If the sheriff cannot secure settlement of the claim between the parties, he shall—

    (a) identify and note on the summons the issues of fact and law which are in dispute;

    (b) note on the summons any facts which are agreed; and

    (c) if possible reach a decision on the whole dispute on the basis of the information before him.

    (d)[1] enquire whether there is or is likely to be a vulnerable witness within the meaning of section 11(1) of the 2004 Act who is to give evidence at any proof or hearing, consider any child witness notice or vulnerable witness application that has been lodged where no order has been made and consider whether any order under section 12(1) of the 2004 Act requires to be made.

(4) Where evidence requires to be led for the purposes of reaching a decision on the dispute, the sheriff shall—

    (a) direct parties to lead evidence on the disputed issues of fact which he has noted on the summons;

    (b) indicate to the parties the matters of fact that require to be proved, and may give guidance on the nature of the evidence to be led; and

    (c) fix a hearing on evidence for a later date for that purpose.

**Conduct of hearings**

**9.3.**—(1) Any hearing in a claim shall be conducted in accordance with the following paragraphs of this rule.

(2) A hearing shall be conducted as informally as the circumstances of the claim permit.

(3) The procedure to be adopted at a hearing shall be such as the sheriff considers—

    (a) to be fair;

    (b) best suited to the clarification and determination of the issues before him; and

    (c) gives each party sufficient opportunity to present his case.

(4) Before proceeding to hear evidence, the sheriff shall explain to the parties the form of procedure which he intends to adopt.

(5) Having considered the circumstances of the parties and whether (and to what extent) they are represented, the sheriff—

    (a) may, in order to assist resolution of the disputed issues of fact, put questions to parties and to witnesses; and

    (b) shall (if he considers it necessary for the fair conduct of the hearing) explain any legal terms or expressions which are used.

(6) Evidence will normally be taken on oath or affirmation but the sheriff may dispense with that requirement if it appears reasonable to do so.

**Inspection of places and objects**

**9.4.**—(1) If, at any hearing, a disputed issue noted by the sheriff is the quality or condition of an object, the sheriff may inspect the object in the presence of the parties or their representatives in court or, if it is not practicable to bring the object to court, at the place where the object is located.

(2) The sheriff may, if he considers it appropriate, inspect any place that is material to the disputed issues in the presence of the parties or their representatives.

**Remit to determine matter of fact**

**9.5.**—(1) The sheriff may, where parties agree, remit to any suitable person to report on any matter of fact.

---

[1] As inserted by the Act of Sederunt (Ordinary Cause, Summary Application, Summary Cause and Small Claim Rules) Amendment (Vulnerable Witnesses (Scotland) Act 2004) 2007 (SSI 2007/463) r.5(3) (effective November 1, 2007).

(2)   Where a remit is made under paragraph (1) above, the report of such person shall be final and conclusive with respect to the matter of fact which is the subject of the remit.

(3)   A remit shall not be made under paragraph (1) of this rule unless parties have previously agreed the basis upon which the fees, if any, of such person shall be met.

### Noting of evidence

**9.6.**   The sheriff must make notes of the evidence at a hearing for his own use and must retain these notes until after any appeal has been disposed of.

### Application for time to pay direction or time order in defended claim

**9.7.**   A defender in a claim which proceeds as defended may, where it is competent to do so, make an incidental application or apply orally at any hearing, at any time before decree is granted, for a time to pay direction (including where appropriate, an order recalling or restricting an arrestment on the dependence) or a time order.

### Pronouncement of decision

**9.8.**—(1)   The sheriff must, where practicable, give his decision and a brief statement of his reasons at the end of the hearing of a claim, or he may reserve judgment.

(2)   If the sheriff reserves judgment, he must, within 28 days of the hearing, give his decision in writing together with a brief note of his reasons, and the sheriff clerk must send a copy to the parties.

(3)   After giving his judgment, the sheriff must—

  (a)   deal with the question of expenses and, where appropriate, make an award of expenses; and

  (b)   grant decree as appropriate.

(4)   The decree of the sheriff shall be a final decree.

### CHAPTER 10

#### INCIDENTAL APPLICATIONS AND SISTS

### General

**10.1.**—(1)   Except where otherwise provided, any incidental application in a claim may be made—

  (a)   orally with the leave of the sheriff during any hearing of the claim; or

  (b)   by lodging the application in written form with the sheriff clerk.

(2)   An application lodged in accordance with paragraph (1)(b) may only be heard after not less than two days' notice has been given to the other party.

(3)   A party who is not—

  (a)   a partnership or a body corporate; or

  (b)   acting in a representative capacity, and is not represented by a solicitor, may require the sheriff clerk to intimate to the other party a copy of an incidental application.

(4)   Where the party receiving notice of an incidental application lodged in accordance with paragraph (1)(b) intimates to the sheriff clerk and the party making the application that it is not opposed, the application shall not require to call in court unless the sheriff so directs.

(5)   Any intimation under paragraph (4) shall be made not later than noon on the day before the application is due to be heard.

### Application to sist claim

**10.2.**—(1)   Where an incidental application to sist a claim is made, the reason for the sist—

  (a)   shall be stated by the party seeking the sist; and

  (b)   shall be recorded in the Register of Small Claims and on the summons.

(2)   Where a claim has been sisted, the sheriff may, after giving parties an opportunity to be heard, recall the sist.

### CHAPTER 11

#### COUNTER CLAIM

### Counterclaim

**11.1.**—(1)   If a defender intends to state a counterclaim he must—

  (a)   indicate that on the form of response; and

  (b)   state the counterclaim—

      (i)   in writing on the form of response; or

      (ii)   orally at the Hearing.

(2)   Where a defender states a counterclaim in accordance with paragraph (1)(b)(i) he must at the same time send a copy of the form of response to—

> (a) the pursuer; and
> (b) any other party.

(3) *[Repealed by the Act of Sederunt (Sheriff Court Rules) (Miscellaneous Amendments) 2009 (SSI 2009/294) r.12 (effective October 1, 2009).]*

(5) Where a defender has indicated in terms of paragraph (1)(a) that he intends to state a counterclaim orally at the Hearing the sheriff may continue the Hearing to allow an answer to the counterclaim to be stated.

(6) The defender may state a counterclaim after—

> (a) the Hearing; or
> (b) any continuation of the Hearing,

as the case may be, only with the leave of the sheriff.

(7) If a counterclaim has been stated orally at any hearing at which the pursuer fails to appear or be represented the sheriff may continue that hearing after noting the counterclaim and the factual basis of it to allow the pursuer to appear.

(8) Intimation of a continued hearing fixed under paragraph (7) shall be given to the pursuer by the sheriff clerk in Form 14 advising him that if he fails to appear or be represented at the continued hearing decree may be granted in terms of the counterclaim.

### CHAPTER 12

#### ALTERATION OF SUMMONS ETC.

**Alteration of summons etc.**

**12.1.**—(1) The sheriff may, on the incidental application of a party allow amendment of the summons, form of response or any counterclaim, and adjust the note of disputed issues at any time before final judgment is pronounced on the merits.

(2) In an undefended claim, the sheriff may order the amended summons to be re-served on the defender on such period of notice as he thinks fit.

### CHAPTER 13

#### ADDITIONAL DEFENDER

**Additional defender**

**13.1.**—(1) Any person who has not been called as a defender may apply by incidental application to the sheriff for leave to enter a claim as a defender, and to state a defence.

(2) An application under this rule must specify—

> (a) the applicant's title and interest to enter the claim; and
> (b) the grounds of the defence which he proposes to state.

(3) On the lodging of an application under this rule—

> (a) the sheriff must fix a date for hearing the application; and
> (b) the applicant must forthwith serve a copy of the application and of the order for a hearing on the parties to the claim.

(4) After hearing the applicant and any party to the claim the sheriff may, if he is satisfied that the applicant has shown title and interest to enter the claim, grant the application.

(5) Where an application is granted under paragraph (4)—

> (a) the applicant shall be treated as a defender; and
> (b) the claim shall proceed against him as if was the Hearing in terms of rule 9.2.

### CHAPTER 13A[1]

#### INTERVENTIONS BY THE COMMISSION FOR EQUALITY AND HUMAN RIGHTS

**Interpretation**

**13A.1.** In this Chapter "the CEHR" means the Commission for Equality and Human Rights.

**Interventions by the CEHR**

**13A.2.**—(1) The CEHR may apply to the sheriff for leave to intervene in any small claim in accordance with this Chapter.

---

[1] As inserted by the Act of Sederunt (Sheriff Court Rules) (Miscellaneous Amendments) 2008 (SSI 2008/223) r.7(2) (effective July 1, 2008).

(2) This Chapter is without prejudice to any other entitlement of the CEHR by virtue of having title and interest in relation to the subject matter of any proceedings by virtue of section 30(2) of the Equality Act 2006 or any other enactment to seek to be sisted as a party in those proceedings.

(3) Nothing in this Chapter shall affect the power of the sheriff to make such other direction as he considers appropriate in the interests of justice.

(4) Any decision of the sheriff in proceedings under this Chapter shall be final and not subject to appeal.

### Applications to intervene

**13A.3.**—(1) An application for leave to intervene shall be by way of minute of intervention in Form 14A and the CEHR shall—

    (a)   send a copy of it to all the parties; and

    (b)   lodge it in process, certifying that subparagraph (a) has been complied with.

(2) A minute of intervention shall set out briefly—

    (a)   the CEHR's reasons for believing that the proceedings are relevant to a matter in connection with which the CEHR has a function;

    (b)   the issue in the proceedings which the CEHR wishes to address; and

    (c)   the propositions to be advanced by the CEHR and the CEHR's reasons for believing that they are relevant to the proceedings and that they will assist the sheriff.

(3) The sheriff may—

    (a)   refuse leave without a hearing;

    (b)   grant leave without a hearing unless a hearing is requested under paragraph (4);

    (c)   refuse or grant leave after such a hearing.

(4) A hearing, at which the applicant and the parties may address the court on the matters referred to in paragraph (6)(c) may be held if, within 14 days of the minute of intervention being lodged, any of the parties lodges a request for a hearing.

(5) Any diet in pursuance of paragraph (4) shall be fixed by the sheriff clerk who shall give written intimation of the diet to the CEHR and all the parties.

(6) The sheriff may grant leave only if satisfied that—

    (a)   the proceedings are relevant to a matter in connection with which the CEHR has a function;

    (b)   the propositions to be advanced by the CEHR are relevant to the proceedings and are likely to assist him; and

    (c)   the intervention will not unduly delay or otherwise prejudice the rights of the parties, including their potential liability for expenses.

(7) In granting leave the sheriff may impose such terms and conditions as he considers desirable in the interests of justice, including, subject to section 36B of the Sheriff Courts (Scotland) Act 1971, making provision in respect of any additional expenses incurred by the parties as a result of the intervention.

(8) The sheriff clerk shall give written intimation of a grant or refusal of leave to the CEHR and all the parties.

### Form of intervention

**13A.4.**—(1) An intervention shall be by way of a written submission which (including any appendices) shall not exceed 5000 words.

(2) The CEHR shall lodge the submission and send a copy of it to all the parties by such time as the sheriff may direct.

(3) The sheriff may in exceptional circumstances—

    (a)   allow a longer written submission to be made;

    (b)   direct that an oral submission is to be made.

(4) Any diet in pursuance of paragraph (3)(b) shall be fixed by the sheriff clerk who shall give written intimation of the diet to the CEHR and all the parties.

INTERVENTIONS BY THE SCOTTISH COMMISSION FOR HUMAN RIGHTS

**Interpretation**

**13B.1.**    In this Chapter—

"the Act of 2006" means the Scottish Commission for Human Rights Act 2006; and
"the SCHR" means the Scottish Commission for Human Rights.

**Applications to intervene**

**13B.2.**—(1)    An application for leave to intervene shall be by way of minute of intervention in Form 14B and the SCHR shall—

    (a)    send a copy of it to all the parties; and

    (b)    lodge it in process, certifying that subparagraph (a) has been complied with.

(2)    In granting leave the sheriff may impose such terms and conditions as he considers desirable in the interests of justice, including, subject to section 36B of the Sheriff Courts (Scotland) Act 1971, making provision in respect of any additional expenses incurred by the parties as a result of the intervention.

(3)    The sheriff clerk shall give written intimation of a grant or refusal of leave to the SCHR and all the parties.

(4)    Any decision of the sheriff in proceedings under this Chapter shall be final and not subject to appeal.

**Invitations to intervene**

**13B.3.**—(1)    An invitation to intervene under section 14(2)(b) of the Act of 2006 shall be in Form 14C and the sheriff clerk shall send a copy of it to the SCHR and all the parties.

(2)    An invitation under paragraph (1) shall be accompanied by—

    (a)    a copy of the pleadings in the proceedings; and

    (b)    such other documents relating to those proceedings as the sheriff thinks relevant.

(3)    In issuing an invitation under section 14(2)(b) of the Act of 2006, the sheriff may impose such terms and conditions as he considers desirable in the interests of justice, including, subject to section 36B of the Sheriff Courts (Scotland) Act 1971, making provision in respect of any additional expenses incurred by the parties as a result of the intervention.

**Form of intervention**

**13B.4.**—(1)    An intervention shall be by way of a written submission which (including any appendices) shall not exceed 5000 words.

(2)    The SCHR shall lodge the submission and send a copy of it to all the parties by such time as the sheriff may direct.

(3)    The sheriff may in exceptional circumstances—

    (a)    allow a longer written submission to be made;

    (b)    direct that an oral submission is to be made.

(4)    Any diet in pursuance of paragraph (3)(b) shall be fixed by the sheriff clerk who shall give written intimation of the diet to the SCHR and all the parties.

CHAPTER 14

APPLICATIONS FOR SIST OF PARTY AND TRANSFERENCE

**Application for sist of party and transference**

**14.1.**—(1)    If a party dies or becomes legally incapacitated while a claim is depending, any person claiming to represent that party or his estate may apply by incidental application to be sisted as a party to the claim.

---

[1] As inserted by the Act of Sederunt (Sheriff Court Rules) (Miscellaneous Amendments) 2008 (SSI 2008/223) r.7(2) (effective July 1, 2008).

(2)  If a party dies or becomes legally incapacitated while a claim is depending and the provisions of paragraph (1) are not invoked, any other party may apply by incidental application to have the claim transferred in favour of or against, as the case may be, any person who represents that party or his estate.

## CHAPTER 15

### TRANSFER AND REMIT OF CLAIMS

**Transfer to another court**

**15.1.**—(1)  The sheriff may transfer a claim to any other sheriff court, whether in the same sheriffdom or not, if the sheriff considers it expedient to do so.

(2)  If the sheriff is satisfied that the court has no jurisdiction, he may transfer the claim to any sheriff court in which it appears to the sheriff that it ought to have been brought.

(3)  A claim so transferred shall proceed in all respects as if it had been brought originally in the court to which it is transferred.

**Remit between procedures**

**15.2.**—(1)  If the sheriff makes a direction that a claim is to be treated as an ordinary cause, he must, at the time of making that direction—

(a)  direct the pursuer to lodge an initial writ, and intimate it to every other party, within 14 days of the date of the direction;

(b)  direct the defender to lodge defences within 28 days of the date of the direction; and

(c)  fix a date and time for an Options Hearing and that date shall be the first suitable court day occurring not sooner than ten weeks, or such lesser period as he considers appropriate, after the last date for lodging the initial writ.

(2)  If the sheriff directs that a claim is to be treated as a summary cause he must specify the next step of procedure to be followed.

(3)  If the sheriff directs that an ordinary cause or a summary cause is to be treated as a claim under these rules it shall call for the Hearing held in terms of rule 9.1(2).

## CHAPTER 16

### PRODUCTIONS AND DOCUMENTS

**Lodging of productions**

**16.1.**—(1)  A party who intends to rely at a hearing at which evidence is to be led, upon any documents or articles in his possession, which are reasonably capable of being lodged with the court, must—

(a)  lodge them with the sheriff clerk together with a list detailing the items no later than 14 days before the hearing; and

(b)  at the same time send a copy of the list to the other party.

(2)  The documents referred to in paragraph (1) include any affidavit or other written statement admissible under section 2(1) of the Civil Evidence (Scotland) Act 1988.

(3)  Subject to paragraph (4), only documents or articles produced—

(a)  in accordance with paragraph (1);

(b)  at an earlier hearing; or

(c)  under rule 17.2(3) or (4), may be used or put in evidence.

(4)  Documents other than those mentioned in paragraph (3) may be used or put in evidence only with the—

(a)  consent of the parties; or

(b)  permission of the sheriff on cause shown, and on such terms as to expenses or otherwise as to him seem proper.

**Borrowing of productions**

**16.2.**—(1)  Any productions borrowed must be returned not later than noon on the day preceding the date of any hearing.

(2)  A receipt for any production borrowed must be entered in the list of productions and that list must be retained by the sheriff clerk.

(3)  Subject to paragraph (4), productions may be borrowed only by—

(a)  a solicitor; or

(b)  his authorised clerk for whom he shall be responsible.

(4)  A party litigant or an authorised lay representative may borrow a production only with permission of the sheriff and subject to such conditions as the sheriff may impose.

(5)  Productions may be inspected within the office of the sheriff clerk during normal business hours, and copies may be obtained by a party litigant, where practicable, from the sheriff clerk.

**Documents lost or destroyed**

**16.3.**—(1)   This rule applies to any—

    (a)   summons;

    (b)   form of response;

    (c)   counterclaim;

    (d)   Register of Small Claims; or

    (e)   other document lodged with the sheriff clerk in connection with a claim.

  (2)   Where any document mentioned in paragraph (1) is—

    (a)   lost; or

    (b)   destroyed,

a copy of it, authenticated in such manner as the sheriff may require, may be substituted and shall, for the purposes of the claim including the use of diligence, be equivalent to the original.

**Documents and productions to be retained in custody of sheriff clerk**

**16.4.**—(1)   This rule applies to all documents or other productions which have at any time been lodged or referred to during a hearing.

  (2)   The sheriff clerk must retain in his custody any document or other production mentioned in paragraph (1) until—

    (a)   after the expiry of the period during which an appeal is competent; and

    (b)   any appeal lodged has been disposed of.

  (3)   Each party who has lodged productions in a claim shall—

    (a)   after the final determination of the claim, where no appeal has been lodged, within 14 days after the appeal period has expired; or

    (b)   within 14 days after the disposal of any appeal lodged on the final determination of the claim, uplift the productions from the sheriff clerk.

  (4)   Where any production has not been uplifted as required by paragraph (3), the sheriff clerk shall intimate to—

    (a)   the solicitor who lodged the production; or

    (b)   where no solicitor is acting, the party himself or such other party as seems appropriate, that if he fails to uplift the production within 28 days after the date of such intimation, it will be disposed of in such manner as the sheriff directs.

CHAPTER 17

RECOVERY OF DOCUMENTS AND ATTENDANCE OF WITNESSES

**Diligence for recovery of documents**

**17.1.**—(1)   At any time after a summons has been served, a party may make an incidental application in writing to the sheriff to grant commission and diligence to recover documents.

  (2)   A party who makes an application in accordance with paragraph (1) must list in the application the documents which he wishes to recover.

  (3)   The sheriff may grant commission and diligence to recover those documents in the list mentioned in paragraph (2) which he considers relevant to the claim.

**Optional procedure before executing commission and diligence**

**17.2.**—(1)   Any party who has obtained a commission and diligence for the recovery of documents may, at any time before executing it, serve by first class recorded delivery post on the person from whom the documents are sought to be recovered (or on his known solicitor or solicitors) an order with certificate attached in Form 15.

  (2)   If in a claim the party in whose favour the commission and diligence has been granted is not—

    (a)   a partnership or body corporate; or

    (b)   acting in a representative capacity, and is not represented by a solicitor, service under paragraph (1) must be effected by the sheriff clerk posting a copy of the order together with a certificate in Form 15 by first class recorded delivery post or, on payment of the fee prescribed by the Scottish Ministers by order, by sheriff officer.

  (3)   Documents recovered in response to an order under paragraph (1) must be sent to, and retained by, the sheriff clerk who shall, on receiving them, advise the parties that the documents are in his possession and may be examined within his office during normal business hours.

  (4)   If the party who served the order is not satisfied that—

    (a)   full production has been made under the specification; or

987

(b) that adequate reasons for non-production have been given, he may execute the commission and diligence in normal form, notwithstanding his adoption in the first instance of the procedure in paragraph (1) above.

(5) Documents recovered under this rule may be submitted as evidence at any hearing without further formality, and rule 17.3(3) and (4) shall apply to such documents.

**Confidentiality of documents**

**17.3.**—(1) In any claim where a party has obtained a commission and diligence to recover documents and the documents have been produced either—

(a) before the execution of the commission and diligence; or

(b) following execution of the commission and diligence, confidentiality may be claimed for any document produced.

(2) Where confidentiality is claimed under paragraph (1), the documents in respect of which confidentiality is claimed shall be enclosed in a separate, sealed packet.

(3) A sealed packet referred to in paragraph (2) shall not be opened except by authority of the sheriff obtained on the application of the party who sought the commission and diligence.

(4) Before the sheriff grants an application made in accordance with paragraph (3), he shall offer to hear the party or parties from whose possession the documents specified in the commission and diligence were obtained.

**Witnesses**

**17.4.**—(1) A party shall be responsible for securing the attendance of his witnesses or havers at a hearing and shall be personally liable for their expenses.

(2) The summons or the copy served on the defender shall be sufficient warrant for the citation of witnesses or havers.

(3) The citation of a witness or haver must be in Form 16 and the certificate of execution of citation must be in Form 16a.

(4) The period of notice given to witnesses or havers cited in terms of paragraph (3) must be not less than seven days.

(5) A witness or haver shall be cited—

(a) by registered post or the first class recorded delivery service by the solicitor for the party on whose behalf he is cited;

(b) by a sheriff officer—

(i) personally;

(ii) by a citation being left with a resident at the person's dwelling place or an employee at his place of business;

(iii) by depositing it in that person's dwelling place or place of business;

(iv) by affixing it to the door of that person's dwelling place or place of business; or

(v) by registered post or the first class recorded delivery service.

(6) Where service is effected under paragraph 5(b)(iii) or (iv), the sheriff officer shall, as soon as possible after such service, send by ordinary post to the address at which he thinks it most likely that the person may be found, a letter containing a copy of the citation.

**Citation of witnesses by party litigants**

**17.5.**—(1) Where a party to a claim is a party litigant he shall—

(a) not later than 28 days before any hearing on evidence apply to the sheriff to fix caution for expenses in such sum as the sheriff considers reasonable having regard to the number of witnesses he proposes to cite and the period for which they may be required to attend court; and

(b) before instructing a solicitor or a sheriff officer to cite a witness, find the sum fixed in accordance with paragraph (1)(a).

(2) A party litigant who does not intend to cite all the witnesses referred to in his application under paragraph (1)(a) may apply for variation of the amount of caution.

**Witnesses failing to attend**

**17.6.**—(1) A hearing must not be adjourned solely on account of the failure of a witness to appear unless the sheriff, on cause shown, so directs.

(2) A witness or haver who fails without reasonable excuse to answer a citation after having been properly cited and offered his travelling expenses if he has asked for them may be ordered by the sheriff to pay a penalty not exceeding £250.

(3) The sheriff may grant decree for payment of a penalty imposed under paragraph (2) above in favour of the party on whose behalf the witness or haver was cited.

(4)   The sheriff may grant warrant for the apprehension of the witness or haver and for bringing him to court.

(5)   A warrant mentioned in paragraph (4) shall be effective in any sheriffdom without endorsation and the expenses of it may be awarded against the witness or haver.

CHAPTER 17A[1]

VULNERABLE WITNESSES (SCOTLAND) ACT 2004

**Interpretation**

**17A.1.**   In this Chapter—

"child witness notice" has the meaning given in section 12(2) of the 2004 Act;
"review application" means an application for review of arrangements for vulnerable witnesses pursuant to section 13 of the 2004 Act;
"vulnerable witness application" has the meaning given in section 12(6) of the 2004 Act.

**Child Witness Notice**

**17A.2.**   A child witness notice lodged in accordance with section 12(2) of the 2004 Act shall be in Form 16B.

**Vulnerable Witness Application**

**17A.3.**   A vulnerable witness application lodged in accordance with section 12(6) of the 2004 Act shall be in Form 16C.

**Intimation**

**17A.4.**—(1)   The party lodging a child witness notice or vulnerable witness application shall intimate a copy of the child witness notice or vulnerable witness application to all the other parties to the proceedings and complete a certificate of intimation.

(2)   A certificate of intimation referred to in paragraph (1) shall be in Form 16D and shall be lodged with the child witness notice or vulnerable witness application.

**Procedure on lodging child witness notice or vulnerable witness application**

**17A.5.**—(1)   On receipt of a child witness notice or vulnerable witness application, the sheriff may—

    (a)   make an order under section 12(1) or (6) of the 2004 Act without holding a hearing;
    (b)   require further information from any of the parties before making any further order;
    (c)   fix a date for a hearing of the child witness notice or vulnerable witness application.

(2)   The sheriff may, subject to any statutory time limits, make an order altering the date of the proof or other hearing at which the child or vulnerable witness is to give evidence and make such provision for intimation of such alteration to all parties concerned as he deems appropriate.

(3)   An order fixing a hearing for a child witness notice or vulnerable witness application shall be intimated by the sheriff clerk—

    (a)   on the day the order is made; and
    (b)   in such manner as may be prescribed by the sheriff,

to all parties to the proceedings and such other persons as are named in the order where such parties or persons are not present at the time the order is made.

**Review of arrangements for vulnerable witnesses**

**17A.6.**—(1)   A review application shall be in Form 16E.

(2)   Where the review application is made orally, the sheriff may dispense with the requirements of paragraph (1).

**Intimation of review application**

**17A.7.**—(1)   Where a review application is lodged, the applicant shall intimate a copy of the review application to all other parties to the proceedings and complete a certificate of intimation.

(2)   A certificate of intimation referred to in paragraph (1) shall be in Form 16F and shall be lodged together with the review application.

**Procedure on lodging a review application**

**17A.8.**—(1)   On receipt of a review application, the sheriff may—

---

[1] As inserted by the Act of Sederunt (Ordinary Cause, Summary Application, Summary Cause and Small Claim Rules) Amendment (Vulnerable Witnesses (Scotland) Act 2004) 2007 (SSI 2007/463) r.5(5) (effective November 1, 2007).

(a) if he is satisfied that he may properly do so, make an order under section 13(2) of the 2004 Act without holding a hearing or, if he is not so satisfied, make such an order after giving the parties an opportunity to be heard;

(b) require of any of the parties further information before making any further order;

(c) fix a date for a hearing of the review application.

(2) The sheriff may, subject to any statutory time limits, make an order altering the date of the proof or other hearing at which the child or vulnerable witness is to give evidence and make such provision for intimation of such alteration to all parties concerned as he deems appropriate.

(3) An order fixing a hearing for a review application shall be intimated by the sheriff clerk—

(a) on the day the order is made; and

(b) in such manner as may be prescribed by the sheriff,

to all parties to the proceedings and such other persons as are named in the order where such parties or persons are not present at the time the order is made.

### Determination of special measures

**17A.9.** When making an order under section 12(1) or (6) or 13(2) of the 2004 Act the sheriff may, in light thereof, make such further orders as he deems appropriate in all the circumstances.

### Intimation of an order under section 12(1) or (6) or 13(2)

**17A.10.** An order under section 12(1) or (6) or 13(2) of the 2004 Act shall be intimated by the sheriff clerk—

(a) on the day the order is made; and

(b) in such manner as may be prescribed by the sheriff,

to all parties to the proceedings and such other persons as are named in the order where such parties or persons are not present at the time the order is made.

### Taking of evidence by commissioner

**17A.11.**—(1) An interlocutor authorising the special measure of taking evidence by a commissioner shall be sufficient authority for the citing the witness to appear before the commissioner.

(2) At the commission the commissioner shall—

(a) administer the oath *de fideli administratione* to any clerk appointed for the commission; and

(b) administer to the witness the oath, or where the witness elects to affirm, the affirmation.

(3) The commission shall proceed without interrogatories unless, on cause shown, the sheriff otherwise directs.

### Commission on interrogatories

**17A.12.**—(1) Where interrogatories have not been dispensed with, the party citing or intending to cite the vulnerable witness shall lodge draft interrogatories in process.

(2) Any other party may lodge cross-interrogatories.

(3) The interrogatories and cross-interrogatories, when adjusted, shall be extended and returned to the sheriff clerk for approval and the settlement of any dispute as to their contents by the sheriff.

(4) The party who cited the vulnerable witness shall—

(a) provide the commissioner with a copy of the pleadings (including any adjustments and amendments), the approved interrogatories and any cross-interrogatories and a certified copy of the interlocutor of his appointment;

(b) instruct the clerk; and

(c) be responsible in the first instance for the fee of the commissioner and his clerk.

(5) The commissioner shall, in consultation with the parties, fix a diet for the execution of the commission to examine the witness.

### Commission without interrogatories

**17A.13.** Where interrogatories have been dispensed with, the party citing or intending to cite the vulnerable witness shall—

(a) provide the commissioner with a copy of the pleadings (including any adjustments and amendments) and a certified copy of the interlocutor of his appointment;

(b) fix a diet for the execution of the commission in consultation with the commissioner and every other party;

(c) instruct the clerk; and

(d) be responsible in the first instance for the fees of the commissioner and his clerk.

**Lodging of video record and documents**

**17A.14.**—(1)   Where evidence is taken on commission pursuant to an order made under section 12(1) or (6) or 13(2) of the 2004 Act the commissioner shall lodge the video record of the commission and relevant documents with the sheriff clerk.

(2)   On the video record and any documents being lodged the sheriff clerk shall—

    (a)   note—

        (i)   the documents lodged;

        (ii)   by whom they were lodged; and

        (iii)   the date on which they were lodged, and

    (b)   intimate what he has noted to all parties concerned.

**Custody of video record and documents**

**17A.15.**—(1)   The video record and documents referred to in rule 17A.14 shall, subject to paragraph (2), be kept in the custody of the sheriff clerk.

(2)   Where the video record of the evidence of a witness is in the custody of the sheriff clerk under this rule and where intimation has been given to that effect under rule 17A.14(2), the name and address of that witness and the record of his evidence shall be treated as being in the knowledge of the parties; and no party shall be required, notwithstanding any enactment to the contrary—

    (a)   to include the name of that witness in any list of witnesses; or

    (b)   to include the record of his evidence in any list of productions.

**Application for leave for party to be present at the commission**

**17A.16.**   An application for leave for a party to be present in the room where the commission proceedings are taking place shall be by incidental application..

(4)   In Appendix 1—

    (a)   for Form 16 there shall be set out the form in Part 1 of Schedule 3 to this Act of Sederunt; and

    (b)   after Form 16A there shall be inserted the forms set out in Part 2 of Schedule 3 to this Act of Sederunt.

CHAPTER 18

EUROPEAN COURT

**Interpretation of rules 18.2 to 18.5**

**18.1.**—[1](1)   In rules 18.2 to 18.5—

"the European Court" means the Court of Justice of the European Communities;

"reference" means a reference to the European Court for—

    (a)   a preliminary ruling under Article 267 of the Treaty on the Functioning of the European Union, Article 150 of the Euratom Treaty or Article 41 of the E.C.S.C. Treaty; or

    (b)   a ruling on the interpretation of the Conventions, as defined in section 1(1) of the Civil Jurisdiction and Judgments Act 1982, under Article 3 of Schedule 2 to that Act.

(2)   The expressions "Euratom Treaty" and "E.C.S.C. Treaty" have the meanings assigned respectively in Schedule 1 to the European Communities Act 1972.

(3)[2]   In paragraph (1), "the Treaty on the Functioning of the European Union" means the treaty referred to in section 1(2)(s) of the European Communities Act 1972.

**Application for reference**

**18.2.**—(1)   The sheriff may, on the incidental application of a party, or of his own accord, make a reference.

(2)   A reference must be made in the form of a request for a preliminary ruling of the European Court in Form 17.

---

[1] As amended by the Act of Sederunt (Sheriff Court Rules) (Miscellaneous Amendments) (No.3) 2012 (SSI 2012/271) para.8 (effective November 1, 2012).

[2] As inserted by the Act of Sederunt (Sheriff Court Rules) (Miscellaneous Amendments) (No.3) 2012 (SSI 2012/271) para.8 (effective November 1, 2012).

### Preparation of case for reference

**18.3.**—(1)  If the sheriff decides that a reference shall be made, he must within four weeks draft a reference.

(2)  On the reference being drafted, the sheriff clerk must send a copy to each party.

(3)  Within four weeks after the date on which copies of the draft have been sent to parties, each party may—

    (a)  lodge with the sheriff clerk; and

    (b)  send to every other party, a note of any adjustments he seeks to have made in the draft reference.

(4)  Within 14 days after the date on which any such note of adjustments may be lodged, the sheriff, after considering any such adjustments, must make and sign the reference.

(5)  The sheriff clerk must forthwith intimate the making of the reference to each party.

### Sist of claim

**18.4.**—(1)  Subject to paragraph (2), on a reference being made, the claim must, unless the sheriff when making the reference otherwise orders, be sisted until the European Court has given a preliminary ruling on the question referred to it.

(2)  The sheriff may recall a sist made under paragraph (1) for the purpose of making an interim order which a due regard to the interests of the parties may require.

### Transmission of reference

**18.5.**  A copy of the reference, certified by the sheriff clerk, must be transmitted by the sheriff clerk to the Registrar of the European Court.

### CHAPTER 19

#### ABANDONMENT

### Abandonment of claim

**19.1.**—(1)  At any time prior to decree being granted, the pursuer may offer to abandon the claim.

(2)  If the pursuer offers to abandon, the sheriff clerk must assess the expenses payable by the pursuer to the defender on such basis as the sheriff may direct subject to the provisions of section 36B of the 1971 Act and rule 21.6, and the claim must be continued to the first appropriate court occurring not sooner than 14 days thereafter.

(3)  If before the continued diet the pursuer makes payment to the defender of the amount fixed under paragraph (2), the sheriff must dismiss the action unless the pursuer consents to absolvitor.

(4)  If before the continued diet the pursuer fails to pay the amount fixed under paragraph (2), the defender shall be entitled to decree of absolvitor with expenses.

### CHAPTER 20

#### DECREE BY DEFAULT

### Decree by default

**20.1.**—(1)  If, after the sheriff has fixed a hearing on evidence under rule 9.2(4), any party fails to appear or be represented at a hearing, the sheriff may grant decree by default.

(2)  If all parties fail to appear or be represented at a hearing referred to at paragraph (1) the sheriff must, unless sufficient reason appears to the contrary, dismiss the claim and any counterclaim.

(3)  If, after a defence has been stated, a party fails to implement an order of the court, the sheriff may, after giving him an opportunity to be heard, grant decree by default.

(4)  The sheriff shall not grant decree by default solely on the ground that a party has failed to appear at the hearing of an incidental application.

### CHAPTER 21

#### DECREES, EXTRACTS, EXECUTION AND VARIATION

### Decree

**21.1.**—(1)  The sheriff must not grant decree against—

    (a)  a defender in respect of a claim; or

    (b)  a pursuer in respect of a counterclaim,

under any provision of these Rules unless satisfied that a ground of jurisdiction exists.

### Decree for alternative claim for payment

**21.2.**—(1)  If the sheriff has granted decree for—

    (a)    delivery;

    (b)    recovery of possession of moveable property; or

    (c)    implement of an obligation,

and the defender fails to comply with that decree, the pursuer may lodge with the sheriff clerk an incidental application for decree in terms of the alternative claim for payment.

    (2)    If the pursuer lodges an incidental application in terms of paragraph (1), he must intimate it to the defender at or before the time it is lodged with the sheriff clerk.

    (3)    The pursuer must appear at the hearing of an incidental application under paragraph (1).

### Taxes on funds under control of the court

    **21.3.**    In a claim in which money has been consigned into court under the Sheriff Court Consignations (Scotland) Act 1893, no decree, warrant or order for payment to any person shall be granted until there has been lodged with the sheriff clerk a certificate by an authorised officer of the Inland Revenue stating that all taxes or duties payable to the Commissioners of Inland Revenue have been paid or satisfied.

### Correction of interlocutor or note

    **21.4.**    At any time before extract, the sheriff may correct any clerical or incidental error in an interlocutor or note attached to it.

### Extract of decree

    **21.5.**—(1)    Unless the sheriff on application authorises earlier extract, extract of a decree signed by the sheriff clerk may be issued only after the lapse of 14 days from the granting of the decree.

    (2)    An application for early extract shall be made by incidental application.

    (3)    In a claim where an appeal has been lodged, the extract may not be issued until the appeal has been disposed of.

    (4)    The extract decree—

        (a)    may be written on the summons or on a separate paper;

        (b)    may be in one of Forms 18 to 18i; and

        (c)    shall be warrant for all lawful execution.

### Expenses

    **21.6.**—(1)[1]    This rule applies, subject to section 36B of the 1971 Act, to the determination of expenses—

        (a)    in a claim, where the defender has—

            (i)    not stated a defence;

            (ii)    having stated a defence, has not proceeded with it; or

            (iii)    having stated a defence, has not acted in good faith as to its merits;

        (b)    in a claim where there has been unreasonable conduct on the part of a party to that claim in relation to the proceedings or the claim; or

        (c)    in an appeal to the sheriff principal.

    (2)[2]    Subject to paragraphs (3) to (5), the sheriff clerk must, with the approval of the sheriff, assess the amount of expenses including the fees and outlays of witnesses awarded in any claim, in accordance with the applicable statutory table of fees.

    (3)[3]    Paragraph (4) applies to a party who—

        (a)    represents himself;

        (b)    is represented by an authorised lay representative or a person authorised under any enactment to conduct proceedings in the sheriff court; or

        (c)    is not an individual and—

            (i)    is represented by an authorised lay representative or a person authorised under any enactment to conduct proceedings in the sheriff court; and

            (ii)    if unrepresented could not represent itself.

---

[1] As substituted by Act of Sederunt (Ordinary Cause, Summary Application, Summary Cause and Small Claim Rules) Amendment (Miscellaneous) 2005 (SSI 2005/648) r.5(2) (effective January 2, 2006).

[2] As amended by the Act of Sederunt (Sheriff Court Rules Amendment) (Sections 25 to 29 of the Law Reform (Miscellaneous Provisions) (Scotland) Act 1990) 2009 (SSI 2009/164) r.5(3) (effective May 20, 2009).

[3] As amended by the Act of Sederunt (Ordinary Cause, Summary Application, Summary Cause and Small Claim Rules) Amendment (Miscellaneous) 2007 (SSI 2007/6) r.5(c) (effective January 29, 2007).

(4)   A party mentioned in paragraph (3) who, if he had been represented by a solicitor or advocate would have been entitled to expenses, may be awarded any outlays or expenses to which he might be found entitled by virtue of the 1975 Act or any enactment under that Act.

(5)   In every case including an appeal where expenses are awarded, the sheriff clerk shall hear the parties or their solicitors on the claims for expenses including fees, if any, and outlays.

(6)   Except where the sheriff principal or the sheriff has reserved judgment or where he orders otherwise, the hearing on the claim for expenses must take place immediately upon the decision being pronounced.

(7)   When that hearing is not held immediately, the sheriff clerk must—

    (a)   fix the date, time and place when he shall hear the parties or their solicitors; and

    (b)   give all parties at least 14 days' notice in writing of the hearing so fixed.

(8)   The party awarded expenses must—

    (a)   lodge his account of expenses in court at least seven days prior to the date of any hearing fixed under paragraph (7); and

    (b)   at the same time forward a copy of that account to every other party.

(9)   The sheriff clerk must—

    (a)   fix the amount of the expenses; and

    (b)   report his decision to the sheriff principal or the sheriff in open court for his approval at a diet which the sheriff clerk has intimated to the parties.

(10)   The sheriff principal or the sheriff, after hearing parties or their solicitors if objections are stated, must pronounce final decree including decree for payment of expenses as approved by him.

(11)   In an appeal, the sheriff may pronounce decree under paragraph (10) on behalf of the sheriff principal.

(12)   Failure by—

    (a)   any party to comply with any of the foregoing provisions of this rule; or

    (b)   the successful party or parties to appear at the hearing on expenses, must be reported by the sheriff clerk to the sheriff principal or the sheriff at a diet which the sheriff clerk has intimated to the parties.

(13)   In either of the circumstances mentioned in paragraphs (12)(a) or (b), the sheriff principal or sheriff must, unless sufficient cause be shown, pronounce decree on the merits of the claim and find no expenses due to or by any party.

(14)   A decree pronounced under paragraph (13) shall be held to be the final decree for the purposes of these Rules.

(15)   The sheriff principal or sheriff may, if he thinks fit, on the application of the solicitor of any party to whom expenses may be awarded, made at or before the time of the final decree being pronounced, grant decree in favour of that solicitor for the expenses of the claim.

### Charge

**21.7.**—(1)   The period for payment specified in any charge following on a decree for payment granted in a claim shall be—

    (a)   14 days if the person on whom it is served is within the United Kingdom; and

    (b)   28 days if he is outside the United Kingdom or his whereabouts are unknown.

(2)   The period in respect of any other form of charge on a decree granted in a claim shall be 14 days.

### Service of charge where address of defender is unknown

**21.8.**—(1)   If the address of a defender is not known to the pursuer, a charge shall be deemed to have been served on the defender if it is—

    (a)   served on the sheriff clerk of the sheriff court district where the defender's last known address is located; and

    (b)   displayed by the sheriff clerk on the walls of court for the period of the charge.

(2)   On receipt of such a charge, the sheriff clerk must display it on the walls of court and it must remain displayed for the period of the charge.

(3)   The period specified in the charge shall run from the first date on which it was displayed on the walls of court.

(4)   On the expiry of the period of charge, the sheriff clerk must endorse a certificate in Form 19 on the charge certifying that it has been displayed in accordance with this rule and must thereafter return the charge to the sheriff officer by whom service was executed.

### Diligence on decree in claim for delivery

**21.9.**—(1)   In a claim for delivery, the court may, when granting decree, grant warrant to search for and take possession of goods and to open shut and lockfast places.

(2)   A warrant granted under paragraph (1) shall only apply to premises occupied by the defender.

**Applications in same claim for variation, etc. of decree**

**21.10.**—(1)   If by virtue of any enactment the sheriff, without a new action being initiated, may order that—

(a)   a decree granted be varied, discharged or rescinded; or

(b)   the execution of that decree in so far as it has not already been executed be sisted or suspended, the party requesting the sheriff to make such an order must do so by lodging a minute to that effect, setting out briefly the reasons for the application.

(2)   On the lodging of such a minute by the pursuer, the sheriff clerk must grant warrant for service upon the defender (provided that the pursuer has returned the extract decree).

(3)   On the lodging of such a minute by the defender, the sheriff clerk must grant warrant for service upon the pursuer ordaining him to return the extract decree and may, where appropriate, grant interim sist of execution of the decree.

(4)   Subject to paragraph (5), the minute shall not be heard in court unless seven days' notice of the minute and warrant has been given to the other parties by the party lodging the minute.

(5)   The sheriff may, on cause shown, alter the period of seven days referred to in paragraph (4) but may not reduce it to less than two days.

(6)   This rule shall not apply to any proceedings under the Debtors (Scotland) Act 1987 or to proceedings which may be subject to the provisions of that Act.

CHAPTER 22

RECALL OF DECREE

**Recall of decree**

**22.1.**—[1](1)   A party may apply for recall of a decree granted under any of the following provisions—

(a)   rule 8.1(3);

(b)   paragraph (6), (7) or (8) of rule 9.1; or

(c)   rule 11.1(8).

(2)   The application is to be by minute in Form 20, which must be lodged with the sheriff clerk.

(3)   The application must include where appropriate (and if not already lodged with the sheriff clerk), the proposed defence or the proposed answer to the counterclaim.

(4)   A party may apply for recall of a decree in the same claim on one occasion only.

(5)   A minute for recall of a decree of dismissal must be lodged within 14 days of the date of decree.

(6)   Subject to paragraphs (7) and (8), a minute for recall of any other kind of decree may be lodged at any time before the decree is fully implemented.

(7)   Subject to paragraph (8), where a charge or arrestment has been executed following the decree, the minute must be lodged within 14 days of that execution (or the first such execution where there has been more than one).

(8)   In the case of a party seeking recall who was served with the action under rule 6.5, the minute must be lodged—

(a)   within a reasonable time of such party having knowledge of the decree against him or her; but

(b)   in any event, within one year of the date of decree.

(9)   On the lodging of a minute for recall of a decree, the sheriff clerk must fix a date, time and place for a hearing of the minute.

(10)   Where a hearing has been fixed under paragraph (9), the party seeking recall must, not less than 7 days before the date fixed for the hearing, serve on the other party—

(a)   a copy of the minute in Form 20a; and

(b)   a note of the date, time and place of the hearing.

(11)   Paragraph (12) applies if the party seeking recall—

(a)   is not a partnership or body corporate;

(b)   is not acting in a representative capacity; and

(c)   is not represented by a solicitor.

(12)   The sheriff clerk must assist such party to complete and lodge the minute for recall and arrange service of the minute for recall—

---

[1] As substituted by the Act of Sederunt (Sheriff Court Rules) (Miscellaneous Amendments) 2011 (SSI 2011/193) r.17 (effective April 4, 2011).

(a)  by first class recorded delivery post; or

(b)  on payment of the fee prescribed by the Scottish Ministers by order, by sheriff officer.

(13)  At a hearing fixed under paragraph (9), the sheriff must recall the decree so far as not implemented and the hearing must then proceed as a hearing held under rules 9.1(4) to (8) and 9.2.

(14)  A minute for recall of a decree, when lodged and served in terms of this rule, will have the effect of preventing any further action being taken by the other party to enforce the decree.

(15)  On receipt of the copy minute for recall of a decree, any party in possession of an extract decree must return it forthwith to the sheriff clerk.

(16)  If it appears to the sheriff that there has been any failure or irregularity in service of the minute for recall of a decree, the sheriff may order re-service of the minute on such conditions as the sheriff thinks fit.

## CHAPTER 23

### APPEALS

**Appeals**

**23.1.**—(1)  An appeal to the sheriff principal, other than an appeal to which rule 23.4 applies, must be by note of appeal in Form 21 and lodged with the sheriff clerk not later than 14 days after the date of final decree—

(a)  requesting a stated case; and

(b)  specifying the point of law upon which the appeal is to proceed.

(2)  The appellant must, at the same time as lodging a note of appeal, intimate a copy of it to every other party.

(3)  The sheriff must, within 28 days of the lodging of a note of appeal, issue a draft stated case containing—

(a)  findings in fact and law or, where appropriate, a narrative of the proceedings before him;

(b)  appropriate questions of law; and

(c)  a note stating the reasons for his decisions in law, and the sheriff clerk must send a copy of the draft stated case to the parties.

(4)  Within 14 days of the issue of the draft stated case—

(a)  a party may lodge with the sheriff clerk a note of any adjustments which he seeks to make;

(b)  a respondent may state any point of law which he wishes to raise in the appeal; and

(c)  the note of adjustment and, where appropriate, point of law must be intimated to every other party.

(5)  The sheriff may, on the motion of a party or of his own accord, and must where he proposes to reject any proposed adjustment, allow a hearing on adjustments and may provide for such further procedure under this rule prior to the hearing of the appeal as he thinks fit.

(6)  The sheriff must, within 14 days after—

(a)  the latest date on which a note of adjustments has been or may be lodged; or

(b)  where there has been a hearing on adjustments, that hearing, and after considering such note and any representations made to him at the hearing, state and sign the case.

(7)  If the sheriff is temporarily absent from duty for any reason, the sheriff principal may extend any period specified in paragraphs (3) or (6) for such period or periods as he considers reasonable.

(8)  The stated case signed by the sheriff must include questions of law, framed by him, arising from the points of law stated by the parties and such other questions of law as he may consider appropriate.

(9)  After the sheriff has signed the stated case, the sheriff clerk must—

(a)  place before the sheriff principal all documents and productions in the case together with the stated case; and

(b)  send to the parties a copy of the stated case together with a written note of the date, time and place of the hearing of the appeal.

**Effect of and abandonment of appeal**

**23.2.**—(1)  When a note of appeal has been lodged, it may be insisted on by all other parties in the claim although they may not have lodged separate appeals.

(2)  After a note of appeal has been lodged, the appellant shall not be at liberty to withdraw it, except—

(a)  with the consent of the other parties which may be incorporated in a joint minute; or

(b)  by leave of the sheriff principal and on such terms as to expenses or otherwise at to him seem proper.

## Hearing of appeal

**23.3.**—(1)  The sheriff principal shall hear the parties or their solicitors orally on all matters connected with the appeal including liability for expenses, but if any party moves that the question of liability for expenses be heard after the sheriff principal has given his decision the sheriff principal may grant that motion.

(2)  In the hearing of an appeal, a party shall not be allowed to raise questions of law of which notice has not been given except on cause shown and subject to such conditions as to expenses or otherwise as the sheriff principal may consider appropriate.

(3)  The sheriff principal may permit a party to amend any question of law or to add any new question in accordance with paragraph (2).

(4)  The sheriff principal may—

    (a)  adhere to or vary the decree appealed against;

    (b)  recall the decree appealed against and substitute another therefor; or

    (c)  remit, if he considers it desirable, to the sheriff, for any reason other than to have further evidence led.

(5)  At the conclusion of the hearing, the sheriff principal may either pronounce his decision or reserve judgment in which case he must give his decision in writing within 28 days and the sheriff clerk must forthwith intimate it to the parties.

## Appeal in relation to a time to pay direction

**23.4.**—(1)  This rule applies to appeals to the sheriff principal or to the Court of Session which relate solely to any application in connection with a time to pay direction.

(2)  Rules 23.1, 23.2 and 23.3(2) and (3) shall not apply to appeals under this rule.

(3)  An application for leave to appeal against a decision in an application for a time to pay direction or any order connected therewith must—

    (a)  be made in Form 22, within seven days of that decision, to the sheriff who made the decision; and

    (b)  must specify the question of law upon which the appeal is to proceed.

(4)  If leave to appeal is granted, the appeal must be lodged in Form 23 and intimated by the appellant to every other party within 14 days of the order granting leave and the sheriff must state in writing his reasons for his original decision.

(5)  An appeal under this rule to the sheriff principal shall proceed in accordance with paragraphs (1), (4) and (5) of rule 23.3.

## Sheriff to regulate interim possession

**23.5.**—(1)  Notwithstanding an appeal, the sheriff shall have power—

    (a)  to regulate all matters relating to interim possession;

    (b)  to make any order for the preservation of any property to which the claim relates or for its sale, if perishable;

    (c)  to make any order for the preservation of evidence; or

    (d)  to make in his discretion any interim order which a due regard for the interests of the parties may require.

(2)  An order under paragraph (1) shall not be subject to review except by the appellate court at the hearing of the appeal.

CHAPTER 24

MANAGEMENT OF DAMAGES PAYABLE TO PERSONS UNDER LEGAL DISABILITY

## Orders for payment and management of money

**24.1.**—(1)  In a claim of damages in which a sum of money becomes payable, by virtue of a decree or an extra-judicial settlement, to or for the benefit of a person under legal disability (other than a person under the age of 18 years), the sheriff shall make such order regarding the payment and management of that sum for the benefit of that person as he thinks fit.

(2)  Any order required under paragraph (1) shall be made on the granting of decree for payment or of absolvitor.

## Methods of management

**24.2.**  In making an order under rule 24.1 (1), the sheriff may—

    (a)  order the money to be paid to—

        (i)  the Accountant of Court, or

        (ii)  the guardian of the person under legal disability, as trustee, to be applied,

997

invested or otherwise dealt with and administered under the directions of the sheriff for the benefit of the person under legal disability;

(b)    order the money to be paid to the sheriff clerk of the sheriff court district in which the person under legal disability resides, to be applied, invested or otherwise dealt with and administered, under the directions of the sheriff of that district, for the benefit of the person under legal disability; or

(c)    order the money to be paid directly to the person under legal disability.

**Subsequent orders**

**24.3.**—(1)  If the sheriff has made an order under rule 24.1(1), any person having an interest may apply for an order under rule 24.2, or any other order for the payment or management of the money, by incidental application.

(2)  An application for directions under rule 24.2(a) or (b) may be made by any person having an interest by incidental application.

**Management of money paid to sheriff clerk**

**24.4.**—(1)  A receipt in Form 24 by the sheriff clerk shall be a sufficient discharge in respect of the amount paid to him under rules 24.1 to 24.3.

(2)  The sheriff clerk shall, at the request of any competent court, accept custody of any sum of money in an claim of damages ordered to be paid to, applied, invested or otherwise dealt with by him, for the benefit of a person under legal disability.

(3)  Any money paid to the sheriff clerk under rules 24.1 to 24.3 must be paid out, applied, invested or otherwise dealt with by the sheriff clerk only after such intimation, service and enquiry as the sheriff may order.

(4)  Any sum of money invested by the sheriff clerk under rules 24.1 to 24.3 must be invested in a manner in which trustees are authorised to invest by virtue of the Trustee Investments Act 1961.

**Management of money payable to children**

**24.5.**  If the sheriff has made an order under section 13 of the Children (Scotland) Act 1995, an application by a person for an order by virtue of section 11(1)(d) of that Act must be made in writing.

CHAPTER 25

ELECTRONIC TRANSMISSION OF DOCUMENTS

**Extent of provision**

**25.1.**—(1)  Any document referred to in these rules which requires to be—

(a)    lodged with the sheriff clerk;

(b)    intimated to a party; or

(c)    sent by the sheriff clerk, may be in electronic or documentary form, and if in electronic form may be lodged, intimated or sent by e-mail or similar means.

(2)  Paragraph (1) does not apply to any certificate of execution of service, citation or arrestment, or to a decree or extract decree of the court.

(3)  Where any document is lodged by e-mail or similar means the sheriff may require any principal document to be lodged.

**Time of lodgement**

**25.2.**  The time of lodgement, intimation or sending shall be the time when the document was sent or transmitted.

CHAPTER 26[1]

THE EQUALITY ACT 2010

**Interpretation and application**

**26.1.**—[2](1)  In this Chapter—

"the Commission" means the Commission for Equality and Human Rights; and

---

[1] As inserted by the Act of Sederunt (Ordinary Cause, Summary Application, Summary Cause and Small Claim Rules) Amendment (Equality Act 2006 etc.) 2006 (SSI 2006/509) r.5(2) (effective November 3, 2006). Chapter title amended by the Act of Sederunt (Sheriff Court Rules) (Equality Act 2010) 2010 (SSI 2010/340) para.5 (effective October 1, 2010).

[2] As substituted by the Act of Sederunt (Sheriff Court Rules) (Equality Act 2010) 2010 (SSI 2010/340) para.5 (effective October 1, 2010).

"the 2010 Act" means the Equality Act 2010.

(2)    This Chapter applies to claims made by virtue of section 114(1) of the 2010 Act including a claim for damages.

### Intimation to Commission

**26.2.**[1]    The pursuer shall send a copy of the summons to the Commission by registered or recorded delivery post.

### Assessor

**26.3.**—(1)    The sheriff may, of his own motion or on the incidental application of any party, appoint an assessor.

(2)    The assessor shall be a person who the sheriff considers has special qualifications to be of assistance in determining the cause.

### Taxation of Commission expenses

**26.4.**    *[Omitted by the Act of Sederunt (Sheriff Court Rules) (Miscellaneous Amendments) 2008 (SSI 2008/223) para.7(3)(c) (effective July 1, 2008).]*

### National security

**26.5.**—[2](1)    Where, on an incidental application under paragraph (3) or of the sheriffs own motion, the sheriff considers it expedient in the interests of national security, the sheriff may—

    (a)    exclude from all or part of the proceedings—
            (i)    the pursuer;
            (ii)   the pursuer's representatives;
            (iii)  any assessors;
    (b)    permit a pursuer or representative who has been excluded to make a statement to the court before the commencement of the proceedings or the part of the proceedings, from which he or she is excluded;
    (c)    take steps to keep secret all or part of the reasons for his or her decision in the proceedings.

(2)    The sheriff clerk shall, on the making of an order under paragraph (1) excluding the pursuer or the pursuer's representatives, notify the Advocate General for Scotland of that order.

(3)    A party may make an incidental application for an order under paragraph (1).

(4)    The steps referred to in paragraph (1)(c) may include the following—

    (a)    directions to the sheriff clerk; and
    (b)    orders requiring any person appointed to represent the interests of the pursuer in proceedings from which the pursuer or the pursuer's representatives are excluded not to communicate (directly or indirectly) with any persons (including the excluded pursuer)—
            (i)    on any matter discussed or referred to;
            (ii)   with regard to any material disclosed, during or with reference to any part of the proceedings from which the pursuer or the pursuer's representatives are excluded.

(5)    Where the sheriff has made an order under paragraph (4)(b), the person appointed to represent the interests of the pursuer may make an incidental application for authority to seek instructions from or otherwise communicate with an excluded person.

(6)    The sheriff may, on the application of a party intending to lodge an incidental application in written form, reduce the period of notice of two days specified in rule 10.1(2) or dispense with notice.

(7)    An application under paragraph (6) shall be made in the written incidental application, giving reasons for such reduction or dispensation.

### Transfer to Employment Tribunal

**26.6.**—[3](1)    On transferring proceedings to an employment tribunal under section 140(2) of the 2010 Act, the sheriff —

    (a)    shall state his or her reasons for doing so in the interlocutor; and
    (b)    may make the order on such conditions as to expenses or otherwise as he or she thinks fit.

---

[1]  As substituted by the Act of Sederunt (Sheriff Court Rules) (Miscellaneous Amendments) 2008 (SSI 2008/223) r.7(3)(b) (effective July 1, 2008).
[2]  As inserted by the Act of Sederunt (Sheriff Court Rules) (Equality Act 2010) 2010 (SSI 2010/340) para.5 (effective October 1, 2010).
[3]  As inserted by the Act of Sederunt (Sheriff Court Rules) (Equality Act 2010) 2010 (SSI 2010/340) para.5 (effective October 1, 2010).

(2) The sheriff clerk must, within 7 days from the date of such order—

    (a) transmit the relevant process to the Secretary of the Employment Tribunals (Scotland);

    (b) notify each party to the proceedings in writing of the transmission under subparagraph (a); and

    (c) certify, by making an appropriate entry in the Register of Small Claims, that he or she has made all notifications required under subparagraph (b).

(3) Transmission of the process under paragraph (2)(a) will be valid notwithstanding any failure by the sheriff clerk to comply with paragraph (2)(b) and (c).

**Transfer from Employment Tribunal**

**26.7.**— (1) On receipt of the documentation in proceedings which have been remitted from an employment tribunal under section 140(3) of the 2010 Act, the sheriff clerk must—

    (a) record the date of receipt on the first page of the documentation;

    (b) fix a hearing to determine further procedure not less than 14 days after the date of receipt of the process; and

    (c) forthwith send written notice of the date of the hearing fixed under subparagraph (b) to each party.

(2) At the hearing arranged under paragraph (1)(b), the sheriff may make such order as he or she thinks fit to secure so far as practicable that the cause thereafter proceeds in accordance with these Rules.

CHAPTER 27[2]

LIVE LINKS

**27.1.**—(1) On cause shown, a party may apply by incidental application for authority for the whole or part of—

    (a) the evidence of a witness or the party to be given; or

    (b) a submission to be made,

through a live link.

(2) in paragraph (1)—

"witness"[3] means a person who has been or may be cited to appear before the court as a witness, except a vulnerable witness within the meaning of section 11(1) of the 2004 Act;

"submission" means any oral submission which would otherwise be made to the court by the party or his representative in person including an oral submission in support of an incidental application; and

"live link" means a live television link or such other arrangement as may be specified in the incidental application by which the witness, party or representative, as the case may be, is able to be seen and heard in the proceedings or heard in the proceedings and is able to see and hear or hear the proceedings while at a place which is outside the courtroom.

Appendix 1

FORMS

**Rule 1.1(4)**

Form A1[4]

Rule 2A.2(2)(b)

Statement by prospective lay representative for Pursuer/Defender*

Case Ref. No.:

in the cause

SHERIFFDOM OF (*insert name of sheriffdom*)

AT (*insert place of sheriff court*)

---

[1] As inserted by the Act of Sederunt (Sheriff Court Rules) (Equality Act 2010) 2010 (SSI 2010/340) para.5 (effective October 1, 2010).

[2] As inserted by the Act of Sederunt (Ordinary Cause, Summary Application, Summary Cause and Small Claim Rules) Amendment (Miscellaneous) (SSI 2007/6) r.5(e) (effective January 29, 2007).

[3] As amended by the Act of Sederunt (Ordinary Cause, Summary Application, Summary Cause and Small Claim Rules) Amendment (Vulnerable Witnesses (Scotland) Act 2004) 2007 (SSI 2007/463) r.5(4) (effective November 1, 2007).

[4] As inserted by the Act of Sederunt (Sheriff Court Rules) (Lay Representation) 2013 (SSI 2013/91) r.5 (effective April 4, 2013).

[A.B.], (*insert designation and address*), Pursuer
against
[C.D.], (*insert designation and address*), Defender
Court ref. no:

| | Name and address of prospective lay representative who requests to make oral submissions on behalf of party litigant: |
|---|---|
| | Identify hearing(s) in respect of which permission for lay representation is sought: |
| | The prospective lay representative declares that: |
| (a) | I have no financial interest in the outcome of the case *or* I have the following financial interest in it:* |
| (b) | I am not receiving remuneration or other reward directly or indirectly from the litigant for my assistance and will not receive directly or indirectly such remuneration or other reward from the litigant. |
| (c) | I accept that documents and information are provided to me by the litigant on a confidential basis and I undertake to keep them confidential. |
| (d) | I have no previous convictions *or* I have the following convictions: (list convictions)* |
| (e) | I have not been declared a vexatious litigant under the Vexatious Actions (Scotland) Act 1898 *or* I was declared a vexatious litigant under the Vexatious Actions (Scotland) Act 1898 on [insert date].* |

(*Signed*)
[Name of prospective lay representative]
[Date]

(*Insert Place/Date*)
The Sheriff grants/refuses* the application.

[*Signed*]
Sheriff Clerk
[Date]

Rule 4(1)(c)
(**delete as appropriate*)

Form 1[1]
*Summons*

FORM 1

OFFICIAL USE ONLY
SUMMONS No.

# Small Claim Summons

**Action for/of**
(state type, e.g., payment of money)

| Sheriff Court (name, address, e-mail and telephone no.) | 1 | |
|---|---|---|
| Name and address of person making the claim (**pursuer**) | 2 | |
| Name and address of person against whom claim made (**defender**) | 3 | |
| Claim (form of decree or other order | 4 | |

---

[1] As amended by the Act of Sederunt (Sheriff Court Rules Amendment) (Diligence) (SSI 2008/121) r.7(6) (effective April 1, 2008). This form as it applied immediately before April 1, 2008 continues to have effect for the purpose of any application for arrestment on the dependence made before that date.

sought)

| | | |
|---|---|---|
| Name, full address, telephone no, and e-mail address of pursuer's solicitor or authorised lay representative (if any) acting in the claim | 5 | |
| Fee Details (Enter these only if forms sent electronically to court) | 5a | |

| 6 | **RETURN DAY** | **20** |
|---|---|---|
| | **HEARING DATE** | 20 at am. |

*Sheriff Clerk to delete as appropriate*

The pursuer is authorised to serve a copy summons in Form *1a/1b, on the defender(s) not less than *21/42 days before the **RETURN DAY** shown in the box above. The summons is warrant for service, and for citation of witnesses to attend court on any future date at which evidence may be led.

*Court Authentication*

**NOTE: The pursuer should complete boxes 1 to 5a, and the statement of claim on page 2. The sheriff clerk will complete box 6.**

---

7.     **STATE DETAILS OF CLAIM HERE (all cases) and PARTICULARS OF ARREST-MENT (furthcoming actions only)**

**(To be completed by the pursuer. If space is insufficient, a separate sheet may be attached)**

The details of the claim are:

**FOR OFFICIAL USE ONLY**

Sheriffs notes as to:

1. Issues of fact and law in dispute

2. Facts agreed

3. Reasons for any final disposal at the hearing held on the calling date.

---

(note 1,2)FORM 1a

*Defender's copy summons—claim for or including claim for payment of money where time to pay direction or time order may be applied for*

| |
|---|
| OFFICIAL USE ONLY |
| SUMMONS No. |

**Small Claim Summons**

**Action for/of**

(state type, e.g. payment of money)

**DEFENDER'S COPY: Claim for or including payment of money (where time to pay direction or time order may be applied for)**

| | | |
|---|---|---|
| Sheriff Court<br>(name, address, e-mail and telephone no.) | 1 | |
| Name and address of person making the claim (**pursuer**) | 2 | |
| Name and address of person against whom claim made (**defender**) | 3 | |
| Claim (form of decree or other order sought—complete as in section 4 of Form 1) | 4 | |
| Name, full address, telephone no., and e-mail address of pursuer's solicitor or authorised lay representative (if any) acting in the claim | 5 | |

| | |
|---|---|
| 6 | **RETURN DAY** 20 |
| | **HEARING DATE** 20 at am. |

**NOTE: You will find details of claim on page 2.**

---

**7.** **STATE DETAILS OF CLAIM HERE OR ATTACH A STATEMENT OF CLAIM**

(To be completed by the pursuer. If space is insufficient, a separate sheet may be attached)

The details of the claim are:

---

**8.** **SERVICE ON DEFENDER**

(Place)                                 (Date)

To:                                       (Defender)

You are hereby served with a copy of the above summons.

Solicitor / sheriff officer

*delete as appropriate*

NOTE: The pursuer should complete boxes 1 to 6 on page 1, the statement of claim in box 7 on page 2 and section A on page 7 before service on the defender. The person serving the Summons will complete box 8, above.

### WHAT MUST I DO ABOUT THIS SUMMONS?

The RETURN DAY (on page 1 of this summons) is the deadline by which you need to reply to the court. You must send the correct forms back (see below for details) by this date if you want the court to hear your case. If you do not do this, in most cases there will not be a hearing about your case and the court will make a decision in your absence.

The HEARING DATE (on page 1 of this summons) is the date for the court hearing.

**You should decide whether you wish to dispute the claim, admit liability for the claim and whether you owe any money or not, and how you wish to proceed.** Then, look at the 5 options listed below. Find the one that covers your decision and follow the instructions given there.

If you are not sure what you need to do, contact the sheriff clerk's office before the return day. Written guidance can also be obtained from the Scottish Court Service website (www.scot-courts.gov.uk).

### OPTIONS

**1. ADMIT LIABILITY FOR THE CLAIM and settle it with the pursuer now.**

**If you wish to avoid the possibility of a court order passing against you, you should settle the claim (including any question of expenses) with the pursuer or his representative in good time before the return day.** Please do not send any payment direct to the court. Any payment should be made to the pursuer or his representative.

**2. ADMIT LIABILITY FOR THE CLAIM and make written application to pay by instalments or by deferred lump sum.**

Complete Box 1 of section **B** on page 7 of this form and return pages 7, 9 and 10 to the court **to arrive on or before the return day**. You should then contact the court to find out whether or not the pursuer has accepted your offer. If he has not accepted it, the case will then call in court on the calling date, when the court will decide how the amount claimed is to be paid.

If your claim is for delivery, or implement of an obligation, and you wish to pay the alternative amount claimed, you may also wish to make an application about the method of payment. If so, follow the instructions in the previous paragraph.

**NOTE: If you fail to return pages 7, 9 and 10 as directed, or if, having returned them, you fail to attend or are not represented at the calling date if the case is to call, the court may decide the claim in your absence.**

**3. ADMIT LIABILITY FOR THE CLAIM and attend at court to make application to pay by instalments or deferred lump sum.**

Complete Box 2 on page 7. Return page 7 to the court so that it arrives **on or before the return day.**

**If the claim for delivery, or implement of an obligation, you may wish to pay the alternative amount claimed and attend at court to make an application about the method of payment.**

**You must attend personally, or be represented, at court on the hearing date.** Your representative may be a solicitor, or someone else having your authority. It may be helpful if you or your representative bring pages 1 and 2 of this form to the court.

**NOTE: If you fail to return page 7 as directed, or if, having returned it, you fail to attend or are not represented at the hearing date, the court may decide the claim in your absence.**

**4. DISPUTE THE CLAIM and attend at court to do any of the following:**

- Challenge the jurisdiction of the court
- State a defence
- State a counterclaim
- Dispute the amount of the claim

Complete Box 3 on page 7. Return page 7 to the court so that it arrives **on or before the return day. You must attend personally, or be represented, at court on the hearing date.**

Your representative may be a solicitor, or someone else having your authority. It may be helpful if you or your representative bring pages 1 and 2 of this form to the court.

**NOTE: If you fail to return page 7 as directed, or if, having returned it, you fail to attend or are not represented at the hearing date, the court may decide the claim in your absence.**

**WRITTEN NOTE OF PROPOSED COUNTERCLAIM**

**You must send to the court a written note of any counterclaim. If you do, you should also send a copy to the pursuer. You must also attend or be represented at court on the hearing date.**

**5. ADMIT LIABILITY FOR THE CLAIM and make written application for a time order under the Consumer Credit Act 1974.**

Complete Box 4 on page 8 and return pages 7 and 8 and 11 to 13 to the court to arrive on or before the return day. You should then contact the court to find out whether or not the pursuer has accepted your offer. Where you have been advised that the pursuer has not accepted your offer then the case will call in court on the hearing date. You should appear in court on the hearing date as the court will decide how the amount claimed is to be paid.

**NOTE: If you fail to return pages 8 and 9 and 11 to 13 as directed, or if, having returned them, you fail to attend or are not represented at the hearing date, if the case is to call, the court may decide the claim in your absence.**

**Please Note**

If you do nothing about this summons, the court will almost certainly, where appropriate, grant decree against you and order you to pay the pursuer the sum claimed, including any interest and expenses found due.

If the summons is for delivery, or implement of an obligation, the court may order you to deliver the article or perform the duty in question within a specified period. If you fail to do so, the court may order you to pay to the pursuer the alternative amount claimed, including interest and expenses.

**You Are Advised to Keep Pages 1 And 2, as They May Be Useful at a Later Stage of the Case.**

**Notes**

**(1) Time to pay directions**

The Debtors (Scotland) Act 1987 gives you the right to apply to the court for a "time to pay direction". This is an order which allows you to pay any sum which the court orders you to pay either in instalments or by deferred lump sum. A "deferred lump sum" means that you will be ordered by the court to pay the whole amount at one time within a period which the court will specify.

If the court makes a time to pay direction it may also recall or restrict any arrestment made on your property by the pursuer in connection with the action or debt (for example, your bank account may have been frozen).

No court fee is payable when making an application for a time to pay direction.

If a time to pay direction is made, a copy of the court order (called an extract decree) will be sent to you by the pursuer telling you when payment should start or when it is you have to pay the lump sum.

If a time to pay direction is not made, and an order for immediate payment is made against you, an order to pay (called a charge) may be served on you if you do not pay.

**(2) Determination of application**

Under the 1987 Act, the court is required to make a time to pay direction if satisfied that it is reasonable in the circumstances to do so, and having regard in particular to the following matters—

- The nature of and reasons for the debt in relation to which decree is granted
- Any action taken by the creditor to assist the debtor in paying the debt
- The debtor's financial position
- The reasonableness of any proposal by the debtor to pay that debt
- The reasonableness of any refusal or objection by the creditor to any proposal or offer by the debtor to pay the debt.

**(3) Time Orders**

The Consumer Credit Act 1974 allows you to apply to the court for a "time order" during a court action, to ask the court to give you more time to pay a loan agreement. **A time order is similar to a time to pay direction, but can only be applied for where the court action is about a credit agreement regulated by the Consumer Credit Act.** The court has power to grant a time order in respect of a regulated agreement to reschedule payment of the sum owed. This means that a time order can change:

- the amount you have to pay each month
- how long the loan will last
- in some cases, the interest rate payable

A time order can also stop the creditor taking away any item bought by you on hire purchase or conditional sale under the regulated agreement, so long as you continue to pay the instalments agreed.

No court fee is payable when making an application for a time order.

| **SECTION A** This section must be be completed complete before service | | Summons No |
| --- | --- | --- |
| | | Return Day |
| | | Hearing Date |

SHERIFF COURT (Including address)

PURSUER'S FULL NAME
AND ADDRESS

DEFENDER'S FULL
NAME AND ADDRESS

## SECTION B DEFENDER'S RESPONSE TO THE SUMMONS
### ** Delete those boxes which do not apply

**\*\*Box 1**

**ADMIT LIABILITY FOR THE CLAIM and make written application to pay by instalments or by deferred lump sum.**

I do not intend to defend the case but admit liability for the claim and wish to pay the sum of money claimed.

I wish to make a written application about payment.

I have completed the application form on pages 9 and 10.

**\*\*Box 2**

**ADMIT LIABILITY FOR THE CLAIM and attend at court.**

I admit liability for the claim.

I wish to make an application to pay the sum claimed by instalments or by deferred lump sum.

I intend to appear or be represented at court.

**\*\*Box 3**

**DISPUTE THE CLAIM (or the amount due) and attend at court**

*I wish to dispute the amount due only.

*I intend to challenge the jurisdiction of the court.

*I intend to state a defence.

*I intend to state a counterclaim.

*I intend to appear or be represented in court.

...............

*I attach a note of my proposed counterclaim which has been copied to the pursuer.

*delete as necessary*

**\*\*Box 4**

**ADMIT LIABILITY FOR THE CLAIM and apply for a time order under the Consumer Credit Act 1974.**

I do not intend to defend the case but admit liability for the claim.

I wish to apply for a time order under the Consumer Credit Act 1974.

I have completed the application form on pages 11 to 13.

**NOTE: Please remember to send your response to the court to arrive on or before the return day if you have completed any of the responses above.**

I WISH TO APPLY FOR A *TIME TO PAY DIRECTION

**I WISH TO APPLY FOR A *TIME TO PAY DIRECTION**

**I admit the claim** and make application to pay as follows:

(1) by instalments of £...............per *week / fortnight / month

**OR**

(2) in one payment within...............*weeks / months from the date of the court order.

The debt is for *(specify the nature of the debt)* and has arisen *(here set out the reasons the debt has arisen)*

Please also state why you say a time to pay direction should be made. In doing so, please consider Notes (1) and (2) on page 5.

To help the court please provide details of your financial position in the boxes below.

I am employed / self-employed / unemployed

***Please also indicate whether payment/receipts are weekly, fortnightly or monthly**

| My outgoings are: | *Weekly / fortnightly/ monthly | | My net income is | *Weekly / fortnightly/ monthly |
|---|---|---|---|---|
| Rent/mortgage | £ | | Wages/pensions | £ |
| Council tax | £ | | State benefits | £ |
| Gas/electricity etc | £ | | Tax credits | £ |
| Food | £ | | Other | £ |
| Loans and credit agreements | £ | | | |
| Phone | £ | | | |
| Other | £ | | | |
| Total | £ | | Total | £ |

People who rely on your income (e.g. spouse/civil partner/ partner/children)— how many

**Please list details of all capital held, e.g. value of house; amount in savings account, shares or other investments:**

I am of the opinion that the payment offer is reasonable for the following reason(s):

*Here set out any information you consider relevant to the court's determination of the application. In doing so, please consider Note (2) on page 5.*

**\*APPLICATION FOR RECALL OR RESTRICTION OF AN ARRESTMENT**

I seek the recall or restriction of the arrestment of which the details are as follows:

Date:

*\*Delete if inapplicable*

**Application for a Time Order under the Consumer Credit Act 1974**

By

Defender

**In an action raised by**

Pursuer

Please Write In Ink Using Block Capitals

If you wish to apply to pay by instalments enter the amount at box 3.

If you wish the court to make any additional orders, please give details at box 4. Please give details of the regulated agreement at box 5 and details of your financial position in the space provided below at box 5.

Sign and date the application where indicated.

You should ensure that your application arrives at the court along with completed pages 7 and 8 on or before the return day.

1. The Applicant is a defender in the action brought by the above named pursuer.

**I/we Wish to Apply for a Time Order under the Consumer Credit Act 1974**

**2. Details of order(s) sought**

The defender wishes to apply for a time order under section 129 of the Consumer Credit Act 1974.

The defender wishes to apply for an order in terms of section..........of the Consumer Credit Act 1974.

**3. Proposals for payment**

I admit the claim and apply to pay the arrears and future instalments as follows:..............

By instalments of £..........per *week/fortnight/month

No time to pay direction or time to pay order has been made in relation to this debt.

**4. Additional orders sought**

The following additional order(s) is (are) sought: (*specify*)

The order(s) sought in addition to the time order is (are) sought for the following reasons:

**5. Details of regulated agreement**

(*Please attach a copy of the agreement if you have retained it and insert details of the agreement where known*)

    (a)    Date of agreement

    (b)    Reference number of agreement

    (c)    Names and addresses of other parties to agreement

    (d)    Name and address of person (if any) who acted as surety (guarantor) to the agreement

    (e)    Place where agreement signed (e.g. the shop where agreement signed, including name and address)

    (f)    Details of payment arrangements

        i.    The agreement is to pay instalments of £..........per week/ month

        ii.    The unpaid balance is £........../ I do not know the amount of arrears

        iii.    I am £..........in arrears / I do not know the amount of arrears

**Defender's financial position**

I am employed /self employed / unemployed

**Defender's financial position**

I am employed /self employed / unemployed

| My net income is: | weekly, fortnightly or monthly | My outgoings are: | weekly, fortnightly or monthly |
|---|---|---|---|
| Wages | £ | Mortgage/rent | £ |
| State benefits | £ | Council tax | £ |
| Tax credits | £ | Gas/electricity etc | £ |
| Other | £ | Food | £ |
| | | Credit and loans | £ |
| | | Phone | £ |
| | | Other | £ |
| Total | £ | Total | £ |

People who rely on your income (e.g. spouse/civil partner/partner/children)—how many

Here list all assets (if any) e.g. value of house; amounts in bank or building society accounts; shares or other investments:

Here list any outstanding debts:

Therefore the defender asks the court to make a time order

Date: .............. Signed: ..............

Defender: ..............

1. As amended by SSI 2008/121 and substituted by the Act of Sederunt (Sheriff Court Rules) (Miscellaneous Amendments) 2009 (SSI 2009/294) r.5 (effective December 1, 2009).

2. As amended by the Act of Sederunt (Sheriff Court Rules) (Miscellaneous Amendments) 2011 (SSI 2011/193) r.12 (effective April 4, 2011).

Rule 4.3(b)

FORM 1b

*Defender's copy summons - all other claims*

**FORM 1b**

# Small Claim Summons
## Action for/of
(state type, e.g., payment of money)

OFFICIAL USE ONLY
SUMMONS No.

**DEFENDER'S COPY: (Claim other than claim for or including payment of money where time to pay direction or time order may be applied for)**

Sheriff Court
(name, address, e-mail and telephone no.)

1

Name and address of person making the claim (**pursuer**)

2

Name and address of person against whom claim made (**defender**)

3

Claim (form of decree or other order sought — *complete as in section 4 of Form 1*)

4

Name, full address, telephone no., and e-mail address of pursuer's solicitor or authorised lay representative (if any)

5

| 6 | RETURN DAY | 20 |
|---|---|---|
| | HEARING DATE | 20 at am. |

**NOTE: You will find details of claim on page 2.**

**7. STATE DETAILS OF CLAIM HERE OR ATTACH A STATEMENT OF CLAIM**
**(To be completed by the pursuer. If space is insufficient, a separate sheet may be attached)**

The details of the claim are:

**8. SERVICE ON DEFENDER**

(Place)..............        (Date)..............

To:..............        (defender).........

You are hereby served with a copy of the above summons.

<table>
<tr><td></td><td>Solicitor / sheriff officer<br>delete as appropriate</td></tr>
</table>

The pursuer should complete boxes 1 to 6 on page 1, the statement of claim in box 7 on page 2 and section A on page 4 before service on the defender. The person serving the summons will complete box 8.

### WHAT MUST I DO ABOUT THIS SUMMONS?

**Decide whether you wish to dispute the claim and/or whether you owe any money or not, and how you wish to proceed.** Then, look at the 2 options listed below. Find the one which covers your decision and follow the instructions given there. You will find the RETURN DAY and the HEARING DATE on page one of the summons.

**Written guidance on small claims procedure can be obtained from the sheriff clerk at any Sheriff Clerk's office.**

**Further advice can also be obtained by contacting any of the following:**

**Citizen's Advice Bureau, Consumer Advice Centre, Trading Standards or Consumer Protection Department or a solicitor. (Addresses can be found in the guidance booklets).**

### OPTION

1. **ADMIT LIABILITY FOR THE CLAIM and settle it with the pursuer now.**

If you wish to avoid the possibility of a court order passing against you, you should settle the claim (including any question of expenses) with pursuer or his representative **in good time before the return day**. Please do not send any payment direct to the court. Any payment should be made to the pursuer or his representative.

2. **DISPUTE THE CLAIM and attend at court to do any of the following:**
   - Challenge the jurisdiction of the court
   - State a defence
   - State a counterclaim
   - Dispute the amount of the claim

Complete Section B on page 4. Return page 4 to the court so that it arrives **on or before the return day. You must attend personally, or be represented, at court on the hearing date.**

Your representative may be a solicitor, or someone else having your authority. It may be helpful if you or your representative bring pages 1 and 2 of this form to the court.

**NOTE: If you fail to return page 4 as directed, or if, having returned it, you fail to attend or are not represented at the hearing date, the court will almost certainly decide the claim in your absence.**

**Written Note of Proposed Counterclaim**

You may send to the court a written note of any counterclaim. If you do, you should also send a copy to the pursuer. You must also attend or be represented at court on the hearing date.

### Please Note

If you do nothing about this summons, the court will almost certainly, where appropriate, grant decree against you and order you to pay to the pursuer the sum claimed, including any interest and expenses found due.

If the summons is for delivery, or implement of an obligation, the court may order you to deliver the article or perform the duty in question within a specified period. If you fail to do so, the court may order you to pay to the pursuer the alternative amount claimed, including interest and expenses.

**You Are Advised to Keep Pages 1 And 2, as They May Be Useful at a Later Stage of the Case.**

| **SECTION A**<br>This section must be completed before service | | Summons No |
| --- | --- | --- |
| | | Return Day |
| | | Hearing Date |
| | SHERIFF COURT (Including address) | |

| | |
|---|---|
| PURSUER'S FULL NAME AND ADDRESS | DEFENDER'S FULL NAME AND ADDRESS |

**SECTION B**  **DEFENDER'S RESPONSE TO THE SUMMONS**

> DISPUTE THE CLAIM (or the amount due) and attend at court
>
> \* I wish to dispute the amount due only.
>
> \* I intend to challenge the jurisdiction of the court.
>
> \* I intend to state a defence.
>
> \* I intend to state a counterclaim.
>
> I intend to appear or be represented in court.
>
> \* I attach a note of my proposed counterclaim which has been copied to the pursuer.
>
> \* delete as necessary

**PLEASE REMEMBER:** You must send this page to the court **to arrive on or before the return day** if you have completed Section B above.

If you have admitted the claim, please do not send any payment direct to the court. Any payment should be made to the pursuer or his solicitor.

FORM 2

Form of claim in a summons for payment of money

Rule 4.1(2)

The pursuer claims from the defender(s) the sum of £.......... with interest on that sum at the rate of ..........% annually from the date of service, together with the expenses of bringing the claim.

FORM 3

Rule 4.1(2)

Form of claim in a summons for delivery

The pursuer claims that, in the circumstances described in the statement contained on page 2 of this copy summons, he has right to the possession of the article(s) described therein.

He therefore asks the court to grant a decree ordering you to deliver the said articles to the pursuer.

*Alternatively*, if you do not deliver said articles, the pursuer asks the court to grant a decree ordering you to pay to him the sum of £.......... with interest on that sum at the rate of ..........% annually from ..........until payment.

The pursuer also claims from you the expenses of bringing the claim.

FORM 4

Rule 4.1(2)

Form of claim in a summons for implement of an obligation

The pursuer claims that, in the circumstances described in the statement contained on page 2 of the summons, you are obliged to...............

He therefore asks the court to grant a decree ordering you to implement the said obligation.

*Alternatively*, if you do not fulfil the obligation, the pursuer asks the court to grant a decree ordering you to pay to him the sum of £.......... with interest on that sum at the rate of ..........% annually from until payment.

The pursuer also claims from you the expenses of bringing the claim.

FORM 5

Rule 6.2(1)

Form of service

XY, you are hereby served with a copy of the above (or attached) summons.

*(signature of solicitor or sheriff officer)*

FORM 6

Form of certificate of execution of service

1011

Rule 6.2(2)

(*place and date*)

I,........... , hereby certify that on the.......... day of......... 20, I duly cited XY to answer the foregoing summons. This I did by (*set forth the mode of service*)

(*signature of solicitor or sheriff officer*)

## FORM 7

### Postal service—form of notice

Rule 6.3(2)

This letter contains a citation to or intimation from the sheriff court at

If delivery cannot be made the letter must be returned immediately to the sheriff clerk at (*insert full address*).

## FORM 8

### Service on person whose address is unknown—form of advertisement.

Rule 6.6(1)(a)

A small claim has been raised in the sheriff court at.........., by AB., pursuer, against CD, defender, whose last known address was...............

If the said CD wishes to defend the claim he should immediately contact the sheriff clerk's office at the above court, from whom the defender's copy summons may be obtained.

Address of court:...............

Telephone no:...............

Fax no:..............

E mail address:...............

## FORM 9

### Service on person whose address is unknown

Rule 6.6(1)(b)

### Form of notice to be displayed on the walls of court

A small claim has been raised in this court by AB, pursuer against CD, defender, whose last known address was...............

If the said CD wishes to defend the claim he should immediately contact the sheriff clerk's office, from whom the defender's copy summons may be obtained.

(*date*)Displayed on the walls of court of this date.

Sheriff clerk depute

## FORM 9A[1]

### Statement to accompany application for interim diligence

Rule 7 A2(2)

### DEBTORS (SCOTLAND) ACT 1987 Section 15D[or DEBT ARRANGEMENT AND ATTACHMENT (SCOTLAND) ACT 2002 Section 9C]

Sheriff Court.........

In the Cause (Cause Reference No. )

[A.B.] (*designation and address*)

Pursuer

against

[C.D.] (*designation and address*)

Defender

### Statement

1. The applicant is the pursuer [or defender] in the action by [A.B] (*design*) against [C.D.] (*design*).

2. [The following persons have an interest [specify names and addresses]]

3. The application is [or is not] seeking the grant under section 15E(1) of the 1987 Act of warrant for diligence [or section 9D(1) of the 2002 Act of interim attachment] in advance of a hearing on the application.

4. [Here provide such other information as may be prescribed by regulations made by the Scottish Ministers under section 15D(2)(d) or 9C(2)(d) of the 1987 Act]

(*Signed*)

---

[1] As inserted by the Act of Sederunt (Sheriff Court Rules Amendment) (Diligence) 2008 (SSI 2008/121) r.7(8) (effective April 1, 2008).

Solicitor [*or* Agent] for A.B. [or C.D.]
*(include full designation)*

**Rule 7.A8**

FORM 9B[1]
Form of schedule of arrestment on the dependence
**SCHEDULE OF ARRESTMENT ON THE DEPENDENCE**

Date: *(date of execution)*............ ...
Time: *(time arrestment executed)*..............
To: *(name and address of arrestee)*..............
IN HER MAJESTY'S NAME AND AUTHORITY AND IN NAME AND AUTHORITY OF THE
SHERIFF, I, *(name)*, Sheriff Officer, by virtue of:

- a summons containing warrant which has been granted for arrestment on the dependence of the action at the instance of *(name and address of pursuer)* against *(name and address of defender)* and dated *(date)*;
- a counterclaim containing a warrant which has been granted for arrestment on the dependence of the claim by *(name and address of creditor)* against *(name and address of debtor)* and dated *(date of warrant)*;
- an order of the Sheriff at *(place)* dated *(date of order)* granting warrant [for arrestment on the dependence of the action raised at the instance of *(name and address of pursuer)* against *(name and address of defender)*] [or for arrestment on the dependence of the claim in the counterclaim by *(name and address of creditor)* against *(name and address or debtor)*],

arrest in your hands (i) the sum of *(amount)*, in excess of the Protected Minimum Balance, where applicable *(see Note 1)*, more or less, due by you to *(defender's name)* [or name and address of common debtor if common debtor is not the defender] or to any other person on his [or her] [or its][or their] behalf; and (ii) all moveable things in your hands belonging or pertaining to the said *(name of common debtor)*, to remain in your hands under arrestment until they are made forthcoming to *(name of pursuer)* [or name and address of creditor if he is not the pursuer] or until further order of the court.
This I do in the presence of *(name, occupation and address of witness)*.

*(Signed)*
Sheriff Officer
*(Address)*

**NOTE**

1. This Schedule arrests in your hands (i) funds due by you to *(name of common debtor)* and (ii) goods or other moveables held by you for him. **You should not pay any funds to him or hand over any goods or other moveables to him without taking legal advice.**

2. This Schedule may be used to arrest a ship or cargo. If it is, you should consult your legal adviser about the effect of it.

3. The Protected Minimum Balance is the sum referred to in section 73F(4) of the Debtors (Scotland) Act 1987. This sum is currently set at [*insert current sum*]. The Protected Minimum Balance applies where the arrestment attaches funds standing to the credit of a debtor in an account held by a bank or other financial institution and the debtor is an individual. The Protected Minimum Balance does not apply where the account is held in the name of a company, a limited liability partnership, a partnership or an unincorporated association or where the account is operated by the debtor as a trading account.

4. Under section 73G of the Debtors (Scotland) Act 1987 you must also, within the period of 3 weeks beginning with the day on which the arrestment is executed, disclose to the creditor the nature and value of the funds and/or moveable property which have been attached. This disclosure must be in the form set out in Schedule 8 to the Diligence (Scotland) Regulations 2009. Failure to comply may lead to a financial penalty under section 73G of the Debtors (Scotland) Act 1987 and may also be dealt with as a contempt of court. You must, at the same time, send a copy of the disclosure to the debtor and to any person known to you who owns (or

---

[1] As inserted by the Act of Sederunt (Sheriff Court Rules Amendment) (Diligence) 2008 (SSI 2008/121) r.7(8) (effective April 1, 2008) and substituted by the Act of Sederunt (Sheriff Court Rules Amendment) (Diligence) 2009 (SSI 2009/107) (effective April 22, 2009).

claims to own) attached property and to any person to whom attached funds are (or are claimed to be due), solely or in common with the debtor.

**IF YOU WISH FURTHER ADVICE CONTACT ANY CITIZENS ADVICE BUREAU/ LOCAL ADVICE CENTRE/SHERIFF CLERK OR SOLICITOR**

Rule 6.A8

FORM 9C[1]

Form of certificate of execution of arrestment on the dependence

**CERTIFICATE OF EXECUTION**

I, (*name*), Sheriff Officer, certify that I executed an arrestment on the dependence, by virtue of an interlocutor of the Sheriff at (*place*) on (*date*) obtained at the instance of (*name and address of party arresting*) against (*name and address of defender*) on (*name of arrestee*)—

\* by delivering the schedule of arrestment to (*name of arrestee or other person*) at (*place*) personally on (*date*).

\* by leaving the schedule of arrestment with (*name and occupation of person with whom left*) at (*place*) on (*date*) [and by posting a copy of the schedule to the arrestee by registered post or first class recorded delivery to the address specified on the receipt annexed to this certificate].

\* by depositing the schedule of arrestment in (*place*) on (*date*). (*Specify that enquiry made and reasonable grounds exist for believing that the person on whom service is to be made resides at the place but is not available*) [and by posting a copy of the schedule to the arrestee by registered post or first class recorded delivery to the address specified on the receipt annexed to this certificate].

\* by affixing the schedule of arrestment to the door at (*place*) on (*date*). (*Specify that enquiry made and that reasonable grounds exist for believing that the person on whom service is to be made resides at the place but is not available*) [and by posting a copy of the schedule to the arrestee by registered post or first class recorded delivery to the address specified on the receipt annexed to this certificate].

\* by leaving the schedule of arrestment with (*name and occupation of person with whom left*) at (*place of business*) on (*date*) [and by posting a copy of the schedule to the arrestee by registered post or first class recorded delivery to the address specified on the receipt annexed to this certificate].

\* by depositing the schedule of arrestment at (*place of business*) on (*date*). (*Specify that enquiry made and that reasonable grounds exist for believing that the person on whom service is to be made carries on business at that place.*) [and by posting a copy of the schedule to the arrestee by registered post or first class recorded delivery to the address specified on the receipt annexed to this certificate].

\* by affixing the schedule of arrestment to the door at (*place of business*) on (*date*). (*Specify that enquiry made and that reasonable grounds exist for believing that the person on whom service is to be made carries on business at that place.*) [and by posting a copy of the schedule to the arrestee by registered post or first class recorded delivery to the address specified on the receipt annexed to this certificate].

\* by leaving the schedule of arrestment at (*registered office*) on (*date*), in the hands of (*name of person*) [and by posting a copy of the schedule to the arrestee by registered post or first class recorded delivery to the address specified on the receipt annexed to this certificate].

\* by depositing the schedule of arrestment at (*registered office*) on (*date*) [and by posting a copy of the schedule to the arrestee by registered post or first class recorded delivery to the address specified on the receipt annexed to this certificate].

\* by affixing the schedule of arrestment to the door at (*registered office*) on (*date*) [and by posting a copy of the schedule to the arrestee by registered post or first class recorded delivery to the address specified on the receipt annexed to this certificate].

I did this in the presence of (*name, occupation and address of witness*).

(*Signed*)
Sheriff Officer
(*Address*)
(*Signed*)
(*Witness*)

\*Delete where not applicable

**NOTE**

A copy of the Schedule of arrestment on the dependence is to be attached to this certificate

---

[1] As inserted by the Act of Sederunt (Sheriff Court Rules Amendment) (Diligence) 2008 (SSI 2008/ 121) r.7(8) (effective April 1, 2008) and substituted by the Act of Sederunt (Sheriff Court Rules Amendment) (Diligence) 2009 (SSI 2009/107) (effective April 22, 2009).

FORM 10

Rule 7.3(4)(a)

Recall or restriction of arrestment Certificate authorising the release of arrested funds or property

Sheriff court at (*place*)

Court ref. no.:...............

AB (pursuer) against CD (defender)

I, (*name*), hereby certify that the sheriff on (*date*) authorised the release of the funds or property arrested on the *dependence of the action / counterclaim to the following extent:

(*details of sheriff's order*)

(*date*)

Sheriff clerk depute

*delete as appropriate*

Copy to:

Party instructing arrestment

Party possessing arrested funds/property

FORM 11

Rule 8.1(2)

Form of minute—no form of response lodged by defender

Sheriff court at (*place*)

Hearing date:...............

In respect that the defender(s) has/have failed to lodge a form of response to the summons, the pursuer requests the court to make the orders specified in the following case(s):

Court ref. no.: .......... Name(s) of defender(s) .......... Minute(s) ..........

FORM 12[1]

Rule 8.2(2)

Form of minute—pursuer not objecting to application for a time to pay direction or time order

Sheriff court at (*place*)

Court ref. no.: ...............

Name(s) of defender(s) ...............

Hearing date: ...............

I do not object to the defender's application for

*    a time to pay direction
*    recall or restriction of an arrestment
*    a time order

The pursuer requests the court to grant decree or other order in terms of the following minute(s)

*delete as appropriate*

FORM 13[2]

Rule 8.2(4)

Form of minute—pursuer opposing an application for a time to pay direction or time order

**Sheriff court (place): ...............**

**Court ref no: ...............**

Name(s) of defender(s): ...............

Hearing date: ...............

I oppose the defender's application for

*    a time to pay direction
*    recall or restriction of arrestment
*    a time order

*delete as appropriate*

   1.   The debt is (*please specify the nature of the debt and any reason known to the pursuer for the debt*).

---

[1] As amended by the Act of Sederunt (Ordinary Cause, Summary Application, Summary Cause and Small Claim Rules) Amendment (Miscellaneous) 2003 (SSI 2003/26), para.5(2)(b) (effective January 24, 2003).

[2] As substituted by the Act of Sederunt (Sheriff Court Rules) (Miscellaneous Amendments) 2009 (SSI 2009/294) r.5 (effective December 1, 2009).

2. The debt was incurred on (*specify date*) and the pursuer has contacted the defender in relation to the debt on (*specify date(s)*).

*3. The contractual payments were (*specify amount*).

*4. (*Specify any action taken by the pursuer to assist the defender to pay the debt*).

*5. The defender has made payment(s) towards the debt of (*specify amount(s)*) on (*specify date(s)*).

*6. The debtor has made offers to pay (*specify amount(s)*) on (*specify date(s)*) which offer(s) was [were] accepted] [*or* rejected] and (*specify amount*) was paid on (*specify date(s)*).

7. (*Here set out any information you consider relevant to the court's determination of the application*).

8. The pursuer requests the court to grant decree.

*delete as appropriate*

(*Signed*)

Pursuer [*or* Solicitor for Pursuer]

(*Date*)

FORM 14

Rule 11.1(8)

Counterclaim—form of intimation by sheriff clerk where pursuer fails to appear

Court ref. no.: ...............

(AB) (*insert address*), pursuer

against

(CD) (*insert address*), defender

When the above case called in court on (*insert date*), the defender appeared (or was represented) and stated a counterclaim to the claim made by you against him.

The court continued the case until (*date*) at (*time*).

**Please note that, if you fail to appear or be represented at the continued diet, the court may grant decree against you in terms of the counterclaim.**

(*date*)

Sheriff clerk depute

Rule 13A.3(1)

Paragraph 7(4)

FORM 14A[1]

Form of minute of intervention by the Commission for Equality and Human Rights

Sheriff Court at (*place*) ............... Court ref. no...............

APPLICATION FOR LEAVE TO INTERVENE BY THE COMMISSION FOR EQUALITY AND HUMAN RIGHTS

in the cause

[A.B.] (*designation and address*), Pursuer

against

[C.D.] (*designation and address*), Defender

[*Here set out briefly:*

(a) *the Commission's reasons for believing that the proceedings are relevant to a matter in connection with which the Commission has a function;*

(b) *the issue in the proceedings which the Commission wishes to address; and*

(c) *the propositions to be advanced by the Commission and the Commission's reasons for believing that they are relevant to the proceedings and that they will assist the court.]*

FORM 14B[2]

Rule 13B.2(1)

Form of minute of intervention by the Scottish Commission for Human Rights

Sheriff Court at (*place*) ............... Court ref. no.

APPLICATION FOR LEAVE TO INTERVENE BY THE SCOTTISH COMMISSION FOR HUMAN RIGHTS

in the cause

---

[1] As inserted by the Act of Sederunt (Sheriff Court Rules) (Miscellaneous Amendments) 2008 (SSI 2008/223) para.7(4) (effective July 1, 2008).

[2] As inserted by the Act of Sederunt (Sheriff Court Rules) (Miscellaneous Amendments) 2008 (SSI 2008/223) para.7(4) (effective July 1, 2008).

[A.B.] (*designation and address*), Pursuer

against

[C.D.] (*designation and address*), Defender

[*Here set out briefly:*

(a)   *the issue in the proceedings which the Commission intends to address;*

(b)   *a summary of the submission which the Commission intends to make.*]

FORM 14C[1]

Rule 13B.3(1)

Invitation to the Scottish Commission for Human Rights to intervene

SHERIFFDOM OF (*insert name of sheriffdom*) ...............Court ref. no.

AT (*insert place of sheriff court*) ..............

INVITATION TO THE SCOTTISH COMMISSION FOR HUMAN RIGHTS TO INTERVENE

in the cause

[A.B.] (*designation and address*), Pursuer

against

[C.D.] (*designation and address*), Defender

[*Here set out briefly:*

(a)   *the facts, procedural history and issues in the proceedings;*

(b)   *the issue in the proceedings on which the court seeks a submission.*]

FORM 15[2]

Rule 17.2(1)

**Sheriff court at** (*place*) ..............

In the claim (*court ref. no.*)

in which

AB (*design*) is the pursuer

and

C.D. (*design*) is the defender

To: (*name and designation of party or haver from whom the documents are sought to be recovered*).

You are hereby required to produce to the sheriff clerk at (*address*) within days of the service upon you of this order:

1.   This order itself (which must be produced intact);

2.   The certificate marked "B" attached;

3.   All documents within your possession covered by the specification which is enclosed; and

4.   A list of those documents.

You can produce the items listed above either:

(a)   by delivering them to the sheriff clerk at the address shown above; or

(b)   sending them to the sheriff clerk by registered or recorded delivery post.

(*date*)

(*signature, name, address and designation of person serving order*)

**PLEASE NOTE:**

If you claim confidentiality for any of the documents produced by you, you must still produce them. However, they may be placed in a separate envelope by themselves, marked "confidential". The court will, if necessary, decide whether the envelope should be opened or not.

Where the person ordering you to produce the document is **not** the sheriff clerk, claims for necessary outlays within certain specified limits may be paid. Claims should be made in writing to the person who has obtained an order that you produce the documents.

**CERTIFICATE**

**B**

Sheriff Court at (*place*)

In the claim (*court ref. no.*)

in which

AB (*design*) is the pursuer

---

[1] As inserted by the Act of Sederunt (Sheriff Court Rules) (Miscellaneous Amendments) 2008 (SSI 2008/223) para.7(4) (effective July 1, 2008).

[2] Substituted by Act of Sederunt (Ordinary Cause, Summary Application, Summary Cause and Small Claim Rules) Amendment (Miscellaneous) 2005 (SSI 2005/648) (effective January 2, 2006).

and

CD (*design*) is the defender

Order for recovery of documents dated (*insert date*).

With reference to the above order and relative specification of documents, I hereby certify:

\* that the documents produced herewith and the list signed by me which accompanies them are all the documents in my possession which fall under the specification.

\* I have no documents in my possession falling under the specification.

\* I believe that there are other documents falling within the specification which are not in my possession. These documents are (*list the documents as described in the specification.*) These documents were last seen by me on (*date*) in the possession of (*name and address of person/ company, if known*).

\* I know of no documents falling within the specification which are in the possession of any other person.

*\* delete as appropriate*

(*name*) (*date*)

<sup></sup>¹ FORM 16

Rule 17.4(3)

Form of citation of witness or haver

(*date*)

CITATION

SHERIFFDOM OF (*insert name of sheriffdom*)

**At (*insert place of sheriff court*)**

**To [A.B.] (*design*)**

(*Name*) who is pursuing/defending a case against (*name*) [*or is a* (*specify*) *in the case of* (*name*) against (*name*)] has asked you to be a witness. You must attend the above sheriff court on (*insert date*) at (*insert time*) for that purpose, [and bring with you (*specify documents*)].

If you

- would like to know more about being a witness
- are a child under the age of 16
- think you may be a vulnerable witness within the meaning of section 11(1) of the Vulnerable Witnesses (Scotland) Act 2004 (that is someone the court considers may be less able to give their evidence due to mental disorder or fear or distress connected to giving your evidence at the court hearing).

you should contact (*specify the solicitor acting for the party or the party litigant citing the witness*) for further information.

If you are a vulnerable witness (including a child under the age of 16) then you should be able to use a special measure (such measures include use of a screen, a live TV link or a supporter, or a commissioner) to help you give evidence.

**Expenses**

You may claim back money which you have had to spend and any earnings you have lost within certain specified limits, because you have to come to court on the above date. These may be paid to you if you claim within specified time limits. Claims should be made to the person who has asked you to attend court. Proof of any loss of earnings should be given to that person.

If you wish your travelling expenses to be paid before you go to court, you should apply for payment to the person who has asked you to attend court.

**Failure to attend**

**It is very important that you attend court and you should note that failure to do so may result in a warrant being granted for your arrest. In addition, if you fail to attend without any good reason, having requested and been paid your travelling expenses, you may be ordered to pay a penalty not exceeding £250.**

If you have any questions about anything in this citation, please contact (*specify the solicitor acting for the party or the party litigant citing the witness*) for further information.

Signed

[P.Q.] Sheriff Officer

or [X.Y.], (*add designation and business address*)

---

¹ As substituted by the Act of Sederunt (Ordinary Cause, Summary Application, Summary Cause and Small Claim Rules) Amendment (Vulnerable Witnesses (Scotland) Act 2004) 2007 (SSI 2007/463) (effective November 1, 2007).

Solicitor for the pursuer [*or* defender][*or (specify)*]

FORM 16A

Rule 17.4(3)

Form cf certificate of execution of witness citation

I certify that on (*date*) I duly cited AB (*design*) to attend at (*name of court*) on (*date*) at (*time*) as a witness for the (*design party*) in the action at the instance of CD (*design*) against EF (*design*) (*and I required him to bring with him...........*). This I did by

(*signature of solicitor or sheriff officer*)

FORM 16B[1]

Form of child witness notice

**Rule 11A.2**

VULNERABLE WITNESSES (SCOTLAND) ACT 2004 SECTION 12

*Received the day .......... of .......... 20*

(*Date of receipt of this notice*)

.............. (*signed*)

Sheriff Clerk

CHILD WITNESS NOTICE

Sheriff court ...............20..........

...............Court Ref. No.

1. The applicant is the pursuer [*cr* defender] in the action by [A.B.] (*design*) against [C.D.] (*design*).

2. The applicant has cited [*or* intends to cite] [E.F.] (*date of birth*) as a witness.

3. [E.F.] is a child witnesses under section 11 of the Vulnerable Witnesses (Scotland) Act 2004 [and was under the age of sixteen on the date of the commencement of proceedings].

4. The applicant considers that the following special measure[s] is [are] the most appropriate for the purpose of taking the evidence of [E.F.][*or* that [E.F.] should give evidence without the benefit of any special measure]:-

(*delete as appropriate and specify any special measure(s) sought*).

5. [(a) The reason[s] this [these] special measure[s] is [are] considered the most appropriate is [are] as follows:-

(*here specify the reason(s) for the special measure(s) sought*)].

OR

[(b) The reason[s] it is considered that [E.F.] should give evidence without the benefit of any special measure is [are]:-

(*here explain why it is felt that no special measures are required*)].

6. [E.F.] and the parent[s] of [*or* person[s] with parental responsibility for] [E.F.] has [have] expressed the following view[s] on the special measure[s] that is [are] considered most appropriate [*or* the appropriateness of [E.F.] giving evidence without the benefit of any special measure]:

(*delete as appropriate and set out the views(s) expressed and how they were obtained*)

7. Other information considered relevant to this application is as follows:—

(*here set out any other information relevant to the child witness notice*).

8. The applicant asks the court to—

(a)    consider this child witness notice;

(b)    make an order authorising the special measure[s] sought; *or*

(c)    make an order authorising the giving of evidence by [E.F.] without the benefit of special measures.

(*delete as appropriate*)

(*Signed*)

[A.B. *or* C.D.]

[*or* Representative of A.B. [*or* C.D.]] (*include full designation*)

*NOTE: This form should be suitably adapted where section 16 of the Act of 2004 applies.*

---

[1] As inserted by the Act of Sederunt (Ordinary Cause, Summary Application, Summary Cause and Small Claim Rules) Amendment (Vulnerable Witnesses (Scotland) Act 2004) 2007 (SSI 2007/463) (effective November 1, 2007).

FORM 16C[1]

Form of vulnerable witness application

Rule 17A.3

VULNERABLE WITNESSES (SCOTLAND) ACT 2004 Section 12

Received the..........day of..........20..........

(*Date of receipt of this notice*)

..........(*signed*)

Sheriff Clerk

VULNERABLE WITNESS APPLICATION

Sheriff Court.................... ..........20..........

Court Ref. No.

1. The applicant is the pursuer [*or* defender] in the action by [A.B] (*design*) against [C.D.] (*design*).

2. The applicant has cited [or intends to cite] [E.F.] (*date of birth*) as a witness.

3. The applicant considers that [E.F.] is a vulnerable witness under section 11(1)(b) of the Vulnerable Witnesses (Scotland) Act 2004 for the following reasons:—

(*here specify reasons witness is considered to be a vulnerable witness*).

4. The applicant considers that the following special measure[s] is [are] the most appropriate for the purpose of taking the evidence of [E.F.].

(*specify any special measure(s) sought*)

5. The reason[s] this [these] special measure[s] is [are] considered the most appropriate is [are] as follows:—

(*here specify the reason(s) for the special measures(s) sought*).

6. [E.F.] has expressed the following view[s] on the special measure[s] that is [are] considered most appropriate:—

(*set out the views expressed and how they were obtained*).

7. Other information considered relevant to this application is as follows:—

(*here set out any other information relevant to the vulnerable witness application*).

8. The applicant asks the court to—

(a)   consider this vulnerable witness application;

(b)   make an order authorising the special measure[s] sought.

(*Signed*)

[A.B. *or* C.D.]

[ *or* Representative of A.B. [ *or* C.D. ]] (*include full designation*)

NOTE: *This form should be suitably adapted where* section 16 of the Act of 2004 *applies.*

FORM 16D[2]

FORM OF CERTIFICATE OF INTIMATION

**Rule 17A.4(2)**

VULNERABLE WITNESSES (SCOTLAND) ACT 2004 Section 12

CERTIFICATE OF INTIMATION

Sheriff Court.......... ..........20..........

Court Ref. No.

I certify that intimation of the child witness notice [*or* vulnerable witness application] relating to (*insert name of witness*) was made to (*insert names of parties or solicitors for parties, as appropriate*) by (*insert method of intimation: where intimation is by facsimile transmission, insert fax number to which intimation sent*) on (*insert date of intimation*).

Date:..........

(*Signed*)

Solicitor [*or* Sheriff Officer]

(*include full business designation*)

---

[1] As inserted by the Act of Sederunt (Ordinary Cause, Summary Application, Summary Cause and Small Claim Rules) Amendment (Vulnerable Witnesses (Scotland) Act 2004) 2007 (SSI 2007/463) (effective November 1, 2007).

[2] As inserted by the Act of Sederunt (Ordinary Cause, Summary Application, Summary Cause and Small Claim Rules) Amendment (Vulnerable Witnesses (Scotland) Act 2004) 2007 (SSI 2007/463) (effective November 1, 2007).

FORM 16E[1]

FORM OF APPLICATION FOR REVIEW

**Rule 17A.6(1)**

VULNERABLE WITNESSES (SCOTLAND) ACT 2004 Section 13

Received the...............day of...............20..........
*(date of receipt of this notice)*
....................*(signed)*
Sheriff Clerk

APPLICATION FOR REVIEW OF ARRANGEMENTS FOR VULNERABLE WITNESS

Sheriff Court..................... ..........20..........

Court Ref. No.

1. The applicant is the pursuer |or defender| in the action by |A.B.| *(design)* against |C.D.| (design).
2. A proof |or hearing| is fixed for *(date)* at *(time)*.
3. [E.F.] is a witness who is to give evidence at, or for the purposes of, the proof [or hearing]. [E.F.] is a child witness [or vulnerable witness] under section 11 of the Vulnerable Witnesses (Scotland) Act 2004.
4. The current arrangements for taking the evidence of [E.F.] are *(here specify current arrangements)*.
5. The current arrangements should be reviewed as *(here specify reasons for review)*.
6. [E.F.] [and the parent[s] of [or person[s] with parental responsibility for] [E.F.]] has [have] expressed the following view[s] on [the special measure[s] that is [are] considered most appropriate] [or the appropriateness of [E.F] giving evidence without the benefit of any special measure]:—
*(delete as appropriate and set out the view(s) expressed and how they were obtained)*.
7. The applicant seeks (here specify the order sought).
*(Signed)*
|A.B. *or* C.D.|
[*or* Representative of A.B. [*or* C.D.]] *(include full designation)*
*NOTE: This form should be suitably adapted where* section 16 of the Act of 2004 applies.

FORM 16F[2]

FORM OF CERTIFICATE OF INTIMATION

**Rule 17A.7(2)**

VULNERABLE WITNESSES (SCOTLAND) ACT 2004 Section 13
CERTIFICATE OF INTIMATION

Sheriff Court......... ..........20...... ...

Court Ref. No.

I certify that intimation of the review application relating to *(insert name of witness)* was made to *(insert names of parties or solicitors far parties, as appropriate)* by *(insert method of intimation; where intimation is by facsimile transmission, insert fax number to which intimation sent) on (insert date of intimation)*.
Date:..........

*(Signed)*
Solicitor [*or* Sheriff Officer]
*(include full business designation)*

FORM 17

FORM OF REFERENCE TO THE EUROPEAN COURT

**Rule 18.2(2)**

REQUEST
for
PRELIMINARY RULING
of

---

[1] As inserted by the Act of Sederunt (Ordinary Cause, Summary Application, Summary Cause and Small Claim Rules) Amendment (Vulnerable Witnesses (Scotland) Act 2004) 2007 (SSI 2007/463) (effective November 1, 2007).
[2] As inserted by the Act of Sederunt (Ordinary Cause, Summary Application, Summary Cause and Small Claim Rules) Amendment (Vulnerable Witnesses (Scotland) Act 2004) 2007 (SSI 2007/463) (effective November 1, 2007).

THE COURT OF JUSTICE OR THE EUROPEAN COMMUNITIES
from
THE SHERIFFDOM OF (*insert name of sheriffdom*) at (*insert place of court*)
in the cause
AB (*insert designation and address*), pursuer
against
CD (*insert designation and address*), defender

(Here set out a clear and succinct statement of the case giving rise to the request for a ruling of the European Court in order to enable the European Court to consider and understand the issues of Community law raised and to enable governments of Member states and other interested parties to submit observations. The statement of the case should include:

- (a)  particulars of the parties;
- (b)  the history of the dispute between the parties;
- (c)  the history of the proceedings;
- (d)  the relevant facts as agreed by the parties or found by the court or, failing such agreement or finding, the contentions of the parties on such facts;
- (e)  the nature of the issues of law and fact between the parties;
- (f)  the Scots law, so far as relevant;
- (g)  the Treaty provisions or other acts, instruments or rules of Community law concerned;
- (h)  an explanation of why the reference is being made).

The preliminary ruling of the Court of Justice of the European Communities is accordingly requested on the following questions:

1,2, etc. (*Here set out the question (s) on which the ruling is sought, identifying the Treaty provisions or other acts, instruments or rules of Community law concerned.*)

Dated the.......... day of..........20

## FORM 18

### FORM OF EXTRACT DECREE (BASIC)

**Rule 21.5(4)(b)**

Sheriff court.................... Court ref. no.:
Date of decree....................*in absence
Pursuer(s).................... Defender(s)
The sheriff
and granted decree against the.................... for payment of expenses of £.......... against the (name of party).
This extract is warrant for all lawful execution thereon.
Date.................... Sheriff clerk depute
*delete as appropriate

## FORM 18A

### FORM OF EXTRACT DECREE FOR PAYMENT

**Rule 21.5(4)(b)**

Sheriff court .................... Court ref. no.
Date of decree .................... *in absence
Pursuer(s) .................... Defender(s)
The sheriff granted decree against the .................... for payment to the .................... of the undernoted sums:

- (1)  Sum(s) decerned for: £
- (2)  Interest atper cent per year from (*date*) until payment.
- (3)  Expenses of £.......... against the (*name of party*).

*A time to pay direction was made under section 1(1) of the Debtors (Scotland) Act 1987.
*A time order was made under section 129 (1) of the Consumer Credit Act 1974.
*The amount is payable by instalments of £.......... per .......... commencing within .......... *days/weeks/months of intimation of this extract decree.
*The amount is payable by lump sum within .......... *days/weeks/months of intimation of this extract decree.
This extract is warrant for all lawful execution thereon.
Date .................... Sheriff clerk depute

*delete as appropriate

## FORM 18B

### FORM OF EXTRACT DECREE IN AN ACTION OF DELIVERY

**Rule 21.5(4)(b)**

Sheriff court .................... Court ref. no.:
Date of decree .................... *in absence
Pursuer(s)
Defender(s)
The sheriff granted decree against the defender
    (1)    for delivery to the pursuer of (*specify articles*)
    (2)    for expenses of £..........
* Further, the sheriff granted warrant to officers of court to (1) open shut and lockfast places occupied by the defender and (2) search for and take possession of said goods in the possession of the defender.
**delete as appropriate*
This extract is warrant for all lawful execution thereon.
Date .................... Sheriff clerk depute

## FORM 18C

### FORM OF EXTRACT DECREE IN AN ACTION OF DELIVERY — PAYMENT FAILING DELIVERY

**Rule 21.5(4)(b)**

Sheriff court .................... Court ref. no.:
Date of decree .................... *in absence
Pursuer(s)
Defender(s)
The sheriff, in respect that the defender has failed to make delivery in accordance with the decree granted in this court on (*date*), granted decree for payment against the defender of the undernoted sums:
    (1)    Sum(s) decerned for: £.........., being the alternative amount claimed.
    (2)    Interest at .......... per cent per year from (*date*) until payment.
    (3)    Expenses of £.......... against the (*name of party*).
*A time to pay direction was made under section 1 (1) of the Debtors (Scotland) Act 1987.
The amount is payable by instalments of £.......... per .......... commencing within .......... *days/weeks/monthsof intimation of this extract decree.
The amount is payable by lump sum within .......... *days/weeks/months of intimation of this extract decree.
**delete as appropriate*
This extract is warrant for all lawful execution thereon.
Date .................... Sheriff clerk depute

## FORM 18D

### FORM OF EXTRACT DECREE RECOVERY OF POSSESSION OF MOVEABLE PROPERTY

**Rule 21.5(4)(b)**

Sheriff court .................... Court ref. no.:
Date of decree .................... *in absence
Pursuer(s) .................... Defender(s)
The sheriff granted decree against the defender:
    (1)    Finding the pursuer entitled to recovery of possession of the article(s) (*specify*)
    (2)    for expenses of £
* Further, the sheriff granted warrant to officers of court to (1) open shut and lockfast places occupied by the defender and (2) search for and take possession of said goods in the possession of the defender.
**delete as appropriate*
This extract is warrant for all lawful execution thereon.
Date .................... Sheriff clerk depute

## FORM 18E

### FORM OF EXTRACT DECREE

**Rule 21.5(4)(b)**

Recovery of possession of moveable property—payment failing recovery

Sheriff court ................... Court ref. no.:

Date of decree ................... *in absence

Pursuer(s) ................... Defender(s)

The sheriff, in respect that the defender has failed to recover possession in accordance with the decree granted in this court on (*date*), granted decree for payment against the defender of the undernoted sums:

Sum(s) decerned for: £.........., being the alternative amount claimed.

Interest at ......... per cent per year from (*date*) until payment.

Expenses of £......... against the (*name of party*).

*A time to pay direction was made under section 1 (1) of the Debtors (Scotland) Act 1987.

*The amount is payable by instalments of £......... per ......... commencing within ......... *days/weeks/monthsof intimation of this extract decree.

*The amount is payable by lump sum within ......... *days/weeks/months of intimation of this extract decree.

* *delete as appropriate*

This extract is warrant for all lawful execution thereon.

Date ......... ......... Sheriff clerk depute

## FORM 18F

### FORM OF EXTRACT DECREE AD FACTUM PRAESTANDUM

**Rule 21.5(4)(b)**

Sheriff ................... court Court ref. no.:

Date of decree ................... *in absence

Pursuer(s)

Defender(s)

The sheriff

    (1)    ordained the defender(s)

    (2)    granted decree for payment of expenses of £......... against the defender(s).

This extract is warrant for all lawful execution thereon.

Date ................... Sheriff clerk depute

## FORM 18G

### FORM OF EXTRACT DECREE AD FACTUM PRAESTANDUM—PAYMENT UPON FAILURE TO IMPLEMENT OBLIGATION

**Rule 21.5(4)(b)**

Sheriff court ................... Court ref. no.:

Date of decree ................... *in absence

Pursuer(s)

Defender(s)

The sheriff, in respect that the defender has failed to implement the obligation contained in and in accordance with the decree granted in this court on (*date*), granted decree for payment against the defender of the undernoted sums:

    (1)    Sum(s) decerned for: £........., being the alternative amount claimed.

    (2)    Interest at ......... per cent per year from (*date*) until payment.

    (3)    Expenses of £......... against the (*name of party*).

*A time to pay direction was made under section 1(1) of the Debtors (Scotland) Act 1987.

The amount is payable by instalments of £......... per ......... commencing within ............... *days/weeks/monthsof intimation of this extract decree.

*The amount is payable by lump sum within ......... *days/weeks/months of intimation of this extract decree.

* *delete as appropriate*

This extract is warrant for all lawful execution thereon.

Date ................... Sheriff clerk depute

## FORM 18H

### FORM OF EXTRACT DECREE OF ABSOLVITOR

**Rule 21.5(4)(b)**

Sheriff court ................... Court ref. no.:

Date of decree ................... *in absence

Pursuer(s)

Defender(s)

The sheriff

    (1)    absolved the defender(s).

    (2)    granted decree for payment of expenses of £.......... against the

This extract is warrant for all lawful execution thereon.

Date .................... Sheriff clerk depute

## FORM 18I

### FORM OF EXTRACT DECREE OF DISMISSAL

**Rule 21.5(4)(b)**

Sheriff court .................... Court ref. no.:

Date of decree .................... *in absence

Pursuer(s)

Defender(s)

The sheriff

    (1)    dismissed the action against the defender(s).

    (2)    granted decree for payment of expenses of £.......... against the

This extract is warrant for all lawful execution thereon.

Date .................... Sheriff clerk depute

## FORM 19

### FORM OF CERTIFICATE BY SHERIFF CLERK

**Rule 21.8(4)**

Service of charge where address of defender is unknown

    I certify that the foregoing charge was displayed on the walls of court on (*date*) and that it remained so displayed for a period of (*period of charge*) from that date.

    (date) .................... Sheriff clerk depute

## FORM 20[1]

### MINUTE FOR RECALL OF DECREE

**Rule 21.1(1)**

Sheriff court: (*place*)

Court ref. no.:

AB (*pursuer*) against CD (*defender(s)*)

    The *(*pursuer / defender*) moves the court to recall the decree pronounced on (*date*) in this case * and in which execution of a charge/arrestment was effected on (*date*).

    *Proposed defence/answer:

Date

*delete as appropriate*

## FORM 20A[2]

### MINUTE FOR RECALL OF DECREE—SERVICE COPY

**Rule 22.1(6)**

Sheriff court: (*place*)

Court ref. no.:

AB (*pursuer*) against CD (*defender(s)*)

    The *(*pursuer / defender*) moves the court to recall the decree pronounced on (*date*) in this case * and in which execution of a charge/arrestment was effected on (*date*).

    *Proposed defence/answer:

Date

*delete as appropriate*

---

[1] As amended by the Act of Sederunt (Sheriff Court Rules) (Miscellaneous Amendments) 2011 (SSI 2011/193) r.17 (effective April 4, 2011).

[2] As amended by the Act of Sederunt (Sheriff Court Rules) (Miscellaneous Amendments) 2011 (SSI 2011/193) r.17 (effective April 4, 2011).

**NOTE: You must return the summons to the sheriff clerk at the court mentioned at the top of this form by (insert date 2 days before the date of the hearing).**

FORM 21

FORM OF NOTE OF APPEAL TO THE SHERIFF PRINCIPAL

**Rule 23.1(1)**

Sheriff court (*place*)
Court ref. no:
AB (pursuer) against CD (defender(s))
The pursuer/defender appeals the sheriffs interlocutor of (*date*) to the sheriff principal and requests the sheriff to state a case.
The point(s) of law upon which the appeal is to proceed is/are: (*give brief statement*).
(*date*)

FORM 22

APPLICATION FOR LEAVE TO APPEAL AGAINST TIME TO PAY DIRECTION

**Rule 23.4(3)(a)**

Sheriff court (*place*)
Court ref. no.:
AB (pursuer) against CD (defender(s))
The pursuer/defender requests the sheriff to grant leave to appeal the decision made on (*date*) in respect of the defender's application for a time to pay direction to the sheriff principal/Court of Session.
The point(s) of law upon which the appeal is to proceed is/are: (give brief statement).
(*date*)

FORM 23

APPEAL AGAINST TIME TO PAY DIRECTION

**Rule 23.4(4)**

Sheriff court (*place*)
Court ref. no.:
AB (pursuer) against CD (defender(s))
The pursuer/defender appeals the decision made on (*date*) in respect of the defender's application for a time to pay direction to the sheriff principal/Court of Session.
(*date*)

FORM 24

FORM OF RECEIPT FOR MONEY PAID TO SHERIFF CLERK

**Rule 24.4(1)**

In the sheriff court of (*name of sheriffdom*) at (*place of sheriff court*).
In the claim (*state names of parties or other appropriate description*)
AB (*designation*) has this day paid into court the sum of £.........., being a payment made in terms of Chapter 24 of the Small Claim Rules 2002.
*Custody of this money has been accepted at the request of (*insert name of court making the request*).
*delete as appropriate

(Date)

Sheriff clerk depute

**Appendix 2**

**GLOSSARY**

**Rule 1.1(5)**

*Absolve*
To find in favour of and exonerate the defender.
*Absolvitor*

1026

An order of the court granted in favour of and exonerating the defender which means that the pursuer is not allowed to bring the same matter to court again.

*Appellant*

A person making an appeal against the sheriff's decision. This might be the pursuer or the defender.

*Arrestee*

A person subject to an arrestment.

*Arrestment on the dependence*

A court order to freeze the goods or bank account of the defender until the court has heard the case.

*Arrestment to found jurisdiction*

A court order used against a person who has goods or other assets in Scotland to give the court jurisdiction to hear a claim. This is achieved by preventing anything being done with the goods or assets until the case has been disposed of

*Authorised lay representative*

A person other than a lawyer who represents a party to a small claim.

*Cause*

Another word for case or claim, used for cases under the summary cause procedure.

*Caution (pronounced kay-shun)*

A security, usually a sum of money, given to ensure that some obligation will be carried out.

*Certificate of execution of service*

The document recording that an application to, or order or decree of, the court for service of documents has been effected.

*Charge*

An order to obey a decree of a court. A common type is one served on the defender by a sheriff officer on behalf of the pursuer who has won a case demanding payment of a sum of money.

*Commission and diligence*

Authorisation by the court for someone to take the evidence of a witness who cannot attend court or to obtain the production of documentary evidence. It is combined with a diligence authorising the person appointed to require the attendance of the witness and the disclosure of documents.

*Consignation*

The deposit in court, or with a third party, of money or an article in dispute.

*Continuation*

An order made by the sheriff postponing the completion of a hearing until a later date or dates.

*Counterclaim*

A claim made by a defender in response to the pursuer's claim and which is not a defence to that claim. It is a separate but related claim against the pursuer which is dealt with at the same time as the pursuer's claim.

*Damages*

Money compensation payable for a breach of contract or some other legal duty.

*Decree*

An order of the court containing the decision of the claim in favour of one of the parties and granting the remedy sought or disposing of the claim.

*Defender*

Person against whom a claim is made.

*Deliverance*

A decision or order of a court.

*Depending*

A case is said to be depending when it is going through a court procedure. Technically, this begins with citation of the defender and ends with any final appeal.

*Diet*

Date for a court hearing.

*Diligence*

The collective term for the procedures used to enforce a decree of a court. These include arrestment of wages, goods or a bank account.

*Dismissal*

An order bringing to an end the proceedings in a claim. It is usually possible for a new claim to be brought if not time barred.

*Domicile*

The place where a person is normally resident or where, in the case of a company, it has its place of business or registered office.

1027

*Execution of service*

See Certificate of execution of service.

*Execution of a charge*

The intimation of the requirement to obey a decree or order of a court.

*Execution of an arrestment*

The carrying out of an order of arrestment.

*Expenses*

The costs of a court case.

*Extra-judicial settlement*

An agreement between the parties to a case to settle it themselves rather than to await a decision by the sheriff.

*Extract decree*

The document containing the order of the court made at the end of the claim. For example, it can be used to enforce payment of a sum awarded.

*Haver*

A person who holds documents which are required as evidence in a case.

*Huissier*

An official in France and some other European countries who serves court documents.

*Incidental application*

An application that can be made during the course of a small claim for certain orders. Examples are applications for the recovery of documents or to amend the statement of claim.

*Interlocutor*

The official record of the order or judgment of a court.

*Intimation*

Giving notice to another party of some step in the small claim.

*Jurisdiction*

The authority of a court to hear particular cases.

*Messenger at arms*

Officers of court who serve documents issued by the Court of Session.

*Minute*

A document produced in the course of a case in which a party makes an application or sets out his position on some matter.

*Minute for recall*

A form lodged with the court by one party asking the court to recall a decree.

*Options Hearing*

A preliminary stage in an ordinary cause action.

*Ordinary cause*

Another legal procedure for higher value claims available in the sheriff court.

*Party litigant*

A person who conducts his own case.

*Productions*

Documents or articles which are used in evidence.

*Pursuer*

The person making a claim.

*Recall of an arrestment*

A court order withdrawing an arrestment.

*Restriction of an arrestment*

An order releasing part of the money or property arrested.

*Recall of a decree*

An order revoking a decree which has been granted.

*Recovery of documents*

The process of obtaining documentary evidence which is not in the possession of the person seeking it (e.g. hospital records necessary to establish the extent of injuries received in a road accident).

*Remit between procedures*

A decision of the sheriff to transfer the claim to another court procedure e.g. summary cause or ordinary cause procedure.

*Respondent*

When a decision of the sheriff is appealed against, the person making the appeal is called the appellant. The other side in the appeal is called the respondent.

*Return day*

The date by which the defender must send a written reply to the court and, where appropriate, the pursuer must return the summons to court.

*Schedule of arrestment*

The list of items which may be arrested.

*Serve/Service*

Sending a copy of the summons or other court document to the defender or another party.

*Sheriff clerk*

The court official responsible for the administration of the sheriff court.

*Sheriff officer*

A person who serves court documents and enforces court orders.

*Sist of action*

The temporary suspension of a court case by court order.

*Sist as a party*

To add another person as a litigant in a case.

*Stated case*

An appeal procedure where the sheriff sets out his findings and the reasons for his decision and states the issues on which the decision of the sheriff principal is requested.

*Statement of claim*

The part of the summons in which pursuers set out details of their claims against defenders.

*Summary cause*

Another legal procedure available in the Sheriff Court. It is used for certain types of claim usually having a higher value than small claims though less than those dealt with as ordinary causes.

*Summons*

The form which must be filled in to begin a small claim.

*Time to pay direction*

A court order for which a defender who is an individual may apply permitting a sum owed to be paid by instalments or by a single payment at a later date.

*Time order*

A court order which assists debtors who have defaulted on an agreement regulated by the Consumer Credit Act 1974 (c.39) and which may be applied for during a court action.

*Warrant for diligence*

Authority to carry out one of the diligence procedures.

*Writ*

A legally significant writing.

SCHEDULE 2

REVOCATIONS

**Paragraph 4**

| (1)<br>**Act of Sederunt** | (2)<br>**Reference** | (3)<br>**Extent of revocation** |
|---|---|---|
| Act of Sederunt (Small Claim Rules) 1988 | S.I. 1988/1976 | The whole Act of Sederunt |
| Act of Sederunt (Amendment of Sheriff Court Ordinary Cause, Summary Cause and Small Claim, Rules) 1990 | S.I. 1990/661 | Paragraph 4 |
| Act of Sederunt (Amendment of Sheriff Court Ordinary Cause, Summary Cause and Small Claim, Rules) (No. 2) 1990 | S.I. 1990/2105 | Paragraph 4 |
| Act of Sederunt (Amendment of | S.I. 1991/821 | Paragraph 3 |

| (1) Act of Sederunt | (2) Reference | (3) Extent of revocation |
|---|---|---|
| Summary Cause and Small Claim Rules) 1991 | | |
| Act of Sederunt (Amendment of Ordinary Cause, Summary Cause and Small Claim Rules) 1992 | S.I. 1992/249 | Paragraph 3 |
| Act of Sederunt (Sheriff Court Ordinary Cause Rules) 1993 | S.I. 1993/1956 | Paragraph 4 |

# ACT OF SEDERUNT (DEBT ARRANGEMENT AND ATTACHMENT (SCOTLAND) ACT 2002) 2002

## (SSI 2002/560)

The Lords of Council and Session, under and by virtue of the powers conferred by section 247(2) of the Local Government (Scotland) Act 1947, section 63(1) of the Taxes Management Act 1970, section 32 of the Sheriff Courts (Scotland) Act 1971, paragraph 3(3) of Schedule 1 to the Car Tax Act 1983, paragraph 7(2) of Schedule 2 to the Abolition of Domestic Rates Etc. (Scotland) Act 1987, section 5 of the Court of Session Act 1988, paragraph 2(2) of Schedule 8 to the Local Government Finance Act 1992, paragraph 2(2) of Schedule 10 to the Local Government etc. (Scotland) Act 1994, paragraph 13(2) of Schedule 5 to the Finance Act 1996, section 52 of the Finance Act 1997, and sections 12, 17, 18, 32, 56 and 64 of the Debt Arrangement and Attachment (Scotland) Act 2002 and of all other powers enabling them in that behalf, having approved draft rules submitted to them by the Sheriff Court Rules Council in accordance with section 34 of the Sheriff Courts (Scotland) Act 1971, do hereby enact and declare:

## Citation, commencement and interpretation

**1.**—(1)   This Act of Sederunt—
- (a)   may be cited as the Act of Sederunt (Debt Arrangement and Attachment (Scotland) Act 2002) 2002;
- (b)   shall come into force on 30th December 2002; and
- (c)   shall be inserted in the Books of Sederunt.

(2)   In this Act of Sederunt, "the 2002 Act" means the Debt Arrangement and Attachment (Scotland) Act 2002.

## Rules for Applications in the Sheriff Court under the 2002 Act

**2.**   Schedule 1 to this Act of Sederunt provides rules for applications in the sheriff court under the 2002 Act.

## Summary warrants

**3.**—(1)   Schedule 2 to this Act of Sederunt provides forms for summary warrants, and any reference in this article to a form means the form so specified in Schedule 2.

(2)   A summary warrant for recovery of any sum shall be in form A or B, as the case may be.

## Minor and consequential amendments

**4.**   Schedule 3 to this Act of Sederunt (which contains minor amendments and amendments consequential upon the provisions of the 2002 Act) shall have effect.

## Revocation and savings

**5.**   The Acts of Sederunt mentioned in column (1) of Schedule 4 to this Act of Sederunt are revoked to the extent specified in column (3) of that Schedule except—
- (a)   in relation to a debt in respect of which a warrant sale has been completed before the date on which section 58 of the 2002 Act comes into force ("the commencement date");

(b) in relation to a debt in respect of which a poinding was executed before the commencement date if—

(i) the poinding was executed at a place other than a dwellinghouse; and

(ii) a warrant sale is completed in respect of the poinding on or before 31st March 2003; or

(c) in relation to an application for sequestration for rent on which warrant was granted on or before the commencement date.

SCHEDULE 1

RULES FOR APPLICATIONS IN THE SHERIFF COURT UNDER THE DEBT ARRANGEMENT AND ATTACHMENT (SCOTLAND) ACT 2002

Article 2

**Arrangement of Rules**

Chapter 1
General

*Chapter 4*

*The Debt Arrangement Scheme (Scotland) Regulations 2004*

**Appendix 1**

**FORMS**

**Appendix 2**

**GLOSSARY**

Chapter 1

General

**Citation and interpretation**

**1.**—(1)  These Rules may be cited as the Rules for Applications in the Sheriff Court under the Debt Arrangement and Attachment (Scotland) Act 2002.

(2)  In these Rules—

"the 2002 Act" means the Debt Arrangement and Attachment (Scotland) Act 2002;

"authorised lay representative" means a person to whom section 32(1) of the Solicitors (Scotland) Act 1980 (offence for unqualified persons to prepare certain documents) does not apply by virtue of section 32(2)(a) of that Act;

"decree" and "document of debt" have the meanings given to them in section 10(5) of the 2002 Act; and

"exceptional attachment order" has the meaning given to it by section 47(1) of the 2002 Act;

(3)  Any reference in these Rules—

(a)  to a section is to be construed as the section bearing that number in the 2002 Act;

(b)  to a specified paragraph is to be construed as a reference to the paragraph so numbered or lettered in the provision in which that reference occurs; or

(c)  to a numbered form means the form so numbered in Appendix 1 to these Rules, or a form of substantially the same effect with such variation as circumstances may require.

(4)  The glossary in Appendix 2 to these Rules is a guide to the meaning of certain legal expressions, but is not to be taken as giving those expressions any meaning that they do not have in law generally.

**Dispensing power of sheriff**

**2.**—(1)  The sheriff may relieve any party from the consequences of any failure to comply with the provisions of these Rules which is shown to be due to mistake, oversight or other excusable cause, on such conditions as the sheriff thinks fit.

(2)  Where the sheriff so relieves a party the sheriff may make such order as the sheriff thinks fit to enable the application to proceed as if the failure to comply had not taken place.

**Lay representation**

**3.**—(1) A party to any proceedings before the sheriff under Parts 2 and 3 of the 2002 Act may be represented by an advocate, a solicitor or, subject to paragraph (3), an authorised lay representative.

(2) An authorised lay representative may in representing a party do everything for the preparation and conduct of any proceedings as may be done by that party.

(3) If the sheriff finds that an authorised lay representative is—

(a) not a suitable representative; or

(b) not duly authorised to represent a party,

that person shall cease to represent the party.

**Conduct of hearings**

**4.**—(1) Any hearing before the sheriff in an application under the 2002 Act shall be conducted as informally as the sheriff considers the circumstances permit.

(2) The procedure to be adopted at a hearing shall be such as the sheriff considers—

(a) to be fair;

(b) best suited to the clarification and determination of the issues; and

(c) gives each party sufficient opportunity to put across the party's position.

**Intimation**

**5.**—(1) A warrant for intimation referred to in these Rules shall be in form 1.

(2) The sheriff may order intimation to such persons other than those to whom intimation is required under these Rules as the sheriff considers appropriate.

(3) Intimation shall be made by sheriff clerk or by officer of court.

(4) The sheriff clerk or officer of court on making intimation shall complete a certificate of intimation in form 2.

**Electronic transmission of documents**

**6.**—(1) Any document referred to in these Rules which requires to be—

(a) lodged with the sheriff clerk;

(b) intimated to a party; or

(c) sent by the sheriff clerk,

may be in electronic or documentary form, and if in electronic form may be lodged, intimated or sent by e-mail or similar means.

(2) Paragraph (1), so far as it permits any document to be in electronic form, or if in electronic form to be lodged, intimated or sent by e-mail or similar means, does not apply to—

(a) a certificate of intimation of service;

(b) a citation;

(c) a decree or extract decree of the court;

(d) a report of an attachment;

(e) a report of an auction; or

(f) an attachment schedule.

(3) Where any document is lodged by e-mail or similar means the sheriff may require any principal document to be lodged.

(4) The time of lodgement, intimation or sending shall be the time when the document was sent or transmitted.

**Vulnerable witnesses**

**6A.**—[1](1) At any hearing on an application under these rules the sheriff shall ascertain whether there is or is likely to be a vulnerable witness who is to give evidence at or for the purposes of any proof or hearing, consider any child witness notice or vulnerable witness application that has been lodged where no order has been made under section 12(1) or (6) of the Vulnerable Witnesses (Scotland) Act 2004, and consider whether any order under section 12(1) of that Act requires to be made.

(2) Except where the sheriff otherwise directs, where a vulnerable witness is to give evidence at or for the purposes of any proof or hearing in an application under these rules any application in relation to

---

[1] As inserted by the Act of Sederunt (Debt Arrangement and Attachment (Scotland) Act 2002) Amendment (Vulnerable Witnesses (Scotland) Act 2004) (SSI 2007/466) art.2(2) (effective November 1, 2007).

the vulnerable witness or special measure that may be ordered shall be dealt with in accordance with the rules within Chapter 45 of the Ordinary Cause Rules in the First Schedule to the Sheriff Courts (Scotland) Act 1907.

(3)    In this rule, "vulnerable witness" means a witness within the meaning of section 11(1) of the Vulnerable Witnesses (Scotland) Act 2004.

CHAPTER 1A[1]

INTERIM ATTACHMENT

### Application for extension of hours of attachment

**6B.**—(1)    An application by an officer of court under section 12(2) to extend the hours of an interim attachment shall be made by minute, which shall be lodged in the process of the action in which the warrant for interim attachment was granted.

(2)    The minute shall specify—

(a)    the extension sought; and

(b)    the reason for the extension.

(3)    The minute does not need to be intimated to any party and the sheriff may grant or refuse it without a hearing.

### Procedure for executing attachment

**6C.**—(1)    When executing an interim attachment the officer of court shall be accompanied by another person who shall witness the whole proceedings.

(2)    Before attaching any article the officer of court shall—

(a)    show to every person present a certified copy of the interlocutor authorising the interim attachment; and

(b)    make enquiries as to the ownership in common of that article (and in particular ownership in common of that article by the debtor and any other person).

(3)    The officer of court shall prepare a schedule (the "schedule of interim attachment") in Form 2a.

(4)    The officer of court and the witness shall sign the schedule of interim attachment.

(5)    The officer of court shall—

(a)    deliver a copy of the signed schedule of interim attachment to any person then in possession of the articles or leave it at the premises occupied by that person; and

(b)    if the person in possession of the articles is not the debtor and it is reasonably practicable to do so, serve a copy of the signed schedule of interim attachment by first class post on the debtor.

### Application of rules 10, 11 and 12 in relation to interim attachment

**6D.**—(1)    Rules 10, 11 and 12 apply in relation to interim attachment as they apply in relation to attachment.

(2)    The application of rule 11 is subject to the following modifications—

(a)    for Part C of Form 6 there is substituted—

"An action has been raised by the Creditor against the Debtor in the Court of Session/Sheriff Court at on. On the court granted warrant for interim attachment."; and

(b)    in Part D of that form, for "attachment" there is substituted "interim attachment".

### Report of attachment

**6E.**—(1)    A report under section 17(1) by an officer of court of the execution of an interim attachment shall be in Form 2b.

(2)    The sheriff clerk shall retain the report of the attachment.

---

[1] As inserted by the Act of Sederunt (Sheriff Court Rules Amendment) (Diligence) (SSI 2008/ 121) r.8 (effective April 1, 2008).

(3) An application by an officer of court under section 17(1) to extend the time for lodging the report shall be made by minute stating the reasons for the extension, which shall be lodged in the process of the action in which the warrant for interim attachment was granted.

CHAPTER 2

ATTACHMENT: GENERAL PROVISIONS

### Applying for an extension of hours of attachment

**7.**—(1) An application by an officer of court under section 12(2) to extend the hours of attachment shall be made by minute, which may be endorsed on the decree or document of debt (or extract decree or document of debt) upon which the attachment has proceeded.

(2) The minute shall specify—

    (a) the extension sought; and

    (b) the reason for the extension.

(3) The minute does not need to be intimated to any party and the sheriff may grant or refuse it without a hearing.

(4) The terms of the sheriffs decision shall be endorsed on the decree or document of debt (or extract decree or document of debt), and may be authenticated by the sheriff clerk.

### Procedure for executing attachment

**8.**—(1) When executing an attachment the officer of court shall be accompanied by another person who shall witness the whole proceedings.

(2) Before attaching any article the officer of court shall—

    (a) show to every person present—

        (i) the decree or document of debt (or an extract of the decree or document) authorising the attachment; and

        (ii) where the decree or document of debt is not a summary warrant, the certificate of execution of the charge to which that decree or document of debt relates;

    (b) demand payment of the sum recoverable from the debtor (or if the debtor is not present, any other person who appears to the officer to be authorised to act for the debtor); and

    (c) make enquiries as to the ownership in common of that article (and in particular ownership in common of that article by the debtor and any other person).

(3)[1] An attachment schedule under section 13A shall be in Form 3.

(4) The officer of court and the witness shall sign the attachment schedule.

(5) The officer of court shall—

    (a) deliver a copy of the signed attachment schedule to any person then in possession of the articles or leave it at the premises occupied by that person;

    (b) if the person then in possession of the articles is not the debtor and it is reasonably practicable to do so, serve a copy of the signed attachment schedule by post on the debtor;

    (c) inform the debtor (if present) of the debtor's right to redeem attached articles under sections 18(1) or 56(1);

    (d) inform any person present who claims to own any attached article in common with the debtor of the right to—

        (i) make a claim for the purposes of section 35(2)(a);

        (ii) apply for an order under section 35(2)(b); and

        (iii) pay the value of the debtor's interest in the attached article in terms of section 35(2)(c); and

    (e) where, after making enquiries of any person present, it appears that the article attached is a mobile home which is the only or principal residence of a person other than the debtor, inform the debtor and that person, by leaving in the mobile home a copy of the attachment schedule, of their right to apply for release of the mobile home from attachment under section 16(1).

### Applying for the attachment to cease to have effect because value fixed is too low

**9.**—(1) An application by the debtor under section 23(2) for an order that the attachment cease to have effect because the value fixed is too low shall be in form 4.

(2) On the lodging of such an application the sheriff clerk shall—

    (a) fix a date for a hearing;

---

[1] As substituted by the Act of Sederunt (Sheriff Court Rules Amendment) (Diligence) 2009 (SSI 2009/107) r.7 (effective April 22, 2009).

(b)    grant a warrant for intimation;

(c)    intimate the application and warrant to the applicant, the creditor and the officer of court who executed the attachment; and

(d)    complete a certificate of intimation.

(3)    The officer of court who executed the attachment shall lodge with the sheriff clerk a copy of the attachment schedule before the date fixed for the hearing.

### Notice of theft after attachment

**10.**—(1)    A notice by the debtor under section 21(7) that an attached article has been stolen shall be in form 5.

(2)    Any notice shall be sent by the debtor to the sheriff clerk, the creditor, and the officer of court.

### Applying for further attachment where articles removed, damaged, destroyed or stolen

**11.**—(1)    The following applications shall be made in form 6:—

(a)    an application under section 21(2)(b) for authority to attach other articles where an article has been moved;

(b)    an application under section 21(10)(a) for authority to attach other articles where an article has been damaged, destroyed or stolen; and

(c)    an application under section 21(10)(b) for the revaluation of any damaged article.

(2)    On the lodging of an application under paragraph (1) the sheriff clerk shall—

(a)    fix a date for a hearing;

(b)    grant a warrant for intimation;

(c)    intimate the application and warrant to the applicant, the debtor and (as appropriate) the creditor or the officer of court who executed the attachment; and

(d)    complete a certificate of intimation.

(3)    The officer of court who executed the attachment shall lodge with the sheriff clerk a copy of the attachment schedule before the date fixed for the hearing.

### Applying for consignation where article damaged, destroyed, lost, stolen or disposed of

**12.**—(1)    An application under section 21(11) for an order against a debtor or third party to consign a sum of money in relation to an article which has been damaged, destroyed, lost, stolen or disposed of for value shall be in form 7.

(2)    On the lodging of such an application the sheriff clerk shall—

(a)    fix a date for a hearing;

(b)    grant a warrant for intimation;

(c)    intimate the application and warrant to the applicant, the officer of court who executed the attachment, the person in respect of whom an order for consignation is sought and (as appropriate) the debtor; and

(d)    complete a certificate of intimation.

(3)    The officer of court who executed the attachment shall lodge with the sheriff clerk a copy of the attachment schedule before the date fixed for the hearing.

### Report of attachment

**13.**—(1)    A report under section 17(1) by an officer of court of the execution of a attachment shall be in form 8.

(2)    The sheriff clerk shall retain the report of attachment.

(3)    An application by an officer of court under section 17(1) to extend the time for lodging the report shall be made by minute stating the reasons for seeking the extension, which may be endorsed on the decree or document of debt (or extract decree or document of debt) upon which the attachment has proceeded.

(4)    The terms of the sheriffs decision on any application shall be endorsed on the decree or document of debt (or extract decree or document of debt), and may be authenticated by the sheriff clerk.

### Receipt for redemption of an attached article

**14.**    A receipt granted by an officer of court for payment for an attached article redeemed under section 18(1) shall be in form 9.

### Applying for security of an attached article or sale of a perishable etc. article

**15.**—(1)    An application for an order under section 20(1) for the security of an attached article, or for the sale of an article which is perishable or likely to deteriorate substantially and rapidly in condition or value, shall be in form 10.

(2)   The sheriff shall on the lodging of such an application decide what further procedure is appropriate and may dispose of it without intimation to any party or without a hearing.

(3)   Where the sheriff considers it appropriate, a date for a hearing shall be fixed.

(4)   Where a hearing is fixed the sheriff clerk shall—

    (a)   intimate the application and warrant for intimation to the applicant and (as appropriate) to the debtor, the creditor and the officer of court who executed the attachment; and

    (b)   complete a certificate of intimation.

(5)   The officer of court who executed the attachment shall lodge with the sheriff clerk a copy of the attachment schedule before the date of the hearing.

### Applying for release of vehicle or mobile home from attachment, or for sale of vehicle

**16.**—(1)   The following applications shall be in form 11:—

    (a)   an application by the debtor or a third party under section 16(1) for the attachment of a mobile home to cease to have effect;

    (b)   an application by the debtor under section 22(1) for the attachment of a vehicle to cease to have effect because the auction of the vehicle would be unduly harsh; or

    (c)   an application by the debtor under section 22(3) for the immediate sale of a vehicle because the auction of the vehicle would be unduly harsh.

(2)   On the lodging of an application under paragraph (1) the sheriff clerk shall—

    (a)   fix a date for a hearing;

    (b)   grant a warrant for intimation;

    (c)   intimate the application and the warrant to the creditor, the officer of court who executed the order, the debtor and (where appropriate) the third party; and

    (d)   complete a certificate of intimation.

(3)   The officer of court who executed the attachment shall lodge with the sheriff clerk a copy of the attachment schedule before the date fixed for the hearing.

### Applying for extension of duration of attachment

**17.**—(1)   An application by a creditor or an officer of court under section 24(2) for an extension of the duration of an attachment shall be in form 12.

(2)   On the lodging of such an application the sheriff clerk shall—

    (a)   fix a date for a hearing;

    (b)   grant a warrant for intimation;

    (c)   intimate the application and warrant to the applicant, the debtor, and (as appropriate) the creditor or the officer of court who executed the attachment; and

    (d)   complete a certificate of intimation.

(3)   The officer of court who executed the attachment shall lodge with the sheriff clerk a copy of the attachment schedule before the date fixed for the hearing.

(4)   The sheriff clerk shall intimate the sheriffs decision on such an application to the debtor.

### Invalidity and cessation of attachment

**18.**—(1)   An application by a debtor for an order under section 26(1)(a) or (b) declaring the attachment to be invalid or to have ceased to have effect shall be in form 13.

(2)   On the lodging of such an application the sheriff clerk shall—

    (a)   fix a date for a hearing;

    (b)   grant a warrant for intimation;

    (c)   intimate the application and warrant to the applicant, the creditor, the officer of court who executed the attachment, and any other person having an interest; and

    (d)   complete a certificate of intimation.

(3)   The officer of court who executed the attachment shall lodge with the sheriff clerk a copy of the attachment schedule before the date fixed for the hearing.

(4)   The sheriff may declare an attachment to be invalid or to have ceased to have effect without an application having been made under paragraph (1).

(5)   The sheriff clerk shall intimate any declaration under paragraph (4) to the debtor.

### Notice of removal and auction of an attached article

**19.**—(1)   An officer of court shall make the following notices in form 14:—

    (a)   a notice under section 27(4) of the date and location of an auction, and the date of removal of an attached article from the place at which it is kept; and

    (b)   a notice under section 53(2) of the date of removal of an attached article from the dwellinghouse at which it is kept.

(2)   A notice under paragraph (1) shall be given to the debtor, and to any other person in possession of an article which is the subject of that notice, no later than 7 days before the proposed date of removal.

### Agreement on payment, and cancellation or renewal of auction

**20.**—(1)   A report by an officer of court to the sheriff under section 29(3)(a) of any agreement on payment between the creditor and the debtor that results in the cancellation of the arrangements for an auction of attached articles shall be in form 15.

(2)   An application by a creditor for an order under section 29(4) that a debtor is in breach of any agreement on payment with the creditor shall be in form 16.

(3)   On the lodging of an application under paragraphs (1) or (2) the sheriff clerk shall—
- (a)   fix a date for a hearing;
- (b)   grant a warrant for intimation;
- (c)   intimate the application and warrant to the applicant, the debtor, the officer of court, and any other person having an interest; and
- (d)   complete a certificate of intimation.

### Report of auction

**21.**—(1)   A report of auction under section 32(1) shall be in form 17.

(2)   There shall be lodged with the report of auction—
- (a)   the decree or document of debt upon which diligence proceeded (or an extract of the decree or document);
- (b)   any executions or certificates of intimation and service;
- (c)   copies of notices required by the 2002 Act; and
- (d)   vouchers for relevant outlays.

(3)   The sheriff clerk shall retain the report of auction.

### Modification of sale balance or declaration that auction void

**22.**—[1](1)   Before making an order under section 33(4)(b) or (c) the sheriff shall—
- (a)   order representations to be lodged by the persons mentioned in section 33(7)(a) within such period as he considers appropriate; or
- (b)   fix a date for a hearing.

(2)   The sheriff clerk shall intimate any order of the sheriff under paragraph (1) to the persons mentioned in section 33(7)(a) and to the officer of court who prepared the report of the auction.

(3)   Where the sheriff makes an order under section 33(4)(b) or (c) the sheriff clerk shall intimate it to the officer of court who prepared the report of the auction.".

### Applications in relation to articles belonging to a third party or in common ownership

**23.**—(1)   An application by a third party—
- (a)   under section 34(1)(b)(ii) for an order that the sheriff is satisfied that the third party owns an attached article shall be in form 18;
- (b)   under section 35(2)(b)(ii) for an order that the sheriff is satisfied that the third party owns an attached article in common with the debtor shall be in form 19; or
- (c)   under section 35(3) for the attachment of an article owned in common to cease to have effect because the sale of the article would be unduly harsh shall be in form 20.

(2)   On the lodging of an application under paragraph (1) the sheriff clerk shall—
- (a)   fix a date for a hearing;
- (b)   grant a warrant for intimation;
- (c)   intimate the application and warrant to the applicant, the creditor, the debtor, the officer of court who executed the attachment, and any person having possession of the article; and
- (d)   complete a certificate of intimation.

(3)   The officer of court who executed the attachment shall lodge with the sheriff clerk a copy of the attachment schedule before the date fixed for the hearing.

### Third party claim after auction

**24.**—(1)   An application by a third party under section 36(1)(e)(ii) for a finding after auction that a claim to an attached article is valid shall be in form 21.

(2)   On the lodging of such an application the sheriff clerk shall—

---

[1] As substituted by the Act of Sederunt (Sheriff Court Rules Amendment) (Diligence) 2009 (SSI 2009/107) r.7 (effective April 22, 2009).

(a) fix a date for a hearing;

(b) grant a warrant for intimation;

(c) intimate the application and warrant to the applicant, the debtor, the creditor and (where appropriate) the officer of court who executed the attachment; and

(d) complete a certificate of intimation.

CHAPTER 3

ATTACHMENT: ARTICLES KEPT WITHIN DWELLINGHOUSES

**Applying for attachment of articles kept within a dwellinghouse**

**25.**—(1)   An application by a creditor under section 47(1) for an exceptional attachment order shall be in form 22.

(2)   On such an application being lodged the sheriff clerk shall—

(a) fix a date for a hearing;

(b) grant a warrant for intimation;

(c) intimate the application and warrant to the debtor, together with—

(i) a form of service in form 23; and

(ii) a copy of form 24 (declaration of financial circumstances); and

(d) complete a certificate of intimation.

(3)   The date fixed for the hearing of the application shall be no earlier than a date that is 21 days after the date when the hearing was fixed.

**Making a declaration of financial circumstances**

**26.**—(1)   A debtor who wishes to make a declaration of financial circumstances for the purpose of section 47(4)(g) shall complete form 24 and lodge it with the sheriff clerk no later than ten days before the date on which the hearing is to take place.

(2)   The sheriff clerk shall send a copy of any declaration to the creditor.

**Appearance at the hearing by the creditor**

**27.**—(1)   A creditor who applies for an exceptional attachment order shall appear or be represented at the hearing of the application.

(2)   Where the creditor does not appear and is not represented at the hearing, the sheriff may dismiss the application.

**Notice of making of exceptional attachment order**

**28.**   The sheriff clerk on the making of an exceptional attachment order shall—

(a) intimate the order to the debtor by notice in form 25;

(b) attach a copy of the order to the notice; and

(c) complete a certificate of intimation.

**Money advice**

**29.**—(1)   A report of a visit to give money advice under section 47(5) shall be in form 26.

(2)   Any report shall be lodged with the sheriff clerk by the money adviser no later than 3 days before the date fixed for the hearing of the application to which the report relates.

(3)   The sheriff clerk shall send a copy of the report to the debtor and the creditor before the date fixed for the hearing of the application to which the report relates.

**Access to premises**

**30.**—(1)   An application by an officer of the court under section 49(3) to dispense with service of a notice of entry shall be made by motion in the process of the application for the exceptional attachment order.

(2)   The motion shall specify the reason why notice might prejudice the execution of the attachment.

(3)   The motion does not need to be intimated to any party and the sheriff may grant or refuse it without a hearing.

**Unlawful acts before attachment**

**31.**—(1)   The following applications shall be in form 27:—

(a) an application by a debtor or a third party under section 50(1)(a) for consent to move any article which forms part of the assets to which an exceptional attachment order relates from the dwellinghouse in which it is kept; or

(b) an application by the debtor under section 50(1)(b) for consent to sell, make a gift of, or otherwise relinquish ownership of any such article.

1040

(2) On the lodging of an application under paragraph (1) the sheriff clerk shall—

(a) fix a date for a hearing;

(b) grant a warrant for intimation;

(c) intimate the application and the warrant to the applicant, the creditor and (as appropriate) the debtor; and

(d) complete a certificate of intimation.

### Notice of theft before attachment

**32.**—(1) A notice by the debtor under section 50(3) that an attached article has been stolen shall be in form 5.

(2) Any notice shall be sent by the debtor to the sheriff who granted the exceptional attachment order, the creditor, and (if appropriate) the officer of court.

### Applying for consignation where article damaged, destroyed, lost, stolen or disposed of

**33.**—(1) An application under section 50(5) for an order against a debtor or third party to consign a sum of money in relation to an article which has been damaged, destroyed, lost, stolen or disposed of for value shall be in form 7.

(2) On the lodging of such an application the sheriff clerk shall—

(a) fix a date for a hearing;

(b) grant a warrant for intimation;

(c) intimate the application and warrant to the applicant, the officer of court who executed the attachment, the person in respect of whom an order for consignation is sought and (as appropriate) the debtor or creditor; and

(d) complete a certificate of intimation.

(3) The officer of court who executed the attachment shall lodge with the sheriff clerk a copy of the attachment schedule before the date fixed for the hearing.

### Applying for return of article removed where attachment not competent, sale unduly harsh, or article of sentimental value

**34.**—(1) An application by a debtor under section 55(2) for an order that an attachment shall cease to have effect, and to require the officer of court to return an article to the dwellinghouse from which it was removed, shall be in form 28.

(2) On the lodging of such an application the sheriff clerk shall—

(a) fix a date for a hearing;

(b) grant a warrant for intimation;

(c) intimate the application and the warrant to the applicant, the creditor, and the officer of court who executed the order; and

(d) complete a certificate of intimation.

(3) The officer of court who executed the order shall lodge with the sheriff clerk a copy of the attachment schedule before the date fixed for the hearing.

### Receipt for redemption of an attached article

**35.** A receipt granted by an officer of court for payment for an attached article redeemed under section 56(1) shall be in form 9.

### Applying for leave to appeal

**36.**—(1) An application for leave to appeal against a decision of the sheriff under section 57 of the 2002 Act shall—

(a) be made in writing to the sheriff clerk within 14 days of the making of the decision; and

(b) specify the question of law upon which the appeal is to proceed.

(2) The sheriff may consider such an application without hearing parties unless it appears to him to be necessary to hold a hearing, and if so the sheriff clerk shall intimate the date, place and time of the hearing to the parties.

The Debt Arrangement Scheme (Scotland) Regulations 2004

**Interpretation**

**37.**—(1)  In this Chapter, "the Regulations" means the Debt Arrangement Scheme (Scotland) Regulations 2004.

(2)  Any reference in this Chapter to a "regulation" shall be a reference to a regulation of the Regulations.

**Applications for approval by sheriff of debt payment programme**

**38.**—(1)  An application to the sheriff for approval of a debt payment programme under regulation 27 of the Regulations shall be in Form 29.

(2)  An application to which paragraph (1) applies shall be lodged with the sheriff clerk who shall—

    (a)  fix a date for the hearing of the application (which date shall be not less than 7 days from the date of intimation made under sub-paragraph (c));

    (b)  obtain from the sheriff a warrant to intimate the application to the debtor and the creditors;

    (c)  intimate the application and warrant to the debtor and the creditors;

    (d)  intimate the warrant to the applicant; and

    (e)  complete a certificate of intimation.

(3)  A warrant for intimation referred to in this rule shall be in Form 30.

(4)  A certificate of intimation referred to in this rule shall be in Form 31.

(5)  An interlocutor granted by the sheriff determining the application for approval of a debt payment programme shall be in Form 32.

**39.**—(1)  At a hearing fixed under rule 38(2)(a), the sheriff having heard interested parties—

    (a)  shall grant the application in terms of regulation 27(1) if he is satisfied that the programme is fair and reasonable;

    (b)  may require of any of the parties further information before making any determination; or

    (c)  may adjourn the hearing and make the determination at the adjourned hearing.

(2)  In determining whether a programme is fair and reasonable, the sheriff shall have regard to the matters referred to in regulation 26(2).

(3)  An approval under rule 39(1)(a) may be made subject to a condition under regulation 30.

**Applications for approval by sheriff of variation of debt payment plan**

**40.**—(1)  An application to the sheriff for approval of a variation of a debt payment programme under regulation 39(3) shall be in Form 33.

(2)  An application to which paragraph (1) applies shall be lodged with the sheriff clerk who shall—

    (a)  fix a date for the hearing of the application (which date shall be not less than 7 days from the date of intimation made under sub-paragraph (c));

    (b)  obtain from the sheriff a warrant to intimate the application to the debtor and the creditors;

    (c)  intimate the application and warrant to the debtor and the creditors;

    (d)  intimate the warrant to the applicant; and

    (e)  complete a certificate of intimation.

(3)  A warrant for intimation referred to in this rule shall be in Form 30.

(4)  A certificate of intimation referred to in this rule shall be in Form 31.

(5)  An interlocutor granted by the sheriff determining an application for variation shall be in Form 34.

**41.**—(1)  At a hearing fixed under rule 40(2)(a), the sheriff having heard interested parties—

    (a)  shall grant the application in terms of regulation 39(3) if, having regard to the matters referred to in regulation 39(4), he is satisfied that the programme is fair and reasonable;

    (b)  may require of any of the parties further information before making any determination; or

    (c)  may adjourn the hearing and make the determination at the adjourned hearing.

(2)  An approval under rule 41(1)(a) may be made subject to a condition under regulation 30.

---

[1] As inserted by the Act of Sederunt (Debt Arrangement and Attachment (Scotland) Act 2002) Amendment (The Debt Arrangement Scheme (Scotland) Regulations 2004) 2004 (SSI 2004/505), art.2(2) (effective November 30, 2004).

List of Forms

| Form | No Description | Rule No |
|------|----------------|---------|
| 1 | Warrant for intimation | 5(1) |
| 2 | Certificate of intimation | 5(4) |
| 3 | Attachment schedule | 8(3) |
| 4 | Application for attachment to cease to have effect because the value fixed is too low | 9(1) |
| 5 | Notice of theft of attached articles | 10(1) & 32(1) |
| 6 | Application for further attachment in same place and/or revaluation when articles moved, stolen, damaged or destroyed | 11(1) |
| 7 | Application for consignation where articles have been damaged, destroyed, lost, stolen or disposed of | 12(1) & 33(1) |
| 8 | Report of attachment | 13(1) |
| 9 | Receipt for redemption of attached articles | 14 & 35 |
| 10 | Application for security of attached articles or sale of articles that are perishable or likely to deteriorate | 15(1) |
| 11 | Application for (1) release of vehicle or mobile home from attachment (2) immediate sale of a vehicle | 16(1) |
| 12 | Application for extension of duration of an attachment | 17(1) |
| 13 | Application for an order declaring the attachment invalid or has ceased to have effect | 18(1) |
| 14 | Notice of removal of attached articles and public auction | 19(1) |
| 15 | Report of agreement resulting in cancellation of auction | 20(1) |
| 16 | Application for an order for a new auction | 20(2) |
| 17 | Report of auction | 21(1) |
| 18 | Application in relation to articles belonging to a third party | 23(1)(a) |
| 19 | Application in relation to articles belonging to a third party in common with the debtor | 23(1)(b) |
| 20 | Application for attachment to cease as sale would be unduly harsh | 23(1)(c) |
| 21 | Application in relation to articles belonging to a third party in common with the debtor that have been sold at auction | 24(1) |
| 22 | Application for exceptional attachment order | 25(1) |
| 23 | Form of service | 25(2)(c)(i) |
| 24 | Declaration by debtor of financial circumstances | 25(2)(c)(ii) & 26(1) |
| 25 | Notice of exceptional attachment order | 28 |
| 26 | Report of visit to give money advice | 29(1) |
| 27 | Application for consent to move any article, to sell, make a gift or otherwise relinquish ownership | 31(1) |
| 28 | Application for return of articles (1)removed where attachment not competent (2) where auction unduly harsh or (3) of sentimental value | 34(1) |
| 29 | Debt Arrangement Scheme (Scotland) Regulations 2004 | 38(1) |
| 30 | Debt Arrangement Scheme (Scotland) Regulations 2004 | 38(3) and 40(3) |
| 31 | Debt Arrangement Scheme (Scotland) Regulations 2004 | 38(4) and 40(4) |

| Form | No Description | Rule No |
|------|----------------|---------|
| 32 | Debt Arrangement Scheme (Scotland) Regulations 2004 | 38(5) |
| 33 | Debt Arrangement Scheme (Scotland) Regulations 2004 | 40(1) |
| 34 | Debt Arrangement Scheme (Scotland) Regulations 2004 | 40(5) |

Form 1

Rule 5(1)

Debt of Arrangement and Attachment (Scotland) Act 2002

**Court Ref. No..........**

### Warrant for Intimation

(*Place and date*)

The Sheriff grants warrant to intimate a copy of the application and this warrant to the applicant, to the other person(s) stated in the application as having an interest (*specify*), Officer of Court referred to in the application and to (*insert any other person the sheriff considers appropriate*).

Fixes as a hearing (*date*) at (*time*) **within the Sheriff Court House** (*address of court*)

1. **Requires the applicant to appear to be represented at the hearing to show why the application should be granted;**

2. **Requires the other persons to whom intimation is given to appear or be represented at the hearing if they intend to oppose the application or make representations about it; and**

3. **Directs the Officer of Court to send a copy of the attachment schedule/exceptional attachment schedule to the Sheriff clerk before the date of the hearing.**

**Sheriff Clerk/Depute**

To (*name of person receiving intimation*)

**This application and warrant is intimated to you.**

Sheriff Clerk/Depute..........
Date..........

Please note

*To the applicant*

If you fail to appear or be represented at the hearing fixed your application may be dismissed

*To the other persons to whom intimation is given*

If you fail to appear or be represented at the hearing fixed the application may be dealt with in your absence

**IF YOU WISH FURTHER ADVICE CONTACT ANY CITIZENS ADVICE BUREAU/ LOCAL ADVICE CENTRE/SHERIFF CLERK OR SOLICITOR**

Rule 5(4)                                               Form 2

*Debt Arrangement and Attachment (Scotland) Act 2002*

Court Ref No..........

### Certificate of intimation

(Place, date).......... This application was intimated by me Sheriff Clerk/Depute by posting to.................................. on.......... a copy of the application (together with a copy of Form(s)..........) in a first class recorded delivery/registered letter addressed as follows—

Sheriff Clerk Depute

(Attach receipt for letter)

Note

Where intimation made by Officer of Court, form to be adapted as appropriate.

Form 3

Rule 8(3)

Debt Arrangement and Attachment (Scotland) Act 2002

Sheriff Court...............

### ATTACHMENT SCHEDULE

To (*name and address of debtor, person in possession of attached articles or any person who claims to own attached articles*)

On.......... a decree was granted in the Sheriff Court.......... /Court of Session in an action by...............

CREDITOR

against

DEBTOR

1044

in which the Debtor(s) were ordered to pay to the Creditor(s)

(*specify amounts*)

(**or give details of other document upon which the attachment proceeded*)

*On.......... a charge for payment of these sums (under deduction of £.......... paid to account since the date of decree) was served on the said (*name of debtor*)

(*delete where attachment proceeded on summary warrant*)

OR

On.......... an exceptional attachment order was made on application by

**CREDITOR**

against

**DEBTOR**

I, (*name and address*), Officer of Court on the instruction of the said (*name of creditor*) attach at (*address*) the articles belonging to the debtor specified in the list attached.

The sum now due by
the debtor is

Principal sum    £

Interest    £    (Further interest
may accrue if the
debt is not immedi-
ately)

Expenses    £

Less paid to    £
account

Charge fee    £

Attachment    £
fee

Other outlays    £
(specify)

**If this sum is not paid arrangements will be made for the auction of the attached article(s).**

**Payment should be made to (name and address)**

*I have removed the attached article(s).

*You may move the attached article(s) to another location only if the creditor or the officer of court has consented in writing to this or the sheriff has authorised their removal.

You (the debtor) have the right to redeem an attached article within *7/14 days on payment to me of the value fixed and referred to in this schedule.

*You (insert name of person present claiming to own article in common with debtor) have the right to apply to the sheriff for an order that an attached article is owned in common, and if an order is made the debtor's interest will be transferred to you on payment to me of a sum equal to the value of debtor's interest in that article.

*You (insert name of person other than the debtor where mobile home is their principal residence) have the right to apply to the sheriff within 14 days of the attachment for an order that the attachment of the mobile home is to cease to have effect.

*I did not attach the following articles on the basis that—

(a)    they were of sentimental value to the debtor; and

(b)    were likely to realise, on sale by auction, an aggregate amount not exceeding £150 (list articles and value).

* delete as appropriate

This attachment is carried out by me today (*date*) and is witnessed by (*name and address*)

**I deliver/leave this attachment schedule to/for you (name) today at (address)**

(*signature*)                    (*signature*)

*Witness*                    *Officer of court*

(designation)                    (designation)

**PLEASE NOTE**

1045

1.  Any unauthorised removal of the attached articles or any wilful damage or destruction of them by the debtor or persons who know the articles have been attached shall be a breach of attachment and may be dealt with as a contempt of court.
2.  The theft of any attached article should be notified to the creditor and to me together with details of any claim on insurance. Failure to do so is also a breach of the attachment and may be dealt with as a contempt of court. A form is available for this purpose and may be obtained from the sheriff clerk or any citizens advice bureau or local advice centre.

### LIST SPECIFYING ATTACHED ARTICLE(S)

ARTICLES ATTACHED                                            VALUE FIXED

Witness                             Officer of court

### IF YOU WISH FURTHER ADVICE CONTACT ANY CITIZENS ADVICE BUREAU/ LOCAL ADVICE CENTRE/SHERIFF CLERK OR SOLICITOR

Form 4

Rule 8(3)

Debt Arrangement and Attachment (Scotland) Act 2002, section 23(2)

Sheriff Court, (name)................

| APPLICATION FOR THE ATTACHMENT TO CEASE TO HAVE EFFECT BECAUSE THE VALUE FIXED IS TOO LOW | .........../20..........<br>*(Court Ref No)*<br>(1)...............APPLICANT |
| --- | --- |

|  | A | The Applicant is the Debtor |
| --- | --- | --- |
| *(1) Insert name and address* | B | Other persons having an interest The Creditor (1)<br><br>Officer of Court who executed the attachment (1) |
| *(2) Insert name* | C | Decree was granted in an action by the Creditor(s)(2) in the Court of Session/Sheriff Court at.......... on.......... 20.......... against the Debtor(s) (2)<br>*(or give details of other document or summary warrant on which the attachment proceeded)* |
|  | D | An attachment was executed on |
| *give details of the article(s) and valuation by Officer of Court* | E | The * article(s) attached was/were the following:— |

The(se) article(s) should be released from attachment as the value of the article(s) fixed by the officer of court is too low for the following reasons:—

This application is made under Section 23(2) of the Debt Arrangement and Attachment (Scotland) Act 2002The Applicant asks the court:—

1   To fix a Hearing

2   To order the Sheriff Clerk to intimate this application and the date of the hearing to the Applicant, the Creditor and the Officer of Court who executed the attachment

3   To order attachment of the article(s) to cease to have effect because the (aggregate of) the value(s) of the attached article(s) is substantially below the (aggregate of) the price(s) which it is/they are likely to fetch if sold on the open market.

4   To award expenses (if competent)

(*Date*)

IF YOU WISH FURTHER ADVICE CONTACT ANY CITIZENS ADVICE BUREAU/ LOCAL ADVICE CENTRE/SHERIFF CLERK OR SOLICITOR

Form 5

Rules 10(1) and 32(1)

Debt Arrangement and Attachment (Scotland) Act 2002, sections 21(7) and 50(3)

NOTICE OF THEFT OF ATTACHED ARTICLES

NOTICE OF THEFT OF  .........../20.........
ATTACHED ARTICLES

(Court Ref No)

| | |
|---|---|
| *Insert name and address of* Creditor | |
| Insert name and address | |
| *(2) Insert name(3) Insert address*<br><br>*Please note the details requested can be found on the attachment Schedule* | An attachment was carried out by (2)Officer of Court on the instructions of the Creditor on 20 at (3) |

The article(s) noted below were stolen on (*insert date*)

\* The article(s) was/were insured and I intend to make a claim

\* The article(s) was/were not insured

\* The insurance company is (*specify name and address*)

\* Insurance Claim Reference Number (please specify)

\* The theft was reported to the police on (specify date) and the report reference number is (*please specify*)

Date.......... Debtor..........Copies of this notice to be sent by the Debtor to the Creditor, Officer of Court, and the Sheriff/Sheriff Clerk (delete as appropriate)

IF YOU WISH FURTHER ADVICE CONTACT ANY CITIZENS ADVICE BUREAU/ LOCAL ADVICE CENTRE/SHERIFF CLERK OR SOLICITOR

Form 6

Rule 11(1)

Debt Arrangement and Attachment (Scotland) Act 2002, sections 21(2)(b), 10(a), and 10(b)

Sheriff Court, (name).........

|  | | |
|---|---|---|
| APPLICA-TION FOR FURTHER ATTACH-MENT IN SAME PLACE AND/OR RE-VALUA-TION WHEN ARTICLES MOVED, STOLEN DAMAGED OR DE-STROYED | | ............/20......<br>*(Court Ref No)*<br>(1).........APPLICANT |

|  |  |  |
|---|---|---|
| | A | The Applicant is* The Creditor* An Officer of Court on behalf of the Creditor |
| *(1)  Insert name and address* | B | Other persons having an interestThe Debtor (1)Third Party (1) |
| *(2)  Insert name* | C | Decree was granted in an action by the Creditor(s) (2)In the Court of Session/Sheriff Court at.............. on.............. 20.......... against the Debtor(s) (2).............. *(or give details of other document or summary warrant on which the attachment proceeded)* |
| *(3) Insert address* | D | An attachment was executed by (2)..............Officer of Court on the instructions of the Creditor on.............. 20.......... at.............. (3) |
| *Add reasons for making these statements and specify damage and give details of the alleged reduction in value of the damaged articles* | E | Among the articles attached were the following:—* The(se) articles were moved from the premises at (3) in breach of the attachment and authority should be given for attachment of other articles belonging to the debtor at the same premises.* The(se) articles were damaged, destroyed or stolen and authority should be given for attachment of other articles belonging to the Debtor and/or the revaluation of damaged articles. |

This application is made under Section *21(2)(b)/ 21(10) of the Debt Arrangement and Attachment (Scotland) Act 2002The Applicant asks the Court:—

1 To fix a Hearing

2 To order the Sheriff Clerk to intimate this application and the date of the hearing to the Applicant, the Debtor and the Officer of Court who carried out the attachment (if not the applicant)

3 To Authorise the attachment of other goods belonging to the Debtor at the premises in which the original attachment took place/ *To Authorise the revaluation of the damaged articles

*delete as appropriate

4 To award expenses (if competent).

*(Date)*

1048

IF YOU WISH FURTHER ADVICE CONTACT ANY CITIZENS ADVICE BUREAU/LOCAL ADVICE CENTRE/SHERIFF CLERK OR SOLICITOR

Form 7

Rule 12(1)

Debt Arrangement and Attachment (Scotland) Act 2002, sections 21(11) and 50(5)

Sheriff Court, (name)..........

| APPLICA-TION FOR CONSIGNA-TION WHERE AR-TICLES HAVE BEEN DAMAGED, DE-STROYED, LOST, STO-LEN OR DIS-POSED OF | | ........../20......<br>*(Court Ref No)*<br>(1).........APPLICANT |
|---|---|---|
| *\* give details of creditor if Applicant is Officer of court* | A | The Applicant is\* The Creditor/An Officer of Court on behalf of the Creditor |
| *(1) Insert name and ad-dress* | B | Other persons having an interestThe Debtor (1)The person in respect of whom an order for consignation is sought (1) |
| *(2) Insert name* | C | Decree was granted in an action by the Creditor(s) (2)in the Court of Session/Sheriff Court at.............. on.............. 20.......... against the Debtor(s) (2).............. *(or give details of other document or summary warrant on which the attachment pro-ceeded)* |
| *(3) Insert ad-dress* | D | \* An attachment was executed on (date) by (1) Of-ficer of Court at (3).\* An exceptional attachment order was granted on 20.........., and executed on (date) by (2) Officer of Court at (3). |
| *\*delete as ap-propriateGive details as far as known of circumstances in which the article(s) was/were dam-aged, lost, sto-len or disposed of* | E | Among the articles attached was/were the following which was/were valued at £.......... and which the said (2) knew had been attached.\* The article(s) having been removed from the premises in breach of attach-ment has/have been \*damaged/\*destroyed/\*lost/ \*passed onto another without knowledge of the at-tachment and for value.\* The said damaged article(s) is/are now valued at £ |

This application is made under Section 21(11)/50(5) of the Debt Arrangement and Attachment (Scotland) Act 2002The Application asks the court:—

1   To fix a Hearing

1049

2 To order the Sheriff Clerk to intimate this application and the date of the hearing to the Applicant, to those persons stated above as having an interest and the Officer of Court who carried out the attachment.

3 To order the said (2).......... to consign £.......... in court being:
    (i) the difference between the value of the article fixed on attachment and the value of the article as damaged
        or
    (iI) the value fixed on attachment, and/or the value of the article(s).

4 To award expenses (if competent).

*(Date)*

IF YOU WISH FURTHER ADVICE CONTACT ANY CITIZENS ADVICE BUREAU/LOCAL ADVICE CENTRE/SHERIFF CLERK OR SOLICITOR

Form 8

Rule 13(1)

Debt Arrangement and Attachment (Scotland) Act 2002, section 17(1)

Sheriff Court (*place*)..............

Report of Attachment

Date of execution of attachment...............

On ... ......a decree was granted in the Sheriff Court.......... /Court of Session in an action by...............

**(Name and address)**                                            **CREDITOR**

against

**(Name and address)**                                           DEBTOR

in which the Debtor(s) were ordered to pay to the Pursuer(s)
    (*specify amounts*)
    (**or give details of other document or order upon which the attachment proceeded*)
    *On (date).......... a charge for payment of these sums (under deduction of £......... paid to account since the date of decree) was served on the debtor)
    (*delete where attachment proceeded on summary warrant*)

The sum now due by the debtor is

| | |
|---|---|
| Principal sum | £ |
| Interest | £ |
| Expenses | £ |
| Less paid to account | £ |
| Charge fee | £ |
| Attachment fee | £ |
| Other outlays (specify) | £ |

I (*name and address*)............... Officer of Court attended at (*address*)............... along with the witness (*name and address*) ..........on the instructions of.......... the creditor(s) (*name and address*);............... showed the warrant to attach *(delete if appropriate) (with certificate of execution of charge) to every person present and demanded payment of the sum due from the debtor/a person who in the debtor's absence appeared to be authorised to act for him/her.

The sum due not being paid, and having made enquiry of those present as to the ownership of the articles I proposed to attach, and in particular whether there were any persons who owned any of the articles in common with the debtor. I attached the articles belong to the said (*name of debtor*) specified in the list attached at the valuation shown.

I advised the person(s) present (if appropriate) of their rights to redeem attached articles or to apply for the attachment to cease to have effect in terms of section 16, 18, 22, 23, 34, 35, 55 or 56) of The Debt Arrangement and Attachment Act 2002.

The following articles were not attached by me on the basis that—

(a) they were of sentimental value to the debtor; and

(b) were likely to realise, on sale by auction, an aggregate amount not exceeding £150.

List of articles and value

I warned those present that any unauthorised removal of the attached article(s) or any wilful damage or destruction of them by the debtor or person(s) who knew the article(s) had been attached would be a breach of attachment and could be dealt with as a contempt of court.

ARTICLES ATTACHED                                    VALUE FIXED

I *delivered/left an attachment schedule signed by myself and the witness to the attachment to/ for (name of debtor/person in possession of the articles) at.............. on the.............. day of.............

*and served a copy of it by first class post on the said debtor(s).

*(signature)*                            *(signature)*

*Witness*                               *Officer of court*

(designation)                           (designation)

Notes

1. Any assertion made before the submission of this report to the Sheriff, that any attached article does not belong to the debtor(s) must be noted in this report.

2. Any redemption of attached articles by the debtor before the submission of the report to the sheriff must be noted in this report.

3. Where the report relates to a further or second attachment to enforce the same debt the officer of court must specify in the report the circumstances justifying the further or second attachment.

*delete as appropriate

Form 9

Rules 14 and 35

Debt Arrangement and Attachment (Scotland) Act 2002, sections 18(1) and 56(1)

**RECEIPT FOR REDEMPTION OF ATTACHED ARTICLES**

In respect of the attachment carried out on.............. at the instance of (name and address of creditor).............. against.......... (name and address of debtor)

Received the sum of £.......... in redemption of the following article(s);

(Specify)

Date..............Officer of Court..............

**Note: Copy to be retained for purpose of report to Court**

Form 10

Rule 15(1)

Debt Arrangement and Attachment (Scotland) Act 2002, section 20(1)

Sheriff Court, (name)..............

| APPLICA-TION FOR SECURITY OF AT-TACHED ARTICLES A THAT OR SALE OF ARTICLES THAT ARE PERISH-ABLE OR ARE LIKELY TO DETE-RIORATE | ............/20...... |
| --- | --- |
| | *(Court Ref No)* |
| | (1)..........APPLICANT |
| | The Applicant is* The Creditor/An Officer of Court on behalf of the Creditor/the Debtor |

| | | |
|---|---|---|
| *(1)     Insert* name and ad-dress | B | Other persons having an interestThe Debtor (1)The Creditor (1)Officer of Court (1) who executed the at-tachment |
| *(2)     Insert* name | C | Decree was granted in an action by the Creditor(s) (2)in the Court of Session/Sheriff Court at.............. on.............     20.........     against     the Debtor(s)(2)............... *(or give details of other docu-ment or summary warrant on which the attachment proceeded)* |
| *(3) Insert ad-dress* | D | An attachment was executed by (2)Officer of Court on the instructions of the Creditor on......... 20......... at (3) |
| *\*delete\*\*give reasons why such an order should be made and pro-posed security arrangements\*\*\*give reasons for making appli-cation* | E | Among the articles attached were the following:—\* It is necessary that an order be made for the security of the attached article(s)\*\*\* The(se) article(s) are of a perishable nature or are likely to deteriorate substan-tially and rapidly in condition or value\*\*\* |
| | F | I have intimated this application to debtor/creditor/ officer of court who executed the attachment\* |

This application is made under Section 20(1) of the Debt Arrangement and Attachment (Scotland) Act 2002The Application asks the court:—

1 \*To order such intimation (if any) and fur-ther procedure as the court considers appropriate

2 \*To make such order as thought appropriate for the security of the attached article(s) referred to

*\*delete*

3 \*To make an order for the immediate sale of the article(s) referred to

4 \*If the article(s) is/are sold, to order consig-nation of the proceeds in court until the diligence is completed or otherwise ceases to have effect

5 To award expenses (if competent)

*(Date)*

IF YOU WISH FURTHER ADVICE CONTACT ANY CITIZENS ADVICE BUREAU/LOCAL ADVICE CENTRE/SHERIFF CLERK OR SOLICITOR

Form 11

Rule 16(1)

Debt Arrangement and Attachment (Scotland) Act 2002, sections 16(1) and 22(1) and (3) Sheriff Court, (name)..............

| | | |
|---|---|---|
| APPLICA-TION FOR (1) RELEASE OF VEHICLE OR MOBILE HOME FROM AT-TACH-MENT(2) IM-MEDIATE SALE OF A VEHICLE | A | ............/20...... *(Court Ref No)* (1)..........APPLICANT The Applicant is* The Debtor* A person whose only or principal residence is an attached mobile home |
| *(1)  Insert name and address* | B | Other persons having an interest* The Debtor (1)* The Creditor (1)* Officer of court who carried out attachment (1) |
| *(2)  Insert name* | C | Decree was granted in an action by the Creditor(s) (2)in the Court of Session/Sheriff Court at.............. on.............. 20......... against the Debtor(s)(2).............. *(or give details of other document or summary warrant on which the attachment proceeded)* |
| *(3) Insert address* | D | An attachment was carried out by (2)Officer of Court on the instructions of the Creditor on 20 at (3) |
| *delete**state reasons why sale would be unduly harsh* | E | Among the articles attached was a mobile home (state whether caravan, houseboat or other moveable structure)/*vehicleThe vehicle was valued on attachment at £.........This is the only or principal residence of the applicant* Sale of the vehicle would be unduly harsh** |

This application is made under Section 16(1)/22(1)(3) of the Debt Arrangement and Attachment (Scotland) Act 2002The Applicant asks the court:—

1 To fix a Hearing

2 To order the Sheriff Clerk to intimate this application and the date of the hearing to the Applicant, and to those persons stated above as having an interest

*3 To order that attachment of the vehicle shall cease to have effect

*4 To order that attachment of the mobile home is to cease to have effect

*5 To order the officer of court(2) to arrange the immediate sale of the vehicle, and to pay the sum of (insert amount) to the debtor from the proceeds of sale and to consign any surplus with the sheriff clerk

6 To award expenses (if competent)

*(Date)*

IF YOU WISH FURTHER ADVICE CONTACT ANY CITIZENS ADVICE BUREAU/LOCAL ADVICE CENTRE/SHERIFF CLERK OR SOLICITOR

Form 12

Rules 17(1)

Debt Arrangement and Attachment (Scotland) Act 2002, section 24(2)

Sheriff Court, (name) .........

| | | |
|---|---|---|
| APPLICA-TION FOR EXTENSION OF DURA-TION OF AN ATTACH-MENT | A | ............/20...... *(Court Ref No)* (1)..........APPLICANT |

|  |  |
|---|---|
| A | The Applicant is* The Creditor* An Officer of Court on behalf of the Creditor |

*(1) Insert name and address*  B  Other persons having an interestThe Debtor (1)The Creditor (1)Officer of court who carried out the attachment (1)

*(2) Insert name*  C  Decree was granted in an action by the Creditor(s) (2)in the Court of Session/Sheriff Court at............... on............... 20.......... against the Debtor(s)(2)............... *(or give details of other document or summary warrant on which the attachment proceeded)*

*(3) Insert address*  D  An attachment was carried out by (2)Officer of Court on the instructions of the Creditor.......... on.......... 20.......... at (3)

*\*deleteGive details to justify the application*  E  *The attachment ceases to have effect onor* An extension of duration of attachment was granted on extending the attachment so that it ceases to have effect on* The debtor is likely to comply with the agreement between the creditor and debtor for payment of the sum recoverable by instalments or otherwise if the date on which the attachment is to cease to have effect were to be substituted with a later dateOr* The auction of the attached article(s) cannot take place before the date on which the attachment is to cease to have effect due to circumstances for which the creditor cannot be held responsible (specify) and the attachment ceasing to have effect on that date would prejudice the creditor.

This application is made under Section 24(2) of the Debt Arrangement and Attachment (Scotland) Act 2002The Applicant asks the court:—

1. To fix a Hearing
2. To order the Sheriff Clerk to intimate this application and the date of the hearing to the Applicant, the Debtor and the Officer of Court who carried out the attachment order (if not the applicant)
3. To extend/further extend the duration of the attachment until*
4. To award expenses (if competent)

*\*state date proposed*  *(Date)*

Place, date    I certify that the Sheriffs decision in respect of the application has been intimated to the Debt orSheriff Clerk Depute

IF YOU WISH FURTHER ADVICE CONTACT ANY CITIZENS ADVICE BUREAU/LOCAL ADVICE CENTRE/SHERIFF CLERK OR SOLICITOR

Form 13

Rule 18(1)

Debt Arrangement and Attachment (Scotland) Act 2002, section 26(1) (a) and (b)

Sheriff Court, (name) .........

| | | |
|---|---|---|
| APPLICA-TION FOR AN ORDER DECLARING THE AT-TACHMENT INVALID OR HAS CEASED TO HAVE EF-FECT | | ........./20.........<br>*(Court Ref No)*...................<br>(1)...............APPLICANT |
| | A | The Applicant is the Debtor................... |
| *(1) Insert name and address* | B | Other persons having an interestThe Creditor (1)..................................Officer of Court (1)................................ |
| *(2) Insert name* | C | Decree was granted in an action by the Creditor(s) (2)..........in the Court of Session/Sheriff Court at..........on..........20..........against the Debtor(s)(2).............................*(or give details of other document or summary warrant on which the attachment proceeded)* |
| *(3) Insert address* | D | An attachment was executed by (2).............................Officer of Court on the instructions of the Creditor..........on..........20..........at (3).............. |
| *\*delete as appropriate\*\*Give reasons for application* | E | The following article(s) was/were attached\* the attachment has ceased to have effect \*\*\* the purported attachment is invalid \*\* |

This application is made under Section 26(1)(a)(b) of the Debt Arrangement and Attached (Scotland) Act 2002The Applicant asks the court:—

1    To fix a Hearing

2    To order the Sheriff Clerk to intimate this application and the date of the hearing to the Applicant, the Creditor and the Officer of Court who carried out the attachment

3    To make an order declaring that the attachment is invalid or has ceased to have effect

\*4    To order to the Officer of Court (2) to return the article(s) to the place from which it was/they were removed

5    To award expenses (if competent)

*(Date)*

IF YOU WISH FURTHER ADVICE CONTACT ANY CITIZENS ADVICE BUREAU/LOCAL ADVICE CENTRE/SHERIFF CLERK OR SOLICITOR

Form 14

Rules 19(1)

Debt Arrangement and Attachment (Scotland) Act 2002, sections 27(4) and 53(2)

NOTICE OF RE-
MOVAL OF AT-
TACHED ARTI-
CLES AND
PUBLIC ATTEN-
TION

........../20..........

*(Court Ref No)*

*Insert name and
address of Creditor*

*Insert name and
address of Debtor/
other person in
possession of at-
tached articles*

*(2) Insert name*

*(3) Insert address*

An attachment was carried out by (2)
Officer of Court on the instructions of the Creditor on 20 at (3)

Please note the attached article(s) (specify where
appropriate) will be removed from your premises
on.........., [at am/pm]. You should arrange for
access to your premises at that time. The Officer
of Court may, if access is denied, open shut and
lockfast places for the purpose of removing the
article(s).A public auction of the attached arti-
cle(s) will be held on (date) at (insert place of
auction).

Date

Designation of Officer of Court

IF YOU WISH FURTHER ADVICE CONTACT ANY CITIZENS ADVICE BUREAU/LOCAL
ADVICE CENTRE/SHERIFFCLE RKOR SOLICITOR

Form 15

Rules 20(1)

Debt Arrangement and Attachment (Scotland) Act 2002, section 29(3) (a)

**Sheriff Court, (name)**..........

**Court Ref No**...........

**REPORT OF AGREEMENT RESULTING IN CANCELLATION OF AUCTION**

**The auction arranged at the Instance of**..............

....................

(1)...............**CREDITOR**..........

...............against...............

(1)...............**DEBTOR**..........

**and due to take place at..........on...............has been cancelled for the purposes of enabling the
sum recoverable to be paid in accordance with an agreement between the creditor and the debtor.**

This is the first/second time auction arrangements have been cancelled.

*(delete)

The agreement is to the following effect (set out terms of agreement or attach copy, if in writing)

**OFFICER OF COURT**

(1) (*Insert name and address*)

*delete as appropriate

Form 16

Rule 20(2)

Debt Arrangement and Attachment (Scotland) Act 2002, section 29(4)

Sheriff Court, (name) ..........

APPLICATION FOR AN ORDER FOR A NEW AUCTION

|  | |
|---|---|
| | ............/20.......... |
| | (Court Ref No)................... |
| | (1)............... APPLICANT |

A

The Applicant is the Creditor

(1) *Insert name and address*    B

Other persons having an interestThe Debtor (1)Officer of Court (1)

(2) *Insert name*    C

Decree was granted in an action by the Creditor(s) (2)..........in the Court of Session/Sheriff Court at..........on..........20..........against the Debtor(s) (2)..........(*or give details of other document or summary warrant on which the attachment proceeded*)

(3) *Insert address*    D

An attachment was carried out by (2)Officer of Court on the instructions of the Creditor on..........20 at..........(3)..........

E

*State nature of the breach*

The auction due to take place at (3)............... on (insert date) was cancelled for the purposes of enabling the sum recoverable to be paid in accordance with an agreement between the Creditor and DebtorA report of the agreement was reported to the Sheriff on..........The Debtor has failed to carry out the agreed terms and is now in breach of the agreement because

This application is made under Section 29(4) of the Debt Arrangement and Attachment (Scotland) Act 2002The Applicant asks the Court:—

1   To fix a Hearing

2   To order the Sheriff Clerk to intimate this application and the date of the hearing to the Applicant, the Debtor and the Officer of Court who carried out the attachment

*3   To order that the Debtor is in breach of the agreement made on (insert date) and to authorise the Officer of Court to resume arrangements for the auction of the attached article(s)

*delete as appropriate*

*4   To order that as the auction cannot be implemented in accordance with the provisions of the Act, that those provisions which prevent such implementation are not to apply for the purposes of the attachment and auction of the article(s)

5 To award expenses (if competent)

*(Date)*

IF YOU WISH FURTHER ADVICE CONTACT ANY CITIZENS ADVICE BUREAU/LOCAL ADVICE CENTRE/SHERIFF CLERK OR SOLICITOR

(note 1) Form 17

Rule 21(1)

Debt Arrangement and Attachment (Scotland) Act 2002, section 32(1)

Sheriff Court, (name) ..........

## Report of Auction

|   | Details of parties and prior steps in diligence | :*(name and address)* |
|---|---|---|
| 1 | The Creditor | |
| 2 | The Debtor | :*(name and address)* |
| 3 | The person who had possession of the attached articles, if not the debtor | :*(name and address)* |
| 4 | Date of decree etc or document of debt | : |
| 5 | List Prior steps of diligence | : |
|   |   | : |
|   |   | : |
|   |   | : |
|   |   | : |

*Extract decree and other documents on which the diligence proceeded to be produced.*

Details of auction arrangements

| 6 | Date of auction | : |
|---|---|---|
| 7 | Location of auction | : |
| 8 | Officer of court who made arrangements | :*(name and address)* |
| 9 | Person who conducted auction | :*(name and address)* |
| 10 | Person who witnessed sale (if applicable) | :*(name and address)* |
| 11 | Notices given by officer of court in respect of auction (*copies to be produced*) | |

*Disposal of attached articles and auction proceeds*

LIST—

| 12 | Articles sold and amount for which sold |
|---|---|
| 13 | Articles unsold |
| 14 | Articles whose ownership passed to creditor |
| 15 | Articles whose ownership reverted to debtor |
| 16 | Articles otherwise disposed of (*specify*) |

*(Specify)* each item under 12-16 and amount debtor was credited with

17 Articles released/redeemed from attachment and value fixed at attachment with explanation of circumstances

DETAIL

18 Disposal of auction proceeds including any surplus paid to debtor

19 Any monies consigned in court

Statement of Debt And Expenses

Sums due by debtor

1 Sums in de-cree etc

| | Principal | .......... |
|---|---|---|
| | | — |
| | Expenses | .......... |
| | | — |
| | Interest | .......... |
| | | — |
| | | .......... |
| | | — |

| | | | | |
|---|---|---|---|---|
| | 2 | Diligence ex-penses | | .......... |
| Outlays to be produced | | Charge At-tachment | .......... | |
| | | | .......... | |
| | | | .......... | |
| | | | .......... | |
| | | | .......... | |
| | | | | .......... |
| | 3 | Auction ex-penses | .......... | .......... |
| | | | .......... | |
| | | | .......... | |
| | | Paid to ac-count | | .......... |
| | | | | .......... |
| | | Proceeds of auction (12-17) | | .......... |
| | | Consignation on/by | | .......... |
| | | Balance due to/by debtor | | .......... |
| | | | | .......... |
| | | | | .......... |

I, (insert name and address) declare that all the information contained within this report is, to the best of my knowledge, true.

(Date)

Signed....................
Officer of Court

....................
Witness

(Place, date) The Sheriff Remits this Report to the Auditor of Court.

Sheriff Clerk/Depute

Rule 23(1)(a)                          Form 18

Debt Arrangement and Attachment (Scotland) Act 2002, section 34(1)\(b)(ii)

Sheriff Court, (name)..........

APPLICATION IN RELA-
TION TO ARTICLES BE-
LONGING TO A THIRD
PARTY

| ........../20.......... |
|---|
| *(Court Ref No)* |
| (1)...............APPLICANT |

*delete      A

> The Applicant is a...............
>
> person claiming ownership of attached article(s)

*(1) Insert name and address*  B

> Other persons having an interest
>  The Creditor (1)...............
>  The Debtor (1)...............
>
> * Any person (other than the Debtor) having possession of the attached article(s) for which release is sought (1).........

*(2) Insert name*    C

> Decree was granted in an action by the Creditor(s) (2)..............................in the Court of Session/Sheriff Court at..........on..........20..........against the Debtor(s) (2).........
>
> (*or give details of other document or summary warrant on which the attachment proceeded*)

*(3) Insert address*   D

> An attachment was carried out by (2)..............................Officer of Court on the instructions of the Creditor on..........20..........at (3).........

*(specify details of where and* E
*when an auction is to be held*
*if this has been fixed)*

> Among the articles attached was/were the following:—
>
> Auction of the attached article(s) has not yet taken place

*(give details of ownership)*

> The article(s) belong to the applicant and the attachment should cease to have effect

> This application is made under Section 34(1)(b)(ii) of the Debt Arrangement and Attachment (Scotland) Act 2002The Applicant asks the Court:—
> 1 To fix a Hearing
> 2 To order the Sheriff Clerk to intimate this application and the date of the hearing to the Applicant to those persons stated above as having an interest and the Officer of Court who carried out the attachment order

3   To find that the applicant owns the article(s) and the article(s) should be released from attachment

4   To award of expenses (if competent)

*(Date)*

IF YOU WISH FURTHER ADVICE CONTACT ANY CITIZENS ADVICE BUREAU/LOCAL ADVICE CENTRE/SHERIFF CLERK OR SOLICITOR

Rule 23(1)(b)                              Form 19

Debt Arrangement and Attachment (Scotland) Act 2002, section 35(2)(b)(ii)

Sheriff Court, (name) .........

| | |
|---|---|
| APPLICATION IN RELATION TO ARTICLES BE- LONGING TO A THIRD PARTY IN COMMON WITH THE DEBTOR | .........../20.........<br>*(Court Ref No)*...................<br>(1)..............APPLICANT |

A       The Applicant is a..............person claiming common ownership of attached article(s)

*(1) Insert name and address*    B

Other persons having an interest
   The Creditor (1)..............
   The Debtor (1)..............

\* Any person (other than the Debtor) having possession of the attached article(s) for which release is sought (1)

*(2) Insert name*    C

Decree was granted in an action by the Creditor(s)(2)...........................in the Court of Session/ Sheriff Court at.........on.........20.........against the Debt- or(s) (2).........
*(or give details of other document or summary warrant on which the attachment proceeded)*

*(3) Insert address*    D

An attachment was carried out by (2).........Officer of Court on the instructions of the Creditor on.........20.........at (3).. .......

E

*(specify details of where and when an auction is to be held if this has been fixed)*

Among the articles attached was/were the following:—

Auction of the attached article(s) has not yet taken place\*

| | |
|---|---|
| *(give details of ownership including extent)* | The applicant owns the article(s) in common with the Debtor |
| *(give details of value of the Article(s) and sum proposed)* | The applicant *has given/gives an undertaking to pay a sum equal to the value of the debtor's interest in the article |

*\*delete as appropriate*

The Applicant asks the Court:—

1 To fix a Hearing
2 To order the Sheriff Clerk to intimate this application and the date of the hearing to the Applicant, to those persons stated above as having an interest, and the Officer of Court who carried out the attachment
3 To find that the applicant has common ownership of the article(s)
4 To order that the said article(s) be released from attachment and transferred to the Applicant on payment of a sum equal to the debtor's interest
5 To award expenses (if competent)

*(Date)*

IF YOU WISH FURTHER ADVICE CONTACT ANY CITIZENS ADVICE BUREAU/LOCAL ADVICE CENTRE/SHERIFF CLERK OR SOLICITOR

**Rule 23(1)(c)**        Form 20

*Debt Arrangement and Attachment (Scotland) Act 2002, section 35(3)*

Sheriff Court, (name) .........

| | |
|---|---|
| APPLICATION FOR ATTACHMENT TO CEASE AS SALE WOULD BE UNDULY HARSH | ........./20.........<br>*(Court Ref No)*<br>(1)...............APPLICANT |

| | | |
|---|---|---|
| | A | The Applicant is a...............person claiming common ownership of attached article(s) |
| *(1) Insert name and address* | B | Other persons having an interestThe Creditor (1)...............The Debtor (1)...............<br>\* Any person (other than the Debtor) having possession of the attached article(s) for which release is sought (1) |
| *(2) Insert name* | C | Decree was granted in an action by the Creditor(s) (2)..........in the Court of Session/Sheriff Court at.........on.........20.........against the Debtor(s) (2).........<br>*(or give details of other document or summary warrant on which the attachment proceeded)* |

*(3) Insert address*  D

An attachment was carried out by (2).........Officer of Court on the instructions of the Creditor on..........20.........at (3)..........

E

Among the articles attached and removed from the place of attachment was/were the following:—

*(specify details of where and when an auction is to be held if this has been fixed)*

Auction of the attached article(s) has not yet taken place

*(give details of ownership including extent)*

The Applicant owns the article(s) in common with the Debtor

*(give reasons for claim that auction would be unduly harsh)*

The auction of the article(s) specified would be unduly harsh to the applicant in the circumstances

*\*delete as appropriate*

This application is made under Section 35(3) of the Debt Arrangement and Attachment (Scotland) Act 2002The Applicant asks the Court:—

1    To fix a Hearing
2    To order the Sheriff Clerk to intimate this application and the date of the hearing to the Applicant, to those persons stated above as having an interest, and the Officer of Court who carried out the attachment
3    To find that the applicant has common ownership in the article(s) 4 To find that auction of the article(s) would be unduly harsh to the applicant and order that the article(s) be released from attachment
5    To award expenses (if competent)

(Date)

IF YOU WISH FURTHER ADVICE CONTACT ANY CITIZENS ADVICE BUREAU/LOCAL ADVICE CENTRE/SHERIFF CLERK OR SOLICITOR

**Rule 24(1)**                         Form 21

*Debt Arrangement and Attachment (Scotland) Act 2002, section 36(1)(e)(ii)*

Sheriff Court, (name) .........

APPLICATION IN RELATION TO ARTICLES BELONGING TO A THIRD PARTY IN COMMON WITH THE DEBTOR THAT HAVE BEEN SOLD AT AUCTION

........./20.........
*(Court Ref No)*
(1)...............APPLICANT

A

The Applicant is a...............person claiming common

| | | ownership of attached article(s) | |

| | | |
|---|---|---|
| *(1) Insert name and address* | B | Other persons having an interestThe Creditor (1)...............* The Debtor (1)............... * Any person (other than the Debtor) having possession of the attached article(s) for which release is sought (1).......... |
| *(2) Insert name* | C | Decree was granted in an action by the Creditor(s) (2).............................in the Court of Session/Sheriff Court at..........on..........20..........against the Debtor(s) (2)............................ (*or give details of other document or summary warrant on which the attachment proceeded*) |
| *(3) Insert address* | D | An attachment was carried out by (2).............................Officer of Court on the instructions of the Creditor..........on..........20..........at (3).......... |
| *(give details of claim)* | E | Among the articles attached was/were the following:— Auction of the attached article(s) took place on..........at..........when the article was/were sold for £..........or transferred to the creditor for that sumThe Applicant claimed ownership of the article(s) in common with the Debtor prior to the auction (*state extent to which ownership claimed*)The Applicant's interest in the article has following the auction of the article been transferred to another person |

*delete as appropriate*

This application is made under Section 36(1)(e)(ii) ) of the Debt Arrangement and Attachment (Scotland) Act 2002The Applicant asks the Court:—

1 To fix a Hearing
2 To order the Sheriff Clerk to intimate this application and the date of the hearing to the Applicant, to those persons stated above as having an interest, and the Officer of Court who carried out the attachment
3 To find that the applicant has common ownership in the article(s)
4 To make an order that the Creditor pay to the Applicant the fraction of the proceeds of the sale/value of the article(s) which corresponds to the Applicant's interest in the article(s)
5 To award expenses (if competent)

(*Date*)

IF YOU WISH FURTHER ADVICE CONTACT ANY CITIZENS ADVICE BUREAU/LOCAL ADVICE CENTRE/SHERIFF CLERK OR SOLICITOR

**Rule 25(1)**                  Form 22

*Debt Arrangement and Attachment (Scotland) Act 2002, section 47(1)*

Sheriff Court, (name) .........

# Act of Sederunt (Debt Arrangement and Attachment (Scotland) Act 2002) 2002

APPLICATION FOR EXCEPTIONAL ATTACHMENT ORDER

> ............/20.........
>
> *(Court Ref No)*....................
>
> (1)..............APPLICANT

A

> The Applicant is the Creditor...................

*(1) Insert name and address*

B

> Other persons having an interest
> The Debtor (1)...............
> ....................

*(2) Insert name*

C

> Decree was granted in an action by the Creditor(s) (2).............................in the Court of Session/Sheriff Court at..........on..........20..........against the Debtor(s) (2)..............................
>
> *(or give details of other document or summary warrant)*

*Give details of the nature of the debt particularly whether it relates to tax, duty or any trade or business carried on by the Debtor and produce an extract*

*(3) Insert address*

D

> Address of dwelling-house where exceptional attachment order Is to be executed (3)The debtor does/*not reside at dwelling-houseThe debtor does/*not carry on a trade or business in this dwelling-house
>
> The creditor has taken steps to negotiate (or seek to negotiate) a settlement of the debt*
>
> The creditor has taken steps to execute (or attempt to execute) an arrestment and action of furthcoming or sale, and an earnings arrestment in order to secure payment of the debt
>
> A Time to Pay Direction/Time to Pay Order was made/not made in respect of this *debt/another debt. If made it has lapsed/ is still in force
>
> *The Debtor has been provided with a debt advice and information package

*(give details)*

*(give details)*

*(\* delete as appropriate and give details if necessary)*

*\* delete as appropriate and give details if necessary*

> There is a reasonable prospect that the sum recovered from auction of non essential assets of the debtor kept in the dwellinghouse would be at least equal to the aggregate of chargeable expenses and £100
>
> *(include details of any other matters that you wish the sheriff to take into account)*

*\*delete as appropriate*

This application is made under Section 47(1) of the Debt Arrangement and Attachment (Scotland) Act 2002The Applicant asks the court:—

1 To fix a Hearing

2 To order the Sheriff Clerk to intimate this application and the date of the hearing to the Creditor and Debtor

3 To serve the debtor with a copy of form (*insert number*)

4* To order the debtor to receive a visit for the purpose of money advice

5 To make an exceptional attachment order authorising within (*specify time*) the attachment, removal and auction of non essential assets of the debtor which are, at the time when an attachment is executed, kept in the dwellinghouse specified above

6 To appoint (*insert name*), officer of court, to arrange for such attachment, removal and auction, and to grant authority to open shut and lockfast places for these purposes

(*Date*)

NOTE: IF NECESSARY ATTACH A SEPARATE SHEET FOR DETAILS IN SECTION D

IF YOU WISH FURTHER ADVICE CONTACT ANY CITIZENS ADVICE BUREAU/LOCAL ADVICE CENTRE/SHERIFF CLERK OR SOLICITOR

**Rule 25(2)(c)(i)**                              Form 23

*Debt Arrangement and Attachment (Scotland) Act 2002, section 35(2)(b)(ii)*

APPLICATION UNDER SECTION 47(1) OF THE DEBT ARRANGEMENT AND ATTACHMENT (SCOTLAND) ACT 2002 FOR EXCEPTIONAL ATTACHMENT ORDER
Form of Service

(Place). .............                                                    (Date).........
To...................                                                      (debtor).........

You are served with a copy of the above application together with a copy of Form 24 (*declaration by Debtor*)

If you want the court to take account of your financial circumstances prior to the hearing you must complete the declaration in Form 24 and lodge it with the Sheriff Clerk at (*address*) no later than*

You may appear or be represented (by an advocate, solicitor or other authorised person) at the hearing of the application but if you fail to do so the application may be considered and granted in your absence.

Signed Sheriff Clerk/Depute

<u>Sheriff Clerk to insert dates before service</u>
*\*insert date that is 10 days before the date of the hearing*

IF YOU WISH FURTHER ADVICE CONTACT ANY CITIZENS ADVICE BUREAU/ LOCAL ADVICE CENTRE/SHERIFF CLERK OR SOLICITOR

**Rule 25(2)(c)(ii)**                             Form 24

*Debt Arrangement and Attachment (Scotland) Act 2002, section 47(4)(g)*

**DECLARATION BY DEBTOR OF FINANCIAL CIRCUMSTANCES IN AN APPLICATION FOR AN EXCEPTIONAL ATTACHMENT ORDER**

| SECTION A This section must be completed before service | (1) | Sheriff Court (including address) | Court Ref No |
| | | | |
| | | | Hearing Date |

| CREDITOR'S FULL | DEBTOR'S FULL |
|---|---|
| NAME AND ADDRESS | NAME AND ADDRESS |
| | |
| | |

I, (name).........debtor in the foregoing application would like the court to consider my financial circumstances in considering whether to make an exceptional attachment order. And/or..............I, Declare that I own the following non essential assets. These assets are located at..............(*insert address*)...............and are valued at (*insert estimated value of each article*)

| My outgoings are *weekly/monthly/fortnightly | My outgoings are *weekly/monthly/fortnightly |
|---|---|
| Rent/Mortgage £ | Wages £ |
| Council Tax £ | Benefits (specify) £ |
| Gas/electricity etc £ | Other (details) £ |
| Food £ | |
| Loans and credit £ | |
| Agreements £ | |
| Other (details) £ | |
| Total £ | Total £ |
| If you wish to provide more details please | |
| Attach a separate sheet | |

| Number of Dependant children | | Number of Dependent relatives | |
|---|---|---|---|

Please list details of all capital held, eg equity on house, amount in savings account, shares or other investments as necessary on a separate sheet

If appropriate, give details of any money adviser who has advised in the completion of this declaration

IF YOU WISH FURTHER ADVICE CONTACT ANY CITIZENS ADVICE BUREAU/LOCAL ADVICE CENTRE/SHERIFF CLERK OR SOLICITOR

**Rule 28**                                      Form 25

*Debt Arrangement and Attachment (Scotland) Act 2002, section 47*

**Important Notice**

With these papers is a copy of an Exceptional Attachment Order made by the court.

It shall be regarded as a breach of an Exceptional Attachment Order if you, the debtor, or any other person who knows that the Exceptional Attachment Order has been made—

1.    moves any article that forms part of the debtor's non-essential assets from the dwellinghouse in which it is kept, or

2.    or for the debtor to sell, make a gift of or otherwise relinquish ownership of any such article,

without the consent of the sheriff.

Any person who knows that an Exceptional Attachment Order has been made who wilfully damages or destroys any article(s) which forms part of the debtor's non-essential assets before an attachment is executed shall be regarded as acting in breach of the order.

If at any time after an Exceptional Attachment Order has been made, an article which forms part of the debtor's non-essential assets is stolen, the debtor shall give notice to the creditor, the officer of court (if known) and the sheriff who granted the order of that fact and of any related claim which the debtor makes, or intends to make, under a contract of insurance. Any failure by the debtor to give notice shall be regarded as a breach of the order.

**IF YOU WISH FURTHER ADVICE CONTACT ANY CITIZENS ADVICE BUREAU/LOCAL ADVICE CENTRE/SHERIFF CLERK OR SOLICITOR**

**Rule 29**                                          Form 26

*Debt Arrangement and Attachment (Scotland) Act 2002, section 47(5)*

Sheriff Court, (name) .........

## REPORT OF VISIT TO GIVE MONEY ADVICE

1
> On (date) the sheriff made an order for a visit to (name) the debtor at (address).

2
> The application for an Exceptional Attachment Order was continued until (date).

3
> (State here that visit made to debtor or give details of attempts to make visit. also confirm whether money advice given to debtor. Unless confidential, state advice given to debtor)

4
> (Report here on any matters ordered by the sheriff).

5
> The debtor indicated that he intends to attend court at the next hearing./The debtor will not attend the next hearing./I will attend the next hearing.

(Designation of money adviser and date of report)

* delete as appropriate

**Rule 31(1)**                                       Form 27

*Debt Arrangement and Attachment (Scotland) Act 2002, section 50(1)*

Sheriff Court, (name) .........

APPLICATION FOR CONSENT TO MOVE ANY ARTICLES, SELL, MAKE A GIFT OF OTHERWISE RELINQUISH OWNERSHIP

> .........../20..........
> *(Court Ref No)*
> (1)...............                    APPLICANT

*delete*                A
> The Applicant is* The Debtor
> * A person who knows the exceptional attachment Order was made

*(1) Insert name and address*    B
> Other persons having an interestThe Creditor (1)* The Debtor (1)* The Officer of Court (1)

*(2) Insert name*       C
*(3) Insert address*
> An exceptional attachment order was executed by (2)
> Officer of Court on the instructions of the Creditor on 20 at (3)

                        D
> Among the articles attached was/were the following:—
> An auction of the attached article(s) has not yet taken place

*(specify details of where and when auction to be held if this has been fixed)*

<table>
<tr><td></td><td>* The applicant seeks consent to move the above article(s) from the dwellinghouse<br>* The applicant seeks consent to *sell/make a gift of or otherwise relinquish ownership of the above article(s)</td></tr>
</table>

|  |  |
|---|---|
| *(give reasons for application)* | * The applicant seeks consent to move the above article(s) from the dwellinghouse<br>* The applicant seeks consent to *sell/make a gift of or otherwise relinquish ownership of the above article(s) |

*(give reasons for application)*

This application is made under Section 50(1)(a)/(b) of the Debt Arrangement and Attachment (Scotland) Act 2002

The Applicant asks the court:—1 To fix a Hearing2 To order the Sheriff Clerk to intimate this application and the date of the hearing to the Applicant, and to those persons stated above as having an interest, and the Officer of Court who carried out the attachment

*\*delete as appropriate*

3* To consent to the removal of the article(s) from the dwellinghouse4* To consent to the sale/making a gift of/or to relinquishing of ownership of the article(s)

5 To award expenses (if competent)

*(Date)*

IF YOU WISH FURTHER ADVICE CONTACT ANY CITIZENS ADVICE BUREAU/LOCAL ADVICE CENTRE/SHERIFF CLERK OR SOLICITOR

**Rule 34(1)**                                        Form 28

*Debt Arrangement and Attachment (Scotland) Act 2002, section 55(2)*

Sheriff Court, (name) .........

APPLICATION FOR RETURN OF ARTICLES SUBJECT TO EXCEPTIONAL ATTACHMENT (1) REMOVED WHERE ATTACHMENT NOT COMPETENT (2) WHERE AUCTION UNDULY HARSH OR (3) SENTIMENTAL VALUE

|  | ........../20......... |
|---|---|
|  | *(Court Ref No)* |
| (1)............ | APPLICANT |

A  The Applicant is the Debtor

*(1) Insert name and address*  B  Other persons having an interestThe Creditor (1)...............Officer of Court (1)...............

*(2) Insert name*  C  An exceptional attachment order was carried out by (2).........
*(3) Insert address*      Officer of Court on the instructions of the Creditor on..........20..........at (3).........

*\*delete as appropriate*  D  Among the articles attached was/were the following:—

The(se) articles should be released from attachment
* (a) as the attachment is not competent
*(b) sale of the articles would be unduly harsh

1069

> \* (c) the article(s) is/are of sentimental value to the debtor and is/ are likely to realise, on sale by auction, an aggregate amount not exceeding £150
>
> (state reasons why application should be granted)

This application is made under Section 55(2) of the Debt Arrangement and Attachment (Scotland) Act 2002.

The Applicant asks the court:—

1 To fix a Hearing
2 To order the Sheriff Clerk to intimate this application and the date of the hearing to the Applicant, and the other persons having an interest
3 To order that attachment of the said article(s) is to cease to have effect
4. To order Officer of Court (2) to return the said articles(s) to the dwellinghouse at which it was/ they were attached 5 To award expenses (if competent)

(*Date*)

IF YOU WISH FURTHER ADVICE CONTACT ANY CITIZENS ADVICE BUREAU/LOCAL ADVICE CENTRE/SHERIFF CLERK OR SOLICITOR

**Rule 38(1)**                    Form 29 [1]

*Debt Arrangement Scheme (Scotland) Regulations 2004*

Regulation 27

Sheriff Court    ...............                ..........20 ..........
                                              (Court Ref. No.)

**Part A**

APPLICATION BY DAS ADMINISTRATOR   DEBTOR IN RESPECT OF WHOM DEBT PAY-
FOR APPROVAL OF DEBT PAYMENT PRO-   MENT PROGRAMME IS PROPOSED
GRAMME

                    ...............

                    ...............

                    ..........the "debtor"

                    DAS Administrator Ref. No.

                    ...............

**PART B**

1. The applicant is the DAS Administrator to whom application has been made by (*insert details of the debtor's money adviser*) ("the money adviser") on behalf of the debtor for approval of a debt payment programme under regulation 20 of the Debt Arrangement Scheme (Scotland) Regulations 2004 ("the Regulations").

2. The known creditors of the debtor are: (*insert details of all known creditors or attach list thereof*).

3. The applicant states that a request for consent to the application for approval was sent to each known creditor in terms of regulation 22 of the Regulations. In respect of the requests for consent—

(a) the following creditor[s] [has/have] not consented and the applicant is unable to dispense with such consent under regulation 22(4) of the Regulations:

(*list creditors who have not consented or attach separate list thereof*);

(b) the following creditor[s] [has/have] objected to the debt payment programme under regulation 23 of the Regulations:

(*list creditors who have objected or attach separate list thereof*).

4. The applicant attaches a copy of the application made by the money adviser on behalf of the debtor together with a copy of each response received from a creditor to whom a request for consent was sent under regulation 22 of the Regulations.

**PART C**

---

[1] As inserted by the Act of Sederunt (Debt Arrangement and Attachment (Scotland) Act 2002) Amendment (the Debt Arrangement Scheme (Scotland) Regulations 2004) (SSI 2004/505) Sch.1, para.1 (effective November 30, 2004).

5. The applicant asks the court—

(a)    to fix a hearing;

(b)    to order the sheriff clerk to intimate this application and the date of the hearing to the applicant, the debtor and to all known creditors of the debtor; and

(c)    to determine the application for approval of the proposed debt payment programme.

...............(Signed)                                      ..........20..........

Applicant                                             (Date)

**Rule 38(3) and 40(3)**                         Form 30 [1]

*Debt Arrangement Scheme (Scotland) Regulations 2004*

Regulation 27 and 39(3)

**Court Ref. No.**

**WARRANT FOR INTIMATION**

*(Place and date)*

The Sheriff grants warrant to intimate a copy of the application and this warrant to the applicant, the debtor, the debtor's money adviser and to all known creditors of the debtor as set out in the application (*specify creditors*) and to (*insert any other person the sheriff considers appropriate*);

Fixes a hearing (*date*) at (*time*) **within the Sheriff Court House** (*address of court*);

1.    Requires the debtor to appear or to be represented at the hearing to show why the application should be granted;

2.    Requires the debtor's money adviser to appear at the hearing if he/she intends to represent the debtor at that hearing; and

3.    Requires the other persons to whom intimation is given to appear or be represented at the hearing if they intend to oppose the application or make representations about it.

**Sheriff**...............

**To** (*name of person receiving intimation*)...............

**This application and warrant is intimated to you.**

Sheriff Clerk/Depute...............

Date...............

Please note (*to the debtor and other persons to whom intimation is given*)..........

If you fail to appear or be represented at the hearing fixed the application may be determined in your absence.

**IF YOU WISH FURTHER ADVICE CONTACT ANY CITIZENS ADVICE BUREAU/LOCAL ADVICE CENTRE/SHERIFF CLERK OR SOLICITOR**

**Rule 38(4) and 40(4)**                         Form 31 [2]

*Debt Arrangement Scheme (Scotland) Regulations 2004*

Regulation 27 and 39(3)

**Court Ref. No.**

**Certificate of Intimation**

*(Place, date)*..........This application was intimated by me Sheriff Clerk/Depute by posting to the applicant, the debtor, the debtor's money adviser and all creditors as specified in the warrant for intimation on (*insert date*) a copy of the application (together with a copy of Form(s)) in a first class recorded delivery/registered letter addressed as follows—

..........(signed)

Sheriff Clerk/Depute

(Attach recorded delivery or registered post receipt for letter)

---

[1] As inserted by the Act of Sederunt (Debt Arrangement and Attachment (Scotland) Act 2002) Amendment (the Debt Arrangement Scheme (Scotland) Regulations 2004) (SSI 2004/505) Sch.1, para.1 (effective November 30, 2004).

[2] As inserted by the Act of Sederunt (Debt Arrangement and Attachment (Scotland) Act 2002) Amendment (the Debt Arrangement Scheme (Scotland) Regulations 2004) (SSI 2004/505) Sch.1, para.1 (effective November 30, 2004).

**Rule 38(5)**                                              Form 32[1]

*Debt Arrangement Scheme (Scotland) Regulations 2004*

Regulation 27

**Court Ref. No.**

**INTERLOCUTOR**

..........(Debtor)..........(DAS Administrator Ref No.)

*(Place, date)* The sheriff [*having heard *(insert details of parties who attended the hearing)* and] having considered the application,

*1. Approves the debt payment programme.

*2. Refuses to approve the debt payment programme on the following grounds:—

*(insert reasons for refusal)*

..............

..............

..............

..............

*3. Approves the debt payment programme subject to the following conditions:—

That the debtor shall—

(a) realise, and distribute amongst creditors the value of the following asset[s], being asset[s] of the debtor other than asset[s] that are excepted by regulation 30(3) of the Debt Arrangement Scheme (Scotland) Regulations ("the Regulations"):—

*(insert details of assets)*

..............

..............

..............

..............

(b) sign and deliver a payment instruction to an employer;

(c) seek agreement from a creditor to pay a continuing liability under regulation 34 of the Regulations;

(d) complete, and submit when due, a tax or duty return or declaration;

(e) maintain an emergency fund in accordance with regulation 30(4) of the Regulations; or

(f) be bound by the following condition(s) intended to serve completion of the programme which the sheriff considers to be reasonable:—(specify further conditions)

**\*delete as appropriate**

..........(signed)

Sheriff

**Rule 39**                                                 Form 33 [2]

*Debt Arrangement Scheme (Scotland) Regulations 2004*

Regulation 39

Sheriff Court ...............                    ..........20 ..........

                                                  (Court Ref. No.)

**PART A**

APPLICATION BY DAS ADMINISTRATOR FOR VARIATION OF DEBT PAYMENT PROGRAMME

DEBTOR IN RESPECT OF WHOSE DEBT PAYMENT PLAN A VARIATION IS BEING PROPOSED

..............

..............

.......... the "debtor"

---

[1] As inserted by the Act of Sederunt (Debt Arrangement and Attachment (Scotland) Act 2002) Amendment (the Debt Arrangement Scheme (Scotland) Regulations 2004) (SSI 2004/505) Sch.1, para.1 (effective November 30, 2004).

[2] As inserted by the Act of Sederunt (Debt Arrangement and Attachment (Scotland) Act 2002) Amendment (the Debt Arrangement Scheme (Scotland) Regulations 2004) (SSI 2004/505) Sch.1, para.1 (effective November 30, 2004).

**PART A**

DAS Administrator Ref. No.

................

**PART B**

**1.** A copy of the debtor's debt payment programme [as approved by the Applicant]/[and the interlocutor approving the debt payment programme] (*delete as appropriate*) is/are attached.

**2.** The Applicant is the DAS Administrator to whom application was made by *[(debtor's money adviser) on behalf of the debtor]/[a creditor under the approved debt payment programme (insert creditor details)]* for variation (under regulation 37 of the Debt Arrangement Scheme (Scotland) Regulations 2004 ("the Regulations")) of the debtor's debt payment programme.

**3.** The creditors under the debtor's debt payment programme whose debts under that programme have not, at the date of this application, been satisfied in full are: (*insert details of outstanding creditors or attach separate list thereof*).

**4.** The Applicant seeks a variation of the debt payment programme on the following grounds:—(*refer to regulation 38 of the Regulations as appropriate*)

....................

....................

....................

**5.** The applicant attaches a copy of—

(a) the application for variation and all relevant supporting documentation;

(b) any documentation received from any creditor in relation to the application for variation; and

(c) any relevant supporting documentation.

**6.** The applicant considers it appropriate for the sheriff to determine this application for the following reasons [*set out reasons*]:

**PART C**

The applicant asks the court—

**1.** To fix a hearing;

**2.** To order the sheriff clerk to intimate this application and the date of the hearing to the applicant, the debtor and the outstanding creditors listed in paragraph 3 of Part B of this application; and

**3.** To approve the variation of the debt payment programme.

...............(Signed)                    ..........20 .........

Applicant                                  (Date)

**Rule 40(5)**                             Form 34 [1]

*Debt Arrangement Scheme (Scotland) Regulations 2004*

Regulation 39

**Court Ref. No.**

**INTERLOCUTOR**

..........(Debtor)..........(DAS Administrator Ref No.)

(*Place, date*) The sheriff [having heard (*insert details of parties who attended the hearing*) and] (delete if no parties attended the hearing) having considered the application,

*****1.** Approves the following variation of the debt payment programme:—

[*insert details of variation*]

....................

....................

....................

*****2.** Refuses to approve the variation of the debt payment programme on the following grounds:—

[*insert reasons for refusal*]

....................

....................

....................

---

[1] As inserted by the Act of Sederunt (Debt Arrangement and Attachment (Scotland) Act 2002) Amendment (the Debt Arrangement Scheme (Scotland) Regulations 2004) (SSI 2004/505) Sch.1, para.1 (effective November 30, 2004).

**\*3.** Approves the following variation of the debt payment programme:—

[*insert details of variation*]

....................

....................

....................

subject to the following conditions:—

That the debtor shall—

(a) realise, and distribute amongst creditors the value of the following asset[s], being asset[s] of the debtor other than asset[s] that are excepted by regulation 30(3) of the Debt Arrangement Scheme (Scotland) Regulations 2004 ("the Regulations"):—

[*insert details of assets*]

....................

....................

....................

(b) sign and deliver a payment instruction to an employer;

(c) seek agreement from a creditor to pay a continuing liability under regulation 34 of the Regulations;

(d) complete, and submit when due, a tax or duty return or declaration;

(e) maintain an emergency fund in accordance with regulation 30(4) of the Regulations; or

(f) be bound by the following condition(s) intended to secure completion of the programme which the sheriff considers to be reasonable:—(specify further conditions).

\* delete as appropriate

..........(signed)

Sheriff

**Appendix 2**

**GLOSSARY**

**Rule 1(4)**

### Absolve

To find in favour of and exonerate the defender.

### Absolvitor

An order of the court granted in favour of and exonerating the defender which means that the pursuer is not allowed to bring the same matter to court again. See also dismissal below.

### Action of count, reckoning and payment

A legal procedure for requiring someone to account for their dealings with assets under their stewardship. For example, a trustee might be subject to such an action.

### Action of furthcoming

A final stage of diligence or enforcement. It results in whatever has been subject to arrestment being made over to the person who is suing. For example, where a bank account has been arrested this results in the appropriate amount being transferred to the pursuer.

### Appellant

A person making an appeal against the sheriff's decision. This might be the pursuer or the defender.

### Arrestee

A person with whom an arrestment is lodged, and therefore subject to the arrestment.

### Arrestment on the dependence

A court order granting until a final court decision a temporary security over goods, or funds in a bank account, held on behalf of the defender by someone else (for example, a bank).

### Arrestment to found jurisdiction

An order to give the court jurisdiction to hear a case against a person who has goods or other assets in Scotland. This is achieved by arresting the goods or assets on the dependence of the action.

**Lay representative**

A person other than a solicitor or advocate who represents a party to a cause or application. In particular, in these Rules such a person unless employed as a lay representative must receive no fee, gain or reward (directly or indirectly) for their actions.

**Calling date**

The date on which a summary cause action will first be held in court.

**Cause**

Another word for case or claim.

**Caution (pronounced kay-shun)**

A security given to ensure that some obligation will be carried out. This will be either a sum of money, or a guarantee of payment by someone other than the parties to a case (for example, an insurance company).

**Certificate of execution of service**

The document recording that an application to, or order or decree of, the court for service of documents has been effectively served.

**Charge**

A notice to obey a decree of a court. A common type is one served on the defender by a sheriff officer on behalf of the pursuer who has won a case demanding payment of a sum of money.

**Claim**

The part of the writ or summons which sets out the legal remedy which the pursuer is seeking.

**Commission and diligence**

An order appointing a solicitor or advocate (the Commissioner) to supervise on behalf of the court the disclosure of documents relating to a case. It is combined with a diligence authorising the Commissioner to require attendance as a witness of the person alleged to be holding any particular document (the haver).

**Consign, or consignation**

The deposit in court, or with a third party, of money or an article in dispute.

**Continuation**

An order made by the sheriff postponing the completion of a hearing until a later date or dates.

**Contribution, Right of**

The right of one person who is legally liable to pay money to someone to claim a proportionate share from others who are also liable.

**Counterclaim**

A claim made by a defender in response to the pursuer's case and which is not necessarily a defence to that case. It is a separate but related case against the pursuer, which is dealt with at the same time as the pursuer's case.

**Damages**

Money compensation payable for a breach of contract or some other legal duty.

**Declarator of irritancy of a lease**

A decision of a court finding that a tenant has failed to observe a term of a lease, and that the landlord is therefore entitled to insist that the tenant shall leave the property.

**Decree**

An order of the court containing the decision of the case in favour of one of the parties and granting the remedy sought or disposing of the case.

**Decree of ejection**

A decree ordering someone to leave land or property which they are occupying. For example, it is used to remove tenants in arrears with their rent.

**Decree of removing**

A court order entitling someone to recover possession of heritable property and ordering a person to leave land which he is occupying. For example, it is used to remove tenants in arrears with their rent.

**Defender**

Person against whom a court action is started.

**Deliverance**

A decision or order of a court.

**Diet**

Date for a court hearing.

**Diligence**

The collective term for the procedures used to enforce a decree of a court. These include attachment of moveable items and arrestment of wages.

**Dismissal**

An order bringing to an end the proceedings in an action. Unlike an order for absolvitor (see above), it is usually possible for a new action to be brought.

**Domicile**

The place where a person is normally resident or where, in the case of a company, it has its place of business or registered office.

**Execution of service**

See *Certificate of execution of service*

**Execution of a charge**

The service by sheriff officers of a formal notice requiring that a decree or order of a court be obeyed. See also Charge.

**Execution of an arrestment**

The carrying out of an order of arrestment.

**Expenses**

The costs of a court case.

**Ex proprio motu**

A decision or order of the court on the sheriffs own initiative, and not requested by a party to a claim or application

**Extract decree**

The actual decree (or interlocutor) is recorded in the court registers. The extract is the official document, which is proof of any order of the court, although usually it is used as proof of the final decision in the action. It is used, for example, to enforce payment of a sum awarded.

**Fund in medio**

See *Multiplepoinding*.

**Haver**

A person who holds documents which are required as evidence in a case (see Commission and Diligence above).

**Hearing date**

The date on which a small claim action will first be held in court.

**Heritable property**

Land and buildings.

**Incidental application**

An application that can be made during the course of a small claim or summary cause for certain orders. Examples are applications for the recovery of documents or to amend the statement of claim.

**Interlocutor**

The official record of the order or judgement of a court.

**Interrogatories**

Written questions put to someone in the course of a court case, and answered on oath.

**Intimation**

Giving notice to another party of some step in a cause.

**Jurisdiction**

The authority of a court to hear particular cases.

**Ish**

The date on which a lease terminates.

**Letter of request**

A document issued by the sheriff court requesting a foreign court to take evidence from a specified person within its jurisdiction or to serve Scottish Court documents on that person.

**Messenger at arms**

Officers of court who serve documents issued by the Court of Session.

**Minute**

A document produced in the course of a case in which a party makes an application or sets out his position on some matters.

**Minute for recall**

A form lodged with the court by one party asking the court to recall a decree.

**Motion**

An application that can be made during the course of an action for certain orders. This type of application is called an incidental application in small claim or summary cause actions (see above).

**Multiplepoinding (pronounced "multiple pinding")**

A special type of action in which the holder of property, etc. (referred to as the fund in medio) requires claimants upon it to appear and settle claims in court. For example, where the police come into possession of a stolen car of which two or more people claim to be owner this procedure could be used.

**Officer of court**

A sheriff officer, messenger at arms, advocate, solicitor or sheriff clerk.

**Options Hearing**

A preliminary stage in an ordinary cause action.

**Ordinary cause**

Another legal procedure for higher value cases available in the sheriff court.

**Party litigant**

A person who conducts his own case.

**Process**

The court file containing the collection of documents relating to a case.

**Productions**

Documents or articles which are used in evidence.

**Pursuer**

The person who starts a claim or cause.

**Recall of an arrestment**

A court order withdrawing an arrestment.

**Restriction of an arrestment**

An order releasing part of the money or property arrested.

**Recall of a decree**

An order cancelling a decree which has been granted.

**Recovery of documents**

The process of obtaining documentary evidence which is not in the possession of the person seeking it (eg hospital records necessary to establish the extent of injuries received in a road accident). See also *Commission and Diligence* above.

**Remit between procedures**

A decision of the sheriff to transfer an action to another court procedure eg a summary cause to either the small claim or ordinary cause procedure.

**Respondent**

When a decision of the sheriff is appealed against, the person making the appeal is called the appellant. The other side in the appeal is called the respondent.

**Return day**

The date by which the defender must send a written reply to the court in a small claim or summary cause and, where appropriate, the date by which the pursuer must return the summons to court.

**Schedule of arrestment**

A list of items which has been arrested.

**Serve/service**

Sending a copy of the summons or other court document to the defender or another party.

**Sheriff clerk**

The court official responsible for the administration of the sheriff court.

**Sheriff officer**

The officer of court who serve sheriff court documents and enforces sheriff court orders.

**Sist of action**

The temporary suspension of a court case by court order.

**Sist as a party**

To add another person as a litigant in a case.

**Small claim**

Another legal procedure in the sheriff court for claims having a lower value than summary cause.

**Specification of documents**

A list lodged in court of documents for the recovery of which a party seeks a court order (see Commission and Diligence).

**Stated case**

An appeal procedure where the sheriff sets out his findings and the reasons for his decision and states the issues on which the decision of the sheriff principal is requested.

**Statement of claim**

The part of the summons in which pursuers set out details of their cases against defenders.

**Summary cause**

Another legal procedure available in the sheriff court. It is used for certain types of claim usually having a higher value than a small claim, and a lesser value than those dealt with as ordinary actions.

**Summons**

The form which must be filled in to begin a small claim or summary cause.

**Time to pay direction**

A court order for which a defender who is an individual may apply permitting a sum owed to be paid by instalments, or by a single payment at a later date.

## Time order

A court order that assists debtors who have defaulted on an agreement regulated by the Consumer Credit Act 1974 (c.39), and which may be applied for during a court action.

## Warrant for diligence

Authority to carry out one of the diligence procedures.

## Writ

A legally significant writing. An example is an Initial Writ, which is used to begin an ordinary action in the same way that a summons is used to begin a small claim or a summary cause action.

SCHEDULE 2[1]

Article 3

**Forms of Summary Warrant**

| Form No | Description | Rule No |
|---------|-------------|---------|
| A | Warrant for recovery of rates etc. | 3(2) |
| B | Warrant under section 128(6) of the Finance Act 2008 | 3(2) |

Article 3(2)                                   Form A

### SUMMARY WARRANT FOR THE RECOVERY OF

*(insert type of sum due eg, Rates, Community Charge, Council Tax etc under (insert section and statute under which sum due)*
*(Place and date)*

The Sheriff having considered the application dated (date) by (name and address of applicant) along with the certificate produced, and it being stated in the application that an action has not been commenced for the recovery of any amount due, grants a summary warrant authorising recovery of the amount remaining due and unpaid by each person specified in the application along with a surcharge of 10 per cent of that amount, by all lawful execution.

Sheriff

Article 3(2)                                   Form B

### SUMMARY WARRANT UNDER SECTION 128(6) OF THE FINANCE ACT 2008 FOR THE RECOVERY OF SUMS PAYABLE TO THE COMMISSIONERS FOR HER MAJESTY'S REVENUE AND CUSTOMS
*(Place and date)*

The Sheriff having considered the application dated (date) by (name and address of applicant) along with the certificate produced, grants a summary warrant authorising recovery of the amount payable by each person specified in the application by all lawful execution.

---

[1] As substituted by the Act of Sederunt (Debt Arrangement and Attachment (Scotland) Act 2002) Amendment 2009 (SSI 2009/403) (effective November 23, 2009).

## SCHEDULE 3

MINOR AND CONSEQUENTIAL AMENDMENTS

**Article 4**

*Omitted.*

## SCHEDULE 4

REVOCATIONS

**Article 5**

| (1)<br>Act of Sederunt | (2)<br>Reference | (3)<br>Extent of revocation |
|---|---|---|
| Act of Sederunt (Proceedings in the Sheriff Court under the Debtors (Scotland) Act 1987) 1988 | S.I. 1988/2013 | The whole of Part III and in the Schedule, Forms 4 to 29 |
| Act of Sederunt (Proceedings in the Sheriff Court under the Debtors (Scotland) Act 1987) (Amendment) 1996 | S.I. 1996/2709 | The whole instrument |

# ACT OF SEDERUNT (TAKING OF EVIDENCE IN THE EUROPEAN COMMUNITY) 2003

(SSI 2003/601)

*1 January 2004.*

The Lords of Council and Session, under and by virtue of the powers conferred by section 32 of the Sheriff Courts (Scotland) Act 1971, and of all other powers enabling them in that behalf, having approved draft rules submitted to them by the Sheriff Court Rules Council in accordance with section 34 of the said Act of 1971, do hereby enact and declare:

## Citation, commencement and interpretation

**1.**—(1)   This Act of Sederunt may be cited as the Act of Sederunt (Taking of Evidence in the European Community) 2003, and shall come into force on 1st January 2004.

(2)   This Act of Sederunt shall be inserted in the Books of Sederunt.

(3)   In this Act of Sederunt—

"Council Regulation" means the Council Regulation (EC) No. 1206/2001 of 28th May 2001 on cooperation between the courts of the Member States in the taking of evidence in civil or commercial matters;

"Ordinary Cause Rules" means Schedule 1 to the Sheriff Courts (Scotland) Act 1907; and

"Summary Cause Rules" means the Act of Sederunt (Summary Cause Rules) 2002.

## Directions by the sheriff principal

**2.**—(1)   The sheriff principal of any sheriffdom on receipt of a request referred to in paragraph (2), may make a direction specifying—

(a)   the sheriff responsible for execution of that request;

(b)   the manner in which that request is to be executed; and

(c)   the manner in which any representative of a requesting court may participate under Article 12 of the Council Regulation in the performance of the taking of evidence.

(2)   A request is—

(a)   under Article 1 of the Council Regulation by a court of a Member State that a sheriff court shall take evidence; or

(b)   under Article 17 of the Council Regulation by the Scottish central body that a sheriff court shall take part in the performance of the taking of evidence by a court of a Member State.

## Hearing on a request

**3.**—(1)   The sheriff responsible for executing a request under rule 2(1) shall, where appropriate, fix a diet for a hearing on that request.

(2)   The sheriff shall grant a warrant for intimation of a hearing under paragraph (1) to such persons as the sheriff shall consider appropriate.

(3)   The sheriff clerk shall, on a hearing being fixed under paragraph (1), intimate that hearing to the persons specified in paragraph (2) in any of the manners prescribed by rules 5.3 to 5.6 of the Ordinary Cause Rules.

[Amendments to the Ordinary Cause Rules and Summary Cause Rules by paras 4–5 and the Schedule of this Act of Sederunt have been taken into the respective rules and are, therefore, not reproduced here.]

# ACT OF SEDERUNT (SHERIFF COURT EUROPEAN ENFORCEMENT ORDER RULES) 2005

(SSI 2005/523)

*21 October 2005.*

The Lords of Council and Session, under and by virtue of the powers conferred by section 32 of the Sheriff Courts (Scotland) Act 197, and of all other powers enabling them in that behalf, having approved draft rules submitted to them by the Sheriff Court Rules Council in accordance with section 34 of the said Act of 1971, do hereby enact and declare:

### Citation, commencement and interpretation

**1.**—(1)   This Act of Sederunt may be cited as the Act of Sederunt (Sheriff Court European Enforcement Order Rules) 2005 and shall come into force on 21st October 2005.

(2)   This Act of Sederunt shall be inserted in the Books of Sederunt.

(3)   In this Act of Sederunt—

"authentic instrument" has the meaning assigned in Article 4(3) of the Regulation;

"Council Regulation (EC) No. 44/2001" means Council Regulation (EC) No. 44/2001 of 22 December 2000 on jurisdiction and the recognition and enforcement of judgments in civil and commercial matters as amended from time to time and as applied by the Agreement of 19th October 2005 between the European Community and the Kingdom of Denmark on jurisdiction and the recognition and enforcement of judgments in civil and commercial matters;[1]

"court of origin" has the meaning assigned in Article 4(6) of the Regulation;

"court settlement" means a settlement where the debtor has expressly agreed to a claim within the meaning of Article 4(2) of the Regulation by admission or by means of a settlement which has been approved by a court or concluded before a court in the course of proceedings; and

"judgment" has the meaning assigned by Article 4(1) of the Regulation; and

"the Regulation" means Regulation (EC) No. 805/2004 of the European Parliament and of the Council of 21 April 2004 creating a European Enforcement Order for uncontested claims.

(4)   Any reference in this Act of Sederunt to a numbered form shall, unless the context otherwise requires, be construed as a reference to the form so numbered in the Schedule to this Act of Sederunt and includes a form substantially to the same effect with such variation as circumstances may require.

### Application etc.

**2.**—(1)   These Rules shall apply to applications under the Regulation where the sheriff court is the court of origin.

(2)   An application shall—

---

[1] As substituted by the Act of Sederunt (Sheriff Court European Enforcement Order Rules) Amendment (Extension to Denmark) (SSI 2007/351) r.2(2) (effective July 1, 2007).

(a) be made in writing to the sheriff clerk of the sheriff court in which the judgment was delivered or authentic instrument was registered; and

(b) subject to rule 8(1) (rectification or withdrawal of European Enforcement Order certificate) be made by letter.

### Certification of decree in absence or decree by default

**3.**—(1) An application for certification under Article 6(1) (judgment on uncontested claim) or Article 8 (partial European Enforcement Order) of the Regulation shall be accompanied by an affidavit—

(a) verifying that the judgment was of an uncontested claim within the meaning of Article 3(1)(b) or (c) of the Regulation and the court proceedings met the requirements set out in Chapter III of the Regulation;

(b) providing the information required by the form of certificate in Annex I to the Regulation (European Enforcement Order—judgment);

(c) verifying that the judgment is enforceable in Scotland and does not conflict with the rules of jurisdiction laid down in sections 3 and 6 of Chapter II of Council Regulation (EC) No. 44/2001; and

(d) stating that where the debtor was a consumer and the judgment related to a contract concluded by the debtor for a purpose outside his trade or profession the judgment was given in the Member State of the debtor's domicile within the meaning of Article 59 of Council Regulation (EC) No. 44/2001,

and an execution of service of the judgment under sub-paragraph (3).

(2) Before an application is made under Article 6(1) (application for certificate as European Enforcement Order) or Article 8 (partial European Enforcement Order certificate) of the Regulation, the party wishing to enforce the judgment shall serve the judgment on all parties against whom the judgment has been given in accordance with the requirements of Article 13 (service with proof of receipt by the debtor) or Article 14 (service without proof of receipt by the debtor) of the Regulation accompanied by a notice in Form 1.

(3) An execution of service of the judgment shall be in Form 2 unless a form of execution of service is provided by a person effecting service in another Member State.

(4) A certificate under Article 9(1) of the Regulation (European Enforcement Order certificate) shall be signed by the sheriff clerk.

### Certification of court settlement

**4.**—(1) An application for certification under Article 24 of the Regulation (court settlement) shall be accompanied by an affidavit—

(a) verifying that the debtor admitted the claim or entered into a court settlement that was approved by the court or concluded before the court in the course of proceedings and is enforceable in Scotland;

(b) verifying that the settlement concerned a claim within the meaning of Article 4(2) of the Regulation (payment of money); and

(c) providing the information required by the form of certificate in Annex II to the Regulation (European Enforcement Order—court settlement).

(2) A certificate under Article 24 of the Regulation (court settlement) shall be signed by the sheriff clerk.

## Certificate of authentic instrument

**5.**—(1)   An application for certification under Article 25(1) of the Regulation (authentic instrument) shall be accompanied by an affidavit—

(a)   verifying that the authentic instrument concerns a claim within the meaning of Article 4(2) of the Regulation (payment of money);

(b)   verifying that the authentic instrument is enforceable in Scotland; and

(c)   providing the information required by the form of certificate in Annex III to the Regulation (European Enforcement Order— authentic instrument).

(2)   A certificate under Article 25(1) of the Regulation (authentic instrument) shall be signed by the sheriff clerk.

## Certificate of lack or limitation of enforceability

**6.**—(1)   An application for certification under Article 6(2) of the Regulation (lack or limitation of enforceability) shall be accompanied by an affidavit—

(a)   stating the date on which the judgment, court settlement or authentic instrument was certified as a European Enforcement Order; and

(b)   providing the information required by the form of certificate in Annex IV to the Regulation (certificate of lack or limitation of enforceability).

(2)   A certificate under Article 6(2) of the Regulation (lack or limitation of enforceability) shall be signed by the sheriff clerk.

## Replacement certificate

**7.**—(1)   An application under Article 6(3) of the Regulation (replacement certificate) shall be accompanied by an affidavit providing the information required by the form of certificate in Annex V to the Regulation (European Enforcement Order—replacement certificate following a challenge).

(2)   A certificate under Article 6(3) of the Regulation (replacement certificate) shall be signed by the sheriff clerk.

## Rectification or withdrawal of European Enforcement Order certificate

**8.**—(1)   An application under Article 10(1) of the Regulation (rectification or withdrawal of European Enforcement Order certificate) shall be in the form set out in Annex VI to the Regulation and shall be lodged with the sheriff clerk.

(2)   An application under paragraph (1) shall be determined by the sheriff in chambers and shall not require any appearance for the applicant unless the sheriff otherwise directs.

(3)   Where the sheriff requires to hear parties on an application the sheriff clerk shall—

(a)   fix a date, time and place for the parties to be heard, and

(b)   inform the parties—

(i)   of that date, time and place; and

(ii)   of the reasons for the sheriff wishing to hear parties.

SCHEDULE

**Rule 3(2)**

FORM 1
**Form of notice to accompany service copy of judgment**

To [A.B.] (*address*)

You are hereby served with a copy of the interlocutor of the Sheriff of ......... at ......... given on the day of ......... 20 ........... [In terms of this interlocutor you are required to (*state requirements of interlocutor*). Your failure to do so may result in further steps being taken to enforce the interlocutor.]

(*Signed*)
(*Address*)
Solicitor [*or* Sheriff Officer]

(*Place and date*)

**Rule 3(3)**

FORM 2

**Execution of service of judgment where service effected by officer of court or solicitor in Scotland**

(*place and date*)

I, [A.B.] (*address*), hereby certify that upon the ......... day of ......... 20 ........., I duly served a copy of this judgment together with a notice under rule 3(2) of the Act of Sederunt (Sheriff Court European Enforcement Order Rules) 2005 upon [CD.], defender. This I did by posting (*set forth mode of service; if by officer and not by post, add* in presence of [E.F.] (*address*) witness, hereto with me subscribing).

(*Signed*)
(*Address*)
Solicitor for Pursuer
[*or* Defender]
[*or*
(*Signed*)
Sheriff Officer
(*Signed*)
Witness]

*28 April 2006.*

The Lords of Council and Session, under and by virtue of the powers conferred by section 32 of the Sheriff Courts (Scotland) Act 1971 and of all other powers enabling them in that behalf, having approved draft rules submitted to them by the Sheriff Court Rules Council in accordance with section 34 of the Sheriff Courts (Scotland) Act 1971, do hereby enact and declare:

## Citation and commencement

**1.**—(1)   This Act of Sederunt may be cited as the Act of Sederunt (Sheriff Court Caveat Rules) 2006 and shall come into force on 28th April 2006.

(2)   This Act of Sederunt shall be inserted into the Books of Sederunt.

## Orders against which caveats may be lodged

**2.**—(1)   Subject to paragraphs (2) and (3), a person may lodge a caveat against only—

(a)   an interim interdict sought against the person in an ordinary cause before the person has lodged a notice of intention to defend;

(b)   an interim order sought against the person in an ordinary cause before the expiry of the period within which the person could lodge a notice of intention to defend;

(c)   an interim order sought against the person in a summary application before service of the initial writ;

(d)   an order for intimation, service and advertisement of a petition to wind up, or appoint an administrator to, a company in which he has an interest;

(e)   an order for intimation, service and advertisement of a petition for his sequestration; and

(f)   the disposal of a commissary application.

(2)   In this rule—

(a)   "interim order" does not include an order under section 1 of the Administration of Justice (Scotland) Act 1972 (orders for inspection of documents and other property etc.); and

(b)   "commissary application" means an application for—

(i)   confirmation;

(ii)   appointment of an executor; or

(iii)   restriction of caution in respect of an executor.

(3)   A person may lodge a caveat against an order mentioned in paragraph (1)(d) only where the person is a company, debenture holder, holder of a floating charge, receiver, shareholder of the company or other person claiming an interest.

## Form, lodging and renewal of caveats

**3.**—(1)   A caveat shall be in the form set out in the Schedule to this Act of Sederunt, or a form substantially to the same effect with such variation as circumstances may require, and shall be lodged with the sheriff clerk.

(2)   A caveat shall remain in force for a period of one year from the date on which it was lodged and may be renewed on its expiry for a further period of one year and yearly thereafter.

(3)   An application for the renewal of a caveat shall be made in writing to the sheriff clerk not less than 7 days before its expiry.

(4)   Where a caveat has been lodged and has not expired, no order in respect of which the caveat was lodged may be pronounced unless the sheriff is satisfied that all reasonable steps have been taken to afford the person lodging the caveat an opportunity of being heard; and the sheriff may continue the hearing on such an order until he is satisfied that such steps have been taken.

## Amendments

**4.**—(1)   Rule 20 of the Act of Sederunt (Sheriff Court Company Insolvency Rules) 1986 shall be omitted.

(2)   Chapter 4 of, and Form G2 in Appendix 1 to, the Ordinary Cause Rules 1993 in Schedule 1 to the Sheriff Courts (Scotland) Act 1907 shall be omitted.

(3)   Rules 2.8 and 2.9 of, and Form 8 in Schedule 1 to, the Act of Sederunt (Summary Applications, Statutory Applications, and Appeals etc. Rules) 1999 shall be omitted.

## Transitional and savings provision

**5.**—(1)   Subject to paragraph (2), nothing in this Act of Sederunt shall affect a caveat lodged prior to 28th April 2006.

(2)   A caveat lodged prior to 28th April 2006 may not be renewed unless the caveat complies with the requirements of this Act of Sederunt.

SCHEDULE

Rule 3(1)

### Form of Caveat

SHERIFFDOM OF (*insert name of sheriffdom*)

AT (*insert place of sheriff court*)

CAVEAT for A.B. (*insert designation and address\**)

Should any application be made for (*here specify, under reference to sub-paragraphs of* rule 2(1), *the application(s) to which this caveat is to apply*) [before the lodging of a notice of intention to defend *[or (specify for each application which of the following alternatives is to apply*: the expiry of the period within which a notice of intention to defend may be lodged; before service of the initial writ or petition)]], it is requested that intimation be made to the caveator before any order is pronounced.

Date (*insert date*)....................Signed

...............[A.B.]...............

　　　　　　　　or [X.Y.] Solicitor for [A.B.] (*add designation, business address and email address*)

Caveator's telephone and fax number (*insert where caveat is not lodged by solicitors*)

Solicitor (*insert name and address, telephone and fax number and reference*)

Out of hours contacts:

1. (*insert name and telephone number*)

2. (*insert name and telephone number*)

\* State whether the caveat is lodged in an individual capacity, or a specified representative capacity (e.g. as a trustee of a named trust) or both. Where appropriate, state the nature of the caveator's interest (e.g. shareholder, debenture holder).

# ACT OF SEDERUNT (JURISDICTION, RECOGNITION AND ENFORCE-MENT OF JUDGMENTS IN MATRIMONIAL MATTERS AND MATTERS OF PARENTAL RESPONSIBILITY RULES) 2006

(SI 2006/397)

**D2.46**

*1 August 2006.*

The Lords of Council and Session, under and by virtue of the powers conferred by section 32 of the Sheriff Courts (Scotland) Act 1971, and of all other powers enabling them in that behalf, having approved draft rules submitted to them by the Sheriff Court Rules Council in accordance with section 34 of that Act, do hereby enact and declare:

## Citation and commencement

**1.** This Act of Sederunt may be cited as the Act of Sederunt (Jurisdiction, Recognition and Enforcement of Judgments in Matrimonial Matters and Matters of Parental Responsibility Rules) 2006 and shall come into force on 1st August 2006.

## Interpretation

**2.**—(1) In this Act of Sederunt—

"central authority" means an authority designated under Article 53 of the Council Regulation;

"the Council Regulation" means Council Regulation (EC) No. 2201/2003 of 27th November 2003 concerning jurisdiction and the recognition and enforcement of judgments in matrimonial matters and matters of parental responsibility;

"foreign court" means a court in a Member State other than the United Kingdom;

"Member State" has the same meaning as in Article 2(3) of the Council Regulation;

"parental responsibility" has the same meaning as in Article 2(7) of the Council Regulation; and

"these Rules" means the rules set out in this Act of Sederunt.

(2) A form referred to in these Rules by number means the form so numbered in the Schedule to this Act of Sederunt or a form substantially to the same effect, with such variation as circumstances may require.

(3) A reference in these Rules to a numbered Article is a reference to the Article of the Council Regulation so numbered.

(4) Except as provided for in these Rules or any order made by a sheriff hereunder, any action to which these Rules apply shall proceed as an ordinary cause under the First Schedule to the Sheriff Courts (Scotland) Act 1907.

## Transfer of case involving matters of parental responsibility to sheriff court

**3.**—(1) A request to a sheriff court under Article 15(1)(a) (request by parties to transfer case involving parental responsibilities) shall be made by initial writ under these Rules.

(2) Where a sheriff court receives a request from a foreign court under Article 15(1)(b) (request by court to assume jurisdiction)—

    (a) the sheriff clerk shall forthwith—

   (i) acknowledge receipt of the request to the foreign court;

   (ii) intimate the request to the parties to the action, their Scottish agents, if known, and any other party to whom the sheriff considers that intimation should be made; and

   (iii) intimate to the parties and, if known, their Scottish agents, the requirement to lodge an initial writ under subparagraph (b) within the time limit set by the foreign court under Article 15(4) (time limit for seising the court); and

  (b) one of the parties shall lodge an initial writ under these Rules.

(3) Where no initial writ has been lodged within the time limit set by the foreign court under Article 15(4), the sheriff clerk shall advise the foreign court that the sheriff court has not been seised under Article 16 (seising of a court).

## General provisions for transfer to sheriff court

**4.**—(1) An initial writ under these Rules shall—

  (a) include the following heading printed above the instance—

    "ACT OF SEDERUNT (JURISDICTION, RECOGNITION AND ENFORCE-MENT OF JUDGMENTS IN MATRIMONIAL MATTERS AND MATTERS OF PARENTAL RESPONSIBILITY RULES) 2006"; and

  (b) include averments stating—

   (i) the full name, designation, postal address, telephone and facsimile numbers and, where appropriate, e-mail address of each of the parties to the action involving parental responsibilities, including any Scottish agent instructed to represent any of the parties;

   (ii) the postal address and telephone and facsimile numbers of the foreign court and the name and, where appropriate, e-mail address of any official of the court to whom any document may be sent by the sheriff clerk;

   (iii) the full name, postal address and date of birth of the child;

   (iv) the status of the proceedings in the foreign court;

   (v) the particular connection the child has with Scotland;

   (vi) why it is in the best interests of the child that the case should be heard in the sheriff court;

   (vii) the time limit set by the foreign court under Article 15(4);

(2) There shall be lodged with an initial writ under these Rules any document considered by the pursuer to be relevant to the action involving parental responsibilities including any papers forming part of the process of the case in the foreign court.

(3) A warrant for citation in respect of an initial writ under these Rules shall be signed by the sheriff.

(4) The sheriff may make such order as to intimation or service, fixing a hearing to determine jurisdiction or otherwise as he thinks fit.

(5) On the fixing of a date for a hearing to determine jurisdiction the pursuer shall—

  (a) intimate to every other party a notice in Form 1;

  (b) lodge a certificate of intimation in Form 2,

within any time limit specified by the sheriff.

### Acceptance of jurisdiction by sheriff court in matters of parental responsibility

**5.**—(1) An interlocutor accepting or refusing to accept jurisdiction to hear an action commenced by initial writ under these Rules shall be signed by the sheriff.

(2) After the expiry of the time limit for any appeal the sheriff clerk shall intimate the decision of the sheriff court to the foreign court by sending to the foreign court—

    (a)    a copy interlocutor by electronic mail or facsimile transmission; and

    (b)    a certified copy interlocutor by first class recorded delivery or registered post.

### Application by sheriff court to foreign court for transfer of case involving matters of parental responsibility

**6.**—(1) Where in any action a sheriff decides to make an application to a foreign court under Article 15(2)(c) (application for transfer of case involving parental responsibilities to sheriff court) he shall append to the interlocutor a note containing—

    (a)    the full name, designation and postal address, telephone and facsimile numbers and, where appropriate, e-mail address of all the parties to the case involving parental responsibilities, including any agent instructed to represent the parties in the foreign court;

    (b)    details of the particular connection the child is considered to have with Scotland; and

    (c)    such other matters as he considers would be of assistance to the foreign court in deciding whether or not to seek a transfer of the case under Article 15(1) (transfer to a court better placed to hear the case).

(2) The sheriff clerk shall forthwith send to the foreign court—

    (a)    a copy interlocutor and note under paragraph (1) by electronic mail or by facsimile transmission; and

    (b)    a certified copy interlocutor and note by first class recorded delivery or registered post.

### Application by foreign court to sheriff court for transfer of case involving matters of parental responsibility

**7.** On receipt of an application by a foreign court under Article 15(2)(c) (application for transfer of case involving parental responsibilities to foreign court) the sheriff clerk shall—

    (a)    give written intimation of the application and any accompanying documents to each party to the case;

    (b)    fix a time and date for a hearing to consider the application; and

    (c)    intimate the hearing to each party to the action.

### Transfer by sheriff court of case involving matters of parental responsibility

**8.**—(1) An interlocutor pronounced by a sheriff sisting a case and inviting parties to make a request to a foreign court under Article 15(1)(a) or requesting a foreign court to assume jurisdiction under Article 15(1)(b) shall—

    (a)    specify the particular connection the child has to the Member State of the foreign court;

(b) set a time limit within which the foreign court may be seised in terms of Article 15(4);

(c) specify which of sub-paragraphs (a) to (c) of Article 15(2) applies and, where appropriate, which of the parties to the action have accepted the transfer.

(2) The sheriff shall append to the interlocutor a note stating—

(a) the reasons why he considers that it would be in the best interests of the child that the foreign court should hear the case; and

(b) such other matters as he considers would be of assistance to the foreign court in deciding whether or not to accept jurisdiction under Article 15(5) (acceptance of jurisdiction).

(3) Where an interlocutor under Article 15(1)(b) has been pronounced on the sheriffs own motion or on an application from the foreign court, the sheriff clerk shall send a certified copy of the interlocutor and note to each of the parties.

(4) Within seven days of any interlocutor pronounced under Article 15(1)(b) (request by court to assume jurisdiction), the sheriff clerk shall send to the foreign court—

(a) a copy of the interlocutor and note under paragraph (2) by electronic mail or by facsimile transmission;

(b) a certified copy of the interlocutor and note by first class recorded delivery or registered post.

(5) The party who effects seisure of the foreign court shall no later than seven days after the expiry of the time limit specified by the sheriff under paragraph (1)(b) lodge in process a certificate stating the date on which the seisure was effected.

(6) Within 14 days of the date of the decision of the foreign court whether or not to accept jurisdiction in accordance with Article 15(5), the party who effected seisure of that court shall lodge in process a certified copy of the order of the foreign court or other document confirming its decision.

**Translation of documents**

**9.** Where any document received from a foreign court or otherwise under these Rules is in a language other than English, the sheriff may order that there shall be lodged with that document a translation into English certified as correct by the translator; and the certificate shall include his full name, address and qualifications.

**Enforcement in another Member State of sheriff court judgments etc.**

**10.**—(1) Where a person seeks to apply under the Council Regulation for recognition or enforcement in another Member State of a judgment given by a sheriff court, he shall apply by letter to the sheriff clerk of that court for—

(a) a certificate under Article 39 of the Council Regulation (certificates concerning judgments in matrimonial matters or matters of parental responsibility); and

(b) a certified copy of the judgment (incorporating the sheriffs interlocutor and note).

(2) The sheriff clerk shall not issue a certificate under paragraph (1)(a) unless there is produced to him an execution of service of the judgment on the person against whom it is sought to be enforced.

(3)　Where a judgment granting rights of access delivered by the sheriff court acquires a cross-border character after the judgment has been delivered and a party seeks to enforce the judgment in another Member State, he shall apply by letter to the sheriff clerk for—

(a)　a certificate under Article 41 of the Council Regulation (certificate concerning rights of access); and

(b)　a certified copy of the judgment (incorporating the sheriffs interlocutor and note).

## Placement of child in another Member State

**11.**　Where the sheriff requires under Article 56 of the Council Regulation to obtain the consent of a competent authority in another Member State to the placement of a child he shall send a request in Form 3 and any other documents he considers to be relevant to the Scottish central authority for transmission to the central authority in the other Member State.

SCHEDULE

**Rule 4(5)**

### FORM 1
**Form of notice of intimation of a hearing to determine jurisdiction under Article 15 of Council Regulation (EC) No.2201/2003 of 27th November 2003**

Date: (*date of posting or other method of intimation*)

To: (*name and address*)

TAKE NOTICE

(*Name and address of pursuer*) has lodged an initial writ in the Sheriff Court at (*place*) against (*name and address of defender*).

The parties are presently engaged in proceedings involving matters of parental responsibility in (*specify court in other Member State where proceedings have been raised*) and a request has been made to the sheriff court to accept jurisdiction of these proceedings and for the action to be dealt with in the Sheriff Court.

A hearing has been fixed on (*date*) at (*time*) within the Sheriff Court to determine the issue of jurisdiction.

You may appear or be represented by a person having a right of audience before the Sheriff Court at the hearing.

You or your representative will be asked whether you agree to jurisdiction being accepted by the Sheriff Court and the proceedings involving matters of parental responsibility being dealt with in the Sheriff Court.

If you do not appear or are not represented at the hearing the court may decide whether to accept jurisdiction in your absence.

(signed)
*Solicitor for pursuer*
(add name and business address)

**Rule 4(5)**

FORM 2
**Certificate of Intimation of a hearing to determine jurisdiction under** Article 15 of Council Regulation (EC) No.2201/2003 of 27th November 2003

*in causa*
AB Pursuer
against
CD Defender

I certify that intimation of a hearing to determine jurisdiction under Article 15 of Council Regulation (EC) No.2201/2003 of 27 November 2003 was made to:

Date: (*date of posting or other method of intimation*)

To: (*name and address*)
Date: (*date of posting or other method of intimation*)
To: (*name and address*)
Date: (*date of posting or other method of intimation*)
To: (*name and address*)

Date: (*insert date*)                                    (*signed*)

                                              Solicitor for pursuer
                                              (*add name and business address*)

**Rule 11**

FORM 3

**Form of request for consent to placement of child under** Article 56 of Council Regulation (EC)
No.2201/2003 of 27th November 2003

Date: (*date of request*)
To: (*name and address of competent authority in other Member State*)

The Sheriff Court has jurisdiction in matters of parental responsibility under the Council Regulation
(EC) No.2201/2003 of 27th November 2003 in respect of (*name and address of child*). The court is
contemplating the placement of (*name of child*) in (*name and address of institution*) [*or* with (*name and
address of foster family*)] and requests your consent to the placement in accordance with Article 56 of
Council Regulation.

                                                            (*Signed*)
                                                         Sheriff Clerk

# ACT OF SEDERUNT (SHERIFF COURT EUROPEAN SMALL CLAIMS PROCEDURE RULES) 2008

(SSI 2008/435)

*12 January 2009.*

The Lords of Council and Session, under and by virtue of the powers conferred by section 32 of the Sheriff Courts (Scotland) Act 1971, and of all other powers enabling them in that behalf, having approved draft rules submitted to them by the Sheriff Court Rules Council in accordance with section 34 of that Act, do hereby enact and declare:

## Citation and commencement, etc

1.—(1) This Act of Sederunt—
    (a) may be cited as the Act of Sederunt (Sheriff Court European Small Claims Procedure Rules) 2008; and
    (b) comes into force on 12th January 2009.
(2) This Act of Sederunt is to be inserted in the Books of Sederunt.

## Interpretation

2.—(1) In this Act of Sederunt—

"the Regulation" means Regulation (EC) No.861/2007 of the European Parliament and the Council of 11th July 2007 creating a European Small Claims Procedure;
"the Ordinary Cause Rules" means the First Schedule to the Sheriff Courts (Scotland) Act 1907;
"the Summary Cause Rules" means the Summary Cause Rules in Schedule 1 to the Act of Sederunt (Summary Cause Rules) 2002;
"the Small Claim Rules" means the Small Claim Rules in Schedule 1 to the Act of Sederunt (Small Claim Rules) 2002;

(2) Expressions used in both the Regulation and this Act of Sederunt have the same meaning here as there.
(3) A form referred to in this Act of Sederunt by number means the form so numbered in the Schedule to this Act of Sederunt or a form to substantially the same effect, with such variation as circumstances may require.
(4) A reference in this Act of Sederunt to a numbered Article is a reference to the Article of the Regulation so numbered.

## Communication by the court

3.—(1) This rule applies where—
    (a) under the Regulation or this Act of Sederunt the court requires to send a document to a person; and
    (b) the Regulation does not require otherwise.
(2) The document is to be sent by the sheriff clerk.
(3) The document is to be sent—
    (a) where it is being sent to an address within the United Kingdom, by first class recorded delivery;
    (b) where it is being sent to an address outside the United Kingdom, by registered post.

(4)　The sheriff clerk must complete a certificate of posting to which must be attached the relevant postal receipt.

## Transfer to domestic procedure

**4.**—(1)　This rule applies where, under paragraph 3 of Article 4 (commencement of the procedure) it is determined that a claim presented under the procedure established by the Regulation is outside the scope of the Regulation.

(2)　The sheriff clerk must, within 21 days of the determination, send to the claimant a notice in Form 1.

(3)　Where the claimant does not withdraw the claim, the proceedings shall proceed under the Ordinary Cause Rules, the Summary Cause Rules or the Small Claim Rules, as the case may be, and the sheriff is to make an order containing such provision as the sheriff thinks fit for the purpose of bringing the proceedings into line with an appropriate stage of proceedings under those rules.

(4)　The provision which may be made in an order under paragraph (2) includes—

　　(a)　provision dispensing with any provision of the rules concerned; or
　　(b)　provision deeming any document lodged in the proceedings under the Regulation to constitute a document in proceedings under those rules.

(5)　The sheriff clerk must, within 21 days of the making of the order, send to the claimant a notice in Form 2.

## Ancillary applications

**5.**—(1)　An application under paragraph 1 of Article 18 (review of judgment) is to be in Form 3.

(2)　An application under paragraph 1 of Article 22 (refusal of enforcement) is to be in Form 4.

(3)　An application under Article 23 (stay or limitation of enforcement) is to be in Form 5.

(4)　The sheriff may make such order as the sheriff thinks fit for the progress of any such application.

SCHEDULE

Form 1

Rule 4(2)

**Form of notice that claim presented under European Small Claims Procedure outside scope of Regulation**

**EUROPEAN SMALL CLAIMS PROCEDURE**

Notice under Article 4(3) of Regulation (EC) No. 861/2007 of 11th July 2007

NOTICE

THAT CLAIM PRESENTED UNDER EUROPEAN SMALL CLAIMS PROCEDURE OUTSIDE SCOPE OF REGULATION

UNDER ARTICLE 4(3) OF REGULATION (EC) NO 861/2007

To [A.B.] [*address*]

You are hereby notified that the claim presented by you under the European Small Claims Procedure is outside the scope of the Regulation. Unless you withdraw the claim, it shall now proceed under [*the ordinary cause procedure*] [*the small claim procedure*] [*the summary cause procedure*]\*. If you wish to withdraw the claim, you should write to me to this effect to reach me no later than [*insert date of day 21 days after date of posting*].

\* *delete as appropriate*

**Further advice can be obtained by contacting a Citizen's Advice Bureau or a Solicitor.**

*(Signed)*
*(Address)*
Sheriff Clerk [Depute]

*(Place and date)*

FORM 2

Rule 4(5)

**Form of notice that claim presented under European Small Claims Procedure transferred to domestic procedure**

**EUROPEAN SMALL CLAIMS PROCEDURE**

Notice under Article 4(3) of Regulation (EC) No. 861/2007 of 11th July 2007

NOTICE

THAT CLAIM PRESENTED UNDER EUROPEAN SMALL CLAIMS PROCEDURE TRANSFERRED TO DOMESTIC PROCEDURE

UNDER ARTICLE 4(3) OF REGULATION (EC) NO 861/2007

To [A.B.] *[address]*

You were previously notified that the claim presented by you under the European Small Claims Procedure is outside the scope of the Regulation. There having been no indication that you wish to withdraw the claim, it shall now proceed under *[the ordinary cause procedure] [the small claim procedure] [the summary cause procedure]**. Under rule 4(3) of the Act of Sederunt (Sheriff Court European Small Claims Procedure Rules) 2008, the sheriff has made an order for the purpose of bringing the proceedings into line with an appropriate stage of the proceedings under the rules which apply to such a cause or claim. A copy of the sheriff's order is attached.

* *delete as appropriate*

**Further advice can be obtained by contacting a Citizen's Advice Bureau or a Solicitor.**

*(Signed)*
*(Address)*
Sheriff Clerk [Depute]

*(Place and date)*

FORM 3

Rule 5(1)

**Form of application for review of a judgment given in the European Small Claims Procedure under Article 18(1) of Regulation (EC) No 861/2007 of 11th July 2007**

**EUROPEAN SMALL CLAIMS PROCEDURE**

Application under Article 18(1) of Regulation (EC) No. 861/2007 of 11th July 2007

APPLICATION FOR

REVIEW OF JUDGMENT GIVEN IN THE EUROPEAN SMALL CLAIMS PROCEDURE

UNDER ARTICLE 18(1) OF REGULATION (EC) NO 861/2007

Sheriff Court at *[insert court]*

Court ref:

I, *[insert name and address]*, apply under Article 18(1) of Regulation (EC) No 861/2007 for a review of the judgment given in the European Small Claims Procedure by the court on *[insert date]* in favour of *[name and address of claimant]*, for the following reasons:

- Service was not effected in sufficient time to enable me to arrange for my defence, without any fault on my part *
- I was prevented from objecting to the claim by reason of force majeure or due to extraordinary circumstances, without any fault on my part *

* *delete as appropriate*

I ask the court to intimate this application on the claimant.

*(Signed)*

FORM 4

Rule 5(2)

**Form of application for refusal of enforcement of a judgment given in the European Small Claims Procedure under Article 22(1) of Regulation (EC) No 861/2007 of 11th July 2007**

**EUROPEAN SMALL CLAIMS PROCEDURE**

Application under Article 22(1) of Regulation (EC) No. 861/2007 of 11th July 2007

APPLICATION FOR

REFUSAL OF ENFORCEMENT OF A JUDGMENT GIVEN IN THE EUROPEAN SMALL CLAIMS PROCEDURE

UNDER ARTICLE 22(1) OF REGULATION (EC) NO 861/2007

Sheriff Court at [*insert court*]

Court ref:

I, [*insert name and address*], apply under Article 22(1) of Regulation (EC) No 861/2007 for the court to make an order refusing enforcement of a judgment given in the European Small Claims Procedure by the court on [*insert date*] in favour of [*name and address of claimant*], as the order is irreconcilable with an earlier judgment given in a Member State or a third country. [*Give details here of decision or order made and in which Member State or third country*], and:

- the earlier judgment involved the same cause of action and the same parties;
- the earlier judgment was given in the Member State of enforcement or fulfils the conditions necessary for its recognition in the Member State of enforcement; and
- the irreconcilability was not and could not have been raised as an objection in the court or tribunal proceedings in the United Kingdom.

I ask the court to intimate this application on the claimant.

(*Signed*)

FORM 5

Rule 5(3)

**Form of application for stay or limitation of enforcement of a judgment given in the European Small Claims Procedure under Article 23(1) of Regulation (EC) No 861/2007 of 11th July 2007**

**EUROPEAN SMALL CLAIMS PROCEDURE**

Application under Article 23(1) of Regulation (EC) No. 861/2007 of 11th July 2007

APPLICATION FOR

STAY OR LIMITATION OF A JUDGMENT GIVEN IN THE EUROPEAN SMALL CLAIMS PROCEDURE

UNDER ARTICLE 23(1) OF REGULATION (EC) NO 861/2007

Sheriff Court at [*insert court*]

Court ref:

I, [*insert name and address*], apply under Article 23(1) of Regulation (EC) No 861/2007 for the court to [*limit / stay*]* the enforcement of the judgment given in the European Small Claims Procedure granted by the court on [*insert date*] in favour of [*insert name and address of claimant*].

* *delete as appropriate*

I ask the court to intimate this application on the claimant.

(*Signed*)

# ACT OF SEDERUNT (SHERIFF COURT EUROPEAN ORDER FOR PAYMENT PROCEDURE RULES) 2008

(SSI 2008/436)

*12 January 2009.*

The Lords of Council and Session, under and by virtue of the powers conferred by section 32 of the Sheriff Courts (Scotland) Act 197, and of all other powers enabling them in that behalf, having approved draft rules submitted to them by the Sheriff Court Rules Council in accordance with section 34 of that Act, do hereby enact and declare:

## Citation and commencement, etc.

1.—(1)  This Act of Sederunt—
  (a)  may be cited as the Act of Sederunt (Sheriff Court European Order for Payment Procedure Rules) 2008; and
  (b)  comes into force on 12th January 2009.
(2)  This Act of Sederunt is to be inserted in the Books of Sederunt.

## Interpretation

2.—(1)  In this Act of Sederunt—

"the Regulation" means Regulation (EC) No. 1896/2006 of the European Parliament and of the Council of 12th December 2006 creating a European order for payment procedure;

"the Ordinary Cause Rules" means the First Schedule to the Sheriff Courts (Scotland) Act 1907;

"the Summary Cause Rules" means the Summary Cause Rules in Schedule 1 to the Act of Sederunt (Summary Cause Rules) 2002;

"the Small Claim Rules" means the Small Claim Rules in Schedule 1 to the Act of Sederunt (Small Claim Rules) 2002;

(2)  Expressions used in both the Regulation and this Act of Sederunt have the same meaning here as there.

(3)  A form referred to in this Act of Sederunt by number means the form so numbered in the Schedule to this Act of Sederunt or a form substantially to the same effect, with such variation as circumstances may require.

(4)  A reference in this Act of Sederunt to a numbered Article is a reference to the Article of the Regulation so numbered.

## Communication by the court

3.—(1)  This rule applies where, under the Regulation or this Act of Sederunt, the court requires to send a document to a person.
(2)  The document is to be sent by the sheriff clerk.
(3)  The document is to be sent—
  (a)  where it is being sent to an address within the United Kingdom, by first class recorded delivery;
  (b)  where it is being sent to an address outside the United Kingdom, by registered post.
(4)  The sheriff clerk must complete a certificate of posting to which must be attached the relevant postal receipt.

### Service on a representative

**4.**—(1) This rule applies where service is effected by virtue of Article 15 (service on a representative).

(2) The claimant must lodge a document signed by the person who effected service indicating the basis on which it was believed that the person on whom service was effected was the defendant's representative.

(3) The document must be accompanied by any written material which the person effecting service relied upon in forming that belief.

### Opposition to European order for payment

**5.**—(1) This rule applies where—

    (a) the defendant lodges a statement of opposition to a European order for payment in accordance with Article 16 (opposition to European order for payment); and

    (b) the claimant has not explicitly requested that the proceedings be terminated in that event.

(2) The proceedings shall continue under the Ordinary Cause Rules, the Summary Cause Rules or the Small Claim Rules, as the case may be, and the sheriff is to make an order containing such provision as the sheriff thinks fit for the purpose of bringing the proceedings into line with an appropriate stage of proceedings under those rules.

(3) The provision which may be made in an order under paragraph (2) includes—

    (a) provision dispensing with any provision of the rules concerned; or

    (b) provision deeming any document lodged in the proceedings for the European order for payment to constitute a document in proceedings under those rules.

(4) The court must, within 21 days after the statement of opposition was lodged—

    (a) send to the claimant a notice in Form 1; and

    (b) send a copy of that form to the defendant.

### Review in exceptional cases

**6.**—(1) An application under paragraph 1 of Article 20 (review in exceptional cases: defective service, etc.) is to be in Form 2.

(2) An application under paragraph 2 of Article 20 (review in exceptional cases: other grounds) is to be in Form 3.

(3) The sheriff may make such order as the sheriff thinks fit for the progress of an application under paragraph (1) or (2) of Article 20.

(4) An application under Article 23 (stay or limitation of enforcement) is to be made by motion.

(5) A motion under paragraph (4) is to be made in accordance with, and is regulated by, Chapter 15 of the Ordinary Cause Rules.

### Refusal of enforcement

**7.**—(1) An application under paragraph (1) of Article 22 (refusal of enforcement) is to be in Form 4.

(2)    The sheriff may make such order as the sheriff thinks fit for the progress of such an application.

SCHEDULE

Rule 5(4)

FORM 1

**Form of notice of statement of opposition to European order for payment**
STATEMENT OF OPPOSITION TO A EUROPEAN ORDER FOR PAYMENT
Sheriff Court at [*insert court*]
To: [*insert name and address of claimant*]
Date: [*insert date*]
Please note that on [*insert date*] a statement of opposition to the European order of payment issued in your favour on [*insert date* was lodged. A copy is attached. In accordance with Article 17(1) of Regulation (EC) No. 1896/2006 of 12th December 2006, the proceedings shall now continue as [*an ordinary cause*][*a summary cause*] [*a small claim*]\*. Under rule 5(2) of the Act of Sederunt (Sheriff Court European Order for Payment Procedure Rules) 2008, the sheriff has made an order for the purpose of bringing the proceedings into line with an appropriate stage of the proceedings under the rules which apply to such a cause or claim. A copy of the sheriff's order is attached.
    **Further advice can be obtained by contacting a Citizen's Advice Bureau or a Solicitor.**
    \* *delete as appropriate*
    Date: [*insert date*]

[*signed*] ..........
Sheriff Clerk [Depute]

FORM 2

**Rule 6(1)**

**Form of application for a review of a European order for payment under Article 20(1) of Regulation (EC) No. 1896/2006 of 12th December 2006**
**EUROPEAN ORDER FOR PAYMENT**
Application for review under Article 20(1) of Regulation (EC) No. 1896/2006 of 12th December 2006
APPLICATION FOR REVIEW OF A EUROPEAN ORDER FOR PAYMENT UNDER ARTICLE 20(1) OF REGULATION (EC) NO 1896/2006
Sheriff Court at [*insert court*]
Court ref:
    I, [insert name and address], apply under Article 20(1) of Regulation (EC) No 1896/2006 for a review of the European order for payment granted by the court on [insert date] in favour of [insert name and address of claimant] for the following reasons:
    •    Service was not effected in sufficient time to enable me to arrange for my defence, without any fault on my part\*
    •    I was prevented from objecting to the claim by reason of force majeure or due to extraordinary circumstances without any fault on my part\*
\* *delete as appropriate*
I ask the court to intimate the application on the claimant.
[*signed*] ..........

FORM 3

**Rule 6(2)**

**Form of application for a review of a European order for payment under Article 20(2) of Regulation (EC) No. 1896/2006 of 12th December 2006**
**EUROPEAN ORDER FOR PAYMENT**
Application for review under Article 20(2) of Regulation (EC) No. 1896/2006 of 12th December 2006
APPLICATION FOR REVIEW OF A EUROPEAN ORDER FOR PAYMENT UNDER ARTICLE 20(2) OF REGULATION (EC) NO 1896/2006
Sheriff Court at [*insert court*]
Court ref:

I, [*insert name and address*], apply under Article 20(2) of Regulation (EC) No 1896/2006 for a review of the European order for payment granted by the court on [*insert date*] in favour of [*insert name and address of claimant*] as:

- the order for payment was clearly wrongly issued having regard to the requirements laid down in the Regulation*
- there are exceptional circumstances for doing so*

* *delete as appropriate*

My reasons are: [*state reasons for seeking review, under reference to the ground on which the review is sought*].

I ask the court to intimate the application on the claimant.

[*signed*] .........

FORM 4

**Rule 7(1)**

**Form of application for refusal of enforcement of a European order for payment under Article 22(1) of Regulation (EC) No. 1896/2006 of 12th December 2006**

**EUROPEAN ORDER FOR PAYMENT**

Application for refusal of enforcement under Article 22(1) of Regulation (EC) No. 1896/2006 of 12th December 2006

APPLICATION FOR REFUSAL OF ENFORCEMENT OF A EUROPEAN ORDER FOR PAYMENT UNDER ARTICLE 22(1) OF REGULATION (EC) NO 1896/2006

Sheriff Court at [*insert court*]

Court ref:

I, [*insert name and address*], apply under Article 22(1) of Regulation (EC) No 1896/2006 for the court to make an order refusing to enforce the European order for payment granted by the court on [*insert date*] in favour of [*insert name and address of claimant*] as:

- the order for payment is irreconcilable with an earlier decision or order given. [*Give details here of decision or order made and in which Member State or third country*].*
- I paid the claimant the amount awarded in the order for payment on [*insert date*].*

* *delete as appropriate*

I ask the court to intimate the application on the claimant.

[*signed*] .........

# ACT OF SEDERUNT (SANCTION FOR THE EMPLOYMENT OF COUNSEL IN THE SHERIFF COURT) 2011

(SSI 2011/404)

*1 January 2012.*

The Lords of Council and Session, under and by virtue of the powers conferred by section 32 of the Sheriff Courts (Scotland) Act 1971 and of all other powers enabling them in that behalf, having approved draft rules submitted to them by the Sheriff Court Rules Council in accordance with section 34 of the said Act of 1971, do hereby enact and declare:

## Citation and commencement

**1.**—(1)  This Act of Sederunt may be cited as the Act of Sederunt (Sanction for the Employment of Counsel in the Sheriff Court) 2011 and comes into force on 1st January 2012.

(2)  A certified copy of this Act of Sederunt is to be inserted in the Books of Sederunt.

## Sanction for the purpose of general regulation 12

**2.**—(1)  This rule applies in relation to any civil proceedings in the sheriff court.

(2)  For the purposes of this rule, proceedings at first instance are to be regarded as separate from proceedings on appeal.

(3)  The sheriff, or as the case may be, the sheriff principal, may, on the motion or incidental application of a party or of his or her own accord, grant sanction for the purpose of general regulation 12 (employment of counsel) of Schedule 1 to the Act of Sederunt (Fees of Solicitors in the Sheriff Court) (Amendment and Further Provisions) 1993 in relation to—

    (a)  appearance at any hearing in the proceedings; or

    (b)  preparation of any document to be lodged in relation to the proceedings.

(4)  Sanction may be granted under paragraph (3)—

    (a)  before, at, or after the hearing or, before or after the preparation of the document concerned; and

    (b)  at the time of, or at any time prior to, the disposal of the proceedings.

(5)  Refusal to grant sanction before the hearing has taken place or before the document has been prepared does not prevent such sanction being granted at or after the hearing, or after the preparation of the document.

(6)  In granting sanction under paragraph (3), the sheriff or, as the case may be, the sheriff principal may—

    (a)  sanction the employment of one or more pleader;

    (b)  grant sanction in relation to one or more hearings in the proceedings or in relation to the preparation of one or more documents to be lodged in the proceedings; and

    (c)  impose such restrictions in respect of the extent of such sanction as he or she thinks fit.

# ACTS OF COURT AND PRACTICE NOTES

NOTE - This section reprints the current Acts of Court and Practice Notes of the sheriffdoms of Scotland, so far as notified to the publishers, other than transient measures relating to court sessions and holidays, etc. Measures now spent although not formally repealed, such as those relating to small debt courts or the suspension of court business during industrial action, have not been reprinted.

# PRACTICE NOTES

[JUNE 5, 2005]

## Contents

## Consolidated Practice Notes

I, EDWARD FARQUHERSON BOWEN, Queens Counsel, Sheriff Principal of Glasgow and Strathkelvin, in respect that many of the Practice Notes in force within the Sheriffdom are spent or in need of modernisation, hereby repeal all Practice Notes presently in force; for the purpose of regulating practice in the Sheriff Court at Glasgow and for convenient reference, in pursuance of the powers conferred under Section 15(2) of the Sheriff Courts (Scotland) Act 1971 and all common law powers enabling in that behalf order and direct as follows:

(Sgd) E F Bowen

## PART I

## CIVIL PROCEDURE

### Records

**1.01** When records are prepared, the answers for the defender and any third party should be inset from the margin used for the pleadings for the pursuer. Lines should be double spaced and pages should be numbered. It will be helpful if every fifth line on each page is numbered.

## Social Security (Recovery of Benefits) Act 1997

**1.02**   In all cases to which the Social Security (Recovery of Benefits) Act 1997 applies, parties seeking decree (except where that decree is sought of consent, for instance, as a result of a joint minute) should lodge in process a *Schedule of Damages* stating the amount of any compensation which is claimed in respect of the relevant period under any of the headings in Column 1 of Schedule 2 to the Act.

**1.03**   For the avoidance of doubt, it should be noted that this requirement will apply not only to final decrees after proof but to decrees in absence, decrees by default, summary decrees, interim decrees and decrees for provisional damages.

## Extracts

**1.04**   All orders for extracts shall be made by written application. Applications for extracts in cases in the ordinary court will be lodged in the general civil department and in other cases in the office of the appropriate department and shall specify the dates of the interlocutors to be extracted. Extracts may be ordered at any time after decree has been pronounced but will not be issued until after the appropriate statutory period has elapsed. The party applying for extract shall be responsible for lodging the process if it is not in the custody of the sheriff clerk at the time when extract may lawfully be issued. The extractor shall not be bound to issue extract if the whole process is not in his hands, but he may do so if he thinks fit.

## Appeals

**1.05**   If an appeal is taken against an interlocutor to which the sheriff has not appended a note, the person taking the appeal shall, at the time when he marks the appeal, add a request that the sheriff write a note.

**1.06**   When, following a proof, an appeal is marked against an interlocutor of a sheriff which has been issued before the notes of evidence are extended and lodged in process, the appellant's solicitor shall, except in a case to which Para 1.08 below applies, inform the shorthand writer forthwith that the notes of evidence are required, and ascertain from him the date when they will be available. When the appeal is to the sheriff principal, the appellant's solicitor shall thereafter inform the sheriff principal's clerk of the date when the notes of evidence will be available in order that an appropriate diet may be fixed for hearing the appeal.

**1.07**   Failure by the appellant or his solicitor to comply with the terms of the two preceding rules, so that there is undue delay in hearing the appeal, or a diet fixed for a hearing is rendered abortive, may be taken into account in determining liability for payment of the expenses of the appeal.

**1.08**   When it appears to the appellant or his solicitor that the grounds of appeal are such that it is unnecessary to have the notes of evidence available for the hearing of the appeal, a written application may be made to the Sheriff Principal to dispense with the requirement of Para 1.06 above. Such application shall be intimated to the other parties to the appeal. The Sheriff Principal will determine the application with or without hearing parties and his decision shall be final in the proceedings before him.

**1.09**   Within 7 days of an appeal being marked, any party who considers that the time required for hearing of the appeal is likely to exceed one day shall indicate that fact in writing to the Sheriff Principal's Personal Secretary, and shall provide an estimate of the number of days required.

**1.10** When it is intended to refer to, or rely on, authorities or list books at the appeal hearing, parties shall lodge not later than 5 working days before the date of the hearing *either* a list of such authorities and textbooks, or a bundle containing photocopies of such authorities and relevant textbooks passages. Parties should consult with each other when preparing such bundles to avoid duplication.

**1.11** At the hearing of the appeal parties may hand up written submissions or skeleton arguments where they would expedite the hearing of the appeal. Copies of such submissions or arguments must be immediately available to opponents. Submissions which include figures or mathematical calculations should be reduced to writing and handed up.

**1.12** Where amendments to findings-in-fact are proposed, a written note of proposals should always be provided, either as part of a written submission as provided by Para 1.11 above, or separately.

# PART II
## AFFIDAVITS IN FAMILY ACTIONS

### When affidavits may be lodged

**2.01** Once the period within which a notice of intention to defend (in the Sheriff Court) or defences (in Court of Session) require to be lodged has expired, without such notice or defences having been lodged, affidavits may be prepared and lodged without such notice or defences having been lodged, affidavits may be prepared and lodged without any order of the court.

### Person before whom sworn or affirmed

**2.02** An affidavit is admissible if it is sworn (or affirmed) before a notary public, justice of the peace, or any person having authority to administer oaths for the place where the affidavit is sworn, such as a commissioner for oaths or a British diplomatic officer or consul abroad. A solicitor acting for a party to the action may act in a notarial capacity when an affidavit is sworn. Any person before whom an affidavit is sworn (referred to below as "the notary") must observe all the normal rules in this connection and must satisfy himself or herself as to the capacity of the witness to swear an affidavit.

### Importance of affidavits

**2.03** The witness should be made to appreciate the importance of the affidavit and that the affidavit constitutes his or her evidence in the case. The possible consequences of giving false evidence should be explained to the witness. Before the witness signs the affidavit he or she must have read it or the notary must have read it over to the witness.

### Oath or affirmation

**2.04** The witness must be placed on oath or must affirm.

### Form and signature of the affidavit

**2.05** The document should be on A4 paper. The affidavit should commence with the words "At the (insert date) day of (insert month) 20, in the presence of 1 (insert name) having been solemnly sworn/having affirmed give evidence as follows:" The affidavit should be drafted in the first person and should take the form of numbered paragraphs. The full name, age, address and occupation of the witness should be given in the first paragraph. The affidavit should end with the words "All of which is the truth as I shall answer to God" or "All of which is affirmed by me to be true", as appropriate. Any blanks in the affidavit must be filled in. Any insertion, deletion or other amendment to the affidavit requires to be initialled by the witness and the notary. Each page must be signed by both the witness and the notary. It is not necessary for the affidavit to be sealed by the notary.

### Drafting the affidavit

**2.06**  An affidavit should be based on a reliable and full precognition of the witness.

**2.07**  The drafter of an affidavit should provide himself or herself, before drawing it, with an up-to-date copy of the pleadings, a copy of the appropriate precognition and the relative productions. The affidavit should be drawn so as to follow the averments in the pleadings to the extent that these are within the knowledge of that particular witness and in the same order.

**2.08**  Affidavits should be expressed in the words of the person whose affidavit it is, should be accurate as at the date of the affidavit and should not consist of a repetition of passages in the pleadings. It should be clear from the terms of the affidavit whether the witness is speaking from his other own knowledge, as to when the witness was present and saw what happened, or whether the witness is relying on what he or she was told by a particular person.

### Productions

**2.09**  Productions already lodged in process must be borrowed up, and put to the party or to the witness who refers to them in his or her affidavit. Each production will require to be referred to in the affidavit by its number of process and must be docqueted and signed by the witness and the notary. If a production has not yet been lodged when the affidavit is sworn, it will require to be identified by the witness in the affidavit, should be docqueted with regard to the affidavit and signed by the witness and the notary. It must then be lodged as a production. Some productions will necessarily be docqueted with regard to more than one affidavit.

**2.10**  In consent cases, the defender's written consent form will have to be put to the pursuer in his or her affidavit, and be identified, docqueted and signed in the same way as other productions.

**2.11**  In adultery cases, photographs of both the pursuer and the defender may require to be produced, put to the appropriate witness and be identified, docqueted and signed in the manner already described.

### Date of affidavit

**2.12**  All affidavits lodged must be of recent date. This factory is particularly important in cases involving children, cases in which financial craves are involved and in other circumstances where the evidence of a witness or circumstances to which the witness speaks are liable to change through the passage of time. The notary must take particular care in such cases to ensure that the affidavit evidence as to such matters is correct as at the time the affidavit is sworn. Affidavits relating to the welfare of children which have been sworn more than three months prior to lodging a minute for decree are likely to be rejected by the court as out of date.

## Applications relating to parental responsibilities and rights (see RCS 49.28. OCR 33.28)

**2.13** In actions in which an application in terms of Section 11 of the Children (Scotland) Act 1995 is before the court not fewer than two affidavits dealing with the welfare of the child(ren) should be provided, at least one of them from a person who is neither a parent nor a party to the action. These affidavits should present the court with a full picture of the arrangements for the care of the child(ren) along the lines set out in paragraph 15, adapted to suit the circumstances of the particular case. The affidavits should set out reasons why it is better that the Section 11 order be made than not. The pursuer's affidavit should deal fully with the arrangements which have been made for their care, so far as within his or her knowledge. If the pursuer cannot give substantial evidence as to that it is likely to be necessary to obtain such evidence from the person who is responsible for their care.

**2.14** In actions of divorce, judicial separation or nullity of marriage in which there are children of the marriage or children treated by the parties as a child of their family but in which no order in terms of Section 11 of the Children (Scotland0) Act 1995 is sought, the court, in terms of Section 12, requires to consider whether to exercise the powers set out in Sections 11 or 54 of that Act in light of the information before it as the arrangements for the child(ren)'s upbringing,. Information accordingly requires to be before the court as to these arrangements. As a minimum, the affidavits of the witnesses should include the information set out in paragraphs 15(a) to (e) below.

**2.15** An affidavit dealing with the arrangements for the care of children should, where relevant, include the following:
- (a) the qualification of the witness, if not a parent, to speak about the child; how often, and in what circumstances the witness normally sees the child;
- (b) the ability of those with whom the child lives to provide proper care for him or her;
- (c) observations as to the relationship between the child and the other members of the household, the child's general appearance, interests, state of health and well-being;
- (d) a description of the home conditions in which the child lives;
- (e) the arrangements for contact between the child and any parent (and siblings) who do not live in the same household as the child;
- (f) information about the school the child attends; whether the child attends school regularly; and
- (g) details of child care arrangements during working hours, including the arrangements for such are outwith school hours.

## Affidavits relating to disclosure of the whereabouts of children

**2.16** An affidavit sworn or affirmed in compliance with an order to disclose the whereabouts of children (in terms of the Family Law Act 1986, Section 33 and RCS 49.24 or OCR 33.23) will require to be drafted in such a way as to meet the requirements of the court in the circumstances of the particular case. The form of the affidavit should be as above.

## Financial and other ancillary craves

**2.17** Affidavit evidence in support of financial craves is necessary in an undefended action. (See *Ali v Ali* , 2001 S.L.T. 602). Where financial craves are involved, the evidence should be as full, accurate and up-to-date as possible. If the evidence is insufficient the court may require supplementary evidence to be provided. If, after an affidavit has been sworn and the solicitor concerned has parted with it, a material change of circumstances occurs before decree has been granted the court must be informed forthwith. A further affidavit may have to be sworn.

**2.18**   The pursuer should give evidence as to his or her own financial position at the date of the affidavit. Where the pursuer gives evidence in an affidavit as to the financial position of the defender, the affidavit should state the date, as precisely as possible, at which the information was valid. The court must be provided with information which is as up-to-date as possible as to the defender's ability to pay the sums the pursuer is seeking. Where the pursuer cannot obtain recent information as to the defender's means the affidavit should that that is the case but should contain as much material information relating to the defender's means as possible. If the pursuer is unable to provide sufficient evidence to justify the orders concluded for or craved in full, in the minute for decree, after the words "in terms of conclusion(s)/ crave(s) (number(s)…) of the summons/initial writ, there may be added words such as "or such other sum (or sums) as the court may think proper.

**2.19**   Where the pursuer has concluded for or craved a capital sum, an order for the same of the matrimonial home, a periodical allowance, interdict or expenses, for example, and in the minute for decree does not seek decree for one or more of these, the reasons for that should be given in his or her affidavit.

### Joint Minutes

**2.20**   When parties record their agreement in a joint minute as to how financial and other ancillary conclusions or craves should be dealt with by the court, the pursuer's affidavit should refer to the joint minute and indicate that he or she is content that the agreement set out in it should be given effect.

### Minute for Decree

**2.21**   The minute for decree must be signed by counsel or by a solicitor who has examined the affidavits and other documents. That counsel or solicitor takes responsibility therefor, whether or not he or she is the person who drew the summons, initial writ or affidavits. The minute of decree should not be signed seeking decree of divorce, separation or declarator of marriage or nullity of marriage unless the evidence consists of or includes evidence other than that of a party to the marriage (or alleged or purported marriage). [Civil Evidence (Scotland) Act 1988, Section 8(3), *Taylor v Taylor* , 2001 S.C.L.R. 16].

## PART III

## A. ADOPTION OF CHILDREN ETC

### Purpose

**3.01**   The purpose of this Practice Note is to secure the efficient management of contested proceedings in applications for orders declaring children free for adoption, applications for the revocation of such orders, applications for adoption orders, applications for parental responsibilities orders and applications for the variation and discharge of such orders. It is intended to provide Sheriffs and practitioners with practical guidance about the operation of the Adoption (Scotland) Act 1978 ("the 1978 Act"), the Children (Scotland) Act 1995 ("the 1995 Act") and the Act of

Sederunt (Child Care and Maintenance Rules) 1997 ("the Rules") relative to such proceedings. It will be revised in the light of experience and any new primary or secondary legislation.

## Commencement

**3.02** This Practice Note applies to all applications lodged after 5 June 2005.

## Minimum of delay

**3.03** It is the duty of the court to secure that applications for freeing orders are dealt with "as expeditiously as possible with the minimum of delay" (*Lothian Regional Council v A* , 1992 S.L.T. 858 at 861). Such applications require the co-operation of all concerned and firm case management by the Sheriff (*Strathclyde Regional Council v MF* 1997 S.C.L.R. 142 at 143). The same considerations apply to the other applications dealt with in this Practice Note. This Practice Note indicates how Sheriffs and practitioners may best fulfil those responsibilities.

## Identity of Sheriff

**3.04** In the interests of continuity and consistency in management, every stage of each case must, whenever possible, call before the same Sheriff on dates and at times assigned by him or her. If a diet of proof has to be fixed, it will normally be assigned to the sheriff who has conducted the previous hearings unless, exceptionally, an early diet can be made available at which another sheriff is free to preside.

## Representatives

**3.05** At every calling of each case any representative of any party must be familiar with the case and must have sufficient authority to deal with any issues that are likely to arise.

## Record of discussion to be kept

**3.06** At every hearing prior to any proof it is the responsibility of the Sheriff not only to pronounce an interlocutor regulating further procedure but also to prepare and keep with the process a brief written record of the main points of the discussion at that hearing.

## B. APPLICATION FOR AN ORDER DECLARING A CHILD FREE FOR ADOPTION

**3.1.1** Section 25A of the 1978 Act provides that in proceedings in which the question arises as to whether the court is satisfied that the agreement of a parent or guardian should be dispensed with, the court must do the following "with a view to determining the question without delay". First, it must draw up a timetable specifying periods within which certain steps must be taken. Secondly, it must give such directions as it considers appropriate for the purpose of ensuring, so far as reasonably practicable, that the timetable is adhered to.

**3.1.2** This Practice Note emphasises the duty of the Sheriff to draw up timetables and the importance of adherence to these timetables. However, the programming of all classes of business in the courts remains exclusively the responsibility of the Sheriff Principal. In this respect he generally acts through the Sheriff Clerk. It is therefore essential that the drawing up of timetables and the assigning of diets by the Sheriff should be undertaken only after consultation with, and with the agreement of, the Sheriff Clerk. Any timetable that is drawn up must be adhered to, unless in exceptional circumstances.

**3.1.3**   Rule 2.4 of the Rules requires the court to draw up the timetable "forthwith" in three situations: (1) where the petition craves the agreement of a parent or guardian to be dispensed with; or (2) where it appears from a report by an adoption agency, local authority or reporting officer that a question as to dispensing with such agreement arises; or (3) such agreement previously given is withdrawn. Where the parent or guardian agrees to the making of an adoption order in terms of section 18(1)(a) of the Act, no timetable is necessary. A timetable is necessary, however, where the agreement of the parent or guardian has not been secured, even if he or she takes no part in the proceedings (as in *T, Petitioner* , 1997 S.L.T. 724).

**3.1.4**   In many freeing cases situation (1) will apply. In such a case, in order to comply with rule 2.4 the timetable should be drawn up at the same time as the interlocutor appointing the curator ad litem and the reporting officer in terms of rule 2.7(1) which must be pronounced after the petition is lodged. It will usually be too early, however, to draw up a detailed timetable at this stage because the areas of dispute, the availability of legal aid, documents and witnesses, and other matters with a bearing on the progress of the case will not yet be known. The timetable at this stage should therefore only specify the date by which the reports of the curator ad litem and the reporting officer should be lodged. The curator ad litem and the reporting officer must generally report within four weeks of the date of the interlocutor appointing them (rule 2.8(1), (2)).

**3.1.5**   The Sheriff may select a period other than four weeks since he or she has a discretion to select a period other than four weeks for the lodging of the reports. Before selecting any other period the Sheriff may wish to consult the curator ad litem and the reporting officer. If selecting any other period it is necessary to keep in view the court's duty to determine "without delay" the question whether consent should be dispensed with.

**3.1.6**   When the reports of the curator ad litem and the reporting officer have been received, the Sheriff must order a diet of hearing to be fixed (rule 2.11(1)). This is the hearing referred to below (see paragraph 3.1) as "the first hearing". It should be fixed after consultation with, and with the agreement of, the Sheriff Clerk (see paragraph 2.2), for a date some two weeks ahead. The Sheriff should consider the advisability of ordering intimation by sheriff officer in order to avoid any possible delay due to ineffective postal service.

**3.1.7**   The Sheriff Clerk should advise the petitioners' solicitors forthwith of the terms of the interlocutor appointing the date of the first hearing in order that they may intimate it as soon as possible.

### First hearing

**3.2.1**   The first hearing provides the first opportunity for all interested parties to be present or represented and for the court to fix a further timetable. The drawing up of a further firm and realistic timetable or timetables and the need for adherence to them will be of central importance to the efficient management of the later stages of the case, as will appear from later paragraphs.

**3.2.2**   The object of the first hearing is to enable the Sheriff to make preliminary inquiries with a view to ascertaining the likely scope of the dispute, encouraging early preparation for the proof and drawing up a timetable and giving such directions as he or she considers appropriate for the purpose of ensuring, so far as reasonably practicable, that the timetable is adhered to.

### Before the first hearing

**3.2.3** Before the first hearing, and throughout the proceedings, the Sheriff should be prepared to engage in active management of the case. He or she should maintain control over the proceedings while exercising flexibility in doing so.

**3.2.4** He or she should have read the report lodged by the local authority which accompanies the petition, and checked that it contains the information required by rule 2.5(2)(b).

**3.2.5** The Sheriff should also have read the reports of the curator ad litem and the reporting officer and checked that they similarly comply with rule 2.8(1) and (2).

**3.2.6** The Sheriff should also have read any other documents lodged by the petitioners in terms of rule 2.5(2)(c). These may include a report by a children's hearing received in terms of section 73(14) of the 1995 Act.

**3.2.7** The Sheriff should have checked that intimation of the hearing has been made as required by rule 2.11(2).

**3.2.8** Where the child has indicated a wish to express a view, the Sheriff should consider ordering appropriate procedural steps in terms of rule 2.9(1)(a). Such steps may include interviewing the child.

**3.2.9** The solicitor for a party who has received intimation of the first hearing may apply to the court for access before the first hearing to any document which has been lodged. (See also paragraph 3.3.4 below.)

### At the first hearing

**3.2.10** At the first hearing the attention of the Sheriff and all parties should be devoted to securing that the issues at the proof will be as sharply focused as possible. The parties should therefore have considered in general terms how they intend to prove their respective cases.

**3.2.11** The Sheriff should ask the respondent or his or her solicitor to indicate in general terms the grounds of his or her opposition to the petition, without prejudice to the right of the respondent to state further or different grounds later.

**3.2.12** The Sheriff should ask the respondent or his or her solicitor whether the respondent has applied, or proposes to apply, for legal aid. If so, the respondent should be able to give the Sheriff at least as much information about the grounds of opposition as has been or will be given to the Scottish Legal Aid Board.

**3.2.13** The Sheriff should ask the respondent or his or her solicitor whether it is intended to instruct counsel or any expert witness and, if so, whether legal aid for that purpose has been or is to be applied for.

**3.2.14** The Sheriff should ensure that the parties have sufficient access to all the documents lodged in process (see also paragraph 3.2.6 above). A party's solicitor is entitled to copies of such documents so long as he or she complies with rule 2.12 by treating the documents and any copies as confidential.

**3.2.15** The Sheriff should ask the respondent or his or her solicitor whether they will be seeking to recover other documents and, if so, which documents. The Sheriff should ask the petitioners' solicitor if the petitioners will make these available to the respondent informally without the need for a commission and diligence, and if so, should fix a date by which those documents should be lodged with the court.

**3.2.16** It is now for the Sheriff to draw up the timetable and determine further procedure after consultation with, and with the agreement of, the Sheriff Clerk. In many cases it will be advantageous to appoint a second hearing and thereafter a pre-proof hearing, as recommended in the following paragraphs. In other cases, however, the Sheriff may in the exercise of his or her discretion dispense with either or both of those hearings. For example, in a very simple case the Sheriff may instead continue the first hearing for a short period in order that any outstanding matters may be addressed and then, if satisfied that the issues in dispute have been clearly identified and the preparations for proof will be simple and straightforward, obtain the parties' estimates of the duration of the proof and assign a diet of proof (as in paragraphs 3.3.4 to 3.3.6 below).

**3.2.17** If the Sheriff decides that a second hearing is appropriate, he or she should advise the parties that he or she is now going to fix a second hearing; and that before the second hearing they must have lodged the minute of disputed issues and joint minute referred to in paragraphs 3.2.1 and 3.2.2, and must be prepared to give the Sheriff the information referred to below.

**3.2.18** The date fixed for the second hearing should normally be no more than six weeks after the date of the first hearing. If it has not been possible for the Sheriff to identify with the Sheriff Clerk, before the first hearing, a suitable date and time for the second hearing, the Sheriff should now adjourn briefly for that purpose.

### Second hearing

**3.3.1** The object of the second hearing is to make further preparations for the proof, to identify clearly the issues in dispute and to avoid having a lengthy and poorly focused proof. "The principal duty of representatives in adoption proceedings is to identify the issues in dispute, and to lead evidence in relation to those issues." (Macphail, *Sheriff Court Practice* (2nd ed), vol 1, p.931, para.28. 111.) The following guidance assists the parties' representatives to carry out that duty.

### Before the second hearing

*The statement of disputed issues*

**3.3.2** Before the hearing the respondent's solicitor should have prepared a statement of disputed issues. It should be signed and lodged at least seven working days before the hearing. It should specify the matters in the local authority's report which the respondent disputes, and should refer to the numbered paragraphs of the report in which these matters are stated. It should also specify any other issues which are not mentioned in the report but which the respondent intends to raise at the proof.

*The Joint Minute*

**3.3.3** Before the hearing the parties should have entered into a joint minute. It is the responsibility of the petitioners' solicitor to draft the joint minute and send it to the respondent's solicitor for revisal. The petitioners' solicitor may use as a basis of the joint minute the material facts in the local authority's report which are considered not to be controversial. The parties' solicitors are expected to co-operate in the framing of the joint minute. It should be signed and lodged at least two working days before the hearing.

*Consideration of legal issues, evidence and proof dates*

**3.3.4**   Before the hearing the parties' solicitors should consider the matters mentioned in paragraphs 3.3.1 to 3.3.5 below in order that they may provide the Sheriff with sufficient information to enable him or her to conduct the second hearing as provided for in these paragraphs. A solicitor who intends to raise a legal issue at the second hearing should intimate it to the other parties' solicitors beforehand.

## At the second hearing

*Consideration of joint minute and statement*

**3.3.5**   At the hearing the Sheriff should consider with the parties the contents of the joint minute and the statement of disputed issues. If necessary, the Sheriff will ask whether further facts can be agreed by joint minute. He or she may also seek clarification of any matter in the statement of disputed issues. If it appears to the Sheriff that a matter identified in the statement is not a relevant issue, although it is disputed, he or she may indicate that evidence on that matter will not be admitted at the proof.

### Legal issues

**3.3.6**   The Sheriff should ask the parties if there are any questions of admissibility of evidence or any other legal issues, including any questions under the European Convention on Human Rights, that are likely to arise at the proof. If so, the Sheriff should consider whether they could with advantage be determined at this hearing rather than at the proof. Alternatively, the Sheriff may continue the second hearing to another date in order to enable any such issue to be argued and determined. If a legal issue is not raised at the second hearing, the Sheriff may refuse to allow it to be raised at the proof except on cause shown.

### Evidence

**3.3.7**   It should be noted that evidence may be presented in the form of affidavits or other written documents (Civil Evidence (Scotland) Act 1988, section 2; *McVinnie v McVinnie* , 1995 S.L.T. (Sh Ct) 81; *Glaser v Glaser* , 1997 S.L.T. 456). The Sheriff is bound to consider reports placed before him or her even if the authors are not called to speak to them, and the strict rules of evidence do not apply (*T, Petitioner* , 1997 S.L.T. 724 at 730L). Such considerations may render the attendance of certain witnesses unnecessary, although for other reasons it may be preferable to call the author of a document. The parties should therefore apply their minds to the question whether any evidence might be appropriately presented in the form of an affidavit or other document and encourage them to decide that question at this hearing. The Sheriff should encourage the use of affidavits to cover contentious issues where that would save the time of witnesses and the court.

**3.3.8**   Where the author of a report or the maker of a statement which has been or is to be lodged is to be called as a witness, the Sheriff should order that the report is to be held to be equivalent to the witness's examination-in-chief, unless for special reasons he or she otherwise directs.

**3.3.9**   The Sheriff should discourage the unnecessary use of expert witnesses. If expert evidence is essential, the Sheriff should encourage the joint instruction of a single expert by all parties. If one party instructs an expert report, it should be disclosed to the other parties with a view to the agreement of as much of its contents as possible.

**3.3.10**  The Sheriff should ask the parties what further productions, if any, they intend to lodge. Any difficulties over the obtaining or lodging of documents should be raised and if possible resolved.

### Estimate of duration of proof

**3.3.11**  "It is essential ... that the Sheriff should be given at the outset a carefully considered forecast of the time which the proof is expected to take." (*Lothian Regional Council v A*, at 861L.) It is therefore very important that the parties should pay close attention to this matter. The Sheriff should ask each party to specify in detail how long he expects to take in the presentation of his own evidence and in the cross-examination of the other side's witnesses. On the basis of that information the Sheriff will assess how many days should be set aside for the proof (including closing submissions). At the proof, parties may expect to be held to the estimates given at this hearing, unless in exceptional circumstances

### Assigning the diet of proof

**3.3.12**  Having assessed how many days are needed for the proof, the Sheriff will assign the diet. He or she should do so at the hearing after consultation with, and with the agreement of, the Sheriff Clerk. The Sheriff may adjourn briefly for that purpose. The dates assigned should be consecutive working days. The Sheriff should consider whether he or she is likely to require any writing days in order to produce the judgment. If so, the dates assigned should include writing time. The reason for such arrangements is that the Sheriff should "be released from other duties so that he can give priority to the case without interruption and until it has been completed by the issuing of his interlocutor. Special arrangements of that kind are clearly necessary if the sheriff is to maintain the continuity of thought throughout the proceedings which is so necessary to a proper disposal of the case." (*Lothian Regional Council v A*, at 862A-B).

**3.3.13**  The parties should have come to the hearing with a list of dates when their witnesses, including any expert witnesses, and counsel, if any, will be available. It is not generally a valid ground for postponing a proof that a party wishes to instruct particular counsel. The Sheriff should not, unless in highly exceptional circumstances, pronounce an interlocutor allowing a proof on dates to be afterwards fixed. If the dates cannot be fixed at the hearing, it will usually be preferable to continue the hearing for a few days and fix the dates at the continued hearing.

### Assigning the pre-proof hearing

**3.3.14**  The Sheriff should also assign a pre-proof hearing on a date some two weeks before the proof. The date and time of the hearing should be selected after consultation with, and with the agreement of, the Sheriff Clerk.

**3.3.15**  In addition to assigning the pre-proof hearing the Sheriff should assign a date two weeks prior to the pre-proof hearing by which the parties must have lodged their productions and exchanged list of the witnesses who are to give oral evidence.

*Pre-proof hearing*

**3.4.1**   The purpose of the pre-proof hearing is to ascertain whether the parties are still in dispute and, if so, whether they are fully prepared for proof. The timetable must, however, be respected and a proof will be discharged only in highly exceptional circumstances.

*The Proof*

**3.5.1**   If the guidance above is followed, the proof should not be unduly long. In any event, "there is a heavy responsibility on the parties' representatives to exercise all reasonable economy and restraint in their presentation of the evidence and in their submissions to the court." (*Lothian Regional Council v A* at 862B).

**3.5.2**   Parties may expect to be held to their estimates of time taken for examination and cross-examination which they gave at the second hearing.

**3.5.3**   The Sheriff may exercise his or her existing common law power to intervene to discourage prolixity, repetition, the leading of evidence of unnecessary witnesses and the leading of evidence on matters which are unlikely to assist the court to reach a decision.

**3.5.4**   If the proof is not completed on the last day assigned, it is very desirable that it should continue on the following day.

**3.5.5**   Before the hearing on evidence, the Sheriff may require the parties to submit, in electronic form or otherwise, draft findings in fact, or skeleton arguments, or both.

*The Judgment*

**3.6.1**   The judgment should be issued within four weeks of the date of the making of *avizandum*.

## C. REVOCATION OF FREEING ORDERS

**3.7.1**   Part A of this Practice Note applies to contested applications for the revocation of freeing orders.

**3.7.2**   Paragraphs 3.2.1 to 3.6.1 of this Practice Note, with the exception of paragraph 3.2.4, apply to contested applications for the revocation of freeing orders mutatis mutandis, subject to paragraphs 3.7.3 to 3.7.5.

**3.7.3**   In paragraph 3.2.1 there shall be inserted at the beginning:
"Rule 2.18(1) requires the Sheriff to order a diet of hearing to be fixed when answers have been lodged under rule 2.15(3)."

**3.7.4**   For paragraph 3.2.5 there shall be substituted:
"The Sheriff should have read the report by any curator ad litem appointed in terms of ule 2.16(1) and checked that it complies with that rule."

**3.7.5**   In paragraph 3.2.7, for the reference to rule 2.11(2) there shall be substituted a reference to rule 2.15(2).

## D. ADOPTION ORDERS

**3.8.1**   Part A of this Practice Note applies to contested applications for adoption orders.

**3.8.2**   Part B of this Practice Note applies to contested applications for adoption orders, mutatis mutandis, subject to paragraphs 3.8.3 to 3.8.7.

**3.8.3**   In paragraph 3.1.2 there shall be added at the end:
"If no report by an adoption agency or local authority has been lodged with the petition, the Sheriff must pronounce an interlocutor requiring such a report to be lodged within four weeks or such other period as the Sheriff may allow: rule 2.21(5)."

**3.8.4**   In paragraph 3.1.4, for the reference to rule 2.7(1) there shall be substituted a reference to rule 2.25(1), and for the reference to rule 2.8(1),(2) a reference to rule 2.26(1),(2).

**3.8.5**   In paragraph 3.2.1 there shall be inserted at the beginning:
"Rule 2.28(1) requires the Sheriff to fix 'a diet of hearing' on receipt of the reports of the reporting officer and curator ad litem in respect of a child who is not free for adoption. Rule 2.28(2) provides that the Sheriff may fix 'a diet of hearing' on receipt of the report of the curator ad litem in respect of a child who is free for adoption. The hearing referred to above as 'the first hearing' is any diet of hearing fixed in terms of either of these rules."

**3.8.6**   For paragraph 3.2.4 there shall be substituted:
"3.2.4 He or she should have read all the reports and other papers lodged with the petition and will have checked that a report by the local authority or adoption agency contains the information required by rule 2.21(3). The other papers may include a report by a children's hearing received in terms of section 73(14) of the 1995 Act and, where the child has not been placed for adoption with the applicant by an adoption agency, a medical report (rule 2.21(2)(c))."

**3.8.7**   In paragraph 3.2.5, for the reference to rule 2.8(1) and (2) there shall be substituted a reference to rule 2.26(1) and (2).

**3.8.8**   In paragraph 3.2.7, for the reference to rule 2.11(2) there shall be substituted a reference to rule 2.28(3).

**3.8.9**   In paragraph 3.2.14 for the reference to rule 2.12 there shall be substituted a reference to rule 2.30.

### E. PARENTAL RESPONSIBIIITIES ORDERS

**3.9.1**   Part A of this Practice Note applies to contested applications for parental responsibilities orders.

**3.9.2**   Part B of this Practice Note applies to contested applications for parental responsibilities orders, mutatis mutandis, subject to paragraphs 3.9.3 to 3.9.7.

**3.9.3**   In paragraph 3.1.4, for the reference to rule 2.7(1) there shall be substituted a reference to rule 2.39(1), and for the reference to rule 2.8(1),(2) a reference to rule 2.40(1),(2).

**3.9.4**   In paragraph 3.2.1 there shall be inserted at the beginning:
"Rule 2.42(1) requires the Sheriff to fix a 'diet of hearing' on receipt of the reports of the reporting officer and curator ad litem."

**3.9.5**   For paragraph 3.2.4 there shall be substituted:

"3.2.4 He or she should have read any report by a children's hearing received in terms of section 73(14) of the 1995 Act and any reports and other papers lodged by the local authority with the application."

**3.9.6** In paragraph 3.2.5, for the reference to rule 2.8(1),(2) there shall be substituted a reference to rule 2.40(1),(2).

**3.9.7** In paragraph 3.2.7, for the reference to rule 2.11(2) there shall be substituted a reference to rule 2.42(2).

## F. VARIATION AND DISCHARGE OF PARENTAL RESPONSIBILITIES ORDERS

**3.10.1** Part A of this Practice Note applies to contested applications for the variation and discharge of parental responsibilities orders.

**3.10.2** Paragraphs 3.2.1 to 3.6.1 of this Practice Note, with the exception of paragraph 3.2.4, applies to contested applications for the variation and discharge of parental responsibilities orders mutatis mutandis, subject to paragraphs 3.10.3 to 3.10.5.

**3.10.3** In paragraph 3.2.1 there shall be inserted at the beginning:
"Rule 2.42(1), as applied by rule 2.44(5), requires the Sheriff to order a diet of hearing to be fixed when the report of any curator ad litem appointed under rule 2.44(3) has been received."

**3.10.4** For paragraph 3.2.5 there shall be substituted:
"The Sheriff should have read the report of any curator ad litem appointed in terms of rule 2.44(3) and checked that it complies with that rule."

**3.10.5** In paragraph 3.2.7, for the reference to rule 2.11(2) there shall be substituted a reference to rule 2.44(6).

## PART IV
## FATAL ACCIDENT INQUIRIES

**4.01** When fixing a time and place for the holding by him of an inquiry in terms of Section 3(1)(a) of the Fatal Accidents and Sudden Deaths Inquiry (Scotland) Act 1976, the sheriff shall assign a date for a preliminary hearing which will be held four weeks before the date fixed for the inquiry

**4.02** The preliminary hearing shall be intimated at the same time and in the same manner as intimation of the date for the inquiry in terms of Section 3(2)(b) of the above mentioned Act and Rule 4 of the Fatal Accident and Sudden Deaths Inquiry Rules 1977.

**4.03** At the preliminary hearing the sheriff shall ascertain from the parties or their representatives, so far as is reasonably practicable, whether the inquiry is likely to proceed on the date assigned and in addition shall take steps to identify:

(a) the likely length of the inquiry and whether it can be concluded within the time allocated;
(b) the state of preparation of the parties or their representatives;
(c) the availability of witnesses;
(d) the issues which are likely to be raised at the Inquiry;
(e) evidence that may be led by affidavit in terms of Rule 10 of the above mentioned Rules and any evidence that can be agreed;

(f)    special arrangements for bulky/voluminous productions;

(g)    whether evidence should be recorded by mechanical means or by use of a shorthand writer;

(h)    the order of parties' cross-examination of witnesses;

(i)    whether there are any other parties on whom intimation of proceedings should be made;

(j)    any other matter any party wishes to raise.

**4.04**    At the conclusion of the preliminary hearing the sheriff may either continue the case to the diet fixed for the inquiry or discharge the diet fixed for inquiry and fix a new diet. In the event that a new diet is fixed the sheriff may assign a further preliminary hearing.

## PROOF ASSIGNMENT ARRANGEMENTS IN ORDINARY ACTIONS

D3.2

### [JULY 29, 1999]

With effect from 4 October 1999, the practice of assigning all diets of proof in ordinary actions administratively, shall be discontinued. From that date, diets of proof requiring 5 days or less shall be fixed in court at the time proof is allowed. Parties or their legal representatives will in consequence require to attend an options hearing (under OCR 9.12) or a procedural hearing (under OCR 10.6) in a position ready to provide the court with a meaningful estimate of the duration of the proof and such other information, for example on the availability of witnesses, necessary to enable a diet to be fixed.

In cases where the court is satisfied that a diet in excess of 5 days is necessary, the Sheriff Clerk will fix and intimate a diet within 2 weeks of the allowance of proof having regard to any information provided by parties at the options or procedural hearing.

In cases where diets of proof are allowed prior to 4 October, proof assignment sheets should be returned in accordance with existing practice.

This practice shall also apply to diets of proof in summary applications.

## COMMERCIAL CASES

D3.3

### [OCTOBER 4, 1999]

Notwithstanding the general requirement that solicitors appearing professionally at the bar of all courts in Open Session are expected to wear a gown, there shall be no such requirement in relation to commercial cases during options hearings and other hearings of a procedural nature. Those appearing at such hearings may be seated unless the presiding sheriff otherwise directs. For the avoidance of doubt gowns should continue to be worn during the hearing of debates and proofs in commercial cases.

This practice takes effect on 6 October 1999 and supplements the provisions made in respect of commercial cases continued in the Practice Note of July 1999.

# ACT OF COURT (CONSOLIDATION) 2005

[JUNE 5, 2005]

I, EDWARD FARQUHARSON BOWEN, Queen's Counsel, Sheriff Principal of Glasgow and Strathkelvin, in respect that many of the Acts of Court in force within this Sheriffdom are spent or in need of modernisation, hereby repeal all Acts of Court other than those listed in the Schedule hereto and direct that the following will be given effect on or after 5 June 2005.

(Sgd) E F Bowen

## PART 1

## STANDING ADVISORY COMMITTEE

### Functions of the Committee

**1.01**  The Committee shall give consideration to any matter affecting the efficiency of the administrative arrangements of the Sheriff Court in Glasgow, which they are asked by any of the Constituents or by any member of the Committee to take into consideration, and shall make such recommendations as they think proper from time to time with regard to such matters to the Constituents or to any of them. Any such recommendation shall be communicated in writing by the Secretary to the Constituents or Constituent concerned.

### Constitution

**1.02**  The Committee shall consist of three sheriffs nominated by the Sheriff Principal of Glasgow and Strathkelvin, two solicitors nominated by the Dean of the Royal Faculty of Procurators in Glasgow, two solicitors nominated by the President of the Glasgow Bar Association, one solicitor nominated by the Dean of Strathkelvin Association of Solicitors, two persons of the rank of Assistant Procurator Fiscal or Procurator Fiscal Depute nominated by the Area Procurator Fiscal of Glasgow and Strathkelvin, two persons of the rank of Sheriff Clerk Depute nominated by the Sheriff Clerk of Glasgow and Strathkelvin, one person of the rank of Inspector nominated by the Chief Constable of Strathclyde Police, one person of the rank of Authority Reporter nominated by the Reporter Manager, Glasgow, one person nominated by the Director of Social Work, Glasgow and the co-ordinator of the Glasgow Sheriff Court Witness Service. The Chairman shall be the senior sheriff present at any meeting and, failing the attendance of a sheriff, the person elected to as Chairman by the members present at the meeting. In the event of equality of votes with regard to any proposed recommendations, the Chairman for the time being shall have a casting vote. The Secretary of the Committee shall be a Sheriff Clerk Depute appointed by the Sheriff Clerk of Glasgow and Strathkelvin to perform that office. The Sheriff Principal of Glasgow and Strathkelvin, the Dean of the Royal Faculty of Procurators in Glasgow, the President of the Glasgow Bar Association, the Dean of Strathkelvin Association of Solicitors, the Area Procurator Fiscal of Glasgow and Strathkelvin, the Sheriff Clerk of Glasgow and Strathkelvin, the Chief Constable of Strathclyde Police and the Reporter Manager, Glasgow are hereinafter referred to as "the Constituents".

**Appointment of Secretary and Nomination and period of service of members:**

**1.03** The name of the person appointed to be the Secretary shall be intimated to the Constituents by the Sheriff Clerk of Glasgow and Strathkelvin, and similar intimation will be made on the occasion of any change in an appointment. The names and addresses of the persons nominated as members of the Committee shall be sent to the Secretary by the Constituents on or before 31 March, in each year. The members will serve for one year from the first day of May following their nomination and they may be re-nominated for further periods of service. In the event of the death or resignation of a member during his/her period of service, another person shall be nominated by his/her Constituents to replace him/her for the remainder of the period. So far as the nominated solicitors are concerned, the appointees may authorise another solicitor to attend a meeting of the Committee on their behalf.

### Dates and place of meetings etc:

**1.04** Meetings will be held during each Session of the Court at times and places to be determined by the Committee. Members of the Committee will inform the Secretary, a fortnight before each meeting, of matters to be included in the agenda, and the Secretary will send a copy of the agenda, together with a draft minute of any previous meeting, to each member a week before the meeting. Additional meetings may be held if the Committee so resolves, and the Committee may appoint subcommittees from time to time which will exercise the functions delegated to them by the Constituents. Persons other than members may be invited to meetings of the Committee or of sub-committees and to take part in their discussions.

## PART 2

## SIGNING OF INTERLOCUTORS

### Signing of interlocutors

**2.01** The classes of interlocutor which a sheriff clerk may write and sign in terms of rule 12 of the Rules contained in the First Schedule annexed to the Act of Sederunt (Sheriff Court Ordinary Cause Rules) 1993 shall not include any final interlocutor or any interlocutor which the sheriff concerned directs to be written or signed by him or her. Subject to the foregoing, an interlocutor dealing with a motion which has been determined by a sheriff clerk in terms of rule 15.4(2) shall be written and signed by that sheriff clerk.

**2.02** The classes of unopposed motions which a sheriff clerk may determine in terms of the said rule 15.4(2) are set out below.
   (a)   A motion to authorise re-service of an initial writ in terms of rule 5.9.
   (b)   A motion to recall a sist and to re-enrol a cause for further procedure.
   (c)   A motion, made under rule 10.3(1), to close the record before the expiry of the adjustment period provided by rule 10.1(1).
   (d)   A motion to allow an amendment of a kind specified in rule 18.1.
   (e)   A motion to allow a minute of amendment to be received and answered within a specified period in terms of rule 18.3(1)(a) and (b)(ii).
   (f)   A motion for an order for service of a third party notice, made under rule 20.1(1) and (2).
   (g)   A motion for the fixing of a peremptory diet following withdrawal from agency under Rule 24.2.(1).

## PART 3
### PRACTICE BY SOLICITORS

**3.01** Solicitors who appear professionally at the Bar of all courts in open session, other than before the nominated Commercial Sheriff in a commercial action so defined by OCR 40.5 or in any appeal to the Sheriff Principal in such cause, shall wear gowns.

### Schedule

Any Act of Court anent Court Holidays.
Any Act of Court anent Sessions and Vacation Courts.

# PRACTICE NOTE NO.1 OF 2006: COMMUNICATION WITH COURT

I, James Alastair Taylor, Sheriff Principal of Glasgow and Strathkelvin, for the purpose of regulating practice in the Sheriff Court at Glasgow in pursuance of the powers conferred under Section 15(2) of the Sheriff Courts (Scotland) Act 1971 and all common law powers enabling in that behalf Order and Direct as follows—

1. Should all parties to an action be in agreement as to the procedure which should be followed at an options hearing or a continued options hearing they should lodge in process a letter or send an email to the sheriff clerk (glasgow@scotcourts.gov.uk) setting out their proposals for further procedure and, where appropriate, showing cause. If such a communication is received by the sheriff clerk on or before 9.30 am on the working day preceding the date for the options hearing or continued options hearing, the communication will be placed before the sheriff assigned to the next day's ordinary court who may give effect to the proposals without the need for a formal hearing. Should the sheriff wish to be addressed, the parties will be informed by the sheriff clerk no later than 3.00 pm on the working day preceding the hearing.

2. Should parties to an action agree upon settlement terms in advance of a hearing (be that a proof, small claim or summary cause hearing, debate, options or continued options hearing) which terms will not be implemented prior to the hearing, they may lodge a joint motion in process or email the sheriff clerk (glasgow@scotcourts.gov.uk) moving that the hearing be discharged and that no further order be made in the case. Should such a motion or email be lodged or sent, and should the sheriff still wish to be addressed, the parties will be so informed by the sheriff clerk no later than 3.00 pm on the working day preceding the hearing.

3. With effect from Monday, 4 September 2006 there will be no miscellaneous procedure roll for civil business in Glasgow Sheriff Court. If it is intimated to the court at or in advance of a hearing (be that a proof, small claim or summary cause hearing, debate, options or continued options hearing) that settlement terms have been agreed but for whatever reason a final interlocutor cannot be pronounced, the court will discharge the hearing and shall pronounce an interlocutor making no further order in the case.

4. If after the closing of the record a party wishes to amend its pleadings, the minute of amendment may take the form of a closed record with the amendment which the party seeks to make indicated by red lining, striking out or some other electronic means. Any answers to a minute of amendment may be presented to the court in the same manner.

5.     If in any action affidavits require to be lodged in process (eg when seeking a power of arrest) such affidavits and the Initial Writ must be lodged in process by 9.30 am on the working day preceding any hearing at which such affidavits will be referred to. Should such affidavits and Initial Writ not be lodged in accordance with this provision, the sheriff will be entitled to adjourn the hearing to a future date.

6.     In all summary applications under the Adults with Incapacity (Scotland) Act 2000—

(a)     the crave of the writ must specify the current address and date of birth of the adult;

(b)     where application is made for the grant of both welfare and financial powers, these must be grouped separately from each other;

(c)     where application is being made for the appointment of Joint Guardians, the writ must contain averments which satisfy the requirements of Section 62(2) of the Act, or enable the court to be so satisfied, as the case may be;

(d)     the writ must contain details of the names and addresses of all known next of kin of the adult, or, if there are no known next of kin, averments to that effect;

(e)     where application is being made for the grant of financial powers, the writ must contain averments as to the known existence or otherwise of any existing Power of Attorney granted by the adult;

(f)     where application is being made for the grant of financial powers, the writ must contain details of the extent and value, if known, of all heritable and moveable property belonging to the adult;

(g)     where an application seeks powers in relation to heritable property, a reference to the Land Registry number, failing which a full conveyancing description, must be provided in the crave of the writ;

(h)     where interim powers are being sought, the writ must contain averments specifying the reasons therefor;

(i)     except in cases where the application seeks the appointment of the Chief Social Worker of a Local Authority, the writ must contain such details as to the character, background, and any relevant financial or investment experience of, any person whose appointment is sought as a guardian, accompanied by such letters of reference as may be thought appropriate, in order that the court can be satisfied as to suitability for appointment;

(j)     pleas in law are not necessary;

(k)     there must be a schedule itemising the names and designations of all those on whom intimation of the application is sought;

(1)     where the court may require the applicant to find caution, steps must be taken in advance of the hearing fixed by the court to make application for such caution and to attempt to secure the processing of any such application, in so far as possible.

July 3, 2006

# PRACTICE NOTE NO.2 OF 2006: SPECIFICATION FOR RECOVERY OF MEDICAL RECORDS

D3.6

*[Revoked by Practice Note No.1 of 2008 (effective April 28, 2008).]*

# PRACTICE NOTE NO.1 OF 2008: SPECIFICATION FOR RECOVERY OF MEDICAL RECORDS

[APRIL 28, 2008]

I, James Alastair Taylor, Sheriff Principal of Glasgow and Strathkelvin, for the purpose of regulating practice in the Sheriff Court at Glasgow in pursuance of the powers conferred under Section 15(2) of the Sheriff Courts (Scotland) Act 1971 and all common law powers enabling in that behalf Order and Direct as follows:
1.  This practice note has effect from 28 April 2008.
2.  For the purpose of Rules 28.2(3)(c) of the Ordinary Cause Rules 1993 and 18.1(3)(b) and 34(2)(6) of the Summary Cause Rules 2002 it is no longer necessary for a copy of a specification or an incidental application for the recovery of medical records to be intimated to the Lord Advocate.
3.  The Practice Note dated 23 October 2006 is hereby revoked.

# PRACTICE NOTE NO.1 OF 2009: DIET ROLL

I, James Alastair Taylor, Sheriff Principal of Glasgow and Strathkelvin, for the purpose of regulating practice in the Sheriff Court at Glasgow in pursuance of the power conferred under Section 15(2) of the Sheriff Courts (Scotland) Act 1971 and all common law powers enabling in that behalf Order and Direct as follows—
1.  With effect from 7 September 2009 there will be no diet roll for civil business in Glasgow Sheriff Court. There will continue to be a roll for Rule 18.3 hearings and for peremptory diet cases. If a diet is not fixed in the course of the hearing when the diet is allowed, agents should write to the Sheriff Clerk intimating suitable dates for the diet within a 3 month period. The Sheriff Clerk will take all reasonable steps to assign the diet to one of the days nominated.

July 6, 2009

# PRACTICE NOTE NO.1 OF 2009: ADOPTION AND CHILDREN (SCOTLAND) ACT 2007: GUIDANCE FOR SHERIFFS AND PRACTITIONERS

## Purpose

1.  The purpose of this Practice Note is to secure the efficient management of contested applications and other proceedings under the Adoption and Children (Scotland) Act 2007 ("the Act"). It should be read subject to the detailed rules of procedure to be found in the Sheriff Court Adoption Rules 2009 ("the Rules")—see the Act of Sederunt (Sheriff Court Rules Amendment) (Adoption and Children (Scotland) Act 2007) 2009 (SSI 2009/284). It will be revised in light of experience and any new primary or secondary legislation.

## Commencement

2.  This Practice Note applies to all applications lodged, or proceedings commenced, on or after 28 September 2009.

## Minimum of delay

**3.** It shall be the duty of the court to secure that all applications and other proceedings under the Act are dealt with as expeditiously as possible and with the minimum of delay. Such applications and proceedings require the co-operation of all concerned and active and firm case management by the sheriff throughout their course.

## Identity of sheriff

**4.** Unless the sheriff principal otherwise agrees, the sheriff presiding at any stage in the proceedings must be a sheriff of this sherrifdom. In the interests of continuity and consistency in management, every stage of each case must, whenever possible, call before the same sheriff.

**5.** In the event that a proof has to be taken by a sheriff other than the sheriff who has conducted the previous hearings, the whole process in the case must be made available to the sheriff who is to take the proof not less than three working days before the date upon which the proof is scheduled to commence.

## Representatives

**6.** At every calling of a case any representative of any party must be familiar with the case and must have sufficient authority to deal with any issues that are likely to arise at that calling.

## Record of discussion to be kept

**7.** At every hearing prior to any proof the sheriff should not only pronounce an interlocutor regulating further procedure but should append a note to the interlocutor providing a brief record of the main points of the discussion at the hearing.

## The application

**8.** Subject to any issue of confidentiality that may arise, wherever possible a copy of the petition or application (as the case may be) should be sent to the sheriff clerk in electronic form on the same date as the date upon which it is lodged. The solicitors in the process should give to the sheriff clerk their respective email addresses.

## The preliminary and pre-proof hearings

**9.** Any preliminary or pre-proof hearing fixed in terms of the Rules should be of sufficient duration to allow for a proper consideration of the issues likely to be canvassed at it. Consideration should be given to the advisability of intimating any such hearing by sheriff officer in order to avoid any possible delay due to ineffective postal service.

**10.** Where the date of a hearing requires to be intimated otherwise than by the sheriff clerk, the sheriff clerk should advise the applicant or petitioner or his or her solicitors forthwith of the terms of the interlocutor appointing the date of the hearing in order that they may intimate it as soon as possible. If so requested (and subject to any issue of confidentiality that may arise), the sheriff clerk should be prepared to send to the applicant or petitioner or his or her solicitors a copy of the interlocutor by fax or in electronic form as soon as it has been signed. Any such request should be accompanied by the appropriate fax, telephone number or email address as the case may be.

**11.** At any preliminary hearing the sheriff should ask the respondent or his or her solicitor whether the respondent has applied, or proposes to apply, for legal aid. The sheriff should also enquire whether it is intended to instruct counsel or any expert witness and, if so, whether legal aid for that purpose has been or is to be applied for.

**12.** The sheriff should ensure that the parties have sufficient access to all the documents lodged in process. The sheriff should ask the parties whether they will be seeking to recover any documents and, if so, which documents. The sheriff should ask the other parties if they will make these available informally without the need for a commission and diligence and, if so, should fix a date by which those documents should be lodged with the court.

**13.** At a preliminary hearing, which failing a pre-proof hearing, the sheriff should give consideration to ordering parties to intimate to every other party and to lodge in process (i) a list of witnesses, including any expert witnesses, on whose evidence it is intended to rely at proof, and (ii) a list of the documents or other productions which it is intended should be used or put in evidence at proof.

### Assigning a diet of proof

**14.** Where it appears that a proof will be necessary, the parties should be in a position to give the sheriff a carefully considered forecast of the time which the proof is expected to take. The sheriff should ask each party to specify in detail how long he expects to take in the presentation of his own evidence and in the cross-examination of the witnesses of the other party or parties. On the basis of this information the sheriff should assess how many days should be set aside for the proof (including closing submissions). At the proof itself, parties may expect to be held to the estimates previously given by them, unless in exceptional circumstances.

**15.** In the fixing of a diet of proof it is not generally a valid ground of objection to a date proposed by the court that a party wishes to instruct particular counsel. If need be, that party can always instruct another counsel.

**16.** Consideration should always be given at an early stage in the proceedings to where the proof will take place and whether the evidence at the proof should be recorded. The holding of a proof elsewhere than at the courthouse may be anticipated to cause administrative problems, for example for the sheriff clerk. But such administrative problems must not be permitted to get in the way of the expeditious disposal of an application or other proceeding under the Act.

### Legal issues

**17.** At a pre-proof hearing the sheriff should ask the parties if there are any questions of admissibility of evidence or any other legal issues, including any questions under the European Convention on Human Rights, which are likely to arise at the proof. If so, the sheriff should consider whether they could with advantage be determined at this hearing rather than at the proof. Alternatively, the sheriff may adjourn the pre-proof hearing to another date in order to enable any such issue to be argued and determined. If a legal issue is not raised at the pre-proof hearing, the sheriff may refuse to allow it to be raised at the proof except on cause shown. A solicitor who intends to raise a legal issue at a pre-proof hearing should intimate it to the other parties' solicitors beforehand.

## Evidence

**18.**  It should be noted that evidence may be presented in the form of affidavits or other written evidence (Civil Evidence (Scotland) Act 1988, section 2; *McVinnie v McVinnie* , 1995 S.L.T. (Sh. Ct) 81; *Glaser v Glaser* , 1997 S.L.T. 456). The sheriff is bound to consider reports placed before him or her even if the authors are not called to speak to them, and the strict rules of evidence do not apply (*T, Petitioner* , 1997 S.L.T. 724 at 730L). Such considerations may render the attendance of certain witnesses unnecessary, although for other reasons it may be preferable to call the author of a document. The parties should therefore apply their minds to the question whether any evidence might be appropriately presented in the form of an affidavit or other document and the sheriff should encourage them to decide that question at the pre-proof hearing. The sheriff should also encourage the use of affidavits to cover non-contentious (or indeed contentious) issues where that would save the time of witnesses and the court. Notwithstanding that an affidavit has been lodged, its author may be called to give evidence at the proof (see paragraph 3 of the judgment of Lady Smith in *Petitions of Aberdeenshire Council to declare A, B and C free for adoption*, Court of Session, 22 June 2004).

**19.**  Where the author of a report or the maker of a statement which has been or is to be lodged is to be called as a witness, the sheriff shall order that the report or statement is to be held to be equivalent to the witness' examination in chief, unless for special reasons he or she otherwise directs.

**20.**  The sheriff should discourage the unnecessary use of expert witnesses. If expert evidence is essential, the sheriff should encourage the joint instruction of a single expert witness by all parties. If one party instructs an expert report, it should be disclosed to the other parties with a view to the agreement of as much of its content as possible.

**21.**  The sheriff should ask the parties what further productions, if any, they intend to lodge. Any difficulties over the obtaining or lodging of documents should be raised and if possible resolved at the pre-proof hearing.

## The proof

**22.**  At a proof it should be borne in mind that "there is a heavy responsibility on the parties' representatives to exercise all reasonable economy and restraint in their presentation of the evidence and in their submissions to the court" (*Lothian Regional Council v A* at page 862B). The sheriff may therefore exercise his or her existing common law power to intervene to discourage prolixity, repetition, the leading of evidence of unnecessary witnesses and the leading of evidence on matters which are unlikely to assist the court to reach a decision.

**23.**  At the conclusion of the evidence parties must be heard orally thereon by the sheriff. In anticipation of this the sheriff may require the parties to submit, in electronic form or otherwise, draft findings in fact, skeleton arguments, or both.

## The Consolidated Practice Note dated 5 June 2005

**24.**  Part III sections A, B, C and D of the Consolidated Practice Note dated 5 June 2005 are revoked subject to the qualification that they shall continue to have effect for the purpose of any application to which they apply which has been made and not determined before 28 September 2009.

20 October 2009

# PRACTICE NOTE NO.1 OF 2012

## FAMILY AND CIVIL PARTNERSHIP ACTIONS: GUIDANCE FOR SHERIFFS AND PRACTITIONERS

### Purpose

1.   The purpose of this Practice Note is to secure the efficient management of procedure in Family and Civil Partnership Actions. It should be read subject to the detailed rules of procedure to be found in Chapter 33 of the Ordinary Cause Rules 1993. It will be revised in light of experience and any new primary or secondary legislation.

### Commencement

2.   This Practice Note applies to all applications lodged or proceedings commenced, on or after 1 March 2012.

### PART I

### DEFINITION OF FAMILY ACTIONS (OCR 33.1)

3.   The definition of a family action does not include applications under Sections 28 and 29 of the Family Law (Scotland) Act 2006 in respect of financial provision for former cohabitants nor does it include interdict actions between spouses/civil partners and former cohabitants/partners. Agents should not submit such actions to the family section for warranting unless the action includes a crave or craves for orders under Sections 1, 2 or 11 of the Children (Scotland) Act 1995.

4.   All applications under the Matrimonial Homes (Family Protection) (Scotland) Act 1981 Act fall within the definition of family actions including applications under Section 2(3) of the said 1981 Act. Agents should send all such applications to the family section for warranting.

### PART II

### DESIGNATIONS OF PARTIES IN INITIAL WRITS

#### Non-disclosure of address

5.   If agents consider it is appropriate not to disclose the address of a party, they must aver fully why the address is not being disclosed. It is insufficient simply to aver that the party seeking to withhold their address does not wish the other party to know her/his whereabouts. In those circumstances the party is not properly designed and the Initial Writ is not in proper form and will not be accepted by the court.

6.   The party seeking to withhold her/his address must adduce reasons in support of that position which satisfy the court and allow it to exercise its discretion in favour of the party seeking non-disclosure of her/his address.

7.   If there are no averments to support the non-disclosure of a party's address the Initial Writ is not in proper form and should not be warranted. If the writ is warranted in error the action will not be allowed to proceed until the rules of procedure have been complied with.

**8.** Agents are required to justify a party's attempt to withhold her/his address at any stage of the proceedings particularly if the averments upon which they seek to found are of some age or are vague or have been diluted in some way, for example, during amendment procedure.

(*A.W.B. v J.P.* (*www.scotcourts.gov.uk/opinions/F99 07.html*) reported as *B v P* , 2010 G.W.D. 19-371. See also *Murdoch v Young* , 1909 2 S.L.T. 450; *Stein v Stein* 1936 S.C. 268; *McColl v McColl* , 1949 S.L.T. (Notes) 11; and *Daughton v Doughton* , 1958 S.L.T. (notes) 34.)

## PART III

## CERTIFICATES OF CITATION IN FAMILY AND CIVIL PARTNERSHIP ACTIONS

**9.** The increasing incidence of certificates of citation which are being lodged in improper form is creating an unnecessary additional administrative burden. Many agents are routinely omitting reference in their certificates of citation to the notices which have been served on the defender along with the service copy Initial Writ. Such certificates will be returned by the Sheriff Clerk's office for clarification as to whether the appropriate notices have been served on the defender.

**10.** The certificate of citation must be in form F16 or form CP17 (as appropriate) and must state which notice(s) was/were attached to the service copy Initial Writ when service was effected on the defender. If the necessary notices have been served on the defender then amendment of the certificate by agents may be sufficient. However, if no reference is made in the certificate of citation to service of the required notices on the defender, the sheriff may order re-service of the action to ensure the necessary notices are served. (OCR 33.11–33.14 and OCR 33A.11–33A.14)

## PART IV

## AFFIDAVITS IN FAMILY AND CIVIL PARTNERSHIP ACTIONS

### When affidavits may be lodged (see OCR 33.29 and OCR 33A.29)

**11.** Once the period within which a notice of intention to defend requires to be lodged has expired, without such a notice having been lodged, affidavits may be prepared and lodged without any order of the court.

**12. Person before whom sworn or affirmed**

An affidavit is admissible if it is sworn (or affirmed) before a notary public, justice of the peace or any person having authority to administer oaths for the place where the affidavit is sworn, such as a commissioner for oaths or a British diplomatic officer or consul abroad. A solicitor acting for a party to the action may act in a notarial capacity when an affidavit is sworn. Any person before whom an affidavit is sworn (referred to below as "the notary") must observe all the normal rules in this connection and must satisfy himself or herself as to the capacity of the witness to swear an affidavit.

### Importance of affidavits

**13.** The witness should be made to appreciate the importance of the affidavit and that the affidavit constitutes his or her evidence in the case. The possible consequences of giving false evidence should be explained to the witness. Before the witness signs the affidavit he or she must have read it or the notary must have read it over to the witness.

### Oath or affirmation

**14.** The witness must be placed on oath or must affirm.

### Form and Signature of the affidavit

**15.** The document should be on A4 paper. The affidavit should commence with the words "At (insert place) on the (insert date) day of (insert month) 20** in the presence of (insert name of notary, justice of the peace etc) compeared (insert name of witness) who having been solemnly sworn or having affirmed gives evidence or depones as follows:" The affidavit should be drafted in the first person and should take the form of numbered paragraphs. The full name, age, address and occupation of the witness should be given in the first paragraph. The affidavit should end with the words "All of which is the truth as I shall answer to God" or "All of which is affirmed by me to be true", as appropriate. Any blanks in the affidavit must be filled in. Any insertion, deletion or other amendment to the affidavit requires to be initialled by the witness and the notary. Each page must be signed by both the witness and the notary. It is not necessary for the affidavit to be sealed by the notary.

### Drafting the affidavit

**16.** An affidavit should be based on a reliable and full precognition of the witness.

**17.** The drafter of an affidavit should provide himself or herself, before drawing it, with an up-to-date copy of the pleadings, a copy of the appropriate precognition and the relative productions. The affidavit should be drawn so as to follow the averments in the pleadings to the extent that these are within the knowledge of that particular witness and in the same order. The affidavits must contain sufficient evidence to establish that the court has jurisdiction.

**18.** Affidavits should be expressed in the words of the person whose affidavit it is, should be accurate as at the date of the affidavit and should not consist of a repetition of passages in the pleadings. It should be clear from the terms of the affidavit whether the witness is speaking from his or her own knowledge or whether the witness is relying on what he or she was told by a particular person.

### Productions

**19.** Productions already lodged in process must be borrowed up and put to the party or to the witness who refers to them in his or her affidavit. Each production will require to be referred to in the affidavit by its number of process and must be docqueted and signed by the witness and the notary. If a production has not yet been lodged when the affidavit is sworn, it will require to be identified by the witness in the affidavit, should be docqueted with regard to the affidavit and signed by the witness and the notary. It must then be lodged as a production.

Some productions will necessarily be docqueted with regard to more than one affidavit.

**20.** In consent cases, the defender's written consent form will have to be put to the pursuer in his or her affidavit and be identified, docqueted and signed in the same way as other productions.

**21.** In adultery cases, photographs of both the pursuer and the defender may require to be produced, put to the appropriate witness and be identified, docqueted and signed in the manner already described.

### Date of affidavit

**22.** All affidavits lodged must be of recent date. This factor is particularly important in cases involving children, cases in which financial craves are involved and in other circumstances where the evidence of a witness or circumstances to which the witness speaks are liable to change through the passage of time. The notary must take particular care in such cases to ensure that the affidavit evidence as to such matters is correct as at the time the affidavit is sworn. Affidavits relating to the welfare of children which have been sworn more than three months prior to lodging a minute for decree are likely to be rejected by the court as out of date.

### Applications relating to parental responsibilities and rights (OCR 33.28 & 33A.29)

**23.** In actions in which an application in terms of Section II of the Children (Scotland) Act 1995 is before the court, not fewer than two affidavits dealing with the welfare of the child(ren) should be provided with at least one of them being from a person who is neither a parent nor a party to the action. These affidavits should present the court with a full picture of the arrangements for the care of the child(ren) along the lines set out in paragraph 25, adapted to suit the circumstances of the particular case. The affidavits should set out reasons why it is better that the Section II order be made than not. The pursuer's affidavit should deal fully with the arrangements which have been made for the care of the child(ren), so far as within his or her knowledge. If the pursuer cannot give substantial evidence as to that, it may be necessary to obtain such evidence from the person who is responsible for their care.

**24.** In actions of divorce, judicial separation, declarator of nullity of marriage or dissolution or declarator of nullity of a civil partnership or separation of civil partners in which there are children of the family or children treated by the parties as children of their family but in which no order in terms of Section 11 of the Children (Scotland) Act 1995 is sought, the court, in terms of Section 12 of said 1995 Act, requires to consider whether to exercise the powers set out in Sections II or 54 of that Act in light of the information before it as to the arrangements for the child(ren)'s upbringing. Information accordingly requires to be before the court as to these arrangements. As a minimum, the affidavits of the witnesses should include the information set out in paragraphs 25(a) to (g) below.

**25.** An affidavit dealing with the arrangements for the care of children should, where relevant, include the following;
- (a) the qualification of the witness, if not a parent, to speak about the child; how often, and in what circumstances the witness normally sees the child;
- (b) the ability of those with whom the child Jives to provide proper care for him or her;
- (c) observations as to the relationship between the child and the other members of the household, the child's general appearance, interests, state of health and well-being;
- (d) a description of the home conditions in which the child lives;
- (e) the arrangements for contact between the child and any parent (and siblings) not resident within the same household as the child;

(f) information about the school or nursery or other establishment the child attends; whether the child attends regularly; and the child's progress there; and

(g) details of child care arrangements during working hours, including the arrangements for such as are outwith school hours.

### Affidavits relating to disclosure of the whereabouts of children

**26.** An affidavit sworn or affirmed in compliance with an order to disclose the whereabouts of children (in terms of the Family Law Act 1986, Section 33 and OCR 33.23 & 33A.24) will require to be drafted in such a way as to meet the requirements of the court in the circumstances of the particular case. The form of the affidavit should be as above.

### Financial and other ancillary craves

**27.** Affidavit evidence in support of financial craves is necessary in an undefended action. (*Ali v Ali (No.2)* 2001 S.L.T. 602). Where financial craves are involved, the evidence should be as full, accurate and up-to-date as possible. If the evidence is insufficient the court may require supplementary evidence to be provided. If, after an affidavit has been sworn and the solicitor concerned has parted with it, a material change of circumstances occurs before decree has been granted, the court must be informed forthwith. A further affidavit may have to be sworn.

**28.** The pursuer should give evidence as to his or her own financial position as at the date of the affidavit. Where the pursuer gives evidence in an affidavit as to the financial position of the defender, the affidavit should state the date, as precisely as possible, at which the information was valid. The court must be provided with information which is as up-to-date as possible as to the defender's ability to pay the sums the pursuer is seeking. Where the pursuer cannot obtain recent information as to the defender's means the affidavit should state that that is the case but should contain as much material information relating to the defender's means as possible. If the pursuer is unable to provide sufficient evidence to justify the orders concluded for or craved in full, in the minute for decree, after the words "in terms of conclusion(s)/crave(s) (number(s) … ) of the summons/initial writ" there may be added words such as "or such other sum (or sums) as the court may think proper."

**29.** Where the pursuer has concluded for or craved a capital sum, an order for the sale of the matrimonial home, a periodical allowance, interdict or expenses, for example, and in the minute for decree does not seek decree for one or more of these, the reasons for that should be given in his or her affidavit.

### Joint minutes

**30.** When parties record their agreement in a joint minute as to how financial and other ancillary conclusions or craves should be dealt with by the court, the pursuer's affidavit should refer to the joint minute and indicate that he or she is content that the agreement set out in it should be given effect.

### Minute for decree

**31.** The minute for decree must be signed by counsel or by a solicitor who has examined the affidavits and other documents. That counsel or solicitor takes responsibility therefor, whether or not he or she is the person who drew the summons, initial writ or affidavits. The minute for decree should not be signed seeking decree of divorce, separation, declarator of marriage or nullity of marriage or dissolution or declarator of nullity of a civil partnership or separation of civil partners unless the evidence consists of or includes evidence other than that of a party to the marriage (or alleged or purported marriage) or other than that of a partner in the civil partnership (or purported civil partnership).

(Civil Evidence (Scotland) Act 1988, Sections 8(3) and 8(3A) and *Taylor v Taylor* , 2001 SCLR 161.)

## PART V

## SECTION 11 REPORTS—APPOINTMENT OF SOLICITOR REPORTERS

**32.** The sheriff clerk will retain a register of solicitors willing to prepare Section 11 reports in family cases. The sheriff clerk will retain a note of the contact details of such solicitors. Each solicitor on the register must provide the sheriff clerk with written confirmation of any changes to those contact details. In the event of the contact details changing and the sheriff clerk not being advised in writing, the solicitor's name may be deleted from the register.

**33.** From time to time, to ensure that the said register contains a sufficient number of solicitors to meet operational requirements, the sheriff clerk may invite applications from suitably qualified solicitors to be considered for inclusion on the said register. Applications submitted outwith the period specified by the sheriff clerk for submission of such applications will not be considered.

**34.** In every case where the sheriff orders such a report (whether the sheriff orders an initial or supplementary report) reporters must obtain information from the Data Protection Office of Strathclyde Police regarding the previous convictions of the parties to the action. In some cases it will be appropriate to obtain details of any previous convictions of their respective partners or indeed any other adults with whom they are living or who will have a potential involvement in the care of the child(ren) concerned. Reporters must request this information from Strathclyde Police at the earliest possible opportunity after receiving instructions.

**35.** Any response from Strathclyde Police must be appended to the report. Even if there are no previous convictions, or there are no convictions which the reporter considers relevant to the issues before the court, the reply from Strathclyde Police must be annexed to the report. Any information provided by Strathclyde Police which is not in written form should normally be included in the report unless, exceptionally, Strathclyde Police provide information to the reporter on a confidential basis on condition that it is not disclosed to the parties in which case the information should be contained in a separate confidential report to the sheriff.

**36.** In the event of the reporter having received no response from Strathclyde Police prior to completion of the report, the reporter should, when submitting the report, advise the court of the up-to-date position, providing a brief summary of the position (such as the outcome of any chase up enquiries) and confirming that the Strathclyde Police response will follow. The police response must be forwarded to the court immediately upon receipt.

## PART VI

## CITATION OF SECTION 11 REPORTERS AS WITNESSES IN FAMILY PROOFS

**37.** The reporter is the court's reporter and is in a different position to that of witnesses of fact and expert witnesses instructed by the parties. No reporter should be cited as a witness by any party to an action without an application having first been made to the court for authority to have the reporter appear before the court for examination on oath regarding any matter dealt with in the report.

(Section 11(4) of the Matrimonial Proceedings (Children) Act 1958. See also *Kristiansen v Kristiansen* , 1987 SCLR 462 and *Oliver v Oliver* , 1988 SCLR 285.)

## PART VII

## ALLOCATION OF CHILD WELFARE HEARINGS

**38.** Agents seeking an urgent child welfare hearing must set out in full the reasons for seeking such a hearing to enable the sheriff properly to consider the request.

**39.** In the event that agents consider that a child welfare hearing should be fixed at the time of warranting an initial writ they must set out in full the reasons for seeking such a hearing to enable the sheriff properly to consider the request.

**40.** Agents must append to any motion seeking the allocation of a child welfare hearing a note of the reasons for fixing such a hearing to enable the sheriff to give proper consideration to the motion whether or not the motion is opposed or joint.

## PART VIII

## MOTIONS

**41.** Where a motion to allow a part of process to be received late or to fix a child welfare hearing is made, either orally or in writing, the reason for the lateness or need for child welfare hearing shall be stated by the party making the motion, and that reason shall be recorded in the interlocutor.

## PART IX

## UNDEFENDED FAMILY ACTIONS—APPLICATION OF THE YEAR AND A DAY RULE

**42.** The year and a day period is calculated from the end of the period of notice.

**43.** If no minute for decree has been received during said period (and there has been no other procedure during that period and no judicial step has been taken during that period) then the action falls and the sheriff has no power to make any further order. Any interim orders previously granted have also fallen after the expiry of said period.

**44.** If a minute for decree has been received during said period but decree cannot be granted for some reason, the intervention of the court has been invoked and the court's response has been that the minute has been refused, the submission of the minute will be treated as a judicial step in the process which interrupts the running of the said period. The action will not therefore fall after a year and a day in these circumstances.

(See inter alia *Cringean v McNeil* , 1996 S.L.T. (Sh. Ct) 136 and the decision of Sheriff Principal Macleod in *The Royal Bank of Scotland plc v Mason* , 1995 S.L.T. (Sh. Ct) 32.)

## PART X

## MINUTES IN FAMILY AND CIVIL PARTNERSHIP ACTIONS

**45.** In depending cases, upon receipt of a minute averring contempt of court the sheriff will issue an interlocutor providing for service on the alleged contemnor and the fixing of a procedural hearing.

**46.** Where the original proceedings have concluded, a summary application must be lodged in respect of any alleged contempt of court such as by failing to obtemper a contact order.

**47.** Where the minute is to vary Section 11 orders, the sheriff may issue an interlocutor which provides for answers to be lodged by the respondent and the fixing of a child welfare hearing.

**48.** A minute to vary is generally not competent where the original action has been dismissed. There are no existing orders which can be varied and the court has not determined that it would be in the interests of the child(ren) for no orders to be pronounced. An application for Section 11 orders must be made by initial writ in those circumstances.

**49.** Where an action of divorce, separation or nullity of marriage has been raised previously and final decree has been granted, a party seeking Section 11 orders or the variation, recall or enforcement of Section 11 orders will require to lodge a minute to vary in the process of the original action even if no Section 11 orders were sought or granted in the original action. Where an action of dissolution or declarator of nullity of civil partnership or separation of civil partners has been raised previously and final decree has been granted, a party seeking Section 11 orders or the variation, recall or enforcement of Section 11 orders will require to lodge a minute to vary in the process of the original action even if no Section 11 orders were sought or granted in the original action. If no Section 11 orders were made when decree was granted then at that time the Sheriff decided that it was in the best interests of the child(ren) that no orders be made.

**50.** After final decree in any of the actions referred to in para.49 above, where a party does not seek to have the other party found in contempt and punished by the court but considers that the other party is not obtempering the court order then he should consider whether the appropriate minute to be enrolled is a minute to enforce the existing order.

**51.** In other cases where Section 11 orders have been granted or refused, applications after final decree for variation or recall of a Section 11 order shall be made by minute to vary in the process of the original action.

[OCR 33.38 and OCR 33.44 and OCR 33.60 and OCR 33.65. See also OCR 33A.38 and OCR 33A.41 and OCR 33A.54 and OCR 33A.57. See section 42(3) of the Family Law Act 1986 which states that matrimonial proceedings in Scotland with respect to a child shall be treated as continuing until the child concerned reaches the age of 16 unless the proceedings have been dismissed or decree of absolvitor has been granted therein. See also *McEwen v McEwen* (Sheriff Principal McInnes, QC at Hamilton—25 August 2000) at *http://www.scotcourts.gov.uk/opinionsID270__00.html*]

## PART XI

## PREPARATIONS FOR PROOF AND PRE PROOF HEARINGS

**52.** When the court allows parties a proof of their respective averments, an interlocutor will be pronounced in such terms but the court will not assign a proof diet until the following procedures have been complied with. The purpose of these procedures is to determine more accurately the number of days which should be allocated to the proof and to ensure that parties have focussed the issues.

**53.** Where parties intend to lead evidence from expert witnesses they must lodge in process and exchange copies of the reports. In addition there must be a meeting of the experts following which the agents must lodge in process a minute of said meeting recording those issues upon which the experts disagree.

**54.** Parties must also lodge in process and exchange lists of the witnesses whom they intend to lead in evidence. In addition to the list of witnesses parties must lodge summaries of the witness statements. The summaries must contain sufficient information to identify the issues which it is anticipated the witnesses will speak to.

**55.** At pre-proof hearings parties shall ensure that they are in a position to provide the sheriff with sufficient information to enable the sheriff to conduct the hearing as provided for in OCR 28A.1. In particular, parties shall ensure that they can provide the sheriff with sufficient information regarding the matters set out in OCR 28A.1(3).

30 January 2012

# PRACTICE NOTE NO.1 OF 2013

## CHILDREN'S REFERRALS

## PART I

## INTRODUCTION

**1.1** The overriding purpose of this Practice Note is to ensure that children's referral proceedings are conducted as fairly, expeditiously and efficiently as possible. By definition, such proceedings concern children who appear to be vulnerable and may be in need of compulsory supervision.

**1.2** It is vital in the interests of the child that such referral proceedings are conducted and concluded as fairly, expeditiously and efficiently as possible. This requires the accurate estimation and allocation of hearings, the reduction of repeated appearances, and the elimination of unnecessary or repetitive evidence at hearings. This will be achieved by active judicial management, together with a requirement on all parties to work to achieve the foregoing aim.

**1.3** The Practice Note applies to the following, all of which are collectively referred to as children's referral proceedings:

— proof applications by the children's reporter;
— applications for place of safety warrants by the children's reporter;
— applications to recall child protection orders;
— appeals against decisions by children's hearings; and
— applications for review of previously established grounds for referral.

The requirements applicable to proof applications (Parts 3 and 4) will also apply, subject to any necessary adjustment, to any other children's referral matter in which it is anticipated that evidence will be led.

**1.4**   This Practice Note will come into effect on 20th May 2013. It s recognised that some flexibility will be required in the application of these arrangements to children's referral proceedings lodged prior to, but still current, as of that date. Full compliance will be expected in relation to all proceedings lodged on or after that date.

**1.5**   All statutory references are to the Children (Scotland) Act 1995. A revised version will be issued on implementation of the Children's Hearings (Scotland) Act 2011

## PART II

## ORGANISATION OF REFERRAL PROCEEDINGS

**2.1**   Children's referral proceedings will now be organised into substantive hearings on Mondays, Tuesdays and Wednesdays, and procedural callings on Thursdays and Fridays.

**2.2**   The only matters to be allocated to the 3 substantive days will be: proofs where it is anticipated that evidence will then be led; appeal hearings where it is anticipated that the substance of the appeal will be argued (or, if agreed by the court, that evidence will be led); and other matters requiring to be heard as a result of statutory timescales, such as an application to recall a child protection order.

**2.3**   All other matters will call on Thursdays or Fridays. For the avoidance of doubt, that includes: first callings of proof applications and appeals; subsequent hearings where evidence is not to be led, including case management hearings and pre-proof hearings; and warrant applications except where the court determines it would be more appropriate to consider the application alongside a proof diet allocated to another day. Unless specified otherwise, it is thus not expected that witnesses will be cited for any calling on a Thursday or Friday.

**2.4**   Business on Thursdays and Fridays will be allocated into 3 half-day slots on Thursday afternoon, Friday morning and Friday afternoon.

**2.5**   All sheriffs will continue to be allocated for substantive matters on Mondays, Tuesdays and Wednesdays. It is expected that sheriffs allocated to sit on Thursdays and Fridays will be drawn from a pool of sheriffs who will undertake judicial case management functions as set out in this Practice Note.

## PART III

## PROOF APPLICATIONS: GENERAL

### Lodging of Application

**3.1**   When lodging an application to establish grounds for referral under section 65(7) or (9), the children's reporter must at the same time lodge a provisional list of witnesses.

**3.2**   At the time of lodging the application, the children's reporter should draw to the sheriff clerk's attention any factors indicating that a long proof, or complex procedure, may be required.

## Cooperation of Parties

**3.3**   Parties are expected to assist the court in achieving the fair and expeditious determination of the application with the minimum of delay. In particular, parties are expected as a matter of routine to
— cooperate in agreeing evidence wherever possible;
— make full and frank disclosure of their position, well in advance;
— provide any additional information on the progress of the application required by the sheriff;
— be informed as to the availability of witnesses; and
— lead only relevant evidence and do so in an efficient manner.

## First Hearing

**3.4**   A first hearing in respect of the application will be fixed for a Thursday or Friday court. At that hearing, the sheriff will seek to progress the application expeditiously and, to that end, will expect parties to be able to address:
— any legal aid application on behalf of a party;
— (if not already determined) whether a curator ad litem or safeguarder should be appointed;
— whether the reporter has disclosed relevant information and, if not, what arrangements will be made for disclosure
— whether the requirement on the child to attend that or subsequent hearings should be dispensed with in terms of section 68(5);
— in the case of an application falling within section 68(8), whether to dispense with the hearing of evidence and deem the grounds for referral to be established;
— whether the scope of any proof hearing can be restricted through the agreement of evidence or the use of affidavit evidence;
— whether the case should be treated as a complex case in terms of Part 4 below;
— any other matters which, in the circumstances of the case, appear likely to enable it to be determined quickly and justly and in accordance with the interests of the child.

**3.5**   If the application is not disposed of at the first hearing, unless the application falls to be considered as a complex case, the sheriff will fix a second procedural hearing, which will normally be fixed as a pre-proof hearing.

**3.6**   At this or any subsequent hearing, the sheriff will fix a proof hearing when satisfied that the parties are or ought to be ready to proceed to proof at the proof hearing, and that the hearing of evidence is likely to be required.

## Subsequent Hearings

**3.7**   Where a second hearing is fixed, the sheriff will consider the matters listed at paragraph 3.3 insofar as not already determined. The sheriff will consider whether a hearing of evidence is likely to be required and, if so, the parties' state of preparation for proof. If the application cannot be determined at the second hearing, the sheriff will fix a proof hearing unless satisfied, on cause shown, that a further procedural hearing should be fixed.

**3.8**   Where a third or further procedural hearing is fixed and the application still cannot be determined at that hearing, the sheriff will fix a proof unless satisfied, on exceptional cause shown, that a further procedural hearing should be fixed.

## Proof Hearing

**3.9**   Where a proof hearing is fixed, the expectation is that the proof will proceed at that hearing. Once fixed, in normal circumstances, the court will grant an adjournment of the proof hearing only where satisfied on cause shown that to do so is in the interests of the child and is likely to result in the fair and expeditious determination of the application.

## PART IV

## PROOF APPLICATIONS: COMPLEX CASES

**4.1**   A complex case is any matter where the court reasonably anticipates either that a hearing of more than 3 days may be required, or that 2 or more parties will seek to lead competing expert evidence.

**4.2**   Throughout the progress of a complex case, all parties are under a duty to cooperate to achieve efficient management of the proceedings and the best use of court time. In particular, parties are expected to
— make full and frank disclosure of their position;
— be prepared for each case management or pre-proof hearing;
— agree evidence wherever possible;
— comply with the requirements set out below regarding expert evidence; and
— lead only relevant evidence and do so in an efficient manner.

### Case Management Hearings

**4.3**   At the first procedural hearing, or as soon thereafter as an application is identified as likely to be a complex case, after considering the matters listed at paragraph 3.4 above the sheriff will fix a case management hearing.

**4.4**   The purpose of the case management hearing is to clarify the likely scope and duration of proof required, and any other logistical or procedural matters likely to affect the progress of the case.

**4.5**   In advance of the case management hearing, each party shall lodge a copy report from any expert witness, and a case summary. Parties shall also lodge a joint minute of admissions in relation to any statements of facts, or any evidence, that is agreed.

**4.6**   A case summary is a document which gives fair notice of a party's position and state of preparation by setting out in concise terms:
— a note of the identity of those who will represent the party at proof;
— (for each party other than the reporter) the extent to which the grounds for referral and statement of facts are disputed;
— (for the reporter) what disclosure has been effected and, if full disclosure has not been made, why not a list of witnesses;
— the nature and scope of the evidence to be led (1 succinct but informative paragraph per witness);
— the manner of the party's compliance with the requirements regarding expert evidence at paragraphs 4.10 to 4.12 below;
— a list of productions lodged or to be lodged by that party or, wherever possible, by parties jointly;
— an estimate of the number of days likely to be required to hear that party's evidence (including cross-examination and re-examination); and

— a note of any other logistical, procedural or legal issues to be raised by that party that may affect the progress of the case.

**4.7** At the case management hearing, parties shall cooperate so as to allow the sheriff to identify

— the scope of the dispute between the parties;
— the nature and duration of the evidence to be led, and why such evidence is required;
— the extent to which evidence may be presented in the form of affidavits or other written evidence;
— whether any procedure other than proof is likely to be required, and the reason for that; and
— any logistical, procedural or legal issues and the extent to which they may affect the progress of the case.

**4.8** The sheriff will not fix a diet of proof, or a pre-proof hearing, until satisfied that the parties have substantially complied with the above requirements and that it is possible to identify with some confidence the length and timing of proof hearing reasonably required. Where, however, the sheriff considers that one or more parties has failed to comply timeously with the above requirements, the sheriff may nevertheless fix a diet of proof where satisfied that to do so would be in the interests of the child and of the fair and expeditious determination of the application.

**4.9** When fixing a diet of proof in a complex case, the sheriff will also fix a pre-proof hearing.

### Expert Evidence

**4.10** Expert opinion evidence should be kept to the minimum necessary. It is the parties' responsibility to instruct experts who are able to meet the ordinary demands of court appearance, including holiday arrangements. It is the responsibility of each party to ascertain that every appointed expert:

— represents an established and respectable body of relevant professional opinion;
— is appropriately informed as to the facts;
— is appropriately qualified and competent to address the relevant issues; and does address the issues.

**4.11** The court will consider joint instruction of a single expert witness to be the norm. Parties who wish to instruct and lead competing experts will require the approval of the court to do so.

**4.12** Where such approval is granted and 2 or more parties intend to lead directly competing expert evidence, these parties must cooperate to ensure that the competing experts exchange views in order to identify areas of agreement and to clarify the scope of and basis for any areas of disagreement, for instance by arranging a joint consultation. Parties must lodge in court a note setting out the areas of agreement and disagreement thus identified.

**4.13** Failure to comply with these requirements in respect of expert evidence may result in the court refusing to hear that evidence.

## Pre-Proof Hearing

**4.14**   In advance of the pre-proof hearing, each party must lodge
— a list of witnesses;
— an updated case summary;
— a proposed running order and timetable for the calling of witnesses;
— any productions to be relied upon;
— and any other matters specified by the sheriff at the case management hearing.

**4.15**   Parties should bring to the sheriff's attention any logistical, procedural or legal matters liable to affect the progress of the case and ensure that the sheriff is enabled to determine such matters.

**4.16**   Parties will be expected to have a clear grasp of the issues in the case and to be able to demonstrate their compliance with the requirements of this Practice Note.

**4.17**   The interlocutor arising from the pre-proof hearing will have attached to it a timetable for the progress and completion of the proof as agreed by the parties or, failing such agreement, as determined by the sheriff.

## Proof

**4.18**   During the proof hearing, the court is likely to sit continuously between 10am and 1pm, and again between 2pm and 4pm. At the court's discretion, parties may be asked to lead evidence beyond 4pm each day, in order to assist the early resolution of the referral.

**4.19**   The referral procedure is summary and intended to be succinct where possible. Accordingly, it will be necessary to justify any request for (i) a shorthand writer; (ii) any further procedure; (iii) any adjournments once the proof has commenced.

**4.20**   Parties must bear in mind at all times their responsibility to exercise reasonable economy and restraint in their presentation of evidence and submissions to the court. The sheriff will not hesitate to use common law powers to discourage prolixity, repetition, or the leading of evidence that is unlikely to assist the court in reaching a decision.

**4.21**   No party will be allowed to lead evidence or to follow a substantive line of examination not previously disclosed to other parties and the court, except with the leave of the court.

## Additional Evidence and/or Court Time

**4.22**   Once a diet of proof is allocated, parties should have no expectation that additional evidence will be allowed or that additional days will be allocated.

**4.23**   Any motion to allow additional evidence or to allocate additional days to the hearing of the proof will be granted only on cause shown, taking account of the responsibilities of parties under this Practice Note and the terms of discussions during case management or pre-proof hearings.

## PART V

## WARRANT APPLICATIONS

**5.1** An application for a warrant to keep a child in a place of safety should be accompanied by a written statement setting out in concise terms the procedural history of the case, and the basis on which the reporter considers there is cause shown for the issue of the warrant sought.

## PART VI

## APPEALS: LEGAL AID

**6.1** An application to the sheriff for the grant of legal aid in respect of an appeal should be accompanied by a copy of the decision to be appealed and a statement from the appellant setting out the basis of the proposed appeal.

**6.2** On cause shown, the sheriff may accept an oral explanation of the basis of the proposed appeal in lieu of a statement from the appellant.

**6.3** For the avoidance of doubt, there is no requirement that the appeal itself should be lodged before or at the same time as the application for legal aid.

## PART VII

## APPOINTMENT OF SAFEGUARDERS OR CURATORS AD LITEM

**7.1** On lodging an application to establish grounds for referral, the reporter must advise the court of the identity of any safeguarder appointed by the children's hearing in respect of the child.

**7.2** Any party lodging an application to recall a child protection order, an appeal against a decision of a children's hearing or an application for review of previously established grounds for referral must advise the court of the identity of any safeguarder or curator ad litem currently or recently appointed in respect of the child.

**7.3** In deciding whether to appoint a safeguarder or curator ad litem, the sheriff may take into account: the age or ages of the child(ren); the nature of the grounds for referral; whether the grounds for referral are accepted or not by any relevant person; whether there is a conflict of interest between the child and any other party such that the court cannot otherwise protect the interests of the child; and any other relevant information provided by the reporter or any other party.

# SHERIFFDOM OF NORTH STRATHCLYDE

## Act of Court (Consolidation, etc.) 1992

*20 October 1992.*

ARRANGEMENT OF RULES

PART I CIVIL PROCEDURE

PART II AFFIDAVITS AND FAMILY ACTIONS

*[Repealed]*

PART III MISCELLANEOUS

*[Repealed]*

Schedule

I, Robert Colquhoun Hay, C.B.E., W.S., Sheriff Principal of North Strathclyde, in respect that many of the Acts of Court and practice notes in force within the Sheriffdom are spent or are in need of modernisation, hereby repeal all Acts of Court and practice notes presently in force within the Sheriffdom other than those listed in the Schedule hereto, and direct that the following will be given effect on or after 20th October 1992:[1]

## PART I

### CIVIL PROCEDURE

**Process**

**1.01.**[2]   No process or any part thereof may be borrowed within the period from 12 noon on the second working day preceding any diet at which it is required until after the said diet.

**1.02–1.05.**   [Repealed by the Act of Court (Consolidation etc.) 1998.]

**Legal representation**

**1.06.**[3]   When, in the course of litigation, a solicitor either withdraws from acting for a party to a cause or accepts instructions to act for a party to a cause, he shall notify immediately that fact **in writing** to the sheriff clerk of the relevant court. Such notice shall specify (a) the process number; (b) the names of the litigants; and (c) the particular litigant to whom the notice relates.

**1.07.**[4]   On receipt of such notice the sheriff clerk shall attach it to the interlocutor sheets, failing which to the initiating document, i.e. the initial writ, summary application, petition, summary cause summons, small claims summons, etc.

**Productions**

**1.08.**[5]   Whenever practicable, where documentary productions have been lodged in process, and are to be referred to in the course of a proof or debate, copies of all such productions, for use by the sheriff, shall be lodged with the sheriff clerk not less than two days prior to the diet of proof or debate.

**1.09.–1.10.**[6]   *[Repealed by the Act of Court (Consolidation etc.) 1998.]*

---

[1] The whole Act of Court (Consolidation etc.) 1992 has been repealed by the Act of Court (Consolidation etc.) 1998, except for: Rules 1.01, 1.06, 1.07, 1.08, 1.11, 1.17 in respect of Ordinary Actions and Summary Applications raised before January 1, 1994; and for Rules 1.06, 1.07 and 1.08 of the said Act of Court in respect of Summary Cause Actions.

[2] Repealed by the Act of Court (Consolidation etc.) 1998, except in respect of Ordinary Actions and Summary Applications raised before January 1, 1994.

[3] Repealed by the Act of Court (Consolidation etc.) 1998, except in respect of Ordinary Actions and Summary Applications raised before January 1, 1994 and in respect of Summary Cause Actions.

[4] Repealed by the Act of Court (Consolidation etc.) 1998, except in respect of Ordinary Actions and Summary Applications raised before January 1, 1994 and in respect of Summary Cause Actions.

[5] Repealed by the Act of Court (Consolidation etc.) 1998, except in respect of Ordinary Actions and Summary Applications raised before January 1, 1994 and in respect of Summary Cause Actions.

[6] Repealed by the Act of Court (Consolidation etc.) 1998 except in respect of Ordinary Actions and Summary Applications raised before January 1994.

## Closed records

**1.11.**[1]   When records are prepared, the answers for the defender should be inset from the margin used for the pleadings for the pursuer and all interlocutors in the cause to the date of making up the record should be reproduced.

**1.12.–1.16.**[2]   *[Repealed by the Act of Court (Consolidation etc.) 1998.]*

## Sterling equivalent of foreign currency

**1.17.**[3]   Where in any action payment is craved of a sum of money in a foreign currency or the sterling equivalent thereof at the date of payment or at the date of extract, whichever is the earlier, with or without interest, and decree has been granted in these terms, an extract may proceed upon a minute by the party in whose favour decree has been granted or his agent, endorsed on or annexed to the summons or initial writ, stating the rate of exchange prevailing at the close of business on the preceding day and the sterling equivalent at that rate of the sum decerned for in foreign currency, craving extract accordingly and accompanied by a certificate, which may be in the form provided in the schedule hereto, from one of the Scottish clearing banks certifying the said rate and sterling equivalent; and the extract shall bear a reference to said certificate.

**1.18–4.01.**   *[Repealed by the Act of Court (Consolidation etc.) 1998.]*

SCHEDULE*[Repealed by the Act of Court (Consolidation etc.) 1998.]*

**Act of Court (Consolidation etc.) 1998**  D3.12

(SI 1998/)

*14 September 1998.*

ARRANGEMENT OF RULES

PART 1 CIVIL PROCEDURE

---

[1] Repealed by the Act of Court (Consolidation etc.) 1998 except in respect of Ordinary Actions and Summary Applications raised before January 1994.
[2] Repealed by the Act of Court (Consolidation etc.) 1998 except in respect of Ordinary Actions and Summary Applications raised before January 1994.
[3] Repealed by the Act of Court (Consolidation etc.) 1998 except in respect of Ordinary Actions and Summary Applications raised before January 1994.

I, Robert Colquhoun Hay, C.B.E., W.S., Sheriff Principal of North Strathclyde, hereby repeal all Acts of Court and Practice Notes presently in force within the Sheriffdom other than those listed in the Schedule hereto, and direct that the following will be given effect on or after 2nd November 1998.

PART 1

CIVIL PROCEDURE

## Process

**1.01.** No process or any part thereof may be borrowed within the period from 12 noon on the second working day preceding any diet other than a diet of proof at which it is required until after the said diet.

**1.02.** All processes must be returned to the sheriff clerk not later than 12 noon of the second working day preceding any diet or the date on which they appear on the rolls of the court.

**1.03.** Where an ordinary cause or summary application process is required for an ordinary court diet, that process will not be available for inspection during the period from 12 noon on the second working day preceding the ordinary court diet in question until after that diet.

## Citation

**1.04.** No document shall be served on or transmitted to the defender or respondent along with the service document other than such notice as is prescribed or required by law.

## Legal representation

**1.05.** The name, address, telephone, fax and document exchange numbers and the reference of the principal agent(s) shall be stated on each part of process lodged in court by any party.

## Ordinary Cause Motions

**1.06.** Where a motion is to be heard in terms of rule 15.5(5) of the Ordinary Cause Rules, any document referred to in the motion or to which a party intends to refer at the hearing of the motion and which is not already lodged in process shall be lodged as a production and a copy thereof intimated to every other party not later than noon on the working day before the date assigned for the hearing of the motion. A document which is not so lodged and intimated shall not be used at the hearing unless with leave of the sheriff on cause shown and on such conditions, if any, as to expenses or otherwise as the sheriff thinks fit.

**1.07.** Except in the event of an unforeseeable emergency, a motion to discharge a diet of proof, whether made of consent or not, shall be lodged in time to be heard not less than 10 working days before the diet of proof.

## Ordinary Cause Motions—Determination and Signature of Interlocutors by Sheriff Clerks

**1.08.** For the purpose of Rules 12.1 and 15.5(2) of the Rules contained in the First Schedule annexed to the Act of Sederunt (Sheriff Court Ordinary Cause Rules), 1993, it is hereby directed as follows: "the sheriff clerk" shall not include a sheriff clerk below the rank of higher executive officer save that, in any sheriff court within the sheriffdom where the senior resident sheriff clerk holds the rank of executive officer, it shall include that sheriff clerk.

**1.09.** The classes of interlocutor which a sheriff clerk may write and sign in terms of the said Rule 12.1 shall not include any final interlocutor or any interlocutor which the sheriff concerned directs to be written or signed by him or her. Subject to the foregoing, any interlocutor dealing with a motion which has been determined by a sheriff clerk in terms of the said Rule 15.5(2) shall be written and signed by that sheriff clerk.

**1.10.** The classes of unopposed motion which a sheriff clerk may determine in terms of the said Rule 15.5(2) are as undernoted. However, if the granting of any such motion might also involve any order relating to expenses, it shall be referred to the sheriff who shall deal with it in accordance with Rule 15.5(2).

(a)   A motion to recall a sist and to re-enrol a cause for further procedure.
(b)   A motion, made under Rule 10.3(1), to close the record before the expiry of the adjustment period provided by Rule 10.1(1).
(c)   A motion to allow an amendment of a kind specified in Rule 18.1.
(d)   A motion to allow a minute of amendment to be received and answered within a specified period in terms of Rule 18.3(1)(a) and (b)(ii).
(e)   A motion for an order for service of a third party notice, made under Rule 20.1(1) and (2).
(f)   A motion for the fixing of a peremptory diet following withdrawal from agency under Rule 24.2(1).
(g)   A motion to allow the late lodging of a notice of intention to defend and a motion to allow the late lodging of defences provided in both cases that the notice of intention to defend or the defences as the case may be is not more than three working days overdue.

## Child Welfare Hearings

**1.11.**   Where a date for a child welfare hearing is fixed in terms of rule 33.22A(1) of the Ordinary Cause Rules, any document to which a party intends to refer at the child welfare hearing and which is not already lodged in process shall be lodged as a production and a copy thereof intimated to every other party not later than noon on the working day before the date fixed for the child welfare hearing. A document which is not so lodged and intimated shall not be used at the hearing unless with leave of the sheriff on cause shown and on such conditions, if any, as to expenses or otherwise as the sheriff thinks fit.

## Interim Hearings

**1.12.**   Where the court has fixed a date, time and place for parties to be heard on an application for an interim order:—
(a)   the initial writ, if borrowed, shall be returned to the sheriff clerk, and
(b)   any document to which a party intends to refer at the hearing and which is not already lodged in process shall be lodged as a production and a copy thereof intimated to every other party,
not later than noon on the working day before the date fixed for the hearing. A document which is not so lodged and intimated shall not be used at the hearing unless with leave of the sheriff on cause shown and on such conditions, if any, as to expenses or otherwise as the sheriff thinks fit.

## Productions

**1.13.**   All productions and copies thereof shall be clearly marked with their process number by the party lodging same. Where copies of productions are lodged with the sheriff clerk in terms of rule 1.06 above, he shall forthwith docquet the inventory of productions to show that copies have been lodged and the date of lodging.

## Records

**1.14.** When records are prepared, the answers for the defender and any third party should be inset from the margin used for the pleadings for the pursuer. Lines should be double-spaced and pages should be numbered. It will be helpful if every fifth line on each page is numbered.

## Notice of Authorities for proofs or debates

**1.15.** Not later than two clear working days before the diet the solicitor for each party to an action in which a proof or debate has been fixed shall lodge with the sheriff clerk a note of all authorities to which reference is to be made in the course of the argument for the party whom he represents.

## Undefended Consistorial Proofs—recording of Evidence

**1.16.** In any undefended consistorial action it shall not be necessary to have the evidence recorded unless the sheriff in his interlocutor allowing proof appoints the evidence to be so recorded either *ex proprio motu* or on the motion of the pursuer. The provisions of Rule 29.15 of the Ordinary Cause Rules 1993 with regard to the ordering of shorthand writers shall apply.

## Summary applications—Recording of Evidence

**1.17.** In any summary application the sheriff may consider at the first hearing whether it is appropriate to have the evidence recorded. To that end, parties should be prepared to indicate the nature and extent of the evidence likely to be adduced, and to state whether or not they consider it desirable to have the evidence recorded. The sheriff in his interlocutor allowing proof may appoint the evidence to be so recorded, either *ex proprio motu* or on the motion of a party. The provisions of Rule 29.15 and 29.18 of the Ordinary Cause Rules with regard to the ordering and payment of shorthand writers shall apply.

## Settlement of actions

**1.18.** When a settlement has been reached in any case and as a result of that settlement a proof or debate or appeal will not proceed on the date which has been listed, the solicitors acting in the case should forthwith intimate the position by telephone to the sheriff clerk and immediately thereafter confirm such intimation in writing.

## Social Security (Recovery of Benefits) Act 1997

**1.19.** In all cases to which the Social Security (Recovery of Benefits) Act 1997 applies, parties seeking decree (except where that decree is sought of consent, for instance, as the result of a Joint Minute) should lodge in process a schedule of damages stating the amount of any compensation which is claimed in respect of the relevant period under any of the headings in Column 1 of Schedule 2 to the Act. For the avoidance of doubt, it should be noted that this requirement will apply not only to final decrees after proof but to decrees in absence, decrees by default, summary decrees, interim decrees and decrees for professional damages.

## Summary cause—expenses

**1.20.** In an action of delivery the value of the article should be stated at market value having regard to depreciation or appreciation from the value as new.

**1.21.** The reduction of 50 per cent of fees shall apply in all cases of delivery where the value of the article is not stated.

**1.22.** In summonses where the crave for delivery is accompanied by alternative or ancillary craves for payment and the value of the article or articles sought to be delivered is not specified, the basis for calculation of fees shall be the amount of the alternative or ancillary craves.

**1.23.** Where the value of the article is specified and there are in addition craves for payment the basis for calculation of fees shall be the aggregate of the value of the article and the total of the sum on the additional craves.

## Small Claims procedure

**1.24.** Hearings under the Small Claims Rules 1998 should be conducted with no more formality than is necessary for the orderly disposal of business by the sheriff in terms of rule 19 of said Rules. To this end,
(a) the number of persons allowed within the bar of the court should normally be restricted to those involved in the current case; and
(b) solicitors are not required to wear gowns.

## Appeals to the Sheriff Principal

**1.25.** When an appeal is marked, the note of appeal or the entry in the interlocutor sheet should specify all the interlocutors which are to be brought under review.

**1.26.** When, following a proof, an appeal is marked against an interlocutor which has been issued by the sheriff before the notes of evidence are extended and lodged in process, the appellant or his solicitor shall, except in a case to which rule 1.28 below applies, inform the shorthand writer forthwith that the notes of evidence are required, and ascertain from him the date when the notes of evidence will be available. The appellant or his solicitor shall thereafter inform the Sheriff Principal's Personal Secretary at Paisley Sheriff Court of the date when the notes of evidence will be available in order that an appropriate diet may be assigned for hearing the appeal.

**1.27.** Failure by the appellant or his solicitor to comply with the above provisions, so that there is undue delay in hearing the appeal, or a diet fixed for the hearing is rendered abortive, may affect the question of expenses.

**1.28.** Where it appears to the appellant or his solicitor that the ground of appeal is such that it may be unnecessary to have the notes of evidence available for the hearing of the appeal, a written application to dispense with the requirements of Rule 1.26 above may be made to the Sheriff Principal and intimated to the other parties in the appeal. The Sheriff Principal's decision on any such application shall be final in the proceedings before him.

**1.29.** Within 10 working days of an appeal being marked, the parties shall provide the Sheriff Principal's Personal Secretary at Paisley Sheriff Court with a note of any dates within the following 12 weeks on which they, or their legal representatives, do not wish the appeal to be heard. When assigning diets of appeal the Sheriff Principal will take into account, but will not be bound by, such note, particularly as regards urgent matters.

**1.30.** Not less than two clear working days before the diet of appeal, the solicitor for each party shall lodge a note of all authorities to which reference is to be made in the course of argument for the party he represents with **(1)** the Sheriff Principal's Personal Secretary at Paisley Sheriff Court, and **(2)** in the case of appeals to be heard at courts other than Paisley, the sheriff clerk of the court where the appeal is to be heard.

**1.31.** Any parts of process in the hands of parties must be returned to the Sheriff Principal's Personal Secretary at Paisley Sheriff Court not later than 10 a.m. on the third working day before the diet assigned for hearing the appeal.

PART 2[1]

AFFIDAVITS IN FAMILY ACTIONS

**When affidavits may be lodged**

**2.01.** Once the period within which a notice of intention to defend requires to be lodged has expired without such notice having been lodged, affidavits may be prepared and lodged without any order of the court.

**Person before whom sworn or affirmed**

**2.02.** An affidavit is admissible if it is sworn (or affirmed) before a notary public, justice of the peace, or any person having authority to administer oaths for the place where the affidavit is sworn, such as a commissioner for oaths or a British diplomatic officer or consul abroad. A solicitor acting for a party to the action may act in a notarial capacity when an affidavit is sworn. Any person before whom an affidavit is sworn (referred to below as "the notary") must observe all the normal rules in this connection and must satisfy himself or herself as to the capacity of the witness to swear an affidavit.

**Importance of affidavits**

**2.03.** The witness should be made to appreciate the importance of the affidavit and that the affidavit constitutes his or her evidence in the case. The possible consequences of giving false evidence should be explained to the witness. Before the witness signs the affidavit he or she must have read it or the notary must have read it over to the witness.

**Oath or affirmation**

**2.04.** The witness must be placed on oath or must affirm.

---

[1] Substituted by Act of Court: Affidavits in Family Actions, May 13, 2003 (effective June 2, 2003).

## Form and signature of the affidavit

**2.05.** The document should be on A4 paper. The affidavit should commence with the words "At ..........the ..........day of ..........20.......... , in the presence of I having been solemnly sworn/having affirmed give evidence as follows:". The affidavit should be drafted in the first person and should take the form of numbered paragraphs. The full name, age, address and occupation of the witness should be given in the first paragraph. The affidavit should end with the words "All of which is the truth as I shall answer to God" or "All of which is affirmed by me to be true", as appropriate. Any blanks in the affidavit must be filled in. Any insertion, deletion or other amendment to the affidavit requires to be initialed by the witness and the notary. Each page must be signed by both the witness and the notary. It is not necessary for the affidavit to be sealed by the notary.

## Drafting the affidavit

**2.06.** An affidavit should be based on a reliable and full precognition of the witness.

**2.07.** The drafter of an affidavit should provide himself or herself, before drawing it, with an up to date copy of the pleadings, a copy of the appropriate precognition and the relative productions. The affidavit should be drawn so as to follow the averments in the pleadings to the extent that these are within the knowledge of that particular witness and in the same order.

**2.08.** Affidavits should be expressed in the words of the person whose affidavit it is, should be accurate as at the date of the affidavit and should not consist of a repetition of passages in the pleadings. It should be clear from the terms of the affidavit whether the witness is speaking from his or her own knowledge, as when the witness was present and saw what happened, or whether the witness is relying on what he or she was told by a particular person.

## Productions

**2.09.** Productions already lodged in process must be borrowed up, and put to the party or to the witness who refers to them in his or her affidavit. Each production will require to be referred to in the affidavit by its number of process and must be docqueted and signed by the witness and the notary. If a production has not yet been lodged when the affidavit is sworn, it will require to be identified by the witness in the affidavit, should be docqueted with regard to the affidavit and signed by the witness and the notary. It must then be lodged as a production. Some productions will necessarily be docqueted with regard to more than one affidavit.

**2.10.** n consent cases, the defender's written consent form will have to be put to the pursuer in his or her affidavit, and be identified, docqueted and signed in the same way as other productions.

**2.11.** In adultery cases, photographs of both the pursuer and the defender may require to be produced, put to the appropriate witnesses and be identified, docqueted and signed in the manner already described.

**Date of Affidavit**

**2.12.** All affidavits lodged must be of recent date. This factor is particularly important in cases involving children, cases in which financial craves are involved and in any other circumstances where the evidence of a witness or circumstances to which the witness speaks are liable to change through the passage of time. The notary must take particular care in such cases to ensure that the affidavit evidence as to such matters is correct as at the time the affidavit is sworn. Affidavits relating to the welfare of children which have been sworn more than three months prior to lodging a minute for decree are likely to be rejected by the court as out of date.

**Applications relating to parental responsibilities and rights (See OCR 33.28)**

**2.13.** In actions in which an application in terms of section 11 of the Children (Scotland) Act 1995 is before the court not fewer than two affidavits dealing with the welfare of the child(ren) should be provided, at least one of them from a person who is neither a parent nor a party to the action. These affidavits should present the court with a full picture of the arrangements for the care of the child(ren) along the lines set out in paragraph 15, adapted to suit the circumstances of the particular case. The affidavits should set out reasons why it is better that the section 11 order be made than not. The pursuer's affidavit should deal fully with the arrangements which have been made for their care, so far as within his or her knowledge. If the pursuer cannot give substantial evidence as to that it is likely to be necessary to obtain such evidence from the person who is responsible for their care.

**2.14.** In actions of divorce or judicial separation in which there are children of the marriage or children treated by the parties as a child of their family but in which no order in terms of section 11 in terms of the Children (Scotland) Act 1995 is sought, the court, in terms of section 12, requires to consider whether to exercise the powers set out in sections 11 or 54 of that Act in light of the information before it as the arrangements for the child(ren)'s upbringing. Information accordingly requires to be before the court as to these arrangements. As a minimum, the affidavits of the witnesses should include the information set out in paragraphs 15 (a) to (e) below.

**2.15.** An affidavit dealing with the arrangements for the care of children should, where relevant, include the following:
- (a) the qualifications of the witness, if not a parent, to speak about the child; how often, and in what circumstances the witness normally sees the child;
- (b) the ability of those with whom the child lives to provide proper care for him or her;
- (c) observations as to the relationship between the child and the other members of the household, the child's general appearance, interests, state of health and well-being;
- (d) a description of the home conditions in which the child lives;
- (e) the arrangements for contact between the child and any parent (and siblings) who do not live in the same household as the child;
- (f) information about the school the child attends; whether the child attends school regularly; and
- (g) details of child care arrangements during working hours, including the arrangements for such care outwith school hours.

### Affidavit relating to disclosure of the whereabouts of children

**2.16.** An affidavit sworn or affirmed in compliance with an order to disclose the whereabouts of children (in terms of the Family Law Act 1986, section 33 and OCR 33.23) will require to be drafted in such a way as to meet the requirements of the court in the circumstances of the particular case. The form of the affidavit should be as above.

### Financial and other ancillary craves

**2.17.** Affidavit evidence in support of financial craves is necessary in an undefended action. (See *Ali v Ali*, 2001 S.C. 618, 2001 S.L.T. 602, 2001 S.C.L.R. 485). Where financial craves are involved, the evidence should be as full, accurate and up-to-date as possible. If the evidence is insufficient the court may require supplementary evidence to be provided. If, after an affidavit has been sworn and the solicitor concerned has parted with it, a material change of circumstances occurs before decree has been granted the court must be informed forthwith. A further affidavit may have to be sworn.

**2.18.** The pursuer should give evidence as to his or her own financial position at the date of the affidavit. Where the pursuer gives evidence in an affidavit as to the financial position of the defender, the affidavit should state the date, as precisely as possible, at which the information was valid. The court must be provided with information which is as up-to-date as possible as to the defender's ability to pay the sums the pursuer is seeking. Where the pursuer cannot obtain recent information as to the defender's means the affidavit should state that that is the case but should contain as much material information relating to the defender's means as possible. If the pursuer is unable to provide sufficient evidence to justify the orders craved in full, in the minute for decree, after the words "in terms of crave(s) (number(s)...) of the initial writ", there may be added words such as "or such other sum (or sums) as the court may think proper".

**2.19.** Where the pursuer has craved a capital sum, an order for the sale of the matrimonial home, a periodical allowance, interdict or expenses, for example, and in the minute for decree does not seek decree for one or more of these, the reasons for that should be given in his or her affidavit.

### Joint Minutes

**2.20.** When parties record their agreement in a joint minute as to how financial and other ancillary craves should be dealt with by the court, the pursuer's affidavit should refer to the joint minute and indicate that he or she is content that the agreement set out in it should be given effect.

### Minute for decree

**2.21.** The minute for decree must be signed by a solicitor who has examined the affidavits and other documents. That solicitor takes responsibility therefor, whether or not he or she is the person who drew the initial writ or affidavits. The minute for decree should not be signed seeking decree of divorce or separation unless the evidence consists of or includes evidence other than that of a party to the marriage (Civil Evidence (Scotland) Act 1988, section 8(3); *Taylor v Taylor*, 2000 S.L.T. 1419; 2001 S.C.L.R. 16).

PART 3

MISCELLANEOUS

## Commissary Business

**3.01.** The inventories of the estates of deceased persons should be presented to the sheriff court of the sheriff court district in which they were last ordinarily resident; or if presented elsewhere, forwarded to that court for issue of confirmation and recording. The exceptions to the foregoing general direction are in respect of the sheriff court districts of Dunoon, Rothesay, Oban and Campbeltown. Inventories of the estates of deceased persons who resided in the sheriff court districts of Dunoon and Rothesay should be lodged at Greenock Sheriff Court; inventories of the estates of deceased persons who resided in the sheriff court districts of Campbeltown and Oban should be lodged at Dumbarton Sheriff Court, or, if such inventories are presented elsewhere, forwarded to the appropriate court as above for issue of confirmation and recording.

**3.02.** Petitions for appointment of executors-dative should be lodged and published in the sheriff court of the district in which the deceased last ordinarily resided.

**3.03.** Subject to the following provisions of this order, all additional and corrective inventories, inventories *ad non executa*, inventories *ad omissa* and additional oaths shall be considered as steps in the original confirmation and shall be lodged in the sheriff court in the commissariat in which the confirmation was granted, or the sheriff court which holds the records of the original application for confirmation.

**3.04.** The sheriff of any court in which a commissary application is made may (a) remit that application to another court, and (b) require an applicant who has applied as executor-dative in any other court within the sheriffdom to produce an extract decree of the appointment.

**3.05.** In the oath to an inventory or in a petition for appointment of executor it shall be sufficient to refer to the deceased's domicile as being within the Sheriffdom of North Strathclyde in Scotland.

## Registration of protests of bills of exchange and deeds

**3.06.** Protests of bills of exchange and deeds shall be registered relative to the sheriff court district of Paisley at Paisley Sheriff Court; to the sheriff court districts of Greenock, Dunoon and Rothesay at Greenock Sheriff Court; to the sheriff court districts of Campbeltown, Dumbarton and Oban at Dumbarton Sheriff Court; and to the sheriff court district at Kilmarnock at Kilmarnock Sheriff Court.

## Reports of poinding, warrants of sale and reports of sale

**3.07.** Every report of a poinding and all applications for orders or warrants relating to poinded moveables and the report of any sale thereof shall be lodged with or made to the court of the sheriff court district in which the poinded moveables are situated.

PART 4

ADMINISTRATION

## Representation and wearing of gowns

**4.01.** Subject to rule 1.24 (hearings in Small Claims) any solicitor appearing professionally at the Bar of any sheriff court in the sheriffdom shall wear a gown.

**4.02.** Except in accordance with rule 1.3 of the Ordinary Cause Rules 1993 or rule 17 of the Schedule to the Act of Sederunt (Summary Cause Rules, Sheriff Court) 1976, or rule 30 of the Schedule to the Act of Sederunt (Small Claim Rules) 1988, no person other than a member of the Faculty of Advocates or a qualified solicitor holding a practising certificate shall be permitted to appear on behalf of a litigant at any stage or procedure.

**4.03.** When a trainee solicitor is allowed to represent a party in terms of the said rule 17 or the said rule 30 he or she shall not wear a gown.

**4.04.** Any party not personally present or represented in accordance with these directions at any diet shall be deemed to be absent.

## Avoidance of congestion in corridors

**4.05.** In courts where interview rooms are provided, interviews between solicitors and clients should take place there and not in the halls and corridors of the sheriff court.

**4.06.** Members of the public attending court must not loiter in corridors, but should proceed to court rooms.

**4.07.** Witnesses must proceed as directed by court staff to the witness room allocated and must remain there unless authorised to leave by a court official.

## No smoking areas

**4.08.** All persons attending court must obey the "no smoking" signs as displayed within the court precincts.

## Sheriff Court car parks

**4.09.** Where car parking has been provided for public use at any of the sheriff courts within the sheriffdom, such car parks will be under the day to day management of the sheriff clerk or an officer appointed by him.

1160

**4.10** Vehicles may be left in the car park only while the occupant is in attendance within the sheriff court house.

**4.11.** The sheriff clerk or the officer nominated by him may at his discretion
    (a)   admit or deny access to the car park to any vehicle;
    (b)   require any vehicle to be removed;
    (c)   reserve space for any vehicle; and
    (d)   regulate where, when and for how long any vehicle may be parked.

### PART 5

### EXTENT

**Extent**

**5.01.** The foregoing rules shall apply in all the sheriff courts within the sheriffdom.

### PART 6

### INTERPRETATION

**6.1.** References in this Act of Court to "the Ordinary Cause Rules" are to the Ordinary Cause Rules 1993 set out in the Act of Sederunt (Sheriff Court Ordinary Cause Rules) 1993.

I appoint this Act of Court to be inserted in the Act Books of all the sheriff courts in the Sheriffdom of North Strathclyde and to be posted on the notice boards in said sheriff courts for publication to the lieges.

### SCHEDULE

**Savings**

The following Acts of Court are not repealed by this Act of Court:
Any Act of Court anent Court Holidays.
Any Act of Court anent Sessions and Vacation Courts.
Rules 1.01, 1.06, 1.07, 1.08, 1.11, 1.17 of the Act of Court (Consolidation etc.) of 20th October 1992 in respect of Ordinary Actions and Summary Applications raised before 1st January 1994.
Rules 1.06, 1.07 and 1.08 of the said Act of Court in respect of Summary Cause Actions.

# ACT OF COURT

D3.13

## AFFIDAVITS IN FAMILY ACTIONS

### [MAY 13, 2003]

I, Bruce Alexander Kerr, Queen's Counsel, Sheriff Principal of North Strathclyde, hereby direct that as and from 2 June 2003 there shall be substituted for Part 2 (Affidavits and Family Actions) of the Act of Court (Consolidation, etc) 1998 the provisions set forth in the Schedule hereto; and I Appoint this act of court to be inserted in the act books of all the sherif f courts of the sheriffdom and to be posted on the notice boards in all the sheriff courthouses for publication to the lieges.

Sheriff Principal of North Strathclyde

## Schedule

*Part 2 Affidavits in Family Actions*

[*See* Act of Court (Consolidation, etc) 1998]

**D3.14**

# PRACTICE NOTE NO. 1, 2006

[JANUARY 31, 2006]

**Adoption of Children, etc: Guidance for Sheriffs and Practitioners**

[*Revoked by Practice Note No.1 of 2009.*]

**D3.15**

# PRACTICE NOTE NO.2 OF 2006: SPECIFICATIONS FOR RECOVERY OF MEDICAL RECORDS

1.  This practice note has effect from 1 November 2006.
2.  For the purpose of rules 28.2(3)(c) of the Ordinary Cause Rules 1993 and 18.1(3)(b) of the Summary Cause Rules 2002 it is no longer necessary for a copy of a specification or an incidental application for the recovery of medical records to be intimated to the Lord Advocate.

October 24, 2006

**D3.16**

# PRACTICE NOTE NO.1 OF 2009: ADOPTION AND CHILDREN (SCOTLAND) ACT 2007: GUIDANCE FOR SHERIFFS AND PRACTITIONERS

### Purpose

1.  The purpose of this Practice Note is to secure the efficient management of contested applications and other proceedings under the Adoption and Children (Scotland) Act 2007 ("the Act"). It should be read subject to the detailed rules of procedure to be found in the Sheriff Court Adoption Rules 2009 ("the Rules")—see the Act of Sederunt (Sheriff Court Rules Amendment) (Adoption and Children (Scotland) Act 2007) 2009 (SSI 2009/284). It will be revised in light of experience and any new primary or secondary legislation.

### Commencement

2.  This Practice Note applies to all applications lodged, or proceedings commenced, on or after 28 September 2009.

### Minimum of delay

3.  It shall be the duty of the court to secure that all applications and other proceedings under the Act are dealt with as expeditiously as possible and with the minimum of delay. Such applications and proceedings require the co-operation of all concerned and active and firm case management by the sheriff throughout their course.

## Identity of sheriff

**4.** Unless the sheriff principal otherwise agrees, the sheriff presiding at any stage in the proceedings must be a sheriff of this sherrifdom. In the interests of continuity and consistency in management, every stage of each case must, whenever possible, call before the same sheriff.

**5.** In the event that a proof has to be taken by a sheriff other than the sheriff who has conducted the previous hearings, the whole process in the case must be made available to the sheriff who is to take the proof not less than three working days before the date upon which the proof is scheduled to commence.

## Representatives

**6.** At every calling of a case any representative of any party must be familiar with the case and must have sufficient authority to deal with any issues that are likely to arise at that calling.

## Record of discussion to be kept

**7.** At every hearing prior to any proof the sheriff should not only pronounce an interlocutor regulating further procedure but should also prepare and keep with the process a brief written record of the main points of the discussion at that hearing.

## The application

**8.** Subject to any issue of confidentiality that may arise, wherever possible a copy of the petition or application (as the case may be) should be sent to the sheriff clerk in electronic form on the same date as the date upon which it is lodged.

## Court programming

**9.** The programming of all classes of business in the courts of the sheriffdom remains exclusively the responsibility of the sheriff principal. In this respect he generally acts through the sheriff clerk. It is therefore essential that the assigning of diets by the sheriff should be undertaken only after consultation with, and with the agreement of, the sheriff clerk.

## The preliminary and pre-proof hearings

**10.** Any preliminary or pre-proof hearing fixed in terms of the Rules should be of sufficient duration to allow for a proper consideration of the issues likely to be canvassed at it. Consideration should be given to the advisability of intimating any such hearing by sheriff officer in order to avoid any possible delay due to ineffective postal service.

**11.** Where the date of a hearing requires to be intimated otherwise than by the sheriff clerk, the sheriff clerk should advise the applicant or petitioner or his or her solicitors forthwith of the terms of the interlocutor appointing the date of the hearing in order that they may intimate it as soon as possible. If so requested (and subject to any issue of confidentiality that may arise), the sheriff clerk should be prepared to send to the applicant or petitioner or his or her solicitors a copy of the interlocutor by fax or in electronic form as soon as it has been signed. Any such request should be accompanied by the appropriate fax telephone number or e-mail address as the case may be.

**12.** At any preliminary hearing the sheriff should ask the respondent or his or her solicitor whether the respondent has applied, or proposes to apply, for legal aid. The sheriff should also enquire whether it is intended to instruct counsel or any expert witness and, if so, whether legal aid for that purpose has been or is to be applied for.

**13.** The sheriff should ensure that the parties have sufficient access to all the documents lodged in process. The sheriff should ask the parties whether they will be seeking to recover any documents and, if so, which documents. The sheriff should ask the other parties if they will make these available informally without the need for a commission and diligence and, if so, should fix a date by which those documents should be lodged with the court.

**14.** At a preliminary hearing, which failing at a pre-proof hearing, the sheriff should give consideration to ordering parties to intimate to every other party and to lodge in court (i) a list of witnesses, including any expert witnesses, on whose evidence it is intended to rely at proof, and (ii) a list of the documents or other productions which it is intended should be used or put in evidence at proof.

## Assigning a diet of proof

**15.** Where it appears that a proof will be necessary, the parties should be in a position to give the sheriff a carefully considered forecast of the time which the proof is expected to take. The sheriff should ask each party to specify in detail how long he expects to take in the presentation of his own evidence and in the cross-examination of the witnesses of the other party or parties. On the basis of this information the sheriff should assess how many days should be set aside for the proof (including closing submissions). At the proof itself, parties may expect to be held to the estimates previously given by them, unless in exceptional circumstances.

**16.** In the fixing of a diet of proof it is not generally a valid ground of objection to a date proposed by the court that a party wishes to instruct particular counsel. If need be, that party can always instruct another counsel.

**17.** Consideration should be given at an early stage in the proceedings to where the proof will take place and whether the evidence at the proof should be recorded. The holding of a proof elsewhere than at the courthouse may be anticipated to cause administrative problems, for example for the sheriff clerk. But such administrative problems must not be permitted to get in the way of the expeditious disposal of an application or other proceeding under the Act.

**18.** It will be seen that rules 20 and 37 of the Rules provide that a proof is to be taken continuously so far as possible, but the sheriff may adjourn the diet from time to time. To allow for this, in particular in the smaller courts in the sheriffdom, consideration should be given to the possibility of holding the proof elsewhere than at the courthouse—see the preceding paragraph. Bearing in mind the time limits in rules 22 and 38, the sheriff should consider too whether he or she is likely to require any writing days in order to produce the judgement. If so, provision for this should be made when a diet of proof is fixed. As in the case of an application to free a child for adoption under the Adoption (Scotland) Act 1978, the reason for such provision is that the sheriff should "be released from other duties so that he can give priority to the case without interruption and until it has been completed by the issuing of his interlocutor. Special arrangements of that kind are clearly necessary if the sheriff is to maintain the continuity of thought throughout the proceedings which is so necessary to a proper disposal of the case" (*Lothian Regional Council v A* , 1992 S.L.T. 858 at page 862A-B).

## Legal issues

**19.** At a pre-proof hearing the sheriff should ask the parties if there are any questions of admissibility of evidence or any other legal issues, including any questions under the European Convention on Human Rights, that are likely to arise at the proof. If so, the sheriff should consider whether they could with advantage be determined at this hearing rather than at the proof. Alternatively, the sheriff may adjourn the pre-proof hearing to another date in order to enable any such issue to be argued and determined. If a legal issue is not raised at the pre-proof hearing, the sheriff may refuse to allow it to be raised at the proof except on cause shown. A solicitor who intends to raise a legal issue at a pre-proof hearing should intimate it to the other parties' solicitors beforehand.

## Evidence

**20.** It should be noted that evidence may be presented in the form of affidavits or other written documents (Civil Evidence (Scotland) Act 1988, section 2; *McVinnie v McVinnie* , 1995 S.L.T. (Sh. Ct) 81; *Glaser v Glaser* , 1997 S.L.T. 456). The sheriff is bound to consider reports placed before him or her even if the authors are not called to speak to them, and the strict rules of evidence do not apply (*T, Petitioner* , 1997 S.L.T. 724 at 730L). Such considerations may render the attendance of certain witnesses unnecessary, although for other reasons it may be preferable to call the author of a document. The parties should therefore apply their minds to the question whether any evidence might be appropriately presented in the form of an affidavit or other document and the sheriff should encourage them to decide that question at the pre-proof hearing. The sheriff should also encourage the use of affidavits to cover non-contentious (or indeed contentious) issues where that would save the time of witnesses and the court. Notwithstanding that an affidavit has been lodged, its author may be called to give evidence at the proof (see paragraph 3 of the judgment of Lady Smith in *Petitions of Aberdeenshire Council to declare A, B and C free for adoption*, Court of Session, 22 June 2004).

**21.** Where the author of a report or the maker of a statement which has been or is to be lodged is to be called as a witness, the sheriff may order that the report or statement is to be held to be equivalent to the witness's examination-in-chief, unless for special reasons he or she otherwise directs.

**22.** The sheriff should discourage the unnecessary use of expert witnesses. If expert evidence is essential, the sheriff should encourage the joint instruction of a single expert by all parties. If one party instructs an expert report, it should be disclosed to the other parties with a view to the agreement of as much of its contents as possible.

**23.** The sheriff should ask the parties what further productions, if any, they intend to lodge. Any difficulties over the obtaining or lodging of documents should be raised and if possible resolved at the pre-proof hearing.

## The proof

**24.** At a proof it should be borne in mind that "there is a heavy responsibility on the parties' representatives to exercise all reasonable economy and restraint in their presentation of the evidence and in their submissions to the court" (*Lothian Regional Council v A* at page 862B). The sheriff may therefore exercise his or her existing common law power to intervene to discourage prolixity, repetition, the leading of evidence of unnecessary witnesses and the leading of evidence on matters which are unlikely to assist the court to reach a decision.

**25.** At the conclusion of the evidence parties must be heard orally thereon by the sheriff. In anticipation of this the sheriff may require the parties to submit, in electronic form or otherwise, draft findings in fact, or skeleton arguments, or both.

## The Practice Note No 1, 2006: Adoption of Children, etc.

**26.** The Practice Note No 1, 2006: Adoption of Children, etc. is revoked subject to the qualification that it shall continue to have effect for the purpose of any application to which it applies which has been made and not yet determined before 28 September 2009.

1 October 2009

# ACT OF COURT NO. 1 OF 1977

[23RD NOVEMBER 1977]

### Practice—Conveyancing and feudal reform (scotland) act 1970

I, Charles Hampton Johnston, Q.C., Sheriff Principal of South Strathclyde,
Dumfries and Galloway, hereby direct as follows:—
1.   The initial writ in any application under Part II of the above-mentioned Act
     shall be headed and backed with the name of the Act, and shall be dealt
     with as a summary application.
2.   An initial writ bearing to be under the said Part of the above-mentioned Act
     but containing a crave for interdict or interim interdict alone or along with
     other craves shall not be accepted for warranting without the approval of
     the sheriff.

# ACT OF COURT NO. 4 OF 1981

[18TH AUGUST 1981]

### Practice—Sterling Equivalent of Foreign Currency

I, Frederick William Fitzgerald O'Brien, Q.C., Interim Sheriff Principal of South
Strathclyde, Dumfries and Galloway, in view of the decision of the First Division of
the Court of Session in the case of *Commerzbank Aktiengesellschaft v. Large* , 1977
S.L.T. 219, hereby direct as follows:

   Where in any action payment is craved of a sum of money in a foreign currency
or the sterling equivalent thereof at the date of payment or at the date of extract,
whichever is the earlier, with or without interest, and decree has been granted in
these terms, an extract may proceed upon a minute by the party in whose favour
decree has been granted or his agent, endorsed on or annexed to the summons or
initial writ, stating the rate of exchange prevailing at the close of business on the
preceding day and the sterling equivalent at that rate of the sum decerned for in
foreign currency, craving extract accordingly and accompanied by a certificate,
which may be in the form provided in the schedule hereto, from one of the Scottish
clearing banks certifying the said rate and sterling equivalent; and the extract shall
bear a reference to said certificate.

### Schedule

*Form of Certificate*

   I (*designation and address*) certify that the rate current in London for the purchase
of (state the unit of the foreign currency in which the decree is expressed) at the
close of business on the.....day of........19..........(being the date preceding that on
which extract of the decree is requested) was.....to the £ sterling and at this rate the
sum of (state the amount of the sum in the decree) amounts to £....

   Dated the....day of..........198..........
   Signed for or on behalf of the Bank
   Manager or other official

**D3.19**

# ACT OF COURT NO. 5 OF 1982

[MAY 25, 1982]

### Reports of Sale of Poinded Effects

I, Ronald Alistair Bennett, Q.C., Sheriff Principal of South Strathclyde, Dumfries and Galloway, hereby direct that upon a report of sale being lodged, the sheriff shall remit the account of expenses of the poinding and sale to the sheriff clerk for assessment and report and no fee shall be exigible from any party in respect of such assessment and report.

**D3.20**

# ACT OF COURT NO. 7 OF 1982

[JUNE 4, 1982]

### Summary Cause—Form Q—Inquiries from Solicitors

I, Ronald Alistair Bennett, Q.C., Sheriff Principal of South Strathclyde, Dumfries and Galloway, hereby direct that there shall be no obligation upon sheriff clerks to make provision for dealing with telephone inquiries from solicitors in relation to the lodging of Forms Q in summary causes, but it shall be within the discretion of the sheriff clerk to answer such inquiries where he is satisfied that to do so would not impair the service normally provided to solicitors and to the public.

**D3.21**

# PRACTICE NOTE

[JUNE 25, 1982]

I, Ronald Alistair Bennett, Q.C., Sheriff Principal of South Strathclyde, Dumfries and Galloway, direct that the rules contained in the schedule annexed hereto, shall come into force and have effect in all sheriff courts in the Sheriffdom of South Strathclyde, Dumfries and Galloway from and including 1st July 1982; and I hereby revoke all practice notes issued prior to the date of this order.

### Schedule

*General—Civil and Criminal Causes*

#### Gowns to be worn

**1.** Solicitors appearing at the bar of all courts (other than summary cause courts) shall wear gowns.

*Civil Causes—Ordinary Actions*

#### Return of process

**1.** All processes must be returned to the sheriff clerk not later than 12 o'clock noon of the second day preceding any diet or the date on which they appear on the rolls of the court.

### Anticipated duration of proof or trial

**2.**    When moving for a date to be fixed for a proof or debate, solicitors shall be prepared to inform the court of the anticipated duration of the proof or debate.

### Retirals and settlements

**3.—**
- (1)    When, in any action in which a diet of proof, or debate, has been fixed, the solicitor of any party decides to retire from the action, he shall at once intimate in writing the fact of his retirement to the solicitors for all other parties to the action and also to the sheriff clerk.
- (2)    When in any such case a settlement has been reached or it is probable that the proof or debate will not proceed on the date which has been fixed, the solicitors acting in the case shall at once intimate the position, in writing, to the sheriff clerk.

### Note of authorities for debate

**4.**    The solicitor for each party to an action in which a debate has been fixed shall, not later than 10 a.m. on the day of the debate, lodge with the sheriff clerk a note of all authorities to which reference is to be made in the course of the argument for the party whom he represents.

### Copies of productions to be provided

**5.**    Solicitors shall, at the time they lodge documentary productions in process, lodge for the use of the court one copy of each production clearly marked with the number of process.

### *Appeals-Ordinary Actions*

**6.**    [Revoked by Practice Note No. 1 of 1989.]

### Note of authorities for hearing of appeal

**7.**    The solicitors for each party to an action under appeal shall, not later than two clear working days prior to the day of the diet of hearing, lodge with the sheriff clerk of the court where the hearing of the appeal is to take place, a note of all authorities to which reference is to be made in the course of the argument for the party he represents, and shall send a copy of said note to the sheriff clerk at Airdrie.

## NOTES BY THE SHERIFF PRINCIPAL FOR THE GUIDANCE OF SOLICITORS IN RELATION TO AFFIDAVIT EVIDENCE IN UNDEFENDED DIVORCE ACTIONS OTHER THAN SIMPLIFIED DIVORCES

D3.22

[JANUARY 30, 1984]

[The terms of the Notes are identical to Section 5 of the Practice Notes of Glasgow and Strathkelvin (p. D 604), supra.]

**D3.23**

# ACT OF COURT NO. 6 OF 1988

[AUGUST 18, 1988]

### Transfer of Administrative Responsibility

I, Maurice Gordon Gillies, Q.C., Sheriff Principal of South Strathclyde, Dumfries and Galloway, hereby direct that as from 1st September 1988 the sheriff court at Kirkcudbright shall, for administrative purposes, cease to be a depute court of Stranraer and shall become a depute court attached to the sheriff court at Dumfries.

**D3.24**

# PRACTICE NOTE NO. 1 OF 1989

[DECEMBER 14, 1989]

### Appeal Against an Interlocutor to which the Sheriff has not Appended a Note

I, John Stuart Mowat, Q.C., Sheriff Principal of South Strathclyde, Dumfries and Galloway, hereby direct as follows:

Where an appeal is marked against an interlocutor to which the sheriff has not appended a note as required by rule 89(1) of the First Schedule to the Sheriff Courts (Scotland) Act 1907, the sheriff clerk, or one of his deputes, shall ascertain from the sheriff concerned, before transmission of the process to the sheriff principal, whether the sheriff wishes to add to such interlocutor a note setting out the grounds upon which he has proceeded.

This practice note supersedes para. 6 of the practice note dated 25th June 1982 and comes into force on 3rd January 1990 and applies to the whole sheriffdom.

**D3.25**

# ACT OF COURT NO. 1 OF 1993

[APRIL 6, 1993]

### Hamilton Sheriff Court Standing Advisory Committee

I, John Stuart Mowat Esquire, Q.C., Sheriff Principal of South Strathclyde, Dumfries and Galloway, after consultation with the Dean of the Society of Solicitors of Hamilton, the Regional Procurator Fiscal and the Sheriff Clerk of Hamilton, hereby re-constitute the committee known as the "Hamilton Sheriff Court Standing Advisory Committee", which shall have the constitution, functions and procedural rules prescribed in the schedule annexed hereto.

I Recall the Act of Court No. 1 of 1978 and I Appoint this Order to be inserted in the Act Book of the Sheriff Court at Hamilton for publication to the lieges.

#### Schedule

*Constitution*

1.  The committee shall consist of two sheriffs nominated by the sheriff principal, one of whom shall be designated as chairman; two solicitors nominated by the Dean of the Society of Solicitors of Hamilton; two persons of the rank of assistant procurator fiscal or procurator fiscal depute nominated by the regional procurator fiscal; and the heads of each of the criminal and civil departments, for the time being, of the sheriff clerk at Hamilton. Failing the attendance of the chairman at any meeting, a person shall be elected to act as chairman by the members present at the meeting. In

the event of equality of votes with regard to any proposed recommendation, the chairman for the time being shall have a casting vote in addition to his deliberative vote. The secretary of the committee shall be a sheriff clerk depute not being already a member of the committee and shall be appointed by the sheriff clerk to perform that office. It shall be open to the sheriff clerk to nominate a sheriff clerk depute other than the secretary to attend to the functions of secretary if the secretary is for any reason not available. The sheriff principal, the Dean of the Society of Solicitors of Hamilton, the regional procurator fiscal and the sheriff clerk of Hamilton are hereinafter referred to as "the constituents".

### Appointment of secretary and nomination and period of service of members

**2.** The name of the person appointed to be the secretary shall be intimated to the constituents by the sheriff clerk of Hamilton, and similar intimation will be made on the occasion of any change in the appointment.

The names and addresses of the persons nominated as members of the committee shall be sent to the secretary by the constituents. The nominated members will serve for two years from 1st May following their nomination and they may be renominated for further periods of service. In the event of the death or resignation of a member during such period of service, another person shall be nominated by the appropriate constituent to replace such member for the remainder of the period. In the event of a member being unable to attend any meeting, such member may be represented by a nominee of the affected constituent for the purposes of that meeting only and shall have the same rights at that meeting as if such nominee were a full member of the committee.

### Dates and place of meetings etc.

**3.** Meetings of the committee will be held as necessary and at least once a year.

Members of the committee will inform the secretary, a fortnight before each meeting, of matters to be included in the agenda, and the secretary will send a copy of the agenda, together with a draft minute of any previous meeting, to each member a week before the meeting. The committee may appoint sub-committees from time to time to perform specific functions delegated to them by the committee. It shall be competent for the chairman to invite other court users to attend meetings on an ad hoc basis when an item on the agenda appears to affect their interests.

### Functions of the committee

**4.** The committee shall take into consideration any matter affecting the efficiency of the administrative arrangements of the sheriff court in Hamilton, which they are asked by any of the constituents or by any member of the committee to take into consideration, and shall make such recommendations as they think proper from time to time with regard to such matters to the constituents or to any of them. A recommendation of the committee shall require the approval of a meeting attended by at least one nominee of each constituent. Any such recommendation shall be communicated in writing by the secretary to constituents.

D3.26

# ACT OF COURT NO. 4 OF 1995

[OCTOBER 25, 1995]

I, Graham Loudon Cox Esquire, Queen's Counsel, Sheriff Principal of the Sheriffdom of South Strathclyde, Dumfries and Galloway, hereby revoke the Act of Court, No 4 of 1982 with effect from this date.

I Appoint this Order to be inserted in the Act Book of every Court within the Sheriffdom, all for publication to the lieges.

D3.27

# PRACTICE NOTE NO. 1 OF 1998

[FEBRUARY 23, 1998]

In all cases to which the Social Security (Recovery of Benefits) Act 1997 applies, parties seeking decree (except where that decree is sought of consent, for instance, as the result of a Joint Minute) should lodge in process a *schedule of damages* stating the amount of any compensation which is claimed in respect of the relevant period under any of the headings in Column 1 of Schedule 2 to the Act.

For the avoidance of doubt, it should be noted that this requirement will apply not only to final decrees after proof but to decrees in absence, decrees by default, summary decrees, interim decrees and decrees for provisional damages.

This Practice Note comes into force on 1 March 1998 and applies to the whole Sheriffdom.

D3.28

# PRACTICE NOTE NO. 2 OF 1998

[DECEMBER 2, 1998]

This Practice Note revokes Practice Note No 2 of 25 November 1988

**1.** The Practice Note No 2 of 25 November 1988 is hereby revoked.

**2.** In the course of a hearing which if decided in favour of the motion of at least one of the parties would, but for the question of expenses, result in a final interlocutor within the meaning of section 27 of the Sheriff Courts (Scotland) Act 1907 the sheriff shall hear submissions on the appropriate award of expenses depending upon the sheriff's decision on the merits.

**3.** The sheriff having heard such submissions shall dispose of the question of expenses wherever possible in the interlocutor dealing with the merits.

**4.** If however a party shows cause why the question of expenses ought not to be disposed of without a separate hearing on expenses following receipt of the sheriff's judgment on the merits or if that be the view of the sheriff because of exceptional circumstances then the interlocutor disposing of the merits shall (a) appoint parties to be heard on the question of expenses within 14 days of its date and (b) suspend extract until after the hearing on expenses.

NOTE

The purpose of this Note is to encourage a practice whereby the merits and expenses are dealt with in the same interlocutor. In the exceptional case where this is not possible the hearing on expenses will take place within 14 days of the decision on the merits.

# PRACTICE NOTE NO.1 OF 2003

[MARCH 27, 2003]

I, JOHN COLIN McINNES, Queen's Counsel, Sheriff Principal of South Strathclyde Dumfries and Galloway, in pursuance of the powers conferred by Section 15(2) of the Sheriff Courts (Scotland) Act 1971, and all common law powers enabling in that behalf, Repeal the Practice Note dated January 30, 1984 in relation to affidavit evidence in undefended divorce actions; Order and Direct that the Practice Note set out in the Schedule hereto shall take effect immediately and subsist until countermanded by me.

Sheriff Principal of South Strathclyde,
Dumfries and Galloway
SHERIFF PRINCIPAL'S CHAMBERS
AIRDRIE: 27 March 2003

### Schedule

*Affidavits in Family Actions*

When affidavits may be lodged

**1.** Once the period within which a notice of intention to defend (in the Sheriff Court) or defences (in the Court of Session) require to be lodged has expired, without such notice or defences having been lodged, affidavits may be prepared and lodged without any order of the court.

Person before whom sworn or affirmed

**2.** An affidavit is admissible if it is sworn (or affirmed) before a notary public, justice of the peace, or any person having authority to administer oaths for the place where the affidavit is sworn, such as a commissioner for oaths or a British diplomatic officer or consul abroad. A solicitor acting for a party to the action may act in a notarial capacity when an affidavit is sworn. Any person before whom an affidavit is sworn (referred to below as "the notary") must observe all the normal rules in this connection and must satisfy himself or herself as to the capacity of the witness to swear an affidavit.

Importance of affidavits

**3.** The witness should be made to appreciate the importance of the affidavit and that the affidavit constitutes his or her evidence in the case. The possible consequences of giving false evidence should be explained to the witness. Before the witness signs the affidavit he or she must have read it or the notary must have read it over to the witness.

Oath or affirmation

**4.** The witness must be placed on oath or must affirm.

Form and signature of the affidavit

**5.** The document should be on A4 paper. The affidavit should commence with the words "At the day of 20 , in the presence of I having been solemnly sworn/having affirmed give evidence as follows:". The affidavit should be drafted in the first person and should take the form of numbered paragraphs. The full name, age, address and occupation of the witness should be given in the first paragraph. The affidavit should end with the words "All of which is the truth as I shall answer to God" or "All of which is affirmed by me to be true", as appropriate. Any blanks in the affidavit must be filled in. Any insertion, deletion or other amendment to the affidavit requires to be initialed by the witness and the notary. Each page must be signed by both the witness and the notary. It is not necessary for the affidavit to be sealed by the notary.

### Drafting the affidavit

6.    An affidavit should be based on a reliable and full precognition of the witness.

7.    The drafter of an affidavit should provide himself or herself, before drawing it, with an up to date copy of the pleadings, a copy of the appropriate precognition and the relative productions. The affidavit should be drawn so as to follow the averments in the pleadings to the extent that these are within the knowledge of that particular witness and in the same order.

8.    Affidavits should be expressed in the words of the person whose affidavit it is, should be accurate as at the date of the affidavit and should not consist of a repetition of passages in the pleadings. It should be clear from the terms of the affidavit whether the witness is speaking from his or her own knowledge, as when the witness was present and saw what happened, or whether the witness is relying on what he or she was told by a particular person.

### Productions

9.    Productions already lodged in process must be borrowed up, and put to the party or to the witness who refers to them in his or her affidavit. Each production will require to be referred to in the affidavit by its number of process and must be docqueted and signed by the witness and the notary. If a production has not yet been lodged when the affidavit is sworn, it will require to be identified by the witness in the affidavit, should be docqueted with regard to the affidavit and signed by the witness and the notary. It must then be lodged as a production. Some productions will necessarily be docqueted with regard to more than one affidavit.

10.    In consent cases, the defender's written consent form will have to be put to the pursuer in his or her affidavit, and be identified, docqueted and signed in the same way as other productions.

11.    In adultery cases, photographs of both the pursuer and the defender may require to be produced, put to the appropriate witnesses and be identified, docqueted and signed in the manner already described.

### Date of affidavit

12.    All affidavits lodged must be of recent date. This factor is particularly important in cases involving children, cases in which financial craves are involved and in any other circumstances where the evidence of a witness or circumstances to which the witness speaks are liable to change through the passage of time. The notary must take particular care in such cases to ensure that the affidavit evidence as to such matters is correct as at the time the affidavit is sworn. Affidavits relating to the welfare of children which have been sworn more than three months prior to lodging a minute for decree are likely to be rejected by the court as out of date.

Applications relating to parental responsibilities and rights (See RCS 49.28, OCR 33.28)

**13.** In actions in which an application in terms of section 11 of the Children (Scotland) Act 1995 is before the court not fewer than two affidavits dealing with the welfare of the child(ren) should be provided, at least one of them from a person who is neither a parent nor a party to the action. These affidavits should present the court with a full picture of the arrangements for the care of the child(ren) along the lines set out in paragraph 15, adapted to suit the circumstances of the particular case. The affidavits should set out reasons why it is better that the section 11 order be made than not. The pursuer's affidavit should deal fully with the arrangements which have been made for their care, so far as within his or her knowledge. If the pursuer cannot give substantial evidence as to that it is likely to be necessary to obtain such evidence from the person who is responsible for their care.

**14.** In actions of divorce, judicial separation or nullity of marriage in which there are children of the marriage or children treated by the parties as a child of their family but in which no order in terms of section 11 in terms of the Children (Scotland) Act 1995 is sought, the court, in terms of section 12, requires to consider whether to exercise the powers set out in sections 11 or 54 of that Act in light of the information before it as the arrangements for the child(ren)'s upbringing. Information accordingly requires to be before the court as to these arrangements. As a minimum, the affidavits of the witnesses should include the information set out in paragraphs 15 (a) to (e) below.

**15.** An affidavit dealing with the arrangements for the care of children should, where relevant, include the following:
  (a)  the qualifications of the witness, if not a parent, to speak about the child; how often, and in what circumstances the witness normally sees the child;
  (b)  the ability of those with whom the child lives to provide proper care for him or her;
  (c)  observations as to the relationship between the child and the other members of the household, the child's general appearance, interests, state of health and well-being;
  (d)  a description of the home conditions in which the child lives;
  (e)  the arrangements for contact between the child and any parent (and siblings) who do not live in the same household as the child;
  (f)  information about the school the child attends; whether the child attends school regularly; and
  (g)  details of child care arrangements during working hours, including the arrangements for such care outwith school hours.

Affidavit relating to disclosure of the whereabouts of children

**16.** An affidavit sworn or affirmed in compliance with an order to disclose the whereabouts of children (in terms of the Family Law Act 1986, section 33 and RCS 49.24 or OCR 33.23) will require to be drafted in such a way as to meet the requirements of the court in the circumstances of the particular case. The form of the affidavit should be as above.

Financial and other ancillary craves

**17.** Affidavit evidence in support of financial craves is necessary in an undefended action. (See *Ali v Ali* , 2001 S.L.T. 602). Where financial craves are involved, the evidence should be as full, accurate and up-to-date as possible. If the evidence is insufficient the court may require supplementary evidence to be provided. If, after an affidavit has been sworn and the solicitor concerned has parted with it, a material change of circumstances occurs before decree has been granted the court must be informed forthwith. A further affidavit may have to be sworn.

**18.** The pursuer should give evidence as to his or her own financial position at the date of the affidavit. Where the pursuer gives evidence in an affidavit as to the financial position of the defender, the affidavit should state the date, as precisely as possible, at which the information was valid. The court must be provided with information which is as up-to-date as possible as to the defender's ability to pay the sums the pursuer is seeking. Where the pursuer cannot obtain recent information as to the defender's means the affidavit should state that that is the case but should contain as much material information relating to the defender's means as possible. If the pursuer is unable to provide sufficient evidence to justify the orders concluded for or craved in full, in the minute for decree, after the words "in terms of conclusion(s)/crave(s) (number(s)...) of the summons/initial writ", there may be added words such as "or such other sum (or sums) as the court may think proper".

**19.** Where the pursuer has concluded for or craved a capital sum, an order for the sale of the matrimonial home, a periodical allowance, interdict or expenses, for example, and in the minute for decree does not seek decree for one or more of these, the reasons for that should be given in his or her affidavit.

### Joint Minutes

**20.** When parties record their agreement in a joint minute as to how financial and other ancillary conclusions or craves should be dealt with by the court, the pursuer's affidavit should refer to the joint minute and indicate that he or she is content that the agreement set out in it should be given effect.

### Minute for decree

**21.** The minute for decree must be signed by counsel or by a solicitor who has examined the affidavits and other documents. That counsel or solicitor takes responsibility therefor, whether or not he or she is the person who drew the summons, initial writ or affidavits. The minute for decree should not be signed seeking decree of divorce, separation or declarator of marriage or nullity of marriage unless the evidence consists of or includes evidence other than that of a party to the marriage (or alleged or purported marriage). [Civil Evidence (Scotland) Act 1988, section 8(3), *Taylor v Taylor*, 2001 S.C.L.R. 16]

**D3.30**

# PRACTICE NOTE NO.1 OF 2004

[DECEMBER 15, 2004]

### Adoption of Children, etc: Guidance for Sheriffs and Practitioners

[*Revoked by Practice Note No.1 of 2009.*]

# ACT OF COURT NO. 6 OF 2005

[JULY 6, 2005]

I John Colin McInnes QC, Sheriff Principal of South Strathclyde Dumfries and Galloway hereby enact as follows:

## Applications under the Proceeds of Crime Act 2002

### 1. Introduction

This Act of Court supersedes Act of Court No 1/2005 which is hereby revoked.

### Purpose

**1.1**  The purpose of this Act of Court is to secure the timeous and efficient management of hearings under section 295 (2) of the Proceeds of Crime Act 2002 based upon agreed protocols between the agencies concerned as outlined below.

**1.2**  This Act of Court applies to all applications lodged on or after 1 July 2005.

### 2. Cash Seizures under the Proceeds of Crime Act 2002

**2.1**  Hearings under section 295(2) of the Proceeds of Crime Act 2002 will take place within the respective Sheriff Courthouses of the Sheriffdom as set out in column 1 of *Table A* below, at the times set out in column 2 of said Table.

### TABLE A:

| COLUMN 1 SHERIFF COURT | COLUMN 2 MONDAY to FRIDAY |
|---|---|
| *HAMILTON* | *2.00 pm* |
| *AIRDRIE* | *2.00 pm* |
| *LANARK* | *2.00 pm* |
| *AYR* | *10.00 am* |
| *DUMFRIES* | *9.45 am* |
| *STRANRAER* | *12 noon* |
| *KIRCUDBRIGHT* | *2.00 pm* |

**2.2.**  When completing the form of receipt/intimation to be given to the affected person(s) in exchange for the cash seized, the seizing officers should select (1) the time for any hearing from column 2 above at the courthouse of the sheriff court district within which the cash has been seized and (2) a date within 48 hours of that time. Where that date is a Saturday, Sunday, Christmas Day, Good Friday, or bank holiday or a prescribed court holiday in the area where the cash is seized, the hearing should be assigned for the first available court date occurring thereafter. *In addition to normal reporting procedures the seizing officer should forthwith intimate details of the hearing to the local Sheriff Clerk.*

**2.3.**  If the Procurator Fiscal subsequently elects to make an application for continued detention of the cash, the Procurator Fiscal should advise the Sheriff Clerk of that decision forthwith in order that programmed business may be rearranged to best accommodate the Hearing. Not less than 30 minutes prior to the appointed time for the Hearing the affected person or his or her representative will be able to obtain a copy of the Summary Application which will be provided to the Sheriff Clerk by the Procurator Fiscal.

I appoint this Order to be inserted in the Act Book of every Court within the Sheriffdom, all for publication to the lieges.

Sheriff Principal of South Strathclyde,
Dumfries and Galloway

D3.32

# ACT OF COURT NO. 3 OF 2006[1]

## [AUGUST 17, 2006]

I, Brian Alexander Lockhart, Esquire, Sheriff Principal of the Sheriffdom of South Strathclyde Dumfries and Galloway, by virtue of the powers conferred upon me by Section 17(1)(b) of the Sheriff Courts (Scotland) Act 1971 and Section 8(2) and (3) of the Criminal Procedure (Scotland) Act 1995, do hereby prescribe that with effect from the 4 September 2006, the Civil Court Sitting days at Hamilton Sheriff Court will be as follows:

| | |
|---|---|
| *Ordinary Court* | *Every Wednesday at 10.00 am* |
| *Sequestrations and Miscellaneous Debtors Applications* | *Every Monday at 10.00 am* |
| *Summary Cause Heritable Court* | *Every Monday at 11.00 am* |
| *Gas Safety Applications* | *Every Monday at 2.00 pm* |
| *Summary Cause and Small Claims Courts (other than heritable actions)* | *Every Thursday at 10.00 am* |
| *Summary Cause Proofs* | *Every alternate Thursday at 11.30 am* |
| *Small Claims Hearings* | *Every alternate Thursday at 11.30 am* |

I Appoint this Order to be inserted in the Act Book of that Court, all for publication to the lieges.

Sheriff Principal of South Strathclyde,
Dumfries and Galloway

D3.33

# PRACTICE NOTE NO.1 OF 2009 (REVOKING PRACTICE NOTE NO.1 OF 2004): ADOPTION AND CHILDREN (SCOTLAND) ACT 2007: GUIDANCE FOR SHERIFFS AND PRACTITIONERS

## Purpose

**1.** The purpose of this Practice Note is to secure the efficient management of contested applications and other proceedings under the Adoption and Children (Scotland) Act 2007 ("the Act"). It should be read subject to the detailed rules of procedure to be found in the Sheriff Court Adoption Rules 2009 ("the Rules")—see the Act of Sederunt (Sheriff Court Rules Amendment) (Adoption and Children (Scotland) Act 2007) 2009 (SSI 2009/284). It will be revised in the light of experience and any new primary or secondary legislation.

---

[1] As amended by Act of Court No.1 of 2007, May 16, 2007.

## Commencement

**2.** This Practice Note applies to all applications lodged, or proceedings commenced, on or after 28 September 2009.

## Minimum of delay

**3.** It shall be the duty of the court to secure that all applications and other proceedings under the Act are dealt with as expeditiously as possible and with the minimum of delay. Such applications and proceedings require the co-operation of all concerned and active and firm case management by the sheriff throughout their course.

## Identity of sheriff

**4.** Unless the sheriff principal otherwise agrees, the sheriff presiding at any stage in the proceedings must be a sheriff of this sheriffdom. In the interests of continuity and consistency in management, every stage of each case must, whenever possible, call before the same sheriff.

**5.** In the event that a proof has to be taken by a sheriff other than the sheriff who has conducted the previous hearings, the whole process in the case must be made available to the sheriff who is to take the proof not less than three working days before the date upon which the proof is scheduled to commence.

## Representatives

**6.** At every calling of a case any representative of any party must be familiar with the case and must have sufficient authority to deal with any issues that are likely to arise at that calling.

## Record of discussion to be kept

**7.** At every hearing prior to any proof the sheriff should not only pronounce an interlocutor regulating further procedure but should also prepare and keep with the process a brief written record of the main points of the discussion at that hearing.

## The application

**8.** Subject to any issue of confidentiality that may arise, it would assist the sheriff clerk wherever possible to receive a copy of the petition or application (as the case may be) in electronic form on the same date as the date upon which it is lodged.

## Court programming

**9.** The programming of all classes of business in the courts of the sheriffdom remains exclusively the responsibility of the sheriff principal. In this respect he generally acts through the sheriff clerk. It is therefore essential that the assigning of diets by the sheriff should be undertaken only after consultation with, and with the agreement of, the sheriff clerk.

## The preliminary and pre-proof hearings

**10.** Any preliminary or pre-proof hearing fixed in terms of the Rules should be of sufficient duration to allow for a proper consideration of the issues likely to be canvassed at it. Consideration should be given to the advisability of intimating any such hearing by sheriff officer in order to avoid any possible delay due to ineffective postal service.

**11.** Where the date of a hearing requires to be intimated otherwise than by the sheriff clerk, the sheriff clerk should advise the applicant or petitioner or his or her solicitors forthwith of the terms of the interlocutor appointing the date of the hearing in order that they may intimate it as soon as possible. If so requested (and subject to any issue of confidentiality that may arise), the sheriff clerk should be prepared to send to the applicant or petitioner or his or her solicitors a copy of the interlocutor by fax or in electronic form as soon as it has been signed. Any such request should be accompanied by the appropriate fax telephone number or e-mail address as the case may be.

**12.** At any preliminary hearing the sheriff should ask the respondent or his or her solicitor whether the respondent has applied, or proposes to apply, for legal aid. The sheriff should also enquire whether it is intended to instruct counsel or any expert witness and, if so, whether legal aid for that purpose has been or is to be applied for.

**13.** The sheriff should ensure that the parties have sufficient access to all the documents lodged in process. The sheriff should ask the parties whether they will be seeking to recover any documents and, if so, which documents. The sheriff should ask the other parties if they will make these available informally without the need for a commission and diligence and, if so, should fix a date by which those documents should be lodged with the court.

**14.** At a preliminary hearing, which failing at a pre-proof hearing, the sheriff should give consideration to ordering parties to intimate to every other party and to lodge in court (i) a list of witnesses, including any expert witnesses, on whose evidence it is intended to rely at proof, and (ii) a list of the documents or other productions which it is intended should be used or put in evidence at proof.

### Assigning a diet of proof

**15.** Where it appears that a proof will be necessary, the parties should be in a position to give the sheriff a carefully considered forecast of the time which the proof is expected to take. The sheriff should ask each party to specify in detail how long he expects to take in the presentation of his own evidence and in the cross-examination of the witnesses of the other party or parties. On the basis of this information the sheriff should assess how many days should be set aside for the proof (including closing submissions). At the proof itself, parties may expect to be held to the estimates previously given by them, unless in exceptional circumstances.

**16.** In the fixing of a diet of proof it is not generally a valid ground of objection to a date proposed by the court that a party wishes to instruct a particular legal representative.

**17.** Consideration should be given at an early stage in the proceedings to where the proof will take place and whether the evidence at the proof should be recorded. The holding of a proof elsewhere than at the courthouse may be anticipated to cause administrative problems, for example for the sheriff clerk. But such administrative problems must not be permitted to get in the way of the expeditious disposal of an application or other proceeding under the Act.

**18.** It will be seen that rules 20 and 37 of the Rules provide that a proof is to be taken continuously so far as possible, but the sheriff may adjourn the diet from time to time. To allow for this, in particular in the smaller courts in the sheriffdom, consideration should be given to the possibility of holding the proof elsewhere than at the courthouse—see the preceding paragraph. Bearing in mind the time limits in rules 22 and 38, the sheriff should consider too whether he or she is likely to require any writing days in order to produce the judgement. If so, provision for this should be made when a diet of proof is fixed. As in the case of an application to free a child for adoption under the Adoption (Scotland) Act 1978, the reason for such provision is that the sheriff should "be released from other duties so that he can give priority to the case without interruption and until it has been completed by the issuing of his interlocutor. Special arrangements of that kind are clearly necessary if the sheriff is to maintain the continuity of thought throughout the proceedings which is so necessary to a proper disposal of the case" (*Lothian Regional Council v A* , 1992 S.L.T. 858 at page 862A-B).

## Legal issues

**19.** At a pre-proof hearing the sheriff should ask the parties if there are any questions of admissibility of evidence or any other legal issues, including any questions under the European Convention on Human Rights, that are likely to arise at the proof. If so, the sheriff should consider whether they could with advantage be determined at this hearing rather than at the proof. Alternatively, the sheriff may adjourn the pre-proof hearing to another date in order to enable any such issue to be argued and determined. If a legal issue is not raised at the pre-proof hearing, the sheriff may refuse to allow it to be raised at the proof except on cause shown. A solicitor who intends to raise a legal issue at a pre-proof hearing should intimate it to the other parties' solicitors beforehand.

## Evidence

**20.** It should be noted that evidence may be presented in the form of affidavits or other written documents (Civil Evidence (Scotland) Act 1988, section 2; *McVinnie v McVinnie* , 1995 S.L.T. (Sh. Ct) 81; *Glaser v Glaser* , 1997 S.L.T. 456). The sheriff is bound to consider reports placed before him or her even if the authors are not called to speak to them, and the strict rules of evidence do not apply (*T, Petitioner* , 1997 S.L.T. 724 at 730L). Such considerations may render the attendance of certain witnesses unnecessary, although for other reasons it may be preferable to call the author of a document. The parties should therefore apply their minds to the question whether any evidence might be appropriately presented in the form of an affidavit or other document and the sheriff should encourage them to decide that question at the pre-proof hearing. The sheriff should also encourage the use of affidavits to cover non-contentious (or indeed contentious) issues where that would save the time of witnesses and the court. Notwithstanding that an affidavit has been lodged, its author may be called to give evidence at the proof (see paragraph 3 of the judgment of Lady Smith in *Petitions of Aberdeenshire Council to declare A, B and C free for adoption*, Court of Session, 22 June 2004).

**21.** Where the author of a report or the maker of a statement which has been or is to be lodged is to be called as a witness, the sheriff may order that the report or statement is to be held to be equivalent to the witness's examination-in-chief, unless for special reasons he or she otherwise directs.

**22.** The sheriff should discourage the unnecessary use of expert witnesses. If expert evidence is essential, the sheriff should encourage the joint instruction of a single expert by all parties. If one party instructs an expert report, it should be disclosed to the other parties with a view to the agreement of as much of its contents as possible.

**23.** The sheriff should ask the parties what further productions, if any, they intend to lodge. Any difficulties over the obtaining or lodging of documents should be raised and if possible resolved at the pre-proof hearing.

### The proof

**24.** At a proof it should be borne in mind that "there is a heavy responsibility on the parties' representatives to exercise all reasonable economy and restraint in their presentation of the evidence and in their submissions to the court" (*Lothian Regional Council v A* at 862B). The sheriff may therefore exercise his or her existing common law power to intervene to discourage prolixity, repetition, the leading of evidence of unnecessary witnesses and the leading of evidence on matters which are unlikely to assist the court to reach a decision.

**25.** At the conclusion of the evidence parties must be heard orally thereon by the sheriff. In anticipation of this the sheriff may require the parties to submit, in electronic form or otherwise, draft findings in fact, or skeleton arguments, or both.

### The Practice Note No 1/2004: Adoption of Children, etc.

**26.** The Practice Note No 1/2004: Adoption of Children, etc is revoked subject to the qualification that it shall continue to have effect for the purpose of any application to which it applies which has been made and not yet determined before 28 September 2009.

21 October 2009

# PRACTICE NOTE

[26TH JANUARY 1983]

## Duration of poinding

If warrant to sell is applied for within six months of the date of execution of the poinding, it may be granted, if otherwise lawful, without special enquiry as to whether there has been undue delay in applying for the warrant.

If warrant to sell is applied for more than six months after the date of execution of the poinding, it shall be done by the creditor or his solicitor in the form of a minute which shall set forth the reasons for the delay. The first deliverance on such a minute shall require service on the debtor and appoint objections, if so advised, within seven days. If so required by the sheriff, the solicitor instructing the diligence, or an accredited representative for the creditor, shall appear personally before the sheriff to give such additional information as may be necessary in support of the application.

## Second poinding

A sheriff officer shall not execute a second poinding in the same premises under the same decree on the instructions of the same creditor unless of poindable goods which were not in the premises when the first poinding was executed.

## Noting of poindings by sheriff clerk—ordinary action

The sheriff clerk will cause the backing of each extract decree accompanying a report of poinding to be marked with the date of the poinding to which the report relates, and an entry recording the date of the poinding and the "A" number of the case will also be made in a register of poindings, indexed by defenders' names which will be kept for this purpose. Before presenting for approval, the sheriff clerk will verify that no earlier poinding has occurred following the decree, and, if there has been such an earlier poinding, he will report the fact to the Sheriff.

## Appointment of auctioneer

When the sheriff grants a warrant of sale, the auctioneer appointed by him shall be a person who, alone or with others, carries on business as an auctioneer, and who is not a whole time employee of the sheriff officer executing the diligence or of any partner or employer of such sheriff officer or of the creditor. If such a person is not available, or in warrants of sale proceeding on a decree in a summary cause, the sheriff may appoint the sheriff officer acting as judge of the roup or such person as seems to him to be suitably qualified to perform the duties of auctioneer.

## Appointment of judge of roup

When the sheriff grants a warrant of sale he may appoint as the judge of the roup a sheriff officer and the sheriff officer so appointed may be the sheriff officer who has executed the poinding.

## Unsold poinded goods

When poinded goods of a debtor are exposed for sale and are not sold and are adjudged to the poinding creditor, the debt shall be reduced by the appraised value of such goods, albeit such goods are not removed from the premises by the poinding creditor.

## Date of sale

The report of sale in an ordinary action will state the date when the sale took place.

## Report of sale—ordinary action

When a report of sale is lodged with the sheriff clerk, there shall be written upon the report of sale and signed by the sheriff an interlocutor in the following or similar terms:—

> "The Sheriff remits the report of sale and the documents attached thereto to the Auditor of Court to tax the account contained therein, to state the balance due to or by the defender as a result of the sale and/or delivery of the poinded goods, and to report."

The remit to the auditor of court which, under existing practice, is included at the end of the warrant of sale, shall in future be deleted therefrom. If, after considering the report of sale, and the auditor's report and any objections thereto, the sheriff approves of the report of sale as taxed, he will sign a docquet "Approved as taxed" which will be written upon the report of sale. A record of the sale will be made in the register of poindings.

## Warrants of concurrence

It is not necessary to obtain a warrant of concurrence under section 13 of the Debtors (Scotland) Act 1838 on a decree granted by a court within the sheriffdom for the purpose of poinding moveables of the defender named in said decree where the moveables are situated in another sheriff court district of the sheriffdom.

## Reports of poindings and sales—where to be made

Every report of a poinding and all applications for orders or warrants relating to poinded moveables and the report of any sale thereof shall be lodged with or made to the court of the sheriff court district in which the poinded moveables are situated.

There shall be discontinued any practice whereby the sheriff clerk of a court which has received the report of a poinding proceeding on a decree granted outwith the sheriffdom is required to notify the court which granted the decree of the receipt of the report.

R. R. Taylor,
Sheriff Principal of Tayside,
Central and Fife.

**D3.35**

# PRACTICE NOTE

### [FEBRUARY 1984]

Notes by the Sheriff Principal for the guidance of solicitors in relation to affidavit evidence in undefended divorce actions other than simplified divorces.

[The terms of the Notes are identical to Section 5 of the Practice Notes of Glasgow and Strathkelvin (p. D602, supra).]

# DIRECTION

D3.36

## [29TH NOVEMBER 1993]

I, John Joseph Maguire, Q.C., Sheriff Principal of the Sheriffdom of Tayside Central and Fife, by virtue of the powers conferred by rules 12.1 and 15.4(2) of the Rules contained in the First Schedule annexed to the Act of Sederunt (Sheriff Court Ordinary Cause Rules) 1993, do hereby direct:

**1.**  For the purpose of said rules 12.1 and 15.4(2) "the sheriff clerk" shall not include a sheriff clerk or depute below the rank of higher executive officer save that, in any sheriff court within the sheriffdom where the senior resident sheriff clerk holds the rank of executive officer, it shall include that sheriff clerk.

**2.**  The classes of interlocutor which a sheriff clerk may write and sign in terms of the said rule 12.1 shall not include any final interlocutor or any interlocutor which the sheriff concerned directs to be written or signed by him or her. Subject to the foregoing, an interlocutor dealing with a motion which has been determined by a sheriff clerk in terms of the said rule 15.4(2) shall be written and signed by that sheriff clerk.

**3.**  The classes of unopposed motion which a sheriff clerk may determine in terms of the said rule 15.4(2) are set out in the appendix to this direction. However, if the granting of any such motion might also involve any order relating to expenses, it shall be referred to the sheriff who shall deal with it in accordance with rule 15.4(1).

**4.**  This direction shall take effect from 1st January 1994.

## APPENDIX

Classes of motion which may be determined by a sheriff clerk in terms of rule 15.4(2):—

(a)  A motion to authorise re-service of an initial writ in terms of rule 5.9.

(b)  A motion to recall a sist and to re-enrol a cause for further procedure.

(c)  A motion, made under rule 10.3(1), to close the record before the expiry of the adjustment period provided by rule 10.1(1).

(d)  A motion to allow an amendment of a kind specified in rule 18.1.

(e)  A motion to allow a minute of amendment to be received and answered within a specified period in terms of rule 18.3(1)(a) and (b)(ii).

(f)  A motion for an order for service of a third party notice, made under rule 20.1(1) and (2).

# PRACTICE NOTE

D3.37

## [FEBRUARY 6, 1998]

I, John Joseph Maguire, Queen's Counsel, Sheriff Principal of the Sheriffdom of Tayside Central and Fife, *HEREBY DIRECT* that from the date hereof in all cases to which the Social Security (Recovery of Benefits) Act 1997 applies, parties seeking decree (except where that decree is sought of consent, for instance, as the result of a Joint Minute) shall lodge in process a *schedule of damages* stating the amount of any compensation which is claimed in respect of the relevant period under any of the headings in Column 1 of Schedule 2 to the Act.

For the avoidance of doubt, it should be noted that this requirement will apply not only to final decrees after proof but to decrees in absence, decrees by default, summary decrees, interim decrees and decrees for provisional damages.

**D3.38**

# PRACTICE NOTE NO.1 OF 2005: ADOPTION OF CHILDREN, ETC: GUIDANCE FOR SHERIFFS AND PRACTITIONERS

[*Revoked by* Practice Note No.1 of 2009.]

**D3.39**

# PRACTICE NOTE NO.1 OF 2006: SPECIFICATION FOR RECOVERY OF MEDICAL RECORDS

[*Revoked by* Practice Note No.1 of 2008.]

**D3.40**

# PRACTICE NOTE NO.1 OF 2008: SPECIFICATION FOR RECOVERY OF MEDICAL RECORDS

[MAY 6, 2008]

**1.**   This practice note has effect from the date hereof.

**2.**   For the purpose of rules 2S.2(3)( c) of the Ordinary Cause Rules 1993 and IS.I(3)(b) and 34.2(6) of the Summary Cause Rules 2002 it is no longer necessary for a copy of a specification or an incidental application for the recovery of medical records to be intimated to the Lord Advocate.

**3.**   The Practice Note No.1 of 2006 dated 27 October 2006 is hereby revoked.

**D3.41**

# PRACTICE NOTE NO.1 OF 2009: ADOPTION AND CHILDREN (SCOTLAND) ACT 2007: GUIDANCE FOR SHERIFFS AND PRACTITIONERS

## Purpose

**1.**   The purpose of this Practice Note is to secure the efficient management of contested applications and other proceedings under the Adoption and Children (Scotland) Act 2007 ("the Act"). It should be read subject to the detailed rules of procedure to be found in the Sheriff Court Adoption Rules 2009 ("the Rules")—see the Act of Sederunt (Sheriff Court Rules Amendment) (Adoption and Children (Scotland) Act 2007) 2009 (SSI 2009/284). It will be revised in the light of experience and any new primary or secondary legislation.

## Commencement

**2.**   This Practice Note applies to all applications lodged, or proceedings commenced, on or after 28 September 2009.

## Minimum of delay

**3.**   It shall be the duty of the court to secure that all applications and other proceedings under the Act are dealt with as expeditiously as possible and with the minimum of delay. Such applications and proceedings require the cooperation of all concerned and active and firm case management by the sheriff throughout their course.

### Identity of sheriff

**4.** Unless the sheriff principal otherwise agrees, the sheriff presiding at any stage in the proceedings must be a sheriff of this sheriffdom. In the interests of continuity and consistency in management, every stage of each case must, whenever possible, call before the same sheriff.

**5.** In the event that a proof has to be taken by a sheriff other than the sheriff who has conducted the previous hearings, the whole process in the case must be made available to the sheriff who is to take the proof not less than three working days before the date upon which the proof is scheduled to commence.

### Representatives

**6.** At every calling of a case any representative of any party must be familiar with the case and must have sufficient authority to deal with any issues that are likely to arise at that calling.

### Record of discussion to be kept

**7.** At every hearing prior to any proof the sheriff should not only pronounce an interlocutor regulating further procedure but should also prepare and keep with the process a brief written record of the main points of the discussion at that hearing.

### The application

**8.** Subject to any issue of confidentiality that may arise, wherever possible a copy of the petition or application (as the case may be) should be sent to the sheriff clerk in electronic form on the same date as the date upon which it is lodged.

### Court programming

**9.** The programming of all classes of business in the courts of the sheriffdom remains exclusively the responsibility of the sheriff principal. In this respect he generally acts through the sheriff clerk. It is therefore essential that the assigning of diets by the sheriff should be undertaken only after consultation with, and with the agreement of, the sheriff clerk.

### The preliminary and pre-proof hearings

**10.** Any preliminary or pre-proof hearing fixed in terms of the Rules should be of sufficient duration to allow for a proper consideration of the issues likely to be canvassed at it. Consideration should be given to the advisability of intimating any such hearing by sheriff officer in order to avoid any possible delay due to ineffective postal service.

**11.** Where the date of a hearing requires to be intimated otherwise than by the sheriff clerk, the sheriff clerk should advise the applicant or petitioner or his or her solicitors forthwith of the terms of the interlocutor appointing the date of the hearing in order that they may intimate it as soon as possible. If so requested (and subject to any issue of confidentiality that may arise), the sheriff clerk should be prepared to send to the applicant or petitioner or his or her solicitors a copy of the interlocutor by fax or in electronic form as soon as it has been signed. Any such request should be accompanied by the appropriate fax telephone number or e-mail address as the case may be.

**12.** At any preliminary hearing the sheriff should ask the respondent or his or her solicitor whether the respondent has applied, or proposes to apply, for legal aid. The sheriff should also enquire whether it is intended to instruct counsel or any expert witness and, if so, whether legal aid for that purpose has been or is to be applied for.

**13.** The sheriff should ensure that the parties have sufficient access to all the documents lodged in process. The sheriff should ask the parties whether they will be seeking to recover any documents and, if so, which documents. The sheriff should ask the other parties if they will make these available informally without the need for a commission and diligence and, if so, should fix a date by which those documents should be lodged with the court.

**14.** At a preliminary hearing, which failing at a pre-proof hearing, the sheriff should give consideration to ordering parties to intimate to every other party and to lodge in court (i) a list of witnesses, including any expert witnesses, on whose evidence it is intended to rely at proof, and (ii) a list of the documents or other productions which it is intended should be used or put in evidence at proof.

### Assigning a diet of proof

**15.** Where it appears that a proof will be necessary, the parties should be in a position to give the sheriff a carefully considered forecast of the time which the proof is expected to take. The sheriff should ask each party to specify in detail how long he expects to take in the presentation of his own evidence and in the cross-examination of the witnesses of the other party or parties. On the basis of this information the sheriff should assess how many days should be set aside for the proof (including closing submissions). At the proof itself, parties may expect to be held to the estimates previously given by them, unless in exceptional circumstances.

**16.** In the fixing of a diet of proof it is not generally a valid ground of objection to a date proposed by the court that a party wishes to instruct particular counsel. If need be, that party can always instruct another counsel.

**17.** Consideration should be given at an early stage in the proceedings to where the proof will take place and whether the evidence at the proof should be recorded. The holding of a proof elsewhere than at the courthouse may be anticipated to cause administrative problems, for example for the sheriff clerk. But such administrative problems must not be permitted to get in the way of the expeditious disposal of an application or other proceeding under the Act.

**18.** It will be seen that rules 20 and 37 of the Rules provide that a proof is to be taken continuously so far as possible, but the sheriff may adjourn the diet from time to time. To allow for this, in particular in the smaller courts in the sheriffdom, consideration should be given to the possibility of holding the proof elsewhere than at the courthouse—see the preceding paragraph. Bearing in mind the time limits in rules 22 and 38, the sheriff should consider too whether he or she is likely to require any writing days in order to produce the judgement. If so, provision for this should be made when a diet of proof is fixed. As in the case of an application to free a child for adoption under the Adoption (Scotland) Act 1978, the reason for such provision is that the sheriff should "be released from other duties so that he can give priority to the case without interruption and until it has been completed by the issuing of his interlocutor. Special arrangements of that kind are clearly necessary if the sheriff is to maintain the continuity of thought throughout the proceedings which is so necessary to a proper disposal of the case" (*Lothian Regional Council v A* , 1992 S.L.T. 858 at page 862A-B).

## Legal issues

**19.**   At a pre-proof hearing the sheriff should ask the parties if there are any questions of admissibility of evidence or any other legal issues, including any questions under the European Convention on Human Rights, which are likely to arise at the proof. If so, the sheriff should consider whether they could with advantage be determined at this hearing rather than at the proof. Alternatively, the sheriff may adjourn the pre-proof hearing to another date in order to enable any such issue to be argued and determined. If a legal issue is not raised at the pre-proof hearing, the sheriff may refuse to allow it to be raised at the proof except on cause shown. A solicitor who intends to raise a legal issue at a pre-proof hearing should intimate it to the other parties' solicitors beforehand.

## Evidence

**20.**   It should be noted that evidence may be presented in the form of affidavits or other written documents (Civil Evidence (Scotland) Act 1988, section 2; *McVinnie v McVinnie* 1995 S.L.T. (Sh. Ct) 81; *Glaser v Glaser* , 1997 S.L.T. 456). The sheriff is bound to consider reports placed before him or her even if the authors are not called to speak to them, and the strict rules of evidence do not apply (*T, Petitioner* , 1997 S.L.T. 724 at 730L). Such considerations may render the attendance of certain witnesses unnecessary, although for other reasons it may be preferable to call the author of a document. The parties should therefore apply their minds to the question of whether any evidence might be appropriately presented in the form of an affidavit or other document and the sheriff should encourage them to decide that question at the pre-proof hearing. The sheriff should also encourage the use of affidavits to cover non-contentious (or indeed contentious) issues where that would save the time of witnesses and the court. Notwithstanding that an affidavit has been lodged, its author may be called to give evidence at the proof (see paragraph 3 of the judgment of Lady Smith in *Petitions of Aberdeenshire Council* to declare A, B and C free for adoption, Court of Session, 22 June 2004).

**21.**   Where the author of a report or the maker of a statement which has been or is to be lodged is to be called as a witness, the sheriff may order that the report or statement is to be held to be equivalent to the witness's examination-in-chief, unless for special reasons he or she otherwise directs.

**22.**   The sheriff should discourage the unnecessary use of expert witnesses. If expert evidence is essential, the sheriff should encourage the joint instruction of a single expert by all parties. If one party instructs an expert report, it should be disclosed to the other parties with a view to the agreement of as much of its contents as possible.

**23.**   The sheriff should ask the parties what further productions, if any, they intend to lodge. Any difficulties over the obtaining or lodging of documents should be raised and if possible resolved at the pre-proof hearing.

## The proof

**24.**   At a proof it should be borne in mind that "there is a heavy responsibility on the parties' representatives to exercise all reasonable economy and restraint in their presentation of the evidence and in their submissions to the court" (*Lothian Regional Council v A* at 862B). The sheriff may therefore exercise his or her existing common law power to intervene to discourage prolixity, repetition, the leading of evidence of unnecessary witnesses and the leading of evidence on matters which are unlikely to assist the court to reach a decision.

**25.** At the conclusion of the evidence parties must be heard orally thereon by the sheriff. In anticipation of this the sheriff may require the parties to submit, in electronic form or otherwise, draft findings in fact, or skeleton arguments, or both.

### The Practice Note No.1, 2005: Adoption of Children, etc.

**26.** The *Practice Note No.1, 2005: Adoption of Children, etc.* is revoked subject to the qualification that it shall continue to have effect for the purpose of any application to which it applies which has been made and not yet determined before 28 September 2009.

25 September 2009

# ACT OF COURT (CONSOLIDATION, ETC.) 1990 NO.1

D3.42

[4TH APRIL 1990]

## Arrangement of Directions

### Part I
### Civil Procedure

### Part II
### Criminal Procedure

### Part III
### Edinburgh Sheriff Court: Standing Advisory Committee

### Part IV
### Miscellaneous

### Part V
### Extent

### Part VI
### Interpretation
### Schedule

I, Gordon Nicholson, Q.C., Sheriff Principal of Lothian and Borders, in respect that many of the Acts of Court in force within the Sheriffdom are spent or are in need of modernisation, hereby repeal all acts of court presently in force within the Sheriffdom other than those listed in the Schedule hereto, and direct that the following will be given effect on and after 1st May 1990:

## PART I—
## CIVIL PROCEDURE

### Civil jurisdiction

**1.—**

(1)  Where a pursuer in an ordinary cause, summary cause or small claim is unaware of any agreement to prorogate jurisdiction over the subject matter of the cause to another court, no averment to that effect need be made in the initial writ or summons as the case may be.

(2)  Where a pursuer in an ordinary cause, summary cause or small claim is unaware of any proceedings pending before another court involving the same cause of action and between the same parties as those named in the initial writ or summons as the case may be, no averment to that effect need be made in the initial writ or summons.

### Borrowing, return and inspection of processes

**2.—**

(1)  Where a process or a part thereof has been borrowed it must be returned to the sheriff clerk not later than 4 p.m. on the second working day before the date on which it is required in court.[1],[2]

(2)  No process or part thereof may be borrowed, nor will it be available for inspection, during the period from the foresaid time and day until the day after the date on which it is required in court.

(3)  The directions in sub-paragraph (1) above do not apply where a process or a part thereof is due to be returned prior to a diet of proof in which case the process or part thereof must be returned in accordance with the provisions of rule 29.13 of the Ordinary Cause Rules.[3]

### Lodging of initial writs, etc.

**3.**  All initial writs, petitions, summonses, motions and minutes must be lodged with the sheriff clerk not later than 4 p.m. on the second working day before the date on which they are to appear on the appropriate rolls of the court. This direction applies only to causes commenced prior to 1st January 1994.[4], [5]

### Summary cause and small claim causes—incidental applications and sist of procedure

**4.—**

(1)  Any incidental application under Rule 93 of the Act of Sederunt, (Summary Cause Rules, Sheriff Court) 1976, or under Rule 33 of the Act of Sederunt

---

[1] Amended by substituting Rule 3 for Rule 2, Act of Court 1997 No.1, 26th August 1997.
[2] Substituted, 15th August 1991.
[3] Inserted, 18th November 1993.
[4] Inserted, 15th August 1991. As amended, 18th November 1993.
[5] Amended by substituting Rule 3A for Rule 3, Act of Court 1997 No.1, 26th August 1997.

(Small Claim Rules) 1988, shall be lodged with the sheriff clerk along with two copies thereof. The sheriff clerk shall appoint the application to be heard at a sitting of the summary cause court or, as the case may be, the small claim court on a date which will allow notice to be given before the hearing to the other party or parties as required by said Rules, and shall mark the date and time appointed on the backing of the application and on the copies. The application and one copy will then be returned to the applicant or his representative, the remaining copy being retained by the sheriff clerk.

(2) Not later than the time fixed for the hearing of the application the applicant or his representative shall, except in a case where intimation has been made by the sheriff clerk under Rule 33(2) of the Act of Sederunt (Small Claim Rules) 1988, return the application to the sheriff clerk along with evidence of notice having been duly given which may be

    (a) a certificate by a solicitor of posting a copy by (i) ordinary first class post, or (ii) recorded delivery first class post, or

    (b) a holograph acceptance of notice.

(3) Failure to follow the above procedure may result in dismissal of the application.

(4) Any motion to sist procedure in a summary cause or in a small claim shall be considered by the sheriff, and the sheriff clerk shall if necessary arrange for the cause to be called in court for that purpose.

### Ordinary cause—motions

**5.—**

(1) The following provisions will apply in regard to cases where all parties to an action are legally represented:

    (a) In all defended ordinary actions a party, before presenting any motion at the sheriff clerk's office, may transmit the principal motion to all the other parties in the action inviting them, if so advised, to mark the motion as consented to or to mark it as unopposed. Upon the motion being so marked, dated and signed, it must be returned to the originator. The motion, so docquetted, may then be presented at the civil department of the sheriff clerk's office to be laid before a sheriff in chambers.

    (b) The sheriff when considering the motion may grant the same and sign the appropriate interlocutor, or, if he sees fit, direct that the presenter appear in support of the motion.

    (c) Where the sheriff instructs a hearing, the motion will be put on the motion roll of the first convenient ordinary court and the date thereof be given to the presenter by a member of the sheriff clerk's staff. The presenter of the motion shall advise all other parties to the action of the date fixed for the hearing.

(2) Except as provided in paragraph (1)(b) above the following motions shall not be enrolled for calling in the ordinary court, but shall be considered in chambers:

    (a) Any motion in an undefended action, (other than a motion in terms of Rule 22 of the first schedule to the Sheriff Courts (Scotland) Act 1907);

    (b) Any motion which is endorsed as unopposed in accordance with paragraph (1)(a) above other than a motion under paragraph (5) below;

    (c) Any joint motion which disposes of an action including all questions of expenses.

(3) Any other written motion presented in an ordinary action shall be enrolled for calling in an appropriate ordinary court. The solicitor presenting the motion shall intimate the date of calling to all other interested parties in the action by lodging the motion with the sheriff clerk, obtaining a date for calling, and intimating said date to all other interested parties in the action.

(4) All motions under paragraph (3) above must be intimated to all other interested parties in the action before noon on the day before the motion is called in court.

(5) Except in the event of an unforeseeable emergency, a motion to discharge a diet of proof, whether made of consent or not, shall be lodged in time to be heard not less than two clear working days before the diet of proof.[1]

(6) The directions contained in this paragraph apply only to causes commenced prior to 1st January 1994.[2]

## Ordinary cause motions under the Ordinary Cause Rules 1993

**6.—**

(1) Where a motion is to be heard in terms of rule 15.5(5) of the Ordinary Cause Rules, any document referred to in the motion or to which a party intends to refer at the hearing of the motion and which is not already lodged in process shall be lodged as a production and a copy thereof intimated to every other party not later than noon on the working day before the date assigned for the hearing of the motion.[3]

(2) A document which is not lodged in accordance with paragraph (1) above shall not be used at the hearing unless with leave of the sheriff on cause shown and on such conditions, if any, as to expenses or otherwise as the sheriff thinks fit.

(3) Except in the event of an unforeseeable emergency, a motion to discharge a diet of proof, whether made of consent or not, shall be lodged in time to be heard not less than two clear working days before the diet of proof.

## Ordinary cause motions—determination and signature by sheriff clerks

**7.** By virtue of the powers conferred by rules 12.1 and 15.4(2) of the Ordinary Cause Rules it is hereby directed as follows:[4]

(1) For the purpose of said rules 12.1 and 15.4(2) "the sheriff clerk" shall not include a sheriff clerk below the rank of higher executive officer save that, in any sheriff court within the sheriffdom where the senior resident sheriff clerk holds the rank of executive officer, it shall include that sheriff clerk.

(2) The classes of interlocutor which a sheriff clerk may write and sign in terms of the said rule 12.1 shall not include any final interlocutor or any interlocutor which the sheriff concerned directs to be written or signed by him or her. Subject to the foregoing, any interlocutor dealing with a motion which has been determined by a sheriff clerk in terms of the said rule 15.4(2) shall be written and signed by that sheriff clerk.

(3) The classes of unopposed motion which a sheriff clerk may determine in terms of the said rule 15.4(2) are set out below. However, if the granting of

---

[1] As amended by Act of Court 1997 No.1, 26th August 1997.
[2] Inserted, 18th November 1993.
[3] Inserted by Act of Court 1997 No.1, 26th August 1997.
[4] Inserted, 18th November 1993; as amended by Act of Court 1997 No.1, 26th August 1997.

any such motion might also involve any order relating to expenses, it shall be referred to the sheriff who shall deal with it in accordance with rule 15.4(1).

Classes of motion which may be determined by a sheriff clerk in terms of rule 15.4(2):

(a) A motion to authorise re-service of an initial writ in terms of rule 5.9.

(b) A motion to recall a sist and to re-enrol a cause for further procedure.

(c) A motion, made under rule 10.3(1), to close the record before the expiry of the adjustment period provided by rule 10.1(1).

(d) A motion to allow an amendment of a kind specified in rule 18.1.

(e) A motion to allow a minute of amendment to be received and answered within a specified period in terms of rule 18.3(1)(a) and (b)(ii).

(f) A motion for an order for service of a third party notice, made under rule 20.1(1) and (2).

(g) A motion to allow the late lodging of a notice of intention to defend and a motion to allow the late lodging of defences provided in both cases that the notice of intention to defend or the defences as the case may be is not more than three working days overdue.[1]

## Child welfare hearings

**8.—**

(1) Where a date for a child welfare hearing is fixed in terms of rule 33.22A(1) of the Ordinary Cause Rules, any document to which a party intends to refer at the child welfare hearing and which is not already lodged in process shall be lodged as a production and a copy thereof intimated to every other party not later than noon on the working day before the date fixed for the child welfare hearing.[2]

(2) A document which is not lodged in accordance with paragraph (1) above shall not be used at the hearing unless with leave of the sheriff on cause shown and on such conditions, if any, as to expenses or otherwise as the sheriff thinks fit.

## Interim hearings

**9.—**

(1) Where the court has fixed a date, time and place for parties to be heard on an application for an interim order—[3]

(a) the initial writ, if borrowed, shall be returned to the sheriff clerk, and

(b) any document to which a party intends to refer at the hearing and which is not already lodged in process shall be lodged as a production and a copy thereof intimated to every other party,

not later than noon on the working day before the date fixed for the hearing.

(2) A document which is not lodged in accordance with paragraph (1)(b) above shall not be used at the hearing unless with leave of the sheriff on cause shown and on such conditions, if any, as to expenses or otherwise as the sheriff thinks fit.

---

[1] Inserted by Act of Court 1997 No.1, 26th August 1997.
[2] Inserted by Act of Court 1997 No.1, 26th August 1997.
[3] Inserted by Act or Court 1997 No.1, 26th August 1997.

### Affidavit evidence in undefended actions of divorce, other than simplified divorces, and in undefended actions of separation and aliment

**10.—**

(1) An affidavit is no substitute for a reliable and adequate precognition though a precognition may eventually be the basis for an affidavit.

(2) The affidavit should be typed on substantial paper, and should be stitched or stapled. It must commence with the words "At.........., the..........day of.......... 19.........., in the presence of.......... Compeared.........., who being solemnly sworn, Depones as follows..........,". The full name, age, address and occupation must be given, and it must thereafter proceed in the first person and should take the form of numbered paragraphs. The witness should be made to appreciate the importance of the affidavit. The witness must be placed on oath, or must affirm, and each page will require to be signed by both the witness and the notary. It is not essential that it should be sealed by the notary. The document should be of a shape and size convenient to be lodged as part of the process. The affidavit should end with the words "All of which is truth as the deponent shall answer to God", or "All of which is affirmed to be true" as appropriate.[1],[2]

(3) Affidavits of parties and witnesses should follow step by step the averments in the initial writ. The drafter of an affidavit should provide himself, before drawing it, with a copy of the initial writ, a copy of the appropriate precognition, and the relative productions. The affidavit to be taken from a witness should follow the averments in the initial writ to the extent that these are within the knowledge of that particular witness. It is not a requirement that the wording of an affidavit should follow exactly the wording of the initial writ.

(4) On the matter of the qualifications of the person before whom the affidavit is taken, the Ordinary Cause Rules provide that the affidavit is admissible if it is duly emitted before a notary public or other competent authority. This means a notary public, Justice of the Peace, Commissioner of Oaths, or other statutory authority within the meaning of the Statutory Declarations Act 1835. In the examples given hereafter, it is assumed that the affidavit is in fact taken before a solicitor who is a notary public, and thereafter the references to the party before whom the affidavit is sworn are to "the notary". The solicitor acting in the action may well be called on also to act in a notarial capacity when the affidavit is subsequently sworn. This is permissible. In acting in a notarial capacity he must, however, as a competent authority, observe all the normal rules in this connection, and must satisfy himself as to the capacity of the witness to make the statement, and ensure that the witness understands that it constitutes his or her evidence in the case.

(5) On the matter of productions, those required, when an affidavit is being taken, may already have been lodged in process, but there may be some productions (such as photographs) which are produced by the witness to the notary when the affidavit is sworn, and which may not by that time have been lodged in process.

(6) Productions already lodged in process must be borrowed up, and put to the party or the witness who makes them part of his or her evidence in the appropriate part of the affidavit. Each production will require to be referred to in the affidavit by its number of process and must be docquetted and signed by

---

[1] See sub-para. (19).
[2] Amended by Act of Court 1997 No.1, 26th August 1997.

the party or witness and the notary. If a production has not yet been lodged when the affidavit is being taken, it will require to be identified by the witness in his evidence in the affidavit, and will then be docquetted with regard to the affidavit and signed by the party or witness and the notary. It will then be lodged as a production. Obviously, certain productions will be docquetted with regard to more than one affidavit.

(7) In adultery cases, photographs of both the pursuer and the defender normally require to be produced, put to the appropriate party or witnesses in the affidavit, and signed and docquetted with reference thereto in the manner already described. In certain circumstances, a photograph may have to be identified and docquetted by more than one person, as in the case of the photograph of a party requiring to be spoken to by the pursuer and two inquiry agents.

(8) After the expiry of the period of notice and no notice of intention to defend having been lodged, affidavits may be prepared and lodged without first seeking the authority of the court. All affidavits lodged must be of as recent a date as is possible in the circumstances. This factor is particularly important in (1) cases involving children, (2) those cases in which financial craves are involved or (3) any other cases where the evidence of a party or witness is liable to change through the passage of time. The notary will require to ensure, therefore, that an affidavit represents the deponent's evidence on such matters at the time the affidavit is sworn. Any affidavit which is more than three months old is likely to be regarded as unacceptable.[1]

(9) In cases involving residence or contact with children, an affidavit or affidavits providing corroborating evidence about the welfare of the children should be provided. The evidence of that witness must present the court with a full picture of the position regarding the child or children. It is, however, clear that such independent evidence in no way relieves the pursuer from testifying fully to the position regarding the children in his or her own affidavit, so far as within his or her knowledge. Whatever else the affidavits of the pursuer and the independent witness contain, their evidence should certainly include the following:[2]

   (a) the qualifications of the witness, if not a parent, to speak about the child; how often, for example, and in what circumstances, does the witness normally see the child;

   (b) a description of the home conditions in which the child lives;

   (c) observations upon the child's general appearance, interests, state of health and well being;

   (d) information, where relevant, about the school the child attends; whether and to what extent he has contact with other children and relatives;

   (e) observations on the relationship between the child and the person in whose care he or she lives, on the child's attitude towards each of the parents, and on the extent of contact with the parent or parents with whom the child is not living;

   (f) details of child care arrangements at all times including arrangements during working hours (outwith school hours);

   (g) the means and status of the person craving residence with a view to enabling him or her to maintain and bring up the child in a suitable manner.

---

[1] Amended by Act of Court 1997 No.1, 26th August 1997.
[2] Amended by Act of Court 1997 No.1, 26th August 1997.

(10) Where financial craves are involved, it is even more important that the evidence is full, accurate and up-to-date. In parole proofs the evidence of the pursuer and the witnesses on these matters can be supplemented at the proof by questions from the bench or from the solicitor for the pursuer. This will not be possible where evidence is taken by affidavit, and the affidavit must be so framed as to exclude the necessity for supplementary questions. Failure to do so may result in the sheriff requiring the attendance of the solicitor in court. If, after an affidavit has been taken, and the solicitor concerned has parted with it, a material change of circumstances occurs, it is essential that the court be immediately informed, and where necessary, that a further affidavit be sworn.[1]

(11) Where the pursuer in an action is speaking in the affidavit of the financial position of the defender, it is essential that the affidavit should state the date, as precisely as possible, at which that information was valid. Otherwise it may be assumed by the court that the pursuer is speaking to the defender's position at the date of the affidavit. The court must be provided with as up-to-date information as possible about the defender's ability to pay the sums the pursuer is seeking, and these sums should be such as that evidence justifies. The pursuer must, of course, speak also to his or her own financial position, at the date of the affidavit. Where the pursuer cannot obtain recent information as to the defender's means, it is suggested that, if the pursuer's advisers approve, assessment may be left to the sheriff, and in such cases it may be that the solicitors representing the pursuer would be willing to incorporate in the terms of the minute for decree, after the words "in terms of the crave of the initial writ" the words "or such other sum (or sums) as the court may think proper".[2]

(12) Where the pursuer has craved a capital sum, a periodical allowance, aliment for the child or children, or expenses, and in the minute for decree does not seek decree for one or any of these, it is essential that the reasons for this are fully narrated in the affidavit. Where these reasons are capable of corroboration by witnesses, they should be dealt with in the witnesses' affidavits.[3]

(13) The minute for decree must be signed by a solicitor who has examined the affidavits and other documents and takes responsibility therefor, whether or not he is the person who drew the initial writ or affidavits.[4]

(14) In consent cases, the defender's written consent form will also have to be borrowed up, put to the pursuer in his or her affidavit, and docquetted and identified in the same way as other productions.[5]

(15) Affidavit procedure will not prevent the parties to the action agreeing the financial or other ancillary craves by joint minute. For so long as these ancillary craves are opposed, the affidavit procedure cannot be used for them, but it can be used for the merits of the action. If a joint minute is signed before an affidavit or supplementary affidavit is emitted by the pursuer, that affidavit must refer to the arrangements in the joint minute. Decree of divorce will not be granted before any issues relating to financial provisions consequent upon the divorce which require to be decided by the court have been so decided.[6]

---

[1] Amended by Act of Court 1997 No.1, 26th August 1997.
[2] Amended by Act of Court 1997 No.1, 26th August 1997.
[3] Amended by Act of Court 1997 No.1, 26th August 1997.
[4] Amended by Act of Court 1997 No.1, 26th August 1997.
[5] Amended by Act of Court 1997 No.1, 26th August 1997.
[6] Amended by Act of Court 1997 No.1, 26th August 1997.

(16)  While it is no longer necessary to corroborate any fact, proof of which is required to establish a ground of divorce or any other matter, solicitors are nonetheless reminded that any affidavit or affidavits must satisfy the requirements of section 8 of the Civil Evidence (Scotland) Act 1988.[1]

(17)  The foregoing provisions shall apply mutatis mutandis to undefended actions of separation and aliment as they apply to undefended actions of divorce.[2]

**Notes**

[2]Inserted, 18th November 1993.

### Conveyancing and Feudal Reform (Scotland) Act 1970

**11.**  An initial writ bearing to be under Part II of the abovementioned Act but containing a crave for interdict or interim interdict alone or along with other craves shall not be accepted for warranting without the approval of the sheriff.[3]

### Social Security (Recovery of Benefits) Act 1997

**11A.—**

(1)  On or after 5th October 1998, in all cases to which the Social Security (Recovery of Benefits) Act 1997 applies, parties seeking decree (except where that decree is sought of consent, for instance as the result of a joint minute) should lodge in process a schedule of damages stating the amount of any compensation which is claimed in respect of the relevant period under any of the headings in Column 1 of Schedule 2 to the Act.[4]

(2)  For the avoidance of doubt, it should be noted that this requirement will apply not only to final decrees after proof but to decrees in absence, decrees by default, summary decrees, interim decrees and decrees for provisional damages.

### Copy productions for use by sheriff

**12.—**

(1)  Where documentary productions have been lodged in process, and are to be referred to in the course of a proof or a debate, copies of all such productions, for use by the sheriff, shall, whenever practicable, be lodged with the sheriff clerk not less than two days prior to the diet of proof or debate.[5]

(2)  All such copy productions shall be clearly marked with their process number.

(3)  Where copies of productions are lodged with the sheriff clerk in terms of paragraph (1) above, he shall forthwith docquet the inventory of productions to show that copies have been lodged and to show the date of their lodging.

### Authorities to be referred to at proof or debate

**13.**  Where authorities are to be referred to in the course of a proof or a debate, a list of those authorities shall, whenever practicable, be given to the sheriff clerk at

---

[1] Amended by Act of Court 1997 No.1, 26th August 1997.
[2] Amended by Act of Court 1997 No.1, 26th August 1997.
[3] As amended by Act of Court 1997 No.1, 26th August 1997.
[4] As amended by Act of Court 1998 No.1, 5th October 1998.
[5] As amended by Act of Court 1997 No.1, 26th August 1997.

least 24 hours prior to the diet in question so that copies of those authorities may be made available for use by the sheriff principal or sheriff in the court where the hearing is to take place.[1]

## Appeals

**14.—**

(1)–(2)*Repealed by Act of Court 2005, No.2, March 1, 2005.*][2]

# PART II—

# CRIMINAL PROCEDURE

### Judicial examinations

**15.—**

(1)     All judicial examinations should be put out before a full time or floating sheriff, and not before an honorary or temporary sheriff.[3]

(2)     In the event of a full time sheriff not being available, application should be made to the sheriff clerk at Edinburgh, who will endeavour to arrange for a full time sheriff from another court, whom failing a floating sheriff, to attend the court in question.

(3)     In the last resort the sheriff principal should be notified with a view to dispensing with the foregoing requirements if so advised.

(4)     In this context the expression "full time" sheriff includes an honorary sheriff who holds or has held office as a full time sheriff.

# PART III—

# EDINBURGH SHERIFF COURT STANDING ADVISORY COMMITTEE

**The Edinburgh Sheriff Court Standing Advisory Committee shall have the following constitution, functions and procedural rules:**

### *Constitution*

16.—(1)     [4]The committee shall consist of three sheriffs nominated by the Sheriff Principal of Lothian and Borders, three solicitors nominated by the President of the Edinburgh Bar Association, two persons of the rank of assistant procurator fiscal or procurator fiscal-depute nominated by the Regional Procurator Fiscal of Lothian and Borders, two persons nominated by the Chief Constable of Lothian and Borders Police, those persons to be the Chief Inspector in charge of the Court and Records Department and the Sheriff Court Sergeant, and three persons of the rank of assistant sheriff clerk or sheriff clerk-depute nominated by the Regional Sheriff Clerk of Lothian and Borders. The chairman shall be the senior sheriff present at any meeting and, failing the attendance of a sheriff, the person elected to act as chairman by the members present at the meeting. In the event of equality of votes with regard to any proposed recommendation, the chairman for the time being shall have a casting vote. The secretary of the committee shall be a member of the sheriff clerk's staff

---

[1] As amended by Act of Court 1997 No.1, August 26, 1997 and Act of Court 2005 No.2, March 1, 2005.

[2] As amended by Act of Court 1997 No.1, August 26, 1997.

[3] As amended by Act of Court 1997 No.1, August 26, 1997.

[4] As amended by Act of Court 1997 No.1, 26th August 1997.

appointed by the Regional Sheriff Clerk of Lothian and Borders to perform that office. The Sheriff Principal of Lothian and Borders, the President of the Edinburgh Bar Association, the Regional Procurator Fiscal of Lothian and Borders, the Chief Constable of Lothian and Borders Police, and the Regional Sheriff Clerk of Lothian and Borders are hereinafter referred to as "the constituents".[1]

### Appointment of Secretary and Nomination and Period of Service of Members

(2)     Whenever there is any change in the appointment as secretary, the Regional Sheriff Clerk of Lothian and Borders shall intimate to the other constituents the name of the person appointed to act as secretary.

The names and addresses of the persons nominated as members of the committee shall be sent to the secretary by the constituents on or before 31st October each year. The members will serve for one year from the first day of November following their nomination and they may be re-nominated for further periods of service. In the event of the death or resignation of a member during his period of service, another person shall be nominated by his constituent to replace him for the remainder of the period.

### Dates and Place of Meetings, etc.

(3)     Meetings of the committee will be held during each session of the court on such day, at such time, and in such place as shall be agreed by the members of the committee. Members of the committee will inform the secretary, a fortnight before each meeting, of matters to be included in the agenda, and the secretary will send a copy of the agenda, together with a draft minute of any previous meeting, to each member a week before the meeting. Additional meetings may be held if the committee so resolves, and the committee may appoint sub-committees from time to time which will exercise the functions delegated to them by the committee. Persons other than members may be invited to attend meetings of the committee or of subcommittees and to take part in their discussions but shall have no voting rights.

### Functions of the Committee

(4)     The committee shall take into consideration any matter affecting the efficiency of the administrative arrangements of the sheriff court in Edinburgh which they are asked by any of the constituents or by any member of the committee to take into consideration, and shall make such recommendations as they think proper from time to time with regard to such matters to the constituents or to any of them. A recommendation of the committee shall require the approval of a meeting attended by at least one nominee of each constituent. Any such recommendation shall be communicated in writing by the secretary to the constituents or constituent concerned.

---

[1] Amended, 15th August 1991.

## PART IV —

## MISCELLANEOUS

### Representation and wearing of gowns

**17.—**

(1) Any solicitor appearing professionally at the Bar of any sheriff court in the sheriffdom shall wear a gown.[1]

(2) Except in accordance with rule 1.3 of the Ordinary Cause Rules, rule 17(2) of the Schedule to the Act of Sederunt (Summary Cause Rules, Sheriff Court) 1976, or rule 30 of the Schedule to the Act of Sederunt (Small Claim Rules) 1988, no person other than a qualified solicitor holding a practising certificate, or a member of the Faculty of Advocates, shall be permitted to appear on behalf of a litigant at any stage of procedure.

(3) When a trainee solicitor is allowed to represent a party in terms of the said rule 17(2) or the said rule 30 he shall not wear a gown.

(4) Any party not personally present or represented in accordance with these directions at any diet shall be deemed to be absent.

### Commissary: Applications

**18.** Where a deceased had his last place of residence within a Sheriff Court District of the Sheriffdom of Lothian and Borders, any commissary application, including an application for the appointment of executor dative relative to the said death, shall, if presented to the Commissariot of the said sheriffdom, be presented only at the sheriff court of the said district.[2]

## PART V —

## EXTENT

**19.** The forgoing Directions, with the exception of Direction number 12, shall apply in all the sheriff courts within the sheriffdom. Direction number 12 shall apply in the sheriff court at Edinburgh only.[3]

## PART VI —

## INTERPRETATION[4]

**20.** References in this Act of Court to "the Ordinary Cause Rules" are references to the Ordinary Cause Rules 1993 contained in the Act of Sederunt (Sheriff Court Ordinary Cause Rules) 1993. Any Directions in this Act of Court which are expressed as applying only to causes commenced prior to 1st January 1994 relate to causes proceeding under the Ordinary Cause Rules which were in force prior to that date.[5]

## Schedule

The following Acts of Court are not repealed by this Act of Court:

---

[1] As amended by Act of Court 1997 No.1, 26th August 1997.
[2] As amended by Act of Court 1997 No.1, 26th August 1997.
[3] As amended by Act of Court 1997 No.1, 26th August 1997.
[4] Inserted, 18th November 1993.
[5] As amended by Act of Court 1997 No.1, 26th August 1997.

[The Acts of Court specified relate to the then current dates of court sittings and holidays.]

# NON-AVAILABILITY OF TEMPORARY SHERIFFS

D3.43

[NOVEMBER 11, 1999]

I, Gordon Nicholson, Queen's Counsel, Sheriff Principal of Lothian and Borders, in pursuance of the powers conferred by Section 15(2) of the Sheriff Courts (Scotland) Act 1971, and all common law powers enabling me in that Behalf, Order and Direct as follows:—

1.    With immediate effect the business of the courts in the Sheriffdom of Lothian and Borders shall, so far as is practicable, be programmed and dealt with in accordance with the following order of priority:—

    (1)    Cases involving a person or persons appearing from custody.
          Trials, both solemn and summary, in which a statutory time limit is imminent.
          Trials involving witnesses who are children or otherwise vulnerable.
          Pleas courts.
          First diet courts and intermediate diet courts.

    (2)    Referrals and appeals from children's hearings.
          Mental health applications.

    (3)    Family actions involving disputes about children.
          Adoption and freeing for adoption cases.
          Ordinary courts, options hearings courts, and motions courts.
          Sequestrations and liquidations.
          Summary cause and small claim courts (excluding proofs and full hearings).

    (4)    Trials, both solemn and summary, which are not covered by the provisions of sub-paragraph (1) hereof.

    (5)    Ordinary proofs and debates (other than those in family actions involving children).
          Summary cause proofs and small claim full hearings. Fatal accident inquiries (unless the subject matter is of considerable public importance).

    (6)    Any other business not specified above.

2.    Sheriff clerks shall have regard to the above order or priorities when allocating business.

3.    Where a court is unable to complete all of the business allocated on any given day, business having the lowest order of priority shall be discharged in order to ensure that business having higher priority is completed.

4.    This direction shall subsist until further notice.

I appoint this Practice Note to be inserted in the Act Book at Edinburgh and to be published on the Notice Boards of all Sheriff Courts within the Sheriffdom of Lothian and Borders.

**D3.44**

# JURY TRIAL SITTINGS AT EDINBURGH SHERIFF COURT

### [MARCH 13, 2000]

With a view to reducing delays in commencing trials on the first day of a jury trial sitting at Edinburgh Sheriff Court, and in order to reduce, so far as possible, inconvenience to potential jurors, the following arrangements will come into force with effect from Monday, 15 May 2000.

1. As at present all witnesses will be cited to attend court at 9.45 a.m.
2. On the first day of a sitting jurors will be cited to attend at 10.30 a.m.
3. A main trial and, where appropriate, a back-up trial will both be indicted for the first day of the sitting.
4. The court will sit at 10 a.m. sharp, and counsel, solicitors, accused and the procurator fiscal must be in court at that time.
5. Any pleas and/or motions will be dealt with by the sheriff at 10 am., and some time will be allowed thereafter for the procurator fiscal and defence counsel or solicitors to engage in such discussions as may be appropriate regarding the day's business.
6. Every effort will be made to ensure that the first trial which is to proceed will be ready to do so at 11 a.m. If for any reason a trial is not ready to proceed at that time the sheriff will nonetheless sit then, and he or she will expect an explanation in open court as to why a trial is not ready to proceed.

Gordon Nicholson,
Q.C.
Sheriff Principal,
Lothian and Borders

**D3.45**

# SHERIFFDOM OF LOTHIAN AND BORDERS PRACTICE NOTE NO. 1, 2004

### FATAL ACCIDENT INQUIRIES: PRELIMINARY HEARINGS

#### Commencement

**1.** This Practice Note shall apply to any inquiry under the Fatal Accidents and Sudden Deaths Inquiry (Scotland) Act 1976 ("the Act") for the holding of which an application is lodged after 29 February 2004.

#### Holding of preliminary hearing

**2.**
(1) The Sheriff, when making an order in terms of section 3(1)(a) of the Act fixing a time and place for the holding of an inquiry under the Act ("the inquiry"), may also make, on the application of the Procurator Fiscal, an order fixing a time and place for the holding of a preliminary hearing.
(2) The preliminary hearing should normally be held some four weeks before the date fixed for the inquiry.
(3) The Sheriff who presides at the preliminary hearing shall be the Sheriff who is to preside at the inquiry, except in special circumstances.

## Notice of holding of preliminary hearing

**3.** Not less than 21 days before the date of the preliminary hearing,—

(1) intimation of the holding of the preliminary hearing and the time and place fixed for it shall be made at the same time, in the same manner and to the same persons as intimation of the holding of the inquiry and the time and place fixed for it in terms of section 3(2)(a) of the Act and rule 4(1) and (2) of the Fatal Accidents and Sudden Deaths Inquiry Procedure (Scotland) Rules 1977 ("the Rules"); and

(2) public notice of the holding of the preliminary hearing and the time and place fixed for it shall be given at the same time and in the same manner as public notice of the holding of the inquiry and the time and place fixed for it in terms of section 3(2)(b) of the Act and rule 4(3) of the Rules.

## Representation

**4.** Rule 7 of the Rules shall apply to the preliminary hearing.

## Conduct of the preliminary hearing

**5.** At the preliminary hearing the Sheriff—

(1) shall ascertain from the parties or their representatives, so far as is reasonably practicable—

    (a) whether the inquiry is likely to proceed on the date assigned;

    (b) the issues which are likely to be raised at the inquiry;

    (c) whether there are any other parties on whom intimation of the proceedings should be made;

    (d) the likely length of the inquiry and whether it can be concluded within the time allocated;

    (e) the state of preparation of the parties or their representatives;

    (f) the availability of witnesses and productions;

    (g) whether there is any evidence that may be admitted in the form of a written statement in terms of rule 10 of the Rules;

    (h) whether there is any evidence that is capable of agreement;

    (i) whether any special arrangements are needed for bulky or voluminous productions;

    (J) whether there is any other matter which any party wishes to raise;

(2) may, after hearing the parties or their representatives,

    (a) direct the order in which the parties are to cross-examine the witnesses;

    (b) make an order in terms of section 4(4) of the Act;

    (c) summon a person to act as an assessor at the inquiry in terms of section 4(6) of the Act;

(3) may raise with the parties or their representatives any other matter which could in his opinion with advantage be discussed and, if appropriate, resolved, before the inquiry.

**6.—**

(1) At the conclusion of the preliminary hearing the Sheriff may—

    (a) continue the preliminary hearing to a date prior to the diet fixed for the inquiry;

    (b) continue the case to the diet fixed for the inquiry; or

    (c) discharge the diet fixed for the inquiry and fix a new diet therefor.

(2)    If the Sheriff fixes a new diet for the inquiry in terms of paragraph 6(1)(c) above, he may assign a further preliminary hearing.

Sheriff Principal of Lothian and Borders
11 February 2004

**D3.46**

## PRACTICE NOTE NO. 2, 2004

### ADOPTION OF CHILDREN ETC.: GUIDANCE FOR SHERIFFS AND PRACTITIONERS

*[Revoked by Practice Note No.1 of 2009.]*

**D3.47**

## PRACTICE NOTE NO.3 OF 2004

### DATIVE PETITIONS: PERSONS WITH PARENTAL RESPONSIBILITIES AND RIGHTS

[DECEMBER 20, 2004]

**1.**   Where the parent of a child has died and a person has obtained an order under section 11(1)(a) and (b) of the Children (Scotland) Act 1995 ("the Act") conferring on him or her parental responsibilities and parental rights in relation to the child, that person has the right to act as the child's legal representative unless the order otherwise provides (Act, sections 1(1)(d) and 2(1)(d)). He or she may therefore petition for appointment as executor-dative or executrix-dative to the deceased qua legal representative of the child. It is incorrect for such a person to petition for appointment qua "guardian" of the child.

**2.**   The following style may be employed:

**Instance** A B *[design]*, legal representative of C D *[design]*, conform to decree of the Sheriff of *[specify sheriffdom]* at *[place]* on *[date]*..........Pursuer.
**Crave** The pursuer craves the court—
To decern the pursuer executor-dative to the deceased E F *[design]* qua legal representative of her son [or as *appropriate*].
**Condescendence** The condescendence should include the following averments:
The said C D is the child of the said E F and has right to her intestate estate. The pursuer is his legal representative conform to an official certified copy interlocutor conferring on him parental responsibilities and rights which is produced herewith. Reference is made to the Children (Scotland) Act 1995, sections 1(1)(d) and 2(1)(d)
**Plea-in-law** The pursuer, being the legal representative of the child of the said E F, is entitled to be decerned her executor-dative.

*Iain Macphail*
Sheriff Principal of Lothian and Borders

# PRACTICE NOTE NO.1 OF 2005

D3.48

APPEALS TO THE SHERIFF PRINCIPAL

**Contents**

A. Preliminary

## A. Preliminary

### 1. Introduction

**1.1 Contents**

This Practice Note is in four parts: A—Preliminary; B—Appeals in Ordinary Causes; C—Appeals by Stated Case; D—Appeals in Summary Applications.

## 1.2 Purpose

The object of this Practice Note is to provide guidance about the conduct of appeals to the Sheriff Principal of Lothian and Borders. The rules about appeals are prescribed by statute, Act of Sederunt and judicial decisions, and are expounded in standard textbooks. This Practice Note supplements the rules and the textbooks with advice on a variety of matters, some of which have recently caused difficulty.

## 1.3 Commencement

This Practice Note applies to all appeals lodged on or after 1 March 2005. Directions 13 (in so far as it relates to appeals) and 14 of Act of Court (Consolidation, etc) 1990 No 1 are repealed by Act of Court 2005 No 2 which also comes into effect on 1 March 2005.

## 1.4 Interpretation

In this Practice Note—
(1) "OCR" means the Ordinary Cause Rules 1993, as amended up to 28 February 2005;
(2) "SCP" means *Sheriff Court Practice* by I D Macphail, second edition by C G B Nicholson and A L Stewart, vol 1 (1998), vol 2 (2002);
(3) any reference to a party means either that party or the solicitor acting in the cause for that party;
(4) cases cited only by date are unreported decisions of the Sheriff Principal which are available online on the Scottish Courts website, *www.scotcourts.gov.uk.*

### B. Appeals in Ordinary Causes

#### 2. *Competency of appeal*

## 2.1 General

A practitioner who is contemplating an appeal to the Sheriff Principal should consider whether the proposed appeal is competent. The competency of appeals from the Sheriff to the Sheriff Principal is primarily regulated by the provisions of section 27 of the Sheriff Courts (Scotland) Act 1907 ("the 1907 Act"). These provisions are discussed in chapter 18 of SCP. Two matters, in particular, are sometimes overlooked. It is important to notice the definition of "final judgment" in section 3(h) of the Act: see SCP paras 18.32 to 18.37. It is also important to check whether it is necessary to apply to the Sheriff for leave to appeal. Whether leave is necessary is usually apparent from the discussion of the relevant interlocutor in SCP.

## 2.2 Opinions of Sheriff Principal

The present Sheriff Principal has expressed the following views on various questions of competency.

### 2.3 Contact Order

An interlocutor making a contact order which does not require the other party to do anything is not an interlocutor "making an order *ad factum praestandum*" (1907 Act, section 27(b)). An appeal against such an order therefore requires the leave of the Sheriff (*Fergus v Eadie* 16 August 2004, following *Black v Black* 1991 S.L.T. (Sh Ct) 5, 1990 S.C.L.R. 817.)

*2.4   Incompetent Interlocutor*

An appeal may be taken to the Sheriff Principal, without the leave of the Sheriff, against an interlocutor which is incompetent in the sense that the Sheriff had no power or right to pronounce it (*Kirk v Kirk* 14 March 2003, following *V AG Finance Ltd v Smith* 1988 S.L.T. (Sh Ct) 59, 1988 S.C.L.R. 598).

*2.5   Summary Decree*

An appeal against an interlocutor granting a summary decree in terms of OCR Chapter 17 does not require the leave of the Sheriff. While section 28(1)(b) of the 1907 Act refers to an "interim decree for payment of money" and not to a summary decree, the substance and effect of a summary decree and an interim decree are the same. Cf *Hughes's Trustee v Hughes* 1925 S.C. 25 at 27–28.

*2.6   Warrant For Citation*

No appeal is competent against the refusal of a warrant for citation (*Fitzpatrick v Advocate General for Scotland* 2004 S.L.T. (Sh Ct) 93). A party aggrieved by the refusal of a warrant should apply to the Sheriff Principal by letter for a direction that a warrant be granted.

**2.7   Leave to appeal**

Where leave to appeal is required, the application for leave may be made either—
(1)   by a motion made orally, with leave of the court (as required by OCR rule 15.1(1)(a)) and in the presence of any other party, to the Sheriff immediately after the Sheriff has pronounced the decision against which it is sought to appeal; or
(2)   by lodging a written motion timeously in terms of OCR rule 31.2(1).

**2.8**   An oral motion made at the time of the decision is preferable because
(1)   the matter is fresh in the minds of the Sheriff and the party or parties,
(2)   the Sheriff is available,
(3)   there is none of the delay and expense involved in proceeding by a written motion, and
(4)   if the Sheriff grants leave and the applicant later decides not to proceed with the appeal, no harm is done.

**2.9**   Where the application is made by lodging a written motion as mentioned in paragraph 2.7, the procedure in OCR Chapter 15 should be followed. It is immaterial that the motion is not heard and disposed of until more than 7 days after the date of the interlocutor against which it is sought to appeal.

**2.10**   Any application for leave to appeal should be heard by the Sheriff who pronounced the interlocutor against which it is sought to appeal, unless in wholly exceptional circumstances.

**2.11**   The object of requiring leave to appeal is to filter out unmeritorious appeals, thus protecting both parties from unnecessary delay and expense. The applicant for leave to appeal should therefore be prepared to indicate to the Sheriff the grounds of the proposed appeal in order that the Sheriff may assess whether it has any realistic prospect of success. See SCP paragraphs 18.50–18.54.

## 2.12 Time-limits

If the time-limit in OCR rule 31.2(1) is not met, the applicant in his written motion should apply to the Sheriff not only for leave to appeal but also for relief in terms of OCR rule 2.1.

**2.13** If the time-limit in OCR rule 31.1 or rule 31.2(2) is not met, the applicant should lodge a written motion applying to the Sheriff Principal for leave to appeal out of time and for relief in terms of OCR rule 2.1.

**2.14** In computing the time-limits in the provisions of OCR rules 31.1 and 31.2 no allowance is made for any day on which the Sheriff Clerk's Office is closed. If, however, the last day of a period within which a provision requires a document to be lodged is a day on which the Office is closed, the period shall be extended to include the next day on which the Office is open.

### 3. Marking of Appeal

## 3.1 Note of appeal

An appeal is marked by lodging a note of appeal in Form A1 (OCR, rule 31.4(1)).

### 3.2 Request For Note Of Reasons

Where the Sheriff has not appended to the interlocutor appealed against a note setting out the reasons for his or her decision, the appellant should take care to comply with rule 31.4(2)(d) by including in the note of appeal a request that the Sheriff write such a note. A failure to request a note may result in the postponement of the hearing of the appeal while a note is obtained and may be taken into account in the determination of any question of expenses.

### 3.3 Grounds of Appeal

Form A1 requires the appellant to state the grounds on which the appeal is to proceed. Rule 31.4(3) provides that the grounds of appeal must consist of brief specific numbered propositions stating the grounds on which it is proposed to submit that the appeal shall be allowed or as the case may be. It is helpful to mention the authorities on which each proposition is based. The purpose of the grounds of appeal is to give notice to the other party or parties and to the Sheriff Principal of the points which will be in issue at the hearing of the appeal, the nature of the argument in relation to those points and the remedy or other order which the appellant seeks. A mere statement that the Sheriff "erred in law" will not suffice (*Smyth v Pearce* 13 July 2004).

3.4 At the hearing of the appeal a party may not rely on a matter not stated in his note of appeal unless the Sheriff Principal gives permission. He may do so of consent or on cause shown, and on such conditions as to adjournment, expenses or otherwise as he sees fit (*McCaskill v McCaskill* 22 September 2004).

### 3.5 Amendment Of Grounds Of Appeal

OCR rule 31.4(5) allows an appellant to amend the grounds of appeal at any time up to 14 days before the date assigned for the hearing of the appeal. The Sheriff Principal may dispense with that time-limit on cause shown (OCR rule 31.4(7)). It is preferable, however, that any amendment of the grounds of appeal should be made as soon as possible. If the amendment makes material additions or alterations to the grounds already stated, the Sheriff Principal may put the case out by order and invite submissions as to whether he should remit the cause to the Sheriff and ask him or her to provide a note (*Richardson v Rivers* 1 May 2004). The allowance to the Sheriff of a reasonable time in which to provide the note may require the postponement of the hearing of the appeal. If it appears that the amendment should have been lodged early enough to avoid the postponement of the hearing, questions may arise as to liability for the expenses of the by order hearing and the postponement.

3.6    Amendment of the grounds of appeal may be necessary where the Sheriff has not appended a note to the interlocutor against which the appeal is taken and it has not therefore been possible for the appellant to state in the note of appeal propositions which are sufficiently specific. In such a case the appellant should lodge amended grounds as soon as reasonably practicable after the provision by the Sheriff of the note requested in terms of OCR rule 31.4(2)(d).

### 3.7   Cross-Appeal

The appeal is available to and may be insisted in by all other parties in the cause (1907 Act, section 29; SCP paragraph 18.71). Any party who wishes the Sheriff Principal to vary the interlocutor of the Sheriff should cross-appeal. A party wishing to crossappeal must lodge and intimate a note of the grounds of appeal (OCR r 31.4(6)). The note should comply with rule 31.4(1), (2) and (3). The provisions of paragraphs 3.3 and 3.4 also apply to a note in a cross-appeal. There is no provision for amendment of the grounds of appeal in such a note.

3.8    OCR rule 31.4(6)(a) requires the note in the cross-appeal to be lodged not less than 7 days before the date assigned for the hearing of the appeal. The Sheriff Principal may shorten or dispense with this time-limit on cause shown (OCR rule 31.4(7)). The time-limit is, however, very short. It is desirable that any party wishing to cross-appeal should lodge a note of the grounds of appeal as soon as possible in order to elide any question of the postponement of the hearing of the appeal.

3.9    If the grounds in the note in the cross-appeal have not been dealt with by the Sheriff in the note appended to his or her interlocutor or in a note already provided in response to a request by the appellant in terms of rule 31.4(2)(d), the note in the crossappeal should include a request that the Sheriff write a note.

3.10    A respondent who wishes to ask the Sheriff Principal to adhere to the Sheriffs interlocutor for reasons different from or additional to those given by the Sheriff should lodge a note stating these reasons not less than 7 days before the date assigned for the hearing of the appeal.

### 4.   Action on marking of appeal

**Initial action by Sheriff Principal's Appeals Clerk**

### 4.1   Note on Interlocutor Sheet

On a note of appeal being lodged, the Appeals Clerk must note on the interlocutor sheet that an appeal has been marked and the date of the appeal (OCR, rule 31.4(8)).

### 4.2   Appeal Questionnaires

At the same time the Appeals Clerk must
(a)    send to the appellant a questionnaire in Form A in the Appendix to this Practice Note; and

(b)    send to every other party a questionnaire in Form B in the Appendix to this Practice Note.

### 4.3   Appeal Correspondence

The Appeals Clerk must maintain a file of copies of all correspondence relative to the appeal and retain the file within the process envelope.

## Initial action by parties

### 4.4   Appeal Questionnaire

A party to whom a questionnaire is sent in terms of paragraph 4.2 must complete it and return it to the Appeals Clerk within 21 days of the date of the letter enclosing the questionnaire. If that is not done, the Sheriff Principal may appoint the case to be put out by order for a hearing on further procedure.

### 4.5   Instruction Of Counsel

The completed questionnaire must state whether the party intends to instruct counsel for the appeal. If counsel is to be instructed, that should be done as soon as possible in order to obtain without undue haste counsel's advice on the preparation or amendment of the grounds of appeal (see paragraphs 3.3–3.10) and on the preparation and presentation of documents and authorities for the hearing (see paragraphs 5.3–5.9).

### 4.6   Time Estimate

The completed questionnaire must also state the party's estimate of the duration of the hearing of the appeal. This information is necessary to enable the Court to assign a diet for the hearing.

### 4.7   Legal Aid

The completed questionnaire must also state whether the party intends to apply, or has applied, for legal aid in respect of the appeal; and if so, whether legal aid is sought for
(a)    the extension of the shorthand notes;
(b)    the instruction of counsel.

4.8    An application for legal aid should be lodged as soon as possible. The result of the application should be communicated to the Appeals Clerk at once.

### 4.9   Shorthand Notes

When, following a procf, an appeal is marked against an interlocutor which has been issued by the sheriff before the notes have been extended and lodged in process, the appellant must, except in a case to which paragraph 4.10 applies,
(1)    inform the shorthand writers forthwith that the notes of evidence are required, and ascertain from them the date when the notes of evidence will be available; and
(2)    thereafter state that date in the questionnaire.

4.10 Failure by the appellant to comply with paragraph 4.8 above so that the hearing of the appeal is unduly delayed or a diet fixed for the hearing is rendered abortive, may be taken into account in the determination of any question of expenses.

4.11 Where it appears to the appellant that the grounds of appeal are such that it may be unnecessary to have the notes of evidence, or a part of the notes of evidence relating to a particular issue, available for the hearing of the appeal, a motion to dispense with the requirements of paragraph 4.8 may be made to the Sheriff Principal. Any such motion must be made as soon as possible after the marking of the appeal and must be intimated to all other parties.

4.12 On appealing without the notes of evidence see SCP paragraphs 16.33, 18.63.

### 4.13 Venue

Appeals from interlocutors pronounced in Edinburgh Sheriff Court are heard in the Sheriff Principal's Appeal Court in Edinburgh. Appeals from interlocutors pronounced in Linlithgow Sheriff Court are also heard in the Sheriff Principal's Appeal Court in Edinburgh in view of the shortage of accommodation in the courthouse in Linlithgow.

4.14 An appeal from an interlocutor pronounced in any of the other courts in the Sheriffdom (the sheriff courts of Haddington, Peebles, Selkirk, Jedburgh and Duns) may be heard either in the Sheriff Principal's Appeal Court in Edinburgh or in the court in which the interlocutor was pronounced (the original court). Each party to such an appeal is invited to state in the questionnaire any preference he or she may have as to the venue for the hearing of the appeal. If no preference is expressed by any party, the appeal will normally be heard in the original court.

### 5. Action prior to hearing of appeal

### 5.1 Assigning diet

After the expiry of the time for the return of the appeal questionnaires, the Sheriff Principal will assign a diet for the hearing of the appeal or appoint the case to be put out by order (see paragraph 4.3).

**5.2** The Appeals Clerk will send to each party notification of the date, time and venue of the hearing.

### 5.3 Lodging of authorities and documents

To enable the Sheriff Principal to study the case before the hearing, each party is asked to lodge, seven days before the hearing, bundles containing photocopies of the authorities and documents to which he intends to refer at the hearing. The parties should consult together when preparing their bundles in order to avoid duplication. Any failure to lodge bundles timeously may be taken into account in the determination of any question of expenses.

### 5.4 Presentation

Where possible the photocopies should be in A4 format. They should be bound together in a lever arch file, ring binder or plastic folder, and may be separated by dividers where appropriate. An index should be included at the front of the bundle, listing all the contents.

## 5.5   Authorities

Each party's bundle of authorities should be bound in chronological order. The index should state the page numbers of the passages on which the party intends to rely.

5.6   If a case is reported in Session Cases or in the official Law Reports published by the Incorporated Council of Law Reporting for England and Wales, that report should be photocopied and lodged (*McGowan v Summit at Lloyds* 2002 S.C. 638 at 660G–661E).

5.7   The passages in each case on which the party intends to rely should be marked or highlighted.

## 5.8   Documents

Each party's bundle of documents should be bound in chronological order. The bundle should be paginated, each page being numbered individually and consecutively. The page numbers should be inserted in bold figures at the top of the page, in a form that can be clearly distinguished from any other pagination on the document.

5.9   The passages in each document on which the party intends to rely should be marked or highlighted.

### 5.10   Return of process

Any parts of process which have been borrowed should be returned to the Appeals Clerk seven days before the hearing.

### 5.11   Pre-reading by Sheriff Principal

Before the hearing of the appeal the Sheriff Principal will normally have read—
(1)   the record;
(2)   all the interlocutors pronounced in the case, including the interlocutor complained of;
(3)   any note by the Sheriff which is appended to the interlocutor complained of or which has been written by request;
(4)   the note of appeal;
(5)   the note of the grounds of any cross-appeal;
(6)   any note lodged in terms of paragraph 3.10; and
(7)   the authorities and documents lodged and highlighted as requested in paragraphs 5.3–5.9 above.

### 5.12   Limitation of scope of appeal

If the appellant intends to limit the scope of the appeal by making no submissions on any ground stated in the note of appeal, he should so intimate as soon as possible to the Appeals Clerk and to the other party or parties.

5.13   Any such limitation of the scope of the appeal does not qualify the powers of the Sheriff Principal in dealing with the appeal, or the availability of the appeal to the other party or parties.

### 5.14   Withdrawal of solicitor

If a solicitor for any party is no longer prepared to act for his client in the appeal he should, at the same time as he so informs his client, intimate his withdrawal from acting for his client by letter to the Appeals Clerk and to the other party or parties to the appeal.

**5.15** OCR Chapter 24 shall apply, mutatis mutandis, to the procedure subsequent to the intimation of the solicitor's withdrawal to the Court.

## Motions

### 5.16 General

The Sheriff Principal may entertain any motion which is competent in the action. OCR Chapter 15 shall apply mutatis mutandis to motions made to the Sheriff Principal.

5.17 Before the hearing of the appeal, a party may lodge with the Appeals Clerk and intimate to every other party any motion which he wishes the Sheriff Principal to hear. The party lodging the motion should indicate to the Appeals Clerk whether he wishes the Sheriff Principal to deal with the motion at or before the hearing.

### 5.18 Motion To Adjourn

If a party does not wish the hearing of the appeal to proceed at the diet assigned, he should lodge with the Appeals Clerk and intimate to every other party a motion for an adjournment of the diet. The motion should state the reason or reasons for seeking the adjournment. OCR rules 15.1 to 15.5 shall apply, mutatis mutandis, to such a motion.

5.19 All the parties to an appeal may lodge a joint motion in Form G6 for an adjournment of the diet. The joint motion should state the reason or reasons for seeking the adjournment. OCR rules 15.5(4) and (9) shall apply, mutatis mutandis, to such a joint motion.

### 5.20 Motion To Sist

OCR Chapter 15 shall apply, mutatis mutandis, to a motion to sist which is made to the Sheriff Principal.

## Disposal of appeal before hearing

### 5.21 General

The Sheriff Principal may dispose of an appeal without a hearing if the appeal is abandoned (see paragraph 5.22) or if the parties are agreed by joint minute as to the mode of disposal (see paragraphs 5.23–5.26).

### 5.22 Abandonment

An appellant is not entitled to abandon his appeal unless (a) of consent of all other parties (see paragraphs 5.23 to 5.26) or (b) with leave of the Sheriff Principal (OCR rule 31.11). An appellant who seeks the leave of the Sheriff Principal to abandon his appeal should lodge with the Appeals Clerk and intimate to every other party a motion to that effect. The motion should specify the order the appellant seeks as to the expenses of the appeal.

### 5.23 Disposal By Consent

If the parties have reached agreement as to how the appeal should be disposed of, they may prepare and lodge a joint minute setting out their agreement in clear and comprehensive terms, including terms as to expenses. The joint minute should also state the terms of the interlocutor they wish the Sheriff Principal to pronounce. A motion asking the Sheriff Principal to interpone authority to the joint minute and to pronounce an interlocutor in the terms stated may be lodged and intimated. If the motion is unopposed or endorsed as consented to, the Sheriff Principal may determine it in chambers without the appearance of parties. A joint motion need not be intimated and may be likewise determined.

5.24    If the parties are agreed that the appeal should be allowed and the interlocutor of the Sheriff should be recalled or varied, the joint minute should set out not only the terms of the interlocutor they wish the Sheriff Principal to pronounce but also the matters relied on as justifying the proposed interlocutor.

5.25    The Sheriff Principal will not allow an appeal on the ground that the decision of the Sheriff was wrong, merely because the parties are agreed that it was wrong (SCP paragraph 18.100). If the parties are so agreed, the joint minute should include

(a)    detailed submissions to that effect with appropriate reference to authority and

(b)    a motion in terms of OCR rule 31.7(b) asking the Sheriff Principal to dispose of the appeal without ordering an oral hearing.

5.26    The parties may agree that the appeal should be allowed, not because the decision of the Sheriff was wrong, but because they now wish his interlocutor to be set aside or varied for practical reasons. These should be explained in the joint minute. The joint minute should make it clear that the parties do not seek a determination of the merits of the appeal. The Sheriff Principal may then of consent pronounce an interlocutor interponing authority to the joint minute and recalling or varying the Sheriff's interlocutor.

*5.    The hearing of the appeal*

## 6.1    Attendance

If either party fails to appear or to be represented at the hearing of the appeal, the Sheriff Principal may fix a peremptory diet, but he is not obliged to do so (*Canmore Housing Association Ltd v Scott* 2003 S.L.T. (Sh Ct) 68 at [7], 69F-J).

6.2    If the appellant fails to appear or to be represented, the Sheriff Principal may dismiss the appeal in respect that it is not insisted in and find the appellant liable to the respondent or respondents in the expenses of the appeal.

6.3    If the respondent fails to appear or to be represented, the Sheriff Principal will call on the appellant to show cause why the appeal should be sustained (SCP paragraph 18.100).

6.4    If a party fails to attend the hearing or is not prepared to proceed with the appeal, the Sheriff Principal may decern against that party for payment of such expenses as he considers reasonable (Act of Sederunt (Fees of Solicitors in the Sheriff Court) (Amendment and Further Provisions) 1993, Sched 1, General Regulations, reg 5(c)).

## 6.4    Written submissions

At the hearing of the appeal the parties may hand up written submissions or skeleton arguments if they would find that convenient. It is recommended that submissions which include figures or mathematical calculations should be reduced to writing and handed up.

**6.5 Expenses**

Each party should either include in his speech submissions as to expenses or move the Sheriff Principal to reserve all questions of expenses and appoint a hearing on expenses after he has issued his interlocutor.

**6.6** If a party wishes the Sheriff Principal to certify the appeal as suitable for the employment of counsel, he should make a motion to that effect at the hearing of the appeal.

**6.7** Where the Sheriff Principal awards expenses in a final judgment he will normally allow an account of the expenses to be given in, remit it when lodged to the Auditor of Court to tax and to report, and remit the cause to the Sheriff to proceed as accords. It will then be for the Sheriff to dispose of any objections to the Auditor's report and to decern for the taxed amount of expenses. If the party liable in expenses is an assisted person, the Sheriff will decern for such proportion of the taxed amount as he may determine. 6.8 Where the Sheriff Principal awards expenses in a judgment other than a final judgment he may make a finding as to liability for expenses, allow an account thereof to be given in and remit the cause to the Sheriff to proceed as accords. The process will be returned to the original court. At the conclusion of the case the Sheriff will remit to the Auditor the account of those expenses along with the account of the expenses awarded by the Sheriff at the conclusion of the case. It will then be for the Sheriff to dispose of any objections and decern for the taxed amount of expenses or a proportion thereof if the party liable is an assisted person. The object of this course is to avoid the inconvenience of more than one taxation.

## C. Appeals By Stated Case

### 1. General

**7.1** The provisions of parts 4, 5 and 6 of this Practice Note apply to appeals to the Sheriff Principal by way of stated case, in the absence of statutory provision to the contrary, with the following modifications:

(1)    paragraph 4.1 does not apply; and
(2)    in paragraph 5.11, "(1) the stated case" is substituted for subparagraphs (1) to (6).

### 2. Specification of points of law, etc

**7.2** Where provision is made for appeal to the Sheriff Principal by way of stated case and the appellant is required to specify, in his application for a stated case, the point of law or other issue upon which the appeal is to proceed, great care should be taken to focus that issue as precisely as possible. If it is proposed to instruct counsel for the appeal, it would be prudent to consult counsel about the formulation of the issue and of any proposed adjustments to the draft stated case. Similar care should be taken by a respondent who is entitled to state any point of law or other issue which he wishes to raise in the appeal. In the absence of any statutory provision or authority to the contrary, the Sheriff Principal will not allow a party to raise issues of which notice has not been given except on cause shown and subject to such conditions as he may consider appropriate (*Cunningham v M* 25 November 2004 at [7]-[11]).

### 3. Disputes about events in the court below

**7.3** If the parties are at variance as to the occurrence of events in the court or tribunal below, the Sheriff Principal will normally accept the account of the matter which is given in the stated case (*T G Norman (Timber) Ltd v Warwick* 10 January 2003 at [8]; *University of Edinburgh v Onifade* 24 December 2004 at [7]).

### 4. Taxation in summary causes

**7.4** Rule 23A of the Summary Cause Rules 2002 provides that an account of expenses may be taxed by the Auditor of Court instead of being assessed by the Sheriff Clerk.

### 5. Expenses in small claims

**7.5** The restrictions on awards of expenses in small claims prescribed by section 36B(1) and (2) of the Sheriff Courts (Scotland) Act 1971 do not apply in relation to an appeal to the Sheriff Principal (see section 36B(3)).

**7.6** Section 36B(3)(b), unlike the other provisions of section 36B(3), has not been repeated in rule 21.6(1) of the Small Claim Rules 2002.

### D. Appeals In Summary Applications

#### 1. General

**8.1** The provisions of parts 4, 5 and 6 of this Practice Note apply to appeals to the Sheriff Principal in summary applications, in the absence of statutory provision to the contrary.

#### 2. Note of appeal

**8.2** In the absence of any statutory provision as to the form of the note of appeal, it is recommended that the provisions of OCR rule 31.4 should be followed (*City of Edinburgh Council v Z 23* December 2004 at [18]).

Sheriff Principal of Lothian and Borders
Edinburgh, 9 February 2005.

### APPENDIX

### Form A

*SHERIFFDOM OF LOTHIAN AND BORDERS APPEAL TO THE SHERIFF PRINCIPAL*
*Appellant's Questionnaire*
*To be completed by the appellant or the appellant's solicitor*
Please complete this questionnaire and return it to reach the address below by
..........20..........

Sheriff Principal's Appeals Clerk
Sheriff Clerk's Office
Sheriff Court House
27 Chambers Street
Edinburgh
EH1 1LB
Tel: 0131 225 2525

DX 550308 EDINBURGH-37
E-mail: edinburgh@scotcourts.gov.uk
*NAME OF CASE:* ...............
*COURT REF NO:* ...............
Name, address, telephone number and e-mail address of appellant's solicitor:
...............
...................

Name: ...............
Address: ...............
...................

Tel: ...............
E-mail: ...............
...................

Name of solicitor dealing with the appeal: ..........
Tel (if different from above): ..........
E-mail (if different from above): ..........
*Questions*
1.     Is counsel to be instructed for the appeal? *Yes/No\**
2.     Please give your estimate of the duration of the hearing of the appeal:
       ...................
3.     Is legal aid to be applied for in respect of—

    (a)   the appeal? *Yes/No\**
    (b)   the extension of shorthand notes of evidence? *Yes/No\**
    (c)   the instruction of counsel? *Yes/No\**

       *Note:* An application for legal aid should be lodged as soon as possible. The result of the application should be communicated at once to the Sheriff Principal's Appeals Clerk at the address printed above. See Lothian and Borders Practice Note No 1, 2005, paragraph 4.7.

4.

    (a)   Are shorthand notes to be extended and lodged? *Yes/No\**
    (b)   If Yes, please state the date by which they will be available: ...................
       Note: You must inform the shorthand writer forthwith that the notes are required, and ascertain from him the date when they will be available. See Lothian and Borders Practice Note No 1, 2005, paragraph 4.8.
5.     If the appeal is from the sheriff court at Haddington, Peebles, Selkirk, Jedburgh or Duns, would you like the hearing of the appeal to take place in that court (the original court) or in the Sheriff Principal's Appeal Court in Edinburgh? *Original court/Edinburgh.\**

       Note: If no party expresses a preference, the appeal will normally be heard in the original court. See Lothian and Borders Practice Note No 1, 2005, paragraph 4.13.

   *\*Please delete as appropriate.*

   *Guidance about the conduct of appeals to the Sheriff Principal is provided in Lothian and Borders Practice Note No 1, 2005. The Practice Note is available online at www.scotcourts.gov.uk on the Sheriff Courts page. The Sheriff Clerk will provide hard copies to party litigants on request.*

## Form B

*SHERIFFDOM OF LOTHIAN AND BORDERS APPEAL TO THE SHERIFF
PRINCIPAL*

*Respondent's Questionnaire*

*To be completed by the respondent or the respondent's solicitor*

*Please complete this questionnaire and return it to reach the address below by
.........20 ..............*

> Sheriff Principal's Appeals Clerk
> Sheriff Clerk's Office
> Sheriff Court House
> 27 Chambers Street
> Edinburgh
> EH1 1LB
> Tel: 0131 225 2525
> DX 550308 EDINBURGH-37
> E-mail: edinburgh@scotcourts.gov.uk

*NAME OF CASE:* ...............

*COURT REF NO:* ...............

Name, address, telephone number and e-mail address of respondent's solicitor:

...............

Name: ...............

Address: ...............

...................

Tel: ...............

E-mail: ...............

Name of solicitor dealing with the appeal: ..........

Tel (if different from above): ..........

E-mail (if different from above): ..........

*Questions*

1.  Is counsel to be instructed for the appeal? *Yes/No\**

2.  Please give your estimate of the duration of the hearing of the appeal:
    ...................

3.  Is legal aid to be applied for in respect of—

    (a)  the appeal? *Yes/No\**
    (b)  the instruction of counsel? *Yes/No\**

    *Note:* An application for legal aid should be lodged as soon as possible. The
    result of the application should be communicated at once to the Sheriff
    Principal's Appeals Clerk at the address printed above. See Lothian and
    Borders Practice Note No 1, 2005, paragraph 4.7.

4.  If the appeal is from the sheriff court at Haddington, Peebles, Selkirk, Jedburgh
    or Duns, would you like the hearing of the appeal to take place in that court
    (the original court) or in the Sheriff Principal's Appeal Court in Edinburgh?
    *Original court/Edinburgh\**

    *Note:* If no party expresses a preference, the appeal will normally be heard
    in the original court. See Lothian and Borders Practice Note No 1, 2005,
    paragraph 4.13.

*\*Please delete as appropriate.*

Guidance about the conduct of appeals to the Sheriff Principal is provided in Lothian and Borders Practice Note No 1, 2005. The Practice Note is available online at www.scotcourts.gov.uk on the Sheriff Courts page. The Sheriff Clerk will provide hard copies to party litigants on request.

D3.49

# ACT OF COURT NO.2 OF 2005

### [FEBRUARY 9, 2005]

I, Iain Duncan Macphail, QC, Sheriff Principal of Lothian and Borders, hereby direct as follows:
1.  This Act of Court will come into effect on 1 March 2005.
2.  TheAct of Court (Consolidation, etc) 1990 No 1 is amended as follows:

    (1)  Direction 13 is repealed in so far as it related to appeals; and
    (1)  Direction 14 is repealed.

I appoint this Order to be inserted in the Act Book at Edinburgh and to be published on the Notice Boards of all Sheriff Courts within the Sheriffdom of Lothian and Borders.

Sheriff Principal of Lothian and Borders
Sheriff Principal's Chambers
EDINBURGH
9 February 2005

D3.50

# PRACTICE NOTE NO.1 OF 2006: SPECIFICATION FOR RECOVERY OF MEDICAL RECORDS

*[Revoked by Practice Note No.1 of 2008.]*

D3.51

# PRACTICE NOTE NO.1 OF 2008: SPECIFICATIONS FOR RECOVERY OF MEDICAL RECORDS

1.  This practice note has effect from 9 June 2008

2.  For the purpose of rules 28.2(3)(c) of the Ordinary Cause Rules 1993 and 18.1(3)(b) and 34.2(6) of the Summary Cause Rules 2002 it is no longer necessary for a copy of a specification or an incidental application for the recovery of medical records to be intimated to the Lord Advocate.

from 9 June 2008
The Practice Note No.1 of 2006 dated 13 November 2006 is hereby revoked.
5 June 2008

D3.52

# PRACTICE NOTE NO.1 OF 2009: ADOPTION AND CHILDREN (SCOTLAND) ACT 2007: GUIDANCE FOR SHERIFFS AND PRACTITIONERS

### Purpose

1.  The purpose of this Practice Note is to secure the efficient management of contested applications and other proceedings under the Adoption and Children (Scotland) Act 2007 ("the Act"). It should be read subject to the detailed rules of procedure to be found in the Sheriff Court Adoption Rules 2009 ("the Rules")—see

the Act of Sederunt (Sheriff Court Rules Amendment) (Adoption and Children (Scotland) Act 2007) 2009 (SSI 2009/284). It will be revised in the light of experience and any new primary or secondary legislation.

## Commencement

**2.** This Practice Note applies to all applications lodged, or proceedings commenced, on or after 28 September 2009.

## Minimum of delay

**3.** It shall be the duty of the court to secure that all applications and other proceedings under the Act are dealt with as expeditiously as possible and with the minimum of delay. Such applications and proceedings require the cooperation of all concerned and active and firm case management by the sheriff throughout their course.

## Identity of sheriff

**4.** Unless the sheriff principal otherwise agrees, the sheriff presiding at any stage in the proceedings must be a sheriff of this sheriffdom. In the interests of continuity and consistency in management, every stage of each case must, whenever possible, call before the same sheriff. Where Interim Orders or Contact Orders are sought, if the presiding Sheriff is unavailable then the Duty Sheriff should deal with such orders.

**5.** In the event that a proof has to be taken by a sheriff other than the sheriff who has conducted the previous hearings, the whole process in the case must be made available to the sheriff who is to take the proof not less than three working days before the date upon which the proof is scheduled to commence.

## Representatives

**6.** At every calling of a case any representative of any party must be familiar with the case and must have sufficient authority to deal with any issues that are likely to arise at that calling.

## Record of discussion to be kept

**7.** At every hearing prior to any proof the sheriff should not only pronounce an interlocutor regulating further procedure but should also prepare and keep with the process a brief written record of the main points of the discussion at that hearing.

## The application

**8.** Subject to any issue of confidentiality that may arise, it would assist the sheriff clerk wherever possible to receive a copy of the petition or application (as the case may be) in electronic form on the same date as the date upon which it is lodged. In cases where Serial numbers have been provided by the court, and the Sheriff Clerk is required to intimate any step in procedure, it would assist the court if the relevant forms of intimation were provided.

## Court programming

**9.** The programming of all classes of business in the courts of the sheriffdom remains exclusively the responsibility of the sheriff principal. In this respect he generally acts through the sheriff clerk. It is therefore essential that the assigning of diets by the sheriff should be undertaken only after consultation with, and with the agreement of, the sheriff clerk.

## The preliminary and pre-proof hearings

**10.** Any preliminary or pre-proof hearing fixed in terms of the Rules should be of sufficient duration to allow for a proper consideration of the issues likely to be canvassed at it. Consideration should be given to the advisability of intimating any such hearing by sheriff officer in order to avoid any possible delay due to ineffective postal service.

**11.** Where the date of a hearing requires to be intimated otherwise than by the sheriff clerk, the sheriff clerk should advise the applicant or petitioner or his or her solicitors forthwith of the terms of the interlocutor appointing the date of the hearing in order that they may intimate it as soon as possible. If so requested (and subject to any issue of confidentiality that may arise), the sheriff clerk should be prepared to send to the applicant or petitioner or his or her solicitors a copy of the interlocutor by fax or in electronic form as soon as it has been signed. Any such request should be accompanied by the appropriate fax telephone number or e-mail address as the case may be.

**12.** At any preliminary hearing the sheriff should ask the respondent or his or her solicitor whether the respondent has applied, or proposes to apply, for legal aid. The sheriff should also enquire whether it is intended to instruct counsel or any expert witness and, if so, whether legal aid for that purpose has been or is to be applied for.

**13.** The sheriff should ensure that the parties have sufficient access to all the documents lodged in process. The sheriff should ask the parties whether they will be seeking to recover any documents and, if so, which documents. The sheriff should ask the other parties if they will make these available informally without the need for a commission and diligence and, if so, should fix a date by which those documents should be lodged with the court.

**14.** At a preliminary hearing, which failing at a pre-proof hearing, the sheriff should give consideration to ordering parties to intimate to every other party and to lodge in court (i) a list of witnesses, including any expert witnesses, on whose evidence it is intended to rely at proof, and (ii) a list of the documents or other productions which it is intended should be used or put in evidence at proof.

## Assigning a diet of proof

**15.** Where it appears that a proof will be necessary, the parties should be in a position to give the sheriff a carefully considered forecast of the time which the proof is expected to take. The sheriff should ask each party to specify in detail how long he expects to take in the presentation of his own evidence and in the cross-examination of the witnesses of the other party or parties. On the basis of this information the sheriff should assess how many days should be set aside for the proof (including closing submissions). At the proof itself, parties may expect to be held to the estimates previously given by them, unless in exceptional circumstances.

**16.** In the fixing of a diet of proof it is not generally a valid ground of objection to a date proposed by the court that a party wishes to instruct particular counsel. If need be, that party can always instruct another counsel.

**17.** Consideration should be given at an early stage in the proceedings to where the proof will take place and whether the evidence at the proof should be recorded. The holding of a proof elsewhere than at the courthouse may be anticipated to cause administrative problems, for example for the sheriff clerk. But such administrative problems must not be permitted to get in the way of the expeditious disposal of an application or other proceeding under the Act.

**18.** It will be seen that rules 20 and 37 of the Rules provide that a proof is to be taken continuously so far as possible, but the sheriff may adjourn the diet from time to time. To allow for this, in particular in the smaller courts in the sheriffdom, consideration should be given to the possibility of holding the proof elsewhere than at the courthouse—see the preceding paragraph. Bearing in mind the time limits in rules 22 and 38, the sheriff should consider too whether he or she is likely to require any writing days in order to produce the judgement. If so, provision for this should be made when a diet of proof is fixed. As in the case of an application to free a child for adoption under the Adoption (Scotland) Act 1978, the reason for such provision is that the sheriff should "be released from other duties so that he can give priority to the case without interruption and until it has been completed by the issuing of his interlocutor. Special arrangements of that kind are clearly necessary if the sheriff is to maintain the continuity of thought throughout the proceedings which is so necessary to a proper disposal of the case" (*Lothian Regional Council v A* , 1992 S.L.T. 858 at page 862A–B).

### Legal issues

**19.** At a pre-proof hearing the sheriff should ask the parties if there are any questions of admissibility of evidence or any other legal issues, including any questions under the European Convention on Human Rights, which are likely to arise at the proof. If so, the sheriff should consider whether they could with advantage be determined at this hearing rather than at the proof. Alternatively, the sheriff may adjourn the pre-proof hearing to another date in order to enable any such issue to be argued and determined. If a legal issue is not raised at the pre-proof hearing, the sheriff may refuse to allow it to be raised at the proof except on cause shown. A solicitor who intends to raise a legal issue at a pre-proof hearing should intimate it to the other parties' solicitors beforehand.

### Evidence

**20.** It should be noted that evidence may be presented in the form of affidavits or other written documents (Civil Evidence (Scotland) Act 1988, section 2; *McVinnie v McVinnie* , 1995 S.L.T. (Sh. Ct) 81; *Glaser v Glaser* , 1997 S.L.T. 456). The sheriff is bound to consider reports placed before him or her even if the authors are not called to speak to them and the strict rules of evidence do not apply (*T, Petitioner* , 1997 S.L.T. 724 at 730L). Such considerations may render the attendance of certain witnesses unnecessary; although for other reasons it may be preferable to call the author of a document. The parties should therefore apply their minds to the question whether any evidence might be appropriately presented in the form of an affidavit or other document and the sheriff should encourage them to decide that question at the pre-proof hearing. The sheriff should also encourage the use of affidavits to cover non-contentious (or indeed contentious) issues where that would save the time of witnesses and the court. Notwithstanding that an affidavit has been lodged, its author may be called to give evidence at the proof (see paragraph 3 of the judgment of Lady Smith in *Petitions of Aberdeenshire Council to declare A, B and C free for adoption*, Court of Session, 22 June 2004).

**21.** Where the author of a report or the maker of a statement which has been or is to be lodged is to be called as a witness, the sheriff may order that the report or statement is to be held to be equivalent to the witness's examination-in-chief, unless for special reasons he or she otherwise directs.

**22.** The sheriff should discourage the unnecessary use of expert witnesses. If expert evidence is essential, the sheriff should encourage the joint instruction of a single expert by all parties. If one party instructs an expert report, it should be disclosed to the other parties with a view to the agreement of as much of its contents as possible.

**23.** The sheriff should ask the parties what further productions, if any, they intend to lodge. Any difficulties over the obtaining or lodging of documents should be raised and if possible resolved at the pre-proof hearing.

### The proof

**24.** At a proof it should be borne in mind that "there is a heavy responsibility on the parties' representatives to exercise all reasonable economy and restraint in their presentation of the evidence and in their submissions to the court" (*Lothian Regional Council v A* at 862B). The sheriff may therefore exercise his or her existing common law power to intervene to discourage prolixity, repetition, the leading of evidence of unnecessary witnesses and the leading of evidence on matters which are unlikely to assist the court to reach a decision.

**25.** At the conclusion of the evidence parties must be heard orally thereon by the sheriff. In anticipation of this the sheriff may require the parties to submit, in electronic form or otherwise, draft findings in fact, or skeleton arguments, or both.

### The Practice Note No 1, 2004: Adoption of Children, etc.

**26.** The Practice Note No 2, 2004: Adoption of Children, etc.: guidance for sheriffs and practitioners is revoked subject to the qualification that it shall continue to have effect for the purpose of any application to which it applies which has been made and not yet determined before 28 September 2009.

30 September 2009

D3.53

# PRACTICE NOTE NO. 1 OF 2011

## COMMERCIAL ACTIONS

I, Edward Farquharson Bowen, CBE TD QC, Sheriff Principal of Lothian and Borders by virtue of the power conferred upon me by Rule 40.1(3) of the Ordinary Cause Rules 1993 hereby direct that, with effect from Monday 21 February 2011, commercial actions may be raised in the sheriff courts at Jedburgh, Selkirk, Duns and Peebles

In terms of Rule 40.2 I further direct that all proceedings in any such action shall be brought before Sheriff T A K Drummond QC and Sheriff D S Corke or, where they are not available, before any other sheriff of the Sheriffdom of Lothian and Borders.

I appoint this Practice Note to be instered in the Act Books of all the sheriff courts in the Sheriffdom of Lothian and Borders and to be posted on the notice boards in said sheriff courts for publication to the lieges.

February 16, 2001

# PRACTICE NOTE

[DECEMBER 9, 1993]

I, Douglas James Risk, Q.C., Sheriff Principal of Grampian, Highland and Islands, by virtue of the powers conferred by rules 12.1 and 15.4(2) of the Rules contained in the First Schedule annexed to the Act of Sederunt (Sheriff Court Ordinary Cause Rules) 1993 do hereby direct:

**1.** For the purpose of said rules 12.1 and 15.4(2) "the Sheriff Clerk" shall not include a sheriff clerk below the rank of higher executive officer save that, in any sheriff court within the Sheriffdom where the resident sheriff clerk in charge of a court holds the rank of executive officer, it shall include that sheriff clerk or his temporary replacement provided he is of the same or higher rank.

**2.** The classes of interlocutor which a sheriff clerk may write and sign, in terms of the said rule 12.1 shall not include any final interlocutor or any interlocutor which the sheriff concerned directs to be written or signed by him or her. Subject to the foregoing, any interlocutor dealing with a motion which has been determined by a sheriff clerk in terms of the said rule 15.4(2) shall be written and signed by that sheriff clerk.

**3.** The classes of unopposed motion which a sheriff clerk may determine in terms of the said rule 15.4(2) are set out in the Appendix to this direction. However, if the granting of any such motion might also involve any order relating to expenses, it shall be referred to the sheriff who shall deal with it in accordance with rule 15.4(1).

**4.** This direction shall take effect from 1st January 1994.

## APPENDIX

Classes of motion which may be determined by a sheriff clerk in terms of rule 15.4(2):

(a) A motion to authorise re-service of an initial writ in terms of rule 5.9.

(b) A motion to recall a sist and to re-enroll a cause for further procedure.

(c) A motion, made under rule 10.3(1), to close the record before the expiry of the adjustment period provided by rule 10.1(1).

(d) A motion to allow an amendment of a kind specified in rule 18.1

(e) A motion to allow a minute of amendment to be received and answered within a specified period in terms of rule 18.3(1)(a) and (b)(ii).

(f) A motion for an order for service of a third party notice, made under rule 20.1(1) and (2).

# PRACTICE NOTE NO.1 OF 2003: AFFIDAVITS IN FAMILY ACTIONS

[JUNE 10, 2003]

I, Sir Stephen S T Young Bt, QC, Sheriff Principal of Grampian, Highland and Islands, hereby direct as follows:

## When affidavits may be lodged

**1.** Once the period within which a notice of intention to defend requires to be lodged has expired without such notice having been lodged, affidavits may be prepared and lodged without any order of the court.

## Person before whom sworn or affirmed

**2.** An affidavit is admissible if it is sworn (or affirmed) before a notary public, justice of the peace, or any person having authority to administer oaths for the place where the affidavit is sworn, such as a commissioner for oaths or a British diplomatic officer or consul abroad. A solicitor acting for a party to the action may act in a notarial capacity when an affidavit is sworn. Any person before whom an affidavit is sworn (referred to below as "the notary") must observe all the normal rules in this connection and must satisfy himself or herself as to the capacity of the witness to swear an affidavit.

## Importance of affidavits

**3.** The witness should be made to appreciate the importance of the affidavit and that the affidavit constitutes his or her evidence in the case. The possible consequences of giving false evidence should be explained to the witness. Before the witness signs the affidavit he or she must have read it or the notary must have read it over to the witness.

## Oath or affirmation

**4.** The witness must be placed on oath or must affirm.

## Form and signature of the affidavit

**5.** The document should be on A4 paper. The affidavit should commence with the words "At the day of 20, in the presence of I having been solemnly sworn/having affirmed give evidence as follows:". The affidavit should be drafted in the first person and should take the form of numbered paragraphs. The full name, age, address and occupation of the witness should be given in the first paragraph. The affidavit should end with the words "All of which is the truth as I shall answer to God" or "All of which is affirmed by me to be true", as appropriate. Any blanks in the affidavit must be filled in. Any insertion, deletion or other amendment to the affidavit requires to be initialed by the witness and the notary. Each page must be signed by both the witness and the notary. It is not necessary for the affidavit to be sealed by the notary.

## Drafting the affidavit

**6.** An affidavit should be based on a reliable and full precognition of the witness.

**7.** The drafter of an affidavit should provide himself or herself, before drawing it, with an up to date copy of the pleadings, a copy of the appropriate precognition and the relative productions. The affidavit should be drawn so as to follow the averments in the pleadings to the extent that these are within the knowledge of that particular witness and in the same order.

**8.** Affidavits should be expressed in the words of the person whose affidavit it is, should be accurate as at the date of the affidavit and should not consist of a repetition of passages in the pleadings. It should be clear from the terms of the affidavit whether the witness is speaking from his or her own knowledge, as when the witness was present and saw what happened, or whether the witness is relying on what he or she was told by a particular person.

## Productions

**9.** Productions already lodged in process must be borrowed up, and put to the party or to the witness who refers to them in his or her affidavit. Each production will require to be referred to in the affidavit by its number of process and must be docqueted and signed by the witness and the notary. If a production has not yet been lodged when the affidavit is sworn, it will require to be identified by the witness in the affidavit, should be docqueted with regard to the affidavit and signed by the witness and the notary. It must then be lodged as a production. Some productions will necessarily be docqueted with regard to more than one affidavit.

**10.** In consent cases, the defender's written consent form will have to be put to the pursuer in his or her affidavit, and be identified, docqueted and signed in the same way as other productions.

**11.** In adultery cases, photographs of both the pursuer and the defender may require to be produced, put to the appropriate witnesses and be identified, docqueted and signed in the manner already described.

## Date of affidavit

**12.** All affidavits lodged must be of recent date. This factor is particularly important in cases involving children, cases in which financial craves are involved and in any other circumstances where the evidence of a witness or circumstances to which the witness speaks are liable to change through the passage of time. The notary must take particular care in such cases to ensure that the affidavit evidence as to such matters is correct as at the time the affidavit is sworn. Affidavits relating to the welfare of children which have been sworn more than three months prior to lodging a minute for decree are likely to be rejected by the court as out of date.

## Applications relating to parental responsibilities and rights (See OCR 33.28)

**13.** In actions in which an application in terms of section 11 of the Children (Scotland) Act 1995 is before the court not fewer than two affidavits dealing with the welfare of the child(ren) should be provided, at least one of them from a person who is neither a parent nor a party to the action. These affidavits should present the court with a full picture of the arrangements for the care of the child(ren) along the lines set out in paragraph 15, adapted to suit the circumstances of the particular case. The affidavits should set out reasons why it is better that the section 11 order be made than not. The pursuer's affidavit should deal fully with the arrangements which have been made for their care, so far as within his or her knowledge. If the pursuer cannot give substantial evidence as to that it is likely to be necessary to obtain such evidence from the person who is responsible for their care.

**14.** In actions of divorce or judicial separation in which there are children of the marriage or children treated by the parties as a child of their family but in which no order in terms of section 11 in terms of the Children (Scotland) Act 1995 is sought, the court, in terms of section 12, requires to consider whether to exercise the powers set out in sections 11 or 54 of that Act in light of the information before it as the arrangements for the child(ren)'s upbringing. Information accordingly requires to be before the court as to these arrangements. As a minimum, the affidavits of the witnesses should include the information set out in paragraphs 15 (a) to (e) below.

**15.** An affidavit dealing with the arrangements for the care of children should, where relevant, include the following:
- (a) the qualifications of the witness, if not a parent, to speak about the child; how often, and in what circumstances the witness normally sees the child;
- (b) the ability of those with whom the child lives to provide proper care for him or her;
- (c) observations as to the relationship between the child and the other members of the household, the child's general appearance, interests, state of health and well-being;
- (d) a description of the home conditions in which the child lives;
- (e) the arrangements for contact between the child and any parent (and siblings) who do not live in the same household as the child;
- (f) information about the school the child attends; whether the child attends school regularly; and
- (g) details of child care arrangements during working hours, including the arrangements for such care outwith school hours.

### Affidavit relating to disclosure of the whereabouts of children

**16.** An affidavit sworn or affirmed in compliance with an order to disclose the whereabouts of children (in terms of the Family Law Act 1986, section 33 and OCR 33.23) will require to be drafted in such a way as to meet the requirements of the court in the circumstances of the particular case. The form of the affidavit should be as above.

### Financial and other ancillary craves

**17.** Affidavit evidence in support of financial craves is necessary in an undefended action. (See *Ali v Ali* 2001 SC 618, 2001 SLT 602, 2001 SCLR 485). Where financial craves are involved, the evidence should be as full, accurate and up-to-date as possible. If the evidence is insufficient the court may require supplementary evidence to be provided. If, after an affidavit has been sworn and the solicitor concerned has parted with it, a material change of circumstances occurs before decree has been granted the court must be informed forthwith. A further affidavit may have to be sworn.

**18.** The pursuer should give evidence as to his or her own financial position at the date of the affidavit. Where the pursuer gives evidence in an affidavit as to the financial position of the defender, the affidavit should state the date, as precisely as possible, at which the information was valid. The court must be provided with information which is as up-to-date as possible as to the defender's ability to pay the sums the pursuer is seeking. Where the pursuer cannot obtain recent information as to the defender's means the affidavit should state that that is the case but should contain as much material information relating to the defender's means as possible. If the pursuer is unable to provide sufficient evidence to justify the orders craved in full, in the minute for decree, after the words "in terms of crave(s) (number(s)...) of the initial writ", there may be added words such as "or such other sum (or sums) as the court may think proper".

**19.** Where the pursuer has craved a capital sum, an order for the sale of the matrimonial home, a periodical allowance, interdict or expenses, for example, and in the minute for decree does not seek decree for one or more of these, the reasons for that should be given in his or her affidavit.

### Joint Minutes

**20.** When parties record their agreement in a joint minute as to how financial and other ancillary craves should be dealt with by the court, the pursuer's affidavit should refer to the joint minute and indicate that he or she is content that the agreement set out in it should be given effect.

### Minute for decree

**21.** The minute for decree must be signed by a solicitor who has examined the affidavits and other documents. That solicitor takes responsibility therefor, whether or not he or she is the person who drew the initial writ or affidavits. The minute for decree should not be signed seeking decree of divorce or separation unless the evidence consists of or includes evidence other than that of a party to the marriage (Civil Evidence (Scotland) Act 1988, section 8(3); *Taylor v Taylor* 2000 S.L.T. 1419; 2001 S.C.L.R. 16).

(Sgd) Stephen Young
Aberdeen, 10th June 2003

# PRACTICE NOTE NO.1 OF 2004: ADOPTION OF CHILDREN, ETC: GUIDANCE FOR SHERIFFS AND PRACTITIONERS

D3.56

*[Revoked by Practice Note No.1 of 2009.]*

# PRACTICE NOTE NO.1 OF 2005

D3.57

ADULTS WITH INCAPACITY (SCOTLAND) ACT 2000: GUIDANCE FOR SHERIFFS AND PRACTITIONERS

[APRIL 4, 2005]

### Purpose

**1.** The purpose of this Practice Note is to secure the efficient management of contested applications and other proceedings under the Adults with Incapacity (Scotland) Act 2000 ("the Act").

### Commencement

**2.** This Practice Note applies to all applications lodged, or proceedings commenced, on or after 18 April 2005.

### Minimum of delay

**3.** It shall be the duty of the court to secure that all applications and other proceedings under the Act are dealt with as expeditiously as possible and with the minimum of delay. Such applications and proceedings require the cooperation of all concerned and firm case management by the sheriff.

## Identity of sheriff

**4.** Unless the sheriff principal otherwise agrees, the sheriff presiding at any stage in the proceedings must be a sheriff of this sheriffdom. In the interests of continuity and consistency in management, every stage of each case must, whenever possible, call before the same sheriff on dates and at times assigned by him or her. If a diet of proof has to be fixed, it should normally be assigned to the sheriff who has conducted the previous hearings unless, exceptionally, an early diet can be made available at which another sheriff is free to preside.

**5.** In the event that a proof is to be taken by a sheriff other than the sheriff who has conducted the previous hearings, the whole process in the case must be made available to the sheriff who is to take the proof not less than three working days before the date upon which the proof is scheduled to commence.

## Representatives

**6.** At every calling of a case any representative of any party must be familiar with the case and must have sufficient authority to deal with any issues that are likely to arise at that calling.

## Record of discussion to be kept

**7.** At every hearing prior to any proof the sheriff should not only pronounce an interlocutor regulating further procedure but should also prepare and keep with the process a brief written record of the main points of the discussion at that hearing.

## The sheriff's role

**8.** Section 3 of the Act and rule 3.16.6(2) of the Act of Sederunt (Summary Applications, Statutory Applications and Appeals etc. Rules) 1999 confer upon the sheriff a very wide discretion to determine the procedure to be followed in an application or other proceeding under the Act. Before the first hearing fixed under rule 3.16.2(a), and throughout the proceedings, the sheriff should be prepared to engage in active management of the case. He or she should maintain firm control over the proceedings while exercising flexibility in doing so.

## The application

**9.** In terms of rule 3.16.7(1) an application submitted to the sheriff under or in pursuance of the Act, other than an appeal or remitted matter, shall be in Form 23. It should be written, typed or printed on A4 size paper of durable quality and should not be backed or folded. Subject to any issue of confidentiality that may arise, it would assist the sheriff clerk wherever possible to receive a copy of the application in electronic form on the same date as the date upon which it is lodged.

## Court programming

**10.** The programming of all classes of business in the courts of the sheriffdom remains exclusively the responsibility of the sheriff principal. In this respect he generally acts through the sheriff clerk. It is therefore essential that the drawing up of timetables (where the sheriff considers this to be appropriate) and the assigning of diets by the sheriff should be undertaken only after consultation with, and with the agreement of, the sheriff clerk. Any timetable that is drawn up must be adhered to, unless in exceptional circumstances.

## The initial hearing

**11.** The hearing fixed in terms of rule 3.16.2(a) must take place within twenty eight days of the interlocutor fixing the hearing unless any person upon whom the application is to be served is outside Europe—see rule 3.16.6(1). The date of this hearing should be fixed after consultation with, and with the agreement of, the sheriff clerk (see the preceding paragraph), and should be of sufficient duration to allow for a proper consideration of the issues likely to be canvassed at it. The sheriff should consider the advisability of ordering intimation by sheriff officer in order to avoid any possible delay due to ineffective postal service.

**12.** The sheriff clerk should advise the applicant or his or her solicitors forthwith of the terms of the interlocutor appointing the date of the hearing in order that they may intimate it as soon as possible. If so requested (and subject to any issue of confidentiality that may arise), the sheriff clerk should be prepared to send to the applicant or his or her solicitors a copy of the interlocutor by fax or in electronic form as soon as it has been signed. Any such request should be accompanied by the appropriate fax telephone number or e-mail address as the case may be.

## Assigning a diet of proof

**13.** Where it appears that a proof will be necessary, the parties should be in a position to give the sheriff a carefully considered forecast of the time which the proof is expected to take. The sheriff should ask each party to specify in detail how long he expects to take in the presentation of his own evidence and in the cross-examination of the witnesses of the other party or parties. On the basis of this information the sheriff should assess how many days should be set aside for the proof (including closing submissions). At the proof itself, parties may expect to be held to the estimates previously given by them, unless in exceptional circumstances.

**14.** Consideration should be given at an early stage in the proceedings to where the proof will take place (which, subject to rule 3.16.3, may be elsewhere than at the courthouse) and whether the evidence at the proof should be recorded. The holding of a proof elsewhere than at the courthouse may be anticipated to cause administrative problems, for example for the sheriff clerk. But such administrative problems must not be permitted to get in the way of the expeditious disposal of an application or other proceeding under the Act.

**15.** Having assessed how many days are needed for the proof, the sheriff should assign the diet, but only after consultation with, and with the agreement of, the sheriff clerk (see paragraph 10 above). The dates assigned should, unless the sheriff otherwise directs, be consecutive working days, and to allow for this, in particular in the smaller courts in the sheriffdom, consideration should be given to the possibility of holding the proof elsewhere than at the courthouse—see the preceding paragraph. The sheriff should consider too whether he or she is likely to require any writing days in order to produce the judgement. If so, the dates assigned should include writing time. As in the case of an application to free a child for adoption, the reason for such arrangements is that the sheriff should "be released from other duties so that he can give priority to the case without interruption and until it has been completed by the issuing of his interlocutor. Special arrangements of that kind are clearly necessary if the sheriff is to maintain the continuity of thought throughout the proceedings which is so necessary to a proper disposal of the case" (*Lothian Regional Council v A* 1992 SLT 858 at page 862A-B).

**16.** If a proof is not completed on the last day assigned to it, it should wherever possible continue on the following day or days until it is concluded.

**17.** At the conclusion of the evidence parties must be heard orally thereon by the sheriff. In anticipation of this the sheriff may require the parties to submit, in electronic form or otherwise, draft findings in fact, or skeleton arguments, or both.

### The judgment

**18.** Any application to the sheriff under the Act requires to be made by summary application—see section 2(2). The sheriff is obliged accordingly in terms of section 50 of the Sheriff Courts (Scotland) Act 1907 to give his or her judgement in writing. In every case the judgement should be issued within four weeks of the date of the making of avizandum.

### The Practice Note No 1, 2004: Adoption of Children, Etc.

**19.** In determining the procedure to be followed in a contested application or other proceeding under the Act, the sheriff may elect to follow the procedure set out in Parts B and C of the Practice Note No 1, 2004: Adoption of Children, Etc. suitably adapted for the purposes of the application or proceeding.

April 4, 2005

D3.58

# PRACTICE NOTE NO.2 OF 2006: SPECIFICATION FOR RECOVERY OF MEDICAL RECORDS

**1.** This practice note has effect from 1st November 2006.

**2.** For the purpose of rules 28.2(3)(c) of the Ordinary Cause Rules 1993 and 18.1(3)(b) of the Summary Cause Rules 2002it is no longer necessary for a copy of a specification or an incidental application for the recovery of medical records to be intimated to the Lord Advocate.

25th October 2006

D3.59

# PRACTICE NOTE NO.1 OF 2009: ADOPTION AND CHILDREN (SCOTLAND) ACT 2007: GUIDANCE FOR SHERIFFS AND PRACTITIONERS

### Purpose

**1.** The purpose of this Practice Note is to secure the efficient management of contested applications and other proceedings under the Adoption and Children (Scotland) Act 2007 ("the Act"). It should be read subject to the detailed rules of procedure to be found in the Sheriff Court Adoption Rules 2009 ("the Rules")—see the Act of Sederunt (Sheriff Court Rules Amendment) (Adoption and Children (Scotland) Act 2007) 2009 (SSI 2009/284). It will be revised in the light of experience and any new primary or secondary legislation.

### Commencement

**2.** This Practice Note applies to all applications lodged, or proceedings commenced, on or after 28 September 2009.

### Minimum of delay

**3.** It shall be the duty of the court to secure that all applications and other proceedings under the Act are dealt with as expeditiously as possible and with the minimum of delay. Such applications and proceedings require the co-operation of all concerned and active and firm case management by the sheriff throughout their course.

### Identity of sheriff

**4.** Unless the sheriff principal otherwise agrees, the sheriff presiding at any stage in the proceedings must be a sheriff of this sheriffdom. In the interests of continuity and consistency in management, every stage of each case must, whenever possible, call before the same sheriff.

**5.** In the event that a proof has to be taken by a sheriff other than the sheriff who has conducted the previous hearings, the whole process in the case must be made available to the sheriff who is to take the proof not less than three working days before the date upon which the proof is scheduled to commence.

### Representatives

**6.** At every calling of a case any representative of any party must be familiar with the case and must have sufficient authority to deal with any issues that are likely to arise at that calling.

### Record of discussion to be kept

**7.** At every hearing prior to any proof the sheriff should not only pronounce an interlocutor regulating further procedure but should also prepare and keep with the process a brief written record of the main points of the discussion at that hearing.

### The application

**8.** Subject to any issue of confidentiality that may arise, wherever possible a copy of the petition or application (as the case may be) should be sent to the sheriff clerk in electronic form on the same date as the date upon which it is lodged.

### Court programming

**9.** The programming of all classes of business in the courts of the sheriffdom remains exclusively the responsibility of the sheriff principal. In this respect he generally acts through the sheriff clerk. It is therefore essential that the assigning of diets by the sheriff should be undertaken only after consultation with, and with the agreement of, the sheriff clerk.

### The preliminary and pre-proof hearings

**10.** Any preliminary or pre-proof hearing fixed in terms of the Rules should be of sufficient duration to allow for a proper consideration of the issues likely to be canvassed at it. Consideration should be given to the advisability of intimating any such hearing by sheriff officer in order to avoid any possible delay due to ineffective postal service.

**11.** Where the date of a hearing requires to be intimated otherwise than by the sheriff clerk, the sheriff clerk should advise the applicant or petitioner or his or her solicitors forthwith of the terms of the interlocutor appointing the date of the hearing in order that they may intimate it as soon as possible. If so requested (and subject to any issue of confidentiality that may arise), the sheriff clerk should be prepared to send to the applicant or petitioner or his or her solicitors a copy of the interlocutor by fax or in electronic form as soon as it has been signed. Any such request should be accompanied by the appropriate fax telephone number or e-mail address as the case may be.

**12.** At any preliminary hearing the sheriff should ask the respondent or his or her solicitor whether the respondent has applied, or proposes to apply, for legal aid. The sheriff should also enquire whether it is intended to instruct counsel or any expert witness and, if so, whether legal aid for that purpose has been or is to be applied for.

**13.** The sheriff should ensure that the parties have sufficient access to all the documents lodged in process. The sheriff should ask the parties whether they will be seeking to recover any documents and, if so, which documents. The sheriff should ask the other parties if they will make these available informally without the need for a commission and diligence and, if so, should fix a date by which those documents should be lodged with the court.

**14.** At a preliminary hearing, which failing at a pre-proof hearing, the sheriff should give consideration to ordering parties to intimate to every other party and to lodge in court (i) a list of witnesses, including any expert witnesses, on whose evidence it is intended to rely at proof, and (ii) a list of the documents or other productions which it is intended should be used or put in evidence at proof.

### Assigning a diet of proof

**15.** Where it appears that a proof will be necessary, the parties should be in a position to give the sheriff a carefully considered forecast of the time which the proof is expected to take. The sheriff should ask each party to specify in detail how long he expects to take in the presentation of his own evidence and in the cross-examination of the witnesses of the other party or parties. On the basis of this information the sheriff should assess how many days should be set aside for the proof (including closing submissions). At the proof itself, parties may expect to be held to the estimates previously given by them, unless in exceptional circumstances.

**16.** In the fixing of a diet of proof it is not generally a valid ground of objection to a date proposed by the court that a party wishes to instruct particular counsel. If need be, that party can always instruct another counsel.

**17.** Consideration should be given at an early stage in the proceedings to where the proof will take place and whether the evidence at the proof should be recorded. The holding of a proof elsewhere than at the courthouse may be anticipated to cause administrative problems, for example for the sheriff clerk. But such administrative problems must not be permitted to get in the way of the expeditious disposal of an application or other proceeding under the Act.

**18.** It will be seen that rules 20 and 37 of the Rules provide that a proof is to be taken continuously so far as possible, but the sheriff may adjourn the diet from time to time. To allow for this, in particular in the smaller courts in the sheriffdom, consideration should be given to the possibility of holding the proof elsewhere than at the courthouse—see the preceding paragraph. Bearing in mind the time limits in rules 22 and 38, the sheriff should consider too whether he or she is likely to require any writing days in order to produce the judgement. If so, provision for this should be made when a diet of proof is fixed. As in the case of an application to free a child for adoption under the Adoption (Scotland) Act 1978, the reason for such provision is that the sheriff should "be released from other duties so that he can give priority to the case without interruption and until it has been completed by the issuing of his interlocutor. Special arrangements of that kind are clearly necessary if the sheriff is to maintain the continuity of thought throughout the proceedings which is so necessary to a proper disposal of the case" (*Lothian Regional Council v A* , 1992 S.L.T. 858 at page 862A-B).

### 19.  Legal issues

At a pre-proof hearing the sheriff should ask the parties if there are any questions of admissibility of evidence or any other legal issues, including any questions under the European Convention on Human Rights, which are likely to arise at the proof. If so, the sheriff should consider whether they could with advantage be determined at this hearing rather than at the proof. Alternatively, the sheriff may adjourn the pre-proof hearing to another date in order to enable any such issue to be argued and determined. If a legal issue is not raised at the pre-proof hearing, the sheriff may refuse to allow it to be raised at the proof except on cause shown. A solicitor who intends to raise a legal issue at a pre-proof hearing should intimate it to the other parties' solicitors beforehand.

### Evidence

**20.**   It should be noted that evidence may be presented in the form of affidavits or other written documents (Civil Evidence (Scotland) Act 1988, section 2; *McVinnie v McVinnie* , 1995 S.L.T. (Sh. Ct) 81; *Glaser v Glaser* , 1997 S.L.T. 456). The sheriff is bound to consider reports placed before him or her even if the authors are not called to speak to them, and the strict rules of evidence do not apply (*T, Petitioner* , 1997 S.L.T. 724 at 730L). Such considerations may render the attendance of certain witnesses unnecessary, although for other reasons it may be preferable to call the author of a document. The parties should therefore apply their minds to the question whether any evidence might be appropriately presented in the form of an affidavit or other document and the sheriff should encourage them to decide that question at the pre-proof hearing. The sheriff should also encourage the use of affidavits to cover non-contentious (or indeed contentious) issues where that would save the time of witnesses and the court. Notwithstanding that an affidavit has been lodged, its author may be called to give evidence at the proof (see paragraph 3 of the judgment of Lady Smith in *Petitions of Aberdeenshire Council to declare A, B and C free for adoption*, Court of Session, 22 June 2004).

**21.**   Where the author of a report or the maker of a statement which has been or is to be lodged is to be called as a witness, the sheriff may order that the report or statement is to be held to be equivalent to the witness's examination-in-chief, unless for special reasons he or she otherwise directs.

**22.**   The sheriff should discourage the unnecessary use of expert witnesses. If expert evidence is essential, the sheriff should encourage the joint instruction of a single expert by all parties. If one party instructs an expert report, it should be disclosed to the other parties with a view to the agreement of as much of its contents as possible.

**23.**   The sheriff should ask the parties what further productions, if any, they intend to lodge. Any difficulties over the obtaining or lodging of documents should be raised and if possible resolved at the pre-proof hearing.

## The proof

**24.** At a proof it should be borne in mind that "there is a heavy responsibility on the parties' representatives to exercise all reasonable economy and restraint in their presentation of the evidence and in their submissions to the court" (*Lothian Regional Council v A* at page 862B). The sheriff may therefore exercise his or her existing common law power to intervene to discourage prolixity, repetition, the leading of evidence of unnecessary witnesses and the leading of evidence on matters which are unlikely to assist the court to reach a decision.

**25.** At the conclusion of the evidence parties must be heard orally thereon by the sheriff. In anticipation of this the sheriff may require the parties to submit, in electronic form or otherwise, draft findings in fact, or skeleton arguments, or both.

### The Practice Note No 1, 2004: Adoption of Children, etc.

**26.** The Practice Note No 1, 2004: Adoption of Children, etc. is revoked subject to the qualification that it shall continue to have effect for the purpose of any application to which it applies which has been made and not yet determined before 28 September 2009.

22 September 2009

**D3.60**

# PRACTICE NOTE NO.1 OF 2012

SIMPLIFIED DISSOLUTION OF CIVIL PARTNERSHIP APPLICATIONS: GUIDANCE FOR SHERIFFS AND PRACTITIONERS

**1.** Section 8 of the Civil Evidence (Scotland) Act 1988 ("the Act") provides:

**D3.61**

**Evidence in actions concerning family relationships, etc.**
(1) In any action to which this subsection applies (whether or not appearance has been entered for the defender), no decree or judgment in favour of the pursuer shall be pronounced until the grounds of action have been established by evidence.
(2) Subsection (1) above applies to actions for divorce, for dissolution of civil partnership, for separation of spouses or of civil partners, for declarator of marriage or of nullity of marriage or of civil partnership or for parentage or non-parentage.
(3) Subject to subsection (4) below, in any action for divorce, separation or declarator of marriage or nullity of marriage, the evidence referred to in subsection (1) above shall consist of or include evidence other than that of a party to the marriage (or alleged or purported marriage).
(3A) Subject to subsection (4) below, in any action for dissolution of civil partnership, separation of civil partners or declarator of nullity of civil partnership, the evidence referred to in subsection (1) above shall consist of or include evidence other than that of a partner in the civil partnership (or purported civil partnership).
(4) The Lord Advocate may by order made by statutory instrument provide that subsection (3) or (3A) above shall not apply, or shall apply subject to such modifications as may be specified in the order, in respect of such class or classes of action as may be so specified.
(5) No order shall be made under this section unless a draft of the order has been laid before Parliament and has been approved by resolution of each House.

**2.** In terms of paragraphs 2 and 3 of the Evidence in Divorce Actions (Scotland) Order 1989 (SI 1989/582) the Lord Advocate disapplied section 8(3) of the Act in simplified divorce applications to which Part XI of Chapter 33 of the Ordinary Cause Rules 1993 ("the 1993 Rules") refers. So no corroboration is required in the case of these applications.

**3.** Part XI of Chapter 33A of the 1993 Rules ignores the fact that no order has been made by the Lord Advocate to disapply section 8(3A) of the Act in the case of simplified dissolution of civil partnership applications. It follows that, despite the terms of Chapter 33A, in the case of such an application the evidence in support of the ground of action must consist of or include evidence other than that of a partner in the civil partnership which is the subject of the application.

**4.** In order to comply with section 8(1) and (3A) of the Act a simplified dissolution of civil partnership application should be signed by the applicant in accordance with rule 33A.67(1) or (2) (as the case may be) of the 1993 Rules and should be supported by an affidavit by a witness who is not a partner in the civil partnership which is the subject of the application. This additional affidavit should be as nearly as may be in the form set out in the schedule to this Practice Note.

**5.** When completed the affidavit should be sent to the sheriff clerk either along with the simplified dissolution of civil partnership application to which it relates or as soon as possible after the application itself has been sent.

**6.** In this context "affidavit" has the same meaning as in rule 1.2(2)(a) of the 1993 Rules.

February 20, 2012

## SCHEDULE

I, *(Insert full name of witness)* .............. residing at *(insert present home address of witness)* .................... SWEAR that to the best of my knowledge and belief the facts stated in the paragraph headed PERIOD OF SEPARATION in the simplified dissolution of civil partnership application by *(insert applicant's full name and address)* are true.

Signature of witness ...............

To be completed by Justice of the Peace, Notary Public or Commissioner for Oaths:

SWORN at *(insert place)*

this .......... day

of............... 20 .......... .

before me *(insert full name)* ...............

*(insert full address)*....................

Signature ..............

*(Justice of the Peace/ Notary Public/Commissioner for Oaths

(* *Delete as appropriate)*

# NOTES FOR GUIDANCE

# SHERIFF COURT OF CHANCERY

## Guidance

**1.1.** The following notes, which have the general approval of the Sheriff of Chancery, are designed to give guidance to solicitors dealing with chancery petitions.

## Advisory service

**2.1.** The depute sheriff clerk of chancery (tel. 031-226 7181, ext. 207) is available to discuss particular cases and will suggest revisals to any petitions submitted in draft. Advice will be given as to the type of petition best suited to particular circumstances.

## Publication

**3.1.** An abstract of the particulars in each chancery petition is published on the walls of the appropriate court having jurisdiction over the subjects or over the domicile of the ancestor. No further procedure will take place until the induciae, which varies according to where the deceased died, has expired. It is generally inadvisable to take evidence from witnesses before the expiry of the induciae.

## Proof form

**4.1.** The normal form of proof is by corroborated affidavit evidence. The affidavits should not be sworn before a notary public, acting as a commissioner, who is a partner or employee of the firm acting for the petitioner.

## Designation

**5.1.** The full name, age and occupation of the witness must be given and the full designations of both the ancestor and petitioner must be included in the depositions, the heading to the affidavit being no part of the depositions.

**5.2.** In special services, the designation and address of the ancestor, as stated in the deed founded on, must be given as well as a designation and address as stated in the petition, when they differ.

## Subscription

**6.1.** The usual practice is for the first deponent to testify to the facts in detail signing each page of his deposition, while the second deponent signs a form of concurrence. The second deponent must sign each page of the deposition of the first deponent as well as his own, unless both are wholly contained on one page. The deponents are, however, speaking to the facts within the knowledge of each, and where their evidence does not coincide there should be separate depositions.

## Evidence

**7.1.** The evidence in the proof should speak to all material facts in the petition. It is not necessary or advisable for deponents to speak to such facts as intestacy or as to the contents of deeds. Probative deeds are their own evidence.

### Difficulty in obtaining evidence

**7.2.** Where there is difficulty in obtaining the evidence of two independent witnesses the Sheriff of Chancery has discretion to allow the evidence of a single witness and, under the Civil Evidence (Scotland) Act 1988, to allow hearsay evidence to be led. It may be that the only witness available is the petitioner, and in that event his evidence is admissible. In all these circumstances the evidence will only be accepted provided that cause is shown why the normal level of proof is unavailable (cf. *Burke v. Burke* , 1983 S.L.T. 331 at p. 332).

### Mandate

**8.1.** At present mandates are required where solicitors are to sign petitions. If a mandate is not produced the petitioner must sign the petition. Mandates need not be tested or holograph but should be specific to the purpose of the petition.

### Productions—inventory

**9.1.** A complete inventory of documents produced must be made out. This should be lodged, together with the productions, along with the affidavits. The inventory does not require to be signed by the petitioner or his mandatory. A property search should be produced in petitions for special service and in petitions under s. 10 of the Conveyancing (Scotland) Act 1874.

### Minutes of amendment

**10.1.** Minutes of amendment may be lodged. Depending on the extent of the amendment, republication may be necessary or the sheriff may on cause shown dispense with republication.

### Error in type of petition

**10.2.** Amendment is inappropriate if the wrong type of petition has been lodged, e.g., if a petition for service has been presented in place of a petition for completion of title. Under these circumstances the petition should be withdrawn and a fresh one lodged. If publication of the original petition has already taken place there will have to be publication of new in respect of the second petition.

### Decree

**11.1.** When decree has been granted, the petitioner's agent will be informed by letter. Productions will be returned at this point but the process will be transmitted to the Keeper of the Registers of Scotland.

### Extract decree

**12.1.** Extracts are prepared for the petition by the Keeper of the Registers. The extract is issued, along with a fee note, to the petitioner's agent.

### Process

**13.1** All parts of process, petitions, mandates, affidavits and inventory of productions should be stiff-backed and headed up "Sheriff Court of Chancery".

### Fee

**14.1** The correct fee for lodging a chancery petition is £36.